Alison Balter's Mastering Microsoft® Access 2002 Desktop Development

Alison Balter

D1361248

SAMS

201 West 103rd St., Indianapolis, Indiana, 46290 USA

Alison Balter's Mastering Microsoft® Access 2002 Desktop Development

Copyright © 2002 by Sams Publishing

International Standard Book Number: 0-672-32101-7

Library of Congress Catalog Card Number: 00-109716

Printed in the United States of America

First Printing: August 2001

03   02   01   4   3   2   1

Trademarks

Warning and Disclaimer

EXECUTIVE EDITOR
Rosemarie Graham

MANAGING EDITOR
Charlotte Clapp

PROJECT EDITOR
Carol Bowers

COPY EDITOR
Mary Ellen Stephenson

INDEXER
Tom Dinse

PROOFREADER
Linda Seifert

TECHNICAL EDITORS
Jon Price
Chris Thibodeaux

TEAM COORDINATOR
Lynne Williams

MEDIA DEVELOPER
Dan Scherf

INTERIOR DESIGN
Anne Jones

COVER DESIGN
Aren Howell

Contents at a Glance

Contents

3   Relationships: Your Key to Data Integrity   79

4   What Every Developer Needs to Know About Query Basics   103

PART II   What To Do When Things Don't Go As Planned

15   Debugging: Your Key to Successful Development   675

Part V   Adding Polish To Your Application

27   Database Security Made Easy   1049

About the Author

Alison Balter is the president of InfoTechnology Partners, Inc., a computer consulting firm based in Westlake Village, California. Alison is a highly experienced independent trainer and consultant specializing in Windows applications training and development. During her 18 years in the computer industry, she has trained and consulted with many corporations and government agencies. Since Alison founded InfoTechnology Partners, Inc. (formerly Marina Consulting Group) in 1990, its client base has expanded to include major corporations and government agencies such as Shell Oil, Accenture, Northrop, the Drug Enforcement Administration, Prudential Insurance, Transamerica Insurance, Fox Broadcasting, the United States Navy, and others.

InfoTechnology Partners, Inc. is a Microsoft Certified Partner. Alison is a Microsoft Certified Professional. Alison was one of the first professionals in the computer industry to become a Microsoft Certified Solutions Developer (MCSD).

Alison is the author of more than 300 internationally marketed computer-training videos for KeyStone Learning Systems Corporation, including seven Access 2.0 videos, eleven Access 95 videos, thirteen Access 97 videos, eighteen Access 2000 videos, nine Visual Basic for Applications videos, and three VBScript videos. She travels throughout North America giving training seminars in Microsoft Access, Visual Basic, Microsoft SQL Server, Visual Studio.NET, Visual InterDev, and Visual Basic for Applications. She is also featured in several live satellite television broadcasts for National Technological University.

Alison is a regular contributing columnist for *Access/Office/VB Advisor* as well as other computer publications. She is also a regular on the Access, Visual Basic, SQL Server, and Visual InterDev national speaker circuits. She was one of four speakers on the Visual Basic 4.0 and 5.0 World Tours, a seminar series co-sponsored by Application Developers Training Company and Microsoft.

Alison is also a co-author of three other Access books published by Sams Publishing: *Essential Access 95*, *Access 95 Unleashed*, and *Access 97 Unleashed*.

An active participant in many user groups and other organizations, Alison is a past president of the Independent Computer Consultants Association of Los Angeles and of the Los Angeles Clipper Users' Group.

On a personal note, Alison keeps herself busy skiing, running, lifting weights, hiking, traveling, flying, and dancing. She most enjoys spending time with her husband, Dan, their daughter Alexis, and their son Brendan.

Alison's firm, InfoTechnology Partners, Inc., is available for consulting work and on-site training in Microsoft Access, Visual Basic, SQL Server, Visual Studio.NET, and Visual InterDev, as well as for Windows NT, Windows 95/98, Windows 2000, Windows XP, Windows 2002 Server, PC networking, and Microsoft Exchange Server. Contact Alison by electronic mail at `Alison@InfoTechnologyPartners.com`, or visit InfoTechnology Partners' Web site at `www.InfoTechnologyPartners.com`.

Dedication

I dedicate this book to my husband Dan, my daughter Alexis, my son Brendan, my parents Charlotte and Bob, and to my real father, Herman. Dan, you are my partner in life and the wind beneath my wings. You are a true partner in every sense of the word. I am so lucky to be traveling the path of life with such a spectacular person. Alexis, you are the sweet little girl that I always dreamed of. You are everything that I could have ever wanted and so very much more. You make every one of my days a happy one! Brendan, you are the one that keeps me on my toes. There is never a dull moment with you around. I wish I had just a small portion of your energy. I thank you for the endless laughter that you bring to our family, and for reminding me about all of the important things in life. Mom and Dad, without all that you do to help out with life's chores, the completion of this book could never have been possible. Words cannot express my gratitude!

To my real father, Herman, I credit my ability to soar in such a technical field to you. I hope that I inherited just a small part of your intelligence, wit, and fortitude. I am sorry that you did not live to see this accomplishment. I hope that you can see my work and that you are proud of it. I also hope that in some way you share in the joy that Dan, Alexis, and Brendan bring to me. More than anyone else, I dedicate this book to you.

Finally, I want to thank God for giving me the gift of gab, a wonderful career, an incredible husband, two beautiful children, and an awesome life. Through your grace, I am truly blessed.

Acknowledgments

Writing a book is a monumental task. Without the support and understanding of those close to me, my dreams for this book would have never come to fruition. Special thanks go to the following special people who helped to make this book possible:

Dan Balter (My Incredible Husband) for his ongoing support, love, encouragement, friendship, and for being patient with me while I wrote this book. Dan, words cannot adequately express the love and appreciation that I feel for all that you are and all that you do for me. You treat me like a princess! Thank you for being the phenomenal person you are. I enjoy sharing not only our career successes, but even more I enjoy sharing the life of our beautiful children, Alexis and Brendan. I look forward to continuing to reach highs we never dreamed of. There is no one I'd rather spend forever with than you.

Alexis Balter (My Precious Daughter) for giving life a special meaning. Your intelligence, compassion, caring, and perceptiveness are far beyond your years. Alexis, you make all my hard work worth it. No matter how bad my day, when I look at you, sunshine fills my life. You are the most special gift that anyone has ever given me.

Brendan Balter (My Adorable Son) for showing me the power of persistence. Brendan, you are small, but, boy, are you mighty! I have never seen such tenacity and fortitude in such a little person. I never imagined that one little guy could render hours of expensive baby-proofing worthless! Most of all, thank you for reminding me how important it is to have a sense of humor.

Charlotte and Bob Roman (Mom & Dad) for believing in me and sharing in both the good times and the bad. Mom and Dad, without your special love and support, I never would have become who I am today. Without all your help, I could never get everything done. Words can never express how much I appreciate all that you do!

Sue Terry for being the most wonderful best friend anyone could possibly have. You inspire me with your music, your love, your friendship, and your faith in God. Whenever I am having a bad day, I picture you singing "Dear God" or "Love My Neighbor Blues", and suddenly my day gets better. Thank you for the gift of friendship.

Roz, Ron, and Charlie Carriere for supporting my endeavors and for encouraging me to pursue my writing. It means a lot to know that you guys are proud of me for what I do.

Steven Chait for being a special brother. I want you to know how much you mean to me. When I was a little girl, I was told about your gift to write. You may not know this, but my desire to write was started as a little girl wanting to be like her big brother.

Sonia Aguilar for being the best nanny that anyone could ever dream of having. You are a person far too special to describe in words. I can't tell you how much it means to know that Alexis and Brendan have someone so loving and caring to spend their days with. You are an amazing model of love, kindness, and charity. Hugo, Claudia, Gaby, and Hugito, you are all special, too. Dan, Alexis, Brendan, and I are so very lucky to have you in our family.

Doug and Karen Sylvester for being the best neighbors and friends a couple could have. You are loads of fun to be with and are always there when we need you. We are so glad you are such an integral part of our lives. We look forward to watching Alexis, Brendan, Nathaniel, and Noah grow up together.

Greggory Peck, Clint Argle, and the Folks at Keystone Learning Systems for their contribution to my success in this industry. I believe that the opportunities you have given me have helped me reach a level in this industry that would have been much more difficult for me to reach on my own.

Scott Barker for being such a great business and personal support. Thanks for handling many of my programming projects while I wrote this book. Thanks for listening to my trials and tribulations in writing and in consulting projects. Most of all, thanks for being a wonderful friend and support.

Rosemarie Graham for making my experience with Sams a truly positive one. I have really enjoyed working with you over these past several months. I am so glad that we finally got to meet. I had a blast with you. You are lots of fun on a roller coaster! On a serious note, I appreciate your thoughtfulness and your sensitivity to my schedule and commitments outside of this book. It is nice to work with someone who appreciates me as a person, not just as an author.

Sindy Vargas for putting lots of time and effort into taking the screen shots for this book. I also want to thank you for making my daily tasks at the office much easier.

Chuck Hinkle, Joyce Milner, and David Cummins (my pals at Shell Oil) for your great friendship and inspiration. Chuck, you have always been a great support and encouragement to me. I hope that we stay in touch regardless of where our paths may lead. Joyce, you are very special to me. I love our long talks. I feel so close to you, as if I have known you for a very long time. I hope that we remain friends forever! David, you are one of the smartest men I have met. You are witty and fun. I really enjoyed working with you on SCURS. Elaine is a beautiful person. I appreciate you bringing her into my life. I hope that you and Elaine remain my friends for a long time to come.

Tell Us What You Think!

As the reader of this book, *you* are our most important critic and commentator. We value your opinion and want to know what we're doing right, what we could do better, what areas you'd like to see us publish in, and any other words of wisdom you're willing to pass our way.

As an Executive Editor for Sams Publishing, I welcome your comments. You can fax, e-mail, or write me directly to let me know what you did or didn't like about this book—as well as what we can do to make our books stronger.

Please note that I cannot help you with technical problems related to the topic of this book, and that due to the high volume of mail I receive, I might not be able to reply to every message.

When you write, please be sure to include this book's title and author as well as your name and phone or fax number. I will carefully review your comments and share them with the author and editors who worked on the book.

> Fax: 317-581-4770
>
> E-mail: rosemarie.graham@samspublishing.com
>
> Mail: Rosemarie Graham
>   Executive Editor
>   Sams Publishing
>   201 West 103rd Street
>   Indianapolis, IN 46290 USA

Introduction

Many excellent books about Access are available, so why write another one? In talking to the many students I meet in my travels around the country, I have heard one common complaint. Instead of the several great books available for the user community or the host of wonderful books available to expert Access developers, my students yearn for a book targeted toward the intermediate-to-advanced developer. They yearn for a book that starts at the beginning, ensures that they have no gaps in their knowledge, and takes them through some of the most advanced aspects of Access development. Along the way, they want to acquire volumes of practical code that they can easily port into their own applications. I wrote *Alison Balter's Mastering Access 2002 Desktop Development* with those requests in mind.

This book begins by providing you with an introduction to Access development. It alerts you to the types of applications that you can develop in Access and introduces you to the components of an Access application. After you understand what an Access application is and when it is appropriate to develop one, you will explore the steps involved in building an actual Access application. The book covers several strategies before you build the first application component. This ensures that you, as the developer of the application, are aware of the design issues that might affect you in your particular environment.

After you have discovered the overall picture, you will be ready to venture into the specific details of each object within an Access database. Chapters 2 through 6 cover the basics of tables, relationships, queries, forms, and reports. The intent of these chapters is to provide you with an approach to developing these database objects from a developer's perspective. Although this text starts at the beginning, it provides many tips, tricks, and caveats not readily apparent from the documentation or from books targeted toward end users.

When you have a strong foundation of knowing how to build tables, queries, forms, and reports, you will be ready to plunge full-force into coding. Chapters 7 and 8 provide you with an extremely strong grasp of the VBA language. Once again, starting with the basics, the book takes you gently through some of the most complex intricacies of the VBA language and Access object model. The text provides you with many practical examples to ensure that you thoroughly digest each topic.

Chapters 9 through 11 provide you with an advanced discussion of queries, forms, and reports. By the time you reach this point in the book, you should be familiar with all the basics of creating database objects. These chapters combine the basics of table, query, form, and report design with the VBA and object techniques covered in Chapters 7 and 8. The power techniques covered in Chapters 9 through 11 provide you with the expertise that you need to design the most complex types of queries, forms, and reports required by your applications.

After you cover the basics, you will be ready to delve into more advanced techniques. Chapter 12 covers advanced VBA techniques. It is followed by an in-depth discussion of class modules in Chapter 13. Many practical examples of how and why to utilize class modules are included in the chapter.

Before you ride through the frontier of the many intricacies of the Access development environment, one basic topic remains. Chapter 14 introduces you to ActiveX Data Objects and Data Access Objects, and explains their differences. You will see how you can move away from bound objects, manipulating the data within your database using code.

Unfortunately, things don't always go as planned. No matter what your level of expertise, you will often find yourself stumped over a piece of code and looking for answers. Chapter 15 shows you how to effectively employ the debugger to solve any coding problem you might run into. Even after your application has been thoroughly debugged, you still must provide a responsible means of handling errors within your applications. Chapter 16 shows you everything you must know to implement error handling. Included in the text and on the sample code CD-ROM is a generic error handler that you can easily build in to any of your own applications.

Even the fanciest of applications will not please its users if it is sluggish. Chapter 17 covers optimization, that is, all the techniques you should incorporate into your programming code to ensure that your application runs as efficiently as possible.

With the foundation provided by the first 17 chapters, you will be ready to move into the more rich and complex aspects of the VBA language and the Access development environment. Chapters 18 through 20 cover the basics of developing applications for a multiuser or a client/server environment. You can explore locking strategies, how to interact with non-native Access file formats, and the alternatives for designing client/server applications.

As an Access developer, your world is not limited to just Access. To be effective and productive as an Access developer, you must know how to interact with other applications and how to use ActiveX controls, libraries, menu add-ins, wizards, and builders to assist you with the application development process. Chapters 21 through 26 cover ActiveX controls, automation, the Windows API, library and add-in techniques, and an introduction to Access and the Internet. After reading these chapters, you will understand how to employ the use of external objects and functionality to add richness to your applications without too much effort on your part.

Having reached the final part of the book, you will be ready to put the final polish on your application. Chapters 27 through 32 cover security, documentation, maintenance, the Microsoft Office Developer edition, the use of third-party tools, and distribution. You will learn how to properly secure your application so that you do not in any way compromise the investment you have put into the application development process. You will also discover how easy it is to put into your application the final touches that give it a professional polish and make it stand out from the rest.

If, after reading this book, you are thirsty for more, *Alison Balter's Mastering Access 2002 Enterprise Development* is for you. It focuses on Access' role as a client/server development tool. It covers the various methodologies you can use to design a client/server application with an Access front end. It also delves into the process of setting up and maintaining a SQL Server database, including the process of building tables, views, stored procedures, and database diagrams. In addition to the plethora of client/server topics included in the book, it covers transaction processing, replication, source code control, and Access as an Internet or intranet development tool. Internet- and intranet-related topics include data access pages, publishing data to the Web, and SQL Server and the Web.

The Access development environment is robust and exciting. With the keys to deliver all that it offers, you can produce applications that provide much satisfaction as well as many financial rewards. After poring over this hands-on guide and keeping it nearby for handy reference, you too can become masterful at Access 2002 development. This book is dedicated to demonstrating how you can fulfill the promise of making Access 2002 perform up to its lofty capabilities. As you will see, you have the ability to really make Access 2002 shine in the everyday world!

The Basics of Access Development

PART

I

IN THIS PART

Access as a Development Tool

IN THIS CHAPTER

Why This Chapter Is Important

In talking to users and developers, I find that Access is a very misunderstood product. Many people think that it is just a toy to be used by managers or secretaries wanting to play with data. Others feel that it is a serious developer product intended for no one but experienced application developers. This chapter dispels the myths of Access. It helps you to decipher what Access is and what it isn't. After reading the chapter, you will know when Access is the tool for you, and when it makes sense to explore other products.

What Types of Applications Can You Develop in Access?

I often find myself explaining exactly what types of applications can be built with Microsoft Access. Access offers a variety of features for different database needs. It can be used to develop six general types of applications:

- Personal applications
- Small-business applications
- Departmental applications
- Corporation-wide applications
- As a front end for enterprise-wide client/server applications
- Intranet/Internet applications

Access as a Development Platform for Personal Applications

At its most basic level, Access can be used to develop simple personal database-management systems. I caution people against this idea, though. People who buy Access hoping to automate everything from their wine collections to their home finances are often disappointed. The problem is that Access is deceptively easy to use. Its wonderful built-in wizards make Access look like a product that anyone can use. After answering a series of questions, you have finished applications—switchboards, data-entry screens, reports, and the underlying tables that support them. In fact, when Access was first released, many people asked if I was concerned that my business as a computer programmer and trainer would diminish because Access seemed to let absolutely anyone write a database application. Although it's true that the simplest of Access applications can be produced without any thought of design and without a single line of code written by the user, most applications require at least some designing and custom code.

As long as you're satisfied with a wizard-generated personal application with only minor modifications, no problems should occur. It's when you want to substantially customize a personal application that problems can happen.

Access as a Development Platform for Small-Business Applications

Access is an excellent platform for developing an application that can run a small business. Its wizards let developers quickly and easily build the application's foundation. The ability to build code modules allows developers to create code libraries of reusable functions, and the ability to add code behind forms and reports allows them to create powerful custom forms and reports.

The main limitation of using Access for developing a custom small-business application is the time and money involved in the development process. Many people use Access wizards to begin the development process but find they need to customize their application in ways they can't accomplish on their own. Small-business owners often experience this problem on an even greater scale. The demands of a small-business application are usually much higher than those of a personal application. I have been called in many times after a doctor, attorney, or other professional reached a dead end in the development process. They're always dismayed at how much money it will cost to make their application usable.

Access as a Development Platform for Departmental Applications

Access is perfect for developing applications for departments in large corporations. It's relatively easy to upgrade departmental users to the appropriate hardware—for example, it's much easier to buy additional RAM for 15 users than it is for 4,000! Furthermore, Access's performance is adequate for most departmental applications without the need for client/server technology. Finally, most departments in large corporations have the development budgets to produce well-designed applications.

Fortunately, most departments usually have a PC guru, who is more than happy to help design forms and reports. This gives the department a sense of ownership because they have contributed to the development of their application. It also makes my life as a developer much easier. I can focus on the hard-core development issues, leaving some of the form and report design tasks to the local talent.

Access as a Development Platform for Corporation-Wide Applications

Although Access might be best suited for departmental applications, it can also be used to pro-duce applications that are distributed throughout the organization. How successful this endeavor is depends on the corporation. There's a limit to the number of users who can concur-rently share an Access application while maintaining acceptable performance, and there's also a limit to the number of records that each table can contain without a significant performance drop. These numbers vary depending on factors such as the following:

- How much traffic already exists on the network?
- How much RAM and how many processors does the server have?
- How is the server already being used? For example, are applications such as Microsoft Office being loaded from the server or from local workstations?
- What types of tasks are the users of the application performing? Are they querying, entering data, running reports, and so on?
- Where are Access and your Access application run from (the server or the workstation?
- What network operating system is in place?

My general rule of thumb for an Access application that's not client/server is that poor perfor-mance generally results with more than 10–15 concurrent users and more than 100,000 records. Remember, these numbers vary immensely depending on the factors mentioned, as well as on the definition of acceptable performance by you and your users. The basics of when to move to a client/server database are covered in Chapter 20, "Developing Multiuser and Enterprise Applications." The details of this topic are covered in a separate book, *Alison Balter's Mastering Access 2002 Enterprise Development*, also published by Sams.

Developers often misunderstand what Access is and what it isn't when it comes to being a client/server database platform. I'm often asked, "Isn't Access a 'client/server' database?" The answer is that Access is an unusual product because it's a file server application out of the box, but it can act as a front end to a client/server database. In case you're lost, here's an explana-tion: If you buy Access and develop an application that stores the data on a file server in an Access database, all data processing is performed on the workstation. This means that every time the user runs a query or report, all the data is brought over to the workstation. The query is then run on the workstation machine, and the results are displayed in a datasheet or on a report. This process generates a significant amount of network traffic, particularly if multiple users are running reports and queries at the same time on large Access tables. In fact, such operations can bring the entire network to a crawl.

Access as a Development Platform for Enterprise-Wide Client/Server Applications

A client/server database, such as Microsoft SQL Server or Oracle, processes queries on the server machine and returns results to the workstation. The server software itself can't display data to the user, so this is where Access comes to the rescue. Acting as a front end, Access can display the data retrieved from the database server in reports, datasheets, or forms. If the user updates the data in an Access form, the update is sent to the back-end database. This can either be accomplished by linking to these external databases so that they appear to both you and the user as Access tables, or by using techniques that access client/server data directly.

Using Access project files (not to be confused with Microsoft Project files), you can build an application specifically for a client/server environment. These project files, known as ADP files (Access Data Project), contain the program's forms, reports, macros, modules, and data access pages. The project is connected to the back-end database that contains the tables, stored procedures, views, and database diagrams that the program accesses. From within a project file, you can easily modify and manipulate objects stored on the server, using Access's friendly graphical user interface. ADP files help to bring rapid application development to the process of building client/server applications. Because Access 2002 ships with an integrated data store (the SQL Server 2000 Desktop Engine), you can develop a client/server application on the desktop and then easily deploy it to an enterprise SQL Server database. The alternatives and techniques for developing client/server applications are covered briefly in Chapter 20. The details of how to develop Access projects are covered in a separate book, *Alison Balter's Mastering Access 2002 Enterprise Development.*

NOTE

Access Projects (ADPs) were introduced in Access 2000. They were considered by many to be version 1.0 technology in that product. Microsoft did significant work with ADP files in Access 2002. Today, they are a very viable solution for client/server application development.

When you reduce the volume of network traffic by moving the processing of queries to the back end, Access becomes a much more powerful development solution. It can handle huge volumes of data and a large number of concurrent users. The main issues usually faced by developers who want to deploy such a wide-scale Access application are

- The variety of operating systems used by each user
- Difficulties with deployment

- The method by which each user is connected to the application and data
- The type of hardware each user has

Although processing of queries in a client/server application is done at the server, which significantly reduces network traffic, the application itself still must reside in the memory of each user's PC. This means that each client machine must be capable of running the appropriate operating system and the correct version of Access. Even when the correct operating system and version of Access are in place, your problems are not over. DLL conflicts often result in difficult-to-diagnose errors and idiosyncrasies in an Access application. Furthermore, Access is not the best solution for disconnected users who must access an application and its data over the Internet. Finally, Access 2002 is hardware hungry! The hardware requirements for an Access application are covered later in this chapter. The bottom line is that, before you decide to deploy a wide-scale Access application, you need to know the hardware and software configurations of all your system's users. You must also decide if the desktop support required for the typical Access application is feasible given the number of people who will use the system that you are building.

Access as a Development Platform for Intranet/Internet Applications

Using data access pages, intranet and Internet users can update your application data from within a browser. Data access pages are HTML documents that are bound directly to data in a database. They are stored outside your database and are used just like standard Access forms except that they are designed to run in Microsoft Internet Explorer 5.5 or higher, rather than in Microsoft Access. Data access pages use dynamic HTML in order to accomplish their work. Because they are supported only in Internet Explorer 5.5 or higher, data access pages are much more appropriate as an intranet solution than as an Internet solution. In addition to using data access pages, you can also publish your database objects as either Static or Dynamic HTML pages. Static pages are standard HTML and can be viewed in any browser. Database objects can be published dynamically to either the HTX/IDC file format or to the ASP (Active Server Page) file format. HTX/IDC files are published dynamically by the Web server and are browser independent. ASP files published by Microsoft Access are also published dynamically by the Web server, but require Internet Explorer 4.0 or higher on the client machine.

New to Access 2002 is the ability to create XML data and schema documents from Jet or SQL Server structures and data. Data and data structures can also be imported into Access from XML documents. This can all be accomplished either using code, or via the user interface.

> **NOTE**
>
> Some coverage of intranet and Internet development using Microsoft Access is provided in the book. Detailed coverage of intranet and Internet development using Microsoft Access is available in *Alison Balter's Mastering Access 2002 Enterprise Development.*

Access as a Scalable Product

One of Access's biggest strong points is its scalability. An application that begins as a small-business application running on a standalone machine can be scaled to an enterprise-wide client/server application. If you design your application properly, scaling can be done with little to no rewriting of your application. This feature makes Access an excellent choice for growing businesses, as well as for applications being tested at a departmental level with the idea that they might eventually be distributed corporation-wide.

The great thing about Access is that, even acting as both the front end and back end with data stored on a file server in Access tables, it provides excellent security and the ability to establish database rules previously available only on back-end databases. As you will see in Chapters 27, "Database Security Made Easy," and 28, "Advanced Security Techniques," security can be assigned to every object in a database at either a user or group level. Referential integrity rules can be applied at the database level, ensuring that (for example) orders aren't entered for customers who don't exist. Data validation rules can be enforced at either a field or record level, maintaining the integrity of the data in your database. In other words, many of the features previously available only on high-end database servers are now available by using Access's own proprietary data-storage format.

What Exactly Is a Database?

The term *database* means different things to different people. For many years, in the world of xBase (dBASE, FoxPro, CA-Clipper), *database* was used to describe a collection of fields and records. (This type of collection is called a *table* in Access.) In a client/server environment, *database* refers to all the data, schema, indexes, rules, triggers, and stored procedures associated with a system. In Access terms, a database is a collection of all the tables, queries, forms, data access pages, reports, macros, and modules that compose a complete system.

Getting to Know the Database Objects

As mentioned previously, Access databases are made up of tables, queries, forms, reports, data access pages, macros, and modules. Each of these objects has a special function. An Access application also includes several miscellaneous objects, including relationships, command bars, database properties, and import/export specifications. With these objects, you can create a powerful, user-friendly, integrated application. Figure 1.1 shows the Access Database window. Notice the seven categories of objects listed in the database container. The following sections take you on a tour of the objects that make up an Access database.

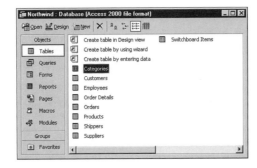

FIGURE 1.1

The Access Database window, with icons for each type of database object.

Tables: A Repository for Your Data

Tables are the starting point for your application. Whether your data is stored in an Access database or you are referencing external data by using linked tables, all the other objects in your database either directly or indirectly reference your tables.

To view all the tables that are contained in the open database, click the Tables icon in the Objects list. (Note that you won't see any hidden tables unless you have checked the Hidden Objects check box in the Tools, Options dialog box's View page.) If you want to view the data in a table, double-click the name of the table you want to view. (You can also select the table, and then click the Open button.) The table's data is displayed in a datasheet, which includes all the table's fields and records. (See Figure 1.2.) You can modify many of the datasheet's attributes and even search for and filter data from within the datasheet. If the table is linked to another table (like the Northwind Customers and Orders tables), you can also expand and collapse the subdatasheet to view data stored in child tables. These techniques aren't covered in this book but can be found in the Access user manual or any introductory Access book, such as *Sams Teach Yourself Access 2002 in 21 Days*.

FIGURE 1.2

Datasheet view of the Customers table in the Northwind database.

As a developer, you most often want to view the table's design, which is the blueprint or template for the table. To view a table's design, click the Design icon with the table selected. (See Figure 1.3.) In Design view, you can view or modify all the field names, data types, and field and table properties. Access gives you the power and flexibility you need to customize the design of your tables. These topics are covered in Chapter 2, "What Every Developer Needs to Know About Tables."

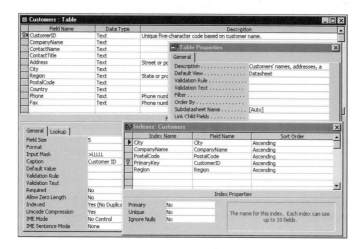

FIGURE 1.3

The design of the Customers table.

> **NOTE**
>
> In an Access project (ADP), although tables are shown in the Database window, they are not stored in the Access project file. Instead, they are stored in the SQL Server database to which the ADP is connected.

Relationships: Tying the Tables Together

To properly maintain your data's integrity and ease the process of working with other objects in the database, you must define relationships among the tables in your database. This is accomplished using the Relationships window. To view the Relationships window, with the Database window active, select Tools|Relationships, or click Relationships on the toolbar. (See Figure 1.4.) In this window, you can view and maintain the relationships in the database. If you or a fellow developer have set up some relationships, but you don't see any in the Relationships dialog box, select Relationships|Show All to unhide any hidden tables and relationships (you might need to click to expand the menu for this option to appear).

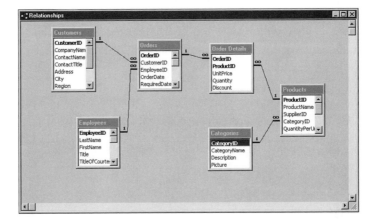

FIGURE 1.4

The Relationships window, where you view and maintain the relationships in the database.

Notice that many of the relationships in Figure 1.4 have a join line between tables with a number *1* and an infinity symbol. This indicates a one-to-many relationship between the tables. If you double-click on the join line, the Edit Relationships dialog box opens. (See Figure 1.5.) In this dialog box, you can specify the exact nature of the relationship between tables. The relationship between Customers and Orders, for example, is a one-to-many relationship with referential integrity enforced. This means that orders can't be added for customers who don't exist.

Notice that the check box to Cascade Update Related Fields is checked. This means that if a CustomerID is updated, all records containing that CustomerID in the Orders table are also updated. Because Cascade Delete Related Records is not checked, customers cannot be deleted from the Customers table if they have corresponding orders in the Orders table.

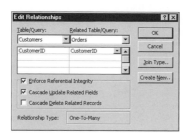

FIGURE 1.5

The Relationships dialog box, which lets you specify the nature of the relationship between tables.

Chapter 3, "Relationships: Your Key to Data Integrity," extensively covers the process of defining and maintaining relationships. It also covers the basics of relational database design. For now, remember that relationships should be established both conceptually and literally as early in the design process as possible. They are integral to successfully designing and implementing your application.

NOTE

In an Access project (ADP), relationships appear in the Database window as Database Diagrams. They are not stored in the Access project file. They are instead stored in the SQL Server database to which the ADP is connected.

Queries: Stored Questions or Actions to Be Applied to Your Data

Queries in Access are powerful and multifaceted. Select queries allow you to view, summarize, and perform calculations on the data in your tables. Action queries let you add to, update, and delete table data. To run a query, select Queries from the Objects list and then double-click the query you want to run, or click to select the query you want to run, and then click Open. When you run a select query, a datasheet appears, containing all the fields specified in the query and all the records meeting the query's criteria. (See Figure 1.6.) When you run an action query, the specified action is run, such as making a new table or appending data to an existing table. In general, the data in a query result can be updated because the result of a query is actually a dynamic set of records, called a *dynaset*, based on your tables' data.

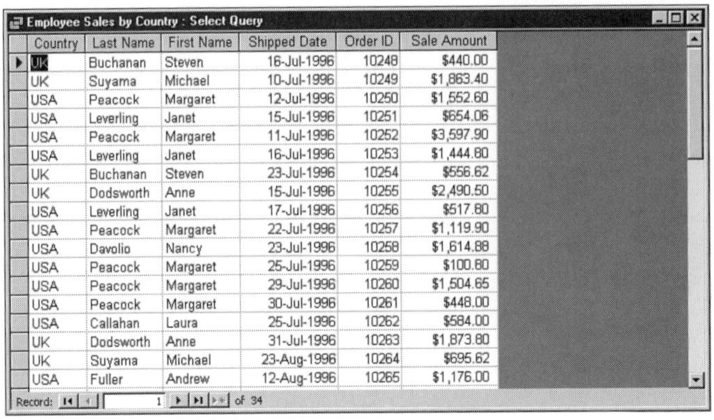

FIGURE 1.6
The result of running the Employee Sales by Country query.

When you store a query, only its definition, layout or formatting properties, and datasheet are actually stored in the database. Access offers an intuitive, user-friendly tool for you to design your queries. Figure 1.7 shows the Query Design window. To open this window, select the Queries from the Objects list in the Database window, choose the query you want to modify, and click Design. The query pictured in the figure selects data from Employees, Orders, and Order Subtotals. It displays the Country, LastName, and FirstName from the Employees table, the ShippedDate and OrderID from the Orders table, and the Subtotal from the Order Subtotals query. Only records within a specific Shipped Date range are displayed in the query's output. This special type of query is called a *parameter query*. It prompts for criteria at runtime, using the criteria entered by the user to determine which records are included in the output. Queries are covered in Chapters 4, "What Every Developer Needs to Know About Query Basics," and 11, "Advanced Query Techniques." Because queries are the foundation for most forms and reports, they're covered throughout this book as they apply to other objects in the database.

NOTE

In an Access project (ADP), queries appear in the Database window as views and stored procedures. They are not stored in the Access project file. They are instead stored in the SQL Server database to which the ADP is connected.

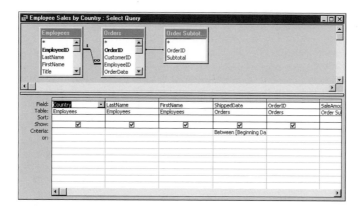

FIGURE 1.7

The design of a query that displays data from the Employees and Orders tables and the Order Subtotals query.

Forms: A Means of Displaying, Modifying, and Adding Data

Although you can enter and modify data in a table's Datasheet view, you can't control the user's actions very well, nor can you do much to facilitate the data-entry process. This is where forms come in. Access forms can take on many traits, and they're very flexible and powerful.

To view any form, select Forms from the Objects list. Then double-click the form you want to view, or click to select the form you want to view, and then click Open. Figure 1.8 illustrates a form in Form view. This form is actually three forms in one: one main form and two subforms. The main form displays information from the Customers table, and the subforms display information from the Orders table and the Order Details table. As the user moves from customer to customer, the orders associated with that customer are displayed. When the user clicks to select an order, the products included on that order are displayed.

Like tables and queries, forms can also be viewed in Design view. To view the design of a form, select the Forms icon from the Objects list (refer to Figure 1.1), choose the form whose design you want to modify, and then click Design. Figure 1.9 shows the Customer Orders form in Design view. Notice the two subforms within the main form. Forms are officially covered in Chapters 5, "What Every Developer Needs to Know About Forms," and 9, "Advanced Form Techniques." They're also covered throughout this text as they apply to other examples of building an application.

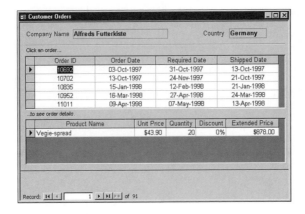

FIGURE 1.8

The Customer Orders form includes customer, order, and order detail information.

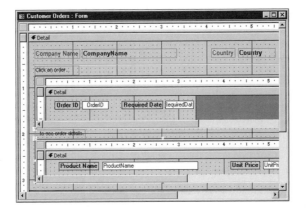

FIGURE 1.9

The design of the Customer Orders form, showing two subforms.

Reports: Turning Data into Information

Forms allow you to enter and edit information, but, with reports, you can display information, usually to a printer. Figure 1.10 shows a report being previewed. To preview any report, select Reports from the Objects list. Double-click the report you want to preview or choose the report you want to preview, and then click Preview. Notice the graphic in the report, as well as other details, such as the shaded line. Like forms, reports can be elaborate and exciting, yet can contain valuable information.

FIGURE 1.10

A preview of the Catalog report.

If you haven't guessed yet, reports can be viewed in Design view, as shown in Figure 1.11. To view the design of any report, select Reports from the Objects list and click Design after selecting the report you want to view. Figure 1.11 illustrates a report with many sections; you can see a Report Header, Page Header, CategoryName Group Header, and Detail section—just a few of the many sections available on a report. Just as a form can contain subforms, a report can contain subreports. Reports are covered in Chapters 6, "What Every Developer Needs to Know About Reports," and 10, "Advanced Report Techniques," and throughout the book as they apply to other examples.

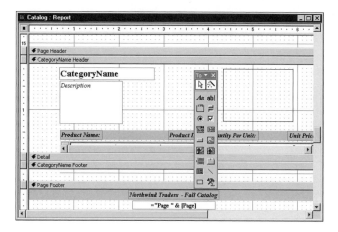

FIGURE 1.11

Design view of the Catalog report.

Data Access Pages: Forms Viewed in a Browser

Data access pages, discussed earlier in the chapter, appeared in Access 2000. They allow you to view and update the data in your database from within a browser. Although they are stored outside the Access database (.mdb) file, they are created and maintained in a manner similar to that of forms. Figure 1.12 shows a data access page being viewed within Access. Although data access pages are targeted toward a browser, they can also be previewed within the Access application environment.

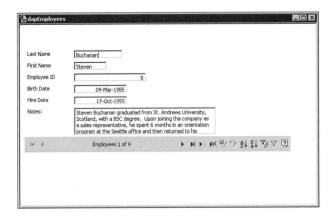

FIGURE 1.12

An example of a data access page based on the Employees table.

Data access pages can also be viewed and modified in Design view. Figure 1.13 shows a data access page in Design view. As you can see, the Design view of a data access page is similar to that of a form. This makes working with data access pages, and the deployment of your application over an intranet, very easy.

> **TIP**
>
> New in Access 2002 is the ability to save an Access form as a data access page. This new feature makes it easier to develop forms used by Access users and browser-based users simultaneously.

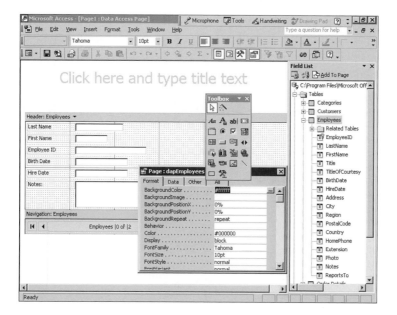

FIGURE 1.13
A data access page shown in Design view.

Macros: A Means of Automating Your System

Macros in Access aren't like the macros in other Office products. They can't be recorded, as they can in Microsoft Word or Excel, and they aren't saved as VBA (Visual Basic for Applications) code. With Access macros, you can perform most of the tasks that you can manually perform from the keyboard, menus, and toolbars. Macros allow you to build logic into your application flow. Generally, you use VBA code contained in modules, rather than macros, to do the tasks your application must perform. This is because VBA code modules give you more flexibility and power than macros do. Although in earlier versions of Access certain tasks could be performed only by using macros, they are rarely used by developers today. The development of applications using macros is therefore not covered in this book.

To run a macro, select Macros from the Objects list, click the macro you want to run, and then click Run. The actions in the macro are then executed. To view a macro's design, select Macros from the Objects list, select the macro you want to modify, and click Design to open the Macro Design window. (See Figure 1.14.) The macro pictured has four columns. The first column is the Macro Name column, where you can specify the name of a subroutine within a macro. The second column allows you to specify a condition. The action in the macro's third column won't execute unless the condition for that action evaluates to true. The fourth column lets you document the macro. In the bottom half of the Macro Design window, you specify the arguments that apply to the selected action. In Figure 1.14, the selected action is MsgBox, which accepts four arguments: Message, Beep, Type, and Title.

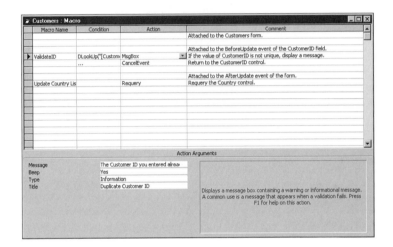

FIGURE 1.14

The design of the Customers macro, containing macro names, conditions, actions, and comments.

Modules: The Foundation to the Application Development Process

Modules, the foundation of any application, let you create libraries of functions that can be used throughout your application. Modules are usually made up of subroutines and functions. Functions always return a value; subroutines do not. By using code modules, you can do the following:

- Perform error handling
- Declare and use variables
- Loop through and manipulate recordsets
- Call Windows API and other library functions
- Create and modify system objects, such as tables and queries
- Perform transaction processing
- Perform many functions not available with macros
- Test and debug complex processes
- Create library databases

These are just a few of the tasks you can accomplish with modules. To view the design of an existing module, click Modules in the Objects list, choose the module you want to modify, and click Design to open the Module Design window. (See Figure 1.15.) The global code module in Figure 1.15 contains a General Declarations section and one function called IsLoaded. Modules and VBA are discussed in Chapters 7, "VBA: An Introduction," and 12, "Advanced VBA Techniques," respectively, and are covered extensively throughout this book.

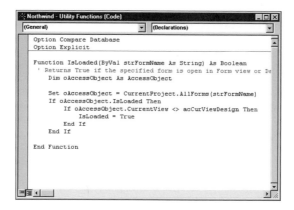

FIGURE 1.15

The global code module in Design view, showing the General Declarations section and IsLoaded function.

Object Naming Conventions

Finding a set of naming conventions—and sticking to it—is one of the keys to successful development in Access or any other programming language. When you're choosing a set of naming conventions, look for three characteristics:

- Ease of use
- Readability
- Acceptance in the developer community

The Reddick naming convention, proposed by Greg Reddick, is by far the best set of naming conventions currently published in the development world.

The Reddick naming conventions supply a standardized approach for naming objects. They were derived from the Leszynski/Reddick naming conventions that were prominent in Access versions 1.x and 2.0. These standards were adopted and used extensively by the development community and can be found in most good development books and magazine articles written in the past couple of years. The new Reddick naming conventions have been revised to deal with issues faced by people developing concurrently in Access, Visual Basic, Excel, and other Microsoft products that use the VBA language. These conventions give you an easy-to-use, consistent methodology for naming the objects in all these environments.

A summarized and slightly modified version of the Reddick conventions for naming objects is published in Appendix B, "Naming Conventions." I'll be using them throughout the book and highlighting certain aspects of them as they apply to each chapter.

Hardware Requirements

One of the downsides of Access is the amount of hardware resources it requires. The requirements for a developer are different from those for an end user, so I have broken the system requirements into two parts. As you read through these requirements, be sure to note actual versus recommended requirements.

What Hardware Does the Developer's System Require?

According to Microsoft documentation, these are the *official* minimum requirements to run Microsoft Access 2002:

- x86—processor
- Windows 98, Windows NT 4 (with at least Service Pack 6a), Windows 2000, or Windows Millennium Edition or later
- 32MB of RAM on a Windows 98 machine
- 64MB of RAM on a Windows NT or Windows 2000 machine
- 445MB of free hard disk space for the Office XP Developer and 285MB of free hard disk space for Office XP Professional
- 285MB of additional hard disk space for the Microsoft Office Developer tools
- 4MB of available registry space (Windows NT only)
- 50MB of extra hard disk space for each extra language interface
- VGA or higher resolution (SVGA 256-color recommended)
- CD-ROM drive
- A pointing device

As if all that hardware isn't enough, my personal recommendations for a development machine are much higher because you'll probably be running other applications along with Microsoft Access. You also want to greatly reduce the chance of hanging or other problems caused by low-memory conditions. I recommend the following for a development machine (in addition to Microsoft's requirements):

- P5 90MHz processor or higher
- 128MB of RAM for Windows 98 and 256MB for Windows NT or Windows 2000
- A high-resolution monitor—the larger, the better, and SVGA, if possible

> **CAUTION**
>
> If you're developing on a high-resolution monitor, you should design your forms so that they will display properly on the lowest common denominator monitor. Although you can take advantage of the high resolution in your development endeavors, don't forget that many of your users might be running your application at a lower resolution.

The bottom line for hardware is the more, the better. You just can't have enough memory or hard drive capacity. The more you have, the happier you will be using Access.

What Hardware Does the User's System Require?

Although the user's PC doesn't need to be as sophisticated as the developer's, I still recommend the following in addition to Microsoft's requirements:

- P3 or higher processor
- 64MB of RAM for Windows 98 and 128MB for Windows NT or Windows 2000 (or even higher if your application supports OLE or your user will be running your application along with other programs)

How Do I Get Started Developing an Access Application?

Many developers believe that because Access is such a rapid application-development environment, there's absolutely no need for system analysis or design when creating an application. I couldn't disagree more. As mentioned earlier in this chapter, Access applications are deceptively easy to create, and, without proper planning, they can become a disaster.

Task Analysis

The first step in the development process is *task analysis*, or considering each and every process that occurs during the user's workday—a cumbersome but necessary task. When I first started working for a large corporation as a mainframe programmer, I was required to carefully follow a task-analysis checklist. I had to find out what each user of the system did to complete his or her daily tasks, document each procedure, determine the flow of each task to the next, relate each task of each user to his or her other tasks as well as to the tasks of every other user of the system, and tie each task to corporate objectives. In this day and age of rapid application development and changing technology, task analysis in the development process seems to have gone out the window. I maintain that if care isn't taken to complete this process at least at some level, the developer will have to rewrite large parts of the application.

Data Analysis and Design

After you have analyzed and documented all the tasks involved in the system, you're ready to work on the data analysis and design phase of your application. In this phase, you must identify each piece of information needed to complete each task. These data elements must be assigned to subjects, and each subject will become a separate table in your database. For example, a subject might be a client; every data element relating to that client—the name, address, phone, credit limit, and any other pertinent information—would become fields within the client table.

You should determine the following for each data element:

- Appropriate data type
- Required size
- Validation rules

You should also determine whether each data element can be updated and whether it's entered or calculated; then you can figure out whether your table structures are normalized.

Normalization Made Easy

Normalization is a fancy term for the process of testing your table design against a series of rules that ensure that your application will operate as efficiently as possible. These rules are based on set theory and were originally proposed by Dr. E. F. Codd. Although you could spend years studying normalization, its main objective is an application that runs efficiently with as little data manipulation and coding as possible. Normalization and database design are covered in detail in Chapter 3, "Relationships: Your Key to Data Integrity." For now, here are six of the basic normalization rules:

1. Fields should be atomic—that is, each piece of data should be broken down as much as possible. For example, rather than creating a field called Name, you would create two fields: one for the first name and the other for the last name. This method makes the data much easier to work with. If you need to sort or search by first name separately from the last name, for example, you can do so without any extra effort.

2. Each record should contain a unique identifier so that you have a way of safely identifying the record. For example, if you're changing customer information, you can make sure you're changing the information associated with the correct customer. This unique identifier is called a *primary key*.

3. The primary key is a field or fields that uniquely identifies the record. Sometimes you can assign a natural primary key. For example, the social security number in an employee table should serve to uniquely identify that employee to the system. At other times, you might need to create a primary key. Because two customers could have the same name, for example, the customer name might not uniquely identify the customer to the system. It might be necessary to create a field that would contain a unique identifier for the customer, such as a customer ID.

4. A primary key should be short, stable, and simple. *Short* means it should be small in size (not a 50-character field). *Stable* means the primary key should be a field whose value rarely, if ever, changes. For example, although a customer ID would rarely change, a company name is much more likely to change. *Simple* means it should be easy for a user to work with.

5. Every field in a table should supply additional information about the record that the primary key serves to identify. For example, every field in the customer table describes the customer with a particular customer ID.

6. Information in the table shouldn't appear in more than one place. For example, a particular customer name shouldn't appear in more than one record.

Take a look at an example. The datasheet shown in Figure 1.16 is an example of a table that hasn't been normalized. Notice that the CustInfo field is repeated for each order, so if the customer address changes, it has to be changed in every order assigned to that customer. In other words, the CustInfo field is not atomic. If you want to sort by city, you're out of luck because the city is in the middle of the CustInfo field. If the name of an inventory item changes, you need to make the change in every record where that inventory item was ordered. Probably the worst problem in this example involves items ordered. With this design, you must create four fields for each item the customer orders: name, supplier, quantity, and price. This design would make it extremely difficult to build sales reports and other reports your users need to effectively run the business.

Figure 1.17 shows the same data normalized. Notice that it's been broken out into several different tables: tblCustomers, tblOrders, tblOrderDetails, and tblSuppliers. The tblCustomers table contains data that relates only to a specific customer. Each record is uniquely identified by a contrived CustID field, which is used to relate the orders table, tblOrders, to tblCustomers. The tblOrders table contains only information that applies to the entire order, rather than to a particular item that was ordered. This table contains the CustID of the customer who placed the order and the date of the order, and it's related to the tblOrderDetails table based on the OrderID. The tblOrderDetails table holds information about each item ordered for a particular OrderID. There's no limit to the potential number of items that can be ordered. As many items can be ordered as needed, simply by adding more records to the tblOrderDetails table. Finally, supplier information has been placed in a separate table, tblSuppliers, so that if any of the supplier information changes, it has to be changed in only one place.

Order#	CustInfo	OrderTotal	OrderDate	Item1Name	Item1Supplier	Item1Quantity	Item1Price
1	12 Any Street Anywhere, CA	$350.00	5/1/2001	Widget	Good Supplier	5	$1.50
2	12 Any Street Anywhere, CA	$0.00		Gadget	Bad Supplier	2	$2.25
3	12 Any Street Anywhere, CA	$0.00		Nut	Okay Supplier	7	$7.70
4	12 Any Street Anywhere, CA	$0.00		Bolt	Another Supplier	9	$3.00
5	45 Any Street Somewhere	$0.00		Pencil	Good Supplier	2	$1.50
6	45 Any Street Somewhere	$0.00		Eraser	Someone	4	$2.20
* (AutoNumber)		$0.00				0	$0.00

Record: 6 of 6

FIGURE 1.16

A table that hasn't been normalized.

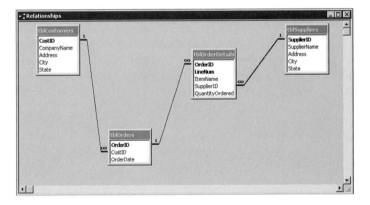

FIGURE 1.17

Data normalized into four separate tables.

Prototyping

Although the task analysis and data analysis phases of application development haven't changed much since the days of mainframes, the prototyping phase has changed. In working with mainframes or DOS-based languages, it was important to develop detailed specifications for each screen and report. I remember requiring users to sign off on every screen and report. Even a change such as moving a field on a screen meant a change order and approval for additional hours. After the user signed off on the screen and report specifications, the programmers would go off for days and work arduously to develop each screen and report. They would return to the user after many months only to hear that everything was wrong. This meant back to the drawing board for the developer and many additional hours before the user could once again review the application.

The process is quite different now. As soon as the tasks have been outlined and the data analysis finished, the developer can design the tables and establish relationships among them. The form and report prototype process can then begin. Rather than the developer going off for weeks or months before having further interaction with the user, the developer needs only a few days, using the Access wizards to quickly develop form prototypes.

Testing

As far as testing goes, you just can't do enough. I recommend that, if your application is going to be run in Windows 98, Windows NT, Windows 2000, and Windows Millennium Edition, you test in all environments. I also suggest you test your application extensively on the lowest common denominator piece of hardware—the application might run great on your machine but show unacceptable performance on your users' machines.

It usually helps to test your application both in pieces and as an integrated application. Recruit several people to test your application and make sure they range from the most savvy of users to the least computer-adept person you can find. These different types of users will probably find completely different sets of problems. Most importantly, make sure you're not the only tester of your application because you're the least likely person to find errors in your own programs.

Implementation

Your application is finally ready to go out into the world, or at least you hope so! Distribute your application to a subset of your users and make sure they know they're performing the test case. Make them feel honored to participate as the first users of the system, but warn them that problems might occur, and it's their responsibility to make you aware of them. If you distribute your application on a wide-scale basis and it doesn't operate exactly as it should, it will be difficult to regain the confidence of your users. That's why it is so important to roll out your application slowly.

Maintenance

Because Access is such a rapid application-development environment, the maintenance period tends to be much more extended than the one for a mainframe or DOS-based application. Users are much more demanding; the more you give them, the more they want. For a consultant, this is great. Just don't get into a fixed-bid situation—because of the scope of the application changing, you could very well end up on the losing end of that deal.

There are three categories of maintenance activities: bug fixes, specification changes, and frills. Bug fixes need to be handled as quickly as possible. The implications of specification changes need to be clearly explained to the user, including the time and cost involved in making the requested changes. As far as frills go, try to involve the users as much as possible in adding frills by teaching them how to enhance forms and reports and by making the application as flexible and user defined as possible. Of course, the final objective of any application is a happy group of productive users.

What's New in Access 2002

Access 2002 sports a number of new features, all worth taking a look at. Although the majority of the new features are targeted at client/server and Web integration, there are many other useful enhancements in the product. This section provides an overview of the new features. Each feature is covered in more detail in the appropriate chapter of this book.

What's New with Forms

You'll find several new features available for Access forms. The following is an overview of these features. They are covered in detail in Chapter 5 and Chapter 9.

Four new events make forms easier to work with. They include the form-level and control-level OnUndo events, the OnRecordExit event, and the OnDirty event. The form-level OnUndo event occurs when a user undoes all edits on a form. Like its form-level counterpart, the control-level OnUndo event occurs when a user undoes changes to an individual control. The OnRecordExit event occurs just before a user navigates away from a record, immediately before the current event. It is intended to simplify form/subform validations. Finally, controls now have OnDirty events. This means that you can react to a control being dirty just as you can react to a form being dirty.

In addition to all the new events available for forms, one new property and one new method are included in Access 2002. The new property is the Movable property. It is available for both forms and controls, and is used to designate whether the form or control is movable. The new method is the Move method. It allows you to programmatically move a form.

Finally, the design-time manipulation of subforms is dramatically improved in Access 2002. Scrolling through a subform in Design view is much less clumsy in Access 2002. Most importantly, you can right-click a subform control and select View|Subform in Own Window. This much-needed command opens the subform in Design view in its own window.

What's New with Reports

Just as there are several new features available for forms, there are several new features available for reports. They are covered in detail in Chapter 6 and Chapter 10.

Several new properties are available for reports. They include Modal, PopUp, BorderStyle, AutoResize, AutoCenter, MinMaxButtons, CloseButton, and ControlBox. These properties all work like their form counterparts, and act to give reports much of the same flexibility as found in forms.

Two new arguments are included with the OpenReport method. A WindowMode argument allows the user to control how the report window behaves (for example, modally). An OpenArgs argument and property allow you to easily pass information to a report as it is opened and to retrieve that information from within the report.

Just as a Movable property and Move method were added for forms, they were also added for reports. They allow you to designate whether a report is movable, and to easily write code to move the report window.

The Exciting World of PivotTables and PivotCharts

Access 2002 allows the user to view any table, query, form, ADP table, ADP view, ADP stored procedure, or ADP function in PivotTable or PivotChart view. PivotTables and PivotCharts allow users to easily perform rather complex data analyses. This means that many of the data analysis tasks once left to Microsoft Excel can now be performed directly within Microsoft Access. PivotTables and PivotCharts are available in data access pages and subforms, you can programmatically react to the events that they raise.

Welcome to the Programmability Enhancements in Access 2002

Several new programmability enhancements are included in Access 2002. They include the following:

- You can now pass a database password on the Access command line.
- DateCreated and DateModified are properties that are programmatically accessible for all Access objects.

- The Expression Builder is available in the VBE.
- A new `Printer` object and a Printers collection allow you to easily and programmatically interact with printers.
- `AddItem` and `RemoveItems` methods are *finally* available for list boxes and combo boxes.
- `CompactRepair` and `ConvertAccessProject` methods were added.
- A BrokenReference property allows you to easily detect if any of your references are broken.
- Saving and compilation of code is streamlined, improving performance when developing large applications.

As you can see, several of these features improve what a developer can do at runtime. Others enhance or improve the performance of the development environment. All help you to get your job done more efficiently and effectively. Each feature is covered in additional detail in the appropriate chapter of this book.

Access 2002 and XML

A significant amount of XML support is included in Access 2002. Both data and schema can easily be exported to XML or imported from XML, either programmatically or via the user interface. Data and schema are exported as a snapshot of the persisted table or query. Schema are exported in the W3C XSD standard. The presentation, or the format for the output, is based on an XSL document that generates HTML 4.0. The XSL presentation document and the XML data document are bound with a .htm file that executes on the user machine. XML support in Access 2002 is covered briefly in this text, and is covered in detail *in Alison Balter's Mastering Access 2002 Enterprise Development.*

What's New with ADP Projects

The new SQL Server 2000 Desktop Engine replaces what was formerly known as MSDE (Microsoft Database Engine). This robust desktop engine offers the same features that are new to SQL Server 2000. Several new features are available in the SQL Server 2000 Desktop Engine:

- The ability to create custom functions
- Extended property support (for example, lookup relationships, validation text, sub-datasheets, and so on)
- Updateable views
- A copy database and transfer database support

What's New with Data Access Pages

Data access pages in Access 2000 were limited and somewhat difficult to work with. They have been greatly improved in Access 2002. For example, the Data Access Page Designer in Access 2002 supports multiple levels of undo and redo. The Designer also allows you to select and manipulate multiple objects either with the mouse or with the keyboard. Many new sizing and drag-and-drop options are included in the new and improved Designer. The Designer supports right-click options that you would expect, and the Properties window is now limited to properties applicable to the selected object(s). In a nutshell, the Access 2002 Designer is much more like its form counterpart, rather than like a neglected stepchild.

In Access 2000 banded data access pages were very limited. In Access 2002 banded data access pages are updatable. Many new properties are available at the band level. They include AllowAdditions, AllowDeletions, and AllowEdits. A new Autosum feature facilitates the process of creating aggregate calculations.

In addition to the standard data access page layouts, Access 2002 offers Tablular, PivotChart, and Spreadsheet options. This allows you to easily customize the look and feel of your data access pages to your needs.

Finally, Access 2002 data access pages are much easier to deploy than their Access 2000 predecessors are. A page-level script notifies users who do not have a compatible browser. Relative paths (rather than absolute paths) can be set to Access databases, and Office Data Connections (ODCs) and Universal Data Links (UDLs) allow you to centralize database connection information. To top it off, the Link property of the page is exposed programmatically and can therefore be easily accessed at runtime.

In summary, data access pages in Access 2002 have the functionality that you would expect from a "form-designer." They are very easy to work with and include a very rich set of features. Data access pages are covered in detail in *Alison Balter's Mastering Access 2002 Enterprise Development*.

Other New Features Found in Access 2002

As if everything mentioned thus far is not enough, well, there's more. Other new features include increased robustness, conversion error logging, worldwide access, accessibility features, and speech recognition.

Two main pieces of functionality improve the robustness of Access 2002. The first is a much-improved compact and repair utility; the second is a better search mechanism and error-resolution process for broken references. To help with the conversion of Access 2000 applications to Access 2002, Access 2002 provides a table of information about problems that might be encountered during the conversion process.

Access 2002 adds many features that improve its ability to compete in the international market. These features include the capability to

- Display multilingual text in tables, forms, and reports
- Select language-specific spell-checking options
- Switch reading direction

In terms of accessibility, Access 2002 adds several keyboard shortcuts, as well as additional zoom powers. Finally, new speech options allow the user to dictate text and navigate menus using speech and voice commands!

PRACTICAL EXAMPLES

A Practical Example of Application Design: A Computer Consulting Firm

Consider a hypothetical computer consulting firm that wishes to track its time and billing with an Access application. First, look at the application from a design perspective.

 The system will track client contacts and the projects associated with those clients. It will allow the users to record all hours billed to, and expenses associated with, each client and project. It will also let users track pertinent information about each employee or subcontractor. The tables in the system are based on the tables produced by the Database Wizard. They have been modified somewhat, and their names have been changed to follow the Reddick naming conventions. Twenty-one tables will be included in the system. Some of these tables are built in Chapter 2, and they can all be found in the application databases on the sample code CD-ROM that accompanies this book:

- tblClients—This table contains all the pertinent information about each client; it's related to tblProjects, the table that will track the information about each project associated with a client.
- tblClientAddresses—This table contains all addresses for each client; it's related to tblClients and tblAddressTypes.
- tblAddressTypes—This table is a lookup table. It contains all valid address types for a client; it's related to tblClientAddresses.
- tblClientPhones—This table contains all phone numbers for each client; it's related to tblClients and tblPhoneTypes.
- tblPhoneTypes—This table is a lookup table. It contains all valid phone types for a client; it's related to tblClientPhones.

- tblTerms—This table is a lookup table. It contains all valid payment terms for a client; it's related to tblClients.

- tblContactType—This table is a lookup table. It contains all valid contact types for a client; it's related to tblClients.

- tblProjects—This table holds all the pertinent information about each project; it's related to several other tables: tblClients, tblPayments, tblEmployees, tblTimeCardHours, and tblTimeCardExpenses.

- tblTimeCardHours—This table is used to track the hours associated with each project and employee; it's related to tblProjects, tblTimeCards, and tblWorkCodes.

- tblPayments—This table is used to track all payments associated with a particular project; it's related to tblProjects and tblPaymentMethods.

- tblTimeCardExpenses—This table is used to track the expenses associated with each project and employee; it's related to tblProjects, tblTimeCards, and tblExpenseCodes.

- tblEmployees—This table is used to track employee information; it's related to tblTimeCards and tblProjects.

- tblTimeCards—This table is used to track each employee's hours; it's actually a bridge between the many-to-many relationship between Employees and Time Card Expenses, as well as between Employees and Time Card Hours. It's also related to tblEmployees, tblTimeCardHours, and tblTimeCardExpenses.

- tblExpenseCodes—This table is a lookup table for valid expense codes; it's related to tblTimeCardExpenses.

- tblWorkCodes—This table is a lookup table for valid work codes; it's related to tblTimeCardHours.

- tblPaymentMethods—This table is a lookup table for valid payment methods; it's related to tblPayments.

- tblCorrespondence—This table is used to track the correspondence related to a project; it's related to tblProjects and tblCorrespondenceType.

- tblCorrespondenceTypes—This table is a lookup table for valid correspondence types; it's related to tblCorrespondence.

- tblCompanyInfo—This table is a system table. It is used to store information about the company. This information is found on forms and reports throughout the system.

- tblErrorLog—This table is a system table. It is used to store runtime errors that occur.

- tblErrors—This table is a system table. It is used to store valid error codes and descriptions.

The relationships among the tables are covered in more detail in Chapter 3, but they're shown in Figure 1.18.

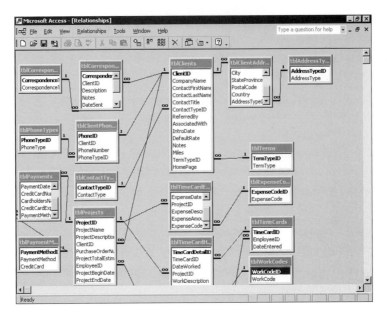

FIGURE 1.18

Relationships among tables in the time and billing system.

Summary

Before you learn about the practical aspects of Access development, you need to understand what Access is and how it fits into the application development world. Access is an extremely powerful product with a wide variety of uses; Access applications can be found on everything from the home PC to the desks of many corporate PC users going against enterprise-wide client/server databases.

After you understand what Access is and what it does, you're ready to learn about its many objects. Access applications are made up of tables, queries, forms, reports, data access pages, macros, modules, command bars, ActiveX controls, relationships, and other objects. When designed properly, an Access application effectively combines these objects to give the user a powerful, robust, utilitarian application.

What Every Developer Needs to Know About Tables

IN THIS CHAPTER

Why This Chapter Is Important

It is useful to think of table design as similar to the process of building a foundation for your house. Just as a house with a faulty foundation will fall over, an application with a poor table design will be difficult to build, maintain, and use. This chapter covers all of the ins and outs of table design in Access 2002. After reading this chapter, you will be ready to build the other components of your application, knowing that the tables you design provide the application with a strong foundation.

Building a New Table

There are several ways to add a new table to an Access 2002 database: using a wizard to help you with the design process, designing the table from scratch, building the table from a spreadsheet-like format, importing the table from another source, and linking to an external table. The process of designing a table from scratch is discussed in this chapter; importing and linking are covered extensively throughout this book. Because the other two options are not appropriate for most business solutions, they are not discussed here.

Regardless of which method you choose, start by selecting the Tables icon from the list of objects in the Database window. Icons appear allowing you to create a table in Design view, create a table using a wizard, and create a table by entering data. (See Figure 2.1.)

FIGURE 2.1

To create a new table, click the Tables icon of the Database window.

NOTE

Access 2002 natively supports the Access 2000 file format so that you can read and write to Access 2000 files under Access 2002 without converting the file format. Access 2002 gives you the option of choosing which file format to use as its default.

> From the menu bar, click Tools|Options, and select the Advanced tab. Select either Access 2000 or Access 2002 as the Default File Format that you prefer from the drop-down list box.

Designing a Table from Scratch

Designing tables from scratch offers flexibility and encourages good design principles. It is almost always the best choice when creating a custom business solution. To design a table from scratch, select Tables from the list of objects, and double-click the Create Table in Design View icon. The Table Design view window, pictured in Figure 2.2, appears. Follow these steps:

1. Define each field in the table by typing its name in the Field Name column. If you prefer, you can click the Build button on the toolbar (the button with the ellipsis) to open the Field Builder dialog box, shown in Figure 2.3. This builder lets you select from predefined fields with predefined properties. Of course, the properties can be modified at any time.

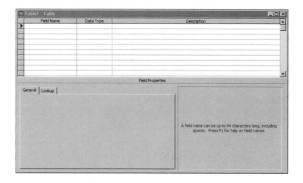

FIGURE 2.2

The Table Design view window is used to enter field names, data types, and descriptions for all the fields in a table.

FIGURE 2.3

The Field Builder dialog box lets you select from predefined fields with predefined properties.

2

TABLES

2. Tab to the Data Type column. Select the default field type, which is Text, or use the drop-down combo box to select another field type. You can find details on which field type is appropriate for your data in the "Selecting the Appropriate Field Type for Your Data" section of this chapter. Note that if you use the Field Builder, it sets a data type value for you that you can modify.

3. Tab to the Description column. What you type in this column appears on the status bar when the user is entering data into the field. This column is also great for documenting what data is actually stored in the field.

4. Continue entering fields. If you need to insert a field between two existing fields, click the Insert Rows button on the toolbar. The new field is inserted above the field you were on. To delete a field, select it and click the Delete Rows button.

5. To save your work, click the Save tool on the toolbar. The Save As dialog shown in Figure 2.4 appears. Enter a table name and click OK. A dialog appears, recommending that you establish a primary key. Every table should have a primary key. Primary keys are discussed in the section "The All-Important Primary Key," later in this chapter.

FIGURE 2.4

Use the Save As dialog box to name a table.

> **NOTE**
>
> The naming conventions for table names are similar to those for field names, except that the standard for table names is that they should begin with the tag *tbl*. Naming conventions are covered in detail in Chapter 1, "Access as a Development Tool," and in Appendix B, "Naming Conventions."

> **NOTE**
>
> Field names can be up to 64 characters long. For practical reasons, you should try to limit them to 10–15 characters—enough to describe the field without making the name difficult to type.

Field names can include any combination of letters, numbers, spaces, and other characters, excluding periods, exclamation points, accents, and brackets. I recommend that you stick to letters. Spaces in field names can be inconvenient when you're building queries, modules, and other database objects. Don't be concerned that your users will see the field names without the spaces. The Caption property of a field, discussed later in this chapter, allows you to designate the text that is displayed for your users.

Field names can't begin with leading spaces. As mentioned, field names shouldn't contain any spaces, so this shouldn't be a problem. Field names also cannot include ASCII control characters (ASCII values 0 through 31).

Try not to duplicate property names, keywords, function names, or the names of other Access objects when naming your fields. Although your code might work in some circumstances, you'll get unpredictable results in others.

To make a potential move to the client/server platform as painless as possible, you should be aware that not all field types are supported by every back-end database. Furthermore, most back-end databases impose stricter limits than Access does on the length of field names and the characters that are valid in field names. To reduce the number of problems you'll encounter if you migrate your tables to a back-end database server, these issues should be considered when you're naming the fields in your Access tables.

NOTE

Adding descriptions to your table, query, form, report, macro, and module objects goes a long way toward making your application self-documenting. This helps you, or anyone who modifies your application, perform any required maintenance on the application's objects. Documenting your application is covered in detail in Chapter 29, "Documenting Your Application."

UPSIZING TIP

It is important to be aware of the effects of the field names that you select on the potential for upsizing your tables to a client/server database. Database servers often have much more stringent rules than Access does regarding the naming of fields. For example, most back ends do not allow spaces in field names. Furthermore, most back ends limit the length of object names to 30 characters or fewer. If you create Access field names that cannot upsize, and later need to move your data to a back-end database server, you will increase the amount of work involved in the upsizing process.

This is because any queries, forms, reports, macros, and modules that use the invalid field names must be changed to reference the new field names when you move your tables to a back-end database server.

Selecting the Appropriate Field Type for Your Data

The data type you select for each field can greatly affect the performance and functionality of your application. Several factors can influence your choice of data type for each field in your table:

- The type of data that's stored in the field
- Whether the field's contents need to be included in calculations
- Whether you need to sort the data in the field
- The way you want to sort the data in the field
- How important storage space is to you

The type of data you need to store in a field has the biggest influence on which data type you select. For example, if you need to store numbers beginning with leading zeros, you can't select a Number field because leading zeros entered into a Number field are ignored. This rule affects data such as ZIP Codes (some begin with leading zeros) and department codes.

NOTE

If it is unimportant that leading zeros are stored in a field, and you simply need them to appear on forms and reports, this can be accomplished using the Format property of the field. The Format property is covered in the "Working with Field Properties" section of this chapter.

If the contents of a field need to be included in calculations, you must select a Number or Currency data type. You can't perform calculations on the contents of fields defined with the other data types. The only exception to this rule is the Date field, which can be included in date/time calculations.

You also must consider whether you will sort or index the data in a field. OLE and Hyperlink fields can't be sorted, so don't select these field types if the data in the field must be sorted or indexed. Furthermore, you must think about the *way* you want the data to be sorted. For example, in a Text field, a set of numbers would be sorted in the order of their leftmost character, then the second character from the left, and so on (that is, 1, 10, 100, 2, 20, 200) because data in the Text field is sorted in a standard ASCII sequence. On the other hand, in a Number or Currency field the numbers would be sorted in ascending value order (that is, 1, 2, 10, 20, 100, 200). You might think you would never want data sorted in a standard ASCII sequence, but sometimes it makes sense to sort certain information, such as department codes, in this fashion. Access 2002 now gives you the ability to sort or group based on a Memo field, but it only performs the sorting or grouping based on the first 255 characters. Finally, you should consider how important disk space is to you. Each field type takes up a different amount of storage space on your hard disk, which could be a factor when you're selecting a data type for a field.

Nine field types are available in Access: Text, Memo, Number, Date/Time, Currency, AutoNumber (known as Counter in Access 2.0), Yes/No, OLE Object, and Hyperlink. Table 2.1 summarizes information on the appropriate uses for each field type and the amount of storage space each type needs.

TABLE 2.1   Appropriate Uses and Storage Space for Access Field Types

Field Type	Appropriate Uses	Storage Space
Text	Data containing text, a combination of text and numbers, or numbers that don't need to be included in calculations. Examples are names, addresses, department codes, and phone numbers.	Based on what's actually stored in the field; ranges from 0 to 255 bytes.
Memo	Long text and numeric strings. Examples are notes and descriptions.	Ranges from 0 to 65,536 bytes.
Number	Data that's included in calculations (excluding money). Examples are ages, codes, such as employee ID, or payment methods.	1, 2, 4, or 8 bytes, depending on the field size selected (or 16 bytes for replication ID).
Date/Time	Dates and times. Examples are date ordered and birthdate.	8 bytes.
Currency	Currency values. Examples are amount due and price.	8 bytes.

TABLE 2.1 Continued

Field Type	Appropriate Uses	Storage Space
AutoNumber	Unique sequential or random numbers. Examples are invoice numbers and project numbers.	4 bytes (16 bytes for replication ID).
Yes/No	Fieldsthat contain one of two values (yes/no, true/false). Sample uses are indicating bills paid and tenure status.	1 bit.
OLE Object	Objects like Word documents or Excel spreadsheets. Examples are employee reviews and budgets.	0 bytes to 1 gigabyte, depending on what's stored within the field.
Hyperlink	Text, or a combination of text and numbers, stored as text and used as a hyperlink for a Web address (URL) or a UNC path. Examples are Web pages or network files.	0 to 2,048 bytes for each of the three parts that compose the address (up to 64,000 characters total).
Lookup Wizard	Used to create a field that allows theuser to select a value from another table or from a list of values via a combo box that the wizard helps to define for you.	4 bytes generally required; it needs the same storage size as the primary key for the lookup field.

NOTE

The Hyperlink field type contains a hyperlink object. The hyperlink object consists of three parts. The first part is called the *displaytext*; it's the text that appears in the field or control. The second part is the actual *file path* (UNC) or *page* (URL) the field is referring to. The third part is the *subaddress*, a location within the file or page.

The most difficult part of selecting a field type is knowing which type is best in each situation. The following detailed descriptions of each field type and when they are used should help you with this process.

Text Fields: The Most Common Field Type

Most fields are Text fields. Many developers don't realize that it's best to use Text fields for any numbers not used in calculations. Examples are phone numbers, part numbers, and ZIP Codes. Although the default size for a Text field is 50 characters, up to 255 characters can be stored in a Text field. Because Access allocates disk space dynamically, a large field size doesn't use hard disk space, but you can improve performance if you allocate the smallest field size possible. The maximum number of characters allowed in a Text field can be controlled by the FieldSize property.

Memo Fields: For Those Long Notes and Comments

Memo fields can store up to 65,536 characters of text, which can hold up to 16 pages of text for each record. Memo fields are excellent for any types of notes you want to store with table data. Remember, now you can sort by a Memo field under Access 2002.

Number Fields: For When You Need to Calculate

Number fields are used to store data that must be included in calculations. If currency amounts are included in calculations or if your calculations require the highest degree of accuracy, you should use a Currency field rather than a Number field. The Number field is actually several types of fields in one because Access 2002 offers seven sizes of numeric fields. Byte can store integers from 0–255, Integer can hold whole numbers from –32768–32767, and Long Integer can hold whole numbers ranging from less than –2 billion to just over 2 billion. Although all three of these sizes offer excellent performance, each type requires an increasingly larger amount of storage space. Two of the other numeric field sizes, Single and Double, offer floating decimal points and, therefore, much slower performance. Single can hold fractional numbers to seven significant digits; Double extends the precision to 14 significant digits. Decimal is a numeric data type new to Access 2002. The Decimal data type allows storage of very large numbers and provides decimal precision up to 28 digits! The final size, Replication ID, supplies a unique identifier required by the data synchronization process.

Date/Time Fields: Tracking When Things Happened

The Date/Time field type is used to store valid dates and times. Date/Time fields allow you to perform date calculations and make sure dates and times are always sorted properly. Access actually stores the date or time internally as an 8-byte floating point number. Time is represented as a fraction of a day.

> **NOTE**
>
> Any date and time settings you establish in the Windows Control Panel are reflected in your data. For example, if you modify the Short Date Style in Regional Settings within the Control Panel, your forms, reports, and datasheets will immediately reflect those changes.

Currency Fields: Storing Money

The Currency field type is a special type of number field used when currency values are being stored in a table. Currency fields prevent rounding off data during calculations. They hold 15 digits of whole dollars, plus accuracy to the hundredths of a cent. Although very accurate, this type of field is quite slow to process.

> **NOTE**
>
> Any changes to the currency format made in the Windows Control Panel are reflected in your data. Of course, Access doesn't automatically perform any actual conversion of currency amounts. As with dates, if you modify the currency symbol in Regional Settings within Control Panel, your forms, reports, and datasheets will immediately reflect those changes.

AutoNumber Fields: For Unique Record Identifiers

The AutoNumber field in Access 2002 is equivalent to the Counter field in Access 2.0. AutoNumber field values are automatically generated when a record is added. In Access 2.0, counter values had to be sequential. The AutoNumber field type in Access 2002 can be either sequential or random. The random assignment is useful when several users are adding records offline because it's unlikely that Access will assign the same random value to two records. A special type of AutoNumber field is a Replication ID. This randomly produced, unique number helps with the replication process by generating unique identifiers used to synchronize database replicas.

You should note a few important points about sequential AutoNumber fields. If a user deletes a record from a table, its unique number is lost forever. Likewise, if a user is adding a record but cancels the action, the unique counter value for that record is lost forever. If this behavior is unacceptable, you can generate your own counter values.

UPSIZING TIP

As with field names, if you plan to upsize your Access database to a client/server database, you must be cognizant of the field types that you select. For example, AutoNumber fields are exported as Long Integers. Because some non-Microsoft database servers do not support autonumbering, you have to create an insert trigger on the server that provides the next key value. You also can achieve autonumbering by using form-level events, but this is not desirable because the numbering will not be enforced if other applications access the data. If you are upsizing to Microsoft SQL Server, the Upsizing Wizard for Access 2002 converts all AutoNumber fields to Identity fields (the SQL Server equivalent to Autonumber).

Yes/No Fields: When One of Two Answers Is Correct

You should use Yes/No fields to store a logical true or false. What's actually stored in the field is -1 for Yes, 0 for No, or Null for no specific choice. The display format for the field determines what the user actually sees (normally Yes/No, True/False, On/Off, or a third option—Null—if you set the TripleState property of the associated control on a form to True). Yes/No fields work efficiently for any data that can have only a true or false value. Not only do they limit the user to valid choices, but also they take up only one bit of storage space.

OLE Object Fields: The Place to Store Just About Anything

OLE Object fields are designed to hold data from any OLE server application registered in Windows, including spreadsheets, word processing documents, sound, and video. There are many business uses for OLE fields, such as storing resumes, employee reviews, budgets, or videos. However, in many cases, it is more efficient to use a Hyperlink field to store a link to the document rather than store the document itself in an OLE Object field.

Hyperlink Fields: Your Link to the Internet

Hyperlink fields are used to store uniform resource locator addresses (URLs), which are links to Web pages on the Internet or on an intranet, or Universal Naming Convention paths (UNCs), which are links to a file location path. The Hyperlink field type is broken into three parts:

- What the user sees,
- The URL or UNC, and
- A subaddress, such as a range name or bookmark.

After an entry is placed in a Hyperlink field, the entry serves as a direct link to the file or page it's referring to. Hyperlinks are covered in more detail later in this chapter, in the section "Access Tables and the Internet."

Working with Field Properties

After you have added fields to your table, you need to customize their properties. Field properties let you control how data is stored as well as what data can be entered into the field. The available properties differ depending on which field type is selected. The most comprehensive list of properties is found under the Text field type. (See Figure 2.5.) The following sections describe each field property.

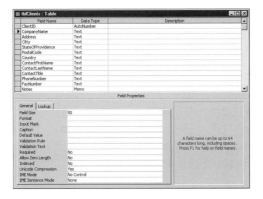

FIGURE 2.5

Field properties available for a Text field.

Field Size: Limiting What's Entered into a Field

The first property is Field Size, available for Text and Number fields only. As mentioned previously, it's best to set the Field Size to the smallest value possible. For Number fields, a small size means lower storage requirements and faster performance.

TRY IT   Build a table with the following fields and types:

CompanyID: AutoNumber

CompanyName: Text

State: Text

PhoneNumber: Text

ContactDate: Date/Time

CreditLimit: Currency

1. To set the Field Size property of the State field to two characters, click anywhere in the field, and then type 2 in the Field Size property.

2. Switch to Datasheet view. You are prompted to save the table. Name it tblCustomers. Because you have not assigned a primary key, you are prompted. When you try to enter data into the State field, notice that only two characters can be entered.

NOTE

 This example, and all others in this chapter, can be found in the Chap2TryIt.MDB file included on the book's sample code CD-ROM. Refer to this file if you want to verify that your table structures are correct.

2

TABLES

Format: Determining How Data Is Displayed

The second property is Format, available for all but OLE Object fields. It allows you to specify how Access displays your data. Access lets you select from predefined formats or create your own custom formats. The available formats differ, depending on the field's data type. For example, with Access you can select from a variety of Date/Time formats, including Short Date (7/7/96); Long Date (Sunday, July 7, 1996); Short Time (7:17); and Long Time (7:17:11AM). The formats for a Currency field include Currency ($1,767.25); Fixed (1767.25); and Standard (1,767.25).

TRY IT Set the Format property of the ContactDate field to Medium Date. Switch to Datasheet view and enter some dates in different formats, such as 07/08/96 and July 8, 1996. Notice that, no matter how you enter the dates, as soon as you tab away from the field, they appear in the format dd/mm/yy as 08-Jul-96.

NOTE

The behavior of the Short Date and Long Date formats is dictated by the Regional Options designated in the Control Panel.

TIP

Access 2002 now supports Multiple Undo and Multiple Redo actions. You can undo and redo multiple actions in Design view for MDB (Microsoft Database) tables and queries; ADP (Access Data Project) views, stored procedures, and functions; and MDB and ADP forms; reports; data access pages; macros; and modules. This feature allows you to roll forward or roll back your changes in Design view in a similar fashion to working with documents under Microsoft Word or Excel.

TIP

New to Access 2002 are shortcut keys that allow you to easily toggle between the various table views. Ctrl+>, Ctrl+Period, Ctrl+<, and Ctrl+Comma. Ctrl+> and Ctrl+Period take you to the next view. Ctrl+< and Ctrl+Comma take you to the previous view.

Input Mask: Determining What Data Goes into a Field

Another important property is Input Mask, available for Text, Number, Date/Time, and Currency fields. The Format property affects how data is displayed, but the Input Mask property controls what data is stored in a field. You can use the Input Mask property to control, on a character-by-character basis, what type of character (numeric, alphanumeric, and so on) can be stored, and whether a particular character is required. The Input Mask Wizard, shown in Figure 2.6, helps you create commonly used input masks for Text and Date fields only. To access the Input Mask Wizard, click the button to the right of the Input Mask field.

NOTE

The Input Mask Wizard is available only if you selected the Additional Wizards component during setup. If you do not, you are prompted to install the option on-the-fly the first time it is used.

For example, the input mask `000-00-0000;;_` (converted to `000\-00\-0000;;_` as soon as you tab away from the property) forces the entry of a valid social security number. Everything that precedes the first semicolon designates the actual mask. The zeros force the entry of the digits 0 through 9. The dashes are literals that appear within the control as the user enters data. The character you enter between the first and second semicolon determines whether literal characters (the dashes in this case) are stored in the field. If you enter a `0` in this position, literal characters are stored in the field; if you enter a `1` or leave this position blank, the literal characters aren't stored. The final position (after the second semicolon) indicates what character is displayed to indicate the space where the user types the next character (in this case, the underscore).

FIGURE 2.6

The Input Mask Wizard helps you enter an input mask.

Here's a more detailed example: In the mask \(999") "000\-0000;;_, the first backslash causes the character that follows it (the open parenthesis) to be displayed as a literal. The three nines allow optional numbers or spaces to be entered. The close parenthesis and space within the quotation marks are displayed as literals. The first three zeros require values 0 through 9. The dash that follows the next backslash is displayed as a literal. Four additional numbers are then required. The two semicolons have nothing between them, so the literal characters aren't stored in the field. The second semicolon is followed by an underscore, so an underscore is displayed to indicate the space where the user types the next character.

TRY IT Use the Input Mask Wizard to add a mask for the PhoneNumber field, which you should have set up as a Text field.

1. To do this, click anywhere in the PhoneNumber field, and then click the Input Mask property.

2. Click the ellipsis to the right of the Input Mask property.

3. Select Phone Number from the list of available masks and choose not to store the literal characters in the field when the wizard asks you "How do you want to store the data?"

4. Switch to Datasheet view and enter a phone number. Notice how your cursor skips over the literal characters. Try leaving the area code blank; Access should allow you to do this.

5. Now try to enter a letter in any position—Access should prohibit you from doing this.

6. Next, try to leave any character from the seven-digit phone number blank. Access shouldn't let you do this, either.

> **TIP**
>
> When you use an input mask, the user is always in Overtype mode. This behavior is a feature of the product and can't be altered.

Caption: A Great Timesaver

The next available property is Caption. The text placed in this property becomes the caption for fields in Datasheet view. It's also used as the caption for the attached label added to data-bound controls when you add them to forms and reports. The Caption property becomes important whenever you name your fields without spaces. Whatever is in the Caption property overrides the field name for use in Datasheet view, on forms, and on reports.

> **NOTE**
>
> The term *data-bound control* refers to a control that is bound to a field in a table or query. The term *attached label* refers to the label attached to a data-bound control.

> **TIP**
>
> It's important to set the Caption property for fields *before* you build any forms or reports that use them. When a form or report is produced, Access looks at the current caption. If the caption is added or modified at a later time, captions for that field on existing forms and reports aren't modified.

Default Value: Saving Data-Entry Time

Another important property is the Default Value property, used to specify the default value that Access will place in the field when the user adds new records to the table. Default values, which can be either text or expressions, can save the data-entry person a lot of time. However, they do not in any way validate what's entered into a field.

TIP

Default values are automatically carried into any queries and forms containing the field. Unlike what happens with the Caption property, this occurs whether the default value was created before or after the query or form is created.

UPSIZING TIP

If you plan to upsize your Access database to a client/server database, you must be aware that default values are not always moved to the server, even if the server supports them. You can set up default values directly on the server, but these values do *not* automatically appear when new records are added to the table unless the record is saved without data being added to the field containing the default value. As in autonumbering, default values can be implemented at the form level, with the same drawbacks. If the Upsizing Wizard for Access 2002 is used to move the data to Microsoft SQL Server, default values are exported to your server database.

TRY IT Enter the following default values for the State, ContactDate, and CreditLimit fields:

State: **CA**

ContactDate: **=Date()**

CreditLimit: **1000**

Switch to Datasheet view and add a new record. Notice that default values appear for the State, ContactDate, and CreditLimit fields. You can override these defaults, if you want.

UPSIZING TIP

Date() is a built-in VBA function that returns the current date and time. When used as a default value for a field, the current date is entered into the field when a new row is added to the table.

2

TABLES

Validation Rule: Controlling What's Entered in a Field

The Default Value property suggests a value to the user, but the Validation Rule property actually limits what the user can place in the field. Validation rules can't be violated; the database engine strictly enforces them. As with the Default Value property, this property can contain either text or a valid Access expression, but user-defined functions can't be included in the Validation Rule property. You also can't include references to forms, queries, or tables in the Validation Rule property.

> **TIP**
>
> If you set the Validation Rule property but not the Validation Text property, Access automatically displays a standard error message whenever the validation rule is violated. To display a custom message, you must enter your message text in the Validation Text property.

> **UPSIZING TIP**
>
> If you plan to upsize your Access database to a database server, you should be aware that validation rules are not always exported to the server. They must be re-created using triggers on the server. No Access-defined error messages are displayed when a server validation rule is violated. Your application should be coded to provide the appropriate error messages. You also can perform validation rules at the form level, but they are not enforced if the data is accessed by other means. If the Upsizing Wizard for Access 2002 is used to move the data to Microsoft SQL Server, validation rules are exported to the server database.

TRY IT Add the following validation rules to the fields in your table (Access will place quotes around the state abbreviations as soon as you tab away from the property):

State: `In (CA, AZ, NY, MA, UT)`

ContactDate: `<= Date()`

CreditLimit: `Between 0 And 5000`

1. Switch to Datasheet view. If the table already contains data, when you save your changes, the message shown in Figure 2.7 appears.

NOTE

In this example, the expression <= Date() is used to limit the value entered into the field to a date that is on or before the current date. Because the Date() expression always returns the current date, the validation rule applies whether the user is adding a new row, or is modifying an existing row.

FIGURE 2.7

The message box asking whether you want to validate existing data.

If you select Yes, Access tries to validate all existing data using the new rules. If any errors are found, you're notified that errors occurred, but you aren't informed of the offending records. (See Figure 2.8.) You have to build a query to find all the records violating the new rules.

FIGURE 2.8

A warning that all data did not validate successfully.

If you select No, Access doesn't try to validate your existing data, and you aren't warned of any problems.

2. After you have entered Datasheet view, try to enter an invalid state in the State field; you should see the message box displayed in Figure 2.9. As you can see, this isn't the most friendly message, which is why you should create a custom message by using the Validation Text property.

FIGURE 2.9

The message displayed when a validation rule is violated, and no validation text has been entered.

TIP

Validation rules entered at a table level are automatically applied to forms and queries built from the table. This occurs whether the rule was entered before or after the query or form was built. If you create a validation rule for a field, Access won't allow Null values to be entered in the field, which means the field can't be left blank. If you want to allow the field to be left Null, you must add the Null to the validation expression:

```
In (CA, AZ, NY, MA, UT) or Is Null
```

Validation Text: Providing Error Messages to the User

Use the Validation Text property to specify the error message users see when they violate the validation rule. The Validation Text property must contain text; expressions aren't valid in this property.

TRY IT Add the following to the Validation Text properties of the State, ContactDate, and CreditLimit fields:

State: **The State Must Be CA, AZ, NY, MA, or UT**

ContactDate: **The Contact Date Must Be On or Before Today**

CreditLimit: **The Credit Limit Must Be Between 0 and 5000**

Try entering invalid values for each of the three fields, and observe the error messages.

Required: Making the User Enter a Value

The Required property is very important—it determines whether you require that a value be entered into a field. This property is useful for foreign key fields, when you want to make sure data is entered into the field. It's also useful for any field containing information that's needed for business reasons (company name, for example).

> **NOTE**
>
> A *foreign key field* is a field that is looked up in another table. For example, in the case of a Customers table and an Orders table, both might contain a CustomerID field. In the Customers table, the CustomerID is the primary key field. In the Orders table, the CustomerID is the foreign key field because its value is looked up in the Customer table.

TRY IT   Set the Required property of the CompanyName and PhoneNumber fields to Yes. Switch to Datasheet view and try to add a new record, leaving the CompanyName and PhoneNumber fields blank. Make sure you enter a value for at least one of the other fields in the record. When you try to move off the record, the error message shown in Figure 2.10 appears.

FIGURE 2.10
A message appears when you leave blank a field blank that has the Required property set to Yes.

Allow Zero Length: Accommodating Situations with Nonexistent Data

The Allow Zero Length property is similar to the Required property. Use it to determine whether you allow the user to enter a zero-length string (""). A zero-length string isn't the same as a Null (which represents the absence of an entry); a zero-length string indicates that the data doesn't exist for that particular field. For example, a foreign employee might not have a social security number. By entering a zero-length string, the data-entry person can indicate that the social security number doesn't exist.

TRY IT   Add a new field called ContactName and set its Required property to Yes. Try to add a new record and enter two quotes ("") in the ContactName field. You should not get an error message because, in Access 2002, the Allow Zero Length property defaults to Yes. Your zero-length string will appear blank when you move off the field. Return to the Design view of the table. Change the setting for the Allow Zero Length property to No. Go back to Datasheet view and once again enter two quotes in the ContactName field. This time you should not be successful. You should get the error message shown in Figure 2.11.

FIGURE 2.11

The result of entering " " when the Allow Zero Length property is set to No.

CAUTION

In previous versions of Access, the default setting for the Allow Zero Length property was No. Under Access 2002, Microsoft has changed this default setting to Yes. Pay close attention to this new default behavior, especially if you're accustomed to working with prior releases of the product.

TIP

Don't forget that if you want to cancel changes to the current field, press Esc once. To abandon all changes to a record, press Esc twice.

TIP

The Required and Allow Zero Length properties interact with each other. If the Required property is set to Yes and the Allow Zero Length property is set to No, you're being as strict as possible with your users. Not only must they enter a value, but also that value can't be a zero-length string.

If the Required property is set to Yes and the Allow Zero Length property is set to Yes, you're requiring users to enter a value, but that value can be a zero-length string. However, if the Required property is set to No and the Allow Zero Length property is set to No, you're allowing users to leave the field Null (blank), but not allowing them to enter a zero-length string.

Finally, if you set the Required property to No and the Allow Zero Length property to Yes, you're being the most lenient with your users. In this case, they can leave the field Null or enter a zero-length string.

Indexes: Speeding Up Searches

Indexes are used to improve performance when the user searches a field. Although it's generally best to include too many indexes rather than too few, indexes do have downsides (see the Tip following the Try It example). A general rule is to provide indexes for all fields regularly used in searching and sorting, and as criteria for queries.

> **TRY IT** Set the Indexed property of the CompanyName, ContactName, and State fields to `Yes - (Duplicates OK)`. Click the Indexes button on the toolbar. Your screen should look like Figure 2.12.

FIGURE 2.12

The Indexes window shows you all the indexes defined for a table.

> **TIP**
>
> To create non–primary-key, multifield indexes, you must use the Indexes window. You create an index with one name and more than one field. See Figure 2.13, which shows an index called StateByCredit that's based on the combination of the CreditLimit and State fields. Notice that only the first field in the index has an index name. The second field, State, appears on the line below the first field but doesn't have an index name.
>
> Indexes speed up searching, sorting, and grouping data. The downside is that they take up hard disk space and slow down the process of editing, adding, and deleting data. Although the benefits of indexing outweigh the detriments in most cases, you should not index every field in each table. Create indexes only for fields, or combinations of fields, on which the user will search or sort. Do not create indexes for fields that contain highly repetitive data, such as a field that can contain only two different values. Finally, never index Yes/No fields. They are only 1 bit in storage size and furthermore apply to the previous rule in that they can take on only one of two values. For these reasons, indexes offer no benefits with Yes/No fields.

FIGURE 2.13

A multifield index called StateByCredit, based on a combination of the CreditLimit and State fields.

UPSIZING TIP

Indexes are equally important on a database server. When upsizing an Access database to a non-Microsoft server, no indexes are created. All indexes need to be re-created on the back-end database server. If your database server is running Microsoft SQL Server, you can use the Access Upsizing Wizard for Access 2002 to upsize your Access database. This tool creates indexes for server tables in the place where the indexes exist in your Access tables.

Unicode Compression

Another important property is Unicode Compression. The Unicode Compression property applies to Text and Memo fields only. This property is used to designate whether you want the data in the field to be compressed using Unicode compression. Prior to Access 2000, data was stored in the DBCS (double-byte character set) format, which was designed to store character data for certain languages such as Chinese. With Access 2000 and Access 2002, all character data is stored in the Unicode 2-byte representation format. Although this format requires more space for each character (2 bytes, rather than 1 byte), the Unicode Compression property allows the data to be compressed if possible. If the character set being used allows compression, and the Unicode Compression property is set to Yes, the data in the column is stored in a compressed format.

The All-Important Primary Key

The most important index in a table is called the Primary Key index; it ensures uniqueness of the fields that make up the index and also gives the table a default order. You must set a primary key for the fields on the one side of a one-to-many relationship. To create a Primary Key index, select the fields you want to establish as the primary key, and then click the Primary Key button on the toolbar.

Figure 2.14 shows the tblCustomer table with a Primary Key index based on the CompanyID field. Notice that the Index Name of the field designated as the primary key of the table is called PrimaryKey. Note that the Primary and Unique properties for this index are both set to Yes (true).

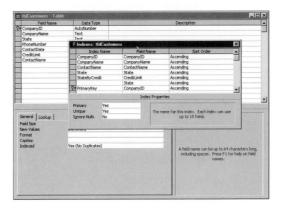

FIGURE 2.14

A Primary Key index based on the CompanyID field.

Working with the Lookup Feature

Using the Lookup Wizard, you can instruct a field to look up its values in another table or query or from a fixed list of values. You can also display the list of valid values in a combo or list box. A lookup is generally created from the foreign key (the "many" side) to the primary key (the "one" side) of a one-to-many relationship.

The Lookup Wizard can be invoked by selecting Lookup Wizard from the list of data types for the field. The first wizard dialog box asks whether you want to look up the values in a table or query or whether you want to input the values. I recommend that you always look up the values in a table or query; this makes your application easier to maintain. The second dialog box asks you to indicate the table or query used to look up the values. Select a table or query and click Next to open the third dialog box. This step of the Lookup Wizard asks you which field in the table or query will be used for the lookup. The fourth step of the Lookup Wizard, shown in Figure 2.15, gives you the opportunity to control the width of the columns in your combo or list box.

2

TABLES

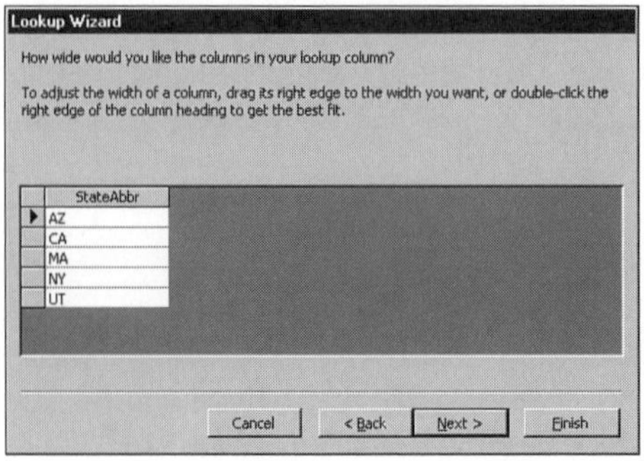

FIGURE 2.15

In the fourth step of the Lookup Wizard, you can adjust the column widths.

TIP

To work through the previous example, it is best that you use the Chap2.MDB sample database file. All the lookup tables have already been added to the sample database.

NOTE

If you select more than one field for your lookup and one is a key column, such as an ID, the Hide Key Column check box appears. You should leave this checked; it automatically hides the key column in the lookup, even though the end result will be bound to the key field.

Finally, the wizard lets you specify a title for your lookup column. When you click Finish, you will be prompted to save the table and all the appropriate properties are filled in by the wizard; they appear on the Lookup tab of the field. (See Figure 2.16.) The Display Control property is set to Combo Box, indicating that the valid values will be displayed in a combo box. This occurs whether the user is in Datasheet view or in a form. The Row Source Type indicates that the source for the combo box is a table or query and shows the actual SQL Select statement used to populate the combo box. Other properties show which column in the combo box is bound to data, how many columns are in the combo box, the width of the combo box, and the width of each column in the combo box. These properties are covered in more detail in Chapter 5, "What Every Developer Needs to Know About Forms." You can modify the SQL statement for the combo box later, if necessary.

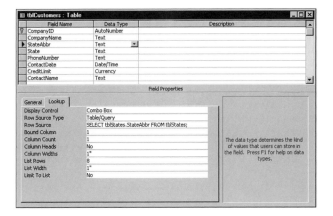

FIGURE 2.16
The field properties set by the Lookup Wizard.

NOTE

In my opinion, the lookup feature is more of a hindrance than a help. Once the lookup feature is invoked, you and the users will no longer have easy access to the underlying numeric values stored in the foreign key field. You will see only the lookup value displayed in the combo box. This makes troubleshooting application problems very difficult.

The main advantage of the lookup feature is that it facilitates the process of building forms by automatically adding a combo box to a form whenever a field with a lookup is placed on a form. Personally, I find it so easy to build a combo box on a form that I do not find the lookup feature to be much of a timesaver. After evaluating the pros and cons of this user-related feature, I opted to eliminate it from the applications that I build.

Working with Table Properties

In addition to field properties, you can specify properties that apply to a table as a whole. To access the table properties, click the Properties button on the toolbar while in a table's Design view. The available table properties are shown in Figure 2.17. The Description property is used mainly for documentation purposes. The Default View property designates the view in which the table appears when the user first opens it. The Validation Rule property specifies validations that must occur at a record level, instead of a field level. For example, credit limits might differ depending on what state a customer is in. In that case, what's entered in one field depends on the value in another field. By entering a table-level validation rule, it doesn't matter in what order the user enters the data. A table-level validation rule ensures that the proper dependency between fields is enforced. The validation rule might look something like this:

```
[State] In ("CA","NY") And [CreditLimit]<=2500 Or _
    [State] In ("MA","AZ") And [CreditLimit]<=3500 Or _
    [State] Not In ("CA", "NY", "MA", "AZ")
```

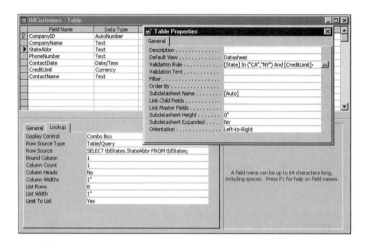

FIGURE 2.17

Viewing the available table properties.

This validation rule requires a credit limit of $2,500 or less for applicants in California and New York and a limit of $3,500 or less for applicants in Massachusetts and Arizona, but it doesn't specify a credit limit for residents of any other states. Table-level validation rules can't be in conflict with field-level validation rules.

The Validation Text property determines the message that appears when the user violates the validation rule. If this property is left blank, a default message appears.

The Filter property is used to indicate a subset of records that appears in a datasheet, form, or query. The Order By property is used to specify a default order for the records. The Filter and Order By properties aren't generally applied as properties of a table.

The Subdatasheet Name property identifies the name of a table used as a drill-down. If set to Auto, the drill-down table is automatically detected, based on relationships established in the database. The Link Child Fields and Link Master Fields properties are implemented to designate the fields, which are used to link the current table with the table specified in the Subdatasheet Name property. These properties should be left blank when Auto is selected for the Subdatasheet Name. The Subdatasheet Height is used to specify the maximum height of the subdatasheet, and the Subdatasheet Expanded property is used to designate whether the subdatasheet is automatically displayed in an expanded state.

The Orientation property determines the layout direction for the table when it is displayed. The default setting for USA English is obviously Left-to-Right. This property is language-specific, and the Right-to-Left setting is only available if you are using a language version of Microsoft Access that supports right-to-left language displays. Arabic and Hebrew are examples of right-to-left languages. You must run a 32-bit Microsoft operating system that offers right-to-left support, such as the Arabic version of Windows 2000, to take advantage of this feature in Access. By installing the Microsoft Office Multilanguage Pack and the Microsoft Office Proofing Tools for a specific language, and by enabling the specific right-to-left language under the Microsoft Office Language Settings, you can also turn on right-to-left support.

Using Indexes to Improve Performance

As previously mentioned, indexes can help you improve your application's performance. You should create indexes on any fields you sort, group, join, or set criteria for, unless those fields contain highly repetitive data. Queries can greatly benefit from indexes, especially when indexes are created for fields included in your criteria, fields used to order the query, and fields used to join two tables that are not permanently related but are joined in a query. In fact, you should always create indexes for fields on both sides of a join. If your users are using the Find dialog box, indexes can help reduce the search time. Remember, the downsides to indexes are the disk space they require and the amount of time it takes to update them when adding, deleting, and updating records. You should always perform benchmarks with your own applications, but you will probably find indexes helpful in many situations.

> **NOTE**
>
> When you establish a relationship between two tables, an index for the table on the many side of the relationship (the foreign key field) is automatically created. For example, if you relate tblOrders to tblCustomers based on the CustomerID field, an internal index is automatically created for the CustomerID field in the tblOrders table. It is therefore not necessary for you to explicitly create a foreign key index. Relationships are covered in Chapter 3, "Relationships: Your Key to Data Integrity."

Access Tables and the Internet

Microsoft has made it easier to develop Internet-aware applications by including the Hyperlink field type and by allowing users to save table data as HTML. The Hyperlink field type lets your users easily store UNC or URL addresses within their tables. The ability to save table data as HTML makes it easy for you or your users to publish table data on an Internet or intranet site. These features are covered in the following sections.

The Hyperlink Field Type

By using the Hyperlink field type, your users can store a different UNC or URL address for each record in the table. Although a UNC or URL address can be typed directly into a field, it's much easier to enter the address by using the Insert Hyperlink dialog box. (See Figure 2.18.) Here, users can graphically browse hyperlink addresses and subaddresses, and the address is entered automatically when they exit the dialog box. To invoke the Insert Hyperlink dialog box, choose Insert|Hyperlink with the cursor placed in the Hyperlink field, or click the Insert Hyperlink button.

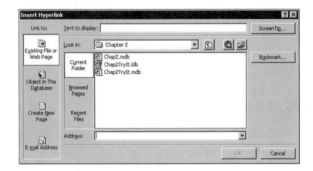

FIGURE 2.18

With the Insert Hyperlink dialog box, users can select or create a hyperlink object for the field.

The Text to Display text box is used to enter the text the user will see when viewing the field data in Datasheet view, in a form, or on a report. The hyperlink can be to any of the following:

- An existing file or Web page
- Another object in the current database
- A new data access page
- An e-mail address

To select an existing file or Web page, click the appropriate Link To icon and either type the file or Web page name or select it from the list of Recent Files, Browsed Pages, or the Current Folder. The Browse for File button is used to browse for an existing file, and the Browse the Web button is used to browse for an existing Web page.

To link to an object in the current database, click the appropriate Link To icon. Click a plus (+) sign to expand the list of tables, queries, forms, reports, pages, macros, or modules. Then click the database object to which you want to link.

To link to a new data access page that you create, click the appropriate Link To icon. Enter the name of the new page and designate whether you want to edit the new page now or later.

To designate an e-mail address you want to link to, click the appropriate Link To icon. Enter the e-mail address and subject, or select from the list of recently used email addresses.

After all the required information has been entered, the link is established, and the hyperlink is entered in the field. If a UNC was entered, clicking the hyperlink invokes the application associated with the file. The selected file is opened, and the user is placed in the part of the document designated in the subaddress. If a URL is entered, and the user is logged on to the Internet or connected to his or her company's intranet, the user is taken directly to the designated page. If the user isn't currently connected to the Internet or an intranet, the Connect To dialog appears, allowing her to log on to the appropriate network.

Saving Table Data as HTML

Table data can be easily saved as HTML so that it can be published on an Internet or intranet site. You can save a file as HTML by using the File|Export menu item. The steps are as follows:

1. Choose File|Export.
2. Select HTML Documents (*.html; *.htm) from the Save as Type combo box.
3. Select a name and location for the .htm file and click Save. Saving a file as HTML with this procedure does not load the browser.

Figure 2.19 shows you how your published Access table might look, and Figure 2.20 displays the underlying HTML that can be edited by using any HTML editor.

> **NOTE**
>
> Building applications for the Internet is covered extensively in *Alison Balter's Mastering Access 2002 Enterprise Development.*

2

TABLES

FIGURE 2.19

Viewing an HTML document in Internet Explorer after a table was saved as HTML. (Note the ugly gaps for fields lacking data.)

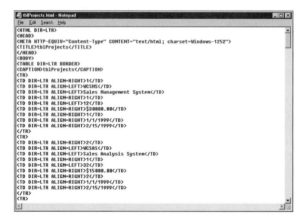

FIGURE 2.20

Viewing HTML generated when a table is saved as HTML.

Saving Table Data as XML

Access 2002 allows you to export Jet or SQL data to XML, and to import data from XML. Using either code or the Access user interface to export XML data, you can generate data (XML), schema (XSD), and presentation (XSL) files. Although in-depth coverage of Access and XML is included in *Alison Balter's Mastering Access 2002 Enterprise Development*, this section provides you with basic information about the import and export processes. To export a table to XML, follow these steps:

1. Select the table you want to export.

2. Select Export from the File menu, or right-click the table and then select Export. The Export table dialog appears.

3. Select XML documents from the Save as Type drop-down.

4. Enter a filename and location and click Export. The XML Export dialog appears. (See Figure 2.21.)

5. Select whether you want to export Data (XML), Schema of the Data, and/or a Presentation of your Data. Click OK. The appropriate files are generated (based on which of the three options you selected).

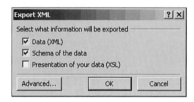

FIGURE 2.21

The XML Export dialog allows you to designate the specifics of the export process.

Just as you can export data to XML, you can import XML data into Access. To import XML data into an Access table, follow these steps:

1. Select File | Get External Data | Import, or right-click within the Database window and select Import. The Import dialog appears.

2. Select XML Document from the Files of Type drop-down list.

3. Select the file you want to import and click Import. The Import XML dialog appears. (See Figure 2.22.)

4. Click Options to designate import options (for example, whether you want to append to or overwrite existing data).

5. Click OK to perform the import.

FIGURE 2.22

The Import XML dialog allows you to designate options used for the import process. You also have the ability to save table data under the XML format.

Working with PivotTable and PivotChart Views

Access 2002 now supports two very useful views borrowed from Microsoft Excel for analyzing data: PivotTable and PivotChart views. You can now view any MDB table or query; ADP table, view, stored procedure, or function; or a form within a PivotTable or PivotChart view. If you are familiar with Microsoft Excel, you probably know how beneficial these views can be for analyzing data. To set up and display a PivotTable view, click either the View menu or the View icon on the toolbar and select PivotTable view. To work with a PivotChart view, click either the View menu or the View icon on the toolbar and select PivotChart view.

You can save both PivotTable views and PivotChart views as data access pages that others can view using Microsoft Internet Explorer 5.0 or later. You can use forms in PivotTable and PivotChart views as subforms in the same way as you use forms under Datasheet view. As a developer, you can take advantage of writing code behind forms within PivotTable and PivotChart views to trigger actions based on new events that are available with these views.

To switch to PivotTable view, follow these steps:

1. Use the View button on the toolbar to select PivotTable view. The view will change to appear as in Figure 2.23.

2. Drag and drop fields to be used as column headings, row headings, totals or detail fields, and filter fields to the various parts of the PivotTable.

3. Move fields around as needed to analyze the data.

FIGURE 2.23

Using PivotTable view, you can quickly and easily analyze your table data any way that you'd like. You also have the ability to save table data under the XML format.

To switch to PivotChart view, follow these steps:

1. Use the View button on the toolbar to select PivotChart view. The view will change to appear as in Figure 2.24.

2. Drag and drop fields to be used as data series, categories, data fields, and filter fields to the various parts of the pivot chart.

3. Move fields around as needed to customize the chart.

4. Change any chart options to customize the look of the chart.

FIGURE 2.24

Using PivotChart view, you can build charts that represent the data stored in your application tables. You also have the ability to save table data under the XML format.

Designing the Tables Needed for the Computer Consulting Firm's Time and Billing Application

Now, create a new database and try designing a few of the tables needed by the computer consulting firm's Time and Billing application. You will build tblClients and tblProjects. The main table for the application, tblClients will be used to track the key information about each client. The second table, tblProjects, will hold all the key information users need to store on the projects they're working on for each client. Table 2.2 shows the field names, data types, and sizes for each field in tblClients. You should include indexes for all fields except Notes. Table 2.3 shows the properties that need to be set for these fields. Table 2.4 shows the fields, data types, and sizes for the fields in tblProjects, and Table 2.5 shows the properties that need to be set for these fields. You should include indexes for all fields except ProjectDescription.

TABLE 2.2   Field Names, Data Types, and Sizes for the Fields in tblClients

Field Name	Data Type	Size
ClientID	AutoNumber	Long Integer (Stored as 4)
CompanyName	Text	50
ContactFirstName	Text	30
ContactLastName	Text	50
ContactTitle	Text	50
ContactTypeID	Number	Long Integer (Stored as 4)
ReferredBy	Text	30
AssociatedWith	Text	30
IntroDate	Date/Time	Stored as 8
DefaultRate	Currency	Stored as 8
Notes	Memo	-
Miles	Number	Long Integer (Stored as 4)
TermTypeID	Number	Long Integer (Stored as 4)
HomePage	Hyperlink	-

TABLE 2.3   Properties That Need to Be Set for the Fields in tblClients

Field Name	Property	Value
ClientID	Caption	Client ID
ClientID	Set as primary key	-
CompanyName	Caption	Company Name
CompanyName	Required	Yes
ContactFirstName	Caption	Contact First Name
ContactLastName	Caption	Contact Last Name
ContactTitle	Caption	Contact Title
ContactTypeID	Caption	Contact Type ID
ReferredBy	Caption	Referred By
AssociatedWith	Caption	Associated With
IntroDate	Input Mask	99/99/0000
IntroDate	Caption	Intro DateIntroDate
	Default Value	=Date()
IntroDate	Validation Rule	<=Date()
IntroDate	Validation Text	Date Entered Must Be On Or Before Today
IntroDate	Required	Yes
DefaultRate	Caption	Default Rate
DefaultRate	Default Value	150
DefaultRate	Validation Rule	Between 75 and 200
DefaultRate	Validation Text	Rate Must Be Between 75 and 200
DefaultRate	Format	Currency
Miles	Validation Rule	>=0
Miles	Validation Text	Miles Must Be Greater Than or Equal to Zero
TermTypeID	Caption	Term Type ID
HomePage	Caption	Home Page

TABLE 2.4   Field Names, Data Types, and Sizes for the Fields in tblProjects

Field Name	Data Type	Size
ProjectID	AutoNumber	Long Integer (Stored as 4)
ProjectName	Text	50
ProjectDescription	Memo	-
ClientID	Number	Long Integer (Stored as 4)
PurchaseOrderNumber	Text	30
ProjectTotalEstimate	Currency	8
EmployeeID	Number	Long Integer (Stored as 4)
ProjectBeginDate	Date/Time	Stored as 8
ProjectEndDate	Date/Time	Stored as 8

TABLE 2.5   Properties That Need to Be Set for the Fields in tblProjects

Field Name	Property	Value
ProjectID	Caption	Project ID
ProjectID	Set as primary key	-
ProjectName	Caption	Project Name
ProjectName	Required	Yes
ProjectDescription	Caption	Project Description
ClientID	Caption	Client ID
ClientID	Default Value	Remove default value of 0
ClientID	Required	Yes
PurchaseOrderNumber	Caption	Purchase Order Number
ProjectTotalEstimate	Caption	Project Total Estimate
ProjectTotalEstimate	Format	Currency
EmployeeID	Caption	Employee ID
ProjectBeginDate	Input Mask	99/99/0000
ProjectBeginDate	Caption	Project Begin Date
	Input Mask	99/99/0000
ProjectEndDate	Caption	Project End Date

The rest of the tables needed by the Time and Billing application are listed in Appendix A, "Table Structures." The finished table structures can be found in

CHAP2.MDB. This file, and all files referred to in this book, can be found on the book's sample code CD-ROM.

Summary

Tables are the foundation for your application. A poorly designed table structure can render an otherwise well-designed application useless. This chapter begins by walking you through several methods for creating tables. It then discusses theoretical issues, such as selecting the correct field type and effectively using field properties. Each property, and its intended use, is discussed in detail. Finally, table properties and indexes are covered. After reading this chapter, you should be ready to harness the many features the Access table designer has to offer.

2

TABLES

Relationships: Your Key to Data Integrity

IN THIS CHAPTER

Why This Chapter Is Important

A *relationship* exists between two tables when one or more key fields from one table are matched to one or more key fields in another table. The fields in both tables usually have the same name, data type, and size. Relationships are a necessary by-product of the data normalization process. Data normalization was introduced in Chapter 1, "Access as a Development Tool" it is covered in additional detail in this chapter. *Normalization* is the process of eliminating duplicate information from your system by splitting information into several tables, each containing a unique value (primary key). Although data normalization brings many benefits, you need to relate your application's tables to each other so that your users can view the data in the system as a single entity. After you define relationships between tables, you can build queries, forms, reports, and data access pages that combine information from multiple tables. In this way, you can reap all the benefits of data normalization while ensuring that your system provides users with all the information they need.

Introduction to Relational Database Design

Many people believe that Access is such a simple product to use, that database design is something they don't need to worry about. I couldn't disagree more! Just as a house without a foundation will fall over, a database with poorly designed tables and relationships will fail to meet the needs of the users.

The History of Relational Database Design

Dr. E.F. Codd first introduced formal relational database design in 1969 while he was at IBM. It is based on set theory and predicate logic. Relational theory applies to both databases and database applications. Codd developed 12 rules that determine how well an application and its data adhere to the relational model. Since Codd first conceived these 12 rules, the number of rules has expanded into the hundreds!

You should be happy to learn that, as an application development environment, although not perfect, Microsoft Access measures up quite well as a relational database system.

Goals of Relational Database Design

The number one goal of relational database design is to, as closely as possible, develop a database that models some real-world system. This involves breaking the real-world system into tables and fields, and determining how the tables relate to each other. Although, on the surface, this might appear to be a trivial task, it can be an extremely cumbersome process to translate a real-world system into tables and fields.

A properly designed database has many benefits. The process of adding, editing, deleting, and retrieving table data is greatly facilitated by a properly designed database. Reports are easy to build. Most importantly, the database becomes easy to modify and maintain.

Rules of Relational Database Design

To adhere to the relational model, certain rules must be followed. These rules determine what is stored in a table, and how the tables are related.

The Rules of Tables

Each table in a system must store data about a single entity. An entity usually represents a real-life object or event. Examples of objects are customers, employees, and inventory items. Examples of events include orders, appointments, and doctor visits.

The Rules of Uniqueness and Keys

Tables are composed of rows and columns. To adhere to the relational model, each table must contain a unique identifier. Without a unique identifier, it becomes programmatically impossible to uniquely address a row. You guarantee uniqueness in a table by designating a *primary key*, which is a single column or a set of columns that uniquely identifies a row in a table.

Each column or set of columns in a table that contains unique values is considered a *candidate key*. One candidate key becomes the *primary key*. The remaining candidate keys become *alternate keys*. A primary key made up of one column is considered a *simple key*. A primary key comprised of multiple columns is considered a *composite key*.

It is generally a good idea to pick a primary key that is

- Minimal (has as few columns as possible)
- Stable (rarely changes)
- Simple (familiar to the user)

Following these rules greatly improves the performance and maintainability of your database application, particularly if you are dealing with large volumes of data.

Consider the example of an employee table. An employee table is generally composed of employee-related fields such as social security number, first name, last name, hire date, salary, and so on. The combination of the first name and the last name fields could be considered a primary key. This choice might work, until the company hires two employees with the same name. Although the first and last names could be combined with additional fields to constitute uniqueness (for example, hire date), this would violate the rule of keeping the primary key minimal. Furthermore, an employee might get married and her last name might change.

Using a name as the primary key violates the principle of stability. The social security number might be a valid choice, but a foreign employee might not have a social security number. This is a case where a derived, rather than a natural, primary key is appropriate. A *derived key* is an artificial key that you create. A *natural key* is one that is already part of the database.

I would suggest adding EmployeeID as an AutoNumber field. Although the field would violate the rule of simplicity (because an employee number is meaningless to the user), it is both small and stable. Because it is numeric, it is also efficient to process. In fact, I use AutoNumber fields (an identity field in SQL Server) as primary keys for most of the tables that I build.

Foreign Keys and Domains

A *foreign key* in a table is the field that relates to the primary key in a second table. For example, the CustomerID is the primary key in the Customers table. It is the foreign key in the Orders table.

A *domain* is a pool of values from which columns are drawn. A simple example of a domain is the specific data range of employee hire dates. In the case of the Order table, the domain of the CustomerID column is the range of values for the CustomerID in the Customers table.

Normalization and Normal Forms

One of the most difficult decisions that you face as a developer is what tables to create, and what fields to place in each table, as well as how to relate the tables that you create. *Normalization* is the process of applying a series of rules to ensure that your database achieves optimal structure. *Normal forms* is a progression of these rules. Each successive normal form achieves a better database design than the previous form did. Although there are several levels of normal forms, it is generally sufficient to apply only the first three levels of normal forms. They are described in the following sections.

First Normal Form

To achieve first normal form, all columns in a table must be atomic. This means, for example, that you cannot store first name and last name in the same field. The reason for this rule is that data becomes very difficult to manipulate and retrieve if multiple values are stored in a single field. Using the full name as an example, it would become impossible to sort by first name or last name independently if both values are stored in the same field. Furthermore, extra work must be done to extract just the first name or the last name from the field.

Another requirement for first normal form is that the table must not contain repeating values. An example of repeating values is a scenario in which Item1, Quantity1, Item2, Quantity2, Item3, and Quantity3 fields are all found within the Orders table (see Figure 3.1). This design introduces several problems. What if the user wants to add a fourth item to the order? Furthermore, finding the total ordered for a product requires searching several columns.

In fact, all numeric and statistical calculations on the table become extremely cumbersome. The alternative, shown in Figure 3.2, achieves first normal form. Notice that each item ordered is located in a separate row.

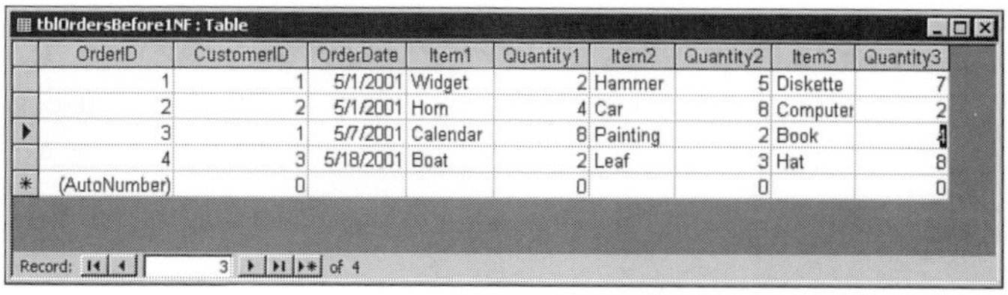

FIGURE 3.1

This table contains repeating groups. Repeating groups make it difficult to summarize and manipulate table data.

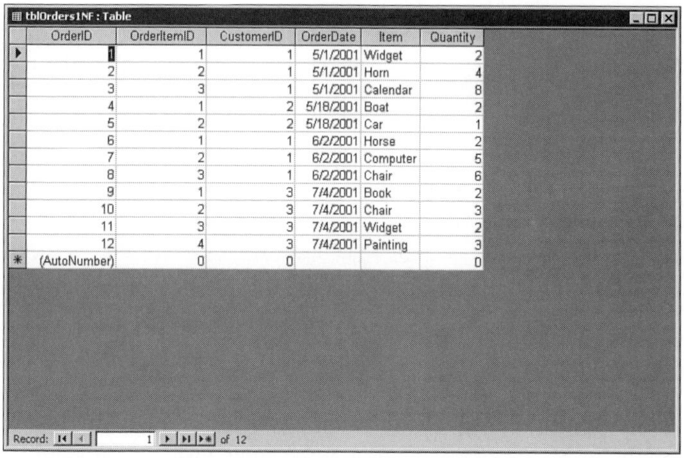

FIGURE 3.2

This table achieves first normal form. Notice that all fields are atomic, and that it contains no repeating groups.

Second Normal Form

To achieve second normal form, all non-key columns must be fully dependent on the primary key. In other words, each table must store data about only one subject. Notice the table shown in Figure 3.2. It includes information about the order (OrderID, CustomerID, and OrderDate) and information about the items being ordered (Item and Quantity). To achieve second normal form, this data must be broken into two tables, an order table and an order detail table. The process of breaking the data into two tables is called *decomposition*. It is considered to be *non-loss* decomposition because no data is lost during the decomposition process. Once the data is broken into two tables, you can easily bring the data back together by joining the two tables in a query. Figure 3.3 shows the data broken up into two tables. These two tables achieve second normal form.

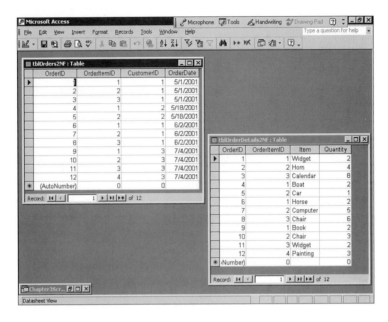

FIGURE 3.3

These tables achieve second normal form. The fields in each table pertain to the primary key of the table.

Third Normal Form

To attain third normal form, a table must meet all the requirements for first and second normal form, and all non-key columns must be mutually independent. This means that you must eliminate any calculations, and you must break out data into lookup tables.

An example of a calculation stored in a table is the product of price multiplied by quantity. Rather than storing the result of this calculation in the table, instead you would generate the calculation in a query, or in the control source of a control on a form or a report.

The example in Figure 3.3 does not achieve third normal form because the description of the inventory items is stored in the order details table. If the description changes, all rows with that inventory item need to be modified. The order detail table, shown in Figure 3.4, shows the item descriptions broken into an inventory table. This design achieves third normal form. All fields are mutually independent. The description of an inventory item can be modified in one place.

Denormalization—Purposely Violating the Rules

Although the developer's goal is normalization, there are many times when it makes sense to deviate from normal forms. This process is referred to as *denormalization*. The primary reason for applying denormalization is to enhance performance.

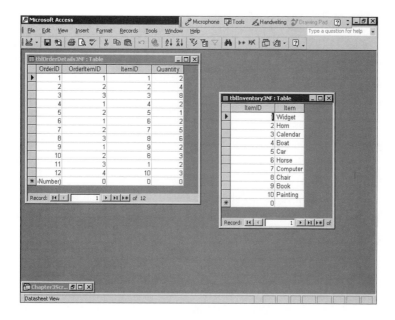

FIGURE 3.4

This table achieves third normal form. The description of the inventory items is moved to an inventory table, and the ItemID is stored in the order details table.

An example of when denormalization might be the preferred tact could involve an open invoices table and a summarized accounting table. It might be impractical to calculate summarized accounting information for a customer when it is needed. The summary calculations are maintained in a summarized accounting table so that they are easily retrieved as needed. Although the upside of this scenario is improved performance, the downside is that the summary table must be updated whenever changes are made to the open invoices. This imposes a definite trade-off between performance and maintainability. You must decide whether the trade-off is worth it.

If you decide to denormalize, document your decision. Make sure that you make the necessary application adjustments to ensure that the denormalized fields are properly maintained. Finally, test to ensure that performance is actually improved by the denormalization process.

Integrity Rules

Although integrity rules are not part of normal forms, they are definitely part of the database design process. Integrity rules are broken into two categories. They include overall integrity rules and database-specific integrity rules.

Overall Rules

The two types of overall integrity rules are *referential integrity rules* and *entity integrity rules*. Referential integrity rules dictate that a database does not contain any orphan foreign key values. This means that

- Child rows cannot be added for parent rows that do not exist. In other words, an order cannot be added for a nonexistent customer.

- A primary key value cannot be modified if the value is used as a foreign key in a child table. This means that a CustomerID cannot be changed if the orders table contains rows with that CustomerID.

- A parent row cannot be deleted if child rows are found with that foreign key value. For example, a customer cannot be deleted if the customer has orders in the order table.

Entity integrity dictates that the primary key value cannot be Null. This rule applies not only to single-column primary keys, but also to multi-column primary keys. In fact, in a multi-column primary key, no field in the primary key can be Null. This makes sense because, if any part of the primary key can be Null, the primary key can no longer act as a unique identifier for the row. Fortunately, Access does not allow a field in a primary key to be Null.

Database-Specific Rules

The other set of rules applied to a database are not applicable to all databases, but are, instead, dictated by business rules that apply to a specific application. Database-specific rules are as important as overall integrity rules. They ensure that only valid data is entered into a database. An example of a database-specific integrity rule is that the delivery date for an order must fall after the order date.

Examining the Types of Relationships

Three types of relationships can exist between tables in a database: one-to-many, one-to-one, and many-to-many. Setting up the proper type of relationship between two tables in your database is imperative. The right type of relationship between two tables ensures

- Data integrity
- Optimal performance
- Ease of use in designing system objects

The reasons behind these benefits are covered throughout this chapter. Before you can understand the benefits of relationships, though, you must understand the types of relationships available.

One-to-Many

A one-to-many relationship is by far the most common type of relationship. In a *one-to-many relationship*, a record in one table can have many related records in another table. A common example is a relationship set up between a Customers table and an Orders table. For each customer in the Customers table, you want to have more than one order in the Orders table. On the other hand, each order in the Orders table can belong to only one customer. The Customers table is on the *one side* of the relationship, and the Orders table is on the *many side*. In order for this relationship to be implemented, the field joining the two tables on the one side of the relationship must be unique.

In the Customers and Orders tables example, the CustomerID field that joins the two tables must be unique within the Customers table. If more than one customer in the Customers table has the same customer ID, it is not clear which customer belongs to an order in the Orders table. For this reason, the field that joins the two tables on the one side of the one-to-many relationship must be a primary key or have a unique index. In almost all cases, the field relating the two tables is the primary key of the table on the one side of the relationship. The field relating the two tables on the many side of the relationship is called a *foreign key*.

One-to-One

In a *one-to-one relationship*, each record in the table on the one side of the relationship can have only one matching record in the table on the many side of the relationship. This relationship is not common and is used only in special circumstances. Usually, if you have set up a one-to-one relationship, you should have combined the fields from both tables into one table. The following are the most common reasons why you should create a one-to-one relationship:

- The amount of fields required for a table exceeds the number of fields allowed in an Access table.

- Certain fields that are included in a table need to be much more secure than other fields included in the same table.

- Several fields in a table are required for only a subset of records in the table.

The maximum number of fields allowed in an Access table is 255. There are very few reasons why a table should ever have more than 255 fields. In fact, before you even get close to 255 fields, you should take a close look at the design of your system. On the rare occasion when having more than 255 fields is appropriate, you can simulate a single table by moving some of the fields to a second table and creating a one-to-one relationship between the two tables.

The second reason to separate into two tables data that logically would belong in the same table involves security. An example is a table containing employee information. Certain information, such as employee name, address, city, state, ZIP Code, home phone, and office extension, might need to be accessed by many users of the system. Other fields, including the hire date, salary, birth date, and salary level, might be highly confidential. Field-level security is not available in Access. You can simulate field-level security by using a special attribute of queries called *Run with Owner's permissions*. This feature is covered in Chapter 11, "Advanced Query Techniques."

The alternative to this method is to place all the fields that can be accessed by all users in one table and the highly confidential fields in another. Only a special Admin user (a user with special security privileges, not one actually named Admin) is given access to the table containing the confidential fields. *ActiveX Data Objects* (ADO) code is used to display the fields in the highly confidential table when needed. This is done using a query with Run with Owner's permissions, based on the special Admin user's permission to the highly secured table. This technique is covered in Chapter 28, "Advanced Security Techniques."

> **NOTE**
>
> If your application utilizes data stored in a SQL Server database, you can use views to easily accomplish the task of implementing field-level security. In such an environment, the process of splitting the data into two tables is unnecessary.

The last situation in which you would want to define one-to-one relationships is when certain fields in a table are going to be used for only a relatively small subset of records. An example is an Employee table and a Vesting table. Certain fields are required only for employees who are vested. If only a small percentage of a company's employees are vested, it is not efficient, in terms of performance or disk space, to place all the fields containing information about vesting in the Employee table. This is especially true if the vesting information requires a large volume of fields. By breaking the information into two tables and creating a one-to-one relationship between them, you can reduce disk-space requirements and improve performance. This improvement is particularly pronounced if the Employee table is large.

Many-to-Many

In a *many-to-many relationship*, records in both tables have matching records in the other table. A many-to-many relationship cannot be directly defined in Access; you must develop this type of relationship by adding a table called a *junction table*. The junction table is related to each of the two tables in one-to-many relationships. An example is an Orders table and a Products table. Each order probably will contain multiple products, and each product is found on many different orders. The solution is to create a third table called Order Details. The Order Details table is related to the Orders table in a one-to-many relationship based on the OrderID field. It is related to the Products table in a one-to-many relationship based on the ProductID field.

Establishing Relationships in Access

Relationships between Access tables are established in the Relationships window, as shown in Figure 3.5. To open the Relationships window, click Relationships on the toolbar with the Database window active or choose Relationships from the Tools menu. If no relationships have been established, the Show Table dialog appears. The Show Table dialog allows you to add tables to the Relationships window.

Looking at the Relationships window, you can see the type of relationships that exists for each table. All the one-to-many and one-to-one relationships defined in a database are represented with a join line. If referential integrity has been enforced between the tables involved in a one-to-many relationship, the join line between the tables appears with the number *1* on the one side of the relationship and with an infinity symbol (∞) on the many side of the relationship. One-to-one relationships appear with a 1 on both ends of the join lines.

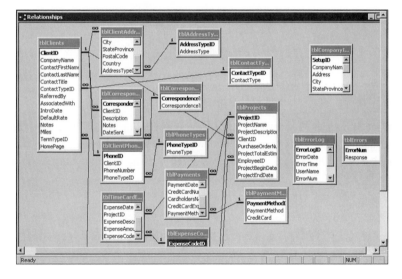

FIGURE 3.5
The Relationships window enables you to view, add, modify, and remove relationships between tables

Establishing a Relationship Between Two Tables

To establish a relationship between two tables, follow these six steps:

1. Open the Relationships window.
2. If it is the first time that you open the Relationships window of a particular database, the Show Table dialog box appears. Select each table you want to relate and click Add.

3. If you have already established relationships in the current database, the Relationships window appears. If the tables you want to include in the relationship do not appear, click the Show Table button on the toolbar or choose Show Table from the Relationships menu. To add the desired tables to the Relationships window, select a table, and then click Add. Repeat this process for each table you want to add. To select multiple tables at once, press Shift while clicking to select contiguous tables or press Ctrl while clicking to select noncontiguous tables; then click Add. Click Close when you are done.

4. Click and drag the field from one table to the matching field in the other table. The Edit Relationships dialog box appears, as shown in Figure 3.6.

FIGURE 3.6

The Edit Relationships dialog box enables you to view and modify the relationships between the tables in a database.

5. Determine whether you want to establish referential integrity, and whether you want to cascade update related fields or cascade delete related records by enabling the appropriate check boxes. These topics are covered in the section, "Establishing Referential Integrity."

6. Click Create.

Looking at Guidelines for Establishing Relationships

You must remember a few important things when establishing relationships. If you are not aware of these important gotchas, you could find yourself in some pretty hairy situations.

- It is important to understand the correlation between the Relationships window and the actual relationships you have established within the database. The Relationships window lets you view and modify the existing relationships. When you establish relationships, the actual relationship is created the moment you click Create. You can delete the tables from the Relationships window (by selecting them and pressing Delete), but the relationships still will exist (permanently removing relationships is covered in the "Modifying an Existing Relationship" section of this chapter). The Relationships window provides a visual blueprint of the relationships that have been established. If you modify the layout of the window by moving around tables, adding tables to the window, or removing tables from the window, you are prompted to save the layout after you close the Relationships window. Access is not asking whether you want to save the relationships you have established; it is simply asking whether you want to save the visual layout of the window.

- When adding tables to the Relationships window using the Show Tables dialog box, it is easy to accidentally add the same table to the window many times. This is because the tables you are adding can hide behind the Show Tables dialog box, or they can appear below the portion of the Relationships window that you are viewing. If this occurs, you'll see multiple occurrences of the same table when you close the Show Tables dialog box. Each occurrence of the table is given a different alias. You must remove the extra occurrences.

- You also can add queries to the Relationships window by using the Show Tables dialog box. Although rarely used, this might be useful if you regularly include the same queries within other queries and want to permanently establish a relationship between them.

- If you remove tables from the Relationships window (this does not delete the relationships) and you want to once again show all relationships that exist in the database, click Show All Relationships on the toolbar or choose Show All from the Relationships menu. This button shows all existing relationships.

- To delete a relationship, click the join line and press Delete.

TRY IT Create a new database and add a table called tblCustomers, another called tblOrders, and another called tblOrderDetails. The table should have the following fields:

> tblCustomers: CustomerID, CompanyName, Address, City, State, ZipCode
>
> tblOrders: OrderID, CustomerID, OrderDate, ShipVIA
>
> tblOrderDetails: OrderID, LineNumber, ItemID, Quantity, Price

1. In the tblCustomers table, set the CustomerID field as the primary key. Set the size of the field to 5. All other fields can be left with their default properties.

2. In the tblOrders table, set OrderID to the AutoNumber field type. Make the OrderID the primary key field. Set the length of the CustomerID field to 5. Set the field type of the OrderDate field to Date.

3. In the tblOrderDetails table, set the field type of the OrderID field to Number and make sure that the size is Long Integer. Set the type of the LineNumber field to Number with a size of Long Integer. The primary key of the table should be based on the combination of the OrderID and LineNumber fields. The ItemID and Quantity fields should be Number type with a size of Long Integer. The Price field should be Currency type.

4. To open the Relationships window, click Relationships on the toolbar with the Database window active. With the tblCustomers table in the Show Table dialog box selected, hold down your Shift key and click to select the tblOrders table. Click Add. All three tables

should be added to the Relationships window. Click Close. Click and drag from the CustomerID field in the tblCustomers table to the CustomerID field in the tblOrders table. After the Relationships dialog box appears, click Create. Repeat the process, clicking and dragging the OrderID field from the tblOrders table to the OrderID field in the tblOrderDetails table.

> **NOTE**
>
> You can find this example, and all examples included in this chapter, in the Chap3TryIt.MDB file included with the sample code on the accompanying CD-ROM.

Modifying an Existing Relationship

Modifying an existing relationship is easy. Access gives you the capability to delete an existing relationship or to simply modify the nature of the relationship. To permanently remove a relationship between two tables, follow these three steps:

1. With the Database window active, click Relationships on the toolbar.
2. Click the line joining the two tables whose relationship you want to delete.
3. Press Delete. You are asked to verify your actions. Click Yes.

You often will want to modify the nature of a relationship rather than remove it. To modify a relationship, follow these four steps:

1. With the Database window active, click Relationships on the toolbar.
2. Double-click on the line joining the two tables whose relationship you want to modify.
3. Make the required changes.
4. Click OK. All the normal rules regarding the establishment of relationships will apply.

Establishing Referential Integrity

As you can see, establishing a relationship is quite easy. Establishing the right kind of relationship is a little more difficult. When you attempt to establish a relationship between two tables, Access makes some decisions based on a few predefined factors:

- A one-to-many relationship is established if one of the related fields is a primary key or has a unique index.

- A one-to-one relationship is established if both the related fields are primary keys or have unique indexes.

- An indeterminate relationship is created if neither of the related fields is a primary key, and neither has a unique index. Referential integrity cannot be established in this case.

As covered earlier in the chapter, *referential integrity* consists of a series of rules that are applied by the Jet Engine to ensure that the relationships between tables are maintained properly. At the most basic level, referential integrity rules prevent the creation of orphan records in the table on the many side of the one-to-many relationship. After establishing a relationship between a Customers table and an Orders table, for example, all orders in the Orders table must be related to a particular customer in the Customers table. Before you can establish referential integrity between two tables, the following conditions must be met:

- The matching field on the one side of the relationship must be a Primary Key field or must have a unique index.

- The matching fields must have the same data types (for linking purposes, AutoNumber fields match Long Integer fields). With the exception of Text fields, they also must have the same size. Number fields on both sides of the relationship must have the same size (Long Integer, for example).

- Both tables must be part of the same Access database.

- Both tables must be stored in the proprietary Access file (.MDB) format (they cannot be external tables from other sources).

- The database containing the two tables must be open.

- Existing data within the two tables cannot violate any referential integrity rules. All orders in the Orders table must relate to existing customers in the Customers table, for example.

> **CAUTION**
>
> Although Text fields involved in a relationship do not have to be the same size, it is prudent to make them the same size. Otherwise, you will degrade performance as well as risk the chance of unpredictable results when creating queries based on the two tables.

After referential integrity is established between two tables, the following rules are applied:

- You cannot enter a value in the foreign key of the related table that does not exist in the primary key of the primary table. For example, you cannot enter a value in the CustomerID field of the Orders table that does not exist in the CustomerID field of the Customers table.

- You cannot delete a record from the primary table if corresponding records exist in the related table. For example, you cannot delete a customer from the Customers table, if related records exist in the Orders table (records with the same value in the CustomerID field).

- You cannot change the value of a primary key on the one side of a relationship if corresponding records exist in the related table. For example, you cannot change the value in the CustomerID field of the Customers table if corresponding orders exist in the Orders table.

If any of the previous three rules are violated and referential integrity is being enforced between the tables, an appropriate error message is displayed, as shown in Figure 3.7.

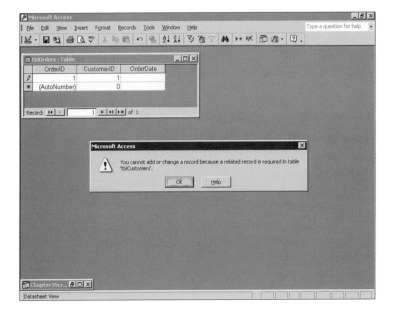

FIGURE 3.7

An error message when attempting to add an order for a customer who doesn't exist.

Access's default behavior is to prohibit the deletion of parent records that have associated child records and to prohibit the change of a primary key value of a parent record when that parent has associated child records. You can override these restrictions by using the two check boxes available in the Relationships dialog box when you establish or modify a relationship.

> **TRY IT** The following example enforces referential integrity between the tblCustomers table and the tblOrders table. It illustrates how this affects the process of adding and deleting records.

1. To open the Relationships window, select the Database window and click Relationships on the toolbar. Double-click on the join line between tblCustomers and tblOrders. Enable the Enforce Referential Integrity check box. Click OK. Repeat the process for the relationship between tblOrders and tblOrderDetails.

2. Go into tblCustomer and add a couple of records. Take note of the CustomerIDs. Go into tblOrders. Add a couple of records, taking care to assign customer IDs of customers that exist in the tblCustomers table. Now try to add an order for a customer whose customer ID does not exist in tblCustomers. You should get an error message.

3. Attempt to delete a customer from tblCustomers who does not have any orders. You should get a warning message, but you should be allowed to complete the process. Now try to delete a customer who does have orders. You should be prohibited from deleting the customer. Attempt to change the customer ID of a customer who has orders. You should not be able to do this.

Cascade Update Related Fields

The Cascade Update Related Fields option is available only if referential integrity has been established between the tables. With this option selected, the user can change the primary key value of the record on the one side of the relationship. Instead, when an attempt is made to modify the field joining the two tables on the one side of the relationship, the change is cascaded down to the Foreign Key field on the many side of the relationship. This is useful if the primary key field is modifiable. For example, a purchase number on a purchase order master record might be updateable. If the user modifies the purchase order number of the parent record, you would want to cascade the change to the associated detail records in the purchase order detail table.

> **NOTE**
>
> There is no need to select the Cascade Update Related Fields option when the related field on the one side of the relationship is an AutoNumber field. An AutoNumber field can never be modified. The Cascade Update Related Fields option has no effect on AutoNumber fields.

3

RELATIONSHIPS:
YOUR KEY TO
DATA INTEGRITY

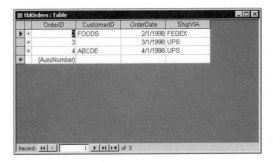

FIGURE 3.8

An orphan record with Null in the Foreign Key field.

Cascade Delete Related Records

The Cascade Delete Related Records option is available only if referential integrity has been established between the tables. With this option selected, the user can delete a record on the one side of a one-to-many relationship, even if related records exist in the table on the many side of the relationship. A customer can be deleted even if the customer has existing orders, for example. Referential integrity is maintained between the tables because Access automatically deletes all related records in the child table.

If you attempt to delete a record from the table on the one side of a one-to-many relationship and no related records exist in the table on the many side of the relationship, you get the usual warning message, as shown in Figure 3.9. On the other hand, if you attempt to delete a record from the table on the one side of a one-to-many relationship and related records exist in the child table, you are warned that you are about to delete the record from the parent table as well as any related records in the child table (see Figure 3.10).

FIGURE 3.9

A message that appears after the user attempts to delete a parent record without related child records.

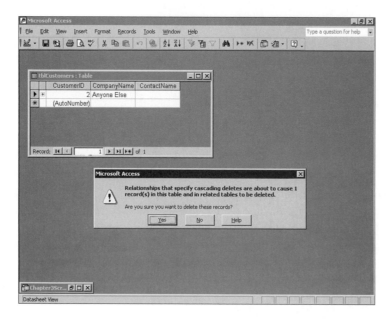

FIGURE 3.10

A message that appears after the user attempts to delete a parent record with related child records.

3

RELATIONSHIPS:
YOUR KEY TO
DATA INTEGRITY

TIP

The Cascade Delete Related Records option is not always appropriate. It is an excellent feature, but you should use it prudently. Although it is usually appropriate to cascade delete from an Orders table to an Order Details table, for example, it generally is not appropriate to cascade delete from a Customers table to an Orders table. This is because you generally do not want all your order history deleted from the Orders table if for some reason you wanted to delete a customer. Deleting the order history causes important information, such as your profit and loss history, to change. It therefore is appropriate to prohibit this type of deletion and handle the customer in some other way, such as marking him as inactive, or archiving his data. On the

> other hand, if you delete an order because it was canceled, you probably want the corresponding order detail information to be removed as well. In this case, the Cascade Delete Related Records option is appropriate. You need to make the appropriate decision in each situation, based on business needs. The important thing is to carefully consider the implications of each option before making your decision.

TRY IT With the Cascade Update feature enabled, you are able to update the primary key value of a record that has associated child records. With the Cascade Delete feature enabled, you can delete a parent record that has associated child records. This exercise illustrates the use of Cascade Update and Cascade Delete.

1. Modify the relationship between tblCustomers and tblOrders. Enable the Cascade Update Related Fields check box. Modify the relationship between tblOrders and tblOrderDetails. Enable the Cascade Delete Related Records check box. There is no need to enable Cascade Update Related Fields because the OrderID field in tblOrders is an AutoNumber field.

2. Attempt to delete a customer who has orders. You still should be prohibited from doing this because you did not enable Cascade Delete Related Records. Change the customer ID in tblCustomers of a customer who has orders. This change should be allowed. Take a look at the tblOrders table. The customer ID of all corresponding records in the table now should be updated to reflect the change in the parent record.

3. Add some order details to the tblOrderDetails table. Try to delete any order that has details within the tblOrderDetails table. You should receive a warning, but you should be allowed to complete the process.

Looking at the Benefits of Relationships

The primary benefit of relationships is the data integrity they provide. Without the establishment of relationships, users are free to add records to child tables without regard to entering required parent information. After referential integrity is established, you can enable Cascade Update Related Fields or Cascade Delete Related Records, as appropriate, which will save you quite a bit of code in maintaining the integrity of the data in your system. Most relational database management systems require that you write the code to delete related records when a parent record is deleted or to update the foreign key in related records when the primary key of the parent is modified. By enabling the Cascade Update and Cascade Delete check boxes, you are sheltered from having to write a single line of code to perform these tasks when they are appropriate.

> **NOTE**
>
> SQL Server 2000 offers Cascade Update and Cascade Delete features similar to those found in Microsoft Access. This means that you no longer need to write your own T-SQL statements when it is appropriate to implement Cascade Update and Delete functionality.

Relationships automatically are carried into your queries. This means that, each time you build a new query, the relationships between the tables within it automatically are established, based on the relationships you have set up in the Relationships window. Furthermore, each time you build a form or report, relationships between the tables included on the form or report are used to assist with the design process. Whether you delete or update data using a datasheet or a form, all referential integrity rules automatically apply, even if the relationship is established after the form is built.

Examining Indexes and Relationships

The field that joins two tables on the one side of a one-to-many relationship must be a Primary Key field or must have a unique index so that referential integrity can be maintained. If the index on the one side of the relationship is not unique, there is no way to determine to which parent a child record belongs.

In Access 2002, it is not necessary to create an index for the field on the many side of the relationship. Access 2002 will create an internal index for you. If you do create an index on the many side of the relationship, make sure that you set the index to Yes (Duplicates OK); otherwise, you will have a one-to-one, rather than a one-to-many, relationship.

> **PRACTICAL EXAMPLES**

Establishing the Relationships Between the Tables Included in the Time and Billing Database

In this example, you'll establish some of the relationships you need to set up for the tables included in a hypothetical time and billing database. If you would like to build the relationships yourself, open the database that you created in Chapter 2.

- tblClients to tblProjects—tblClients and tblProjects need to be related in a one-to-many relationship based on the ClientID field. You must enforce referential integrity to ensure that projects cannot be added for nonexistent clients. There is no need to set Cascade

Update Related Fields because the client ID that relates the two tables is an AutoNumber field in tblClients. You do not want to enable Cascade Delete Related Records because you do not want any billing information to change if a client is deleted. Instead, you want to prohibit the deletion of clients who have projects by establishing referential integrity between the two tables.

- tblProjects to tblPayments—tblProjects and tblPayments need to be related in a one-to-many relationship based on the ProjectID field. You must enforce referential integrity to ensure that payments cannot be added for nonexistent projects. There is no need to set Cascade Update Related Fields because the ProjectID that relates the two tables is an AutoNumber field in tblProjects. You do not want to enable Cascade Delete Related Records because you do not want any payment information to change if a client is deleted. Prohibit the deletion of clients who have payments by establishing referential integrity between the two tables.

- tblProjects to tblTimeCardHours—tblProjects and tblTimeCardHours need to be related in a one-to-many relationship based on the ProjectID field. You must enforce referential integrity to ensure that hours cannot be added for nonexistent projects. There is no need to set Cascade Update Related Fields because the ProjectID that relates the two tables is an AutoNumber field in tblProjects. Enable Cascade Delete Related Records so that hours are deleted if a project is deleted.

- tblProjects to tblTimeCardExpenses—tblProjects and tblTimeCardExpenses need to be related in a one-to-many relationship based on the ProjectID field. You must enforce referential integrity to ensure that expenses cannot be added for nonexistent projects. There is no need to set Cascade Update Related Fields because the ProjectID that relates the two tables is an AutoNumber field in tblProjects. Enable Cascade Delete Related Records so that expenses are deleted if a project is deleted.

- tblEmployees to tblTimeCards—tblEmployees and tblTimeCards need to be related in a one-to-many relationship based on the EmployeeID field. You must enforce referential integrity to ensure that time cards cannot be added for nonexistent employees. There is no need to set Cascade Update Related Fields because the EmployeeID that relates the two tables is an AutoNumber field in tblEmployees. You do not want to enable Cascade Delete Related Records because, if an employee is deleted, all the employee's time cards are deleted.

- tblEmployees to tblProjects—tblEmployees and tblProjects need to be related in a one-to-many relationship based on the EmployeeID field. You must enforce referential integrity to ensure that projects cannot be assigned to nonexistent employees. There is no need to set Cascade Update Related Fields because the employee ID that relates the two tables is an AutoNumber field in tblEmployees. You do not want to enable Cascade Delete Related Records because, if an employee is deleted, all the employee's projects would be deleted, which is generally not desirable.

- tblTimeCards to tblTimeCardHours—tblTimeCards and tblTimeCardHours need to be related in a one-to-many relationship based on the TimeCardID field. You must enforce referential integrity to ensure that time card hours cannot be added for nonexistent time cards. There is no need to set Cascade Update Related Fields because the time card ID that relates the two tables is an AutoNumber field in tblTimeCards. You do want to enable Cascade Delete Related Records because, if a time card is deleted, you want the corresponding hours to be deleted.

- tblTimeCards to tblTimeCardExpenses—tblTimeCards and tblTimeCardExpenses need to be related in a one-to-many relationship based on the TimeCardID field. You must enforce referential integrity to ensure that time card expenses cannot be added for nonexistent time cards. There is no need to set Cascade Update Related Fields because the time card ID that relates the two tables is an AutoNumber field in tblTimeCards. You do want to enable Cascade Delete Related Records because, if a time card is deleted, you want the corresponding expenses to be deleted.

- tblExpenseCodes to tblTimeCardExpenses—tblExpenseCodes and tblTimeCardExpenses need to be related in a one-to-many relationship based on the ExpenseCodeID field. You must enforce referential integrity to ensure that time card expenses cannot be added with nonexistent expense codes. There is no need to set Cascade Update Related Fields because the expense code ID that relates the two tables is an AutoNumber field in tblExpenseCodes. You do not want to enable Cascade Delete Related Records because, if an expense code is deleted, you do not want the corresponding expenses to be deleted.

- tblWorkCodes to tblTimeCardHours—tblWorkCodes and tblTimeCardHours need to be related in a one-to-many relationship based on the WorkCodeID field. You must enforce referential integrity to ensure that time card hours cannot be added with invalid work codes. There is no need to set Cascade Update Related Fields because the work code ID that relates the two tables is an AutoNumber field in tblWorkCodes. You do not want to enable Cascade Delete Related Records because, if a work code is deleted, you do not want the corresponding hours to be deleted.

- tblPaymentMethods to tblPayments—tblPaymentMethods and tblPayments need to be related in a one-to-many relationship based on the PaymentMethodID field. You must enforce referential integrity to ensure that payments cannot be added with an invalid payment method. There is no need to set Cascade Update Related Fields because the PaymentMethodID that relates the two tables is an AutoNumber field in tblPaymentMethods. You do not want to enable Cascade Delete Related Records because, if a payment method is deleted, you do not want the corresponding payments to be deleted.

Summary

Relationships enable you to normalize your database. Using relationships, you can divide your data into separate tables, once again combining the data at runtime. This chapter began by explaining relational database design principles. It described the types of relationships that can be defined. It then covered the details of establishing and modifying relationships between tables and described all the important aspects of establishing relationships.

The capability to easily establish and maintain referential integrity between tables is an important strength of Microsoft Access. This chapter described the referential integrity options and highlights when each option is appropriate. Finally, this chapter summarized the benefits of relationships.

What Every Developer Needs to Know About Query Basics

IN THIS CHAPTER

Why This Chapter Is Important?

Although tables act as the ultimate foundation for any application that you build, queries are very important as well. Most of the forms and reports that act as the user interface for your application are based on queries. An understanding of queries, what they are, and when and how to use them is imperative for your success as an Access application developer. This chapter teaches you the basics of working with queries. After reading this chapter, you will know how to build queries, add tables and fields to the queries that you create, sort the query output, and apply criteria to limit the data that appears in the query output. You will also be familiar with tips and tricks and important "gotchas" of working with queries.

What Is a Query, and When Should You Use One?

A *Select query* is a stored question about the data stored in your database's tables. Select queries are the foundation of much of what you do in Access. They underlie most of your forms and reports, allowing you to view the data you want, when you want. You use a simple Select query to define the tables and fields whose data you want to view and also to specify the criteria to limit the data the query's output displays. A Select query is a query of a table or tables that just displays data; it doesn't modify data in any way. More advanced Select queries are used to summarize data, supply the results of calculations, or cross-tabulate your data. You can use Action queries to add, edit, or delete data from your tables, based on selected criteria, but this chapter covers Select queries. Other types of queries are covered in Chapter 11, "Advanced Query Techniques."

Everything You Need to Know About Query Basics

Creating a basic query is easy because Microsoft has given us a user-friendly, drag-and-drop interface. There are two ways to start a new query in Access 2002. The first way is to select the Queries icon from the Objects list in the Database window; then double-click the Create Query in Design View icon or the Create Query by Using Wizard icon. (See Figure 4.1.) The second method is to select the Queries icon from the Objects list in the Database window and then click the New command button on the Database window toolbar. The New Query dialog appears. (See Figure 4.2.) This dialog box lets you select whether you want to build the query from scratch or use one of the wizards to help you. The Simple Query Wizard walks you through the steps for creating a basic query. The other wizards help you create three specific types of queries: Crosstab, Find Duplicates, or Find Unmatched.

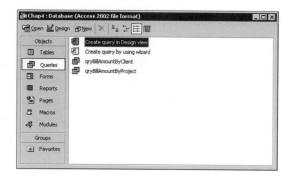

FIGURE 4.1

Select the Queries icon from the Objects list to create a query in Design view or to create one using a wizard.

FIGURE 4.2

Use the New Query dialog box to select a wizard for the query you want to create, or choose Design view to make a query on your own.

Adding Tables to Your Queries

If you select Design view rather than one of the wizards, the Show Table dialog box appears. (See Figure 4.3.) Here, you can select the tables or queries that supply data to your query. Access doesn't care whether you select tables or queries as the foundation for your queries. You can select them by double-clicking on the name of the table or query you want to add or by clicking on the table and then clicking Add. You can select multiple tables or queries by using the Shift key to select a contiguous range of tables or the Ctrl key to select noncontiguous tables. When you have selected the tables or queries you want, click Add and then click Close. This brings you to the Query Design window shown in Figure 4.4.

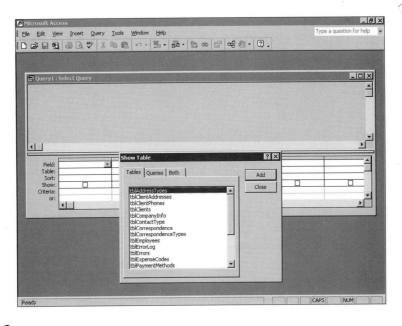

FIGURE 4.3
Selecting Design view displays the Show Table dialog that allows you to select the tables and queries on which your query is based.

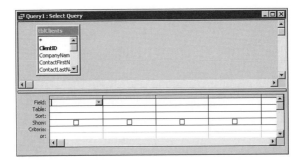

FIGURE 4.4
The Query Design window presents an easy-to-use (and learn) query design grid.

TIP

An alternative way to add a table is to first select Tables from the Objects list in the Database window. Then select the table on which you want the query to be based. With the table selected, select New Query from the New Object drop-down list on the toolbar or choose Query from the Insert menu. The New Query dialog appears.

This is an efficient method of starting a new query based on only one table because the Show Table dialog box never appears.

Adding Fields to Your Query

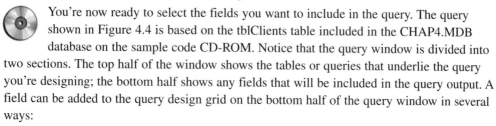 You're now ready to select the fields you want to include in the query. The query shown in Figure 4.4 is based on the tblClients table included in the CHAP4.MDB database on the sample code CD-ROM. Notice that the query window is divided into two sections. The top half of the window shows the tables or queries that underlie the query you're designing; the bottom half shows any fields that will be included in the query output. A field can be added to the query design grid on the bottom half of the query window in several ways:

- Double-click the name of the field you want to add.

- Click and drag a single field from the table in the top half of the query window to the query design grid below.

- Select multiple fields at the same time by using your Shift key (for a contiguous range of fields) or your Ctrl key (for a noncontiguous range). You can double-click the title bar of the field list to select all fields; then click and drag any one of the selected fields to the query design grid.

TIP

You can double-click the asterisk to include all fields within the table in the query result. Although this is very handy, in that changes to the table structure magically affect the query's output, I believe that this "trick" is dangerous. When the asterisk is selected, all table fields are included in the query result whether or not they are needed. This can cause major performance problems in a LAN, WAN, or client/server application.

4

QUERY BASICS

TRY IT

Open the Northwind database that comes with Access (this database is not installed unless you designate that you want to install sample files during the install). If you want to prevent the Startup form from appearing, hold down your Shift key as you open the database. Click the Query icon and then click New. Select Design view from the New Query dialog. Add the Customers table to the query. Follow these steps to select six fields from Customers:

1. Click the CustomerID field.

2. Hold down your Shift key and click the ContactTitle field. This should select the CustomerID, CompanyName, ContactName, and ContactTitle fields.

3. Scroll down the list of fields, using the vertical scrollbar, until the Region field is visible.

4. Hold down your Ctrl key and click the Region field.

5. With the Ctrl key still held down, click the Phone field. All six fields should now be selected.

Click and drag any of the selected fields from the table on the top half of the query window to the query design grid on the bottom. All six fields should appear in the query design grid. You might need to use the horizontal scrollbar to view some of the fields on the right.

TIP

The easiest way to run a query is to click the Run button on the toolbar (which looks like an exclamation point). You can click the Query View button to run a query, but this method works only for Select queries, not for Action queries. The Query View button has a special meaning for Action queries (explained in Chapter 11). Clicking Run is preferable because you don't have to worry about what type of query you're running. After running a Select query, you should see what looks like a datasheet, with only the fields you selected. To return to the query's design, click the Query View button.

TIP

New to Access 2002 are shortcut keys that allow you to easily toggle between the various query views: Ctrl+>, Ctrl+Period, Ctrl+<, and Ctrl+Comma. Ctrl+> and Ctrl+Period take you to the next view; Ctrl+< and Ctrl+Comma take you to the previous view.

Removing a Field from the Query Design Grid

To remove a field from the query design grid, follow these steps:

1. Find the field you want to remove.

2. Click the small horizontal gray button (column selector) immediately above the name of the field. The entire column of the query design grid should become black. (See Figure 4.5.)

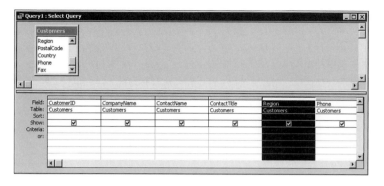

FIGURE 4.5

Removing a field from the query design grid.

3. Press the Delete key or select Delete from the Edit menu.

> **TRY IT** Assume that you have decided to remove the Region field from the query design grid. Use the horizontal scrollbar to see the Region field on the query design grid.

1. Click the column selector immediately above the Region field. The entire column of the query design grid should become black, and the cursor turns into a downward-pointing arrow.

2. Press the Delete key to remove the Region field from the query design grid.

Inserting a Field After the Query Is Built

The process for inserting a field after a query is built differs, depending on where you want the new field to be inserted. If you want it inserted after the existing fields, it's easiest to double-click the name of the field you want to add. If you prefer to insert the new field between two existing fields, it's best to click and drag the field you want to add, dropping it onto the field you want to appear to the right of the inserted field.

> **TRY IT** To insert the Country field between the ContactTitle and Phone fields, click and drag the Country field from the table until it's on top of the Phone field. This inserts the field in the correct place. To run the query, click Run on the toolbar.

Moving a Field to a Different Location on the Query Design Grid

Although the user can move a column while in a query's Datasheet view, sometimes you want to permanently alter the position of a field in the query output. This can be done as a convenience to the user or, more importantly, because you will use the query as a foundation for forms and reports. The order of the fields in the query becomes the default order of the fields

4

on any forms and reports you build using any of the wizards. You can save yourself quite a bit of time by ordering your queries effectively.

To move a single column, follow these steps:

1. Select a column while in the query's Design view by clicking its column selector (the button immediately above the field name).

2. Click the selected column a second time, and then drag it to a new location on the query design grid.

Follow these steps to move more than one column at a time:

1. Drag across the column selectors of the columns you want to move.

2. Click any of the selected columns a second time, and then drag them to a new location on the query design grid.

TRY IT   Move the ContactName and ContactTitle fields so that they appear before the CompanyName field. Do this by clicking and dragging from ContactName's column selector to ContactTitle's column selector. Both columns should be selected. Click again on the column selector for either column, and then click and drag until the thick black line jumps to the left of the CompanyName field.

NOTE

Moving a column in the Datasheet view doesn't modify the query's underlying design. If you move a column in Datasheet view, subsequent reordering in the Design view isn't reflected in the Datasheet view. In other words, Design view and Datasheet view are no longer synchronized, and you must reorder both by hand. This actually serves as an advantage in most cases. As you will learn later, if you want to sort by the Country field and then by the CompanyName field, the Country field must appear to the left of the CompanyName field in the design of the query. If you want the CompanyName to appear to the left of the Country in the query's result, you must make that change in Datasheet view. The fact that the order of the columns is maintained separately in both views allows you to easily accomplish both objectives.

Saving and Naming Your Query

To save your query at any time, click the Save button on the toolbar. If the query is a new one, you're then prompted to name your query. Query names should begin with the tag *qry* so that you can easily recognize and identify them as queries. It's important to understand that, when you save a query, you're saving only the query's definition, not the actual query result.

TRY IT Return to the design of the query. To save your work, click Save on the toolbar. When prompted for a name, call the query qryCustomers.

Ordering Your Query Result

When you run a new query, notice that the query output appears in no particular order, but generally, you want to order it. You can do this by using the Sort row of the query design grid.

To order your query result, follow these steps:

1. In Design view, click within the query design grid in the Sort cell of the column you want to sort. (See Figure 4.6.)

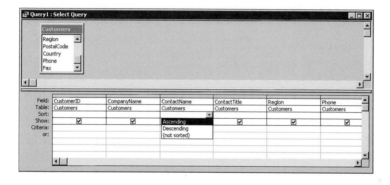

FIGURE 4.6

Changing the order of the query result.

2. Use the drop-down combo box to select an ascending or descending sort.

TRY IT To sort in ascending order by the ContactTitle field, follow these steps:

1. In Design view, click in the Sort row of the query design grid for the ContactTitle field.
2. Open the Sort drop-down combo box.
3. Select Ascending.
4. Run your query and view the results. Your records should now be in order by the ContactTitle field.
5. If you want to return to the query's design, click View on the toolbar.

Sorting by More than One Field

Quite often, you want to sort your query output by more than one field. The columns you want to sort must be placed in order from left to right on the query design grid, with the column you

4

QUERY BASICS

want to act as the primary sort on the far left and the secondary, tertiary, and any additional sorts following to the right. If you want the columns to appear in a different order in the query output, they need to be moved manually in Datasheet view after the query is run.

TRY IT   Sort the query output by the Country field and, within individual country groupings, by the ContactTitle field. Because sorting always occurs from left to right, you must place the Country field before the ContactTitle field. Therefore, you must move the Country field. Follow these steps:

1. Select the Country field from the query design grid by clicking the thin gray button above the Country column.

2. After you have selected the Country field, move your mouse back to the thin gray button and click and drag to the left of ContactTitle. A thick gray line should appear to the left of the ContactTitle field.

3. Release the mouse button.

4. Change the sort of the Country field to Ascending.

5. Run the query. The records should be in order by country and, within the country grouping, by contact title.

Refining Your Query with Criteria

So far, you have learned how to select the fields you want and how to indicate the sort order for your query output. One of the important features of queries is the ability to limit your output by selection criteria. Access allows you to combine criteria by using any of several operators to limit the criteria for one or more fields. The operators and their meanings are covered in Table 4.1.

TABLE 4.1   Access Operators and Their Meanings

Operator	Meaning	Example	Result
=	Equal to	="Sales"	Finds only those records with "Sales" as the field value.
<	Less than	<100	Finds all records with values less than 100 in that field.
<=	Less than or equal to	<=100	Finds all records with values less than or equal to 100 in that field.
>	Greater than	>100	Finds all records with values greater than 100 in that field.

TABLE 4.1   Continued

Operator	Meaning	Example	Result
>=	Greater than or equal to	>=100	Finds all records with values greater than or equal to 100 in that field.
<>	Not equal to	<>"Sales"	Finds all records with values other than Sales in the field.
And	Both conditions must be true	Created by adding criteria on the same line of the query design grid to more than one field	Finds all records where the conditions in both fields are true.
Or	Either condition can be true	"CA" or "NY" or "UT"	Finds all records with the value of "CA", "NY", or "UT" in the field.
Like	Compares a string expression to a pattern	Like "Sales*"	Finds all records with the value of "Sales" at the beginning of the field.
Between	Finds a range of values	Between 5 and 10	Finds all records with the values of 5–10 (inclusive) in the field.
In	Same as Or	In("CA", "NY","UT")	Finds all records with the value of "CA", "NY", or "UT" in the field.
Not	Same as not equal	Not "Sales"	Finds all records with values other than Sales in the field.
Is Null	Finds Nulls	Is Null	Finds all records where no data has been entered in the field.
Is Not Null	Finds all records not Null	Is Not Null	Finds all records where data has been entered the field.

Criteria entered for two fields on a single line of the query design grid are considered an And, which means that both conditions need to be true for the record to appear in the query output.

Entries made on separate lines of the query design grid are considered an Or, which means that either condition can be true for the record to be included in the query output. Take a look at the example in Figure 4.7; this query would output all records in which the ContactTitle field begins with either Marketing or Owner, regardless of the customer ID. It outputs the records in which the ContactTitle field begins with Sales only for the customers whose IDs begin with the letters *M* through *R* inclusive.

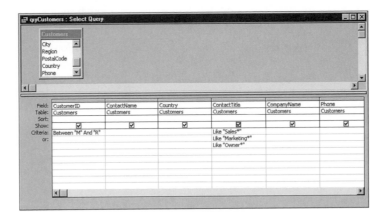

FIGURE 4.7

Adding AND and OR conditions to a query.

TRY IT Design a query to find all the sales agents in Brazil or France. The criteria you build should look like those in Figure 4.8.

1. Notice that the criterion for the Country field is "Brazil" Or "France" because you want both Brazil and France to appear in the query output. The criterion for the ContactTitle field is "Sales Agent". Because the criteria for both the Country and ContactTitle fields are entered on the same line of the query design grid, both must be true for the record to appear in the query output. In other words, the customer must be in either Brazil or France and must also be a sales agent.

2. Modify the query so that you can output all the customers for whom the contact title begins with Sales. Try changing the criteria for the ContactTitle field to Sales. Notice that no records appear in the query output because no contact titles are just Sales. You must enter "Like Sales*" for the criteria. Now you get the Sales Agents, Sales Associates, Sales Managers, and so on. You still don't see the Assistant Sales Agents because their titles don't begin with Sales. Try changing the criteria to "Like *Sales*". Now all the Assistant Sales Agents appear.

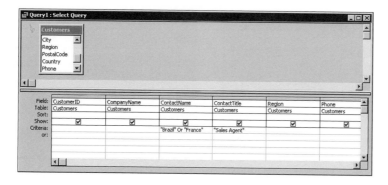

FIGURE 4.8

The criterion to select sales agents whose country is either Brazil or France.

Working with Dates in Criteria

Access gives you significant power for adding date functions and expressions to your query criteria. Using these criteria, you can find all records in a certain month, on a specific weekday, or between two dates. Table 4.2 lists several examples.

TABLE 4.2 Sample Date Criteria

Expression	Meaning	Example	Result
Date()	Current date	Date()	Records with the current date within a field.
Day(Date)	The day of a date	Day ([OrderDate])=1	Records with the order date on the first day of the month.
Month(Date)	The month of a date	Month ([OrderDate])=1	Records with the order date in January.
Year(Date)	The year of a date	Year ([OrderDate]) =1991	Records with the order date in 1991.
Weekday(Date)	The weekday of a date	Weekday ([OrderDate])=2	Records with the order date on a Monday.

4

QUERY BASICS

TABLE 4.2 Continued

Expression	Meaning	Example	Result
Between Date And Date	A range of dates	Between #1/1/95# and #12/31/95#	All records in 1995.
DatePart (Interval, Date)	A specific part of a date	DatePart ("q", [OrderDate])=2	All records in the second quarter.

The Weekday(Date, [FirstDayOfWeek]) function works based on your locale and how your system defines the first day of the week. Weekday() used without the optional FirstDayOfWeek argument defaults to vbSunday as the first day. A value of 0 defaults the FirstDayOfWeek to the system definition. Other values can be set also.

Figure 4.9 illustrates the use of a date function. Notice that DatePart("q",[OrderDate]) is entered as the expression, and the value of 2 is entered for the criteria. Year([OrderDate)] is entered as another expression with the number 1995 as the criteria. Therefore, this query outputs all records in which the order date is in the second quarter of 1995.

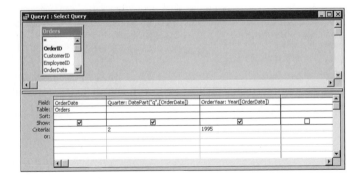

FIGURE 4.9
Using the DatePart() *and* Year() *functions in a query.*

Understanding How Query Results Can Be Updated

If you haven't realized it yet, the results of your query can usually be updated. This means that if you modify the data in the query output, the data in the tables underlying the query is permanently modified.

Build a query based on the Customers table. Add the CustomerID, CompanyName, Address, City, and Region fields to the query design grid; then run the query. Change the address of a particular customer, and make a note of the customer ID of the customer whose address you changed. Make sure you move off the record so that the change is written to disk. Close the query, open the actual table in Datasheet view, and find the record whose address you modified. Notice that the change you made was written to the original table—this is because a query result is a dynamic set of records that maintains a link back to the original data. This happens whether you're on a standalone machine or on a network.

CAUTION

It's essential that you understand how query results are updated; otherwise, you might mistakenly update table data without even realizing you did so. Updating multitable queries is covered later in this chapter in the sections "Pitfalls of Multitable Queries" and "Row Fix-Up in Multitable Queries."

Building Queries Based on Multiple Tables

If you have properly normalized your table data, you probably want to bring the data from your tables back together by using queries. Fortunately, you can do this quite easily with Access queries.

The query in Figure 4.10 joins the Customers, Orders, and Order Details tables, pulling fields from each. Notice that the CustomerID and CompanyName fields are selected from the Customers table, the OrderID and OrderDate from the Orders table, and the UnitPrice and Quantity from the Order Details table. After running this query, you should see the results shown in Figure 4.11. Notice that you get a record in the query's result for every record in the Order Details table. In other words, there are 2,155 records in the Order Details table, and that's how many records appear in the query output. By creating a multitable query, you can look at data from related tables, along with the data from the Order Details table.

4

QUERY BASICS

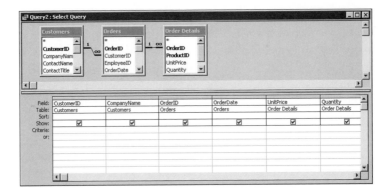

FIGURE 4.10

A query joining the Customers, Orders, and Order Details tables.

Customer ID	Company Name	Order ID	Order Date	Unit Price	Quantity
ALFKI	Alfreds Futterkiste	10643	25-Aug-1997	$45.60	15
ALFKI	Alfreds Futterkiste	10643	25-Aug-1997	$18.00	21
ALFKI	Alfreds Futterkiste	10643	25-Aug-1997	$12.00	2
ALFKI	Alfreds Futterkiste	10952	16-Mar-1998	$25.00	16
ALFKI	Alfreds Futterkiste	10952	16-Mar-1998	$45.60	2
ALFKI	Alfreds Futterkiste	10692	03-Oct-1997	$43.90	20
ALFKI	Alfreds Futterkiste	10835	15-Jan-1998	$55.00	15
ALFKI	Alfreds Futterkiste	10835	15-Jan-1998	$13.00	2
ALFKI	Alfreds Futterkiste	11011	09-Apr-1998	$13.25	40
ALFKI	Alfreds Futterkiste	11011	09-Apr-1998	$21.50	20
ALFKI	Alfreds Futterkiste	10702	13-Oct-1997	$10.00	6
ALFKI	Alfreds Futterkiste	10702	13-Oct-1997	$18.00	15
ANATR	Ana Trujillo Emparedados y helados	10759	28-Nov-1997	$32.00	10
ANATR	Ana Trujillo Emparedados y helados	10926	04-Mar-1998	$21.00	2
ANATR	Ana Trujillo Emparedados y helados	10926	04-Mar-1998	$6.00	10
ANATR	Ana Trujillo Emparedados y helados	10926	04-Mar-1998	$9.20	7
ANATR	Ana Trujillo Emparedados y helados	10926	04-Mar-1998	$34.80	10
ANATR	Ana Trujillo Emparedados y helados	10308	18-Sep-1996	$28.80	1

Record: 14 ◄ | 1 | ► ►I ►* | of 2155

FIGURE 4.11

The results of querying multiple tables.

TRY IT Build a query that combines information from the Customers, Orders, and Order Details tables. To do this, build a new query by following these steps:

1. Select the Query tab from the Database window.

2. Click New.

3. Select Design view.

4. From the Show Table dialog box, select Customers, Orders, and Order Details by holding down the Ctrl key and clicking on each table name. Then select Add.

5. Click Close.

6. Some of the tables included in the query might be hiding below. If so, scroll down with the vertical scrollbar to view any tables that aren't visible. Notice the join lines between the tables; they're based on the relationships set up in the Relationships window.

7. Select the following fields from each table:

   Customers: Country, City

   Orders: Order Date

   Order Details: UnitPrice, Quantity

8. Sort by Country and then City. Your finished query design should look like the one in Figure 4.12.

9. Run the query. Data from all three tables should be included in the query output.

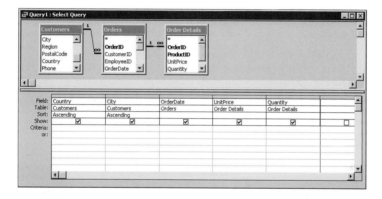

FIGURE 4.12

The query design from the example.

4

QUERY BASICS

NOTE

To remove a table from a query, click anywhere on the table in the top half of the query design grid and press the Delete key. You can add tables to the query at any time by clicking the Show Table button from the toolbar. If you prefer, you can select the Database window and then click and drag tables directly from the Database window to the top half of the query design grid.

Pitfalls of Multitable Queries

You should be aware of some pitfalls of multitable queries; they involve updating as well as which records you see in the query output.

It's important to remember that certain fields in a multitable query can't be updated. These are the join fields on the "one" side of a one-to-many relationship (unless the Cascade Update referential integrity feature has been activated). You also can't update the join field on the "many" side of a relationship after you've updated data on the "one" side. More importantly, which fields can be updated, and the consequences of updating them, might surprise you. If you update the fields on the "one" side of a one-to-many relationship, you must be aware of that change's impact. You're actually updating that record in the original table on the "one" side of the relationship; several records on the "many" side of the relationship will be affected.

For example, Figure 4.13 shows the result of a query based on the Customers, Orders, and Order Details tables. I have changed "Alfreds Futterkiste" to "Waldo Futterkiste" on a specific record of my query output. You might expect this change to affect only that specific order detail item. Pressing the down-arrow key to move off the record shows that all records associated with Alfreds Futterkiste have been changed. (See Figure 4.14.) This happened because all the orders for Alfreds Futterkiste were actually getting their information from one record in the Customers table—the record for customer ID ALFKI. This is the record I modified while viewing the query result.

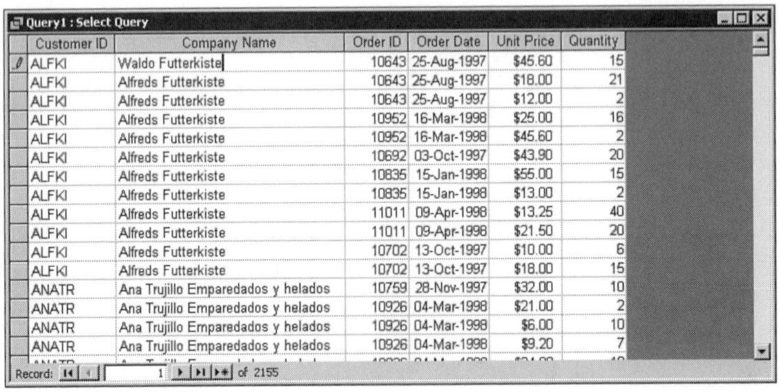

FIGURE 4.13

Changing a record on the "one" side of a one-to-many relationship. After updating the company name, all records with the same customer ID are affected.

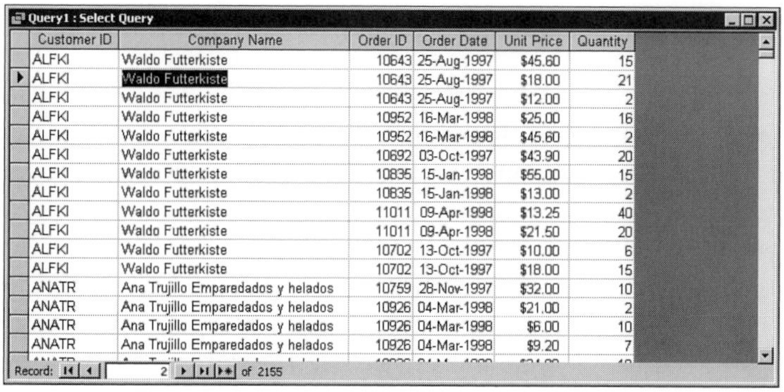

FIGURE 4.14

The result of changing a record on the "one" side of a one-to-many relationship. Notice that the Company Name field has been updated for all records with ALFKI *as the customer ID.*

TRY IT   To get this experience firsthand, try changing the data in the City field for one of the records in the query result. Notice that the record (as well as several other records) is modified. This happens because the City field actually represents data from the "one" side of the one-to-many relationship. In other words, when you're viewing the Country and City fields for several records in the query output, the data for the fields might originate from one record. The same goes for the Order Date field because it's also on the "one" side of a one-to-many relationship. The only field in the query output that can't be modified is TotalPrice, a calculated field. Practice modifying the data in the query result, and then returning to the original table and noticing which data has changed.

The second pitfall of multitable queries is figuring out which records result from such a query. So far, you have learned how to build only inner joins. Join types are covered in detail in Chapter 11, but for now, it's important to understand that the query output contains only customers who have orders and orders that have order detail. This means that not all the customers or orders might be listed. In Chapter 11, you learn how to build queries in which you can list all customers, regardless of whether they have orders. You'll also learn how to list only the customers without orders.

Row Fix-Up in Multitable Queries

The row fix-up feature is automatically available to you in Access. As you fill in key values on the "many" side of a one-to-many relationship in a multitable query, the non-key values are automatically looked up in the parent table. Most database developers refer to this as *enforced referential integrity*. A foreign key must first exist on the "one" side of the query to be entered successfully on the "many" side. As you can imagine, you don't want to be able to add an order to your database for a nonexistent customer.

4

QUERY BASICS

For example, the query in Figure 4.15 is based on the Customers and Orders tables. The fields included in the query are CustomerID from the Orders table; CompanyName, Address, and City from the Customers table; and OrderID and OrderDate from the Orders table. If the CustomerID associated with an order is changed, the CompanyName, Address, and City are looked up from the Customers table and immediately displayed in the query result. Notice in Figure 4.16 how the information for Alfreds Futterkiste is displayed in the query result. Figure 4.17 shows that the CompanyName, Address, and City change automatically when the CustomerID is changed. Don't be confused by the combo box used to select the customer ID. The presence of the combo box within the query is a result of Access's auto-lookup feature, covered in Chapter 2, "What Every Developer Needs to Know About Tables." The customer ID associated with a particular order is actually being modified in the query. If a new record is added to the query, the customer information is filled in as soon as the customer ID associated with the order is selected.

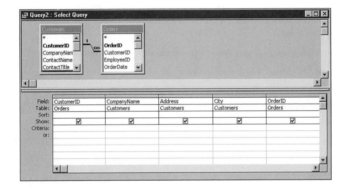

FIGURE 4.15
This query illustrates the use of Row Fix Up in a query with multiple tables.

Query2 : Select Query

Customer	Company Name	Address
Alfreds Futterkiste	Alfreds Futterkiste	Obere Str. 57
Alfreds Futterkiste	Alfreds Futterkiste	Obere Str. 57
Alfreds Futterkiste	Alfreds Futterkiste	Obere Str. 57
Alfreds Futterkiste	Alfreds Futterkiste	Obere Str. 57
Alfreds Futterkiste	Alfreds Futterkiste	Obere Str. 57
Alfreds Futterkiste	Alfreds Futterkiste	Obere Str. 57
Ana Trujillo Emparedados y hela	Ana Trujillo Emparedados y helados	Avda. de la Constitución 2222
Ana Trujillo Emparedados y hela	Ana Trujillo Emparedados y helados	Avda. de la Constitución 2222
Ana Trujillo Emparedados y hela	Ana Trujillo Emparedados y helados	Avda. de la Constitución 2222
Ana Trujillo Emparedados y hela	Ana Trujillo Emparedados y helados	Avda. de la Constitución 2222
Antonio Moreno Taquería	Antonio Moreno Taquería	Mataderos 2312
Antonio Moreno Taquería	Antonio Moreno Taquería	Mataderos 2312
Antonio Moreno Taquería	Antonio Moreno Taquería	Mataderos 2312
Antonio Moreno Taquería	Antonio Moreno Taquería	Mataderos 2312
Antonio Moreno Taquería	Antonio Moreno Taquería	Mataderos 2312
Antonio Moreno Taquería	Antonio Moreno Taquería	Mataderos 2312

Record: 1 of 830

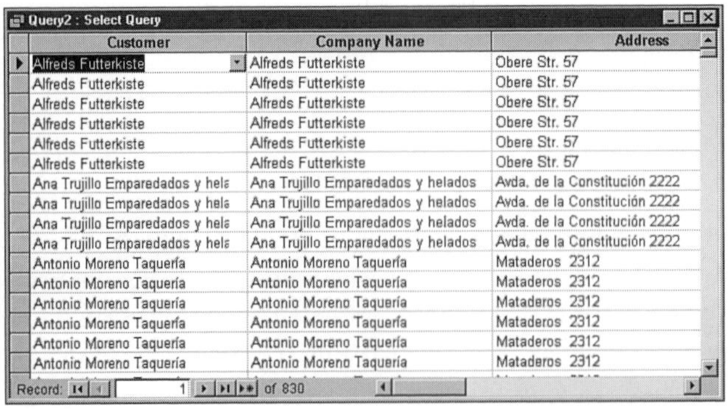

FIGURE 4.16
The query result before selecting another customer ID.

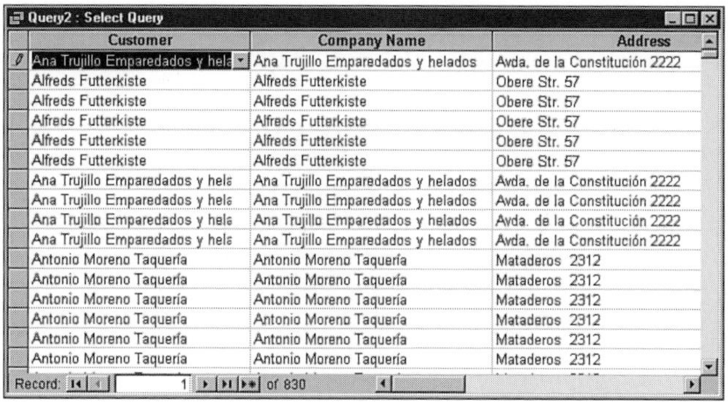

FIGURE 4.17

The result of an auto-lookup after the customer ID is changed. The information on the "one" side of the relationship is "fixed up" to display information for the appropriate customer.

Creating Calculated Fields

One of the rules of data normalization is that the results of calculations shouldn't be included in your database. You can output the results of calculations by building those calculations into your queries, and you can display the results of the calculations on forms and reports by making the query the foundation for a form or report. You can also add controls to your forms and reports containing the calculations you want. In certain cases, this can improve performance. (This topic is covered in more depth in Chapter 15, "Debugging: Your Key to Successful Development.")

The columns of your query result can hold the result of any valid expression, including the result of a user-defined function. This makes your queries extremely powerful. For example, the following expression could be entered:

```
Left([FirstName],1) & "." & Left([LastName],1) & "."
```

This expression would give you the first character of the first name followed by a period, the first character of the last name, and another period. An even simpler expression would be this one:

```
[UnitPrice]*[Quantity]
```

This calculation would simply take the UnitPrice field and multiply it by the Quantity field. In both cases, Access would automatically name the resulting expression. For example, the calculation that results from concatenating the first and last initials is shown in Figure 4.18. Notice that in the figure, the expression has been given a name (often referred to as an "alias"). To give the expression a name, such as Initials, you must enter it as follows:

```
Initials:Left([FirstName],1) & "." & Left([LastName],1) & "."
```

4

QUERY BASICS

The text preceding the colon is the name of the expression—in this case, Initials. If you don't explicitly give your expression a name, it defaults to Expr1.

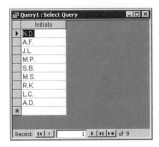

The result of the expression Initials:Left([FirstName],1) & "." & Left([LastName],1) & "." *in the query.*

TRY IT   Follow these steps to add a calculation that shows the unit price multiplied by the quantity:

1. Scroll to the right on the query design grid until you can see a blank column.

2. Click in the Field row for the new column.

3. Type **TotalPrice:UnitPrice*Quantity**. If you want to see more easily what you're typing, press Shift+F2 (Zoom). The dialog box shown in Figure 4.19 appears. (Access will supply the space after the colon and the square brackets around the field names if you omit them.)

FIGURE 4.19
Expanding the field with the Zoom function (Shift+F2).

4. Click OK to close the Zoom window.

5. Run the query. The total sales amount should appear in the far-right column of the query output. The query output should look like the one in Figure 4.20.

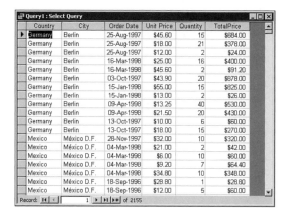

FIGURE 4.20
The result of the total price calculation.

NOTE

You can enter any valid expression in the Field row of your query design grid. Notice that field names included in an expression are automatically surrounded by square brackets, unless your field name has spaces. If a field name includes any spaces, you must enclose the field name in brackets; otherwise, your query won't run properly. This is just one of the many reasons why field and table names shouldn't contain spaces.

Getting Help from the Expression Builder

The Expression Builder is a helpful tool for building expressions in your queries, as well as in many other situations in Access. To invoke the Expression Builder, click in the Field cell of your query design grid and then click Build on the toolbar. (See Figure 4.21.) Notice that the Expression Builder is divided into three columns. The first column shows the objects in the database. After selecting an element in the left column, select the elements you want to paste from the middle and right columns.

The example in Figure 4.22 shows Functions selected in the left column. Within Functions, both user-defined and built-in functions are listed; here, the Functions object is expanded with Built-In Functions selected. In the center column, Date/Time is selected. After you select

4

QUERY BASICS

`Date/Time`, all the built-in date and time functions appear in the right column. If you double-click a particular function—in this case, the `DatePart` function—the function and its parameters are placed in the text box at the top of the Expression Builder window. Notice that the `DatePart` function has four parameters: `Interval`, `Date`, `FirstWeekDay`, and `FirstWeek`. If you know what needs to go into each of these parameters, you can simply replace the parameter place markers with your own values. If you need more information, you can invoke help on the selected function and learn more about the required parameters. In Figure 4.23, two parameters are filled in: the interval and the name of the field being evaluated. After clicking OK, the expression is placed in the Field cell of the query.

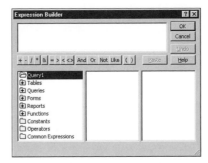

FIGURE 4.21

The Expression Builder makes it easier for you to create expressions in your query.

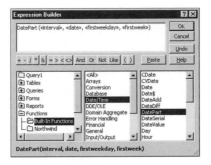

FIGURE 4.22

The Expression Builder with the `DatePart` function selected and pasted in the expression box.

FIGURE 4.23

A function pasted by Expression Builder with the parameters updated with appropriate values.

Summarizing Data with Totals Queries

By using Totals queries, you can easily summarize numeric data. Totals queries can be used to calculate the Sum, Average, Count, Minimum, Maximum, and other types of summary calculations for the data in your query result. These queries let you calculate one value for all the records in your query result or group the calculations as desired. For example, you could determine the total sales for every record in the query result, as shown in Figure 4.24, or you could output the total sales by country and city. (See Figure 4.25.) You could also calculate the total, average, minimum, and maximum sales amounts for all customers in the United States. The possibilities are endless.

FIGURE 4.24

Total sales for every record in the query result.

4

QUERY BASICS

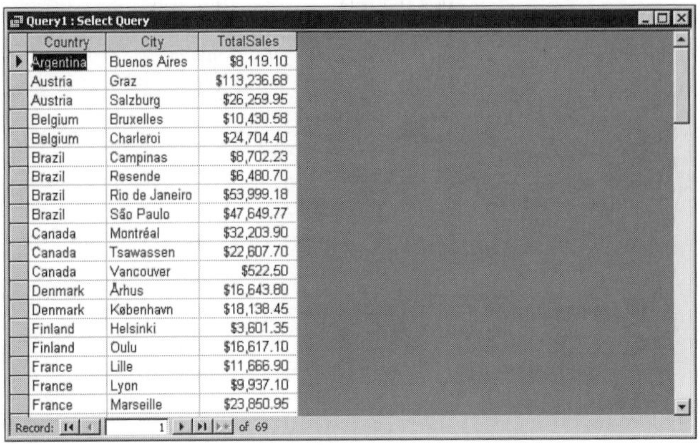

FIGURE 4.25

Total sales by country and city.

To create a Totals query, follow these steps:

1. Add to the query design grid the fields or expressions you want to summarize. It's important that you add the fields in the order in which you want them grouped. For example, Figure 4.26 shows a query grouped by country, and then city.

2. Click Totals on the toolbar or select View|Totals to add a Total row to the query. By default, each field in the query has Group By in the total row.

3. Click in the Total row on the query design grid.

4. Open the combo box and choose the calculation you want. (See Figure 4.26.)

5. Leave Group By in the Total cell of any fields you want to group by, as shown in Figure 4.26. Remember to place the fields in the order in which you want them grouped. For example, if you want the records grouped by country, and then by sales representative, the Country field must be placed to the left of the Sales Representative field on the query design grid. On the other hand, if you want records grouped by sales representative, and then by country, the Sales Representative field must be placed to the left of the Country field on the query design grid.

6. Add the criteria you want to the query.

Figure 4.27 shows the design of a query that finds the total, average, maximum, and number of sales by country and city; Figure 4.28 shows the results of running the query. As you can see, Totals queries can give you valuable information.

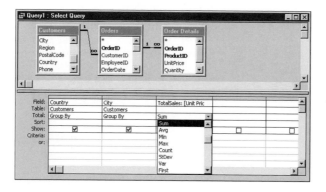

FIGURE 4.26

Selecting the type of calculation for the Total row from a drop-down list.

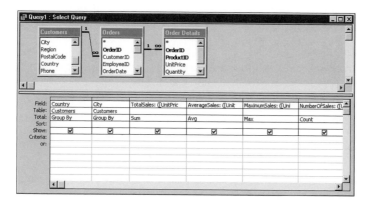

FIGURE 4.27

A query that finds the total, average, maximum, and number of sales by country and city.

If you save this query and reopen it, you'll see that Access has made some changes to its design. The Total cell for the Sum is changed to Expression, and the Field cell is changed to the following:

```
TotalSales: Sum([UnitPrice]*[Quantity])
```

If you look at the Total cell for the Avg, it's also changed to Expression. The Field cell is changed to the following:

```
AverageSales: Avg([UnitPrice]*[Quantity])
```

Access modifies the query in this way when it determines that you're using an aggregate function on an expression having more than one field. You can enter the expression either way. Access stores and resolves the expression as noted.

4

QUERY BASICS

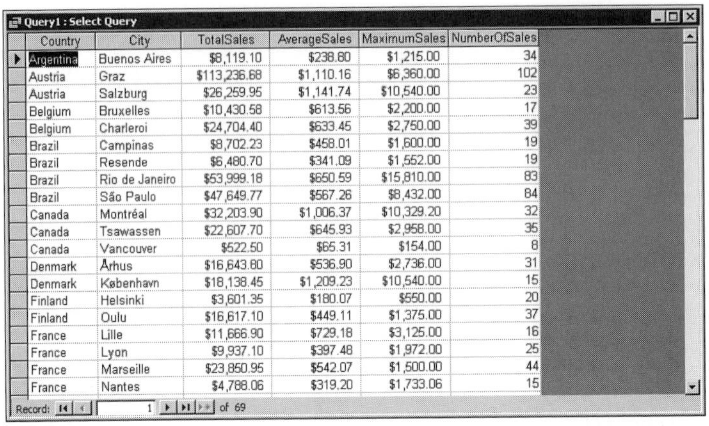

FIGURE 4.28

The result of running a query with many aggregate functions.

TRY IT Modify the query to show the total sales by country, city, and order date. Before you continue, save your query as qryCustomerOrderInfo, and then close it. With the Query tab of the Database window visible, click qryCustomerOrderInfo. Choose Copy from the toolbar and then Paste. Access should prompt you for the name of the new query. Type **qryCustomerOrderSummary** and click OK. With qryCustomerOrderSummary selected, click the Design command button. Delete both the UnitPrice and Quantity fields from the query output. To turn your query into a Totals query, follow these steps:

1. Click Totals on the toolbar. Notice that an extra line, called the Total line, is added to the query design grid; this line says Group By for all fields.

2. Group by country, city, and order date but total by the total price (the calculated field). Click the Total row for the TotalPrice field and use the drop-down list to select Sum. (Refer to Figure 4.26.)

3. Run the query. Your result should be grouped and sorted by country, city, and order date, with a total for each unique combination of the three fields.

4. Return to the query's design and remove the order date from the query design grid.

5. Rerun the query. Notice that now you're summarizing the query by country and city.

6. Change the Total row to Avg. Now you're seeing the average price times quantity for each combination of country and city. Change it back to Sum and save the query.

As you can see, Totals queries are both powerful and flexible. Their output can't be edited, but you can use them to view the sum, minimum, maximum, average, and count of the total price, all at the same time. You can easily modify how you're viewing this information—by country, country and city, and so on—all at the click of your mouse.

Excluding Fields from the Output

At times, you need to include a column in your query that you don't want displayed in the query output; this is often the case with columns used solely for criteria. Figure 4.29 shows an example. If this query were run, you would get the total, average, and maximum sales grouped by both country and order date. However, you want to group only by country and use the order date only as criteria. Therefore, you need to set the Total row of the query to `Where`, as shown in Figure 4.30. The column used in the `Where` has been excluded from the query result. This is easily determined by noting that the check box in the Show row of the OrderDate column is unchecked.

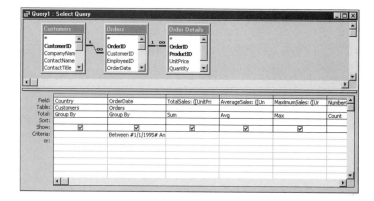

FIGURE 4.29

A query with criteria for the order date, before excluding fields from the query output.

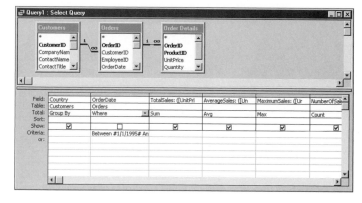

FIGURE 4.30

The Total row of the OrderDate field is set to `Where`, excluding the field from the query result.

Nulls and Query Results

Null values in your table's fields can noticeably affect query results. A Null value is different from a zero or a zero-length string, which indicates that the data doesn't exist for a particular field; a field contains a Null value when no value has yet been stored in the field. (As discussed in Chapter 2, a zero-length string is entered in a field by typing two quotation marks.)

Null values can affect the results of multitable queries, queries including aggregate functions (Totals queries), and queries with calculations. By default, when a multitable query is built, only records that have non-Null values on the "many" side of the relationship appear in the query result (discussed earlier in this chapter, in the "Pitfalls of Multitable Queries" section).

Null values can also affect the result of aggregate queries. For example, if you perform a count on a field containing Null values, only records having non-Null values in that field are included in the count. If you want to get an accurate count, it's best to perform the count on a Primary Key field or some other field that can't have Null values.

Probably the most insidious problem with Nulls happens when they're included in calculations. A Null value, when included in a calculation containing a numeric operator (+, -, /, *, and so on), results in a Null value. In Figure 4.31, for example, notice that the query includes a calculation that adds the values in the Parts and Labor fields. These fields have been set to have no default value and, therefore, contain Nulls unless something has been explicitly entered into them. Running the query gives you the results shown in Figure 4.32. Notice that all the records having Nulls in either the Parts or Labor fields contain a Null in the result.

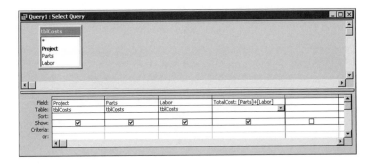

FIGURE 4.31
The Design view of a query that propagates Nulls in the query result.

The solution to this problem is constructing an expression that converts the Null values to zero. The expression looks like this:

```
TotalCost: NZ([Parts])+NZ([Labor])
```

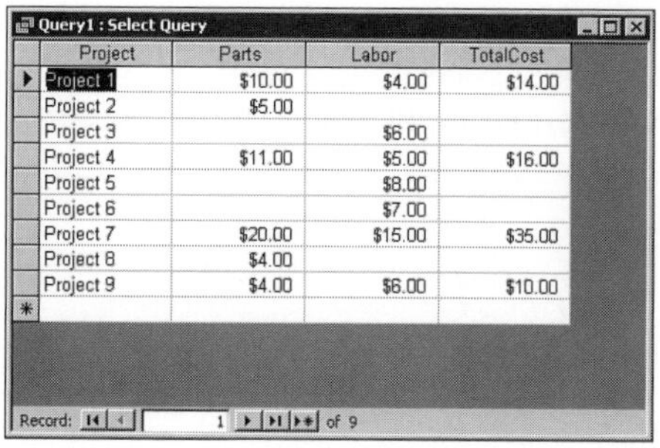

FIGURE 4.32

The result of running a query illustrating Nulls.

The NZ() function determines whether the Parts field contains a Null value. If the Parts field contains a Null value, it's converted to a zero and included in the calculation; otherwise, the field's value is used in the calculation. The same expression is used to evaluate the Labor field. The result of the modified query is shown in Figure 4.33.

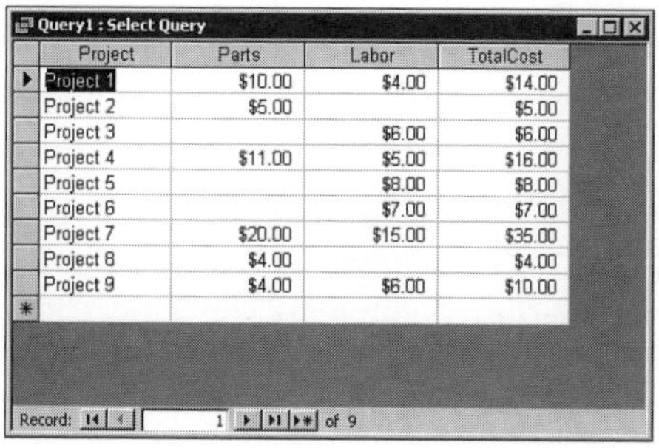

FIGURE 4.33

The query with an expression to convert Nulls to zero.

CAUTION

Nulls really cause trouble when the results of one query containing Nulls are used in another query—a snowball effect occurs. It's easy to miss the problem and output reports with inaccurate results. Using the NZ() function eliminates this kind of problem. You can use the NZ() function to replace the Null values with zeros or zero-length strings. Be careful when doing this, though, because it might affect other parts of your query that use this value for another calculation. Also, be sure to use any function in a query on the top level of the query tree only because functions at lower levels might hinder query performance. A *query tree* refers to the fact that a query can be based on other queries. Placing the criteria at the top of the query tree means that, if queries are based on other queries, the criteria should be placed in the highest-level queries.

Refining Your Queries with Field, Field List, and Query Properties

Field and query properties can be used to refine and control the behavior and appearance of the columns in your query and of the query itself. Here's how:

1. Click in a field to select the field, click in a field list to select the field list, or click in the Query Design window anywhere outside a field or the field list to select the query.

2. Click Properties on the toolbar.

3. Modify the desired property.

NOTE

If you click a field within the query design grid that has its Show check box cleared, only the query properties will display when you bring up the properties window for that field, not the field properties. If you mark the Show check box with the properties window open, the field properties will then be displayed.

Field Properties: Changing the Behavior of a Field

The properties of a field in your query include the Description, Format, Input Mask, and Caption of the column. The Description property documents the use of the field and controls what appears on the status bar when the user is in that column in the query result. The Format property is the same as theq Format property in a table's field; it controls the display of the field in the query result. The Input Mask property, like its table counterpart, actually controls how data is entered and modified in the query result. The Caption property in the query does the same thing as a Caption property of a field—sets the caption for the column in Datasheet view and the default label for forms and reports.

You might be wondering how the properties of the fields in a query interact with the same properties of a table. For example, how does the Caption property of a table's field interact with the Caption property of the same field in a query? All properties of a table's field are automatically inherited in your queries. Properties explicitly modified in the query override those same properties of a table's fields. Any objects based on the query inherit the properties of the query, not those of the original table.

> **NOTE**
>
> In the case of the Input Mask property, it is important that the Input Mask in the query not be in conflict with the Input Mask of the table. The Input Mask of the query can be used to further restrict the Input Mask of the table, but not to override it. If the query's Input Mask conflicts with the table's Input Mask, the user will not be able to enter data into the table.

Field List Properties: Changing the Properties of the Field List

Field List properties specify attributes of each table participating in the query. The two Field List properties are Alias and Source. The Alias property is used most often when the same table is used more than once in the same query. This is done in self-joins, covered in Chapter 11. The Source property specifies a connection string or database name when you're dealing with external tables that aren't linked to the current database.

Query Properties: Changing the Behavior of the Overall Query

Microsoft offers many properties, shown in Figure 4.34, that allow you to affect the behavior of the overall query. Some of the properties are discussed here; the rest are covered as applicable throughout this book.

The Description property documents what the query does. The Default View property is new in Access 2002. This property determines which view will display by default whenever the query is run. Datasheet is the default setting; PivotTable or PivotChart are the other two Default View settings that are available. Output All Fields shows all the fields in the query results, regardless of the contents of the Show check box in each field. Top Values lets you specify the top x number or x percent of values in the query result. The Unique Values and Unique Records properties are used to determine whether only unique values or unique records are displayed in the query's output. (These properties are also covered in detail in Chapter 11.)

FIGURE 4.34

Query properties that affect the behavior of a given query.

Several other more advanced properties exist. The Run Permissions property has to do with security and is covered in Chapter 28, "Advanced Security Techniques." Source Database, Source Connect String, ODBC Timeout, and Max Records all have to do with client/server issues and are covered in a separate book, *Alison Balter's Mastering Access 2002 Enterprise Development*. The Record Locks property concerns multiuser issues and is also covered in *Alison Balter's Mastering Access 2002 Enterprise Development*. The Recordset Type property determines whether updates can be made to the query output. By default, this is set to the Dynaset type allowing updates to the underlying data. Filter displays a subset that you determine, rather than the full result of the query. Order By determines the sort order of the query. The Orientation property whether the visual layout of the fields is left-to-right or right-to-left. The Subdatasheet Name property allows you to specify the name of the table or query that will appear as a subdatasheet within the current query. After the Subdatasheet property is set, the Link Child Fields and Link Master Fields properties designate the fields from the child and parent tables or queries that are used to link the current query to its subdatasheet. Finally, the Subdatasheet Height property sets the maximum height for a subdatasheet, and the Subdatasheet Expanded property determines whether the subdatasheet automatically appears in an expanded state.

Building Parameter Queries When You Don't Know the Criteria at Design Time

You, or your application's users, might not always know the parameters for a query output when designing the query. Parameter queries let you specify different criteria at runtime so that you don't have to modify the query each time you want to change the criteria.

For example, say you have a query, like the one shown in Figure 4.35, for which you want users to specify the date range of the data they want to view each time they run the query. The following clause has been entered as the criteria for the OrderDate field:

```
Between [Enter Starting Date] And [Enter Ending Date]
```

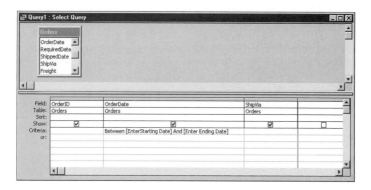

FIGURE 4.35

This Parameter query prompts for a starting date and an ending date.

This criterion causes two dialog boxes to appear when the query is run. The first one, shown in Figure 4.36, prompts the user with the criteria text in the first set of brackets (refer to Figure 4.35). The text the user types is substituted for the bracketed text. A second dialog box appears, prompting the user for whatever is in the second set of brackets. The user's response is used as the criterion for that query.

FIGURE 4.36

This dialog box appears when the Parameter query is run.

4

QUERY BASICS

TRY IT   Add a parameter to the query qryCustomerOrderSummary so that you can view
only TotalPrice summaries within a specific range. Go to the criteria for TotalPrice
and type **Between [Please Enter Starting Value] and [Please Enter Ending Value]**.
This allows you to view all the records in which the total price is within a specific range. The
bracketed text is replaced by actual values when the query is run. Click OK and run the query.
You're then prompted to enter both a starting and an ending value.

To make sure Access understands what type of data should be placed in these parameters, you
must define the parameters. Do this by selecting Parameters from the Query menu to open the
Parameters window. Another way to display the Query Parameters window is to right-click a
gray area in the top half of the query design grid; then select Parameters from the context-sensitive, pop-up menu.

The text that appears within the brackets for each parameter must be entered in the Parameter
field of the Query Parameters dialog. The type of data in the brackets must be defined in the
Data Type column. Figure 4.37 shows an example of a completed Query Parameters dialog box.

FIGURE 4.37
This completed Query Parameters dialog box declares two date parameters.

You can easily create parameters for as many fields as you want, and parameters are added just
as you would add more criteria. For example, the query shown in Figure 4.38 has parameters
for the Title, HireDate, and City fields in the Employees table from the Northwind database.
Notice that all the criteria are on one line of the query design grid, which means that all the
parameters entered must be satisfied for the records to appear in the output. The criterion for
the title is [Please Enter a Title]. This means that the records in the result must match the
title entered when the query is run. The criterion for the HireDate field is >=[Please Enter
Starting Hire Date]. Only records with a hire date on or after the hire date entered when the
query is run will appear in the output. Finally, the criterion for the City field is [Please Enter
a City]. This means that only records with the City entered when the query is run will appear
in the output.

The criteria for a query can also be the result of a function; this technique is covered in
Chapter 11.

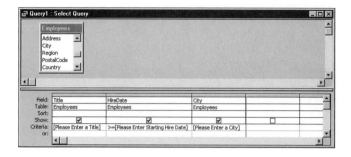

FIGURE 4.38

The Query Design window showing a query with parameters for three fields.

Parameter queries offer significant flexibility; they allow the user to enter specific criteria at runtime. What's typed in the Query Parameters dialog box must exactly match what's typed within the brackets; otherwise, Access prompts the user with additional dialog boxes.

You can add as many parameters as you like to a query, but the user might become bothered if too many dialog boxes appear. Instead, build a custom form that feeds the Parameter query. This technique is covered in Chapter 10, "Advanced Report Techniques."

Building Queries Needed by the Time and Billing Application for the Computer Consulting Firm

Build a query based on tblTimeCardHours. This query gives you the total billing amount by project for a specific date range. The query's design is shown in Figure 4.39. Notice that it's a Totals query that groups by project and totals by using the following expression:

```
BillAmount: Sum([BillableHours]*[BillingRate])
```

The DateWorked field is used as the Where clause for the query with this criteria:

`Between [Enter Start Date] And [Enter End Date]`

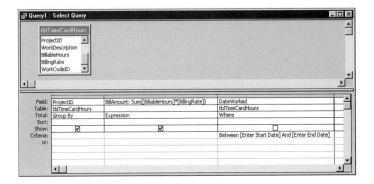

FIGURE 4.39

The design of the qryBillAmountByProject query.

The two parameters of the criteria are declared in the Parameters dialog box. (See Figure 4.40.) Save this query as `qryBillAmountByProject`.

FIGURE 4.40

The Query Parameters window for qryBillAmountByProject.

The second query is based on tblClients, tblProjects, and tblTimeCardHours. This query gives you the total billing amount by client for a specific date range. The query's design is shown in Figure 4.41. This query is a Totals query that groups by the company name from the tblClients table and totals by using the following expression:

`BillAmount: Sum([BillableHours]*[BillingRate])`

As with the first query, the DateWorked field is used as the Where clause for the query, and the parameters are defined in the Query Parameters window. Save this query as `qryBillAmountByClient`.

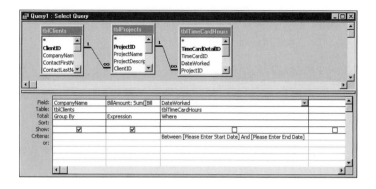

FIGURE 4.41

The design of the qryBillAmountByClient query.

 These queries are included on the sample CD-ROM in a database called CHAP4.MDB. Of course if this were a completed application, you would build many other queries.

Summary

This chapter covers the foundations of perhaps the most important function of a database: getting data from the database and into a usable form. You have learned about the Select query used to retrieve data from a table, how to retrieve data from multiple tables, and how to use functions in your queries to make them more powerful by synthesizing data. In later chapters, you will extend your abilities with Action queries and queries based on other queries (also known as *nested queries*).

What Every Developer Needs to Know About Forms

IN THIS CHAPTER

Why This Chapter Is Important

Most Access applications are centered on forms. Forms are used to collect and display information, navigate about the application, and more. This chapter covers all the basics of creating and working with forms. We'll begin by looking at the various uses of forms. Then we'll delve into the wealth of form and control properties. You'll learn the differences between bound, unbound, and calculated controls, and when it is appropriate to use each. You'll also learn important form techniques, such as how to create forms based on data from more than one table, and when forms should be populated with a query result rather than a table or embedded SQL statement.

Uses of Forms

Developers often think that forms exist solely for the purpose of data entry. To the contrary, forms serve many different purposes in Access 2002:

- Data entry—Displaying and editing data
- Application flow—Navigating through your application
- Custom dialog boxes—Providing messages to your user
- Printing information—Providing hard copies of data-entry information

Probably the most common use of an Access form is as a vehicle for displaying and editing existing data or for adding new data. Fortunately, Access offers many features that allow you to build forms that ease data entry for your users. Access also makes it easy for you to design forms that let your users view and modify data, view data but not modify it, or add new records only.

Although not everyone immediately thinks of an Access form as a means of navigating through an application, forms are quite strong in this area. Figure 5.1 shows a form created with the Switchboard Manager in Access 2002; Figure 5.2 shows a "home-grown" switchboard form. Although the Switchboard Manager makes designing a switchboard form very simple, you will find any type of switchboard easy to develop. You can be creative with switchboard forms by designing forms that are both utilitarian and exciting. Switchboard forms are covered in detail in Chapter 9, "Advanced Form Techniques."

You can also use Access to create custom dialog boxes used to display information or retrieve information from your users. The custom dialog box shown in Figure 5.3 gets the information needed to run a report. The user must fill in the required information before he can proceed.

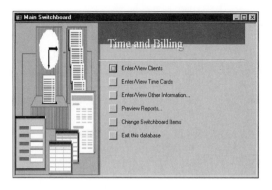

FIGURE 5.1

A form created with the Switchboard Manager.

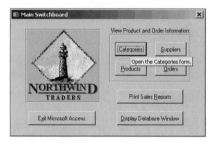

FIGURE 5.2

A custom switchboard with ToolTips and bitmaps.

FIGURE 5.3

A custom dialog box that lets the user specify a date range for a report.

Another strength of Access is its capability to produce professional-looking printed forms. With many other products, it's difficult to print a data-entry form; sometimes the entire form needs to be re-created as a report. In Access, printing a form is simply a matter of clicking a button that has a little code written behind it. You have the option of creating a report that displays the information your user is entering or of printing the form itself.

5

FORMS

Access offers many styles of forms. The data in a form can be displayed one record at a time, or you can let the user view several records at once. Forms can be displayed *modally*, meaning that the user must respond and close the form before continuing, or displayed so that the user can move through the open forms at will. The important thing to remember is that there are many uses and styles of forms. You will learn about them throughout this chapter, in Chapter 9, and throughout the book. As you read this chapter, remember that your forms are limited only by your imagination.

Anatomy of a Form

Access forms are comprised of a few different sections; each one has its own function and behavior. These are the three main sections of an Access form:

- Header
- Detail
- Footer

The Detail section of a form is the main section; it's the one used to display the data of the table or query underlying the form. As you will see, the Detail section can take on many different looks. It's quite flexible and robust.

The Header and Footer sections of the form are used to display information that doesn't change from record to record. Command buttons that control the form—such as one used to let users view all the projects associated with a particular client—are often placed in a form's header or footer. Controls can also be used to help the user navigate around the records associated with the form. In the example shown in Figure 5.4, the user can select from a valid list of clients. After a client has been selected from the combo box, the user is moved to the appropriate record.

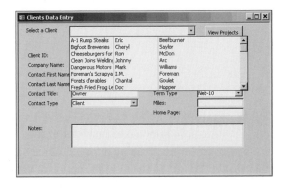

FIGURE 5.4

Record navigation using a combo box placed in the form header.

Creating a New Form

You can create a new form in several ways. The most common way is to select the Forms icon from the Objects list in the Database window. You can then select the Create Form in Design View icon or the Create Form by Using Wizard icon. Another way to create a form is to click Forms in the Objects list and then click the New button on the Database window toolbar. The New Form dialog box will appear, allowing you to select from a multitude of creation options. (See Figure 5.5.) Forms can be created from scratch by using Design view, or they can be created with the help of any one of eight wizards. The wizards will be covered briefly before you move on to the process of creating a form from scratch. Even the most experienced developers use the Form Wizard to perform certain tasks.

FIGURE 5.5
The New Form dialog box lets you specify the table or query to underlie the form and choose the method for creating the form.

Creating a Form with the Form Wizard

To create a form with the Form Wizard, select the Create Form By Using the Wizard icon with the Forms icon selected in the Objects list. You can also select Form Wizard from the New Form dialog and click OK. First, the Form Wizard prompts you for the name of the table or query you want to use as the form's foundation. Whether you're creating a form with Form Wizard or from Design view, it's generally better to base a form on a query or on an embedded SQL statement (a query stored as part of a form). Doing so offers better performance (unless your form requires all fields and all records), allows for more flexibility, and lets you create a form based on data from several tables.

Figure 5.6 shows the Tables/Queries drop-down list. You can see that all the tables are listed, followed by all the queries. After you select a particular table or query, its fields are displayed in the list box on the left. (See Figure 5.7.) To select the fields you want to include on the form, double-click the name of the field or click on the field; then click the > button. In the example shown in Figure 5.7, several fields have been selected from the qryClients query.

FIGURE 5.6

A list of tables and queries available for use in the Form Wizard.

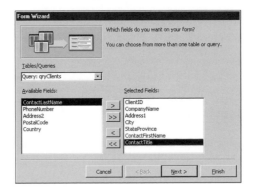

FIGURE 5.7

Selected fields from qryClients.

After you've selected the fields you want, click Next. The second step of the Form Wizard allows you to specify the layout for the form you're designing. You can select from Columnar, Tabular, Datasheet, Justified, PivotTable, or PivotChart; the most common choice is Columnar. Click Next after selecting a form layout.

In the third step of the Form Wizard, you can select a style for your form from several predefined styles. (See Figure 5.8.) Although all the properties set by the wizard can be modified in Design view after the form has been created, to save time, it's best to select the appropriate style now. Click Next after selecting a style.

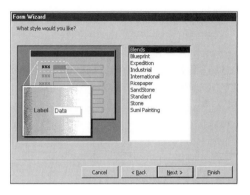

FIGURE 5.8

Selecting a form style.

In the final step of the Form Wizard, supply a title for your form. (If you just accept the default, the form will have the same name as the underlying table or query, which could be confusing.) Unfortunately, the form's title becomes the name of the form as well. For this reason, type the text you want to use as the name of the form. If you want to follow standard naming conventions, you should begin the name of the form with the tag *frm*. You can worry about changing the title in Design view of the form. This last step of the Form Wizard also lets you specify whether you want to view the results of your work or open the form in Design view. It's usually best to view the results and then modify the form's design after you have taken a peek at what the Form Wizard has done.

TIP

Another way to start the Form Wizard is to click the Tables or Queries icon in the Objects list, and then click the table or query you want the form to be based on. Use the New Object drop-down list on the toolbar to select Form; this opens the New Form dialog box. Select Form Wizard. You won't have to use the Tables/Queries drop-down list to select a table or query. The table or query you selected before invoking the wizard is automatically selected for you.

Creating a Form from Design View

Although the Form Wizards are both powerful and useful, in many cases you'll prefer building a form from scratch, especially if you're building a form that's not bound to data. To create a form without using a wizard, click Forms in the Objects list. Double-click the Create Form in Design View icon or click New on the Database window toolbar to open the New Form dialog

5

FORMS

box and select Design View (the default choice). If you clicked New to open the New Form dialog, and your form will be bound to data, use the drop-down list in the New Form dialog box to select the table or query that will serve as the form's foundation. Click OK, and the Form Design window appears. (See Figure 5.9.)

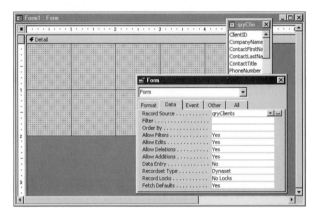

FIGURE 5.9
Use the Form Design window to build and customize a form.

Working with the Form Design Window

The Form Design window is used to build and customize a form. Using this window, you can add objects to a form and customize them by using the Properties window. Microsoft has supplied many form and control properties. After gaining a command of these properties, you can customize the look and feel of your forms.

Understanding and Working with the Form Design Tools

Even the best developer needs the right tools for the job. Fortunately, Microsoft has given you tools to help you build exciting and utilitarian forms. The Form Design window includes a toolbar, a toolbox, and the actual form you're designing. Other tools are available to help you with the design process, including the Field List and Properties window.

By default, two toolbars appear when you're in a form's Design view: the Form Design toolbar and the Formatting toolbar. The Form Design toolbar has buttons you use to save, print, copy, cut, paste, and perform other standard Windows tasks within the form. It also includes buttons that allow you to toggle the different design windows (such as the toolbox). The Format Painter tool allows you to easily apply all formatting from one control to one or more additional controls. The Build tool invokes the Choose Builder dialog box, from which you can invoke the Expression, Macro, or Code builder. The Formatting toolbar contains tools for graphically modifying the form's properties and objects. You can modify the font, font size, and color of selected objects on the form. With the Formatting toolbar, you can also add bold, underline, and italic or change the alignment; you can also add special effects to the selected objects.

Toggling the Tools to Get What You Want

Many windows are available to help you with the design process when you're in a form's Design view. If you don't have a high-resolution monitor, you'll probably find it annoying to have all the windows open at once. In fact, with all the windows open at once on a low-resolution monitor, the form is likely to get buried underneath all the windows. This is why Microsoft has made each window open and close in a toggle-switch–like fashion. The Form Design toolbar has tools for the Field List, Toolbox, and Properties windows, and each of these toolbar buttons is a toggle. Clicking once on the button opens the appropriate window; clicking a second time closes it.

Figure 5.10 shows a form with the Field List, Toolbox, and Properties windows open. Although each of these windows can be sized however you like (and the toolbox can be docked to a window edge), the design environment in this low-resolution display is rather cluttered with all these windows open. One of the tricks in working with Access is knowing when it's appropriate to have each set of tools available. The goal is to have the right windows open at the right time as often as possible.

FIGURE 5.10

The Form Design toolbar with Design windows visible.

NOTE

The Field List, Toolbox, and Properties windows can be closed by using the toolbar buttons. In addition, they can be closed by using the Close button on each window, or they can be toggled with the View menu.

TIP

Access 2002 offers some handy new shortcut keystrokes for working with forms and form properties. In Design view, the F4 key displays the property sheet. When working with a property sheet in Design view, pressing Shift+F7 will shift the focus to the Form Design window while maintaining the focus on the selected control. You can toggle among all available views for a form (Design, Datasheet, Form, PivotTable, PivotChart) by pressing CTRL+> or CTRL+. (period). You can toggle among the different views in the reverse order using CTRL+< or CTRL+, (comma). These shortcut keys are also supported for changing between available views of tables, queries, reports, pages, views, and stored procedures.

Adding Fields to the Form

Fields can be easily added to a form by using the Field List window, which contains all the fields that are part of the form's record source. The *record source* for the form is the table, query, or embedded SQL statement that underlies the form. For example, in Figure 5.10, the form's record source is qryClients. The fields listed in the Field List window are the fields that are part of the query. To add fields to a form, use these two steps:

1. Make sure the Field List window is visible. If it isn't, click the Field List button on the toolbar.
2. Locate the field you want to add to the form; then click and drag the field from the field list to the place on the form where you want it to appear. The location you select becomes the upper-left corner of the text box, and the attached label appears to the left of where you dropped the control.

NOTE

A *control* is an object that you add to a form or report. Types of controls include text boxes, combo boxes, list boxes, and check boxes.

> **NOTE**
>
> To add multiple fields to a form at the same time, select several qryClients fields from the field list. Use the Ctrl key to select noncontiguous fields or the Shift key to select contiguous fields. For example, hold down your Ctrl key and click on three noncontiguous fields. Each field will be selected. Next, click a field, hold down your Shift key, and click another field. All fields between the two fields will be selected. If you want to select all fields, double-click the field list title bar. Click and drag any one of the selected fields to the form, and all of them will be added to the form at once.

Selecting, Moving, Aligning, and Sizing Form Objects

You must know several important tricks of the trade when selecting, moving, aligning, and sizing form objects. These tips will save you hours of frustration and wasted time.

Selecting Form Objects

The easiest way to select a single object on a form is to click it. After the object is selected, you can move it, size it, or change any of its properties. Selecting multiple objects is a bit trickier, but can be done in several ways. Different methods are more efficient in different situations. To select multiple objects, you can hold down the Shift key and click each object you want to select. Each selected object is surrounded by selection handles, indicating that it has been selected.

Figure 5.11 shows a form with four selected objects; it's important to understand which objects are actually selected. The ClientID text box, the Address label and text box, and the Company Name label are all selected; however, the Client ID label and CompanyName text box aren't selected. If you look closely at the figure, you can see that the selected objects are completely surrounded by selection handles. The Client ID label and CompanyName text box each has just a single selection handle because they're attached to objects that are selected. If you change any properties of the selected objects, the Client ID label and CompanyName text box will be unaffected.

You can also select objects by lassoing them. Objects to be lassoed must be located adjacent to one another on the form. Place your mouse pointer on a blank area of the form (not over any objects)and then click and drag your mouse pointer. You can see a thin line around the objects your mouse pointer is encircling. When you let go, any objects that were within the lasso, including those only partially surrounded, are selected. If you want to deselect any of these objects to exclude them, hold down your Shift key and click the object(s) you want to deselect.

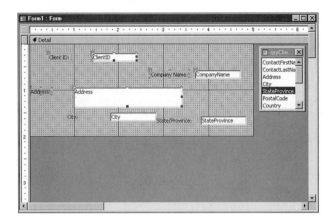

FIGURE 5.11

Selecting objects on a form.

One of my favorite ways to select multiple objects is to use the horizontal and vertical rulers that appear at the edges of the Form Design window. Click and drag within the ruler. Notice that as you click and drag on the vertical ruler, two horizontal lines appear, indicating which objects are selected. As you click and drag across the horizontal ruler, two vertical lines appear, indicating the selection area. When you let go of your mouse, any objects within the lines are selected. As with the process of lassoing, to remove any objects from the selection, hold down your Shift key and click on the object(s) you want to deselect.

Moving Things Around

To move a single control with its attached label, you don't need to select it first. Place your mouse over the object and click and drag. An outline appears, indicating the object's new location. When the object reaches the position you want, release the mouse. The attached label automatically moves with its corresponding control.

To move more than one object at a time, you must first select the objects you want to move. Select the objects using one of the methods outlined in the previous section. Place your mouse over any of the selected objects and click and drag. An outline appears, indicating the proposed new position for the objects. Release the mouse when you have reached the position you want for the objects.

Sometimes you want to move a control independent of its attached label, which requires a special technique. If you click a control, such as a text box, as you move your mouse over the border of the control, a hand icon with five fingers pointing upward appears. If you click and drag, both the control and the attached label move as a unit, and the relationship between them is maintained. If you place your mouse pointer over the larger handle in the upper-left corner of the object, the mouse pointer appears as a hand with only the index finger pointing upward.

If you click and drag here, the control moves independently of its attached label, and the relationship between the objects changes.

Aligning Objects to One Another

Access makes it easy to align objects. Figure 5.12 shows several objects that aren't aligned. Notice that the attached labels of three of the objects are selected. If you align the attached labels, the controls (in this case, text boxes) remain in their original positions. If you select the text boxes as well, they will try to align with the attached labels. Because Access doesn't allow the objects to overlap, the text boxes end up immediately next to their attached labels. To left-align any objects (even objects of different types), select the objects you want to align and then choose Format, Align, Left or right-click one of the objects and select Align, Left. The selected objects are then aligned. (See Figure 5.13.) You can align the left, right, top, or bottom edges of any objects on a form.

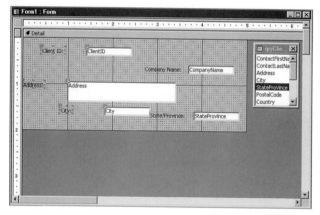

FIGURE 5.12
The form before aligning objects.

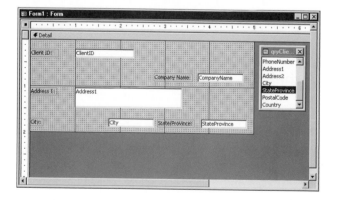

FIGURE 5.13
The form after aligning objects.

NOTE

Don't confuse the Format, Align feature with the Align tools (Align Left, Center, Align Right) on the Formatting toolbar. The Format, Align feature aligns objects one to the other, but the Align tools on the Formatting toolbar provide justification for the text inside of an object.

TIP

It is helpful to add to the toolbar the design tools that you commonly use. For example, you can easily add the Format|Align options to the toolbar. To modify the toolbar, select Tools|Customize. Click to display the appropriate toolbar on the Toolbars tab. You will find the align tools in the Form/Report Design category. Drag and drop the desired tools from the Commands list onto the appropriate toolbar.

Snap to Grid

The Snap to Grid feature determines whether objects snap to the gridlines on the form as you move and size them. This feature is found under the Format menu. If you turn off this feature (it's a toggle), objects can be moved and sized without regard for the gridlines.

TIP

I prefer to leave the Snap to Grid feature on at all times. I use a special trick to temporarily deactivate the feature when needed—hold down your Ctrl key as you click and drag to move objects. The Snap to Grid setting is then ignored.

Power Sizing Techniques

Just as there are several ways to move objects, you have several options for sizing objects. When an object is selected, each handle, except for the handle in the upper-left corner of the object, can be used to size the object. The handles at the top and bottom of the object allow you to change the object's height, and the handles at the left and right of the object let you change the object's width. You can use the handles in the upper-right, lower-right, and lower-left corners of the object to change the width and height of the object simultaneously. To size an object, place your mouse pointer over a sizing handle, click, and drag. You can select several objects and size them all at once. Each of the selected objects increases or decreases in size by the same amount; their relative sizes stay intact.

Access offers several powerful methods of sizing multiple objects, found under the Format, Size menu:

- **To Fit:** Sizes the selected objects to fit the text within them
- **To Grid:** Sizes the selected objects to the nearest gridlines
- **To Tallest:** Sizes the selected objects to the height of the tallest object in the selection
- **To Shortest:** Sizes the selected objects to the height of the shortest object in the selection
- **To Widest:** Sizes the selected objects to the width of the widest object in the selection
- **To Narrowest:** Sizes the selected objects to the width of the narrowest object in the selection

Probably the most confusing of the options is Format, Size, To Fit. This option is somewhat deceiving because it doesn't perfectly size text boxes to the text within them. In today's world of proportional fonts, it isn't possible to perfectly size a text box to the largest possible entry it contains. Generally, however, you can visually size text boxes to a sensible height and width. Use the field's Size property to limit what's typed in the text box. If the entry is too large to fit in the allocated space, the user can scroll to view the additional text. As the following Tip indicates, the Format, Size, To Fit option is much more appropriate for labels than it is for text boxes.

TIP

To quickly size a label to fit the text within it, select the label and then double-click any of its sizing handles, except the sizing handle in the upper-left corner of the label.

Controlling Object Spacing

Access gives you excellent tools for spacing the objects on your form an equal distance from one another. Notice in Figure 5.14 that the ClientID, Address, and City text boxes aren't equally spaced vertically from one another. To make the vertical distance between selected objects equal, choose Format, Vertical Spacing, Make Equal. In Figure 5.15, you can see the result of using this command on the selected objects in Figure 5.14.

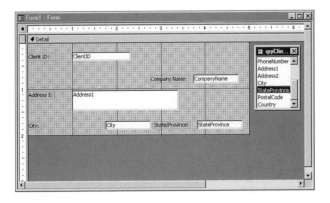

FIGURE 5.14

The form before modifying vertical spacing.

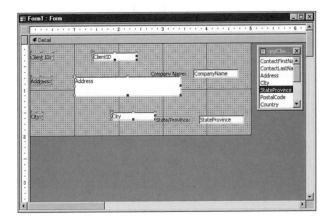

FIGURE 5.15

The form after modifying vertical spacing.

The horizontal distance between objects can be made equal by choosing Format, Horizontal Spacing, Make Equal. Other related commands that are useful are Format, Vertical Spacing, Increase (or Decrease) and Format, Horizontal Spacing, Increase (or Decrease). These commands maintain the relationship between objects while proportionally increasing or decreasing the distance between them.

Modifying Object Tab Order

The tab order for the objects on a form is determined by the order in which you add the objects to the form. However, this order isn't necessarily appropriate for the user. You might need to modify the tab order of the objects on the form. To do so, select View, Tab Order to open the Tab Order dialog box, shown in Figure 5.16. This dialog box offers two options. Use the Auto

Order button to tell Access to set the tab order based on each object's location in a section on the form. However, if you want to customize the order of the objects, click and drag the gray buttons to the left of the object names listed under the Custom Order heading to specify the objects' tab order.

> **NOTE**
>
> You must set the tab order for the objects in each section of the form (that is, header, detail, or footer) separately. To do this, select the appropriate section from the Tab Order dialog box, and then set the order of the objects in the section. If your selected form doesn't have a header or footer, the Form Header and Form Footer sections are unavailable.

FIGURE 5.16
Use the Tab Order dialog box to select the tab order of the objects in each section of a form.

Selecting the Correct Control for the Job

Windows programming in general, and Access programming in particular, isn't limited to just writing code. Your ability to design a user-friendly interface can make or break the success of your application. Access and the Windows programming environment offer a variety of controls, and each one is appropriate in different situations. The following sections discuss each type of control, outlining when and how it should be used.

Labels

Labels are used to display information to your users. Attached labels are automatically added to your form when you add other controls, such as text boxes, combo boxes, and so on, and they can be deleted or modified as necessary. Their default captions are based on the Caption property of the field that underlies the control they're attached to. If nothing has been entered into a field's Caption property, the field name is used for the label's caption.

The Label tool, found in the toolbox, can be used to add any text to the form. Click the Label tool; then click and drag the label to place it on the form. Labels are often used to provide a description of the form or to supply instructions to users. Labels can be customized by modifying their font, size, color, and so on. Although developers can use VBA code to modify label properties at runtime, users don't have this Ability.

> **TIP**
>
> Sometimes attached labels get detached from their associated text boxes. This means that the label will no longer move, size, and become selected with the text box that it applies to. To reassociate the label with the text box, cut the label (Ctrl+X), click to select the text box, and then press Ctrl+V to paste.
>
> If you purposely want to disassociate a label from its attached control, simply cut the label and then paste it back on the form *without* selecting the control that it was attached to. This allows you to perform tasks such as hiding the control without hiding the label.

Text Boxes

Text boxes are used to get information from the user. Bound text boxes display and retrieve field information stored in a table; unbound text boxes gather information from the user that's not related to a specific field in a specific record. For example, a text box can be used to gather information about report criteria from a user.

Text boxes are automatically added to a form when you click and drag a field from the field list to the form. The Display control for the field must be set to Text Box. (The Display control is the default control type for an object; this default is set in the design of the underlying table.). Another way to add a text box is to select the Text Box tool from the toolbox, and then click and drag to place the text box on the form. This process adds an unbound text box to the form. If you want to bind the text box to data, you must set its Control Source property.

Combo Boxes

Combo boxes allow a user to select from a list of appropriate choices. Access offers several easy ways to add a combo box to a form. If a field's Display Control property has been set to Combo Box, a combo box is automatically added to a form when the field is added. The combo box automatically knows the source of its data as well as all its other important properties.

If a field's Display Control property hasn't been set to Combo Box, the easiest way to add a combo box to a form is to use the Control Wizard. When selected, the Control Wizards tool helps you add combo boxes, list boxes, option groups, and subforms to your forms. Although all the properties set by the Combo Box Wizard can be set manually, using the wizard saves both time and energy. If you want the Combo Box Wizard to be launched when you add a combo box to the form, make sure the Control Wizards tool in the toolbox has been clicked (switched on) before you add the combo box.

Then, select the Combo Box tool in the toolbox, and then click and drag to place the combo box on the form. This launches the Combo Box Wizard; its first step is shown in Figure 5.17. You're offered three sources for the combo box's data. Use the first option if your combo box will select the data that's stored in a field, such as the state associated with a particular client. I rarely, if ever, use the second option, which requires that you type the values for the combo box. Populating a combo box this way makes it difficult to maintain. Every time you want to add an entry to the combo box, your application must be modified. The third and final option is appropriate when you want the combo box to be used as a tool to search for a specific record. For example, a combo box can be placed in the form's header to display a list of valid customers. After selecting a customer, the user is then moved to the appropriate record. This option is available only when the form is bound to a record source.

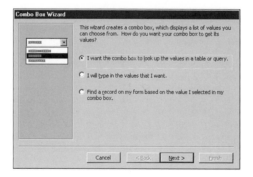

FIGURE 5.17
The first step of the Combo Box Wizard: selecting the source of the data.

In the second step of the Combo Box Wizard, you select a table or query to populate the combo box. For optimal performance, you should select a query. In the third step, you select the fields that appear in your combo box. (See Figure 5.18.) The combo box being built in the example will be used to select the client associated with a particular project. Although the CompanyName field will be the only field visible in the combo box, ClientID and CompanyName have both been selected because ClientID is a necessary element of the combo box. After a company name has been selected from the combo box, the client ID associated with the company name will be stored in the ClientID field of the tblProjects table.

5

FORMS

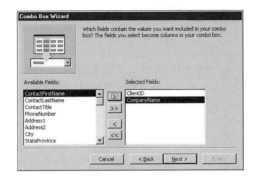

FIGURE 5.18

The third step of the Combo Box Wizard: selecting fields.

The fourth step lets you specify the width of each field in the combo box. Notice in Figure 5.19 that Access recommends that the key column, ClientID, be hidden. The idea is that the user will see the meaningful English description while Access worries about storing the appropriate key value in the record.

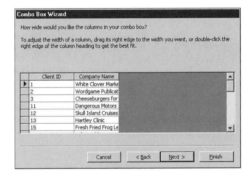

FIGURE 5.19

The fourth step of the Combo Box Wizard: setting column widths.

In the wizard's fifth step, you specify whether you want Access to simply remember the selected value or store it in a particular field in a table. In the example shown in Figure 5.20, the selected combo box value will be stored in the ClientID field of the tblProjects table.

The sixth and final step of the Combo Box Wizard prompts for the text that will become the attached label for the combo box. Pressing the Finish button completes the process, building the combo box and filling in all its properties with the appropriate values.

Although the Combo Box Wizard is a helpful tool, it's important to understand the properties it sets. Figure 5.21 shows the Properties window for a combo box. Many of the Combo Box properties are covered in other chapters, but take a moment to go over the properties set by the Combo Box Wizard in this example.

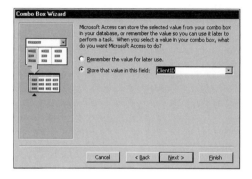

FIGURE 5.20

The fifth step of the Combo Box Wizard: indicating where the selected value will be stored.

The Control Source property indicates the field in which the selected entry is stored. In Figure 5.21, the selected entry will be stored in the ClientID field of the tblProjects table. The Row Source Type property specifies whether the source used to populate the combo box is a table/query, value list, or field list. In the example, the Row Source Type is Table/Query. The Row Source is the name of the actual table or query used to populate the combo box. In the example, the Row Source is tblClients. The Column Count property designates how many columns are in the combo box, and the Column Widths property indicates the width of each column. In the example, the width of the first column is zero, which renders the column invisible. Finally, Bound Column is used to specify which column in the combo box is being used to store data into the Control Source. In the example, this is column 1.

FIGURE 5.21

Properties of a combo box, showing that the ClientID field has been selected as the control source for the Combo5 combo box.

Combo boxes are very powerful controls, but you need to know many other things about them to leverage their power. The advanced aspects of combo boxes are covered in Chapter 9.

List Boxes

List boxes are similar to combo boxes, but differ from them in three major ways:

- They consume more screen space.
- They allow you to select only from the list that's displayed. This means you can't type new values into a list box (as you can with a combo box).
- They can be configured to let you select multiple items.

As with a combo box, the Display Control of a field can be set to List Box, and a list box will be added to the form when the field is clicked and dragged from the field list to the form.

The List Box Wizard is almost identical to the Combo Box Wizard. After running the List Box Wizard, the List Box properties affected by the wizard are the same as the Combo Box properties. Advanced list box techniques are covered in Chapter 9.

Check Boxes

Check boxes are used when you want to limit your user to entering one of two values, such as Yes/No, True/False, or On/Off. You can add a check box to a form in several ways:

- Set the Display Control of the underlying field to Check Box; then click and drag the field from the field list to the form.
- Click the Check Box tool in the toolbox; then click and drag a field from the field list to the form. This method adds a check box to the form even if the Display Control of the underlying field isn't a check box.
- Click the Check Box tool in the toolbox; then click and drag to add a check box to the form. The check box you have added will be unbound. To bind the check box to data, you must set the control's Control Source property.

TIP

Use the `Triple` state property of a check box to add a third value, `Null`, to the possible choices for the check box value.

Option and Toggle Buttons

Option buttons and toggle buttons can be used alone or as part of an option group. An option button or toggle button alone can be used to display a `True`/`False` value, but this isn't a standard use of an option or toggle button. (Check boxes are standard for this purpose.) As part of an option group, option buttons and toggle buttons force the user to select from a mutually exclusive set of options, such as choosing from American Express, MasterCard, Visa, or Discover for a payment type. This use of option buttons and toggle buttons is covered in the section, "Option Groups."

The difference between option buttons and toggle buttons is in their appearance. Personally, I find toggle buttons confusing to users. I find that option buttons provide a much more intuitive interface.

Option Groups

Option groups allow the user to select from a mutually exclusive set of options. They can include check boxes, toggle buttons, or option buttons, but the most common implementation of an option group is option buttons.

The easiest way to add an option group to a form is to use the Option Group Wizard. Make sure the Control Wizards button in the toolbox is selected, click Option Group in the toolbox, and then click and drag to add the option group to the form. This launches the Option Group Wizard.

The first step of the Option Group Wizard, shown in Figure 5.22, allows you to type the text associated with each item in the option group. The second step gives you the option of selecting a default choice for the option group. This choice comes into effect when a new record is added to the table underlying the form. The third step of the wizard lets you select values associated with each option button. (See Figure 5.23.) The text displayed with the option button isn't stored in the record; instead, the underlying numeric value is stored in the record. In Figure 5.23, the number 2 is stored in the field if Check is selected. The fourth step of the Option Group Wizard asks whether you want to remember the option group value for later use or store the value in a field. In Figure 5.24, the option group value is stored in the PaymentMethodID field. In the fifth step, you can select from a variety of styles for the option group buttons, including option buttons, check boxes, and toggle buttons. You can also select from etched, flat, raised, shadowed, or sunken effects for your buttons. The wizard lets you preview each option. The sixth and final step of the wizard allows you to add an appropriate caption to the option group. The completed group of option buttons is shown in Figure 5.25.

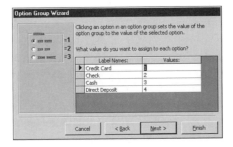

FIGURE 5.22

The first step of the Option Group Wizard: adding text to options.

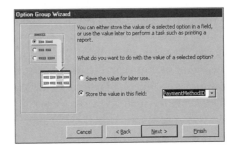

FIGURE 5.23

The third step of the Option Group Wizard: selecting values for options.

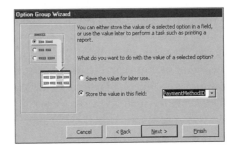

FIGURE 5.24

The fourth step of the Option Group Wizard: tying the group to data.

It's important to understand that the Option Group Wizard sets properties of the frame, the option buttons within the frame, and the labels attached to the option buttons. The properties of the frame are shown in Figure 5.26. The control source of the frame and the default value of the option group are set by the Option Group Wizard. Each individual option button is assigned a value, and the caption of the attached labels associated with each button is set.

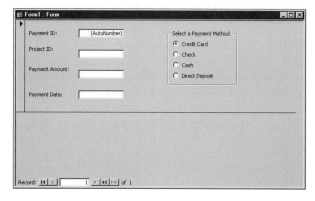

FIGURE 5.25

The results of running the Option Group Wizard.

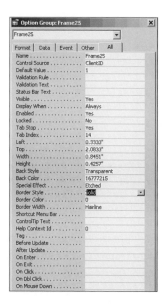

FIGURE 5.26

An option group frame, showing the properties of the selected button.

Control Morphing

When you first build a form, you might not always choose the best type of control to display each field on the form, or you might make what you think is the best choice for the control, only to find out later that it wasn't exactly what your user had in mind. In Access, it's easy to *morph*, or convert, the type of control into another type. For example, you can morph a list box into a combo box.

Morphing a Text Box to a Combo Box

One of the most common types of conversions is from a text box to a combo box. To morph a text box to a combo box, right-click on the text box. Choose Change To, and then select Combo Box. The types of controls available depend on the type of control you're morphing. For example, a text box can be converted to a label, list box, or combo box. (See Figure 5.27.)

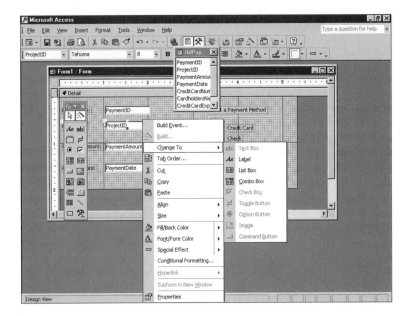

FIGURE 5.27

Morphing a text box.

After morphing a text box to a combo box, you modify the appropriate Control properties. The Row Source, Bound Column, Column Count, and Column Widths properties need to be filled in. For the row source, you must select the appropriate table or query. If you select a table and then click the ellipsis, you are prompted to create a query based on the table. After selecting Yes, you can build a query containing only the fields you want to include in the combo box. You're then ready to select the bound column, which is used to store data in the underlying table. For example, the user might select the name of a project that a payment is being applied to, but the ProjectID will be stored in the Payments table. Set the column count to the number of columns selected in the underlying query; the column widths can be set so that the key column is hidden.

Morphing a Combo Box to a List Box

Morphing a combo box to a list box is a much simpler process than morphing a text box to a combo box or a list box because combo boxes and list boxes share so many properties. To morph a combo box to a list box, simply right-click on the combo box and choose Change To, List Box.

Conditional Formatting

Access 2000 introduced conditional formatting, which displays data meeting specified criteria differently than it displays data meeting other criteria. For example, you can display sales higher than a certain amount in one color and sales less than that amount in another color. To conditionally format data displayed within a control, follow these steps:

1. Select the control you want to conditionally format.
2. Select Format|Conditional Formatting. The Conditional Formatting dialog appears.
3. Select Field Value Is, Expression Is, or Field Has Focus from the first combo box.
4. Select the appropriate operator from the second combo box.
5. Enter the values you are testing for in the text boxes that appear on the right.
6. Select the special formatting (bold, italic, background color, and so on) that you want to apply when the conditional criteria are met.
7. Click Add to add additional formats.
8. Click OK to apply the conditional formatting.

What Form Properties Are Available, and Why Should You Use Them?

Forms have many properties that can be used to affect their look and behavior. The properties are broken down into categories: Format, Data, Event, and Other.

To view a form's properties, you must select the form in one of two ways:

- Click the Form Selector (the small gray button at the intersection of the horizontal and vertical rulers)
- Choose Edit|Select Form

Working with the Properties Window

After a form has been selected, click the Properties button on the toolbar to view its properties. The Properties window, shown in Figure 5.28, consists of five tabs: Format, Data, Event,

5

FORMS

Other, and All. Many developers prefer to view all properties at once on the All tab, but a form can have a total of 107 properties! Rather than viewing all 107 properties at once, try viewing the properties by category. The Format category includes all the physical attributes of the form, the ones that affect the form's appearance (such as background color, for example). The Data category includes all the properties of the data that the form is bound to, such as the form's underlying record source. The Event category contains all the Windows events to which a form can respond. For example, you can write code that executes in response to the form being loaded, becoming active, displaying a different record, and so on. The Other category holds a few properties that don't fit into the other three categories.

FIGURE 5.28
Viewing the Format properties of a form.

Working with the Important Form Properties

As mentioned, forms have 107 properties, and, of those, 52 are Event properties, covered in Chapter 9. This section covers the Format, Data, and Other properties of forms.

Format Properties of a Form

The Format properties of a form affect its physical appearance. Forms have 31 Format properties, described here.

Caption: The Caption property sets the text that appears on the form's title bar. This property can be customized at runtime. For example, you could include the name of the current user or specify the name of the client for whom an invoice is being generated.

Default View: The Default View property allows you to select from five available options:

- SINGLE FORM—Only one record can be viewed at a time.
- CONTINUOUS FORMS—As many records as will fit within the form window are displayed at one time, each presented as the detail section of a single form.

- `DATASHEET`—Displays the records in a spreadsheet-like format, with the rows representing records and the columns representing fields.
- `PIVOTTABLE`—Displays the records in a Microsoft Excel–type PivotTable format.
- `PIVOTCHART`—Displays the records in a Microsoft Excel–type PivotChart format

The selected option becomes the default view for the form.

Allow Form View: Prior to Access 2002, Access forms had a property called Views Allowed. The This Views Allowed property determined whether the user was allowed to switch from Form view to Datasheet view, or vice versa. The Default View property determined the initial default display mode for the form, but Views Allowed determined whether the user was permitted to switch out of the default view.

In Access 2002, Microsoft has separated out each type of view as an additional property for the form. Allow Form View specifies whether the user is permitted to switch to the Form view of a form.

Allow Datasheet View: Allow Datasheet View determines whether the user is permitted to switch to the Datasheet view of a form.

Allow PivotTable View: Allow PivotTable View determines whether the user is allowed to switch to the PivotTable view of a form.

Allow PivotChart View: Allow PivotChart View determines whether the user is allowed to switch to the PivotChart view of a form.

Scroll Bars: The Scroll Bars property determines whether scrollbars appear if the controls on the form don't fit within the form's display area. You can select from vertical and horizontal scrollbars, neither vertical nor horizontal, just vertical, or just horizontal.

Record Selectors: A record selector is the gray bar to the left of a record in Form view, or the gray box to the left of each record in Datasheet view. It's used to select a record to be copied or deleted. The Record Selectors property determines whether the record selectors appear. If you give the user a custom menu, you can opt to remove the record selector to make sure the user copies or deletes records using only the features specifically built in to your application.

Navigation Buttons: Navigation buttons are the controls that appear at the bottom of a form; they allow the user to move from record to record within the form. The Navigation Buttons property determines whether the navigation buttons are visible. You should set it to No for any dialog forms, and you might want to set it to No for data-entry forms, too, and add your own toolbar or command buttons that enhance or limit the standard buttons' functionality. For example, in a client/server environment, you might not want to give users the ability to move to the first or last record because that type of record movement can be inefficient in a client/server architecture.

5

FORMS

Dividing Lines: The Dividing Lines property indicates whether you want a line to appear between records when the default view of the form is set to `Continuous Forms`. It also determines whether dividing lines are placed between the form's sections (header, detail, and footer).

Auto Resize: The Auto Resize property determines whether the form is automatically sized to display a complete record.

Auto Center: The Auto Center property specifies whether you want the form to automatically be centered within the Application window whenever it's opened.

Border Style: The Border Style property is far more powerful than its name implies. The options for the Border Style property are `None`, `Thin`, `Sizable`, and `Dialog`. The border style is often set to `None` for splash screens, which means the form has no border. A `Thin` border is not resizable; the Size command isn't available in the Control menu. This setting is a good choice for pop-up forms, which remain on top even when other forms are given the focus. A `Sizable` border is standard for most forms. It includes all the standard options in the Control menu. A `Dialog` border looks like a `Thin` border. A form with a border style of Dialog can't be maximized, minimized, or resized. Once the border style of a form is set to `Dialog`, the Maximize, Minimize, and Resize options aren't available in the form's Control menu. The `Dialog` border is often used along with the Pop Up and Modal properties to create custom dialog boxes.

Control Box: The Control Box property determines whether a form has a Control menu. You should use this option sparingly. One of your responsibilities as an Access programmer is to make your applications comply with Windows standards. If you look at the Windows programs you use, you'll find very few forms without Control menu boxes. This should tell you something about how to design your own applications.

Min Max Buttons: The Min Max Buttons property indicates whether the form has minimize and maximize buttons. The available options are `None`, `Min Enabled`, `Max Enabled`, and `Both Enabled`. If you remove one or both buttons, the appropriate options also become unavailable in the Control menu. The Min Max property is ignored for forms with a border style of `None` or `Dialog`. As with the Control Box property, I rarely use this property. To make my applications comply with Windows standards, I set the Border Style property, and then inherit the standard attributes for each border style.

Close Button: The Close Button property determines whether the user can close the form by using the Control menu or double-clicking the Control icon. If you set the value of this property to `No`, you must give your user another way to close the form; otherwise, the user might have to reboot his or her computer to close your application.

Whats This Button: The Whats This Button property specifies whether you want the Whats This button added to the form's title bar. This feature works only when the form's Min Max

Buttons property is set to No. When the Whats This Button property is set to Yes, the user can click on the Whats This button and then click on an object on the form to display Help for that object. If the selected object has no Help associated with it, Help for the form is displayed, and if the form has no Help associated with it, Microsoft Access Help is displayed.

Width: The Width property is used to specify the form's width. This option is most often set graphically by clicking and dragging to select an appropriate size for the form. You might want to set this property manually when you want more than one form to be the exact same size.

Picture, Picture Type, Picture Size Mode, Picture Alignment, and Picture Tiling: The Picture properties let you select and customize the attributes of a bitmap used as the background for a form.

Grid X, Grid Y: The Grid X and Grid Y properties can be used to modify the spacing of the horizontal and vertical lines that appear in the form when in Design view. By setting these properties, you can affect how precisely you place objects on the form when the Snap to Grid option is active.

Layout for Print: The Layout for Print property specifies whether screen or printer fonts are used on the form. If you want to optimize the form for printing rather than display, set this property to Yes.

SubdatasheetHeight: The SubdatasheetHeight property is used to designate the maximum height for a subdatasheet.

SubdatasheetExpanded: The SubdatasheetExpanded property allows you to designate whether a subdatasheet is initially displayed in an expanded format. When set to False, the subdatasheet appears collapsed. When set to True, the subdatasheet appears in an expanded format.

Palette Source: The Palette Source property determines the source for selecting colors for a form.

Orientation: The Orientation property allows you to take advantage of language-specific versions of Microsoft Access, such as Arabic. This property can be set to support right-to-left display features for language-specific editions of Access, provided that the underlying operating system supports that language and is 32-bit (for example, Windows 2000).

Moveable: The Moveable property determines whether the user can move the form window around the screen by clicking and dragging the form by its title bar.

Data Properties of a Form

The Data properties of a form are used to control the source for the form's data, what sort of actions the user can take on the data in the form, and how the data in the form is locked in a multiuser environment. There are 11 Data properties of a form.

5

FORMS

Record Source: The Record Source property indicates the Table, Stored Query, or SQL statement on which the form's records are based. After you have selected a record source for a form, the controls on the form can be bound to the fields in the record source.

> **NOTE**
>
> The Field List window is unavailable until the record source of the form has been set.

> **TIP**
>
> The record source of a form can be changed at runtime. Because of this aspect of the Record Source property, you can create generic, reusable forms for many situations.

Filter: The Filter property is used to automatically load a stored filter along with the form. I prefer to base a form on a query that limits the data displayed on the form. The query can be passed parameters at runtime to customize exactly what data is displayed.

Order By: The Order By property specifies in what order the records on a form appear. This property can be modified at runtime.

Allow Filters: The Allow Filters property controls whether records can be filtered at runtime. When this option is set to No, all filtering options become disabled to the user.

Allow Edits, Allow Deletions, Allow Additions: These properties let you specify whether the user can edit data, delete records, or add records from within the form. These options can't override any permissions that have been set for the form's underlying table or queries. Security is covered in Chapters 27, "Database Security Made Easy," and 28, "Advanced Security Techniques."

Data Entry: The Data Entry property determines whether your users can only add records within a form. Set this property to Yes if you don't want your users to view or modify existing records but want them to be able to add new records.

Recordset Type: The Recordset Type property gives you three options: Dynaset, Dynaset (Inconsistent Updates), and Snapshot. Each offers different performance and updating capability. The Dynaset option creates a fully updateable recordset. The only exceptions to this rule involve records or fields that can't be updated for some other reason. An example is a form based on a query involving a one-to-many relationship. The join field on the one side of the relationship can be updated only if the Cascade Update Related Records feature has been enabled. The Dynaset (Inconsistent Updates) option allows all tables and bound data to be edited. This might result in inconsistent updating of data in the tables involved in the query. The Snapshot option doesn't allow any updating.

Record Locks: The Record Locks property specifies the locking mechanism to be used for the data underlying the form's recordset. Three options are available. The No Locks option—the least restrictive locking mechanism—provides *optimistic locking*; that is, Access doesn't try to lock the record until the user moves off it. This option can lead to potential conflicts when two users simultaneously make changes to the same record. The All Records option locks all records underlying the form the entire time the form is open. This is the most restrictive option and should be used only when it's necessary for the form's user to make sure other users can view, but not modify, the form's underlying recordset. The Edited Record option locks a 4KB page of records as soon as a user starts editing the data in the form. This option provides *pessimistic locking*. Although it averts conflicts by prohibiting two users from modifying a record at the same time, it can lead to potential locking conflicts. These three locking options are covered in detail in *Alison Balter's Mastering Access 2002 Enterprise Development*.

Fetch Defaults: The Fetch Defaults property is new in Access 2002. It allows you to specify whether defaults for bound fields underlying the form are retrieved when new records are added. When this property is set to No, default values are not retrieved. When set to Yes, default values are retrieved.

Other Properties of a Form

Pop Up: The Pop Up property indicates whether the form always remains on top of other windows. This property is often set to Yes, along with the Modal property, for custom dialog boxes.

Modal: The Modal property indicates whether focus can be removed from a form while it's open. When the Modal property is set to Yes, the form must be closed before the user can continue working with the application. As mentioned, this property is used with the Pop Up property to create custom dialog boxes.

Cycle: The Cycle property controls the behavior of the Tab key in the form. The options are All Records, Current Record, and Current Page. When the Cycle property is set to All Records, the user moves to the next record on a form when he presses Tab from the last control on the previous record. With Current Record, the user is moved from the last control on a form to the first control on the same record. The Current Page option refers only to multipage forms; when the Cycle property is set to Current Page, the user tabs from the last control on the page to the first control on the same page. All three options are affected by the tab order of the objects on the form.

5

FORMS

Menu Bar: The Menu Bar property specifies a menu bar associated with the form. The menu bar, sometimes referred to as a *command bar* in Access 2002, is created by using the Customize dialog box. Reach this dialog box by choosing Toolbars from the View menu and then selecting Customize. Menus are covered in Chapter 9, "Advanced Form Techniques."

Toolbar: The Toolbar property designates a toolbar associated with the form. The toolbar, sometimes referred to as a *command bar* in Access 2002, is created by using the Customize dialog box. The toolbar you select is displayed whenever the form has the focus. Toolbars are covered in Chapter 9.

Shortcut Menu, Shortcut Menu Bar: The Shortcut Menu property indicates whether a shortcut menu is displayed when the user clicks with the right mouse button over an object on the form. The Shortcut Menu Bar property lets you associate a custom menu with a control on the form or with the form itself. As with a standard menu bar, a shortcut menu bar is created by choosing Toolbars from the View menu and then selecting Customize. Shortcut menus are covered in Chapter 9.

Fast Laser Printing: The Fast Laser Printing property determines whether lines and rectangles print along with the form. When this property is set to Yes, you'll notice a definite improvement when printing the form to a laser printer.

Help File, Help Context ID: The Help File and Help Context ID properties are used to associate a specific Help file and topic with a form.

Tag: The Tag property is an extra property used to store miscellaneous information about the form. This property is often set and monitored at runtime to store necessary information about the form. You could use the Tag property to add a tag to each of several forms that should be unloaded as a group.

Has Module: The Has Module property determines whether the form has a class module. If no code is associated with your form, setting this property to No can noticeably decrease load time and improve your form's performance while decreasing the database's size.

Allow Design Changes: The Allow Design Changes property determines whether changes can be made to the design of the form while viewing form data. If this property is set to All Views, the Properties window is available in Form view, and changes made to form properties while in Form view are permanent if the form is saved.

What Control Properties Are Available, and Why Use Them?

Available Control properties vary quite a bit, depending on the type of control that's been selected. The more common properties are covered in this section; individual properties are covered throughout the book as they apply to a specific topic.

Format Properties of a Control

Format: The Format property of a control determines how the data in the control is displayed. A control's format is automatically inherited from its underlying data source. This property is used in three situations:

- When the Format property is not set for the underlying field
- When you want to override the existing Format setting for the field
- When you want to apply a format to an unbound control

You can select from a multitude of predefined values for a control's format, or you can create a custom format. I often modify this property at runtime to vary the format of a control depending on a certain condition. For example, the format for a Visa card number is different from the format for an ATM card number.

Decimal Places: The Decimal Places property specifies how many decimal places you want to appear in the control. This property is used with the Format property to determine the control's appearance.

Caption: The Caption property is used to specify information helpful to the user. It's available for labels, command buttons, and toggle buttons.

Hyperlink Address: The Hyperlink Address property is available only for command buttons, images, and unattached labels. It contains a string used to specify the a UNC (path to a file) or a URL (Web page address) associated with the control. When the form is active and the cursor is placed over the control, clicking the control displays the specified object or Web page.

Hyperlink SubAddress: Like the Hyperlink Address property, the Hyperlink SubAddress property is available only for command buttons, images, and unattached labels. The Hyperlink SubAddress property is a string representing a location in the document specified in the Hyperlink Address property.

Visible: The Visible property indicates whether a control is visible. This property can be toggled at runtime, depending on specific circumstances. For example, a question on the form might apply only to records in which the gender is set to `Female`; if the gender is set to `Male`, the question shouldn't be visible.

Display When: The Display When property is used when you want certain controls on the form to be sent only to the screen or only to the printer. The three options are `Always`, `Print Only`, or `Screen Only`. An example of the use of the Display When property is a label containing instructions. You might want the instructions to appear on the screen but not on the printout.

Scroll Bars: The Scroll Bars property determines whether scrollbars appear when the data in the control doesn't fit within the control's size. The options are None and Vertical. I often set the Scroll Bars property to Vertical when the control is used to display data from a Memo field. The scrollbar makes it easier for the user to work with a potentially large volume of data in the Memo field.

Can Grow, Can Shrink: The Can Grow and Can Shrink properties apply only to the form's printed version. The Can Grow property, when set to Yes, expands the control when printing so that all the data in the control fits on the printout. When the Can Shrink property is set to Yes and no data has been entered, the control shrinks so that blank lines won't be printed.

Left, Top, Width, Height: These properties are used to set the control's position and size.

Back Style, Back Color: The Back Style property can be set to Normal or Transparent. When set to Transparent, the form's background color shows through the control. This is often the preferred setting for an option group. The control's Back Color property specifies the background color (as opposed to text color) for the control.

CAUTION

If the Back Style of a control is set to Transparent, the control's back color is ignored.

Special Effect: The Special Effect property adds 3D effects to a control. The options for this property are Flat, Raised, Sunken, Etched, Shadowed, and Chiseled. Each of these effects gives the control a different look.

Border Style, Border Color, Border Width: These properties affect the look, color, and thickness of a control's border. The border style options are Transparent, Solid, Dashes, Short Dashes, Dots, Sparse Dots, Dash Dot, and Dash Dot Dot. The Border Color property specifies the color of the border; you can select from a variety of colors. The Border Width property can be set to one of several point sizes.

CAUTION

If the Border Style of a control is set to Transparent, the control's Border Color and Border Width are ignored.

Fore Color, Font Name, Font Size, Font Weight, Font Italic, Font Underline: These properties control the appearance of the text in a control. As their names imply, they let you select a color, font, size, and thickness of the text and determine whether the text is italicized or underlined. These properties can be modified in response to a runtime event, such as modifying a control's text color if the value in that control exceeds a certain amount. The Font Weight selections generally exceed what is actually available for a particular font and printer—normally, you have a choice of only Regular and Bold, in whatever value you select for this property.

Text Align: The Text Align property is often confused with the ability to align controls. The Text Align property affects how the data is aligned *within* a control.

Reading Order: The Reading Order property is new in Access 2002. As its name implies, it allows you to specify the reading order for text in a control. This feature is only available if you are using a version of Microsoft Office that supports right-to-left features.

Keyboard Language: The Keyboard Language property is new to Access 2002. It allows you to override the keyboard language currently in use. This means that when a specific control receives the focus, the language specified in this property becomes the keyboard language in affect while typing data into the control.

Scroll Bar Align: The Scroll Bar Align property is another language-related property new in Access 2002. You use this property to place the vertical scrollbars in the appropriate left-to-right or right-to-left position. If the System option is selected, the position of the scrollbar is based on the selected user interface language. The scrollbar is placed on the right for left-to-right languages and on the left for right-to-left languages. If Left or Right is selected, the scrollbar is placed on the left or right side of the control, respectively.

Numerical Shape: The Numerical Shape property is new to Access 2002. It allows you to designate whether numeric shapes are displayed in the Arabic or Hindi style. The available choices for this property are System, Arabic, National, and Context. System bases the Numerical Shape on the operating system. Arabic and National use the Arabic and Hindi styles, respectively. Context bases the numerical style on the text adjacent to the control.

Left Margin, Top Margin, Right Margin, Bottom Margin: These properties determine how far the text appears from the left, top, right, and bottom of the control. They are particularly useful with controls such as text boxes based on memo fields, which are generally large controls.

5

FORMS

Line Spacing: The Line Spacing property is used to determine the spacing between lines of text in a multiline control. This property is most commonly used with a text box based on a memo field.

Is Hyperlink: This property, when set to Yes, formats the data in the control as a hyperlink. If the data in the control is a relevant link (that is, `http:\\microsoft.com`), the data will function as a hyperlink.

Data Properties of a Control

Control Source: The Control Source property specifies the field from the record source that's associated with a particular control. A control source can also be any valid Access expression.

Input Mask: The Format and Decimal Places properties affect the appearance of a control, but the Input Mask property affects what data can be entered into the control. The input mask of the field underlying the control is automatically inherited into the control. If no input mask is entered as a field property, the input mask can be entered directly in the form. If the input mask of the field is entered, the input mask of the associated control on a form can be used to further restrict what is entered into that field via the form.

NOTE

If a control's Format property and Input Mask property are different, the Format property affects the display of the data in the control until the control gets focus. Once the control gets focus, the Input Mask property prevails.

Default Value: The Default Value property of a control determines the value assigned to new records entered in the form. This property can be set within the field properties. A default value set at the field level is automatically inherited into the form. The default value set for the control overrides the default value set at the field level.

Validation Rule, Validation Text: The validation rule and validation text of a control perform the same functions as they do for a field.

CAUTION

Because the validation rule is enforced at the database engine level, the validation rule set for a control can't be in conflict with the validation rule set for the field to which the control is bound. If the two rules conflict, the user can't enter data into the control.

Enabled: The Enabled property determines whether you allow a control to get focus. If set to No, the control appears dimmed.

Locked: The Locked property determines whether the data in the control can be modified. When the Locked property is set to Yes, the control can get focus but can't be edited. The Enabled and Locked properties of a control interact with one another. Table 5.1 summarizes their interactions.

TABLE 5.1   How Enabled and Locked Properties Interact

Enabled	Locked	Effect
Yes	Yes	The control can get focus; its data can be copied but not modified.
Yes	No	The control can get focus, and its data can be edited.
No	Yes	The control can't get focus.
No	No	The control can't get focus; its data appears dimmed.

Filter Lookup: The Filter Lookup property indicates whether you want the values associated with a bound text box to appear in the Filter By Form window.

Other Properties of a Control

Name: The Name property allows you to name the control. This name is used when you refer to the control in code and is also displayed in various drop-down lists that show all the controls on a form. It's important to name your controls because named controls improve your code's readability and make working with Access forms and other objects easier. The naming conventions for controls are in Appendix B, "Naming Conventions."

IME Hold, IME Mode, IME Sentence Mode: The IME (Input Method Editor) properties are new in Access 2002. IME is a program that converts keystrokes into East Asian character sets. The IME properties are used to designate the settings in effect when an Input Method Editor is used.

Status Bar Text: The Status Bar Text property specifies the text that appears in the status bar when the control gets focus. This property setting overrides the Description property that can be set in a table's design.

Enter Key Behavior: The Enter Key Behavior property determines whether the Enter key causes the cursor to move to the next control or to add a new line in the current control. This setting is often changed for text boxes used to display the contents of Memo fields.

5

Allow AutoCorrect: The Allow AutoCorrect property specifies whether the AutoCorrect feature is available in the control. The AutoCorrect feature automatically corrects common spelling errors and typos.

Vertical: The Vertical property is used to control whether the text in the control is displayed horizontally or vertically. The default is No, or horizontal. When Yes (vertical display) is selected, the text within the control is rotated 90 degrees.

Auto Tab: The Auto Tab property, when set to Yes, automatically advances the cursor to the next control when the last character of an input mask has been entered. Some users like this option, and others find it annoying, especially if they must tab out of some fields but not others.

Default: The Default property applies to a command button or ActiveX control and specifies whether the control is the default button on a form.

Cancel: The Cancel property applies to a command button or ActiveX control. It indicates that you want the control's code to execute when the Esc key is pressed while the form is active.

Auto Repeat: The Auto Repeat property specifies whether you want an event procedure or macro to execute repeatedly while its command button is being pressed.

Status Bar Text: The Status Bar Text property specifies the message that appears in the status bar when the control has the focus.

Tab Stop: The Tab Stop property determines whether the Tab key can be used to enter a control. It's appropriate to set this property to No for controls whose values rarely get modified. The user can always opt to click in the control when necessary.

Tab Index: The Tab Index property sets the tab order for the control. I generally set the Tab Index property by using View, Tab Order, rather than by setting the value directly in the control's Tab Index property.

Shortcut Menu Bar: The Shortcut Menu Bar attaches a specific menu to a control. The menu bar appears when the user right-clicks the control.

ControlTip Text: The ControlTip Text property specifies the ToolTip associated with a control. The ToolTip automatically appears when the user places the mouse pointer over the control and leaves it there for a moment.

Help Context ID: The Help Context ID property designates the Help topic associated with a particular control.

Tag: The Tag property is an extra property you can use to store information about a control. Your imagination determines how you use this property. The Tag property can be read and modified at runtime.

Bound, Unbound, and Calculated Controls

There are important differences between bound and unbound controls. *Unbound controls* display information to the user or gather information from the user that's not going to be stored in your database. Here are some examples of unbound controls:

- A label providing instructions to the user
- A logo placed on a form
- A combo or text box placed on a form so that the user can enter report criteria
- A rectangle placed on the form to logically group several controls

Bound controls are used to display and modify information stored in a database table. A bound control automatically appears in the form specified in its Display Control property; the control automatically inherits many of the attributes assigned to the field that the control is bound to.

> **NOTE**
>
> The Display Control property is set in the design of the underlying table. Located on the Lookup tab of the Table Design window, it determines the default control type that is used when a control is added to a form or report.

A *calculated control* is a special type of control that displays the results of an expression. The data in a calculated control can't be modified by the user. The control's value automatically changes as the values in its expression are changed. For example, the Sales Total changes as the Price or Quantity is changed.

Using Expressions to Enhance Your Forms

As mentioned in the previous section, a control can contain any valid expression as its control source. When entering an expression as a control source, the expression must be preceded by an equal sign. The control source can be manually typed, or you can use the Expression Builder to make the process easier.

To add an expression to a control source, start by adding an unbound control to the form. To use the Expression Builder, click the control's Control Source property, and then click the ellipsis. The Expression Builder appears. (See Figure 5.29.) In the list box on the left, select the type of object you want to include in the expression. The middle and right list boxes let you select the specific element you want to paste into your expression. The Expression Builder is useful when you're not familiar with the specific syntax required for the expression. An expression can also be entered directly into the text box for the Control Source property. To view the expression more easily, you can use the Zoom feature (Shift+F2). The Zoom dialog box for the control source is pictured in Figure 5.30; the expression shown in the figure evaluates the PaymentAmount. If the PaymentAmount is greater than or equal to 1,000, the message "Big Hitter" is displayed; otherwise, nothing is displayed.

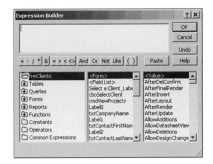

FIGURE 5.29

The Expression Builder helps you add an expression as a control's control source.

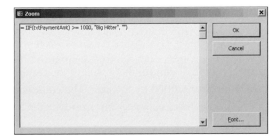

FIGURE 5.30

The Zoom dialog box for a control source.

The Command Button Wizards: Programming Without Typing

With the Command Button Wizard, you can quickly and easily add functionality to your forms. It writes the code to perform more than 30 commonly required tasks. The tasks are separated into record navigation, record operations, form operations, report operations, application operations, and other miscellaneous tasks. The Command Button Wizard is automatically invoked when a command button is added with the Control Wizards tool selected. The first step of the Command Button Wizard is shown in Figure 5.31; here, you specify the category of activity and specific action you want the command button to perform. The subsequent wizard steps vary, depending on the category and action you select.

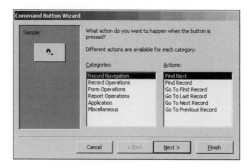

FIGURE 5.31
The first step of the Command Button Wizard.

Figure 5.32 shows the second step of the Command Button Wizard when the Form Operations category and Open Form action are selected in the first step. This step asks which form you want to open. After selecting a form and clicking Next, you're asked whether you want Access to open the form and find specific data to display, or whether you want the form to be opened and all records displayed. If you indicate that you want only specific records displayed, the dialog box shown in Figure 5.33 appears. This dialog box asks you to select fields relating the two forms. In the next step of the wizard, select text or a picture for the button. The final step of the wizard asks you to name the button.

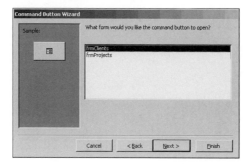

FIGURE 5.32
The Command Button Wizard requesting the name of a form to open.

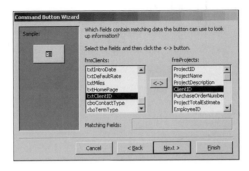

FIGURE 5.33

The Command Button Wizard asking for the fields that relate to each form.

What's surprising about the Command Button Wizard is how much it varies depending on the features you select. It allows you to add somewhat sophisticated functionality to your application without writing a single line of code. The code generated by the example just outlined is shown in Figure 5.34; it will make a lot more sense after you read the next couple chapters. The advantage to the code generated by the Command Button Wizard is that it can be fully modified after it's written; this means that you can have Access do some of the dirty work for you, and then customize the work to your liking.

FIGURE 5.34

The code generated from the Command Button Wizard.

Building Forms Based on More Than One Table

Many forms are based on more than one table. A form, for example, that shows a customer at the top and the orders associated with that customer at the bottom is considered a one-to-many form. Forms can also be based on a query that joins more than one table. Rather than seeing a one-to-many relationship in such a form, you see the two tables displayed as one, with each record on the many side of the relationship appearing with its parent's data.

Creating One-to-Many Forms

There are several ways to create one-to-many forms. As with many other types of forms, you can use a wizard to help you or build the form from scratch. Because all the methods for creating a form are helpful to users and developers alike, the available options are covered in this section.

Building a One-to-Many Form by Using the Form Wizard

Building a one-to-many form by using the Form Wizard is a simple, 10-step process:

1. Click Forms in the Objects list and double-click the Create Form by Using Wizard icon.
2. Use the Tables/Queries drop-down list to select the table or query that will appear on the one side of the relationship.
3. Select the fields you want to include from the one side of the relationship.
4. Use the Tables/Queries drop-down list to select the table or query that will appear on the many side of the relationship.
5. Select the fields you want to include from the many side of the relationship.
6. Click Next.
7. Select whether you want the parent form to appear with subforms or the child forms to appear as linked forms. (See Figure 5.35.) Click Next.
8. If you select the Subform option, indicate whether you want the subform to appear in a tabular format, as a datasheet, as a PivotTable, or as a PivotChart. (This option is not available if Linked forms was selected in step 7,) Click Next.
9. Select a style for the form; then click Next.
10. Name both the form and the subform and click Finish.

The result is a main form that contains a subform. An example is shown in Figure 5.36.

5

FORMS

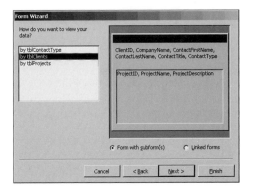

FIGURE 5.35

The Form Wizard creating a one-to-many form.

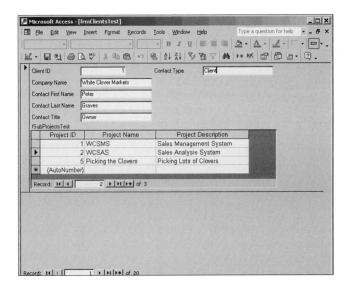

FIGURE 5.36

The result of creating a one-to-many form with the Form Wizard.

Building a One-to-Many Form with the Subform/Subreport Wizard

A one-to-many form can also be created by building the parent form; then adding a Subform/Subreport control, which is found in the toolbox. If you want to use the Subform/Subreport Wizard, make sure that the Control Wizards tool is selected before you add the Subform/Subreport control to the main form. Then follow these steps:

1. Click to select the Subform/Subreport control.

2. Click and drag to place the Subform/Subreport control on the main form; this invokes the Subform/Subreport Wizard.

3. Indicate whether you want to use an existing form as the subform or build a new subform from an existing table or query.

4. If you select Use existing Tables and Queries, the next step of the Subform/Subreport Wizard prompts you to select a table or query and which fields you want to include from it. (See Figure 5.37.) Select the fields; then click Next.

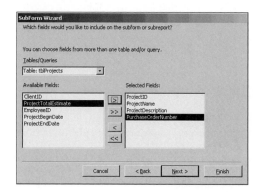

FIGURE 5.37

Selecting fields to include in the subform.

5. The next step of the Subform/Subreport Wizard allows you to define which fields in the main form link to which fields in the subform. You can select from the suggested relationships or define your own. (See Figure 5.38.) Select the appropriate relationship and click Next.

6. Name the subform and click Finish.

The resulting form should look similar to the form created with the Form Wizard. Creating a one-to-many form this way is simply an alternative to the Form Wizard.

TIP

Another way to add a subform to a main form is to click and drag a form from the Database window onto the main form. Access then tries to identify the relationship between the two forms.

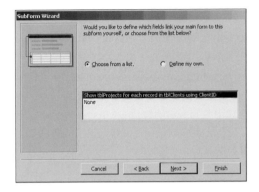

FIGURE 5.38

Defining the relationship between the main form and the subform.

Working with Subforms

Once a subform has been added, you need to understand how to work with it. To begin, familiarize yourself with a few properties of a Subform control:

Source Object: The name of the form that's being displayed in the control.

Link Child Fields: The fields from the child form that link the child form to the master form.

Link Master Fields: The fields from the master form that link the child form to the master form.

You should also understand how to make changes to the subform. One option is to open the subform in a separate window (as you would open any other form). After closing and saving the form, all the changes automatically appear in the parent form. The other choice is to modify the subform from within the main form. With the main form open, the subform is visible. Any changes made to the design of the subform from within the main form are permanent.

The default view of the subform is Datasheet or Continuous Forms, depending on how you added the subform and what options you selected. If you want to modify the default view, simply change the subform's Default View property.

> **NOTE**
>
> When the subform is displayed in Datasheet view, the order of the fields in the subform has no bearing on the datasheet that appears in the main form. The order of the columns in the datasheet depends on the tab order of the fields in the subform. You must therefore modify the tab order of the fields in the subform to change the order of the fields in the resulting datasheet.

5

TIP

Access 2002 now makes it easier to work with subforms and subreports in Design view. Scrolling has been improved so that it's easier to design subforms and subreports. In addition, you can now open subforms in their own separate Design view window by right-clicking the subform and selecting Subform in New Window. Alternatively, instead of right-clicking the subform, you can select the subform and then click View | Subform in New Window from the menu bar.

Basing Forms on Queries: The Why and How

One strategy when building forms is to base them on queries; by doing this, you generally get optimal performance and flexibility. Rather than bringing all fields and all records over the network, you bring only the fields and records you need. The benefits are even more pronounced in a client/server environment where the query is run on the server. Even in an environment where data is stored in the proprietary Access file format (.mdb) on a file server, a form based on a stored query can take better advantage of Access's indexing and paging features. By basing a form on a query, you also have more control over which records are included in the form and in what order they appear. Finally, you can base a form on a query containing a one-to-many join, viewing parent and child information as if it were one record. Notice in Figure 5.39 that the client and project information appear on one form as if they were one record.

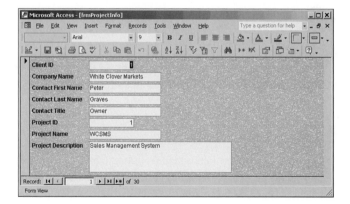

FIGURE 5.39

A form based on a one-to-many query.

Embedding SQL Statements Versus Stored Queries

In earlier versions of Access, stored queries offered better performance than embedded SQL statements. This is because when a query is saved, Access compiles the query and creates a query plan, which has information on the best way to execute the query based on available indexes and the volume of data. In earlier versions of Access, if a form was based on an embedded SQL statement, the SQL statement was compiled and optimized each time the form was opened. With Access 2002 (as with Access 2000), embedded SQL statements are compiled just like stored queries. You might ask whether, with Access 2002, it is better to base a query on a stored query or on a SQL statement. My personal preference is as follows: If I plan to use the same or a similar query with multiple forms and reports, I build a query and base multiple forms and reports on that query. This keeps me from having to duplicate my efforts in building the query. If I have a query that is unique to the form, I build it as an embedded SQL statement. This eliminates the extra "clutter" of the query in the database container.

NOTE

A query plan can sometimes be inaccurate because the query plan optimizes the query based on the amount of data in the underlying tables. If the amount of data in the tables underlying a form changes significantly, it is necessary to rebuild the query plan. This can be accomplished by opening, running, and saving the query, or by compacting the database.

Access Forms and the Internet

Microsoft has made it easier to develop Internet-aware applications by adding hyperlinks to forms and allowing you to save an Access form as HTML, XML, or a Microsoft Active Server Page (.asp), or in the Microsoft IIS 1-2 format. These features are covered in the following sections.

Adding a Hyperlink to a Form

Hyperlinks can be added to unattached labels (labels not attached to a text box or other object), command buttons, and image controls. Once added, they let the user jump to a document (UNC) or Web page (URL) simply by clicking the control containing the hyperlink. To add a hyperlink to a label, command button, or image control, follow these steps:

1. Click to select the control.
2. View the control's properties.

3. Select the Format tab of the Properties window.

4. Click in the Hyperlink Address property.

5. Click the build button (the ellipsis) to open the Insert Hyperlink dialog box. (See Figure 5.40.)

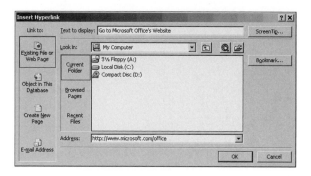

FIGURE 5.40
Establishing a link to a file or URL by using the Insert Hyperlink dialog box.

6. With Existing File or Web Page selected as the Link To option, you can enter a file path or URL in the text box or click Current Folder to locate a file or Web Page in the current folder. You can also click to insert hyperlinks to Browsed Pages or Recent Files. With Object in This Database selected as the Link To option, you can link to an object in the current database (see Figure 5.41). Select Create New Page to create a new data access page, and select Email Address to link to an email address.

FIGURE 5.41
Setting the location within an Access database for your hyperlink.

7. Click OK to finish the process. The contents of the Link to File or URL combo box become the Hyperlink Address, and the object name becomes the Hyperlink SubAddress. (See Figure 5.42.)

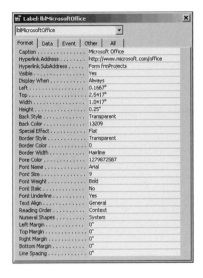

FIGURE 5.42

Hyperlink address and subaddress defined for a label control.

TIP

Using a hyperlink address to open an object in an Access database, rather than using the `Click` event of the command button and VBA code, allows you to remove the class module associated with the form (if that is the only procedure you need for the form), thereby optimizing the form's performance.

Saving a Form as HTML

Forms can be saved as HTML documents in one of two ways. The first method is to save a form as HTML by choosing File, Export (you can also right-click the form in the database container [Database window] and select Export). The Export Form dialog appears. Select HTML Documents (*.html*.htm) from the Save as Type drop-down. Enter a filename for the HTML document. If you want the system's default browser to load after the HTML document is saved, click Autostart. Click Export. The HTML Output Options dialog box appears. If desired, click Browse to locate an HTML template file. Click OK to close the dialog box. Only the datasheet associated with the form is saved as HTML; the format of the form itself isn't saved.

The other method is to choose File, Save As. Select Data Access Page from the As drop-down. Additional information about saving forms as HTML is included in Chapter 26, "An

Introduction to Access and the Internet/Intranet," and in *Alison Balter's Mastering Access 2002 Enterprise Development.*

Saving a Form as XML

Forms can also be saved as XML by selecting the form within the database window (or by having the form open and in focus) and clicking File, Export from the menu bar. Choose XML Documents (*.xml) from the Save As type drop-down. Accept the default filename or specify a different filename and click Export All. Access generates three files: *filename*.htm, *filename*.xsl, and *filename*.xml. The .xsl file is the stylesheet for displaying the XML data. When you open the .htm file within a browser, the form is displayed with the data. If you open the .xml file within a browser, you are viewing the actual XML code.

> **NOTE**
>
> These topics, and others on creating Access applications for the Internet, are covered in more detail in Chapter 26 and in Alison Balter's Mastering Access 2002 Enterprise Development.

Saving a Form as Microsoft Active Server Pages or Microsoft IIS 1-2

Forms can also be saved as Active Server Pages or in the Microsoft IIS 1-2 format. Both of these options create dynamic forms. With Microsoft IIS 1-2, Microsoft Information Server uses the .HTX and .IDC files to build an .HTM file with the current data. The .IDC file contains data source information, including the data source name, username, password, and the query that returns the record source of the form being created. The .HTX file is an HTML file that includes merge codes indicating where the data being returned should be inserted. With Active Server Pages, Microsoft Internet Information Server also builds an .HTM file with the current data.

> **PRACTICAL EXAMPLES**

Designing Forms for Your Application

 Several forms are required by the hypothetical Time and Billing application.

> **NOTE**
>
> The forms created in this section are somewhat complex. If you prefer, you can review the completed forms in CHAP5.MDB, rather than build them yourself. They are called frmClients and frmProjects.

Designing the Clients Form

Here are the steps involved in creating the form:

1. Double-click Create form in Design view.

2. Activate the Data tab of the Properties window. Select the Record Source property and select tblClients as the Record Source. Although we will modify this form later in the book to be based on a query, for now it is based directly on the tblClients table.

3. Select the CompanyName, ContactFirstName, ContactLastName, ContactTitle, ReferredBy, AssociatedWith, IntroDate, DefaultRate, Miles, HomePage, and Notes fields from the field list. Drag and drop them to the form so they appear as shown in Figure 5.43.

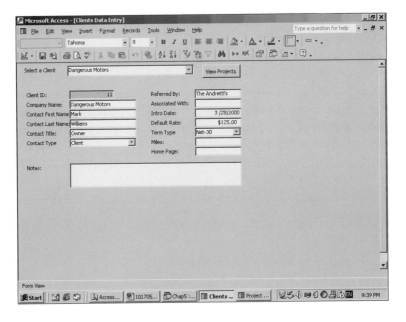

FIGURE 5.43

The frmClients form allows you to select and work with a particular client.

The next step is to add a combo box that allows the user to select the appropriate contact type for the client. The easiest way to accomplish the task is using the control wizards.

1. Make sure that the Control Wizards tool is selected.
2. Click to select a combo box from the toolbox. Then click and drag to add the combo box to the appropriate location in the detail section of the form. The Combo Box wizard launches.
3. Select I Want the Combo Box to Look Up the Values in a Table or Query. Click Next.
4. Select the tblContactType table from the list of available tables and click Next.
5. Select both the ContactTypeID and the ContactType fields and click Next.
6. Leave the Key column hidden, and size the ContactType column, if desired. Click Next.
7. Select Store that value in this field. Select ContactTypeID from the combo box and click Next.
8. Enter Contact Type as the text to appear within the label and click Finish.
9. Click the Data tab of the Properties window. Click the Row Source property and click the ellipsis to invoke the Query Builder.
10. Designate that you want the Contact Type field to appear in ascending order.
11. Close the Query Builder window and designate Yes, you want to save changes made to the SQL statement and update the property.

You can add another combo box to the form, allowing the user to designate the terms for the client, with the following steps:

1. Make sure that the Control Wizards tool is selected.
2. Click to select a combo box from the toolbox, and click and drag to add it to the appropriate location in the detail section of the form. The Combo Box wizard launches.
3. Select I Want the Combo Box to Look Up the Values in a Table or Query. Click Next.
4. Select the tblTerms table from the list of available tables and click Next.
5. Select both the TermTypeID and the TermType fields and click Next.
6. Leave the Key column hidden, and size the TermType column, if desired. Click Next.
7. Select Store that value in this field. Select TermTypeID from the combo box and click Next.
8. Enter Term Type as the text to appear within the label and click Finish.
9. Click the Data tab of the Properties window. Click the Row Source property and click the ellipsis to invoke the Query Builder.

10. Designate that you want the Term Type field to appear in ascending order.

11. Close the Query Builder window and designate Yes, you want to save changes made to the SQL statement and update the property.

Take the following steps to refine the look and feel of the form:

1. Use the appropriate tools to size and align the objects to appear as in Figure 5.43.

2. Rename the objects per the naming conventions found in Appendix B ("txt" for text boxes, "cbo" for combo boxes, and so on).

3. Set the Dividing Line, Navigation Buttons, and Record Selector properties of the form to No. Set the Auto Center property to Yes.

4. Select View|Tab Order and set the tab order of the controls as appropriate.

5. Set the Caption property of the form to Client Data Entry.

6. Because the txtClientID is bound to an AutoNumber field, it is best to set its Locked property to Yes, its Tab Stop property to No, and its Back Color property to the same color as the background of the form.

The next step is to add a combo box to the form that allows the user to select the client whose data they want to view.

1. Select Form Header/Footer from the View menu.

2. Expand the header to make it large enough to hold the combo box and a command button that navigates to the frmProjects form.

3. Make sure that the Control Wizards tool is selected.

4. Click to select a combo box from the toolbox, and click and drag to add it to the header section of the form. The Combo Box wizard launches.

5. Select Find a record on my form based on a value I selected in my combo box. Click Next.

6. Select the ClientID, CompanyName, ContactFirstName, and ContactLastName fields as the Selected fields and click Next.

7. Size the columns as appropriate (keeping the Key column hidden) and click Next.

8. Type Select a Company as the text for the label, and click Finish.

9. Click the Data tab of the Properties window. Select the Record Source property and click the ellipsis to launch the Query Builder.

10. Change the Sort Order to sort the combo box entries by CompanyName, ContactFirstName, and ContactLastName.

11. Close the Query Builder window and designate Yes, you want to save changes made to the SQL statement and update the property.

12. Run the form and make sure that the combo box functions properly.

Designing the Projects Form

The next step is to design the Projects form. The projects form is pictured in Figure 5.44. The form is easily created with the form wizard and then customized. Here are the steps involved:

1. Select Forms from the list of objects in the Database window.

2. Double-click Create Form by Using a Wizard.

3. Select tblProjects from the Tables/Queries drop-down. This record source is modified in Chapter 9.

4. Click to select all fields and click Next.

5. Select Columnar from the list of layouts, and click Next.

6. Select a style of your choice, and click Next.

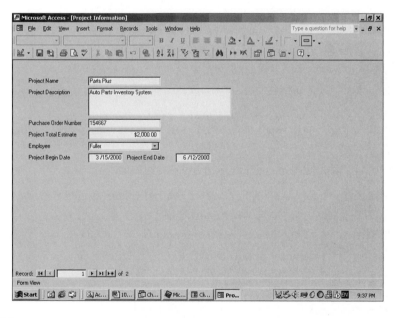

FIGURE 5.44

The frmClients form allows you to select and work with projects associated with a particular client.

7. Title the form frmProjects and click Finish.

8. Switch to the form Design view. Delete the ProjectID and EmployeeID text boxes, and the ClientID combo box. Move and size the form objects so that the form appears as in Figure 5.44.

A combo box must be added for the EmployeeID.

1. Make sure that the Control Wizards tool is selected.

2. Click to select a combo box from the toolbox, and click and drag to add it to the appropriate location in the detail section of the form. The Combo Box wizard launches.

3. Select I Want the Combo Box to Look Up the Values in a Table or Query. Click Next.

4. Select the tblEmployees table from the list of available tables and click Next.

5. Select the EmployeeID, LastName, and FirstName fields and click Next.

6. Leave the Key column hidden, and size the LastName and FirstName columns, if desired. Click Next.

7. Select Store that value in this field. Select EmployeeID from the combo box and click Next.

8. Enter Employee as the text to appear within the label and click Finish.

9. Click the Data tab of the Properties window. Click the Row Source property and click the ellipsis to invoke the Query Builder.

10. Designate that you want the LastName and FirstName fields to appear in ascending order.

11. Close the Query Builder window and designate Yes, you want to save changes made to the SQL statement and update the property.

Take the following steps to refine the look and feel of the form:

1. Rename the objects per the naming conventions found in Appendix B ("txt" for text boxes, "cbo" for combo boxes, and so on).

2. Set the Dividing Line and Record Selector properties of the form to No.

3. Select View|Tab Order and set the tab order of the controls as appropriate.

4. Set the Caption property of the form to Project Information.

Adding a Command Button That Links the Clients and Projects Forms

The final step is to tie the Clients form to the Projects form. The command wizard will help to accomplish the task.

1. Return to the frmClients form in Design view.

2. Make sure the Control Wizards toolbar button is active.

3. Click to select a command button and then click and drag to place it within the Header section of the frmClients form. The Command Button wizard launches.

4. Click Form Operations within the list of categories.

5. Click Open Form within the list of Actions and click Next.

6. Select frmProjects as the name of the form you would like the command button to open. Click Next.

7. Click Open Form and Find Specific Data to Display. Click Next.

8. Click to select the ClientID field from the frmClients form and the ClientID field from the frmProjects form. Click the <-> button to designate the fields are joined. Click Next to continue.

9. Select a picture or enter text for the caption of the command button.

10. Enter the name for the command button. Don't forget to use proper naming conventions (for example, cmdShowProjects). Click Finish.

11. Switch from Design view to Form view and test the command button. The frmProjects form should load, displaying projects for the currently selected client.

What's Ahead

The application you're building is a time and billing application. You will build the application from scratch so that you can learn about all its components. You'll also be adding considerably more functionality to the application as you proceed through the book.

Summary

Microsoft Access gives you rich, powerful tools you can use to build even the most sophisticated form. This chapter gives you an overview of what Access forms are capable of and shows you the many options you have for creating a new form.

Regardless of how a form has been created, you need to know how to modify all the attributes of a form and its controls. This chapter showed you how to work with form objects, modifying both their appearance and how they're tied to data. Each control type and its properties were discussed in detail, and all the properties of the form itself were covered. Using the techniques in this chapter, you can control both the appearance and functionality of a form and its objects.

What Every Developer Needs to Know About Reports

IN THIS CHAPTER

Why This Chapter Is Important

Although forms provide an excellent means for data entry, reports are the primary output device in Access. Reports can be previewed on the screen, output to a printer, displayed in a browser, and more! They are relatively easy to create, and are extremely powerful. This chapter covers the basics of creating and working with reports. After reading the chapter, you'll be familiar with the types of reports available. You'll learn how to build reports with and without a wizard, and how to manipulate the reports that you build. You will understand the report and control properties available, and when it is appropriate to use each. You'll also be familiar with many important report techniques.

Types of Reports Available

The reporting engine of Microsoft Access is very powerful, with a wealth of features. Many types of reports are available in Access 2002:

- Detail reports
- Summary reports
- Cross-tabulation reports
- Reports containing graphics and charts
- Reports containing forms
- Reports containing labels
- Reports including any combination of the preceding

Detail Reports

A Detail report supplies an entry for each record included in the report. As you can see in Figure 6.1, there's an entry for each order in the Orders table during the specified period (1/1/1995-12/31/1996). The report's detail is grouped by country and within country by salesperson and gives you subtotals by salesperson and country. The bottom of the report has grand totals for all records included in the report. The report is based on a Parameter query that limits the data displayed on the report based on criteria supplied by the user at runtime.

Summary Reports

A Summary report gives you summary data for all the records included in the report. In Figure 6.2, only total sales by quarter and year are displayed in the report. The underlying detail records that compose the summary data aren't displayed in the report. The report is based on a query that summarizes the net sales by OrderID. The report itself contains no controls in its Detail section. All controls are placed in report Group Headers and Footers that are grouped on the quarter and year of the ship date. Because no controls are found in the report's Detail section, Access prints summary information only.

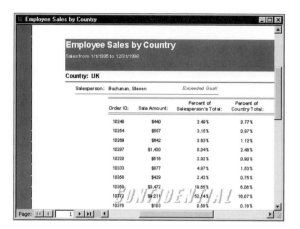

FIGURE 6.1

An example of a Detail report.

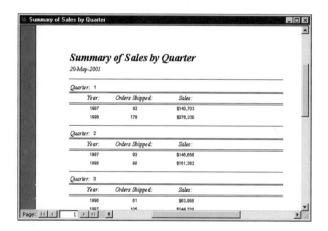

FIGURE 6.2

An example of a Summary report.

Cross-tabulation Reports

Cross-tabulation reports display summarized data grouped by one set of information on the left side of the report and another set across the top. The report shown in Figure 6.3 shows total sales by product name and employee. The report is based on a Crosstab query and is generated using a fair amount of VBA code. This code is required because each time the report is run, a different number of employees might need to be displayed in the report's columns. In other words, the number of columns needed might be different each time the report is run. This report and the techniques needed to produce it are covered in Chapter 10, "Advanced Report Techniques."

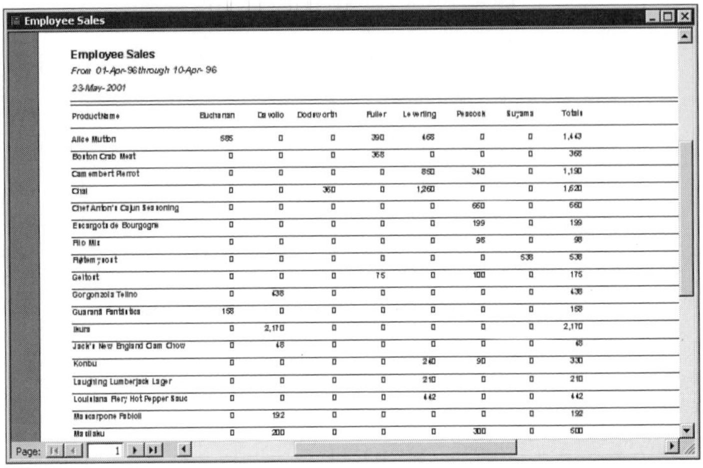

Employee Sales
From 01-Apr-96 through 10-Apr-96
23-May-2001

ProductName	Buchanan	Davolio	Dodsworth	Fuller	Leverling	Peacock	Suyama	Totals
Alice Mutton	585	0	0	390	468	0	0	1,443
Boston Crab Meat	0	0	0	368	0	0	0	368
Camembert Pierrot	0	0	0	0	850	340	0	1,190
Chai	0	0	360	0	1,260	0	0	1,620
Chef Anton's Cajun Seasoning	0	0	0	0	0	660	0	660
Escargots de Bourgogne	0	0	0	0	0	199	0	199
Filo Mix	0	0	0	0	0	98	0	98
Fløtemysost	0	0	0	0	0	0	538	538
Geitost	0	0	0	75	0	100	0	175
Gorgonzola Telino	0	438	0	0	0	0	0	438
Guaraná Fantástica	158	0	0	0	0	0	0	158
Ikura	0	2,170	0	0	0	0	0	2,170
Jack's New England Clam Chow	0	48	0	0	0	0	0	48
Konbu	0	0	0	0	240	90	0	330
Laughing Lumberjack Lager	0	0	0	0	210	0	0	210
Louisiana Fiery Hot Pepper Sauce	0	0	0	0	442	0	0	442
Mascarpone Fabioli	0	192	0	0	0	0	0	192
Mozzarella	0	200	0	0	0	300	0	600

Page: 1

FIGURE 6.3
An example of a Cross-tabulation report.

Reports with Graphics and Charts

Although the statement "A picture paints a thousand words" is a cliché, it's also quite true—research proves that you retain data much better when it's displayed as pictures rather than numbers. Fortunately, Access makes including graphics and charts in your reports quite easy. As shown in Figure 6.4, a report can be designed to combine both numbers and charts. The report in Figure 6.4 shows the sales by product, both as numbers and as a bar chart. The main report is grouped by product category and contains a subreport based on a query that summarizes sales by CategoryID, CategoryName, and ProductName for a specific date range. The chart totals product sales by product name, displaying the information graphically.

Reports with Forms

Users often need a report that looks like a printed form. The Access Report Builder, with its many graphical tools, allows you to quickly produce reports that emulate the most elegant data-entry form. The report shown in Figure 6.5 produces an invoice for a customer. The report is based on a query that draws information from the Customers, Orders, Order Details, Products, Employees, and Shippers tables. The report's Filter property is filled in, limiting the data that appears on the report to the last six records in the Orders table. Using graphics, color, fonts, shading, and other special effects gives the form a professional look.

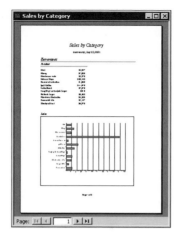

FIGURE 6.4

An example of a report with a chart.

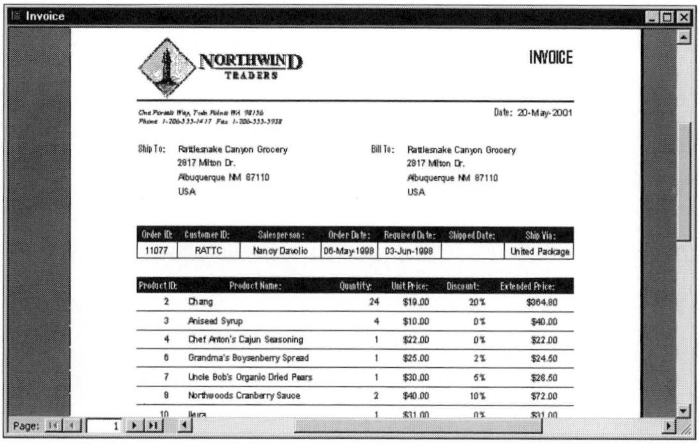

FIGURE 6.5

An example of a report containing a form.

Reports with Labels

Creating mailing labels in Access 2002 is easy using the Label Wizard. Mailing labels are simply a special type of report with a page setup indicating the number of labels across the page and the size of each label. An example of a mailing label report created by using the Label Wizard is shown in Figure 6.6. This report is based on the Customers table but could have just as easily been based on a query that limits the mailing labels produced.

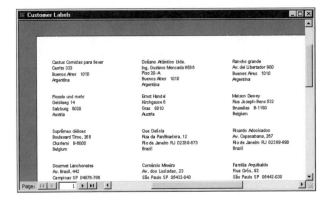

FIGURE 6.6

An example of a report containing mailing labels.

Anatomy of a Report

Reports can have many parts. These parts are referred to as *sections* of the report. A new report is automatically made up of the following three sections, shown in Figure 6.7:

- Page Header section
- Detail section
- Page Footer section

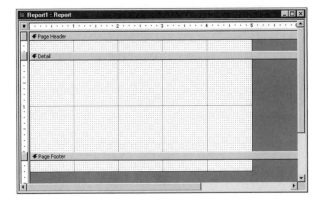

FIGURE 6.7

Sections of a report.

The Detail section is the main section of the report; it's used to display the detailed data of the table or query underlying the report. Certain reports, such as Summary reports, have nothing in the Detail section. Instead, Summary reports contain data in Group Headers and Footers (discussed at the end of this section).

The Page Header is the portion that automatically prints at the top of every page of the report. It often includes information such as the report's title. The Page Footer automatically prints at the bottom of every page of the report and usually contains information such as the page number and date. Each report can have only one Page Header and one Page Footer.

In addition to the three sections automatically added to every report, a report can have the following sections:

- Report Header
- Report Footer
- Group Headers
- Group Footers

A Report Header is a section that prints once, at the beginning of the report; the Report Footer prints once, at the end of the report. Each Access report can have only one Report Header and one Report Footer. The Report Header is often used to create a cover sheet for the report. It can include graphics or other fancy effects, adding a professional look to a report. The most common use of the Report Footer is for grand totals, but it can also include any other summary information for the report.

In addition to Report and Page Headers and Footers, an Access report can have up to 10 Group Headers and Footers. Report groupings separate data logically and physically. The Group Header prints before the detail for the group, and the Group Footer prints after the detail for the group. For example, you can group customer sales by country and city, printing the name of the country or city for each related group of records. If you total the sales for each country and city, you can place the country and city names in the country and city Group Headers and the totals in the country and city Group Footers.

Creating a New Report

You can create a new report in several ways—the most common is to select Reports from the Objects list in the Database window and double-click the Create Report by Using Wizard icon. If you prefer, you can click New on the toolbar for the database window to open the New Report dialog box. (See Figure 6.8.) Here, you can select from many options available for creating reports. Reports can be created from scratch by using Design view; they can also be created with the help of five wizards. Three of the wizards help you build standard reports, one helps you build reports with charts, and the last wizard automates the process of creating mailing labels. The Report Wizards are so powerful that I use one of them to build the initial foundation for almost every report I create.

FIGURE 6.8

In the New Report dialog box, you can designate Design view or select from one of five wizards.

Creating a Report with the Report Wizard

To create a report with the Report Wizard, click Reports in the Objects list and then double-click the Create Report by Using Wizard icon. This launches the Report Wizard. The first step is to select the table or query that will supply data to the report. I prefer to base my reports on queries, or on embedded SQL statements (a query stored as part of a report). This generally improves performance because it returns as small a dataset as possible. In a client/server environment, this is particularly pronounced because the query is usually run on the server and only the results are sent over the network wire. Basing reports on queries also enhances your ability to produce reports based on varying criteria.

After you have selected a table or query, you can select the fields you want to include on the report. The fields included in the selected table or query are displayed in the list box on the left. To add fields to the report, double-click the name of the field you want to add or click the field name and click the > button. In the example in Figure 6.9, five fields have been selected from the tblClients table.

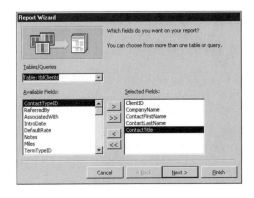

FIGURE 6.9

The first step of the Report Wizard: table/field selection.

After you have selected a table or query and the fields you want to include on the report, click Next. You're then prompted to add group levels, which add report groupings, to the report. Add group levels if you need to visually separate groups of data or include summary calculations (subtotals) in your report. Report groupings are covered later in this chapter. If your report doesn't require groupings, click Next.

In the third step of the Report Wizard, you choose sorting levels for your report. Because the order of a query underlying a report is overridden by any sort order designated in the report, it's a good idea to designate a sort order for the report. You can add up to four sorting levels with the wizard. In the example shown in Figure 6.10, the report is sorted by the ClientID field. After you select the fields you want to sort on, click Next.

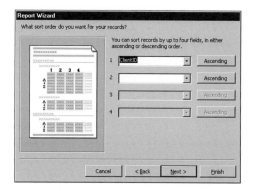

FIGURE 6.10
The third step of the Report Wizard: sorting report data.

In the fourth step of the Report Wizard, you decide on the report's layout and orientation. The layout options vary depending on what selections have been made in the wizard's previous steps. The orientation can be Portrait or Landscape. This step of the Report Wizard also allows you to specify whether you want Access to adjust the width of each field so that all the fields fit on each page. After supplying Access with this information, click Next.

You choose a style for your report in the Report Wizard's fifth step. The choices are Bold, Casual, Compact, Corporate, Formal, and Soft Gray. You can preview each look before you make a decision. Any of the style attributes applied by the Report Wizard, as well as other report attributes defined by the wizard, can be modified in Report Design view any time after the wizard has produced the report. After you have selected a style, click Next.

The final step of the Report Wizard prompts you for the report's title. This title is used as both the name and the caption for the report. I supply a standard Access report name and modify the caption after the Report Wizard has finished its process. You're then given the opportunity to preview the report or modify the report's design. If you opt to modify the report's design, you're placed in Design view. (See Figure 6.11.) The report can then be previewed at any time. You can optionally mark the check box Display Help on working with the Report to have Access display the help window and list the associated report topics.

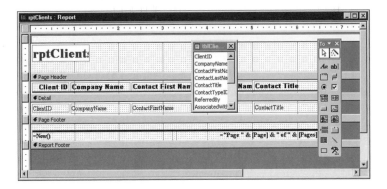

FIGURE 6.11

Design view of a completed report.

NOTE

Another way to start the Report Wizard is to select Tables or Queries from the Objects list in the Database Container, and then click the table or query that you want the report to be based on. Use the New Object drop-down list on the toolbar to select Report. In the New Report dialog box, select Report Wizard. You don't have to use the Tables/Queries drop-down menu to select a table or query because the one you selected before invoking the wizard is automatically selected for you.

Creating a Report from Design View

Although you usually get started with most of your reports by using a Report Wizard, you should understand how to create a new report from Design view. To create a report without using a wizard, click Reports in the Objects list and then double-click the Create Report in Design View icon. The Report Design window appears. You must then set the Record Source of the report to the table or query upon which you want the report to be based. Another way to create a report from Design view is to click Reports in the Objects list and then click New to open the New Report dialog box. Click Design view and use the drop-down list to select the table or query on which the report will be based; then click OK. The Report Design window appears.

Working with the Report Design Window

The Report Design window is used to build and modify a report. Using this window, you can add objects to a report and modify their properties. Microsoft provides numerous Report, Report Grouping, and Control properties. By modifying these properties, you can create reports with diverse looks and functionality.

Understanding the Report Design Tools

To help you design reports, several report design tools are available, including the Properties, Toolbox, Field List, and Sorting and Grouping windows. Two toolbars are also available to make developing and customizing your reports easier: the Report Design toolbar and the Formatting toolbar. The Report Design toolbar offers tools for saving, previewing, and printing your report and for cutting, copying, and pasting report objects. The Formatting toolbar is specifically designed to help you customize the look of your report. It includes tools for changing the font, font size, alignment, color, shading, and other physical attributes of the report objects.

The Properties, Toolbox, Field List, and Sorting and Grouping windows are all designed as toggles. This means that buttons on the Report Design toolbar alternately hide and show these valuable windows. If you have a high-resolution monitor, you might want to leave the windows open at all times. If you have a low-resolution monitor, you need to get a feel for when it's most effective for each window to be opened or closed.

Adding Fields to the Report

Fields can most easily be added to a report by using the Field List window. With the Field List window open, click and drag a field from the field list onto the appropriate section of the report. Several fields can be added at one time, just as they can in forms. Use the Ctrl key to select noncontiguous fields, use the Shift key to select contiguous fields, or double-click the field list's title bar to select all the fields; then click and drag them to the report as a unit.

CAUTION

One problem with adding fields to a report is that both the fields and the attached labels are placed in the same section of the report. This means that, if you click and drag fields from the Field List window to the Detail section of the report, both the fields and the attached labels appear in the Detail section. If you're creating a tabular report, this isn't acceptable, so you must cut the attached labels and paste them into the report's Page Header section.

Selecting, Moving, Aligning, and Sizing Report Objects

Microsoft Access offers several techniques to help you select, move, align, and size report objects. Different techniques are effective in different situations. Experience will tell you which technique you should use and when. Selecting, moving, aligning, and sizing report objects are quite similar to performing the same tasks with form objects. The techniques are covered briefly in this chapter; for a more detailed explanation of each technique, refer to Chapter 5, "What Every Developer Needs to Know About Forms."

Selecting Report Objects

To select a single report object, click it; selection handles appear around the selected object. After the object is selected, you can modify any of its attributes (properties), or you can size, move, or align it.

To select multiple objects so you can manipulate them as a unit, use one of the following techniques:

- Hold down the Shift key as you click multiple objects. Each object you click is then added to the selection.

- Place your mouse pointer in a blank area of the report. Click and drag to lasso the objects you want to select. When you let go of the mouse, any object even partially within the lasso is selected.

- Click and drag within the horizontal or vertical ruler. As you click and drag, lines appear indicating the potential selection area. When you release the mouse, all objects within the lines are selected.

> **NOTE**
>
> Make sure that you understand which objects are actually selected; attached labels can cause some confusion. Figure 6.12 shows a report with four objects selected: the rptClients label, the Contact First Name label, the City text box, and the ContactFirstName text box. The City label is *not* selected. It has one selection handle because it's attached to the City text box. If you were to modify the properties of the selected objects, the City label would be unaffected.

Moving Things Around

If you want to move a single control along with its attached label, click the object and drag it to a new location. The object and the attached label move as a unit. To move multiple objects, use one of the methods explained in the previous section to select the objects you want to move. After the objects are selected, click and drag any of them; the selected objects and their attached labels move as a unit.

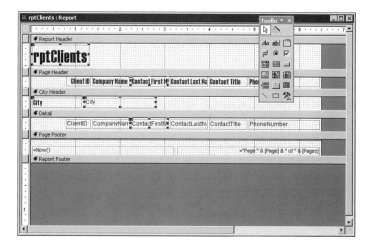

FIGURE 6.12

Selecting objects in an Access report.

Moving an object without its attached label is a trickier process. When placed over the center or border of a selected object (not on a sizing handle), the mouse pointer looks like a hand with all five fingers pointing upward. This indicates that the selected object and its attached label move as a unit, maintaining their relationship to one another. However, if you place your mouse pointer directly over the selection handle in the object's upper-left corner, the mouse pointer looks like a hand with the index finger pointing upward. This indicates that the object and the attached label move independently of one another so that you can alter the distance between them.

Aligning Objects with One Another

To align objects with one another, you must select them first. Choose Format|Align; then select Left, Right, Top, Bottom, or To Grid. The selected objects will align in relation to each other.

CAUTION

Watch out for a few "gotchas" when you're aligning report objects. If you select several text boxes and their attached labels and align them, Access tries to align the left sides of the text boxes with the left sides of the labels. To avoid this problem, you have to align the text boxes separately from their attached labels.

During the alignment process, Access never overlaps objects. For this reason, if the objects you're aligning don't fit, Access can't align them. For example, if you try to align the bottom of several objects horizontally and they don't fit across the report, Access aligns only the objects that fit on the line.

Using Snap to Grid

The Snap to Grid feature is a toggle found under the Format menu. When Snap to Grid is selected, all objects that you're moving or sizing snap to the report's gridlines. To temporarily disable the Snap to Grid feature, hold down your Ctrl key while sizing or moving an object.

Using Power-Sizing Techniques

Access offers many techniques to help you size report objects. A selected object has eight sizing handles, and all of them, except for the upper-left handle, can be used to size the object. Simply click and drag one of the sizing handles. If multiple objects are selected, they are sized by the same amount.

The Format|Size menu can also help you size objects. It has six options: To Fit, To Grid, To Tallest, To Shortest, To Widest, and To Narrowest. These options are discussed in detail in Chapter 5.

TIP

Access offers a great trick that can help size labels fit. Simply double-click any sizing handle, and the object is automatically sized to fit the text within it.

Controlling Object Spacing

Access also makes it easy for you to control object spacing. Both the horizontal and vertical distances between selected objects can be made equal. Select the objects; then choose Format| Horizontal Spacing|Make Equal or Format|Vertical Spacing|Make Equal. You can also maintain the relative relationship between selected objects while increasing or decreasing the space between them. To do this, choose Format|Horizontal Spacing|Increase/Decrease or Format| Vertical Spacing|Increase/Decrease.

Selecting the Correct Control for the Job

Reports usually contain labels, text boxes, lines, rectangles, image controls, and bound and unbound object frames. The other controls are generally used for reports that emulate data-entry forms. The different controls that can be placed on a report, as well as their uses, are discussed briefly in the following sections.

Labels

Labels are used to display information to your users. They're commonly used as report headings, column headings, or group headings for your report. Although the text they display can be modified at runtime by using VBA code, they can't be directly bound to data.

To add a label to a report, select the Label tool in the toolbox; then click and drag to place the label on the report.

Text Boxes

Text boxes are used to display field information or the result of an expression. They are used throughout a report's different sections. For example, in a Page Header, a text box might contain an expression showing the date range that's the criteria for the report. In a Group Header, a text box might be used to display a heading for the group. The possibilities are endless because a text box can hold any valid expression.

To add a text box to a report, select the Text Box tool from the toolbox. Click and drag the text box to place it on the report. A text box can also be added to a report by dragging a field from the field list to a report. This works as long as the field's Display control property is a text box.

Lines

Lines can be used to visually separate objects on your report. For example, a line can be placed at the bottom of a section or underneath a subtotal. To add a line to a report, click the Line tool to select it; then click and drag to place the line on your report. When added, the line has several properties that can be modified to customize its look.

> **TIP**
>
> To make sure that the line you draw is perfectly straight, hold down the Shift key while you click and drag to draw the line.

Rectangles

Rectangles can be used to visually group items that logically belong together on the report. They can also be used to make certain controls on your report stand out. I often draw rectangles around important subtotal or grand total information that I want to make sure that the report's reader notices.

To add a rectangle to a report, select the Rectangle tool from the toolbox; then click and drag to place the rectangle on the report.

CAUTION

The rectangle might obscure objects that have already been added to the report. To rectify this problem, the rectangle's Back Style property can be set to Transparent. This setting is fine unless you want the rectangle to have a background color. If so, choose Format|Send to Back to layer the objects so that the rectangle lies behind the other objects on the report.

Bound Object Frames

Bound object frames let you display the data in OLE fields, which contain objects from other applications, such as pictures, spreadsheets, and word processing documents.

To add a bound object frame to a report, click the Bound Object Frame tool in the toolbox; then click and drag the frame onto the report. Set the Control Source property of the frame to the appropriate field. You can also add a bound object frame to a report by dragging and dropping an OLE field from the field list onto the report.

Unbound Object Frames

Unbound object frames can be used to add logos and other pictures to a report. Unlike bound object frames, however, they aren't tied to underlying data.

To add an unbound object frame to a report, click the Unbound Object Frame tool in the toolbox. Click and drag the object frame to place it on the report. This opens the Insert Object dialog box, shown in Figure 6.13, which you use to create a new OLE object or insert an existing OLE object from a file on disk. If you click Create From File, the Insert Object dialog box changes to look like Figure 6.14. Click Browse and locate the file you want to include in the report. The Insert Object dialog box gives you the option of linking to or embedding an OLE object. If you select Link, a reference is created to the OLE object. Only the bitmap of the object is stored in the report, and the report continues to refer to the original file on disk. If you don't select Link, the object you select is copied and embedded in the report and becomes part of the Access MDB file; no link to the original object is maintained.

NOTE

It's usually preferable to use an image control rather than an unbound object frame for static information like a logo because the image control requires much fewer resources than does an unbound object frame. Image controls are covered in the next section; Figure 6.15 shows a report with an image control.

FIGURE 6.13

Use the Insert Object dialog box to insert a new or existing object into an unbound object frame.

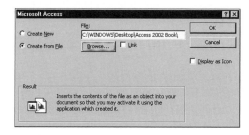

FIGURE 6.14

The Insert Object dialog box with Create from File selected.

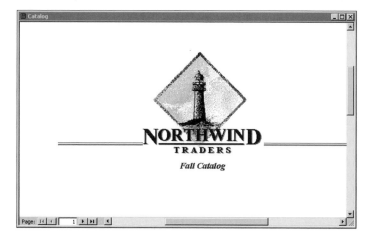

FIGURE 6.15

A report with an image control.

Image Controls

Image controls are your best option for displaying static images, such as logos, on a report. An unbound object can be modified after it is placed on a report, but you can't open the object application and modify an image when it's placed on a report. This limitation, however, means far fewer resources are needed, so performance improves noticeably.

Other Controls

As mentioned earlier in this section, it's standard to include mostly labels and text boxes on your reports, but other controls can be added when appropriate. To add any other type of control, click to select the control; then click and drag to place it on the report.

What Report Properties Are Available and Why Use Them

Reports have many different properties that can be modified to change how the report looks and performs. Like Form properties, Report properties are divided into categories: Format, Data, Event, and Other. To view a report's properties, first select the report, rather than a section of the report, in one of two ways:

- Click the Report Selector, which is the small gray button at the intersection of the horizontal and vertical rulers.
- Select Report from the drop-down in the Properties window.
- Choose Edit|Select Report.

When a report has been selected, you can view and modify its properties.

Working with the Properties Window

When the report is selected, the Properties window shows all the properties associated with the report. To select the report and open the Properties window at the same time, double-click the Report Selector. A report has 47 properties available on the property sheet (there are additional properties available only from code) broken down into the appropriate categories in the Properties window. Forty of the properties relate to the report's format, data, and other special properties; the remaining seven relate to the events that occur when a report is run. The format, data, and other properties are covered here, and the event properties are covered in Chapter 10.

The Report's Format Properties

A report has the following 23 Format properties for changing the report's physical appearance:

Caption: The Caption property of the report is the text that appears in the Report window's title bar when the user is previewing the report. It can be modified at runtime to customize it for a particular situation.

Auto Resize: The Auto Resize property is new in Access 2002. This setting determines whether a report is resized automatically to display all the data on the report.

Auto Center: The Auto Center property is also new in Access 2002. You use the Auto Center property to designate whether you want the Report window to automatically be centered on the screen. Auto Center property is also new in Access 2002. This property specifies whether a report is centered automatically within the application window whenever it is opened.

Page Header, Page Footer: The Page Header and Page Footer properties determine on what pages these sections appear. The options are All Pages, Not with Rpt Hdr, Not with Rpt Ftr, and Not with Rpt Hdr/Ftr. Because you might not want the Page Header or Page Footer to print on the Report Header or Report Footer pages, these properties give you control over where those sections print.

Grp Keep Together: In Access, you can keep a group of data together on the same page by using the Grp Keep Together property. The Per Page option forces the group of data to remain on the same page, and the Per Column option forces the group of data to remain within a column. A *group of data* refers to all the data within a report grouping (for example, all the customers in a city).

Border Style: The Border Style property is a new property for Access 2002 reports. Like its form counterpart, it is far more powerful than its name implies. The options for the Border Style property are None, Thin, Sizable, and Dialog. A border style set to None means the report has no border. A Thin border is not resizable; the Size command isn't available in the Control menu. This setting is a good choice for pop-up reports, which remain on top even when other forms or reports are given the focus. A Sizable border is standard for most reports. It includes all the standard options in the Control menu. A Dialog border looks like a Thin border. A report with a border style of Dialog can't be maximized, minimized, or resized. Once the border style of a report is set to Dialog, the Maximize, Minimize, and Resize options aren't available in the report's Control menu. Border Style property is new in Access 2002. This setting lets you specify the type of border to be used for the Report window under print preview mode. It also determines whether the Report window is sizable and which border elements are available for the Report window such as the title bar, Close button, the Control menu, and the Minimize and Maximize buttons.

Control Box: The Control Box property is new in Access 2002 as well. This property lets you specify the whether the Report window under print preview has the Control menu available. The Control menu is activated by clicking the icon in the upper-left corner of a window and displays options for manipulating the window: Restore, Move, Size, Minimize, Maximize, and Close.

Min Max Buttons: The Min Max Buttons property is also new in Access 2002. This property lets you specify whether the Minimize and/or Maximize options should be available from the Control menu for the Report window in Print Preview mode. You can select from None, Min Enabled, Max Enabled, or Both Enabled.

Close Button: The Close Button property is new in Access 2002. This setting specifies whether to enable or disable the close button on the Print Preview window.

Width: The Width property specifies the width of the report sections.

Picture, Picture Type, Picture Size Mode, Picture Alignment, Picture Tiling, and Picture Pages: The background of a report can be a picture. The Picture properties determine what picture is used as a background for the report and what attributes are applied to it.

Grid X/Grid Y: The Grid X and Grid Y properties determine the density of the gridlines in the Report Design window.

Layout for Print: The Layout for Print property specifies whether screen or printer fonts are used in the report. If you want to optimize reports for preview, select No; if you want to optimize reports for the printer, select Yes. This option is not as important if you select TrueType fonts because TrueType fonts usually print equally well to the screen and printer.

Palette Source: The Palette Source property determines the source for the report's selectable color.

Orientation: The Orientation property is used for taking advantage of language-specific versions of Microsoft Access, such as Arabic. This property can be set to support right-to-left display features for these language-specific editions of Access, provided that the underlying operating system supports that language and is 32-bit (for example, Windows 2000).

Moveable: The Moveable property determines whether the user can move the Report window around the screen by clicking and dragging the report by its title bar.

The Report's Data Properties

A report has the following five Data properties used to supply information about the data underlying the report:

Record Source: The Record Source property specifies the table or query whose data underlies the report. The record source of a report can be modified at runtime. This aspect of the Record

Source property makes it easy for you to create generic reports that use different record sources in different situations.

Filter: The Filter property allows you to open the report with a specific filter set. I usually prefer to base a report on a query rather than apply a filter to it. At other times, it's more appropriate to base the report on a query, but then apply and remove a filter as required, based on the report's runtime conditions.

Filter On: The Filter On property determines whether a report filter is applied. If the value of this property is set to No, the Filter property of the report is ignored.

Order By: The Order By property determines how the records in a report are sorted when the report is opened.

Order By On: The Order By On property determines whether the Order By property of the report is used. If the value of this property is No, the report's Order By property is ignored.

Other Report Properties

A report has 12 other properties; these miscellaneous properties, shown in the following, allow you to control other important aspects of the report:

Record Locks: The Record Locks property determines whether the tables used in producing the report are locked while the report is being run. The two values for this property are No Locks and All Records. No Locks is the default value; it means that no records in the tables underlying the report are locked while the report is being run. Users can modify the underlying data as the report is run, which can be disastrous when running sophisticated reports. The data in the report can be changed as the report is being run, which would make figures for totals and percent of totals invalid. Although the All Records option for this property locks all records in all tables included in the report (thereby preventing data entry while the report is being run), it might be a necessary evil for producing an accurate report.

Date Grouping: The Date Grouping property determines how grouping of dates occurs in your report. The US Defaults option means that Access uses United States' defaults for report groupings; therefore, Sunday is the first day of the week, the first week begins January 1, and so on. The Use System Settings option means that date groupings are based on the locale set in the Control Panel's Regional Settings, rather than on U.S. defaults.

Pop Up: The Pop Up property determines whether the report's print preview window opens as a pop-up window. Within Microsoft Access, pop-up windows always remain on top of other open windows.

Modal: The Modal property instructs Access to open the Report window in a modal or modeless state. The default is No, meaning that the window will not be opened as modal. A modal window retains the application program's focus until the window receives the appropriate user input that it requires.

Menu Bar: The Menu Bar property allows you to associate a custom menu bar with the report that's visible when the user is previewing the report. Adding a custom menu to your report lets you control what the user can do while the report is active.

Toolbar: The Toolbar property lets you associate a custom toolbar with the report that's visible when the user is previewing the report.

Shortcut Menu Bar: The Shortcut Menu Bar property determines what shortcut menu is associated with the report while the report is being previewed. The shortcut menu bar appears when the user clicks the right mouse button over the preview window.

Fast Laser Printing: The Fast Laser Printing property determines whether lines and rectangles are replaced with text character lines when you print a report with a laser printer. If fast printing is your objective and you're using a laser printer, you should set this property to Yes.

Help File, Help Context ID: The Help File and Help Context ID properties let you associate a help file and help topic with the report.

Tag: The Tag property is an extra property for storing information defined by the user at either design time or runtime. It is Microsoft Access's way of giving you an extra property. Access makes no use of this property; if you don't take advantage of it, it will never be used.

Has Module: The Has Module property determines whether the report contains an associated class module. If no code will be included in the report, eliminating the class module can both improve performance and reduce the size of the application database. A report without a class module is considered a "lightweight object," which loads and displays faster than an object with an associated class module.

CAUTION

A couple of the Has Module property's behaviors deserve special attention. When a report is created, the default value for the Has Module property is No. Access automatically sets the Has Module property to Yes as soon as you try to view a report's module. If you set the HasModule property of an existing report to No, Access prompts you if you wish to proceed. If you confirm the change, Access deletes the object's class module and all the code it contains!

What Control Properties Are Available and Why Use Them

Just as reports have properties, so do controls. Most control properties can be changed at design time or at runtime, allowing you to easily build flexibility into your reports. For example, certain controls are visible only when specific conditions are true.

The Control's Format Properties

You can modify several formatting properties of the selected objects by using the formatting toolbar. If you prefer, you can set all the properties in the Properties window:

Format: The Format property determines how the data in the control is displayed. This property is automatically inherited from the underlying field. If you want the control's format on the report to differ from the underlying field's format, you must set the Format property of the control.

Caption: The Caption property specifies the text displayed for labels and command buttons. A caption is a string containing up to 2,048 characters.

Hyperlink Address: The Hyperlink Address property is a string representing the path to a UNC (network path) or URL (Web page). Command buttons, image controls, and labels all contain the Hyperlink Address property.

Hyperlink SubAddress: The Hyperlink SubAddress property is a string representing a location within the document specified in the Hyperlink Address property. Command buttons, image controls, and labels all contain the Hyperlink SubAddress property.

Decimal Places: The Decimal Places property defines the number of decimal places displayed for numeric values.

Visible: The Visible property determines whether a control is visible. In many cases, you will want to toggle the visibility of a control in response to different situations.

Hide Duplicates: The Hide Duplicates property hides duplicate data values in a report's Detail section. Duplicate data values occur when one or more consecutive records in a report contain the same value in one or more fields.

Can Grow, Can Shrink: The Can Grow property, when set to Yes, allows a control to expand vertically to accommodate all the data in it. The Can Shrink property eliminates blank lines when no data exists in a field for a particular record. For example, if you have a second address line on a mailing label, but there's no data in the Address2 field, you don't want a blank line to appear on the mailing label.

Left, Top, Width, Height: These properties set the size and position of the controls on a report.

Back Style, Back Color: The Back Style property can be set to Normal or Transparent. When set to Transparent, the color of the report shows through to the control. When set to Normal, the control's Back Color property determines the object's color.

Special Effect: The Special Effect property adds 3D effects to a control.

Border Style, Border Color, Border Width: These properties set the physical attributes of a control's border.

Fore Color: This property sets the color of the text within the control.

Font Color, Font Name, Font Size, Font Weight, Font Italic, Font Underline: The border properties affect the control's border, but the font properties affect the appearance of the text within the control.

Text Align: The Text Align property sets the alignment of the text within the control. It can be set to Left, Center, Right, or Distribute. When set to Distribute, text is justified.

Reading Order: The Reading Order property determines the visual order in which characters, words, and groups of words are displayed. This property is often used with language-specific editions of Microsoft Access where the reading order needs to be changed. The default setting is Context; Left-to-Right and Right-to-Left are the other available settings.

Scroll Bar Align: The Scroll Bar Align property specifies the visual placement of the control's vertical scrollbars and buttons. This property also works in conjunction with language-specific versions of Access to determine scrollbar placement in either the right-to-left or left-to-right direction. The default setting is System, which lets the operating system determine the scroll-bar alignment.

Numeral Shapes: The Numeral Shapes property determines the format for displaying numeric characters. This property also works in conjunction with language-specific versions of Access to determine the type of numeric character to display. The default setting is System, which lets the operating system determine the numeric character display format. The other settings include Arabic, National, and Context.

Left Margin, Top Margin, Right Margin, Bottom Margin: These properties are used to determine how far the text within the control prints from the left, top, right, and bottom of the control. These properties are particularly useful for large controls containing a lot of text, such as a memo on an invoice.

Line Spacing: The Line Spacing property is used to control the spacing between lines of text within a control. The Line Spacing property is designated in inches.

Is Hyperlink: The Is Hyperlink property is used to determine whether the text within the control is displayed as a hyperlink. If the Is Hyperlink property is set to Yes, and the text within the control is a relevant link, the text will serve as a hyperlink. (This is useful only if you save the report in HTML format.)

The Control's Data Properties

The Data properties of a control specify information about the data underlying a particular report control.

Control Source: The Control Source property specifies the field in the report's record source that's used to populate the control. A control source can also be a valid expression.

Input Mask: The Input Mask property assigns specific formatting to any data that is entered into a particular control. For example, you could use the Input Mask !(999) 000-0000 to format the data entered as a phone number.

Running Sum: The Running Sum property (unique to reports) is quite powerful. It can be used to calculate a record-by-record or group-by-group total. It can be set to No, Over Group, or Over All. When set to Over Group, the value of the text box accumulates from record to record within the group but is reset each time the group value changes. An example is a report that shows deposit amounts for each state with a running sum for the amount deposited within the state. Each time the state changes, the amount deposited is set to zero. When set to Over All, the sum continues to accumulate over the entire report.

The Other Control Properties

The Other properties of a control designate properties that don't fit into any other category, such as:

Name: The Name property gives you an easy and self-documenting way to refer to the control in VBA code and in many other situations. You should name all your controls. Naming conventions for report controls are the same as those for form controls. Refer to Appendix B, "Naming Conventions," for more detailed information.

Vertical: The Vertical property is used to determine whether the text within the control is displayed vertically. The default value for this property is No.

Tag: Like the Tag property of a report, the Tag property of a control gives you a user-defined slot for the control. You can place any extra information in the Tag property.

> **CAUTION**
>
> A common mistake many developers make is giving controls names that conflict with Access names. This type of error is very difficult to track down. Make sure you use distinctive names for both fields and controls. Furthermore, don't give a control the same name as the name of a field within its expression. For example, the expression =ClientName & Title shouldn't have the name "ClientName"; that would cause an #error# message when the report is run. Finally, don't give a control the same name as its control source. Access gives bound controls the same name as their fields, so you need to change them to avoid problems. Following these simple warnings will spare you a lot of grief!

Inserting Page Breaks

Page breaks can be set to occur before, within, or at the end of a section. The way that you set each type of page break is quite different. To set a page break within a section, you must use the Page Break tool in the toolbox. Click the Page Break tool in the toolbox, and then click the report where you want the page break to occur. To set a page break before or after a section, set the Force New Page property of the section to Before Section, After Section, or Before & After. The Force New Page property applies to Group Headers, Group Footers, and the report's Detail section.

> **CAUTION**
>
> Be careful not to place a page break within a control on the report. The page break will occur in the middle of the control's data.

Unbound, Bound, and Calculated Controls

Three types of controls can be placed on a report: Bound, Unbound, and Calculated. Unbound controls, such as logos placed on reports, aren't tied to data. Bound controls are tied to data within a field of the table or query underlying the report. Calculated controls contain valid expressions; they can hold anything from a page number to a sophisticated financial calculation. Most complex reports have a rich combination of Bound, Unbound, and Calculated controls.

Using Expressions to Enhance Your Reports

Calculated controls use expressions as their control sources. To create a Calculated control, you must first add an Unbound control to the report. Expressions must be preceded by an equal sign (=); an example of a report expression is =Sum([BillableHours]). This expression, if placed in the Report Footer, totals the contents of the BillableHours control for all detail records in the report. You can build an expression by typing it directly into the control source or by using the Expression Builder, covered in Chapter 5.

Building Reports Based on More Than One Table

The majority of reports you create will probably be based on data from more than one table. This is because a properly normalized database usually requires that you bring table data back together to give your users valuable information. For example, a report that combines data from a Customers table, an Orders table, an Order Details table, and a Product table can supply the following information:

- Customer information: company name and address
- Order information: order date and shipping method
- Order detail information: quantity ordered and price
- Product table: product description

A multitable report can be based directly on the tables whose data it displays, or it can be based on a query that has already joined the tables, providing a flat table structure.

Creating One-to-Many Reports

You can create one-to-many reports by using a Report Wizard, or you can build the report from scratch. Different situations require different techniques, some of which are covered in the following sections.

Building a One-to-Many Report with the Report Wizard

Building a one-to-many report with the Report Wizard is quite easy; just follow these steps:

1. Click Reports in the Objects list and double-click Create Report by Using Wizard.
2. Use the Tables/Queries drop-down list to select the first table or query whose data will appear on the report.
3. Select the fields you want to include from that table.
4. Select each additional table or query you want to include on the report, selecting the fields you need from each.

5. Click Next. Step 2 of the Report Wizard offers a suggested layout for your data. (See Figure 6.16.) You can accept Access's suggestion, or you can choose from any of the available layout options. Click Next.

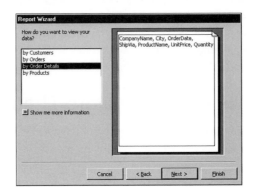

FIGURE 6.16

Step 2 of the Report Wizard: selecting a layout.

6. Step 3 of the Report Wizard asks whether you want to add any grouping levels. Grouping levels can be used to visually separate data and to provide subtotals. In the example in Figure 6.17, the report is grouped by city and company name. After you select grouping levels, click Next.

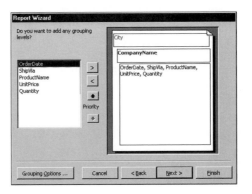

FIGURE 6.17

Step 3 of the Report Wizard: selecting groupings.

7. Step 4 of the Report Wizard lets you select how you want the records in the report's Detail section to be sorted. (See Figure 6.18.) This step of the wizard also allows you to specify any summary calculations you want to perform on the data. (See Figure 6.19.)

Click the Summary Options to specify the summary calculations. Using the button you can even opt to include the percent of total calculations.

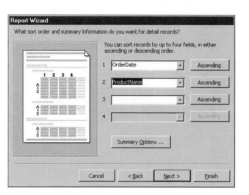

FIGURE 6.18
Step 4 of the Report Wizard: selecting a sort order.

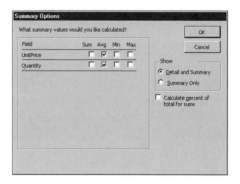

FIGURE 6.19
Adding summary calculations.

8. In step 5 of the Report Wizard, you select the layout and orientation of your report. Layout options include Stepped, Blocked, Outline 1, Outline 2, Align Left 1, and Align Left 2.

9. Step 6 of the Report Wizard lets you select from predefined styles for your report, including Bold, Casual, Compact, Corporate, Formal, and Soft Gray. You can preview each style to see what it looks like.

10. In step 7 of the Report Wizard, you select a title for your report. The title also becomes the name for the report. I like to select an appropriate name and change the title after the wizard is finished. The final step also allows you to determine whether you want to immediately preview the report or to see the report's design first.

The report created in the previous example is shown in Figure 6.20. Notice that the report is sorted and grouped by City and CompanyName. The report's data is in order by OrderDate and ProductName within a CompanyName grouping.

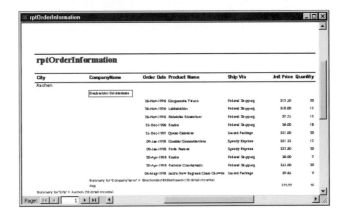

FIGURE 6.20
A completed one-to-many report.

This method of creating a one-to-many report is by far the easiest. In fact, the "background join" technology that the wizards use when they allow you to pick fields from multiple tables—figuring out how to build the complex queries needed for the report or form—was one of the major enhancements in Access 95. It's a huge timesaver and helps hide unnecessary complexity from you as you build a report. Although you should take advantage of this feature, it's important that, as a developer, you know what's happening under the covers. The following two sections give you this necessary knowledge.

Building a Report Based on a One-To-Many Query

Another popular method of building a one-to-many report is from a one-to-many query. A one-to-many report built in this way is constructed as though it were based on the data within a single table. First, you build the query that will underlie the report. (See Figure 6.21.)

When you have finished the query, you can select it rather than select each individual table (as done in the previous section). After the query is selected, creating the report is the same process as the one used for the previous report.

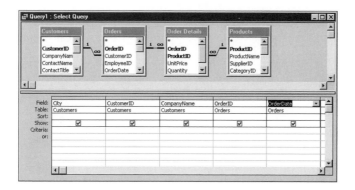

FIGURE 6.21

An example of a query underlying a one-to-many report.

Building a One-to-Many Report with the Subreport Wizard

A one-to-many report can also be created by building the parent report and then adding a Subform/Subreport control. This is often the method used to create reports such as invoices that show the report's data in a one-to-many relationship rather than in a denormalized format (as shown in Figure 6.20). If you want to use the Subform/Subreport Wizard, you must make sure that the Control Wizards tool is selected before you add the Subform/Subreport control to the main report. Here is the process:

1. Click to select the Subform/Subreport control tool.

2. Click and drag to place the Subform/Subreport control on the main report. The Subform/Subreport control is usually placed in the report's Detail section. When you have placed the Subform/Subreport control on the report, the SubReport Wizard is invoked.

3. Indicate whether you want the subreport to be based on an existing report or form or you want to build a new subreport based on a query or table. Click Next.

4. If you select Table or Query, you have to select the table or query on which the subreport will be based. You can then select the fields you want to include on the subreport. You can even select fields from more than one table or query. When you're finished, click Next.

5. The next step of the SubReport Wizard suggests a relationship between the main report and the subreport. (See Figure 6.22.) You can accept the selected relationship, or you can define your own. When you're finished, click Next.

6. The final step of the SubReport Wizard asks you to name the subreport. To follow standards, the name should begin with the prefix *rsub*. Click Finish when you're finished.

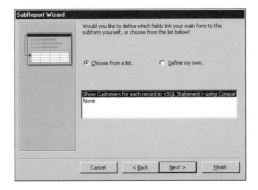

FIGURE **6.22**
The Subreport Wizard: identifying the relationship.

As you can see in Figure 6.23, the one-to-many relationship between two tables is clearly high-lighted by this type of report. In the example, each customer is listed. All the detail records reflecting the orders for each customer are listed immediately following each customer's data.

Customer I	Company Name		Contact Name	Contact Title	
ALFKI	Alfreds Futterkiste		Maria Anders	Sales Representative	

Order ID	Last Name	First Nam	Order Date	Ship Via		Freight
10643	Suyama	Michael	25-Aug-1997	Speedy Express		$29.46
10692	Peacock	Margaret	03-Oct-1997	United Package		$61.02
10702	Peacock	Margaret	13-Oct-1997	Speedy Express		$23.94
10835	Davolio	Nancy	15-Jan-1998	Federal Shipping		$69.53
10952	Davolio	Nancy	16-Mar-1998	Speedy Express		$40.42
11011	Leverling	Janet	09-Apr-1998	Speedy Express		$1.21

ANATR	Ana Trujillo Emparedados y helad		Ana Trujillo	Owner	

Order ID	Last Name	First Nam	Order Date	Ship Via		Freight
10308	King	Robert	18-Sep-1996	Federal Shipping		$1.61
10625	Leverling	Janet	08-Aug-1997	Speedy Express		$43.90
10759	Leverling	Janet	28-Nov-1997	Federal Shipping		$11.99
10926	Peacock	Margaret	04-Mar-1998	Federal Shipping		$39.92

Page: 1

FIGURE **6.23**
A completed one-to-many report created with the Subreport Wizard.

Working with Subreports

When a subreport has been added to a report, it's important to understand what properties have been set by the SubReport Wizard so that you can modify the Subreport control, if needed. You should become familiar with a few properties of a subreport:

Source Object: The name of the report or other object that's being displayed within the control.

Link Child Fields: The fields from the child report that link the child report to the master report.

Link Master Fields: The fields from the master report that link the master report to the child report.

Can Grow: Determines whether the control can expand vertically to accommodate data in the subreport.

Can Shrink: Determines whether the control can shrink to eliminate blank lines when no data is found in the subreport.

Not only should you know how to work with the properties of a Subreport object, but you should also be able to easily modify the subreport from within the main report. You can always modify the subreport by selecting it within the list of reports in the Database window. To do this, click the report you want to modify; then click Design. You can also modify a subreport by selecting its objects directly within the parent report.

TIP

Access 2002 now makes it easier to work with subforms and subreports in Design view. Scrolling has been improved so that it's easier to design subforms and subreports. In addition, you can now open subreports in their own separate Design view window by right-clicking the subreport and selecting Subreport in New Window. Alternately, instead of right-clicking the subreport, you can select the subreport and then click View, Subreport in New Window from the menu bar.

Working with Sorting and Grouping

As opposed to sorting within forms, sorting the data within a report isn't determined by the underlying query. In fact, the underlying query affects the report's sort order only when no sort order has been specified for the report. Any sort order specified in the query is completely overwritten by the report's sort order, which is determined by the report's Sorting and Grouping window. (See Figure 6.24.) The sorting and grouping of the report is affected by what options you select when you run a Report Wizard. The Sorting and Grouping window can then be used to add, remove, or modify sorting and grouping options for the report. Sorting simply affects the order of the records on the report. Grouping adds Group Headers and Footers to the report.

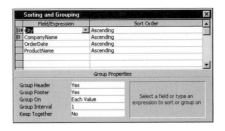

FIGURE 6.24

The Sorting and Grouping window, showing grouping by city and company name and sorting by order date and product name.

Adding Sorting and Grouping

Often, you want to add sorting or grouping to a report. To do so, follow these four steps:

1. Click Sorting and Grouping on the Report Design toolbar to open the Sorting and Grouping window.

2. Click the selector of the line above where you want to insert the sorting or grouping level. In Figure 6.25, a sorting or grouping level is being added above the City grouping. Press the Insert key to insert a blank line in the Sorting and Grouping window.

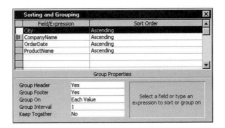

FIGURE 6.25

Inserting a sorting or grouping level.

3. Click in the Field/Expression field and use the drop-down list to select the field on which you want to sort or group.

4. Set the properties to determine the nature of the sorting or grouping (see the next section).

NOTE

To remove a sorting or grouping that has been added, click the selector on the line of the field in the Sorting and Grouping window that you want to delete; then press the Delete key. You will be warned that any controls in the Group Header or Footer will be lost.

Sorting and Grouping Properties

Each grouping in a report has properties that define the group's attributes. Each group has five properties that determine whether the field or expression is used for sorting, grouping, or both. (See Figure 6.26.) They are also used to specify details about the grouping options. Here are the Sorting and Grouping properties:

Group Header: The Group Header property specifies whether the selected group contains a header band. When you set the Group Header property to Yes, an additional band appears in the report that can be used to display information about the group. For example, if you're grouping by country, the Group Header is used to display the name of the country you're about to print. If the Group Header and Group Footer properties are both set to No, the field is used only to determine the sort order of the records in the report.

FIGURE 6.26

The Sorting and Grouping window, showing the five sorting and grouping properties.

Group Footer: The Group Footer property specifies whether the selected group contains a footer band. When you set the Group Footer property to Yes, an additional band appears in the report. The Group Footer band can be used to display summary information about the group; it's often used to display subtotals for the group.

Group On: The Group On property specifies what constitutes a new group. It's often used for situations such as departmental roll-ups. Rather than grouping on the entire department number, you might want to group on the first three digits, for example.

The Group On choices for text fields are Each Value and Prefix Characters. For Date fields, the choices are much more complex. They include Each Value, Year, Qtr, Month, Week, Day, Hour, and Minute. This means you could group by a Date field and have Access subtotal and begin a new group each time the week changes in the field. For AutoNumber, Currency, and Number fields, the choices are Each Value and Interval.

Group Interval: The Group Interval property is used with the Group On property to specify an interval value by which data is grouped. If, for example, the Group On property for a text field is set to Prefix Characters, and the Group Interval is set to 3, the field's data is grouped on the first three characters.

Keep Together: The Keep Together property determines whether Access tries to keep an entire group together on one page. The three choices for the property are No, Whole Group, and With First Detail. The Whole Group option means that Access tries to keep the entire group together on one page. This includes the Group Header, Group Footer, and Detail section. The With First Detail option means that Access prints the group header on a page only if it can also print the first detail record on the same page.

> **NOTE**
>
> If you have set Keep Together to Whole Group, and the group is too large to fit on a page, Access ignores the property setting. Furthermore, if you set Keep Together to With First Detail and either the group header or detail record is too large to fit on one page, that setting is ignored, too.

What Are Group Header and Footer Properties and Why Use Them?

Each Group Header and Footer has its own properties that determine the behavior of the Group Header or Footer:

Force New Page: The Force New Page property can be set to None, Before Section, After Section, or Before & After. When set to None, no page break occurs either before or after the report section. If set to Before Section, a page break occurs before the report section prints; if set to After Section, a page break occurs after the report section prints. When set to Before and After, a page break occurs before the report section prints as well as after it prints.

New Row or Col: The New Row or Col property determines whether a column break occurs whenever the report section prints. This property applies only to multicolumn reports. The choices are None, Before Section, After Section, and Before & After. Like the Force New

Page property, this property determines whether the column break occurs before the report section prints, after it prints, or before and after, or whether it's affected by the report section break at all.

Keep Together: The Keep Together property specifies whether you want Access to try to keep an entire report section together on one page. If this property is set to Yes, Access starts printing the section at the top of the next page if it can't print the entire section on the current page. When set to No, Access prints as much of the section as possible on the current page, inserting each page break as necessary. If a section exceeds the page length, Access starts printing the section on a new page and continues printing it on the following page.

Visible: The Visible property indicates whether the section is visible. It's common to hide the visibility of a particular report section at runtime in response to different situations. This can easily be done by changing the value of the report section's Visible property with VBA code, usually on the Format event.

Can Grow, Can Shrink: The Can Grow property determines whether the section stretches vertically to accommodate the data in it. The Can Shrink property specifies whether you want the section to shrink vertically, eliminating blank lines.

Repeat Section: The Repeat Section property is a valuable property; it lets you specify whether the group header is repeated on subsequent pages if a report section needs more than one page to print.

Improving Performance and Reusability by Basing Reports on Stored Queries or Embedded SQL Statements

Basing your Access reports on stored queries offers you two major benefits:

- The query underlying the report can be used by other forms and reports.
- Sophisticated calculations need to be built only once—they don't need to be re-created for each report (or form).

With earlier versions of Access, reports based on stored queries opened faster than reports based on embedded SQL statements. This is because, when you build and save a query, Access compiles and creates a query plan. This query plan is a plan of execution that's based on the amount of data in the query's tables as well as all the indexes available in each table. In earlier versions of Access, if you ran a report based on an embedded SQL statement, the query was compiled, and the query plan was built at runtime, slowing the query's execution. With Access 2002, query plans are built for embedded SQL statements when the form or report is saved. Query plans are stored with the associated form or report.

So what are the benefits of basing a report on a stored query instead of an embedded SQL statement? Often, you want to build several reports and forms all based on the same information. An embedded SQL statement can't be shared by multiple database objects. At the very least, you must copy the embedded SQL statement for each form and report you build. Basing reports and forms on stored queries eliminates this problem. You build the query once and modify it once if changes need to be made to it. Many forms and reports can all use the same query (including its criteria, expressions, and so on).

Reports often contain complex expressions. If a particular expression is used in only one report, nothing is lost by building the expression into the embedded SQL statement. On the other hand, many complex expressions are used in multiple reports and forms. By building these expressions into queries on which the reports and forms are based, you have to create the expression only one time.

> **TIP**
>
> It's easy to save an embedded SQL statement as a query. This allows you to use the Report Wizard to build a report using several tables; you can then save the resulting SQL statement as a query. With the report open in Design view, bring up the Properties window. Click the Data tab; then click in the Record Source property and click the ellipsis. The embedded SQL statement appears as a query. Select File Save As, enter a name for the query, and click OK. Close the Query window, indicating that you want to update the Record Source property. Your query is now based on a stored query instead of an embedded SQL statement.

Although you can see that basing reports on stored queries offers several benefits, it has its downside as well. If your database contains numerous reports, the database container becomes cluttered with a large number of queries that underlie those reports. Furthermore, queries and the expressions within them are often very specific to a particular report. If that is the case, you should opt for embedded SQL statements rather than stored queries.

Access Reports and the Internet

Microsoft makes it easy to develop Internet-aware applications by adding hyperlinks to reports and by allowing you to save an Access report as an HTML document. These features are covered in the following sections.

Adding a Hyperlink to a Report

Hyperlinks can be added to reports in the form of labels. When added, they serve as a direct link to a UNC or URL. To add a hyperlink to a report, follow these steps:

1. With the report open in Design view, add a label to the report.

2. Set the Hyperlink Address property to the UNC or URL you want to link to. The easiest way to do this is to click in the Hyperlink Address property; then click the ellipsis to open the Insert Hyperlink dialog box.

3. With Existing File or Web Page selected as the Link To, you can enter a file path or URL in the text box or click Current Folder to locate a file or Web Page in the current folder. You can also click to insert hyperlinks to Browsed Pages or Recent Files. With Object in This Database selected as the Link To, you can link to an object in the current database. Select Create New Page to create a new data access page and select Email Address to link to an e-mail address.

4. If you want to enter a Hyperlink SubAddress, click Bookmark. The Hyperlink SubAddress can be a range name, bookmark, slide number, or any other recognized location in the document specified in the Link to File or URL combo box.

5. Click OK. The Hyperlink Address and Hyperlink SubAddress properties are filled in with the information supplied in the Insert Hyperlink dialog box.

The Hyperlink Address and Hyperlink SubAddress properties come into play only when a report is saved as HTML and viewed in a Web browser, such as Internet Explorer 5.0. Saving a report as an HTML document is covered in the following section.

> **NOTE**
>
> Attached labels (those associated with a text box) do not have HyperLink Address or HyperLink SubAddress properties.

Saving a Report as HTML

To save a report as HTML, choose File|Export. Use the Save As Type drop-down list to select HTML documents (*.htm, *.html). Pick a location and name for the file, and then click Export. The document is saved as HTML and assigned the name and location you specified. Click Autostart to display the report in the default Web browser after the HTML is generated.

Saving a Report as XML

Reports can also be saved as XML by selecting the report within the database window (or by having the report open and in focus) and clicking File|Export from the menu bar. Choose XML Documents (*.xml) from the Save As Type drop-down. Accept the default filename or specify a different filename and click Export. Access generates three files: *filename*.htm, *filename*.xsl, and *filename*.xml. The .xsl file is the stylesheet for displaying the XML data. When you open the .htm file within a browser, the report is displayed along with the data. If you open the .xml file within a browser, you are viewing the actual XML code. Saving reports as XML is covered in detail in *Alison Balter's Mastering Access 2002 Enterprise Development*.

PRACTICAL EXAMPLES

Building Reports Needed for Your Application

The sample application requires several reports that you'll design throughout the book. A couple of the simpler ones are built here.

Designing the rptClientListing Report

The rptClientListing report lists all the clients in the tblClients table. The report includes the company name, contact name, intro date, default rate, and term type of each customer. The report is grouped by contact type and sorted by company name. It provides the average default rate by contact type and overall.

The rptClientListing report is based on a query called qryClientListing, which is shown in Figure 6.27. The query includes the CompanyName, IntroDate, and DefaultRatefields from the tblClients table. It joins the tblClients table to the tblContactType table to obtain the ContactType field from tblContactType, and joins the tblClients table to the tblTerms table to obtain the TermType field from the tblTerms table. It also includes an expression called ContactName that concatenates the ContactFirstName and ContactLastName fields. The expression looks like this:

```
ContactName: [ContactFirstName] & " " & [ContactLastName]
```

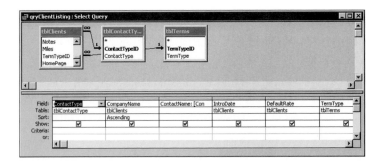

FIGURE 6.27
The qryClientListing query—a foundation for the rptClientListing report.

To build the report, follow these steps:

1. Select Reports from the Objects list and double-click Create Report by Using Wizard.

2. Use the drop-down list to select the qryClientListing query. (See Figure 6.28.) Click OK.

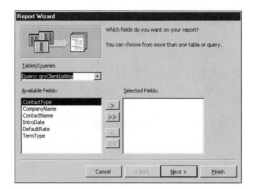

FIGURE 6.28
Selecting the qryClientListing query.

3. Click the >> button to designate that you want to include all the fields in the query within the report. Click Next.

4. Indicate that you want to view your data by tblContactType. Click Next.

5. Do not add any grouping to the report. Click Next.

6. Use the drop-down list to select CompanyName as the sort field. (See Figure 6.29.)

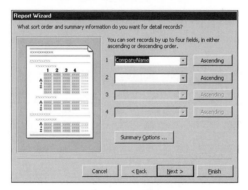

FIGURE 6.29
Selecting CompanyName as the sort order.

7. Click Summary Options and click the Avg check box to add the average default rate to the report. Click OK to close the Summary Options dialog and Next to proceed to the next step of the wizard.

8. Select Landscape for the Orientation and click Next.

9. Select a style for the report and click Next.

10. Give the report the title rptClientListing; then click Finish.

11. The completed report should look like Figure 6.30. Click Design to open the report in Design view. Notice that both the name and title of the report are rptClientListing. Modify the title of the report so that it reads `Client Listing by Contact Type and Company Name`. (See Figure 6.31.)

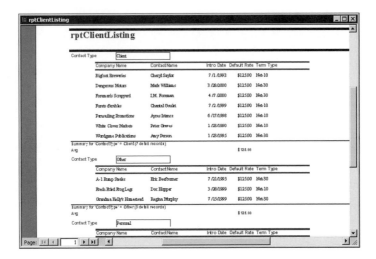

FIGURE 6.30

A preview of the completed report.

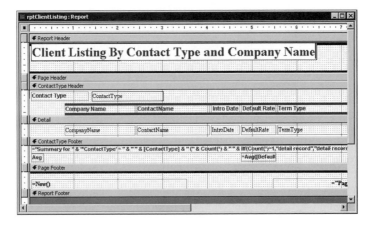

FIGURE 6.31

Changing the report title.

Designing the rptTimeSheet Report

The rptTimeSheet report is much more complex than the rptClientListing report. It includes two subreports: rsubTimeSheet and rsubTimeSheetExpenses.

The rptTimeSheet report is shown in Figure 6.32. It's based on a query called qryTimeSheet. (See Figure 6.33.) It contains fields from both tblTimeCards and tblEmployees.

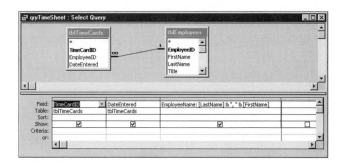

FIGURE 6.32

The rptTimeSheet report in Design view.

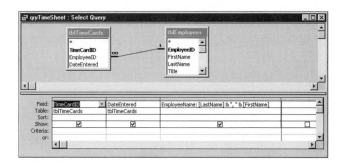

FIGURE 6.33

The qryTimeSheet query in Design view.

The rptTimeSheet report has a Page Header that includes the title of the report, but nothing else is found within the Page Header. The TimeCardID header contains the EmployeeName and DateEntered from the qryTimeSheet query. The report's Detail section contains the two subreports rsubTimeSheet and rsubTimeSheetExpenses. The TimeCardID footer has a text box that contains the grand total of hours and expenses. The expression within the text box is

```
=[rsubTimeSheet].[Report]![txtTotalHourlyBillings]+[rsubTimeSheetExpenses].[Rep
ort]![txtTotalExpenseAmount]
```

It is easiest to build the expression using the expression builder.

The Page Footer holds two expressions, one for the date and another for the page number. They look like this:

```
=Now()
="Page " & [Page] & " of " & [Pages]
```

The rsubTimeSheet report is based on qrySubTimeSheet; this query contains the following fields from the tblProjects and tblTimeCardHours tables:

> tblProjects: ProjectName
>
> tblTimeCardsHours: TimeCardID, TimeCardDetailID, DateWorked, WorkDescription, BillableHours, BillingRate, and the expression HourlyBillings:
> `[tblTimeCardHours].[BillingRate]*[BillableHours]`

The design of rsubTimeSheet is shown in Figure 6.34. This subreport can easily be built from a wizard. Select all fields except TimeCardID and TimeCardDetailID from qrySubTimeSheets. View the data by tblTimeCardHours. Don't add any groupings, and don't sort the report. When you're finished with the wizard, modify the design of the report. Remove the caption from the Report Header, and move everything from the Page Header to the Report Header. Collapse the Page Header, remove everything from the Page Footer, and add a Report Footer with the expression =Sum([HourlyBillings]).

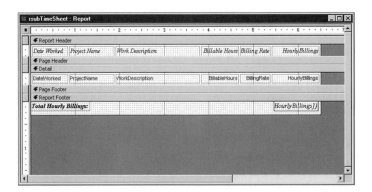

FIGURE 6.34

The rsubTimeSheet report in Design view.

Change the format of the HourlyBillings and the TotalHourlyBillings controls to Currency. Use the Sorting and Grouping window to sort by TimeCardID and TimeCardDetailID.

The rsubTimeSheetExpenses report is based on qrySubTimeSheetExpense, which contains the following fields from the tblProjects, tblExpenseCodes, and tblTimeCardExpenses tables:

> tblProjects: ProjectName
>
> tblTimeCardsExpenses: TimeCardID, TimeCardExpenseID, ExpenseDate, ExpenseDescription, and ExpenseAmount
>
> tblExpenseCodes: ExpenseCode

The design of rsubTimeSheetExpenses is shown in Figure 6.35. This subreport can easily be built from a wizard. Select all fields except TimeCardID and TimeCardExpenseID from qrySubTimeSheetExpense. View the data by tblTimeCardExpenses. Don't add any groupings, and don't sort the report. When you're finished with the wizard, modify the design of the report. Remove the caption from the Report Header, and move everything from the Page Header to the Report Header. Collapse the Page Header, remove everything from the Page Footer, and add a Report Footer with the expression =Sum(ExpenseAmount).

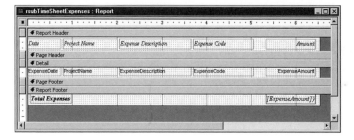

FIGURE 6.35
The rsubTimeSheetExpenses report in Design view.

Change the format of the ExpenseAmount and the TotalExpenseAmount controls to Currency, and use the Sorting and Grouping window to sort by TimeCardID and TimeCardExpenseID.

Summary

Reports give you valuable information about the data stored in your database. Many types of reports can be built in Access 2002, including Detail reports, Summary reports, reports that look like printed forms, and reports containing graphs and other objects. Access offers many properties for customizing the look and behavior of each report to fit your users' needs. Understanding how to work with each property is integral to the success of your application-development projects. For more information about reports and their use, refer to Chapter 10, "Advanced Report Techniques."

VBA: An Introduction

IN THIS CHAPTER

Why This Chapter Is Important

The Visual Basic for Applications (VBA) language is at the heart of every application that you write. It is your key to taking Access beyond the world of wizards into a world where anything is possible. This chapter introduces you to the VBA language. It serves as a foundation for the remainder of the book. After reading the chapter, you will be familiar with the development environment. You will know how to declare variables, utilize control structures, pass and return parameters, work with built—in functions, and more.

VBA Explained

Visual Basic for Applications (VBA) is the development language for Microsoft Access 2002. It offers a consistent language for application development in the Microsoft Office suite. The core language, its constructs, and the environment are the same in Microsoft Access 2002, Microsoft Visual Basic 6.0 and below, Microsoft Excel, Microsoft Word, Microsoft Outlook (for application-wide programming), and Microsoft Project. What differs among these environments are the built-in objects specific to each application. For example, Access has a CurrentProject object, but Excel has a Workbook object. Each application's objects have appropriate properties (attributes) and methods (actions)—and, in some cases, events—associated with them. This chapter gives you an overview of the VBA language and its constructs.

Unlike macros in Word or Excel, Access macros are not subprocedures in modules; instead, they are a different type of database object, with their own interface. Because of this, you can't use Access macros to learn to program in VBA, as you can by recording a Word or Excel macro and then examining its VBA code. Simple Access applications can be written by using macros. Although macros are okay for quick prototyping and very basic application development, most serious Access development is done by using the VBA language. Unlike macros, VBA gives you the ability to do the following:

- Work with complex logic structures (case statements, loops, and so on)
- Use constants and variables
- Take advantage of functions and actions not available in macros
- Loop through and perform actions on recordsets
- Perform transaction processing
- Create database objects programmatically and work with them
- Implement error handling
- Create libraries of user-defined functions
- Call Windows API functions
- Perform complex DDE and OLE automation commands

The VBA language enables you to use complex logic structures. Macros let you perform only simple `If...Then...Else` logic, but the VBA language offers a wealth of logic and looping constructs, which are covered later in this chapter.

The VBA language also lets you declare and work with variables and constants. These variables can be scoped appropriately and passed as parameters to subroutines and functions. As you will see later in this chapter, variables and constants are an integral part of any Access application.

If you try to develop an application using only macros, you can't take advantage of many of the rich features available in the VBA language. In addition, many of the actions available in both macros and modules can be done much more efficiently with VBA code.

Complex Access applications often require you to loop through a recordset, performing some action on each member of the set. There's no way to do this using Access macros. However, with the VBA language and ActiveX Data Objects, you can add, delete, update, and manipulate data. ActiveX Data Objects are covered in Chapter 14, "What Are ActiveX Data Objects and Data Access Objects, and Why Are They Important?"

When manipulating sets of records, you want to ensure that all processing finishes successfully before your data is permanently updated. Macros don't enable you to protect your data with transaction processing. Using the `BeginTrans`, `CommitTrans`, and `Rollback` methods, you can make sure your data is updated only if all parts of a transaction finish successfully. Transaction processing, if done properly, can substantially improve your application's performance because no data is written to disk until the process is finished. Transaction processing and its benefits are covered in *Alison Balter's Mastering Access 2002 Enterprise Development*.

With Access macros, you can't create or modify database objects at runtime. Using VBA, you can create databases, tables, queries, and other database objects; you can also modify existing objects. There are many practical applications of this capability to create or modify database objects (discussed in more detail in Chapter 14). When users are able to build queries on-the-fly, for example, you might want to give them the capability to design a query by using a front-end form that you provide. You can also enable users to store the query so that they can run it again later.

Access macros don't allow you to implement error handling. If an error occurs while an Access macro is executing in Access's runtime version, the user is exited out of the application and is returned to the Windows desktop. By using error-handling techniques, you can determine exactly what will happen when an error occurs during the execution of your application. Error handling is covered in more depth in Chapter 16, "Error Handling: Preparing for the Inevitable."

VBA also makes it easier for you to write code libraries of reusable functions, design and debug complex processes, and even write your own add-ins. If you're developing even moderately complex applications, you want to be able to create generic function libraries that can be used with all your Access applications. It's extremely difficult, if not impossible, to do this using macros.

Many powerful functions not available within the VBA language are available as part of Windows itself. The Windows API (Application Programming Interface) refers to the nearly 1,000 Windows functions that Microsoft exposes for use by Access programmers. You can't take advantage of these functions from an Access macro. However, by using VBA code, you can declare and call these functions, improving both the performance and functionality of your applications. The Windows API is covered in Chapter 23, "Exploiting the Power of the Windows API."

DDE (Dynamic Data Exchange) and Automation enable you to communicate between your Access applications and other applications. Although DDE is an older technology than Automation, it's still used to communicate with a few applications that don't support Automation. Automation is used to control Automation server applications, such as Excel and Project, and their objects (all Microsoft Office applications are Automation servers). Automation is covered in Chapter 22, "Automation: Communicating with Other Applications."

Although macros can offer a quick fix to a simple problem, their limitations make the VBA language the only real option for developing complex solutions. To make the transition from macros to modules easier, Microsoft has given you a feature that enables you to convert any macro to VBA code.

What Are Access Class Modules, Standard Modules, Form Modules, and Report Modules?

VBA code is written in units called *subroutines* and *functions* that are stored in modules. Microsoft Access modules are either Standard modules or Class modules. *Standard modules* are created by selecting the Modules icon in the Database window, and then clicking New. *Class modules* can be standalone objects or can be associated with a form or report. To create a standalone Class module, you choose the Class Module command from the Insert menu. In addition, whenever you add code behind a form or report, Microsoft Access creates a Class module associated with that form or report that contains the code you create.

Modules specific to a form or report are generally called *Form* and *Report Class modules*, and their code is often referred to as *Code Behind Forms* (CBF). CBF is created and stored in that form or report and triggered from events occurring within it.

A *subroutine* (or, *subprocedure*) is a routine that responds to an event or performs some action. An *event procedure* is a special type of subroutine that automatically executes in response to an event such as a mouse click on a command button or the loading of a form. A *function* is a special type of routine because it can return a value; a subroutine can't return a value. Like a subroutine, a function can be triggered from an event.

Where Is VBA Code Written?

All VBA code is written in the Visual Basic Editor, also known as the VBE. You are placed in the VBE any time that you attempt to access the code in a Standard or Class module. The Visual Basic Editor is pictured in Figure 7.1. The VBE environment in Microsoft Access is now consistent with the editor interfaces in other Microsoft Office products. The VBE is a separate window from that of Microsoft Access and comprises a menu bar, toolbar, Project window, Properties window, Immediate window, Locals window, Watch window, Object Browser, and Code windows. The various components of the VBE are discussed as appropriate in this chapter and throughout the book.

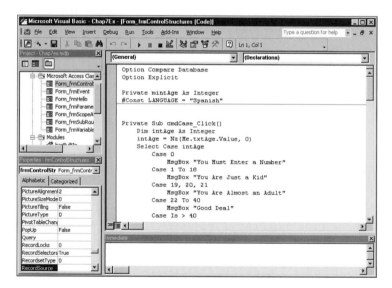

FIGURE 7.1
The Visual Basic Editor (VBE).

The Anatomy of a Module

Whether you're dealing with a Standard module or a Class module, all modules contain a General Declarations section. (See Figure 7.2.) As the name implies, this is where you can declare variables and constants that you want to be visible to all the functions and subroutines in the module. You can also set options in this section. These variables are referred to as *module-level* or *Private variables*. You can also declare Public variables in the General Declarations section of a module. *Public variables* can be seen and modified by any function or procedure in any module in the database.

FIGURE 7.2

The General Declarations section of a module is used to declare Private and Public variables.

NOTE

Public variables in Access 97, 2000, and 2002 replace Access 2.0's Global variables. Although Global variables are still supported in Access 97, 2000, and 2002, today most people use Public variables rather than Global variables.

A module is also made up of user-defined subroutines and functions. Figure 7.3 shows a subroutine called SayHello. Notice the drop-down list in the upper-left portion of the window titled Chap7Ex - Module1 (Code). This is referred to as the Object drop-down list. Subroutines and functions are sometimes associated with a specific object, such as a form or a control within a form. This is where such an association is noted. In this case, the subroutine named SayHello is not associated with any object, so the Object drop-down list contains (General).

FIGURE 7.3

An example of a user-defined subroutine called SayHello.

TIP

Access 2002 has an environment option called Full Module View. This option, when checked, enables you to see several subroutines and functions in a module at one time. Notice the difference between Figure 7.3 and Figure 7.4. In the code window shown in Figure 7.3, only one subroutine is visible at a time. The code window shown in Figure 7.4 illustrates the effects of Full Module View—multiple subroutines are visible, each separated by a thin, horizontal line. Full Module View is the default in Access 2002. To change the Full Module View environment setting, with the Microsoft Visual Basic Editor (VBE) active, choose Tools|Options, click the Editor tab, and check Default to Full Module View. If you want to temporarily change to Procedure view, click the Procedure view button in the lower-left corner of a module window and then click the Full Module View button to return to Full Module View.

FIGURE 7.4

In Full Module View, you can view several procedures simultaneously.

Option Explicit

Option Explicit is a statement that can be included in the General Declarations section of any module, including the Class module of a form, or report. When Option Explicit is used, all variables in that module must be declared before they're used, or an error saying that a variable is undefined will occur when the module is compiled. If an undeclared variable is encountered when compiling a module without Option Explicit, VBA will simply treat it as a new variable and continue without warning. It might appear at first glance that, because Option Explicit can cause compiler errors that would otherwise not occur, it might be better to avoid the use of this option. However, just the opposite is true. You should use Option Explicit in every module, without exception. For example, look at the following code:

```
intAmount = 2
intTotal = intAmont * 2
```

Clearly the intent of this code is to multiply the value contained in the variable intAmount, in this case 2, by 2. Notice, however, that the variable name is misspelled on the second line. If Option Explicit has not been set, VBA views intAmont as a new variable and simply continues its processing. The variable intTotal will be set to 0 instead of 4, and no error indication is given at all. This kind of result can be totally avoided by using Option Explicit.

TIP

In Access 2.0, you had to manually enter the Option Explicit statement into each module, form, and report. Going back to Access 97, developers have had the option of globally instructing Access to insert the Option Explicit statement in all new modules. To do this in Access 2002, with the Visual Basic Editor (VBE) active, choose Tools|Options. Under the Editor tab, click Require Variable Declaration. It's important that the Option Explicit statement be placed in all your modules, so make sure you set this option to True. The default when installing Microsoft Access 2002 is False. Option Explicit will save you hours of debugging and prevent your beeper from going off after your application has been distributed to your users.

In addition to a General Declarations section and user-defined procedures, forms, and reports, Class modules also contain event procedures that are associated with a particular object on a form. Notice in Figure 7.5 that the Object drop-down list says cmdHello. This is the name of the object whose event routines you are viewing. The drop-down list on the right shows all the events that can be coded for a command button; each of these events creates a separate event routine. You will have the opportunity to write many event routines as you read through this book.

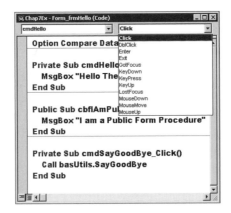

FIGURE 7.5

An event procedure for the Click event of the cmdHello command button.

Creating Event Procedures

Event procedures are automatically created when you write event code for an object. For example, the routine `Private Sub cmdHello_Click` is created when you place code in the `Click` event of the cmdHello command button, shown in Figure 7.5. To get to the event code of an object, follow these steps:

1. Click on the object in Design view and click the Properties button on the toolbar, or right-click on the object and choose Properties from the context-sensitive menu.
2. Click on the Event properties tab.
3. Select the property you want to write code for (for example, the `On Click` event).
4. Select `[Event Procedure]` from the drop-down list.
5. Click on the ellipsis button, which places you in the Visual Basic Editor (VBE) within the event code for that object.

> **NOTE**
>
> As discussed at the beginning of the chapter, the Visual Basic Editor opens in a separate window. It provides a programming environment consistent with that of all the other Microsoft Office applications. Modules added in the VBE will not appear in the database container until they are saved within the VBE.

Creating Functions and Subroutines

You can also create your own procedures that aren't tied to a particular object or event. Depending on how and where they're declared, they can be called from anywhere in your application or from a particular Code module, Form module, or Report module.

Creating a User-Defined Routine in a Code Module

1. Click Modules within the Objects list in the Database window.
2. Click New to create a new module or select an existing module and click Design. The VBE appears.
3. Select Procedure from the Insert drop-down on the toolbar (second icon from the left) or choose Procedure from the Insert menu. The Add Procedure dialog box shown in Figure 7.6 appears.

FIGURE 7.6

In the Add Procedure dialog box, you specify the name, type, and scope of the procedure you're creating.

4. Type the name of the procedure.

5. Select Sub, Function, or Property as the Type of procedure.

6. To make the procedure available to your entire application, select Public as the Scope; to make the procedure private to this module, select Private.

7. Finally, indicate whether you want all the variables in the procedure to be static. (Static variables are discussed in this chapter under "Scope and Lifetime of Variables: Exposing Your Variables as Little as Possible.") Then click OK.

Creating a User-Defined Routine in a Form or Report Class Module

1. While in Design view of a form or report, select View from the menu. Notice the icon beside the Code menu entry. This same icon is also available on the toolbar. You can view the code behind the form or report by clicking on this icon on the toolbar or by selecting Code from the View menu. You are placed in the VBE.

2. Select Procedure from the Insert drop-down list on the toolbar (second icon from the left), or choose Procedure from the Insert menu to open the Insert Procedure dialog box.

3. Type the name of the procedure.

4. Select Sub, Function, or Property as the Type of procedure.

5. To make the procedure available to your entire application, select Public as the Scope; to make the procedure private to this module, select Private.

6. Finally, indicate whether you want all the variables in the procedure to be static. When you're finished, click OK.

TIP

Whether you're creating a procedure in a Standard module or a Class module, you're now ready to enter the code for your procedure. A great shortcut for creating a procedure is to type directly in the code window the name of the new procedure, preceded by its designation as either a Sub or a Function. Example: Sub *Whatever* or Function *Whatever*. This creates a new subroutine or function as soon as you press Return.

Calling Event and User-Defined Procedures

Event procedures are automatically called when an event occurs for an object. For example, when a user clicks a command button, the Click event code for that command button executes.

The standard method for calling user-defined procedures is to use the Call keyword—Call SayHello, for example. You can also call the same procedure without using the Call keyword: SayHello.

Although not required, using the Call keyword makes the statement self-documenting and easier to read. A user-defined procedure can be called from an event routine or from another user-defined procedure or function.

Scope and Lifetime of Procedures

The scope of a procedure can be declared Public or Private. A procedure's scope determines how widely it can be called from other procedures. In addition to a procedure's scope, the placement of a procedure can noticeably affect your application's functionality and performance.

Another attribute of a procedure has to do with the lifetime of any variables that are declared within the procedure. By default, the variables declared within a procedure have a *lifetime*—that is, they have value and meaning only while the procedure is executing. When the procedure completes execution, the variables that it declared are destroyed. This default lifetime can be altered by using the Static keyword.

Public Procedures

A Public procedure placed in a code module can be called from anywhere in the application. Procedures declared in a module are automatically Public. This means that, unless you specify otherwise, procedures you place in any code module can be called from anywhere within your application.

 You might think that two Public procedures can't have the same name. Although this was true in earlier versions of Access, it isn't true in Access 2000 and Access 2002. If two Public procedures share a name, the procedure that calls them must explicitly state which of the two routines it's calling. This is illustrated by the following code snippet found in frmHello's Class module in the sample database, Chap7ex.mdb:

```
Private Sub cmdSayGoodBye_Click()
    Call basUtils.SayGoodBye
End Sub
```

NOTE

This code, and all the sample code in this chapter, is found in Chap7ex.mdb on the sample code CD-ROM.

The SayGoodBye routine is found in two Access code modules; however, the prefix basUtils indicates that the routine you want to execute is in the Standard module named basUtils.

Procedures declared in Form or Report Class modules are also automatically Public, so they can be called from anywhere within the application. The procedure called cbfIAmPublic, shown in Figure 7.7, is found in the form called frmHello. The only requirement for this procedure to be called from outside the form is that the form containing the procedure must be open in Form view. The cbfIAmPublic procedure can be called from anywhere within the application by using the following syntax (found in the Standard module basHello):

```
Sub CallPublicFormProc()
    Call Forms.frmHello.cbfIAmPublic
End Sub
```

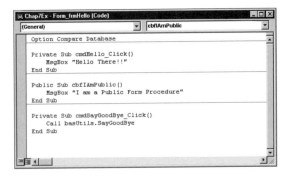

FIGURE 7.7

A Public form procedure is visible to any subroutine or function in the database.

> **TIP**
>
> Although all procedures (except event procedures) are by default Public, the `Public` keyword should be used to show that the procedure is visible to any subroutine or function in the database.

Private Procedures

As mentioned, all user-defined procedures are automatically Public. If you want a procedure declared in a module to have the scope of that module only, meaning that it can be called only from another routine within the module, you must explicitly declare it as Private. (See Figure 7.8.)

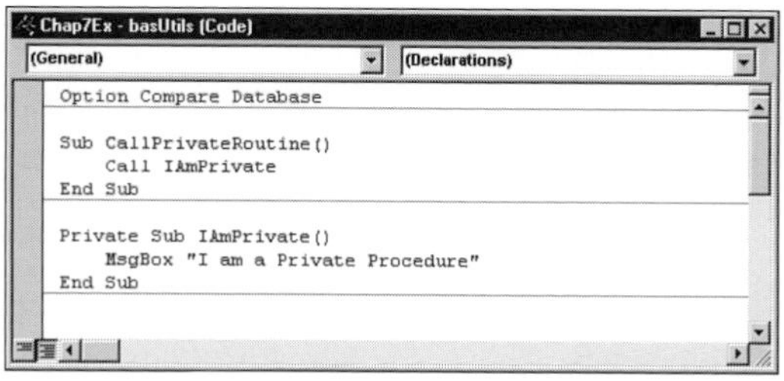

FIGURE 7.8

A Private procedure is visible only to subroutines and functions in the basUtils module.

The procedure shown in Figure 7.8, called `IAmPrivate`, is Private. It can be called only from other procedures in the Standard basUtils module.

Scope Precedence

Private procedures always take precedence over Public procedures. If a Private procedure in one module has the same name as a Public procedure declared in *another* module, the Private procedure's code is executed if it's called by any routine in the module where it was declared. Naming conflicts don't occur between Public and Private procedures (unless you declare a public and private variable with the same name in the same module).

> **TIP**
>
> Developers often wonder where to place code: in Form or Report Class modules or in Standard modules? There are pros and cons to each method. Placing code in Standard

modules means that the code can be easily called from anywhere in your application, without loading a specific form or report. Public routines placed in Standard modules can also be called from other databases. For this reason, Standard modules are a great place to put generic routines that you want readily available as part of a library.

Access 2000 and Access 2002 load modules on a demand-only basis, which means that procedures no longer take up memory unless they're being used. This is especially true if you plan your modules carefully (see Chapter 17, "Optimizing Your Application"). Regardless of when the code is loaded, an advantage of placing code behind forms and reports (rather than within modules) is that the form or report is self-contained and, therefore, portable. You can import the form or report into any other database, and it still operates as expected. This object-oriented approach means that the form requires nothing from the outside world.

As you can see, there are pluses and minuses to each method. As a general rule, if a routine is specific to a particular form or report, place that routine in the form or report; if it's widely used, place it in a module.

Static Procedures

If a procedure is declared as Static, all the variables declared in the procedure maintain their values between calls to the procedure. This is an alternative to explicitly declaring each variable in the procedure as Static. Here's an example of a Static procedure, found in basVariable:

```
Static Sub IncrementThem()
    Dim intCounter1 As Integer
    Dim intCounter2 As Integer
    Dim intCounter3 As Integer
    intCounter1 = intCounter1 + 1
    intCounter2 = intCounter2 + 1
    intCounter3 = intCounter3 + 1
    MsgBox intCounter1 & " - " & intCounter2 & " - " & intCounter3
End Sub
```

Ordinarily, each variable in this procedure would be reinitialized to zero each time the procedure is run. This means that all 1s would appear in the message box each time the procedure is run. Because the procedure is declared as Static, the variables in it retain their values from call to call. That means that each time the procedure is run, the values in the message box increase. This behavior should become much clearer after the discussion of variables later in this chapter.

Working with Variables

You must consider many issues when creating VBA variables. The way that you declare a variable determines its scope, its lifetime, and more. The following topics will help you better understand declaring variables in VBA.

Declaring Variables

There are several ways to declare variables in VBA. Three are nonstandard, and one is standard. For example, you could simply declare x=10. With this method of variable declaration, you really aren't declaring your variables at all; you're essentially declaring them as you use them. This method is quite dangerous. It lends itself to typos and other problems. If you follow the practice, recommended previously—of always using the `Option Explicit` statement—, Access will not allow you to declare variables in this manner.

You could also type `Dim intCounter`; the `Dim` statement declares the variable. The only problem with this method is that you haven't declared the type of the variable to the compiler, so it's declared as a variant variable.

Another common mistake is declaring multiple variables on the same line, as in this example:

```
Dim intCounter, intAge, intWeight As Integer.
```

In this line, only the last variable is explicitly declared as an integer variable. The other variables are implicitly declared as variants. If you're going to declare multiple variables on one line, make sure each variable is specifically declared, as in the following example:

```
Dim intCounter As Integer, intAge As Integer, intWeight As Integer
```

The most efficient and bug-proof way to declare your variables is to strong type them to the compiler and declare only one variable per line of code, as in this example:

```
Dim intCounter As Integer
Dim strName As String
```

As you can see, strong typing declares the name of the variable as well as the type of data it can contain. This enables the compiler to catch errors, such as storing a string in an integer variable, before your program runs. If implemented properly, this method can also reduce the resources needed to run your programs by selecting the smallest practical data type for each variable.

> **NOTE**
>
> You should try to avoid using variants whenever possible. Besides requiring a significant amount of storage space, variants are also slow because they must be resolved by the compiler at runtime. However, certain situations warrant using a variant. One example is when you want the variable to contain different types of data at different times. Another case occurs when you want to be able to differentiate between an empty variable (one that hasn't been initialized) and a variable that has a zero or a zero-length string. Also, variant variables are the only type of variable that can hold the special value of `null`. Empty and `null` values are covered in Chapter 12, "Advanced VBA Techniques."

VBA Data Types

VBA offers several data types for variables. Table 7.1 shows a list of the available data types, the standard for naming them, the amount of storage space they require, the data they can store, and their default values.

TABLE 7.1   Data Types and Naming Conventions

Data Type	Naming Conv Example	Storage of Data	Range	Default Value
Byte	bytValue	1 byte	0 to 255	0
Boolean	boolAnswer	2 bytes	True or False	False
Integer	intCounter	2 bytes	–32768 to 32767	0
Long Integer	lngAmount	4 bytes	–2,147,483,648 to 2,147,483,647	0
Single	sngAmount	4 bytes	–3.402823E38 to –1.401298E-45 for negative values; from 1.401298E-45 to 3.402823E38 for positive values	0
Double	dblValue	8 bytes	–1.79769313486231E308 to –4.94065645841247E-324 for negative values; from 4.94065645841247E-324 to 1.79769313486232E308 for positive values	0

TABLE 7.1   Continued

Data Type	Naming Conv Example	Storage of Data	Range	Default Value
Currency	curSalary	8 bytes	−922,337,203,685,477.5808 to 922,337,203,685,477.5807	0
Date 12/30/1899	dtmStartDate	8 bytes	1/1/100 to 12/31/9999	
Object Reference	objExcel	4 bytes	Any object	N/A
Fixed String	strName	varies	Up to 65,526 characters	" "
Variable String	strName	varies	Up to approximately 2 billion characters	" "
Variant	varData	varies	Can contain any of the other data types except Fixed String	Empty
User- Defined Data Type	typEmp	varies	Based on Elements	N/A
Decimal	decTaxAmount	12 bytes	Stores numbers from $-10^{28}-1$ through $10^{28}-1=20$	0

7

Scope and Lifetime of Variables: Exposing Your Variables as Little as Possible

You have read about the different types of variables available in VBA. Like procedures, variables also have a scope. A variable can be declared as Local, Private (Module), or Public in scope. You should try to use Local variables in your code because they're shielded from being accidentally modified by other routines.

Variables also have an attribute referred to as their lifetime. The *lifetime* of a variable reflects the time during which the variable actually exists and, therefore, the time during which its value is retained. In the following sections, we take a closer look at how you can set the scope and lifetime of variables.

Local Variables

Local variables are available only in the procedure where they are declared. Consider this example (not included in Chap7ex):

```
Private Sub cmdOkay_Click
  Dim strAnimal As String
  strAnimal = "Dog"
  Call ChangeAnimal
  Debug.Print strAnimal ''Still Dog
End Sub

Private Sub ChangeAnimal
  strAnimal = "Cat"
End Sub
```

This code can behave in one of three ways. If Option Explicit were in effect, meaning that all variables must be declared before they're used, this code would generate a compiler error. If the Option Explicit statement isn't used, strAnimal would be changed to Cat only within the context of the subroutine ChangeAnimal. If the Dim strAnimal As String statement is moved to the Declarations Section of the module, the variable's value is changed to "Cat".

> **NOTE**
>
> Notice the Debug.Print statement in the cmdOkay_Click event routine shown previously. The expression that follows the Debug.Print statement is printed in the Immediate window. The Immediate window is a tool that helps you to troubleshoot your applications. You can invoke the Immediate window from almost anywhere within your application. The easiest way to activate the Immediate window is with the Ctrl+G keystroke combination. You are placed in the Visual Basic Editor within the Immediate window. You can then view the expressions that were printed to the Immediate window. The Immediate window is discussed in detail in Chapter 15, "Debugging: Your Key to Successful Development."

Static Variables: A Special Type of Local Variable

The following examples illustrate the difference between Local and Static variables. Local variables are reinitialized each time the code is called. The following procedure can be run by opening the form named frmScopeAndLifeTime and clicking the Local Age button. Notice that each time you run the procedure, the numeral 1 is displayed in the txtNewAge text box.

```
Private Sub cmdLocalAge_Click()
  Dim intAge As Integer
  intAge = intAge + 1
  Me.txtNewAge.Value = intAge
End Sub
```

Each time this code runs, the `Dim` statement reinitializes `intAge` to zero. This is quite different from the following code, which illustrates the use of a Static variable:

```
Private Sub cmdStaticAge_Click()
  Static sintAge As Integer
  sintAge = sintAge + 1
  Me.txtNewAge.Value = sintAge
End Sub
```

Each time this code executes, the variable called `sintAge` is incremented, and its value is retained. You can test this by opening the form named frmScopeAndLifeTime and clicking the Static Age button.

Private Variables

So far, this discussion has been limited to variables that have scope within a single procedure. Private (module-level) variables can be seen by any routine in the module they were declared in, but not from other modules. Thus, they are Private to the module. Private variables are declared by placing a `Private` statement, such as the following, in the General Declarations section of a form, report, or Access module:

```
[General Declarations]
Option Explicit
Private mintAge As Integer
```

The value of a variable declared as Private can be changed by any subroutine or function within that module. For example, the following subroutine increments the value of the Private variable `mintAge` by `1`. You can run this code by opening the form frmScopeAndLifeTime and clicking the Module Age button.

```
Private Sub cmdModuleAge_Click()
  mintAge = mintAge + 1
  Me.txtNewAge.Value = mintAge
End Sub
```

Notice the naming convention of using the letter `m` to prefix the name of the variable, which denotes the variable as a Private module-level variable. You should use Private declarations only for variables that need to be seen by multiple procedures in the same module; aim for making most of your variables Local to make your code modular and more bulletproof.

Public Variables

Public variables can be accessed from any VBA code in your application. They're usually limited to things such as login IDs, environment settings, and other variables that must be seen by your entire application. Declarations of Public variables can be placed in the General Declarations section of a module. The declaration of a Public variable looks like this:

```
Option Explicit
Public gintAge As Integer
```

Notice the prefix g (a relic of the old Global variables), the proper prefix for a Public variable declared in a Standard module. This standard is used because Public variables declared in a Standard module are visible not only to the module they were declared in, but also to other modules. The following code, placed in the Click event of the cmdPublic command button, increments the Public variable gintAge by 1. You can run this code by opening the form frmScopeAndLifeTime and clicking the Public Age button.

```
Private Sub cmdPublicAge_Click()
  gintAge = gintAge + 1
  Me.txtNewAge.Value = gintAge
End Sub
```

Adding Comments to Your Code

Comments, which have been color-coded since the release of Access 97, are added to modules by using an apostrophe ('). The keyword Rem can also be used, but the apostrophe is generally preferred. The apostrophe can be placed at the beginning of the line of code or anywhere within it. Anything following the apostrophe is considered a comment. Figure 7.9 shows code containing comments.

FIGURE 7.9

Code containing comments that clarify what the subroutine is doing.

TIP

Many people ask if it is possible to comment several lines of code at once. Although not easily discoverable, the process is quite simple. Within the VBE, right-click any toolbar or menu bar and display the Edit toolbar. Click the Comment Block tool on the Edit toolbar. To uncomment the block of code, click the Uncomment Block tool.

Using the Line Continuation Character

Access Basic code, used in Access 2.0, didn't have a line continuation character. Therefore, you had to scroll a lot, as well as pull out a bag of tricks to simulate continuing a line of code. With VBA, Access 97, 2000, and 2002 solve this problem; the line continuation character is an underscore. Figure 7.10 illustrates the use of this character.

FIGURE 7.10
The line continuation character is used to improve the readability of a long line of code.

Using the VBA Control Structures

VBA gives the developer several different constructs for looping and decision processing. The most commonly used ones are covered in the following sections and are found in the form called `frmControlStructures`.

If...Then...Else

The `If...Then...Else` construct evaluates whether a condition is `True`. In the following example, anything between `If` and `Else` will occur if the statement evaluates to `True`, and any code between `Else` and `End If` will be executed if the statement evaluates to `False`. The `Else` is optional.

```
Private Sub cmdIfThenElse_Click()
  If IsNull(Me.txtName.Value) or IsNull(Me.txtAge.Value) Then
    MsgBox "Name or Age is Blank"
  Else
    MsgBox "Your Name Is " & Me.txtName.Value _
        & " And Your Age Is " & Me.txtAge.Value
  End If
End Sub
```

This code tests whether the text box called `txtName` or the text box `txtAge` contains a `null`. A different message is displayed depending on whether one of the text boxes contains a `Null` value.

One-line `If` statements are also permitted; they look like this:

```
If IsNull(Me.txtvalue.Value) Then MsgBox "You must Enter a Value"
```

However, this format for an `If` statement isn't recommended because it reduces readability.

Another useful form of an `If` statement is `ElseIf`, which enables you to evaluate an unlimited number of conditions in one `If` statement. The following code gives you an example (this example is not included in Chap7Ex):

```
Sub MultipleIfs(intNumber As Integer)
    If intNumber = 1 Then
        MsgBox "You entered a One"
    ElseIf intNumber = 2 Then
        MsgBox "You entered a Two"
    ElseIf intNumber >= 3 And intNumber <= 10 Then
        MsgBox "You entered a Number Between 3 and 10"
    Else
        MsgBox "You Entered Some Other Number"
    End If
End Sub
```

The conditions in an `If` statement are evaluated in the order in which they appear. For this reason, it's best to place the most common conditions first. After a condition is met, execution continues immediately after `End If`. If no conditions are met, and there's no `Else` statement, execution will also continue immediately after `End If`.

NOTE

If multiple conditions exist, it's almost always preferable to use a `Select Case` statement, described later in this chapter, rather than an `If` statement. `Case` statements generally make your code easier to read and maintain.

Immediate If (`IIf`)

An Immediate If (`IIf`) is a variation of an `If` statement. It's actually a built-in function that returns one of two values, depending on whether the condition being tested is true or false. Here's an example (this code is not included in Chap7Ex):

```
Function EvalSales(curSales As Currency) As String
   EvalSales = IIf(curSales >= 100000, "Great Job", "Keep Plugging")
End Function
```

This function evaluates the curSales parameter to see whether its value is greater than or equal to $100,000. If it is, the string "Great Job" is returned from the function; otherwise, the string "Keep Plugging" is returned.

CAUTION

Both the true and false portions of the IIf are evaluated, so, if there's a problem with either part of the expression (for example, a divide-by-zero condition), an error occurs.

The IIf function is most often used in a calculated control on a form or report, or to create a new field in a query. Probably the most common example is an IIf expression that determines whether the value of a control is null. If it is, you can have the expression return a zero or an empty string; otherwise, you can have the expression return the value in the control. The following expression, for example, evaluates the value of a control on a form:

```
=IIf(IsNull(Forms!frmOrders.txtFreight.Value),0,Forms!frmOrders.
txtFreight.Value)
```

This expression displays either a zero or the value for freight in the control called txtFreight.

NOTE

Although the IIf function can be used to handle Nulls, the built-in Nz function is a more efficient solution to this problem and avoids the inherent pitfalls of IIf.

CAUTION

The IIf function is rather slow. It is best to avoid using it whenever possible.

The Conditional `If`: Conditional Compilation

Conditional compilation enables you to selectively execute blocks of code. This feature is useful in several situations:

- When you want certain blocks of code to execute in the demo version of your product and other blocks to execute in your product's retail version
- When you're distributing your application in different countries and want certain blocks of code to apply to some countries but not to others
- When you want certain blocks of code to execute only during the testing of your application

Conditional compilation is done by using the `#If...Then...#Else` directive, as shown here and found under the Conditional Compilation command button on the frmControlStructures form:

```
Sub cmdConditionalCompilation_Click()
   #If Language = "Spanish" Then
      MsgBox "Hola, Que Tal?"
   #Else
      MsgBox "Hello, How Are You?"
   #End If
End Sub
```

The compiler constant, in this case, `Language`, can be declared in one of two places: in a module's General Declarations section or in the Project Properties dialog box. A compiler constant declared in the General Declarations section of a module looks like this:

```
#Const Language = "Spanish"
```

The disadvantage of this constant is that it can't be declared as Public. It isn't possible to create Public compiler constants by using the `#Const` directive. This means that any compiler constants declared in a module's Declarations section can be used only within that module. The major advantage of declaring this type of compiler constant is that it can contain a string. For example, the compiler constant `Language`, defined in the previous paragraph, is given the value `"Spanish"`.

Public compiler constants can be declared by modifying the Project Properties. Because they are Public in scope, compiler constants declared in the Project Properties can be referred to from anywhere in your application. The major limitation on compiler directives set up in Project Properties is that they can contain only integers. For example, you would have to enter `Language = 1`.

To define compiler constants using the Project Properties dialog box, right-click within the Project window and select *projectx* Properties, wherein *projectx* is the name of the project you are working with. You can now enter the values you need into the text box labeled Conditional Compilation Arguments. You can enter several arguments by separating them with a colon, such as Language = 1 : Version = 2.

With the compiler directive Language=1, the code would look like this:

```
Sub ConditionalIf()
    #If Language = 1 Then
        MsgBox "Hola, Que Tal?"
    #Else
        MsgBox "Hello, How Are You?"
    #End If
End Sub
```

NOTE

For this code to execute properly, you must remove the constant declaration from the previous example.

Notice that ConditionalIf now evaluates the constant Language against the integer of 1.

It's important to understand that using conditional constants isn't the same as using regular constants or variables with the standard If...Then...Else construct. Regular constants or variables are evaluated at runtime, which requires processing time each time the application is run. Conditional constants and conditional If...Then...Else statements control which sections of code are actually compiled. All resolution is completed at compile time; this eliminates the need for unnecessary processing at runtime.

Select Case

Rather than using multiple If...Then...Else statements, it's often much clearer to use a Select Case statement, as shown here and found under the Select Case command button of the frmControlStructures form:

```
Private Sub cmdCase_Click()
    Dim intAge As Integer
    intAge = Nz(Me.txtAge.Value, 0)      Select Case intAge
      Case 0
        MsgBox "You Must Enter a Number"
      Case 1 To 18
        MsgBox "You Are Just a Kid"
      Case 19, 20, 21
        MsgBox "You are Almost an Adult"
      Case 22 to 40
        MsgBox "Good Deal"
```

7

VBA: AN INTRODUCTION

```
        Case Is > 40
          MsgBox "Getting Up There!"
        Case Else
          MsgBox "You Entered an Invalid Number"
      End Select
End Sub
```

This subroutine first uses the Nz function to convert a Null or empty value in the txtAge control to 0; otherwise, the value in txtAge is stored in intAge. The Select Case statement then evaluates intAge. If the value is 0, a message box is displayed with You Must Enter a Number. If the value is between 1 and 18 inclusive, a message box is displayed saying, You Are Just a Kid. If the user enters 19, 20, or 21, the message You are Almost an Adult is displayed. If the user enters a value between 22 and 40 inclusive, the message Good Deal is displayed. If a value greater than 40 is displayed, the message Getting Up There is displayed; otherwise, the user gets a message indicating that he or she entered an invalid number.

Looping

Several looping structures are available in VBA; most are discussed in this section. Take a look at the following example of a looping structure (found under the Do While...Loop command button of the frmControlStructures form):

```
Sub cmdDoWhileLoop_Click()

   Do While Nz(Me.txtAge.Value)< 35

      Me.txtAge.Value = Nz(Me.txtAge.Value) + 1
   Loop
End Sub
```

In this structure, if the value in the txtAge text box is greater than or equal to 35, the code in the loop is not executed. If you want the code to execute unconditionally at least one time, you need to use the following construct (found under the Do...Loop While command button of the frmControlStructures form:

```
Sub cmdDoLoopWhile_Click()

   Do

      Me.txtAge = Nz(Me.txtAge.Value) + 1
   Loop While Nz(Me.txtAge.Value) < 35
End Sub
```

This code will execute one time, even if the value in the txtAge text box is set to 35. The Do While...Loop in the previous example evaluates before the code is executed, so it doesn't ensure code execution. The `Do...Loop While` is evaluated at the end of the loop and it, therefore, guarantees execution.

Alternatives to the `Do While...Loop` and the `Do...Loop While` are `Do Until...Loop` and `Do...Loop Until`. `Do Until...Loop` (found under the `Do Until...Loop` command button of the frmControlStructures form) works like this:

```
Sub cmdDoUntil_Click()

   Do Until Nz(Me.txtAge.Value) = 35

      Me.txtAge.Value = Nz(Me.txtAge.Value) + 1
   Loop
End Sub
```

This loop continues to execute until the value in the `txtAge` text box becomes equal to 35. The `Do...Loop Until` construct (found under the `Do...Loop Until` command button of the frmControlStructures form) is another variation:

```
Sub cmdLoopUntil_Click()

   Do

      Me.txtAge.Value = Nz(Me.txtAge.Value) + 1
   Loop Until Nz(Me.txtAge.Value) = 35
End Sub
```

As with the `Do...Loop While` construct, the `Do...Loop Until` construct doesn't evaluate the condition until the end of the loop, so the code in the loop is guaranteed to execute at least once.

TIP

As covered in Chapter 17, it is not a good idea to reference a control over and over again in a loop. Notice that, in the looping examples, the txtAge control is referenced each time through the loop. This was done to keep the examples simple. To eliminate the performance problem associated with this technique, use the code that follows (found under the cmdEfficient command button on the frmControlStructures form):

```
Private Sub cmdEfficient_Click()
    Dim intCounter As Integer
    intCounter = Nz(Me.txtAge.Value)
    Do While intCounter < 35
       intCounter = intCounter + 1
    Loop
    Me.txtAge.Value = intCounter
End Sub
```

> **CAUTION**
>
> With *any* of the looping constructs, it's easy to unintentionally cause a loop to execute endlessly, as shown in this example and can also be illustrated with the code samples shown previously (this code is not included in Chap7Ex):
>
> ```
> Sub EndlessLoop()
>     Dim intCounter As Integer
>     intCounter = 5
>     Do
>         Debug.Print intCounter
>         intCounter = intCounter + 1
>     Loop Until intCounter = 5
> End Sub
> ```
>
> This code snippet sets `intCounter` equal to 5. The code in the loop increments `intCounter`, and then tests to see whether `intCounter` equals 5. If it doesn't, the code in the loop executes another time. Because `intCounter` will never become equal to 5 (it starts at 6 within the `Do` loop), the loop executes endlessly. You need to use Ctrl+Break to exit the loop; however, Ctrl+Break doesn't work in Access's runtime version.

For...Next

The `For...Next` construct is used when you have an exact number of iterations you want to perform. It looks like this and is found under the `For...Next` command button of the frmControlStructures form:

```
Sub cmdForNext_Click()
    Dim intCounter As Integer
    For intCounter = 1 To 5
        Me.txtAge.Value = Nz(Me.txtAge.Value) + 1
    Next intCounter
End Sub
```

Note that `intCounter` is self-incrementing. The start value and the stop value can both be variables. A `For...Next` construct can also be given a step value, as shown in the following (the counter is incremented by the value of `Step` each time the loop is processed):

```
Sub ForNextStep()
' Note that this code is not in database Chap7ex.mdb
    Dim intCounter As Integer
    For intCounter = 1 To 5 Step 2
        Me.txtAge.Value = Nz(Me.txtAge.Value) + 1
    Next intCounter
End Sub
```

With...End With

The `With...End With` statement executes a series of statements on a single object or user-defined type. Here's an example (found under the `With...End With` command button of the frmControlStructures form:

```
Private Sub cmdWithEndWith_Click()
    With Me.txtAge
        .BackColor = 16777088
        .ForeColor = 16711680
        .Value = "40"
        .FontName = "Arial"
    End With
End Sub
```

This code performs four operations on the txtAge text box, found on the form it's run on. The `BackColor`, `ForeColor`, `Value`, and `FontName` properties of the txtAge text box are all modified by the code.

TIP

The `With...End With` statement offers two main benefits. The first is simply less typing—you don't need to repeat the object name for each action you want to perform on the object. The more important benefit involves performance. Because the object is referred to once rather than multiple times, this code runs much more efficiently. The benefits are even more pronounced when the `With...End With` construct is found in a loop.

For Each...Next

The `For Each...Next` statement executes a group of statements on each member of an array or collection. The following example (found under the `For Each...Next` command button of the frmControlStructures form) illustrates the use of this powerful construct:

```
Private Sub cmdForEachNext_Click()

    Dim ctl As Control
    For Each ctl In Controls
        ctl.FontSize = 8
    Next ctl
End Sub
```

This code loops through each control on the form, modifying the FontSize property of each control.

As in the following example, the `With...End With` construct is often used along with the `For Each...Next` construct.

```
Private Sub cmdForEachWith_Click()
    Dim ctl As Control
    For Each ctl In Controls
        With ctl
            .ForeColor = 16711680
            .FontName = "Arial"
            .FontSize = 14
        End With
    Next ctlEnd Sub
```

This code loops through each control on a form; the `ForeColor`, `FontName`, and `FontSize` properties of each control on the form are modified.

CAUTION

Before you put all this good information to use, remember that no error handling has been implemented in the code yet. If one of the controls on the form in the example doesn't have a `ForeColor`, `FontName`, or `FontSize` property, the code would cause an error. In Chapter 8, you will learn how to determine the type of an object before you perform a command on it. Knowing the type of an object before you try to modify its properties can help you prevent errors.

Passing Parameters and Returning Values

Both subroutines and functions can receive arguments (parameters), but only functions can return values. The following subroutine (found under the Pass Parameters command button of the frmParametersAndReturnValues form) receives two parameters, `txtFirst` and `txtLast`. It then displays a message box with the first character of each of the parameters that was passed.

```
Private Sub cmdPassParameters_Click()
  Call Initials(Nz(Me.txtFirstName.Value), Nz(Me.txtLastName.Value))
End Sub

Sub Initials(strFirst As String, strLast As String)
' This procedure can be found by selecting General in
' the Object drop-down list in the VBE window
  MsgBox "Your Initials Are: " & Left$(strFirst, 1) _
    & Left$(strLast, 1)
End Sub
```

Notice that the values in the controls txtFirstName and txtLastName from the current form (represented by the Me keyword) is passed to the subroutine called Initials. The parameters are received as strFirst and strLast. The first left character of each parameter is displayed in the message box.

The preceding code simply passes values and then operates on those values. This next example (found under the Return Values command button of the frmParametersAndReturnValues form) uses a function to return a value.

```
Private Sub cmdReturnValues_Click()
    Dim strInitials As String
    strInitials = ReturnInit(Nz(Me.txtFirstName.Value), _
        Nz(Me.txtLastName.Value))
    MsgBox "Your initials are: " & strInitials
End Sub

Function ReturnInit(strFName As String, strLName As String) As String
' This procedure can be found by selecting General in
' the Object drop-down list in the VBE window
    ReturnInit = Left$(strFName, 1) & Left(strLName, 1)
End Function
```

Notice that this example calls the function ReturnInit, sending values contained in the two text boxes as parameters. The function sets ReturnInit (the name of the function) equal to the first two characters of the strings. This returns the value to the calling routine (cmdReturnValues _Click) and sets strInitials equal to the return value.

NOTE

Notice that the function ReturnInit is set to receive two string parameters. You know this because of the As String keywords that follow each parameter. The function is also set to return a string. You know this because the keyword As String follows the list of the parameters, outside the parentheses. If you don't explicitly state that the function should return a particular type of data, it returns a variant.

Executing Procedures from the Module Window

It's easy to test procedures from the Module window in Access 2002—simply click anywhere inside the procedure you want to execute, and then press the F5 key or click the Run Sub/UserForm button on the toolbar. The procedure you're in will execute as though you had called it from code or from the Immediate pane of the Debug window.

The DoCmd Object: Performing Macro Actions

The Access environment is rich with objects that have built-in properties and methods. By using VBA code, you can modify the properties and execute the methods. One of the objects available in Access is the DoCmd object, used to execute macro actions in Visual Basic procedures. The macro actions are executed as methods of the DoCmd object. The syntax looks like this:

```
DoCmd.ActionName [arguments]
```

Here's a practical example:

```
DoCmd.OpenReport strReportName, acPreview
```

The OpenReport method is a method of the DoCmd object; it runs a report. The first two parameters that the OpenReport method receives are the name of the report you want to run and the view in which you want the report to appear (Preview, Normal, or Design). The name of the report and the view are both arguments of the OpenReport method.

Most macro actions have corresponding DoCmd methods that can be found in Help, but some don't. They are AddMenu, MsgBox, RunApp, RunCode, SendKeys, SetValue, StopAllMacros, and StopMacro. The SendKeys method is the only one that has any significance to you as a VBA programmer. The remaining macro actions either have no application to VBA code or can be performed more efficiently by using VBA functions and commands. The VBA language includes a MsgBox function, for example, that's far more robust than its macro action counterpart.

Many of the DoCmd methods have optional parameters. If you don't supply an argument, its default value is assumed. You can use commas as place markers to designate the position of missing arguments, as shown here:

```
DoCmd.OpenForm "frmOrders", , ,"[OrderAmount] > 1000"
```

The OpenForm method of the DoCmd object receives seven parameters; the last six parameters are optional. In the example, two parameters are explicitly specified. The first is the name of the form ("FrmOrders"), a required parameter. The second and third parameters have been omitted, meaning that you're accepting their default values. The commas, used as place markers for the second and third parameters, are necessary because one of the parameters following them is explicitly designated. The fourth parameter is the Where condition for the form, which has been designated as the record in which the OrderAmount is greater than 1,000. The remaining parameters haven't been referred to, so default values are used for these parameters.

If you prefer, you can use named parameters to designate the parameters that you are passing. Named parameters, covered later in this chapter, can greatly simplify the preceding syntax.

With named parameters, the arguments don't need to be placed in a particular order, nor do you need to worry about counting commas. The preceding syntax can be changed to the following:

```
DoCmd.OpenForm FormName:="frmOrders", WhereCondition:=
"[OrderAmount] > 1000"
```

Working with Built-In Functions

Visual Basic for Applications has a rich and comprehensive function library as well as tools to assist in their use.

Built-In Functions

Some of the more commonly used functions and examples are listed in the following sections. On some rainy day, go through the online Help to become familiar with the rest.

> **NOTE**
>
> The following examples are located in basBuiltIn in the Chap7Ex database.

Format

The Format function formats expressions in the style specified. The first parameter is the expression you want to format; the second is the type of format you want to apply. Here's an example of using the Format function:

```
Sub FormatData()
    Debug.Print Format$(50, "Currency")
    'Prints $50.00
    Debug.Print Format$(Now, "Short Date")
    'Prints the current date
    Debug.Print Format$(Now, "DDDD")
    'Displays the word for the day
    Debug.Print Format$(Now, "DDD")
    'Displays 3 - CHAR Day
    Debug.Print Format$(Now, "YYYY")
    'Displays 4 - digit Year
    Debug.Print Format$(Now, "WW")
    'Displays the Week Number
End Sub
```

Instr

The `Instr` function returns the position where one string begins within another string:

```
Sub InstrExample()
  Debug.Print InStr("Alison Balter", "Balter") 'Returns 8
  Debug.Print InStr("Hello", "l") 'Returns 3
  Debug.Print InStr("c:\my documents\my file.txt", "\") 'Returns 3
End Sub
```

InStrRev

`InStrRev` begins searching at the end of a string and returns the position where one string is found within another string:

```
Sub InstrRevExample()
    Debug.Print InStrRev("c:\my documents\my file.txt", "\") 'Returns 16
End Sub
```

Notice that the `InStr` function returns 3 as the starting position for the backslash character within `"c:\my documents\my file.txt"`, whereas the `InStrRev` function returns 16 as the starting position for the backslash character in the same string. This is because `InStr` starts searching at the beginning of the string, continuing until it finds a match, whereas `InStrRev` begins searching at the end of the string, continuing until it finds a match.

Left

`Left` returns the left-most number of characters in a string:

```
Sub LeftExample()
  Debug.Print Left$("Hello World", 7) 'Prints Hello W
End Sub
```

Right

`Right` returns the right-most number of characters in a string:

```
Sub RightExample()
 Debug.Print Right$("Hello World", 7) 'Prints o World
End Sub
```

Mid

`Mid` returns a substring of a specified number of characters in a string. This example starts at the fourth character and returns five characters:

```
Sub MidExample()
    Debug.Print Mid$("Hello World", 4, 5) ''Prints lo Wo
End Sub
```

UCase

UCase returns a string that is all uppercase:

```
Sub UCaseExample()
    Debug.Print UCase$("Hello World") 'Prints HELLO WORLD
End Sub
```

DatePart

DatePart returns the specified part of a date:

```
Sub DatePartExample()
    Debug.Print DatePart("YYYY", Now)
    'Prints the Year
    Debug.Print DatePart("M", Now)
    'Prints the Month Number
    Debug.Print DatePart("Q", Now)
    'Prints the Quarter Number
    Debug.Print DatePart("Y", Now)
    'Prints the Day of the Year
    Debug.Print DatePart("WW", Now)
    'Prints the Week of the Year
End Sub
```

DateDiff

DateDiff returns the interval of time between two dates:

```
Sub DateDiffExample()
  Debug.Print DateDiff("d", Now, "12/31/99")
  ''Days until 12/31/99
  Debug.Print DateDiff("m", Now, "12/31/99")
  ''Months until 12/31/99
  Debug.Print DateDiff("yyyy", Now, "12/31/99")
  ''Years until 12/31/99
  Debug.Print DateDiff("q", Now, "12/31/99")
  ''Quarters until 12/31/99
End Sub
```

DateAdd

DateAdd returns the result of adding or subtracting a specified period of time to a date:

```
Sub DateAddExample()
    Debug.Print DateAdd("d", 3, Now)
    'Today plus 3 days
    Debug.Print DateAdd("m", 3, Now)
    'Today plus 3 months
    Debug.Print DateAdd("yyyy", 3, Now)
    'Today plus 3 years
```

```
    Debug.Print DateAdd("q", 3, Now)
    'Today plus 3 quarters
    Debug.Print DateAdd("ww", 3, Now)
    'Today plus 3 weeks
End Sub
```

Replace

Replace replaces one string with another:

```
Sub ReplaceExample()
    Debug.Print Replace("Say Hello if you want to", "hello", "bye")
    'Returns Say Bye if you want to
    Debug.Print Replace("This gets rid of all of the spaces", " ", "")
    'Returns Thisgetsridofallofthespaces
End Sub
```

StrRev

StrRev reverses the order of text in a string:

```
Sub StrReverseExample()
    Debug.Print StrReverse("This string looks very funny when reversed!")
    'Returns !desrever nehw ynnuf yrev skool gnirts sihT
End Sub
```

MonthName

MonthName returns the text string associated with a month number:

```
Sub MonthNameExample()
    Debug.Print MonthName(7)
    'Returns July
    Debug.Print MonthName(11)
    'Returns November
```

Functions Made Easy with the Object Browser

With the Object Browser, you can view members of an ActiveX component's type library. In plain English, the Object Browser enables you to easily browse through a component's methods, properties, and constants. You can also copy information and add it to your code. It even adds a method's parameters for you. The following steps let you browse among the available methods, copy the method you want, and paste it into your code:

1. With the VBE active, select View|Object Browser from the menu (note that the menu line also shows an icon that you can use from the toolbar), or press F2 to open the Object Browser window. (See Figure 7.11.)

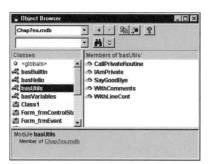

FIGURE 7.11

The Object Browser showing all the classes in the Chap7ex database and all the members in the basUtils module.

2. The Object Browser window is divided into two parts; the upper part of the window and the lower part. The drop-down list at the upper-left of the window is used to filter the items to be displayed in the lower part of the window. Use this drop-down list to select the project or library whose classes and members you want to view in the lower part of the window.

3. In the lower portion of the window, select the class from the left list box, which lists Class modules, templates for new objects, standard modules, and modules containing subroutines and functions.

4. Select a related property, method, event, constant, function, or statement from the Members Of list box. In Figure 7.11, the basUtils module is selected from the list box on the left. Notice that the subroutines and functions included in basUtils appear in the list box on the right.

5. Click the Copy to Clipboard button (third from the right in the upper toolbar within the Object Browser window) to copy the function name and its parameters to the Clipboard so that you can easily paste it into your code.

The example in Figure 7.11 shows choosing a user-defined function selected from a module in a database, but you can also select any built-in function. Figure 7.12 shows an example in which the DatePart function is selected from the Visual Basic for Applications library. The Object Browser exposes all libraries referred to by the database and is covered in more detail in Chapter 8, "Objects, Properties, Methods, and Events Explained," and Chapter 22, "Automation: Communicating with Other Applications."

FIGURE 7.12

The Object Browser with the VBA library selected.

Working with Constants

A *constant* is a meaningful name given to a meaningless number or string. Constants can be used only for values that don't change at runtime. A tax rate or commission rate, for example, might be constant throughout your application. There are three types of constants in Access:

- Symbolic
- Intrinsic
- System defined

Symbolic constants, created by using the Const keyword, are used to improve the readability of your code and make code maintenance easier. Rather than referring to the number .0875 every time you want to refer to the tax rate, you can refer to the constant mccurTaxRate. If the tax rate changes, and you need to modify the value in your code, you'll make the change in only one place. Furthermore, unlike the number .0875, the name mccurTaxRate is self-documenting.

Intrinsic constants are built into Microsoft Access; they are part of the language itself. As an Access programmer, you can use constants supplied by Microsoft Access, Visual Basic, DAO, and Active Data Objects (ADO). You can also use constants provided by any object libraries you're using in your application.

There are only three system-defined constants—True, False, and Null, and they are available to all applications on your computer.

Working with Symbolic Constants

As mentioned, a symbolic constant is declared by using the Const keyword. A constant can be declared in a subroutine or function or in the General section of a Form or Report module.

Constants can be strong-typed in Access 2000 and Access 2002. The declaration and use of a Private constant looks like this:

```
Private Const TAXRATE As Currency = .0875
```

This code, when placed in a module's Declarations section, creates a Private constant called TAXRATE and sets it equal to `.0875`. Here's how the constant is used in code:

```
Function TotalAmount(curSaleAmount As Currency)
   TotalAmount = curSaleAmount * TAXRATE
End Function
```

This routine multiplies the `curSaleAmount`, received as a parameter, by the constant TAXRATE. It returns the result of the calculation by setting the function name equal to the product of the two values. The advantage of the constant in this example is that the code is more readable than `TotalAmount = curSaleAmount * .0875` would be.

Scoping Symbolic Constants

Just as regular variables have scope, user-defined constants have scope. In the preceding example, you created a Private constant. The following statement, when placed in a module's Declarations section, creates a Public constant:

```
Public Const TAXRATE = 0.0875 As Currency
```

Because this constant is declared as Public, it can be accessed from any subroutine or function (including event routines) in your entire application. To better understand the benefits of a Public constant, take a case where you have many functions and subroutines all making reference to the constant TAXRATE. Imagine what would happen if the tax rate were to change. If you hadn't used a constant, you would need to search your entire application, replacing the old tax rate with the new tax rate. However, because your Public constant is declared in one place, you can easily go in and modify the one line of code where this constant is declared.

> **NOTE**
>
> By definition, the values of constants cannot be modified at runtime. If you try to modify the value of a constant, you get this VBA compiler error:
>
> ```
> Assignment to constant not permitted
> ```
>
> Figure 7.13 illustrates this message box. You can see that an attempt is made to modify the value of the constant TAXRATE, which results in a compile error.
>
> If you need to change the value at runtime, you should consider storing the value in a table rather than declaring it as a constant. You can read the value into a variable when the application loads, and then modify the variable if needed. If you choose, you can write the new value back to the table.

7

VBA: An Introduction

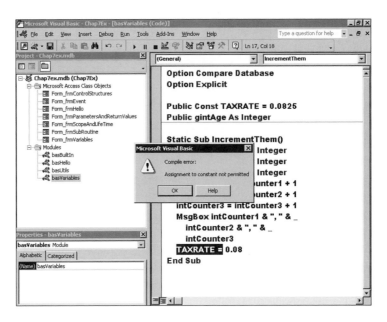

FIGURE 7.13
Trying to modify the value of a constant.

Working with Intrinsic Constants

Microsoft Access declares a number of intrinsic constants that can be used in Code, Form, and Report modules. Because they're reserved by Microsoft Access, you can't modify their values or reuse their names; however, they can be used at any time without being declared.

You should use intrinsic constants whenever possible in your code. Besides making your code more readable, they make your code more portable to future releases of Microsoft Access. Microsoft might change the value associated with a constant, but it isn't likely to change the constant's name. All intrinsic constants appear in the Object Browser; to activate it, simply click the Object Browser tool on the Visual Basic toolbar. To view the constants that are part of the Access library, select Access from the Object Browser's Project/Library drop-down list. Click Constants in the Classes list box, and a list of those constants is displayed in the Members Of 'Constants' list box. (See Figure 7.14.)

In the list shown in Figure 7.14, all the constant names begin with *ac*. All VBA constants are prefixed with *vb*, all Data Access Object constants are prefixed with *db*, and all constants that are part of the Access language are prefixed with *ac*. To view the Visual Basic language constants, select VBA from the Project/Library drop-down list and Constants from the Classes list box. If the project you are working with has a reference to the ActiveX Data Object library, you can view these constants by selecting ADODB from the Project/Library drop-down list. Click <globals>. A list of the ADODB constants appears (these constants have the prefix *ad*).

FIGURE 7.14

Using the Object Browser to view intrinsic constants.

Another way to view constants is within the context of the parameter you're working with in the Code window. Right-click the name of a parameter and select List Constants to display the constants associated with the parameter.

Tools for Working in the Visual Basic Editor

Effectively using the tips and tricks of the trade, many of which are highlighted in this chapter, can save you hours of time. These tricks help you to navigate around the coding environment, as well as to modify your code quickly and easily. They include the capability to easily zoom to a user-defined procedure, search and replace within modules, get help on VBA functions and commands, and split the Code window so that two procedures can be viewed simultaneously.

The Access 97, Access 2000, and Access 2002 development environments are better than those of their predecessors. Several features have been added to make coding easier and more pleasant for you. These enhancements include the capability to do the following:

- List properties and methods
- List constants
- Get quick information on a command or function
- Get parameter information
- Enable Access to finish a word for you
- Get a definition of a function

All these features that help you with coding are available with a right-click when you place your cursor within the Module window.

List Properties and Methods

With the List Properties and Methods feature, you can view all the objects, properties, and methods available for the current object. To invoke this feature, right-click after the name of the object and select List Properties, Methods (you can also press Ctrl+J). The applicable objects, properties, and methods appear in a list box. (See Figure 7.15.) To find the appropriate object, property, or method in the list, use one of these methods:

- Begin typing the name of the object, property, or method.
- Use the up-arrow and down-arrow keys to move through the list.
- Scroll through the list and select your choice.

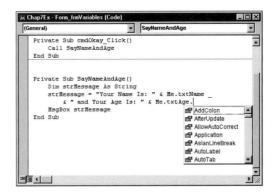

FIGURE 7.15

A list of properties and methods for the TextBox object.

Use one of these methods to insert your selection:

- Double-click the entry.
- Click to select the entry. Then press Tab to insert, or Enter to insert and move to the next line.

TIP

The Auto List Members option, available on the Editor tab of the Options dialog box, causes the List Properties and Methods feature, as well as the List Constants feature, to be invoked automatically each time you type the name of an object or property.

List Constants

The List Constants feature opens a drop-down list displaying valid constants for a property you have typed and for functions with arguments that are constants. It works in a similar manner to the List Properties and Methods feature. To invoke it, right-click after the name of the property or argument (in cases where multiple arguments are available, the previous argument must be delimited with a comma) and select List Constants (or press Ctrl+Shift+J). A list of valid constants appears. (See Figure 7.16.) You can use any of the methods listed in the previous section to select the constant you want.

FIGURE 7.16

A list of constants for the vbMsgBoxStyle *parameter.*

Quick Info

The Quick Info feature gives you the full syntax for a function, statement, procedure, method, or variable. To use this feature, right-click after the name of the function, statement, procedure, method, or variable, and then select Quick Info (or press Ctrl+I). A tip appears, showing the valid syntax for the item. (See Figure 7.17.) As you type each parameter in the item, it's displayed in boldface type until you type the comma that delineates it from the next parameter.

TIP

The Auto Quick Info option, available in the Options dialog box, causes the Quick Info feature to be invoked automatically each time you type the name of an object or property.

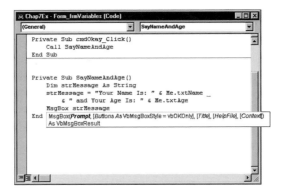

FIGURE 7.17

The syntax for the MsgBox *function.*

Parameter Information

The Parameter Info feature gives you information about the parameters of a function, statement, or method. To use this feature, after the delimiter that denotes the end of the function, statement, or method name, right-click and select Parameter Info (or press Ctrl+Shift+I). A pop-up list appears with information about the parameters of the function or statement. This list doesn't close until all the required parameters are entered, the function is completed without any optional parameters, or the Esc key is pressed.

> **NOTE**
>
> The Parameter Info feature supplies information about the initial function only. If parameters of a function are themselves functions, you must use Quick Info to find information about the embedded functions.

Complete Word

The Complete Word feature completes a word you're typing. To use this feature, you must first type enough characters for Visual Basic to recognize the word you want. Next, right-click and select Complete Word (or press Ctrl+Spacebar). Visual Basic then finishes the word you're typing.

Definition

The Definition feature shows the place in the Code window where the selected variable or procedure is defined. To get a definition of a variable or procedure, right-click in the name of the variable or procedure of interest, and select Definition (or press Shift+F2). Your cursor is moved to the module and location where the variable or procedure was defined.

As you become more proficient with VBA, you can create libraries of VBA functions and subroutines. When you're viewing a call to a particular subroutine or function, you usually want to view the code behind that function. Fortunately, VBA gives you a quick and easy way to navigate from procedure to procedure. Assume that the following code appears in your application:

```
Private Sub cmdOkay_Click()
    Dim intAgeInTen As Integer
    If IsNull(Me.txtNameValue) Or IsNull(Me.txtAge.Value) Then
        MsgBox "You must fill in name and age"
        Exit Sub
    Else
        MsgBox "Your Name Is: " & Me.txtName.Value & " _
        and Your Age Is: " & Nz(Me.txtAge.Value)
        Call EvaluateAge(Nz(Me.txtAge.Value))
        intAgeInTen = AgePlus10(Fix(Val(Me.txtAge.Value)))
        MsgBox "In 10 Years You Will Be " & intAgeInTen
    End If
End Sub
```

If you want to quickly jump to the procedure called EvaluateAge, all you need to do is place your cursor anywhere within the name, EvaluateAge, and then press Shift+F2. This immediately moves you to the EvaluateAge procedure. Ctrl+Shift+F2 takes you back to the routine you came from (in this case, cmdOkay_Click). This procedure works for both functions and subroutines.

TIP

If you prefer, you can right-click the name of the routine you want to jump to and select Definition. To return to the original procedure, right-click again and select Last Position.

NOTE

If the definition is in a referenced library, the Object Browser is invoked, and the definition is displayed.

7

VBA: AN
INTRODUCTION

Mysteries of the Coding Environment Solved

If you're a developer who's new to VBA, you might be confused by the Visual Basic Editor. We will begin by talking about the Code window. The Code window has two combo boxes, shown in Figure 7.18. The combo box on the left lists objects. For a form or report, the list includes all its objects; for a standard module, which has no objects, only (General) appears.

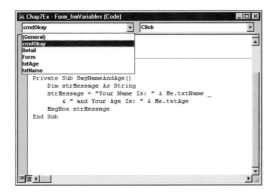

FIGURE 7.18

The Code window with the Object combo box open.

The combo box on the right lists all the event procedures associated with a particular object. Figure 7.19 shows all the event procedures associated with a command button. Notice that the Click event is the only one that appears in bold because it's the only event procedure that has been coded.

FIGURE 7.19

The Code window with the Procedure combo box open.

The Project Window

The Project window, shown in Figure 7.20, enables you to easily maneuver between the modules behind the objects within your database. The elements of your project are displayed hierarchically in a tree view within the Project window. All elements of the project are divided into Microsoft Access Classes and Modules. All Form, Report, and Class modules are found within the Microsoft Access Classes. All Standard modules are found within Modules. To view the code behind an object, simply double-click the object within the Project window. To view the object, such as a form, single-click the name of the form in the Project window and then click the View Object tool (the second icon from the left on the Project Window toolbar). You are returned to Microsoft Access with the selected object active.

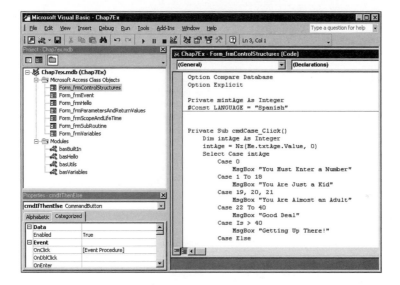

FIGURE 7.20

The Project window showing all the classes and modules contained within the Chap7ex project.

NOTE

You can also right-click the object and then select View Code (the left icon on the Project Window toolbar) to view the code, or View Object to view the object. The context-sensitive menu also enables you to insert modules and Class modules, to import and export files, to print the selected object, and to view the database properties. These features are covered in Chapter 12, "Advanced VBA Techniques."

The Properties Window

The Properties window, pictured in Figure 7.21, enables you to view and modify object properties from within the VBE. At the top of the Properties window is a combo box that allows you to select the object whose properties you wish to modify. The objects listed in the combo box include the parent object selected in the Project window (for example, the form) and the objects contained within the parent object (for example, the controls). After an object is selected, its properties can be modified within the list of properties. The properties can be viewed either alphabetically or categorically. In the example, the command button cmdIfThenElse is selected. The properties of the command button are shown by category.

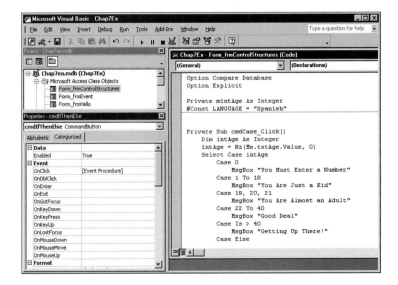

FIGURE 7.21
The Properties window showing the properties of a command button displayed categorically.

The View Microsoft Access Tool

If at any time you want to return to the Access application environment, simply click the View Microsoft Access icon (the left icon) on the toolbar. You can then return to the VBE using the taskbar, or using one of the methods covered earlier in this chapter.

Find and Replace

Often, you name a variable only to decide later that you want to change the name. VBA comes with an excellent find-and-replace feature to help you with this change. You can simply search for data, or you can search for a value and replace it with some other value. To invoke the Find dialog box, shown in Figure 7.22, choose Edit|Find, or use Ctrl+F.

Figure 7.22
The Find dialog box is set up to search for strMessage *in the current module.*

Type the text you want to find in the Find What text box. Notice that you can search in the Current Procedure, Current Module, Current Project, or Selected Text. The option Find Whole Word Only doesn't find the text if it's part of another piece of text. For example, if you check Find Whole Word Only, and then search for *Count*, VBA doesn't find *Counter*. Other options include toggles for case sensitivity and pattern matching.

You can also use the Replace dialog box to search for text and replace it with another piece of text. (See Figure 7.23.) This dialog can be invoked by selecting Edit|Replace from the menu, or by pressing Ctrl+H (or Alt+E, E). It offers all the features of the Find dialog box, but also enables you to enter Replace With text. In addition, you can select Replace or Replace All. Replace asks for confirmation before each replacement, but Replace All replaces text without this prompt. I recommend you take the time to confirm each replacement because it's all too easy to miscalculate the pervasive effects of a global search-and-replace.

Figure 7.23
The Replace dialog box is set to find strMessage *and replace it with* strNewMessage *in the current project.*

Help

A very useful but under-utilized feature of VBA is the ability to get context-sensitive help while coding. With your cursor placed anywhere in a VBA command or function, press the F1 key to get context-sensitive help on that command or function. Most of the help topics let you view practical examples of the function or command within code. Figure 7.24 shows help on the With...End With construct. Notice that the Help window includes the syntax for the command, a detailed description of each parameter included in the command, and remarks about using the command. At the top of the window, you can see hypertext links to related topics (See Also), as well as a link to an example of using the With...End With construct. If you click on Example, a specific example of the construct appears that you can copy and place into a module. (See Figure 7.25.) This feature is a great way to learn about the various parts of the VBA language.

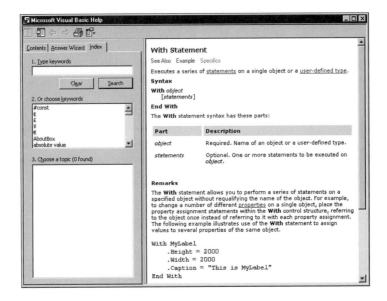

FIGURE 7.24

Help on With...End With.

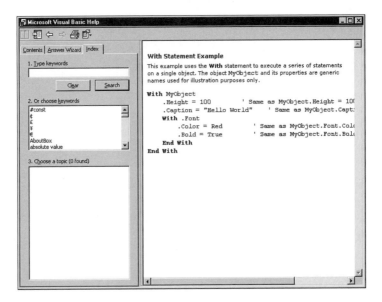

FIGURE 7.25

An example of With...End With.

Splitting the Code Window

The VBA Code window can be split so that you can look at two routines in the same module at the same time. This option is useful if you're trying to solve a problem involving two procedures or event routines in a large module. To split your Code window, as shown in Figure 7.26, choose Window|Split.

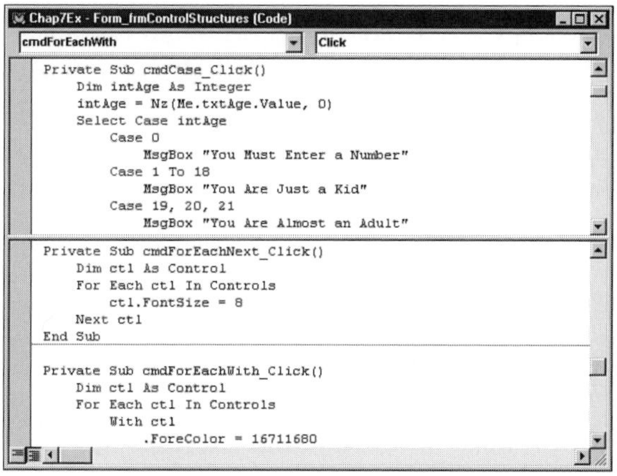

FIGURE 7.26

A split Code window lets you view two routines.

Notice the splitter. Place your mouse cursor on the gray splitter button just above the Code window's vertical scrollbar. By clicking and dragging, you can size each half of the window. The window can be split into only two parts. After it has been split, you can use the Object and Procedure drop-down lists to navigate to the procedure of your choice. The drop-down lists will work for either of the two panes of the split window, depending on which pane was last selected.

NOTE

Only routines in the same module can be viewed in a particular Code window, but several Code windows can be open at the same time. Each time you open an Access, Form, or Report module, you're placed in a different window. Each module window can then be sized, moved, and split.

Using Bookmarks to Save Your Place

The Access 2000 and Access 2002 coding environments enable you to create place markers—called *bookmarks*—so that you can easily return to key locations in your modules. To add a bookmark, right-click on the line of code where the bookmark will be placed and choose Toggle|Bookmark, or choose Bookmarks|Toggle Bookmark from the Edit menu. You can add as many bookmarks as you like.

To navigate between bookmarks, choose Edit|Bookmarks|Next Bookmark, or Edit|Bookmarks|Previous Bookmark. A bookmark is a toggle. To remove one, you simply choose Toggle|Bookmark from the shortcut menu or Bookmarks|Toggle Bookmark from the Edit menu. If you want to clear all bookmarks, choose Edit|Bookmarks|Clear All Bookmarks. Bookmarks are not saved when you close the database.

> **NOTE**
>
> Do not confuse the bookmarks discussed in this section with recordset bookmarks. Recordset bookmarks are covered in Chapter 14, "What Are ActiveX Data Objects and Data Access Objects, and Why Are They Important?"

Customizing the VBE

Access 2000 and Access 2002 provide Access programmers with significant opportunity to customize the look and behavior of the Visual Basic Editor (VBE). To view and customize the environment options, choose Tools|Options with the VBE active. Figure 7.27 shows the Options dialog box; its different aspects are discussed in detail in the rest of this section.

FIGURE 7.27

The Options dialog box.

Coding Options—The Editor Tab

The coding options available to you are found under the Editor tab of the Options dialog box. They include Auto Indent, Tab Width, Auto Syntax Check, Require Variable Declaration, Auto List Members, Auto Quick Info, and Auto Data Tips.

The Auto Indent feature invokes the automatic indenting of successive lines of code. This means that when you indent one line, all other lines are indented to the same position until you specify otherwise.

The Auto Syntax Check feature determines whether Access performs a syntax check each time you press Enter after typing a single line of code. Many developers find this option annoying. It's not uncommon to type a line of code and notice a typo in a previous line of code. You want to rectify the error before you forget, so you move off the incomplete line of code you're typing, only to get an error message that your syntax is incorrect.

The Require Variable Declaration option is a must. If this option is turned on, all variables must be declared before they are used. This important feature, when set, places the Option Explicit line in the Declarations section of every module. You're then forced to declare all variables before they're used. The compiler identifies many innocent typos at compile time, rather than by your users at runtime.

The Auto List Members option determines whether the List Properties/Methods and List Constants features are automatically invoked as you type code in the Code window. They help you in your coding endeavors by presenting a valid list of properties, methods, and constants. For more about these features, see Chapter 8.

The Auto Quick Info feature determines whether the syntax of a procedure or method is automatically displayed. If this option is selected, the syntax information is displayed as soon as you type a procedure or method name followed by a space, period, or opening parenthesis.

The Auto Data Tips feature is used when you're debugging. It displays the current value of a selected value when you place your mouse pointer over the variable in Break mode. This feature is discussed in Chapter 15, "Debugging: Your Key to Successful Development."

Code Color, Fonts, and Sizes—The Editor Format Tab

In Access 2000 and Access 2002, you can customize code colors, font, and size within the coding environment. You can also specify the foreground and background colors for the Code window text, selection text, syntax error text, comment text, keyword text, and more. You can select from any of the Windows fonts and sizes for the text in the Code window. For a more readable Code window, select the FixedSys font.

General Options—The General Tab

The General tab contains miscellaneous options that affect the behavior of the development environment. For example, the Show Grid option determines whether a form grid is displayed, and the Grid Units are used to designate the granularity of the gridlines. The other options on this tab are discussed in Chapter 12, "Advanced VBA Techniques."

Docking Options—The Docking Tab

The Docking tab enables you to specify whether the windows within the VBE are dockable. A window is said to be *dockable* if you can lock it alongside and dock it to another window. It is not dockable when you can move it anywhere and leave it there. The windows you can dock include the Immediate, Locals, Watch, Project, Properties, and Object Browser windows.

CAUTION

All the customization options that have been discussed apply to the entire Access environment. This means that, when set, they affect all your databases.

PRACTICAL EXAMPLES

Event Routines, User-Defined Functions, and Subroutines

The Chap7.MDB database includes two forms: frmClients and frmProjects. The frmClients form contains two command buttons. The first command button is used to save changes to the underlying record source (the tblClients table.) The code looks like this:

```
Private Sub cmdSave_Click()
    'Save changes to the client record
    DoCmd.RunCommand acCmdSaveRecord
End Sub
```

The code, placed under the cmdSave command button on the frmClients form, executes the RunCommand method of the DoCmd object. The acCmdSaveRecord intrinsic constant, when used as a parameter to the RunCommand method, causes changes made to the form to be saved to the underlying data source.

The second command button is used to undo changes made to the current record. The code looks like this:

```
Private Sub cmdUndo_Click()
    'Undo changes
    DoCmd.RunCommand acCmdUndo
End Sub
```

This code is found under the cmdUndo button on the frmClients form. It executes the RunCommand method of the DoCmd object. The acCmdUndo intrinsic constant, when used as a parameter to the RunCommand method, undoes changes made to the form.

The code originally located under the cmdViewProjects was generated by the command button wizard (in Chapter 5, "What Every Developer Needs to Know About Forms.") It looked like this:

```
Private Sub cmd_Click()
On Error GoTo Err_cmd_Click

    Dim stDocName As String
    Dim stLinkCriteria As String

    stDocName = "frmProjects"

    stLinkCriteria = "[ClientID]=" & Me![txtClientID]
    DoCmd.OpenForm stDocName, , , stLinkCriteria

Exit_cmd_Click:
    Exit Sub

Err_cmd_Click:
    MsgBox Err.Description
    Resume Exit_cmd_Click

End Sub
```

The code first declared two variables, one for the name of the form to be opened, and the other to hold the criteria used to open the form. It then assigned a value to the stDocName variable as well as to the stLinkCriteria variable. Finally, it used the OpenForm method of the DoCmd object to open the frmProjects form, passing the value in stLinkCriteria as the where clause for the OpenForm method. This wizard-generated code is inefficient. It utilizes variables that are not necessary. More importantly, the use of the WHERE clause in the OpenForm method causes the form to open, filtering data to the data specified in the WHERE clause. Because the data is filtered, all projects travel over the network wire, even though only the projects that meet the criteria set in the WHERE clause are displayed. Although this is not of particular importance when your data is stored in an Access database (.mdb file), it makes a tremendous difference if the data is moved to a client/server database such as Microsoft SQL Server. To eliminate both problems, the code is changed as follows.

```
Private Sub cmdViewProjects_Click()
On Error GoTo Err_cmdViewProjects_Click

    DoCmd.OpenForm FormName:="frmProjects"

Exit_cmdViewProjects_Click:
    Exit Sub

Err_cmdViewProjects_Click:
    MsgBox Err.Description
    Resume Exit_cmdViewProjects_Click
End Sub
```

Although it appears that the form is now opened without a where clause, this is not the case. The key to the solution is found in the frmProjects form. The code in the Open event of the frmProjects form looks like this:

```
Private Sub Form_Open(Cancel As Integer)
    If Not IsLoaded("frmClients") Then
        MsgBox "You Must Load this Form from the Projects form", _
            vbCritical, "Warning"
        Cancel = True
    Else
        Me.RecordSource = "qryProjects"
    End If
End Sub
```

This code first uses a user-defined function called IsLoaded to determine if the frmClients form is loaded. (The mechanics of the IsLoaded function are discussed in the following text.) The function returns True if the frmClients form is loaded, and False, if it is not. If the frmClients form is not loaded, a message is displayed to the user, and the loading of the frmProjects form is cancelled. If the frmClients form is loaded, the RecordSource property of the frmProjects form is set to a query called qryProjects. The qryProjects query is a parameter query that returns only those projects with a ClientID that matches the ClientID associated with the client displayed on the frmClients form.

The IsLoaded function looks like this:

```
Public Function IsLoaded(strFormName As String) As Boolean
    Const FORMOPEN = -1
    Const FORMCLOSED = 0
```

```
If SysCmd(acSysCmdGetObjectState, acForm, strFormName) <> FORMCLOSED Then
    IsLoaded = True
Else
    IsLoaded = False
End If

'IsLoaded = SysCmd(acSysCmdGetObjectState, acForm, strFormName)
End Function
```

The function declares two user-defined constants. These constants are intended to make the function more readable. The built-in SysCmd function is used to determine if the form whose name is received as a parameter is loaded. The SysCmd function, when passed the intrinsic constant acSysCmdGetObjectState as the first argument and acForm as the second argument, attempts to determine the state of the form whose name is passed as the third argument. The IsLoaded function returns True to its caller if the form is loaded, and False, if it is not. An alternative to this function is the following:

```
Public Function IsLoaded(strFormName As String) As Boolean
    IsLoaded = SysCmd(acSysCmdGetObjectState, acForm, strFormName)
End Function
```

This function is much shorter and more efficient, but is less readable. It simply places the return value from the SysCmd directly into the return value for the function.

In addition to the save and undo that are included in the frmClients form, this version of the frmProjects form contains one other routine. The BeforeUpdate event of the form, covered in Chapter 9, "Advanced Form Techniques," executes before the data underlying the form is updated. The code in the BeforeUpdate event of the frmProjects form looks like this:

```
Private Sub Form_BeforeUpdate(Cancel As Integer)
    If Me.txtProjectBeginDate.Value > _
        Me.txtProjectEndDate.Value Then
        MsgBox "Project Start Date Must Precede " & _
            "Project End Date"
        Cancel = True
    End If
End Sub
```

It tests to see if the project begin date falls after the project end date. If so, a message is displayed to the user, and the update is cancelled.

Summary

A strong knowledge of the VBA language is imperative for the Access developer. This chapter has covered all the basics of the VBA language. You have learned the differences between Code, Form, and Report modules and how to effectively use each. You have also learned the difference between event procedures and user-defined subroutines and functions. To get the most mileage out of your subroutines and functions, you have learned how to pass parameters to, and receive return values from, procedures.

Variables are used throughout your application code. Declaring each variable with the proper scope and lifetime helps make your application bulletproof and easy to maintain. Furthermore, selecting an appropriate variable type ensures that the minimal amount of memory is consumed and that your application code protects itself. Effectively using control structures and built-in functions gives you the power, flexibility, and functionality required by even the most complex of applications. Finally, a strong command of the Visual Basic Editor (VBE) is imperative to a successful development experience!

Objects, Properties, Methods, and Events Explained

IN THIS CHAPTER

Why This Chapter Is Important

Objects, properties, methods, and events are at the heart of all programming that you do within Microsoft Access. Without a strong foundation in objects, properties, methods, and events, and how they are used, your efforts at Access and VBA programming will fail. This chapter introduces you to Access's object model. You will become familiar not only with Access's objects, properties, methods, and events, and how to manipulate them, but you will also learn concepts that will carry throughout the book and throughout your Access and VBA programming career.

> **NOTE**
>
>
> Most of the examples in this chapter are included in the Chap8Ex database located on the sample code CD-ROM.

Understanding Objects, Properties, Events, and Methods

Many people, especially those accustomed to a procedural language, don't understand the concept of objects, properties, and events. As mentioned earlier, you need a thorough knowledge of Access's objects, their properties, and the events that each object can respond to if you want to be a productive and successful Access programmer.

What Exactly Are Objects?

Objects are all the things that make up your database. They include tables, queries, forms, reports, data access pages, macros, and modules, as well as the components of those objects. For example, a Table object contains Field and Index objects. A Form object contains various controls (text boxes, combo boxes, list boxes, and so on). Each object in the database has specific properties that determine its appearance or behavior. Each object also has specific methods, which are actions that can be taken upon it.

What Exactly Are Properties?

A *property* is an attribute of an object, and each object has many properties. Often, different types of objects share the same properties; at other times, an object's properties are specific to that particular object. Forms, combo boxes, and text boxes all have Width properties, for example, but a form has a RecordSource property that the combo box and text box don't have.

Most properties can be set at design time and modified at runtime; however, some can't be modified at runtime, and others can't be accessed at design time (just modified at runtime). Access's built-in Help for each property tells you one of the following:

- You can set the property in the object's property sheet, a macro, or Visual Basic.
- You can set this property only in Design view.
- You can access this property by using Visual Basic or a macro.

Each of these descriptions indicates when the property can be modified.

As a developer, you set the values of many objects' properties at design time; the ones you set at design time are the starting values at runtime. Much of the VBA code you write modifies the values of these properties at runtime in response to different situations. For example, suppose that a text box has a Visible property. If a client is paying by cash, you might not want the text box for the credit card number to be visible. If he's paying by credit card, you might want to set the Visible property of the text box with the credit card number to True. This is just one of the many things you can do to modify the value of an object's property at runtime in response to an event or action that has occurred.

You might wonder how you can determine all the properties associated with a particular object (both those that can be modified at design time and those that can be modified at runtime). Of course, to view the properties that can be set at design time, you can select the object and then view its property sheet. Viewing all the properties associated with an object is actually quite easy to do; just invoke Help by pressing F1. Click the Index tab in the help topics dialog box and type the name of the object whose properties you want to view. In Figure 8.1, Combo box has been typed into the text box. Click Search. Notice that one of the entries in the list box at the bottom of the dialog box is Properties of list boxes, combo boxes, drop-down list boxes, and Lookup fields. If you click that entry, information about the Combo Box Control appears in the right pane. (See Figure 8.2.) To find out about the LimitToList property, type LimitToList in the text box and click Search. Figure 8.3 shows help information on the LimitToList property. You can also use the Object Browser to quickly and easily view all properties associated with an object.

8

OBJECTS,
PROPERTIES,
METHODS

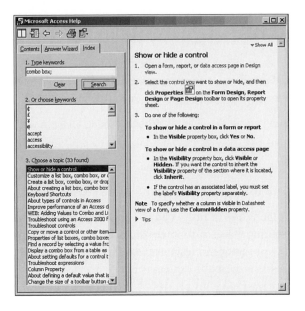

FIGURE 8.1

The Help Topics dialog box.

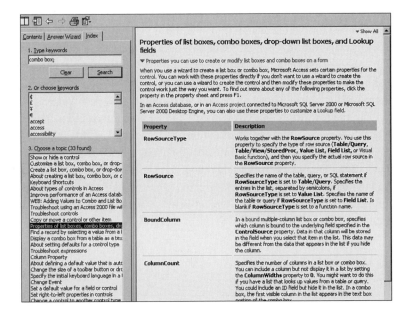

FIGURE 8.2

Information about the combo box control.

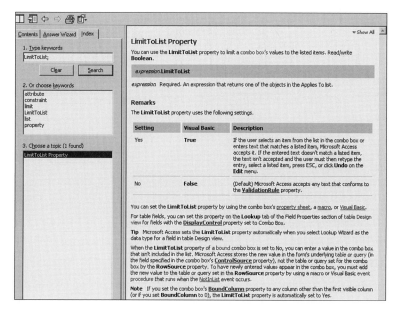

FIGURE 8.3

Help associated with a combo box's LimitToList property.

What Exactly Are Events?

Windows is an event-driven operating system; in other words, the operating system responds to many events that are triggered by actions that the user takes and by the operating system itself. Access exposes many of these events through its Object Model. An *event* in an Access application is something your application can respond to. Events include mouse movements, changes to data, a form opening, a record being added, and much more. Users initiate events, as does your application code. It's up to you to determine what happens in response to the events that are occurring. You respond to events by using macros or VBA code. Each Access object responds to different events. If you want to find out all the events associated with a particular object, take the following steps:

1. Select the object (for example, a text box).
2. Open the Properties window.
3. Click the Event tab, shown in Figure 8.4.
4. Scroll through the available list of events.

FIGURE 8.4

The list of events associated with a text box.

What Exactly Are Methods?

Methods are actions that an object takes on itself. As with properties and events, different objects have different methods associated with them. A method is like a function or subroutine, except that it's specific to the object it applies to. For example, a form has a `GoToPage` method that doesn't apply to a text box or any other object. If you search for help on methods, you see that the Choose a Topic list box fills with a list of topics. (See Figure 8.5.) If you select Undo Method in the list of topics, help appears on the `Undo` method. (See Figure 8.6.)

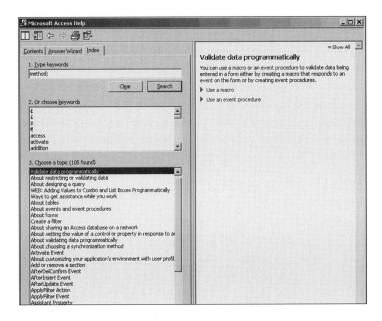

FIGURE 8.5

Getting help on methods.

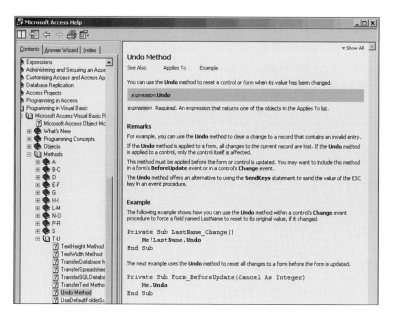

FIGURE 8.6

Help on the Undo *method.*

Using the Object Browser to Learn About Access's Objects

The Object Browser is a powerful tool that can help you learn about and work with the objects that are part of both Access 2002 and the Microsoft Windows environment. The Object Browser displays information about Microsoft Access and other objects and can help you with coding by showing you all the properties and methods associated with a particular object.

Access objects are complex—they have many properties and methods. The Object Browser helps you to understand and use objects, properties, and methods by doing the following:

- Displaying the types of objects available
- Allowing you to quickly navigate between application procedures
- Displaying the properties and methods associated with a particular object
- Finding and pasting code into your application

How to Use the Object Browser

The Object Browser can easily be invoked from the Visual Basic Editor. You can click the Object Browser button on the toolbar, press F2, or choose View|Object Browser. The dialog box shown in Figure 8.7 appears.

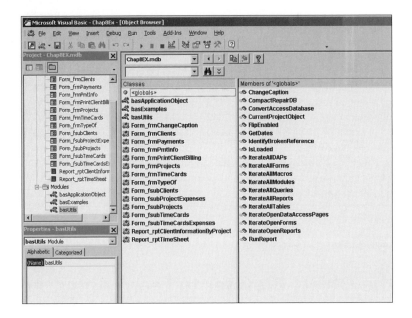

FIGURE 8.7

The Object Browser dialog box with the database object selected.

The Object Browser displays two levels of information about the selected library or database. With the Chap8Ex database open, if you select Chap8Ex.MDB from the Project/Library drop-down (the top drop-down), your screen will look similar to Figure 8.7. The Classes list box displays all modules, including Form and Report modules, in the database. The Members of list box displays any procedures that have been defined in the selected module. Notice the basUtils module, which is part of the CHAP8Ex.MDB database. Looking at the list box on the right, you can see the functions included in the basUtils module. You can click to select each Form and Report module in the list box on the left and view the associated methods and properties in the list box on the right.

You can use the Project/Library drop-down list to select a different object library (provided you have set a reference to it). The Classes list box displays the types of objects available in the selected library or database. The Members Of list box displays the methods, properties, and data elements defined for the selected object. (See Figure 8.8.) The Access item has been selected from the Library combo box, so the list box on the left shows all Access 2002's classes. The list box on the right shows all the members of the selected object—in this case, the `Application` object. You can even add other libraries to the Library drop-down list by referring to other type libraries. This method is covered in Chapter 22, "Automation: Communicating with Other Applications."

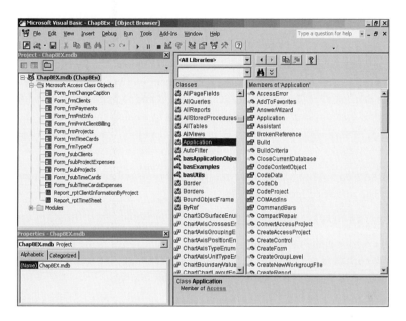

FIGURE 8.8
Selecting the Access 2002 library in the Object Browser.

Pasting Code Templates into a Procedure

After you have located the method or property you're interested in, you have the option of pasting it into your application. With the method or property selected, simply click the Copy to Clipboard button in the Object Browser; then paste it in the appropriate module. If you want to get more information about a particular method or property, click the Help button in the Object Browser or press F1.

Referring to Objects

Access objects are categorized into *collections*, which are groupings of objects of the same type. The Forms collection, for example, is a grouping of all the open forms in a database. Each form has a Controls collection that includes all the controls on that form. Each control is an object, and you must refer to an object through the collection to which it belongs. For example, you refer to a form through the Forms collection. VBA offers three ways to refer to an object; if you want to refer to the `frmProjects` form, for example, you can choose from the following options:

- `Forms.frmProjects` (or `Forms!frmProjects`)
- `Forms("frmProjects")`
- `Forms(0)`

Referring to the form as `Forms(0)` assumes that `frmProjects` was the first form opened. However, you need to understand that although an element number is assigned as each form is loaded, this element number changes as forms are loaded and unloaded at runtime. For example, the third form that's loaded can initially be referred to as element two, but if the second form is unloaded, that third form becomes element one. In other words, you can't rely on the element number assigned to a form; that number is a moving target.

You must refer to a control on a form first through the Forms collection and then through the specific form. The reference looks like this:

`Forms.frmProjects.txtClientID`

In this example, `Forms` is the name of the collection, `frmProjects` is the name of the specific form, and `txtClientID` is the name of a control on the `frmProjects` form. If this code is found in the Code module of `frmProjects`, it could be rewritten like this:

`Me.txtClientID`

`Me` refers to the current form or report. It's generic because the code could be copied to any form having a txtClientID control, and it would still run properly. Referring to a control on a report is very similar to referring to a control on a form. Here's an example:

`Reports.rptTimeSheet.txtHoursBilled`

This example refers to the txtHoursBilled text box on the rptTimeSheet report, part of the Reports collection. After you know how to refer to an object, you're ready to write code that modifies its properties and executes its methods.

Properties and Methods Made Easy

To modify an object's properties and execute its methods, you must refer to the object and then supply an appropriate property or method, as shown in this example:

`Forms.frmHello.cmdHello.Visible = False`

This line of code refers to the Visible property of cmdHello, found in the frmHello form, which is in the Forms collection. Notice that you must identify the object name frmHello as being associated with the Forms collection. If you want to change the Caption property of frmHello to say "Hello World", you would use the following code:

```
Forms.frmHello.Caption = "Hello World"
```

TIP

You might be confused about whether you're looking at an object's property or method, but there are a couple of quick ways to tell. A property is always used in some type of an expression. For example, you might be setting a property equal to some value:

```
Forms.frmClients.txtAddress.Visible = False
```

Here, you're setting the Visible property of the txtAddress text box on the frmClients form from True to False. You also might retrieve the value of a property and place it in a variable:

```
strFirstName = Forms.frmClients.txtFirstName.Value
```

You also might use the value of a property in an expression, as in the following example:

```
MsgBox Forms.frmClients.txtFirstName.Value
```

The pattern here is that a property is always used somewhere in an expression. It can be set equal to something, something can be set equal to its value, or it's otherwise used in an expression.

A method, however, is an action taken on an object. The syntax for a method is *Object.Method*. A method isn't set equal to something; however, you frequently create an object variable and then set it by invoking a method. A method looks like this:

```
Forms.frmHello.txtHelloWorld.SetFocus
```

In this example, the SetFocus method is being executed on the text box called txtHelloWorld.

A method that returns an object variable looks like this:

```
Dim cbr As CommandBar
Set cbr = CommandBars.Add("MyNewCommandBar")
```

In this example, the CommandBars collection's Add method is used to set the value of the CommandBar object variable named cbr. For more information, see the section "Declaring and Assigning Object Variables," later in this chapter.

8

OBJECTS, PROPERTIES, METHODS

> ### NOTE
>
> Many people are confused about when to use a bang (!) and when to use a period. You can use a bang whenever you're separating an object from its collection, as shown in these two examples:
>
> ```
> Forms!frmClients
>
> Forms!frmClients!txtClientID
> ```
>
> In the first example, `frmClients` is part of the Forms collection. In the second example, `txtClientID` is part of the Controls collection of the `frmClients` form.
>
> In most cases, you can also use a period to separate an object from its collection. This is because the expression `Me!txtClientID` is actually a shortcut to the complete reference `Me.Controls!txtClientID`. Because Controls is the default collection for a form, you can omit Controls from the statement. The expression can be abbreviated to `Me.txtClientID`. The advantage of using the dot over the bang is that the dot provides you with Intellisense. To test this, create a form and add a control called `txtFirstName`. Go to the code behind the form and try typing **Me!**. Notice that Intellisense is not invoked. Next type **Me.** and watch Intellisense get invoked. Intellisense facilitates the development process by providing a list box containing valid properties, methods, constants, and so on, as appropriate.
>
> In addition to separating an object from its collection, the period is also used to separate an object from a property or method. The code looks like this:
>
> ```
> Forms.frmClients.RecordSource = "tblClients"
>
> Forms.frmClients.txtClientID.Visible = False
> ```
>
> The first example sets the RecordSource property of `frmClients` to `tblClients`, and the second example sets the Visible property of the `txtClientID` on the `frmClients` form to `False`.

Default Properties

Each object has a default property, and, if you're working with an object's default property, you don't have to explicitly refer to it in code. Take a look at the following two code samples:

```
Forms.frmHello.txtHello.Value = "Hello World"
```

```
Forms.frmHello.txtHello = "Hello World"
```

The Value property is the default property of a text box, so you don't need to explicitly refer to it in code. However, I prefer to explicitly state the property—it is a practice that contributes to the code's readability and keeps novice Access programmers who work with my code from having to guess which property I'm changing.

Declaring and Assigning Object Variables

Object variables are variables that reference an object of a specific type, such as databases, recordsets, forms, controls, and even objects created in other applications. They allow you to create shortcut references to objects and pass objects to subroutines and functions. You can use them to streamline code by using short names to refer to objects with long names and to optimize code by supplying a direct pointer to a particular object.

First, you must declare an object variable; then you assign—or *point*—the object variable to a particular object, as shown in the following code:

```
Private Sub cmdChangeCaption_Click()
    'Declare a CommandButton object
    Dim cmdAny As CommandButton
    'Point the CommandButton object at the cmdHello Command button
    Set cmdAny = Me.cmdHello
    'Change the Caption of the control referenced by the cmdAny variable
    cmdAny.Caption = "Hello"
End Sub
```

This code creates an object variable called `cmdAny` of the type `CommandButton`. You then use the `Set` statement to point your `CommandButton` object variable toward the `cmdHello` object on the current form, using the `Me` keyword. Finally, you modify the caption of the `cmdAny` object variable. Because an object variable is a reference to the original object, you're actually changing the caption of the `cmdHello` command button.

Object Variables Versus Regular Variables

The difference between object variables and regular variables is illustrated by the following code:

```
Dim intVar1 As Integer
Dim intVar2 As Integer
intVar1 = 5
intVar2 = intVar1
intVar1 = 10
Debug.Print intVar1 'Prints 10
Debug.Print intVar2 'Prints 5
```

This code uses ordinary variables. When you dimension these variables, each one is assigned a separate memory location. Although `intVar2` is initially assigned the value of `intVar1`, changing the value of `intVar1` has no effect on `intVar2`. This differs from the following code, which uses an object variable:

8

OBJECTS, PROPERTIES, METHODS

```
Private Sub Command5_Click()
    Dim ctlText As TextBox
    Set ctlText = Forms.frmSales.txtProductID
    ctlText.Text = "New Text"
    Debug.Print Forms.frmSales.txtProductID.Text 'Prints New Text
End Sub
```

This routine creates an object variable called `ctlText` of type `TextBox`. It then associates the object variable with `Forms.frmSales.txtProductID`. Next, it modifies the Text property of the object variable. Because the object variable is actually pointing to the text box on the form, the `Debug.Print` statement prints the new text value.

Generic Versus Specific Object Variables

Access supports the use of generic object variables, including `Application`, `Control`, `Form`, and `Report`. Generic object variables can be used to refer to any object of that generic type:

```
Private Sub ChangeVisible_Click()
    Dim ctlAny As Control
    Set ctlAny = Me.txtCustomerID
    ctlAny.Visible = False
End Sub
```

In this example, `ctlAny` can be used to point to any control. Compare that with the following code:

```
Private Sub cmdChangeVisible_Click()
    Dim txtAny As TextBox
    Set txtAny = Me.txtCustomerID
    txtAny.Visible = False
End Sub
```

Here, your object variable can be used only to point to a text box.

Cleaning Up After Yourself

When you're finished working with an object variable, you should set its value to `Nothing`. As used in the following example, this statement frees up all memory and system resources associated with the object:

```
Set frmNew = Nothing
```

Understanding the Differences Between Objects and Collections

Many people get confused about the differences between an object and a collection. Think of an object as a member of a collection. For example, `frmHello` is a form that's a member of the

Forms collection; `cmdHello`, a command button on `frmHello`, is a member of the Controls collection of `frmHello`. Sometimes you want to manipulate a specific object, but other times you want to manipulate a collection of objects.

Manipulating a Single Object

You have already learned quite a bit about manipulating a single object, such as setting the Enabled property of a text box:

```
Me.txtCustomerID.Enabled = False
```

This line of code affects only one text box and only one of its properties. However, when you're manipulating a single object, you might want to affect several properties at the same time. In that case, it's most efficient to use the `With...End With` construct, explained in the following section.

With...End With: Performing Multiple Commands on an Object

One method you can use to modify several properties of an object is to modify the value of each property, one at a time:

```
Me.txtCustomerID.Enabled = False
Me.txtCustomerID.SpecialEffect = 1
Me.txtCustomerID.FontSize = 16
Me.txtCustomerID.FontWeight = 700
```

Contrast this with the following code:

```
With Me.txtCustomerID
    .Enabled = False
    .SpecialEffect = 1
    .FontSize = 16
    .FontWeight = 700
End With
```

This code uses the `With...End With` statement to assign multiple properties to an object. In addition to improving the readability of your code, the `With...End With` construct results in a slight increase in performance.

Manipulating a Collection of Objects

A *collection* is like an array of objects. What makes the array special is that it's defined and maintained by Access. Every collection in Microsoft Access is an object, each with its own properties and methods. The VBA language makes it easy for you to manipulate Access's collections of objects; you simply use the `For Each...Next` construct, covered in the following section.

8

OBJECTS, PROPERTIES, METHODS

`For...Each`: Performing the Same Command on Multiple Objects

In the "Determining the Type of a Control" section later in this chapter, you learn how to loop through the collection of controls on a form, performing actions on all the command buttons. This illustrates a practical use of a collection. In the following example, you loop through all the open forms, changing the caption of each form:

```
Sub FormCaptions()
    Dim frm As Form
    For Each frm In Forms
        frm.Caption = frm.Caption & " - " & CurrentUser
    Next frm
End Sub
```

This routine uses the `For...Each` construct to loop through each form in the Forms collection, setting the caption of each form to the form's caption concatenated with the current username. As you travel through the loop, the code `frm.Caption` refers to each member of the Forms collection.

Passing Objects to Subroutines and Functions

 Just as you can pass a string or a number to a subroutine or function, you can also pass an object to a subroutine or function. The code, found in the basExamples module in the Chap8Ex database, looks like this:

```
Sub ChangeCaption(frmAny as Form)
    'Change the caption property of the form received
    'to what was already in the caption property,
    'concatenated with a colon and the name of the current user
    frmAny.Caption = frmAny.Caption & ": " & CurrentUser
End Sub
```

The `ChangeCaption` routine receives a reference to a form as a parameter. The caption of the form referenced by the procedure is modified to include the name of the current user. The `ChangeCaption` routine is called like this:

```
Private Sub cmdChangeCaption_Click()
    'Call the ChangeCaption routine, passing a reference to the current form
    Call ChangeCaption(Me)
End Sub
```

In this example, the click event of the cmdChangeCaption command button calls the `ChangeCaption` routine, sending a reference to the form that the command button is contained within. This code is found in the form frmChangeCaption.

Determining the Type of a Control

When writing generic code, you might need to determine the type of a control. For example, you might want to loop through all the controls on a form and flip the Enabled property of all the command buttons. To do this, use the ControlType property of a control. Here's an example of how it's used (you can find this in CHAP8EX.MDB in the module called basExamples):

```
Sub FlipEnabled(frmAny As Form, ctlAny As Control)
    'Declare a control object variable
    Dim ctl As Control
    'Loop through the Controls collection using the For..Each Construct
    ctlAny.Enabled = True
    ctlAny.SetFocus
    For Each ctl In frmAny.Controls
        'Evaluate the type of the control
        If ctl.ControlType = acCommandButton Then
            'Make sure that we don't try to disable the command button _
            that invoked this routine
            If ctl.Name <> ctlAny.Name Then
                ctl.Enabled = Not ctl.Enabled
            End If
        End If
    Next ctl
End Sub
```

The FlipEnabled procedure is called from the form frmTypeOf. Each command button on the form (Add, Edit, Delete, and so on) sends the form and the name of a control to the FlipEnabled routine. The control that it sends is the one that you want to receive the focus after the routine executes. In the example that follows, the cmdSave command button is sent to the FlipEnabled routine. The FlipEnabled routine sets focus to the Save button:

```
Private Sub cmdAdd_Click()
    'Call the FlipEnabled routine, passing references to the current form,
    'and to the cmdSave command button on the current form
    Call FlipEnabled(Me, Me.cmdSave)
End Sub
```

The FlipEnabled routine receives the form and control as parameters. It begins by enabling the command button that was passed to it and setting focus to it. The FlipEnabled routine then uses the VBA construct For...Each to loop through all the controls on a form. The For...Each construct repeats a group of statements for each object in an array or collection—in this case, the Controls collection. The code evaluates each control on the form to determine whether it's a command button. If it is, and it isn't the command button that was passed to the

8

OBJECTS, PROPERTIES, METHODS

routine, the routine flips the control's Enabled property. The following VBA intrinsic controls are used when evaluating the `ControlType` property of a control:

Intrinsic Constant	Type of Control
acLabel	Label
acRectangle	Rectangle
acLine	Line
acImage	Image
acCommandButton	Command button
acOptionButton	Option button
acCheckBox	Check box
acOptionGroup	Option group
acBoundObjectFrame	Bound object frame
acTextBox	Text box
acListBox	List box
acComboBox	Combo box
acSubform	Subform/subreport
acObjectFrame	Unbound object frame or chart
acPageBreak	Page break
acPage	Page
acCustomControl	ActiveX (custom) control
acToggleButton	Toggle button
acTabCtl	Tab

Special Properties That Refer to Objects

VBA offers the convenience of performing actions on the active control, the active form, and other specially recognized objects. The following is a list of special properties that refer to objects in the Access Object Model:

- The ActiveControl property refers to the control that has focus on a screen object, form, or report.
- The ActiveForm property refers to the form that has focus.
- The ActiveReport property refers to the report that has focus.
- The Form property refers to the form that a subform is contained in or to the form itself.
- Me refers to the form or report where code is currently executing.

- Module refers to the module of a form or report.
- The Parent property refers to the form, report, or control that contains a control.
- PreviousControl refers to the control that had focus immediately before the ActiveControl.
- RecordsetClone refers to a clone of the form's underlying recordset.
- The Report property refers to the report that a subform is contained in or to the report itself.
- The Section property refers to the section in a form or report where a particular control is located.

The following example using the Screen.ActiveForm property shows how a subroutine can change the caption of the active form:

```
Sub ChangeCaption()
    Screen.ActiveForm.Caption = Screen.ActiveForm.Caption & _
          " - " & CurrentUser()
End Sub
```

This subroutine modifies the caption of the active form, appending the value of the CurrentUser property onto the end of the existing caption.

Understanding Access's Object Model

Now that I've discussed the concept of objects, properties, methods, and events in a general sense, I'm going to switch the discussion to the objects that are natively part of Microsoft Access. Databases are composed of objects, such as the tables, queries, forms, reports, data access pages, macros, and modules that appear in the database window. They also include the controls (text boxes, list boxes, and so on) on a form or report. The key to successful programming lies in your ability to manipulate the database objects using VBA code at runtime. It's also very useful to be able to add, modify, and remove application objects at runtime.

The `Application` Object

An overview of the superficial Access Object Model is shown in Access help. At the top of the model, you can see the `Application` object, which refers to the active Access application. It contains all Access's other objects and collections, including the Forms collection, the Reports collection, the DataAccessPages collection, the Modules collection, the `CurrentData` object, the `CurrentProject` object, the `CodeProject` object, the `CodeData` object, the `Screen` object, and the `DoCmd` object. The `Application` object can be used to modify the properties of, or execute commands on, the Access application itself, such as specifying whether Access's built—in toolbars are available while the application is running.

> **NOTE**
>
> This object model can be found in the Microsoft Access Visual Basic Reference under the Microsoft Access Object Model.

Application Object Properties

The Application object has a rich list of properties. A new property added to Access 2002 is the BrokenReference property. This property is used to determine whether any broken references exist within the current project. The property is equal to True if broken references exist, and False if no broken references are identified. The property eliminates the need to iterate through each reference, determining if any references are broken. The following code returns the value of the BrokenReference property:

```
Public Function IdentifyBrokenReference() As Boolean
    'Return whether or not broken references are identified
    'within the current project
    IdentifyBrokenReference = Application.BrokenReference
End Function
```

Application Object Methods

Just as the Application object has a rich list of properties, it also has a rich list of methods. A new method added to Access 2002 is the CompactRepair method, which allows you to programmatically compact and repair a database, without declaring ADO objects. The code looks like this:

```
Sub CompactRepairDB()
    Dim strFilePath As String

    'Store path of current database in a variable
    strFilePath = CurrentProject.Path

    'If destination database exists, delete it
    If Len(Dir(strFilePath & "\Chap8Small.mdb")) Then
        Kill strFilePath & "\Chap8Small.mdb"
    End If

    'Use the CompactRepair method of the application object
    'to compact and repair the database
    Application.CompactRepair strFilePath & "\Chap8Big.mdb", _
        strFilePath & "\Chap8Small.mdb", True

End Sub
```

This code uses the Path property of the `CurrentProject` object to extract the path of the current project and place it into a string variable. Covered later in this chapter, the `CurrentProject` object returns a reference to the current database project. The Dir function is then used to evaluate whether the database called Chap8Small.mdb exists. If it does, the `Kill` command is used to delete the file. Finally, the `CompactRepair` method is used to compact the Chap8Big.mdb file into Chap8Small.mdb.

Another new Access 2002 method is the `ConvertAccessProject` method. This method allows you to programmatically convert an Access database from one version of Access to another. Here's an example:

```
Sub ConvertAccessDatabase()
    Dim strFilePath As String

    'Store current file path into variable
    strFilePath = CurrentProject.Path

    'Delete destination database if it exists
    If Len(Dir(strFilePath & "\Chap8V97.mdb")) Then
        Kill strFilePath & "\Chap8V97.mdb"
    End If

    'Convert source database to Access 97 file format
    Application.ConvertAccessProject strFilePath & "\Chap8Big.mdb", _
        strFilePath & "\Chap8V97.mdb", _
        DestinationFileFormat:=acFileFormatAccess97
End Sub
```

This code first places the path associated with the current project into a variable called `strFilePath`. Next, it determines if a file called Chap8V97.mdb exists. If it does, the file is deleted. Finally, the `ConvertAccessProject` method of the `Application` object is used to convert an Access 2002 database called Chap8Big.mdb to the Access 97 file format. The destination file is called Chap8V97.mdb. Different constants are used for the `DestinationFileFormat` parameter to designate conversion of the source file to different versions of Access.

The Forms Collection

The Forms collection contains all the currently open forms in the database. Using the Forms collection, you can perform an action, such as changing the color, on each open form.

8

OBJECTS,
PROPERTIES,
METHODS

> **NOTE**
>
> The Forms collection isn't the same as the list of all forms in the database; that list is part of the `CurrentProject` object discussed later in this chapter.

The code that follows iterates through the Forms collection, printing the name of each form. It is found in the basApplicationObject module within the Chap8Ex database. It begins by establishing a form object variable. It then uses the `For Each...Next` construct to loop through each form in the Forms collection (the collection of open forms), printing its name. Before running the code, open a few forms. Run the code and then take a look in the Immediate window. Close a couple of the forms and rerun the code. The list of forms displayed in the Immediate window should change.

> **NOTE**
>
> The Immediate window and its uses are covered in Chapter 15, "Debugging: Your Key to Successful Development." You can easily invoke it using the Ctrl+G keystroke combination.

```
Sub IterateOpenForms()
    'Declare a form object variable
    Dim frm As Form
    'Use the form object variable to point at each form in the Forms collection
    For Each frm In Forms
        'Print the name of the referenced form to the Immediate window
        Debug.Print frm.Name
    Next frm
End Sub
```

> **NOTE**
>
> Notice that it is not necessary to refer to `Application.Forms`. This is because the `Application` object is always assumed when writing VBA code within Access.

The Reports Collection

Just as the Forms collection contains all the currently open forms, the Reports collection contains all the currently open reports. Using the Reports collection, you can perform an action on each open report.

The code that follows iterates through the Reports collection, printing the name of each open report. It is found in basApplicationObject. It begins by establishing a report object variable. It then uses the `For Each...Next` construct to loop though each report in the Reports collection (the collection of reports open in print preview), printing its name.

```
Sub IterateOpenReports()
    'Declare a report object variable
    Dim rpt As Report
    'Use the report object variable to point at each report in the Reports
collection
    For Each rpt In Reports
        'Print the name of the referenced report to the Immediate window
        Debug.Print rpt.Name
    Next rpt
End Sub
```

The DataAccessPages Collection

Just as the Forms collection contains all the currently open forms and the Reports collection contains all the currently open reports, the DataAccessPages collection contains all the currently open data access pages. Using the DataAccessPages collection, you can perform an action on each open data access page.

The code that follows iterates through the DataAccessPages collection, printing the name of each open data access page. It is found in basApplicationObject. It establishes a DataAccessPage object variable. It then uses the For Each...Next construct, along with the object variable, to point at each data access page in the DataAccessPages collection (the collection of open data access pages). The name of each data access page is printed to the Immediate window.

```
Sub IterateOpenDataAccessPages()
    'Declare a data access page variable
    Dim dap As DataAccessPage
    'Use the data access page object variable to point at
    'each data access page in the data access pages collection
    For Each dap In DataAccessPages
        'Print the name of the referneced data access page
        'to the Immediate window
        Debug.Print dap.Name
    Next dap
End Sub
```

The Modules Collection

The Modules collection contains all the standard and class modules that are open. All open modules are included in the Modules collection, regardless of whether they're compiled and whether they contain code that's currently running.

The `CurrentProject` Object

The `CurrentProject` object returns a reference to the current project. The `CurrentProject` contains properties such as Name, Path, and Connection. It contains the following collections: AllDataAccessPages, AllForms, AllMacros, AllModules, and AllReports. These collections are used to iterate through all the data access pages, forms, macros, modules, and reports stored in the database. These collections differ from the DataAccessPages, Forms, Macros, Modules, and Reports collections in that they refer to all objects stored in the current project, rather than to just the open objects.

The following code retrieves the Name and Path properties of the current project. It uses the `With...End With` construct to retrieve the properties of the `CurrentProject` object.

```
Sub CurrentProjectObject()
    With CurrentProject
        Debug.Print .Name
        Debug.Print .Path
    End With
End Sub
```

The AllForms Collection

As previously mentioned, the `CurrentProject` object contains collections that refer to the various objects in your database. The following code iterates through the AllForms collection of the `CurrentProject`, printing the name of each form.

```
Sub IterateAllForms()

    'Declare iteration variable
    Dim vnt As Variant
    'Loop through each form in the current project,
    'printing the name of each form to the Immediate window
    With CurrentProject
        For Each vnt In .AllForms
            Debug.Print vnt.Name
        Next vnt
    End With
End Sub
```

> **NOTE**
>
> It's easy to confuse the AllForms collection of the `CurrentProject` object with the Forms collection. The AllForms collection of the `CurrentProject` object comprises all the saved forms that are part of the database; the Forms collection comprises only the forms currently running in memory. If you want to see a list of all the forms that

make up a database, you must use the AllForms collection of the `CurrentProject` object. However, if you want to change the caption of all the open forms, you must use the Forms collection.

The AllReports Collection

The AllReports collection allows you to loop through all reports in the current project. The example that follows prints the name of each report stored in the database referenced by the CurrentProject object.

```
Sub IterateAllReports()
    'Declare iteration variable
    Dim vnt As Variant
    'Loop through each report in the current project,
    'printing the name of each report to the Immediate window
    With CurrentProject
        For Each vnt In .AllReports
            Debug.Print vnt.Name
        Next vnt
    End With
End Sub
```

The AllMacros Collection

The AllMacros collection is a collection that allows you to iterate through all macros stored in the current project. The example that follows prints the name of each macro stored in the database referenced by the CurrentProject object.

```
Sub IterateAllMacros()
    'Declare iteration variable
    Dim vnt As Variant
    'Loop through each macro in the current project,
    'printing the name of each macro to the Immediate window
    With CurrentProject
        For Each vnt In .AllMacros
            Debug.Print vnt.Name
        Next vnt
    End With
End Sub
```

The AllModules Collection

The AllModules collection is another collection associated with the CurrentProject object. The code that follows iterates through all modules located in the database referenced by the CurrentProject object. The name of each module is printed to the Immediate window.

```
Sub IterateAllModules()
    'Declare iteration variable
    Dim vnt As Variant
    'Loop through each module in the current project,
    'printing the name of each module to the Immediate window
    With CurrentProject
        For Each vnt In .AllModules
            Debug.Print vnt.Name
        Next vnt
    End With
End Sub
```

The AllDataAccessPages Collection

The AllDataAccessPages collection allows you to programmatically manipulate all data access pages found in the database referenced by the CurrentProject object. The code that follows iterates through the AllDataAccessPages collection, printing the name of each data access page.

```
Sub IterateAllDAPs()
    'Declare iteration variable
    Dim vnt As Variant
    'Loop through each data access page in the current project,
    'printing the name of each data access page to the Immediate window
    With CurrentProject
        For Each vnt In .AllDataAccessPages
            Debug.Print vnt.Name
        Next vnt
    End With
End Sub
```

The CurrentData Object

Whereas the CurrentProject object is used to access and manipulate the application components of your database, the CurrentData object is used to reference the data elements of the database. The CurrentData object contains six collections: AllDatabaseDiagrams, AllQueries, AllStoredProcedures, AllTables, AllViews, and AllFunctions. These collections are used to iterate through and manipulate all the database diagrams, queries, stored procedures, views, and functions stored in the database. The AllTables and AllQueries collections are covered in the sections that follow. The AllDatabaseDiagrams, AllStoredProcedures, AllViews, and AllFunctions collections are available only in Access Data Projects and are discussed in detail in *Alison Balter's Mastering Access 2002 Enterprise Development*.

The AllTables Collection

The AllTables collection is used to iterate through all tables in the database referenced by the CurrentData object as shown in the following code. It prints the name of each table in the database.

```
Sub IterateAllTables()
    'Declare looping variable
    Dim vnt As Variant
    'Loop through each table in the database
    'referenced by the CurrentData object
    With CurrentData
        For Each vnt In .AllTables
            'Print the name of the table
            Debug.Print vnt.Name
        Next vnt
    End With
End Sub
```

The AllQueries Collection

The AllQueries collection is used to iterate through all queries located in the database referenced by the CurrentData object. The following example loops through all queries in the database referenced by the CurrentData object. The name of each query is printed to the Immediate window.

```
Sub IterateAllQueries()
    'Declare looping variable
    Dim vnt As Variant
    'Loop through each query in the database
    'referenced by the CurrentData object
    With CurrentData
        For Each vnt In .AllQueries
            'Print the name of the table
            Debug.Print vnt.Name
        Next vnt
    End With
End Sub
```

The CodeProject Object

The CodeProject object is used when your database implements code libraries. It is similar to the CurrentProject object, but is used to reference the properties and collections stored within the library database. Library databases are covered in Chapter 24, "Creating Your Own Libraries."

The `CodeData` Object

Just as the `CodeProject` is used to reference the application objects stored within a library database, the `CodeData` object is used to reference the data elements of a code library. These include the database diagrams, queries, stored procedures, tables, views, and functions stored within the library.

The `Screen` Object

The `Screen` object can be used to refer to the form, datasheet, report, data access page, or control that has the focus. The `Screen` object contains properties that refer to the active form, active report, active control, and previous control. Using these properties, you can manipulate the currently active form, report, or control, as well as the control that was active just before the current control. If you try to refer to the `Screen` object when no form or report is active, a runtime error occurs.

The `DoCmd` Object

The `DoCmd` object is used to perform macro commands or Access actions from VBA code; it's followed by a period and the name of an action. Most of the `DoCmd` actions—the `OpenQuery` action, for example—also require arguments. The `OpenQuery` action is used to execute an Access query. It receives the following arguments:

- Query Name—The name of the query you want to execute
- View—Datasheet, Design, or Print preview
- Data Mode—Add, edit, or read-only

Here's an example of the `OpenQuery` action of the `DoCmd` object:

```
DoCmd.OpenQuery "qryCustomers", acNormal, acReadOnly
```

The `OpenQuery` action is performed by the `DoCmd` object. The first argument, the query name, is `"qryCustomers"`. This is the name of the query that's opened in Datasheet view (rather than Design view or Print preview). It's opened in read-only mode, meaning the resulting data can't be modified.

New Access 2002 Properties

In addition to the properties listed as new to Access 2002, two other properties are worth mentioning. They are the DateCreated and DateModified properties. They are available for *all* Access objects. Here's an example that shows the use of these properties with the AllTables collection:

```
Public Sub GetDates()
    'Declare looping variable
    Dim vnt As Variant
    'Loop through each table in the database
    'referenced by the CurrentData object
    With CurrentData
        For Each vnt In .AllTables
            'Print the name, date created and the data the table was last
modified
            Debug.Print vnt.Name & ", " & _
                vnt.DateCreated & ", " & _
                vnt.DateModified
        Next vnt
    End With
End Sub
```

This code loops through each table stored in the database referenced by the `CurrentData` object. The name, creation date, and last modification data are all printed to the Immediate window.

PRACTICAL EXAMPLES

Working with Objects

 Objects are used throughout most applications. The example that follows applies the technique you learned to enable and disable command buttons in response to the user making changes to the data on the `frmClients` form, located in Chap8EX.MDB on the sample code CD-ROM.

Enabling and Disabling Command Buttons

When a user is in the middle of modifying form data, there's really no need for her to use other parts of the application. It makes sense to disable other features until the user has opted to save the changes to the Client data. The clean form begins with the View Projects command button enabled and the Save and Cancel buttons disabled. The KeyPreview property of the form is set to Yes so that the form previews all keystrokes before the individual controls process them. In the example, the KeyDown event of the form is used to respond to the user "dirtying" the form. It executes whenever the user types ANSI characters while the form has the focus. The KeyDown event of the form (discussed in detail in Chapter 9) looks like this:

```
Private Sub Form_KeyDown(KeyCode As Integer, Shift As Integer)
    'If the Save command button is not already enabled
    If Not cmdSave.Enabled Then
```

```
        'If a relevant key was pressed
        If ImportantKey(KeyCode, Shift) Then

                'Flip the command buttons on the form,
                'setting focus to the active control
                Call FlipEnabled(Me, Screen.ActiveControl)

                'Disable the cboSelectClient combo box
                Me.cboSelectClient.Enabled = False

        End If

    'If the Save button is already enabled (form is dirty)
    'ignore the PageUp and PageDown keys
    Else
        If KeyCode = vbKeyPageDown Or _
         KeyCode = vbKeyPageUp Then
         KeyCode = 0
        End If
    End If
End Sub
```

The KeyDown event automatically receives the code of the key that was pressed, whether Shift, Alt, or Ctrl was pressed along with that key. The event routine checks to determine whether the Save button is already enabled. If it is, there's no reason to continue; the Enabled property of the command buttons has already been flipped. If Save isn't already enabled, the ImportantKey function (discussed in detail later) is called. It receives the key that was pressed, despite whether Shift, Alt, or Control was used.

The ImportantKey evaluates the key that was pressed to determine whether a keystroke is modifying the data. If it is, the function returns True. Otherwise, it returns False. If ImportantKey returns True, the FlipEnabled routine is executed. FlipEnabled flips the enabled property of command buttons on the form so that Save and Cancel are enabled, and View Projects is disabled.

If the value returned from the ImportantKey function is True, the enabled property cboSelectClient combo is set to False. If you fail to prevent movement to other records while the form is dirty, users' changes are automatically saved (by Access) when the user navigates to another record. Furthermore, the enabled state of the command buttons still reflects a dirty state of the form.

Finally, if Save is already enabled, you know that the form is in a dirty state. If that is the case it is not appropriate for the user to be able to move to another record using the PageUp and

PageDown keys. If the cmdSave command button is enabled, and the key pressed is PageUp or PageDown, the keystoke is ignored.

Now that you understand the role of the KeyDown event of the form, take a look at the functions that underlie its functionality. The ImportantKey function looks like this:

```
Function ImportantKey(KeyCode, Shift)
    'Set return value to false
    ImportantKey = False

    'If Alt key was pressed, exit function
    If Shift = acAltMask Then
        Exit Function
    End If

    'If Delete, Backspace, or a a typeable character was pressed
    If KeyCode = vbKeyDelete Or KeyCode = vbKeyBack Or (KeyCode > 31 _
        And KeyCode < 256) Then
        'If the typeable character was NOT right, left, up
        'or down arrows, page up, or page down, return True
        If KeyCode = vbKeyRight Or KeyCode = vbKeyLeft Or _
            KeyCode = vbKeyUp Or KeyCode = vbKeyDown Or _
            KeyCode = vbKeyPageUp Or KeyCode = vbKeyPageDown Then

        Else
            ImportantKey = True
        End If
    End If
End Function
```

This generic function, found in basUtils, sets its default return value to False. It tests to see whether the Alt key was pressed. If so, the user was accessing a menu or accelerator key, which means that there's no reason to flip the command buttons. The function is exited. If Alt wasn't pressed, the key that was pressed is evaluated. If the Delete key, Backspace key, or any key with an ANSI value between 31 and 256 was pressed (excluding the left, right, up, and down arrow keys, and page up or page down), True is returned from this function. The Keydown event of the form then calls the FlipEnabled routine. It looks like this:

```
Sub FlipEnabled(frmAny As Form, ctlAny As Control)
    'Declare a control object variable
    Dim ctl As Control

    'If the type of control received as a parameter
    'is a command button, enable it and set focus to it
    ctlAny.Enabled = True
    ctlAny.SetFocus
```

```
'Loop through each control in the controls collection
'of the form that was received as a paramter
For Each ctl In frmAny.Controls

    'If the type of the control is a command button
    'and the name of the control does not match the
    'name of the control received as a parameter
    'flip the enabled property of the control
    If ctl.ControlType = acCommandButton Then
        If ctl.Name <> ctlAny.Name Then
            ctl.Enabled = Not ctl.Enabled
        End If
    End If
Next ctl
End Sub
```

This generic routine, also found in basUtils, flips the Enabled property of every command button in the form, except the one that was passed to the routine as the second parameter. The FlipEnabled routine receives a form and a control as parameters. It begins by creating a control object variable; then it enables the control that was passed as a parameter and sets focus to it. The routine then loops through every control on the form that was passed to it. It tests to see whether each control is a command button. If it finds a command button, and the name of the command button isn't the same as the name of the control that was passed to it, it flips the Enabled property of the command button. The idea is this: When the user clicks Save, you can't immediately disable the Save button because it still has focus. You must first enable a selected control (the one that was passed to the routine) and set focus to the enabled control. After the control is enabled, you don't want to disable it again, so you need to eliminate it from the processing loop.

Remember that as long as the cmdSave command button is enabled, the PageUp and PageDown keys are ignored. This is an important step because it is imperative that the user not be able to move from record to record while editing the form data.

You need a way to flip the command buttons back the other way when editing is complete. The Click event of the Save button contains the following code:

```
Private Sub cmdSave_Click()
    'Save changes to the client record
    DoCmd.RunCommand acCmdSaveRecord

    'Enable client selection combo
    Me.cboSelectClient.Enabled = True
```

```
    'Call routine to disable save and cancel and
    'enable view projects
    Call FlipEnabled(Me, Me.cboSelectClient)
End Sub
```

This code saves the current record and enables the cboSelectClient control. It then calls the
FlipEnabled routine, passing a reference to the cboSelectClient control as a parameter. The
FlipEnabled routine flips the command buttons back to their original state.

The form contains a cancel command button with a similar routine. It looks like this:

```
Private Sub cmdUndo_Click()
    'Undo changes
    DoCmd.RunCommand acCmdUndo

    'Enable client selection combo
    Me.cboSelectClient.Enabled = True

    'Call routine to disable save and cancel and
    'enable view projects
    Call FlipEnabled(Me, Me.cboSelectClient)

End Sub
```

This code undoes changes to the current record. It enables the cboSelectClient control and
calls the FlipEnabled routine to once again disable Save and Cancel and enable View Projects.

Summary

The ability to successfully work with objects and understand their properties, methods, and
events is fundamental to your success as an Access programmer. Working with properties
involves setting properties at design time and changing their values in response to events that
occur at runtime. The ability to pass forms and other objects to subroutines and functions
makes the VBA language extremely robust and flexible.

8

**OBJECTS,
PROPERTIES,
METHODS**

Advanced Form Techniques

Why This Chapter Is Important

Given Access's graphical environment, your development efforts are often centered on forms. Therefore, you must understand all the Form and Control events and know which event you should code to perform each task. You should also know what types of forms are available and how you can get the look and behavior you want in them.

Often, you won't need to design your own form because you can make use of one of the built-in dialog boxes that are part of the VBA language or supplied as part of the Microsoft Office 2002 Developer Edition tools. Whatever types of forms you create, you should take advantage of all the tricks and tips of the trade covered throughout this chapter, including adding menu bars and toolbars to your forms.

What Are the `Form` Events, and When Do You Use Them?

Microsoft Access traps for 34 Form events (excluding those specifically related to PivotTables), each of which has a distinct purpose. Access also traps events for Form sections and controls. The following sections cover the Form events and when you should use them.

Current

A form's `Current` event is one of the more commonly coded events. It happens each time focus moves from one record to another. The `Current` event is a great place to put code that you want to execute whenever a record is displayed. For example, you might want the company name to appear with a special background if the client is an important one. The following code is placed in the `Current` event of the frmClients form that's part of the Time and Billing application:

```
Private Sub Form_Current()
    'If user is on a new record,
    'move the focus to the Contact First Name control
    If Me.NewRecord Then
        Me.txtContactFirstName.SetFocus
    End If
End Sub
```

This code moves focus to the txtContactFirstName control if the `txtClientID` of the record that the user is moving to happens to be `Null`; this happens if the user is adding a new record.

BeforeInsert

The `BeforeInsert` event occurs when the first character is typed in a new record, but before the new record is actually created. If the user is typing in a text or combo box, the

BeforeInsert event occurs even before the Change event of the text or combo box. The frmProjects form of the Time and Billing application has an example of a practical use of the BeforeInsert event:

```
Private Sub Form_BeforeInsert(Cancel As Integer)
On Error GoTo Err_Form_BeforeInsert
    'Set the ClientID to the ClientID on the Clients form
    Me.ClientID = Forms.frmClients.txtClientID

Exit_Form_BeforeInsert:
    Exit Sub

Err_Form_BeforeInsert:
    MsgBox Err.Description
    Resume Exit_Form_BeforeInsert
End Sub
```

The frmProjects form is always called from the frmClients form. The BeforeInsert event of frmProjects sets the value of the txtClientID text box equal to the value of the txtClientID text box on frmClients.

AfterInsert

The AfterInsert event occurs after the record has actually been inserted. It can be used to requery a recordset when a new record is added.

NOTE

Here's the order of form events when a user begins to type data into a new record:

BeforeInsert->BeforeUpdate->AfterUpdate->AfterInsert

The BeforeInsert event occurs when the user types the first character, the BeforeUpdate event happens when the user updates the record, the AfterUpdate event takes place when the record is updated, and the AfterInsert event occurs when the record that's being updated is a new record.

BeforeUpdate

The BeforeUpdate event runs before a record is updated. It occurs when the user tries to move to a different record (even a record on a subform) or when the Records|Save Record command is executed. The BeforeUpdate event can be used to cancel the update process when you want to perform complex validations. When a user adds a record, the BeforeUpdate event occurs after the `BeforeInsert` event. The frmClients form in the Chap9Ex sample database provides an example of using a `BeforeUpdate` event:

```
Private Sub Form_BeforeUpdate(Cancel As Integer)

    'If the Contact FirstName, LastName, Company or
    'Phone Number is left blank, display a message
    'and cancel the update
    If IsNull(Me.txtContactFirstName) Or _
        IsNull(Me.txtContactLastName) Or _
        IsNull(Me.txtCompanyName) Or _
        IsNull(Me.txtPhoneNumber) Then
        MsgBox "The Contact First Name, " & vbCrLf & _
            "Contact Last Name, " & vbCrLf & _
            "Company Name, " & vbCrLf & _
            "And Contact Phone Must All Be Entered", _
            vbCritical, _
            "Canceling Update"
        Me.txtContactFirstName.SetFocus
        Cancel = True
    End If
End Sub
```

This code determines whether the first name, last name, company name, or phone number contains `Null`s. If any of these fields contains `Null`, a message is displayed, and the `Cancel` parameter is set to `True`, canceling the update process. As a convenience to the user, focus is placed in the txtFirstName control.

AfterUpdate

The `AfterUpdate` event occurs after the changed data in a record is updated. You might use this event to requery combo boxes on related forms or perhaps to log record changes. Here's an example:

```
Private Sub Form_AfterUpdate()
    Me.cboSelectProduct.Requery
End Sub
```

This code requeries the cboSelectProduct combo box after the current record is updated.

Dirty

The `Dirty` event occurs when the contents of the form, or of the text portion of a combo box, changes. It also occurs when you programmatically change the Text property of a control. Here's an example:

```
Private Sub Form_Dirty(Cancel As Integer)
    'Flip the Enabled properties of the appropriate
    'command buttons
    Call FlipEnabled(Me, ActiveControl)

    'Hide the form navigation buttons
    Me.NavigationButtons = False
End Sub
```

This code, located in the frmClients form of the Time and Billing application, calls
FlipEnabled to flip the command buttons on the form. This has the effect of enabling the Save
and Cancel command buttons and disabling the other command buttons on the form. The code
also removes the navigation buttons, prohibiting the user from moving to other records while
the data is in a "dirty" state.

Undo

The Undo event executes before changes to a row are undone. The Undo event initiates when
the user clicks the Undo button on the toolbar, taps the Esc key, or executes code that attempts
to undo changes to the row. If you cancel the Undo event, the changes to the row are not
undone. Here's an example:

```
Private Sub Form_Undo(Cancel As Integer)

    'Ask user if they meant to undo changes
    If MsgBox("You Have Attempted to Undo Changes " & _
        "to the Current Row.  Would You Like to Proceed " & _
        "with the Undo Process?", _
        vbYesNo) = vbYes Then

        'If they respond yes, proceed with the undo
        Cancel = False

    Else

        'If they respond no, cancel the undo
        Cancel = True
    End If

End Sub
```

This code, located in the frmProjects form of the Time and Billing application, displays a message to the user, asking him if he really wants to undo his changes. If he responds Yes, the
Undo process proceeds. If he responds No, the Undo process is cancelled.

Delete

The `Delete` event occurs when a user tries to delete a record, but before the record is removed from the table. This is a great way to place code that allows deleting a record only under certain circumstances. If the `Delete` event is canceled, the `BeforeDelConfirm` and `AfterDelConfirm` events never execute, and the record is never deleted.

> **TIP**
>
> When the user deletes multiple records, the `Delete` event happens after each record is deleted. This allows you to evaluate a condition for each record and decide whether to delete each record.

BeforeDelConfirm

The `BeforeDelConfirm` event takes place after the `Delete` event, but before the Delete Confirm dialog box is displayed. If you cancel the `BeforeDelConfirm` event, the record being deleted is restored from the delete buffer, and the Delete Confirm dialog box is never displayed.

AfterDelConfirm

The `AfterDelConfirm` event occurs after the record is deleted, or when the deletion is canceled. If the code does not cancel the `BeforeDelConfirm` event, the `AfterDelConfirm` event takes place after Access displays the Confirmation dialog box.

Open

The `Open` event occurs when a form is opened but before the first record is displayed. With this event, you can control exactly what happens when the form first opens. The `Open` event of the Time and Billing application's frmProjects form looks like this:

```
Private Sub Form_Open(Cancel As Integer)
    'If the Clients form is not loaded,
    'Display a message to the user and
    'do not load the form
    If Not IsLoaded("frmClients") Then
        MsgBox "Open the Projects form using the Projects " & _
            "button on the Clients form."
        Cancel = True
    End If
End Sub
```

This code checks to make sure the frmClients form is loaded. If it isn't, it displays a message box, and sets the Cancel parameter to True, which prohibits the form from loading.

Load

The Load event happens when a form opens, and the first record is displayed; it occurs after the Open event. A form's Open event can cancel the opening of a form, but the Load event can't. The following routine is placed in the Load event of the Time and Billing application's frmExpenseCodes form:

```
Private Sub Form_Load()
    'If the form is opened in Data Entry Mode
    'And the OpenArgs property is not null,
    'Set the txtExpenseCode text box equal to
    'the value of the opening arguments
    If Me.DataEntry _
        And Not (IsNull(Me.OpenArgs)) Then
        Me.txtExpenseCode = Me.OpenArgs
    End If
End Sub
```

This routine looks at the string that's passed as an opening argument to the form. If the OpenArgs string is not Null, and the form is opened in data entry mode, the txtExpenseCode text box is set equal to the opening argument. In essence, this code allows the form to be used for two purposes. If the user opens the form from the database container, no special processing occurs. On the other hand, if the user opens the form from the fsubTimeCardsExpenses subform, the form is opened in data entry mode, and the expense code that the user specified is placed in the txtExpenseCode text box.

Resize

The Resize event takes place when a form is opened or whenever the form's size changes.

Unload

The Unload event happens when a form is closed, but before Access removes the form from the screen. It's triggered when the user chooses Close from the File menu, quits the application by choosing End Task from the task list, quits Windows, or when your code closes the form. You can place code that makes sure it's okay to unload the form in the Unload event, and you can also use the Unload event to place any code you want executed whenever the form is unloaded. Here's an example:

```
Private Sub Form_Unload(Cancel As Integer)
    'Determine if the form is dirty
    If Me.cmdSave.Enabled Then
```

```
        'If form is dirty, ask user if they want to save
        Select Case MsgBox("Do You Want To Save", _
            vbYesNoCancel + vbCritical, _
            "Please Respond")

            'If user responds yes, save record and allow unload
            Case vbYes
                DoCmd.RunCommand Command:=acCmdSaveRecord
                Cancel = False

            'If user responds no, undo changes to record and
            'allow unload
            Case vbNo
                On Error Resume Next
                DoCmd.RunCommand Command:=acCmdUndo
                Cancel = False

            'If user clicks cancel, cancel unloading of form
            Case vbCancel
                Cancel = True
        End Select
    End If
End Sub
```

This code is in the Unload event of the frmClients form from the Time and Billing application. It checks whether the Save button is enabled. If it is, the form is in a dirty state. The user is prompted as to whether he wants to save changes to the record. If he responds affirmatively, the code saves the data, and the form is unloaded. If he responds no, the code cancels changes to the record, and the form is unloaded. Finally, if he opts to cancel, the value of the Cancel parameter is set to False, and the form is not unloaded.

Close

The Close event occurs *after* the Unload event, when a form is closed and removed from the screen. Remember, you can cancel the Unload event but not the Close event.

The following code is located in the Close event of the frmClients form that's part of the Time and Billing database:

```
Private Sub Form_Close()
    'If the frmProjects form is loaded,
    'unload it
    If IsLoaded("frmProjects") Then
        DoCmd.Close acForm, "frmProjects"
    End If
End Sub
```

When the frmClients form is closed, the code tests whether the frmProjects form is open. If it is, the code closes it.

Activate

The `Activate` event takes place when the form gets focus and becomes the active window. It's triggered when the form opens, when a user clicks on the form or one of its controls, and when the `SetFocus` method is applied by using VBA code. The following code, found in the `Activate` event of the Time and Billing application's frmClients form, requeries the fsubClients subform whenever the frmClients main form activates:

```
Private Sub Form_Activate()
    'Requery form when it becomes active
    'This ensures that changes made in the projects form
    'are immediately reflected in the clients form
    Me.fsubClients.Requery
End Sub
```

Deactivate

The `Deactivate` event occurs when the form loses focus, which happens when a table, query, form, report, macro, module, or the Database window becomes active. However, the `Deactivate` event isn't triggered when a dialog, pop-up form, or another application becomes active. The following is an example of the use of the `Deactivate` event:

```
Private Sub Form_Deactivate()
    'Use AllowEdits property setting to determine which toolbar to hide.
    'Show Form View toolbar.
    If Me.AllowEdits = True Then
        DoCmd.ShowToolbar "Enter Or Edit Products 2", acToolbarNo
    Else
        DoCmd.ShowToolbar "Enter Or Edit Products 1", acToolbarNo
    End If
    DoCmd.ShowToolbar "Form View", acToolbarWhereApprop
End Sub
```

This code evaluates the AllowEdits property to determine which custom toolbar is currently active. It hides the appropriate toolbar and shows the standard Form View toolbar.

GotFocus

The `GotFocus` event happens when a form gets focus, but only if there are no visible, enabled controls on the form. This event is rarely used for a form.

LostFocus

The LostFocus event occurs when a form loses focus, but only if there are no visible, enabled controls on the form. This event, too, is rarely used for a form.

Click

The Click event takes place when the user clicks on a blank area of the form, on a disabled control on the form, or on the form's record selector.

DblClick

The DblClick event happens when the user double-clicks on a blank area of the form, on a disabled control on the form, or on the form's record selector.

MouseDown

The MouseDown event occurs when the user clicks on a blank area of the form, on a disabled control on the form, or on the form's record selector. However, it happens *before* the Click event fires. You can use it to determine which mouse button was pressed.

MouseMove

The MouseMove event takes place when the user moves the mouse over a blank area of the form, over a disabled control on the form, or over the form's record selector. It's generated continuously as the mouse pointer moves over the form. The MouseMove event occurs *before* the Click event fires.

MouseUp

The MouseUp event occurs when the user releases the mouse button. Like the MouseDown event, it happens before the Click event fires. You can use the MouseUp event to determine which mouse button was pressed.

KeyDown

The KeyDown event happens if there are no controls on the form, or if the form's KeyPreview property is set to Yes. If the latter condition is true, all keyboard events are previewed by the form and occur for the control that has focus. If the user presses and holds down a key, the KeyDown event occurs repeatedly until the user releases the key. Here's an example:

```
Private Sub Form_KeyDown(KeyCode As Integer, Shift As Integer)
    'If the form is dirty and the user presses page up or
    'page down, ignore the keystroke
    If Me.Dirty Then
```

```
        If KeyCode = vbKeyPageDown Or _
            KeyCode = vbKeyPageUp Then
            KeyCode = 0
        End If
    End If
End Sub
```

This code, found in the frmClients form that is part of the Time and Billing application, tests to see if the form is in a dirty state. If it is, and Page Down or Page Up is pressed, the keystroke is ignored. This prevents the user from moving to other records without first clicking the Save or Cancel command buttons.

KeyUp

Like the KeyDown event, the KeyUp event occurs if there are no controls on the form, or if the form's KeyPreview property is set to Yes. The KeyUp event takes place only once, though, regardless of how long the key is pressed. You can cancel the keystroke by setting KeyCode to Zero.

KeyPress

The KeyPress event occurs when the user presses and releases a key or key combination that corresponds to an ANSI code. It takes place if there are no controls on the form or if the form's KeyPreview property is set to Yes. You can cancel the keystroke by setting KeyCode to Zero.

Error

The Error event triggers whenever an error happens while the user is in the form. Microsoft Jet Engine errors are trapped, but Visual Basic errors aren't. You can use this event to suppress the standard error messages. You must handle Visual Basic errors using standard On Error techniques. Both the Error event and handling Visual Basic errors are covered in Chapter 16, "Error Handling: Preparing for the Inevitable."

Filter

The Filter event takes place whenever the user selects the Filter By Form or Advanced Filter/Sort options. You can use this event to remove the previous filter, enter default settings for the filter, invoke your own custom filter window, or prevent certain controls from being available in the Filter By Form window. The later section "Taking Advantage of Built-In, Form-Filtering Features" covers filters in detail.

ApplyFilter

The ApplyFilter event occurs when the user selects the Apply Filter/Sort, Filter By Selection, or Remove Filter/Sort options. It also takes place when the user closes the Advanced

9

ADVANCED FORM TECHNIQUES

Filter/Sort window or the Filter By Form window. You can use this event to make sure that the applied filter is correct, to change the form's display before the filter is applied, or to undo any changes you made when the `Filter` event occurred. The later section "Taking Advantage of Built-In, Form-Filtering Features" covers filters in detail.

Timer

The `Timer` event and a form's TimerInterval property work hand in hand. The TimerInterval property can be set to any value between `0` and `2,147,483,647`. The value used determines the frequency, expressed in milliseconds, at which the `Timer` event will occur. For example, if the TimerInterval property is set to `0`, the `Timer` event will not occur at all; if set to `5000` (5000 milliseconds), the `Timer` event will occur every five seconds. The following example uses the `Timer` event to alternate the visibility of a label on the form. This produces a flashing effect. The TimerInterval property can be initially set to any valid value other than `0`, but will be reduced by 50 milliseconds each time the code executes. This has the effect of making the control flash faster and faster. The `Timer` events continue to occur until the TimerInterval property is finally reduced to `0`.

```
Private Sub Form_Timer()
'If Label1 is visible, hide it, otherwise show it
If Me.Label2.Visible = True Then
    Me.Label2.Visible = False
Else
    Me.Label2.Visible = True
End If

'Decrement the timer interval, causing the
'label to flash more quickly
Me.TimerInterval = Me.TimerInterval - 50

'Once the timer interval becomes zero,
'make the label visible
If Me.TimerInterval = 0 Then
    Me.Label2.Visible = True
End If
End Sub
```

Understanding the Sequence of Form Events

One of the mysteries of events is the order in which they occur. One of the best ways to figure this out is to place `Debug.Print` statements in the events you want to learn about. This technique is covered in Chapter 15, "Debugging: Your Key to Successful Development." Keep in mind that event order isn't an exact science; it's nearly impossible to guess when events will happen in all situations. It's helpful, though, to understand the basic order in which certain events do take place.

What Happens When a Form Is Opened?

When a user opens a form, the following events occur:

```
Open->Load->Resize->Activate->Current
```

After these Form events take place, the `Enter` and `GotFocus` events of the first control occur. Remember that the `Open` event provides the only opportunity to cancel opening the form.

What Happens When a Form Is Closed?

When a user closes a form, the following events take place:

```
Unload->Deactivate->Close
```

Before these events occur, the `Exit` and `LostFocus` events of the active control triggers.

What Happens When a Form Is Sized?

When a user resizes a form, what happens depends on whether the form is minimized, restored, or maximized. When the form minimizes, here's what happens:

```
Resize->Deactivate
```

When a user restores a minimized form, these events take place:

```
Activate->Resize
```

When a user maximizes a form or restores a maximized form, just the `Resize` event occurs.

What Happens When Focus Shifts from One Form to Another?

When a user moves from one form to another, the `Deactivate` event occurs for the first form; then the `Activate` event occurs for the second form. Remember that the `Deactivate` event doesn't take place if focus moves to a dialog box, a pop-up form, or another application.

What Happens When Keys Are Pressed?

When a user types a character, and the form's KeyPreview property is set to `True`, the following events occur:

```
KeyDown->KeyPress->Dirty->KeyUp
```

If you trap the `KeyDown` event and set the `KeyCode` to `Zero`, the remaining events never happen. The `KeyPress` event captures only ANSI keystrokes. This event is the easiest to deal with. However, you must handle the `Keydown` and `KeyUp` events when you need to trap for non-ANSI characters, such as Shift, Alt, and Ctrl.

What Happens When Mouse Actions Take Place?

When a user clicks the mouse button, the following events occur:

```
MouseDown->MouseUp->Click
```

What Are the Section and Control Events, and When Do You Use Them?

Sections have only five events: `Click`, `DblClick`, `MouseDown`, `MouseMove`, and `MouseUp`. These events rarely play significant roles in your application.

Each control type has its own set of events to which it responds. Many events are common to most controls, but others are specific to certain controls. Furthermore, some controls respond to very few events. The following sections cover all the Control events and the controls they apply to.

BeforeUpdate

The `BeforeUpdate` event applies to text boxes, option groups, combo boxes, list boxes, and bound object frames. It occurs before changed data in the control updates. The following code example is found in the `BeforeUpdate` event of the txtProjecttotalBillingEstimate control on the frmProjects form in the sample database:

```
Private Sub CustomerID_BeforeUpdate(Cancel As Integer)
    'If project total billings are less than or equal to zero
    'display a message to the user and cancel the update
    If Me.txtProjectTotalBillingEstimate <= 0 Then
        MsgBox "Project Total Billings Must Be Greater Than " & _
            "or Equal to Zero", vbCritical, "Canceling Update"
        Cancel = True
    End If

End Sub
```

This code tests whether the value of the CustomerID control is less than or equal to zero. If it is, the code displays a message box, and the `Update` event is canceled.

AfterUpdate

The `AfterUpdate` event applies to text boxes, option groups, combo boxes, list boxes, and bound object frames. It occurs after changed data in the control updates. The following code example is from the `AfterUpdate` event of the txtBeginDate control on the frmPrintInvoice form found in the Time and Billing database:

```
Private Sub txtBeginDate_AfterUpdate()
    'Requery the subforms when the begin
    'date changes
    Me.fsubPrintInvoiceTime.Requery
    Me.fsubPrintInvoiceExpenses.Requery
End Sub
```

This code requeries both the fsubPrintInvoiceTime subform and the fsubPrintInvoiceExpenses subform when the txtBeginDate control updates. This ensures that the subforms display the time and expenses appropriate for the selected date range.

Updated

The Updated event applies to a bound object frame only. It occurs when the OLE (Object Linking and Embedding) object's data is modified.

Change

The Change event applies to text and combo boxes and takes place when data in the control changes. For a text box, this event occurs when a character is typed; for a combo box, it happens when a user types a character or selects a value from the list. You use this event when you want to trap for something happening on a character-by-character basis.

NotInList

The NotInList event applies only to a combo box and happens when a user enters a value in the text box portion of the combo box that's not in the combo box list. By using this event, you can allow the user to add a new value to the combo box list. For this event to be triggered, the LimitToList property must be set to Yes. Here's an example from the Time and Billing application's frmPayments form:

```
Private Sub cboPaymentMethodID_NotInList _
    'If payment method is not in the list,
    'ask user if they want to add it
    If MsgBox("Payment Method Not Found, Add?", _
        vbYesNo + vbQuestion, _
        "Please Respond") = vbYes Then

        'If they respond yes, open the frmPaymentMethods form
        'in add mode, passing in the new payment method
        DoCmd.OpenForm "frmPaymentMethods", _
            Datamode:=acFormAdd, _
            WindowMode:=acDialog, _
            OpenArgs:=NewData

        'If form is still loaded, unload it
        If IsLoaded("frmPaymentMethods") Then
            Response = acDataErrAdded
            DoCmd.Close acForm, "frmPaymentMethods"

        'If the user cancels the add, redisplay the existing options
        Else
            Response = acDataErrContinue
```

```
        End If
    Else
        'If the user responds no, redisplay the existing options
        Response = acDataErrContinue
    End If

End Sub
```

This code executes when a user enters a payment method that's not in the cboPaymentMethodID combo box. It asks the user if he wants to add the entry. If he responds yes, the frmPaymentMethods form displays. Otherwise, the user must select another entry from the combo box. The NotInList event is covered in more detail later in the "Handling the NotInList Event" section.

Enter

The Enter event applies to text boxes, option groups, combo boxes, list boxes, command buttons, object frames, and subforms. It occurs *before* a control gets focus from another control on the same form and *before* the GotFocus event. Here's an example from the Time and Billing application's frmTimeCards form:

```
Private Sub fsubTimeCards_Enter()
    'If the user clicks to enter time cards, and the EmployeeID
    'is Null, display a message and set focus back to the
    'cboEmployeeID combo box
    If IsNull(Me.EmployeeID) Then
        MsgBox "Enter employee before entering time or expenses."
        Me.cboEmployeeID.SetFocus
    End If
End Sub
```

When the user moves into the fsubTimeCards subform control, its Enter event tests whether the EmployeeID has been entered on the main form. If it hasn't, a message box displays, and focus is moved to the cboEmployeeID control on the main form.

Exit

The Exit event applies to text boxes, option groups, combo boxes, list boxes, command buttons, object frames, and subforms. It occurs just before the LostFocus event.

GotFocus

The GotFocus event applies to text boxes, toggle buttons, options buttons, check boxes, combo boxes, list boxes, and command buttons. It takes place when focus moves to a control in response to a user action or when the SetFocus, SelectObject, GoToRecord, GoToControl, or GoToPage method is issued in code. Controls can get focus only if they're visible and enabled.

LostFocus

The LostFocus event applies to text boxes, toggle buttons, options buttons, check boxes, combo boxes, list boxes, and command buttons. It occurs when focus moves away from a control in response to a user action, or when your code issues the SetFocus, SelectObject, GoToRecord, GoToControl, or GoToPage methods.

> **NOTE**
>
> The difference between GotFocus/LostFocus and Enter/Exit lies in when they occur. If focus is lost (moved to another form) or returned to the current form, the control's GotFocus and LostFocus events are triggered. The Enter and Exit events don't take place when the form loses or regains focus. Finally, it is important to note that none of these events takes place when the user makes menu selections or clicks toolbar buttons.

Click

The Click event applies to labels, text boxes, option groups, combo boxes, list boxes, command buttons, and object frames. It occurs when a user presses, and then releases, a mouse button over a control. Here's an example from the Time and Billing application's frmProjects form:

```
Private Sub cmdToggleView_Click()
    'If the caption of the control is View Expenses,
    'hide the Projects subform and show the Project Expenses subform
    'Change caption of command button to View Hours
    If Me.cmdToggleView.Caption = "&View Expenses" Then
        Me.fsubProjects.Visible = False
        Me.fsubProjectExpenses.Visible = True
        Me.cmdToggleView.Caption = "&View Hours"
    'If the caption of the control is View Hours,
    'hide the Project Expenses subform and show the Project subform
    'Change caption of command button to View Expenses
    Else
        Me.fsubProjectExpenses.Visible = False
        Me.fsubProjects.Visible = True
        Me.cmdToggleView.Caption = "&View Expenses"
    End If
End Sub
```

This code checks the caption of the cmdToggleView command button. If the caption reads "&View Expenses" (with the ampersand indicating a hotkey), the fsubProjects subform is hid-

9

den, the fsubProjectExpenses subform is made visible, and the caption of the cmdToggleView command button is modified to read "&View Hours". Otherwise, the fsubProjectExpenses subform is hidden, the fsubProjects subform is made visible, and the caption of the cmdToggleView command button is modified to read "&View Expenses".

NOTE

The Click event is triggered when the user clicks the mouse over an object, as well as in the following situations:

- When the user presses the spacebar while a command button has focus
- When the user presses the Enter key, and a command button's Default property is set to Yes
- When the user presses the Escape key, and a command button's Cancel property is set to Yes
- When an accelerator key for a command button is used

DblClick

The DblClick event applies to labels, text boxes, option groups, combo boxes, list boxes, command buttons, and object frames. It occurs when a user presses, and then releases the left mouse button twice over a control. Here's an example from the Time and Billing application's fsubTimeCards form:

```
Private Sub cboWorkCodeID_DblClick(Cancel As Integer)
Dim strWorkCode As String

On Error GoTo Err_cboWorkCodeID_DblClick

    'If the cboWorkCodeID is Null, set the
    'strWorkCode variable to a zero-length string
    'otherwise set it to the text in the combo box
    If IsNull(Me.cboWorkCodeID.Text) Then
        strWorkCode = ""
    Else
        strWorkCode = Me.cboWorkCodeID.Text
    End If

    'If the cboWorkCodeID is Null, set the
    'Text property to a zero-length string
    If IsNull(Me.cboWorkCodeID) Then
```

```
        Me.cboWorkCodeID.Text = ""
    Else

        'Otherwise, set the cboWorkCodeID
        'combo box to Null
        Me.cboWorkCodeID = Null
    End If

    'Open the frmWorkCodes form modally
    DoCmd.OpenForm "frmWorkCodes", _
        DataMode:=acFormAdd, _
        windowmode:=acDialog, _
        OpenArgs:=strWorkCode

    'After the form is closed, requery the combo box
    Me.cboWorkCodeID.Requery

    'Set the text of the combo box to the value added
    Me.cboWorkCodeID.Text = strWorkCode

Exit_cboWorkCodeID_DblClick:
    Exit Sub

Err_cboWorkCodeID_DblClick:

    MsgBox Err.Description
    Resume Exit_cboWorkCodeID_DblClick
End Sub
```

In this example, the code evaluates the cboWorkCodeID combo box control to see whether it's Null. If it is, the text of the combo box is set to a zero-length string. Otherwise, a long integer variable is set equal to the combo box value, and the combo box value is set to Null. The frmWorkCodes form is opened modally. When it's closed, the cboWorkCodeID combo box is requeried. If the long integer variable doesn't contain a zero, the combo box value is set equal to the long integer value.

MouseDown

The MouseDown event applies to labels, text boxes, option groups, combo boxes, list boxes, command buttons, and object frames. It takes place when a user presses the mouse button over a control, *before* the Click event fires.

MouseMove

The MouseMove event applies to labels, text boxes, option groups, combo boxes, list boxes, command buttons, and object frames. It occurs as a user moves the mouse over a control.

9

ADVANCED FORM TECHNIQUES

MouseUp

The MouseUp event applies to labels, text boxes, option groups, combo boxes, list boxes, command buttons, and object frames. It occurs when a user releases the mouse over a control, *before* the Click event fires.

KeyDown

The KeyDown event applies to text boxes, toggle buttons, option buttons, check boxes, combo boxes, list boxes, and bound object frames. It happens when a user presses a key while within a control; the event occurs repeatedly until the key is released. It can be canceled by setting KeyCode equal to Zero.

KeyUp

The KeyUp event applies to text boxes, toggle buttons, option buttons, check boxes, combo boxes, list boxes, and bound object frames. It occurs when a user releases a key within a control. It occurs only once, no matter how long a key is pressed.

KeyPress

The KeyPress event applies to text boxes, toggle buttons, option buttons, check boxes, combo boxes, list boxes, and bound object frames. It occurs when a user presses and releases an ANSI key while the control has focus. It can be canceled by setting KeyCode equal to Zero.

Understanding the Sequence of Control Events

Just as Form events take place in a certain sequence when the form is opened, activated, and so on, Control events occur in a specific sequence. You need to understand this sequence to write the event code for a control.

What Happens When Focus Is Moved to or from a Control?

When focus is moved to a control, the following events occur:

```
Enter->GotFocus
```

If focus is moving to a control as the form is opened, the Form and Control events take place in the following sequence:

```
Open(form)->Activate(form)->Current(form)->Enter(control) GotFocus(control)
```

When focus leaves a control, the following events occur:

```
Exit->LostFocus
```

When focus leaves the control because the form is closing, the following events happen:

```
Exit(control)->LostFocus(control)->Unload(form)->Deactivate(form)
➥Close(form)
```

What Happens When the Data in a Control Is Updated?

When you change data in a control and then move focus to another control, the following events occur:

```
BeforeUpdate->AfterUpdate->Exit->LostFocus
```

After every character that's typed in a text or combo box, the following events take place before focus is moved to another control:

```
KeyDown->KeyPress->Change->KeyUp
```

For a combo box, if the NotInList event is triggered, it occurs after the KeyUp event.

Referring to Me

The Me keyword is like an implicitly declared variable; it's available to every procedure in a Form or Report module. Using Me is a great way to write generic code in a form or report. You can change the name of the form or report, and the code will be unaffected. Here's an example:

```
Me.RecordSource = "qryProjects"
```

It's also useful to pass Me (the current form or report) to a generic procedure in a module, as shown in the following example:

```
Call ChangeCaption(Me)
```

The ChangeCaption procedure looks like this:

```
Sub ChangeCaption(frmAny As Form)
    If IsNull(frmAny.Caption) Then
        frmAny.Caption = "Form For - " & CurrentUser
    Else
        frmAny.Caption = frmAny.Caption & " - " & CurrentUser
    End If
End Sub
```

The ChangeCaption procedure in a Code module receives any form as a parameter. It evaluates the caption of the form that was passed to it. If the caption is Null, ChangeCaption sets the caption to "Form For -", concatenated with the user's name. Otherwise, it takes the existing caption of the form passed to it and appends the user's name.

9

ADVANCED FORM
TECHNIQUES

What Types of Forms Can I Create, and When Are They Appropriate?

You can design a variety of forms with Microsoft Access. By working with the properties available in Access's form designer, you can create forms with many different looks and types of functionality. This chapter covers all the major categories of forms, but remember that you can create your own forms. Of course, don't forget to maintain consistency with the standards for Windows applications.

Single Forms: Viewing One Record at a Time

One of the most common types of forms, the Single form, allows you to view one record at a time. The Single form shown in Figure 9.1, for example, lets the user view one customer record and then move to other records as needed.

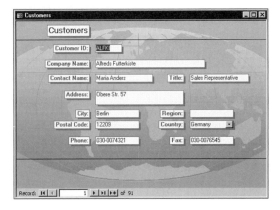

FIGURE 9.1

A single form.

Creating a single form is easy—simply set the form's Default View property to single Form. (See Figure 9.2.)

Continuous Forms: View Multiple Records at a Time

Often, the user wants to be able to view multiple records at a time, which requires creating a Continuous form, like the one shown in Figure 9.3. To do this, just set the Default View property to Continuous Forms.

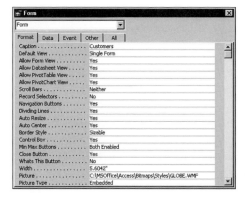

FIGURE 9.2

Setting the form's Default View property.

FIGURE 9.3

A continuous form.

A subform is a common use for a Continuous form; generally, you should show multiple records in a subform. The records displayed in the subform are all the records that relate to the record displayed in the main form. Figure 9.4 shows two subforms, each with its Default View property set to Continuous Forms. One subform shows all the orders relating to a specific customer, and the other shows all the order detail items for the selected order.

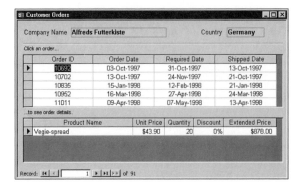

FIGURE 9.4

A form containing two Continuous subforms.

Multipage Forms: When Everything Doesn't Fit on One Screen

Scarcity of screen real estate is a never-ending problem, but a multipage form can be a good solution. Figures 9.5 and 9.6 show the two pages of the multipage Employees form, which can be found in the Northwind.MDB database. When looking at the form in Design view, you can see a Page Break control placed just before the 3-inch mark on the form. (See Figure 9.7.) To insert a Page Break control, select it from the toolbox, and then click and drag to place it on the form.

FIGURE 9.5

The first page of a multipage form.

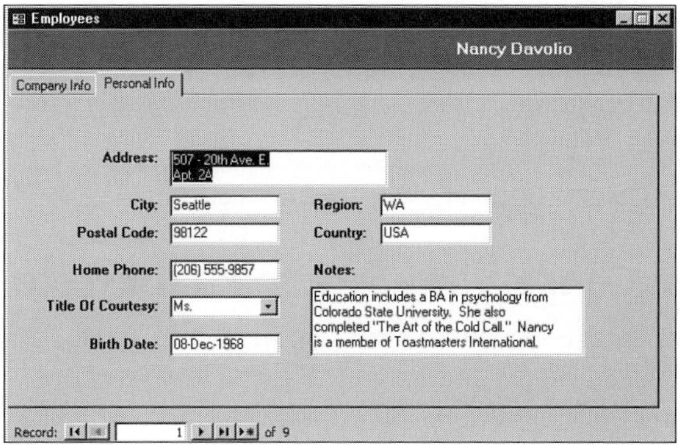

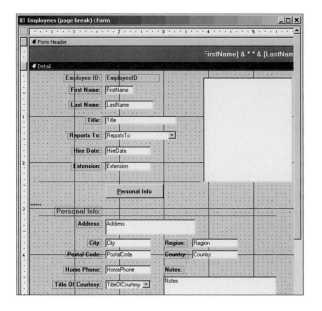

FIGURE 9.6
The second page of a multipage form.

FIGURE 9.7
A multipage form in Design view, showing a Page Break control.

When creating a multipage form, remember a few important steps:

- Set the Default View property of the form to Single Form.
- Set the Scrollbars property of the form to Neither or Horizontal Only.
- Set the Auto Resize property of the form to No.

- Place the Page Break control exactly halfway down the form's Detail section if you want the form to have two pages. If you want more pages, divide the total height of the Detail section by the number of pages and place Page Break controls at the appropriate positions on the form.

- Size the Form window to fit exactly one page of the form.

Tabbed Forms: Conserving Screen Real Estate

A tabbed form is an alternative to a multipage form. Access 97, Access 2000, and Access 2002 all include a built-in Tab control that allows you to easily group sets of controls. A tabbed form could, for example, show customers on one tab, orders for a selected customer on another tab, and order detail items for the selected order on a third tab.

The form shown in Figure 9.8 uses a Tab control. This form, called Employees, is included in the Northwind database. It shows an employee's company information on one tab and her personal information on the second tab. No code is needed to build the example.

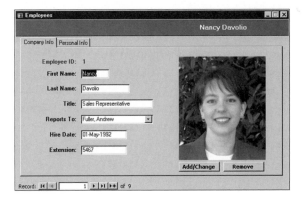

FIGURE 9.8
A tabbed form.

Adding a Tab Control and Manipulating Its Pages

To add a Tab control to a form, simply select it from the toolbox and drag and drop it onto the form. By default, two tab pages appear. To add more tabs, right-click the control and select Insert Page. To remove tabs, right-click the page you want to remove and select Delete Page. To change the order of pages, right-click any page and select Page Order.

Adding Controls to the Pages of a Tab Control

You can add controls to each tab just as you would add them directly to the form. Remember to select a tab by clicking it before you add the controls. If you don't select a specific tab, the controls you add will appear on every tab.

Modifying the Tab Order of Controls

The controls on each page have their own tab order. To modify their tab order, right-click the page and select Tab Order. You can then reorder the controls in whatever way you want.

Changing the Properties of the Tab Control

To change the properties of the Tab control, click to select it rather than a specific page. You can tell whether you've selected the Tab control because the words `Tab Control` appear in the upper-left corner of the title bar of the Properties window. (See Figure 9.9.) A Tab control's properties include its name, the text font on the tabs, and more.

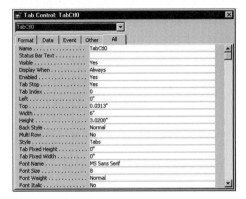

FIGURE 9.9

Viewing properties of a Tab control.

Changing the Properties of Each Page

To change the properties of each page, select a specific page of the Tab control. You can tell whether you've selected a specific page because the word `Page` is displayed in the upper-left corner of the title bar of the Properties window. (See Figure 9.10.) Here you can select a name for the page, the page's caption, a picture for the page's background, and more.

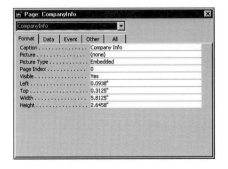

FIGURE 9.10

Viewing properties of a Tab page.

9

ADVANCED FORM
TECHNIQUES

Switchboard Forms: Controlling Your Application

A Switchboard form is a great way to control your application. A Switchboard form is simply a form with command buttons that allow you to navigate to other Switchboard forms or to the forms and reports that make up your system.

The form shown in Figure 9.11 is a Switchboard form. It lets a user work with different components of the database. What differentiates a Switchboard form from other forms is that its purpose is limited to navigating through the application. It usually has a border style of Dialog, and it has no scrollbars, record selectors, or navigation buttons. Other than these characteristics, a Switchboard form is a normal form. There are many styles of Navigation forms; which one you use depends on your users' needs.

FIGURE 9.11
An example of a Switchboard form.

Splash Screen Forms: A Professional Opening to Your Application

Splash screens add professional polish to your applications and give your users something to look at while your programming code is setting up the application. Just follow these steps to create a Splash Screen form:

1. Create a new form.
2. Set the Scrollbars property to Neither, the Record Selectors property to No, the Navigation Buttons property to No, the Auto Resize property to Yes, the Auto Center property to Yes, and the Border Style to None.
3. Make the form pop-up and modal.
4. Add a picture to the form and set the picture's properties.
5. Add any text you want on the form.
6. Set the form's timer interval to the number of seconds you want the splash screen to be displayed.

7. Code the form's `Timer` event for `DoCmd.Close`.

8. Code the form's `Unload` event to open your main Switchboard form.

Because the `Timer` event of the Splash Screen form closes the form after the amount of time specified in the timer interval, the Splash Screen form unloads itself. While it's unloading, it loads a Switchboard form. The Splash Screen form included in CHAP9EX.MDB is called frmSplash. When it unloads, it opens the frmSwitchboard form.

You can implement a Splash Screen form in many other ways. For example, you can call a Splash Screen form from a Startup form; its `Open` event simply needs to open the Splash Screen form. The problem with this method is that if your application loads and unloads the Switchboard while the application is running, the Splash Screen is displayed again.

TIP

You can also display a Splash Screen by including a bitmap file with the same name as your database (MDB) in the same directory as the database file. When the application is loaded, the Splash Screen is displayed for a couple of seconds. The only disadvantage to this method is that you have less control over when, and how long, the Splash Screen is displayed.

Dialog Forms: Gathering Information

Dialog forms are typically used to gather information from the user. What makes them Dialog forms is that they're *modal*, meaning that the user can't go ahead with the application until the form is handled. Dialog forms are generally used when you must get specific information from your user before your application can continue processing. A custom Dialog form is simply a regular form that has a `Dialog` border style and has its Modal property set to `Yes`. Remember to give users a way to close the form; otherwise, they might close your modal form with the famous "Three-Finger Salute" (Ctrl+Alt+Del) or, even worse, by using the PC's Reset button. The frmArchivePayments form in CHAP9EX.MDB is a custom Dialog form.

9

TIP

Although opening a form with its BorderStyle property set to `Dialog` and its Modal property set to `Yes` will prevent the user from clicking outside the form (thereby continuing the application), it does not halt the execution of the code that opened the form. Suppose the intent is to open a dialog form to gather parameters for a report, and then open a report based on those parameters. In this case, the `OpenForm`

> method used to open the form must include the `acDialog` option in its `Windowmode` argument. Otherwise, the code will continue after the `OpenForm` method and open the report before the parameters are collected from the user.

Using Built-In Dialog Boxes

Access comes with two built-in dialog boxes: the standard Windows message box and the input box. New to Access 2002 is the `FileDialog` object. It gives you access to other commonly used dialog boxes.

Message Boxes

A message box is a predefined dialog box that you can incorporate into your applications; however, it can be customized by using parameters. The VBA language has a `MsgBox` statement—that just displays a message—and a `MsgBox` function, which can display a message and return a value based on the user's response.

The message box in the VBA language is the same message box that's standard in most Windows applications, so it's already familiar to most Windows users. Rather than create your own dialog boxes to get standard responses from your users, you can use an existing, standard interface.

The `MsgBox` Function

The `MsgBox` function receives five parameters. The first parameter is the message that you want to display. The second is a numeric value indicating which buttons and icon you want to display. Tables 9.1 and 9.2 list the values that can be numerically added to create the second parameter. The intrinsic constants in the table can be substituted for the numeric values, if you want.

`MsgBox`'s third parameter is the message box's title. Its fourth and fifth parameters are the Help file and context ID that you want available if the user selects Help while the dialog box is displayed. The `MsgBox` function syntax looks like this:

```
MsgBox "This is a Message", vbInformation, "This is a Title"
```

This example displays the message `"This is a Message"` and the information icon. The title for the message box is `"This is a Title"`. The message box also has an OK button that's used to close the dialog box.

The `MsgBox` function is normally used to display just an OK button, but it can also be used to allow a user to select from a variety of standard button combinations. When used in this way, it returns a value indicating which button the user selected.

TABLE 9.1   Values Indicating the Buttons That a Message Box Can Display

Buttons	Value	Intrinsic Constant
OK button only	0	vbOKOnly
OK and Cancel	1	vbOKCancel
Abort, Retry, and Ignore	2	vbAbortRetryIgnore
Yes, No, and Cancel	3	vbYesNoCancel
Yes and No	4	vbYesNo
Retry and Cancel	5	vbRetryCancel

The values in Table 9.1 must be numerically added to one of the values in Table 9.2 if you want to include an icon other than the dialog box's default icon.

TABLE 9.2   Values Indicating the Icons That a Message Box Can Display

Icon	Value	Intrinsic Constant
Critical (Stop Sign)	16	vbCritical
Warning Query (Question)	32	vbQuestion
Warning Exclamation (!)	48	vbExclamation
Information (I)	64	vbInformation

In the following example, the message box displays Yes, No, and Cancel buttons:

```
Sub MessageBoxFunction()
    Dim intAnswer As Integer
    intAnswer = MsgBox("Are You Sure?", vbYesNoCancel + vbQuestion, _
        "Please Respond")
End Sub
```

This message box also displays the Question icon. (See Figure 9.12.) The Function call returns a value stored in the Integer variable intAnswer.

FIGURE 9.12

The dialog box displayed by the MsgBox function.

9

ADVANCED FORM
TECHNIQUES

After you have placed the return value into a variable, you can easily introduce logic into your program to respond to the user's selection, as shown in this example:

```
Sub MessageBoxAnswer()
    Dim intAnswer As Integer
    intAnswer = MsgBox("Are You Sure?", vbYesNoCancel + vbQuestion, _
        "Please Respond")
    Select Case intAnswer
        Case vbYes
            MsgBox "I'm Glad You are Sure!!"
        Case vbNo
            MsgBox "Why Aren't You Sure??"
        Case vbCancel
            MsgBox "You Coward! You Bailed Out!!"
    End Select
End Sub
```

This code evaluates the user's response and displays a message based on her answer. Of course, in a real-life situation, the code in the Case statements would be more practical. Table 9.3 lists the values returned from the MsgBox function, depending on which button the user selected.

TABLE 9.3   Values Returned from the MsgBox Function

Response	Value	Intrinsic Constant
OK	1	vbOK
Cancel	2	vbCancel
Abort	3	vbAbort
Retry	4	vbRetry
Ignore	5	vbIgnore
Yes	6	vbYes
No	7	vbNo

Input Boxes

The InputBox function displays a dialog box containing a simple text box. It returns the text that the user typed in the text box and looks like this:

```
Sub InputBoxExample()
    Dim strName As String
    strName = InputBox("What is Your Name?", _
                "This is the Title", "This is the Default")
    MsgBox "You Entered " & strName
End Sub
```

This subroutine displays the input box shown in Figure 9.13. Notice that the first parameter is the message, the second is the title, and the third is the default value. The second and third parameters are optional.

FIGURE 9.13

An example of using the InputBox *function to gather information.*

The `FileDialog` Object

The `FileDialog` object is new in Access 2002. This object allows you to easily display the common dialog boxes previously available only by using the Common Dialog ActiveX control. Here's an example of how `FileDialog` works:

```
Sub SaveDialog()

    'Declare a FileDialog object
    Dim dlgSaveAs As FileDialog

    'Instantiate the FileDialog object
    'indicating the it will act as a Save dialog
    Set dlgSaveAs = Application.FileDialog( _
        DialogType:=msoFileDialogSaveAs)

    'Display the dialog
    dlgSaveAs.Show

    'Display the specified file name in a message box
    MsgBox dlgSaveAs.SelectedItems(1)

End Sub
```

The code in the example declares a `FileDialog` object. It instantiates the object, setting its type to a File SaveAs dialog box. It shows the dialog box and then displays the first selected file in a message box. Here's another example:

```
Sub OpenDialog()
    'Declare a FileDialog object
    Dim dlgOpen As FileDialog
```

9

ADVANCED FORM
TECHNIQUES

```
    'Instantiate the FileDialog object, setting its
    'type to a File Open dialog
    Set dlgOpen = Application.FileDialog( _
        DialogType:=msoFileDialogOpen)

With dlgOpen

    'Allow multiple selections in the dialog
    .AllowMultiSelect = True

    'Display the dialog
    .Show
End With

    'Display the first file selected in the dialog
    MsgBox dlgOpen.SelectedItems(1)
End Sub
```

This code once again declares a FileDialog object. When the object is instantiated, the dialog box type is designated as a File Open dialog box. The AllowMultiSelect property of the dialog box is set to allow multiple selections in the dialog. The dialog box is displayed, and then the first selected file is displayed in a message box.

Adding Custom Menus, Toolbars, and Shortcut Menus to Your Forms

You can create custom menus to display with your forms and reports; there's no limit as to how many you can use. You can attach each menu to one or more forms or reports. Quite often, you will want to restrict what users can do while they're working with a form or report. By creating a custom menu, you can restrict and customize what users are allowed to do.

Designing a Menu

Prior to Access 97, Access users could create a custom menu bar by setting the MenuBar property to the name of a menu bar macro. This function was supported for backward compatibility only. In Access 97, Access 2000, and Access 2002, custom menu bars, toolbars, and pop-up menus are all referred to as *command bars*. To create any of these three objects, choose View| Toolbars and then select Customize. After a custom menu bar, toolbar, or pop-up menu has been created, you can easily associate it with forms and reports by using the Menubar, Toolbar, and Shortcut Menu Bar properties, respectively.

Follow these steps to create a custom menu bar:

1. Choose View|Toolbars and click Customize, or right-click any command bar and select Customize.

2. When the Customize dialog box opens, click the Toolbars tab and then click New. (See Figure 9.14.)

FIGURE 9.14

Using the Customize dialog box to create a new command bar.

3. Assign a name to the new menu bar, toolbar, or pop-up menu. The new command bar then appears.

4. Click the Properties button on the Customize dialog box to view the properties for your newly created command bar. In the Toolbar Properties dialog box, you name the toolbar, select the toolbar type, indicate the type of docking that's allowed, and set other options for the command bar. The Type drop-down list allows you to select Menu Bar, Toolbar, or Pop-up. The Docking options are Allow Any, Can't Change, No Vertical, and No Horizontal. You can also choose whether the user will be allowed to customize or move the command bar.

5. Select the options you want and click Close.

NOTE

Menu bars, toolbars, and pop-up menus are all referred to generically as *command bars*. The process to create each type of object is very similar. The Type property of the command bar is used to designate the type of object you want to create.

Now you're ready to add items to the new command bar. The process differs slightly, depending on whether you selected a toolbar, menu bar, or pop-up menu. To add items to a command bar, click the Commands tab of the Customize dialog box, shown in Figure 9.15, and drag and drop command icons onto your new command bar.

FIGURE 9.15

Use the Commands tab to add items to a command bar.

Here are some tips to help you to create custom menu bars, toolbars, and pop-up menus:

- To add an entire built-in menu to the menu bar, select Built-in Menus from the Categories list box. Click and drag a menu pad from the Commands list box over to the menu bar to add the entire built-in menu pad to the custom menu.

- To create a custom menu pad, select New Menu from the Categories list box. Click and drag the New Menu option to the menu bar. To modify the text on the menu pad, right-click the menu pad and type a new value in the Name text box.

- To add a built-in command to the menu, select a category from the Categories list box, and then click and drag the appropriate command to the menu pad. The new item will appear underneath the menu pad.

- To add a separator bar to a menu, right-click on the menu item that will follow the separator bar and select Begin a Group. To remove the separator bar, select Begin a Group again.

- Menu items can contain text only or images and text. To select one of these options, right-click a menu item and select Default Style, Text Only (Always), Text Only (in Menus), or Image and Text. To customize an image, right-click a menu item and select Change Button Image. Choose one of the available images. To modify the button image, right-click a menu item and select Edit Button Image; this opens the Button Editor dialog box. (See Figure 9.16.) If you want to reset the button to its original image, right-click the menu item and select Reset Button Image.

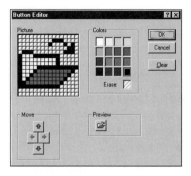

FIGURE 9.16
Modifying or creating button images with the Button Editor.

- If you want to modify several properties of a menu item at once, you can right-click the menu item and select Properties to open the File Control Properties dialog box. (See Figure 9.17.) Here you can select attributes for the menu item, such as the Caption, Screen Tip, Style, Help File, and Help ContextID. You can also associate an action with a custom menu item (covered in the next section).

FIGURE 9.17
Modifying menu item properties with the File Control Properties dialog box.

Associating a Command with a Menu Item

In Access, it's easy to customize your menus with both built-in commands and custom-built functions. For built-in commands, you can simply drag and drop commands onto your command bars. To have a command bar item run a custom-built function, you need to create a custom item and set its properties, as explained in the following steps:

9

ADVANCED FORM TECHNIQUES

1. Select the File category from the Categories list box in the Customize dialog box.

2. Click and drag the Custom option from the Commands list box to the position you want for the menu.

3. Right-click the new menu item and select Properties.

4. Type the name of the function or subroutine you want to call in the On Action drop-down list. If the procedure you're calling is a function, you must precede the function name with an equal sign (=) and include any parameters in parentheses following the function name.

5. Click Close to close the Control Properties dialog box.

6. Click Close to close the Customize dialog box.

Deleting and Renaming Menus

You can also use the Customize dialog box to delete and rename menus by following these steps:

1. Right-click any command bar and select Customize.

2. Click in the Toolbars list box to select the command bar you want to delete or rename.

3. Click Delete to delete the command bar, or Rename to rename it.

Manipulating Command Bars by Using Code

You can add, modify, and remove command bars, all by using VBA code. This allows you to build flexibility into your application. You can easily modify a command bar in response to different conditions in your application. You can even give your user a front end to customize the command bars in your application, as shown in this example located in the basExamples module in Chap9Ex.mdb.

```
Sub CreateCustomCommandBar()
    Dim cbr As CommandBar
    Dim btn As CommandBarButton

    'Attempt to point the command bar object at
    'a command button named My Command Bar
    Set cbr = CommandBars("My Command Bar")

    'If an error occurs, the command bar doesn't exist
    'so create it
    If Err.Number Then
        Set cbr = CommandBars _
        .Add(Name:="My Command Bar", Position:=msoBarTop)
    End If
```

```
'Attempt to add a button "Are You Sure?"
Set btn = cbr.Controls("Are You Sure?")

'If an error occurs, the custom button doesn't exist
'so create it
If Err.Number Then
    Set btn = cbr.Controls.Add(msoControlButton, , , , True)
End If

'Set properties of the button
With btn
    .Caption = "Are You Sure?"
    .BeginGroup = True
    .OnAction = "MessageBoxAnswer"
    .Style = msoButtonCaption
End With
End Sub
```

This code illustrates that, by using the VBA language, you have full control over command bar objects. It begins by creating `CommandBar` and `CommandBarButton` object variables; then it sets the `CommandBar` object variable to a command bar called My Command Bar. If this causes an error, you know that the My Command Bar command bar doesn't exist. The `Add` method is used to add the command bar, which will be placed at the top of the screen. The routine then tries to point at a command bar button called Are You Sure?. If this causes an error, the `Add` method of the Controls collection of the `CommandBar` object is used to add a command button to the collection. The button's caption is set to `Are You Sure?`, a group is added, and the command button's action is set to call the subroutine `MessageBoxAnswer`. The command button's style is set to display just a caption.

Taking Advantage of Built-In, Form-Filtering Features

Access has several form-filtering features that are part of the user interface. You can opt to include these features in your application, omit them from your application entirely, or control their behavior. For your application to control their behavior, it needs to respond to the `Filter` event, which it does by detecting when a filter is placed on the data in the form. When it has detected a filter, the code in the `Filter` event executes.

Sometimes you might want to alter the standard behavior of a filter command. You might want to display a special message to a user, for example, or take a specific action in your code. You might also want your application to respond to a `Filter` event because you want to alter the form's display before the filter is applied. For example, if a certain filter is in place, you might want to hide or disable certain fields. When the filter is removed, you could then return the form's appearance to normal.

Fortunately, Access not only lets you know that the `Filter` event occurred, but it also lets you know how the filter was invoked. Armed with this information, you can intercept and change the filtering behavior as needed.

When a user chooses Filter By Form or Advanced Filter/Sort, the `FilterType` parameter is filled with a value that indicates how the filter was invoked. If the user invokes the filter by selecting Filter By Form, the `FilterType` parameter equals the constant `acFilterByForm`; however, if she selects Advanced Filter/Sort, the `FilterType` parameter equals the constant `acFilterAdvanced`. The following code demonstrates how to use these constants:

```
Private Sub Form_Filter(Cancel As Integer, FilterType As Integer)
    Select Case FilterType
        Case acFilterByForm
            MsgBox "You Just Selected Filter By Form"
        Case acFilterAdvanced
            MsgBox "You Are Not Allowed to Select Advanced Filter/Sort"
            Cancel = True
    End Select
End Sub
```

This code, placed in the form's `Filter` event, evaluates the filter type. If Filter By Form was selected, a message box is displayed, and the filtering proceeds as usual. However, if the user selects Advanced Filter/Sort, she's told she can't do this, and the filter process is canceled.

Not only can you check how the filter was invoked, but you can also intercept the process when the filter is applied. You do this by placing code in the form's `ApplyFilter` event, as shown in this example:

```
Private Sub Form_ApplyFilter(Cancel As Integer, ApplyType As Integer)
    Dim intAnswer As Integer
    If ApplyType = acApplyFilter Then
        intAnswer = MsgBox("You just selected the criteria: & _
                    Chr(13) & Chr(10) & Me.Filter & _
                    Chr(13) & Chr(10) & Are You Sure You Wish _
                    to Proceed?", vbYesNo + vbQuestion)
        If intAnswer = vbNo Then
            Cancel = True
        End If
    End If
End Sub
```

This code evaluates the value of the `ApplyType` parameter. If it's equal to the constant `acApplyFilter`, a message box is displayed, verifying that the user wants to apply the filter. If the user responds `Yes`, the filter is applied; otherwise, the filter is canceled.

Including Objects from Other Applications: Linking Versus Embedding

Microsoft Access is an ActiveX client application, meaning that it can contain objects from other applications. Access 97, Access 2000, and Access 2002 are also ActiveX server applications. Using Access as an ActiveX server is covered in Chapter 22, "Automation: Communicating with Other Applications." Access's ability to control other applications with programming code is also covered in Chapter 22. In the following sections, you learn how to link to and embed objects in your Access forms.

Bound OLE Objects

Bound OLE objects are tied to the data in an OLE field within a table in your database. An example is the Photo field that's part of the Employees table in the Northwind database. The field type of the Employees table that supports multimedia data is OLE object. This means that each record in the table can contain a unique OLE object. The Employees form contains a bound OLE control, whose control source is the Photo field from the Employees table.

If you double-click the photo of an employee, the OLE object can be edited *in-place*. The picture of the employee is actually embedded in the Employees table. This means that the data associated with the OLE object is stored as part of the Access database (MDB) file, within the Employees table. Embedded objects, if they support the OLE 2.0 standard, can be modified In-place. This Microsoft feature is called *In-Place activation*.

To insert a new object, take the following steps:

1. Move to the record that will contain the OLE object.
2. Right-click the OLE Object control and select Insert Object to open the Insert Object dialog box.
3. Select an object type. Select Create New if you want to create an embedded object, or select Create from File if you want to link to or embed an existing file.
4. If you select Create from File, the Insert Object dialog box changes to look like the one shown in Figure 9.18.
5. Select Link if you want to link to the existing file. Don't check Link if you want to embed the existing file. If you link to the file, the Access table will have a reference to the file as well as to the presentation data (a bitmap) for the object. If you embed the file, Access copies the original file, placing the copy in the Access table.
6. Click Browse and select the file you want to link to or embed.
7. Click OK.

If you double-click a linked object, you launch its source application; you don't get In-Place activation. (See Figure 9.19.)

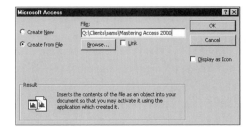

FIGURE 9.18
The Insert Object dialog box as it appears when you select Create from File.

FIGURE 9.19
Editing a linked object.

Unbound OLE Objects

Unbound OLE objects aren't stored in your database. Instead, they are part of the form they were created in. Like bound OLE objects, unbound OLE objects can be linked or embedded. You create an unbound OLE object by adding an unbound object frame to the form.

OpenArgs

The OpenArgs property gives you a way to pass information to a form as it's being opened. The OpenArgs argument of the OpenForm method is used to populate a form's OpenArgs property at runtime. It works like this:

```
DoCmd.OpenForm "frmPaymentMethods", _
        Datamode:=acFormAdd, _
        WindowMode:=acDialog, _
        OpenArgs:=NewData
```

This code is found in the Time and Billing application's frmPayments form. It opens the frmPaymentMethods form when a new method of payment is added to the cboPaymentMethodID combo box. It sends the frmPaymentMethods form an OpenArg of whatever data is added to the combo box. The Load event of the frmPaymentMethods form looks like this:

```
Private Sub Form_Load()
    If Not IsNull(Me.OpenArgs) Then
        Me.txtPaymentMethod.Value = Me.OpenArgs
    End If
End Sub
```

This code sets the txtPaymentMethod text box value to the value passed as the opening argument. This occurs only when the frmPaymentMethods form is opened from the frmPayments form.

Switching a Form's RecordSource

Many developers don't realize how easy it is to switch a form's RecordSource property at runtime. This is a great way to use the same form to display data from more than one table or query containing the same fields. It's also a great way to limit the data that's displayed in a form at a particular moment. Using the technique of altering a form's RecordSource property at runtime, as shown in Listing 9.1, you can dramatically improve performance, especially for a client/server application. This example is found in the frmShowSales form of the Chap9Ex database. (See Figure 9.20.)

FIGURE 9.20

Changing the RecordSource property of a form at runtime.

LISTING 9.1   Altering a Form's RecordSource at Runtime

```
Private Sub cmdShowSales_Click()

    'Check to see that Ending Date is later than Beginning Date.
    If Me.txtEndingDate < Me.txtBeginningDate Then
        MsgBox "The Ending Date must be later than the Beginning Date."
        txtBeginningDate.SetFocus
        Exit Sub
    End If

    'Create an SQL statement using search criteria entered by user and
    'set RecordSource property of ShowSalesSubform.

    Dim strSQL As String
    Dim strRestrict As String
    Dim lngX As Long

    lngX = Me.optSales.Value
    strRestrict = ShowSalesValue(lngX)

    'Create SELECT statement.
    strSQL = "SELECT DISTINCTROW tblCustomers.CompanyName,_
      qryOrderSubtotals.OrderID, "
    strSQL = strSQL & "qryOrderSubtotals.Subtotal ," & _
        "tblOrders.ShippedDate "
    strSQL = strSQL & "FROM tblCustomers INNER JOIN _
      (qryOrderSubtotals INNER JOIN tblOrders ON "
    strSQL = strSQL & "qryOrderSubtotals.OrderID = " & _
        "tblOrders.OrderID) ON "
    strSQL = strSQL & "tblCustomers.CustomerID = tblOrders.CustomerID "
    strSQL = strSQL & "WHERE (tblOrders.ShippedDate _
    Between Forms!frmShowSales!txtBeginningDate "
    strSQL = strSQL & "And Forms!frmShowSales!txtEndingDate) "
    strSQL = strSQL & "And " & strRestrict
    strSQL = strSQL & " ORDER BY qryOrderSubtotals.Subtotal DESC;"

    'Set RecordSource property of ShowSalesSubform.
    Me.fsubShowSales.Form.RecordSource = strSQL

    'If no records match criteria, reset subform's
    'RecordSource property,
    'display message, and move focus to BeginningDate text box.
    If Me.fsubShowSales.Form.RecordsetClone.RecordCount = 0 Then
        Me.fsubShowSales.Form.RecordSource = _
        "SELECT CompanyName FROM tblCustomers WHERE False;"
```

LISTING 9.1 Continued

```
        MsgBox "No records match the criteria you entered.", _
          vbExclamation, "No Records Found"
        Me.txtBeginningDate.SetFocus
    Else
        'Enable control in detail section.
        EnableControls Me, acDetail, True
        'Move insertion point to ShowSalesSubform.
        Me.fsubShowSales!txtCompanyName.SetFocus
    End If

    End Sub

Private Function ShowSalesValue(lngOptionGroupValue As Long) As String

    'Return value selected in Sales option group.

    'Define constants for option group values.
    Const conSalesUnder1000 = 1
    Const conSalesOver1000 = 2
    Const conAllSales = 3

    'Create restriction based on value of option group.
    Select Case lngOptionGroupValue
        Case conSalesUnder1000:
            ShowSalesValue = "qryOrderSubtotals.Subtotal < 1000"
        Case conSalesOver1000:
            ShowSalesValue = "qryOrderSubtotals.Subtotal >= 1000"
        Case Else
            ShowSalesValue = "qryOrderSubtotals.Subtotal = True"
    End Select
End Function
```

Listing 9.1 begins by storing the value of the optSales option group on the frmShowSales main form into a Long Integer variable. It calls the ShowSalesValue function, which declares three constants; then it evaluates the parameter that was passed to it (the Long Integer variable containing the option group value). Based on this value, it builds a selection string for the subtotal value. This selection string becomes part of the SQL statement used for the subform's record source and limits the range of sales values displayed on the subform.

The ShowSales routine builds a string containing a SQL statement, which selects all required fields from the tblCustomers table and qryOrderSubtotals query. It builds a WHERE clause that includes the txtBeginningDate and txtEndingDate from the main form as well as the string returned from the ShowSalesValue function.

9

ADVANCED FORM TECHNIQUES

When the SQL statement has been built, the RecordSource property of the fsubShowSales sub-form control is set equal to the SQL statement. The RecordCount property of the RecordsetClone (the form's underlying recordset) is evaluated to determine whether any records meet the criteria specified in the RecordSource. If the record count is zero, no records are displayed in the subform, and the user is warned that no records met the criteria. However, if records are found, the form's Detail section is enabled, and focus is moved to the subform.

Power Combo Box and List Box Techniques

Combo and list boxes are very powerful. Being able to properly respond to a combo box's NotInList event, to populate a combo box by using code, and to select multiple entries in a list box are essential skills of an experienced Access programmer. They're covered in detail in the following sections.

Handling the `NotInList` Event

As previously discussed, the NotInList event occurs when a user types a value in the text box portion of a combo box that's not found in the combo box list. This event takes place only if the LimitToList property of the combo box is set to True. It's up to you whether you respond to this event.

You might want to respond with something other than the default error message when the LimitToList property is set to True and the user tries to add an entry. For example, if a user is entering an order and she enters the name of a new customer, you could react by displaying a message box asking whether she really wants to add the new customer. If the user responds affirmatively, you can display a customer form.

After you have set the LimitToList property to True, any code you place in the NotInList event is executed whenever the user tries to type an entry that's not found in the combo box. The following is an example:

```
Private Sub cboPaymentMethodID_NotInList(NewData As String, _
    Response As Integer)
    'If payment method is not in the list,
    'ask user if they want to add it
    If MsgBox("Payment Method Not Found, Add?", _
        vbYesNo + vbQuestion, _
        "Please Respond") = vbYes Then

        'If they respond yes, open the frmPaymentMethods form
        'in add mode, passing in the new payment method
        DoCmd.OpenForm "frmPaymentMethods", _
            DataMode:=acFormAdd, _
```

```
            windowmode:=acDialog, _
            OpenArgs:=NewData

        'If form is still loaded, uload it
        If IsLoaded("frmPaymentMethods") Then
            Response = acDataErrAdded
            DoCmd.Close acForm, "frmPaymentMethods"

        'If the user responds no,
        Else
            Response = acDataErrContinue
        End If
    Else
        Response = acDataErrContinue
    End If

End Sub
```

When you place this code in the NotInList event procedure of your combo box, it displays a message asking the user whether she wants to add the payment method. If the user responds No, she is returned to the form without the standard error message being displayed, but she still must enter a valid value in the combo box. If the user responds Yes, she is placed in the frmPaymentMethods form, ready to add the payment method whose name she typed.

The NotInList event procedure accepts a response argument, which is where you can tell VBA what to do *after* your code executes. Any one of the following three constants can be placed in the response argument:

- acDataErrAdded—This constant is used if your code adds the new value into the record source for the combo box. This code requeries the combo box, adding the new value to the list.

- acDataErrDisplay—This constant is used if you want VBA to display the default error message.

- acDataErrContinue—This constant is used if you want to suppress VBA's error message, using your own instead. Access still requires that a valid entry be placed in the combo box.

Working with a Pop-Up Form

The NotInList technique just described employs the pop-up form. When the user opts to add the new payment method, the frmPaymentMethod form displays modally. This halts execution of the code in the form that loads the frmPaymentMethod form (in this case, the frmPayments form). The frmPaymentMethod form is considered a pop-up form because the form is modal, it uses information from the frmPayments form, and the frmPayments form reacts to whether the

OK or Cancel button is selected. The code in the Load event of the frmPaymentMethods form
in the Time and Billing database appears as follows:

```
Private Sub Form_Load()
    Me.txtPaymentMethod.Value = Me.OpenArgs
End Sub
```

This code uses the information received as an opening argument to populate the
txtPaymentMethod text box. No further code executes until the user clicks either the OK or the
Cancel command button. If the OK button is clicked, the following code executes:

```
Private Sub cmdOK_Click()
    Me.Visible = False
End Sub
```

Notice that the preceding code hides, rather than closes, the frmPaymentMethods form. If the
Cancel button is clicked, this code executes:

```
Private Sub cmdCancel_Click()
    DoCmd.RunCommand acCmdUndo
    DoCmd.Close
End Sub
```

The code under the Cancel button first undoes the changes that the user made. It then closes
the frmPaymentMethods form. Once back in the NotInList event of the cboPaymentMethod
combo box on the frmPayments form, the code that follows executes:

```
If IsLoaded("frmPaymentMethods") Then
        Response = acDataErrAdded
        DoCmd.Close acForm, "frmPaymentMethods"
Else
        Response = acDataErrContinue
End If
```

The code evaluates whether the frmPaymentMethods form is still loaded. If it is, the user must
have clicked OK. The Response parameter is set to acDataErrAdded, designating that the new
entry has been added to the combo box and to the underlying data source. The
frmPaymentMethods form is then closed.

If the frmPaymentMethods form is not loaded, the user must have clicked Cancel. The user is
returned to the combo box where she must select another combo box entry. In summary, the
steps are as follows:

1. Open the pop-up form modally (with the WindowMode parameter equal to acDialog).

2. Pass an OpenArgs parameter, if desired.

3. When control returns to the original form, check to see if the pop-up form is still loaded.

4. If the pop-up form is still open, use its information and then close it.

Adding Items to a Combo Box or List Box at Runtime

Prior to Access 2002, it was very difficult to add and remove items from list boxes and combo boxes at runtime. The next section, "Populating a Combo or List Box with a `Callback` Function," illustrates this point. Access 2002 list boxes and combo boxes support two new powerful methods that make it easier to programmatically manipulate these boxes at runtime. The `AddItem` method allows you to easily add items to a list box or a combo box. The `RemoveItem` method allows you to remove items from a list box. Here's an example:

```
Private Sub Form_Load()
    Dim obj As AccessObject

    'Loop through all tables in the current database
    'adding the name of each table to the list box
    For Each obj In CurrentData.AllTables
        Me.lstTables.AddItem obj.Name
    Next obj

    'Loop through all queries in the current database
    'adding the name of each query to the list box
    For Each obj In CurrentData.AllQueries
        Me.lstTables.AddItem obj.Name
    Next obj
End Sub
```

This code is found in the frmSendToExcel form that's part of the Chap9Ex database. It loops through all tables in the database, adding the name of each table to the lstTables list box. It then loops through each query in the database, once again adding each to the list box.

Populating a Combo or List Box with a `Callback` Function

As mentioned in the previous section, prior to Access 2002, the only way to add items to a combo box or list box at runtime was to use a `Callback` function. Although the new `AddItem` method renders the `Callback` function technique nearly extinct, many legacy applications utilize `Callback` functions. The technique is therefore covered in this section.

As you know, it's easy to populate a combo or list box by setting the control's properties. This method is enough for many situations; however, there are times when you might want to populate a combo or list box programmatically—with values from an array, for example. You might also want to populate the box with table or report names or some other database component.

To populate a combo or list box using code, you create a `Callback` function, which tells Access how many rows and columns will be in the combo or list box and what data will be used to fill the box. This function becomes the Row Source type for your combo or list box. Access calls the function; then it uses its information to populate the combo or list box. The example in Listing 9.2 is found in the frmSendToExcelCallBack form that's part of the Chap9Ex database.

LISTING 9.2   Filling a List Box By Using a `Callback` Function

```
Function FillWithTableList(ctl As Control, vntID As Variant, _
        lngRow As Long, lngCol As Long, intCode As Integer) _
        As Variant

    Dim cat As ADOX.Catalog
    Dim tdf As ADOX.Table
    Dim qdf As ADOX.View
    Dim intCounter As Integer
    Static sastrTables() As String
    Static sintNumTables As Integer
    Dim varRetVal As Variant


    varRetVal = Null


    Select Case intCode
        Case acLBInitialize         'Initialize.
        Set cat = New ADOX.Catalog
        cat.ActiveConnection = CurrentProject.Connection
        'Determine the Total Number of Tables + Queries
        sintNumTables = cat.Tables.Count + cat.Views.Count
        ReDim sastrTables(sintNumTables - 2)
        'Loop through each Table adding its name to
        'the List Box
        For Each tdf In cat.Tables
            If Left(tdf.Name, 4) <> "MSys" Then
                sastrTables(intCounter) = tdf.Name
                intCounter = intCounter + 1
            End If
        Next tdf
        'Loop through each Query adding its name to
        'the List Box
        For Each qdf In cat.Views
            sastrTables(intCounter) = qdf.Name
            intCounter = intCounter + 1
        Next qdf
        varRetVal = sintNumTables
        Case acLBOpen               'Open
            varRetVal = Timer           'Generate unique ID for control.
        Case acLBGetRowCount        'Get number of rows.
            varRetVal = sintNumTables
        Case acLBGetColumnCount     'Get number of columns.
            varRetVal = 1
        Case acLBGetColumnWidth     'Get column width.
            varRetVal = -1              '-1 forces use of default width.
```

LISTING 9.2 Continued

```
        Case acLBGetValue              'Get the data.
            varRetVal = sastrTables(lngRow)
    End Select
    FillWithTableList = varRetVal
End Function
```

The function must contain five predetermined arguments. The first argument must be declared as a control, and the remaining arguments must be declared as variants. The function itself must return a variant. The parameters are listed in Table 9.4.

TABLE 9.4 Five Predetermined Arguments of a Callback Function

Argument	Description
fld	A control variable that refers to the combo or list box being filled.
id	A unique value that identifies the control being filled. It's useful when you're using the same function to populate more that one combo or list box.
row	The row being filled (zero-based).
col	The column being filled (zero-based).
code	A value specifying the information being requested.

The List function is called several times. Each time it's called, Access automatically supplies a different value for the code, indicating the information it's requesting. The code item can have the values shown in Table 9.5.

TABLE 9.5 Code Item Values

Code	Intrinsic Constant	Meaning	Returns
0	acLBInitialize	Initialize	Nonzero if the function can fill the list; False or Null if a problem occurs
1	acLBOpen	Open	Nonzero ID value if the function can fill the list; False or Null if a problem occurs
3	acLBGetRowCount	Number of rows	Number of rows in the list

TABLE 9.5   Continued

Code	Intrinsic Constant	Meaning	Returns
4	acLBGetColumnCount	Number of columns	Number of columns in the list
5	acLBGetColumnWidth	Column width	Width of the column specified
6	acLBGetValue	List entry	List entry to be displayed in the column and row specified
7	acLBGetFormat	Format string	Format string used to format the list entry
8	acLBClose	Not used	N/A
9	acLBEnd	End (last call)	Nothing

The function is automatically called once for codes 0, 1, 3, and 4. These calls initiate the process and determine the number of rows and columns that the combo or list box contains. The function is called twice for code 5: once to determine the total width of the box, and again to set the column width. The number of times that codes 6 and 7 are executed varies, depending on the number of rows contained in the box (code 3). Code 9 is called when the form is closed, or the combo or list box is queried.

Armed with this knowledge, you can take a good look at the FillWithTableList function. This Callback function populates the list box with a list of tables and queries contained in the current database. When the user selects a table or query and clicks the Send To Excel command button, the data from the selected table or query is sent to Excel.

The Callback function uses ADO code to count all the tables and queries found in the current database. ADO (ActiveX Data Objects) is covered in Chapter 14, "What Are ActiveX Data Objects and Data Access Objects, and Why Are They Important?" Each element of the case structure seen in the routine is called as each code is sent by Access. Here's what happens:

- When Access sends the code of 0, the tables and views are counted. The code loops through each table and query in the database. If it is not a system table, its name is added to the sastrTables array. The return value of the function is the number of tables and views in the database.
- When Access sends the code 1, the return value is a unique value equal to the return value of the Timer function.
- When Access sends the code 3, the return value is set equal to the count of tables and queries in the database.

- When Access sends the code 4, the return value is set to 1 (one column).

- When Access sends the code 5, the return value is set to -1, forcing a default width for the combo or list box.

- Access then automatically calls code 6 by the number of times that was returned for the number of rows in the combo or list box. Each time code 6 is called, the form object variable is set equal to a different element of the form collection. The table or query name is returned from the function. The table or query name is the value that's added to the list box.

All this work might seem difficult at first. After you have populated a couple of combo or list boxes, though, it's quite easy. In fact, all you need to do is copy the case structure you see in the FillWithTableList function and use it as a template for all your Callback routines.

Handling Multiple Selections in a List Box

Access 97, Access 2000, and Access 2002 list boxes have a Multiselect property. When set to True, this property lets the user select multiple elements from the list box. Your code can then evaluate which elements are selected and perform some action based on the selected elements. The frmReportEngine form, found in the Chap9Ex database, illustrates the use of a multiselect list box. The code under the Click event of the Run Reports button looks like Listing 9.3.

LISTING 9.3   Evaluating Which Items Are Selected in the Multiselect List Box

```
Private Sub cmdRunReports_Click()
    Dim varItem As Variant
    Dim lst As ListBox

    Set lst = Me.lstReports
    'Single select is 0, Simple multi-select is 1,
    'and extended multi-select is 2.
    If lst.MultiSelect > 0 Then
        'Loop through all the elements
        'of the ItemsSelected collection, and use
        'the Column array to retrieve the
        'associated value.
        If lst.ItemsSelected.Count > 0 Then
            For Each varItem In lst.ItemsSelected
                DoCmd.OpenReport lst.ItemData(varItem), acViewPreview
            Next varItem
        End If
    End If

End Sub
```

9

This code first checks to ensure that the list box is a multiselect list box. If it is, and at least one report is selected, the code loops through all the selected items in the list box. It prints each report that is selected.

Power Subform Techniques

Many new Access developers don't know the ins and outs of creating and modifying a subform and referring to subform controls, so let's first look at some important points you should know when working with subforms:

- The easiest way to add a subform to a main form is to open the main form, and then drag and drop the subform onto the main form.
- The subform control's LinkChildFields and LinkMasterFields properties determine which fields in the main form link to which fields in the subform. A single field name, or a list of fields separated by semicolons, can be entered into these properties. When they are properly set, these properties make sure all records in the child form relate to the currently displayed record in the parent form.

Referring to Subform Controls

Many developers don't know how to properly refer to subform controls. You must refer to any objects on the subform through the subform control on the main form, as shown in this example:

```
Forms.frmCustomer.fsubOrders
```

This example refers to the fsubOrders control on the frmCustomer form. If you want to refer to a specific control on the fsubOrders subform, you can then point at its controls collection. Here's an example:

```
Forms.frmCustomer.fsubOrders!txtOrderID
```

You can also refer to the control on the subform implicitly, as shown in this example:

```
Forms!frmCustomer!subOrders!txtOrderID
```

Both of these methods refer to the txtOrderID control on the form in the fsubOrder control on the frmCustomer form. To change a property of this control, you would extend the syntax to look like this:

```
Forms.frmCustomer.fsubOrders!txtOrderID.Enabled = False
```

This code sets the Enabled property of the txtOrderID control on the form in the fsubOrders control to `False`.

Synchronizing a Form with Its Underlying Recordset

A form's RecordsetClone property is used to refer to its underlying recordset. You can manipulate this recordset independently of what's currently being displayed on the form. Here's an example:

```
Private Sub cboCompany_AfterUpdate()
   'Use the recordset behind the form to locate the client
   'Selected in the combo box
   Me.RecordsetClone.FindFirst "[ClientID] = " & cboCompany.Value

   'If the client is not found, display a message
   'Otherwise, synchronize the form with the underlying recordset
   If Me.RecordsetClone.NoMatch Then
      MsgBox "Client Not Found"
   Else
      Me.Bookmark = Me.RecordsetClone.Bookmark
   End If
End Sub
```

This example issues the FindFirst method on the form's RecordsetClone. It searches for a record in the form's underlying recordset whose ClientID is equal to the current combo box value. If a match is found, the form's bookmark is synchronized with the bookmark of the form's underlying recordset. This code can be rewritten, using an object variable to point at the RecordsetClone:

```
Private Sub cboCompany_AfterUpdate()
   'Create a recordset based on the recordset underlying the form
   Dim rst As Recordset
   Set rst = Me.RecordsetClone

   'Search for the client selected in the combo box
   rst.FindFirst "ClientID = " & cboCompany.Value

   'If the client is not found, display an error message
   'If the client is found, move the bookmark of the form
   'to the bookmark in the underlying recordset
   If rst.NoMatch Then
      MsgBox "Client Not Found"
   Else
      Me.Bookmark = rst.Bookmark
   End If
End Sub
```

9

ADVANCED FORM TECHNIQUES

This code creates an object variable that points at the form's `RecordsetClone`. The recordset object variable can then be substituted for `Me.RecordsetClone` because it references the form's underlying recordset.

The RecordSetClone property allows you to navigate or operate on a form's records independently of the form. This is often useful when you want to manipulate the data behind the form without affecting the appearance of the form. On the other hand, when you use the Recordset property of the form, the act of changing which record is current in the recordset returned by the form's Recordset property also sets the current record of the form. Here's an example:

```
Private Sub cboSelectEmployee_AfterUpdate()
    'Find the employee selected in the combo box
    Me.Recordset.FindFirst "EmployeeID = " _
        & Me.cboSelectEmployee

    'If employee not found, display a message
    If Me.Recordset.EOF Then
        MsgBox "Employee Not Found"
    End If
End Sub
```

Notice that it is not necessary to set the Bookmark property of the form equal to the Bookmark property of the recordset. They are one in the same.

Creating Custom Properties and Methods

Forms and reports are *Class modules*, which means they act as templates for objects you create instances of at runtime. Public procedures of a form and report become Custom properties and methods of the form object at runtime. Using VBA code, you can set the values of a form's Custom properties and execute its methods.

Creating Custom Properties

You can create Custom properties of a form or report in one of two ways:

- Create Public variables in the form or report.
- Create `PropertyLet` and `PropertyGet` routines.

Creating and Using a Public Variable as a Form Property

The following steps are used to create and access a Custom form or report property based on a Public variable. The example is included in CHAP9EX.MDB in the forms frmPublicProperties and frmChangePublicProperty.

1. Begin by creating the form that will contain the Custom property (Public variable).

2. Place a Public variable in the General Declarations section of the form or report. (See Figure 9.21.)

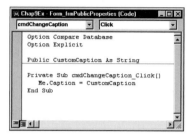

FIGURE 9.21

Creating a Public variable in the General Declarations section of a Class module.

3. Place code in the form or report that accesses the Public variable. The code in Figure 9.21 creates a Public variable called CustomCaption. The code behind the Click event of the cmdChangeCaption command button sets the form's (frmPublicProperties) Caption property equal to the value of the Public variable.

4. Create a form, report, or module that modifies the value of the Custom property. Figure 9.22 shows a form called frmChangePublicProperty.

FIGURE 9.22

Viewing the form frmChangePublicProperty.

5. Add the code that modifies the value of the Custom property. The code behind the ChangeCaption button, as seen in Figure 9.21, modifies the value of the Custom property called CustomCaption that's found on the form called frmPublicProperties.

 To test the Custom property created in the preceding example, run the form called frmPublicProperties, which is in the database CHAP9EX.MDB, found on your sample code CD-ROM. Click the Change Form Caption command button. Nothing happens

9

ADVANCED FORM
TECHNIQUES

because the value of the Custom property hasn't been set. Open the form called frmChangePublicProperty and click the Change Form Property command button. Return to frmPublicProperties and again click the Change Form Caption command button. The form's caption should now change.

Close the frmPublicProperties form and try clicking the Change Form Property command button. A runtime error occurs, indicating that the form you're referring to is not open. You can eliminate the error by placing the following code in the Click event of cmdPublicFormProperty:

```
Private Sub cmdPublicFormProperty_Click()
   Form_frmPublicProperties.CustomCaption = _
         "This is a Custom Caption"
   Forms!frmPublicProperties.Visible = True
End Sub
```

This code modifies the value of the Public property by using the syntax Form_FormName.Property. If the form isn't loaded, this syntax loads the form but leaves it hidden. The next command sets the form's Visible property to True.

Creating and Using Custom Properties with PropertyLet and PropertyGet Routines

A PropertyLet routine is a special type of subroutine that automatically executes whenever the property's value is changed. A PropertyGet routine is another special subroutine that automatically executes whenever the value of the Custom property is retrieved. Instead of using a Public variable to create a property, you insert two special routines: PropertyLet and PropertyGet. This example is found in CHAP9EX.MDB in the frmPropertyGetLet and frmChangeWithLet forms. To insert the PropertyLet and PropertyGet routines, follow these steps:

1. Choose Insert|Procedure. The dialog box shown in Figure 9.23 appears.

FIGURE 9.23

Starting a new procedure with the Add Procedure dialog box.

2. Type the name of the procedure in the Name text box.

3. Select Property from the Type option buttons.

4. Select Public as the Scope so that the property is visible outside the form.

5. Click OK. The `PropertyGet` and `PropertyLet` subroutines are inserted in the module. (See Figure 9.24.)

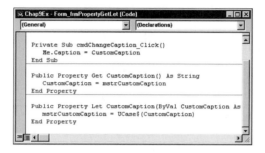

FIGURE 9.24

Subroutines created using the Add Procedure dialog box.

Notice that the `Click` event code for the cmdChangeCaption command button hasn't changed. The `PropertyLet` routine, which automatically executes whenever the value of the CustomCaption property is changed, takes the uppercase value of what it's being sent and places it in a Private variable called `mstrCustomCaption`. The `PropertyGet` routine takes the value of the Private variable and returns it to whomever asked for the value of the property. The sequence of events is as follows—the following code is placed in the form called frmChangeWithLet:

```
Private Sub cmdPublicFormProperty_Click()
   Form_frmPropertyGetLet.CustomCaption = "This is a Custom Caption"
   Forms!frmPropertyGetLet.Visible = True
End Sub
```

This routine tries to set the value of the Custom property called `CustomCaption` to the value `"This is a Custom Caption"`. Because the property's value is being changed, the `PropertyLet` routine in frmPropertyGetLet is automatically executed. It looks like this:

```
Public Property Let CustomCaption(ByVal CustomCaption As String)
   mstrCustomCaption = UCase$(CustomCaption)
End Property
```

The `PropertyLet` routine receives the value `"This is a Custom Caption"` as a parameter. It uses the `UCase` function to manipulate the value it was passed and convert it to uppercase. It then places the manipulated value into a Private variable called `mstrCustomCaption`.

The `PropertyGet` routine isn't executed until the user clicks the cmdChangeCaption button in the frmPropertyGetLet form. The `Click` event of cmdChangeCaption looks like this:

```
Private Sub cmdChangeCaption_Click()
    Me.Caption = CustomCaption
End Sub
```

Because this routine needs to retrieve the value of the Custom property `CustomCaption`, the `PropertyGet` routine automatically executes:

```
Public Property Get CustomCaption() As String
    CustomCaption = mstrCustomCaption
End Property
```

The `PropertyGet` routine takes the value of the Private variable, set by the `PropertyLet` routine, and returns it as the value of the property.

You might wonder why this method is preferable to declaring a Public variable. Using the `UCase` function within `PropertyLet` should illustrate why. Whenever you expose a Public variable, you can't do much to validate or manipulate the value you receive. The `PropertyLet` routine gives you the opportunity to validate and manipulate the value to which the property is being set. By placing the manipulated value in a Private variable and then retrieving the Private variable's value when the property is returned, you gain full control over what happens internally to the property.

> **NOTE**
>
> This section provides an introduction to custom properties and methods. A comprehensive discussion of custom classes, properties, and methods is found in Chapter 13, "Exploiting the Power of Class Modules."

Creating Custom Methods

Custom methods are simply Public functions and subroutines placed in a form module or a report module. As you will see, they can be called by using the `Object.Method` syntax. Here are the steps involved in creating a Custom method; they are found in CHAP9EX.MDB in the forms frmMethods and frmExecuteMethod:

1. Open the form or report that will contain the Custom method.
2. Create a Public function or subroutine. (See Figure 9.25.)

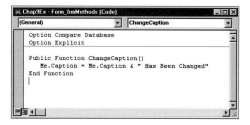

FIGURE 9.25

Using the custom method ChangeCaption.

3. Open the form module, report module, or code module that executes the Custom method.

4. Use the Object.Method syntax to invoke the Custom method. (See Figure 9.26.)

FIGURE 9.26

The Click *event code behind the Execute Method button.*

Figure 9.25 shows the Custom method ChangeCaption found in the frmMethods form. The method changes the form's caption. Figure 9.26 shows the Click event of cmdExecuteMethod found in the frmExecuteMethod form. It issues the ChangeCaption method of the frmMethods form, and then sets the form's Visible property to True.

PRACTICAL EXAMPLES

Applying Advanced Techniques to Your Application

Many examples in this chapter can be used in all the applications that you build. To polish your application, build a startup form that displays a splash screen and then performs some setup functions. The CHAP9EX.MDB file contains these examples.

9

ADVANCED FORM TECHNIQUES

Getting Things Going with a Startup Form

The frmSwitchboard form is responsible both for displaying the splash screen, and for performing necessary setup code. The code in the Load event of the frmSwitchboard form looks like this:

```
Private Sub Form_Load()
    DoCmd.Hourglass True
    DoCmd.OpenForm "frmSplash"
    Call GetCompanyInfo
    DoCmd.Hourglass False
End Sub
```

The Form_Load event first invokes an hourglass. It then opens the frmSplash form. Next, it calls the GetCompanyInfo routine to fill in the CompanyInfo type structure that is eventually used throughout the application. (Type structures are covered in Chapter 12, "Advanced VBA Techniques.") Finally, Form_Load turns off the hourglass.

Building a Splash Screen

The splash screen, shown in Figure 9.27, is called frmSplash. Its timer interval is set to 3,000 milliseconds (3 seconds), and its Timer event looks like this:

```
Private Sub Form_Timer()
    DoCmd.Close acForm, Me.Name
End Sub
```

FIGURE 9.27

Using an existing form as a splash screen.

The Timer event unloads the form. The frmSplash Pop-up property is set to Yes, and its border is set to None. Record selectors and navigation buttons have been removed.

Summary

Forms are the centerpiece of most Access applications, so it's vital that you be able to fully harness their power and flexibility. This chapter showed you how to work with Form and Control events. You saw many examples of when and how to leverage the event routines associated with forms and specific controls. You also learned about the types of forms available, their uses in your applications, and how you can build them. Finally, you learned several power techniques that will help you develop complex forms.

Advanced Report Techniques

IN THIS CHAPTER

Why This Chapter Is Important

Chapter 6, "What Every Developer Needs to Know About Reports," covers all the basics of report design. Reports are an integral part of almost every application, so fortunately for you, the Access 2002 report design tool is very powerful. Although it's easy to create most reports, as you mature as an Access developer, you'll probably want to learn the intricacies of Access report design. This chapter covers report events, advanced techniques, and tips and tricks of the trade.

Events Available for Reports, and When to Use Them

Although report events aren't as plentiful as form events, the report events you can trap for allow you to control what happens as your report runs. This topic discusses report events, and the section "Events Available for Report Sections, and When to Use Them" covers events specific to report sections.

The Open Event

The Open event is the first event that occurs in a report, before the report begins printing or displaying. In fact, it happens even before the query underlying the report is run. Listing 10.1 provides an example of using the Open event.

LISTING 10.1   The Open Event Is the First Event That Occurs for a Report

```
Private Sub Report_Open(Cancel As Integer)
    'Ignore an error if it occurs
    On Error Resume Next

    'Open the report criteria form
    DoCmd.OpenForm "frmReportDateRange", _
        WindowMode:=acDialog, _
        OpenArgs:="rptProjectBillingsbyWorkCode"

    'If the criteria form is not loaded, display an error
    'message and cancel the printing of the report
    '(the form will not be loaded if the user clicks cancel)
    If Not IsLoaded("frmReportDateRange") Then
        MsgBox "Criteria Form Not Successfully Loaded, " & _
            "Canceling Report"
        Cancel = True
    End If
End Sub
```

This code can be found in rptProjectBillingsByWorkCode in CHAP10.MDB on the sample code CD-ROM. It tries to open the frmReportDateRange form, the criteria form that supplies the parameters for the query underlying the report. The report is canceled if the form is not loaded.

The `Close` Event

The `Close` event occurs as the report is closing, before the `Deactivate` event occurs. Listing 10.2 illustrates the use of the `Close` event.

LISTING 10.2   The `Close` Event Is the Last Event That Occurs for a Report

```
Private Sub Report_Close()
    'Close criteria form as report is closing
    DoCmd.Close acForm, "frmReportDateRange"
End Sub
```

 This code is found in the rptProjectBillingsByWorkCode report in CHAP10.MDB on the sample code CD-ROM. It closes the criteria form frmReportDateRange when the report is closing, in case the form is still open.

The `Activate` Event

A report's `Activate` event happens when the report becomes the active window. It occurs after the `Open` event and before the report starts printing. It is often used to display a custom toolbar that will be visible whenever the report is active. Listing 10.3 shows an example.

LISTING 10.3   Using the `Activate` Event to Display Custom Toolbars

```
Private Sub Report_Activate()

    'Hide built-in Print Preview toolbar.
    'Show Custom Print Preview toolbar.
    DoCmd.ShowToolbar "Print Preview", acToolbarNo
    DoCmd.ShowToolbar "Custom Print Preview", acToolbarYes

End Sub
```

This code hides the Print Preview toolbar and shows the custom toolbar called Custom Print Preview. As you will see, this event works with the `Deactivate` event to show and hide the custom report toolbars when the report becomes the active window, and the user moves the focus to another window.

The `Deactivate` Event

The `Deactivate` event occurs when you move to another Access window or close the report, *not* when focus is moved to another application. Listing 10.4 provides an example of how the `Deactivate` event is used.

LISTING 10.4   Using the `Deactivate` Event to Display Custom Toolbars

```
Private Sub Report_Deactivate()

    'Hide Custom Print Preview toolbar.
    'Show built-in Print Preview toolbar.
    DoCmd.ShowToolbar "Custom Print Preview", acToolbarNo
    DoCmd.ShowToolbar "Print Preview", acToolbarWhereApprop

End Sub
```

This routine hides the custom toolbar displayed during the `Activate` event and indicates that the Print Preview toolbar should once again display where appropriate. You don't want to show the Print Preview toolbar here; instead, you just reset it to display whenever Access's default behavior would tell it to display. The `acToolbarWhereApprop` constant accomplishes this task.

> **NOTE**
>
> The sample code used in the sections on the `Activate` and `Deactivate` events illustrates one way to hide and show custom toolbars. The Toolbar property of a report can be used to perform the same task. However, when you need to display more than one toolbar while the report is active, you must place the code to hide and show the toolbars in the `Activate` and `Deactivate` events.

The `NoData` Event

If no records meet the criteria of the recordset underlying a report's `RecordSource`, the report prints without any data and displays `#Error` in the report's Detail section. To eliminate this problem, you can code the `NoData` event of the report, as shown in Listing 10.5.

LISTING 10.5   The NoData Event Executes When No Records Meet the Criteria Specified in the Report's RecordSource

```
Private Sub Report_NoData(Cancel As Integer)
    'Display a message and cancel processing
    MsgBox "There is no data for this report. Canceling report..."
    Cancel = True
End Sub
```

This code is found in the NoData event of rptProjectBillingsByWorkCode in CHAP10.MDB on the sample code CD-ROM. In case no data is returned by the report's underlying recordset, a message is displayed to the user, and Cancel is set equal to True. This exits the report without running it.

The Page Event

The Page event gives you the opportunity to do something immediately before the formatted page is sent to the printer. For example, the Page event can be used to place a border around a page, as shown in Listing 10.6.

LISTING 10.6   The Page EventOccurs Before the Formatted Page Is Sent to the Printer

```
Private Sub Report_Page()
    'Draw a red line starting in the upper left-hand corner
    'and going to the lower right hand corner
    Me.Line (0, 0)-(Me.ScaleWidth - 30, Me.ScaleHeight - 30), _
        RGB(255, 0, 0), B
End Sub
```

This code is found in the rptTimeSheet report, in CHAP10.MDB. It draws a red line on the report, starting in the upper-left corner and going to the lower-right corner. It uses the ScaleWidth and ScaleHeight properties to determine where the lower-right corner of the report's printable area is. The B in the third parameter creates a rectangle by using the coordinates as opposite corners of the rectangle.

The Error Event

If a Jet Engine error occurs when the report is formatting or printing, the Error event is triggered. This error usually occurs if there's no RecordSource for the report or if someone else has exclusive use over the report's RecordSource. Listing 10.7 provides an example.

10

LISTING 10.7   The `Error` Event Executes If a Jet Engine Occurs While the Report Is Formatting or Printing

```
Private Sub Report_Error(DataErr As Integer, Response As Integer)
    'If Data Source Not Found error occurs, display message
    'To test this, rename qryTimeSheet
    If DataErr = 2580 Then
        MsgBox "Record Source Not Available for this Report"
        Response = acDataErrContinue
    End If
End Sub
```

NOTE

If you have Name Autocorrect turned on, the process of renaming the query will not cause the desired error to occur.

This code responds to a `DataErr` of 2580, which means that the report's `RecordSource` isn't available. A custom message is displayed to the user, and the Access error is suppressed.

Order of Events for Reports

It's important to understand the order of events for reports. When the user opens a report, previews it, and then closes it, the following sequence of events occurs:

`Open→Activate→Close→Deactivate`

When the user switches to another report or to a form, the following sequence occurs:

`Deactivate(Current Report)→Activate(Form or Report)`

NOTE

The `Deactivate` event doesn't occur when the user switches to a dialog box, to a form whose `PopUp` property is set to `Yes`, or to a window of another application.

Events Available for Report Sections, and When to Use Them

Just as the report itself has events, so does each section of the report. The three section events are the `Format` event, `Print` event, and `Retreat` event, covered in the following sections.

The Format Event

The Format event happens after Access has selected the data to be included in a report section, but before it formats or prints the data. With the Format event, you can affect the layout of the section or calculate the results of data in the section, before the section actually prints. Listing 10.8 shows an example.

LISTING 10.8 Using the Format Event to Affect the Report Layout

```
Private Sub Detail2_Format(Cancel As Integer, FormatCount As Integer)

    'Determine whether to print detail record or "Continued."

    'Show Continued text box if at maximum number of
    'detail records for page.
    If (Me.txtRow = Me.txtOrderPage * (Me.txtRowsPerPage - 1) + 1) _
        And Me.txtRow <> Me.txtRowCount Then
        Me.txtContinued.Visible = True
    End If

    'Show page break and hide controls in detail record.
    With Me
        If .txtContinued.Visible Then
            .txtDetailPageBreak.Visible = True
            .txtProductID.Visible = False
            .txtProductName.Visible = False
            .txtQuantity.Visible = False
            .txtUnitPrice.Visible = False
            .txtDiscount.Visible = False
            .txtExtendedPrice.Visible = False

            'Increase value in Order Page.
            .NextRecord = False
            .txtOrderPage = Me.txtOrderPage + 1
        Else
            'Increase row count if detail record is printed.
            .txtRow = Me.txtRow + 1
        End If
    End With

End Sub
```

This code is found in the rptInvoice report included in the CHAP10EX.MDB database found on your sample code CD. The report has controls that track how many rows of detail records should be printed on each page. If the maximum number of rows has

been reached, a control with the text `Continued on Next Page...` is visible. If the control is visible, the page break control is also made visible, and all the controls that display the detail for the report are hidden. The report is kept from advancing to the next record.

 Another example of the `Format` event is found in the Page Header of the rptEmployeeSales report, found in the CHAP10EX.MDB database. Because the report is an unbound report whose controls are populated by using VBA code at runtime, the report needs to determine what's placed in the report header. This varies depending on the result of the Crosstab query on which the report is based. The code appears in Listing 10.9.

LISTING 10.9 Using the `Format` Event to Populate Unbound Controls at Runtime

```
Private Sub PageHeader0_Format(Cancel As Integer, FormatCount As Integer)

    Dim intX As Integer

    'Put column headings into text boxes in page header.
    For intX = 1 To mintColumnCount
        Me("Head" + Format(intX)) = mrstReport(intX - 1).Name
    Next intX

    'Make next available text box Totals heading.
    Me("Head" + Format(mintColumnCount + 1)) = "Totals"

    'Hide unused text boxes in page header.
    For intX = (mintColumnCount + 2) To conTotalColumns
        Me("Head" + Format(intX)).Visible = False
    Next intX
End Sub
```

The code loops through each column of the recordset that results from executing the Crosstab query (in the `Open` event of the report). The code populates the controls in the report's Page Header with the name of each column in the query result. The final column header is set equal to `Totals`. Finally, any remaining (extra) text boxes are hidden. This chapter covers several examples of using the `Format` event.

NOTE

The example in Listing 10.9 and several other examples in this chapter use a DAO (Data Access Objects) recordset. DAO is covered in Chapter 14, "What Are ActiveX Data Objects and Data Access Objects, and Why Are They Important?" If you are unfamiliar with DAO and ADO, you might want to review Chapter 14 before reviewing the examples.

> **TIP**
>
> By placing logic in the `Format` event of a report's Detail section, you can control what happens as each line of the Detail section is printed.

The `Print` Event

The code in the `Print` event executes when the data formats to print in the section, but before it's actually printed. The `Print` event occurs at the following times for different sections of the report:

Detail Section: Just before the data is printed.

Group Headers: Just before the Group Header is printed; the Group Header's `Print` event has access to both the Group Header and the first row of data in the group.

Group Footers: Just before the Group Footer is printed; the `Print` event of the Group Footer has access to both the Group Footer and the last row of data in the group.

 Listing 10.10 is in the `Print` event of the rptEmployeeSales report's Detail section; this report is included in the CHAP10EX.MDB database and is called from frmEmployeeSalesDialogBox.

LISTING 10.10   Using the `Print` Event to Calculate Column and Row Totals

```
Private Sub Detail1_Print(Cancel As Integer, PrintCount As Integer)

    Dim intX As Integer
    Dim lngRowTotal As Long

    'If PrintCount is 1, initialize rowTotal variable.
    'Add to column totals.
    If Me.PrintCount = 1 Then
        lngRowTotal = 0

        For intX = 2 To mintColumnCount
            'Starting at column 2 (first text box with crosstab value),
            'compute total for current row in detail section.
            lngRowTotal = lngRowTotal + Me("Col" + Format(intX))
            'Add crosstab value to total for current column.
            mlngRgColumnTotal(intX) = mlngRgColumnTotal(intX) + _
                Me("Col" + Format(intX))
        Next intX
```

LISTING 10.10   Continued

```
            'Place row total in text box in detail section.
            Me("Col" + Format(mintColumnCount + 1)) = lngRowTotal
            'Add row total for current row to grand total.
            mlngReportTotal = mlngReportTotal + lngRowTotal
        End If
End Sub
```

The code begins by evaluating the `PrintCount` property. If it's equal to 1, meaning this is the first time the `Print` event has occurred for the Detail section, the row total is set equal to 0. The code then loops through each control in the section, accumulating totals for each column of the report and a total for the row. After the loop has been exited, the routine places the row total in the appropriate control and adds the row total to the report's grand total. The report's Detail section is now ready to be printed.

> **NOTE**
>
> Many people are confused about when to place code in the `Format` event and when to place code in the `Print` event. If you're doing something that doesn't affect the page layout, you should use the `Print` event. However, if you're doing something that affects the report's physical appearance (the layout), use the `Format` event.

The `Retreat` Event

Sometimes Access needs to move back to a previous section when printing, such as when a group's Keep Together property is set to `With First Detail` or `Whole` in the Sorting and Grouping dialog box. Access needs to format the Group Header and the first detail record or, in the case of `Whole`, the entire group. It then determines whether it can fit the section on the current page. It retreats from the two sections, and then formats and prints them; a `Retreat` event occurs for each section. Here's an example of the `Retreat` event for a report's Detail section:

```
Private Sub Detail1_Retreat()

    'Always back up to previous record when detail section retreats.
    mrstReport.MovePrevious

End Sub
```

This code is placed in the `Retreat` event of the rptEmployeeSales report that's part of the CHAP10EX.MDB. Because the report is an unbound report, it needs to return to the previous record in the recordset whenever the `Retreat` event occurs.

CAUTION

Whenever you're working with an unbound report, you need to be careful that the record pointer remains synchronized with the report. For example, if the record pointer has been advanced and the `Retreat` event occurs, the record pointer must be moved back to the previous record.

Order of Section Events

Just as report events have an order, report sections also have an order of events. All the `Format` and `Print` events for each section happen after the report's `Open` and `Activate` events, but before the report's `Close` and `Deactivate` events. The sequence looks like this:

```
Open(Report)→Activate(Report)→Format(Report Section)→
Print(Report Section)→Close(Report)→Deactivate(Report)
```

Programmatically Manipulating Report Sections

Not only can you create and manipulate report sections at design time, you also can do so at runtime. You must first open the report in Design view. You use the `DoCmd` object to add a report header and footer or a page header and footer. The code appears in Listing 10.11.

LISTING 10.11   Using the `DoCmd` Object to Programmatically Add Sections to Reports at Runtime

```
Private Sub cmdAddHeadersFooters_Click()
    'Open rptAny in Design View
    DoCmd.OpenReport "rptAny", acViewDesign

    'Add a report header and footer
    DoCmd.RunCommand acCmdReportHdrFtr

    'Add a page header and footer
    DoCmd.RunCommand acCmdPageHdrFtr
End Sub
```

You can also add section headers and footers. The code in Listing 10.12 illustrates the process. It is found in frmReportSections on the sample code CD.

LISTING 10.12   Using the DoCmd Object to Programmatically Add Sections to Reports at Runtime

```
Private Sub cmdAddSections_Click()
    Dim boolSuccess As Boolean

    'Use CreateGroupLevel function to create a grouping
    'based on the City field in the report rptAny
    boolSuccess = CreateGroupLevel("rptAny", "City", True, True)
End Sub
```

Note that the CreateGroupLevel function receives four parameters. The first is the name of the report you wish to affect. The second is an expression designating the expression on which the grouping is based. The third parameter allows you to specify whether you wish the group to have a group header, and the final parameters lets you designate whether you wish to include a group footer.

Special Report Properties

Several report properties are available only at runtime. They let you refine your report's processing significantly. These properties are covered in the sections that follow. The later section "Practical Applications of Report Events and Properties" provides examples of these properties.

MoveLayout

The MoveLayout property indicates to Access whether it should move to the next printing location on the page. By setting the property to False, the printing position is not advanced.

NextRecord

The NextRecord property specifies whether a section should advance to the next record. By setting this property to False, you suppress advancing to the next record.

PrintSection

The PrintSection property indicates whether the section is printed. By setting this property to False, you can suppress printing the section.

Interaction of MoveLayout, NextRecord, and PrintSection

By using the MoveLayout, NextRecord, and PrintSection properties in combination, you can determine exactly where, how, and whether data is printed. Table 10.1 illustrates this point.

TABLE 10.1 Interaction of `MoveLayout`, `NextRecord`, and `PrintSection`

MoveLayout	NextRecord	PrintSection	Effect
True	True	True	Move to the next position, get the next record, and print the data.
True	False	True	Move to the next position, remain on the same record, and print the data.
True	True	False	Move to the next position, get the next record, and don't print the data. This has the effect of skipping a record and leaving a blank space.
True	False	False	Move to the next position, remain on the same record, and don't print. This causes a blank space to appear without moving to the next record.
False	True	True	Remain in the same position, get the next record, and print the data. This has the effect of overlaying one record on another.
False	False	True	Not allowed.
False	True	False	Remain in the same position, get the next record, and refrain from printing. This has the effect of skipping a record without leaving a blank space.
False	False	False	Not allowed.

FormatCount

The FormatCount property evaluates the number of times the `Format` event has occurred for the report's current section. The `Format` event happens more than once whenever the `Retreat` event occurs. By checking the FormatCount property, you can make sure that complex code placed in the `Format` event is executed only once.

PrintCount

The PrintCount property identifies the number of times the `Print` event has occurred for the report's current section. The `Print` event happens more than once whenever the `Retreat` event occurs. By checking the value of the PrintCount property, you can make sure that logic in the `Print` event is executed only once.

HasContinued

The HasContinued property determines whether part of the current section is printed on a previous page. You can use this property to hide or show certain report controls (for example, `Continued From...`), depending on whether the section is continued.

WillContinue

The WillContinue property determines whether the current section continues on another page. You can use this property as you do the HasContinued property to hide or display certain controls when a section continues on another page.

Controlling the Printer

Prior to Access 2002, there was no easy way to programmatically control the printer in the applications that you built. Unlike other aspects of Access in which Microsoft provided you with objects, properties, methods, and events that you could easily manipulate, programmatically controlling the printer in versions prior to Access 2002 involved rolling up your sleeves, and talking at a low level to operating system objects.

Fortunately, Access 2002 introduces a new `Printer` object and a Printers collection. The `Printer` object greatly facilitates the process of programmatically manipulating a printer. The Printers collection allows you to loop through all the `Printer` objects and perform a task.

The `Printer` Object

The Printers collection consists of individual `Printer` objects. You use a `Printer` object to control each printer in the Printers collection. Listing 10.13 provides an example of the `Printer` object.

LISTING 10.13   You Can Easily Retrieve and Set Properties of the New Access 2002 `Printer` Object

```
Private Sub cmdPrinterObject_Click()
    'Declare a Printer object
    Dim prt As Printer
```

LISTING 10.13   Continued

```
    'Point the Printer object at the first printer in
    'the Printers collection
    Set prt = Printers(0)

    'Display properties of the printer
    MsgBox "Device Name: " & prt.DeviceName & vbCrLf & _
        "Port: " & prt.Port & vbCrLf & _
        "Color Mode: " & prt.ColorMode & vbCrLf & _
        "Copies: " & prt.Copies
End Sub
```

Listing 10.13 begins by instantiating a `Printer` object. It points the `Printer` object at the first printer in the Printers collection. It then retrieves the DeviceName, Port, ColorMode, and Copies properties of the printer. These are four of the many properties included for the `Printer` object. Other properties include the LeftMargin, RightMargin, TopMargin, BottomMargin, Orientation, and PrintQuality properties. Most properties of the `Printer` object are read/write. This means that you can programmatically manipulate the properties at runtime, easily controlling the behavior of the printer.

The Printers Collection

Using the Printers collection, you can loop through all the printers available for a user, programmatically manipulating each one. Listing 10.14 provides an example. It is found in frmPrinterObjectAndPrintersCollection on the sample code CD.

LISTING 10.14   The Printers Collection Allows You to Programmatically Manipulate `Printer` Objects Available for a User

```
Private Sub cmdPrintersCollection_Click()
    'Declare a Printer object
    Dim prt As Printer

    Dim strPrinterInfo As String

    'Loop through each printer in the user's
    'Printers collection
    For Each prt In Printers

        'Retrieve properties of the printer
        strPrinterInfo = strPrinterInfo & vbCrLf & _
            "Device Name: " & prt.DeviceName & "; " & _
            "Port: " & prt.Port & "; " & _
```

LISTING 10.14   Continued

```
            "Color Mode: " & prt.ColorMode & "; " & _
            "Copies: " & prt.Copies
    Next prt

    'Display the properties of all printers in a
    'message box
    MsgBox strPrinterInfo
End Sub
```

Practical Applications of Report Events and Properties

When developing reports, you should make sure that the report can be used in as many situations as possible—that you build as much flexibility into the report as you can. Instead of managing several similar reports, making changes to each one whenever something changes, you can manage one report that handles different situations. Using the events and properties covered in this chapter will help you do just that. This might involve changing the report's RecordSource at runtime; using the same report to print summary data, detail data, or both; changing the print position; or even running a report based on a Crosstab query with unbound controls. All these aspects of report design are covered in the following sections.

Changing a Report's RecordSource

There are many times when you might want to change a report's RecordSource at runtime. By doing this, you can allow your users to alter the conditions for your report and transparently modify the query on which the report is based. The rptClientListing report in CHAP10.MDB has the code in Listing 10.15 in its Open event.

LISTING 10.15   An Example of Using the Report Open Event to Modify a Report's RecordSource

```
Private Sub Report_Open(Cancel As Integer)
    On Error Resume Next

    'Open the report criteria form
    DoCmd.OpenForm "frmClientListingCriteria", WindowMode:=acDialog

    'Ensure that the form is loaded
    If Not IsLoaded("frmClientListingCriteria") Then
        MsgBox "Criteria form not successfully loaded, " & _
```

Listing 10.15   Continued

```
        "Canceling Report"
        Cancel = True
    Else

        'Evaluate which option button was selected
        'Set the RecordSource property as appropriate
        Select Case Forms!frmClientListingCriteria.optCriteria.Value
            Case 1
                Me.RecordSource = "qryClientListingCity"
            Case 2
                Me.RecordSource = "qryClientListingStateProv"
            Case 3
                Me.RecordSource = "qryClientListing"
        End Select
    End If
End Sub
```

This code begins by opening the frmClientListingCriteria form, if it isn't already loaded. It loads the form modally and waits for the user to select the report criteria. (See Figure 10.1.) After the user clicks to preview the report, the form sets its own Visible property to `False`. This causes execution to continue in the report, but leaves the form in memory so that its controls can be accessed with VBA code. The code evaluates the value of the form's optCriteria option button. Depending on which option button is selected, the report's RecordSource property is set to the appropriate query. The following code is placed in the `Close` event of the report:

```
Private Sub Report_Close()
    DoCmd.Close acForm, "frmClientListingCriteria"
End Sub
```

Figure 10.1

The criteria selection used to determine the RecordSource.

This code closes the criteria form as the report is closing. The frmClientListingCriteria form has some code that's important to the processing of the report. It's found in the `AfterUpdate` event of the `optCriteria` option group. (See Listing 10.16.)

LISTING 10.16   The `AfterUpdate` Event of optCriteriaCombo Hides and Shows Combo Boxes as Appropriate

```
Private Sub optCriteria_AfterUpdate()
    'Evaluate which option button is selected
    'Hide and show combo boxes as appropriate

    Select Case optCriteria.Value
        Case 1
            Me.cboCity.Visible = True
            Me.cboStateProv.Visible = False
        Case 2
            Me.cboStateProv.Visible = True
            Me.cboCity.Visible = False
        Case 3
            Me.cboCity.Visible = False
            Me.cboStateProv.Visible = False
    End Select
End Sub
```

This code evaluates the value of the option group. It hides and shows the visibility of the cboCity and cboStateProv combo boxes, depending on which option button is selected. The cboCity and cboStateProv combo boxes are then used as appropriate criteria for the queries that underlie the rptClientListing report.

The example shown in Listing 10.15 utilizes three stored queries to accomplish the task of switching the report's record source. An alternative to this technique is to programmatically set the RecordSource property of the report to the appropriate SQL statement. This technique is illustrated in Listing 10.17 and is found in rptClientListingAlternate on the sample code CD.

LISTING 10.17   Using the `Report Open` Event to Modify a Report's `RecordSource` to the Appropriate SQL Statement

```
On Error Resume Next

'Open the report criteria form
DoCmd.OpenForm "frmClientListingCriteria", WindowMode:=acDialog

'Ensure that the form is loaded
If Not IsLoaded("frmClientListingCriteria") Then
```

LISTING 10.17   Continued

```
        MsgBox "Criteria form not successfully loaded, " & _
        "Canceling Report"
        Cancel = True
    Else

        'Evaluate which option button was selected
        'Set the RecordSource property as appropriate
        Select Case Forms!frmClientListingCriteria.optCriteria.Value
            Case 1
                Me.RecordSource = "SELECT DISTINCTROW " & _
                "tblClients.CompanyName, " & _
                "ContactFirstName & ' ' & ContactLastName AS ContactName, " & _
                "tblClients.City, tblClients.StateProvince, " & _
                "tblClients.OfficePhone, tblClients.Fax " & _
                "FROM tblClients " & _
                "WHERE tblClients.City = '" & _
                Forms!frmClientListingCriteria.cboCity.Value & _
                "' ORDER BY tblClients.CompanyName;"
            Case 2
                Me.RecordSource = "SELECT DISTINCTROW " & _
                "tblClients.CompanyName, " & _
                "ContactFirstName & ' ' & ContactLastName AS ContactName, " & _
                "tblClients.City, tblClients.StateProvince, " & _
                "tblClients.OfficePhone, tblClients.Fax " & _
                "FROM tblClients " & _
                "WHERE tblClients.StateProvince = '" & _
                Forms!frmClientListingCriteria.cboStateProv.Value & _
                "' ORDER BY tblClients.CompanyName;"
            Case 3
                Me.RecordSource = "SELECT DISTINCTROW " & _
                "tblClients.CompanyName, " & _
                "ContactFirstName & ' ' & ContactLastName AS ContactName, " & _
                "tblClients.City, tblClients.StateProvince, " & _
                "tblClients.OfficePhone, tblClients.Fax " & _
                "FROM tblClients " & _
                "ORDER BY tblClients.CompanyName;"
        End Select
    End If
```

The example programmatically builds a SQL statement based on the option selected on the criteria form. It utilizes the `cboCity` and `cboStateProv` combo boxes to build the WHERE clause in the appropriate SQL strings.

Working with Report Filters

The Filter and FilterOn properties allow you to set a report filter and to turn it on and off. Three possible scenarios can apply:

- No filter is in effect.
- The Filter property is set but is not in effect because the FilterOn property is set to False.
- The filter is in effect. This requires that the Filter property is set, and the FilterOn property is set to True.

You can set filtering properties either at design time or at runtime. This solution provides *another* alternative to the example provided in Listing 10.15. With this alternative, the RecordSource of the report is fixed. The Filter and FilterOn properties are used to display the appropriate data. Listing 10.18 provides an example. The code is found in rptClientListingFiltered on the sample code CD.

LISTING 10.18   The Filter and FilterOn Properties Work Together to Apply Filtering to a Report

```
Private Sub Report_Open(Cancel As Integer)
    On Error Resume Next

    'Open the report criteria form
    DoCmd.OpenForm "frmClientListingCriteria", WindowMode:=acDialog

    'Ensure that the form is loaded
    If Not IsLoaded("frmClientListingCriteria") Then
        MsgBox "Criteria form not successfully loaded, " & _
        "Canceling Report"
        Cancel = True
    Else

        'Evaluate which option button was selected
        'Set the Filter and FilterOn properties as appropriate
        Select Case Forms!frmClientListingCriteria.optCriteria.Value
            Case 1
                Me.Filter = "City = '" & _
                    Forms!frmClientListingCriteria.cboCity & "'"
                Me.FilterOn = True
            Case 2
                Me.Filter = "StateProvince = '" & _
                    Forms!frmClientListingCriteria.cboStateProv & "'"
                Me.FilterOn = True
```

LISTING 10.18 Continued

```
        Case 3
            Me.FilterOn = False
    End Select
  End If
End Sub
```

In the example, the Record Source of the report is the qryClients query. The query returns clients in all cities and all states. The example uses the Open event of the report to filter the data to the appropriate city or state.

CAUTION

Listings 10.15 and 10.17 are much more efficient than the code in Listing 10.18. In a client/server environment, such as Microsoft SQL Server, with the code in Listings 10.15 and 10.17, only the requested data comes over the network wire. For example, only data for the requested city comes over the wire. On the other hand, the Filter property is applied *after* the data comes over the wire. This means that, in the example, all clients come over the wire, and the filter for the requested City or State is applied at the workstation. The exception to this are server-side filters. These filters are available with Access Data Projects (ADP files). ADP files are covered in *Alison Balter's Mastering Access 2002 Enterprise Development*.

Working with the Report Sort Order

The OrderBy and OrderByOn properties are similar to the Filter and FilterOn properties. They allow you to apply a sort order to the report. As with filters, three scenarios apply:

- No sort is in effect.
- The OrderBy property is set but is not in effect because the OrderByOn property is set to False.
- The order is in effect. This requires that the OrderBy property is set, and the OrderByOn property is set to True.

You can set ordering properties either at design time or at runtime. The OrderBy and OrderByOn properties are used to determine the sort order of the report and whether the sort is in effect. Listing 10.19 provides an example. The code is found in rptClientListingSorted on the sample code CD.

LISTING 10.19   Using the `Report` `Open` Event to Modify a the Sort Order of a Report

```
Private Sub Report_Open(Cancel As Integer)
    On Error Resume Next

    'Open the report sort order form
    DoCmd.OpenForm "frmClientListingSortOrder", WindowMode:=acDialog

    'Ensure that the form is loaded
    If Not IsLoaded("frmClientListingSortOrder") Then
        MsgBox "Criteria form not successfully loaded, " & _
        "Canceling Report"
        Cancel = True
    Else

        'Evaluate which option button was selected
        'Set the OrderBy and OrderByOn properties as appropriate
        Select Case Forms!frmClientListingSortOrder.optCriteria.Value
            Case 1
                Me.OrderBy = "City, CompanyName"
                Me.OrderByOn = True
            Case 2
                Me.OrderBy = "StateProvince, CompanyName"
                Me.OrderByOn = True
            Case 3
                Me.OrderBy = "CompanyName"
                Me.OrderByOn = True
        End Select
    End If
End Sub
```

The code appears in the `Open` event of the report. It evaluates which option button is selected on the frmClientListingSortOrder form. It then sets the OrderBy property as appropriate and sets the OrderByOn property to `True` so that the OrderBy property takes effect.

CAUTION

The OrderBy property *augments,* rather than replaces, the existing sort order of the report. If the OrderBy property is in conflict with the sort order of the report, the OrderBy property is ignored. For example, if the sort order in the Sorting and Grouping window is set to CompanyName and the OrderBy property is set to City combined with CompanyName, the OrderBy property is ignored.

Using the Same Report to Display Summary, Detail, or Both

Many programmers create three reports for their users: one that displays summary only, one that displays detail only, and another that displays both. This is unnecessary. Because you can hide and display report sections as necessary at runtime, you can create one report that meets all three needs. The rptClientBillingsByProject report included in the CHAP10.MDB database illustrates this point. Place the code shown in Listing 10.20 in the report's Open event.

LISTING 10.20   The Report Open Event Is Used to Hide and Show Report Sections as Appropriate

```
Private Sub Report_Open(Cancel As Integer)
    'Load the report criteria form
    DoCmd.OpenForm "frmReportDateRange", _
        WindowMode:=acDialog, _
        OpenArgs:="rptClientBillingsbyProject"

    'Ensure that the form is loaded
    If Not IsLoaded("frmReportDateRange") Then
        Cancel = True
    Else

        'Evaluate which option button is selected
        Select Case Forms!frmReportDateRange!optDetailLevel.Value

            'Modify caption and hide and show detail section and summary
            'sections as appropriate
            Case 1
                Me.Caption = Me.Caption & " - Summary Only"
                Me.lblTitle.Caption = Me.lblTitle.Caption & " - Summary Only"
                Me.Detail.Visible = False
            Case 2
                Me.Caption = Me.Caption & " - Detail Only"
                Me.lblTitle.Caption = Me.lblTitle.Caption & " - Detail Only"
                Me.GroupHeader0.Visible = False
                Me.GroupFooter1.Visible = False
                Me.txtCompanyNameDet.Visible = True
            Case 3
                Me.Caption = Me.Caption & " - Summary and Detail"
                Me.lblTitle.Caption = Me.lblTitle.Caption & " - Summary and
Detail"
                Me.txtCompanyNameDet.Visible = False
        End Select
    End If
End Sub
```

The code begins by opening frmReportDateRange included in CHAP10.MDB. (See Figure 10.2.). The form has an option group asking users whether they want a Summary report, Detail report, or report that contains both Summary and Detail. If Summary is selected, the caption of the Report window and the lblTitle label are modified, and the Visible property of the Detail section is set to False. If the user selects Detail Only, the captions of the Report window and the lblTitle label are modified, and the Visible property of the Group Header and Footer sections is set to False. A control in the Detail section containing the company name is made visible. The CompanyName control is visible in the Detail section when the Detail Only report is printed, but it's invisible when the Summary and Detail report is printed. When Both is selected as the level of detail, no sections are hidden. The captions of the Report window and the lblTitle label are modified, and the CompanyName control is hidden.

FIGURE 10.2

The criteria selection used to determine detail level.

The code behind the form's Preview button looks like Listing 10.21.

LISTING 10.21   Code That Validates the Date Range Entered by the User

```
Private Sub cmdPreview_Click()
    'Ensure that both the begin date and end date are populated
    'If not, display a message and set focus to the begin date
    If IsNull(Me.txtBeginDate) Or IsNull(Me.txtEndDate) Then
        MsgBox "You must enter both beginning and ending dates."
        Me.txtBeginDate.SetFocus

    'If begin date and end date are populated, ensure that
    'begin date is before end date
    Else
        If Me.txtBeginDate > Me.txtEndDate Then
            MsgBox "Ending date must be greater than Beginning date."
            Me.txtBeginDate.SetFocus

        'If all validations succeed, hide form, allowing report to print
        Else
```

LISTING 10.21   Continued

```
            Me.Visible = False
        End If
    End If
End Sub
```

This code makes sure that both the beginning date and the ending date are filled in, and that the beginning date comes before the ending date. If both of these rules are fulfilled, the `Visible` property of the form is set to `False`. Otherwise, an appropriate error message is displayed.

Numbering Report Items

Many people are unaware how simple it is to number the items on a report. Figure 10.3 provides an example of a numbered report. This report is called rptClientListingNumbered, and is located on the sample code CD. The process of creating such a report is extremely simple. Figure 10.4 shows the Data properties of the txtNumbering text box. The Control Source property of the text box is set to =1, and the Running Sum property is set to `Over All`. The combination of these two properties causes the report to begin numbering with the number 1 and to continue the numbering throughout the report. Setting the Running Sum property to `Over Group` causes the numbering to reset itself at the beginning of each report grouping.

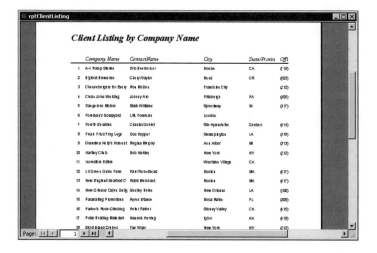

FIGURE 10.3

You can add numbering to items on a report easily.

FIGURE 10.4

The Control Source allows you to designate the starting number for a report and the Running Sum property allows you to specify when the numbering is reset to the starting value.

Printing Multiple Labels

Many times, users want to print multiple copies of the same label. The report's MoveLayout, NextRecord, PrintSection, and PrintCount properties help us to accomplish the task. The form shown in Figure 10.5 is called frmClientLabelCriteria and is found in CHAP10.MDB. It asks that the users select a company and the number of labels they want to print for that company. The code for the Print Labels command button looks like Listing 10.22.

LISTING 10.22 Code That Prints the lblClientMailingLabels Report for the Selected Company

```
Sub cmdPrintLabels_Click()
On Error GoTo Err_cmdPrintLabels_Click

    'Run the mailing labels, showing only those
    'rows where the company name matches
    'the company selected in the combo box
    DoCmd.OpenReport "lblClientMailingLabels", _
        View:=acPreview, _
        WhereCondition:="CompanyName = '" & _
            Me.cboCompanyName.Value & "'"

Exit_cmdPrintLabels_Click:
    Exit Sub

Err_cmdPrintLabels_Click:
    MsgBox Err.Description
    Resume Exit_cmdPrintLabels_Click

End Sub
```

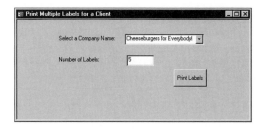

FIGURE 10.5
The criteria selection used to specify company name and number of labels to print.

Notice that the routine uses the company name selected from the combo box as a criterion to run the lblClientMailingLabels report. The Open event of lblClientMailingLabels appears in Listing 10.23.

LISTING 10.23   The Open Event Ensures That the Criteria Form Is Loaded

```
Private Sub Report_Open(Cancel As Integer)
    'Ensure that the criteria form is loaded
    'If not, display message and cancel report
    If Not IsLoaded("frmClientLabelCriteria") Then
        MsgBox "You Must Run This Report From Label Criteria Form"
        Cancel = True
    End If
End Sub
```

This code tests to make sure the frmClientLabelCriteria form is open. If it's not, the code displays a message and cancels the report. The Detail section's Print event, shown in Listing 10.24, is the key to the whole process.

LISTING 10.24   The Code in the Print Event Compares the Requested Number of Labels with the Number of Labels Printed

```
Private Sub Detail_Print(Cancel As Integer, PrintCount As Integer)
    'If the number of times the detail section has been printed is
    'less than the number of labels that has been printed,
    'cancel movement to the next row
    If PrintCount < _
        Forms!frmClientLabelCriteria!txtNumberOfLabels Then
        Me.NextRecord = False
    End If
End Sub
```

This code compares the PrintCount property to the number of labels the user wants to print. As long as the PrintCount is less than the number of labels requested, the record pointer is not advanced. This causes multiple labels to be printed for the same record.

Determining Where a Label Prints

Users often want to print several copies of the same label, but they might also want to print mailing labels in a specific position on the page. Users generally do this so that they can begin the print process on the first unused label. The frmClientLabelPosition form from CHAP10.MDB lets the user specify the first label location on which to print by designating the number of labels that the user wants to skip. (See Figure 10.6.) The Open event of the lblClientMailLabelsSkip appears in Listing 10.25.

LISTING 10.25   The Code in the Open Event of the Report Ensures That the Label frmClientLabelPosition Form Is Loaded

```
Private Sub Report_Open(Cancel As Integer)
    'Ensure that the criteria form is loaded
    'If not, display message and cancel printing
    If Not IsLoaded("frmClientLabelPosition") Then
        MsgBox "You Must Run This Report From Label Criteria Form"
        Cancel = True
    Else
        mboolFirstLabel = True
    End If
End Sub
```

FIGURE 10.6

The criteria selection used to indicate the number of labels to skip.

The code tests to make sure that the frmClientLabelPosition form is loaded. It also sets a private variable, mboolFirstLabel, equal to True. The Detail section's Print event appears in Listing 10.26.

LISTING 10.26 The `Detail Print` Event Suppresses Printing Until the Correct Number of Labels Are Skipped

```
Private Sub Detail_Print(Cancel As Integer, PrintCount As Integer)
    'Check to see if the number of times the detail section was
    'visited is less than the number of labels to skip, AND
    'that the mboolFirstLabel flag is true
    If PrintCount <= _
        Forms!frmClientLabelPosition.txtLabelsToSkip _
        And mboolFirstLabel = True Then

        'Do not move to the next record and do not print anything
        Me.NextRecord = False
        Me.PrintSection = False
    Else
        'Allow printing and turn mboolFirstLabel flag to false
        mboolFirstLabel = False
        End If
End Sub
```

This routine checks to see whether the PrintCount property of the report is less than or equal to the number of the labels to skip. It also checks to make sure that the `mboolFirstLabel` variable is equal to `True`. If both conditions are `True`, the report doesn't move to the next record and doesn't print anything. The print position is advanced. When the PrintCount becomes greater than the number of labels to skip, the `mboolFirstLabel` variable is set to `False` and printing proceeds as usual. If `mboolFirstLabel` is not set to `False`, the designated number of labels is skipped between each record. One additional event makes all this work—the `Format` event of the Report Header:

```
Private Sub ReportHeader_Format(Cancel As Integer, FormatCount As Integer)
    'Set the mboolFirstLabel flag to True when the header
    'formats for the first time
    mboolFirstLabel = True
End Sub
```

The `ReportHeader Format` event sets `mboolFirstLabel` back to `True`. You must include this step in case the user previews and then prints the labels. If the `mboolFirstLabel` variable is not reset to `True`, the selected number of labels isn't skipped on the printout because the condition that skips the labels is never met.

Building a Report from a Crosstab Query

 It's difficult to base a report on the results of a Crosstab query because its number of columns usually varies. Take a look at the example shown in Figure 10.7. Notice that the employee names appear across the top of the report as column headings, and the

products are listed down the side of the report. This report is based on the Crosstab query called qxtabEmployeeSales, part of the CHAP10EX.MDB database found on the sample code CD. (See Figure 10.8.) The problem is that the number of employees—and, therefore, column headings—can vary. This report is coded to handle such an eventuality.

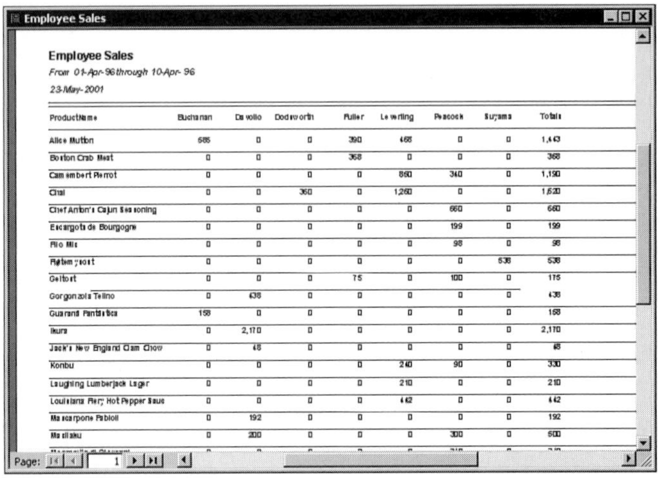

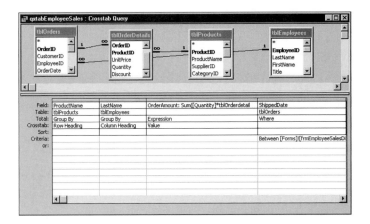

FIGURE 10.7

A report based on a Crosstab query.

FIGURE 10.8

A Crosstab query underlying a report.

When the rptEmployeeSales (located in Chap10Ex) report runs, its Open event executes (see Listing 10.27).

Listing 10.27   Code That Obtains Criteria Information for the Report and Then Builds a Recordset That Underlies the Report

```
Private Sub Report_Open(Cancel As Integer)

    'frmEmployeeSalesDialogBox form.

    Dim intX As Integer
    Dim db As DAO.Database
    Dim qdf As DAO.QueryDef
    Dim frm As Form

    Set db = CurrentDb

    'Cancel printing if frmEmployeeSalesDialogBox form isn't loaded.
    If Not (IsLoaded("frmEmployeeSalesDialogBox")) Then
        Cancel = True
        MsgBox "To preview or print this report, you must open " _
        & "EmployeeSalesDialogBox in Form view.", vbExclamation, _
        "Must Open Dialog Box"
        Exit Sub
    End If

    Set frm = Forms!frmEmployeeSalesDialogBox

    'Point at the qxtabEmployeeSales Query.
    Set qdf = db.QueryDefs("qxtabEmployeeSales")

    'Set parameters for query based on values entered
    'in EmployeeSalesDialogBox form.
    qdf.Parameters("Forms!frmEmployeeSalesDialogBox!txtBeginningDate") _
        = frm!txtBeginningDate
    qdf.Parameters("Forms!frmEmployeeSalesDialogBox!txtEndingDate") _
        = frm!txtEndingDate

    'Open Recordset object.
    Set mrstReport = qdf.OpenRecordset

    'Set a variable to hold number of columns in crosstab query.
    mintColumnCount = mrstReport.Fields.Count

End Sub
```

The Open event points a database object variable to the current database. It then checks to make sure the criteria form, frmEmployeeSalesDialogBox, is open. This form supplies the criteria for the qxtabEmployeeSales query that underlies the report. It opens the qxtabEmployeeSales query definition and passes it the parameters from the frmEmployeeSalesDialogBox criteria form. Next, it opens a recordset based on the query definition, using the criteria found on the frmEmployeeSalesDialogBox form. The number of columns returned from the Crosstab query is very important. This number is stored in a Private variable called mintColumnCount and is used throughout the remaining functions to determine how many columns to fill with data.

> **NOTE**
>
> This book focuses on the use of ADO (ActiveX Data Objects) rather than DAO (Data Access Objects). You might wonder why this example uses DAO rather than ADO. The query that underlies this example is a Crosstab query. The ADO command object does not recognize Crosstab queries. It was therefore necessary to use DAO in this example.

Next, the Report Header Format event occurs. It moves to the first record in the recordset created during the Open event (see Listing 10.28). It also calls an InitVars routine shown in Listing 10.29.

LISTING 10.28 The Report Header Format Routine Moves to the First Record in the Recordset and Calls the InitVars Routine

```
Private Sub ReportHeader3_Format(Cancel As Integer, _
FormatCount As Integer)

    'Move to first record in recordset at beginning of report
    'or when report is restarted. (A report is restarted when
    'you print a report from Print Preview window, or when you return
    'to a previous page while previewing.)
    mrstReport.MoveFirst

    'Initialize variables.
    Call InitVars

End Sub
```

The InitVars routine initializes some variables used in the report.

LISTING 10.29   The `InitVars` Routine Initializes Report Variables

```
Private Sub InitVars()

    Dim intX As Integer

    'Initialize lngReportTotal variable.
    mlngReportTotal = 0

    'Initialize array that stores column totals.
    For intX = 1 To conTotalColumns
        mlngRgColumnTotal(intX) = 0
    Next intX

End Sub
```

The `mlngReportTotal` variable is used for the report grand total (all products, all salespeople), and the `mlngRgColumnTotal` array contains the total for each salesperson. After the `Report Header Format` event occurs, the `Page Header Format` event takes place. (See Listing 10.30.)

LISTING 10.30   The Code in the `Page Header Format` Event Inserts the Appropriate Column Headings and Hides the Appropriate Controls

```
Private Sub PageHeader0_Format(Cancel As Integer, FormatCount As Integer)

    Dim intX As Integer

    'Put column headings into text boxes in page header.
    For intX = 1 To mintColumnCount
        Me("Head" + Format$(intX)) = mrstReport(intX - 1).Name
    Next intX

    'Make next available text box Totals heading.
    Me("Head" + Format$(mintColumnCount + 1)) = "Totals"

    'Hide unused text boxes in page header.
    For intX = (mintColumnCount + 2) To conTotalColumns
        Me("Head" + Format$(intX)).Visible = False
    Next intX
End Sub
```

The `PageHeader Format` event uses the names of the fields in the query results as column headings for the report. This essential routine is "smart" because, after it fills in all the column headings, it hides all the extra controls on the report.

Next, the `Detail Section Format` event, shown is Listing 10.31, occurs.

10

ADVANCED
REPORT
TECHNIQUES

LISTING 10.31   The Code in the `Detail Section Format` Event Inserts Data from the Current Row into the Report and Hides the Appropriate Controls

```
Private Sub DetailSection1_Format(Cancel As Integer, FormatCount As Integer)
 'Place values in text boxes and hide unused text boxes.

    Dim intX As Integer
    'Verify that not at end of recordset.
    If Not mrstReport.EOF Then
        'If FormatCount is 1, place values from recordset into text boxes
        'in detail section.
        If Me.FormatCount = 1 Then
            For intX = 1 To mintColumnCount
                'Convert Null values to 0.
                Me("Col" + Format(intX)) = xtabCnulls(mrstReport(intX - 1))
            Next intX

            'Hide unused text boxes in detail section.
            For intX = mintColumnCount + 2 To conTotalColumns
                Me("Col" + Format(intX)).Visible = False
            Next intX

            'Move to next record in recordset.
            mrstReport.MoveNext
        End If
    End If


End Sub
```

The `Detail Section Format` event checks the recordset's `EOF` property to determine whether the last record in the query has already been read. If not, the section's FormatCount property is tested to see whether it's equal to `1`. If so, each column in the current record of the recordset is read. The code fills each control in the Detail section with data from a column in the recordset, and any unused text boxes in the report's Detail section are hidden. Finally, the code moves to the next record in the recordset, readying the report to print the next line of detail. The `xtabCnulls` function, which converts `Null` values into zeros, is called each time the recordset underlying the report is read:

```
Private Function xtabCnulls(varX As Variant)

    'Test if a value is null.
    XtabCnulls = NZ(varX,0)


End Function
```

The `xtabCnulls` function evaluates each value sent to it to check whether the value is Null. If so, it returns zero from the function; otherwise, it returns the value passed to the function.

After the code executes the `Detail Section Format` event, it executes the `Detail Section Print` (shown in Listing 10.32).

LISTING 10.32 The Code in the `Detail Section Print` Event Accumulates Column Totals and Prints Rows Totals

```
P
rivate Sub DetailSection1_Print(Cancel As Integer, PrintCount As Integer)

    Dim intX As Integer
    Dim lngRowTotal As Long

    'If PrintCount is 1, initialize rowTotal variable.
    'Add to column totals.
    If Me.PrintCount = 1 Then
        lngRowTotal = 0

        For intX = 2 To mintColumnCount
            'Starting at column 2 (first text box with crosstab value),
            'compute total for current row in detail section.
            lngRowTotal = lngRowTotal + Me("Col" + Format(intX))
            'Add crosstab value to total for current column.
            mlngRgColumnTotal(intX) = mlngRgColumnTotal(intX) + _
                Me("Col" + Format(intX))
        Next intX

        'Place row total in text box in detail section.
        Me("Col" + Format(mintColumnCount + 1)) = lngRowTotal
        'Add row total for current row to grand total.
        mlngReportTotal = mlngReportTotal + lngRowTotal
    End If
End Sub
```

The `Detail Section Print` event generates the row total value, placing it in the last column of the report, accumulating column totals, and accumulating the `mlngReportTotal` value, which is the grand total for all columns and rows. It does this by making sure the PrintCount of the section is 1. If so, it resets the `lngRowTotal` variable to 0. Starting at column 2 (column 1 contains the product name), it begins accumulating a row total by looking at each control in the row, adding its value to `lngRowTotal`. As it traverses each column in the row, it also adds the value in each column to the appropriate element of the `mlngRgColumnTotal` private array, which maintains all the column totals for the report. It prints the row total and adds the row total to the report's grand total.

When the Retreat event occurs, the following code executes:

```
Private Sub Detail1_Retreat()

    'Always back up to previous record when Detail section retreats.
    mrstReport.MovePrevious

End Sub
```

This code forces the record pointer to move back to the previous record in the recordset. Finally, the report footer prints, which causes the Report Footer Print event, shown in Listing 10.33, to execute.

LISTING 10.33   The Code in the Report Footer Print Event Prints the Grand Totals and Hides the Appropriate Controls

```
Private Sub ReportFooter4_Print(Cancel As Integer, PrintCount As Integer)

    Dim intX As Integer

    'Place column totals in text boxes in report footer.
    'Start at column 2 (first text box with crosstab value).
    For intX = 2 To mintColumnCount
        Me("Tot" + Format(intX)) = mlngRgColumnTotal(intX)
    Next intX

    'Place grand total in text box in report footer.
    Me("Tot" + Format(mintColumnCount + 1)) = mlngReportTotal

    'Hide unused text boxes in report footer.
    For intX = mintColumnCount + 2 To conTotalColumns
        Me("Tot" + Format(intX)).Visible = False
    Next intX
End Sub
```

The Report Footer Print event loops through each control in the footer, populating each control with the appropriate element of the mlngRgColumnTotal array. This gives you the column totals for the report. Finally, the grand total is printed in the next available column. Any extra text boxes are hidden from display.

Printing the First and Last Page Entries in the Page Header

 Another useful technique is printing the first and last entries from a page in the report's header. The rptCustomerPhoneList report, found in the CHAP10EX.MDB database located on the sample code CD, illustrates this. (See Figure 10.9.) The code for this report relies on Access making two passes through the report. During the first pass, a variable called gboolLastPage is equal to False. The gboolLastPage variable becomes True only when the Report Footer Format event is executed at the end of the first pass through the report. Keep this in mind as you review the code behind the report.

FIGURE 10.9

The first and last entry printed in the report header.

The first routine that affects the report processing is the Page Header Format event routine shown in Listing 10.34.

LISTING 10.34 The Code in the Page Header Format Event Updates the Appropriate Text Boxes with the First and Last Entries on the Page

```
Private Sub PageHeader0_Format(Cancel As Integer, FormatCount As Integer)

    'During second pass, fill in FirstEntry and LastEntry text boxes.
    If gboolLastPage = True Then
        Reports!rptCustomerPhoneList.txtFirstEntry = _
            Reports!rptCustomerPhoneList.txtCompanyName
```

LISTING 10.34   Continued

```
        Reports!rptCustomerPhoneList.txtLastEntry = _
            gstrLast(Reports!rptCustomerPhoneList.Page)
    End If

End Sub
```

The `Page Header Format` routine tests to see whether the `gboolLastPage` variable is equal to `True`. During the first pass through the report, the `gboolLastPage` variable is equal to `False`. During the second pass, the `txtFirstEntry` and `txtLastEntry` text boxes (both of which appear in the report's header) are populated with data. The `txtFirstEntry` text box is filled with the value in the `txtCompanyName` control of the current record (the first record on the page), and the `txtLastEntry` text box is populated with the appropriate element number from the `CustomerPhoneList` array. Each element of the `CustomerPhoneList` array is populated by the `Format` event of the Page Footer for that page during the first pass through the report.

Next, the `Page Footer Format` event is executed (see Listing 10.35).

LISTING 10.35   The Code in the `Page Footer Format` Event Populates the Array with the Last Entry on a Page

```
Private Sub PageFooter2_Format(Cancel As Integer, FormatCount As Integer)

    'During first pass, increase size of array and enter last record on
    'page into array.
    If Not gboolLastPage Then
        ReDim Preserve gstrLast(Reports!rptCustomerPhoneList.Page + 1)
        gstrLast(Reports!rptCustomerPhoneList.Page) = _
            Reports!rptCustomerPhoneList.txtCompanyName
    End If

End Sub
```

The `Page Footer Format` event determines whether the `gboolLastPage` variable is equal to `False`. If so (which it is during the first pass through the report), the code redimensions the `gstrLast` array to add an element. The value from the `txtCompanyName` control of the last record on the page is stored in the new element of the `gstrLast` array. This value eventually appears in the Page Header of that page as the last company name that appears on the page. Finally, the `Report Footer Format` event executes as shown in Listing 10.36.

LISTING 10.36   The Code in the `Report Footer Format` Event Inserts Data from the Last Row in the Recordset into the Last Element of the Array

```
Private Sub ReportFooter4_Format(Cancel As Integer, _
FormatCount As Integer)

    Dim rst As ADODB.Recordset
    Set rst = New ADODB.Recordset

    'Set flag after first pass has been completed.
    gboolLastPage = True

    'Open recordset for report.
    rst.Open "tblCustomers", CurrentProject.Connection, adOpenStatic

    'Move to last record in recordset.
    rst.MoveLast

    'Enter last record into array.
    ReDim Preserve gstrLast(Reports!rptCustomerPhoneList.Page + 1)
    gstrLast(Reports!rptCustomerPhoneList.Page) = rst!CompanyName

End Sub
```

The `Report Footer` routine sets the `gboolLastPage` variable equal to `True` and opens a recordset based on the Customers table. This is the recordset on which the report is based. It moves to the last record in the recordset and adds the `CompanyName` value from the recordset's last record in an additional element of the array.

Now the first pass of the report has finished. As the user moves to each page of the report during a print preview, or as each page is printed to the printer, the `Format` event executes for the Page Header. The company name from the first record on the page is placed in the `txtFirstEntry` control, and the appropriate element from the `gstrLast` array is placed in the `txtLastEntry` control.

Creating a Multifact Crosstab Report

 By nature, Crosstab queries are limited because they don't allow you to place multiple rows of data in the result. For example, you can't display months as column headings and then show the minimum, average, and maximum sales for each employee as row headings. The rptSalesAverages report, found in the Chap10Ex database, and shown in Figure 10.10, solves this problem.

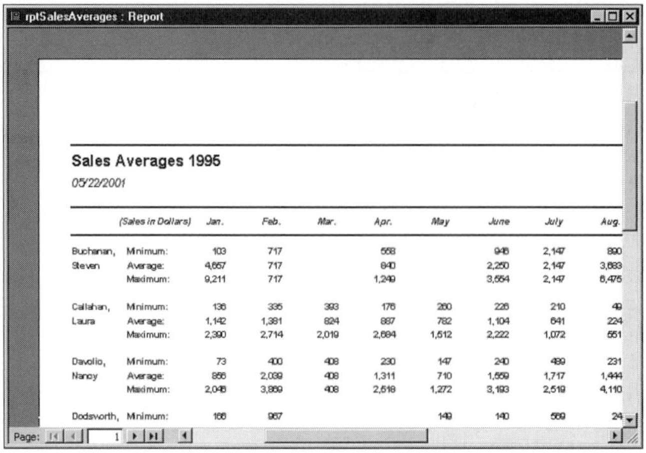

FIGURE 10.10

An example of a multifact crosstab report.

Each time the Format event of the Page Header executes, the variable mboolPrintWhat, is reset to False:

```
Private Sub PageHeader1_Format(Cancel As Integer, FormatCount As Integer)

    'At top of page, initialize mboolPrintWhat variable to False
    mboolPrintWhat = False

End Sub
```

After the Page Header Format event executes, the Group Header Format event launches, as shown in Listing 10.36.

LISTING 10.36 The Code in the Group Header Format Event Hides and Shows the Appropriate Controls

```
Private Sub GroupHeader2_Format(Cancel As Integer, _
FormatCount As Integer)

    'Print SalespersonLastName and FirstName text boxes,
    'hide Minimum, Average, and Maximum labels,
    'set mboolPrintWhat variable to True, and don't advance to next record.
    With Me
        If mboolPrintWhat = False Then
            .txtSalespersonLastName.Visible = True
            .txtFirstName.Visible = True
            .lblMinimum.Visible = False
```

LISTING 10.36   Continued

```
            .lblAverage.Visible = False
            .lblMaximum.Visible = False
            mboolPrintWhat = True
            .NextRecord = False

        'Hide SalespersonLastName and FirstName text boxes,
        'print Minimum, Average, and Maximum labels,
        'and set mboolPrintWhat variable to False
        Else
            .txtSalespersonLastName.Visible = False
            .txtFirstName.Visible = False
            .lblMinimum.Visible = True
            .lblAverage.Visible = True
            .lblMaximum.Visible = True
            mboolPrintWhat = False
        End If
    End With
End Sub
```

The first time the Format event for LastName Group Header (GroupHeader2) executes, the value of the mboolPrintWhat variable is equal to False. The txtSalesPersonLastName and the txtFirstName controls are made visible, and the lblMinimum, lblAverage, and lblMaximum controls are hidden. The mboolPrintWhat variable is set to True, and movement to the next record is suppressed by setting the value of the NextRecord property to False.

The second time the Format event for the LastName Group Header executes, the txtSalespersonLastName and txtFirstName controls are hidden. The lblMinimum, lblAverage, and lblMaximum controls are made visible, and the value of the mboolPrintWhat variable is reset to False.

The only other code for the report, shown in Listing 10.37, is in the Format event of the Shipped Date Header (GroupHeader3).

LISTING 10.37   The Code in the Group Header Format Event Determines When Printing Occurs

```
Private Sub GroupHeader3_Format(Cancel As Integer, _
FormatCount As Integer)
    'Print data in correct column.

    'Don't advance to next record or print next section.
    If Me.Left < Me.txtLeftMargin + _
        (Month(Me.txtShippedDate) + 1) _
```

LISTING 10.37   Continued

```
            * Me.txtColumnWidth Then
            Me.NextRecord = False
            Me.PrintSection = False
        End If
End Sub
```

This code compares the report's Left property to the result of an expression. The Left property is the amount that the current section is offset from the page's left edge. This number is compared with the value in the `txtLeftMargin` control added to the current month plus one, and then it's multiplied by the value in the `txtColumnWidth` control. If this expression evaluates to `True`, the NextRecord and PrintSection properties of the report are both set to `False`. This causes the printer to move to the next printing position, but to remain on the same record and not print anything, which forces a blank space in the report. You might wonder what the complicated expression is all about. Simply put, it's an algorithm that makes sure printing occurs, and that Access moves to the next record only when the data is ready to print.

PRACTICAL EXAMPLES

Report Techniques Used by the Hypothetical Time and Billing Application

Almost every report in the Time and Billing application implements at least one of the techniques discussed in this chapter. In fact, the rptClientListing, rptClientBillingsByProject, lblClientMailingLabels, and lblClientMailingLabelsSkip reports discussed in this chapter are an integral part of the Time and Billing application.

One report not covered in the chapter is the rptEmployeeBillingsByProject report. This report has the following code in its `NoData` event:

```
Private Sub Report_NoData(Cancel As Integer)
    'If no data in the RecordSource underlying the report,
    'display a message and cancel printing
    MsgBox "There is no data for this report. Canceling report..."
    Cancel = True
End Sub
```

If there's no data in the report's `RecordSource`, a message box is displayed, and the report is canceled. The `Open` event of the report looks like this:

```
Private Sub Report_Open(Cancel As Integer)
    'Open the criteria form
    DoCmd.OpenForm "frmReportDateRange", _
```

```
        WindowMode:=acDialog, _
        OpenArgs:="Employee Billings by Project"

    'If the criteria form is not loaded, cancel printing
    If Not IsLoaded("frmReportDateRange") Then
        Cancel = True
    End If
End Sub
```

The report's Open event opens a form called frmReportDateRange. (See Figure 10.11.) This form is required because it supplies criteria to the query underlying the report. If the form isn't loaded successfully, the report is canceled.

FIGURE 10.11

A criteria selection form.

Finally, the report's Close event looks like this:

```
Private Sub Report_Close()
    'Close the criteria form when the report closes
    DoCmd.Close acForm, "frmReportDateRange"
End Sub
```

The report cleans up after itself by closing the criteria form.

Summary

To take full advantage of what the Access reporting tool has to offer, you must understand—and be able to work with—report and section events. This chapter has gone through the report and section events, giving you detailed examples of when to use each event.

In addition to the report events, several special properties are available to you only at runtime. By manipulating these properties, you can have more control over your reports' behavior. After covering the report and section events, this chapter covered the properties you can manipulate only at runtime. Examples highlighted the appropriate use of each property.

There are many tips and tricks of the trade that help you do things you might otherwise think are impossible to accomplish. This chapter gave you several practical examples of these tips and tricks, making it easy for you to use them in your own application development.

10

ADVANCED
REPORT
TECHNIQUES

Advanced Query Techniques

IN THIS CHAPTER

Why This Chapter Is Important

You learned the basics of query design in Chapter 4, "What Every Developer Needs to Know About Query Basics," but Access has a wealth of query capabilities. In addition to the relatively simple `Select` queries covered in Chapter 4, you can create Crosstab queries, Union queries, Self-Join queries, and many other complex selection queries. You can also easily build Access queries that modify information, rather than retrieve it. This chapter covers these topics and the more advanced aspects of query design.

Action Queries

With Action queries, you can easily modify data without writing any code. In fact, using Action queries is often a more efficient method than using code. Four types of action queries are available: Update, Delete, Append, and Make Table. You use Update queries to modify data in a table, Delete queries to remove records from a table, Append queries to add records to an existing table, and Make Table queries to create an entirely new table. Each type of query and its appropriate uses are explained in the following sections.

Update Queries

Update queries are used to modify all records or any records meeting specific criteria. An Update query can be used to modify the data in one field or several fields (or even tables) at one time (for example, a query that increases the salary of everyone in California by 10%). As mentioned, using Update queries is usually more efficient than performing the same task with VBA code, so they're considered a respectable way to modify table data.

To build an Update query, follow these steps:

1. Click Queries in the Objects list from the Database window.

2. Double-click the Create Query in Design view icon.

3. In the Show Table dialog box, select the tables or queries that will participate in the Update query and click Add. Click Close when you're ready to continue.

4. To let Access know you're building an Update query, open the Query Type drop-down list on the toolbar and select Update Query. You can also choose Query|Update Query from the menu.

5. Add fields to the query that will either be used for criteria or be updated as a result of the query. In Figure 11.1, StateProvince has been added to the query grid because it will be used as a criterion for the update. DefaultRate has been included because it's the field that's being updated.

6. Add any further criteria, if you want. In Figure 11.1, the criterion for StateProvince has been set to CA.

7. Add the appropriate Update expression. In Figure 11.1, the DefaultRate is being increased by 10%.

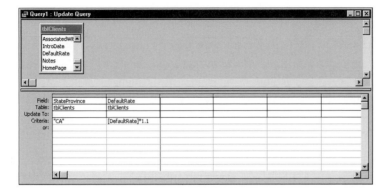

FIGURE 11.1

An Update query that increases the DefaultRate for all clients in California.

8. Click Run on the toolbar. The message box shown in Figure 11.2 appears. (See the section "Special Notes About Action Queries" later in this chapter for how to suppress this message by programming.) Click Yes to continue. All records meeting the selected criteria are updated.

FIGURE 11.2

The confirmation message you see when running an Update query.

Access Update queries should be named with the prefix qupd. To adhere to standard naming conventions, each type of Action query should be given a prefix indicating what type of query it is. Table 11.1 lists all the proper prefixes for Action queries.

TABLE 11.1 Naming Prefixes for Action Queries

Type of Query	Prefix	Example
Update	qupd	qupdDefaultRate
Delete	qdel	qdelOldTimeCards
Append	qapp	qappArchiveTimeCards
Make Table	qmak	qmakTempSales

All Access queries are stored as SQL (Structured Query Language) statements. (Access SQL is discussed later in this chapter in the "Understanding SQL" section.) You can display the SQL for a query by selecting SQL view from the View drop-down on the toolbar. The SQL behind an Access Update query looks like this:

```
UPDATE tblClients SET tblClients._
    DefaultRate = [DefaultRate]*1.1
      WHERE (((tblClients.StateProvince)="CA"));
```

Delete Queries

Rather than simply modify table data, Delete queries permanently removes from a table any records meeting specific criteria; they're often used to remove old records. You might want to delete all orders from the previous year, for example.

To build a Delete query, follow these steps:

1. While in a query's Design view, use the Query Type drop-down list on the toolbar to select Delete Query. You can also choose Query|Delete Query from the menu.

2. Add the criteria you want to the query grid. The query shown in Figure 11.3 deletes all time cards more than 365 days old.

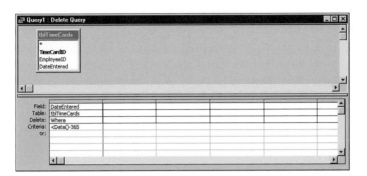

FIGURE 11.3

A Delete query used to delete all time cards entered more than a year ago.

3. Click Run on the toolbar. The message box shown in Figure 11.4 appears. You can suppress this message using the programming techniques explained later in the section "Special Notes About Action Queries."

FIGURE 11.4

The Delete query confirmation message box.

4. Click Yes to permanently remove the records from the table.

The SQL behind a Delete query looks like this:

```
DELETE tblTimeCards.DateEntered
    FROM tblTimeCards
    WHERE (((tblTimeCards.DateEntered)<Date()-365));
```

NOTE

It's often useful to view the results of an Action query before you actually change the records included in the criteria. To view the records affected by the Action query, click the Query view button on the toolbar before you select Run. All records that will be affected by the Action query appear in Datasheet view. If necessary, you can temporarily add key fields to the query to get more information about these records.

CAUTION

Remember that if the Cascade Delete Related Records Referential Integrity setting is turned on, all corresponding records in related tables are deleted. If the Cascade Delete Related Records option isn't turned on and referential integrity is being enforced, the Delete query doesn't allow the offending records to be deleted. If you want to delete the records on the one side of the relationship, first you need to delete all the related records on the many side.

Append Queries

With Append queries, you can add records to an existing table. This is often done during an archive process. First, the records to be archived are appended to the history table by using an Append query. Next, they're removed from the master table by using a Delete query.

To build an Append query, follow these steps:

1. While in Design view of a query, use the Query Type drop-down list on the toolbar to select Append Query or choose Query|Append Query from the menu. The dialog box shown in Figure 11.5 appears.

FIGURE 11.5

Identifying the table to which data will be appended and the database containing that table.

2. Select the table to which you want the data appended.

3. Drag all the fields whose data you want included in the second table to the query grid. If the field names in the two tables match, Access automatically matches the field names in the source table to the corresponding field names in the destination table. (See Figure 11.6.) If the field names in the two tables don't match, you need to explicitly designate which fields in the source table match which fields in the destination table.

4. Enter any criteria in the query grid. Notice in Figure 11.6 that all records with a DateEntered in 1995 are appended to the destination table.

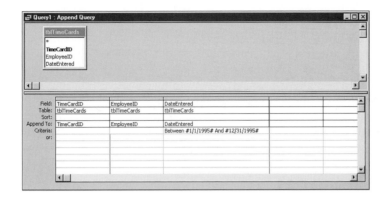

FIGURE 11.6

An Append query that appends the TimeCardID, EmployeeID, and DateEntered of all employees entered in the year 1995 to another table.

5. To run the query, click Run on the toolbar. The message box shown in Figure 11.7 appears.

FIGURE 11.7

The Append Query confirmation message box.

6. Click Yes to finish the process.

The SQL behind an Append query looks like this:

```
INSERT INTO tblTimeCardsArchive ( TimeCardID, EmployeeID, DateEntered )
    SELECT tblTimeCards.TimeCardID, tblTimeCards.EmployeeID,
    tblTimeCards.DateEntered
    FROM tblTimeCards
    WHERE (((tblTimeCards.DateEntered) Between #1/1/95# And #12/31/95#));
```

CAUTION

Append queries don't allow you to introduce any primary key violations. If you're appending any records that duplicate a primary key value, the message box shown in Figure 11.8 appears. If you go ahead with the append process, only those records without primary key violations are appended to the destination table.

FIGURE 11.8

The warning message you see when an Append query and conversion, primary key, lock, or validation rule violation occurs.

Make Table Queries

An Append query adds records to an existing table, but a Make Table query creates a new table, which is often a temporary table used for intermediary processing. A temporary table is frequently created to freeze data while a report is being run. By building temporary tables and running the report from those tables, you make sure users can't modify the data underlying the report during the reporting process. Another common use of a Make Table query is to supply a subset of fields or records to another user.

To build a Make Table query, follow these steps:

1. While in the query's Design view, use the Query Type drop-down list on the toolbar to select Make Table Query or choose Query|Make Table Query from the menu. The dialog box shown in Figure 11.9 appears.

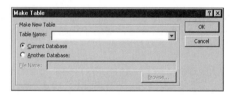

FIGURE 11.9

Enter a name for the new table and select which database to place it in.

2. Enter the name of the new table and click OK.

3. Move all the fields you want included in the new table to the query grid. The result of an expression is often included in the new table. (See Figure 11.10.)

4. Add the criteria you want to the query grid.

5. Click Run on the toolbar to run the query. The message shown in Figure 11.11 appears.

6. Click Yes to finish the process.

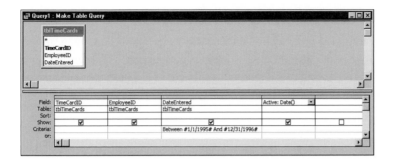

FIGURE 11.10
Add an expression to a Make Table query.

FIGURE 11.11
The Make Table query confirmation message box

CAUTION

If you try to run the same Make Table query more than one time, the table with the same name as the table you're creating is permanently deleted. (See the warning message in Figure 11.12.)

FIGURE 11.12
The Make Table query warning message displayed when a table already exists with the same name as the table to be created.

The SQL for a Make Table query looks like this:

```
SELECT tblTimeCards.TimeCardID, tblTimeCards.EmployeeID,
    tblTimeCards.DateEntered, [DateEntered]+365 AS ArchiveDate
    INTO tblOldTimeCards
    FROM tblTimeCards
    WHERE (((tblTimeCards.TimeCardID) Between 1 And 10));
```

Special Notes About Action Queries

Additional warning messages, such as the one shown in Figure 11.13, appear when you're running Action queries from the Database window or using code. This message, and all other query messages, can be suppressed programmatically by using the `SetWarnings` method of the `DoCmd` object. The code looks like this:

```
DoCmd.SetWarnings False
```

CAUTION

I strongly suggest that `Docmd.SetWarnings True` be used to restore the warning messages immediately after running your Action query. Failure to do so could result in accidental deletion or alteration of data at some later time, without any warning.

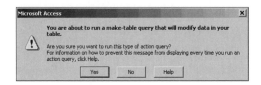

FIGURE 11.13

A warning message you might see when running an Action query from code.

To suppress warnings by modifying the Access environment, choose Tools|Options and click the Edit/Find tab. Remove the check mark from the Action Queries Confirm check box.

NOTE

There's a major difference between suppressing warnings by using the `DoCmd` object and doing so by choosing Tools|Options. Suppressing warnings by using the `DoCmd` object centralizes control within the application. On the other hand, using Tools| Options to suppress warnings affects all applications run by a particular user.

Using Action Queries Versus Processing Records with Code

As mentioned, Action queries can be far more efficient than VBA code. Take a look at this example:

```
Sub ModifyRate()
    Dim rst As ADODB.Recordset

    Set rst = New ADODB.Recordset

    With rst
        .CursorType = adOpenKeyset
        .LockType = adLockOptimistic
        .Open "tblEmployees", CurrentProject.Connection

        Do Until .EOF
            !BillingRate = !BillingRate + 1
            .Update
            .MoveNext
        Loop
    End With
End Sub
```

This subroutine uses ADO code to loop through tblEmployees. It increases the billing rate
by 1. Compare the ModifyRate subroutine to the following code:

```
Sub RunActionQuery()
    DoCmd.OpenQuery "qupdBillingRate"
End Sub
```

As you can see, the RunActionQuery subroutine is much easier to code. The qupdBillingRate
query, shown in Figure 11.14, performs the same tasks as the ModifyRate subroutine. In most
cases, the Action query runs more efficiently.

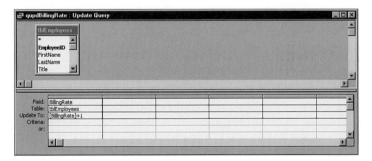

FIGURE 11.14

The qupdBillingRate *query increments the BillingRate by 1.*

> **NOTE**
>
> An alternative to the two techniques shown previously is to use ADO code (rather than
> the DoCmd object) to execute an Action query. This is covered in detail in Chapter 14,
> "What Are ActiveX Data Objects and Data Access Objects, and Why Are They Important?"

Special Query Properties

Access 2002 queries have several properties that can dramatically change their behavior. To look up a query's properties, right-click on a blank area in the top half of the Query window and select Properties to open the Properties window. (See Figure 11.15.) Many of these properties are discussed in Chapter 4, but Unique Values, Unique Records, and Top Values are covered in the following sections.

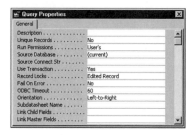

FIGURE 11.15

Viewing the general properties for a query.

Unique Values

When sent to Yes, the Unique Values property causes the query output to contain no duplicates for the combination of fields included in it. Figure 11.16, for example, shows a query that includes the Country and City fields from tblClients. The Unique Values property in this example is set to No, its default value. Notice that many combinations of countries and cities appear more than once. This happens whenever more than one client is found in a particular country and city. Compare this with Figure 11.17, in which the Unique Values property is set to Yes. Each combination of country and city appears only once.

Unique Records

In Access 2000 and Access 2002, the default value for the Unique Records property is No. Setting it to Yes causes the DISTINCTROW statement to be included in the SQL statement underlying the query. When set to Yes, the Unique Records property denotes that only unique rows in the recordset underlying the query are included in the query result—and not just unique rows based on the fields in the query result. The Unique Records property applies only to multitable queries; it's ignored for queries that include only one table.

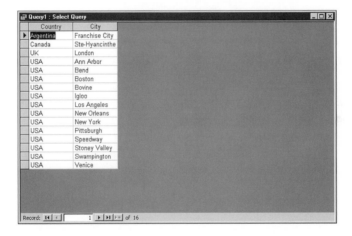

FIGURE 11.16

A query with the Unique Values property set to No.

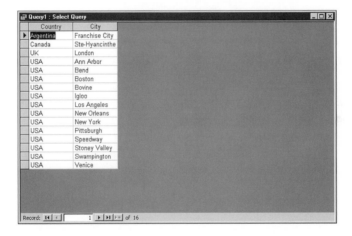

FIGURE 11.17

A query with the Unique Values property set to Yes.

Top Values

The Top Values property enables you to specify a certain percentage or a specific number of
records that the user wants to view in the query result. For example, you can build a query that
outputs the country/city combinations with the top 10 sales amounts. You can also build a
query that shows the country/city combinations whose sales rank in the top 50%. You can
specify the Top Values property in a few different ways. Here are two examples:

- Click the Top Values combo box on the toolbar and choose from the predefined list of choices (this combo box is not available for certain field types).

- Type a number or a number with a percent sign directly into the Top Values property in the Query Properties window, or select one of the predefined entries from the drop-down list for the property.

Figure 11.18 illustrates the design of a query showing the companies with the top 25% of sales. This Total query summarizes the result of the BillableHours multiplied by the BillingRate for each company. Notice that the Top Values property is set to 25%. The output of the query is sorted in descending order by the result of the TotalAmount calculation. (See Figure 11.19.) If the SaleAmount field were sorted in ascending order, the bottom 10% of the sales amount would be displayed in the query result. Remember that the field(s) being used to determine the top values must appear as the left-most field(s) in the query's sort order.

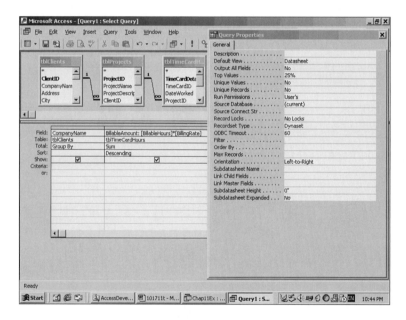

FIGURE 11.18

A Total query that retrieves the top 25% of the billable amounts.

Company Name	BillableAmount
▶ White Clover Markets	$6,380.00
Wordgame Publications	$4,660.00
New England Seafood Cannery	$3,795.00
Dangerous Motors	$2,550.00
New Orleans Cajun Delights	$1,905.00

FIGURE 11.19

The result of a Total query showing the top 25% of the billable amounts.

NOTE

You might be surprised to discover that the Top Values property doesn't always seem to accurately display the correct number of records in the query result. All records with values that match the value in the last record are returned as part of the query result. In a table with 100 records, for example, the query asks for the top 10 values. Twelve records will appear in the query result if the 10th, 11th, and 12th records all have the same value in the field being used to determine the top value.

Optimizing Queries

The Microsoft Jet Engine includes an Optimizer that looks at how long it takes to perform each task needed to produce the required query results. It then produces a plan for the shortest path to get the results that you want. This plan is based on several statistics:

- The amount of data in each table included in the query
- How many data pages are in each table
- The location of each table included in the query
- What indexes are available in each table
- Which indexes are unique
- Other statistics

Understanding the Query Compilation Process

The statistics just listed are updated whenever the query is compiled. For a query to be compiled, it must be flagged as needing to be compiled. The flag can be any of the following occurrences:

- Changes are saved to the query.
- Changes are saved to any tables underlying a query.
- The database is compacted.

After a query has been flagged as needing to be compiled, it isn't compiled until the next time the query is run. During compiling, which takes one to four seconds, all statistics are updated, and a new optimization or Query Plan is produced.

NOTE

Because a Query Plan is based on the number of records in each table included in the query, you should open and save your queries each time the volume of data in a table changes significantly. This is especially true when you're moving your query from a test environment to a production environment. If you test your application with a few records in each table and the table's production data soon grows to thousands of records, your query will be optimized for only a few records and won't run efficiently. I handle this problem by compacting the production database on a regular basis.

Analyzing a Query's Performance

When you're analyzing the time it takes for a particular query to run, it's important to time two tasks:

- How long it takes for the first screen of data to display
- How long it takes to get the last record in the query result

The first measurement is fairly obvious; it measures the amount of time it takes from the moment the Run button is clicked on the toolbar until the first screen of data is displayed. The second measurement is a little less obvious; it involves waiting until the N value in Record 1 of N displays at the bottom of the query result. The two measurements might be the same, if the query returns only a small number of records. The Jet Engine decides whether it's more efficient to run the query and then display the query results, or to display partial query results while the query continues to run in the background.

TIP

The Performance Analyzer can analyze your queries to determine whether additional indexes will improve query performance. It's important to run the Performance Analyzer with the same volume of data that will be present in the production version of your tables. The Performance Analyzer is covered in Chapter 17, "Optimizing Your Application."

Things You Can Do to Improve a Query's Performance

You can do many things to improve a query's performance. These include, but aren't limited to, the following techniques:

- Index fields on both sides of a join. If you establish a permanent relationship between two tables, the foreign key index is automatically created for you.

- Add to the query grid only the fields you actually need in the query results. If a field is required for criteria, but it doesn't need to appear in the query result, clear the Show check box on the query grid.

- Add indexes for any fields that you are using in the sort order of the query result.

- Always index on fields used in the criteria of the query.

- Compact the database often. During compacting, Access tries to reorganize a table's records so that they reside in adjacent database pages, ordered by the table's primary key. The query plans are also rebuilt, based on the current amount of data. These side effects of the compacting process improve performance when the table is being scanned during a query.

- When running a multitable query, test to see whether the query runs faster with the criteria placed on the one side or the many side of the join.

- Avoid adding criteria to calculated or nonindexed fields.

- Select the smallest field types possible for each field. For example, create a Long Integer CustID field rather than specifying the CompanyName field as the primary key for the table.

- Avoid calculated fields in nested queries. It's always preferable to add calculations to the higher-level queries.

- Rather than including all expressions in the query, consider placing some expressions in the control source of form and report controls. If you do this, the expression will need to be repeated and maintained on each form and report.

- Use Make Table queries to build tables out of query results based on tables that rarely change. In a State table, for example, rather than displaying a unique list of states based on all the states currently included in the Customer table, build a separate State table and use that in your queries.

- When using `Like` in the query criteria, try to place the asterisk at the end of the character string rather than at the beginning. When the asterisk is placed at the end of a string, as in `Like Th*`, an index can be used to improve query performance. If the asterisk is placed at the beginning of a string, as in `Like *Sr`, no index can be used.

- Use `Count(*)` rather than `Count([fieldname])` when counting how many records meet a particular set of criteria. `Count(*)` simply tallies up the total number of records, but `Count([fieldname])` actually checks to see whether the value is `Null`, which would exclude the record from the total computation. Furthermore, as mentioned in the next section on Rushmore technology, the `Count(*)` function is highly optimized by Rushmore.

- Use `Group By` as little as possible. When possible, use `First` instead. For example, if you're totaling sales information by order date and order number, you can use `First` for the order date and group by order number. This is because all records for a given order number automatically occur on the same order date.

- Use Rushmore technology to speed query performance whenever possible. Rushmore technology—a data-access technology "borrowed" from Microsoft's FoxPro PC database engine—improves the performance of certain queries. Rushmore technology is discussed in the following section.

Probably one of the most important things to learn about the tips listed here is that they shouldn't be followed blindly. Query optimization is an art rather than a science. What helps in some situations might actually do harm in others, so it's important to perform benchmarks with your actual system and data.

Rushmore Technology

As mentioned, Rushmore is a data-access technology that can help improve processing queries. Rushmore technology can be used only when certain types of expressions are included in the query criteria. It won't automatically speed up all your queries. A query must be constructed in a certain way for the query to benefit from Rushmore.

Rushmore can optimize a query with an expression and a comparison operator as the criteria for an Indexed field. The comparison operator must be <, >, =, <=, >=, <>, `Between`, `Like`, or `In`.

The expression can be any valid expression, including constants, functions, and fields from other tables. Here are some examples of expressions that can be optimized:

```
[Age] > 50
[OrderDate] Between #1/1/98# And #12/31/98#
[State] = "CA"
```

Rushmore can also be used to optimize queries that include complex expressions combining the `And` and `Or` operators. If both expressions can be fully optimized, the query will be fully optimized. However, if only one expression can be fully optimized, and the expressions are combined with an `And`, the query will be partially optimized. If only one expression can be fully optimized, and the expressions are combined with an `Or`, the query won't be optimized.

Important Notes About Rushmore

You should remember a few important concepts about Rushmore:

- Queries containing the Not operator can't be optimized.

- The Count(*) function is highly optimized by Rushmore.

- Descending indexes cannot be used by Rushmore unless the expression is =.

- Queries on ODBC data sources can't use Rushmore.

- Rushmore can use multifield indexes only when the criteria is in the order of the index. For example, if an index exists for the LastName field in combination with the FirstName field, the index can be used to search on LastName or on a combination of LastName and FirstName, but it can't be used in an expression based on the FirstName field.

Crosstab Queries

A Crosstab query summarizes query results by displaying one field in a table down the left side of the datasheet and additional facts across the top of the datasheet. A Crosstab query can, for example, summarize the dollars sold by a salesperson to each company. The name of each company can be placed in the query output's left-most column, and each salesperson can be displayed across the top. The dollars sold appear in the appropriate cell of the query output. (See Figure 11.20.)

Company Name	Balter, Dan	Callahan, Laura	Davolio, Nancy	Fuller, Andrew	Leverling, Janel
A-1 Rump Steaks				$8,500.00	
Bigfoot Breweries			$2,500.00		$4,000.00
Cheeseburgers for Everybody!	$250,000.00				
Clean Joins Welding					
Dangerous Motors				$2,000.00	
Foreman's Scrapyard		$700.00			
Forets d'erables			$3,700.00		
Fresh Fried Frog Legs					$5,250.00
Grandma Kelly's Homestead					
Hartley Clinic		$2,500.00			
Li'l Green Onion Farm					
New England Seafood Cannery	$30,000.00	$5,000.00			
New Orleans Cajun Delights	$15,000.00		$3,000.00		
Parasailing Promotions	$2,700.00				
Parker's Rock-Climbing Adventu		$2,400.00			
Polar Building Materials	$3,000.00				
Skull Island Cruises		$0.00			

FIGURE 11.20

An example of a Crosstab query that shows the dollars sold to each company by salesperson.

Crosstab queries are probably one of the most complex and difficult queries to create. For this reason, Microsoft offers a Crosstab Query Wizard. The methods for creating a Crosstab query with and without the Crosstab Query Wizard are explained in the following sections.

Creating a Crosstab Query with the Crosstab Query Wizard

Follow these steps to design a Crosstab query with the Crosstab Query Wizard:

1. Select Queries from the Objects list in the Database window and click New.

2. Select Crosstab Query Wizard and click OK.

3. Select the table or query that will act as a foundation for the query. If you want to include fields from more than one table in the query, you'll need to base the Crosstab query on another query that has the tables and fields you want. Click Next.

4. Select the fields whose values you want to use as the row headings for the query output. In Figure 11.21, the ProductName and CustomerID fields are selected as the row headings. Click Next.

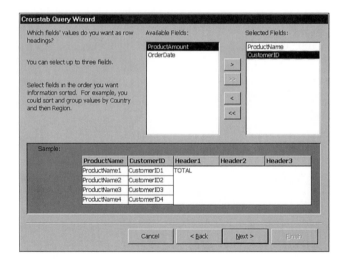

FIGURE 11.21

Specifying the rows of a Crosstab query.

5. Select the field whose values you want to use as the column headings for the query output. In Figure 11.22, the OrderDate field is selected as the column heading. Click Next.

6. If the field you selected for a heading is a Date field, the Crosstab Query Wizard asks that you specify the interval you want to group by. In Figure 11.23, the OrderDate field is grouped by quarter. Select the desired date interval and click Next.

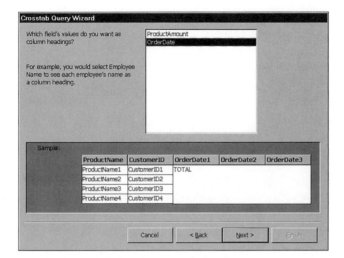

FIGURE 11.22
Specifying the columns of a Crosstab query.

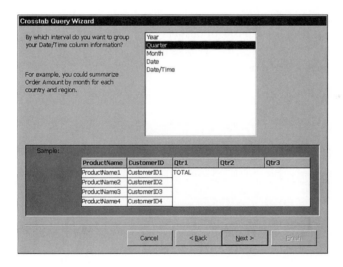

FIGURE 11.23
Specifying the interval for a Date field of a Crosstab query.

7. The Crosstab Query Wizard asks you to specify what field stores the number you want to use to calculate the value for each column and row intersection. In Figure 11.24, the ProductAmount field is totaled by quarter for each product and customer. Click Next.

8. Specify a name for your query. When you're finished, click Finish.

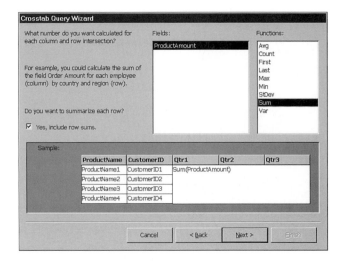

FIGURE 11.24

Specifying the field you want the Crosstab query to use for calculating.

Figure 11.25 shows a completed Crosstab query in Design view; take a look at several important attributes. Notice the Crosstab row of the query grid. The ProductName and CustomerID fields are specified as row headings and are used as Group By columns for the query. The following expression is included as a column heading:

```
"Qtr" & Format([OrderDate], "q")
```

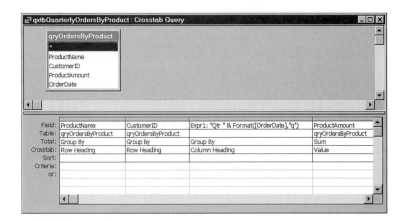

FIGURE 11.25

A completed Crosstab query in Design view.

This expression returns the order date formatted to display only the quarter. This expression is also used as a Group By for the query. The ProductAmount is specified as a value. The Total cell for the column indicates that this field will be summed (as opposed to being counted, averaged, and so on).

Notice the column labeled Total of ProductAmount. This column displays the total of all the columns in the query. It's identical to the column containing the value except for the alias in the field name and the fact that the Crosstab cell is set to Row Heading rather than Value, as shown in Figure 11.26.

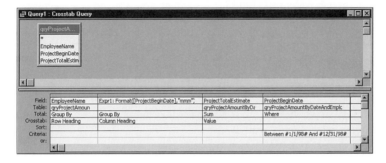

FIGURE 11.26
A Row Total column in a Crosstab query in Design view.

Creating a Crosstab Query Without the Crosstab Query Wizard

Although you can create many of your Crosstab queries by using the Crosstab Query Wizard, you should know how to build one without the wizard. This knowledge lets you modify existing Crosstab queries and gain ultimate control over creating new queries.

To build a Crosstab query without using the Crosstab Query Wizard, follow these steps:

1. Click Queries in the Objects list of the Database window and click New.
2. Double-click Create a Query Design View.

3. Select the table or query that will be included in the query grid. Click Add to add the table or query. Click Close.

4. Use the Query Type drop-down list to select Crosstab Query.

5. Add to the query grid the fields you want to include in the query output.

6. Click the Crosstab row of each field you want to include as a row heading. Select Row Heading from the drop-down list.

7. Click the Crosstab row of the field you want to include as a column heading. Select Column Heading from the drop-down list.

8. Click the Crosstab row of the field whose values you want to cross-tabulate. Select Value from the Crosstab drop-down list.

9. Select the appropriate aggregate function from the Total drop-down list.

10. Add any date intervals or other expressions you want to include.

11. Specify any criteria for the query.

12. Change the sort order of any of the columns, if you like.

13. Run the query when you're ready.

Figure 11.27 shows a query in which the column heading is set to the month of the ProjectBeginDate field; the row heading is set to the EmployeeName field. The sum of the ProjectTotalEstimate field is the value for the query. The OrderDate is also included in the query grid as a WHERE clause for the query. Figure 11.28 shows the results of running the query.

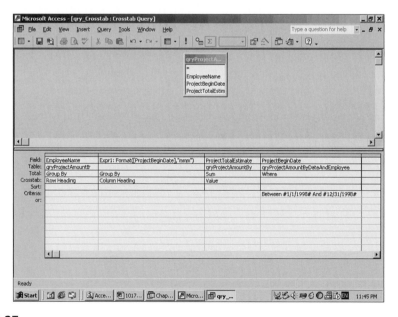

FIGURE 11.27

A Crosstab query, designed without a wizard, showing the project total estimate by employee and month.

EmployeeName	Jan	May	Jul	Sep	Oct
Balter, Dan			$30,000.00		
Callahan, Laura					$5,000.00
Davolio, Nancy	$30,000.00			$3,000.00	
Fuller, Andrew	$15,000.00				
Leverling, Janet	$45,000.00				
Peacock, Marga	$28,000.00	$1,500.00			

FIGURE 11.28

The result of running the Crosstab query shown in Figure 11.27.

Creating Fixed Column Headings

If you don't use fixed column headings, all the columns are included in the query output in alphabetical order. For example, if you include month names in the query result, they appear as Apr, Aug, Dec, Feb, and so on. By using fixed column headings, you tell Access the order in which each column appears in the query result. Column headings can be specified by setting the query's Column Headings property. (See Figure 11.29.)

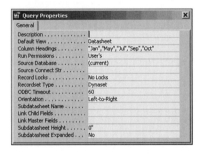

FIGURE 11.29

A query's Column Headings property.

NOTE

All fixed column headings must match the underlying data exactly; otherwise, information will be omitted inadvertently from the query result. For example, if the column heading for the month of June was accidentally entered as June and the data output by the format statement included data for the month of Jun, all June data would be omitted from the query output.

Important Notes About Crosstab Queries

Regardless of how Crosstab queries are created, you should be aware of some special caveats when working with them:

- You can select only one value and one column heading for a Crosstab query, but you can select multiple row headings.

- The results of a Crosstab query can't be updated.

- You can't define criteria on the Value field. If you do, you get the error message `You can't specify criteria on the same field for which you enter Value in the Crosstab row`. If you must specify criteria for the Value field, you must first build another query that includes your selection criteria, and base the Crosstab query on the first query.

- All parameters used in a Crosstab query must be explicitly declared in the Query Parameters dialog box.

TIP

PivotTables, new to Access 2002, have all the functionality of cross-tab queries, and then some! Consider replacing cross-tab queries with select queries stored in PivotTable view.

Outer Joins

Outer joins are used when you want the records on the one side of a one-to-many relationship to be included in the query result, regardless of whether there are matching records in the table on the many side. With a Customers table and an Orders table, for example, users often want to include only customers with orders in the query output. An Inner Join (the default join type) does this. In other situations, users want all customers to be included in the query result, whether or not they have orders. This is when an outer join is necessary.

NOTE

There are two types of outer joins: left outer joins and right outer joins. A left outer join occurs when all records on the one side of a one-to-many relationship are included in the query result, regardless of whether any records exist on the many side. A right outer join means all records on the many side of a one-to-many relationship are included in the query result, regardless of whether there are any records on the one side. A right outer join should never occur if referential integrity is being enforced.

To establish an outer join, you must modify the join between the tables included in the query:

1. Double-click the line joining the tables in the query grid.
2. The Join Properties window appears. (See Figure 11.30.) Select the type of join you want to create. To create a left outer join between the tables, select Option 2 (Option 3 if you want to create a right outer join). Notice in Figure 11.30 that the description is Include ALL Records from tblClients and only Those Records from tblProjects Where the Joined Fields Are Equal.

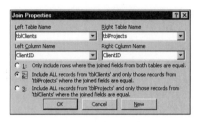

FIGURE 11.30

Establishing a left outer join.

3. Click OK to accept the join. An outer join should be established between the tables. Notice that the line joining the two tables now has an arrow pointing to the many side of the join.

The SQL statement produced when a left outer join is established looks like this:

```
SELECT DISTINCTROW tblClients.ClientID, tblClients.CompanyName
FROM tblClients
LEFT JOIN tblProjects ON tblClients.ClientID = tblProjects.ClientID;
```

A left outer join can also be used to identify all the records on the one side of a join that don't have any corresponding records on the many side. To do this, simply enter Is Null as the criteria for any required field on the many side of the join. A common solution is to place the criteria on the foreign key field. In the query shown in Figure 11.31, only clients without projects are displayed in the query result.

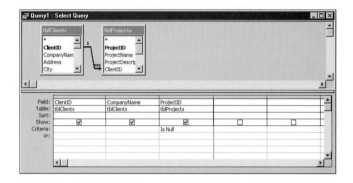

FIGURE 11.31

A query showing clients without projects.

Self Joins

A self join enables you to join a table to itself. This is often done so that information in a single table can appear to exist in two separate tables. A classic example is seen with employees and supervisors. Two fields are included in the Employees table; one field includes the EmployeeID of the employee being described in the record, and the other field specifies the EmployeeID of the employee's supervisor. If you want to see a list of employee names and the names of their supervisors, you'll need to use a self join.

To build a self-join query, follow these steps:

1. Click the Queries tab of the Database window and then click New.

2. Select Design view and click OK.

3. From the Show Tables dialog box, add the table to be used in the self join to the query grid two times. Click Close. Notice that the second instance of the table appears with an underscore and the number 1.

4. To change the alias of the second table, right-click on top of the table in the query grid and select Properties. Change the Alias property as desired. In Figure 11.32, the alias has been changed to Supervisors.

5. To establish a join between the table and its alias, click and drag from the field in one table that corresponds to the field in the aliased table. In Figure 11.33, the SupervisorID field of the tblEmployees table has been joined with the EmployeeID field from the aliased table.

6. Drag the appropriate fields to the query grid. In Figure 11.33, the FirstName and LastName fields are included from the tblEmployees table. The SupervisorName expression (a concatenation of the supervisor's first and last names) is supplied from the copy of the table with the Supervisors alias.

FIGURE 11.32

Building a self join.

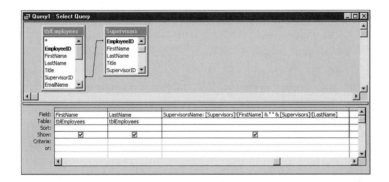

FIGURE 11.33

Establishing a self join between the table and its alias.

> **TIP**
>
> Self-relationships can be permanently defined in the Relationships window. This is often done so that referential integrity can be established between two fields in the same table. In the example of employees and supervisors, a permanent relationship with referential integrity can be established to make sure supervisor ID numbers aren't entered with employee ID numbers that don't exist.

Understanding SQL

Access SQL is the language that underlies Access queries, so you need to understand a little bit about it, where it came from, and how it works. Access SQL enables you to construct queries without using the Access QBE (Query By Example) grid. For example, you must build a SQL statement on-the-fly in response to user interaction with your application. Furthermore, certain operations supported by Access SQL aren't supported by the graphical QBE grid. You must build these SQL statements in the Query Builder's SQL view. In addition, there are many times when you will want to build the record source for a form or report on-the-fly. In those situations, you must have command of the SQL language. Finally, you will want to use SQL statements in your ADO (ActiveX Data Objects) and DAO (Data Access Objects) code. For all these reasons, learning SQL is a valuable skill.

What Is SQL, and Where Did It Come From?

SQL is a standard from which many different dialects have emerged. It was developed at an IBM research laboratory in the early 1970s and first formally described in a research paper released in 1974 at an Association for Computing Machinery meeting. Jet 4.0, the version of the Jet Engine provided with Access 2000 and Access 2002, has two modes, one of which supports Access SQL and the other supports SQL-92. The SQL-92 extensions are not available from the user interface. They can only be accessed using ActiveX Data Objects (ADO). They are covered in a later section of this chapter, "Jet 4.0 ANSI-92 Extensions."

What Do You Need to Know About SQL?

At the very least, you need to understand SQL's basic constructs, which enable you to select, update, delete, and append data by using SQL commands and syntax. Access SQL is made up of very few verbs. The most commonly used verbs are discussed in the following sections.

SQL Syntax

SQL is easy to learn. When retrieving data, you simply build a SELECT statement. SELECT statements are composed of clauses that determine the specifics of how the data is selected. When they're executed, SELECT statements select rows of data and return them as a recordset.

NOTE

In the examples that follow, keywords appear in uppercase. Values that you supply appear italicized. Optional parts of the statement appear in square brackets. Curly braces, combined with vertical bars, indicate a choice. Finally, ellipses are used to indicate a repeating sequence.

The SELECT Statement

The SELECT statement is at the heart of the SQL language. It is used to retrieve data from one or more tables. Its basic syntax is

```
SELECT column-list FROM table-list WHERE where-clause ORDER BY order-by-clause
```

The SELECT Clause

The SELECT clause specifies what columns you want to retrieve from the table whose data is being returned to the recordset. The basic syntax for a SELECT clause is

```
SELECT column-list
```

The simplest SELECT clause looks like this:

```
SELECT *
```

This SELECT clause retrieves all columns from a table. Here's another example that retrieves only the ClientID and CompanyName columns from a table:

```
SELECT ClientID, CompanyName
```

Not only can you include columns that exist in your table, you can include expressions in a SELECT clause. Here's an example:

```
SELECT ClientID, City & ", " & State & "   " & PostalCode AS Address
```

This SELECT clause retrieves the ClientID column as well as an alias called Address, which includes an expression that concatenates the City, State, and PostalCode columns.

The FROM Clause

The FROM clause specifies the tables or queries from which the records should be selected. It can include an alias you use to refer to the table. The FROM clause looks like this:

```
FROM table-list [AS alias]
```

Here's an example of a basic FROM clause:

```
FROM tblClients AS Clients
```

In this case, the name of the table is tblClients, and the alias is Clients. If you combine the SELECT clause with the FROM clause, the SQL statement looks like this:

```
SELECT ClientID, CompanyName FROM tblClients
```

This SELECT statement retrieves the ClientID and CompanyName columns from the tblClients table.

Just as you can alias the fields included in a SELECT clause, you can also alias the tables included in the FROM clause. The alias is used to shorten the name, to simplify a cryptic name, and for a variety of other reasons. Here's an example:

```
SELECT ClientID, CompanyName FROM tblClients AS Customers
```

The WHERE Clause

The WHERE clause limits the records retrieved by the SELECT statement. A WHERE clause can include up to 40 columns combined by the keywords AND and OR. The syntax for a WHERE clause looks like this:

```
WHERE expression1 [{AND|OR} expression2 [...]]
```

A simple WHERE clause looks like this:

```
WHERE Country = "USA"
```

Using an AND to further limit the criteria, the WHERE clause looks like this:

```
WHERE Country = "USA" AND ContactTitle Like "Sales*"
```

This WHERE clause limits the records returned to those in which the country is equal to USA and the ContactTitle begins with Sales. Using an OR, the SELECT statement looks like this:

```
WHERE Country = "USA" OR Country = "Canada"
```

This WHERE clause returns all records in which the country is equal to either USA or Canada. Compare that with the following example:

```
WHERE Country = "USA" OR ContactTitle Like "Sales*"
```

This WHERE clause returns all records in which the country is equal to USA or the ContactTitle begins with Sales. For example, the salespeople in China will be returned from this WHERE clause because their ContactTitle begins with Sales. The WHERE clause combined with the SELECT and FROM clauses looks like this:

```
SELECT ClientID, CompanyName FROM tblClients
    WHERE Country = "USA" OR Country = "Canada"
```

You must follow several rules when building a WHERE clause. The text strings that you are searching for must be enclosed in quotes. Dates must be surrounded by pound (#) signs. Finally, you must include the keyword LIKE when utilizing wildcard characters.

NOTE

Although Access SQL uses quotes to surround text values that you are searching for, the ANSI-92 standard dictates that apostrophes (single quotes) must be used to delimit text values.)

The ORDER BY Clause

The ORDER BY clause determines the order in which the returned rows are sorted. It's an optional clause and looks like this:

```
ORDER BY column1 [{ASC|DESC}], column2 [{ASC|DESC}] [,...]]
```

Here's an example:

```
ORDER BY ClientID
```

The ORDER BY clause can include more than one field:

```
ORDER BY Country, ClientID
```

When more than one field is specified, the left-most field is used as the primary level of sort. Any additional fields are the lower sort levels. Combined with the rest of the SELECT statement, the ORDER BY clause looks like this:

```
SELECT ClientID, CompanyName FROM tblClients
    WHERE Country = "USA" OR Country = "Canada"
    ORDER BY ClientID
```

The ORDER BY clause allows you to determine whether the sorted output appears in ascending or descending order. By default, output appears in ascending order. To switch to descending order, use the optional keyword DESC. Here's an example:

```
SELECT ClientID, CompanyName FROM tblClients ORDER BY ClientID DESC
```

This example selects the ClientID and CompanyName fields from the tblClients table, ordering the output in descending order by the ClientID field.

The JOIN Clause

Often you'll need to build SELECT statements that retrieve data from more than one table. When building a SELECT statement based on more than one table, you must join the tables with a JOIN clause. The JOIN clause differs depending on whether you join the tables with an INNER JOIN, a LEFT OUTER JOIN, or a RIGHT OUTER JOIN.

The SQL-89 and SQL-92 syntax for joins differs. The basic SQL-89 syntax is

```
SELECT column-list FROM table1, table2 WHERE table1.column1 = table2.column2
```

The SQL-92 syntax is preferred. It is

```
SELECT column-list FROM table1 {INNER|LEFT [OUTER]|RIGHT [OUTER]} JOIN table2
    ON table1.column1 = table2.column2
```

Note that the keyword OUTER is optional.

Here's an example of a simple INNER JOIN:

```
SELECT DISTINCTROW tblClients.ClientID,
    tblClients.CompanyName, tblProjects.ProjectName,
    tblProjects.ProjectDescription
    FROM tblClients
    INNER JOIN tblProjects ON tblClients.ClientID = tblProjects.ClientID
```

Notice that four columns are returned in the query result. Two columns are from tblClients and two are from tblProjects. The SELECT statement uses an INNER JOIN from tblClients to tblProjects based on the ClientID field. This means that only clients who have projects are displayed in the query result. Compare this with the following SELECT statement:

```
SELECT DISTINCTROW tblClients.ClientID,
    tblClients.CompanyName, tblProjects.ProjectName,
    tblProjects.ProjectDescription
    FROM tblClients
    LEFT JOIN tblProjects ON tblClients.ClientID = tblProjects.ClientID
```

This SELECT statement joins the two tables using a LEFT JOIN from tblClients to tblProjects based on the ClientID field. All clients are included in the resulting records, whether or not they have projects.

> **NOTE**
>
> The word OUTER is assumed in the LEFT JOIN clause used when building a left outer join.

There are times when you will need to join more than two tables in a SQL statement. The ANSI-92 syntax is

```
FROM table1 JOIN table2 ON condition1 JOIN table3 ON condition2
```

The following example joins the tblClients, tblProjects, and tblPayments tables:

```
SELECT tblClients.ClientID, tblClients.CompanyName,
tblProjects.ProjectName, tblPayments.PaymentAmount
FROM (tblClients
INNER JOIN tblProjects
ON tblClients.ClientID = tblProjects.ClientID)
INNER JOIN tblPayments
ON tblProjects.ProjectID = tblPayments.ProjectID
```

In the example, the order of the joins is unimportant. The exception to this is when inner and outer joins are combined. When combining inner and outer joins, the Jet Engine applies two specific rules. First, the nonpreserved table in an outer join cannot participate in an inner join. The nonpreserved table is the one whose rows may not appear. In the case of a left outer join from tblClients to tblProjects, the tblProjects table is considered the non-preserved table. It therefore cannot participate in an inner join with tblPayments. The second rule is that the non-preserved table in an outer join cannot participate with another nonpreserved table in another outer join.

Self Joins

Self joins were covered earlier in the chapter. The SQL syntax required to create them is similar to a standard join and is covered here.

```
SELECT [FirstName] & " " & [LastName] AS EmployeeName,
[FirstName] & " " & [LastName] AS SupervisorName
FROM tblEmployees
INNER JOIN tblEmployees
AS tblSupervisors
ON tblEmployees.SupervisorID = tblSupervisors.EmployeeID
```

Notice that the tblEmployees table is joined to an alias of the tblEmployees table that is referred to as tblSupervisors. The SupervisorID from the tblEmployees table is joined with the EmployeeID field from the tblSupervisors alias. The fields included in the output are the FirstName and LastName from the tblEmployees table and the FirstName and LastName from the alias of the tblEmployees table.

Non-equi Joins

So far, all the joins that we have covered involve situations where the value of a field in one table is equal to the value of the field in the other table. You can create non-equi joins where the >, >=, <, <=, <>, or Between operator is used to join two tables. Here's an example:

```
SELECT tblClients.CompanyName, tblProjects.ProjectName
FROM tblClients
INNER JOIN tblProjects
ON tblClients.ClientID = tblProjects.ClientID
AND tblProjects.ProjectBeginDate >=  tblClients.IntroDate
```

This example returns only the rows from tblProjects where the ProjectBeginDate is on or after the IntroDate stored in the tblClients table.

ALL, DISTINCTROW, and DISTINCT Clauses

The ALL clause of a SELECT statement means that all rows meeting the WHERE clause are included in the query result. When the DISTINCT keyword is used, Access eliminates duplicate rows, based on the fields included in the query result. This is the same as setting the Unique Values property to Yes in the graphical QBE grid. When the DISTINCTROW keyword is used, Access eliminates any duplicate rows based on all columns of all tables included in the query (whether they appear in the query result or not). This is the same as setting the Unique Records property to Yes in the graphical QBE grid. These keywords in the SELECT clause look like this:

```
SELECT [{ALL|DISTINCT|DISTINCT ROW}] column-list
```

The TOP Predicate

The Top Values property, available via the user interface, is covered in the "Special Query Properties" section of this chapter. The keyword TOP is used to implement this feature in SQL. The syntax looks like this:

```
SELECT [{ALL|DISTINCT|DISTINCTROW}] [TOP n [PERCENT]] column-list
```

The example that follows extracts the five clients whose IntroDate field is most recent.

```
SELECT TOP 5 tblClients.ClientID, tblClients.CompanyName, tblClients.IntroDate
FROM tblClients
ORDER BY tblClients.IntroDate DESC
```

The GROUP BY Clause

The GROUP BY clause is used to calculate summary statistics; it's created when you build a Totals query by using the graphical QBE grid. The syntax of the GROUP BY clause is

```
GROUP BY group-by-expression1 [,group-by-expression2 [,...]]
```

The GROUP BY clause is used to dictate the fields on which the query result is grouped. When multiple fields are included in a GROUP BY clause, they are grouped from left to right. The output is automatically ordered by the fields designated in the GROUP BY clause. In the following example, the SELECT statement returns the country, city, and total freight for each country/city combination. The results are displayed in order by country and city:

```
SELECT DISTINCTROW tblCustomers.Country, tblCustomers.City,
    Sum(tblOrders.Freight) AS SumOfFreight
    FROM tblCustomers
    INNER JOIN tblOrders ON tblCustomers.CustomerID = tblOrders.CustomerID
    GROUP BY tblCustomers.Country, tblCustomers.City
```

The GROUP BY clause indicates that detail for the selected records isn't displayed. Instead, the fields indicated in the GROUP BY clause are displayed uniquely. One of the fields in the SELECT statement must include an aggregate function. This result of the aggregate function is displayed along with the fields specified in the GROUP BY clause.

The HAVING Clause

A HAVING clause is similar to a WHERE clause, but it differs in one major respect: It's applied after the data is summarized rather than before. In other words, the WHERE clause is used to determine which rows are grouped. The HAVING clause determines which groups are included in the output. A HAVING clause looks like this:

```
HAVING expression1 [{AND|OR} expression2[...]]
```

In the following example, the criterion > 1000 will be applied after the aggregate function SUM is applied to the grouping:

```
SELECT DISTINCTROW tblCustomers.Country, tblCustomers.City,
   Sum(tblOrders.Freight) AS SumOfFreight
   FROM tblCustomers
   INNER JOIN tblOrders ON tblCustomers.CustomerID = tblOrders.CustomerID
   GROUP BY tblCustomers.Country, tblCustomers.City
   HAVING (((Sum(tblOrders.Freight))>1000))
```

Applying What You Have Learned

You can practice entering and working with SQL statements in two places:

- In a query's SQL View window
- In VBA code

Now take a look at both these techniques.

Using the Graphical QBE Grid as a Two-Way Tool

A great place to practice writing SQL statements is in the SQL View window of a query. It works like this:

1. Start by building a new query.
2. Add a couple of fields and maybe even some criteria.
3. Use the Query View drop-down list on the Query Design toolbar to select SQL view.
4. Try changing the SQL statement, using what you have learned in this chapter.
5. Use the Query View drop-down list on the Query Design toolbar to select Design view. As long as you haven't violated any Access SQL syntax rules, you can easily switch to the query's Design view and see the graphical result of your changes. If you've introduced any syntax errors into the SQL statement, an error occurs when you try to return to the query's Design view.

Including SQL Statements in VBA Code

SQL statements can also be executed directly from VBA code. You can run a SQL statement from VBA code in two ways:

- You can build a temporary query and execute it.
- You can open a recordset with the SQL statement as the foundation for the recordset.

The VBA language enables you to build a query on-the-fly, execute it, and never store it. The code looks like this:

```
Sub CreateTempQuery()
    Dim cmd As ADODB.Command
    Dim rst As ADODB.Recordset

    Set cmd = New ADODB.Command
    With cmd
        .ActiveConnection = CurrentProject.Connection
        .CommandText = "Select ProjectID, ProjectName from " & _
            "tblProjects Where ProjectTotalEstimate > 30000"
        .CommandType = adCmdText
        .Prepared = True
        Set rst = .Execute
    End With

    Do Until rst.EOF
        Debug.Print rst!ProjectID, rst!ProjectName
        rst.MoveNext
    Loop

End Sub
```

Working with recordsets is covered extensively in Chapter 14. For now, you need to understand that this code creates a temporary query definition using a SQL statement. In this example, the query definition is never added to the database. Instead, the SQL statement is executed but never stored.

A SQL statement can also be provided as part of the recordset's Open method. The code looks like this:

```
Sub OpenRWithSQL()
    Dim rst As ADODB.Recordset

    Set rst = New ADODB.Recordset

    rst.Open "Select ProjectId, ProjectName from " & _
        "tblProjects Where ProjectTotalEstimate > 30000", _
        CurrentProject.Connection

    Do Until rst.EOF
        Debug.Print rst!ProjectID, rst!ProjectName
        rst.MoveNext
    Loop
End Sub
```

Again, this code is discussed more thoroughly in Chapter 14. Notice that the Open method of the recordset object receives two parameters: The first is a SELECT statement, and the second is the Connection object.

Union Queries

A Union query enables you to combine data from two tables with similar structures; data from each table is included in the output. For example, say you have a tblTimeCards table containing active time cards and a tblTimeCardsArchive table containing archived time cards. The problem occurs when you want to build a report that combines data from both tables. To do this, you must build a Union query as the record source for the report. The syntax for a Union query is

```
Select-statement1 UNION [ALL]
Select-statement2 [UNION [ALL]
SelectStatement3] [...]
```

Here's an example:

```
SELECT FirstName, LastName, Department, Salary
FROM tblEmployees
UNION ALL SELECT FirstName, LastName, Department, Salary
FROM tblSummerEmployees
```

The ALL Keyword

Notice the keyword ALL in the previous SQL statement. By default, Access eliminates all duplicate records from the query result. This means that, if an employee is found in both the tblEmployees and tblSummerEmployees tables, he appears only once in the query result. Including the keyword ALL causes any duplicate rows to display.

Sorting the Query Results

When sorting the results of a Union query, the ORDER BY clause must be included at the end of the SQL statement. Here's an example:

```
SELECT FirstName, LastName, Department, Salary
FROM tblEmployees
UNION ALL SELECT FirstName, LastName, Department, Salary
FROM tblSummerEmployees
ORDER BY Salary
```

If the column names that you are sorting by differ in the tables included in the Union query, you must use the column name from the first table.

Using the Graphical QBE to Create a Union Query

You can use the graphical QBE to create a Union query. The process is as follows:

1. Click Queries in the list of objects in the Database window and double-click Create Query in Design view.

2. Click Close from the Show Tables dialog box without selecting a table.

3. Choose Query|SQL Specific|Union to open a SQL window.

4. Type in the SQL UNION clause. Notice that you can't switch back to the query's Design view. (See Figure 11.34.)

5. Click the Run button on the toolbar to execute the query.

CAUTION

If you build a query and then designate the query as an SQL Specific query, you lose *everything* that you did prior to the switch. There is *no* warning, and Undo is not available!

FIGURE 11.34

An example of a Union query that joins tblTimeCards with tblTimeCardsArchive.

Important Notes about Union Queries

It is important to note that the result of a Union query is not updateable. Furthermore, the fields in each SELECT statement are matched only by position. This means that you can get strange results by accidentally listing the FirstName field followed by the LastName field in the first SELECT statement, and the LastName field followed by the FirstName field in the second SELECT statement. Each SELECT statement included in a Union query must contain the same number of columns.

Pass-Through Queries

Pass-Through queries enable you to send uninterpreted SQL statements to your back-end database when you're using something other than the Jet Engine. These uninterpreted statements are in the SQL that's specific to your particular back end. Although the Jet Engine sees these SQL statements, it makes no attempt to parse or modify them. Pass-Through queries are used in several situations:

- The action you want to take is supported by your back-end database server, but not by Access SQL or ODBC SQL.

- Access or the ODBC driver is doing a poor job parsing the SQL statement and sending it in an optimized form to the back-end database.

- You want to execute a stored procedure on the back-end database server.

- You want to make sure the SQL statement is executed on the server.

- You want to join data from more than one table residing on the database server. If you execute the join without a Pass-Through query, the join is done in the memory of the user's PC after all the required data has been sent over the network.

Although Pass-Through queries offer many advantages, they aren't a panacea. They do have a few disadvantages:

- Because you're sending SQL statements specific to your particular database server, you must write the statement in the "dialect" of SQL used by the database server. For example, in writing a Pass-Through query to access SQL Server data, you must write the SQL statement in T-SQL. When writing a Pass-Through query to access Oracle data, you must write the SQL statement in PL-SQL. This means that you'll need to rewrite all the SQL statements if you switch to another back end.

- The results returned from a Pass-Through query can't be updated.

- The Jet Engine does no syntax checking of the query before passing it on to the back end.

Now that you know all the advantages and disadvantages of Pass-Through queries, you can learn how to build one:

1. Click Queries in the list of objects in the Database window, and double-click Create Query in Design view.

2. Click Close from the Show Tables dialog box without selecting a table.

3. Choose Query|SQL Specific|Pass-Through to open the SQL Design window.

4. Type in the SQL statement in the dialect of your back-end database server.

5. View the Query Properties window and enter an ODBC connect string. (See Figure 11.35.)

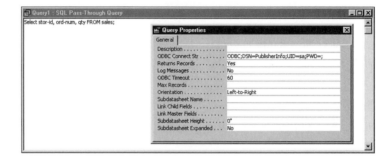

FIGURE 11.35

A SQL Pass-Through query that selects specific fields from the Sales table, which resides in the PublisherInfo data source.

6. Click the Run button on the toolbar to run the query.

NOTE

Using ADO and DAO to execute Pass-Through queries is covered in Chapter 14.

The Propagation of `Null`s and Query Results

`Null` values can wreak havoc with your query results because they propagate. Take a look at the query in Figure 11.36. Notice that when parts and labor are added, and either the Parts field or the Labor field contains a `Null`, the result of adding the two fields is `Null`. In Figure 11.37, the problem is rectified. Notice the expression that adds the two values:

```
TotalPrice: Nz([Parts]) + Nz([Labor])
```

This expression uses the Nz function to convert the Null values to 0 before the two field values are added together.

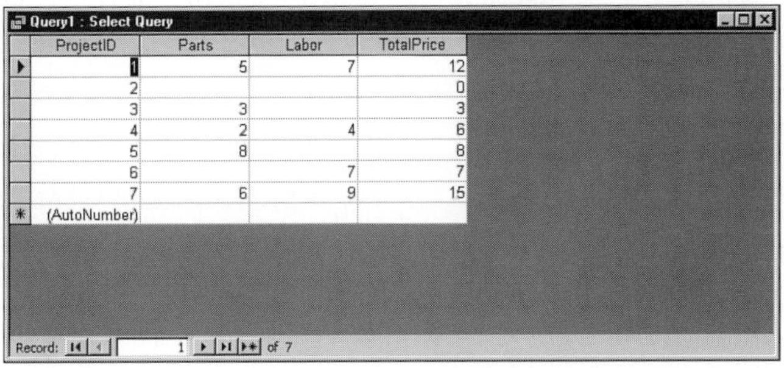

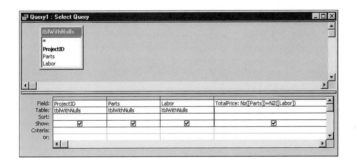

FIGURE 11.36

Propagation of Nulls *in a query result.*

FIGURE 11.37

A solution to eliminate propagation of Nulls.

Subqueries

Subqueries allow you to embed one SELECT statement within another. By placing a subquery in a query's criteria, you can base one query on the result of another. Figure 11.38 shows an example. The query pictured finds all the clients without projects. The SQL statement looks like this:

```
SELECT DISTINCTROW tblClients.ClientID,
    tblClients.CompanyName FROM tblClients
    WHERE tblClients.ClientID Not In (Select ClientID from tblProjects)
```

This query first runs the SELECT statement Select ClientID from tblProjects. It uses the result as criteria for the first query.

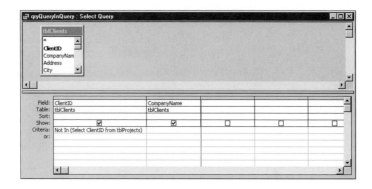

FIGURE 11.38
A query containing a subquery.

Using SQL to Update Data

SQL can be used not only to retrieve data, but to update it as well. This concept was introduced in the section "Action Queries," which focused on the SQL statements behind the Action queries.

The UPDATE Statement

The UPDATE statement is used to modify the data in one or more columns of a table. The syntax for the UPDATE statement is

```
UPDATE table/query
SET column1=expression1 [,column2=expression2] [,...]
[WHERE criteria]
```

The WHERE clause in the UPDATE statement is used to limit the rows that are updated. The following is an example of an UPDATE statement:

```
UPDATE tblClients
SET tblClients.DefaultRate = [DefaultRate]*1.1
WHERE tblClients.DefaultRate<=125
```

This statement updates the DefaultRate column of the tblClients table, increasing it by 10%, for any clients that have a default rate less than or equal to 125.

The DELETE Statement

Whereas the UPDATE statement is used to update all rows that meet specific criteria, the DELETE statement deletes all rows that meet the specified criteria. The syntax for the DELETE statement is

```
DELETE FROM table [WHERE criteria]
```

As with the UPDATE statement, the WHERE clause is used to limit the rows that are deleted. The following is an example of the use of a DELETE statement.

```
DELETE tblClients.*, tblClients.DefaultRate
FROM tblClients
WHERE tblClients.DefaultRate<=125
```

This statement deletes all clients from the tblClients table whose DefaultRate field is less than or equal to 125.

The INSERT INTO Statement

The INSERT INTO statement is used to copy rows from one table to another. The syntax for the INSERT INTO statement is

```
INSERT INTO target-table select-statement [WHERE criteria]
```

Once again ,the optional WHERE clause is used to limit the rows that are copied. Here's an example:

```
INSERT INTO tblCheapClients
(ClientID, CompanyName, ContactFirstName,
ContactLastName, ContactTitle, DefaultRate )
SELECT tblClients.ClientID, tblClients.CompanyName,
tblClients.ContactFirstName,
tblClients.ContactLastName, tblClients.ContactTitle, tblClients.DefaultRate
FROM tblClients
WHERE tblClients.DefaultRate<=125
```

This statement inserts the ClientID, CompanyName, ContactFirstName, ContactLastName, ContactTitle, and DefaultRate fields into the corresponding fields in the tblCheapClients table for any clients whose DefaultRate field is less than or equal to 125.

The SELECT INTO Statement

Whereas the INSERT INTO statement inserts data into an *existing* table, the SELECT INTO statement inserts data into a new table. The syntax looks like this:

```
SELECT column1 [,column2 [,...]] INTO new-table
FROM table-list
[WHERE where-clause]
[ORDER BY orderby-clause]
```

The WHERE clause is used to determine which rows in the source table are inserted into the destination table. The ORDER BY clause is used to designate the order of the rows in the destination table. Here's an example:

```
SELECT tblClients.ClientID, tblClients.CompanyName,
tblClients.ContactFirstName, tblClients.ContactLastName,
tblClients.ContactTitle, tblClients.DefaultRate
INTO tblCheapClients
FROM tblClients
WHERE tblClients.DefaultRate)<=125
```

This statement inserts data from the selected fields in the tblClients table into a new table called tblCheapClients. Only the clients whose DefaultRate field is less than 125 are inserted.

Using SQL for Data Definition

Access 2002 offers two methods of programmatically defining and modifying objects. You can use either ADOX (ActiveX Data Object Extensions for DDL and Security) or DDL (Data Definition Language). DDL is covered in this chapter. ADOX is covered in Chapter 14.

The CREATE TABLE Statement

As its name implies, the CREATE TABLE statement is used to create a new table. The syntax is

```
CREATE TABLE table-name
(column1 type1 [(size1)] [CONSTRAINT column-constraint1]
[,column2 type2 [(size2)] [CONSTRAINT column-constraint2]
[,...]]
[CONSTRAINT table-constraint1 [,table-constraint2 [,]]])
```

You must designate the type of data for each column included in the table. When defining a text field, you can also specify the size parameter. Notice that constraints are available at the table level and at the field level. Here's an example of a CREATE TABLE statement:

```
CREATE TABLE tblCustomers
        (CustomerID LONG, CompanyName TEXT (50), IntroDate DATETIME)
```

The CONSTRAINT clause allows you to create primary and foreign keys. It looks like this:

```
CONSTRAINT name {PRIMARY KEY|UNIQUE|REFERENCES foreign-table [foreign-column]}
```

Here's an example:

```
CREATE TABLE tblCustomers
(CustomerID LONG CONSTRAINT CustomerID PRIMARY KEY,
CompanyName TEXT (50), IntroDate DATETIME)
```

The example creates a primary key index based on the CustomerID field.

The CREATE INDEX Statement

The CREATE INDEX statement is used to add an index to an existing table. It is supported in Access, but is not part of the ANSI standard. It looks like this:

```
CREATE [UNIQUE] INDEX index-name
ON table-name (column1 [,column2 [,...]])
[WITH {PRIARMY|DISALLOW NULL|IGNORE NULL}]
```

Here's an example:

```
CREATE INDEX  CompanyName
ON tblCustomers (CompanyName)
```

The example creates an index called CompanyName, based on the CompanyName field.

The ALTER TABLE Statement

The ALTER TABLE statement is used to modify the structure of an existing table. The syntax has four forms:

```
ALTER TABLE table-name ADD [COLUMN] column-name datatype [(size)]
[CONSTRAINT column-constraint]
```

This form of the ALTER TABLE statement adds a column to an existing table. Here's an example:

```
ALTER TABLE tblCustomers ADD ContactName Text 50
```

Use the following syntax to delete a column from an existing table:

```
ALTER TABLE table-name DROP [COLUMN] column-name
```

Here's an example:

```
ALTER TABLE tblCustomers DROP COLUMN ContactName
```

The ALTER TABLE statement is also used to add a constraint to an existing column. The syntax is

```
ALTER TABLE table-name ADD CONSTRAINT constraint
```

Here's an example:

```
ALTER TABLE tblCustomers ADD CONSTRAINT CompanyName UNIQUE (CompanyName)
```

Finally, to drop a constraint from an existing column, use this syntax:

```
ALTER TABLE table-name DROP CONSTRAINT index
```

Here's an example:

```
ALTER TABLE tblCustomers DROP CONSTRAINT CompanyName
```

The DROP INDEX Statement

The DROP INDEX statement is used to remove an index from a table. The syntax is as follows:

```
DROP INDEX index ON table-name
```

Here's an example:

```
DROP INDEX CompanyName ON tblCustomers
```

The DROP TABLE Statement

The DROP TABLE statement is used to remove a table from the database. The syntax is

```
DROP TABLE table-name
```

Here's an example:

```
DROP TABLE  tblCustomers
```

Using the Result of a Function as the Criteria for a Query

Many people are unaware that the result of a function can serve as an expression in a query or as a parameter to a query. The query shown in Figure 11.39 evaluates the result of a function called Initials. The return value from the function is evaluated with criteria to determine whether the employee is included in the query result. The Initials function shown here (it's also in the basUtils module of CHAP11EX.MDB, found on the sample code CD-ROM) receives two strings and returns the first character of each string followed by a period:

```
Function Initials(strFirstName As String, _
    strLastName As String) As String
  Initials = Left(strFirstName, 1) & "." & _
    Left(strLastName, 1) & "."
End Function
```

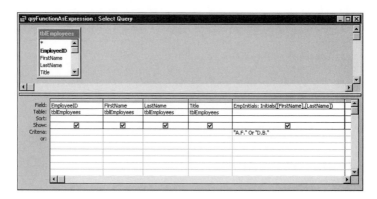

FIGURE 11.39

A query that uses the result of a function as an expression.

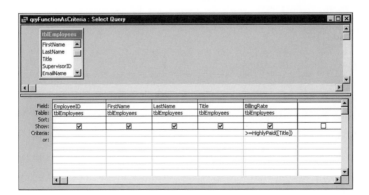

The return value from a function can also be used as the criteria for a query. (See Figure 11.40.) The query in the figure uses a function called `HighlyPaid` to determine which records appear in the query result. Here's what the `HighlyPaid` function looks like. (It's also in the basUtils module of CHAP12EX.MDB, found on the sample code CD-ROM.)

```
Function HighlyPaid(strTitle) As Currency
    Dim curHighRate As Currency
    Select Case strTitle
        Case "Sr. Programmer"
            curHighRate = 60
        Case "Systems Analyst"
            curHighRate = 80
        Case "Project Manager"
            curHighRate = 100
        Case Else
            curHighRate = 50
    End Select
    HighlyPaid = curHighRate
End Function
```

The function receives the employee's title as a parameter. It then evaluates the title and returns a threshold value to the query that's used as the criterion for the query's Billing Rate column.

FIGURE 11.40

A query that uses the result of a function as criteria.

Passing Parameter Query Values from a Form

The biggest frustration with Parameter queries occurs when multiple parameters are required to run the query. The user is confronted with multiple dialog boxes, one for each parameter in the query. The following steps explain how to build a Parameter query that receives its parameter values from a form:

1. Create a new unbound form.

2. Add text boxes or other controls to accept the criteria for each parameter added to your query.

3. Name each control so that you can readily identify the data it contains.

4. Add a command button to the form and instruct it to call the Parameter query. (See Figure 11.41.)

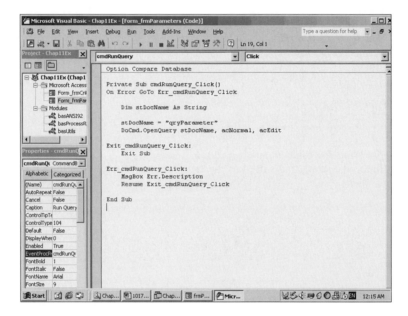

FIGURE 11.41

The Click *event code of the command button that calls the Parameter query.*

5. Save the form.

6. Create the query and add the parameters to it. Each parameter should refer to a control on the form. (See Figure 11.42.)

7. Right-click the top half of the Query Design grid and select Parameters. Define a data type for each parameter in the Parameters dialog box. (See Figure 11.43.)

8. Save and close the query.

9. Fill in the values on the criteria form and click the command button to execute the query. It should execute successfully.

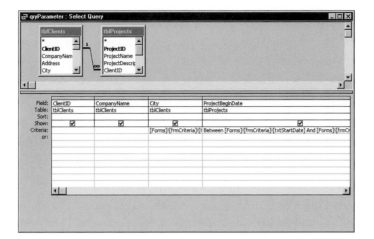

FIGURE 11.42

Parameters that refer to controls on a form.

FIGURE 11.43

The Parameters dialog box lets you select the data type for each parameter in the query.

Jet 4.0 ANSI-92 Extensions

Jet 4.0, the version of Jet that ships with Access 2000 and Access 2002, includes expanded support for the ANSI-92 standard. Although these extensions are not available via the Access user interface, you can tap into them using ADO code. This section covers the extensions and the functionality they afford you. Because I have not yet covered ADO, you might want to refer to Chapter 14 to better understand the examples. For now, you need to understand that the code examples in this section use the ADO Command object to execute SQL statements that create and manipulate database objects.

Table Extensions

Six table extensions are included with Jet 4.0. These extensions provide you with the ability to:

- Create defaults
- Create check constraints
- Set up cascading referential integrity
- Control fast foreign keys
- Implement Unicode string compression
- Better control autonumber fields

Creating Defaults

The DEFAULT keyword can be used with the CREATE TABLE statement. The syntax is

```
DEFAULT (value)
```

Here's an example:

```
Sub CreateDefault()
    Dim cmd As ADODB.Command
    Set cmd = New ADODB.Command

    cmd.ActiveConnection = CurrentProject.Connection
    cmd.CommandText = "CREATE TABLE tblCustomers " & _
        "(CustomerID LONG CONSTRAINT CustomerID PRIMARY KEY, " & _
        "CompanyName TEXT (50), IntroDate DATETIME, " & _
        "CreditLimit CURRENCY DEFAULT 5000)"
    cmd.Execute
End Sub
```

Notice first that ADO is used to execute the SQL statement. This is because the DEFAULT keyword is not accessible via the use interface. The CreditLimit field includes a DEFAULT clause that sets the default value of the field to 5000.

Creating Check Constraints

The CHECK keyword can be used with the CREATE TABLE statement. It allows you to add business rules for a table. Unlike field- and table-level validation rules that are available via the user interface, check constraints can span tables. The syntax for a check constraint is

```
[CONSTRAINT [name]] CHECK (search_condition)
```

Here's an example:

```
Sub CreateCheckConstraint()
    Dim cmd As ADODB.Command
    Set cmd = New ADODB.Command
```

```
    cmd.ActiveConnection = CurrentProject.Connection
    cmd.CommandText = "CREATE TABLE tblCustomers " & _
        "(CustomerID LONG CONSTRAINT CustomerID PRIMARY KEY, " & _
        "CompanyName TEXT (50), IntroDate DATETIME, " & _
        "CONSTRAINT IntroDateCheck CHECK (IntroDate <= Date()), " & _
        "CreditLimit CURRENCY DEFAULT 5000)"
    cmd.Execute
End Sub
```

The example creates a check constraint on the IntroDate field that limits the value entered in the field to a date on or before today's date.

Implementing Cascading Referential Integrity

The ANSI-92 extensions can also be used to establish cascading referential integrity. The syntax is

```
CONSTRAINT name FOREIGN KEY (column1 [,column2 [,...]])
REFERENCES foreign-table [(forign-column1 [, foreign-column2 [,...]])]
[ON UPDATE {NO ACTION|CASCADE}]
[ON DELETE {NO ACTION|CASCADE}]
```

Without the CASCADE options, the primary key field cannot be updated if the row has child records, and the row on the one side of the one-to-many relationship cannot be deleted if it has children.

Controlling Fast Foreign Keys

Whenever you join two tables in a one-to-many relationship, Access automatically creates an index on the foreign key field (the many side of the relationship). This is generally a good thing. It is only bad if the foreign key contains a lot of Nulls. In that case, the index serves only to degrade performance rather than improve it. Fortunately, using the Jet 4.0 ANSI-92 extensions, and the NO INDEX keywords, you can create the foreign key without the index. Here's the syntax:

```
CONSTRAINT name FOREIGN KEY NO INDEX (column1 [,column2 [,...]])
REFERENCES foreign-table [(forign-column1 [, foreign-column2 [,...]])]
[ON UPDATE {NO ACTION|CASCADE}]
[ON DELETE {NO ACTION|CASCADE}]
```

Implementing Unicode String Compression

Just as you can implement Unicode string compression using the user interface, you can also implement it in code. The syntax is

```
Column string-data-type [(length)] WITH COMPRESSION
```

Controlling Autonumber Fields

Using the Jet 4.0 ANSI-92 extensions, you can change both the autonumber seed and increment. The syntax is

```
Column AUTOINCREMENT (seed, increment)
```

Here's an example:

```
Sub CreateAutonumber()
    Dim cmd As ADODB.Command
    Set cmd = New ADODB.Command

    cmd.ActiveConnection = CurrentProject.Connection
    cmd.CommandText = "CREATE TABLE tblCustomers " & _
        "(CustomerID AUTOINCREMENT (100000,1), " & _
        "CompanyName TEXT (50), IntroDate DATETIME, " & _
        "CreditLimit CURRENCY DEFAULT 5000)"
    cmd.Execute
End Sub
```

The code creates an autoincrement field called CustomerID. The starting value is 100000. The field increments by 1. In addition to the added support for seed value and increment value, the Jet 4.0 ANSI-92 extensions allow you to retrieve the last-assigned autonumber value. Here's how it works:

```
Sub LastAutonumber()
    Dim cmd As ADODB.Command
    Dim rst As ADODB.Recordset
    Set cmd = New ADODB.Command
    Set rst = New ADODB.Recordset

    cmd.ActiveConnection = CurrentProject.Connection
    cmd.CommandText = "INSERT INTO tblCustomers " & _
        "(CompanyName, IntroDate, CreditLimit) " & _
        "VALUES ('Test Company', #1/1/2001#, 100) "
    cmd.Execute

    rst.ActiveConnection = CurrentProject.Connection
    rst.Open ("SELECT @@Identity as LastCustomer FROM tblCustomers")
    MsgBox rst("LastCustomer")
End Sub
```

The code first inserts a row into the tblCustomers table. It then opens a recordset and retrieves the @@Identity value. As with SQL Server, this @@Identity variable contains the value of the last assigned autonumber.

View and Stored Procedures Extensions

The Jet 4.0 ANSI-92 extensions allow you to create views and stored procedures similar to those found in SQL Server. Essentially, these views and stored procedures are Access queries that are repackaged to behave like their SQL Server counterparts. Although stored as queries, the views and stored procedures that you create are not visible via the user interface. They can be executed just like saved queries. The syntax to create a view looks like this:

```
CREATE VIEW view-name [(field1 [(,field2 [,...]])] AS select-statement
```

Here's an example:

```
Sub CreateView()
    Dim cmd As ADODB.Command
    Set cmd = New ADODB.Command

    cmd.ActiveConnection = CurrentProject.Connection
    cmd.CommandText = "CREATE VIEW vwClients " & _
        "AS SELECT ClientID, CompanyName " & _
        "FROM tblClients"
    cmd.Execute
End Sub
```

As covered in Chapter 14, use the following code to execute the view:

```
Sub ExecuteView()
    Dim rst As ADODB.Recordset
    Set rst = New ADODB.Recordset

    rst.ActiveConnection = CurrentProject.Connection
    rst.CursorType = adOpenStatic
    rst.Open "vwClients"
    MsgBox rst.RecordCount
End Sub
```

The syntax to create a stored procedure is

```
CREATE PROC[EDURE] procedure [(param1 datatype1 [,param2 datatype2 [,...]])] AS
sql-statement
```

Here's an example:

```
Sub CreateStoredProc()
    Dim cmd As ADODB.Command
    Set cmd = New ADODB.Command

    cmd.ActiveConnection = CurrentProject.Connection
    cmd.CommandText = "CREATE PROCEDURE procClientGet " & _
        "(ClientID long) " & _
```

```
        "AS SELECT ClientID, CompanyName " & _
        "FROM tblClients " & _
        "WHERE ClientID = ClientID"
    cmd.Execute
End Sub
```

Use the EXECUTE statement, as shown in the following code, to execute the stored procedure:

```
Sub ExecuteStoredProc()
    Dim rst As ADODB.Recordset
    Dim cmd As Command
    Set cmd = New ADODB.Command

    cmd.ActiveConnection = CurrentProject.Connection
    cmd.CommandText = "EXECUTE procClientGet 1"
    Set rst = cmd.Execute
    MsgBox rst("CompanyName")
End Sub
```

Transaction Extensions

Using Jet 4.0 ANSI-92 security extensions, you can create transactions that span an ADO connection. These extensions are intended to augment, rather than replace, ADO transactions. You use BEGIN TRANSACTION to start a transaction, COMMIT TRANSACTION to commit a transaction, and ROLLBACK [TRANSACTION] to cancel a transaction. Transactions are covered in detail in *Alison Balter's Mastering Access 2002 Enterprise Development.*

Security Extensions

Jet 4.0 provides numerous ANSI-92 security extensions. These extensions allow you to add and remove users and groups, as well as administer passwords and permissions. The ANSI-92 security extensions are covered in detail in Chapter 28, "Advanced Security Techniques."

PRACTICAL EXAMPLES

Applying These Techniques in Your Application

The following are several practical applications of these advanced techniques.

NOTE

The examples shown in this section are included in the CHAP11EX.MDB database on the sample code CD-ROM.

Archive Payments

After a while, you might need to archive some of the data in the tblPayment table. Two queries archive the payment data. The first, called qappAppendToPaymentArchive, is an Append query that sends all data in a specified date range to an archive table called tblPaymentsArchive. (See Figure 11.44.) The second query, called qdelRemoveFromPayments, is a Delete query that deletes all the data archived from the tblPayments table. (See Figure 11.45.) The archiving is run from a form called frmArchivePayments, where the date range can be specified by the user at runtime. (See Figure 11.46.)

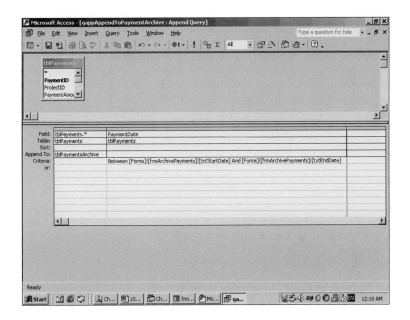

FIGURE 11.44

The Append query qappAppendToPaymentArchive.

Show All Payments

At times, you might want to combine data from both tables. To do this, you'll need to create a Union query that joins tblPayments to tblPaymentsArchive. The query's design is shown in Figure 11.47.

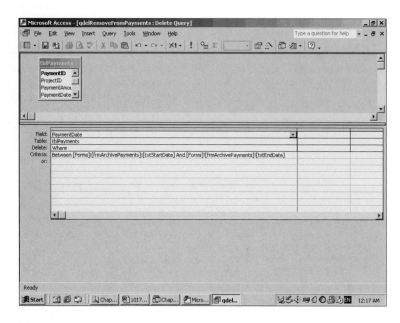

FIGURE 11.45

The Delete query qdelRemoveFromPayments.

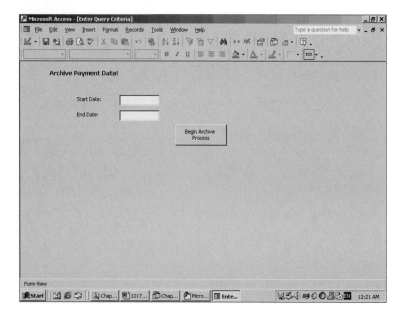

FIGURE 11.46

The form that supplies criteria for the archive process.

FIGURE 11.47

Using a Union query to join tblPayments to tblPaymentsArchive.

Create State Table

Because you'll regularly be looking up the states and provinces, you want to build a unique list of all the states and provinces in which your clients are currently located. The query needed to do this is shown in Figure 11.48. The query uses the tblClients table to come up with all the unique values for the StateProvince field. The query is a `Make Table` query that takes the unique list of values and outputs it to a tblStateProvince table.

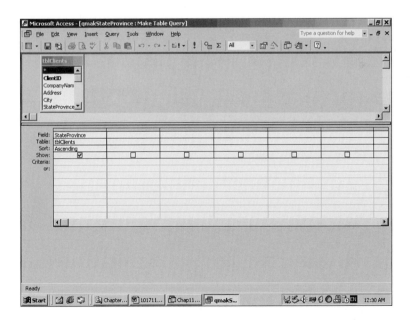

FIGURE 11.48

A Make Table query that creates a tblStateProvince table.

Summary

As you can see, Microsoft gives you a sophisticated query builder for constructing complex and powerful queries. Action queries let you modify table data without writing code; these queries can be used to add, edit, or delete table data. The Unique Values and Top Values properties of a query offer you flexibility in determining exactly what data is returned in your query result.

Many things can be done to improve your queries' efficiency. A little attention to the details covered in this chapter can give you dramatic improvements in your application's performance.

Other special types of queries covered in this chapter include Crosstab queries, outer joins, and self joins. Whatever can't be done by using the graphical QBE grid can be accomplished by typing the required SQL statement directly into the SQL View window. In this window, you can type Access SQL statements or use SQL Pass-Through to type SQL statements in the SQL dialect that's specific to your back-end database. Once you harness the power of the SQL language, you can perform powerful tasks such as modifying the record source of a form or report at runtime.

Advanced VBA Techniques

IN THIS CHAPTER

Why This Chapter Is Important

The Visual Basic for Applications (VBA) language is extremely rich and comprehensive. VBA is covered throughout this book because it applies to different topics, but this chapter focuses on some advanced application development techniques. These topics include user-defined types, arrays, advanced function techniques, and VBA compilation options. The mastering of these topics helps to ensure your success as a VBA programmer.

What Are User-Defined Types, and Why Would You Use Them?

A user-defined type, known as a *struct* or *record*, allows you to create a variable containing several pieces of information. User-defined types are often used to hold information from one or more records in memory. They can also hold related information that would otherwise be stored in several unrelated variables. Because each element of a user-defined type can be instructed to hold a particular type of data, each element in the type can be defined to correspond to the type of data stored in a specific field of a table. A user-defined type might look like this:

```
Public Type TimeCardInfo
    TimeCardDetailID As Long
    TimeCardID As Long
    DateWorked As Date
    ProjectID As Long
    WorkDescription As String * 255
    BillableHours As Double
    BillingRate As Currency
    WorkCodeID As Long
End Type
```

Notice that the type of data stored in each element has been explicitly declared. The element containing the string WorkDescription has been declared with a length of 255. User-defined types make code cleaner by storing related data as a unit. A user-defined type exists only in memory and is, therefore, temporary. It's excellent for information that needs to be temporarily tracked at runtime. Because it's in memory, it can be quickly and efficiently read from and written to.

> **NOTE**
>
> The code snippets shown in the previous example are located in the basDataHandling module.

Declaring a User-Defined Type

You declare a user-defined type by using a Type statement that must be placed in the module's Declarations section. Types can be declared as Public or Private within a standard module. Types can be used, but can't be declared in Form or Report modules.

Creating a Type Variable

A Type variable is an instance of the type in memory; it must be declared before you can use the type. To declare a Type variable, create a Local, Private, Module-Level, or Public variable based on the type. Depending on where you place this declaration and how you declare it (using keywords Dim, Private, or Public), you determine its scope. The same rules for any other kind of variable apply to Type variables. The Dim statement in the code that follows creates a variable called mtypTimeCardData. If you place this Dim statement in the module's General section, it's visible to all routines in that module (notice the m, indicating that it is declared at the module level). If you place it in a subroutine or function, it's local to that particular routine:

```
Dim mtypTimeCardData As TimeCardInfo
```

Storing Information from a Record in a Form into a Type

After a Type variable has been declared, you can store data into each of its elements. The following code in the frmTimeCardHours form stores information from the form into a Type variable called mtypTimeCardData. The Type variable is declared as a Private variable in the General Declarations section of the form. The Type structure is declared in basDataHandling.

```
Private Sub cmdWriteToType_Click()

    'Retrieve control values and place them in the type structure
    mtypTimeCardData.TimeCardDetailID = Me.txtTimeCardDetailID
    mtypTimeCardData.TimeCardID = Me.txtTimeCardID
    mtypTimeCardData.DateWorked = Me.txtDateWorked
    mtypTimeCardData.ProjectID = Me.cboProjectID
    mtypTimeCardData.WorkDescription = Me.txtWorkDescription
    mtypTimeCardData.BillableHours = Me.txtBillableHours
    mtypTimeCardData.BillingRate = Me.txtBillingRate
    mtypTimeCardData.WorkCodeID = Me.cboWorkCodeID
End Sub
```

The code for this chapter can be found in the CHAP12EX.MDB database on the book's CD-ROM. The advantage of this code is that, rather than creating eight variables to store these eight pieces of related information, it creates one variable with eight elements. This method keeps things nice and neat.

Retrieving Information from the Elements of a Type

To retrieve information from your Type variable, simply refer to its name, followed by a period, and then the name of the element. The following code displays a message box containing all the time card–hour information:

```
Private Sub cmdDisplayFromType_Click()
    'Retrieve information from the type structure
    MsgBox "Timecard Detail ID Is " & mtypTimeCardData.TimeCardDetailID &
Chr(13) & _
        "Timecard ID Is " & mtypTimeCardData.TimeCardID & Chr(13) & _
        "Date Worked Is " & mtypTimeCardData.DateWorked & Chr(13) & _
        "Project ID Is " & mtypTimeCardData.ProjectID & Chr(13) & _
        "Work Description Is " & Trim(mtypTimeCardData.WorkDescription) &
Chr(13) & _
        "Billable Hours Is " & mtypTimeCardData.BillableHours & Chr(13) & _
        "Billing Rate Is " & mtypTimeCardData.BillingRate & Chr(13) & _
        "Workcode ID Is " & mtypTimeCardData.WorkCodeID
End Sub
```

> **NOTE**
>
> In Chapter 16, "Error Handling: Preparing for the Inevitable," an exercise shows a user-defined type used to hold pertinent error information. The example then replaces the user-defined type with properties of a custom error class. Although user-defined types are still useful and are, in fact, necessary for many Windows API function calls, custom class modules have replaced much of their functionality.

Working with Constants

A *constant* is a meaningful name given to a meaningless number or string. Constants can be used only for values that don't change at runtime. A tax rate or commission rate, for example, might be constant throughout your application. There are three types of constants in Access:

- Symbolic
- Intrinsic
- System-defined

Symbolic constants, created by using the Const keyword, improve the readability of your code and make code maintenance easier. Rather than referring to the number .0875 every time you want to refer to the tax rate, you can refer to the constant MTAXRATE. If the tax rate changes and you need to modify the value in your code, you'll make the change in only one place. Furthermore, unlike the number .0875, the name MTAXRATE is self-documenting.

Intrinsic constants are built in to Microsoft Access: they are part of the language itself. As an Access programmer, you can use constants supplied by Microsoft Access, Visual Basic, and ActiveX Data Objects (ADO). You can also use constants provided by any object libraries you're using in your application.

There are only three system-defined constants available to all applications on your computer: True, False, and Null.

Defining Your Own Constants

As mentioned, a symbolic constant is declared by using the Const keyword. A constant can be declared in a subroutine or function or in the General section of a Form, Report, or Class module. Unlike in previous versions of Access, constants can be strong-typed in Access 97, Access 2000, and Access 2002. There are several naming conventions for constants. One of them is to use a suitable scoping prefix, the letter c to indicate that you're working with a constant rather than a variable, and then the appropriate tag for the data type. The declaration and use of a Private constant would look like this:

```
Private Const mccurTaxRate As Currency = .0875
```

The naming convention that I prefer is the use of a scoping prefix and typing the name of the constant in all uppercase. The example given previously is changed to appear as follows:

```
Private Const MTAXRATE as Currency = .0875
```

This code, when placed in a module's Declarations section, creates a Private constant called MTAXRATE and sets it equal to .0875. Here's how the constant is used in code:

```
Function TotalAmount(curSaleAmount As Currency)
   TotalAmount = curSaleAmount * MTAXRATE
End Function
```

This routine multiplies the curSaleAmount, received as a parameter, by the constant MTAXRATE. It returns the result of the calculation by setting the function name equal to the product of the two values. The advantage of the constant in this example is that the code is more readable than TotalAmount = curSaleAmount * .0875 would be.

Scoping Symbolic Constants

Just as regular variables have scope, user-defined constants have scope. In the preceding example, you created a Private constant. The following statement, when placed in a module's Declarations section, creates a Public constant:

```
Public Const GTAXRATE As Currency = 0.0875
```

Because this constant is declared as Public, it can be accessed from any subroutine or function (including event routines) in your entire application. To better understand the benefits of a Public constant, suppose that you have many functions and subroutines, all referencing the constant GTAXRATE. Imagine what would happen if the tax rate were to change. If you hadn't used a constant, you would need to search your entire application, replacing the old tax rate with the new tax rate. However, because your Public constant is declared in one place, you can easily go in and modify the one line of code where this constant is declared.

NOTE

By definition, the value of constants can't be modified at runtime. If you try to modify the value of a constant, you get this VBA compiler error:

```
Variable Required - can't assign to this expression
```

Figure 12.1 illustrates this message box. You can see that an attempt was made to modify the value of the constant called GTAXRATE, which resulted in a compile error.

If you must change the value at runtime, you should consider storing the value in a table rather than declaring it as a constant. You can read the value into a variable when the application loads, and then modify the variable if needed. If you choose, you can write the new value back to the table.

FIGURE 12.1

An error message resulting from trying to modify the value of a constant.

Working with Intrinsic Constants

Microsoft Access declares a number of intrinsic constants that can be used in Code, Form, and Report modules. Because they're reserved by Microsoft Access, you can't modify their values or reuse their names; however, they can be used at any time without being declared.

You should use intrinsic constants whenever possible in your code. Besides making your code more readable, they make your code more portable to future releases of Microsoft Access. Microsoft might change the value associated with a constant, but it isn't likely to change the constant's name. All intrinsic constants appear in the Object Browser; to activate it, simply click the Object Browser tool on the Visual Basic toolbar while in the VBE. To view the constants that are part of the VBA language, select VBA from the Object Browser's

Project/Library drop-down list. Click Constants in the Classes list box, and a list of those constants is displayed in the Members of 'Constants' list box. (See Figure 12.2.)

Figure 12.2

Using the Object Browser to view intrinsic constants.

In Figure 12.2, all the constant names begin with vb. All VBA constants are prefixed with vb; all ActiveX Data Object constants, with ad; all Data Access Object (DAO) constants, with db; and all constants that are part of the Access language are prefixed with ac. To view the Access language constants, select Access from the Project/Library drop-down list and Constants from the Classes list box. To view the ActiveX Data Object constants, select ADODB from the Project/Library drop-down list. The constants are categorized by their function into various classes (for example, LockTypeEnum and ExecuteOptionEnum). Select the appropriate class from the Classes list box, and its members appear in the Members Of list box.

Another way to view constants is within the context of the parameter you're working with in the Code window. Right-click after the name of a parameter and select List Constants to display the constants associated with the parameter. This feature is covered in detail in Chapter 7, "VBA: An Introduction" in the section entitled "Tools for Working in the Visual Basic Editor."

Working with Arrays

An *array* is a series of variables referred to by the same name. Each element of the array is differentiated by a unique index number, but all the elements must be of the same data type. Arrays help make coding more efficient. It's easy to loop through each element of an array, performing some process on each element. Arrays have a lower bound, which is zero by default, and an upper bound, and array elements must be contiguous.

The scope of an array can be Public, Module, or Local. As with other variables, this depends on where the array is declared and whether the Public, Private, or Dim keyword is used.

Declaring and Working with Fixed Arrays

When declaring a *fixed array*, you give VBA the upper bound and the type of data that it will contain. The following code creates an array that holds six string variables:

```
Dim astrNames(5) As String
```

Fixed means that this array's size can't be altered at runtime. The following code gives an example of how you can loop through the array:

```
Sub FixedArray()
    'Declare an array of six elements
    Dim astrNames(5) As String
    Dim intCounter As Integer

    'Populate the first four elements of the array
    astrNames(0) = "Dan"
    astrNames(1) = "Alexis"
    astrNames(2) = "Brendan"
    astrNames(3) = "Zachary"

    'Use a For...Next loop to loop through the
    'elements of the array
    For intCounter = 0 To UBound(astrNames)
        Debug.Print astrNames(intCounter)
    Next intCounter
End Sub
```

This code starts by storing values into the first four elements of a six-element array. It then loops through each element of the array, printing the contents. Notice that the For...Next loop starts at zero and goes until the upper bound of the array, which is (5). Because the array is made up of strings, the last two elements of the array contain zero-length strings. If the array was composed of integers, the last two elements would contain zeros.

Another way to traverse the array is to use the For Each...Next construct. Your code would look like this:

```
Sub ArrayWith()
    'Declare an array of six elements
    Dim astrNames(5) As String
    Dim intCounter As Integer
    Dim vntAny As Variant

    'Populate the first four elements of the array
    astrNames(0) = "Dan"
```

```
        astrNames(1) = "Alexis"
        astrNames(2) = "Brendan"
        astrNames(3) = "Zachary"

        'Use a For...Each loop to loop through the
        'elements of the array
        For Each vntAny In astrNames
            Debug.Print vntAny
        Next vntAny
    End Sub
```

This code declares a `Variant` variable called `vntAny`. Instead of using a loop with `Ubound` as the upper delimiter to traverse the array, the example uses the `For Each...Next` construct.

NOTE

Many people do not like the fact that, by default, the elements of an array are zero based. Fortunately, the VBA language allows you to declare both the lower bound and the upper bound of any array. The syntax looks like this:

```
Dir astrNames(1 to 6)
```

Declaring and Working with Dynamic Arrays

Often, you don't know how many elements your array needs to contain. In this case, you should consider declaring a *dynamic array*, which can be resized at runtime. Using this type of array can make your code more efficient because VBA preallocates memory for all elements of a fixed array, regardless of whether data is stored in each of the elements. However, if you aren't sure how many elements your array will contain, preallocating a huge amount of memory can be quite inefficient.

To create a dynamic array, you declare it without assigning an upper bound. You do this by omitting the number between the parentheses when declaring the array, as shown in this example:

```
Sub DynamicArray()
    'Declare a dynamic array
    Dim astrNames() As String
    Dim intCounter As Integer
    Dim vntAny As Variant

    'Resize the array to hold two elements
    ReDim astrNames(1)
```

```
    'Populate the two elements
    astrNames(0) = "Dan"
    astrNames(1) = "Alexis"

    'Use a For...Each loop to loop through the
    'elements of the array
    For Each vntAny In astrNames
        Debug.Print vntAny
    Next vntAny
End Sub
```

However, there's a potential problem when you try to resize the array:

```
Sub ResizeDynamic()
    'Declare a dynamic array
    Dim astrNames() As String
    Dim intCounter As Integer
    Dim vntAny As Variant

    'Resize the array to hold two elements
    ReDim astrNames(1)

    'Populate the two elements
    astrNames(0) = "Dan"
    astrNames(1) = "Alexis"

    'Use a For...Each loop to loop through the
    'elements of the array
    For Each vntAny In astrNames
        Debug.Print vntAny
    Next vntAny
End Sub

Sub ResizeDynamic()
    'Declare a dynamic array
    Dim astrNames() As String
    Dim intCounter As Integer
    Dim vntAny As Variant

    'Resize the array to hold two elements
    ReDim astrNames(1)

    'Populate the two elements
    astrNames(0) = "Dan"
    astrNames(1) = "Alexis"
```

```
    'Resize the array to hold four elements
    ReDim astrNames(3)

    'Populate the last two elements
    astrNames(2) = "Brendan"
    astrNames(3) = "Zachary"

    'Use a For..Each loop to loop through the
    'elements of the array
    For Each vntAny In astrNames
        Debug.Print vntAny
    Next vntAny
End Sub
```

You might expect that all four elements will contain data. Instead, the `ReDim` statement reinitializes all the elements, and only elements 2 and 3 contain values. This problem can be avoided by using the `Preserve` keyword. The following code behaves quite differently:

```
Sub ResizePreserve()
    'Declare a dynamic array
    Dim astrNames() As String
    Dim intCounter As Integer
    Dim vntAny As Variant

    'Resize the array to hold two elements
    ReDim astrNames(1)

    'Populate the two elements
    astrNames(0) = "Dan"
    astrNames(1) = "Alexis"

    'Resize the array to hold four elements
    ReDim Preserve astrNames(3)

    'Populate the last two elements
    astrNames(2) = "Brendan"
    astrNames(3) = "Zachary"

    'Use a For...Each loop to loop through the
    'elements of the array
    For Each vntAny In astrNames
        Debug.Print vntAny
    Next vntAny
End Sub
```

In this example, all values already stored in the array are preserved. The `Preserve` keyword brings its own difficulties, though. It can temporarily require huge volumes of memory because, during the ReDim process, VBA creates a copy of the original array. All the values from the original array are copied to a new array. The original array is removed from memory when the process is complete. The Preserve keyword can cause problems if you're dealing with very large arrays in a limited memory situation.

> **TIP**
>
> Each type of array complements the other's drawbacks. As a VBA developer, you have the flexibility of choosing the right type of array for each situation. Fixed arrays are the way to go when the number of elements doesn't vary widely. But, dynamic arrays should be used when the number varies widely, and you're sure you have enough memory to resize even the largest possible arrays.

Passing Arrays as Parameters

Many people are unaware that you can pass an array as a parameter to a function or subroutine. The following code provides an example:

```
Sub PassArray()
    'Declare a six-element array
    Dim astrNames(5) As String
    Dim intCounter As Integer

    'Call the FillNames function, passing a reference
    'to the array
    Call FillNames(astrNames)

    'Use a For...Next loop to loop through the
    'elements of the array
    For intCounter = 0 To UBound(astrNames)
        Debug.Print astrNames(intCounter)
    Next intCounter
End Sub
```

The code begins by declaring a fixed array called astrNames. The FillNames routine is called. It receives the array as a parameter and then populates all its elements. The PassArray routine is then able to loop through all the elements of the array that was passed, displaying information from each element. The FillNames routine looks like this:

```
Sub FillNames(varNameList As Variant)
    'Populate the elements of the array
    varNameList(0) = "Alison"
    varNameList(1) = "Dan"
```

```
        varNameList(2) = "Alexis"
        varNameList(3) = "Brendan"
        varNameList(4) = "Zachary"
        varNameList(5) = "Sonia"
End Sub
```

Notice that the routine receives the array as a variant variable. It then populates each element of the array.

Advanced Function Techniques

The advanced function techniques covered in this section allow you to get the most out of the procedures you build. First, you learn the difference between passing your parameters by reference and passing them by value, and see that the default method of passing parameters isn't always the most prudent method.

The second part of this section shows you how to work with optional parameters, which help you build flexibility into your functions. They let you omit parameters, but named parameters allow you to add readability to your code. Named parameters also shelter you from having to worry about the order in which the parameters must appear. After reading this section, you can build much more robust and easy-to-use functions.

Passing by Reference Versus Passing by Value

By default, parameters in Access are passed *by reference*. This means that a memory reference to the variable being passed is received by the function. This process is best illustrated by an example:

```
Sub PassByRef()
    'Declare string variables
    Dim strFirstName As String
    Dim strLastName As String

    'Assign values to the string variables
    strFirstName = "Alison"
    strLastName = "Balter"

    'Call a subroutine that receives the two variables as
    'parameters by reference
    Call FuncByRef(strFirstName, strLastName)

    'Print the changed values of the variables
    Debug.Print strFirstName
    Debug.Print strLastName
End Sub
```

```
Sub FuncByRef(strFirstParm As String, strSecondParm As String)
    'Modify the values of the parameters
    strFirstParm = "Bill"
    strSecondParm = "Gates"
End Sub
```

You might be surprised that the Debug.Print statements found in the subroutine PassByRef print "Bill" and "Gates". This is because strFirstParm is actually a reference to the same location in memory as strFirstName, and strSecondParm is a reference to the same location in memory as strLastName. This violates the concepts of *black-box processing*, in which a variable can't be changed by any routine other than the one it was declared in. The following code eliminates this problem:

```
Sub PassByVal()
    'Declare the string variables
    Dim strFirstName As String
    Dim strLastName As String

    'Assign values to the string variables
    strFirstName = "Alison"
    strLastName = "Balter"

    'Call a subroutine that receives the two variables as
    'parameters by value
    Call FuncByVal(strFirstName, strLastName)

    'Print the unchanged values of the variables
    Debug.Print strFirstName
    Debug.Print strLastName
End Sub

Sub FuncByVal(ByVal strFirstParm As String, _
ByVal strSecondParm As String)
    'Change the values of the parameters
    'Since they are received by value,
    'the original variables are unchanged
    strFirstParm = "Bill"
    strSecondParm = "Gates"
End Sub
```

This FuncByVal subroutine receives the parameters *by value*. This means that only the values in strFirstName and strLastName are passed to the FuncByVal routine. The strFirstName and strLastName variables, therefore, can't be modified by the FuncByVal subroutine. The Debug.Print statements print "Alison" and "Balter".

The following example illustrates a great reason why you might want to pass a parameter by reference:

```
Sub GoodPassByRef()
    'Declare variables
    Dim blnSuccess As Boolean
    Dim strName As String

    'Set the value of the string variable
    strName = "Microsoft"

    'Set the boolean variable equal to the value
    'returned from the GoodFunc function
    blnSuccess = GoodFunc(strName)

    'Print the value of the boolean variable
    Debug.Print blnSuccess
End Sub

Function GoodFunc(strName As String)
    'Evaluate the length of the value received
    'as a parameter
    'Convert to Upper Case and return true if not zero-length
    'Return false if zero-length
    If Len(strName) Then
        strName = UCase$(strName)
        GoodFunc = True
    Else
        GoodFunc = False
    End If
End Function
```

In essence, the GoodFunc function needs to return two values. Not only does the function need to return the uppercase version of the string passed to it, but it also needs to return a success code. Because a function can return only one value, you need to be able to modify the value of strName within the function. As long as you're aware of what you're doing and why you're doing it, there's no problem with passing a parameter by reference.

TIP

I use a special technique to help readers of my code see whether I'm passing parameters by reference or by value. When passing parameters by reference, I refer to the parameters by the same name in both the calling routine and the actual procedure that I'm calling. On the other hand, when passing parameters by value, I refer to the parameters by different names in the calling routine and in the procedure that's being called.

After reading this section, you might ask yourself whether it is better to pass parameters by reference or by value. Although in terms of "black-box" processing, it is better to pass by value, code that involves parameters passed by reference actually executes more quickly than those passed by value. As long as you and the programmers that you work with are aware of the potential problems with passing parameters by reference, in general, I feel that it is better to pass parameters by reference.

Optional Parameters: Building Flexibility into Functions

Access 97, Access 2000, and Access 2002 allow you to use optional parameters. In other words, it isn't necessary to know how many parameters will be passed. The ReturnInit function in the following code receives the second two parameters as optional; it then evaluates whether the parameters are missing and responds accordingly:

```
Function ReturnInit(ByVal strFName As String, _
      Optional ByVal strMI, Optional ByVal strLName)
    'If strMI parameter is not received, prompt user for value
    If IsMissing(strMI) Then
        strMI = InputBox("Enter Middle Initial")
    End If


    'If strLName parameter is not received, prompt user for value
    If IsMissing(strLName) Then
        strLName = InputBox("Enter Last Name")
    End If

    'Return concatenation of last name, first name,
    'and middle initial
    ReturnInit = strLName & "," & strFName & " " & strMI
End Function
```

This function could be called as follows:

```
strName = ReturnInit("Bill",,"Gates")
```

As you can see, the second parameter is missing. Rather than causing a compiler error, as in earlier versions of Access, this code compiles and runs successfully. The IsMissing function, built into Access, determines whether a parameter has been passed. After identifying missing parameters, you must decide how to handle the situation in code. In the example, the function prompts for the missing information, but here are some other possible choices:

- Insert default values when parameters are missing.
- Accommodate for the missing parameters in your code.

Listing 12.1 and Listing 12.2 illustrate how to carry out these two alternatives.

LISTING 12.1   Inserting Default Values When Parameters Are Missing

```
Function ReturnInit2(ByVal strFName As String, _
    Optional ByVal strMI, Optional ByVal strLName)
    'If middle initial is not received, set it to "A"
    If IsMissing(strMI) Then
        strMI = "A"
    End If

    'If last name is not received, set it to "Roman"
    If IsMissing(strLName) Then
        strLName = "Roman"
    End If

    'Return concatenation of last name, first name,
    'and middle initial
    ReturnInit2 = strLName & "," & strFName & " " & strMI
End Function
```

This example uses a default value of "A" for the middle initial and a default last name of "Roman". Now take a look at Listing 12.2, which illustrates another method of handling missing parameters.

LISTING 12.2   Accommodating for Missing Parameters in Your Code

```
Function ReturnInit3(ByVal strFName As String, _
    Optional ByVal strMI, Optional ByVal strLName)
    Dim strResult As String

    'If middle initial and last name are missing,
    'return first name
    If IsMissing(strMI) And IsMissing(strLName) Then
        ReturnInit3 = strFName

    'If only the middle initial is missing
    'return last name and first name
    ElseIf IsMissing(strMI) Then
        ReturnInit3 = strLName & ", " & strFName

    'If only the last name is missing
    'return first name and middle initial
    ElseIf IsMissing(strLName) Then
        ReturnInit3 = strFName & " " & strMI

    'Otherwise (If nothing is missing),
    'return last name, first name and middle initial
```

LISTING 12.2   Continued

```
    Else
        ReturnInit3 = strLName & "," & strFName & " " & strMI
    End If
End Function
```

This example manipulates the return value, depending on which parameters it receives. If neither optional parameter is passed, just the first name displays. If the first name and middle initial are passed, the return value contains the first name followed by the middle initial. If the first name and last name are passed, the return value contains the last name, a comma, and the first name. If all three parameters are passed, the function returns the last name, a comma, a space, and the first name.

The declaration of the ReturnInit3 function shown in Listing 12.2 can easily be modified to provide default values for each optional parameter. The following declaration illustrates this:

```
Function ReturnInit4(Optional ByVal strFName As String = "Alison", _
        Optional ByVal strMI As String = "J", _
        Optional ByVal strLName As String = "Balter")
```

ReturnInit4 has three optional parameters. The declaration assigns a default value to each parameter. The function uses the default value if the calling routine does not supply the parameter.

> **NOTE**
>
> It is important to note that the IsMissing function only works with parameters with a data type of variant. This is because the IsMissing function returns true only if the value of the parameter is empty. If the parameter is numeric (for example, an integer), you will need to test for zero. If the parameter is a string, you will need to test for a zero-length string (" ").

Named Parameters: Eliminate the Need to Count Commas

In all the examples you've seen so far, the parameters of a procedure have been supplied positionally. Named parameters allow you to supply parameters without regard for their position, which is particularly useful in procedures that receive optional parameters. Take a look at this example:

```
strName = ReturnInit3("Bill",,"Gates")
```

Because the second parameter isn't supplied, and the parameters are passed positionally, a comma must be used as a placemarker for the optional parameter. This requirement can become unwieldy when you're dealing with several optional parameters. The following example greatly simplifies the process of passing the parameters and also better documents what's happening:

```
strName = ReturnInit3(strFName:= "Bill",strLName:= "Gates")
```

When parameters are passed by name, it doesn't even matter in what order the parameters appear, as shown in the following example:

```
strName = ReturnInit3(strLName:= "Gates",strFName:="Bill")
```

This call to the `ReturnInit3` function yields the same results as the call to the function in the previous example.

> **NOTE**
>
> When using named parameters, each parameter name must be exactly the same as the name of the parameter in the function being called. Besides requiring intimate knowledge of the function being called, this method of specifying parameters has one important disadvantage: If the author of the function modifies a parameter's name, all routines that use the named parameter will fail when calling the function.

Recursive Procedures

A *recursive procedure* is one that calls itself. If a procedure calls itself over and over again, it will eventually render an error. This is because it runs out of stack space. Here's an example:

```
Function Recursive(lngSomeVal)
    'Return value based on another call to the function
    Recursive = Recursive(lngSomeVal)
End Function
```

There are practical reasons why you might want to call a function recursively. Here's an example:

```
Function GetFactorial(intValue as Integer) as Long
    'If value passed is less than or equal to one, we're done
    If intValue <= 1 Then
        GetFactorial = 1

    'If value passed is greater than one,
    'call function again with decremented value
    'and multiply by value
```

```
    Else
        GetFactorial = GetFactorial(intValue - 1) * intValue
    End If
End Function
```

The code receives an input parameter (for example, 5). The value is evaluated to see if it is less than or equal to 1. If it is, the function is exited. If the value is greater than 1, the function is called again, but is passed the previous input parameter minus 1 (for example, 4). The return value from the function is multiplied by the original parameter value (for example, 4*5). The function calls itself over and over again until the value that it passes to itself is 2 minus 1 (1), and the function is exited. In the example where 5 is passed to the function, it multiplies 5*4*3*2*1, resulting in 120, the factorial of 5.

Using Parameter Arrays

Using a parameter array, you can easily pass a variable number of arguments to a procedure. Here's an example:

```
Sub GetAverageSalary(strDepartment As String, _
    ParamArray currSalaries() As Variant)

    Dim sngTotalSalary As Single
    Dim sngAverageSalary As Single
    Dim intCounter As Integer

    'Loop through the elements of the array,
    'adding up all of the salaries
    For intCounter = 0 To UBound(currSalaries())
        sngTotalSalary = sngTotalSalary + currSalaries(intCounter)
    Next intCounter

    'Divide the total salary by the number of salaries in the array
    sngAverageSalary = sngTotalSalary / (UBound(currSalaries()) + 1)

    'Display the department and the average salary in a message box
    MsgBox strDepartment & " has an average salary of " & _
        sngAverageSalary
End Sub
```

The routine is called like this:

```
Call GetAverageSalary("Accounting", 60000, 20000, 30000, 25000, 80000)
```

The beauty of the `ParamArray` keyword is that you can pass a variable number of parameters to the procedure. In the example, a department name and a variable number of salaries are passed to the `GetAverageSalary` procedure. The procedure loops through all the salaries that it receives in the parameter array, adding them together. It then divides the total by the number of salaries contained in the array.

Working with `Empty` and `Null`

`Empty` and `Null` are values that can exist only for Variant variables. They're different from one another and different from zero or a zero-length string. At times, you need to know whether the value stored in a variable is zero, a zero-length string, `Empty`, or `Null`. You can make this differentiation only with Variant variables.

Working with `Empty`

Variant variables are initialized to the value of `Empty`. Often, you need to know whether a value has been stored in a Variant variable. If a Variant has never been assigned a value, its value is `Empty`. As mentioned, the `Empty` value is not the same as zero, `Null`, or a zero-length string.

It's important to be able to test for `Empty` in a runtime environment. This can be done by using the `IsEmpty` function, which determines whether a variable has the `Empty` value. The following example tests a String variable for the `Empty` value:

```
Sub StringVar()
    Dim strName As String
    Debug.Print IsEmpty(strName) 'Prints False
    Debug.Print strName = "" 'Prints True
End Sub
```

The `Debug.Print` statement prints `False`. This variable is equal to a zero-length string because the variable is initialized as a String variable. All String variables are initialized to a zero-length string. The next example tests a Variant variable to see whether it has the `Empty` value:

```
Sub EmptyVar()
    Dim vntName As Variant
    Debug.Print IsEmpty(vntName) 'Prints True
    vntName = ""
    Debug.Print IsEmpty(vntName) 'Prints False
    vntName = Empty
    Debug.Print IsEmpty(vntName) 'Prints True
End Sub
```

A Variant variable loses its `Empty` value when any value has been stored in it, including zero, `Null`, or a zero-length string. It can become `Empty` again only by storing the keyword `Empty` in the variable.

Working with `Null`

`Null` is a special value that indicates unknown or missing data. `Null` is not the same as `Empty`, nor is one `Null` value equal to another one. Variant variables can contain the special value called `Null`.

Often, you need to know whether specific fields or controls have never been initialized. Uninitialized fields and controls have a default value of `Null`. By testing for `Null`, you can make sure fields and controls contain values.

If you want to make sure that all fields and controls in your application have data, you need to test for `Null`s. This can be done by using the `IsNull` function:

```
Sub NullVar()
    Dim vntName As Variant
    Debug.Print IsEmpty(vntName) 'Prints True
    Debug.Print IsNull(vntName) 'Prints False
    vntName = Null
    Debug.Print IsNull(vntName) 'Prints True
End Sub
```

Notice that `vntName` is equal to `Null` only after the value of `Null` is explicitly stored in it. It's important to know not only how variables and `Null` values interact, but also how to test for `Null` within a field in your database. A field contains a `Null` if data hasn't yet been entered in the field, and the field has no default value. In queries, you can test for the criteria `"Is Null"` to find all the records in which a particular field contains a `Null` value. When dealing with recordsets (covered in Chapter 14, "What Are ActiveX Data Objects and Data Access Objects, and Why Are They Important?"), you can also use the `IsNull` function to test for a `Null` value in a field. Here's an example:

```
Sub LoopProjects()
    Dim rst As ADODB.Recordset
    Set rst = New ADODB.Recordset

    'Open a recordset based on the projects table
    rst.Open "tblProjects", CurrentProject.Connection

    'Loop through all of the records in the recordset
    Do Until rst.EOF

        'Print the ProjectID and the ProjectName
        Debug.Print rst!ProjectID, rst!ProjectName

        'If the ProjectBeginDate field is null,
        'display a message to the user
        If IsNull(rst!ProjectBeginDate) Then
```

```
            Debug.Print "Project Begin Date Contains No Value!!"
        End If

        'Move to the next row in the recordset
        rst.MoveNext
    Loop
End Sub
```

Alternatively, you could use the more compact Nz function to detect Nulls and print a special message:

```
Sub LoopProjects2()
    Dim rst As ADODB.Recordset
    Set rst = New ADODB.Recordset

    'Open a recordset based on the projects table
    rst.Open "tblProjects", CurrentProject.Connection

    'Loop through all of the rows in the recordset
    Do Until rst.EOF

        'Print the ProjectID and the ProjectName
        Debug.Print rst!ProjectID, rst!ProjectName

        'Print the ProjectBeginDate, or a message if
        'the ProjectBeginDate is null
        Debug.Print Nz(rst!ProjectBeginDate, _
            "Project Begin Date Contains No Value!!")
        rst.MoveNext
    Loop
End Sub
```

All the concepts of recordset handling are covered in Chapter 14. For now, you need to understand only that this code loops through each record in tblProjects. It uses the IsNull function to evaluate whether the ProjectBeginDate field contains a Null value. If the field does contain a Null, a warning message is printed to the Immediate window. Here is another example:

```
Private Sub Form_Current()

    Dim ctl as Control

    'Loop through each control in the form's
    'Controls collection
    For Each ctl In Controls

        'If the control is a TextBox
        If TypeOf ctl Is TextBox Then
```

```
              'If the value in the control is null,
              'change the BackColor property to cyan
              If IsNull(ctl.Value) Then
                  ctl.BackColor = vbCyan

              'If the value in the control is not null
              'change the BackColor property to white
              Else
                  ctl.BackColor = vbWhite
              End If
          End If
      Next ctl
End Sub
```

The code in this example (found in the frmProjects form in CHAP12EX.MDB) loops through every control on the current form. If the control is a text box, the routine checks to see whether the value in the text box is Null. If it is, the BackColor property of the text box is set to Aqua; otherwise, it's set to White.

You should know about some idiosyncrasies of Null:

- Expressions involving Null always result in Null. (See the next example.)
- A function that's passed a Null usually returns a Null.
- Null values propagate through built-in functions that return variants.

The following example shows how Null values are propagated:

```
Sub PropNulls()
    Dim rst As ADODB.Recordset
    Set rst = New ADODB.Recordset

    'Open a recordset based on the Projects table
    rst.Open "tblProjects", CurrentProject.Connection

    'Loop through the recordset
    Do Until rst.EOF

        'Print the ProjectID and the value of the
        'ProjectBeginDate plus one
        Debug.Print rst!ProjectID, rst!ProjectBeginDate + 1

        'Move to the next row
        rst.MoveNext
    Loop
End Sub
```

Figure 12.3 illustrates the effects of running this routine on a table in which the first and third records contain Null values. Notice that the result of the calculation is Null for those records because the Null propagated within those records.

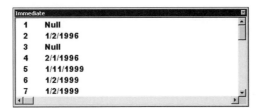

FIGURE 12.3

The result of running the PropNulls routine.

Notice the difference from the previous example if the value in the field is Empty:

```
Sub EmptyVersusNull()
    Dim rst As ADODB.Recordset
    Set rst = New ADODB.Recordset

    'Open a recordset based on the Projects table
    rst.Open "tblProjects", CurrentProject.Connection

    'Loop through the recordset
    Do Until rst.EOF

        'Print the ProjectID and the PurchaseOrderNumber
        'combined with the word "Hello"
        Debug.Print rst!ProjectID, rst!PurchaseOrderNumber + "Hello"

        'Move to the next row
        rst.MoveNext
    Loop
End Sub
```

In this example, the tblProjects table has several records. The PurchaseOrderNumber for the first record contains a Null; for the third record, it contains an Empty. Notice the different effects of the two values, as shown in Figure 12.4.

Looking at Figure 12.4, you can see that Null printed for the first record, and Hello printed for the third record.

FIGURE 12.4

The result of running the EmptyVersusNull *routine.*

NOTE

The EmptyVersusNull routine uses a numeric operator (+). As discussed, the effect of Null used in a calculation is a resulting Null. In text strings, you can use an ampersand (&) instead of a plus (+) to eliminate this problem. Figure 12.5 illustrates the same code with an ampersand to concatenate rather than add. You can see that no Null values result from the concatenation.

FIGURE 12.5

The result of changing plus (+) in the EmptyVersusNull *routine to an ampersand (&).*

It's very common to create a generic routine that receives any value, tests to see whether it's Null, and returns a non-Null value. An example is the CvNulls function:

```
Function CvNulls(vntVar1 As Variant, vntVar2 As Variant) _
    As Variant
    'If first variable is null, return the second variable
    'otherwise, return the first variable
    CvNulls = IIf(IsNull(vntVar1), vntVar2, vntVar1)
End Function
```

This routine would be called as follows:

```
Sub TestForNull(vntSalary As Variant, vntCommission As Variant)
    'Add the result of calling the CVNulls function,
    'passing the salary and zero to the
    'result of calling the CVNulls function
    'passing the commission and zero
    curTotal = CvNulls(vntSalary, 0) + CvNulls(vntCommission, 0)

    'Display the total of salary plus commission
    MsgBox curTotal
End Sub
```

The `TestForNull` routine receives two parameters: `salary` and `commission`. It adds the two values to determine the total of salaries plus commissions. Ordinarily, if the value of either parameter is `Null`, the expression results in `Null`. This problem is eliminated by the `CvNulls` function, which also receives two parameters. The first parameter is the variable being tested for `Null`; the second is the value you want the function to return if the first parameter is determined to be `Null`. The routine combines the `Immediate If` (`IIf`) function and the `IsNull` function to evaluate the first parameter and return the appropriate value.

> **NOTE**
>
> If you simply want to substitute a value for a `Null`, the built-in function `Nz` can be used instead of a user-defined function. The user-defined function offers more functionality, when necessary.

Creating and Working with Custom Collections

Earlier in this chapter, I discussed the problems associated with arrays. If you are unsure of the number of elements that the array will contain, fixed arrays can take up large amounts of memory unnecessarily. On the other hand, the resizing of dynamic arrays is rather inefficient. Finally, all the elements of an array must be contiguous, and the arbitrary identifier for the array element is meaningless. The answer—custom collections. Custom collections can contain values and objects. You can easily add items to, and remove items from, a collection. Each element in the collection is identified by a meaningful unique key.

In summary, custom collections are similar to arrays, but they offer several advantages:

- Collections are dynamically allocated. They take up memory based only on what's in them at a given time. This is different from arrays, whose size must be either predefined or redimensioned at runtime. When an array is redimensioned, Access actually makes a copy of the array in memory, taking up substantial resources. By using custom collections, you can avoid this consumption of extra resources.

- A collection always knows how many elements it has, and elements can easily be added and removed.

- Each element of a collection can contain a different type of data.

- Elements can be added into any element of a collection.

> **NOTE**
>
> The code examples in this section are found in the basCollections module of the Chap12EX.MDB database.

Creating a Collection

A collection is created using a Collection object. After the Collection object is declared, items can be added to the collection. The code necessary to create a custom collection looks like this:

```
Dim colNames as Collection
```

Adding Items to a Collection

The Add method of the Collection object is used to add items to a custom collection. The Add method receives a value or object reference as its first parameter, and a unique key to that element of the collection as a second parameter. The Add method appears as follows:

```
colNames.Add "Alexis", "Alexis"
```

The code shown previously adds the name Alexis to a collection called colNames. The key to the item in the collection is the name Alexis. In the following code example, the collection colNames is first declared and instantiated. Then several names are added to the custom collection colNames.

```
Sub AddToCollection()
    'Declare a Collection object
    Dim colNames As Collection
```

```
        'Instantiate the Collection object
        Set colNames = New Collection

        'Add items to the collection
        colNames.Add "Alison", "Alison"
        colNames.Add "Dan", "Dan"
        colNames.Add "Alexis", "Alexis"
        colNames.Add "Brendan", "Brendan"
        colNames.Add "Sonia", "Sonia"
        colNames.Add "Sue", "Sue"
End Sub
```

12

> **CAUTION**
>
> Unlike almost every other array or collection in VBA, custom collections are one-based rather than zero-based. This is a big change if you're used to thinking of arrays and collections as always zero-based.

Accessing an Item in a Collection

After items have been added to a collection, the `Item` method is used to access them via either their ordinal position, or the key designated when they were added. Accessing an item in a collection using the ordinal position looks like this:

```
Debug.Print colNames.Item(1)
```

Because the `Item` method is the default method of the Collection object, the code can be shortened to this:

```
Debug.Print colNames(1)
```

I usually prefer to refer to an item in a collection using its unique key. The code appears as follows:

```
Debug.Print colNames("Alexis")
```

Removing Items from a Collection

The `Remove` method of the Collection object is used to remove items from a collection. The syntax looks like this:

```
colNames.Remove 2
```

The preceding syntax would remove the second element of the collection. Using the key, the code is changed to this:

```
colNames.Remove "Sonia"
```

You can easily remove all the elements of a collection in two ways:

```
Set colNames = New Collection
```

or

```
Set colNames = Nothing
```

Iterating Through the Elements of a Collection

The For...Each loop is used to iterate through the items in a collection. The code looks like this:

```
Sub IterateCollection()
    'Declare a Collection object
    Dim colNames As Collection

    'Declare a variant variable for looping
    'through the collection
    Dim varItem As Variant

    'Instantiate the Collection object
    Set colNames = New Collection

    colNames.Add "Alison", "Alison"
    colNames.Add "Dan", "Dan"
    colNames.Add "Alexis", "Alexis"
    colNames.Add "Brendan", "Brendan"
    colNames.Add "Sonia", "Sonia"
    colNames.Add "Sue", "Sue"

    'Use the variant variable and a For..Each
    'loop to loop through each element in
    'the collection, printing its value
    For Each varItem In colNames
        Debug.Print colNames(varItem)
    Next varItem
End Sub
```

Notice that in addition to the declaration of the Collection variable, a Variant variable is declared. The Variant variable is used in the For...Each loop to loop through each item in the collection. The Variant variable is the subscript within the For...Each loop for accessing a particular item within the collection.

Low-Level File Handling

On occasion, it is necessary to write data to, or read data from, a text file. This is often referred to as *low-level file handling*. Three types of file access exist: sequential, random, and binary. Only sequential access is covered in this text. Sequential access is used to read and write to a text file, such as an error log. The Open keyword is used to open a text file. The Input # keyword is used to read data. The Write # keyword is used to write data. Finally, the Close keyword is used to close the file. Here's an example:

```
Sub LogErrorText()
    Dim intFile As Integer

    'Store a free file handle into a variable
    intFile = FreeFile

    'Open a file named ErrorLog.txt in the current directory
    'using the file handle obtained above
    Open CurDir & "\ErrorLog.Txt" For Append Shared As intFile

    'Write the error information to the file
    Write #intFile, "LogErrorDemo", Now, Err, Error, CurrentUser()

    'Close the file
    Close intFile
End Sub
```

The FreeFile function is used to locate a free file handle. The Open keyword opens a file located in the current directory, with the name ErrorLog.txt. The file is open in shared mode and for append, using the file handle returned by the FreeFile function. The Write # keyword is then used to write error information to the text file. Finally, the Close keyword closes the text file.

> **NOTE**
>
> This example is taken from Chapter 14. The sample code is located in the CHAP14EX.mdb database.

Understanding and Effectively Using Compilation Options

Microsoft Access gives you a few alternatives for compilation. Understanding them can help you to decide whether compilation speed or trapping compilation errors is more important to you.

12

ADVANCED VBA TECHNIQUES

Compile on Demand

By default, VBA compilesyour code only when the code in the module changes or when a pro-cedure in one module is called by another module. Although this default setting can dramati-cally speed the compilation process, it can leave you wondering whether you have a hidden time bomb lurking somewhere in your application.

Here's a typical scenario: You open a form, make some simple changes, save the changes, and close the form. You repeat this process for a few additional forms. You also open a couple of modules to make some equally simple changes. During the testing process, you forget to test one or more of the forms and one or more of the modules. With the Compile On Demand option set to True (its default value), errors aren't identified until the offending code is accessed.

To disable the Compile On Demand feature, choose Tools|Options from the VBE. Click the General tab and remove the check from Compile On Demand. You might notice some degrada-tion in performance each time your code compiles, but this is time well spent.

Importing and Exporting Code Modules

The Access 2002 VBE allows you to import code or form modules into, and export code mod-ules from, a database. To export a form or code module, take the following steps:

1. Activate the VBE.
2. Within the Project Explorer window, right-click the object you want to export.
3. Select Export File. The Export File dialog appears.
4. Select a location and name for the exported file and then click Save.

When you export a module, it is exported as an ASCII text file. You can import the text file into another Microsoft Access database, into any other Microsoft Office product (for example, Microsoft Excel), or into a Visual Basic project.

NOTE

If you export a Form module from the VBE, only the Class module behind the form is exported. No visual aspects of the form are exported.

Just as you can export a text file, you can import a text file. This allows you to add an existing module or form to a project. The file is copied and imported into the database. The original file is unaffected. To import a file into your Access database:

1. Activate the VBE.
2. Within the Project Explorer window, right-click and select Import File. The Import File dialog appears.
3. Locate and select the file you want to import, and then click Open.

Working with Project Properties

Every database project has user-definable properties. These include:

- The project name
- A description of the project
- The name of the help file associated with the project
- The help context ID associated with the project
- Conditional compilation arguments
- A password associated with the project

To view or modify project properties:

1. Activate the VBE.
2. Select Tools|<*project name*> Properties. The Project Properties dialog appears (see Figure 12.6).

FIGURE 12.6
The Project Properties dialog.

3. Click the General tab to designate or change any of the general project properties.

4. Click the Protection tab to specify a password for the VBA project.

5. Click OK to close the dialog, accepting the options you have set. You must close the database and reopen it for any security options to take effect.

The Protection options deserve special attention. If you click to select Lock Project for Viewing, the VBA project cannot be viewed or edited by someone who does not have the correct password. If you do not select Lock Project for Viewing, the VBA project can be viewed by anyone, but project properties can be changed only by someone with the correct password.

PRACTICAL EXAMPLES

Putting Advanced Techniques to Use

The examples in this section put into practice all that you have learned throughout this chapter. Concepts covered include the use of Null, intrinsic constants, and type structures.

Examples of Null, the DoCmd Object, and Intrinsic Constants

The following event routine illustrates how you could view all the projects associated with the selected client. It illustrates the importance of the ability to work with Null values and intrinsic constants.

```
Private Sub cmdViewProjects_Click()
On Error GoTo Err_cmdViewProjects_Click

    'Evaluate the ClientID text box to determine if it is null
    'If it is null, display a message to the user
    'Otherwise, save the current record and open the
    'projects form (which is set up to only show projects
    'related to the selected client)
    If IsNull(Me.txtClientID.Value) Then
        MsgBox "You Must Enter Client Information Before " & _
            "Viewing the Projects Form"
    Else
        DoCmd.RunCommand acCmdSaveRecord
        DoCmd.OpenForm FormName:="frmProjects"
    End If

Exit_cmdViewProjects_Click:
    Exit Sub
```

```
Err_cmdViewProjects_Click:
    MsgBox Err.Description
    Resume Exit_cmdViewProjects_Click

End Sub
```

The routine first invokes error handling (discussed in Chapter 16, "Error Handling: Preparing for the Inevitable"); then uses the IsNull function to test whether a ClientID has been entered. The IsNull function returns a True if the value in the txtClientID control is Null. If it is, an error message is displayed. If the txtClientID control contains a non-Null value, two methods are performed on the DoCmd object.

The first method performed on the DoCmd object is the RunCommand method. This method receives the constant associated with the name of the menu command you want to execute. The use of intrinsic constants makes this code more readable, and the RunCommand method makes it much easier to call menu commands from code. The second method performed on the DoCmd object is OpenForm, which opens the frmProjects form. The RecordSource property of the frmProjects form is programmatically set to a query that only displays projects associated with the currently selected customer.

An Example of Using a Type Structure

If many parts of an application require the same information that is stored in a specific table, it would be inefficient to read the data from this table each time the application needs it. It would be much more efficient to read this data once, when the application loads, and store it in a type structure. Because it remains in memory at all times, you can efficiently retrieve it whenever needed. The type structure is defined, and a Public Type variable based on the type structure is declared in a module's Declarations section. It looks like this:

```
Type CompanyInfo
    SetUpID As Long
    CompanyName As String * 50
    Address As String * 255
    City As String * 50
    StateProvince As String * 20
    PostalCode As String * 20
    Country As String * 50
    PhoneNumber As String * 30
    FaxNumber As String * 30
    DefaultPaymentTerms As String * 255
    DefaultInvoiceDescription As String
End Type
Public typCompanyInfo As CompanyInfo
```

You must build a subroutine that is invoked when your startup form is first loaded. This routine populates all the elements of the type structure. The routine looks like this:

```
Sub GetCompanyInfo()

    Dim strSubName As String
    Dim rst As ADODB.Recordset

    'Instantiate and open a recordset
    'based on the tblCompanyInfo table
    Set rst = New ADODB.Recordset
    rst.ActiveConnection = CurrentProject.Connection
    rst.Open "Select * from tblCompanyInfo", Options:=adCmdText

    'Populate the elements of the type structure
    'with data from the table
    With typCompanyInfo
        .SetUpID = rst!SetUpID
        .CompanyName = rst!CompanyName
        .Address = rst!Address
        .City = rst!City
        .StateProvince = rst!StateOrProvince
        .PostalCode = rst!PostalCode
        .Country = rst!Country
        .PhoneNumber = rst!PhoneNumber
        .FaxNumber = rst!PhoneNumber
    End With

    'Close the recordset and destoy the object
    rst.Close
    Set rst = Nothing
End Sub
```

Don't be concerned with the recordset handling included in this routine. Instead, notice that the value from each field in the first (and only) record of the tblCompanyInfo table is being loaded into the elements of the Global Type variable. Here's an example of how the Type variable is used:

```
Sub PopulateControls()
    'Populate the text boxes on the report
    'with data from the type structure
    txtCompanyName.Value = Trim(typCompanyInfo.CompanyName)
    txtAddress.Value = Trim(typCompanyInfo.Address)
    txtCityStateZip.Value = Trim(typCompanyInfo.City) & ", " & _
        Trim(typCompanyInfo.StateProvince) & _
```

```
    "   " & Format(Trim(typCompanyInfo.PostalCode), "!&&&&&-&&&&")
    txtPhoneFax.Value = "PHONE: " & _
        Format(Trim(typCompanyInfo.PhoneNumber), "(&&&)&&&-&&&&") & _
        "       FAX: " & _
        Format(Trim(typCompanyInfo.FaxNumber), "(&&&)&&&-&&&&")
End Sub
```

This routine is populates four different controls on a form with the company information retrieved from the elements of the Global Type variable.

Summary

As an Access developer, you spend much of your time writing VBA code. Knowing the tricks and tips of the trade and understanding the more advanced aspects of the language will save you much time and help you streamline your application code.

This chapter showed you tricks and tips you can use to effectively navigate the VBA environment. It delved into more advanced aspects of the VBA language, such as user-defined types, constants, and arrays. You have seen the important difference between passing parameters by reference and passing them by value, and learned about other advanced function techniques, such as optional and named parameters. Other important topics covered in this chapter included collections, Empty versus Null, and compilation options. Understanding these valuable aspects of the VBA language will help you get the most out of the code you write.

12

**ADVANCED VBA
TECHNIQUES**

Exploiting the Power of Class Modules

IN THIS CHAPTER

Exploring the Benefits of Class Modules

Access 2002 offers two types of modules: Standard modules and Class modules. Access 95 introduced Class modules for forms and reports, but Access 97 was the first version of Access to offer the capability to create standalone Class modules.

A Class module is similar to a Code module. The subroutines and functions in the Class module become the methods of the class. The `Property Let` and `Property Get` routines become the properties of the class, and the Class module's name becomes the name of the custom object. A Class module is a great way to encapsulate related functions into a portable, self-contained object. Class modules can help you simplify the process of performing the following tasks:

- Manipulating databases and recordsets
- Calling Windows API functions
- Performing low-level, file-handling tasks
- Accessing and modifying the registry

If you regularly open databases and recordsets and traverse those recordsets by using code, you might decide that you want to simplify these tasks. By building Class modules, you can more easily access table data.

Object Orientation—An Introduction

The world of object orientation is exciting, but it requires a new way of thinking about things. Access 2002 is actually object-based, rather than object-oriented. So, what exactly is the difference? The definitions of the following terms should help you differentiate between these two concepts:

- Class—A template for an object
- Object—An instance of a class
- Instantiation—The process of creating an object based on a class
- Polymorphism—The state of being multifaced; using the same method and property names with different objects, the properties and methods of which are implemented differently for different objects
- Subclassing—Building one class based on another
- Inheritance—In object-oriented programming, the ability for newly created subclasses to take on the behavior of their parent classes

VBA, and therefore Access, supports the creation of custom classes and the instantiation of objects based on those classes. Polymorphism can also be simulated by using the same property and method names within different classes. VBA does not fully support subclassing and inheritance. With the exception of a keyword called Implements, classes cannot be based on other classes and, therefore, cannot elicit the behavior of other classes. True polymorphism can exist only when child classes inherit the properties and methods of their parents. The Implements keyword gets you close, but does not fully exhibit the behavior of polymorphism.

To make sure that you understand the terms, let's use an analogy. Imagine that you are going to bake some cookies. The cookie cutter is the class, the template for a cookie object. When you use the cookie cutter to create an actual cookie, you instantiate the cookie class to create a cookie object. The cookie has some properties, such as a powdered sugar property, and some methods, such as the bake method. A ham class is a template for a ham object. The ham class also has a bake method. The "code" behind the bake method of the cookie object and the bake method of the ham object are different. This is polymorphism (being multifaced) in action. If VBA were fully object-oriented, the cookie class and the ham class would have been derived from the same parent. Now that you are familiar with some object-oriented terms and concepts, take a look at how custom classes work in VBA.

Creating and Using a Class Module

You can insert a Class module in one of three ways:

- With the Database window active, select Insert|Class Module.
- With the Visual Basic Editor active, select Insert|Class Module.
- With the Visual Basic Editor active, right-click the project within the Project Explorer window and select Insert|Class Module from the pop-up menu.

After being inserted, a Class module looks like a Standard Code module. (See Figure 13.1.) The differences lie in how the variables and procedures in the Class module are accessed, as well as in the behavior of the Class module.

Adding Properties

The most basic way to add a property to a Class module is to use a Public variable. For example, the following code shows the declaration of two Public variables, FirstName and LastName. After they are added to a class, both of these variables are considered properties of the class.

```
Public FirstName as String
Public LastName as String
```

FIGURE 13.1

A new Class module.

Adding Methods

A function or subroutine placed within a Class module is considered a method of the class. The `Speak` subroutine that follows acts as a method of the `PublicPerson` class. It accesses the FirstName and LastName properties of the class, displaying them in a message box:

```
Public Function Speak()
    Speak = FirstName & " " & LastName
End Function
```

Instantiating and Using the Class

To utilize the code within a class, you must instantiate an object based on that class. To do that, you first declare an object based on the class. You then instantiate the object using a `Set` statement. Then, you can access the properties and methods of the object. The code looks like this:

```
Sub SingleInstance()
    'Declare and instantiate a Person object
    Dim oPerson As Person
    Set oPerson = New Person

    'Set the first name and last name
    'properties of the person object
```

```
    oPerson.FirstName = "Alison"
    oPerson.LastName = "Balter"

    'Display the return value from the Speak
    'method in a message box
    MsgBox oPerson.Speak
End Sub
```

The code begins by declaring a `Person` object. The `Set` statement is used to create an instance of the `Person` object. The FirstName and LastName properties of the instance are set to `Alison` and `Balter`, respectively. The `Speak` method of the object is then executed. It returns the concatenated name, which is displayed in a message box.

Property Let and Get—Adding Properties the Right Way

Public variables, when used as properties, have the following major disadvantages:

- Using Public variables, you cannot create properties that are read-only or write-only.
- You cannot validate what goes into Public variables.
- You cannot manipulate the value as the Public variable is set.
- You cannot track changes to Public variables.

For these reasons, it is prudent to utilize property procedures rather than Public variables. With property procedures, you can create custom runtime properties of user-defined objects. After you have defined custom properties, you can use `Property Let` and `Get` to assign values to and retrieve values from custom properties. Custom properties give you more flexibility in creating your applications; you can create reusable objects that expose properties to other objects.

Custom properties are Public by default and are placed in Class, Form, or Report modules, making them visible to other modules in the current database. They aren't visible to other databases.

The `Property Let` routine defines a property procedure that assigns a value to a user-defined object's property. Using a `Property Let` is similar to assigning a value to a Public variable, but a Public variable can be written to from anywhere in the database, with little or no control over what's written to it. With a `Property Let` routine, you can control exactly what happens when a value is assigned to the property. Here's an example:

```
Public Property Let FirstName(ByVal strNewValue As String)
    mstrFirstName = UCase(strNewValue)
End Property
```

You might be thinking this code looks just like a subroutine, and you're somewhat correct. It's a special type of subroutine that executes automatically in response to the change in a custom property's value. The example receives the value that the property is changed to as strNewValue. The uppercase version of the value is stored in the Private variable mstrFirstName. The following line of code causes the code in the Property Let to execute:

```
FirstName = "Alison"
```

Property Let sets the value of a custom property, but Property Get defines a property procedure that retrieves a value from a user-defined object's property. This example illustrates how Property Get is used:

```
Public Property Get FirstName() As String
    FirstName = mstrFirstName
End Property
```

The Property Get routine automatically executes whenever the code tries to retrieve the value of the property. The value stored in the Private variable mstrFirstName is returned from the Property Get procedure. This routine can be executed by retrieving the property from anywhere in the database. The following line of code causes the code in the Property Get to execute:

```
MsgBox FirstName
```

The code that follows shows the declaration of the two Private variables mstrFirstName and mstrLastName. The Property Let for FirstName and the Property Let for LastName store values into these two Private variables. The Property Get for FirstName and the Property Get for LastName retrieve the values stored in the Private variables.

```
Private mstrFirstName As String
Private mstrLastName As String

Public Property Get FirstName() As String
    FirstName = mstrFirstName
End Property

Public Property Let FirstName(ByVal strNewValue As String)
    mstrFirstName = UCase(strNewValue)
End Property

Public Property Get LastName() As String
    LastName = mstrLastName
End Property

Public Property Let LastName(ByVal strNewValue As String)
    mstrLastName = UCase(strNewValue)
End Property
```

Unlike with Public variables, you have significant control over a property created with `Property Let` and `Property Get` routines. To create a read-only property, include only a `Property Get`. To create a write-only property, include only a `Property Let`. If you want a read/write property, include both the `Property Get` and the `Property Let` routines.

Setting Values with `Property Set`

Whereas a `Property Let` stores a value in a property, a `Property Set` is used to store a reference to an object in a property. It looks like this:

```
Private mobjCustomer as Customer

Public Property Set GoodCustomer(objCustomer as Customer)
    Set mobjCustomer = objCustomer
End Property
```

`Property Set` and its uses are covered in more detail in the later section "Building Hierarchies of Classes."

Creating Multiple Class Instances

One of the advantages of Class modules is that multiple instances of the class can be created. Each instance maintains its own variables and executes its own code. This is illustrated in the following code:

```
Sub MultipleInstance()
    'Declare both class objects
    Dim oPerson1 As Person
    Dim oPerson2 As Person

    'Instantiate both class objects
    Set oPerson1 = New Person
    Set oPerson2 = New Person

    'Set the first name and last name
    'properties of the oPerson1 object
    oPerson1.FirstName = "Alison"
    oPerson1.LastName = "Balter"

    'Display the return value from the Speak
    'method of the first instance in a message box
    MsgBox oPerson1.Speak

    'Set the first name and last name
    'properties of the oPerson2 object
```

```
oPerson2.FirstName = "Dan"
oPerson2.LastName = "Balter"

'Display the return value from the Speak
'method of the second instance in a message box
MsgBox oPerson2.Speak
```

```
End Sub
```

Two instances of the Person class are created. The first is referred to as oPerson1 and the second, as oPerson2. The FirstName property of oPerson1 is set equal to Alison, and the LastName property of oPerson1 is set equal to Balter. The FirstName property of oPerson2 is set equal to Dan, and the LastName property of oPerson2 is set equal to Balter. The Speak method returns the name of the correct person and is displayed in a message box.

The Initialize and Terminate Events

The Initialize and Terminate events are the two built-in events that execute for a class object. The Initialize event executes as the class is instantiated, and the Terminate event executes as the class is destroyed.

Initialize

The Initialize event is generally used to perform tasks such as establishing a connection to a database and initializing variables. The following is an example of the use of the Initialize event:

```
Private Sub Class_Initialize()
    FirstName = "Alison"
    LastName = "Balter"
End Sub
```

In this example the default values of the FirstName and LastName properties of the class are set equal to Alison and Balter, respectively.

Terminate

The Terminate event is generally used to perform the class's cleanup tasks. An example is closing a recordset used by the class. The following is an example of the use of the Terminate event:

```
Private Sub Class_Terminate()
    rstCustomer.Close
    Set rstCustomer = Nothing
End Sub
```

Working with Enumerated Types

By now, you should be quite familiar with Intellisense and its benefits. One benefit is that, when you type the name of a property or a method whose value should be set to one of a set of constants, the list of appropriate constants automatically appears. For example, when using the OpenForm method of the DoCmd object, a list of six intrinsic constants appears for the View parameter. Using enumerated types, you can benefit from this behavior with your own custom properties and methods. Here's how it works.

For the custom PersonType property, imagine that only four values are appropriate: Client, PersonalContact, Vendor, and Other. Using an enumerated type, you can easily set it up so that the four appropriate types appear in a list whenever you set the PersonType property of the class. Use the Enum keyword to define an enumerated type:

```
'Enumeration for PersonType
Public Enum PersonTypeList
    Client
    PersonalContact
    Vendor
    Other
End Enum
```

To use the enumerated type with the property, you must include it in the definition of the Property Get and Property Let routines:

```
Public Property Get PersonType() As PersonTypeList
    'Retrieve the PersonType property
    PersonType = mlngPersonType
End Property

Public Property Let PersonType(ByVal lngPersonType As PersonTypeList)
    'Set the PersonType property
    mlngPersonType = lngPersonType
End Property
```

Whenever you attempt to set the value of the PersonType property of the class, the list of valid types automatically appears. (See Figure 13.2.)

Notice that a long integer is used to store the person type. This is because *all* enumerated type constants are limited to long integer values. Furthermore, you might wonder what values are stored in the variable when each constant is used. Unless directed otherwise, the first item in the list is assigned the value 0 (zero). Each subsequent item in the list is assigned the next value (1, 2, 3, and so on) In this example, Client is assigned 0, PersonalContact is assigned 1, Vendor is assigned 2, and Other is assigned 3. If you wish to control the long integer value assigned to each item in the list, simply set the constant equal to a value:

```
'Enumeration for PersonType
Public Enum PersonTypeList2
    Client = 10
    PersonalContact = 5
    Vendor = 2
    Other = 999
End Enum
```

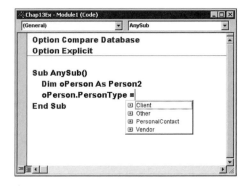

Figure 13.2

The list of types that appears after defining an enumerated type for the PersonType property of the class.

There is one additional aspect of enumerated types that is worth noting. The process of defining an enumerated type does not ensure that only valid values are used for the property or method. Although Intellisense provides a list of the constants included in the enumerated type, any value can be entered.

Building Hierarchies of Classes

It is common to emulate real-life relationships between objects in the classes that you build. This necessitates the building of a class hierarchy. The relationships that you build between classes make up an object model. For example, you might have a Client class that has multiple Order objects associated with it. Each individual Order object can then have multiple Order Detail objects associated with it.

To relate one class to another, place a declaration of the child class in the General Declarations section of the parent. For example, the Order class contains the following declaration:

```
Public OrderDetail as OrderDetail
```

The Initialize event of the Order class contains the code that instantiates the OrderDetail class.

```
Private Sub Class_Initialize()
    Set OrderDetail = New OrderDetail
End Sub
```

When you instantiate the Order class (the parent class), the child is automatically instantiated. You can then set the properties and execute the methods of the child class. Here's an example:

```
Sub CreateOrder()
    'Declare and instantiate the order object
    Dim objOrder As Order
    Set objOrder = New Order

    'Set properties of the child class (OrderDetail)
    With objOrder.OrderDetail
        .ItemNumber = 5
        .OrderNumber = 1
        .Quantity = 3
    End With
End Sub
```

Notice that the code declares and instantiates an Order object. It then uses a With statement to point at the OrderDetail object instantiated in the Initialize event of the Order class. It sets the ItemNumber, OrderNumber and Quantity properties of the OrderDetail object.

This example shows how to have one child associated with a parent. The section titled "Using a Collection to Manipulate Multiple Instances of the File Information Class " shows how to use a Custom collection to emulate a one-to-many relationship with classes.

Adding a Parent Property to Classes

Many Microsoft-generated objects have a Parent property. This property generally provides a reference back to the parent of an object in a hierarchy. You can emulate this behavior in your own classes. Place this code in the child class:

```
Private mobjParent As Order

Public Property Get Parent() As Order
    'Return the pointer stored in mobjParent
    Set Parent = mobjParent
End Property

Public Property Set Parent(ByVal objParent As Order)
    If mobjParent Is Nothing Then
        Set mobjParent = objParent
    End If
End Property
```

Code in the `Initialize` event of the parent class sets the Parent property of the child class. The code looks like this:

```
Private Sub Class_Initialize()
    Set OrderDetail = New OrderDetail
    Set OrderDetail.Parent = Me
End Sub
```

Once the `Initialize` event of the `Order` class sets the Parent property of the `OrderDetail` class, the `Property Set` for the Parent property of the `OrderDetail` class executes. If the `mobjParent` variable is `Nothing`, a `Set` statement points the `mobjParent` variable at the reference to the parent class (`Set OrderDetail.Parent = Me`). Notice the `Set` statement only executes if `mobjParent` is `Nothing`. This renders the property as write-once. The following code illustrates how the Parent property is used:

```
Sub FindParentsName()
    'Declare and instantiate the order object
    Dim objOrder As Order
    Set objOrder = New Order

    'Retrieve Name property of the parent
    MsgBox objOrder.OrderDetail.Parent.Name
End Sub
```

This code declares and instantiates the `Order` object. The `Initialize` event of the `Order` object instantiates the `OrderDetail` object, and sends it a reference to the `Order` object. The code retrieves the Name property of the `Parent` object and displays it in a message box.

The `Implements` Keyword

Using the `Implements` keyword, you can share interfaces between classes. This means that one class can inherit the properties and methods of one or more other classes. The process is quite simple. All you need to do is place the following in the General Declarations section of the class that derives from another class:

```
Implements Person
```

After it is placed in the General Declarations section of the `BabyPerson` class, this code allows you to select the `Person` class from the Objects drop-down. The property and method names of the `Person` class will then appear in the Procedure drop-down. You must write code for each property and method. In other words, the interface of the `Person` class is inherited, but not its code. You can add properties and methods to the derived class (`BabyPerson`), just as you would in any class.

Working with Custom Collections

In addition to the collections built in to the Access and other object libraries, you can create custom collections. Custom collections are similar to arrays, but they offer several advantages:

- Collections are dynamically allocated. They take up memory based only on what's in them at a given time. This is different from arrays, whose size must be either predefined or redimensioned at runtime. When an array is redimensioned, Access actually makes a copy of the array in memory, taking up substantial resources. By using custom collections, you can avoid that.

- A collection always knows how many elements it has, and elements can easily be added and removed.

- Each element of a collection can contain a different type of data.

- Elements can be added into any element of a collection.

Although collections are very powerful and provide several advantages, it is important that you be aware of their disadvantages, which are

- Every item in a collection is stored as a variant.

- Although the capability to store a different type of data in each element of a collection can be an advantage, it can also be a disadvantage. If you attempt to treat each item in the collection the same (for example, by accessing the same property in each element of the collection), your code might render an error.

You might wonder why collections are covered in this section. A common use of collections is to house instances of custom objects. An example of such a use is covered in the section of this chapter titled "Using a Collection to Manipulate Multiple Instances of the File Information Class."

Creating a Collection

Defining a custom collection is easy—simply use the `Dim` keyword to create an object of the type `Collection`, as shown here:

```
Dim colSports As New Collection
```

The `Dim` statement tells the compiler you want to declare a variable, and the `As New` keywords indicate that you're creating a new instance of something. Specifically, you're creating a new instance of a `Collection` object. Let's take a look at how you can add items to and remove items from a custom collection.

Adding Items to a Collection

The `Add` method adds a new item to a custom collection. It looks like this:

```
colSports.Add "Basketball"
```

This line of code adds the text "Basketball" to the colSports collection. The `Add` method has three optional arguments: `Key`, `Before`, and `After`. `Key` is a string name you can use to uniquely identify an element; the `Before` and `After` arguments enable you to specify where in the collection the new item will be placed. Here's an example:

```
Sub NewCollection()
   Dim colSports As New Collection
   colSports.Add "Basketball"
   colSports.Add "Skiing"
   colSports.Add "Skating", Before:=1
   colSports.Add "Hockey", After:=2
End Sub
```

This code creates a new collection called `colSports` and adds two consecutive elements to the collection: `Basketball` and `Skiing`. It then adds `Skating` before `Basketball`. `Skating` becomes Element 1 and `Basketball` becomes Element 2. Finally, it adds `Hockey` after Element 2 (`Basketball`).

> **CAUTION**
>
> Unlike almost every other array or collection in VBA, custom collections are one-based, rather than zero-based. This is a big change if you're used to thinking of arrays and collections as being only zero-based.

Looping Through the Elements of a Custom Collection

Just as you can loop through built-in collections, you can also loop through a custom collection. The code looks like this:

```
Sub LoopThroughCollection()
   Dim colSports As New Collection
   Dim varSport As Variant
   colSports.Add "Basketball"
   colSports.Add "Skiing"
   colSports.Add "Skating", Before:=1
   colSports.Add "Hockey", After:=2
   For Each varSport In colSports
```

```
      Debug.Print varSport
   Next varSport
End Sub
```

This code uses a `For Each...Next` loop to loop through each element of `colSports`. Notice that the routine declares a variant variable as the type of object in the collection. This is done so that different types of values can be stored in each object in the collection.

Referencing Items in a Collection

When you add an item to a collection, you can specify a custom key for the object. This makes it easy to return to the item in the collection whenever necessary. The following code illustrates how to specify a custom key:

```
Sub CustomKey()
   Dim colSports As New Collection
   colSports.Add "Basketball", "B"
   colSports.Add "Skiing", "S1"
   colSports.Add "Skating", "S2"
   colSports.Add "Hockey", "H"
   Debug.Print colSports.Item("S1")
End Sub
```

This code adds several items to the `colSports` collection. As each item is added, it's assigned a unique key. Each item in the collection can then be easily accessed by using its unique key. The `Item` method is often used when adding several instances of a form, such as a Customer form to a collection. The customer ID of each customer is added as the unique key for each form in the collection. This unique identifier enables you to readily return to a specific instance of the Customer form.

Removing Items from a Collection

Removing objects from a custom collection is just as easy as adding them. You use the `Remove` method, which looks like this:

```
Sub RemoveElements()
   Dim colSports As New Collection
   colSports.Add "Basketball"
   colSports.Add "Skiing"
   colSports.Add "Skating"
   colSports.Add "Hockey"
   colSports.Remove 2
End Sub
```

This routine removes Element 2 (`Skiing`) from the collection.

Adding Your Own Events

Just as you can add custom properties and methods to the classes that you build, you can also add custom events. Custom events are often used to return information back to the application code that uses them. For example, if an error occurs in the Class module, it is prudent to raise an event to the user of the class, notifying it that the error occurred. Error handling is one of the *many* uses of a custom event. To declare a custom event, place a `Public Event` statement in the General Declarations section of the Class module:

```
Public Event Speaking(strNameSaid As String)
```

This statement declares a `Speaking` event that passes a string up to its caller. Once you have declared an event, you must then raise it in the appropriate place in the class code. You raise an event with the `RaiseEvent` command. Realize that custom events mean nothing to Access or to the operating system. In other words, they are not triggered by something that the operating system responds to. Instead, you generate them with the code that you write, in the places in your application where you deem appropriate. Although you can only declare an event once, you can raise it as many times as you like. The following is an example of raising the `Speaking` event from the `Speak` method of the class:

```
Public Function Speak()
    Dim strNameSaid As String
    Speak = mstrFirstName & " " & mstrLastName
    strNameSaid = mstrLastName & ", " & mstrFirstName
    RaiseEvent Speaking(strNameSaid)
End Function
```

In this example, the `Speak` method raises the `Speaking` event. It passes the concatenation of the last name and first name spoken back to the caller.

Once you have raised an event, you need to respond to it in some other part of your application. You can only respond to events in Class modules (form, report, or standalone). You must first create an object variable that is responsible for reporting the events of the class to your application:

```
Private WithEvents mobjPerson As Person2
```

You can then select the class from the Objects drop-down, and the event from the Procedures drop-down. The code that follows responds to the `Speaking` event, displaying what was said in a message box.

```
Private Sub mobjPerson_Speaking(strNameSaid As String)
    MsgBox strNameSaid
End Sub
```

> PRACTICAL EXAMPLES

Class Modules

To best understand how to benefit from the use of Class modules, it is beneficial to see them in action. Three examples are covered in this chapter. The first shows the use of a file information class. Each instance of the class is used to house information about a particular file. The second illustrates how the use of a customer class facilitates the process of dealing with customer data. The third is a system information class. It retrieves and then provides information about the computer system. An additional example of the use of Class modules is found in Chapter 16, "Error Handling: Preparing for the Inevitable." It shows how a custom error class facilitates the process of implementing error handling within your application.

The `FileInformation` Class

 It is a common application requirement to be able to extract the drive, path, or short filename from a complete filename. Although obtaining these pieces of information can be accomplished using a Standard Code module and functions, placing the functions in a Class module makes them easier to work with. The `FileInformation` class contained in the Chap13Ex sample database contains four properties: FullFileName, Drive, Path, and Name. The FullFileName property is set by the user of the class. It contains the complete filename and path of the file whose parts the user wishes to extract. The Drive, Path, and Name properties of the class contain the drive, path, and name of the file specified in the FullFileName property. The `Property Let` and `Property Get` procedures, as well as the Private variables associated with these properties, are shown in Listing 13.1.

LISTING 13.1   The Property Declarations for the `FileInformation` Class

```
Private mstrFullFileName As String
Private mstrDrive As String
Private mstrPath As String
Private mstrName As String

Public Property Get FullFileName() As String
   FullFileName = mstrFullFileName
End Property

Public Property Let FullFileName(ByVal strFileName As String)
   Call GetDrive(strFileName)
   Call GetPath(strFileName)
   Call GetName(strFileName)
End Property
```

LISTING 13.1   Continued

```
Public Property Get Drive() As String
    Drive = mstrDrive
End Property

Public Property Get Path() As String
    Path = mstrPath
End Property

Public Property Get Name() As String
    Name = mstrName
End Property
```

Notice that the Drive, Path, and Name properties have no associated Property Let routines. This is because these properties are read-only properties from outside the class. When the FullFileName property is set, the GetDrive, GetPath, and GetName routines are executed. Each of these routines populates the appropriate Private variables so that they can be retrieved in the Property Get routines. The GetDrive, GetPath, and GetName subroutines are shown in Listing 13.2.

LISTING 13.2   The GetDrive, GetPath, and GetName Routines Retrieve the Drive, Path, and Short Filename of the File Designated in the FullFileName Property

```
Private Sub GetDrive(ByVal strFile As String)
    'Everything before the : is the drive
    mstrDrive = Left$(strFile, _
        InStr(strFile, ":"))
End Sub

Private Sub GetPath(ByVal strFile As String)
    'Everything up until the last backslash
    'is the path
    mstrPath = _
        Mid(strFile, 1, InStrRev(strFile, "\"))
End Sub

Private Sub GetName(strFile)
    'Everything after the last backslash
    'is the name
    mstrName = _
        Mid$(strFile, InStrRev(strFile, "\") + 1)
End Sub
```

The GetDrive routine extracts the characters to the left of the colon, including the colon, thereby extracting the drive. The GetPath routine locates the last backslash in the filename.

The string to the left of the last backslash contains the path name. Finally, the `GetName` routine extracts everything to the right of the last backslash.

Note that the `GetDrive`, `GetPath`, and `GetName` routines are private to the Class module. This means that their code cannot be executed from outside the Class module. The code shown in Listing 13.3 illustrates how the code within the Class module is used.

LISTING 13.3   Using the `FileInformation` Class

```
Private Sub cmdGetFileInfo_Click()
    'Declare a FileInformation object
    Dim objFile As FileInformation

    'If the txtFullFileName text box is null,
    'display a message and bail out
    If IsNull(Me.txtFullFileName.Value) Then
        MsgBox "File Name Must Be Entered"

    'If the file name is entered, instantiate the
    'FileInformation class
    Else
        Set objFile = New FileInformation
        With objFile

            'Set the FullFileName property of the class
            'this causes the Drive, Path, and Name properties
            'to be populated
            .FullFileName = Me.txtFullFileName

            'Extract the values of the Drive, Path, and Name
            'properties and display them in text boxes
            Me.txtDrive = .Drive
            Me.txtPath = .Path
            Me.txtName = .Name
        End With
    End If
End Sub
```

This code, found in the frmFileInformation form in Chap13Ex, declares a `FileInformation` variable. As long as the user has entered a filename, the FileInformation class is instantiated. The FullFileName property is set equal to the value contained in the txtFullFileName text box. This causes the `GetDrive`, `GetPath`, and `GetName` routines to execute, thereby populating the Private variables contained within the class. The Drive, Path, and Name property values are then retrieved and placed in text boxes on the form.

Using a Collection to Manipulate Multiple Instances of the `FileInformation` Class

The idea of using a collection to manipulate multiple instances of a class was discussed in the "Working with Custom Collections" section of this chapter. It is illustrated in Listing 13.4.

LISTING 13.4   Using a Collection to Manipulate Multiple Instances of the `FileInformation` Class

```
Sub FileInfoCollection(strDirName As String)
    'Declare a Collection object
    Dim colFiles As Collection

    'Declare a FileInformation object
    Dim objFileInfo As FileInformation

    Dim strFile As String
    Dim vntFile As Variant

    'Instantiate the Collection object
    Set colFiles = New Collection

    'Return the first file that meets the file spec
    strFile = Dir(strDirName)

    'Loop as long as files meet the file spec
    Do Until Len(strFile) = 0

        'Instantiate a FileInformation object
        Set objFileInfo = New FileInformation

        'Set its FullFileName property
        objFileInfo.FullFileName = strDirName & strFile

        'Add that instance of the FileInformation class
        'to the Collection object
        colFiles.Add objFileInfo

        'Find the next file that meets the criteria
        strFile = Dir()

    Loop

    'Loop through the collection, extracting the Drive,
    'Path and Name properties
```

Listing 13.4   Continued

```
For Each vntFile In colFiles
    Debug.Print vntFile.Drive, vntFile.Path, vntFile.Name
Next vntFile

End Sub
```

The code receives a directory path (including a trailing backslash) as a parameter. It creates and instantiates a `Collection` object. The `Dir` function is then executed, retrieving the name of the first file in the specified directory. As long as at least one file is found, the code within the `Do Until` loop is executed. An instance of the FileInformation class is created. The FullFileName property of the instance is then set equal to the directory name concatenated with the filename. The most important line of code in the routine is then executed, adding the instance of the FileInformation class to the collection. This enables the instance to persist. The `Dir` function is then called to retrieve the name of the next file in the specified directory, and the process is repeated until no additional filenames are located.

After all the instances of the `FileInformation` class are added to the collection, the `For...Each` loop is used to iterate through all items in the collection. The Drive, Path, and Name properties of each item in the collection are retrieved and printed to the Debug window. Notice that a variant variable is be used to iterate through the elements of the `Collection` object.

Data Access Class

Building a data access class greatly facilitates the process of dealing with data, particularly when the data within a table is accessed from numerous forms or numerous databases. By encapsulating the data access activities into a Class module, you can better ensure that the data is treated consistently by all the forms and applications. Each field within the table becomes a property of the class. This is illustrated by the private declarations and `Property Let` and `Property Get` routines shown in Listing 13.5.

Listing 13.5   The Private Variables and `Property Let` and `Property Get` Routines Used by the `Data Access` Class

```
Private mlngClientID As Long
Private mstrCompanyName As String
Private mstrAddress As String
Private mstrCity As String
Private mconn As ADODB.Connection
```

LISTING 13.5   Continued

```
Private mrst As ADODB.Recordset
Private mboolAddFlag As Boolean

Public Property Get ClientID() As Long
    ClientID = mlngClientID
End Property

Public Property Get CompanyName() As String
    CompanyName = mstrCompanyName
End Property

Public Property Let CompanyName(ByVal strCompanyName As String)
    mstrCompanyName = strCompanyName
End Property

Public Property Get Address() As String
    Address = mstrAddress
End Property

Public Property Let Address(ByVal strAddress As String)
    mstrAddress = strAddress
End Property

Public Property Get City() As String
    City = mstrCity
End Property

Public Property Let City(ByVal strCity As String)
    mstrCity = strCity
End Property

Public Property Get AddFlag() As Boolean
    AddFlag = mboolAddFlag
End Property

Public Property Let AddFlag(ByVal boolAddFlag As Boolean)
    mboolAddFlag = boolAddFlag
End Property
```

The Initialize event of the class, shown in Listing 13.6, is responsible for establishing a connection with the database and opening a recordset based on the data in the tblClients table. This example uses the ActiveX Data Object (ADO) object library. ADO is covered in detail in Chapter 14, "What Are ActiveX Data Objects and Data Access Objects, and Why Are They Important?" For now, it's only important to understand the basics. The example sets the

LockType of the recordset to adLockOptimistic, and the CursorType of the recordset to adOpenDynamic. The combination of these two property settings renders the recordset's data updateable.

LISTING 13.6   The Initialize Event Establishes a Connection to the Data and Opens a Recordset Based on the tblClients Table

```
Private Sub Class_Initialize()
    'Instantiate the Recordset object
    Set mrst = New ADODB.Recordset

    'Set the LockType and CursorType of the
    'recordset to render it updateable
    mrst.LockType = adLockOptimistic
    mrst.CursorType = adOpenDynamic

    'Open a recordset based on the tblClients table,
    'utilizing the connection associated with the current project
    mrst.Open "tblClients", _
        CurrentProject.Connection, _
        Options:=adCmdTable

    'Call the Scatter routine to populate the controls on the form
    'with the first row from the recordset
    Call Scatter
End Sub
```

After the recordset is open, the contents of the first record in the recordset must be available as properties of the class. This is necessary so that the contents of the first record can be displayed in the frmClients form. The Scatter method, shown in Listing 13.7, accomplishes this task.

LISTING 13.7   The Scatter Method Takes the Contents of the Current Record and Places Them in Module Level Variables

```
Public Sub Scatter()
    'Take the field values from the current row
    'and place them into private variables
    With mrst
        mlngClientID = !ClientID
        mstrCompanyName = !CompanyName
        mstrAddress = !Address
        mstrCity = !City
    End With
End Sub
```

The Scatter method simply takes the contents of the fields in the current record (in this case the first record) and stores them in Private variables that are accessed by the Property Get and Property Let routines within the class. The variables are then used by the Form_Load event of the frmClients form, shown in Listing 13.8.

LISTING 13.8 The Form_Load Routine of the frmClients Form Calls the Scatter Method and Then Populates the Form's Text Boxes

```
Private Sub Form_Load()
    'Instantiate the Client Class
    Set mobjClients = New Client

    'Grab the values out of the class
    'properties to populate the text boxes
    With mobjClients
        Me.txtClientID = .ClientID
        Me.txtCompanyName = .CompanyName
        Me.txtAddress = .Address
        Me.txtCity = .City
    End With
End Sub
```

The Form_Load event instantiates the Client class, causing the Initialize event of the class to execute. The Scatter method of the class executes, and then the text boxes on the form are populated with the contents of the ClientID, CompanyName, Address, and City properties of the class. The frmClient form, populated with data from the first record in the tblClients table, is shown in Figure 13.3.

FIGURE 13.3

The frmClients form is used to display and manipulate data in the tblClients table.

After the first record is displayed, the user can opt to move to the next record in the recordset. Listing 13.9 shows the Click event of the cmdNext command button on the frmClients form.

Listing 13.9 The `Click` Event of the cmdNext Command Button Calls the `MoveNext` Method of the Class and Then Displays the Contents of the Class's Properties

```
Private Sub cmdNext_Click()
    With mobjClients
        'Execute the MoveNext method of the class
        .MoveNext

        'Populate the text boxes with the
        'property values of the class
        Me.txtClientID = .ClientID
        Me.txtCompanyName = .CompanyName
        Me.txtAddress = .Address
        Me.txtCity = .City
    End With
End Sub
```

The cmdNext `Click` event calls the `MoveNext` method of the class. The `MoveNext` method is responsible for moving forward from record to record within the class. It uses the module-level recordset object set in the `Initialize` event of the class. This appears in Listing 13.10.

Listing 13.10 The `MoveNext` Method Is Responsible for Moving to and Displaying the Next Record in the Recordset

```
Public Sub MoveNext()
    With mrst
        'Determine if at EOF
        If Not .EOF Then

            'If not at EOF, move next
            .MoveNext

            'Evalute to see if movement
            'caused us to be at end of file
            'If so, move back to the last row
            If .EOF Then
                .MoveLast
            End If
        End If

        'Once on the correct row,
        'call Scatter routine to populate the properties
        Call Scatter
    End With
End Sub
```

The MoveNext method first tests to see whether the end of the recordset has been reached. If not, the MoveNext method is used to move to the next record in the recordset. If the end of the recordset is encountered, the code moves back to the last record. The Scatter method is called to update the values of the module-level variables. The cmdNext Click event then retrieves these values via the Property Get routines, to update the data displayed on the form.

The cmdPrevious Click event of the frmClients form is similar to the cmdNext click event. It appears in Listing 13.11.

LISTING 13.11   The Click Event of the cmdPrevious Command Button Calls the MovePrevious Method of the Class and Then Displays the Contents of the Class's Properties

```
Private Sub cmdPrevious_Click()
    With mobjClients
        'Execute the MovePrevious method of the class
        .MovePrevious

        'Populate the text boxes with the
        'property values of the class
        Me.txtClientID = .ClientID
        Me.txtCompanyName = .CompanyName
        Me.txtAddress = .Address
        Me.txtCity = .City
    End With
End Sub
```

The Click event of the cmdPrevious command button first calls the MovePrevious method of the class. The MovePrevious method of the class is similar to the MoveNext method. It appears in Listing 13.12.

LISTING 13.12   The MovePrevious Method Moves to and Displays the Previous Record in the Recordset

```
Public Sub MovePrevious()
    With mrst
        'Determine if at BOF
        If Not .BOF Then

            'If not at BOF, move next
            .MovePrevious

            'Evalute to see if movement
            'caused us to be at beginning of file
            'If so, move back to the first row
            If .BOF Then
```

LISTING 13.12 Continued

```
            .MoveFirst
        End If
    End If

    'Once on the correct row,
    'call Scatter routine to populate the properties
    Call Scatter
  End With
End Sub
```

The `MovePrevious` method first tests to see if the record pointer is before the first record in the recordset. If not, the `MovePrevious` method is used to move to the previous record in the recordset. If the beginning of the recordset is encountered, the code moves forward to the first record. The `Scatter` method is called to update the values of the module-level variables. These variables are then retrieved by the `Property Get` routines initiated by the `Click` event of the cmdPrevious command button.

The Client class enables the user to edit the data in the underlying recordset. The user simply enters data into the form's unbound text boxes. After the data is entered, the user clicks Save. The click event of the cmdSave command button is executed as shown in Listing 13.13.

LISTING 13.13 The `Click` Event of the cmdSave Command Button Saves the Form's Data to the Underlying Recordset

```
Private Sub cmdSave_Click()
    'Ensure that the txtCompany text box is populated
    If IsNull(Me.txtCompanyName.Value) Or _
        Len(Me.txtCompanyName.Value) = 0 Then
        MsgBox "Company Name Must be Filled In Before Proceeding"

    Else

        'If txtCompany text box is populated,
        'populate the properties of the class
        'with values in the text boxes
        With mobjClients
            .CompanyName = Me.txtCompanyName
            .Address = Me.txtAddress
            .City = Me.txtCity

            'Execute the Save method of the class to write
            'the record to disk
            .Save
```

LISTING 13.13   Continued

```
                'Reset the Add Flag
                .AddFlag = False

                'Populate the txtClientId text box with the
                'ClientID assigned by the Add method
                Me.txtClientID = .ClientID
            End With
        End If
End Sub
```

The code in the Click event of the cmdSave command button first sets all the properties of the class to the corresponding text box values. It then executes the Save method of the class (see Listing 13.15).

Before we look at the Save method, it is important to explore the code under the Click event of the cmdNew command button (see Listing 13.14). It is very simple. It clears the text boxes on the form, readying them for the entry of the new data. It then sets the value of the AddFlag to True.

LISTING 13.14   The Click Event of the cmdNew Command Clears All the Text Boxes and Sets the Value of the AddFlag Property to True

```
Private Sub cmdNew_Click()
    'Clear the text box values
    Me.txtClientID = ""
    Me.txtCompanyName = ""
    Me.txtAddress = ""
    Me.txtCity = ""

    'Set the Add flag
    mobjClients.AddFlag = True
End Sub
```

In the case of either an edit or an add, the code in the Save method of the class actually writes the data from the new record to disk. This code is shown in Listing 13.15.

LISTING 13.15   The Save Method of the Class Calls the Appropriate Routine to Write the Data to Disk

```
Public Sub Save()
    'If add flag is true, call AddNew routine
    'otherwise, call Edit routine
```

LISTING 13.15   Continued

```
    If mboolAddFlag Then
        Call AddNew
    Else
        Call Edit
    End If
End Sub
```

The Save method of the class first determines whether the user is adding or editing data. This is determined by evaluating the mboolAddFlag. The mboolAddFlag is set to True when the Add button is clicked. When editing, the value of the variable is False. If the user is adding the record, the private routine call AddNew is executed. It appears in Listing 13.16.

LISTING 13.16   The AddNew Method of the Class Adds the New Record

```
Private Sub AddNew()
    With mrst
        'Add a new row to the recordset,
        'populating it with values from the
        'class properties
        .AddNew
            !CompanyName = mstrCompanyName
            !Address = mstrAddress
            !City = mstrCity
        .Update

        'Set the ClientID property equal
        'to the ClientID of the inserted row
        mlngClientID = !ClientID
End Sub
```

The AddNew method of the class uses the AddNew method of an ADO recordset to populate a new record with the values contained in the Private variables. The Update method of the recordset object writes the new data to disk. When the Update method is executed, the value of the AutoNumber field is assigned and stored in the variable called mlngClientID. This variable is retrieved in the Click event of cmdSave so that the txtClientID text box contains the appropriate value.

Whereas the AddNew method of the class adds the record in the recordset, the Edit method of the class updates the data in an existing record. It appears in Listing 13.17.

13

EXPLOITING THE
POWER OF CLASS
MODULES

LISTING 13.17   The `Edit` Method of the Class Updates the Contents of a Record

```
Private Sub Edit()
    'Edit the current row setting the field
    'values equal to the values in the
    'class properties
    With mrst
        !CompanyName = mstrCompanyName
        !Address = mstrAddress
        !City = mstrCity
        .Update
    End With
End Sub
```

The `Edit` method uses the `Update` method of the ADO recordset to take the values in the module-level variables and write them to disk.

The last data task associated with the cmdClients form provides the user with the capability to delete a record from the recordset. The code behind the `Click` event of the cmdDelete command button appears in Listing 13.18.

LISTING 13.18   The `Click` Event of the cmdDelete Command Button Calls the `Delete` Method of the Class

```
Private Sub cmdDelete_Click()
    With mobjClients
        'Execute the delete method of the class
        .Delete

        'Populate the controls on the form with
        'the property values of the class
        Me.txtClientID = .ClientID
        Me.txtCompanyName = .CompanyName
        Me.txtAddress = .Address
        Me.txtCity = .City
    End With
End Sub
```

This code executes the `Delete` method of the class, shown in Listing 13.19. It uses the `Delete` method of an ADO recordset to delete the current record from the recordset. After the delete, the record pointer is sitting on the deleted record. The `MoveNext` method of the class moves the record pointer to the next valid record. The `Click` event of the cmdDelete command button then populates the text boxes on the form with the values of the record that the `MoveNext` method moved to.

LISTING 13.19 The `Delete` Method of the Class Deletes a Record from the Recordset

```
Public Sub Delete()
        'Delete the current row
        .Delete

        'Move off the deleted row
        Call MoveNext
End Sub
```

System Information Class

The process of obtaining system information, such as the amount of drive space free, is usually a somewhat tedious and difficult process. This information is generally available only through the Windows API, covered in Chapter 23, "Exploiting the Power of the Windows API." Executing Windows API functions is best left to more advanced developers. So how can a junior developer access this important information? If the senior developer encapsulates the complex functionality of the Windows API calls in a Class module, the junior developer can obtain the system information as properties of the class.

The class called `SystemInformation` is responsible for obtaining information about the hardware, operating system, and system resources. To obtain this information, the `Declare` statements, type structure declarations, and constant declarations are included in the General Declarations section of the Class module (see Listing 29.20).

LISTING 13.20 The Private Variables and Type Structures Required by the `SystemInformation` Class

```
Private Declare Sub GlobalMemoryStatus _
    Lib "Kernel32" (lpBuffer As MEMORYSTATUS)
Private mlngTotalMemory As Long
Private mlngAvailableMemory As Long
Private mstrOSVersion As String
Private msngOSBuild As Single
Private mstrOSPlatform As String
Private mlngProcessor As Long

Private Type MEMORYSTATUS
    dwLength As Long
    dwMemoryLoad As Long
    dwTotalPhys As Long
    dwAvailPhys As Long
    dwTotalPageFile As Long
    dwAvailPageFile As Long
```

LISTING 13.20   Continued

```
   dwTotalVirtual As Long
   dwAvailVirtual As Long
End Type

Private Declare Function GetVersionEx Lib "Kernel32" _
    Alias "GetVersionExA" (lpOSInfo As OSVERSIONINFO) As Boolean

Private Type OSVERSIONINFO
   dwOSVersionInfoSize As Long
   dwMajorVersion As Long
   dwMinorVersion As Long
   dwBuildNumber As Long
   dwPlatformId As Long
   strReserved As String * 128
End Type

Private Declare Sub GetSystemInfo Lib "Kernel32" _
 (lpSystemInfo As SYSTEM_INFO)

Private Type SYSTEM_INFO
   dwOemID As Long
   dwPageSize As Long
   lpMinimumApplicationAddress As Long
   lpMaximumApplicationAddress As Long
   dwActiveProcessorMask As Long
   dwNumberOrfProcessors As Long
   dwProcessorType As Long
   dwAllocationGranularity As Long
   dwReserved As Long
End Type
```

The SystemInformation class contains six read-only properties: TotalMemory, AvailableMemory, OSVersion, OSBuild, OSPlatform, and Processor. These properties are set within the class and cannot be modified from outside it. The Property Get functions for the six properties are shown in Listing 13.21.

LISTING 13.21   The Property Get and Property Let Routines Required by the SystemInformation Class

```
Public Property Get TotalMemory() As Long
    TotalMemory = mlngTotalMemory
End Property
```

LISTING 13.21   Continued

```
Public Property Get AvailableMemory() As Long
    AvailableMemory = mlngAvailableMemory
End Property

Public Property Get OSVersion() As String
    OSVersion = mstrOSVersion
End Property

Public Property Get OSBuild() As Single
    OSBuild = msngOSBuild
End Property

Public Property Get OSPlatform() As String
    OSPlatform = mstrOSPlatform
End Property

Public Property Get Processor() As Long
    Processor = mlngProcessor
End Property
```

13

EXPLOITING THE
POWER OF CLASS
MODULES

All the work is done in the `Initialize` event of the class. When the class is instantiated, the `Initialize` event executes all the Windows API functions necessary to obtain the required system information. The `Initialize` event of the class is shown in Listing 13.22.

LISTING 13.22   The `Initialize` Event of the System Information Class Executes the Windows API Functions Required to Obtain the System Information

```
Private Sub Class_Initialize()
    'Get Free Memory
    Dim MS As MEMORYSTATUS
    MS.dwLength = Len(MS)
    GlobalMemoryStatus MS

    mlngTotalMemory = Format(MS.dwTotalPhys, "Standard")
    mlngAvailableMemory = Format(MS.dwAvailPhys, "Standard")

    'Get Version Information
    Dim OSInfo As OSVERSIONINFO
    OSInfo.dwOSVersionInfoSize = Len(OSInfo)
    If GetVersionEx(OSInfo) Then
        mstrOSVersion = OSInfo.dwMajorVersion & "." & _
            OSInfo.dwMinorVersion
        msngOSBuild = OSInfo.dwBuildNumber And &HFFFF&
```

LISTING 13.22   Continued

```
      If OSInfo.dwPlatformId = 0 Then
          mstrOSPlatform = "Windows 95"
      Else
          mstrOSPlatform = "Windows NT"
      End If
  End If

  'Get System Information
  Dim SI As SYSTEM_INFO
   GetSystemInfo SI
  mlngProcessor = SI.dwProcessorType

End Sub
```

The `GlobalMemoryStatus` Windows API function populates the TotalMemory and AvailableMemory properties. The `GetVersionEX` function is used to set the OSVersion, OSBuild, and OSPlatform properties. Finally, the `GetSystemInfo` function populates the Processor property.

Summary

In this chapter, you learned how to implement your application's subroutines and functions as methods of Class modules. In doing so, you discovered how complex activities can be encapsulated into Class modules, greatly simplifying the implementation of their functionality. After exploring the basics of object orientation and Class modules, you saw several practical examples of classes in action. These included a File Information class, a Data Access class, and a System Information class. The possible practical application of classes within the business environment is limited only by your imagination!

What Are ActiveX Data Objects and Data Access Objects, and Why Are They Important?

IN THIS CHAPTER

Why This Chapter Is Important

ActiveX Data Objects (ADO) and Data Access Objects (DAO) are used to create, modify, and remove Jet Engine, SQL Server, or other ODBC objects via code. They give you the flexibility to move beyond the user interface to manipulate data stored in the Jet Engine and other formats. Some of the many tasks that you can perform with either ActiveX Data Objects or Data Access Objects include

- Analyzing the structure of an existing database
- Adding or modifying tables and queries
- Creating new databases
- Changing the underlying definitions for queries by modifying the SQL on which the query is based
- Traversing through sets of records
- Administrating security
- Modifying table data

Using ActiveX Data Objects Versus Data Access Objects

The editions of this book prior to Access 2000 referred only to Data Access Objects (DAO). There was no mention of ActiveX Data Objects (ADO) because ActiveX Data Objects were only in their infancy when Access 97 was released. When I began writing this book, I was faced with a decision: Do I cover ADO, DAO, or both? I pondered the question for quite some time. Although I recommend that all new development be done using ADO, it is premature to entirely remove coverage of DAO from this book. I made the decision to cover both ADO and DAO in this chapter. The first half of this chapter covers ADO. If you are developing a new application or have the liberty of rebuilding an existing application, the first half of the chapter is for you. If you are unfamiliar with DAO and need to work with existing applications that use DAO, the second half of the chapter provides you with the basics of DAO. Finally, if you are already familiar with DAO and want to compare and contrast DAO and ADO, this chapter shows you how to perform each task using both data access methodologies.

> **Note**
>
> Although DAO is covered in this chapter, the remainder of the book uses ADO to perform all necessary data access tasks. If you want further information on DAO, consult *Alison Balter's Mastering Access 97 Development*.

What Are ActiveX Data Objects and Data Access Objects and Why Are They Important?

CHAPTER 14

583

Examining the ActiveX Data Object Model

Figure 14.1 shows an overview of the Microsoft ActiveX Data Object (ADO) model. Unlike the Data Access Object (DAO) model, the ADO object model is not hierarchical.

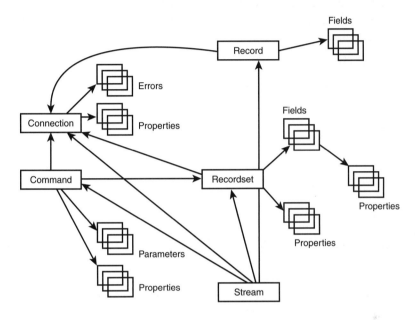

FIGURE 14.1
The ADO object model.

The Connection Object

The Connection object defines a session for a user for a data source. Although the ADO object model is not considered to be hierarchical, the Connection object is considered the highest-level ADO object. After you have established a Connection object, you can use it with multiple recordsets. This improves performance and greatly simplifies your programming code.

A Connection object must be declared before it is used. The declaration looks like this:

```
Dim cnn as ADODB.Connection
```

NOTE

Notice that the declaration specifies ADODB.Connection rather than just Connection. This process is called *disambiguation*. The process of disambiguating a reference ensures that the correct type of object is created. For example, both the ADO and DAO object libraries have Recordset objects. By disambiguating the reference, you explicitly designate the type of recordset object you want to create. If you do not disambiguate the reference, the object library with priority in Tools|References is assumed.

After the `Connection` object has been declared, a new `Connection` object must be instantiated. The code looks like this:

```
Set cnn = New ADODB.Connection
```

The `Connection` must then be opened. The `Open` method of the `Connection` object receives a connection string, and optionally a user ID, password, and options as a parameter. The following is an example of the simplest use of the `Open` method:

```
cnn.Open "Provider=Microsoft.Jet.OLEDB.4.0;" & _
    "Persist Security Info=False;" & _
    "User ID=Admin;" & _
    "Data Source=" & CurrentProject.Path & _
        "\Chap14Ex.mdb;"
```

The Connection string contains three pieces of information:

- The OLEDB Provider that you want to use (in this case, JET 4.0)
- Standard ADO connection properties (for example, User ID)
- Provider-specific connection properties

Table 14.1 lists the most commonly used Connection string properties used by the Jet OLEDB provider.

TABLE 14.1   Connection String Properties Used by the Jet OLEDB Provider

Property Name	Description
Jet OLEDB:Database Locking Mode	Can be set to 0 for page-locking and 1 for row-locking.
Jet OLEDB:Database Password	Used to designate the password for a password-protected database (database security rather than user-level security).

What Are ActiveX Data Objects and Data Access Objects and Why Are They Important?

CHAPTER 14

585

TABLE 14.1   Continued

Property Name	Description
Jet OLEDB:System Database	Full path and filename to the system database (when user-level security is used).
Jet OLEDB:Lock Delay	Used to indicate the number of milliseconds to wait before attempting to acquire a lock after the previous attempt has failed.
Jet OLEDB:Lock Retry	Used to designate how many times an attempt to access a locked page is repeated.

The complete routine required to establish a connection appears in Listing 14.1.

LISTING 14.1   Creating a Connection Object

```
Sub CreateConnection()
    'Declare and instantiate the connection
    Dim cnn As ADODB.Connection
    Set cnn = New ADODB.Connection

    'Open the connection
    cnn.Open "Provider=Microsoft.Jet.OLEDB.4.0;" & _
    "Persist Security Info=False;" & _
    "User ID=Admin;" & _
    "Data Source=" & CurrentProject.Path & _
        "\Chap14Ex.mdb;"

    'Close the connection
    cnn.Close

    'Destroy the connection object
    Set cnn = Nothing
End Sub
```

14

ACTIVEX AND
DATA ACCESS
OBJECTS

TIP

All the examples in this chapter first declare a variable using the keyword Dim, and then instantiate it using the keyword Set. You can remove the Set statement by specifying the New keyword in the Dim statement. For example, you could use

```
Dim rst as New ADODB.Recordset
```

Although this works, it is not considered desirable. This is because you have little control over when the object is placed in memory. For example, if the variable is public, Access places it in memory the moment anything in the module is referenced. Separating the `Dim` and `Set` statements allows you to declare the variable wherever you like, and place it in memory when you need to.

NOTE

 Listing 14.1 and most code in this chapter is located in the CHAP14EX.MDB file included with this book's CD-ROM.

The `Recordset` Object

A `Recordset` object is used to look at records as a group. A `Recordset` object refers to the set of rows returned from a request for data. As with a `Connection` object, to use a `Recordset` object, you must first declare it. The code looks like this:

```
Dim rst as ADODB.Recordset
```

After the `Recordset` object has declared, it must be instantiated. The code looks like this:

```
Set rst = New ADODB.Recordset
```

As with a `Connection` object, the `Open` method is used to point the `Recordset` object at a set of records. The code looks like this:

```
rst.Open "Select * From tblClients", CurrentProject.Connection
```

The first parameter of the `Open` method is the source of the data. The source can be a table name, a SQL statement, a stored procedure name, a `Command` object variable name, or the filename of a persisted recordset. In the example, the source is a SQL `Select` statement.

The second parameter of the `Open` method must be either a valid connection string, or the name of a `Connection` object. In the example, the Connection property of the `CurrentProject` object returns a reference to a copy of the connection associated with the current project. The reference supplies the connection for the `Recordset` object. The completed code appears in Listing 14.2.

What Are ActiveX Data Objects and Data Access Objects and Why Are They Important?

CHAPTER 14

587

LISTING 14.2 Creating a Recordset Using a Connection String

```
Sub CreateRecordset1()
    'Declare and instantiate the recordset
    Dim rst As ADODB.Recordset
    Set rst = New ADODB.Recordset

    'Open the recordset
    rst.Open "Select * From tblClients", CurrentProject.Connection

    'Print its contents
    Debug.Print rst.GetString

    'Close and destroy the recordset
    rst.Close
    Set rst = Nothing
End Sub
```

Notice that after the recordset is opened, the result of the GetString method of the Recordset object is printed to the Immediate window. The GetString method of the Recordset object builds a string based on the data contained in the recordset. For now, this is a simple way of verifying that your code works as expected. Also note that the Close method of the Recordset object is used to close the recordset. The Close method, when applied to either a Connection object, or to a Recordset object, has the effect of freeing the associated system resources. The Close method does *not* eliminate the object from memory. Setting the Recordset object equal to Nothing eliminates the object from memory.

Although this syntax works quite well, I prefer to set the parameters of the Open method as properties of the Recordset object, before the Open method is issued. You will see that this makes your code much more readable as you add parameters to the Open method. The code appears in Listing 14.3.

LISTING 14.3 Creating a Recordset Using the ActiveConnection Property

```
Sub CreateRecordset2()
    'Declare and instantiate the recordset
    Dim rst As ADODB.Recordset
    Set rst = New ADODB.Recordset

    'Set the connection of the recordset to the connection
    'associated with the current project
    rst.ActiveConnection = CurrentProject.Connection
```

14

ACTIVEX AND
DATA ACCESS
OBJECTS

LISTING 14.3 Continued

```
    'Open the recordset and print its contents
    rst.Open "Select * From tblClients"
    Debug.Print rst.GetString

    'Close and destroy the recordset object
    rst.Close
    Set rst = Nothing
End Sub
```

Finally, a Connection object, rather than a copy of the Connection object associated with the CurrentProject object, can be used to provide a connection for the recordset. In fact, the same Connection object can be used for multiple recordsets. The code appears in Listing 14.4.

LISTING 14.4 Creating a Recordset Using a Connection Object

```
Sub CreateRecordset3()
    'Declare and instantiate one connection object
    'and two recordset objects
    Dim cnn As ADODB.Connection
    Dim rst1 As ADODB.Recordset
    Dim rst2 As ADODB.Recordset

    Set cnn = New ADODB.Connection
    Set rst1 = New ADODB.Recordset
    Set rst2 = New ADODB.Recordset

    'Point the Connection object
    'to the Connection associated with the CurrentProject object
    Set cnn = CurrentProject.Connection

    'Utilize the connection just opened as the connection for
    'two different recordsets
    rst1.ActiveConnection = cnn
    rst1.Open "Select * From tblClients"
    rst2.ActiveConnection = cnn
    rst2.Open "Select * From tblPayments"

    'Retrieve data out of the recordsets
    Debug.Print rst1.GetString
    Debug.Print rst2.GetString

    'Close the recordsets and the connection and destroy the objects
    rst1.Close
```

What Are ActiveX Data Objects and Data Access Objects and Why Are They Important?

CHAPTER 14

589

LISTING 14.4   Continued

```
    rst2.Close
    cnn.Close

    Set rst1 = Nothing
    Set rst2 = Nothing
    Set cnn = Nothing

End Sub
```

Notice that both `rst1` and `rst2` use the same `Connection` object.

The `Command` Object

The ADO `Command` object represents a query, SQL statement, or stored procedure that is executed against a data source. Although not always necessary, a `Command` object is particularly useful when executing parameterized queries and stored procedures. Just as with the `Connection` object and the `Recordset` object, the `Command` object must be declared before it is used:

```
Dim cmd as ADODB.Command
```

Next, the `Command` object must be instantiated:

```
Set cmd = New ADODB.Command
```

After the `Command` object has been instantiated, you must set its ActiveConnection property and its CommandText property. As with a `Recordset` object, the ActiveConnection property can be either a connection string or a reference to a `Connection` object. The CommandText property is the SQL statement or stored procedure used by the `Command` object. The ActiveConnection and the CommandText properties look like this:

```
cmd.ActiveConnection = CurrentProject.Connection
cmd.CommandText = "tblClients"
```

The completed code appears in Listing 14.5.

LISTING 14.5   Using a `Command` Object

```
Sub CommandObject()
    'Declare a recordset and a command object
    Dim rst As ADODB.Recordset
    Dim cmd As ADODB.Command
```

14

ACTIVEX AND
DATA ACCESS
OBJECTS

LISTING 14.5   Continued

```
    'Instantiate the command object
    Set cmd = New ADODB.Command

    'Designate where the data comes from
    cmd.CommandText = "Select * from tblClients"

    'Establish the connection information
    cmd.ActiveConnection = CurrentProject.Connection

    'Use the execute method to return a result set
    'into the recordset object
    Set rst = cmd.Execute

    'Display the resulting data
    Debug.Print rst.GetString

    'Close the recordset and destroy the objects
    rst.Close

    Set cmd = Nothing
End Sub
```

In the example, the Command object is instantiated. The CommandText property is set to a SQL Select statement, and the ActiveConnection property is pointed to the connection associated with the current database. The Execute method of the Command object is used to return the results of the SQL statement into the Recordset object.

Understanding ADO Recordset Types

There are three parameters of the Open method of a Recordset object that affect the type of recordset that is created. They are the CursorType, the LockType, and the Options parameters. These parameters combine to determine the types of movements that can be executed within a recordset, when changes that other users make to data underlying the recordset will be seen, and whether the recordset's data is updateable.

The CursorType Parameter

By default, when you open a recordset, the CursorType parameter is set to adOpenForwardOnly. This means that you can only move forward through the records in the recordset. You will not see any adds, edits, or deletions that other users make. Furthermore, many properties and methods, such as the RecordCount property and the MovePrevious method, are unavailable. Listing 14.6 illustrates this.

LISTING 14.6 The RecordCount Property Is Not Supported with a Forward-Only Recordset

```
Sub ForwardOnlyRecordset()

    'Declare and instantiate a recordset object
    Dim rst As ADODB.Recordset
    Set rst = New ADODB.Recordset

    'Establish a connection and open a forward-only recordset
    rst.ActiveConnection = CurrentProject.Connection
    rst.Open "Select * from tblClients"

    'Attempt to retrieve the recordcount
    Debug.Print rst.RecordCount

    'Close and destroy the recordset
    rst.Close
    Set rst = Nothing


End Sub
```

The value -1 displays in the Immediate window because the RecordCount property is not supported with a forward-only recordset. Because you did not explicitly designate the cursor type, a forward-only recordset was created.

Three other values are available for the CursorType. They are adOpenStatic, adOpenKeyset, and adOpenDynamic. The adOpenStatic option allows forward and backward movement through the records in the recordset, but changes that other users make to the underlying data are not seen by the recordset. The adOpenKeyset option offers everything offered by the adOpenStatic option, but in addition, edits that other users make are seen by the recordset. Finally, with the adOpenDynamic option, adds, edits, and deletions made by other users are seen by the recordset. Table 14.2 illustrates each of these options in further detail.

14

ACTIVEX AND DATA ACCESS OBJECTS

TABLE 14.2   Valid Choices for the `CursorType` Parameter

Value	Description
`adOpenForwardOnly`	Copies a set of records as the recordset is created. Therefore, it doesn't show changes made by other users. This is the fastest type of cursor, but only allows forward movement through the recordset.
`adOpenStatic`	Copies a set of records as the recordset is created. Supports bookmarks and allows forward and backward movement through the recordset. Doesn't show changes made by other users. This is the only type of recordset allowed when using client-side cursors.
`adOpenKeyset`	Provides a set of pointers back to the original data. Supports bookmarks. Shows changes made by other users. New records are not shown, and provides no access to deleted rows.
`adOpenDynamic`	Provides access to a set of records. Shows all changes, including additions and deletions, made by other users.

The CursorType property of the recordset can be set in one of two ways. It can be set as a parameter of the `Open` method of the `Recordset` object. Listing 14.7 illustrates this.

LISTING 14.7   Supplying the CursorType as a Parameter of the `Open` Method

```
Sub StaticRecordset1()
    'Declare and instantiate a recordset object
    Dim rst As ADODB.Recordset
    Set rst = New ADODB.Recordset

    'Establish a connection and open a static recordset
    rst.ActiveConnection = CurrentProject.Connection
    rst.Open "Select * from tblClients", _
        CursorType:=adOpenStatic

    'Retrieve the recordcount
    Debug.Print rst.RecordCount

    rst.Close
    Set rst = Nothing



End Sub
```

What Are ActiveX Data Objects and Data Access Objects and Why Are They Important?

CHAPTER 14

593

Notice that, in Listing 14.7, the CursorType appears as a parameter of the Open method. Contrast Listing 14.7 with Listing 14.8.

LISTING 14.8 Supplying the CursorType as a Property of the Recordset Object

```
Sub StaticRecordset2()
    'Declare and instantiate a recordset object
    Dim rst As ADODB.Recordset
    Set rst = New ADODB.Recordset

    'Set the ActiveConnection and CursorType properties
    'of the recordset
    rst.ActiveConnection = CurrentProject.Connection
    rst.CursorType = adOpenStatic

    'Open the recordset
    rst.Open "Select * from tblClients"

    'Retrieve the recordcount
    Debug.Print rst.RecordCount

    rst.Close
    Set rst = Nothing

End Sub
```

In Listing 14.8, the CursorType is set as a property of the Recordset object, prior to the execution of the Open method. Separating the properties from the Open method improves the readability of the code.

The LockType Parameter

Although the CursorType property of a Recordset object determines how movements can occur within the recordset, and whether other users' changes are seen, the CursorType in no way affects the updateability of the recordset's data. In fact, when a recordset is opened, it is opened as read-only by default. It is only by changing the LockType property that you can make the recordset updateable.

The options for lock type are adLockReadOnly, adLockPessimistic, adLockOptimistic, and adLockBatchOptimistic. The default, adLockReadOnly, does not allow changes to the recordset. The other options all provide updateability for the recordset's data. The difference lies in when the records are locked. With the adLockPessimistic option, locking occurs as soon as the editing process begins. With the adLockOptimistic option, the record is locked when the Update method is issued. Finally, with the adLockBatchOptimistic, you can postpone locking until a batch of records are updated. All these options are discussed in extensive detail in *Alison Balter's Mastering Access 2002 Enterprise Development*.

As with the CursorType property, the LockType property can be set as a parameter of the Open method or as a property of the Recordset object. Listing 14.9 shows the configuration of the lock type as a property of the Recordset object.

LISTING 14.9 Configuration of the LockType Property

```
Sub OptimisticRecordset()
    'Declare and instantiate a recordset object
    Dim rst As ADODB.Recordset
    Set rst = New ADODB.Recordset

    'Set the ActiveConnection and CursorType, and
    'LockType properties of the recordset
    rst.ActiveConnection = CurrentProject.Connection
    rst.CursorType = adOpenStatic
    rst.LockType = adLockOptimistic

    'Open the recordset
    rst.Open "Select * from tblClients"

    'Modify the contents of the city field
    rst("City") = "Westlake Village"
    rst.Update
    Debug.Print rst("City")

    rst.Close
    Set rst = Nothing

End Sub
```

In Listing 14.9, the LockType property is set to adLockOptimistic. The record is locked when the Update method of the Recordset object is issued.

NOTE

Listing 14.9 references the field name in the format rst("City"). You can use any one of four syntactical constructs to reference a member of a collection. These include

```
Collection("Name")
Collection(VariableName)
```

```
Collection!Name
Collection(Ordinal)
```

You might wonder which is best. Although all are valid, I most prefer the `Collection("Name")` and `Collection(VariableName)` methods. I like the fact that the syntax is the same whether you are supplying a string or a variable. Furthermore, the same syntax works with Active Server Pages (ASP). The bang does not work with Active Server Pages, and you cannot rely on the ordinal position because it changes. One of the only instances when you must use a bang is when you are supplying a parameter for a query. Besides that, I use the `Collection("Name")` syntax in the ADO and DAO code that I write.

The `Options` Parameter

The `Options` parameter determines how the provider should evaluate the source argument. The valid choices are illustrated in Table 14.1.

TABLE 14.1   Valid Choices for the `Options` Parameter

Value	Description
adCmdText	The provider evaluates the source as a command.
adCmdTable	A SQL query is generated to return all rows from the table named in the source.
adCmdTableDirect	The provider returns all rows in the table named in the source.
adCmdStoredProc	The provider evaluates the source as a stored procedure.
adCmdUnknown	The type of command in the source is unknown.
adCmdFile	The source is evaluated as a persisted recordset.
adAsyncExecute	The source is executed asynchronously.
adAsyncFetch	The initial quantity specified in the Initial Fetch Size property is fetched.
adAsyncFetchNonBlocking	The main thread never blocks when fetching.

The default for the `Options` parameter is `adCmdUnknown`. If you do not explicitly specify the `Options` parameter, the provider attempts to evaluate it while the code is running. This degrades performance. It is therefore important to specify the parameter. Listing 14.9 illustrates the use of the `Options` parameter of the `Open` method.

14

ACTIVEX AND
DATA ACCESS
OBJECTS

LISTING 14.9   The Options Parameter of the Open Method

```
Sub OptionsParameter()
    'Declare and instantiate a recordset object
    Dim rst As ADODB.Recordset
    Set rst = New ADODB.Recordset

    'Set the ActiveConnection and CursorType, and
    'LockType properties of the recordset
    rst.ActiveConnection = CurrentProject.Connection
    rst.CursorType = adOpenStatic
    rst.LockType = adLockOptimistic

    'Open the recordset, designating that the source
    'is a command
    rst.Open "Select * from tblClients", _
        Options:=adCmdText

    'Modify the contents of the city field
    rst("City") = "Westlake Village"
    rst.Update
    Debug.Print rst("City")

    rst.Close
    Set rst = Nothing


End Sub
```

In Listing 14.9, the Options parameter is set to adCmdText. This causes the source to be evaluated as a SQL command.

Consistent Versus Inconsistent Updates

When a recordset is based on data from more than one table, Jet automatically allows you to make changes to the foreign key field. For example, if a recordset is based on data from the Customers table and the Orders table, you are able to make changes to the CustomerID in the Orders table. This is referred to as a *consistent update*. At times you might want to make changes to the primary key field. This could result in a violation of referential integrity and is therefore referred to as an *inconsistent update*.

If you've established referential integrity and have designated that you want to cascade updates, consistent and inconsistent updates yield the same results. On the other hand, without cascade updates activated, a change to the primary key field causes referential integrity to be violated.

What Are ActiveX Data Objects and Data Access Objects and Why Are They Important?

CHAPTER 14

597

Listing 14.10 shows you how to open a recordset with inconsistent updates.

LISTING 14.10   Opening a Recordset with Inconsistent Updates

```
Sub InconsistentUpdates()
    'Declare and instantiate a recordset object
    Dim rst As ADODB.Recordset
    Set rst = New ADODB.Recordset

    'Set the ActiveConnection and CursorType, and
    'LockType properties of the recordset
    rst.ActiveConnection = CurrentProject.Connection
    rst.CursorType = adOpenStatic
    rst.LockType = adLockOptimistic

    'Open the recordset, designating that the source
    'is a SQL statement based on more than one table
    rst.Properties("Jet OLEDB:Inconsistent") = True
    rst.Open Source:="Select * from tblClients " & _
        "INNER JOIN tblProjects " & _
        "ON tblClients.ClientID = tblProjects.ClientID", _
        Options:=adCmdText

    'Modify the contents of the foreign key field
    rst("tblProjects.ClientID") = 1
    rst.Update
    Debug.Print rst("tblProjects.ClientID")

    rst.Close
    Set rst = Nothing

End Sub
```

Notice that the Jet OLEDB: Inconsistent property is set prior to the Open method of the record-set. This causes the recordset to be opened so that you can use inconsistent updates if you want.

NOTE

Very few providers support inconsistent updates. In fact, the Jet provider is one of the few providers that supports this feature.

14

ACTIVEX AND
DATA ACCESS
OBJECTS

Selecting a Cursor Location

A *cursor* refers to the set of rows or row pointers that are returned when you open a recordset. With DAO, the location of the cursor is not an issue. On the other hand, ADO supports two cursor locations. As its name implies, the client manages a client-side cursor. The server manages a server-side cursor.

If you are using Jet, the client machine always manages the cursor because Jet only runs on the client machine. You might think that this means that you should always designate a client-side cursor when working with Jet. Actually, the opposite is true. If you designate a client-side cursor when working with Jet, the data is cached twice on the client machine. When a client-side cursor is specified, the Microsoft Cursor Service for OLE DB requests all the data from the OLEDB provider and then caches it and presents it to the application as a static recordset. For this reason, when working with JET, you should only designate a client-side cursor when you want to take advantage of functionality provided only by a client-side cursor.

Listing 14.11 illustrates how to designate the cursor location.

LISTING 14.11   Designating the Cursor Location

```
Sub CursorLocation()
    'Declare and instantiate a recordset object
    Dim rst As ADODB.Recordset
    Set rst = New ADODB.Recordset

    'Set the ActiveConnection and CursorType, and
    'LockType, and CursorLocation properties of the recordset
    rst.ActiveConnection = CurrentProject.Connection
    rst.CursorType = adOpenStatic
    rst.LockType = adLockOptimistic
    rst.CursorLocation = adUseServer

    'Open the recordset, designating that the source
    'is a SQL statement
    rst.Open Source:="Select * from tblClients ", _
        Options:=adCmdText

    'Modify the contents of the city field
    rst("City") = "New City"
    rst.Update
    Debug.Print rst("City")

    rst.Close
```

What Are ActiveX Data Objects and Data Access Objects and Why Are They Important?

CHAPTER 14

599

LISTING 14.11   Continued

```
    Set rst = Nothing

End Sub
```

In the example, a server-side cursor is designated.

Working with the Supports Method

Depending on which CursorType, LockType, CursorLocation, and Provider are used to open a recordset, the functionality of the recordset varies. The Supports method of a recordset determines which features a particular recordset supports. It returns a Boolean value designating whether the selected feature is supported. Listing 14.12 provides an example.

LISTING 14.12   The Supports Method of the Recordset Object

```
Sub SupportsMethod()
    'Declare and instantiate a recordset object
    Dim rst As ADODB.Recordset
    Set rst = New ADODB.Recordset

    'Set the ActiveConnection and CursorType, and
    'LockType, and CursorLocation properties of the recordset
    rst.ActiveConnection = CurrentProject.Connection
    rst.CursorType = adOpenStatic
    rst.LockType = adLockOptimistic
    rst.CursorLocation = adUseServer

    'Open the recordset, designating that the source
    'is a SQL statement
    rst.Open Source:="Select * from tblClients ", _
        Options:=adCmdText

    'Determine whether the recordset supports certain features
    Debug.Print "Bookmark " & rst.Supports(adBookmark)
    Debug.Print "Update Batch " & rst.Supports(adUpdateBatch)
    Debug.Print "Move Previous " & rst.Supports(adMovePrevious)
    Debug.Print "Seek " & rst.Supports(adSeek)
    rst.Close
    Set rst = Nothing

End Sub
```

14

**ACTIVEX AND
DATA ACCESS
OBJECTS**

Working with ADO Recordset Properties and Methods

The ADO Recordset object is rich with properties and methods. These properties and methods allow you to move through a recordset, sort, filter, and find data, as well as update data contained with the recordset. The sections that follow cover the most commonly used properties and methods.

Examining Record-Movement Methods

When you have a Recordset object variable set, you probably want to manipulate the data in the recordset. Table 14.3 shows several methods you can use to traverse through the records in a recordset.

TABLE 14.3   Methods for Moving Through the Records in a Recordset

Method	Moves
MoveFirst	To the first record in a recordset
MoveLast	To the last record in a recordset
MovePrevious	To the previous record in a recordset
MoveNext	To the next record in a recordset

Listing 14.13 shows an example of using the record-movement methods on a Recordset object.

LISTING 14.13   Recordset Movement Methods

```
Sub RecordsetMovements()
    Dim rst As ADODB.Recordset
    Set rst = New ADODB.Recordset

    'Establish the connection and cursor type and open
    'the recordset
    rst.ActiveConnection = CurrentProject.Connection
    rst.CursorType = adOpenStatic
    rst.Open "Select * from tblProjects"

    'Print the ProjectID of the first row
    Debug.Print rst("ProjectID")
```

What Are ActiveX Data Objects and Data Access Objects and Why Are They Important?

CHAPTER 14

601

LISTING 14.13   Continued

```
    'Move to the next row and print the ProjectID
    rst.MoveNext
    Debug.Print rst("ProjectID")

    'Move to the last row and print the ProjectID
    rst.MoveLast
    Debug.Print rst("ProjectID")

    'Move to the previous row and print the ProjectID
    rst.MovePrevious
    Debug.Print rst("ProjectID")

    'Move to the first row and print the ProjectID
    rst.MoveFirst
    Debug.Print rst("ProjectID")

    rst.Close
    Set rst = Nothing
End Sub
```

This code opens a recordset based on the tblProjects table. When the recordset is open, the ProjectID of the first record is printed to the Immediate window. The MoveNext method of the Recordset object is used to move to the next record in the recordset. The ProjectID of the record is printed. The MoveLast method of the Recordset object is used to move to the last record in the recordset. Once again, the ProjectID is printed. The MovePrevious method moves the record pointer back one record and the ProjectID is printed again. Finally, the MoveFirst method moves the record pointer to the first record and the ProjectID is printed. The recordset is closed, and the Recordset object is destroyed.

Detecting the Limits of a Recordset

Before you begin to traverse through recordsets, you must understand two recordset properties: BOF and EOF. The names of these properties are outdated acronyms that stand for *beginning of file* and *end of file*. They determine whether you have reached the limits of your recordset. The BOF property is True when the record pointer is before the first record, and the EOF property is True when the record pointer is after the last record.

You commonly will use the EOF property when moving forward through your recordset with the MoveNext method. This property becomes True when your most recent MoveNext has moved you beyond the bounds of the recordset. Similarly, BOF is most useful when using the MovePrevious method.

You must keep in mind some important characteristics of the BOF and EOF properties:

- If a recordset contains no records, both the BOF and EOF properties evaluate to True.
- When you open a recordset containing at least one record, the BOF and EOF properties are set to False.
- If the record pointer is on the first record in the recordset and the MovePrevious method is issued, the BOF property is set to True. If you attempt to use MovePrevious again, a runtime error occurs.
- If the record pointer is on the last record in the recordset and the MoveNext method is issued, the EOF property is set to True. If you attempt to use MoveNext again, a runtime error occurs.
- When the BOF and EOF properties are set to True, they remain True until you move to a valid record.
- When the only record in a recordset is deleted, the BOF and EOF properties remain False until you attempt to move to another record.

Listing 14.14 shows an example of using the EOF property to determine the bounds of a recordset.

LISTING 14.14   Determining the Bounds of a Recordset

```
Sub DetermineLimits()
    'Declare and instantiate a recordset object
    Dim rst As ADODB.Recordset
    Set rst = New ADODB.Recordset

    'Establish the connection and cursor type and open
    'the recordset
    rst.ActiveConnection = CurrentProject.Connection
    rst.CursorType = adOpenStatic
    rst.Open "Select * from tblProjects"

    'Loop through the recordset, printing the
    'ClientID of each row
    Do Until rst.EOF
        Debug.Print rst("ClientID")
        rst.MoveNext
    Loop

    rst.Close
End Sub
```

What Are ActiveX Data Objects and Data Access Objects and Why Are They Important?

CHAPTER 14

603

In Listing 14.14, a recordset is opened based on tblProjects. The EOF property is evaluated. As long as the EOF property equals False, the contents of the ClientID field are printed, and the record pointer is advanced to the next record in the recordset.

Counting the Number of Records in a Recordset

The RecordCount property returns the number of rows in the recordset. Not all types of recordsets and providers support the RecordCount property. If the RecordCount property is not supported, no error occurs. Instead, the RecordCount is -1. Listing 14.15 provides an example.

LISTING 14.15   A Recordset That Does Not Support the RecordCount Property

```
Sub CountRecordsBad()
    'Declare and instantiate a recordset
    Dim rst As ADODB.Recordset
    Set rst = New ADODB.Recordset

    'Establish the connection and open a
    'forward-only cursor
    rst.ActiveConnection = CurrentProject.Connection
    rst.Open "Select * from tblProjects"

    'Print the RecordCount property
    Debug.Print rst.RecordCount   'Prints -1

    rst.Close
    Set rst = Nothing
End Sub
```

Because the default CursorType is adOpenForwardOnly, and a forward-only cursor does not support the RecordCount property, -1 prints to the Immediate window. Listing 14.16 rectifies this problem.

LISTING 14.16   A Recordset That Supports the RecordCount Property

```
Sub CountRecordsGood()
    'Declare and instantiate a recordset
    Dim rst As ADODB.Recordset
    Set rst = New ADODB.Recordset

    'Establish the connection and cursor type and open
    'the recordset
    rst.ActiveConnection = CurrentProject.Connection
    rst.CursorType = adOpenStatic
    rst.Open "Select * from tblProjects"
```

14

ACTIVEX AND
DATA ACCESS
OBJECTS

LISTING 14.16 Continued

```
'Print the RecordCount property
Debug.Print rst.RecordCount  'Prints Recordcount

rst.Close
Set rst = Nothing

End Sub
```

Notice that the CursorType is set to adOpenStatic. Because the RecordCount property is supported with static cursors, the correct number of records is printed to the Immediate window.

> **NOTE**
>
> If you are accustomed to the DAO RecordCount property, you might be surprised by the ADO RecordCount property. The DAO RecordCount returns only the number of *visited* records in the recordset. This means that, in using DAO, you must move to the last record in the recordset to obtain an accurate record count. Although this step is unnecessary when using ADO, it is important to note that attempting to retrieve the RecordCount property might result in severe performance degradation. Whether or not obtaining the RecordCount degrades performance depends on the particular database provider.

One of the important uses of the RecordCount property is to determine if a recordset contains any rows. Listing 14.17 illustrates this important use of the RecordCount property.

LISTING 14.17 Checking to See Whether Records Are Returned in a Recordset

```
Sub CheckARecordset()
    'Declare and instantiate the recordset
    Dim rst As ADODB.Recordset
    Set rst = New ADODB.Recordset

    'Establish the connection and cursor type and open
    'the recordset
    rst.ActiveConnection = CurrentProject.Connection
    rst.CursorType = adOpenStatic
    rst.Open "Select * from tblEmpty"

    'Call a routine to determine if the recordset contains
    'any records
```

What Are ActiveX Data Objects and Data Access Objects and Why Are They Important?

CHAPTER 14

605

LISTING 14.17 Continued

```
    If Not AreThereRecords(rst) Then
      MsgBox "Recordset Empty...Unable to Proceed"
    End If

    rst.Close
    Set rst = Nothing
End Sub

Function AreThereRecords(rstAny As ADODB.Recordset) As Boolean
    'Return whether or not there are any rows
    AreThereRecords = rstAny.RecordCount
End Function
```

The CheckARecordset routine opens a recordset based on a table called tblEmpty, which contains no data. The CheckARecordset routine calls the AreThereRecords function, passing a reference to the recordset. The AreThereRecords function evaluates the RecordCount property of the recordset that it is passed. It returns False if the RecordCount is zero, and True, if the RecordCount is non-zero.

Sorting, Filtering, and Finding Records

Sometimes it is necessary to sort, filter, or find data within an existing recordset. The Sort property, Filter property, and Find method of the Recordset object allow you to accomplish these tasks. The sections that follow cover these properties and this method.

Sorting a Recordset

The Sort property of the Recordset object allows you to sort data in an existing recordset. Listing 14.18 illustrates its use.

LISTING 14.18 The Sort Property of the Recordset Object

```
Sub SortRecordset()
    Dim intCounter As Integer

    'Declare and instantiate a recordset
    Dim rst As ADODB.Recordset
    Set rst = New ADODB.Recordset

    'Establish the connection and cursor location and open
    'the recordset
    rst.ActiveConnection = CurrentProject.Connection
```

14

ACTIVEX AND
DATA ACCESS
OBJECTS

LISTING 14.18   Continued

```
    rst.CursorLocation = adUseClient
    rst.Open "Select * from tblTimeCardHours"

    'Loop through the recordset, printing
    'the contents of the DateWorked field
    Debug.Print "NOT Sorted!!!"
    Do Until rst.EOF
        Debug.Print rst("DateWorked")
        rst.MoveNext
    Loop

    'Sort the recordset and the loop through
    'it, printing the contents of the DateWorked field
    Debug.Print "Now Sorted!!!"
    rst.Sort = "[DateWorked]"
    Do Until rst.EOF
        Debug.Print rst("DateWorked")
        rst.MoveNext
    Loop

    rst.Close
    Set rst = Nothing
End Sub
```

The code begins by opening a recordset based on the tblTimeCardHours table. The records in the recordset are printed in their "natural" order. Next, the Sort property of the Recordset object sorts the data by the DateWorked field. Notice that the Sort property is set equal to a field. If you want to sort by more than one field, you must separate the field names with commas. When the records are once again printed, they appear in order by the DateWorked field.

NOTE

To sort in descending order, the field name must be followed by a space and then the keyword DESC.

Filtering a Recordset

Sometimes you might want to select a subset of the data returned in a recordset. The Filter property helps you to accomplish this task. Its use is illustrated in Listing 14.19.

What Are ActiveX Data Objects and Data Access Objects and Why Are They Important?

CHAPTER 14

607

LISTING 14.19   The Filter Property of the Recordset Object

```
Sub FilterRecordSet()
    'Declare and instantiate a recordset
    Dim rst As ADODB.Recordset
    Set rst = New ADODB.Recordset

    'Establish the connection and cursor type,
    'and lock type, and open the recordset
    rst.ActiveConnection = CurrentProject.Connection
    rst.CursorType = adOpenKeyset
    rst.LockType = adLockOptimistic
    rst.Open "Select * from tblTimeCardhours"

    'Loop through the recordset, printing the contents of
    'the DateWorked field
    Debug.Print "Without Filter"
    Do Until rst.EOF
        Debug.Print rst("DateWorked")
        rst.MoveNext
    Loop

    'Filter the recordset and then loop through it, printing the
    'contents of the DateWorked field
    rst.Filter = "DateWorked >= #1/1/1995# and DateWorked <= #1/5/1995#"
    Debug.Print "With Filter"
    Do Until rst.EOF
        Debug.Print rst("DateWorked")
        rst.MoveNext
    Loop

    rst.Close
    Set rst = Nothing
End Sub
```

14

In the example, a recordset is opened based on tblTimeCardHours. The code prints the records without a filter applied. The Filter property is then set to limit the data to only records with a DateWorked value between 1/1/1995 and 1/5/1995. The code prints the records in the recordset again.

> **NOTE**
>
> It is inefficient to build a large recordset and then filter to only those records that you need. If you know that you need only records meeting specific criteria, you should build a recordset using that criteria. The difference in performance can be profound, particularly when dealing with client/server data. In summary, you should use the `Filter` property only when you are initially dealing with a larger set of records and then need to perform an operation on a subset of the records.

> **TIP**
>
> To return to the complete recordset after a filter has been applied, set the Filter property to a zero-length string (" ").

Finding a Specific Record in a Recordset

The `Find` method allows you to locate a particular record in the recordset. It is different from the Filter property in that all records in the recordset remain available. Listing 14.20 illustrates the use of the `Find` method.

LISTING 14.20   The `Find` Method of a `Recordset` Object

```
Sub FindProject(lngValue As Long)
    Dim strSQL As String

    'Declare and instantiate a recordset
    Dim rst As ADODB.Recordset
    Set rst = New ADODB.Recordset

    'Establish the connection and cursor type,
    'and open the recordset
    rst.ActiveConnection = CurrentProject.Connection
    rst.CursorType = adOpenStatic
    rst.Open "Select * from tblProjects"

    'Attempt to find a specific project
    strSQL = "[ProjectID] = " & lngValue
    rst.Find strSQL
```

What Are ActiveX Data Objects and Data Access Objects and Why Are They Important?

CHAPTER 14

609

LISTING 14.20   Continued

```
    'Determine if the specified project was found
    If rst.EOF Then
        MsgBox lngValue & " Not Found"
    Else
        MsgBox lngValue & " Found"
    End If

    rst.Close
    Set rst = Nothing
End Sub
```

> **TIP**
>
> Because the FindProject routine is found in more than one module, the routine must be executed as follows:
>
> ```
> Call basADORecordsets.FindProject(1)
> ```
>
> Preceding the name of the routine with the name of the module removes the ambiguity as to which FindProject routine to execute.

The example opens a recordset based on all the records in the tblProjects table. The Find method is used to locate the first record where the ProjectID is equal to a specific value. If the record is not found, the EOF property of the Recordset object is True.

> **NOTE**
>
> Unlike its DAO counterpart, ADO does not support the FindFirst, FindNext, FindPrevious, and FindLast properties. The default use of the Find method locates the *next* record that meets the specified criteria. This means that, if the record pointer is not at the top of the recordset, records meeting the specified criteria might not be located. The SkipRows, SearchDirection, and Start parameters of the Find method modify this default behavior. The SkipRows parameter allows you to specify the offset from the current row where the search begins. The SearchDirection parameter allows you to designate whether you want the search to proceed forward or backward from the current row. Finally, the Start parameter determines the starting position for the search.

14

**ACTIVEX AND
DATA ACCESS
OBJECTS**

Working with Variables in Strings

When using the Find method, or when building a SQL statement in code, you must be cognizant of the delimiters to use. No delimiters are necessary when working with numeric values. For example,

```
Select * FROM tblClients WHERE ClientID = 1
```

You must use a pound symbol (#) when delimiting dates for Microsoft Access, like this:

```
Select * FROM tblClients WHERE IntroDate = #12/31/2001#
```

> **CAUTION**
>
> If your back-end is Microsoft SQL Server, you must use an apostrophe to delimit dates.

The process of delimiting strings is somewhat more difficult than it initially seems. The basic process is to surround the string with apostrophes:

```
Select * FROM tblClients WHERE City = 'Oak Park'
```

This works unless there is an apostrophe in the string. Listing 14.21 provides the solution.

LISTING 14.21   Handling Apostrophes Within Strings

```
Sub DelimitString()

    Dim strCompanyName As String
    'Declare and instantiate a recordset object
    Dim rst As ADODB.Recordset
    Set rst = New ADODB.Recordset

    'Ask for the company to locate
    strCompanyName = InputBox("Please Enter a Company")

    'Set the ActiveConnection and CursorType, and
    'LockType, and CursorLocation properties of the recordset
    rst.ActiveConnection = CurrentProject.Connection
    rst.CursorType = adOpenStatic
    rst.LockType = adLockOptimistic
    rst.CursorLocation = adUseServer

    'Open the recordset, designating that the source
    'is a SQL statement
```

What Are ActiveX Data Objects and Data Access Objects and Why Are They Important?

CHAPTER 14

611

LISTING 14.21   Continued

```
rst.Open Source:="Select * from tblClients " & _
    "WHERE CompanyName = " & ReplaceApostrophe(strCompanyName), _
        Options:=adCmdText

    'Display a message as to whether the selected company
    'was found
    If rst.EOF Then
        MsgBox strCompanyName & " NOT Found!"
    Else
        MsgBox rst("ClientID")
    End If

    rst.Close
    Set rst = Nothing

End Sub

Public Function ReplaceApostrophe(strCompanyName As String) As String
    'Surround text with apostrophes and replace any
    'apostrophes in the string with two apostrophes
    ReplaceApostrophe = "'" & _
        Replace(strCompanyName, "'", "''") & "'"
End Function
```

The code passes the string to a user-defined function called ReplaceApostrophe, which sur-
rounds the string with apostrophes. If any apostrophes are found within the string, they are
replaced with two apostrophes.

Using the AbsolutePosition Property

The AbsolutePosition property of the Recordset object sets or returns the ordinal position of
the current row in the recordset. Its use is illustrated in Listing 14.22.

LISTING 14.22   The AbsolutePosition Property of a Recordset Object

```
Sub FindPosition(lngValue As Long)
    Dim strSQL As String

    'Declare and instantiate a recordset
    Dim rst As ADODB.Recordset
    Set rst = New ADODB.Recordset

    'Establish the connection and cursor type,
    'and open the recordset
```

LISTING 14.22   Continued

```
    rst.ActiveConnection = CurrentProject.Connection
    rst.CursorType = adOpenStatic
    rst.Open "Select * from tblProjects"

    'Attempt to find a specific project
    strSQL = "[ProjectID] = " & lngValue
    rst.Find strSQL

    'If record is found, print its position
    If rst.EOF Then
        MsgBox lngValue & " Not Found"
    Else
        Debug.Print rst.AbsolutePosition
    End If

    rst.Close
    Set rst = Nothing

End Sub
```

In the example, the Find method is used to locate a project with a specific ProjectID. If the project is found, the ordinal position of the record that is located is printed to the Immediate window.

Using the Bookmark Property

The Bookmark property of a Recordset object returns a variant variable that acts as a unique identifier for that particular record in the recordset. You can use the Bookmark property to save the current position and then quickly and easily return to it at any time. Listing 14.23 illustrates the use of a bookmark.

LISTING 14.23   The Bookmark Property of a Recordset Object

```
Sub UseBookMark()
    Dim strSQL As String
    Dim vntPosition As Variant

    'Instantiate and declare a recordset
    Dim rst As ADODB.Recordset
    Set rst = New ADODB.Recordset

    'Establish the connection and cursor type,
    'and open the recordset
```

What Are ActiveX Data Objects and Data Access Objects and Why Are They Important?

CHAPTER 14

613

LISTING 14.23 Continued

```
rst.ActiveConnection = CurrentProject.Connection
rst.CursorType = adOpenStatic
rst.Open "Select * from tblProjects"

'Store bookmark in a variant variable
vntPosition = rst.Bookmark

'Perform some operation
'on the records in the recordset
Do Until rst.EOF
    Debug.Print rst("ProjectID")
    rst.MoveNext
Loop

'Return to the bookmarked record by setting
'the Bookmark property of the recordset to the
'value stored in the variant variable
rst.Bookmark = vntPosition
Debug.Print rst("ProjectID")

rst.Close
Set rst = Nothing


End Sub
```

In the example, a unique identifier to the current record is stored into a variant variable. The code then loops through the remainder of the records in the recordset. When it is done, the Bookmark property of the Recordset object is set equal to the unique identifier stored in the variant variable.

> **CAUTION**
>
> Not all recordsets support bookmarks. Whether a recordset supports bookmarks depends on the provider as well as the type of recordset created.

Running Parameter Queries

You will not always know the criteria for a recordset at design time. Fortunately, ADO allows you to supply parameters to the CommandText property of the Command object. Listing 14.24 provides an example.

14

ACTIVEX AND
DATA ACCESS
OBJECTS

LISTING 14.24   Running a Parameter Query

```
Sub RunParameterQuery(datStart As Date, datEnd As Date)
    'Declare Command and Recordset objects
    Dim cmd As ADODB.Command
    Dim rst As ADODB.Recordset

    'Instantiate the Command object
    Set cmd = New ADODB.Command

    'Establish the connection, command text,
    'and command type of the Command object
    cmd.ActiveConnection = CurrentProject.Connection
    cmd.CommandText = "Select * from tblTimeCardHours " & _
        "Where DateWorked Between ? and ?"
    cmd.CommandType = adCmdText

    'Use the Execute method of the command object to
    'return results into the recordset object; Notice that
    'an array is passed to the Parameters parameter of
    'the Command object
    Set rst = cmd.Execute(Parameters:=Array(datStart, datEnd))

    'Loop through the resulting recordset, printing the
    'contents of the TimeCardID and DateWorked fields
    Do Until rst.EOF
        Debug.Print rst("TimeCardID"), rst("DateWorked")
        rst.MoveNext
    Loop

    rst.Close
    Set rst = Nothing
    Set cmd = Nothing

End Sub
```

Notice that in the example, the CommandText property contains two question marks. Each of these is considered a parameter. The parameters are supplied when the Execute method of the Command object is used. Notice that the Parameters argument of the Execute method receives an array containing the parameter values. Note that unless you specify basADORecordsets.RunParameterQuery, you get an "ambiguous name detected" error.

Refreshing Recordset Data

Two methods are used to refresh the data in a recordset: Requery and Resync. The Requery method is roughly equivalent to once again opening the recordset. The Requery method forces the OLEDB provider to perform all the steps it performed when first creating the recordset.

New rows are added to the recordset, changes to data made by other users are reflected in the recordset, and deleted rows are removed from the recordset. The `Requery` method requires significant resources to execute. The `Resync` method is much more efficient. It updates the recordset to reflect changes made by other users. It does not show added rows or remove deleted rows from the recordset.

Working with Persisting Recordsets

Using ADO, recordsets cannot only exist in memory, but can also be written to disk. A recordset written to disk is referred to as a *persisted recordset*. Listing 14.25 illustrates how to persist a recordset to disk.

LISTING 14.25 Persisting a Recordset

```
Sub PersistRecordset()

    Dim strFileName As String

    'Prompt user for file name and path
    strFileName = InputBox("Please enter file name and path")

    'Declare and instantiate a recordset object
    Dim rst As ADODB.Recordset
    Set rst = New ADODB.Recordset

    'Set the ActiveConnection and CursorType, and
    'LockType, and CursorLocation properties of the recordset
    rst.ActiveConnection = CurrentProject.Connection
    rst.CursorType = adOpenStatic
    rst.LockType = adLockOptimistic

    'Open the recordset, designating that the source
    'is a SQL statement
    rst.Open Source:="Select * from tblClients ", _
        Options:=adCmdText

    'Destroy existing file with that name
    On Error Resume Next
    Kill strFileName

    'Save the recordset
    rst.Save strFileName, adPersistADTG

    rst.Close
    Set rst = Nothing

End Sub
```

14

ACTIVEX AND
DATA ACCESS
OBJECTS

Notice that the Save method of the Recordset object is used to persist the recordset to disk. The Format parameter of the Save method allows you to designate whether you want to save the recordset in the Microsoft proprietary Advanced Data Tablegram format, or whether you want to save the recordset as XML. Listing 14.26 shows you how to read a persisted recordset.

LISTING 14.26 Reading a Persisted Recordset

```
Sub ReadPersistedRecordset()
    Dim strFileName As String

    'Prompt user for file name and path to read
    strFileName = InputBox("Please enter file name and path")

    'Ensure that the selected file exists
    If Len(Dir(strFileName)) = 0 Then
        MsgBox "File Not Found"
        Exit Sub
    End If

    'Declare and instantiate a recordset object
    Dim rst As ADODB.Recordset
    Set rst = New ADODB.Recordset

    'Set the ActiveConnection and CursorType, and
    'LockType, and CursorLocation properties of the recordset
    rst.ActiveConnection = CurrentProject.Connection
    rst.CursorType = adOpenStatic
    rst.LockType = adLockOptimistic

    'Open the recordset, designating that the source
    'is a SQL statement
    rst.Open Source:=strFileName, _
        Options:=adCmdFile

    'Loop through the recordset, printing ClientIds
    Do Until rst.EOF
        Debug.Print rst("ClientID")
        rst.MoveNext
    Loop

    rst.Close
    Set rst = Nothing

End Sub
```

What Are ActiveX Data Objects and Data Access Objects and Why Are They Important?

CHAPTER 14

617

After prompting the user for a filename, the code ensures that the designated file is found. It then opens a recordset, using the file as the source argument. The adCmdFile constant is used for the Options parameter of the Open method. The adCmdFile value notifies ADO that the source is a persisted recordset.

Modifying Table Data Using ADO Code

So far, this chapter has only covered the process of retrieving data from a recordset. It is common that you might need to update the data in a recordset. The sections that follow show you how to change data one record at a time, update a batch of records, delete records, and add records.

Changing Record Data One Record at a Time

It is possible to loop through a recordset, modifying all the records in the recordset. This technique is shown in Listing 14.27.

LISTING 14.27   Modifying One Record At a Time

```
Sub IncreaseEstimate()

    Dim rst As ADODB.Recordset
    Set rst = New ADODB.Recordset

    Dim strSQL As String
    Dim lngUpdated As Long

    'Establish the connection, cursor type,
    'and lock type, and open the recordset
    rst.ActiveConnection = CurrentProject.Connection
    rst.CursorType = adOpenDynamic
    rst.LockType = adLockOptimistic
    rst.Open ("Select * from tblProjectsChange")

    strSQL = "ProjectTotalEstimate < 30000"
    lngUpdated = 0

    'Find the first row meeting the designated criteria
    rst.Find strSQL

    'Loop through the recordset, locating all rows meeting
    'the designated criteria, increasing the ProjecTotalEstimate
    'field by ten percent
    Do Until rst.EOF
        lngUpdated = lngUpdated + 1
```

LISTING 14.27   Continued

```
        rst("ProjectTotalEstimate") = rst("ProjectTotalEstimate") * 1.1
        rst.Update
        rst.Find strSQL, 1, adSearchForward
    Loop

    'Print how many rows are updated
    Debug.Print lngUpdated & " Records Updated"

    rst.Close
    Set rst = Nothing


End Sub
```

In Listing 14.27, a recordset is opened based on all the records in the tblProjectsChange table. The first record where the ProjectTotalEstimate is less than 30,000 is located. The ProjectTotalEstimate is increased by 10%, and the record is updated. The next record that meets the specified criteria is located. The process is repeated until all records meeting the specified criteria are located.

This code is very inefficient from several standpoints. The first problem is that a recordset is opened based on all the records in the tblProjectsChange table, when only those with a ProjectTotalEstimate less than 30,000 needed to be updated. A more efficient approach is to open a recordset containing only those records that you need to update. Listing 14.28 illustrates this technique.

LISTING 14.28   Improving the Process of Modifying One Record At a Time

```
Sub IncreaseEstimateImproved()

    'Declare and instantiate a recordset
    Dim rst As ADODB.Recordset
    Set rst = New ADODB.Recordset

    Dim lngUpdated As Long

    'Establish the connection, cursor type,
    'and lock type, and open the recordset
    rst.ActiveConnection = CurrentProject.Connection
    rst.CursorType = adOpenDynamic
    rst.LockType = adLockOptimistic
```

What Are ActiveX Data Objects and Data Access Objects and Why Are They Important?

CHAPTER 14

619

LISTING 14.28 Continued

```
rst.Open ("Select * from tblProjectsChange " & _
    "WHERE ProjectTotalEstimate < 30000")

'Loop through the recordset, locating all rows meeting
'the designated criteria, increasing the ProjecTotalEstimate
'field by ten percent
Do Until rst.EOF
    lngUpdated = lngUpdated + 1
    rst("ProjectTotalEstimate") = rst("ProjectTotalEstimate") * 1.1
    rst.Update
    rst.MoveNext
Loop

'Print how many rows are updated
Debug.Print lngUpdated & " Records Updated"

rst.Close
Set rst = Nothing

End Sub
```

Furthermore, it would be more efficient to simply execute an action query that performs the update. This technique is covered in the section that follows.

CAUTION

If you're accustomed to DAO, you might be quite surprised by the behavior of ADO. Whereas, DAO requires that the Edit method be used before field values are assigned, no Edit method is used with ADO. Furthermore, if you forget to issue the Update method on a DAO recordset, the record is not updated. On the other hand, with ADO, the Update method is implied. The update occurs automatically as soon as the record pointer is moved. These behavior differences can lead to big surprises!

14

ACTIVEX AND
DATA ACCESS
OBJECTS

Performing Batch Updates

If you use a client-side cursor, along with a static or keyset cursor, you can take advantage of batch updates. Using batch updates, all changes you make to a recordset are sent to the underlying OLEDB provider as a batch. The process is illustrated in Listing 14.29.

LISTING 14.29   Performing Batch Updates

```
Sub BatchUpdates()
    'Declare and instantiate a recordset
    Dim rst As ADODB.Recordset
    Set rst = New ADODB.Recordset

    Dim strSQL As String
    Dim lngUpdated As Long

    'Establish the connection, cursor type,
    'and lock type, and open the recordset
    rst.ActiveConnection = CurrentProject.Connection
    rst.CursorType = adOpenKeyset
    rst.CursorLocation = adUseClient
    rst.LockType = adLockBatchOptimistic
    rst.Open ("Select * from tblProjectsChange")

    strSQL = "ProjectTotalEstimate < 30000"
    lngUpdated = 0

    'Find the first row meeting the designated criteria
    rst.Find strSQL

    'Loop through the recordset, locating all rows meeting
    'the designated criteria, increasing the ProjecTotalEstimate
    'field by ten percent
    Do Until rst.EOF
        lngUpdated = lngUpdated + 1
        rst("ProjectTotalEstimate") = rst("ProjectTotalEstimate") * 1.1
        rst.Find strSQL, 1, adSearchForward
    Loop

    'Send all changes to the provider
    rst.UpdateBatch

    'Print how many rows are updated
    Debug.Print lngUpdated & " Records Updated"

    rst.Close
    Set rst = Nothing

End Sub
```

In the example, the CursorLocation property of the recordset is set to adUseClient, the CursorType is set to adOpenKeyset, and the LockType is set to adLockBatchOptimistic.

What Are ActiveX Data Objects and Data Access Objects and Why Are They Important?

CHAPTER 14

621

Notice that the Update method is not included in the Do Until loop. Instead, the UpdateBatch method is used to send all of the changes to the server at once.

Making Bulk Changes

As mentioned in the previous section, it is inefficient to open a recordset and then update each record individually. It is much more efficient to execute an action query. Listing 14.30 illustrates this process.

LISTING 14.30   Making Bulk Changes to the Records in a Recordset

```
Sub RunUpdateQuery()
    'Declare and instantiate a Connection object
    Dim cnn As ADODB.Connection
    Set cnn = New ADODB.Connection

    'Establish the connection and execute an action query
    Set cnn = CurrentProject.Connection
    cnn.Execute "qryIncreaseTotalEstimate"
    cnn.Close

End Sub
```

In Listing 14.30, the Execute method of the Connection object executes a stored query called qryIncreaseTotalEstimate. Any criteria contained within the query is applied.

Deleting an Existing Record

You can use ADO code to delete a record in a recordset. The code appears in Listing 14.31. Note that it must be called using basADORecordset.DeleteCusts.

LISTING 14.31   Deleting an Existing Record

```
Sub DeleteCusts(lngProjEst As Long)

    'Declare and instantiate a recordset
    Dim rst As ADODB.Recordset
    Set rst = New ADODB.Recordset

    'Establish the connection, cursor type,
    'and lock type, and open the recordset
    rst.ActiveConnection = CurrentProject.Connection
    rst.CursorType = adOpenDynamic
```

LISTING 14.31   Continued

```
rst.LockType = adLockOptimistic
rst.Open "Select * from tblProjectsChange"

intCounter = 0

'Loop through the recordset, deleting all projects
'with an estimate lower than the specified amount
Do Until rst.EOF
    If rst("ProjectTotalEstimate") < lngProjEst Then
        rst.Delete
        intCounter = intCounter + 1
    End If
    If Not rst.EOF Then
        rst.MoveNext
    End If
Loop

'Designate how many customers were deleted
Debug.Print intCounter & " Customers Deleted"

rst.Close
Set rst = Nothing

End Sub
```

In Listing 14.31, a recordset is opened, based on all the records in the tblProjectsChange table. The code loops through all the records in the recordset. If the ProjectTotalEstimate is less than the value passed as a parameter to the routine, the `Delete` method of the `Recordset` object removes the record from the recordset.

As previously discussed, this example is very inefficient. You should either build a recordset containing only the records you want to delete, or use an action query to accomplish the task.

TIP

If you are using a provider that supports stored procedures, it is most efficient to add, edit, and delete data using a stored procedure. Stored procedures execute on the server, sending no data over the network wire.

What Are ActiveX Data Objects and Data Access Objects and Why Are They Important?

CHAPTER 14

623

Adding a New Record

Not only can you edit and delete data using ADO, but you can also add records as well.
Listing 14.32 illustrates this process.

LISTING 14.32   Adding a New Record to a Recordset

```
Private Sub cmdAddADO_Click()
    Dim rst As ADODB.Recordset

    'Ensure that the project name and clientid are entered
    If IsNull(Me.txtProjectName) Or _
        IsNull(Me.cboClientID) Then

        MsgBox "The Project Name and Client must be Filled In"

    Else

        'Instantiate a recordset
        Set rst = New ADODB.Recordset

        'Set the connection, cursor type and lock type
        'and open the recordset
        With rst
            .ActiveConnection = CurrentProject.Connection
            .CursorType = adOpenKeyset
            .LockType = adLockOptimistic
            .Open "Select * from tblProjectsChange Where ProjectID = 0"

            'Add a new row to the recordset, populating its values with
            'the controls on the form
            .AddNew
                !ProjectName = Me.txtProjectName
                !ProjectDescription = Me.txtProjectDescription
                !ClientID = Me.cboClientID
            .Update

            'Populate the txtProjectID text box with the
            'autonumber value assigned to the new row
            Me.txtProjectID = !ProjectID
        End With

    End If

End Sub
```

14

ACTIVEX AND
DATA ACCESS
OBJECTS

This code, an event procedure for a command button on frmUnbound, begins by setting the CursorType property of the recordset to adOpenKeyset and the LockType property to adLockOptimistic. The AddNew method creates a buffer for a new record. All the field values are assigned, based on values in the text boxes on the form. The Update method writes the data to disk. Because the ProjectID field is an Autonumber field, the txtProjectID text box must be updated to reflect the Autonumber value that was assigned.

> **CAUTION**
>
> With DAO, you are not placed on the new record after it is added. With ADO, you are moved to the new record when the Update method is issued.

Creating and Modifying Database Objects Using ADO Code

Although most of the time you will design your database structure before you deploy your application, there might be times when you will need to design or modify database objects at runtime. Fortunately, you can accomplish these tasks using ADO code. The following sections cover adding and removing tables, modifying relationships, and building queries, all using ADO code. These are only a few of the tasks that you can accomplish.

Adding a Table Using Code

It is relatively easy to add a table using ADO code. Listing 14.33 provides an example.

LISTING 14.33   Adding a Table

```
Sub CreateTable()
   Dim tdf As ADOX.Table
   Dim idx As ADOX.Index

   'Declare and instantiate a Catalog object
   Dim cat As ADOX.Catalog
   Set cat = New ADOX.Catalog

   'Establish a connection
   cat.ActiveConnection = CurrentProject.Connection

   ' Instantiate a Table object
   Set tdf = New ADOX.Table
```

What Are ActiveX Data Objects and Data Access Objects and Why Are They Important?

CHAPTER 14

625

LISTING 14.33 Continued

```
' Name the table and add field to it
With tdf
    .Name = "tblFoods"
    Set .ParentCatalog = cat
    .Columns.Append "FoodID", adInteger
    .Columns("FoodID").Properties("AutoIncrement") = True
    .Columns.Append "Description", adWChar
    .Columns.Append "Calories", adInteger
End With

'Append the table to the Tables collection
cat.Tables.Append tdf

'Instantiate an Index object
Set idx = New ADOX.Index

'Set properties of the index
With idx
    .Name = "PrimaryKey"
    .Columns.Append "FoodID"
    .PrimaryKey = True
    .Unique = True
End With

'Add the index to the Indexes collection
'of the table
tdf.Indexes.Append idx

Set idx = Nothing
Set cat = Nothing


End Sub
```

14

Listing 14.33 begins by instantiating an ADOX table object. It sets the Name and ParentCatalog properties of the Table object. Then it uses the Append method of the Columns collection of the table to append each field to the table. After all the columns are appended, it uses the Append method of the Tables collection of the Catalog object to append the Table object to the database.

After the table is appended to the Catalog, you can add indexes to the table. An Index object is instantiated. The Name property of the index is set. Next, the Append method of the Columns object of the Index adds a column to the Index. The PrimaryKey and Unique properties of the index are both set to `True`. Finally, the `Index` object is appended to the Indexes collection of the `Table` object.

> **CAUTION**
>
> When running code that appends an object, an error occurs if the object already exists. You must either include error handling in your routine to handle this eventuality or delete the existing instance of the object before appending the new object.

Removing a Table Using Code

Sometimes it is necessary to remove a table from a database. Fortunately, this is very easily accomplished using ADO code. Listing 14.34 illustrates the process.

LISTING 14.34   Removing a Table

```
Sub DeleteTable()
    'Ignore error if it occurs
    On Error Resume Next

    'Declare and instantiate a Catalog object
    Dim cat As ADOX.Catalog
    Set cat = New ADOX.Catalog

    'Establish the connection for the Catalog object
    cat.ActiveConnection = CurrentProject.Connection

    'Delete a table from the tables collection
    cat.Tables.Delete "tblFoods"

End Sub
```

First, a `Catalog` object is declared and instantiated. Then the `Delete` method of the Tables collection of the `Catalog` object removes the table from the database.

Establishing Relationships Using Code

If your application adds new tables to a database, it might be necessary to establish relationships between those tables, as demonstrated in Listing 14.35.

What Are ActiveX Data Objects and Data Access Objects and Why Are They Important?

CHAPTER 14

627

LISTING 14.35   Establishing a Relationship

```
Sub CreateRelation()
    Dim tbl As ADOX.Table
    Dim fk As ADOX.Key

    'Declare and instantiate a Catalog object
    Dim cat As ADOX.Catalog
    Set cat = New ADOX.Catalog

    'Establish a connection
    cat.ActiveConnection = CurrentProject.Connection

    'Point the Table object at the tblPeople table
    Set tbl = cat.Tables("tblPeople")

    'Instantiate a Key object
    Set fk = New ADOX.Key

    'Set properties of the Key object to relate the
    'tblPeople table to the tblFoods table
    With fk
        .Name = "PeopleFood"
        .Type = adKeyForeign
        .RelatedTable = "tblFoods"
        .Columns.Append "FoodId"
        .Columns("FoodID").RelatedColumn = "FoodID"
    End With

    'Append the Key object to the Keys collection of
    'the tblPeople table
    tbl.Keys.Append fk

    Set cat = Nothing
    Set tbl = Nothing
    Set fk = Nothing
End Sub
```

14

ACTIVEX AND DATA ACCESS OBJECTS

The code begins by pointing a Table object at the foreign key table in the relationship. A Key object is instantiated. The Name property of the Key object is set. Next, the Type property of the Key object is established. The RelatedTable property is set equal to the name of the primary key table involved in the relationship. The Append method of the Columns collection of the Key object appends the foreign key field to the Key object. Then the RelatedColumn property of the column is set equal to the name of the primary key field. Finally, the Key object is appended to the Keys collection of the Table object.

Creating a Query Using Code

At times, you will want to build a query on-the-fly and permanently store it in the database. Listing 14.36 illustrates this process.

LISTING 14.36   Creating a Query

```
Sub CreateQuery()
    Dim cmd As ADODB.Command
    Dim strSQL As String

    'Declare and instantiate a Catalog object
    Dim cat As ADOX.Catalog
    Set cat = New ADOX.Catalog

    'Establish a connection
    cat.ActiveConnection = CurrentProject.Connection

    'Instantiate a Command object and set its
    'CommandText property
    Set cmd = New ADODB.Command
    cmd.CommandText = "Select * From tblClients Where State='CA'"

    'Append the Command object to the Views collection
    'of the Catalog object
    cat.Views.Append "qryCAClients", cmd
    cat.Views.Refresh

    Set cat = Nothing
    Set cmd = Nothing

End Sub
```

The code begins by creating and instantiating a Catalog object and a Command object. The CommandText property of the Command object is set equal to the SQL statement that underlies the query. The Append method of the Views collection of the Catalog object appends the Command object to a query with the specified name. The View collection of the Catalog object is then refreshed.

Examining the Data Access Object Model

Figure 14.2 shows an overview of the Data Access Object model for the Jet 4.0 Database Engine. At the top of the hierarchy is the Microsoft Jet Database Engine, referred to as the DBEngine object. The DBEngine object contains all the other objects that are part of the hierarchy. The DBEngine object is the only object in the hierarchy that does not have an associated collection.

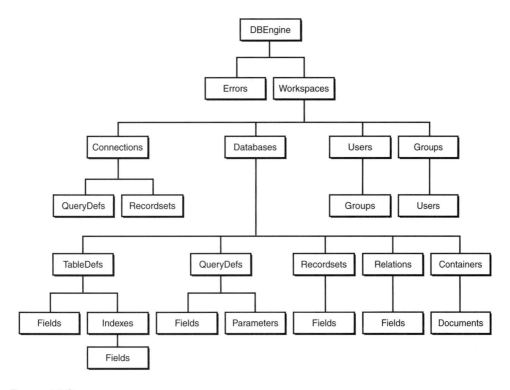

FIGURE 14.2

The Data Access Object model.

Each object within the Data Access Object model is important because you will manipulate the various objects at runtime using code to accomplish the tasks required by your application. The following sections describe each major object and how it affects your programming endeavors.

Workspaces

The Workspaces collection contains Workspace objects. Each Workspace object defines the area in which a particular user operates. All security and transaction processing for a given user takes place within a particular workspace. You can programmatically create multiple workspaces. This is of great value because, by using this technique, you can log in as another user behind the scenes and accomplish tasks not allowed by the security level of the current user. You can log in as a member of the Admins group, for example, change the structure of a table that the current user does not have rights to, and log back out without the user of the system ever knowing that anything happened.

Users

The Users collection contains the User objects for a particular workspace. Each User object is a user account defined by a workgroup database. Because each user is a member of one or more groups, each User object contains a Groups collection that consists of each group of which a particular user is a member. User objects easily can be added and manipulated at runtime.

Groups

The Groups collection contains all Group objects for a particular workspace. Each Group object is a group defined by a workgroup database. Because each group contains users, the Group object contains a Users collection that consists of each user who is a member of the group. Like User objects, Group objects can be added and manipulated at runtime.

Databases

The Databases collection contains all the databases that are currently open within a particular workspace. You can open multiple databases at a time. These open databases can be Jet databases or external databases. A Database object refers to a particular database within the Databases collection. It is easy to loop through the Databases collection, printing the name of each Database object contained in the collection, as shown in Listing 14.37.

LISTING 14.37   Printing the Name of Each Database in a Workspace

```
Sub EnumerateDBs()
    Dim ws As dao.Workspace
    Dim db As dao.Database
    Dim db1 As dao.Database
    Dim db2 As dao.Database

    Set ws = DBEngine(0)

    'Point the db1 database object at a reference to the
    'Current Database
    Set db1 = CurrentDb

    'Point the db2 database object a a reference to a
    'database called Chap2.mdb
    Set db2 = ws.OpenDatabase(CurrentProject.Path & "\Chap2.MDB")
```

What Are ActiveX Data Objects and Data Access Objects and Why Are They Important?

CHAPTER 14

631

LISTING 14.37   Continued

```
    'Loop through all of the databases in the workspace
    'printing their names
    For Each db In ws.Databases
        Debug.Print db.Name
    Next db
End Sub
```

This code loops through the open databases in the current workspace. It prints the name of each open database. It also is easy to perform all the other tasks required to build, modify, and manipulate database objects at runtime.

TableDefs

The TableDefs collection contains all the tables contained in a particular database—whether or not they are open. The TableDefs collection also includes linked tables and detailed information about each table. It is easy to loop through the TableDefs collection, printing various properties (for example, the name) of each `Table` object contained within the collection. Listing 14.38 shows an example of using the TableDefs collection to print the properties of each `Table` object, in addition to printing the properties of each index on the table.

Indexes

Each `TableDef` object contains an Indexes collection, which enumerates all the indexes on the table. Each index contains a Fields collection to describe the fields in the index.

LISTING 14.38   Using the TableDefs and Indexes Collections

```
Sub EnumerateTablesAndIndexes()
    Dim db As dao.Database
    Dim tbl As dao.TableDef
    Dim idx As dao.Index
    Dim fld As dao.Field

    'Point the db object at a reference to the current database
    Set db = CurrentDb

    'Loop through each TableDef object in the TableDefs
    'Collection in this database
    For Each tbl In db.TableDefs

        'Print the name of the table
        Debug.Print "Table: "; tbl.Name
```

14

ACTIVEX AND
DATA ACCESS
OBJECTS

LISTING 14.38   Continued

```
        'Loop through all indexes associated with the table
        For Each idx In tbl.Indexes

            'Print the name, primary, and unique properties of
            'the index
            Debug.Print "  Index: "; idx.Name
            Debug.Print "   Primary="; idx.PRIMARY; ", Unique="; idx.Unique

            'Loop through each field in the index printing its name
            For Each fld In idx.Fields
                Debug.Print "    Field:"; fld.Name
            Next fld
        Next idx
    Next tbl
End Sub
```

This code loops through the TableDefs in the current database and prints the name of each table in the database. It then prints the name of every index on the table and every field in the index. It is easy to write code that adds, deletes, modifies, and otherwise manipulates tables and indexes at runtime.

QueryDefs

The QueryDefs collection includes all the queries contained within a particular database. It contains information about each query. It is easy to loop through the QueryDefs collection, printing various pieces of information about each query, as Listing 14.39 shows.

LISTING 14.39   Printing Information About Each Query Using the QueryDefs Collection

```
Sub EnumerateQueries()
    Dim db As dao.Database
    Dim qry As dao.QueryDef

    'Point the db object at a reference to the current database
    Set db = CurrentDb

    'Loop through each QueryDef object in the QueryDefs
    'collection of the database
    For Each qry In db.QueryDefs

        'Print the name and the SQL statement behind the query
        Debug.Print qry.Name
        Debug.Print qry.SQL
    Next qry
End Sub
```

What Are ActiveX Data Objects and Data Access Objects and Why Are They Important?

CHAPTER 14

633

This code loops through the QueryDefs in the current database and prints the name and SQL statement associated with each QueryDef. It is easy to write code that adds, deletes, modifies, and otherwise manipulates queries at runtime.

Fields

Fields collections are contained within the `TableDef`, `QueryDef`, `Index`, `Relation`, and `Recordset` objects. The Fields collection of an object is the collection of `Field` objects within the parent object. A `TableDef` object contains `Field` objects that are contained in the specific table, for example. Using the parent object, you can get information about its Fields collection, as shown in Listing 14.40.

LISTING 14.40 Getting Information from the Fields Collection

```
Sub EnumerateFields()
    Dim tbl As dao.TableDef
    Dim fld As dao.Field

    'Point the db object at a reference to the current database
    Set db = CurrentDb

    'Loop through each TableDef object in the TableDefs
    'collection of the database
    For Each tbl In db.TableDefs

        'Loop through each Field object in the Fields
        'collection of the table
        For Each fld In tbl.Fields

            'Print the name and type of each field
            Debug.Print fld.Name
            Debug.Print fld.Type
        Next fld
    Next tbl
End Sub
```

This code loops through the TableDefs in the current database. As it loops through each TableDef, it prints the name and type of each field contained within the Fields collection of the TableDef. Code also can be used to add, delete, or change the attributes of fields at runtime. With a large database, this code is likely to output more information than can be contained in the Immediate window buffer. You might want to pause the code at some point to view the contents of the Immediate window.

> **NOTE**
>
> Notice that the Type property is an integer value. Each integer returned from this property represents a different field type. You might want to write a case statement that converts the integer value to a more meaningful text string.

Parameters

Access queries can contain parameters. These parameters are created so that the user can supply information required by the query at runtime. Each `QueryDef` object has a Parameters collection, which consists of `Parameter` objects. You can write code to manipulate these parameters at runtime, as Listing 14.41 shows.

LISTING 14.41   Listing the Parameters of Every Query

```
Sub EnumerateParameters()
    Dim db As dao.Database
    Dim qry As dao.QueryDef
    Dim prm As dao.Parameter

    'Point the db object at a reference to the current database
    Set db = CurrentDb

    'Loop through each QueryDef object in the QueryDefs
    'collection of the database
    For Each qry In db.QueryDefs

        'Print the Name of the Query
        Debug.Print "*****" & qry.Name & "*****"

        'Loop through each Parameter object in the Parameters
        'collection of the query
        For Each prm In qry.Parameters

            'Print the name of the parameter
            Debug.Print prm.Name
        Next prm
    Next qry
End Sub
```

What Are ActiveX Data Objects and Data Access Objects and Why Are They Important?

CHAPTER 14

635

This code loops through the `QueryDefs` object within the current database. It prints the name of the `QueryDef` object and then loops through its Parameters collection, printing the name of each parameter. `Parameter` objects can be added, deleted, and manipulated through code at runtime.

Recordsets

`Recordset` objects exist only at runtime. A `Recordset` object is used to reference a set of records coming from one or more tables. The Recordsets collection contains all the `Recordset` objects that are currently open within the current `Database` object. `Recordset` objects are covered extensively in "Understanding DAO Recordset Types," later in this chapter.

Relations

The Relations collection contains all the `Relation` objects that describe the relationships established within a `Database` object. The code in Listing 14.42 loops through the current database, printing the `Table` and `ForeignTable` of each `Relation` object.

LISTING 14.42   Using the Relations Collection

```
Sub EnumerateRelations()
    Dim db As dao.Database
    Dim rel As dao.Relation

    'Point the db object at a reference to the current database
    Set db = CurrentDb

    'Loop through each Relation object in the Relations
    'collection of the database
    For Each rel In db.Relations

        'Print the names of the Primary and Foreign key tables
        Debug.Print rel.Table & " Related To: " & rel.ForeignTable
    Next rel
End Sub
```

Relationships can be created, deleted, and modified at runtime using VBA code.

Containers

The Containers collection contains information about each saved `Database` object. Using the Containers collection, you can view and modify all the objects contained within the current database, as demonstrated in Listing 14.43.

LISTING 14.43   Listing Every Container in a Database

```
Sub EnumerateContainers()
    Dim db As dao.Database
    Dim cnt As dao.Container

    'Point the db object at a reference to the current database
    Set db = CurrentDb

    'Loop through each Container object in the Containers
    'collection of the database
    For Each cnt In db.Containers

        'Print the name of the container
        Debug.Print cnt.Name
    Next cnt
End Sub
```

This code loops through the Containers collection, printing the name of each `Container` object. The results are `DataAccessPages`, `Databases`, `Forms`, `Modules`, `Relationships`, `Reports`, `Scripts`, `SysRel`, and `Tables` objects.

Documents

A `Document` object represents a specific object in the Documents collection. You can loop through the Documents collection of a `Container` object, as shown in Listing 14.44.

LISTING 14.44   Printing the Names of `Document` Objects

```
Sub EnumerateForms()
    Dim db As dao.Database
    Dim cnt As dao.Container
    Dim doc As dao.Document

    'Point the db object at a reference to the current database
    Set db = CurrentDb

    'Point the Container object at the Forms collection of
    'the Container
    Set cnt = db.Containers!Forms

    'Loop through each Document object in the Documents
    'collection of the container
    For Each doc In cnt.Documents
```

What Are ActiveX Data Objects and Data Access Objects and Why Are They Important?

CHAPTER 14

637

LISTING 14.44   Continued

```
        'Print the name of the document
        Debug.Print doc.Name
    Next doc

End Sub
```

This code points a Container object to the forms in the current database. It then loops through each document in the Container object, printing the name of each Document object (in this case, the name of each form).

> **NOTE**
>
> It is important to understand the difference between the Forms container and the Forms collection. The *Forms container* is part of the Containers collection; it contains all the forms that are part of the database. The *Forms collection* contains all the forms open at runtime. The properties of each form in the Forms container differ from the properties of a form in the Forms collection.

Properties

Each Data Access Object has a Properties collection. The Properties collection of an object is a list of properties associated with that particular object. This gives you a generic way to view and modify the properties of any object, as shown in Listing 14.45.

You can use this collection to create generic routines to handle common tasks. You could write a routine to set the font size of any control to 8 points, for example. Your routine could use the Properties collection to verify that the control has a Font property before attempting to set the size.

LISTING 14.45   Printing Every Property of Document Objects

```
Sub EnumerateProperties()
    Dim db As dao.Database
    Dim cnt As dao.Container
    Dim doc As dao.Document
    Dim prp As dao.Property
```

14

ACTIVEX AND
DATA ACCESS
OBJECTS

LISTING 14.45   Continued

```
    'Point the db object at a reference to the current database
    Set db = CurrentDb


    'Point the Container object at the Forms collection of
    'the Container
    Set cnt = db.Containers!Forms

    'Loop through each Document object in the Documents
    'collection of the container
    For Each doc In cnt.Documents
        Debug.Print doc.Name

        'Loop through each Property object in the
        'Properties collection of the document
        For Each prp In doc.Properties

            'Print the name and value of the property
            Debug.Print prp.Name & " = " & prp.Value
        Next prp
    Next doc
End Sub
```

This code loops through each form in the current database, printing all the properties of each
Form object.

Errors

The Errors collection consists of Error objects. An Error object contains information about
the most recent error that occurred. Each time an operation generates an error, the Errors collection is cleared of any previous errors. Sometimes a single operation can cause more than
one error, so one or more Error objects might be added to the Errors collection when a single
data access error occurs.

Getting to Know DBEngine

As mentioned, the DBEngine object refers to the Jet Database Engine, which is at the top of the
Data Access Object hierarchy. The DBEngine object contains only two collections: Workspaces
and Errors. When referring to the current database, you can use the CurrentDB() function discussed in the next section. When referring to any database other than the current database, you
must refer to the DBEngine object, as in Listing 14.46.

What Are ActiveX Data Objects and Data Access Objects and Why Are They Important?

CHAPTER 14

639

LISTING 14.46 Accessing the Properties of the `DBEngine` Object

```
Sub ReferToCurrentDB()
    Dim ws As dao.Workspace
    Dim db As dao.Database

    Set ws = DBEngine(0)

    'Point the database object at a database
    'opened in the current workspace
    Set db = ws.OpenDatabase(CurrentProject.Path & "\Chap14Ex.mdb")

    'Print the version property of the database
    Debug.Print db.Version
End Sub
```

This code creates a `Workspace` object variable that points at the current workspace. The `OpenDatabase` method of the `Workspace` object then is used to open another database. The version of the database is printed by the routine.

Using `CurrentDB()`

Microsoft offers a shortcut you can use when creating an object variable that points to the current database. Using the `CurrentDB()` function, you do not need to first point at the workspace; nor do you need to issue the `OpenDatabase` method. Instead, you set the `Database` object variable equal to the result from the `CurrentDB()` function, as shown in Listing 14.47.

LISTING 14.47 Listing the Errors in the Current Database

```
Sub UseCurrentDBFunc()
    Dim db As dao.Database

    'Point the database object at a reference to the current
    'database
    Set db = CurrentDb()

    'Print the version property of the database
    Debug.Print db.Version
End Sub
```

This code sets the `Database` object variable so that it points at the current database object. It then prints the version of the database engine and each of the errors in the Errors collection.

The CurrentDB() function cannot be used to refer to objects that are not part of the current database. As with all VBA functions that do not require arguments, the parentheses after CurrentDB are optional.

Understanding DAO Recordset Types

A Recordset object represents the records in a table or the records returned by a query. A Recordset object can be a direct link to the table, a dynamic set of records, or a snapshot of the data at a certain time. Recordset objects are used to directly manipulate data in a database. They enable you to add, edit, delete, and move through data as required by your application. DAO supports three types of Recordset objects: dynasets, snapshots, and tables.

Dynasets

You can use a Recordset object of the dynaset type to manipulate local or linked tables or the results of queries. A *dynaset* is actually a set of references to table data. Using a dynaset, you can extract and update data from multiple tables—even tables from other databases. In fact, the tables containing the data included in a dynaset can even come from databases that are not of the same type (for example, Microsoft SQL Server, Paradox, and dBASE).

True to its name, a dynaset is a dynamic set of records. This means that changes made to the dynaset are reflected in the underlying tables, and changes made to the underlying tables by other users of the system are reflected in the dynaset. Although a dynaset is not the fastest type of Recordset object, it is definitely the most flexible.

Snapshots

A Recordset object of the snapshot type is similar to a dynaset. The major difference is that the data included in the snapshot is fixed at the time it is created. The data within the snapshot, therefore, cannot be modified and is not updated when other users make changes to the underlying tables. This trait can be an advantage or a disadvantage. It is a disadvantage, of course, if it is necessary for the data in the recordset to be updateable. It is an advantage if you are running a report and want to ensure that the data does not change during the time in which the report is being run. You, therefore, can create a snapshot and build the report from the Snapshot object.

> **NOTE**
>
> With small resultsets, snapshots are more efficient than dynasets because a Snapshot object creates less processing overhead. Regardless of their reduced overhead, snapshots actually are less efficient than dynasets when returning a resultset with a large

What Are ActiveX Data Objects and Data Access Objects and Why Are They Important?

CHAPTER 14

641

volume of data (generally more than 500 records). This is because when you create a Snapshot object, all fields are returned to the user as each record is accessed. On the other hand, a Dynaset object contains a set of primary keys for the records in the resultset. The other fields are returned to the user only when they are required for editing or display.

Tables

A Recordset object of the table type often is used to manipulate local or linked tables created using Microsoft Access or the Jet Database Engine. When you open a table-type recordset, all operations are performed directly on the table.

Certain operations, such as a Seek, can be performed only on a table-type recordset. You get the best performance for sorting and filtering records when using a table type of recordset.

The downside of a table-type recordset is that it can contain the data from only one table. It cannot be opened using a join or union query. It also cannot be used with tables created using engines other than Jet (for example, ODBC and other ISAM data sources).

Selecting Among the Types of DAO Recordset Objects Available

Deciding which type of recordset to use involves looking at the task to determine which type is most appropriate. When fast searching is most important and it is not a problem to retrieve all the records, a table is the best choice. If you must retrieve the results of a query and your resultset needs to be editable, a dynaset is the best choice. If there is no need for the results to be updated but the results must consist of a relatively small subset of the data, a snapshot is most appropriate.

Working with DAO Recordset Properties and Methods

Like other objects, Recordset objects have properties and methods. The properties are the attributes of the Recordset objects, and the methods are the actions you can take on the Recordset objects. Some properties are read-only at runtime; others can be read from and written to at runtime.

14

ACTIVEX AND
DATA ACCESS
OBJECTS

Creating a Recordset Variable

When working with a recordset, you first must create a `Recordset` variable. You use the `OpenRecordSet` method to create a `Recordset` object variable. You first must declare a generic `Recordset` variable and then point a specific recordset at the variable using a `Set` statement, as shown in the example in Listing 14.48.

LISTING 14.48 Opening a Recordset

```
Sub OpenTable()
    Dim dbInfo As dao.Database
    Dim rstClients As dao.Recordset

    'Point the database object at a reference to the
    'current database
    Set dbInfo = CurrentDb()

    'Open a recordset based on the tblClients table
    Set rstClients = dbInfo.OpenRecordset("tblClients")

    'Print the Updatable property of the recordset
    Debug.Print rstClients.Updatable
End Sub
```

This code creates a `Database` object variable and a `Recordset` object variable. It then uses the `CurrentDB` function to point the `Database` object variable to the current database. Next, it uses the `OpenRecordSet` method to assign the recordset based on `tblClients` to the object variable `rstClients`.

The type of recordset that is created is determined by the default type for the object or by a second parameter of the `OpenRecordSet` method. If the `OpenRecordSet` method is executed on a table and no second parameter is specified, the recordset is opened as the table type. If the `OpenRecordSet` method is performed on a query and no second parameter is specified, the recordset is opened as the dynaset type. You can override this default behavior by passing a second parameter to the `OpenRecordSet` method, as Listing 14.49 shows.

LISTING 14.49 Opening a Dynaset-Type Recordset on a Table

```
Sub OpenDynaSet()
    Dim dbInfo As dao.Database
    Dim rstClients As dao.Recordset

    'Point the database object at a reference to the
    'current database
    Set dbInfo = CurrentDb()
```

LISTING 14.49   Continued

```
    'Open a dynaset type recordset based on the tblClients table
    Set rstClients = dbInfo.OpenRecordset("tblClients", dbOpenDynaset)

    'Print the Updateable property of the recordset
    Debug.Print rstClients.Updateable
End Sub
```

This code opens the recordset as a dynaset. dbOpenTable, dbOpenDynaset, and dbOpenSnapshot are all intrinsic constants that can be used to open a Recordset object. A query can be opened only as a dynaset or snapshot Recordset object. Listing 14.50 shows the code to open a recordset based on a query.

LISTING 14.50   Opening a Recordset Based on a Query

```
Sub OpenQuery()
    Dim dbInfo As dao.Database
    Dim rstClients As dao.Recordset

    'Point the database object at a reference to the
    'current database
    Set dbInfo = CurrentDb()

    'Open a snapshot type recordset based on the qryHoursByProject query
    Set rstClients = dbInfo.OpenRecordset("qryHoursByProject", dbOpenSnapshot)

    'Print the Updateable property of the recordset
    Debug.Print rstClients.Updatable
End Sub
```

NOTE

As was the case with Access 95, the proper method to create a Recordset object in Access 97, Access 2000, and Access 2002 differs from that of earlier versions of Access. In earlier versions, it was appropriate to dimension a dynaset, snapshot, or table type of object variable and then use the CreateDynaset, CreateSnapshot, and OpenTable methods of the Database object to create the appropriate type of recordset. This method for creating recordsets is included in Access 97, Access 2000, and Access 2002 for backward compatibility only. It should be avoided and replaced with the code included in this section.

14

ACTIVEX AND DATA ACCESS OBJECTS

Using Arguments to Open a Recordset

Microsoft provides several arguments that control the way in which a recordset is opened. The arguments and their uses follow:

- dbAppendOnly—When this option is used, records can be added to the recordset only. Existing data cannot be displayed or modified. This option is useful when you want to ensure that existing data is not affected by the processing. This option applies to dynasets only.

- dbConsistent—This argument applies to dynasets. It allows consistent updates only. This means that in a one-to-many join, you can update only those fields that are not duplicated in other records in the dynaset. This is the default argument for dynasets.

- dbDenyRead—This argument prevents other users from even reading the data contained within the recordset as long as the recordset remains open. You can use this option only on table recordsets.

- dbDenyWrite—When creating a dynaset or snapshot, this option prevents all other users from modifying the records contained in the recordset until the recordset is closed. Other users still are able to view the data contained within the recordset. When this option is applied to a table type of recordset, other users are prevented from opening the underlying table.

- dbForwardOnly—This argument creates a forward-scrolling snapshot. This type of recordset is fast but limited because you can use only the Move and MoveNext methods to move directly through the snapshot.

- dbInconsistent—This argument allows for inconsistent updates. This means that, in a one-to-many join, you can update all columns in the recordset.

- dbReadOnly—This option prevents your recordset from modifying data. If you don't want the data within the recordset to be updateable, but you expect a large number of records to be returned and you want to take advantage of the record paging offered by dynasets, you might want to open the recordset as a dynaset.

- dbSeeChanges—This option ensures that a user receives an error if the code issues an Edit method and another user modifies the data before an Update method is used. This option is useful in a high-traffic environment when it is likely that two users will modify the same record at the same time. This option applies to dynaset and table recordsets only.

- dbSQLPassThrough—When the source of the recordset is a SQL statement, this argument passes the SQL statement to an ODBC database for processing. This option does not completely eliminate Jet; it simply prevents Jet from making any changes to the SQL statement before passing it to the ODBC Drive Manager. You can use the dbSQLPassThrough argument only with snapshots and read-only dynasets.

What Are ActiveX Data Objects and Data Access Objects and Why Are They Important?

CHAPTER 14

645

The arguments described can be used in combination to accomplish the desired objectives. Listing 14.51 shows the use of an `OpenRecordSet` argument.

LISTING 14.51   Using an `OpenRecordset` Argument

```
Sub OpenRecordsetArgs()
    Dim db As dao.Database
    Dim rst As dao.Recordset

    'Point the database object at a reference to the
    'current database
    Set db = CurrentDb

    'Open a dynaset type recordset based on the tblProjects table,
    'but designate that the recordset is read only
    Set rst = db.OpenRecordset("tblProjects", dbOpenDynaset, dbReadOnly)

    'Print the Updateable property of the recordset
    Debug.Print rst.Updateable
End Sub
```

This code opens a recordset as read-only.

Examining Record-Movement Methods

When you have a `Recordset` object variable set, you probably want to manipulate the data in the recordset. Table 14.4 shows several methods you can use to traverse through the records in a recordset.

TABLE 14.4   Methods for Moving Through the Records in a Recordset

Method	Moves
MoveFirst	To the first record in a recordset
MoveLast	To the last record in a recordset
MovePrevious	To the previous record in a recordset
MoveNext	To the next record in a recordset
Move[0]	Forward or backward a specified number of records

Listing 14.52 shows an example of using the record-movement methods on a dynaset.

14

ACTIVEX AND
DATA ACCESS
OBJECTS

LISTING 14.52 Using the Move Methods

```
Sub RecordsetMovements()
    Dim db As dao.Database
    Dim rst As dao.Recordset

    'Point the database object at a reference to the
    'current database
    Set db = CurrentDb

    'Open a dynaset type recordset based on the tblProjects table
    Set rst = db.OpenRecordset("tblProjects", dbOpenDynaset)

    'Print the contents of the ProjectID field
    Debug.Print rst("ProjectID")

    'Move to the next row, printing the ProjectID
    rst.MoveNext
    Debug.Print rst("ProjectID")

    'Move to the last row, printing the ProjectID
    rst.MoveLast
    Debug.Print rst("ProjectID")

    'Move to the previous row, printing the ProjectID
    rst.MovePrevious
    Debug.Print rst("ProjectID")

    'Move to the first row, printing the ProjectID
    rst.MoveFirst
    Debug.Print rst("ProjectID")
    rst.Close
End Sub
```

This code opens a dynaset. The record pointer automatically is placed on the first record of the dynaset when the recordset is opened. The routine prints the contents of the ProjectID field and then moves to the next record, printing its ProjectID. It then moves to the last record of the dynaset, printing its ProjectID; moves to the previous record, printing its ProjectID; and moves to the first record, printing its ProjectID. The Close method is applied to the Recordset object. It is a good idea to always close an open recordset before exiting a routine. After changes are made to the recordset, the Close method properly closes the recordset, ensuring that all changes are written to disk.

What Are ActiveX Data Objects and Data Access Objects and Why Are They Important?

CHAPTER 14

647

Detecting the Limits of a Recordset

All the information discussed in the section about determining the limits of an ADO recordset apply when dealing with a DAO recordset. Listing 14.53 shows a DAO code sample that uses the EOF property with the MoveNext method.

LISTING 14.53   Using the EOF Property with MoveNext

```
Sub DetermineLimits()
    Dim db As dao.Database
    Dim rstClients As dao.Recordset

    'Point the database object at a reference to the
    'current database
    Set db = CurrentDb()

    'Open a snapshot type recordset based on the tblClients table
    Set rstClients = db.OpenRecordset("tblClients", dbOpenSnapshot)

    'Loop through all of the records in the recordset, printing
    'the ClientID
    Do Until rstClients.EOF
        Debug.Print rstClients("ClientID")
        rstClients.MoveNext
    Loop
    rstClients.Close
End Sub
```

This code traverses through a snapshot recordset, printing the value of the ClientID field for each record until it reaches the position after the last record in the recordset. It then exits the loop and closes the recordset.

Counting the Number of Records in a Recordset

The RecordCount property of a recordset returns the number of records in a recordset that have been accessed. The problem with this is evident if you open a recordset and view the RecordCount property. You will discover that the count is equal to 0, if no records exist in the recordset, or equal to 1, if there are records in the recordset. The record count is accurate only if you visit all the records in the recordset, which you can do by using the MoveLast method, as Listing 14.54 shows.

14

ACTIVEX AND DATA ACCESS OBJECTS

Listing 14.54 Demonstrating the Limitations of RecordCount

```
Sub CountRecords()
    Dim rstProjects As dao.Recordset

    'Point the database object at a reference to the
    'current database
    Set db = CurrentDb()

    'Open a snapshot type recordset based on the tblClients table
    Set rstProjects = db.OpenRecordset("tblProjects", dbOpenSnapshot)

    'Print the recordcount
    Debug.Print rstProjects.RecordCount   'Prints 0 Or 1

    'Move to the last row
    rstProjects.MoveLast

    'Print the recordcount
    Debug.Print rstProjects.RecordCount 'Prints an accurate record Count
    rstProjects.Close
End Sub
```

The MoveLast method has its problems, though. It is slow and inefficient, especially in a client/server environment. Furthermore, in a multiuser environment, the RecordCount property becomes inaccurate as other people add and remove records from the table. This means that, if determining the record count is not absolutely necessary, you should avoid it.

The RecordCount property has one good use, though: You can use it to see whether there are any records in a recordset. If you are performing an operation that might return an empty recordset, you easily can use the RecordCount property to determine whether records were returned, as Listing 14.55 shows.

Listing 14.55 Checking for an Empty Recordset Using RecordCount

```
Sub CheckARecordset()
    Dim db As dao.Database
    Dim rstProjects As dao.Recordset

    'Point the database object at a reference to the
    'current database
    Set db = CurrentDb()

    'Open a snapshot type recordset based on the tblEmpty table
    Set rstProjects = db.OpenRecordset("tblEmpty", dbOpenSnapshot)
```

What Are ActiveX Data Objects and Data Access Objects and Why Are They Important?

CHAPTER 14

649

LISTING 14.55   Continued

```
    'Execute the AreThereRecords function to determine if the
    'recordset contains any rows
    If Not AreThereRecords(rstProjects) Then
        MsgBox "Recordset Empty...Unable to Proceed"
    End If
End Sub
Function AreThereRecords(rstAny As Recordset) As Boolean
    'Return the RecordCount property of the recordset
    'received as a parameter
    AreThereRecords = rstAny.RecordCount
End Function
```

The CheckARecordset procedure opens a recordset based on the tblEmpty table. It then calls the AreThereRecords function to determine whether any records are found in the recordset. If the AreThereRecords function returns False, an error message is displayed to the user.

Sorting, Filtering, and Finding Records

Sometimes you might need to sort or filter an existing recordset. You also might want to locate each record in the recordset that meets some specified criteria. The following techniques enable you to sort, filter, and find records within a Recordset object.

Sorting a Recordset

You can't actually change the sort order of an existing dynaset or snapshot. Instead, you create a second recordset based on the first recordset. The second recordset is sorted in the desired order. Listing 14.56 shows how this process works.

14

ACTIVEX AND DATA ACCESS OBJECTS

LISTING 14.56   Sorting an Existing Recordset

```
Sub SortRecordset()
    Dim db As dao.Database
    Dim rstTimeCardHours As dao.Recordset

    'Point the database object at a reference to the
    'current database
    Set db = CurrentDb

    'Open a Dynaset type recordset based on tblTimeCardHours
    Set rstTimeCardHours = db.OpenRecordset("tblTimeCardHours", dbOpenDynaset)

    'Loop through the unsorted recordset
    Debug.Print "NOT Sorted!!!"
    Do Until rstTimeCardHours.EOF
```

LISTING 14.56   Continued

```
        Debug.Print rstTimeCardHours("DateWorked")
        rstTimeCardHours.MoveNext
    Loop

    'Loop through the sorted recordset
    Debug.Print "Now Sorted!!!"
    rstTimeCardHours.Sort = "[DateWorked]"
    Set rstTimeCardHours = rstTimeCardHours.OpenRecordset
    Do Until rstTimeCardHours.EOF
        Debug.Print rstTimeCardHours("DateWorked")
        rstTimeCardHours.MoveNext
    Loop
End Sub
```

In this case, you are sorting a dynaset based on the tblTimeCardHours table. The first time you loop through the recordset and print each date worked, the dates are in the default order (usually the primary key order). After using the Sort method to sort the recordset, the records appear in order by the date worked.

Filtering a Recordset

Filtering a recordset is a useful technique when you want to select a subset of the records in your recordset. This is especially useful for allowing users to drill-down on a set of records to find the subset they need.

The process of filtering an existing recordset is similar to sorting one. Listing 14.57 is a variation of the example in Listing 14.56. Instead of sorting an existing recordset, it filters an existing recordset.

LISTING 14.57   Filtering an Existing Recordset

```
Sub FilterRecordSet()
    Dim db As dao.Database
    Dim rstTimeCardHours As Recordset

    'Point the database object at a reference to the
    'current database
    Set db = CurrentDb

    'Open a Dynaset type recordset based on tblTimeCardHours
    Set rstTimeCardHours = db.OpenRecordset("tblTimeCardHours", dbOpenDynaset)

    'Loop through the unfiltered recordset
    Debug.Print "Without Filter"
```

What Are ActiveX Data Objects and Data Access Objects and Why Are They Important?

CHAPTER 14

651

LISTING 14.57   Continued

```
Do Until rstTimeCardHours.EOF
    Debug.Print rstTimeCardHours("DateWorked")
    rstTimeCardHours.MoveNext
Loop

'Loop through the filtered recordset
rstTimeCardHours.Filter = "[DateWorked] Between #1/1/95# and #1/5/95#"
Debug.Print "With Filter"
Set rstTimeCardHours = rstTimeCardHours.OpenRecordset
Do Until rstTimeCardHours.EOF
    Debug.Print rstTimeCardHours("DateWorked")
    rstTimeCardHours.MoveNext
Loop
End Sub
```

The first time the code loops through the recordset, no filter is set. Then the code sets the filter, and the code loops through the recordset again. The second time, only the records meeting the filter criteria are displayed.

Finding a Specific Record Within a Recordset

The Seek method enables you to find records in a table recordset. It is usually the quickest method of locating data because it uses the current index to locate the requested data. Listing 14.58 shows how the Seek method works.

LISTING 14.58   Using the Seek Method

```
Sub SeekProject(lngProjectID As Long)
    Dim db As dao.Database
    Dim rstProjects As dao.Recordset

    'Point the database object at a reference to the
    'current database
    Set db = CurrentDb()

    'Open a table type recordset based on the tblProjects table
    Set rstProjects = db.OpenRecordset("tblProjects", dbOpenTable)

    'Set the Index property of the recordset and
    'use the Seek method to find a project
    rstProjects.Index = "PrimaryKey"
    rstProjects.Seek "=", lngProjectID
```

14

ACTIVEX AND
DATA ACCESS
OBJECTS

LISTING 14.58   Continued

```
      'Determine if the requested row was found
      If rstProjects.NoMatch Then
          MsgBox lngProjectID & " Not Found"
      Else
          MsgBox lngProjectID & " Found"
      End If
End Sub
```

This code uses the primary key index to locate the first project with the project number that was passed to the function. It then displays a message box to indicate whether the value was found.

You cannot use the Seek method to locate data in a dynaset or snapshot. Furthermore, you cannot use Seek to search for records in a linked table, regardless of whether the linked table is an Access table or a client/server table. In this case, you must use the FindFirst, FindLast, FindNext, and FindPrevious methods. The FindFirst method finds the first occurrence of data that meets the criteria, and FindLast finds the last occurrence of such data. The FindNext and FindPrevious methods enable you to find additional occurrences of the data.

The code in Listing 14.59 uses the FindFirst method to find the first occurrence of the parameter that was passed in. Again, it displays an appropriate message box.

LISTING 14.59   Using the FindFirst Method

```
Sub FindProject(lngValue As Long)
    Dim db As dao.Database
    Dim rstProjects As dao.Recordset
    Dim sSQL As String

    'Point the database object at a reference to the
    'current database
    Set db = CurrentDb()

    'Open a Dynaset type recordset based on tblProjects
    Set rstProjects = db.OpenRecordset("tblProjects", dbOpenDynaset)

    'Find the first row meeting the specified criteria
    sSQL = "[ProjectID] = " & lngValue
    rstProjects.FindFirst sSQL

    'Determine if a match was found
    If rstProjects.NoMatch Then
        MsgBox lngValue & " Not Found"
```

LISTING 14.59 Continued

```
    Else
        MsgBox lngValue & " Found"
    End If
End Sub
```

> **TIP**
>
> You can use another trick to search a linked table. You can open the database that contains the linked table and seek directly on the table data. This works only if the linked table is in another Access database.

Using the AbsolutePosition Property

The AbsolutePosition property returns the position of the current record. It is a zero-based value. You can use it to specify where in a recordset a specific record was found, as shown in Listing 14.60.

LISTING 14.60 Specifying Where a Record Was Found

```
Sub FindPosition(lngValue As Long)
    Dim db As dao.Database
    Dim rstProjects As dao.Recordset
    Dim sSQL As String

    'Point the database object at a reference to the
    'current database
    Set db = CurrentDb()

    'Open a Dynaset type recordset based on tblProjects
    Set rstProjects = db.OpenRecordset("tblProjects", dbOpenDynaset)

    'Find the first row meeting the specified criteria
    sSQL = "[ProjectID] = " & lngValue
    rstProjects.FindFirst sSQL

    'If a match is found, print the position of the row
    If rstProjects.NoMatch Then
        MsgBox lngValue & " Not Found"
    Else
        Debug.Print rstProjects.AbsolutePosition
    End If
End Sub
```

14

ACTIVEX AND
DATA ACCESS
OBJECTS

This code finds the first record with a ProjectID equal to the long integer received as a parameter. If the ProjectID is found, the value in the AbsolutePosition property of the record is printed.

CAUTION

Do not assume that the AbsolutePosition property of a particular record will stay the same. The AbsolutePosition property of a record changes as records are added or deleted or their order is changed as the records are modified.

Using the Bookmark Property

A *bookmark* is a system-generated byte array that uniquely identifies each record in a recordset. The Bookmark property of a recordset changes as you move to each record in the recordset. It often is used if you need to store the current position in the recordset so that you can perform some operation and then return to the position after the operation is completed. Three steps are involved in this process:

1. Storing the current bookmark of the recordset to a `Variant` variable.

2. Performing the desired operation.

3. Setting the Bookmark property of the recordset to the value contained within the `Variant` variable.

Listing 14.61 shows an example of using a bookmark.

LISTING 14.61   Using a Bookmark

```
Sub UseBookMark()
    Dim db As dao.Database
    Dim rstProjects As dao.Recordset
    Dim sSQL As String
    Dim vntPosition As Variant

    'Point the database object at a reference to the
    'current database
    Set db = CurrentDb()

    'Open a Dynaset type recordset based on tblProjects
    Set rstProjects = db.OpenRecordset("tblProjects", dbOpenDynaset)
```

What Are ActiveX Data Objects and Data Access Objects and Why Are They Important?

655

CHAPTER 14

LISTING 14.61 Continued

```
    'Store the current position in a variant variable
    vntPosition = rstProjects.Bookmark

    'Process the recordset
    Do Until rstProjects.EOF
        Debug.Print rstProjects("ProjectID")
        rstProjects.MoveNext
    Loop

    'Move back to the bookmarked row
    rstProjects.Bookmark = vntPosition
    Debug.Print rstProjects("ProjectID")
End Sub
```

This code begins by opening a recordset and storing the bookmark of the first record into a Variant variable. It then loops through each record in the recordset, printing the value in the ProjectID. After the loop completes, the Bookmark property of the recordset is set equal to the Variant variable, setting the current position of the recordset back to where it was before the loop began processing.

Using the RecordsetClone Property

You use the RecordsetClone property of a form to refer to the recordset underlying the form. This property often is used when you want to perform an operation and then synchronize the form with its underlying recordset. Listing 14.62 shows an example of the RecordsetClone property.

LISTING 14.62 Using the RecordsetClone Property

```
Private Sub cmdFindClient_Click()
    'This code is not found in the sample database
    Me.RecordsetClone.FindFirst "ClientID = " & Me.txtClientID
    If Me.RecordsetClone.NoMatch Then
        MsgBox Me.txtClientID & " Not Found"
    Else
        Me.Bookmark = Me.RecordsetClone.Bookmark
    End If
End Sub
```

This routine performs the FindFirst method on the RecordsetClone property of the current form. If the record is found, the Bookmark property of the form is set equal to the bookmark of the recordset. This matches the form's position to the underlying recordset's position.

Running Parameter Queries

Access parameter queries are very powerful. They enable the user to specify criteria at runtime. This capability often is helpful if your user wants to fill out a form at runtime and have the values on that form fed to the query. This also can be a useful way to protect your code from changes in the database schema. Creating a parameterized query is like writing a subroutine, in which the details of implementing that routine are hidden from the caller. This programming technique is called *encapsulation*. Listing 14.63 shows an example of using parameter queries.

LISTING 14.63   *Using Parameter Queries*

```
Sub RunParameterQuery(datStart As Date, datEnd As Date)
    Dim db As dao.Database
    Dim qdf As dao.QueryDef
    Dim rst As dao.Recordset

    'Point the database object at a reference to the
    'current database
    Set db = CurrentDb

    'Point the QueryDef object at the qryBillAmountByClient query
    Set qdf = db.QueryDefs("qryBillAmountByClient")

    'Set the parameters of the QueryDef object
    qdf.Parameters("Please Enter Start Date") = datStart
    qdf.Parameters("Please Enter End Date") = datEnd

    'Open a recordset based on the QueryDef object
    Set rst = qdf.OpenRecordset

    'Loop through the resulting recordset
    Do Until rst.EOF
        Debug.Print rst("CompanyName"), rst("BillAmount")
        rst.MoveNext
    Loop
End Sub
```

This subroutine receives two date variables as parameters. It just as easily could receive form controls as parameters. It opens a query definition called qryBillAmountByClient. It then sets the values of the parameters called Please Enter Start Date and Please Enter End Date to the date variables passed into the subroutine as parameters. The query then is executed by issuing the OpenRecordset method on the Recordset object.

What Are ActiveX Data Objects and Data Access Objects and Why Are They Important?

CHAPTER 14

657

Modifying Table Data Using DAO Code

So far, you have learned how to loop through and work with `Recordset` objects. Now you will learn how to change the data contained in a recordset.

Changing Record Data One Record at a Time

Often, you want to loop through a recordset, modifying all the records that meet a specific set of criteria. Listing 14.64 shows the code required to accomplish this task.

LISTING 14.64 Updating Records That Meet a Set of Criteria

```
Sub IncreaseEstimate()
    Dim db As dao.Database
    Dim rstProjectst As dao.Recordset
    Dim sSQL As String
    Dim intUpdated As Integer

    'Point the database object at a reference to the
    'current database
    Set db = CurrentDb()

    'Open a Dynaset type recordset based on tblProjectsChange
    Set rstProjectst = db.OpenRecordset("tblProjectsChange", dbOpenDynaset)

    'Locate the first project that meets the designated criteria
    sSQL = "ProjectTotalEstimate < 30000"
    intUpdated = 0
    rstProjectst.FindFirst sSQL

    'Loop as long as records meet the designated criteria
    'increasing the ProjectTotalEstimate by 10%
    Do Until rstProjectst.NoMatch
        intUpdated = intUpdated + 1
        rstProjectst.Edit
        rstProjectst("ProjectTotalEstimate") =
rstProjectst("ProjectTotalEstimate") * 1.1
        rstProjectst.Update
        rstProjectst.FindNext sSQL
    Loop

    'Display the number of rows that were updated
    Debug.Print intUpdated & " Records Updated"
    rstProjectst.Close
End Sub
```

14

ACTIVEX AND
DATA ACCESS
OBJECTS

This code finds the first record with a `ProjectTotalEstimate` of less than 30,000. It uses the `Edit` method to prepare the current record in the dynaset for editing. It replaces the `ProjectTotalEstimate` with the `ProjectTotalEstimate` multiplied by 1.1. It then issues the `Update` method to write the changes to disk. Finally, it uses the `FindNext` method to locate the next occurrence of the criteria.

Making Bulk Changes

Many of the tasks that you can perform by looping through a recordset also be can accomplished with an Update query. Executing an Update query often is more efficient than the process of looping through a recordset. If nothing else, it takes much less code. Therefore, it is important to understand how to execute an Update query through code.

Suppose that you have a query called `qryChangeTotalEstimate` that increases the `ProjectTotalEstimate` for all projects where the `ProjectTotalEstimate` is less than 30,000. The query is an Update query. The code in Listing 14.65 executes the stored query definition.

LISTING 14.65 Making Bulk Changes Using a Predefined Update Query

```
Sub RunUpdateQuery()
    Dim db As dao.Database
    Dim qdf As dao.QueryDef

    'Point the database object at a reference to the
    'current database
    Set db = CurrentDb

    'Point the QueryDef object at qryIncreaseTotalEstimate
    Set qdf = db.QueryDefs("qryIncreaseTotalEstimate")

    'Use the Execute method of the QueryDef object to
    'execute the update query
    qdf.Execute
End Sub
```

Notice that the `Execute` method operates on the query definition, executing the Updatequery.

Deleting an Existing Record

The `Delete` method enables you to programmatically delete records from a recordset, as shown in Listing 14.66.

What Are ActiveX Data Objects and Data Access Objects and Why Are They Important?

Chapter 14

659

Listing 14.66   Deleting Records with the `Delete` Method

```
Sub DeleteCusts(lngProjEst As Long)
    Dim db As dao.Database
    Dim rstProjects As dao.Recordset
    Dim intCounter As Integer

    'Point the database object at a reference to the
    'current database
    Set db = CurrentDb

    'Open a Dynaset type recordset based on tblProjectsChange
    Set rstProjects = db.OpenRecordset("tblProjectsChange", dbOpenDynaset)

    'Loop through the entire table, deleting all projects where
    'the ProjectTotalEstimate is less than a designated amount
    intCounter = 0
    Do Until rstProjects.EOF
        If rstProjects("ProjectTotalEstimate") < lngProjEst Then
            rstProjects.Delete
            intCounter = intCounter + 1
        End If
        rstProjects.MoveNext
    Loop

    'Print the number of affected rows
    Debug.Print intCounter & " Customers Deleted"
End Sub
```

This code loops through the rstProjects recordset. If the `ProjectTotalEstimate` amount is less than the value passed in as a parameter, the record is deleted. This task also can be accomplished with a Delete query.

Adding a New Record

The `AddNew` method enables you to programmatically add records to a recordset, as shown in Listing 14.67.

Listing 14.67   Adding Records to a Recordset

```
Private Sub cmdAddDAO_Click()
    Dim db As Database
    Dim rstProject As Recordset
```

LISTING 14.67 Continued

```
'Ensure that the project name and clientid are entered
If IsNull(Me.txtProjectName) Or _
    IsNull(Me.cboClientID) Then

    MsgBox "The Project Name and Client must be Filled In"

Else

    'Point the database object at a reference to the
    'current database
    Set db = CurrentDb()

    'Open a Dynaset type recordset based on tblProjectsChange
    Set rstProject = db.OpenRecordset("tblProjectsChange", dbOpenDynaset)

    'Add a new row to the recordset, populating its values with
    'the controls on the form
    With rstProject
        .AddNew
        !ProjectName = Me.txtProjectName
        !ProjectDescription = Me.txtProjectDescription
        !ClientID = Me.cboClientID
        .Update
    End With

    'Populate the txtProjectID text box with the
    'autonumber value assigned to the new row
    Me!txtProjectID = rstProject!ProjectID

End If
End Sub
```

This code is used on an Unbound form called frmUnbound. The code issues an AddNew method, which creates a buffer ready to accept data. Each field in the recordset then is populated with the values from the controls on the form. The Update method writes the data to disk. If you forget to include the Update method, the record is never written to disk.

The last line of code does not work. The ProjectID field is an AutoNumber field, so Access will assign its value during the update. The offending line is supposed to copy the newly created ProjectID value into a text field on the form. The line is there to illustrate a problem: When an AddNew method is issued, the record pointer is not moved within the dynaset. Even after the Update method is issued, the record pointer remains at the record it was on prior to the AddNew method.

What Are ActiveX Data Objects and Data Access Objects and Why Are They Important?

CHAPTER 14

661

Therefore, this code will add a record, but it will place the ProjectID value of the previously existing record into the txtProjectId text box on the form. To get around this, you must explicitly move to the new record before populating the text box. This can be accomplished easily by using the LastModified property.

Using the LastModified Property

The LastModified property contains a bookmark of the most recently added or modified record. By setting the bookmark of the recordset to the LastModified property, the record pointer is moved to the most recently added record. Listing 14.68 is a modified version of Listing 14.67, using the LastModified property to fix the problem described previously.

LISTING 14.68 Using the LastModified Property After AddNew

```
Private Sub cmdLastModified_Click()
    Dim db As Database
    Dim rstProject As Recordset

    'Point the database object at a reference to the
    'current database
    Set db = CurrentDb()

    'Open a Dynaset type recordset based on tblProjectsChange
    Set rstProject = db.OpenRecordset("tblProjectsChange", dbOpenDynaset)

    'Add a new row to the recordset, populating its values with
    'the controls on the form
    With rstProject
        .AddNew
        !ProjectName = Me.txtProjectName
        !ProjectDescription = Me.txtProjectDescription
        !ClientID = Me.cboClientID
        .Update

        'Move to the row you just added
        .Bookmark = .LastModified
    End With

    'Populate the txtProjectID text box with the
    'autonumber value assigned to the new row
    Me!txtProjectID = rstProject!ProjectID

End Sub
```

Notice that the bookmark of the recordset is set to the LastModified property of the recordset.

14

ACTIVEX AND
DATA ACCESS
OBJECTS

Creating and Modifying Database Objects Using DAO Code

When developing an Access application, it might be useful to add tables or queries, define or modify relationships, change security, or perform other data-definition techniques at runtime. You can accomplish all this by manipulating the various Data Access Objects.

Adding a Table Using Code

Many properties and methods are available for adding and modifying Jet Engine objects. The code in Listing 14.69 creates a table, adds some fields, and then adds a primary key index.

LISTING 14.69   Creating a Table, Adding Fields, and Adding a Primary Key Index

```
Sub CreateTable()
    Dim db As dao.Database
    Dim tbl As dao.TableDef
    Dim fld As dao.Field
    Dim idx As dao.Index

    'Point the database object at a reference to the
    'current database
    Set db = CurrentDb()

    'Point a TableDef object at a new TableDef
    Set tbl = db.CreateTableDef("tblFoods")

    'Add fields to the TableDef object
    Set fld = tbl.CreateField("FoodID", dbLong, 5)
    tbl.Fields.Append fld
    Set fld = tbl.CreateField("Description", dbText, 25)
    tbl.Fields.Append fld
    Set fld = tbl.CreateField("Calories", dbInteger)
    tbl.Fields.Append fld
    db.TableDefs.Append tbl

    'Add an index to the TableDef object
    Set idx = tbl.CreateIndex("PrimaryKey")

    'Add a field to the Index object
    Set fld = idx.CreateField("FoodID")

    'Set properties of the index
    idx.PRIMARY = True
    idx.Unique = True
```

What Are ActiveX Data Objects and Data Access Objects and Why Are They Important?

663

CHAPTER 14

LISTING 14.69   Continued

```
    'Add the field to the Fields collection of the Index object
    idx.Fields.Append fld

    'Add the index to the Indexes collection of the Table object
    tbl.Indexes.Append idx
End Sub
```

This code first creates a table definition called tblFoods. Before it can add the table definition to the TableDefs collection, it must add fields to the table. Three fields are added to the table. Notice that the field name, type, and length are specified. After the table definition is added to the database, indexes can be added to the table. The index added in Listing 14.69 is a primary key index.

> **CAUTION**
>
> When running code that appends an object, an error occurs if the object already exists. You must either include error handling in your routine to handle this or delete the existing instance of the object before appending the new object.

Removing a Table Using Code

Just as you can add a table using code, you can remove a table using code, as shown in Listing 14.70

LISTING 14.70   Removing a Table

```
Sub DeleteTable()
    Dim db As dao.Database

    'Point the database object at a reference to the
    'current database
    Set db = CurrentDb

    'Use the Delete method of the TableDefs collection
    'to delete a table called tblFoods
    db.TableDefs.Delete "tblFoods"
End Sub
```

The Delete method is issued on the TableDefs collection. The table you want to delete is passed to the Delete method as an argument.

14

ACTIVEX AND
DATA ACCESS
OBJECTS

NOTE

If a relationship exists between the table that you are deleting and other tables in the database, an error occurs. You must therefore delete any relationships a table is involved in before deleting a table.

Establishing Relationships Using Code

When you create tables using the Access environment, you normally create relationships between the tables at the same time. If you are creating tables using code, you probably want to establish relationships between those tables using code as well. Listing 14.71 shows an example.

LISTING 14.71   Establishing Relationships Between Database Objects

```
Sub CreateRelation()
    Dim db As dao.Database
    Dim rel As dao.Relation
    Dim fld As dao.Field

    'Point the database object at a reference to the
    'current database
    Set db = CurrentDb

    'Use the CreateRelation method of the database object
    'the create a Relation object
    Set rel = db.CreateRelation()

    'Set properties of the Relation object
    With rel
        .Name = "PeopleFood"
        .Table = "tblFoods"
        .ForeignTable = "tblPeople"
        .Attributes = dbRelationDeleteCascade
    End With

    'Set the Primary Key field of the Relation object
    Set fld = rel.CreateField("FoodID")

    'Set the Foreign Key field of the Relation object
    fld.ForeignName = "FoodID"
```

What Are ActiveX Data Objects and Data Access Objects and Why Are They Important?

CHAPTER 14

665

LISTING 14.71   Continued

```
    'Add the Field object to the Fields collection of
    'the Relation object
    rel.Fields.Append fld

    'Append the Relation object to the Relations
    'collection of the Database object
    db.Relations.Append rel

End Sub
```

This code begins by creating a new `Relation` object. It then populates the Name, Table, Foreign Table, and Attributes properties of the relationship. After the properties of the relationship are set, the field is added to the `Relation` object. Finally, the `Relation` object is appended to the Relations collection.

Creating a Query Using Code

If you are running your application from the Access runtime, your users won't be able to design their own queries unless they have their own full copies of Access. You might want to build your own query designer into your application and then allow the users to save the queries they build. This requires that you build the queries yourself, after the user designs them. Listing 14.72 shows the code needed to build a query.

LISTING 14.72   Building a Query

```
Sub CreateQuery()
    Dim db As dao.Database
    Dim qdf As dao.QueryDef
    Dim strSQL As String

    'Point the database object at a reference to the
    'current database
    Set db = CurrentDb

    'Create a QueryDef object called qryBigProjects
    Set qdf = db.CreateQueryDef("qryBigProjects")

    'Designate the SQL associated with the QueryDef object
    strSQL = "Select ProjectID, ProjectName, ProjectTotalEstimate " _
        & "From tblProjects " _
        & "Where ProjectTotalEstimate >= 30000"
    qdf.SQL = strSQL
End Sub
```

14

ACTIVEX AND
DATA ACCESS
OBJECTS

This code uses the `CreateQueryDef` method of the `Database` object to create a new query definition. It then sets the SQL statement associated with the query definition. This serves to build and store the query.

NOTE

It is important to understand that the `CreateTableDef` method does not immediately add the table definition to the database, unlike the `CreateQueryDef` method of the database object, which immediately adds the query definition to the database. You must use the `Append` method of the TableDefs collection to actually add the table definition to the database.

TIP

You can create a temporary query definition by using a zero-length string for the name argument of the `CreateQueryDef` method.

Using the DAO Containers Collection

A `Container` object maintains information about saved `Database` objects. The types of objects in the Containers collection are data access pages, databases, tables (including queries), relationships, system relationships, forms, reports, scripts (macros), and modules. The `Container` object is responsible for letting Jet know about the user interface objects. Databases, tables, relationships, and system relationships have Jet as their parent object. Forms, reports, scripts, and modules have the Access application as their parent object.

Each `Container` object possesses a collection of `Document` objects. These are the actual forms, reports, and other objects that are part of your database. The `Document` objects contain only summary information about each object (date created, owner, and so on); they do not contain the actual data of the objects. To refer to a particular document within a container, you must use one of two techniques:

```
Containers("Name")
```

or

```
Containers!Name
```

What Are ActiveX Data Objects and Data Access Objects and Why Are They Important?

CHAPTER 14

667

To list each `Container` object and its associated `Document` objects, you need to use the code shown in Listing 14.73.

LISTING 14.73   Listing Each `Container` Object and Its Associated `Document` Objects

```
Sub ListAllDBObjects()
    Dim db As dao.Database
    Dim con As dao.Container
    Dim doc As dao.Document

    'Point the database object at a reference to the
    'current database
    Set db = CurrentDb

    'Loop through each Container object in the
    'Containers collection, printing the name of each object
    For Each con In db.Containers
        Debug.Print "*** " & con.Name & " ***"

        'Loop through each Document object in the
        'Documents collection of the Container,
        'Printing its name
        For Each doc In con.Documents
            Debug.Print doc.Name
        Next doc
    Next con
End Sub
```

This code loops through all the documents in all the containers, listing each one.

PRACTICAL EXAMPLES

Applying These Techniques to Your Application

The potential applications for the methodologies learned in this chapter are endless. This section explores just a few of the ways you can apply these techniques. The examples here are located in CHAP14Ex.MDB.

Using Recordset Methods on a Data-Entry Form

At times, you might want to disable the default record movement and add, edit, or delete functionality from a form and code all the functionality yourself. You might want to perform these actions if you are going against client/server data and want to execute additional control over the data-entry environment. You also might want to use these techniques when you are developing applications for both the Access and Visual Basic environments and are striving for maximum code compatibility. Regardless of your reasons for using the following techniques, it is a good idea to know how to assign a Recordset object to a form and then use the form's underlying recordset to display and modify data.

Figure 14.3 shows a form in which the navigation buttons and record selectors have been removed. The form contains six command buttons: Move Previous (<), Move Next (>), Add, Delete, Find, and Exit. All the buttons use the recordset underlying the form to move from record to record in the form and modify the data contained within the form.

FIGURE 14.3

The frmRecordsets dialog box.

The RecordSource property of the form is not set. The Load event of the form is responsible for assigning a Recordset object to the form. Listing 14.74 shows the Load event of the form.

LISTING 14.74   The Load Event Assigning a Recordset Object to the Form

```
Private Sub Form_Load()
    'Declare and instantiate a recordset
    Dim rst As ADODB.Recordset
    Set rst = New ADODB.Recordset

    'Establish the Connection, Cursor Type, and
    'Lock Type and open the recordset
    rst.ActiveConnection = CurrentProject.Connection
    rst.CursorType = adOpenKeyset
    rst.LockType = adLockOptimistic
    rst.Open "Select * from tblClients", Options:=adCmdText

    'Set the form's recordset to the recordset just created
    Set Me.Recordset = rst
End Sub
```

What Are ActiveX Data Objects and Data Access Objects and Why Are They Important?

CHAPTER 14

669

The code begins by declaring and instantiating an ADODB `Recordset` object. It then sets three properties of the `Recordset` object: the ActiveConnection, the CursorType, and the LockType. The `Open` method is used to open a recordset, based on the tblClients table. Finally, a `Set` statement is used to assign the recordset to the recordset underlying the form.

NOTE

When an ADO recordset is assigned to a form, and the form is based on Jet data, the form is rendered read-only. If an ADO recordset is assigned to a form based on SQL data, the form is rendered read/write.

Listing 14.75 shows the code for the Move Previous button.

LISTING 14.75 Code for the Move Previous Button

```
Private Sub cmdPrevious_Click()
    'Move to the next record in the recordset
    Me.Recordset.MovePrevious

    'If at BOF, move to the next record
    If Me.Recordset.BOF Then
        Me.Recordset.MoveNext
        MsgBox "Already at First Record!!"
    End If

    'Set the bookmark of the form to the bookmark
    'of the recordset underlying the form
    Me.Bookmark = Me.Recordset.Bookmark
End Sub
```

This routine performs the `MovePrevious` method on the Recordset property of the form. If the BOF property becomes `True`, indicating that the record pointer is before the first valid record, the `MoveNext` method is performed on the Recordset property of the form to return the record pointer to the first record in the recordset. Finally, the bookmark of the form is synchronized with the bookmark of the Recordset property. Listing 14.76 shows the code for the Move Next button.

14

**ACTIVEX AND
DATA ACCESS
OBJECTS**

LISTING 14.76   Code for the Move Next Button

```
Private Sub cmdNext_Click()
    'Move to the next record in the recordset
    Me.Recordset.MoveNext

    'If at EOF, move to the previous record
    If Me.Recordset.EOF Then
        Me.Recordset.MovePrevious
        MsgBox "Already at Last Record!!"
    End If

    'Set the bookmark of the form to the bookmark
    'of the recordset underlying the form
    Me.Bookmark = Me.Recordset.Bookmark
End Sub
```

The code for the Add button is a little tricky, as Listing 14.77 shows.

LISTING 14.77   Code for the Add Button

```
Private Sub cmdAdd_Click()
    'Add a new row to the recordset
    Me.Recordset.AddNew
    Me.Recordset("CompanyName") = "New Company"
    Me.Recordset.Update

    'Move to the row that was added
    Me.Bookmark = Me.Recordset.Bookmark
End Sub
```

The AddNew method is performed on the Recordset property of the form. This method creates a buffer in memory that is ready to accept the new data. When the Update method is issued, the record pointer is moved to the new record. Because the CompanyName field is a required field, you must populate it with data before issuing the Update method on the Recordset property.

By setting the bookmark of the form to the Bookmark property of the recordset, you synchronize the form with the new record. In a production environment, you would want to clear out all the text boxes and force the user to save or cancel before the AddNew or Update methods are issued.

The process of deleting a record is quite simple, as Listing 14.78 shows.

LISTING 14.78   Deleting a Record

```
Private Sub cmdDelete_Click()
    'Ask user if they really want to delete the row
    intAnswer = MsgBox("Are You Sure???", _
        vbYesNo + vbQuestion, _
        "Delete Current Record?")

    'If they respond yes, delete the row and
    'move to the next row
    If intAnswer = vbYes Then
        Me.Recordset.Delete
        Call cmdNext_Click
        Me.Refresh
    End If
End Sub
```

CAUTION

Because the tblClients table is linked to the tblProjects table, the process of deleting a client will render an error if that client has associated projects. This must be handled using standard error handling techniques.

This code verifies that the user actually wants to delete the record and then issues the Delete method on the Recordset property of the form. Because the current record no longer is valid, the code calls the Click event of the cmdNext button.

The last piece of code involved in the form is the code for the Find button, as shown in Listing 14.79.

LISTING 14.79   Code for the Find Button

```
Private Sub cmdFind_Click()
    Dim strClientID As String
    Dim varBookmark As Variant

    'Store the book of the current record
    varBookmark = Me.Recordset.Bookmark

    'Attempt to locate another client
    strClientID = InputBox("Enter Client ID of Client You Want to Locate")
    Me.Recordset.Find "ClientID = " & strClientID, Start:=1
```

LISTING 14.79   Continued

```
    'If client not found, display a message and return to
    'the original record
    If Me.Recordset.EOF Then
        MsgBox "Client ID " & strClientID & " Not Found!!"
        Me.Recordset.Bookmark = varBookmark

    'If client found, synchronize the form with the
    'underlying recordset
    Else
        Me.Bookmark = Me.Recordset.Bookmark
    End If
End Sub
```

This routine begins by storing the bookmark of the current record to a Variant variable. Users are prompted for the client ID they want to locate, and then the Find method is issued on the Recordset property of the form. If the EOF property is True, the user is warned, and the bookmark of the recordset is set to the value within the Variant variable, returning the record pointer to the position it was in prior to the search. If the client ID is found, the bookmark of the form is synchronized with the bookmark of the Recordset property.

Summary

In this chapter, you learned how to manipulate recordsets via code. The chapter began by contrasting ActiveX Data Objects with Data Access Objects. It continued by introducing you to the ActiveX Data Object model. It explored the different types of ADO recordsets available, highlighting why you would want to use each type.

Next, you learned how to manipulate recordsets using code. The capability to manipulate recordsets behind the scenes is an important aspect of the VBA language. It frees you from the user interface and enables you to control what is going on programmatically. Finally, you learned how to create and modify database objects using code. This is important if the application you are creating requires you to create or modify tables, queries, or other objects at runtime.

The techniques required for ActiveX Data Objects were covered as well as the different coding techniques that are needed for Data Access Objects.

What to Do When Things Don't Go As Planned

IN THIS PART

Debugging: Your Key to Successful Development

IN THIS CHAPTER

Why This Chapter Is Important

A good programmer is not necessarily one who can get things right the first time. To be fully effective as a VBA programmer, you need to master the art of debugging—the process of troubleshooting your application. Debugging involves locating and identifying problem areas within your code and is a mandatory step in the application-development process. Fortunately, the Access 2002 Visual Basic Editor provides excellent tools to help you with the debugging process. Using the Access 2002 debugging tools, you can step through your code, setting watchpoints and breakpoints as needed.

Using the VBA debugging tools is significantly more efficient than taking random stabs at fixes to your application. A strong command of the Access 2002 debugging tools can save you hours of trial and error. In fact, it can be the difference between a successfully completed application-development process and one that continues indefinitely with problems left unsolved.

Avoiding Bugs

The best way to deal with bugs is to avoid them in the first place. Proper coding techniques can really aid you in this process. Using `Option Explicit`, strong typing, naming standards, and tight scoping can help you eliminate bugs in your code.

Option Explicit

`Option Explicit` requires that all your variables be declared before they are used. Including `Option Explicit` in each Form, Code, and Report module helps the VBA compiler find typos in the names of variables.

As discussed in detail in Chapter 7, "VBA: An Introduction," the `Option Explicit` statement is a command that can be inserted manually into the General Declarations section of any Code, Form, or Report module. If you prefer, it can be inserted automatically by selecting Require Variable Declaration from the Editor tab after choosing Tools|Options from within the Visual Basic Editor. After it is inserted, Option Explicit is placed in the General Declarations section of all *new* modules. Existing modules are not affected.

Strong-Typing

Strong-typing your variables is discussed in Chapter 7. *Strong-typing* a variable means indicating what type of data is stored in a variable at the time it is declared. For example, `Dim intCounter As Integer` initializes a variable that contains integers. If elsewhere in your code you assign a character string to `intCounter`, the compiler will catch the error.

Naming Standards

Naming standards can also go a long way toward helping you eliminate errors. The careful naming of variables makes your code easier to read and makes the intended use of the variable more obvious. Problem code tends to stand out when naming conventions have been followed judiciously. Naming standards are covered in Chapter 1, "Access as a Development Tool," and are outlined in detail in Appendix B, "Naming Conventions."

Variable Scoping

Finally, giving your variables the narrowest scope possible reduces the chances of one piece of code accidentally overwriting a variable within another piece of code. You should use local variables whenever possible. Use module-level and global variables only when it is necessary to see the value of a variable from multiple subroutines or multiple modules. For more information about the issues surrounding variable scoping, see Chapter 7.

Bugs Happen!

Unfortunately, no matter what you do to prevent problems and errors, they still creep into your code. Probably the most insidious type of error is a logic error. A *logic error* is sneaky because it escapes the compiler; your code compiles but simply does not execute as planned. This type of error might become apparent when you receive a runtime error or when you don't get the results you expected. This is where the debugger comes to the rescue.

Harnessing the Power of the Immediate Window

The Immediate window serves several purposes. It provides you with a great way to test VBA and user-defined functions, it enables you to inquire about and change the value of variables while your code is running, and it enables you to view the results of `Debug.Print` statements. To open the Immediate window while in the Visual Basic Editor, do one of three things:

- Click the Immediate Window tool on the Debug toolbar.
- Choose View|Immediate window.
- Press Ctrl+G.

NOTE

An advantage of pressing Ctrl+G is that it invokes the Immediate window without a Code window being active. You can click the Immediate Window toolbar button or choose View|Immediate Window only from within the VBE.

The Immediate window is shown in Figure 15.1.

15

DEBUGGING

FIGURE 15.1

The Immediate window enables you to test functions and to inquire about and change the value of variables.

NOTE

The Debug tools are available on a separate toolbar. To show the Debug toolbar, right-click any toolbar or menu bar and select Debug from the list of available tool-bars.

Testing Values of Variables and Properties

The Immediate window enables you to test the values of variables and properties as your code executes. This can be quite enlightening as to what is actually happening within your code.

To practice with the Immediate window, you do not even need to be executing code. To invoke the Immediate window while in a form, report, or module, press Ctrl+G. To see how this works, follow these steps:

1. Run the frmClients form from the CHAP15EX.MDB database on the accompanying CD-ROM.

2. Press Ctrl+G to open and activate the Immediate window. You are placed in the Visual Basic Editor (VBE) within the Immediate window.

3. Type **?Forms!frmClients.txtClientID.Value** and press Enter. The client ID of the current client appears on the next line.

4. Type **?Forms!frmClients.txtCompanyName.Visible** and press Enter. The word True appears on the next line, indicating that the control is visible.

5. Type **?Forms!frmClients.txtContactTitle.BackColor** and press Enter. The number associated with the BackColor of the Contact Title text box appears on the next line.

Your screen should look like the one shown in Figure 15.2. You can continue to request the values of properties or variables within your VBA code.

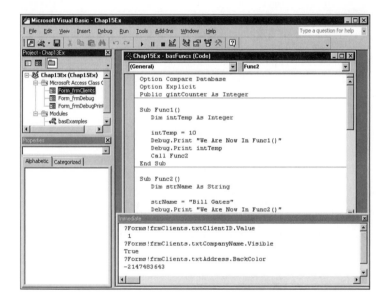

FIGURE 15.2
Using the Immediate window to test the values of properties.

Setting Values of Variables and Properties

Not only can you display things in the Immediate window, you can use the Immediate window to modify the values of variables and controls as your code executes. This feature becomes even more valuable when you realize that you can re-execute code within a procedure after changing the value of a variable. Here's how this process works:

1. Invoke the Immediate window, if necessary. Remember that you can do this by pressing Ctrl+G.

2. Type **Forms!frmClients.txtContactTitle.Value** = "Hello" in the immediate pane. Press Enter. The contact title of the current record changes to Hello.

15

3. Type **Forms!frmClients.txtCompanyName.Visible = False**. Press Enter. The txtCompanyName control on the frmClients form becomes hidden.

4. Type **Forms!frmClients.txtClientID.BackColor = 123456**. Press Enter. The background color of the txtClientID control on the frmClients forms turns green. The Immediate window and your form now look like those shown in Figure 15.3.

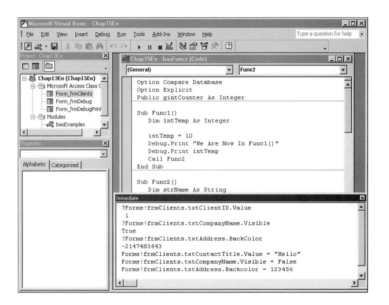

FIGURE 15.3

Setting the values of properties using the Immediate window.

The Immediate window is an extremely valuable testing and debugging tool. The examples here barely begin to illustrate its power and flexibility.

CAUTION

Changes you make to data while working in the Immediate window are permanent. On the other hand, changes you make to the properties of controls or the values of variables are not saved with the form or report.

Some people think that data changes made in the Immediate window are not permanent. In other words, if you modify the last name of a customer, she believes that the change will not be permanent (but, of course, it is). Other people think that if they change the backcolor property of a control, the change will persist in the design environment (but, of course, it won't).

Clearing the Immediate Window

The Immediate window displays the last 200 lines of output. As additional lines of code are added to the Immediate window, older lines disappear. When you exit completely from Access and return to the Immediate window, it is cleared. If you want to clear the Immediate window at any other time, follow these three steps:

1. With the Immediate window active, press Ctrl+Home to go to the top of the Immediate window.
2. Hold down your Shift key and press Ctrl+End to go to the last statement in the Immediate window.
3. Press Delete.

Practicing with the Built-In Functions

In addition to being able to test and set the values of properties and variables using the Immediate window, you can test any VBA function. To do so, type the function and its arguments in the Immediate window, preceded by a question mark. This code returns the month of the current date, for example:

```
?datepart("m",date)
```

This tells you the date one month after today's date:

```
?dateadd("m",1,date)
```

This tells you how many days exist between the current date and the end of the millennium:

```
?datediff("d",date(),#12/31/2999#)
```

Executing Subroutines, Functions, and Methods

 In addition to enabling you to test any VBA function, the Immediate window lets you test any user-defined subroutine, function, or method. This is a great way to debug your user-defined procedures. To see how this works, follow these steps:

1. Open the basExamples module found in the CHAP15EX.MDB database on the accompanying CD-ROM.
2. Invoke the Immediate window if it is not already visible.
3. Type **?ReturnInitsFunc("Bill","Gates")**. This calls the user-defined function ReturnInitsFunc, sending "Bill" as the first parameter and "Gates" as the second parameter. The value B.G. appears in the Immediate window. This is the return value from the function.

15

4. Type **Call ReturnInitsSub("Bill","Gates")**. This calls the user-defined subroutine ReturnInitsSub, sending "Bill" as the first parameter and "Gates" as the second parameter. The value B.G. appears in a message box.

Notice the difference between how you call a function and how you call a subroutine. Because the function returns a value, you must call it using a question mark. On the other hand, when calling a subroutine, you use the Call keyword.

NOTE

You also can call a subroutine from the Immediate window using this syntax:

    RoutineName Parameter1, Parameter2, ...

Notice that, when you omit the Call keyword, the parameters do not need to be enclosed in parentheses.

Printing to the Immediate Window at Runtime

The capability to print to the Immediate window is useful because you can test what is happening as your code executes without having to suspend code execution. It also is valuable to be able to print something to a window when you are testing, without interfering with the user-interface aspect of your code. You can test a form without being interrupted and then go back and view the values of variables and so on. Here's how the process works:

1. Type **Call LoopThroughCollection**. This calls the user-defined subroutine LoopThroughCollection. The values Skating, Basketball, Hockey, and Skiing appear. These values are printed to the Immediate window by the routine.

2. Open the form frmDebugPrint in Form view.

3. Press Tab to move from the First Name field to the Last Name field.

4. Press Tab to move back to the First Name field.

5. Type your first name.

6. Open the Immediate window. Notice that all the statements are printed to the Immediate window. (See Figure 15.4.) These Debug.Print statements are coded in all the appropriate form and control events.

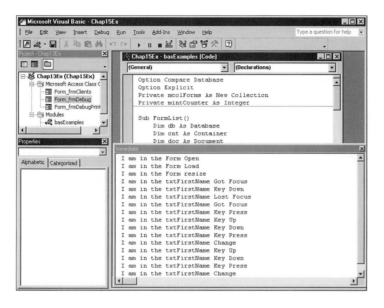

FIGURE 15.4

Using `Debug.Print` *statements to print values to the Immediate window.*

NOTE

Although it is good practice to remove `Debug.Print` statements when the debugging process is complete, you can safely deploy your applications without removing them. Your users will never know that the statements are in your code unless they view the Immediate window. The `Debug.Print` statements result in only a minor degradation in performance.

Invoking the Debugger

You can invoke the Access debugger in several ways:

- Place a breakpoint in your code.
- Place a watch in your code.
- Press Ctrl+Break while the code is running.
- Insert a `Stop` statement in your code.

15

DEBUGGING

A *breakpoint* is an unconditional point at which you want to suspend code execution. It is temporary because it is in effect only while the database is open. In other words, breakpoints are not saved with the database.

A *watch* is a condition under which you want to suspend code execution. You might want to suspend code execution when a counter variable reaches a specific value, for example. A watch also is temporary; it is removed after you close the database.

A Stop statement is permanent. In fact, if you forget to remove Stop statements from your code, your application stops execution while the user is running it.

Using Breakpoints to Troubleshoot

As mentioned, a breakpoint is a point at which execution of code will be unconditionally halted. You can set multiple breakpoints in your code. You can add and remove breakpoints as your code executes.

A breakpoint enables you to halt your code execution at a suspicious area of code. This enables you to examine everything that is going on at that point in your code execution. By strategically placing breakpoints in your code, you quickly can execute sections of code that already are debugged, stopping only at problem areas.

To set a breakpoint, follow these steps:

1. Place your cursor on the line of code where you want to invoke the debugger.

2. You can insert a breakpoint in one of four ways:

   - Press your F9 function key.
   - Click in the gray margin area to the left of the line of the code that will contain the breakpoint.
   - Click the Toggle Breakpoint button on the Debug toolbar.
   - Choose Debug | Toggle Breakpoint.

   The line of code containing the breakpoint appears in a different color, and a dot appears, indicating the breakpoint.

3. Run the form, report, or module containing the breakpoint. VBA suspends execution just before executing the line of code where you placed the breakpoint. The statement that is about to execute appears in a contrasting color (the default is yellow).

Now that your code is suspended, you can step through it one line at a time, change the value of variables, and view your call stack, among other things.

Keep in mind that a breakpoint is actually a toggle. If you want to remove a breakpoint, click in the gray margin area, press F9, or click Toggle Breakpoint on the Debug toolbar.

Breakpoints are removed when the database is closed, when another database is opened, or when you exit Access.

It is easiest to get to know the debugger by actually using it. The following example gives you hands-on experience in setting and stopping code execution at a breakpoint. The example is developed further later in the chapter.

TRY IT Start by creating a form called frmDebug that contains a command button called cmdDebug. Give the button the caption Start Debug Process. Place the following code in the Click event of the command button:

```
Sub cmdDebug_Click ()
    Call Func1
End Sub
```

Create a module called basFuncs. Enter three functions into the module:

```
Sub Func1 ()
    Dim intTemp As Integer

    intTemp = 10
    Debug.Print "We Are Now In Func1()"
    Debug.Print intTemp
    Call Func2
End Sub

Sub Func2 ()
    Dim strName As String

    strName = "Bill Gates"
    Debug.Print "We Are Now In Func2()"
    Debug.Print strName
    Call Func3

End Sub

Sub Func3 ()
    Debug.Print "We Are Now In Func3()"
    MsgBox "Hi There From The Func3() Sub Procedure"
End Sub
```

Now you should debug. Start by placing a breakpoint within the Click event of cmdDebug on the line called Call Func1. Here are the steps:

1. Click anywhere on the line of code that says Call Func1.

2. Click in the gray margin area, press the F9 function key, click the Toggle Breakpoint button on the Debug toolbar, or choose Debug|Toggle Breakpoint. The line with the breakpoint turns a different color (red by default).

15

DEBUGGING

3. Go into Form view and click the Start Debug Process button. Access suspends execution just before executing the line where you placed the breakpoint. VBA displays the line that reads Call Func1 in a different color (by default, yellow), indicating that it is about to execute that line. (See Figure 15.5.)

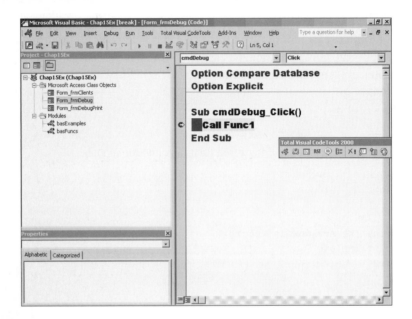

FIGURE 15.5
Code execution halted at a breakpoint.

Stepping Through Code

Access 2002 gives you three main options for stepping through your code. Each one is slightly different. The Step Into option enables you to step through each line of code within a subroutine or function, whereas the Step Over option executes a procedure without stepping through each line of code within it. The Step Out option runs all code in nested procedures and then returns you to the procedure that called the line of code you are on. Knowing the right option to use to solve a particular problem is an acquired skill that comes with continued development experience.

Using Step Into

When you reach a breakpoint, you can continue executing your code one line at a time or continue execution until another breakpoint is reached. To step through your code one line at a time, click Step Into on the Debug toolbar, press F8, or choose Debug|Step Into.

The following example illustrates the process of stepping through your code, printing the values of variables to the Immediate window, and modifying the values of variables using the Immediate window.

TRY IT You can continue the debug process from the breakpoint you set in the previous example. Step two times (press F8). You should find yourself within Func1, about to execute the line of code intTemp = 10. (See Figure 15.6.) Notice that VBA did not stop on the line Dim intTemp As Integer. The debugger does not stop on variable declarations.

The Debug statements are about to print to the Immediate window. Take a look by opening the Immediate window. None of your code has printed anything to the Immediate window yet. Press F8 (step) three more times until you have executed the line Debug.Print intTemp. Your screen should look like Figure 15.7. Notice the results of the Debug.Print statements.

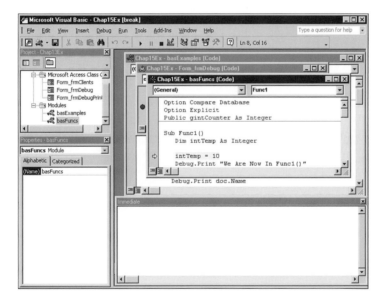

FIGURE 15.6
The Immediate window with code halted within Func1.

Now that you have seen how you can display variables and the results of expressions to the Immediate window, take a look at how you can use the Immediate window to modify values of variables and controls. Start by changing the value of intTemp. Click the Immediate window and type **intTemp = 50**. When you press Enter, you actually modify the value of intTemp. Type **?intTemp**, and you'll see that Access returns the value of 50. You also can see the value of intTemp in the Locals window. Notice in Figure 15.8 that the intTemp variable appears along with its value and type.

15

DEBUGGING

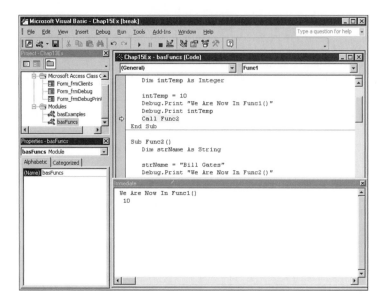

FIGURE 15.7

The Immediate window with entries generated by Debug.Print *statements.*

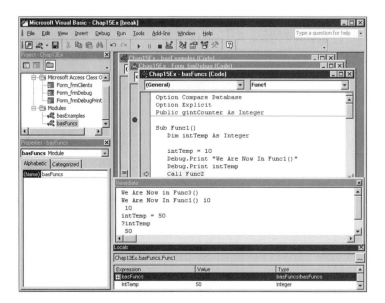

FIGURE 15.8

The Immediate and Locals windows after modifying the value of intTemp.

Executing Until the Next Breakpoint Is Reached

Suppose that you have reached a breakpoint, but you realize that your problem is farther down in the code execution. In fact, the problem is actually in a different function. You might not want to continue to move one step at a time down to the offending function. Use the Procedure drop-down menu to locate the questionable function, and then set a breakpoint on the line where you want to continue stepping. You now are ready to continue code execution until Access reaches this line. To do this, click Continue on the Debug toolbar, press F5, or choose Run|Continue. Your code continues to execute, stopping at the next breakpoint. To see how this works, continue the Debug process with the next example.

> **NOTE**
>
> You also can opt to resume code execution to the point at which your cursor is located. To do this, select Run to Cursor from the Debug menu, or press Ctrl+F8.

TRY IT Suppose that you realize your problem might be in Func3. You do not want to continue to move one step at a time down to Func3. No problem. Use the Procedure drop-down menu to view Func3, as shown in Figure 15.9. Set a breakpoint on the line that reads Debug.Print "We Are Now In Func3()". You are ready to continue code execution until Access reaches this line. Click Continue on the Debug toolbar, press F5, or choose Run| Continue. Your code continues to execute, stopping on the breakpoint you just set. Press F5 again. The code finishes executing. Return to the Form View window.

Using Step Over

Sometimes you already have a subroutine fully tested and debugged. You want to continue stepping through the routine that you are in, but you don't want to watch the execution of subroutines. In this case, you use Step Over. To step over a subroutine or function, click Step Over on the Debug toolbar, press Shift+F8, or choose Debug|Step Over. The code within the subroutine or function you are stepping over executes, but you do not step through it. To experiment with the Step Over feature, follow the next example.

TRY IT Click the open form and click the Start Debug Process button one more time. Because your breakpoints are still set, you are placed on the line of code that reads Call Func1. Select Clear All Breakpoints from the Debug menu, or use the Ctrl+Shift+F9 keystroke combination to remove all breakpoints. Step (press F8) five times until you are about to execute the line Call Func2. Suppose that you have tested Func2 and Func3 and know that they are not the cause of the problems in your code. With Func2 highlighted as the next line to be executed, click Step Over on the toolbar. Notice that Func2 and Func3 are both executed but that you now are ready to continue stepping in Func1. In this case, you are placed on the End Sub line immediately following the call to Func2.

15

DEBUGGING

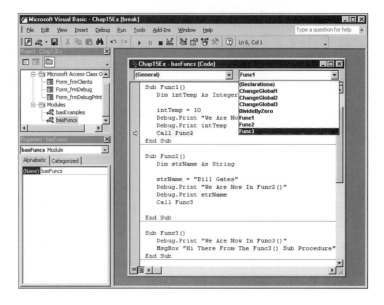

FIGURE 15.9

Using the Procedure drop-down menu to view another function.

Using Step Out

TRY IT   The Step Out feature is used to step out of the procedure you are in and to return to the procedure that called the line of code you are on. You use this feature when you have accidentally stepped into a procedure that you realize is fully tested. You want to execute all the code called by the procedure you are in and then step out to the calling procedure so that you can continue with the debugging process. To test how this works, follow this example.

1. Place a breakpoint on the call to Func2.

2. Click the Reset button on the toolbar to halt code execution.

3. Activate the frmDebug form and click the Start Debug Process command button.

4. Step once to place yourself in the first line of Func2.

5. Supposethat you realize you just stepped one step too far. You really intended to step over Func2 and all the procedures it calls. No problem! Click the Step Out button to step out of Func2 and return to the line following the line of code that called Func2. In this case, you should find yourself on the End Sub statement of Func1.

Setting the Next Statement to Execute

After you have stepped through your code, watched the logical flow, and modified some variables, you might want to re-execute the code beginning at a prior statement. The easiest way to do this is to click and drag the yellow arrow in the margin to the statement on which you want to continue execution. If you prefer, you can click anywhere in the line of code where you want to commence execution and then choose Debug|Set Next Statement. Regardless of the method you chose, notice that the contrasting color (usually yellow)—indicating the next line of code to be executed—is now placed over that statement. You then can step through the code by pressing F8, or you can continue normal code execution by pressing F5. Access enables you to set the next line to be executed within a procedure only. This feature can be used to re-execute lines of code or to skip over a problem line of code.

The following example walks you through the process of changing the value of a variable and then re-executing code after the value is changed.

> **TRY IT** The preceding example left you at the last line of code (the End Sub statement) within Func1. You want to change the value of intTemp and re-execute everything.

1. Go to the Immediate window and type **intTemp = 100**.

2. You need to set the next statement to print on the line that reads Debug.Print "We Are Now in Func1()". To do this, click and drag the yellow arrow from the End Sub statement to the Debug.Print "We Are Now In Func1()" line. Notice the contrasting color (yellow), indicating that the next line of code to be executed is now over that statement.

3. Press F8 (step) two times. The code now executes with intTemp set to 100. Observe the Immediate window again. Notice how the results have changed.

Using the Calls Window

You have learned how to set breakpoints, step through and over code, use the Immediate window, set the next line to be executed, and continue to run until the next breakpoint is reached. When you reach a breakpoint, it often is important to see which functions were called to bring you to this point. This is where the Calls feature can help.

To bring up the Call Stack window, click the Call Stack button on the toolbar or choose View| Call Stack. The window in Figure 15.10 appears. If you want to see the line of code that called a particular function or subroutine, double-click that particular function or click the function and then click Show. Although your execution point is not moved to the calling function or subroutine, you are able to view the code within the procedure. If you want to continue your code execution, press F8. You move back to the procedure through which you were stepping,

15

DEBUGGING

and the next line of code executes. If you press F5, your code executes until another breakpoint or watch is reached. If you want to return to where you were without executing additional lines of code, choose Debug|Show Next Statement.

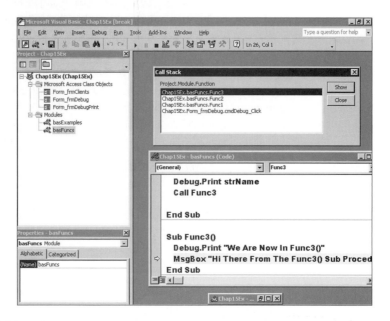

FIGURE 15.10

Viewing the stack with the Call Stack window.

TRY IT   To test this process, perform the next example.

1. Click the Reset button to stop your code execution if you are still in Break mode.

2. Remove the breakpoint on the call to Func2.

3. Move to the procedure called Func3 in basFuncs. Set a breakpoint on the line
   `Debug.Print "We Are Now in Func3()"`.

4. Run the frmDebug form and click the command button. You are placed in Func3 on the line where the breakpoint is set.

5. Bring up the Call Stack window by clicking the Call Stack button on the toolbar. If you want to see the line of code that called Func2 from Func1, double-click Func1. Although your execution point is not moved to Func1, you are able to view the code within the procedure. To return to the next line of code to execute, choose Debug|Show Next Statement.

6. Press F5, and the rest of your code executes.

Working with the Locals Window

The Locals window enables you to see all the variables on the current stack frame and to view and modify their values. To access the Locals pane, click Locals Window on the toolbar, or select Locals Window from the View menu. Three columns appear: Expression, Value, and Type. The Expression column shows you the variables, user-defined types, arrays, and other objects visible within the current procedure. The Value column displays the current value of a variable or expression. The Type column tells you what type of data a variable contains. Variables that contain hierarchical information—arrays, for example—are displayed with an Expand/Collapse button.

The information contained within the Locals window is dynamic. It is updated automatically as the code executes and as you move from routine to routine. Figure 15.11 illustrates how you can use the Locals window to view the variables available with the Func2 subroutine. To try this example yourself, remove all existing breakpoints. Place a breakpoint in Func2 on the line of code that reads Debug.Print strName. Click Reset if code is still executing, and click the Start Debug Process command button to execute code until the breakpoint. Click the Locals Window button on the Debug toolbar. Click the plus sign to view the contents of the public variable gintCounter.

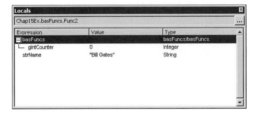

FIGURE 15.11

Viewing the Locals window.

> **NOTE**
>
> You can change the value of a variable in the Locals window, but you cannot change its name or type.

Working with Watch Expressions

Sometimes it is not enough to use the Immediate window to test the value of an expression or variable. You might want to keep a constant eye on the expression's value. Access 95 introduced the capability to set watches before running a procedure or while code execution is suspended. After a Watch expression is added, it appears in the Watch window. As you'll see, you can create several types of watches.

Using Auto Data Tips

The quickest and easiest way to view the value contained within a variable is to use Auto Data Tips, which is an option for working with modules. This feature is available only when your code is in Break mode. While in Break mode, simply move your mouse over the variable or expression whose value you want to check. A tip appears with the current value. To set the Auto Data Tips option from the Visual Basic Editor (VBE), choose Tools|Options, click the Editor tab, and check the option for Auto Data Tips, which is under the Code Settings options.

Using a Quick Watch

A *quick watch* is the most basic type of watch. To add a quick watch, highlight the name of the variable or expression you want to watch and click the Quick Watch button on the toolbar. The Quick Watch dialog box, shown in Figure 15.12, appears. You can click Add to add the expression as a permanent watch or choose Cancel to view the current value without adding it as a watch. If you click Add, the Watches window appears, like the one in Figure 15.13. This window is discussed in more detail in the next section.

Figure 15.12

The Quick Watch dialog box enables you to quickly view the value of a variable or add an expression as a permanent watch.

Figure 15.13

The Watches window with a Watch expression.

Adding a Watch Expression

As you saw, you can add a Watch expression using a quick watch. Adding a watch this way does not give you full control over the nature of the watch, however. If you need more control over the watch, you must choose Debug|Add Watch. The Add Watch dialog box appears, as shown in Figure 15.14.

> **TIP**
>
> If you add a quick watch or you add a watch by choosing Debug|Add Watch, you easily can customize the specifics of the watch by clicking with the right mouse button over the watch in the Watches window. Then select Edit Watch.

> **TIP**
>
> A quick way to add a watch to the Watches window is to click and drag a variable or expression from a Code module into the Watches window. The watch is added with default settings.

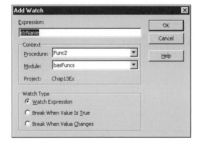

FIGURE 15.14

The Add Watch dialog box enables you to easily designate all the specifics of a Watch expression.

In the Expression text box, enter a variable, property, function call, or any other valid expression. It is important to select the procedure and module in which you want the expression to be watched. Next, indicate whether you want to simply watch the value of the expression in the Immediate window, break when the expression becomes True, or break whenever the value of the expression changes. The two latter options are covered in detail in the following sections.

15

DEBUGGING

TRY IT   The next example walks you through the process of adding a watch and viewing the Watch variable as you step through your code. It illustrates how a variable goes in and out of scope, and changes value, during code execution.

1. To begin, stop code execution if your code is running, and remove any breakpoints you have set.

2. Click within the strName variable in Func2.

3. Right-click and choose Add Watch.

4. Click OK to accept the Func2 procedure as the context for the variable and basFuncs as the module for the variable.

5. Set a breakpoint on the line strName = "Bill Gates".

6. Run the frmDebug form and click the command button. View the Watches window and notice that strName has the value of a zero-length string.

7. Step one time and notice that strName is equal to Bill Gates.

8. Step three more times. Notice that, although you are in the Func3 routine, strName still has the value Bill Gates. This is because the variable is still in memory in the context of basFuncs.Func2.

9. Step four more times until you are back on the End Sub statement of Func2. The strName variable is still in context.

10. Step one more time. The strName variable is finally out of context because Func2 has been executed.

Editing a Watch Expression

After you add a watch, you might want to edit the nature of the watch or remove it entirely. You use the Edit Watch dialog box to edit or delete a Watch expression. Follow these steps:

1. Activate the Watches window.

2. Select the expression you want to edit.

3. Choose Debug|Edit Watch, or right-click and choose Edit Watch. The dialog box in Figure 15.15 appears.

4. Make changes to the watch or click Delete to remove it.

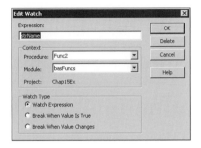

FIGURE 15.15

You can use the Edit Watch dialog box to modify the specifics of a watch after you add it.

Breaking When an Expression Is True

A powerful aspect of a Watch expression is that you can break whenever an expression becomes True. You can break whenever a Public variable reaches a specific value, for example. You might want to do this when a Public or Private variable somehow is being changed, and you want to find out where. Consider the following code, located in the basFuncs module of CHAP15EX.MDB:

```
Sub ChangeGlobal1()
    gintCounter = 50
    Call ChangeGlobal2
End Sub

Sub ChangeGlobal2()
    gintCounter = gintCounter + 10
    Call ChangeGlobal3
End Sub

Sub ChangeGlobal3()
    Dim intCounter As Integer
    For intCounter = 1 To 10
        gintCounter = gintCounter + intCounter
    Next intCounter
End Sub
```

You might find that gintCounter somehow is reaching a number greater than 100, and you are not sure how. To solve the problem, add the watch shown in Figure 15.16. Notice that the expression you are testing for is gintCounter > 100. You have set the breakpoint to break the code whenever the expression becomes True. To test the code, type **ChangeGlobal1** in the Immediate window and press Enter. The code should break in the ChangeGlobal3 routine, indicating that this routine is the culprit.

15

FIGURE 15.16
Defining a watch that will cause the code execution to break whenever the expression is True.

Breaking When an Expression Changes

Instead of breaking when an expression becomes True, you might want to break whenever the value of the expression changes. This is a great way to identify the place where the value of a variable is mysteriously altered. Like Break When Value Is True, the Break When Value Changes option is great for tracking down problems with Public and Private variables. Notice the watch being set in Figure 15.17. It is in the context of all procedures within all modules. It is set to break whenever the value of gintCounter changes. If you execute the ChangeGlobal1 routine, you'll find that the code halts execution within ChangeGlobal1 immediately after the value of gintCounter is set to 50. If you press F5 to continue execution, the code halts within ChangeGlobal2 immediately after gintCounter is incremented by 10. In other words, every time the value of gintCounter is modified, the code execution breaks.

FIGURE 15.17
Creating a watch that will cause code execution to break whenever the value of an expression changes.

Continuing Execution After a Runtime Error

As you are testing, you often discover runtime errors that are quite easy to fix. When a runtime error occurs, a dialog box similar to the one shown in Figure 15.18 appears.

FIGURE 15.18

The Runtime Error dialog box.

If you click Debug, you are placed in the Code window on the line that generated the error. After rectifying the problem, click the Continue button on the toolbar, or choose Run | Continue.

Figure 15.19 shows the locals window after Debug was clicked from the Runtime Error dialog box and the value of int2 was set to 20. Code execution now can continue without error.

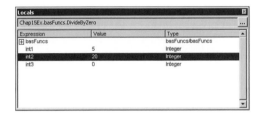

FIGURE 15.19

Debug mode after a divide-by-zero error.

Often, after an error occurs, VBA displays a message giving you the option of resetting your code. If you opt to reset your code, all variables (including Publics and Statics) lose their values. You also can click Reset on the toolbar. You must decide whether it is better to proceed with your variables already set or to reset the variables and then proceed.

> **NOTE**
>
> The General tab of the Options dialog box allows you to configure how VBA error handling and the debugger interact. The available options are discussed in Chapter 16, "Error Handling: Preparing for the Inevitable."

Looking At Gotchas with the Immediate Window

Although the Access debugger is excellent, the debugging process itself is wrought with an array of potential problems, as follows:

- The debugging process can interrupt code execution, especially when forms are involved. When this occurs, the best bet is to place `Debug.Print` statements in your code and examine what happens after the code executes.

- Along the lines of the previous problem, it is difficult to debug code where `GotFocus` and `LostFocus` events are coded. Moving to the VBE triggers the `LostFocus` event of the control. Returning to the form causes the `GotFocus` event of the control to be triggered. Once again, a great solution is `Debug.Print`. You also might consider writing information to an error log for perusal after the code executes.

- Many methods of the DoCmd object cannot be successfully executed during debugging. An example is `DoCmd.RunCommand accmdSaveRecord`. When executed in the debugger, this line of code renders the error shown in Figure 15.20.

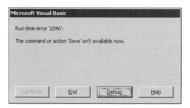

FIGURE 15.20

Error that results when executing the `RunCommand` method of the `DoCmd` object while the debugger is active.

- Code that uses `Screen.ActiveForm` and `Screen.ActiveControl` wreaks havoc on the debugging process. When the VBE is active, there is no active form and no active control. Avoiding these lines in your code wherever possible alleviates this problem.

- Finally, be aware that resetting code can cause problems. If you are modifying environmental settings, you are left with whatever environmental settings your application code changed. If you continue execution after the error without resetting, all sorts of other problems can occur. It is a good idea to code a special utility routine that resets your environment.

Using Assertions

Assertions are used to ensure that, if a certain state is encountered, the debugger is invoked. The following code, found in basExamples, is an example:

```
Sub Assertion()
    Dim intAge As Integer
    intAge = InputBox("Please Enter Your Age")
    Debug.Assert (intAge >= 0)
    MsgBox "You are " & intAge
End Sub
```

In this example, a variable called `intAge` is set equal to the value entered into an Input Box. The `Debug.Assert` statement "asserts" that the value entered is greater than or equal to zero. If it is, code execution proceeds as expected. If the assertion is *incorrect,* the debugger is invoked.

It is a good idea to include a comment as to why an assertion might fail. By doing this you will facilitate the process of responding to the situation when it occurs. Also, it is important to realize that, if you deploy your application with `Debug.Assert` statements intact, you will receive a technical support call when an assertion fails, and your user is placed in the debugger without warning!

Debugging Tips

The following tips will make your life much simpler and easier when debugging:

- Before starting to debug, be clear about what the problem is. Make sure that you get all of the necessary information from the user as to what they did to generate the problem. Without this vital information, you can spend countless hours trying to reproduce the problem rather than solve it.

- Make changes one line of code at a time. I have seen many hot-shot developers attempt to change multiple lines of code simultaneously. Instead of correcting the problem they initially set out to solve, they generate a multitude of additional problems.

- Talk the problem out with other developers. Sometimes the process of simply verbalizing the problem can be enough to help you to figure it out. If verbalizing the problem doesn't provide you with the answer, the person that you are verbalizing to might know the answer.

- When all else fails, take a break. Many times I have stayed up into the wee hours of the night, attempting to solve a problem. After finally giving up, I surrender and go to bed. It's amazing how many times I solve the "unsolvable" problem from the night before while in the shower the next morning!

15

DEBUGGING

PRACTICAL EXAMPLES

Debugging Real Applications

As you develop your own applications, use the techniques you learned to help solve any problems you encounter. For now, use the debugger to step through and learn more about the debugging process with one of the routines found in the sample database.

Summary

If programming were a perfect science, there would be no reason to use a debugger. Given the reality of the challenges of programming, a thorough understanding of the use of the debugger is imperative. Fortunately, the Access 2002 VBE provides an excellent tool to assist in the debugging process.

This chapter began by showing you how you can reduce the chance of bugs within your application in the first place. It then taught you how to use the Immediate window to test and change the values of variables and properties. You learned how to use watches and breakpoints, as well as how to view the call stack. All these techniques help make the process of testing and debugging your application a pleasant experience.

Error Handling: Preparing for the Inevitable

IN THIS CHAPTER

Why This Chapter Is Important

Errors happen, even in the absence of programmer error. You need to protect your programs and your data from the adverse effects of errors by practicing error handling.

Error handling (also known as *error trapping*) is the process of intercepting Jet's or VBA's response to an error. It enables the developer to determine the severity of an error and to take the appropriate action in response to the error. This chapter shows you the techniques required to successfully implement error handling within your applications.

Implementing Error Handling

Without error handling, the user of your application is forced to exit abruptly from your application code. Consider the example in Listing 16.1.

LISTING 16.1   An Example of Code Without Error Handling

```
Private Sub cmdNoErrorHandler_Click()
    'Call TestError1, passing the values in the txtValue1
    'and txtValue2 text boxes
    Call TestError1(Me.txtValue1.Value, Me.txtValue2.Value)
End Sub


Sub TestError1(Numerator As Integer, Denominator As Integer)
    'Divide the value received as the first parameter
    'by the value received as the second parameter
    Debug.Print Numerator / Denominator
    'If successful, display a message to the user
    MsgBox "I am in Test Error"
End Sub
```

The click event behind the command button calls the routine TestError1, passing it the values from two text boxes. TestError1 accepts those parameters and attempts to divide the first parameter by the second parameter. If the second parameter is equal to 0, a runtime error occurs. Because no error handling is in effect, the program terminates.

Figure 16.1 shows the error message the user receives. As you can see, the choices are Continue, End, Debug, and Help. If users click Debug, the module window appears, and they are placed in Debug mode on the line of code causing the error. Clicking Continue (this is not always available) tells Access to ignore the error and continue with the execution of the program. End terminates execution of the programming code. If the application is running with the runtime version of Access, it shuts down, and users are returned to Windows.

Error Handling: Preparing for the Inevitable

CHAPTER 16

705

16

ERROR HANDLING:
PREPARING FOR
THE INEVITABLE

With error handling in effect, you can attempt to handle the error in a more appropriate way whenever possible.

FIGURE 16.1

The default error handling message.

You can add error-handling code to the error event procedure of a form or report. You also can add it to any VBA subroutine, function, or event routine. You easily can modify the code in Listing 16.1 to handle the error gracefully. The code in Listing 16.2 shows a simple error-handling routine.

LISTING 16.2 A Simple Error-Handling Routine

```
Sub TestError2(Numerator As Integer, Denominator As Integer)
On Error GoTo TestError2_Err
    'Divide the value received as the first parameter
    'by the value received as the second parameter
    Debug.Print Numerator / Denominator
    'If successful, display a message to the user
    MsgBox "I am in Test Error"

    Exit Sub

TestError2_Err:
    'If a divide by zero (error 11) occurs, display an
    'appropriate message to the user
    If Err = 11 Then
        MsgBox "Variable 2 Cannot Be a Zero", , "Custom Error Handler"
    End If
    Exit Sub

End Sub
```

This code is located in the basError module, which is in the CHAP16EX.MDB database on the accompanying CD-ROM.

The routine now invokes error handling. If a divide-by-zero error occurs, a message box alerts the user to the problem, as Figure 16.2 shows.

FIGURE 16.2

A custom error handler message.

Using On Error Statements

On Error statements activate error handling. Each routine must contain its own On Error statement if you want that routine to do its own error handling. Otherwise, error handling is cascaded up the call stack. If no On Error statements are found in the call stack, VBA's own error handling is invoked.

Suppose that Func1 calls Func2, and Func2 calls Func3. Only Func1 contains error handling. An error occurs in Func3. Func3 passes control up to Func2. Func2 has no error handling, so it passes control up to Func1. Func1 handles the error. Needless to say, the error handler found in Func1 is not necessarily appropriate to handle the error that occurred in Func3.

Using an On Error statement, you can cause the application to branch to error-handling code, resume code execution on the line immediately following the error, or attempt to re-execute the problem line of code.

You must decide the most appropriate response to a particular error. Sometimes it is most appropriate for your application to halt in response to an error. At other times, it is best if the routine skips the offending line entirely. By combining the use of On Error Goto, On Error Resume Next, and the Resume statement, you can handle each error appropriately.

Using On Error Goto

The statement On Error Goto <label> tells VBA that, from this point forward in the subroutine or function, if an error occurs, it should jump to the label specified in the statement. This is the most common form of error handling.

The label specified in the On Error statement must be located in the current procedure. Listing 16.3 shows a simple example of error handling.

LISTING 16.3 An Example of Error Handling Using the On Error GoTo Statement

```
Sub SimpleErrorHandler(iVar1 As Integer, iVar2 As Integer)
    'Invoke error handling
    On Error GoTo SimpleErrorHandler_Err

    'Declare a variable to hold the result
    Dim sngResult As Single
    'Divide the first parameter received by the
    'second parameter received
    sngResult = iVar1 / iVar2

    'Exit the subroutine if all went as planned
    Exit Sub

SimpleErrorHandler_Err:
    'If an error occurs, display a message and exit
    'the subroutine
    MsgBox "Oops!"
    Exit Sub

End Sub
```

You can learn some important things from this simple routine. The routine receives two integer values. It then invokes the error handler. When an error occurs, execution continues at the label. Notice that this routine contains two Exit Sub statements. If you remove the first Exit Sub statement, the code falls through to the label regardless of whether an error occurred. The Exit Sub statement at the bottom gracefully exits the procedure, setting the error code back to 0.

Including the Error Number and Description in the Error Handler

The error-handling code in Listing 16.3 did not give a very descriptive message to users. The Description and Number properties of the Err object give users more meaningful error messages. The Err object is covered in detail later in this chapter in the section "Using the Err Object." For now, take a look at the Description and Number properties to see how you can use them to enhance an error-handling routine. To display the error number and description, you must modify the error-handling code to look like this:

```
SimpleErrorHandler_Err:
    'If an error occurs, display a message and exit
    'the subroutine
    MsgBox "Error #" & Err.Number & ": " & Err.Description
    Exit Sub
```

This time, instead of hard-coding the error message, you display the error number and VBA's internal error string. Figure 16.3 shows the resulting error message. The `SimpleErrorHandler` routine and all the following examples are located in the basError module of the CHAP16EX.MDB database.

FIGURE 16.3

An error message with an error number and error string.

Using `On Error Goto 0`

You use `On Error Goto 0` for two purposes:

- When you want Access to return to its default error handler
- When you have other error handling in a routine, but want Access to return to the calling routine when a specific condition occurs

Generally, you don't want Access to return to its default error handler. You might do this only if you are unable to handle the error or if you are in the testing phase and not yet ready to implement your own error handler.

The reason why you want Access to return the error to a higher-level routine is much clearer. You do this if you want to *centralize* the error handling, meaning that one routine might call several others. Instead of placing error-handling code in each routine that is called, it is appropriate in certain situations to place the error handling in the calling routine.

Using `On Error Resume Next`

`On Error Resume Next` continues program execution on the line immediately following the error. This construct generally is used when it is acceptable to ignore an error and continue code execution. Listing 16.4 shows an example of such a situation.

LISTING 16.4   Ignoring an Error and Continuing Execution

```
Sub TestResumeNext()
    'Instruct VBA to continue on the next line if an error
    'occurs
    On Error Resume Next

    'Attempt to delete a file
    Kill "AnyFile"
```

LISTING 16.4   Continued

```
    'If no error occurred, do nothing. Otherwise, display
    'a message with the description of the error that occurred
    If Err.Number = 0 Then
    Else
        MsgBox "We Didn't Die, But the Error Was: " & Err.Description
    End If
End Sub
```

You use the Kill statement to delete a file from disk. If the specified file is not found, an error results. You delete the file only if it exists, so you are not concerned about an error. On Error Resume Next is very appropriate in this situation because resuming execution after the offending line of code does no harm. The example illustrates that, although code execution proceeds, the properties of the error object are still set.

Using Resume Statements

While you are in your error-handling code, you can use the Resume, Resume Next, and Resume <LineLabel> statements to specify how you want VBA to respond to the error. Resume attempts to re-execute the offending line of code, Resume Next resumes execution after the offending line of code, and Resume <LineLabel> continues execution at a specified line label. The following sections cover these statements in detail.

The Resume Statement

The Resume statement resumes code execution on the line of code that caused the error. You must use this statement with extreme care because it can throw the code into an unrecoverable endless loop. Listing 16.5 shows an example of an inappropriate use of the Resume statement.

LISTING 16.5   Using Resume Inappropriately

```
Function BadResume(strFileName As String)
    'Invoke error handling
    On Error GoTo BadResume_Err
    Dim strFile As String

    'Perform the Dir function to determine if
    'the file passed as a parameter exists
    strFile = Dir(strFileName)

    'If the file doesn't exist, return False
    'Otherwise, return True
    If strFile = "" Then
```

LISTING 16.5   Continued

```
    BadResume = False
  Else
    BadResume = True
  End If

  'Exit the function if all goes well
  Exit Function

BadResume_Err:
  'Display an error message with the
  'description of the error that occurred
  MsgBox Error.Description

  'Attempt to re-execute the offending line of code
  Resume
End Function
```

This function is passed a filename. The `Dir` function searches for a file with that name and returns `True` or `False`, depending on whether the specified file is found. The problem occurs when the drive requested is not available or does not exist. This code throws the computer into an endless loop. To remedy the problem, you should modify your code to look like the code in Listing 16.6.

LISTING 16.6   Using `Resume` Conditionally Based on User Feedback

```
Function GoodResume(strFileName As String)
    'Invoke error handling
    On Error GoTo GoodResume_Err
    Dim strFile As String

    'Perform the Dir function to determine if
    'the file passed as a parameter exists
    strFile = Dir(strFileName)

    'If the file doesn't exist, return False
    'Otherwise, return True
    If strFile = "" Then
      GoodResume = False
    Else
      GoodResume = True
    End If

    'Exit the function if all goes well
    Exit Function
```

LISTING 16.6   Continued

```
GoodResume_Err:
    Dim intAnswer As Integer

    'Ask user if they want to try again
    intAnswer = MsgBox(Error & ", Would You Like to Try Again?", vbYesNo)

    'If they respond yes, attempt to re-execute the offending line
    'of code. Otherwise, exit the function
    If intAnswer = vbYes Then
        Resume
    Else
        Exit Function
    End If
End Function
```

In this example, the error handler enables the user to decide whether to try again. The `Resume` occurs only if the user's response is affirmative.

The `Resume Next` Statement

Just as you can invoke error handling using an `On Error Resume Next` statement, you can place a `Resume Next` statement in your error handler, as Listing 16.7 shows.

LISTING 16.7   Placing a `Resume Next` Statement in Your Error Handler

```
Sub TestResumeNextInError()

    'Invoke error handling
    On Error GoTo TestResumeNextInError_Err

    'Attempt to delete a file
    Kill "AnyFile"

    'If no error occurred, do nothing. Otherwise, display
    'a message with the description of the error that occurred
    If Err.Number = 0 Then
    Else
        MsgBox "We Didn't Die, But the Error Was: " & Err.Description
    End If

    Exit Sub
```

LISTING 16.7   Continued

```
TestResumeNextInError_Err:
    'Reset error information and resume execution on the
    'line of code following the line on which the error cocurred
    Resume Next
End Sub
```

In this example, the code is instructed to go to the label called `TestResumeNextInError_Err` when an error occurs. The `TestResumeNextInError_Err` label issues a `Resume Next` statement. This clears the error and causes execution to continue on the line after the line on which the error occurred.

> **NOTE**
>
> Note the difference between `On Error Resume Next` and `Resume Next`. `On Error Resume Next` is placed in the body of the routine. It causes code execution to continue on the line of code following the line that caused the error. It does *not* reset any error information.
>
> `Resume Next` is placed *within* the error handler. It also causes code execution to continue on the line of code following the line that caused the error. It *does* reset the error information.

The `Resume <LineLabel>` Statement

The `Resume <LineLabel>` statement enables you to specify a line of code where you want code execution to continue after an error occurs. This is a great way to eliminate the two `Exit Sub` or `Exit Function` statements required by the error-handling routines you have looked at so far. Listing 16.8 shows an example.

LISTING 16.8   Using the `Resume <LineLabel>` Statement to Specify Where Execution Continues After an Error Occurs

```
Sub TestResumeLineLabel(intVar1 As Integer, intVar2 As Integer)
    'Invoke error handling
    On Error GoTo TestResumeLineLabel_Err

    Dim sngResult As Single
    'Divide the value received as the first parameter
    'by the value received as the second parameter
    sngResult = intVar1 / intVar2
```

Error Handling: Preparing for the Inevitable

CHAPTER 16

713

16

ERROR HANDLING:
PREPARING FOR
THE INEVITABLE

LISTING 16.8   Continued

```
TestResumeLineLabel_Exit:
    'Exit subroutine
    Exit Sub

TestResumeLineLabel_Err:
    'If an error occurs, display message with the error
    'number and description
    MsgBox "Error #" & Err.Number & ": " & Err.Description

    'Resume execution at the TestResumeLineLable_Exit label
    Resume TestResumeLineLabel_Exit

End Sub
```

Notice that this routine contains only one Exit Sub statement. If no error occurs, Access drops through the TestResumeLineLabel_Exit label to the Exit Sub statement. If an error *does* occur, the code in the TestResumeLineLabel_Err label executes. Notice that the last line of the error label resumes execution at the TestResumeLineLabel_Exit label.

This method of resolving an error is useful because any code required to execute as the routine is exited can be written in one place. Object variables might need to be set equal to Nothing as the routine is exited, for example. You can place these lines of code in the exit routine.

Clearing an Error

When an error occurs, the Err object remains set with the error information until one of the following clears the error:

- Resume, Resume Next, or Resume <LineLabel>
- Exit Sub, Exit Function, or Exit Property
- Any Goto statement
- Explicitly using the Clear method on the Err object

Until the error is cleared somehow, all the information remains set in the Err object. After the error is cleared, no information is found in the Err object.

Examining the Cascading Error Effect

As mentioned earlier in the section "Using On Error Statements," if Access does not find any error handling in a particular subroutine or function, it looks up the call stack for a previous error handler. Listing 16.9 shows an example of this process.

LISTING 16.9   Looking Up the Call Stack for a Previous Error Handler

```
Sub Func1()

    'Invoke error handling
    On Error GoTo Func1_Err

    'Print to the immediate window
    Debug.Print "I am in Function 1"

    'Execute the Func2 routine
    Call Func2

    'Print to the immediate window
    Debug.Print "I am back in Function 1"

    'Exit the subroutine
    Exit Sub

Func1_Err:
    'Display a message to the user,
    'indicating that an error occurred
    MsgBox "Error in Func1"

    'Resume execution
    Resume Next
End Sub

Sub Func2()
    'No error handling in this routine!
    'Print to the immediate window
    Debug.Print "I am in Func2"

    'Execute Func3
    Call Func3

    'Print to the immediate window
    Debug.Print "I am still in Func2"
End Sub

Sub Func3()
    'No error in this routine either!
    Dim sngAnswer As Single

    'Print to the immediate window
    Debug.Print "I am in Func3"
```

LISTING 16.9 Continued

```
    'Opps, an error occurred
    sngAnswer = 5 / 0

    'This line of code will never execute
    Debug.Print "I am still in Func3"
End Sub
```

In this situation, the error occurs in Func3. Because Func3 does not have its own error handling, it refers back to Func2. Func2 does not have any error handling either, so Func2 relinquishes control to Func1. VBA executes the error code in Func1. The real problem occurs because of the Resume Next statement. The application continues executing within Func1 on the Debug.Print "I am back in Function 1" statement. This type of error handling is dangerous and confusing. Therefore, it is best to develop a generic error-handling routine that is accessed throughout your application. The creation of a generic error handler is discussed in the section "Creating a Generic Error Handler."

Using the Err Object

The Err object contains information about the most recent error that occurred. As with all Access objects, it has its own built-in properties and methods. Table 16.1 lists the properties of the Err object.

TABLE 16.1 Properties of the Err Object

Property	Description
Description	Description of the error that occurred
HelpContext	Context ID for the Help file
HelpFile	Path and filename of the Help file
LastDLLError	Last error that occurred in a 32-bit DLL
Number	Number of the error that was set
Source	System in which the error occurred (which is extremely useful when you are using OLE automation to control another application, such as Excel)

The Err object has only two methods: Clear and Raise. The Clear method enables you to clear an error condition explicitly. This is used primarily when you write code that uses the On Error Resume Next statement. This statement does not clear the error condition. Remember that there is no reason to issue the Clear method explicitly with any type of Resume, Exit Sub,

Exit Function, Exit Property, or On Error Goto statement. The Clear method is implicitly issued when these constructs are used. The Raise method of the Err object is covered in the next section.

Raising an Error

You use the Raise method of the error object in these situations:

- When you want to generate an error on purpose (for example, in testing)
- When you want to generate a user-defined error
- When no code in the error routine handles the current error, and you want to allow other parts of the call stack to attempt to handle the error
- When you want to nest an error handler

Using the Raise method to generate an error on purpose and creating a user-defined error are covered in the following sections.

Generating an Error on Purpose

Many times during testing, you want to generate an error so that you can check your own error handling. Instead of figuring out how to cause the error condition, you can use the Raise method of the Err object to accomplish this task, as Listing 16.10 shows.

LISTING 16.10   Raising an Error

```
Sub TestRaiseError()
    'Invoke error handling
    On Error GoTo TestRaiseError_Err

    Dim sngResult As String

    'Raise a divide-by-zero error
    Err.Raise 11

    'Exit the subroutine
    Exit Sub

TestRaiseError_Err:
    'Display a message with the error number and description
    MsgBox "Error #" & Err.Number & ": " & Err.Description

    'Exit the subroutine
    Exit Sub

End Sub
```

This code invokes an error 11 (divide by 0).

Creating User-Defined Errors

Another important use of the `Raise` method of the `Err` object is the generation of a custom error condition. This is useful when you want to *force* an error in response to something that the user did. For example, assume that the user must enter five characters into an unbound text box. Entering only two characters would not generate an Access error. Rather than handling this *user-generated* error in some other manner, you can raise the error and have your standard error handler respond to the error condition. Because the `Raise` method enables you to set all the properties of the `Err` object, you can create a user-defined error complete with a number, description, source, and so on, as shown in Listing 16.11.

LISTING 16.11   Creating a User-Defined Error

```
Sub TestCustomError()
    'Invoke error handling
   On Error GoTo TestCustomError_Err
   Dim strName As String

   'Prompt the user to enter their name
   strName = InputBox("Please Enter Your Name")

   'If the length of the name is less than five
   'characters, raise an error number 11111
   If Len(strName) < 5 Then
      Err.Raise Number:=11111, _
               Description:="Length of Name is Too Short"
   Else
      MsgBox "You Entered " & strName
   End If

   Exit Sub

TestCustomError_Err:
    'Display a message with the error number
    'and description
    MsgBox "Error # " & Err.Number & _
       " - " & Err.Description
    Exit Sub
End Sub
```

Although it is very simple, Listing 16.11 illustrates an important use of generating user-defined errors. The code tests to see whether the value entered has less than five characters. If it does, a user-defined error message (number 11111) is generated. The routine drops into the normal error-handling routine. The section "Creating a Generic Error Handler," later in this chapter, explores how to put together a generic error handler. By passing user-defined errors through your generic error handler, all errors—user-defined or not—are handled in the same way.

Using the Errors Collection

The Errors collection is part of Access's Jet Engine. It stores the most recent set of DAO errors that have occurred. This is important when dealing with DAO (Data Access Objects) and ODBC (Open Database Connectivity), in which one operation can result in multiple errors. If you are concerned with each error that was generated by one operation, you need to look at the Errors collection. Each error object in the Errors collection contains information about an error that occurred. If you want to view the errors stored in the Errors collection, you must loop through it, viewing the properties of each Err object. Listing 16.12 shows the code you can use to accomplish this.

LISTING 16.12   Viewing the Errors Stored in the Errors Collection

```
Sub TestErrorsCollection()
    'Invoke error handling
    On Error GoTo TestErrorsCollection_Err

    'Declare a DAO database object
    Dim db As DAO.Database

    'Point the database object at the database
    'referenced by the CurrentDB object
    Set db = CurrentDb

    'Attempt to execute a query that doesn't exist
    db.Execute ("qryNonExistent")

    Exit Sub

TestErrorsCollection_Err:

    Dim ErrorDescrip As DAO.Error

    'Loop through the errors collection,
    'sending the error number and description to
    'the Immediate window
    For Each ErrorDescrip In Errors
        Debug.Print ErrorDescrip.Number
        Debug.Print ErrorDescrip.Description
    Next ErrorDescrip
    Exit Sub
End Sub
```

This routine loops through each `Error` object in the Errors collection, printing the description of each error contained in the collection.

Creating a Generic Error Handler

A *generic* error handler can be called from every procedure in your application to respond to any type of error.

A generic error handler prevents you from having to write specific error handling in each of your subroutines and functions. This enables you to invoke error handling throughout your application in the most efficient manner possible.

You can take many approaches to create a generic error handler. It should give users information about the error, enable users to print this information, and log the information to a file.

The `On Error` routine (in this case, the label `AnySub_Err`) of every procedure that performs error handling should look like the error-handling routine contained in the subroutine in Listing 16.13.

LISTING 16.13   A Generic Error Handler for All Your Functions and Subroutines

```
Sub AnySub()
'Declare constant with the name of the routine
Const SUBNAME As String = "AnySub"

'Invoke error handling
On Error GoTo AnySub_Err

    'Beginning of any routine
    MsgBox "This is the rest of your code...."

    'Oops! Something causes an error!
    Err.Raise 11

    'Code after the error
    MsgBox "We are Past the Error!!"

AnySub_Exit:
    'Generic exit point for routine
    Exit Sub

AnySub_Err:
    Dim intAction As Integer
```

LISTING 16.13   Continued

```
    'Call generic error handler, passing it the error
    'number and description, as well as the module name
    'and subroutine name
    intAction = ErrorHandler(lngErrorNum:=Err.Number, _
                  strErrorDescription:=Err.Description, _
                  strModuleName:=MODULENAME, _
                  strRoutineName:=SUBNAME)

    'Evaluate return value to determine what action to take
    Select Case intAction
        Case ERR_CONTINUE
            Resume Next
        Case ERR_RETRY
            Resume
        Case ERR_EXIT
            Resume AnySub_Exit
        Case ERR_QUIT
            Quit
    End Select
End Sub
```

This error-handling routine in AnySub creates an Integer variable that holds the return value from the error system. The intAction variable holds an appropriate response to the error that occurred. The error routine calls the generic error-handling function ErrorHandler, passing it the error number (Err.Number), a description of the error (Err.Description), the name of the module containing the error, and the name of the subroutine or function containing the error. The name of the module is stored in a Private constant called MODULENAME. The Private constant is declared in the General section of the module and needs to be created for every module you make. The name of the subroutine or function is stored in a local constant called SUBNAME. With this approach, you create a local constant and assign it the name of the sub at the beginning of each procedure. This requires upkeep because procedure names can change, and you need to remember to change your string. Unfortunately, because the VBA environment does not expose the subroutine and module names to you when an error occurs, this sort of brute force is necessary if you want your error handler to track the subroutine and module. When the code returns from the ErrorHandler function, a return value is placed in the intAction variable. This return value is used to determine the fate of the routine.

> **TIP**
>
> The process of adding error handling to every routine that you create is a tedious one. Fortunately, a tool is available that makes the process much more palatable. The tool is produced by FMS Software and is called FMS Total Access Code Tools. This tool is covered in detail in Chapter 31, "Third-Party Tools That Can Help You to Get Your Job Done Effectively." Amongst its many features, it allows you to create a custom error template that you can use to quickly and easily add error handling to all the routines that you create. A scaled-down version of FMS Total Access Code Tools is built into the Microsoft Office Developer.

Now that you have seen how to implement error handling in your procedures, take a look at the function that is called when an error occurs, as shown in Listing 16.14.

LISTING 16.14   A Type Structure Declaration to Be Used for Generic Error Handling

```
'Type structure used to hold error information
Type typErrors
    lngErrorNum As Long
    strMessage As String
    strModule As String
    strRoutine As String
    strUserName As String
    datDateTime As Variant
End Type

'Declaration of public type structure variable
Public gtypError As typErrors

'Constants used by global error handler
Public Const ERR_CONTINUE = 0  'Resume Next
Public Const ERR_RETRY = 1 'Resume
Public Const ERR_QUIT = 2  'End
Public Const ERR_EXIT = 3  'Exit Sub or Func
```

This code is placed in the General section of basHandleErrors. The type structure declared holds all the pertinent information about the error. A *type structure* is a special kind of variable that is made up of various parts, each of which stores a different piece of information. (Type structures are covered in Chapter 12, "Advanced VBA Techniques.")

In Listing 16.14, the public variable gtypError holds all the information from the type structure. The constants are used to help determine the fate of the application after an error occurs. Listing 16.15 shows the ErrorHandler function.

LISTING 16.15   Using the ErrorHandler Function

```
Function ErrorHandler(lngErrorNum As Long, _
                strErrorDescription As String, _
                strModuleName As String, _
                strRoutineName As String) As Integer


    'Populate elements of the type structure variable
    'with information about the error that occurred
    gtypError.lngErrorNum = lngErrorNum
    gtypError.strMessage = strErrorDescription
    gtypError.strModule = strModuleName
    gtypError.strRoutine = strRoutineName
    gtypError.strUserName = CurrentUser()
    gtypError.datDateTime = Now

    'Log the error
    Call LogError

    'Locate the error number in tblErrors to
    'determine how you should respond to the error
    Dim rst As adodb.Recordset
    Set rst = New adodb.Recordset
    rst.Open "Select Response from tblErrors Where ErrorNum = " & _
    lngErrorNum, CurrentProject.Connection, adOpenStatic

    'If the error number that occurred is not found
    'in tblErrors, display the error form and return
    'ERR_QUIT to the problem routine
    If rst.EOF Then
        DoCmd.OpenForm "frmError", WindowMode:=acDialog, _
            OpenArgs:="ErrorHandler"
        ErrorHandler = ERR_QUIT

    'If the error is in tblErrors, evaluate the contents of
    'the Response field. Response appropriately, displaying the appropriate
    'form and returning the appropriate value to the offending routine
    Else
        Select Case rst!Response
```

LISTING 16.15   Continued

```
        Case ERR_QUIT
            DoCmd.OpenForm "frmError", WindowMode:=acDialog, _
                OpenArgs:="Critical Error:  Application will Terminate"
            ErrorHandler = ERR_QUIT
        Case ERR_RETRY
            ErrorHandler = ERR_RETRY
        Case ERR_EXIT
            DoCmd.OpenForm "frmError", WindowMode:=acDialog, _
                OpenArgs:="Severe Error:  Processing Did Not Complete"
            ErrorHandler = ERR_EXIT
        Case ERR_CONTINUE
            ErrorHandler = ERR_CONTINUE
    End Select
End If

End Function
```

The ErrorHandler function receives the error number, error description, module name, and subroutine or function name as parameters. It then fills in the gtypError type structure with the information that it was passed, as well as the current user and date. Next, it calls a routine that logs the error into an Access table. The routine looks up the severity of the error code in an Access table called tblErrors to decide the most appropriate way to handle the error. If the error code is not found in the error table, an error form is displayed, and a return value is sent to the calling function, indicating that application execution is to be terminated. If the error code is found in the tblErrors table and determined to be critical or severe, an error form appears before control is returned to the calling routine. In any case, a severity code for the error is returned to the calling function. The following section discusses the details involved in each step of the process.

Logging the Error

The LogError routine is responsible for logging all the error information into an Access table. Because users often decide not to print the error form or provide you with inaccurate information about what was happening when the error occurred (or neglect to tell you about the error), it is important that you log each error so that you can review the error log at any time. Errors can be logged to a text file or a data table. This section shows you both methods of logging your errors. Start with logging your errors to a table, as shown in Listing 16.16 with the LogError routine.

Listing 16.16   Using the `LogError` Routine

```
Sub LogError()

    'Declare a Connection object
    Dim cnn As adodb.Connection
    Dim strSQL As String

    'Point the Connection object at the connection
    'associated with the current project
    Set cnn = CurrentProject.Connection

    'Build a SQL statement that inserts error information
    'into the tblErrorLog table
    strSQL = "INSERT INTO tblErrorLog ( ErrorDate, ErrorTime, UserName,
ErrorNum, ErrorString, ModuleName, RoutineName) "
    strSQL = strSQL & "Select #" & gtypError.datDateTime & "#, #" _
                            & gtypError.datDateTime & "#, '" _
                            & gtypError.strUserName & "', " _
                            & gtypError.lngErrorNum & ", '" _
                            & gtypError.strMessage & "', '" _
                            & gtypError.strModule & "', '" _
                            & gtypError.strRoutine & "'"

    'Execute the SQL statement
    cnn.Execute strSQL, , adExecuteNoRecords

End Sub
```

This routine uses the `Execute` method of the `ADO Connection` object to add a record to your error table. The record contains all the information from the structure called `gtypError`. The information is logged to a table called tblErrorLog. Figure 16.4 shows the structure of this table.

The alternative error-logging method is to write the information to a textual error log file, as shown in Listing 16.17.

Listing 16.17   Writing Information to a Textual Error Log File

```
Sub LogErrorText()
    Dim intFile As Integer

    'Store a free file handle into a variable
    intFile = FreeFile
```

Error Handling: Preparing for the Inevitable

CHAPTER 16

725

16

ERROR HANDLING:
PREPARING FOR
THE INEVITABLE

LISTING 16.17 Continued

```
    'Open a file named ErrorLog.txt in the current directory
    'using the file handle obtained above
    Open CurDir & "\ErrorLog.Txt" For Append Shared As intFile

    'Write the error information to the file
    Write #intFile, "LogErrorDemo", Now, Err, Error, CurrentUser()

    'Close the file
    Close intFile
End Sub
```

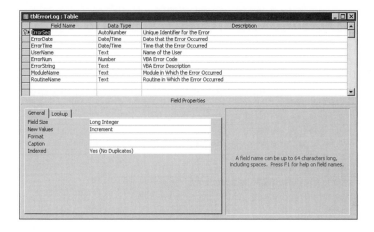

FIGURE 16.4
The structure of the tblErrorLog table.

This code uses low-level file functions to `Open` and `Write` to an ASCII text file. All the pertinent information about the error is written to this text file. The routine then uses the `Close` command to close the text file. The potential advantage of this routine is that, if the problem is with the database (for example, the network is down), the error logging process still succeeds.

Determining the Appropriate Response to an Error

After the error is logged, you are ready to determine the best way to respond to the error. By making your error system data driven, you can handle each error a little differently. Figure 16.5 shows the structure of the tblErrors table. This table should contain a list of all the error numbers that you want to trap. It contains three fields: ErrorNum, ErrorDescription, and Response. When an error occurs, the `ErrorHandler` function searches for a record with a value in the ErrorNum field that matches the number of the error that occurred.

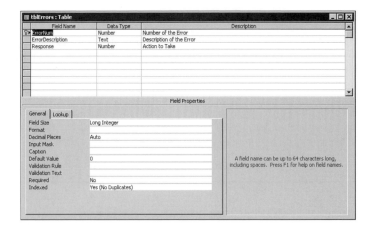

FIGURE 16.5

The structure of the tblErrors table.

The `ErrorHandler` function, as shown in Listing 16.15, uses the code in Listing 16.18 to locate the error code in the tblErrors table.

LISTING 16.18   Locating the Error Code in the tblErrors Table

```
'Locate the error number in tblErrors to
'determine how you should respond to the error
Dim rst As adodb.Recordset
Set rst = New adodb.Recordset
rst.Open "Select Response from tblErrors Where ErrorNum = " & lngErrorNum, _
    CurrentProject.Connection, adOpenStatic

'If the error number that occurred is not found
'in tblErrors, display the error form and return
'ERR_QUIT to the problem routine
If rst.EOF Then
    DoCmd.OpenForm "frmError", WindowMode:=acDialog, _
        OpenArgs:="ErrorHandler"
    ErrorHandler = ERR_QUIT

'If the error is in tblErrors, evaluate the contents of
'the Response field. Respond appropriately, displaying the appropriate
'form and returning the appropriate value to the offending routine
Else
    Select Case rst!Response
        Case ERR_QUIT
```

LISTING 16.18   Continued

```
            DoCmd.OpenForm "frmError", WindowMode:=acDialog, _
                OpenArgs:="Critical Error:  Application will Terminate"
            ErrorHandler = ERR_QUIT
        Case ERR_RETRY
            ErrorHandler = ERR_RETRY
        Case ERR_EXIT
            DoCmd.OpenForm "frmError", WindowMode:=acDialog, _
                OpenArgs:="Severe Error:  Processing Did Not Complete"
            ErrorHandler = ERR_EXIT
        Case ERR_CONTINUE
            ErrorHandler = ERR_CONTINUE
    End Select
End If
```

The part of the `ErrorHandler` function shown in Listing 16.18 creates an ADO `Recordset` object variable. It opens a recordset using a `Select` statement, which in turn searches a table called tblErrors. If a match is found, the Response column is used to determine the response to the error. Notice in Listing 16.18 that, if the error number is not found in tblErrors, default error handling occurs, which means that the code handles all other errors as a group. (This is my default error handling, not Access's.) If the error number is found, the Response field is evaluated and the appropriate action is taken (via the `Case` statement). If it is not found, the frmError form is opened, and the `ERR_QUIT` constant value is returned from the `ErrorHandler` function. When using this method, you need to add to the table only specific errors that you want to trap.

If the error number is found in tblErrors, the Response field from the recordset is evaluated. If the Response field contains the constant value `ERR_QUIT` or `ERR_EXIT`, the frmError form appears before the constant value is returned to the offending function or subroutine. If the Response field contains the constant value for `ERR_RETRY` or `ERR_CONTINUE`, the constant value is returned without displaying the frmError form.

NOTE

The tblErrors table is included in CHAP16EX.MDB on the sample code CD-ROM. To take full advantage of this table, you must add all errors that you want to trap, along with the actions that you want the error handler to take when that error occurs.

Listing 16.19 shows how the return value from the `ErrorHandler` function is used.

Listing 16.19   Using the Return Value from the `ErrorHandler` Function

```
Sub AnySub()
'Declare constant with the name of the routine
Const SUBNAME As String = "AnySub"

'Invoke error handling
On Error GoTo AnySub_Err

    'Beginning of any routine
    MsgBox "This is the rest of your code...."

    'Oops! Something causes an error!
    Err.Raise 11

    'Code after the error
    MsgBox "We are Past the Error!!"

AnySub_Exit:
    'Generic exit point for routine
    Exit Sub

AnySub_Err:
    Dim intAction As Integer

    'Call generic error handler, passing it the error
    'number and description, as well as the module name
    'and subroutine name
    intAction = ErrorHandler(lngErrorNum:=Err.Number, _
                strErrorDescription:=Err.Description, _
                strModuleName:=MODULENAME, _
                strRoutineName:=SUBNAME)

    'Evaluate return value to determine what action to take
    Select Case intAction
        Case ERR_CONTINUE
            Resume Next
        Case ERR_RETRY
            Resume
        Case ERR_EXIT
            Resume AnySub_Exit
        Case ERR_QUIT
            Quit
    End Select
End Sub
```

Error Handling: Preparing for the Inevitable

CHAPTER 16

729

16

ERROR HANDLING:
PREPARING FOR
THE INEVITABLE

In Listing 16.19, the `AnySub` routine generates an error 11 (divide by 0). Because tblErrors contains the number 3 in the Response column and the `ERR_CONTINUE` constant is equal to 3, the error form is displayed, and the `AnySub` routine is exited with an `Exit Sub` statement.

NOTE

To test what happens when the error code is not found in the tblErrors table, run the `SubWithUnknownError` routine found in basError. To test what happens when the `ERR_CONTINUE` code is returned, execute the `SubWithContinue` routine.

Creating an Error Form

The code in the error form's `Load` event calls two subroutines: `GetSystemInfo` and `GetErrorInfo`, as shown here:

```
Private Sub Form_Load()

    'Call routine to obtain system information
    Call GetSysInfo(Me)

    'Call routine to obtain error information
    Call GetErrorInfo(Me)

    'If FormCaption property contains a value, use the
    'value as the caption for the form
    If Not IsNull(Me.OpenArgs) Then
        Me.lblAction.Caption = Me.OpenArgs
    End If
End Sub
```

The first subroutine is called `GetSysInfo`. It performs several Windows API calls to fill in the system information on your form. The code is shown in Listing 16.20, and it is discussed in Chapter 23, "Exploiting the Power of the Windows API."

LISTING 16.20   Getting System Information Through Code

```
Sub GetSysInfo(frmAny As Form)

    'Get Free Memory
    Dim MS As MEMORYSTATUS
    MS.dwLength = Len(MS)
    GlobalMemoryStatus MS
```

LISTING 16.20   Continued

```
    frmAny.lblMemoryTotal.Caption = Format(MS.dwTotalPhys, "Standard")
    frmAny.lblMemoryAvail.Caption = Format(MS.dwAvailPhys, "Standard")

    'Get Version Information
    Dim OSInfo As OSVERSIONINFO
    OSInfo.dwOSVersionInfoSize = Len(OSInfo)
    If GetVersionEx(OSInfo) Then
        frmAny.lblOSVersion.Caption = OSInfo.dwMajorVersion & "." &
OSInfo.dwMinorVersion
        frmAny.lblBuild.Caption = OSInfo.dwBuildNumber And &HFFFF&
        If OSInfo.dwPlatformId = 0 Then
            frmAny.lblPlatform.Caption = "Windows 95"
        Else
            frmAny.lblPlatform.Caption = "Windows NT"
        End If
    End If

    'Get System Information
    Dim SI As SYSTEM_INFO
     GetSystemInfo SI
    frmAny.lblProcessor.Caption = SI.dwProcessorType

End Sub
```

These API calls require the Declare statements and constants shown in Listing 16.21. They are placed in a module called basAPI.

LISTING 16.21   Declaring Windows API Calls

```
'Declarations required by WinAPI Calls
Option Compare Database
Option Explicit

Private Declare Sub GlobalMemoryStatus Lib "Kernel32"_
(lpBuffer As MEMORYSTATUS)

Private Type MEMORYSTATUS
    dwLength As Long
    dwMemoryLoad As Long
    dwTotalPhys As Long
    dwAvailPhys As Long
    dwTotalPageFile As Long
    dwAvailPageFile As Long
    dwTotalVirtual As Long
```

LISTING 16.21   Continued

```
   dwAvailVirtual As Long
End Type

Private Declare Function GetVersionEx Lib "Kernel32" _
   Alias "GetVersionExA" (lpOSInfo As OSVERSIONINFO) As Boolean

Type OSVERSIONINFO
   dwOSVersionInfoSize As Long
   dwMajorVersion As Long
   dwMinorVersion As Long
   dwBuildNumber As Long
   dwPlatformId As Long
   strReserved As String * 128
End Type

Private Declare Sub GetSystemInfo Lib "Kernel32"_
   (lpSystemInfo As SYSTEM_INFO)

Private Type SYSTEM_INFO
   dwOemID As Long
   dwPageSize As Long
   lpMinimumApplicationAddress As Long
   lpMaximumApplicationAddress As Long
   dwActiveProcessorMask As Long
   dwNumberOrfProcessors As Long
   dwProcessorType As Long
   dwAllocationGranularity As Long
   dwReserved As Long
End Type
```

The second subroutine, GetErrorInfo, fills in the labels on the error form with all the information from your structure, as shown in Listing 16.22.

LISTING 16.22   Using the GetErrorInfo Subroutine

```
Sub GetErrorInfo(frmAny As Form)
    'Populate form controls with error information
    'contained in the type variable
    frmAny.lblErrorNumber.Caption = gtypError.lngErrorNum
    frmAny.lblErrorString.Caption = gtypError.strMessage
    frmAny.lblUserName.Caption = gtypError.strUserName
    frmAny.lblDateTime.Caption = Format(gtypError.datDateTime, "c")
    frmAny.lblModuleName.Caption = gtypError.strModule
    frmAny.lblRoutineName.Caption = gtypError.strRoutine
End Sub
```

Finally, the disposition of the error, sent as an `OpenArg` from the `ErrorHandler` function, is displayed in a label on the form. Figure 16.6 shows the error form.

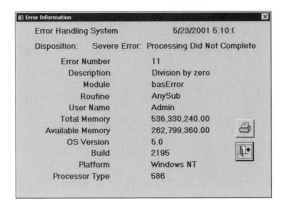

FIGURE 16.6

The frmErrors form displays important information about the error that occurred.

Printing the Error Form

Users often are not very accurate in describing an error and corresponding error message. It therefore is important to give them the capability to print their error message. The code in Listing 16.23 prints your error form. It is found behind the click event of the Print button on the error form.

LISTING 16.23   Printing an Error Form

```
Sub cmdPrint_Click()
On Error GoTo Err_cmdPrint_Click

    'Use the PrintOut method to print the form
    DoCmd.PrintOut

Exit_cmdPrint_Click:
    Exit Sub

Err_cmdPrint_Click:
    MsgBox Err.Description
    Resume Exit_cmdPrint_Click

End Sub
```

Preventing Your Own Error Handling from Being Invoked

When you are testing your application, you do not want your own error handling to be triggered. Instead, you want VBA's error handling to be activated. The trick is in the Options dialog box of the VBE. Choose Tools|Options and click the General tab. Enable the option Break on All Errors located in the Error Trapping section. As long as this option is set, your error handling is ignored, and Access's default error handling is invoked. Using this setting, you can turn error handling on and off from one central location.

Other settings for error trapping are Break in Class Module and Break on Unhandled Errors (the default). With the latter setting, handled errors do not cause the application to enter break mode. Unhandled errors do cause the project to enter break mode and place you, or the user, on the line of code that invoked the error handler. The Break in Class Module option causes *only* unhandled errors in a *class module* to invoke break mode.

Creating a Call Stack

While in the debugger, it is very easy to view the call stack. Unfortunately, the call stack information cannot be accessed programmatically when an error occurs. If you wish to keep track of the sequence of procedures that brought you to the error condition, you must do it yourself. The code in Listing 16.24 shows three routines. Func1 calls Func2, and then Func2 calls Func3. Func3 renders an error.

LISTING 16.24   Routines That Call One Another

```
Sub Func1()

    'Invoke error handling
    On Error GoTo Func1_Err

    'Put routine in call stack
    ERH_PushStack_TSB ("Func1")

    'Print to the immediate window
    Debug.Print "I am in Function 1"

    'Execute the Func2 routine
    Call Func2

    'Print to the immediate window
    Debug.Print "I am back in Function 1"
```

Listing 16.24   Continued

```
Func1_Exit:

    'Pop error stack
    ERH_PopStack_TSB

    'Exit the subroutine
    Exit Sub

Func1_Err:
    'Display a message to the user,
    'indicating that an error occurred
    MsgBox "Error in Func1"

    'Resume execution
    Resume Func1_Exit
End Sub

Sub Func2()
    'Put routine in call stack
    ERH_PushStack_TSB ("Func2")

    On Error GoTo Func2_Err

    Debug.Print "I am in Func2"

    'Execute Func3
    Call Func3

    'Print to the immediate window
    Debug.Print "I am still in Func2"

Func2_Exit:

    'Pop error stack
    ERH_PopStack_TSB

    'Exit the subroutine
    Exit Sub

Func2_Err:
    'Display a message to the user,
    'indicating that an error occurred
    MsgBox "Error in Func1"
```

Error Handling: Preparing for the Inevitable

CHAPTER 16

735

16

ERROR HANDLING:
PREPARING FOR
THE INEVITABLE

LISTING 16.24 Continued

```
    'Resume execution
    Resume Func2_Exit

End Sub

Sub Func3()
    Dim sngAnswer As Single

    'Put routine in call stack
    ERH_PushStack_TSB ("Func3")

    On Error GoTo Func3_Err

    'Print to the immediate window
    Debug.Print "I am in Func3"

    'Opps, an error occurred
    sngAnswer = 5 / 0

    'This line of code will never execute
    Debug.Print "I am still in Func3"

Func3_Exit:

    'Pop error stack
    ERH_PopStack_TSB

    'Exit the subroutine
    Exit Sub

Func3_Err:
    Dim intCounter As Integer
    Dim strCallStack As String

    For intCounter = LBound(gaERH_Stack_TSB) To UBound(gaERH_Stack_TSB)
        If Len(gaERH_Stack_TSB(intCounter)) Then
            strCallStack = strCallStack & _
                gaERH_Stack_TSB(intCounter) & vbCrLf
        End If
    Next intCounter

    MsgBox Err.Number & ": " & Err.Description & _
        vbCrLf & strCallStack

    Resume Func3_Exit
End Sub
```

Notice that at the beginning of each routine, the ERH_PushStack_TSB subroutine is called, as shown in Listing 16.25.

LISTING 16.25 The ERH_PushStack_TSB Function Pushes the Error into the Stack

```
Sub ERH_PushStack_TSB(strProc As String)
  ' Comments  : Pushes the supplied procedure name onto the error handling
stack
  ' Parameters: strProc - name of the currently executing procedure
  ' Returns   : Nothing
  '

  gintERH_Pointer_TSB = gintERH_Pointer_TSB + 1

  If gintERH_Pointer_TSB <= ERH_MAXITEMS_TSB Then
    gaERH_Stack_TSB(gintERH_Pointer_TSB) = strProc
  Else
    gaERH_Stack_TSB(gintERH_Pointer_TSB + 2) = strProc
  End If

End Sub
```

The code adds the name of the procedure to the gaERH Stack_TSB array. The ERH_PopStack_TSB subroutine, shown in Listing 16.26, is executed in the exit code for each procedure.

LISTING 16.26 The ERH_PopStack_TSB Function Removes the Error from the Stack

```
Sub ERH_PopStack_TSB()
  ' Comments  : Pops the current procedure name off the error handling stack
  ' Parameters: None
  ' Returns   : Nothing
  '

  If gintERH_Pointer_TSB <= ERH_MAXITEMS_TSB Then
    gaERH_Stack_TSB(gintERH_Pointer_TSB) = ""
  End If

  gintERH_Pointer_TSB = gintERH_Pointer_TSB - 1

  If gintERH_Pointer_TSB < 0 Then
    gintERH_Pointer_TSB = 0
  End If

End Sub
```

The ERH_PopStack_TSB subroutine removes the text in the largest array element.

Error Handling: Preparing for the Inevitable

CHAPTER 16

737

16

ERROR HANDLING:
PREPARING FOR
THE INEVITABLE

> **NOTE**
>
> The `ERH_PushStack_TSB` and `ERH_PullStack_TSB` subroutines are found in the FMS SourceBook library. For more information about the FMS SourceBook, see Chapter 32.

As the code goes in and out of routines, entries are added to and then removed from the array. Because the array is Public, you can review its contents at any time. Notice in Func3 in Listing 16.24 that the error handler iterates through the array, pulling out the error information.

Building a Custom Error Handler Class

Implementing error handling within an application can be very tedious, especially if you attempt to place specific error-handling logic in each routine that you write. Although implementing a generic error handler does not mandate the use of a class module, using a class module greatly facilitates the process of implementing error handling within your applications. Listing 6.27 illustrates this point.

LISTING 16.27 An Example of an Access Subroutine

```
Sub AnySub2()
'Declare constant with the name of the routine
Const SUBNAME As String = "AnySub"

'Invoke error handling
On Error GoTo AnySub2_Err

    'Beginning of any routine
    MsgBox "This is the rest of your code...."

    'Oops! Something causes an error!
    Err.Raise 11

    'Code after the error
    MsgBox "We are Past the Error!!"

AnySub2_Exit:
    'Generic exit point for routine
    Exit Sub

AnySub2_Err:
    Dim intAction As Integer
```

LISTING 16.27   Continued

```
    'Instantiate the error handler class
    Set gobjErrorHandler = New ErrorHandler

    'Execute the ErrorProcess method,
    'passing the error information
    intAction = gobjErrorHandler.ErrorProcess(ModuleName, _
        SUBNAME, Err.Number, Err.Description)

    'Evaluate return value to determine what action to take
    Select Case intAction
        Case ERR_CONTINUE
            Resume Next
        Case ERR_RETRY
            Resume
        Case ERR_EXIT
            Resume AnySub2_Exit
        Case ERR_QUIT
            Quit
    End Select
End Sub
```

When an error occurs, the ErrorHandler class is instantiated. The Initialize event of the class executes, as shown in Listing 16.28.

LISTING 16.28   The Initialize Event of the ErrorHandler Class

```
Private Sub Class_Initialize()
    'Place user name into private variable
    mstrUsername = CurrentUser

    'Place current date and time into private variable
    mdatDateTime = Now
End Sub
```

The Initialize event of the class sets the module-level variables mstrUserName and mdatDateTime equal to the CurrentUser and the current date and time, respectively. The Username and DateTime properties of the class use these variables.

The ErrorProcess method of the ErrorHandler class is then executed. It appears in Listing 16.29.

Error Handling: Preparing for the Inevitable

CHAPTER 16

739

16

ERROR HANDLING:
PREPARING FOR
THE INEVITABLE

LISTING 16.29   The `ErrorProcess` Method of the `ErrorHandler` Class Logs the Error and Then Takes Appropriate Action in Response to the Error

```
Public Function ErrorProcess(strRoutine As String, _
    strModule As String, _
    lngErrorNumber As Long, _
    strErrorMessage As String) As Integer

    'Store error information into module-level variables
    mstrRoutine = strRoutine
    mstrModule = strModule
    mlngErrorNumber = lngErrorNumber
    mstrErrorMessage = strErrorMessage

    'Log error
    Call LogError

    'Locate the error number in tblErrors to
    'determine how you should respond to the error
    Dim rst As ADODB.Recordset
    Set rst = New ADODB.Recordset
    rst.Open "Select Response from tblErrors Where ErrorNum = " &
lngErrorNumber, _
        CurrentProject.Connection, adOpenStatic

    'If the error number that occurred is not found
    'in tblErrors, display the error form and return
    'ERR_QUIT to the problem routine
    If rst.EOF Then
        DoCmd.OpenForm "frmError2", WindowMode:=acDialog, _
            OpenArgs:="ErrorHandler"
        ErrorProcess = ERR_QUIT

    'If the error is in tblErrors, evaluate the contents of
    'the Response field. Respond appropriately, displaying the appropriate
    'form and returning the appropriate value to the offending routine
    Else
        Select Case rst!Response
            Case ERR_QUIT
                DoCmd.OpenForm "frmError2", WindowMode:=acDialog, _
                    OpenArgs:="Critical Error:  Application will Terminate"
                ErrorProcess = ERR_QUIT
            Case ERR_RETRY
                ErrorProcess = ERR_RETRY
            Case ERR_EXIT
                DoCmd.OpenForm "frmError2", WindowMode:=acDialog, _
```

LISTING 16.29   Continued

```
                OpenArgs:="Severe Error:  Processing Did Not Complete"
            ErrorProcess = ERR_EXIT
        Case ERR_CONTINUE
            ErrorProcess = ERR_CONTINUE
      End Select
   End If

End Function
```

The routine first sets the `ModuleName`, `Routine`, `ErrorMessage`, and `ErrorNumber` variables within the class to the values of the parameters passed to the `ErrorProcess` method. The `Property Get` routines for the ModuleName, Routine, ErrorMessage, and ErrorNumber properties appear in Listing 16.30. Because we only want the properties to be set via the `ErrorProcess` method, no `Property Let` routines exist.

LISTING 16.30   The `Property Get` Routines of the Class Are Responsible for Manipulating Error Information

```
Public Property Get ModuleName() As String
    ModuleName = mstrModule
End Property

Public Property Get Routine() As String
    Routine = mstrRoutine
End Property

Public Property Get ErrorMessage() As String
    ErrorMessage = mstrErrorMessage
End Property

Public Property Get ErrorNumber() As Integer
    ErrorNumber = mlngErrorNumber
End Property

Public Property Get UserName() As String
    UserName = mstrUsername
End Property

Public Property Get DateTime() As Date
    DateTime = mdatDateTime
End Property
```

As you can see, the `Property Get` routines retrieve the values from their associated module-level variables.

Error Handling: Preparing for the Inevitable

CHAPTER 16

741

16

ERROR HANDLING:
PREPARING FOR
THE INEVITABLE

Next, the function calls a routine that logs the error that occurred. This LogError routine is shown in Listing 16.31. The LogError routine utilizes ADO code to add a record to the tblErrorLog table. The record contains all the information about the error that occurred. Notice that the error information is retrieved from the module level variables populated by the ErrorHandler class's ErrorProcess method.

After the error is logged, the number of the error that occurred is looked up in the tblErrors table. If it is not found in the tblErrors table, a form is displayed, containing all the critical information about the error that occurred. The value contained in the constant ERR_QUIT is returned from the ErrorHandler function. If the error number is found in the tblErrors table, the value contained in the Response field is evaluated. If it is the value contained in the constant ERR_QUIT, the frmError form is displayed, and the value in the constant ERR_QUIT is returned from the ErrorHandler method. If the Response field contains the value of the ERR_RETRY constant, that value is returned from the method, without the frmError form being displayed. If the Response field contains the value associated with the ERR_EXIT constant, the frmError form is displayed, and the ERR_EXIT value is returned from the ErrorHandler method. Finally, if the value in the Response field is the value associated with the ERR_CON-TINUE constant, no error information is displayed, and the ERR_CONTINUE value is returned from the ErrorHandler method.

LISTING 16.31   The LogError Subroutine Uses ADO Code to Add the Error Information to tblErrorLog

```
Sub LogError()

    'Declare a Connection object
    Dim cnn As ADODB.Connection
    Dim strSQL As String

    'Point the Connection object at the connection
    'associated with the current project
    Set cnn = CurrentProject.Connection

    'Build a SQL statement that inserts error information
    'into the tblErrorLog table
    strSQL = "INSERT INTO tblErrorLog ( ErrorDate, ErrorTime, UserName,
ErrorNum, ErrorString, ModuleName, RoutineName) "
    strSQL = strSQL & "Select #" & Me.DateTime & "#, #" _
                            & Me.DateTime & "#, '" _
                            & Me.UserName & "', " _
                            & Me.ErrorNumber & ", '" _
                            & Me.ErrorMessage & "', '" _
```

LISTING 16.31   Continued

```
                                 & Me.ModuleName & "', '" _
                                 & Me.Routine & "'"

    'Execute the SQL statement
    cnn.Execute strSQL, , adExecuteNoRecords

End Sub
```

All the code contained in the `ErrorHandler` class is similar to that contained in the basErrorHandler module. The code has been modified so that it is implemented using properties and methods of a `Class` object.

The other code that is changed to utilize classes is the code behind the error form. Listing 16.32 shows the load event of the error form.

LISTING 16.32   The `Form_Load` Event Is Modified to Call Methods of the Appropriate Classes

```
Private Sub Form_Load()

    Dim objSys As SystemInformation
    Set objSys = New SystemInformation

    'Call routine to obtain system information
    Call objSys.GetSysInfo(Me)

    'Call routine to obtain error information
    Call gobjErrorHandler.GetErrorInfo(Me)

    'If FormCaption property contains a value, use the
    'value as the caption for the form
    If Not IsNull(Me.OpenArgs) Then
        Me.lblAction.Caption = Me.OpenArgs
    End If
End Sub
```

Notice that instead of calling the `GetSysInfo` function and the `GetErrorInfo` function, the load event executes the `GetSysInfo` method of the `SystemInformation` object and the `GetErrorInfo` method of the `ErrorHandler` object.

The `GetSystemInfo` function and associated declarations were moved to a SystemInformation class. No other changes were made to the code.

The `GetErrorInfo` function was moved to the `ErrorHandler` class and modified as shown in Listing 16.33.

LISTING 16.33   The GetErrorInfo method of the `ErrorHandler` Class Retrieves Properties of the Class

```
Sub GetErrorInfo(frmAny As Form)
    'Populate form controls with error information
    'contained in the type  variable
    frmAny.lblErrorNumber.Caption = Me.ErrorNumber
    frmAny.lblErrorString.Caption = Me.ErrorMessage
    frmAny.lblUserName.Caption = Me.UserName
    frmAny.lblDateTime.Caption = Format(Me.DateTime, "c")
    frmAny.lblModuleName.Caption = Me.ModuleName
    frmAny.lblRoutineName.Caption = Me.Routine
End Sub
```

Notice that instead of using a type structure, the code references its own properties. The `Private` variables associated with these properties were set by the `ErrorProcess` method of the class.

Working with Error Events

Every form and report contains an error event procedure. This event is triggered by any interface or Jet Database Engine error. It is not triggered by a programming error made by the Access developer.

Errors often occur in the interface of a form or report, as well as in the Jet Database Engine. A user might try to enter an order for a customer who doesn't exist, for example. Instead of displaying Access's default error message, you might want to intercept and handle the error in a particular way.

After an error occurs within a form, its error event is triggered. In Listing 16.34, you can see `Sub Form_Error`. It contains two parameters. The first parameter is the number of the error. The second is the way you want to respond to the error. The error number is an Access-generated number.

This code, which is located in the frmOrders form in the CHAP16EX.MDB database, tests to see whether a referential integrity error has occurred. If it has, a message box asks whether the user wants to add the customer. If the user answers Yes, the customer form is displayed.

LISTING 16.34   Viewing Sub Form_Error From the Form frmOrders

```
Private Sub Form_Error(DataErr As Integer, Response As Integer)
    Dim intAnswer As Integer
    If DataErr = 3201 Then  'Referential Integrity Error
        intAnswer = MsgBox("Customer Does Not Exist... _
                Would You Like to Add Them Now", vbYesNo)
        If intAnswer = vbYes Then
            DoCmd.OpenForm "frmCustomer", , , , acAdd, acDialog
        End If
    End If
    Response = acDataErrContinue
End Sub
```

> **CAUTION**
>
> Be aware that the code in Listing 16.34 only traps referential integrity errors. It does not handle any other error.

The Response = acDataErrContinue line is very important. It instructs Access to continue the code execution without displaying the standard error message. The other option for Response is AcDataErrDisplay. It tells Access to display the default error message.

Creating a List of Error Codes and Descriptions

Many people ask me how to create a list of error numbers and descriptions. The code in Listing 16.35 creates a table of all the errors that can occur in your VBA code, with a description of what each error number means. You can copy this code into any module and run it.

LISTING 16.35   Code That Creates a Table of Errors and Descriptions

```
Sub CreateErrorsTable()
    Dim cnn As ADODB.Connection
    Dim rst As New ADODB.Recordset
    Dim lngCode As Long
    Const conAppObjectError = "Application-defined or object-defined error"

    Set cnn = CurrentProject.Connection
    ' Open recordset on Errors table.
    rst.Open "tblErrorMessages", cnn, adOpenStatic, adLockOptimistic
    ' Loop through first 10000 Visual Basic error codes.
    For lngCode = 1 To 10000
```

Error Handling: Preparing for the Inevitable

CHAPTER 16

745

16

ERROR HANDLING:
PREPARING FOR
THE INEVITABLE

LISTING 16.35   Continued

```
        On Error Resume Next
        ' Raise each error.
        Err.Raise lngCode
        DoCmd.Hourglass True
        ' Skip error codes that generate application or object-defined errors.
        If Err.Description <> conAppObjectError Then
            ' Add each error code and string to Errors table.
            rst.AddNew
            rst!ErrorCode = Err.Number
            rst!ErrorString = Err.Description
            rst.Update
        End If
        ' Clear Err object.
        Err.Clear
    Next lngCode
    ' Close recordset.
    rst.Close
    DoCmd.Hourglass False
    MsgBox "Errors table created."
End Sub
```

The code opens a recordset based on the tblErrorMessages table. It loops through from 1 to 10000, raising an error with each number. Each time through the loop, it appends the error number and the associated error description to the tblErrorMessages table.

PRACTICAL EXAMPLES

Incorporating Error Handling

Error-handling code should be added throughout the applications that you build. The following example shows you how to incorporate a generic error handler into the hypothetical Time and Billing application.

The Time and Billing application contains a routine called GetCompanyInfo. This routine reads all the company information from the tblCompanyInfo table. The information is read from the public class instance, as needed, while the application is running. This routine, like any routine, has the potential for error. The original routine has been modified to incorporate the generic error handler, as shown in Listing 16.36.

LISTING 16.36   Incorporating the Generic Error Handler into Your Code

```
Sub GetCompanyInfo()
    Dim strSubName As String
    Dim rst As ADODB.Recordset
```

LISTING 16.36   Continued

```
'Declare constant with the name of the routine
Const SUBNAME As String = "GetCompanyInfo"

'Invoke error handling
On Error GoTo GetCompanyInfo_Err

'Instantiate the CompanyInformation class
Set gobjCompanyInfo = New CompanyInformation
Set rst = New ADODB.Recordset

'Open a recordset based on the tblCompanyInfo table
rst.Open "tblCompanyInfo", CurrentProject.Connection

'Populate the properties of the public class instance
'with values from the tblCompanyInfo table
With gobjCompanyInfo
    .SetupID = rst!SetupID
    .CompanyName = rst!CompanyName
    .Address = rst!Address
    .City = rst!City
    .StateProvince = rst!StateProvince
    .PostalCode = rst!PostalCode
    .Country = rst!Country
    .PhoneNumber = rst!PhoneNumber
    .FaxNumber = rst!PhoneNumber
End With

rst.Close

GetCompanyInfo_Exit:
    'Generic exit point for routine
    Exit Sub

GetCompanyInfo_Err:
    Dim intAction As Integer

    'Instantiate the error handler class
    Set gobjErrorHandler = New ErrorHandler

    'Execute the ErrorProcess method,
    'passing the error information
    intAction = gobjErrorHandler.ErrorProcess(ModuleName, _
        SUBNAME, Err.Number, Err.Description)
```

Error Handling: Preparing for the Inevitable

CHAPTER 16

747

16

ERROR HANDLING:
PREPARING FOR
THE INEVITABLE

LISTING 16.36   Continued

```
    'Evaluate return value to determine what action to take
    Select Case intAction
        Case ERR_CONTINUE
            Resume Next
        Case ERR_RETRY
            Resume
        Case ERR_EXIT
            Resume GetCompanyInfo_Exit
        Case ERR_QUIT
            Quit
    End Select
End Sub
```

Notice the On Error Goto statement at the beginning of the routine and that the local constant SUBNAME is declared and set equal to GetCompanyInfo. The generic error handler uses the value in the constant to display the routine within which the error occurred. The error handler GetCompanyInfo_Err instantiates the ErrorHandler class. It executes the ErrorProcess method of the class and then evaluates its return value.

Summary

In this chapter, you learned the alternatives for handling errors in your Access applications. This chapter covered how you can use the error event to trap for application and Jet Engine errors in forms and reports. You also learned how to use the On Error statement. Finally, you learned how to build a generic error system. Regardless of the amount of testing done on an application, errors will occur. It is important that you properly trap for those errors.

Optimizing Your Application

IN THIS CHAPTER

Why This Chapter Is Important

In a world where it is often difficult for hardware to keep up with software, it is important to do everything you can to improve the performance of your application. This chapter helps you optimize your application's speed and reduce its memory and hard disk space requirements.

Introducing Optimization

Optimization is the process of reviewing your operating environment, VBA code, application objects, and data structures to ensure that they are providing optimum performance. In a nutshell, optimization is the process of making your application leaner and meaner.

Users become frustrated when an application runs slowly. In fact, if a user is not warned about a slow process, he often will reboot or shut down the power on the machine while a process is running. This can have dire results on the integrity of the data.

TIP
To help reduce the chance of users rebooting the computer during a lengthy process, it generally is a good idea to provide them with some sort of indication that a process will take a while. You can do this by using a message box that appears before processing begins, or by providing a status bar or progress meter that shows the progress of the task being completed.

You can do many things to optimize an application's performance, ranging from using a front-end tool such as the Performance Analyzer to fastidiously adhering to certain coding techniques. This chapter highlights the major things you can do to optimize the performance of your applications.

Modifying Hardware and Software Configurations

The Access *environment* refers to the combination of hardware and software configurations under which Microsoft Access runs. These environmental settings can greatly affect the performance of an Access application.

The easiest way to improve an application's performance is to upgrade its hardware and software configuration. This form of optimization requires no direct intervention from the developer. Plus, a side benefit of most of the environmental changes you can make is that any improvements made to the environment are beneficial to users in all their Windows applications.

Improving the environment involves more than just adding some RAM. It also can mean optimally configuring the operating system and the Access application.

Hardware, Hardware, More Hardware, Please!

The bottom line is that Windows 95, Windows 98, Windows NT, and Access 2002 all crave hardware—the more, the better. The faster your users' machines are, and the more memory they have, the better your applications will run. Obtaining additional hardware might not be the least expensive solution, but it certainly is the quickest and easiest thing you can do to improve the performance of your application.

RAM, RAM—That's All I Need!

Memory is what Access craves most, whether you are running under the full version of Microsoft Access or using the runtime version of the product. Microsoft Access requires 32MB of RAM just to run under Windows 98 and 64MB of RAM to run under Windows 2000. These minimums are considered Access' standard operating environments. Although 32MB of RAM is required, the recommended RAM is even higher. Both requirements for Windows 98 and Windows 2000 can climb dramatically if your user is running other applications or if your application uses OLE automation to communicate with other applications. Put in a very straightforward way, the more RAM you and the users of your application have, the better. RAM measuring 128MB is a great environment for Access 2002. In fact, if every one of your users has at least 128MB of RAM, you can stop reading this chapter because everything else covered here is going to provide you with minor benefits compared to adding more RAM. If you are like most of us, though, meaning that not every one of your users has a Pentium III 666Mhz with 512MB of RAM, read on.

> **NOTE**
>
> Developers should have a bare minimum of 128MB of RAM installed on their machines. Remember that this is a minimum! Most developers agree that 256MB of RAM or more is ideal if you intend to do any serious development work, especially if you plan to develop client/server or Internet/intranet applications.

Defragment Your User's Hard Disk

As your computer writes information to disk, it attempts to find contiguous space on which to place data files. As the hard disk fills up, files are placed in fragmented pieces on the hard disk. Each time your application attempts to read data and programs, it must locate the information scattered over the disk. This is a very time-consuming process. It therefore is helpful to defragment the hard disk on which the application and data tables are stored, using a utility such as the Disk Defragmenter that ships with Windows 95, 98, and Windows 2000.

TIP

The process of defragmenting a hard disk easily can be automated by using the System Agent, which is included as part of the Microsoft Plus! Pack. This package is sold as an add-on to Windows 95. The System Agent is a useful tool that enables you to schedule when and how often the defragmentation process occurs. Windows 98 ships with the Maintenance Wizard, which is used to schedule various system tasks to run automatically, such as the Disk Defragmenter and the ScanDisk utility. Windows 2000 ships with a very basic defragmenter utility. If you are using Windows NT or Windows 2000, numerous third-party tools can assist you with the process of automating the defragmentation process.

Compact Your Database

Just as the operating system fragments your files over time, Access itself introduces its own form of fragmentation. Each time you add and modify data, your database grows. The problem is that, when you delete data or objects within your database, it does not shrink. Instead, Access leaves empty pages available in which new data will be placed. The problem is that these empty pages are not necessarily filled with data. The empty space can be freed using the Compact utility, included in the Microsoft Access software. The compact utility frees this excess space and attempts to make all data pages contiguous. You should compact your database frequently, especially if records or database objects (for example, forms and reports) are regularly added and deleted. The Compact utility can be accessed only when no database is open. Choose Tools|Database Utilities. Then choose the Compact and Repair Database option.

NOTE

It is worth noting that, if you plan to distribute an Access application to other users, possibly via the runtime module, it is a good idea to include some means of compacting the database. The runtime module does not allow access to the Compact menu item. The CompactDatabase method enables you to compact a database from within an Access database, but you cannot call this command from within the current application. A second application must be created to use the CompactDatabase method on the original application.

Don't Use Compressed Drives

Regardless of the compression utility you are using, disk compression will significantly degrade performance with Access 2002.

Tune Virtual Memory: Tweak the Swap File

Although Windows 95, Windows 98, Windows NT, and Windows 2000 attempt to manage virtual memory on their own, you might find it useful to provide them with some additional advice. To modify the physical location of the swap file under Windows 95 and Windows 98, right-click My Computer. Choose Properties and then select the Performance tab. Click the Virtual Memory button. Under Windows 2000, right-click My Computer, choose Properties, and click the Advanced tab. Then click Performance Options and Change. It might be useful to move the swap file to a faster disk drive or a drive connected to a separate controller card. Any changes you make might adversely affect performance. It is important that you evaluate whether any changes you make will help the situation—or, perhaps, make things worse! In general, it is advisable to let Windows dynamically manage the size of the swap file unless the system is running very low on disk space.

17

OPTIMIZING YOUR
APPLICATION

> **TIP**
>
> If Access 2002 or Windows is running on a compressed drive, you can improve performance by moving the swap file to an uncompressed drive. If possible, the swap file should be located on a drive or partition solely dedicated to the swap file, or on a drive or partition that is accessed rarely by other applications. This helps to ensure that the entire swap file remains in a contiguous location on a disk.

Run Access and Your Application Locally

In Chapter 20, "Developing Multiuser and Enterprise Applications," you will learn that it is best to install both the Access software and your application objects on each user's local machine. Only the data tables should be stored on a network file server. Otherwise, you will be sending DLLs, OLE objects, help files, type libraries, executables, and database objects all over the network wire.

> **TIP**
>
> One very viable option is to run Access 2002 using Windows 2000 Terminal Services. In this scenario, Access is installed on a very powerful server machine running Windows 2000 Server Terminal Services. Workstations connect to the terminal server using the

Terminal Services Client utility. No data travels over the network wire. Each user becomes a session running on the server machine. All processing is done on the server machine. Keystrokes and mouse movements are sent from the client machine to the server, which processes them and sends a screen image back to the client.

Do Everything You Can to Make Windows Itself Faster

It always amuses me that the users with the slowest machines and the least memory have the most accessories running. These accessories include multimedia, fancy wallpapers, and other nifty utilities. If performance is a problem, you might try to see whether eliminating some of the frivolous niceties improves the performance of your application. If it does, encourage the user to eliminate the frills, get more memory, or accept your application's performance. Furthermore, if you are finished using other applications, such as Microsoft Excel, close them. This frees up system memory for Access.

Another tip to make Windows 95 and Windows 98 run faster is to shut down and restart on a regular basis. Memory tends to get fragmented, making applications run more slowly. Although I can go weeks or months in Windows NT or Windows 2000 without rebooting, I find it beneficial to reboot my Windows 95 and Windows 98 machines a couple of times a day.

Change Access's Software Settings

In addition to the more obvious measures just outlined, some minor software tweaking can go a long way toward improving performance. Adjusting several settings in the Windows registry can dramatically improve performance. These changes all involve the registry's ISAM section. The properties you might want to change include `MaxBufferSize` and `ReadAheadPages`. Both these settings determine how the Jet Engine uses memory.

`MaxBufferSize` controls the maximum size of the Jet Engine's internal cache. By default, it is set to optimize performance on most machines. It does this by reading data in 2KB pages, placing the data in a memory cache. The data in the cache is readily available to forms, reports, tables, and queries. Lowering the value for `MaxBufferSize` frees memory for other tasks. This might be helpful on a machine with a minimum memory configuration.

`ReadAheadPages` controls the number of 4KB data pages that the Jet Engine reads ahead when performing sequential page reads. This number can range from 0–31, with the default at 16. The higher the number, the more efficient Access is at reading ahead so that data is available when you need it. The lower this number, the more memory is freed up for other tasks.

As you configure any of these settings, remember that what is good for one machine is not necessarily good for the next. The settings for each machine must be optimized with its unique hardware configuration in mind.

What Jet 3.5 Did to Improve Performance

Specific improvements that appeared with Jet 3.5 (Access 97) include the following:

- Faster delete operations. Portions of a page can be removed at once, instead of having to be removed row by row.
- Better multiuser concurrency on indexed columns. More users can read and update indexed columns without experiencing locking conflicts; indexed columns no longer contain read locks.
- Implicit transaction processing. Whereas many people wrapped processing loops in the BeginTrans...CommitTrans construct in earlier versions of Access to limit the number of disk writes, the Jet 3.5 Engine handled this quite well on its own.
- Large queries run faster. This is because of improvements in the transactional behavior for SQL data manipulation language (DML) statements as well as new registry settings that force transactions to commit when a certain lock threshold is reached.
- Queries containing the inequality operator (<>) run faster.
- Sequential reads are faster. Up to 64K of disk space can be allocated at a time.
- Temporary queries run faster.
- Deleting a table is faster when you use SQL DROP or SQL DELETE.
- The amount of space occupied by indexes is reduced.
- When you compact a database, all indexes are optimized for performance.
- Improved page allocation mechanism. This better ensures that data from a table is stored on adjacent pages and improves the read-ahead capability.
- Dynamically configured cache. The cache is configured at startup based on the amount of system memory available and contains the most recently used data, thereby enhancing performance.
- ISAM support for HTML files.
- The MaxLocksPerFile registry setting enables you to force records to commit when a certain lock threshold is hit. This speeds up the completion of large queries when data is stored on NetWare- and Windows NT–based servers.

Understanding What Jet 4.0 Does to Improve Performance

Improvements made to the Jet 4.0 Engine, which is included with Access 2000 and Access 2002, have dramatically improved its performance over that of its predecessors. Some of these improvements appeared with the Jet 3.0 Engine that shipped with Access 95 or the Jet 3.5

Engine that shipped with Access 97, but many are new to Jet 4.0. The Jet 4.0 Engine is thoroughly 32-bit. It takes advantage of multiple execution threads, providing significant performance benefits.

The following are improvements introduced in Jet 4.0:

- Data page size is now 4KB instead of 2KB. This increases the maximum database size from 1.07GB to 2.14GB, and provides better performance for many operations because of a decrease in I/O.

- The native OLEDB Provider offers superior performance to ODBC data.

- The first 255 characters of memo fields can be indexed. This significantly improves performance when searching and sorting memo fields.

Letting the Performance Analyzer Determine Problem Areas

You can do many things to improve the performance of an application. Most of them require significant attention and expertise on your part. The Performance Analyzer is a tool that does some of that work for you. This tool analyzes the design of an Access application in order to suggest techniques you can use to improve the application's performance. Many of the techniques the Performance Analyzer suggests can be implemented automatically.

To use the Performance Analyzer, choose Tools|Analyze|Performance. The dialog box in Figure 17.1 appears.

FIGURE 17.1

The Performance Analyzer dialog box.

Select the individual tables, queries, forms, reports, macros, modules, and relationships you want the Performance Analyzer to scrutinize. If you want Access to analyze the relationships, you must click the Current Database tab and then select Relationships. Make all your selections and click OK. When the Performance Analyzer completes the analysis process, the second part of Performance Analyzer dialog box appears, as shown in Figure 17.2. This window provides you with a list of suggested improvements to the selected objects. The results are broken down into Recommendations, Suggestions, Ideas, and Items (meaning items that were automatically fixed). Suggested improvements will include enhancements such as the addition of an index or the conversion of an OLE object. After analyzing the Northwind database that ships with Access, for example, the Performance Analyzer suggested that fewer controls should be placed on the Employees form.

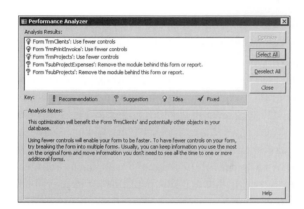

FIGURE 17.2
The second part of the Performance Analyzer dialog box.

Designing Tables to Optimize Performance

Now that you have seen the changes you can make to your environment to improve performance, take a look at the changes you can make to your data structures to optimize performance. Such changes include eliminating redundant data, using indexes, selecting appropriate field data types, and using various query techniques.

Tweaking the data structure is imperative for good performance. No matter what else you do, poor data design can dramatically degrade the performance of your application. All other optimization attempts are futile without proper attention to this area.

Days and days can be spent optimizing your data. These changes must be well thought out and carefully analyzed. Changes often are made over time as problems are identified. Such changes can include those in the following sections.

Why Be Normal?

In essence, "be normal" means normalize your tables—that is, consolidate common data in related tables. Processing the same data that appears in multiple places can significantly slow down your application. This is due to both the volume of data that is generated, as well as the need to update all copies of the data whenever the data changes. Suppose a company address appears in both the Customer table and the Orders table. If the company address changes, it must be changed in both the Customer table and in the Orders table. This information should be included only in the Customer table. Queries should be used to combine the address and order data when needed.

I Thought You Just Told Me to Normalize

When it comes to performance, unfortunately, there are no hard-and-fast rules. Although, most of the time, you gain performance by normalizing your data structure, denormalizing your structure can help at times. This generally is the case when you find yourself creating a particular join over and over again. Another example is an accounting application in which you need to be able to readily see the total amount that a customer owes. Rather than evaluating all the open invoices each time you move to a customer record, you can store the total amount that the customer owes on the customer record. Of course, this requires that you update the summarized figure whenever the customer is billed or makes a payment. In summary, you can try denormalizing the data to see whether dramatic performance improvements result. Remember that denormalization has definite downsides regarding data integrity and maintenance.

Index, Index, Index!

It is amazing how far an index can go in improving performance. Any fields or combination of fields on which you search should be included in an index. You should create indexes for all columns used in query joins, searches, and sorts. You should create primary key indexes rather than unique indexes, and unique indexes rather than non-unique indexes. It is not necessary to create an index for the foreign key field in a one-to-many relationship. The index is created automatically by Access when the relationship is established. Furthermore, there is no benefit to creating an index on a field containing highly repetitive data. An example is a state field in a customer table where all the customers are located in one of two states. Although indexes can be overused, when used properly, the performance improvements rendered by indexes are profound.

CAUTION

Although indexes can dramatically improve performance, you should not create an index for every field in a table. Indexes do have their downside. Besides taking up disk space, they also slow down the process of adding, editing, and deleting data.

> **TIP**
>
> In a multiple-field index, index on as few fields as possible. Searching through multiple-field indexes can dramatically degrade performance.

> **NOTE**
>
> Client/server optimization strategies are covered in detail in *Alison Balter's Mastering Access 2002 Enterprise Development*.

Select the Correct Data Type

When defining a field, select the shortest data type available for the storage of the data. If you will be storing a code between 1 and 10 within the field, for example, there is no reason to select Double for a numeric field.

Designing Queries to Optimize Performance

Optimizing your queries requires a great deal of practice and experimentation. Some queries involving a one-to-many relationship run more efficiently if the criteria is placed on the one side of the relationship, for example. Others run more efficiently if the criteria are placed on the many side. Understanding some basics can go a long way toward improving the performance of your queries and your application as a whole, as listed in the following:

- Include as few columns in the resultset as possible.
- Try to reduce the number of complex expressions contained in the query. Although including a complex expression in a query eliminates the need to build the expression into each form and report, the performance benefits gained sometimes are worth the trouble.
- Use the Between operator rather than greater than (>) and less than (<) operators.
- Use Count(*) rather than Count([column]).
- Group Totals queries by the field that is in the same table you are totaling. In other words, if you are totaling cost multiplied by price for each order in the Order Detail table, group by the order ID within the Order Detail table, not by the order ID within the Orders table.

Now that you have seen what you can do with the design of your queries to improve performance, take a look at a couple simple techniques you can use to improve the performance of your queries.

A simple but often neglected method of optimizing queries is to deliver your queries compiled. A query compiles when you open it in Datasheet view and then simply close it. If you modify a query and then save it, it is not compiled until the query runs. All queries are compiled when you compact a database. Delivering precompiled queries ensures that they run as quickly as possible. It is therefore a good idea to compact a database before you distribute it to your users.

Finally, it is important that you compile your queries using the same amount of data that your application will contain. This is because Jet's Query Optimizer optimizes the query differently, depending on the amount of data it finds. If you build a query using 100 records that will run on a live table containing 100,000 records, the query will not be optimized properly. You must rerun and resave your query using the correct quantity of data if you want the query to be optimized properly, or compact the database after the live data has been entered.

Making Coding Changes to Improve Performance

No matter what you do to optimize the operating system environment and improve your data design, poor code can continue to bog you down. A properly optimized application is optimized in terms of the environment, data design, and code. Just as poor table design can degrade performance, poor coding techniques also can have a dramatic negative effect on performance. Changes to your code include eliminating variants and dead code, using built-in collections, and using specific object types. An important code-related optimization is to deliver your modules precompiled.

The following changes and techniques can aid in the improvement of performance. It is important to recognize that any one change won't make much of a difference. However, an accumulation of all the changes, especially where code is being re-executed in a loop, can make a significant impact on your application's performance.

Eliminate Variants and Use the Smallest Data Type Possible

Variant variables are the slowest for the operating system to process; they carry a lot of overhead because they are resolved at runtime. Remember that this statement declares a variant type of variable:

```
Dim intCounter
```

To strong-type this variable as an integer, for example, your code must be modified to look like this:

```
Dim intCounter As Integer
```

Not only should you strong-type your variables, but you also should use the smallest data type possible. Remember that data types such as Boolean, Byte, Integer, and Long are the smallest and therefore the fastest to resolve. These are followed by Single, Double, Currency, and (finally) Variant. Of course, if you must store very large numbers with decimal points in a variable, you cannot pick Single. Just keep in mind that it is wise to select the smallest data type appropriate for the use of the variable. Listing 17.1 provides code that illustrates the difference between using a variant and a long integer.

LISTING 17.1   Data Type Benchmark

```
Private Sub cmdVariantBenchMark_Click()
    Dim vntAny
    Dim intCounter As Long
    Dim dblStartTime As Double
    Dim dblTime1 As Double
    Dim dblTime2 As Double

    'Execute loop with variant
    dblStartTime = Timer

    Do Until vntAny = 500000
        vntAny = vntAny + 1
    Loop

    dblTime1 = Timer - dblStartTime

    'Execute loop with integer
    dblStartTime = Timer

    Do Until intCounter = 500000
        intCounter = intCounter + 1
    Loop

    dblTime2 = Timer - dblStartTime

    'Display time and percent differences
    Me.txtSlow = dblTime1
    Me.txtOptimized = dblTime2
    Me.txtPercent = (1 - (dblTime1 / dblTime2)) * 100

End Sub
```

The code, found in the form frmBenchmark in the Chap17Ex.mdb sample database, loops using a variant, and then a long integer. The amount of time required to execute each loop is displayed, along with the percent difference between the two techniques.

Use Specific Object Types

Just as using the General variant data type is inefficient, using generic object variables also is inefficient. This is because the compiler needs to evaluate their type at runtime. The MakeItBold subroutine uses a generic object variable, as shown in Listing 17.2.

LISTING 17.2   The MakeItBold Subroutine

```
Private Sub cmdMakeBold_Click()
    Call MakeItBold(Screen.PreviousControl)
End Sub

Sub MakeItBold(ctlAny As Control)
    ctlAny.FontBold = True
End Sub
```

On the other hand, the SpecificBold subroutine uses a specific object variable, as Listing 17.3 shows.

LISTING 17.3   The SpecificBold Subroutine

```
Private Sub cmdSpecificBold_Click()
    Call SpecificBold(Screen.PreviousControl)
End Sub

Sub SpecificBold(txtAny As TextBox)
    txtAny.FontBold = True
End Sub
```

The difference is that the SpecificBold routine expects to receive only text boxes. It does not need to resolve the type of object it receives and therefore is more efficient.

 This code is contained in the CHAP17EX.MDB database on the accompanying CD-ROM. You can find the example in frmObjVar.

The best way to truly compare using a specific control versus a generic control is to benchmark the techniques, as shown in Listing 17.4.

LISTING 17.4   Object Type Benchmark

```
Private Sub cmdObjectTypes_Click()
    Dim intCounter As Long
    Dim dblStartTime As Double
    Dim dblTime1 As Double
    Dim dblTime2 As Double

    'Execute loop with generic control
    dblStartTime = Timer

    For intCounter = 1 To 5000
        Call MakeItBold(Me.txtOptimized)
    Next intCounter

    dblTime1 = Timer - dblStartTime

    'Execute loop with specific control
    dblStartTime = Timer

    For intCounter = 1 To 5000
        Call SpecificBold(Me.txtOptimized)
    Next intCounter

    dblTime2 = Timer - dblStartTime

    'Display time and percent differences
    Me.txtSlow = dblTime1
    Me.txtOptimized = dblTime2
    Me.txtPercent = (1 - (dblTime1 / dblTime2)) * 100

End Sub
```

The code, found in frmBenchmark, passes a text box to two different routines. The first routine receives any control as a parameter. The second routine receives only text boxes as a parameter. The benchmarks prove that routines that utilize specific object types take less time and therefore are more efficient.

Use Inline Code

There is a tendency to call out to procedures for everything. This is good from a maintenance standpoint but not from an efficiency standpoint. Each time VBA calls out to a procedure, additional time is taken to locate and execute the procedure. This is particularly evident when the procedure is called numerous times. The alternative is to use inline code. Executing inline code is more efficient than calling out to procedures because Access does not need to locate the code. The downside of inline code is that it is more difficult to maintain. You must decide how important maintainability is compared to speed.

Listing 17.5 shows the same code called as a routine and executed in-line. The benchmark shows that the inline code executes much more quickly.

LISTING 17.5   Inline Code Benchmark

```
Private Sub cmdInLine_Click()
    Dim dblAny As Double
    Dim intCounter As Long
    Dim dblStartTime As Double
    Dim dblTime1 As Double
    Dim dblTime2 As Double

    'Execute loop calling out to procedure
    dblStartTime = Timer

    For intCounter = 1 To 50000
        Call SmallRoutine
    Next intCounter

    dblTime1 = Timer - dblStartTime

    'Execute loop with in-line code
    dblStartTime = Timer

    For intCounter = 1 To 50000
        dblAny = 5 / 3
    Next intCounter

    dblTime2 = Timer - dblStartTime

    'Display time and percent differences
    Me.txtSlow = dblTime1
    Me.txtOptimized = dblTime2
    Me.txtPercent = (1 - (dblTime1 / dblTime2)) * 100
End Sub

Private Sub SmallRoutine()
    Dim dblAny As Double
    dblAny = 5 / 3
End Sub
```

Toggle Booleans Using Not

This code is very inefficient:

```
If bFlag = True Then
  bFlag = False
Else
    bFlag = True
End If
```

It should be modified to look like this:

```
bFlag = Not bFlag
```

Besides requiring fewer lines of code, this expression evaluates much more quickly at runtime. Listing 17.6 proves that toggling the Boolean variable is a much more efficient approach to the problem than having to test each condition separately. This code is found in frmBenchmarks on the CD-ROM accompanying this book.

LISTING 17.6   Toggling Boolean Benchmark

```
Private Sub cmdBooleans_Click()
    Dim boolAny As Boolean
    Dim intCounter As Long
    Dim dblStartTime As Double
    Dim dblTime1 As Double
    Dim dblTime2 As Double

    'Execute loop with If statement
    dblStartTime = Timer

    For intCounter = 1 To 100000
        If boolAny = True Then
            boolAny = False
        Else
            boolAny = True
        End If
    Next intCounter

    dblTime1 = Timer - dblStartTime

    'Execute loop toggling boolean
    dblStartTime = Timer
```

LISTING 17.6   Continued

```
    For intCounter = 1 To 100000
        boolAny = Not boolAny
    Next intCounter

    dblTime2 = Timer - dblStartTime

    'Display time and percent differences
    Me.txtSlow = dblTime1
    Me.txtOptimized = dblTime2
    Me.txtPercent = (1 - (dblTime1 / dblTime2)) * 100

End Sub
```

Use the Built-In Collections

The built-in collections are there whether or not you use them. By using `For Each...Next` and a collection of objects, you can write very efficient code, as shown in Listing 17.7.

LISTING 17.7   Using `For Each...Next`

```
Sub FormCaption()
   Dim frm As Form
   For Each frm In Forms
      frm.Caption = frm.Caption & " - " & CurrentUser()
   Next
End Sub
```

In this example, you use the Forms collection to quickly and efficiently loop through each form, changing the caption on its title bar. The code shown in Listing 17.8 illustrates the use of the Forms collection, as well as an alternative method of accomplishing the same task.

LISTING 17.8   `For Each...Next` Benchmark

```
Private Sub cmdCollections_Click()
    Dim frm As Form
    Dim intNumForms As Integer
    Dim intLoop As Integer
    Dim intCounter As Long
    Dim dblStartTime As Double
    Dim dblTime1 As Double
    Dim dblTime2 As Double
```

LISTING 17.8   Continued

```
    'Execute loop with For Next
    dblStartTime = Timer

    For intCounter = 1 To 50
        intNumForms = Forms.Count - 1
        For intLoop = 0 To intNumForms
            Forms(intLoop).Caption = "Hello"
        Next intLoop
    Next intCounter

    dblTime1 = Timer - dblStartTime

    'Execute loop with For Each
    dblStartTime = Timer

    For intCounter = 1 To 50
        For Each frm In Forms
            frm.Caption = "Hello"
        Next frm
    Next intCounter

    dblTime2 = Timer - dblStartTime

    'Display time and percent differences
    Me.txtSlow = dblTime1
    Me.txtOptimized = dblTime2
    Me.txtPercent = (1 - (dblTime1 / dblTime2)) * 100
End Sub
```

Without the For Each..Next loop, a variable must be used to loop through the forms. Notice that intNumForms is set equal to the number of forms in the Forms collection minus one. The loop goes from zero to the value stored in intNumForms, changing the caption of the specified form. Although the performance gains realized by using the Forms collection are not dramatic, you'll probably agree that the Forms collection technique is much simpler to implement.

Use the Len Function

Using the Len function (as shown in Listing 17.9) is more efficient than testing for a zero-length string (as shown in Listing 17.10).

LISTING 17.9   Using the Len Function

```
Sub SayNameLen(strName As String)
   If Len(strName) Then
      MsgBox strName
   End If
End Sub
```

LISTING 17.10   Testing for a Zero-Length String

```
Sub SayNameZero(strName As String)
   If strName <> "" Then
      MsgBox strName
   End If
End Sub
```

Listing 17.9 is easier for VBA to evaluate and therefore runs more quickly and efficiently. This is emphasized by the code shown in Listing 17.11 (located in frmBenchmark). The code shows two loops. One utilizes the Len function and the other does not. The benchmark proves that the routine that utilizes the Len function executes more quickly.

LISTING 17.11   Len Benchmark

```
Private Sub cmdLen_Click()
    Dim dblStartTime As Double
    Dim dblTime1 As Double
    Dim dblTime2 As Double
    Dim strTextBoxValue As String

    strTextBoxValue = Me.txtOptimized

    'Execute loop with zero-length string
    dblStartTime = Timer

    For intCounter = 1 To 50000
        If strTextBoxValue <> "" Then
        End If
    Next intCounter

    dblTime1 = Timer - dblStartTime

    'Execute loop with Len
    dblStartTime = Timer

    For intCounter = 1 To 50000
        If Len(strTextBoxValue) Then
```

Listing 17.11   Continued

```
        End If
    Next intCounter

    dblTime2 = Timer - dblStartTime

    'Display time and percent differences
    Me.txtSlow = dblTime1
    Me.txtOptimized = dblTime2
    Me.txtPercent = (1 - (dblTime1 / dblTime2)) * 100

End Sub
```

Use `True` and `False` Instead of `0`

This example is similar to the preceding one. It is better to evaluate for `True` and `False` (as shown in Listing 17.12) instead of `0` (as shown in Listing 17.13).

Listing 17.12   Evaluating for `True` and `False`

```
Sub SaySalaryTrue(lngSalary As Long)
    If lngSalary Then
        MsgBox "Salary is " & lngSalary
    End If
End Sub
```

Listing 17.13   Evaluating for `0`

```
Sub SaySalaryZero(lngSalary As Long)
    If lngSalary <> 0 Then
        MsgBox "Salary is " & lngSalary
    End If
End Sub
```

The code in Listing 17.12 runs more efficiently. The benchmark shown in Listing 17.14 provides an example. The lngSalary is evaluated against zero in the top loop. The bottom loop tests lngSalary against `True`. The second loop runs more quickly.

Listing 17.14   True/False Benchmark

```
Private Sub cmdTrueFalse_Click()
    Dim intCounter As Long
    Dim lngSalary As Long
```

LISTING 17.14 Continued

```
Dim dblStartTime As Double
Dim dblTime1 As Double
Dim dblTime2 As Double

'Execute loop with zero
dblStartTime = Timer

For intCounter = 1 To 50000
    If lngSalary <> 0 Then
    End If
Next intCounter

dblTime1 = Timer - dblStartTime

'Execute loop with True/False
dblStartTime = Timer

For intCounter = 1 To 50000
    If lngSalary Then
    End If
Next intCounter

dblTime2 = Timer - dblStartTime

'Display time and percent differences
Me.txtSlow = dblTime1
Me.txtOptimized = dblTime2
Me.txtPercent = (1 - (dblTime1 / dblTime2)) * 100

End Sub
```

NOTE

Although both the Len function, and the use of True/False, provided consistently better results in Access 2000 and earlier versions of Access, they appear to provide inconsistent results in Access 2002. This leads me to believe that there might have been changes to how these functions, or their alternatives, execute in Access 2002. I suggest that you test both the Len function and the use of True/False in your own environments to determine if they result in improved performance.

Use Transactions...Sometimes?

In versions of Access prior to Access 95, transactions dramatically improved performance. Using explicit transactions, the data is written to disk only once, after the `CommitTrans`. All changes between a `BeginTrans` and a `CommitTrans` are buffered in memory. Because disk access has the slowest throughput on a computer, this technique offered major performance benefits when it was introduced. The difference between Access 95 and all subsequent versions of Access is that the Jet 3.0, 3.5, 3.6 and 4.0 engines in the later versions implicitly buffer transactions. Most of the time, Jet's own transaction-handling offers better performance than your own. At other times, you can improve on what Jet does. The only way you will know what works for your code is to do your own benchmarking. Each situation is different.

Eliminate Unused `Dim` and `Declare` Statements

As you modify your subroutines and functions, you often declare a variable and then never use it. Each `Dim` statement takes up memory, whether or not you are using it. Furthermore, `Declare` statements, which are used to call external library functions, also take up memory and resources. You should remove these statements if they are not being used.

Eliminate Unused Code

Most programmers experiment with various alternatives for accomplishing a task. This often involves creating numerous test subroutines and functions. The problem is that most people do not remove this code when they are done with it. This dead code is loaded with your application and therefore takes up memory and resources. Several third-party tools are available that can help you find both dead code and variable declarations. One tool that many people use is called Total Access Analyzer, by FMS, Inc.

Use Variables to Refer to Properties, Controls, and Data Access Objects

If you are going to repeatedly refer to an object, you should declare an object and refer to the object variable rather than the actual control, as shown in Listing 17.15.

LISTING 17.15   Declaring an Object and Referring to the Object Variable

```
Forms!frmAny.txtHello.FontBold = True
Forms!frmAny.txtHello.Enabled = True
Forms!frmAny.txtHello.Left = 1
Forms!frmAny.txtHello.Top = 1
```

17

OPTIMIZING YOUR APPLICATION

This is a very scaled-down example, but, if numerous properties are being changed, or if this code is being called recursively, an object variable can make the code more efficient, as Listing 17.16 shows.

LISTING 17.16   Using an Object Variable to Make Your Code More Efficient

```
Private Sub cmdChangeObject_Click()
    Dim txt As TextBox
    Set txt = Forms!frmHello.txtHello1
    txt.FontBold = True
    txt.Enabled = True
    txt.Left = 100
    txt.Top = 100
End Sub
```

The benchmark shown in Listing 17.17 contains two loops. The first loop sets four properties of the same control, explicitly referencing the control as each property is set. The second loop uses an object variable to accomplish the same task. The difference in performance between the two loops is somewhat dramatic.

LISTING 17.17   Object Variable Benchmark

```
Private Sub cmdObjectVariable_Click()
    Dim intCounter As Long
    Dim dblStartTime As Double
    Dim dblTime1 As Double
    Dim dblTime2 As Double

    'Execute loop without object variable
    dblStartTime = Timer

    For intCounter = 1 To 1000
        Forms.frmBenchMark.txtOptimized.FontBold = True
        Forms.frmBenchMark.txtOptimized.Enabled = True
        Forms.frmBenchMark.txtOptimized.Locked = False
        Forms.frmBenchMark.txtOptimized.BackStyle = vbNormal
    Next intCounter

    dblTime1 = Timer - dblStartTime

    'Execute loop with object variable
    dblStartTime = Timer

    For intCounter = 1 To 1000
        Dim txt As TextBox
```

LISTING 17.17   Continued

```
        Set txt = Forms.frmBenchMark.txtOptimized
        txt.FontBold = True
        txt.Enabled = True
        txt.Locked = False
        txt.BackStyle = vbNormal
    Next intCounter

    dblTime2 = Timer - dblStartTime

    'Display time and percent differences
    Me.txtSlow = dblTime1
    Me.txtOptimized = dblTime2
    Me.txtPercent = (1 - (dblTime1 / dblTime2)) * 100


End Sub
```

Use `With...End With`

Another way to optimize the code in the preceding example is to use a `With...End With` construct, as shown in Listing 17.18.

LISTING 17.18   Using `With...End With`

```
Private Sub cmdChangeObjectWith_Click()
    With Forms!frmHello.txtHello2
        .FontBold = True
        .Enabled = True
        .Left = 100
        .Top = 100
    End With
End Sub
```

The code in Listing 17.19 shows two different loops. The first loop explicitly references the text box four different times to set four different properties. The second loop uses a `With` statement to reference the same control and set the four properties. The code in the second loop executes much more efficiently.

LISTING 17.19   Object Variable Resolution Benchmark

```
Private Sub cmdWith_Click()
    Dim intCounter As Long
    Dim dblStartTime As Double
```

LISTING 17.19   Continued

```
Dim dblTime1 As Double
Dim dblTime2 As Double

'Execute loop without With statement
dblStartTime = Timer

For intCounter = 1 To 1000
    Forms.frmBenchMark.txtOptimized.FontBold = True
    Forms.frmBenchMark.txtOptimized.Enabled = True
    Forms.frmBenchMark.txtOptimized.Locked = False
    Forms.frmBenchMark.txtOptimized.BackStyle = vbNormal
Next intCounter

dblTime1 = Timer - dblStartTime

'Execute loop with With statement
dblStartTime = Timer

For intCounter = 1 To 1000
    With Forms.frmBenchMark.txtOptimized
        .FontBold = True
        .Enabled = True
        .Locked = False
        .BackStyle = vbNormal
    End With
Next intCounter

dblTime2 = Timer - dblStartTime

'Display time and percent differences
Me.txtSlow = dblTime1
Me.txtOptimized = dblTime2
Me.txtPercent = (1 - (dblTime1 / dblTime2)) * 100

End Sub
```

Resolve Variable Outside a Loop

Although both the object variable reference and the With statement significantly improve performance, Listings 17.17 and 17.19 can be further improved by resolving the object variable outside the loop. Listing 17.20 provides an example.

LISTING 17.20   Object Variable Resolution Benchmark

```
Private Sub cmdVariable_Click()
    Dim txtAny As TextBox
    Dim intCounter As Long
    Dim dblStartTime As Double
    Dim dblTime1 As Double
    Dim dblTime2 As Double

    'Execute loop without object resolution
    dblStartTime = Timer

    For intCounter = 1 To 1000
        Forms.frmBenchmark.txtOptimized.FontBold = True
        Forms.frmBenchmark.txtOptimized.Enabled = True
        Forms.frmBenchmark.txtOptimized.Locked = False
        Forms.frmBenchmark.txtOptimized.BackStyle = vbNormal
    Next intCounter

    dblTime1 = Timer - dblStartTime

    'Execute loop with object resolution
    dblStartTime = Timer

    Set txtAny = Forms.frmBenchmark.txtOptimized
    For intCounter = 1 To 1000
        With txtAny
            .FontBold = True
            .Enabled = True
            .Locked = False
            .BackStyle = vbNormal
        End With
    Next intCounter

    dblTime2 = Timer - dblStartTime

    'Display time and percent differences
    Me.txtSlow = dblTime1
    Me.txtOptimized = dblTime2
    Me.txtPercent = (1 - (dblTime1 / dblTime2)) * 100
End Sub
```

Notice that the object variable is resolved outside the loop. This loop executes significantly faster than the loops in Listings 17.17 and 17.19.

Use the Me Keyword

In the preceding example, you used `Forms!frmHello.txtHello` to refer to a control on the current form. It is more efficient to refer to the control as `Me.txtHello` because VBA searches only in the local name space. Although this makes your code more efficient, the downside is that the `Me` keyword only works within form, report, and class modules. It won't work within standard code modules. This means that you cannot include the `Me` keyword in generic functions that are accessed by all your forms.

Use String Functions When VBA Provides a Variant and String Alternative

Several VBA functions come in two forms: one with a dollar sign ($) and one without. An example is `Left(sName)` versus `Left$(sName)`. Whenever it is acceptable to return a string, it is more efficient to use the version with the dollar sign, which return strings rather than variants. When a string variable is returned, VBA doesn't need to perform type conversions.

Use Dynamic Arrays

Array elements take up memory, whether or not they are being used. It therefore is sometimes preferable to use dynamic arrays. You can increase the size of a dynamic array as necessary. If you want to reclaim the space used by all the elements of the array, you can use the `Erase` keyword, as in this example:

```
Erase aNames
```

If you want to reclaim some of the space being used by the array without destroying data in the elements you want to retain, use `Redim Preserve`:

```
Redim Preserve aNames(5)
```

This statement sizes the array to six elements. (It is zero-based.) Data within those six elements is retained.

CAUTION

You must be careful when using dynamic arrays with `Redim Preserve`. When you resize an array using `Redim Preserve`, the entire array is copied in memory. If you are running in a low-memory environment, this can mean that virtual disk space is used, which slows performance—or worse than that, the application can fail if both physical and virtual memory are exhausted.

Use Constants When They Are Available

Constants improve both readability and performance. A constant's value is resolved after compilation. The value the constant represents is written to code. A normal variable has to be resolved as the code is running because VBA needs to obtain the current value of the variable.

Use Bookmarks

A bookmark provides you with the most rapid access to a record. If you are planning to return to a record, set a variable equal to that record's bookmark, making it very easy to return to that record at any time. Listing 17.21 shows an example that uses a bookmark.

LISTING 17.21   Using a Bookmark

```
Sub BookMarkIt()
    Dim rst As ADODB.Recordset
    Set rst = New ADODB.Recordset

    Dim varBM As Variant

    rst.Open "tblProjects", CurrentProject.Connection, adOpenStatic
    varBM = rst.Bookmark
    Do Until rst.EOF
        Debug.Print rst!ProjectID
        rst.MoveNext
    Loop
    rst.Bookmark = varBM
    Debug.Print rst!ProjectID
End Sub
```

 You can find this code in basOptimize of CHAP17EX.MDB. The bookmark is stored in a variable until the `Do...Until` loop executes. Then, the recordset's bookmark is set equal to the value contained within the variable.

Set Object Variables Equal to `Nothing`

Object variables take up memory and associated resources. Their value should be set to `Nothing` when you are finished using them, for example,

```
Set oObj = Nothing
```

This conserves memory and resources.

Use Action Queries Instead of Looping Through Recordsets

Besides being easier to code, executing a stored query is much more efficient than looping through a recordset, performing some action on each record. Listing 17.22 shows an example that loops through a recordset.

LISTING 17.22 Looping Through a Recordset

```
Sub LoopThrough()
    Dim rst As ADODB.Recordset
    Set rst = New ADODB.Recordset

    rst.Open "tblProjects", CurrentProject.Connection, adOpenDynamic, _
    adLockOptimistic
    Do Until rst.EOF
        rst!ProjectTotalEstimate = rst!ProjectTotalEstimate + 1
        rst.UPDATE
        rst.MoveNext
    Loop
End Sub
```

 This code, which is located in basOptimize of CHAP17EX.MDB, loops through a recordset, adding 1 to each project's total estimate. Contrast this with the code in Listing 17.23.

LISTING 17.23 Executing a Stored Query

```
Sub ExecuteQuery()
    Dim adoCat As ADOX.Catalog
    Dim cmd As ADODB.Command
    Set adoCat = New ADOX.Catalog
    Set cmd = New ADODB.Command

    Set adoCat.ActiveConnection = CurrentProject.Connection
    Set cmd = adoCat.Procedures("qupdLowerEstimate").Command
    cmd.Execute

End Sub
```

This code uses a command object to execute a stored query called `qupdLowerEstimate`. The query runs much more efficiently than the `Do...Until` loop shown in Listing 17.22.

NOTE

The most efficient method to update records is with a stored procedure. You can utilize stored procedures with a client/server database engine such as Microsoft SQL Server. This is covered in detail in *Alison Balter's Mastering Access 2002 Enterprise Development*.

Deliver Your Application with the Modules Compiled

Applications run slower when they are not compiled. Forms and reports load slower, and the application requires more memory. If you deliver your application with all the modules compiled, they do not need to be compiled on the user's machine before they run.

To easily recompile all modules, choose Debug|Compile with the Visual Basic Editor (VBE) active. This command opens and compiles all code in the application, including the code behind forms and reports. It then saves the modules in the compiled state, preserving the compiled state of the application.

Retaining the Compiled State

Don'tbother choosing the Debug|Compile command if you plan to make additional changes to the application. An application becomes decompiled whenever the application's controls, forms, reports, or modules are modified. Even something as simple as adding a single control to a form causes the application to lose its compiled state. It therefore is important to choose the Debug|Compile command immediately before you distribute the application.

CAUTION

Renaming a database file causes the code contained in the database to decompile. It therefore is important to always choose the Compile command after renaming a database.

Distribute Your Application as an MDE

The process of creating an MDE file compiles all modules, removes editable source code, and compacts the destination database. All Visual Basic code will run, but cannot be viewed or edited. This improves performance, reduces the size of the database, and protects your intellectual property. Memory use also is improved. The process of saving an application as an MDE, and the implications of doing so, are covered in Chapter 27, "Database Security Made Easy," and Chapter 32, "Distributing Your Application."

Organize Your Modules

VBA code theoretically can be placed in any module within your application. The problem is that a module is not loaded until a function within it is called. After a single procedure in a module is called, the entire module is loaded into memory. Furthermore, if a single variable within a module is used, the entire module is loaded into memory. As you might imagine, if you design your application without much thought, every module in your application will be loaded.

If you place similar routines all in one module, that module will be loaded, and others will not. This means that if people are using only part of the functionality of your application, they will never be loading other code modules. This conserves memory and therefore optimizes your application.

Designing Forms and Reports to Improve Performance

You can do several things to forms and reports to improve your application's performance. These include techniques to quickly load the forms and reports, tips and tricks regarding OLE objects, and special coding techniques that apply only to forms and reports.

Designing Forms

Because forms are your main interface to your user, making them as efficient as possible can go a long way toward improving the user's perception of your application's performance. Additionally, many of the form techniques are extremely easy to implement.

Form-optimization techniques can be categorized in two ways: those that make the forms load more quickly, and those that enable you to more efficiently manipulate objects within the form.

The larger a form and the more controls and objects you have placed on it, the less efficient that form is. Make sure that controls on the form do not overlap. It also is extremely beneficial to group form data onto logical pages. This is especially important if your users have insufficient video RAM. Objects on subsequent pages should not be populated until the user moves to that page.

Forms and their controls should be based on saved queries or embedded SQL statements. Include only fields required by the form in the form's underlying query. Avoid using `Select *` queries. Because Access is so efficient at internally optimizing the manipulation of query results, this improves the performance of your forms. To further take advantage of the power of queries, reduce the number of records that the query returns, loading only the records you need to at a particular time.

If you will use a form solely to add new records, set the `DataEntry` property of the form to `Yes` so that it opens to a blank record. This is necessary because, otherwise, Access must read all records to display the blank record at the end of the recordset.

Avoid bitmaps and other graphic objects if possible. If you must display an image, it is important to remember that OLE objects take far more resources than images. If an OLE bitmapped object does not need to be changed, convert it to an image. To accomplish this, right-click the object and choose Change To|Image.

Avoid the use of subforms whenever possible. Access treats a subform as a separate form. It therefore takes up significant memory. Make sure that all fields in a subform that are either linked to the main form or used for criteria are indexed. Make sure that only necessary fields are included in the record source of the subform. If the data in the subform does not need to be edited, set its `AllowEdits`, `AllowAdditions`, and `AllowDeletions` properties to `No`, or set its `RecordsetType` property to `Snapshot`.

Make sure that the `RowSource` for a combo box includes only the columns needed for the combo box. Index on the first field that appears in the combo box. This has a dramatic effect on the speed at which a user can move to an element of the combo box. Also, whenever possible, make the first visible field of a combo box a text field. Access converts numeric fields to text as it searches through the combo box to find a matching value. Finally, don't base list boxes or combo boxes on linked data if that data rarely, if ever, changes. Instead, make the static table local, updating it whenever necessary.

As a general rule regarding the performance of forms, place all database objects, except data, on each user's machine. This eliminates the need for Access to constantly pull object definitions over the network.

Close forms that no longer are being used. This is necessary because open forms take up memory and resources, degrading performance.

Another tip that can help you dramatically improve the performance of your forms is to use the default formatting and properties for as many controls as possible. This significantly improves performance because only the form and control properties that differ from the default properties are saved with the form.

17

OPTIMIZING YOUR
APPLICATION

> **TIP**
>
> If most controls have a set of properties that are different from those of the default control for the form, you should change the default control and then add controls based on the default. Access saves only the properties of the default control and does not need to store the properties for each control placed on the form. This can result in dramatic performance improvements. Changing the default control is covered in Chapter 9, "Advanced Form Techniques."

Finally, eliminate the code module from forms that don't need it. A form without a code module loads more quickly and occupies less disk space. You still can call function procedures from an event property using an expression, or you can navigate about your application from the form using hyperlinks. You can remove the module associated with a form by setting the HasModule property to No.

Designing Reports

Many of the report-optimization techniques are the same as the form-optimization techniques. Reducing the number of controls, avoiding overlapping controls, basing reports on queries, avoiding OLE objects, and converting unbound object frames that display graphics to image controls are all techniques that improve the performance of reports as well as forms.

You can use a few additional techniques to specifically improve the performance of reports. Eliminate any unnecessary sorting and grouping expressions, and index all fields on which you sort or group. Base subreports on queries rather than on tables, and include only necessary fields in the queries. Make sure that the queries underlying the report are optimized and that you index all fields in the subreport that are linked to the main report.

A special technique that you can use to improve the performance of reports was introduced with Access 95. It involves the No Data event and the HasData property. The No Data event is fired when a report is opened, and no data is returned by the record source of the report. The HasData property is used to determine whether a report is bound to an empty recordset. If the HasData property of a subreport is False, you can hide the subreport, thereby improving performance.

PRACTICAL EXAMPLES

Improving the Performance of Your Applications

To ensure that your applications are optimized, you can do several things:

- Make sure that the database is compacted.
- Use the Performance Analyzer to analyze the application and make recommendations for improvement.
- Choose Debug|Compile from the VBE before distributing the application.

Summary

The most attractive application can be extremely frustrating to use if its performance is less than acceptable. Because Access itself requires significant resources, you must take the responsibility of making your code as lean and efficient as possible.

This chapter focused on several techniques for improving performance. Probably one of the easiest ways to improve performance is by modifying the hardware and software environment within which Access operates. You learned about adding RAM, defragmenting a hard disk, and tuning virtual memory and other settings to dramatically improve the performance of your applications. You also looked at using the Performance Analyzer to quickly and easily identify problem areas in your application. Finally, the chapter focuses on data-design fundamentals, coding techniques, and techniques to optimize forms and reports.

By following the guidelines covered in this chapter, you can help ensure that you are not inadvertently introducing bottlenecks into your application. Although any one of the suggestions included in this chapter might not make a difference by itself, the combined effects of these performance enhancements can be quite dramatic.

Developing Multiuser and Enterprise Applications

IN THIS PART

A Strategy to Developing Access Applications

IN THIS CHAPTER

Why This Chapter Is Important

You should know about several tricks of the trade that can save you a lot of time in the development process and help ensure that your applications are as optimized as possible for performance. This chapter addresses these strategies and also explains several commonly misunderstood aspects of the Jet Engine, Access Runtime Engine, and security. All the topics covered in this chapter should be kept in mind when developing your Access applications. When reading this chapter, think of the general strategy outlined rather than the details of each topic. Each topic is covered in depth in other chapters of the book.

Splitting Databases into Tables and Other Objects

When earlier versions of Access ran in a multiuser environment, it was imperative to place the system's tables in one database and the rest of the system objects in another database. With Access 95 and the advent of replication, you could either split the tables from the other objects or use replication to deploy design changes without comprising live data. Access 2000 and Access 2002 take this a step further with the Access Data Project (ADP), in which tables, views, stored procedures, and data diagrams are stored in a SQL Server database or by the SQL Server 2000 Desktop Engine (formerly the Microsoft Data Engine, or MSDE). forms, reports, macros, and modules are stored in the ADP file.

As mentioned earlier, splitting tables from other system objects is still a very viable solution. For simplicity, I'll refer to the database containing the tables as the Table database and the database with the other objects as the Application database. Linking from the Application database to the Table database connects the two databases. This strategy enhances

- Maintainability
- Performance
- Scalability

Assume for a moment that you distribute your application as one MDB file. Your users work with your application for a week or two, writing down all problems and changes. It's time for you to make modifications to your application. Meanwhile, live data has been entered into the application for two weeks. You make a copy of the database (which includes the live data) and make all the fixes and changes. This process takes a week. You're ready to install your copy of the database on the network. Now what? The users of the application have been adding, editing, and deleting records all week. Data replication, which is covered in *Alison Balter's Mastering Access 2002 Enterprise Development*, could help you with this problem, but replication isn't always feasible.

The simplest solution is to split the database objects so that the tables containing your data are in one MDB file, and the rest of your database objects (your application) are in a second MDB file. When you're ready to install the changes, all you would need to do is copy the Application database to the file server. The new Application database could then be installed on each client machine from the file server. In this way, users could run new copies of the application from their machines. The database containing your data tables would remain intact and be unaffected by the process. (Of course, this is possible only if you finalize your table structure before splitting the database.)

The second benefit of splitting the database objects is performance. Your Table database obviously needs to reside on the network file server, so the data can be shared among the system's users; however, there's no good reason why the other database components need to be shared. Access gives you optimal performance if the Application database is stored on each local machine. This method also significantly reduces network traffic, and it decreases the chance of database corruption. If the Application database is stored on the file server, the application objects and code will need to be sent over the network each time an object in the database is opened. If the Application database is stored on each local machine, then only the data will need to be sent over the network. The only complication to this scenario is that, each time the Application database is updated, it will need to be redistributed to the users. On an already overtaxed network, this is a small inconvenience compared to the performance benefits gained from this structural split.

The third benefit of splitting tables from the other database objects is scalability. Because the tables are already linked, it's easy to change from a link to a table stored in Access's own proprietary format to any ODBC database, such as Microsoft SQL Server. This capability gives you quick-and-dirty access to client/server databases. If you have already thought through your system's design with linked tables in mind, the transition will be that much easier. Don't be fooled, though, by how easy this sounds. There are many issues associated with using Access as a front end to client/server data that go far beyond simply linking to the external tables. Some of these issues are covered in this chapter, and others are covered in Chapter 20, "Developing Multiuser and Enterprise Applications." Client/server techniques are covered in extensive detail in *Alison Balter's Mastering Access 2002 Enterprise Development*.

18

DEVELOPING
ACCESS
APPLICATIONS

> **TIP**
>
> A few special types of tables should be stored in the Application database rather than the Table database. Tables that rarely change should be stored in the Application database on each user's local machine. For example, a State table rarely, if ever, changes, but it's continually accessed to populate combo boxes, participate in queries, and so on. Placing the State table on each local machine, therefore, improves performance and reduces network traffic. Lookup tables containing localized information such as department codes should also be placed in the Application database.

Temporary tables should also be placed on each local machine—this is more a necessity than an option. If two users are running the same process at the same time and that process uses temporary tables, a conflict occurs when one user overwrites the other's temporary tables. Placing temporary tables on each local machine improves performance and eliminates the chance of potentially disastrous conflicts.

If you have already designed your application and included all the tables in the same database as the rest of your database objects, don't despair; Access 2002 includes the Database Splitter Wizard. You can find this valuable tool by choosing Tools|Database Utilities|Database Splitter. The Database Splitter, as well as linked tables, is covered in Chapter 19, "Using External Data."

NOTE

I split all the applications I build into two databases. However, you might notice when looking at the sample databases in this book that, until you reach Chapter 19, none of the chapters show databases split in the manner I recommend. This is because, until you learn all you need to know about splitting database objects, I don't think it's helpful to be working with a split sample database. From Chapter 19 on, however, each chapter offers some sample databases split according to the strategy recommended here.

Basing Forms and Reports on Queries or Embedded SQL Statements

The record source for a form or report can be based on a table object, a query object, or a SQL statement. By basing forms and reports on stored queries or embedded SQL statements, you can improve the performance and flexibility of your applications. In most cases, you don't need to display all fields and all records on a form or report. By basing a form or report on a query or embedded SQL statement, you can better limit the data transferred over the network. These benefits are most pronounced in a client/server environment. When you base a form or report on a table object, Access sends a SQL statement that retrieves all fields and all records from the database server. On the other hand, if the record source for the form or report is a query or embedded SQL statement, just the fields and records specified within the query are returned to the workstation.

In Access 2.0, a form or report based on a stored query was more efficient than a form or report based on a SQL statement. This was the case because when you save a query, the Access database Jet Engine creates a Query Plan. This plan contains information on the most efficient method of executing the query. When the query is saved, the Jet Engine looks at the volume of data and the available indexes, determines the optimal method of executing the query, and stores the method as the Query Plan. This plan is used whenever a form or report based on that query is executed. With Access 2.0, when a form or report was based on a SQL statement, the optimization process happened when the form or report was opened, and the Query Plan was executed on-the-fly. With Access 97, Access 2000, and Access 2002, an embedded SQL statement is optimized just like a stored query. It is therefore up to you whether you prefer to use a stored query or an embedded SQL statement as the foundation for your forms and reports.

On the other hand, when basing a form on table data, you can't control the order of the records in the form, nor can you base the form on more than one table. You can't limit the records displayed on the form until after the form is opened. By basing a form on a query or an embedded SQL statement, you can control the criteria for the form as well as the default order in which the records are displayed.

Everything just mentioned applies to reports as well, except the order of the records, which is determined by the sorting and grouping of the report itself.

TIP

Many other techniques are available to you when displaying a form based on a large recordset. My favorite involves basing the form on only a single record at a time and changing the form's RecordSource property each time the user wants to view a different record. Another technique that I use is to base the form's RecordSource property on the value selected in a combo box in the Header section of the form. I use the After_Update event of the combo box to requery the form. Because the form's RecordSource uses the combo box value for criteria, the desired record is displayed. These techniques, and others, are covered in detail in *Alison Balter's Mastering Access 2002 Enterprise Development*.

Understanding the Access Runtime Engine

Many developers don't understand what Access has to offer out of the box and what the Microsoft Office Developer (MOD) tools can add to the picture. They often tell me, "I can't develop applications in Access because my company refuses to buy each user a copy of

Access," or "I'm going to buy the MOD so that I can compile my applications with the MOD tools." These are just two of the many misconceptions about exactly what the MOD tools do and don't have to offer.

Features of the MOD

You no longer need to buy a separate product to create runtime versions of your Access applications. As a developer, you will likely buy the MOD tools, which include Office Premium and all the features from the old Office Developer Environment (ODE), plus many new components. An important feature of the MOD tools is a royalty-free distribution license. It allows you to distribute unlimited copies of your Access application; your users don't have to own separately licensed copies of Access. By using the MOD tools, you can create applications and distribute them to your users, along with the necessary runtime engine. The MOD tools includes numerous additional tools that are covered in *Alison Balter's Mastering Access 2002 Enterprise Development.*

Differences Between the Standard and Runtime Versions of Access

It's important to understand the differences between the standard and runtime versions of Access. The following differences have definite implications for the way you develop any applications you expect to run from the runtime version:

- The Database, Macro, and Module windows aren't available in the runtime environment.
- No Design views are available in the runtime environment.
- No built-in toolbars are available in the runtime environment.
- Many windows, menus, and commands are invisible in the runtime environment. For example, the Window|Hide and Window|Unhide commands are invisible. Although these and other commands aren't visible, their functions are generally accessible by using code.
- You must build error handling into your runtime applications. If you don't, when an error occurs, the application displays a standard Access dialog box indicating an irrecoverable error and then exits to the desktop.
- You must build your own custom help files for each runtime application.
- Some keystrokes aren't available in the runtime application.

Some of the disabled features protect your applications. For example, the absence of the Database and Design windows means that your users can't modify your application while running it under Access's runtime version. Other disabled features translate into additional coding chores for you, such as the absence of command bars. If you want your application to offer toolbars, you have to build your own and then assign them to the forms and reports in your database.

Steps for Preparing an Application for Distribution

With all the features absent from the runtime version of Access, it's not surprising you must take some special steps to prepare your application for distribution. Most are steps you'll probably want to take so that your application seems professional to the user. The following are preparations specific to running Access from the runtime version:

- Base your application around forms.
- Add startup options to your database.
- Secure the objects in your application.
- Build error handling into your application.
- Add some level of custom help.
- Build custom command bars to be associated with your application's forms and reports.

Basing Your Application Around Forms

Your application should be based on and controlled through forms. It should generally begin with a main switchboard that lets the user get to the other components of your application. Or, it can start with a core data-entry form around which the rest of the application is based. If you opt to go with an application switchboard, the main switchboard can direct the user to additional switchboards, such as a data-entry switchboard, a report switchboard, or a maintenance switchboard. You can build switchboards with an add-in called the Switchboard Manager. Alternatively, you can design them as custom dialog boxes. Building custom dialog boxes is covered in Chapter 9, "Advanced Form Techniques"; using the Switchboard Manager is covered in Chapter 32, "Distributing Your Application." The main advantage of using the Switchboard Manager is that it lets you quickly and easily create a polished application interface. The primary advantage of custom switchboards is the flexibility and freedom they offer.

An alternative to the switchboard approach is to build the application around a core data-entry form, such as a contact management application based around a contacts form. All other forms and reports that make up the application are accessed via custom menu bars and toolbars on the contacts form.

Adding Start-Up Options to Your Database

Regardless of the approach that you take, you designate a form as the starting point for your application by modifying the database's startup options. Choose Tools|Startup to open the Startup dialog box. (See Figure 18.1.) In this dialog box, you can set options, such as a startup form, an application title, and an icon that appears when your application is minimized. These options are covered in detail in Chapter 32.

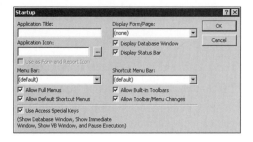

FIGURE 18.1

The Startup dialog box lets you control many aspects of your application environment.

Securing Your Application

As you will learn in the next section, a database isn't secure just because you're running it from a runtime version of Access. Without security, your application can be modified by anyone with a full copy of Access, so securing your database objects is an important step in preparing your application for distribution. Security is covered in Chapters 27, "Database Security Made Easy," and 28, "Advanced Security Techniques."

Access 2000 and Access 2002 also offer you the ability to remove the source code from your applications. This protects your intellectual property and improves the performance of your application. The resulting database is called an MDE (covered in Chapter 32).

Building Error Handling in to Your Applications

If error handling isn't built into your application and an error occurs while your user is running your application from Access's runtime version, the user will be rudely exited out of the program. She won't get an appropriate error message and will be left wondering what happened. Hence, it's essential that you add error handling to your application's procedures. Error handling is covered in Chapter 16, "Error Handling: Preparing for the Inevitable." The VBA Error Handler, included with the Microsoft Office Developer (MOD) tools, can also assist in building error handling into your application.

Adding Custom Help

In most cases, you want your users to have at least some level of custom help specific to your application. You can use the ControlTip Text property of controls and the Description property of fields to add the most basic level of help to your application. The ControlTip Text property provides a description of a control when a user hovers his mouse pointer over the control. The Description property of a field appears on the status bar when a control based on that field has the focus. If you are more ambitious, and if the scope and budget for the application warrant it, you can build a custom help file for your application. To add custom help to your application, you must build a help file; then attach parts of it to application's forms and controls. The HTML Help Workshop, included with the Microsoft Office Developer (MOD) tools, can assist with the process.

Building Custom Command Bars

Finally, because built-in toolbars aren't available in the runtime version of Access and most of the features on the standard built-in menus are disabled, you should build your own command bars associated with specific forms and reports. Creating custom command bars adds both polish and functionality to your application.

After you complete these steps, you'll be ready for the final phase of preparing your application for distribution, which includes the following steps:

- Test your application by using the /Runtime switch.
- Create setup disks or perform a network install with the Package and Deployment Wizard.
- Install your application on a machine that has never run a copy of either the standard or runtime version of Access.
- Test your application on the machine; make sure it runs as expected.

Before you bother running the Package and Deployment Wizard (a somewhat lengthy process), it's best that you run your application with the /Runtime switch. This switch simulates the runtime environment, allowing you to mimic user actions under the runtime version of Access. Taking this step saves you a lot of time and energy. It will find most, if not all, of the problems associated with the runtime version.

After you test your application with the /Runtime switch, you're ready to run the Package and Deployment Wizard (covered in Chapter 32). It lets you create setup disks or perform a network install. Selecting A:Setup (or the appropriate network drive and path) provides a professional-looking, familiar setup program similar to those included with most Microsoft products.

After you run the Package and Deployment Wizard, you must test your application by running the install on a machine that has never contained a copy of either the standard or runtime version of Access. The whole idea is to test your application on a machine containing no Access-related files. This ensures that all the required files are included on your setup disks.

I suggest you use a "ghosting" utility such as Symantec Ghost to create a complete image of your operating system and application drives. Install and fully test your application; make sure you experiment with every feature. When you're done testing, restore the original machine from the Ghost image, so that you can use it to test your next installation.

> **TIP**
>
> Symantec Ghost allows you to restore individual files, selected directories, or entire hard drives as needed. When a backup image file is created, it can be compressed by up to 70%, greatly reducing transfer times and storage requirements. Amongst its many other uses, Symantec Ghost greatly facilitates the testing process by allowing you to easily restore a test machine to its pretesting state. Learn more about Symantec Ghost at http://www.ghostsoft.com.

The Access Runtime Engine: Summing It Up

You have just read an overview of the differences between the full and runtime versions of Access. The process of preparing an application for distribution with the runtime version of Access is covered in detail in Chapter 32. If you plan to distribute an application with the runtime version of Access, remember which features will be available to your users; otherwise, you and your users will be in for some big surprises.

Using an EXE Versus Access Database: What It Means to You

Many developers mistakenly think that distributing an application with the runtime version of Access is equivalent to distributing an EXE. An unsecured database distributed with the runtime version of Access can be modified just like any other database.

Users can run your application n, and all the rules of running an application under the runtime version apply. This means that users can't go into Design view, can't create their own objects, don't have access to the built-in toolbars, and so on.

Using their own copies of the standard version of Access, users can open the same database. If the objects in the database haven't been secured, users can modify the application at will.

In short, a database prepared with the Package and Deployment Wizard is no different from any other database. The wizard doesn't modify an MDB file in any way. It simply compresses all the files needed to run your application, including the database and runtime engine, and creates a network install folder or distribution disks containing the compressed files. Two ways to protect the design of your application are to set up security and to distribute your application as an MDE file.

Understanding the Importance of Securing Your Database

By now, you should understand the importance of securing your application. Setting up security is a complex but worthwhile process that can be done at either a group or user level. You can assign rights to objects, and those rights can be assigned to either individual users or a group of users. Figure 18.2 shows the User and Group Permissions dialog box. As you can see, rights can be assigned for each object. For a table, the user or group can be assigned rights to read, insert, update, and delete data as well as to read, modify, or administer the table's design. Different groups of users can be assigned different rights to an object. For example, one group can be assigned rights to add, edit, and delete data. Another group can be assigned rights to edit only, another group to view only, and another can be denied the right to even view the data.

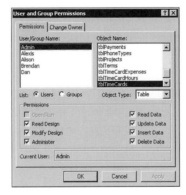

FIGURE 18.2
The User and Group Permissions dialog box lets you assign user and group rights to each database object.

Available rights differ for tables, queries, forms, reports, macros, and modules. The types of rights that can be assigned are appropriate to each particular type of object. When security has been properly invoked, it is difficult to violate, no matter how someone tries to access the database objects (including using the runtime version of Access, a standard copy of Access, programming code, or even a Visual Basic application). If properly secured, the database is as difficult to illegally access as an executable file.

> **NOTE**
>
> Web site businesses exist that remove Access security for a fee. Although Access security protects you against "honest" people, it doesn't completely protect you against those who are out to get you, your application, or the data that your application stores.

Using Access as a Front End

If you're planning to use Access as a front end to other databases, you need to consider a few issues. In fact, the whole design methodology of your system will differ depending on whether you plan to store your data in an Access database or on a back-end database server.

In a system where your data is stored solely in Access tables, the Jet Engine supplies all data retrieval and management functions and handles security, data validation, and enforcement of referential integrity.

In a system where Access acts as a front end to client/server data, the server handles the data management functions. It's responsible for retrieving, protecting, and updating data on the back-end database server. In this scenario, the local copy of Access is responsible only for sending requests and getting either data or pointers to data back from the database server. If you're creating an application in which Access acts as a front end, capitalizing on the strengths of both Access and the server can be a challenging endeavor.

Things You Need to Worry About in Converting to Client/Server

The transition to client/server technology isn't always a smooth one. You need to consider the following factors if you're developing a client/server application or planning to eventually move your application from an Access database to a back-end structured query language (SQL) database server:

- Not all field types supported in Access are supported in every back-end database.
- Any security you set up in Access won't be converted to your back-end database.
- Validation rules you set up in Access need to be re-established on the back end.
- Referential integrity isn't supported on all back ends. If it is on yours, it won't automatically be carried over from Access.
- Queries involving joins that could be updated in Access can't be updated on the back-end server.

This list is just an overview of what you need to think about when moving an application from an Access database with linked tables to a back-end server or when developing an application specifically for a back end. Many of these issues have far-reaching implications. For example, if you set up validation rules and validation text in your application, the rules will need to be rewritten as triggers on the back end. If a validation rule is violated on the back end, you will get a returnable error code. You have to respond to this code by using error handling in your application, displaying the appropriate message to your user. The Validation Text property can't be used.

> **TIP**
>
> The Access 2000 and Access 2002 Upsizing Wizards address most of the transitioning issues covered in this chapter. These tools, included as part of Access 2000 and Access 2002, respectively, automate the migration of data from the native Access data format to Microsoft SQL Server. The Upsizing Wizard is covered in *Alison Balter's Mastering Access 2002 Enterprise Development*.

18

Benefits and Costs of Client/Server Technology

With all the issues discussed in the previous section, you might ask, "Why bother with client/server?" In each case, you need to evaluate whether the benefits of client/server technology outweigh its costs. The major benefits include the following:

- Greater control over data integrity
- Increased control over data security
- Increased fault tolerance
- Reduced network traffic
- Improved performance
- Centralized control and management of data

These are some of the major expenses:

- Increased development costs
- Hardware costs for the server machine
- Setup costs for the server database
- The cost of employing a full- or part-time database administrator (DBA)

These and other issues are covered in more detail in Chapter 20, "Developing Multiuser and Enterprise Applications."

Your Options When Using Access as a Front End

Client/server applications are not an all-or-none proposition, nor is there only one way to implement them through Access. One option is to use Access as a true front end, which means that all data is stored on the server and all queries are processed on the server. This is done by using pass-through queries and stored procedures, rather than stored Access queries. With pass-through queries, a back-end–specific SQL statement is passed to the back end instead of being processed by Access. With stored procedures, SQL statements are stored on the back end and are executed using DAO or ADO code. (Both scenarios are covered briefly in Chapter 20 and in detail in *Alison Balter's Mastering Access 2002 Enterprise Development.*)

To make Access a true front end, you must also disable its natural ability to bind data to forms and reports. Doing so, however, eliminates all the features that make Access a strong product in the first place. Unfortunately, you haven't eliminated all the overhead associated with the functionality you removed. If you want to use this approach, you're better off developing the entire application in a lower-overhead environment, such as Visual Basic, or instead developing a Web—based solution.

Another approach is a hybrid method in which you use a combination of linked tables, SQL pass-through queries, stored procedures, and local Access tables. The idea is that you take advantage of Access's features and strong points whenever possible. Pass-through queries and stored procedures are used to perform functions that are done more efficiently by communicating directly to the back end or that aren't available at all with Access SQL. To further improve performance, many tasks can be performed locally and then communicated to the server as one transaction, after any initial validation has been done. Access Project files, introduced in Access 2000, allow you to communicate with the back-end database without loading the Microsoft Jet Engine. With Access Projects, commonly referred to as *ADP files*, you can improve both the performance and functionality of a client/server application. The basics of ADP files are covered in Chapter 20. The ins and outs of working with ADP files are covered in *Alison Balter's Mastering Access 2002 Enterprise Development*. In addition to the solutions just discussed, data can also be downloaded to Access in bulk so that additional processing can be done locally. Many possibilities exist, and each is appropriate in different situations. It takes experience and experimentation to determine the combination of methods that will optimize performance in a given situation.

What Are the Considerations for Migrating to a Client/Server Environment?

The preceding sections have given you an overview of the issues you need to consider when building a client/server application or considering moving to a client/server environment in the future. More detailed information is given in Chapter 20. If you're using Access as a front end, make sure that, as you read through this book, particularly the more advanced chapters, you take special note of any cautions about developing client/server applications. If you want in-depth coverage of client/server development techniques, refer to *Alison Balter's Mastering Access 2002 Enterprise Development*.

PRACTICAL EXAMPLES

Applying the Strategy to the Computer Consulting Firm Application

The Time and Billing application for the computer consulting firm introduced in Chapter 1, "Access as a Development Tool," could be comprised of two databases: one containing the majority of the tables, and the other with the remainder of the database objects, including static and temporary tables. If developed properly, the application would be developed with the idea that the data might eventually be moved to a back-end database server and designed so that the transition to client/server would be as smooth as possible. The forms and reports that make up the application would be based on stored queries or embedded SQL statements to maximize their flexibility and efficiency. Finally, the application would be designed so that it can easily run from Access's runtime version and will be secured so that its data and other objects couldn't be accessed by unauthorized users.

Summary

It's important that you have a strategy before you begin the application development process. This chapter introduced many strategic issues, such as splitting a database into tables and other objects and using Access as a front end. It also covered converting to a client/server environment, explored the benefits and costs involved in such a conversion, and discussed the different options available to you. These concepts were then tied together by the explanation of what you can do to prepare your applications for future growth.

Many people don't fully understand the Access runtime engine, so this chapter explained what it is and what it isn't. It also explained what you need to be concerned about in preparing an application for distribution, including the importance of properly securing your databases.

18

DEVELOPING ACCESS APPLICATIONS

Using External Data

IN THIS CHAPTER

Why This Chapter Is Important

Microsoft Access is very capable of interfacing with data from other sources. It can use data from any OLEDB or ODBC data source, as well as data from FoxPro, dBASE, Paradox, Lotus, Excel, and many other sources. In this chapter, you will learn how to interface with external data sources, with the user interface, and by using code.

External data is data stored outside the current database. It can refer to data stored in another Microsoft Access database, as well as data stored in a multitude of other file formats—including ISAM, spreadsheet, ASCII, and more. This chapter focuses on accessing data sources other than ODBC and OLE DB data sources. ODBC and OLEDB data sources are discussed briefly in Chapter 20, "Developing Multiuser and Enterprise Applications." They are covered in extensive detail in *Alison Balter's Mastering Access 2002 Enterprise Development*.

Access is an excellent *front-end* product, which means that it provides a powerful and effective means of presenting data—even data from external sources. Data is stored in places other than Access for many reasons. Large databases, for example, can be managed more effectively on a back-end database server such as Microsoft SQL Server. Data often is stored in a FoxPro, dBASE, or Paradox file format because the data is being used by a legacy application written in one of those environments. Text data often has been downloaded from a mainframe. Regardless of the reason why data is stored in another format, it is necessary that you understand how to manipulate this external data in your VBA modules. With the capability to access data from other sources, you can create queries, forms, and reports.

When accessing external data, you have three choices. You can import the data into an Access database, access the data by linking to it from your Access database, or open a data source directly. Importing the data is the optimum route (except with ODBC data sources) but not always possible. If you can't import external data, you should link to external files because Microsoft Access maintains a lot of information about these linked files. This optimizes performance when manipulating the external files. Sometimes a particular situation warrants accessing the data directly. You therefore should know how to work with linked files, as well as how to open and manipulate files directly.

Importing, Linking, and Opening Files: When and Why

When you import data into an Access table, a copy is made of the data and is placed in an Access table. After data is imported, it is treated like any other native Access table. In fact, neither you nor Access has any way of knowing from where the data came. As a result, imported data offers the same performance and flexibility as any other Access table.

Linking to external data is quite different from importing data. Linked data remains in its native format. By establishing a link to the external data, you can build queries, forms, and reports that present the data. After you create a link to external data, the link remains permanently established unless you explicitly remove it. The linked table appears in the database window just like any other Access table, except that its icon is different. In fact, if the data source permits multiuser access, the users of your application can modify the data as can the users of the applications written in the data source's native database format (such as FoxPro, dBASE, or Paradox). The main difference between a linked and a native table is that you cannot modify the linked table's structure from within Access.

Opening an external table is similar to linking to the table, except that a permanent relationship is not created. When you *link* to an external table, connection information is maintained from session to session. When you *open* a table, you create a recordset from the table, and no permanent link is established.

Selecting an Option

It is important that you understand when to import external data, when to link to external data, and when to open an external table directly. You should import external data in either of these circumstances:

- You are migrating an existing system into Access.
- You want to use external data to run a large volume of queries and reports, and you will not update the data. You want the added performance that native Access data provides.

When you are migrating an existing system to Access and you are ready to permanently migrate test or production data into your application, you import the tables into Access. You might also want to import external data if the data is downloaded from a mainframe into ASCII format on a regular basis, and you want to use the data for reports. Instead of attempting to link to the data and suffering the performance hits associated with such a link, you can import the data each time it is downloaded from the mainframe.

You should link to external data in any of the following circumstances:

- The data is used by a legacy application requiring the native file format.
- The data resides on an ODBC-compliant database server.
- You will access the data on a regular basis (making it prohibitive to keep the data up-to-date if it is not linked).

Often, you won't have the time or resources to rewrite an application written in FoxPro, Paradox, or some other language. You might be developing additional applications that will share data with the legacy application, or you might want to use the strong querying and reporting capabilities of Access instead of developing queries and reports in the native environment.

By linking to the external data, users of existing applications can continue to work with the applications and their data. Your Access applications can retrieve and modify data without concern for corrupting, or in any other way harming, the data.

If the data resides in an ODBC database such as Microsoft SQL Server, you want to reap the data-retrieval benefits provided by a database server. By linking to the ODBC data source, you can take advantage of Access's ease of use as a front-end tool, while taking advantage of client/server technology.

Finally, if you intend to access data on a regular basis, linking to the external table instead of temporarily opening the table directly provides you with ease of use and performance benefits. After you create the link, in most cases, Access treats the table just like any other Access table.

You should open an external table directly in either of these circumstances:

- You rarely need to establish a connection to the external data source.
- You have determined that performance actually improves by opening the data source directly.

If you rarely need to access the external data, it might be appropriate to open it directly. Links increase the size of your MDB file. This size increase is not necessary if you rarely will access the data. Furthermore, in certain situations, when accessing ISAM (indexed sequential access method) data, you might find that opening the table directly provides better performance than linking to it.

Although this chapter covers the process of importing external data, this is essentially a one-time process and doesn't require a lot of discussion. It is important to note, however, that after data is imported into an Access table, it no longer is accessed by the application in its native format. The majority of this chapter focuses on linking to or directly opening external data tables.

Looking at Supported File Formats

Microsoft Access enables you to import, link to, and open files in these formats:

- Microsoft Jet databases (including previous versions of Jet)
- Access projects (ADP and ADE files)
- ODBC databases
- HTML documents
- XML documents (import and open only)

- Microsoft Exchange/Outlook
- dBASE III, dBASE IV, and dBASE 5.0
- Paradox 3.*x*, 4.*x*, and 5.*x*
- Microsoft Excel spreadsheets, versions 3.0, 4.0, 5.0, and 8.0
- Lotus WKS, WK1, WK3, and WK4 spreadsheets (import and open only)
- ASCII text files stored in a tabular format

Importing External Data

The process of importing external data is quite simple. You can import external data by using the user interface or by using VBA code. If you are planning to import the data only once or twice, you should use the user interface. If you are importing data on a regular basis (for example, from a downloaded mainframe file), you should write code that accomplishes the task transparently to the user.

Using the User Interface

To import an external data file using the user interface, follow these steps:

1. Right-click anywhere within the database window.
2. Choose Import (or choose File|Get External Data|Import). The Import dialog box appears, as shown in Figure 19.1.

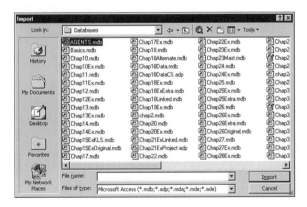

FIGURE 19.1

The Import dialog box.

3. From the Files of Type drop-down list, select the type of file you are importing.
4. Select the file you want to import and click Import.

5. Depending on the type of file you select, the import process finishes, or you see additional dialog boxes. If you select Excel Spreadsheet, for example, the Import Spreadsheet Wizard appears, as shown in Figure 19.2. This wizard walks you through the process of importing spreadsheet data.

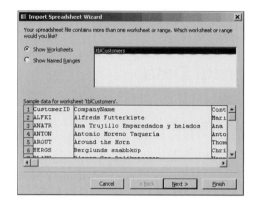

FIGURE 19.2

The Import Spreadsheet Wizard.

CAUTION

If you find that you can't bring a large (4M–5M) text file directly into an Access database, change the text file into an Excel spreadsheet first and then import that file.

Using Code

The DoCmd object has three methods that assist you with importing external data. They are TransferDatabase, TransferText, and TransferSpreadsheet, each of which is covered in this section.

Importing Database Data Using Code

You use the TransferDatabase method of the DoCmd object to import data from a database such as FoxPro, dBASE, Paradox, or another Access database. Listing 19.1, included in basImport, shows an example that uses the TransferDatabase method.

LISTING 19.1   Using the `TransferDatabase` Method

```
Sub ImportDatabase()
  DoCmd.TransferDatabase _
    TransferType:=acImport, _
    DatabaseType:="dBASE III", _
    DatabaseName:= CurrentProject.Path, _
    ObjectType:=acTable, _
    Source:="Customer", _
    Destination:="tblCustomers", _
    StructureOnly:=False
End Sub
```

NOTE

This code and all the code in this chapter are located in the CHAP19EX.MDB file on the sample code CD-ROM.

Table 19.1 lists the arguments for the `TransferDatabase` method.

TABLE 19.1   `TransferDatabase` Arguments

Argument	Specifies
`TransferType`	Type of transfer being performed.
`DatabaseType`	Type of database being imported.
`DatabaseName`	Name of the database. If the table is a separate file (as is the case with dBASE, Paradox, and earlier versions of FoxPro), the database name is the name of the directory that contains the table file. Do *not* include a backslash after the name of the directory.
`ObjectType`	Type of object you want to import. This argument is ignored for all but Access objects.
`Source`	Name of the object you are importing. Do *not* include the file extension.
`Destination`	Name of the imported object.
`StructureOnly`	Whether you want the structure of the table only or the structure and data.
`StoreLogin`	Whether you want to save the login ID and password for an ODBC database in the connection string for linked tables.

19

USING EXTERNAL
DATA

Importing Text Data Using Code

You use the `TransferText` method of the `DoCmd` object to import text from a text file. Listing 19.2 shows an example of this method.

LISTING 19.2   Using the `TransferText` Method

```
Sub ImportText()
  DoCmd.TransferText _
    TransferType:=acImportDelim, _
    TableName:="tblCustomerText", _
    FileName:=CurrentProject.Path & "\Customer.Txt"
End Sub
```

Table 19.2 lists the arguments for the `TransferText` method.

TABLE 19.2   `TransferText` Arguments

Argument	Specifies
TransferType	Type of transfer you want to make.
SpecificationName	Name for the set of options that determines how the file is imported.
TableName	Name of the Access table that will receive the imported data.
FileName	Name of the text file to import from.
HTMTableName	Name of the table or list in the HTML file that you want to import or link to
CodePage	A long integer used to indicate the character set of the code page
HasFieldHeadings	Whether the first row of the text file contains field headings.

Importing Spreadsheet Data Using Code

You use the `TransferSpreadsheet` method of the `DoCmd` object to import data from a spreadsheet file. Listing 19.3 shows an example that uses the `TransferSpreadsheet` method.

LISTING 19.3   Using the `TransferSpreadsheet` Method

```
Sub ImportSpreadsheet()
  DoCmd.TransferSpreadsheet _
    TransferType:=acImport, _
    SpreadsheetType:=acSpreadsheetTypeExcel9, _
    TableName:="tblCustomerSpread", _
    FileName:=CurrentProject.Path & "\Customer.Xls", _
    HasFieldNames:=True
End Sub
```

Table 19.3 lists the arguments for the `TransferSpreadsheet` method.

TABLE 19.3   `TransferSpreadsheet` Arguments

Argument	*Specifies*
`TransferType`	Type of transfer you want to make.
`SpreadsheetType`	Type of spreadsheet to import from. The default is Excel 3.0.
`TableName`	Name of the Access table that will receive the imported data.
`FileName`	Name of the spreadsheet file to import from.
`HasFieldNames`	Whether the first row of the spreadsheet contains field headings.
`Range`	Range of cells to import.

Creating a Link to External Data

If you need to keep the data in its original format but want to treat the data just like any other Access table, linking is the best solution. All the information required to establish and maintain the connection to the remote data source is stored within the linked table definition. You can create links through the user interface and by using code. This section covers both alternatives.

One of the most common types of links is a link to another Access table. This type of link is created so that the application objects (queries, forms, reports, macros, and modules) can be placed in a local database and the tables can be stored in another database on a file server. Numerous benefits are associated with such a configuration. Chapter 20 discusses these benefits in more detail.

Using the User Interface

It is very common to create a link using the user interface. If you know what links you want to establish at design time, this is probably the easiest way to establish links to external data. You can establish links using the Database Splitter or by establishing them manually.

Using the Database Splitter to Create Links

The Database Splitter was designed to split databases that already have been built with the tables and other database objects all in one physical MDB database file. It automates the process of moving the data tables to another database. The Database Splitter is covered in detail in Chapter 20.

19

> **NOTE**
>
> You can create links to tables only from an Access database, not from an Access project.

Creating Links to Access Tables

To create a link to an Access table, follow these steps:

1. Right-click anywhere within the Database window.

2. Choose Link Tables. The Link dialog box appears, as shown in Figure 19.3.

FIGURE 19.3

The Link dialog box.

3. Select the name of the database containing the table to which you want to link.

4. Click the Link button. The Link Tables dialog box appears, as shown in Figure 19.4.

FIGURE 19.4

The Link Tables dialog box.

5. Select the tables to which you want to establish a link.

6. Click OK. The link process finishes. Notice the arrows in Figure 19.5, which indicate that the tblCustomer, tblOrders, and tblOrderDetails tables are linked tables instead of tables stored in the current database.

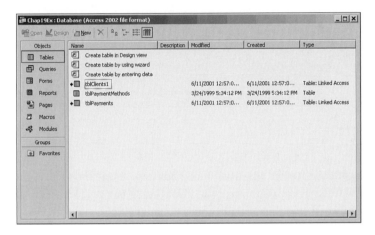

FIGURE 19.5
Linked tables in the Database window.

Creating Links to Other Types of Tables

The process of creating links to other types of database files is a little different. It works like this:

1. Right-click anywhere within the Database window.

2. Choose Link Tables. The Link dialog box appears.

3. In the Files of Type drop-down list, select the type of table to which you are linking.

4. Select the external file containing the data to which you will be linking.

5. Click the Link button. The next dialog box varies, depending on the type of table to which you want to link. With a dBASE file, for example, the Select Index Files dialog box appears, as shown in Figure 19.6. It is important that you select any index files associated with the data file. These indexes are updated automatically by Access as you add, change, and delete table data from within Access.

6. You receive a message indicating that the index was added successfully and that you can add other indexes if you choose. Click OK.

7. Add any additional indexes and click Close.

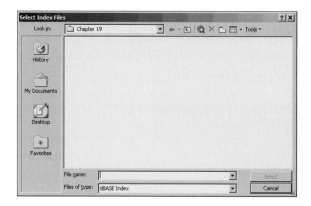

FIGURE 19.6
The Select Index Files dialog box.

8. The Select Unique Record Identifier dialog box appears, as shown in Figure 19.7 (see Note below if the dialog doesn't appear). This dialog box enables you to select a unique identifier for each record in the table. Select a unique field and click OK.

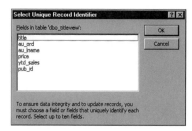

FIGURE 19.7
The Select Unique Record Identifier dialog box.

> **NOTE**
>
> You must install the Jet 4.0 Service Pack 5 or have the BDE (Borland Database Engine) for the Select Unique Record Identifier dialog box to appear. If you do not have one of these tools, the data in the database cannot be edited. For more information, see the Microsoft knowledge base article Q283294.

Notice the icon indicating the type of file you linked to, as shown in Figure 19.8.

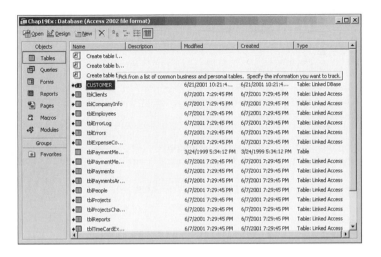

FIGURE 19.8

An icon indicating that the file database is linked to a dBASE database file.

> **NOTE**
>
> Earlier versions of Access supported links to FoxPro files using the FoxPro ISAM driver. With Jet 4.0, you must link to FoxPro tables using the Visual FoxPro ODBC Driver.

Using Code

Creating a link to an external table using code is a six-step process. Here are the steps involved in establishing the link:

1. Create a reference to the Microsoft ADO Extension 2.6 for DDL and Security (ADOX) library.
2. Create a `Catalog` object.
3. Set the Connection property of the `Catalog` object to the database that will contain the linked table.
4. Create a new `Table` object.
5. Set properties of the `Table` object.
6. Append the `Table` object to the `Catalog`.

Listing 19.4 shows the code for linking to an external table, which, in this case, exists in another Microsoft Access database.

LISTING 19.4   Linking to an External Table

```
Sub LinkToAccessTableProps()
    Dim cat As ADOX.Catalog
    Dim tbl As ADOX.Table

    'Instantiate a Catalog Object
    Set cat = New ADOX.Catalog

    'Set the connection of the Catalog object
    'to the connection associated with the current
    'project
    cat.ActiveConnection = CurrentProject.Connection

    'Instantiate a table object
    Set tbl = New ADOX.Table

    'Establish the name of the new table object
    tbl.Name = "tblLinkedTable"

    'Point the catalog of the new table at the
    'catalog object established above
    Set tbl.ParentCatalog = cat

    'Set necessary properties of the new table object
    tbl.Properties("Jet OLEDB:Create Link") = True
    tbl.Properties("Jet OLEDB:Link Datasource") = _
        CurrentProject.Path & "\Chap19Data.mdb"
    tbl.Properties("Jet OLEDB:Link Provider String") = ";pwd=password"
    tbl.Properties("Jet OLEDB:Remote Table Name") = "tblClients"

    'Append the new table object to the tables collection
    'of the catalog object
    cat.Tables.Append tbl
End Sub
```

In Listing 19.4, a `Catalog` object is created. The ActiveConnection property of the `Catalog` object is pointed at the connection associated with the current database. Next, a `Table` object is created. The Name property of the `Table` object is set equal to `tblLinkedTable`. The ParentCatalog property of the `Table` object is set to point at the `Catalog` object. Four properties in the properties collection of the `Table` object are set to the appropriate values, and the `Table` object is appended to the `Catalog` object. This process is discussed in further detail in the following sections.

Providing Connection Information

When you link to an external table, you must provide information about the type, name, and location of the external database. This is accomplished by setting the following properties in the Properties collection of the Table object:

- Jet OLEDB:Link Provider String
- Jet OLEDB:Remote Table Name
- Jet OLEDB:Link Datasource

The following three lines of code illustrate the process of setting the provider string, name, and location of the source table:

```
tbl.Properties("Jet OLEDB:Link Provider String") = ";pwd=password"
tbl.Properties("Jet OLEDB:Remote Table Name") = "tblClients"
tbl.Properties("Jet OLEDB:Link Datasource") = CurrentProject.Path &
"\Chap19Data.mdb"
```

The Jet OLEDB:Link Provider is the ISAM format that will be used for the link. Each source database type is a different folder in the Windows registry. The folders are located in the HKEY_LOCAL_MACHINE\SOFTWARE\Microsoft\Jet\4.0\ISAM Formats section of the registry. Valid source database types are as follows:

dBASE	dBASE III, dBASE IV, and dBASE 5.0
Excel	Excel 3.0, Excel 4.0, Excel 5.0, and Excel 8.0
HTML	HTML Export and HTML Import
Jet	Jet 2.x, Jet 3.x
Lotus	Lotus WK1, Lotus WK3, Lotus WK4, Lotus WJ2, and Lotus WJ3
Exchange	Exchange 4.0
Outlook	Outlook 9.0
Paradox	Paradox 3.x, Paradox 4.x, Paradox 5.x, and Paradox 7.x
Text	N/A

The Jet OLEDB:Link Datasource must include a fully qualified path to the file. You can specify the path with a drive letter and directory path or by using *universal naming conventions* (UNCs). For a local database, you must specify the path like this:

```
tbl.Properties("Jet OLEDB:Link Datasource") = "c:\Databases\Chap19Data"
```

For a file server, you can specify the UNC path or the drive letter path. The UNC path looks like this:

```
tbl.Properties("Jet OLEDB:Link Datasource") = _
    "\\FILESERVERNAME\Databases\Chap19Data"
```

In this case, the database called Chap19Data is stored on the databases share of a particular file server.

Creating the Link

Listing 19.5 shows how you put all the connection information together to establish a link to an external table.

LISTING 19.5   Establishing a Link to an External Table

```
Sub LinkToDBase(strDirName As String, strTableName As String, _
   strAccessTable)
   Dim cat As ADOX.Catalog
   Dim tbl As ADOX.Table

    'Instantiate a Catalog  object
    Set cat = New ADOX.Catalog
    cat.ActiveConnection = CurrentProject.Connection

    'Instantiate a Table object
    Set tbl = New ADOX.Table
    tbl.Name = strAccessTable
    Set tbl.ParentCatalog = cat

    'Set necessary properties of the new Table object
    tbl.Properties("Jet OLEDB:Create Link") = True
    tbl.Properties("Jet OLEDB:Link Datasource") = strDirName
    tbl.Properties("Jet OLEDB:Link Provider String") = & _
    "dBASE III;HDR=NO;IMEX=2;"
    tbl.Properties("Jet OLEDB:Remote Table Name") = strTableName

    'Append the new table object to the tables collection
    'of the catalog object
    cat.Tables.Append tbl
End Sub
```

Here is an example of how this subroutine is called:

```
Call LinkToDBase("c:\customer\data","customer","tblCustomers")
```

The LinkToDBase subroutine receives three parameters:

- The name of the directory in which the dBASE file is stored.
- The name of the file (the name of the table, without the DBF extension) to which you want to connect.
- The name of the Access table that you are creating.

The subroutine creates two object variables: a `Catalog` object variable and a `Table` object variable. It points the ActiveConnection property of the `Catalog` object variable at the connection associated with the current database. Next, it establishes properties of the `Table` object. The Link Datasource is the name of the directory within which the dBASE file is stored. The Link Provider String specifies that the type of table you are linking to is a dBASE III file. The Remote Table Name is the name of the dBASE file that you are linking to. After setting these properties, you are ready to append the table definition to the database.

You have seen how you can link to a dBASE table. Listing 19.6 puts together everything you have learned thus far in this chapter by creating a link to an Access table stored in another database.

LISTING 19.6   Creating a Link to an Access Table Stored in Another Database

```
Sub LinkToAccess(strDBName As String, strTableName As String, _
    strAccessTable)
    Dim cat As ADOX.Catalog
    Dim tbl As ADOX.Table

    'Instantiate a Catalog object
    Set cat = New ADOX.Catalog

    'Set the ActiveConnection property of the Catalog object
    'to the connection associated with the current project
    cat.ActiveConnection = CurrentProject.Connection

    'Instantiate a Table object
    Set tbl = New ADOX.Table

    'Set the Name property of the Table object to the name
    'you wish to give to the linked table
    tbl.Name = strAccessTable

    'Set the ParentCatalog property of the Table object
    'to the Catalog object
    Set tbl.ParentCatalog = cat

    'Set all necessary properties of the Table object
    tbl.Properties("Jet OLEDB:Create Link") = True
    tbl.Properties("Jet OLEDB:Link Datasource") = strDBName
    tbl.Properties("Jet OLEDB:Link Provider String") = ";pwd=password"
    tbl.Properties("Jet OLEDB:Remote Table Name") = strTableName

    'Append the Table object to the Tables collection
    'associated with the CatalogObject
    cat.Tables.Append tbl
End Sub
```

19

USING EXTERNAL
DATA

Notice that the Jet OLEDB Link Provider string no longer specifies the type of database to which you are connecting. Everything else in this routine is the same as the routine that connected to dBASE. Also, notice the parameters passed to this routine:

```
Call LinkToAccess("C:\databases\northwind.mdb","Customers","tblCustomers")
```

The database passed to the routine is an actual Access database (as opposed to a directory), and the table name is the name of the Access table in the other database (instead of the DBF filename).

> **NOTE**
>
> Whether you link to an external database using the user interface or code, you should always use the UNC path, rather than a drive letter. This ensures that all users with access to the network share are able to see the data, regardless of their drive letter mappings.

Opening an External Table

There are times when you will want to open—rather than link to—an external table. Linking provides ease of use when dealing with external tables. After you link to a table, it is treated just like any other Access table. The disadvantage of linking is that it uses ODBC. ODBC is not the most efficient means of interacting with a database for which you have a native OLEDB provider. Therefore, you might want to programmatically open an external table without creating a link to it. Opening an external table is a two-step process:

1. Establish a connection to the external data source.
2. Point a `Recordset` object at the result of executing a SQL statement against the `Connection` object.

Providing Connection Information

The connection information you provide when you open an external table is similar to the information you provide when you link to the table. The connection information is provided as the `ConnectionString` argument of the `Open` method of the `Connection` object. Here's an example:

```
cnn.Open "Providersqlodedb;" & _
        "Data Source=(local);" & _ _
        "Initial Catalog=Pubs;" & _
        "User ID=sa;Password=;"
```

Here, the connection string is to the SQL Server database called Pubs on the local machine.

Opening the Table

The Recordset object is pointed at the result of executing a Select statement against the Connection object:

```
Set rst = cnn.EXEcute("Select * from Authors")
```

Listing 19.7 shows what the entire process looks like in code.

LISTING 19.7   Using the OpenDatabase Method

```
Sub OpenExternalSQL(strDBName As String, strTableName As String)
    Dim cnn As ADODB.Connection
    Dim rst As ADODB.Recordset

    'Instantiate Connection and Recordset objects
    Set cnn = New ADODB.Connection
    Set rst = New ADODB.Recordset

    'Use the Open method of the Connection object to establish
    'a connection to the SQL Server database
    cnn.Open "Provider=sqloledb;" & _
        "Data Source=(local);" & _
        "Initial Catalog=" & strDBName & ";" & _
        "User Id=sa;Password=; "


    'Use the Execute method of the Connection object to execute
    'a Select statement and return the result as a Recordset
    Set rst = cnn.Execute("Select * from " & strTableName)

    'Loop through the resulting recordset,
    'printing the value of the first field
    Do Until rst.EOF
        Debug.Print rst.Fields(0).Value
        rst.MoveNext
    Loop

    'Close the Connection
    cnn.Close
End Sub
```

Listing 19.7 is called with this code:

```
Call OpenExternalSQL("Pubs","authors")
```

Notice that you are not appending a table definition here. Instead, you are creating a temporary recordset that refers to the external data. After the external table is opened as a recordset, the code traverses through each record of the table, printing the value of the first field. Of course,

19

USING EXTERNAL
DATA

after the recordset is opened, you can manipulate it in any way you want. The table does not show up as a linked table in the database window. In fact, when the routine completes and the local variable goes out of scope, the recordset no longer exists.

Now that you have seen how you can link to external tables as well as open them, you are ready to take a look at how you can refine both these processes. This involves learning the Windows registry settings that affect the linking process, learning more about the parameters that are available to you when specifying connection information, learning how to specify passwords, learning how to refresh and remove links, and learning how to create an external table using VBA code.

Understanding Windows Registry Settings

Each ISAM driver has a separate key in the Windows registry. These keys are located in the appropriate ISAM driver in the HKEY_LOCAL_MACHINE\SOFTWARE\Microsoft\Jet\4.0\ISAM Formats section of the registry. These keys are used to configure the driver after initialization. As you can see in Figure 19.9, the setup program has created keys for several data sources. If you look at a specific data source (in this case, dBASE III), you can see all the settings that exist for the dBASE driver. The IndexFilter is set to dBASE Index(*.ndx), for example. At times, you will need to modify one of the registry settings to customize the behavior of the ISAM driver; this is covered later in this chapter in the section "Looking at Special Considerations."

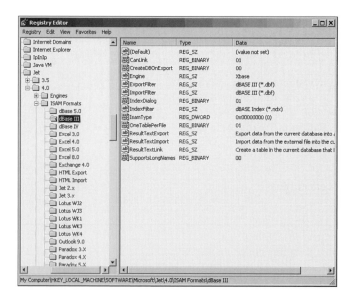

FIGURE 19.9

The Windows registry with keys for ISAM drivers.

Using the Jet OLEDB:Link Provider String

The Jet OLEDB:Link Provider String is used when linking to external tables. It includes the source database type, user ID, and password. A semicolon must be used to separate each part of the connection string.

Each source database type has a valid name. This is the name that must be used when accessing that type of data. These database types are found in the Windows registry under HKEY_LOCAL_MACHINE\Software\Microsoft\Jet\4.0\ISAM Formats. You must accurately specify the source database type, or you will be unable to access the external data.

The user ID is used whenever a username must be specified in order to successfully log on to the data source. This is most common when dealing with back-end databases such as Oracle, Sybase, or Microsoft SQL Server. This part of the provider string can be required to log on the user to the system where the source data resides. The UID keyword refers to the user ID.

As with the user ID, the password most often is included when dealing with back-end data. It also can be used on other database types that support passwords, such as Paradox, or when linking to an external Access table. The PWD keyword is used when specifying the password.

Finally, the dataset name refers to a defined ODBC data source. The DSN keyword refers to the dataset name in the connection string. The following is an example of a Jet OLEDB Link Provider String:

```
tbl.Properties("Jet OLEDB:Link Provider String") = "ODBC" & _
        ";DATABASE=Pubs" & _
        ";UID=Alison" & _
        ";PWD=MyPass" & _
        ";DSN=PublisherData"
```

In the example, the SQL Server database being accessed is Pubs, the user ID is Alison, the Password is MyPass, and the data source name is PublisherData.

Working with Passwords

In working with passwords, you probably won't want to hard-code the password into your application because that defeats the purpose of placing a password on your database. In Listing 19.8, the database's password is included in the code, allowing the link to be made to the secured table without any password validation.

LISTING 19.8 Embedding a Database Password in Code

```
Sub LinkToSecured()
    Dim cat As ADOX.Catalog
    Dim tbl As ADOX.Table
```

LISTING 19.8   Continued

```
    'Instantiate a Catalog object
    Set cat = New ADOX.Catalog

    'Set the ActiveConnection property of the Catalog
    'object to the connection associated with the
    'current project
    cat.ActiveConnection = CurrentProject.Connection

    'Instantiate a Table object
    Set tbl = New ADOX.Table

    'Set the Name property of the Table object
    tbl.Name = "tblLinkedTable"

    'Associate the ParentCatalog of the Table object
    'with the Catalog object
    Set tbl.ParentCatalog = cat

    'Set properties of the Table object
    tbl.Properties("Jet OLEDB:Create Link") = True
    tbl.Properties("Jet OLEDB:Link Provider String") = "ODBC" & _
        ";DATABASE=Pubs" & _
        ";UID=SA" & _
        ";PWD=" & _
        ";DSN=PublisherData"
    tbl.Properties("Jet OLEDB:Remote Table Name") = "Authors"

    'Append the Table object to the Tables collection
    'associated with the Catalog object
    cat.Tables.Append tbl
End Sub
```

An invalid password results in a message appearing, requiring the user to log on. Unless you are using integrated Windows NT security to log on to your database server, it is best to require the user to supply the password at runtime. In Listing 19.9, the code prompts the user for a password. The password entered by the user is used as part of the connection string.

LISTING 19.9   Requiring Password Validation

```
Sub ReallySecure()
    Dim cat As ADOX.Catalog
    Dim tbl As ADOX.Table
    Dim strPassword As String
```

Listing 19.9   Continued

```
    'Instantiate a Catalog object
    Set cat = New ADOX.Catalog

    'Set the ActiveConnection property of the Catalog
    'object to the connection associated with the
    'current project
    cat.ActiveConnection = CurrentProject.Connection

    Set tbl = New ADOX.Table

    'Set the Name property of the Table object
    tbl.Name = "tblLinkedTable"

    'Associate the ParentCatalog of the Table object
    'with the Catalog object
    Set tbl.ParentCatalog = cat

    'Prompt the user for the password
    strPassword = InputBox("Please Enter Your Password", "Database" & _
    "Security!!!")

    'Set properties of the Table object
    tbl.Properties("Jet OLEDB:Create Link") = True
    tbl.Properties("Jet OLEDB:Link Provider String") = "ODBC" & _
        ";DATABASE=Pubs" & _
        ";UID=SA" & _
        ";PWD=" & strPassword & _
        ";DSN=PublisherData"
    tbl.Properties("Jet OLEDB:Remote Table Name") = "Authors"

    'Append the Table object to the Tables collection
    'associated with the Catalog object
    cat.Tables.Append tbl
End Sub
```

Notice that the password is retrieved from the user and stored in a variable called strPassword. This strPassword variable is included in the connection string at runtime.

Refreshing and Removing Links

Refreshing links refers to updating the link to an external table. It is done when the location of an external table has changed. *Removing links* refers to permanently removing a link to an external table.

Access cannot find external tables if their locations have moved. You need to adjust for this in your VBA code. Furthermore, there might be times when you want to remove a link to external data—when it is no longer necessary to use the data, or when the data has been imported permanently into Access.

Updating Links That Have Moved

To refresh a link using VBA code, simply redefine the Jet OLEDB:Link Datasource. Listing 19.10 shows the code to refresh a link.

LISTING 19.10   Refreshing a Link

```
Sub RefreshLink()
    Dim cat As ADOX.Catalog
    Dim tdf As ADOX.Table

    Set cat = New ADOX.Catalog
    Set cat.ActiveConnection = CurrentProject.Connection
    tdf.Properties("Jet OLEDB:Link Datasource") = _
        strNewLocation
End Sub
```

You can modify this routine to prompt the user for the directory containing the data tables, as Listing 19.11 shows.

LISTING 19.11   Prompting the User for the Database Path and Name

```
Sub RefreshLink()
    'Initiate error handling
    On Error GoTo RefreshLink_Err
    Dim cat As ADOX.Catalog
    Dim tdf As ADOX.Table
    Dim strNewLocation As String
    Dim strTemp As String

    'Instantiate a Catalog object
    Set cat = New ADOX.Catalog

    'Set the ActiveConnection property of the Catalog
    'object to the connection associated with the
    'current project
    Set cat.ActiveConnection = CurrentProject.Connection
```

LISTING 19.11 Continued

```
    'Point the TableeDef object at the tblClients table
    Set tdf = cat.Tables("tblClients")

    'Attempt to retrieve the Name property of the table
    strTemp = tdf.Columns(0).Name

    'Exit the routine if all goes well
    Exit Sub

RefreshLink_Err:

    'If an error occurs, prompt the user for the new name
    'and location
    strNewLocation = InputBox("Please Enter Database Path and Name")

    'Set the properties of the TableDef object to the
    'information provided by the user
    tdf.Properties("Jet OLEDB:Link Datasource") = _
        strNewLocation
    Set cat.ActiveConnection = CurrentProject.Connection
    Set tdf = cat.Tables("tblClients")

    'Try to grab the name property again
    Resume
End Sub
```

This routine points a Table object to the tblClients table. It then attempts to access the name of the first column in the table. If an error occurs, an input box prompts the user for the new location of the database. The Jet OLEDB:Link Datasource property for the database is modified to incorporate the new location. The code then resumes on the offending line of code. You should modify this routine to give the user a way out. Resume throws the user into an endless loop if the database is not available. An enhanced routine (see Listing 19.13) is presented later in the "Practical Examples" section of this chapter.

Deleting Links

To remove a link using VBA code, simply execute a Delete method of the Tables collection of a Catalog object connected to the database, as shown in Listing 19.12.

LISTING 19.12   Removing a Link

```
Sub RemoveLink()
    Dim cat As Catalog

    Set cat = New ADOX.Catalog
    cat.ActiveConnection = CurrentProject.Connection

    cat.Tables.Delete ("tblClients")

End Sub
```

Looking at Special Considerations

When dealing with different types of external files, various problems and issues arise. If you understand these stumbling blocks before they affect you, you will get a great head start in dealing with these potential obstacles.

dBASE

The major concerns you will have when dealing with dBASE files surround deleted records, indexes, data types, and memo fields. When you delete a record from a dBASE table, it is not actually removed from the table. Instead, it is just marked for deletion. You must Pack the database (a process in a dBASE table that removes deleted rows) must be completed in order for the records to actually be removed from the table. If records are deleted from a dBASE table using an Access application, the records are not removed. Because you cannot pack a dBASE database from within an Access application, the records still remain in the table. In fact, they are not automatically filtered from the Access table. In order to filter deleted records so that they cannot be seen within the Access application, the Deleted value in the \HKEY_LOCAL_MACHINE\SOFTWARE\Microsoft\Jet\4.0\Engines\Xbase section of the registry must be set to 01 (True).

Access can use the dBASE indexes to improve performance (Jet 4.0 Service Pack 5 the Borland Database Engine must be installed). After you link to a dBASE table and select an index, an INF file is created. This file has the same name as your dBASE database with an INF extension. It contains information about all the indexes being used. Here's an example of an INF:

```
[dBASE III]
NDX1=CUSTID.NDX
UNDX1=CUSTID.NDX
```

dBASE III is the database type identifier. NDX1 is an index number for the first index. The UNDX1 entry specifies a unique index.

The data types available in dBASE files are different from those available in Access files. It is important to understand how the field types are mapped. Table 19.4 shows how each dBASE data type is mapped to a Jet data type.

TABLE 19.4   Mapping of dBASE Data Types

dBASE Data Type	Jet Data Type
Character	Text
Numeric, Float	Double
Logical	Boolean
Date	Date/Time
Memo	Memo
OLE	OLE Object

Finally, make sure that the dBASE memo files are stored in the same directory as the table. Otherwise, Access is unable to read the data in the memo file.

Text Data

When linking to an ASCII text file, Jet can determine the format of the file directly, or it can use a schema information file, which resides in the same directory as the text file. It always is named SCHEMA.INI, and it contains information about the format of the file, the column names, and the data types. The schema information file is optional for delimited files, but it is required for fixed length files. It is important to understand that ASCII files can never be opened for shared use.

Troubleshooting

Unfortunately, working with external data is not always a smooth process. Many things can go wrong, including connection problems and a lack of temporary disk space.

Connection Problems

Difficulties with accessing external data can be caused by any of the following circumstances:

- The server on which the external data is stored is down.
- The user does not have rights to the directory in which the external data is stored.
- The user does not have rights to the external data source.
- The external data source was moved.
- The UNC path or network share name was modified.

- The connection string is incorrect.
- The installable ISAM driver has not been installed.

Temp Space

Access requires a significant amount of disk space in order to run complex queries on large tables. This disk space is required whether the tables are linked tables stored remotely in another format, or they reside on the local machine. The application behaves unpredictably if not enough disk space is available to run the query. It therefore is necessary to make sure that all users have enough disk space to meet the requirements of the queries that are run.

Looking at Performance Considerations and Links

Because your application has to go through an extra translation layer, the installable ISAM, performance is not nearly as good with ISAM files as it is with native Jet data. It always is best to import ISAM data whenever possible. If it is not possible to import the data, you need to accept the performance that linking offers or consider linking the best solution to an otherwise unsolvable problem.

Working with HTML Documents

Access 2002 enables you to import, export, and link to HTML documents. Although working with HTML documents is similar to working with other files types, HTML documents deserve special mention. To import an HTML document, follow these steps:

1. Right-click anywhere within the Database window and choose Import.
2. From the Files of Type drop-down list, select HTML Documents.
3. Select the document you want to import and click Import. The Import HTML Wizard appears, as shown in Figure 19.10.
4. The first step of the wizard attempts to parse the HTML document into fields. You can accept what the wizard has done or click Advanced. The Import Specification dialog box that appears enables you to designate field names, data types, and indexes for each field; and to select any fields you want to eliminate from the imported file. (See Figure 19.11.) This dialog box also enables you to modify the date order, date delimiter, and more.
5. After you make any required changes to the import specifications, click OK to return to the Import HTML Wizard. Click Next to advance to the next step of the wizard, which enables you to select whether the imported data is stored in a new table or in an existing table. Make your selection and then click Next.

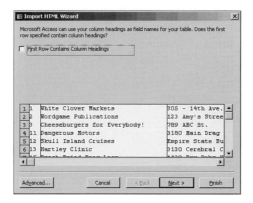

FIGURE 19.10

The first step of the Import HTML Wizard.

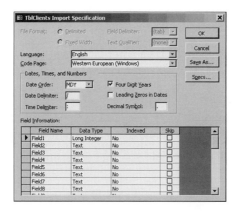

FIGURE 19.11

The Import Specification dialog box enables you to designate the specifics of the import.

6. Designate a field name, data type, and index for each field, as shown in Figure 19.12. Make any desired changes here and click Next.

7. The fourth step of the wizard enables you to indicate that you want Access to add a primary key to the table, that you want to select your own primary key, or that you don't want the imported table to have a primary key. Make your selection and click Next.

8. The final step of the wizard enables you to assign a name to the table. You even can have the wizard analyze the table after importing it. Click Finish after you make your selection.

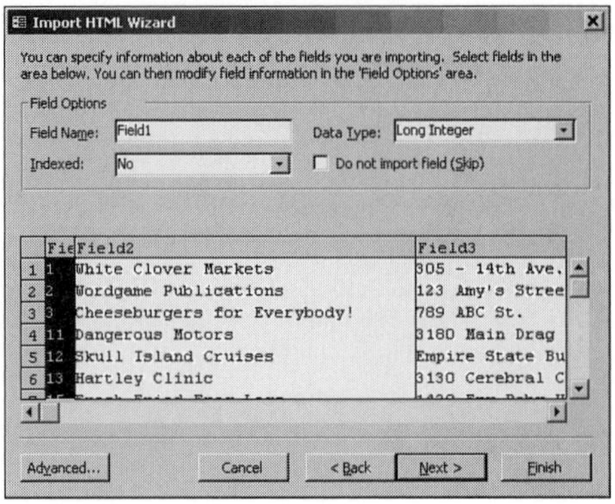

FIGURE 19.12

Customizing the properties of each imported field.

Not only can you import an HTML document, but you also can link to one. To link to an HTML document, follow these steps:

1. Right-click anywhere within the Database window and choose Link Tables.

2. From the Files of Type drop-down list, select HTML Documents.

3. Select the table you want to link to and click Link. The Link HTML Wizard appears.

4. Click the Advanced button to modify any link specifications and return to the first step of the wizard. Click Next to move to the second step of the wizard.

5. Specify information about each field you are linking to. Make any required changes and click Next.

6. Supply a name for the linked table and click Finish.

Whereas an imported HTML document acts like any other Access table, the data in a linked HTML document cannot be modified from within Access. You can use the linked document to create queries, reports, and forms.

PRACTICAL EXAMPLES

Working with External Data from within Your Application

It's time to split the data tables from the remainder of the application objects. You easily can accomplish this using the Database Splitter. After you split the tables from the rest of the database objects, you need to write code to refresh links. Both these topics are covered in this section.

Splitting the Database Using the Database Splitter

Begin by using the Database Splitter (covered in Chapter 20, "Developing Multiuser and Enterprise Applications") to separate the tables from the rest of the database objects. The CHAP19EX.MDB and CHAP19DATA.MDB files are included on the sample code CD-ROM. The CHAP19DATA.MDB file contains all the tables, and CHAP19EX.MDB contains the rest of the database objects.

Refreshing Links

If you distribute your application and all users did not have the same path to the CHAP19DATA.MDB file, the application would not load successfully. The LinkTables routine, located in the Switchboard startup form, ensures that the tables are successfully linked, as Listing 19.13 shows.

Listing 19.13   Loading the Application and Checking Table Attachments

```
Sub LinkTables()
    Dim objFileDialog As FileDialog

    On Error GoTo LinkTables_Err:

    DoCmd.Hourglass True

    'Determine if links are ok
    If Not VerifyLink Then

        'If not ok, attempt to relink with expected file name
        If Not ReLink(CurrentProject.FullName, True) Then

            'If still not ok, ask user to locate file
            Set objFileDialog = FileDialog(msoFileDialogOpen)

            With objFileDialog
                .AllowMultiSelect = False
                .Show
            End With

            'Attempt to link to file that user selected
            If Not ReLink(objFileDialog.SelectedItems(1), False) Then

                'If not successful, display a message a quit app
                MsgBox "You Cannot Run This App Without " & _
                    "Locating Data Tables"
                DoCmd.Close acForm, "frmSplash"
```

19

USING EXTERNAL
DATA

Listing 19.13   Continued

```
            DoCmd.Quit
        End If
    End If
End If

DoCmd.Hourglass False
Exit Sub

LinkTables_Err:
    DoCmd.Hourglass False
    MsgBox "Error # " & Err.Number & ": " & Err.Description
    Exit Sub
End Sub
```

Notice that the VerifyLink routine is called from the LinkTables routine. The VerifyLink routine appears in Listing 19.14.

Listing 19.14   The VerifyLink Routine Tests to See Whether Any Table Links Are Broken

```
Function VerifyLink() As Boolean
    'Verify connection information in linked tables.

    'Declare Required Variables
    Dim cat As ADOX.Catalog
    Dim tdf As ADOX.Table
    Dim strTemp As String

    'Point Database object variable at the current database
    Set cat = New ADOX.Catalog

    With cat
        Set .ActiveConnection = CurrentProject.Connection

        'Continue if links are broken.
        On Error Resume Next

        'Open one linked table to see if connection
        'information is correct.
        For Each tdf In .Tables
            If tdf.Type = "LINK" Then
                strTemp = tdf.Columns(0).Name
                If Err.Number Then
```

LISTING 19.14 Continued

```
                Exit For
            End If
        End If

    Next tdf
End With

VerifyLink = (Err.Number = 0)

End Function
```

The routine begins by pointing the ActiveConnection property of the `Catalog` object to the connection associated with the current database. It then loops through each table in the Tables collection of the `Catalog` object. If the table is a linked table, it attempts to access the name of the first column in the table. If any of the links are broken, an error occurs, and the `For...Each` loop is exited. If no error occurs, the function returns `True`; otherwise, the function returns `False`.

If the `VerifyLink` routine returns `False`, the `ReLink` routine is called. Listing 19.15 shows the `ReLink` routine.

LISTING 19.15 The `ReLink` Routine Attempts to Re-establish the Broken Links

```
Function ReLink(strDir As String, DefaultData As Boolean) _
    As Boolean

    ' Relink a broken linked Access table.

    Dim cat As ADOX.Catalog
    Dim tdfRelink As ADOX.Table
    Dim oDBInfo As DBInfo
    Dim strPath As String
    Dim strName As String
    Dim intCounter As Integer
    Dim vntStatus As Variant

    'Prepare status bar
    vntStatus = SysCmd(acSysCmdSetStatus, "Updating Links")

    Set cat = New ADOX.Catalog

    'Instantiate database information class
    Set oDBInfo = New DBInfo
```

19

USING EXTERNAL DATA

LISTING 19.15 Continued

```
With cat
    .ActiveConnection = CurrentProject.Connection

    'Extract the name and path from the passed database
    oDBInfo.FullName = strDir
    strPath = oDBInfo.FilePathOnly
    strName = Left(oDBInfo.FileName, InStr(oDBInfo.FileName, ".") - 1)

    On Error Resume Next
    'Update progress meter
    Call SysCmd(acSysCmdInitMeter, "Linking Data Tables", .Tables.Count)

    'Loop through each table, attempting to update the link
    For Each tdfRelink In .Tables
        intCounter = intCounter + 1
        Call SysCmd(acSysCmdUpdateMeter, intCounter)
        If .Tables(tdfRelink.Name).Type = "LINK" And _
            Left(tdfRelink.Name, 3) = "tbl" Then
            tdfRelink.Properties("Jet OLEDB:Link Datasource") = _
            strPath & strName & IIf(DefaultData, "Data.Mdb", ".mdb")
        End If
        If Err.Number Then
            Exit For
        End If
    Next tdfRelink
End With

'Reset the progress meter
Call SysCmd(acSysCmdRemoveMeter)

vntStatus = SysCmd(acSysCmdClearStatus)

ReLink = (Err = 0)
End Function
```

The ReLink function receives two parameters. The first parameter is the name of the database the function will attempt to link to. The second parameter is a Boolean variable that designates whether the database is considered the default database.

The function begins by modifying the status bar. It then creates a Catalog object and an instance of a custom class called DBInfo. This custom class is covered in further detail in Chapter 32, "Distributing Your Application." Class modules are covered in Chapter 13, "Exploiting the Power of Class Modules." The ActiveConnection property of the catalog object is set equal to the Connection property of the current project. Next, the FullName property of the DBInfo class is set equal to the name of the file that is passed as a parameter to the function. The DBInfo class extracts the path and the filename from the full filename. Just as with the VerifyLink function, the ReLink function uses a For...Next loop to loop through all the tables in the database. As it loops through each table, it attempts to establish a link to a database with the name passed as parameter to the ReLink function.

This ReLink function is called twice from the LinkTables routine, shown in Listing 19.13. The first time it is passed, the FullName property of the CurrentProject object and the boolean is True, indicating that it will try to locate the table in a database with the same location as the application database. If that attempt is not successful, the LinkTables routine uses the FileDialog object to display the File Open dialog, allowing the user to attempt to locate the database. The ReLink function is called again, searching for the table in the database selected by the user. If it is still unsuccessful, the routine quits the application.

Summary

The capability to link to external data is one of Access 2002's strongest attributes. It is important that you understand how to link to external data via the user interface and by using VBA code. This chapter taught you how to link to external tables, open external data sources directly, refresh and remove links, and create external tables using VBA code. Many of the techniques covered in this chapter are covered extensively in *Alison Balter's Mastering Access 2002 Enterprise Development*.

Developing Multiuser and Enterprise Applications

IN THIS CHAPTER

Why This Chapter Is Important

Many people forge right into the application development process with little worry about the scalability of the application. Even a simple application that begins as a single-user application can develop into a multiuser application. It can even be used throughout the enterprise. Unfortunately, the techniques you can get away with in the single-user application can wreak havoc in a network or client/server environment. It is therefore necessary to think about the future when you design any application. Although the initial development process might be more complex, if written properly, the application will survive any growth that it experiences. This chapter focuses on writing applications that transition easily from the single-user environment through the enterprise client/server environment.

Designing Your Application with Multiuser Issues in Mind

When you develop applications that will be accessed over the network by multiple users, you must make sure they effectively handle sharing data and other application objects. Many options are available for developers when they design multiuser applications, and this chapter covers the pros and cons of these options.

Multiuser issues revolve around locking data; they include deciding where to store database objects, when to lock data, and how much data to lock. In a multiuser environment, having several users simultaneously trying to modify the same data can cause conflicts. As a developer, you need to handle these conflicts. Otherwise, your users will experience unexplainable errors.

Multiuser Design Strategies

There are many methods for handling concurrent access to data and other application objects by multiple users; each one offers both solutions and limitations. It's important to select the best solution for your particular environment.

Strategies for Installing Access

There are two strategies for installing Access:

- Run Access from a file server across a network
- Run a separate copy of Access on each workstation

The advantages of running Access from a file server are that it

- Allows for central administration of the Access software.
- Reduces hard disk requirements.

- Potentially reduces the licensing requirements.

- Allows Access applications to be installed on diskless workstations.

- Reduces hard disk requirements.

> **NOTE**
>
> The Access software takes up a significant amount of disk space. Although using the Access runtime engine can reduce disk space requirements, local hard-disk space can definitely be a problem. Installing Access on the file server at least partially eliminates this problem. It can totally eliminate the problem if dynamic link libraries (DLLs) are also installed on the file server.

File server installations also have serious drawbacks, including the following:

- Every time the user launches an Access application, the Access EXE, DLLs, and any other files required to run Access are *all* sent over the network wire to the local machine. Obviously, this generates a significant volume of network traffic.

- Performance is generally degraded to unacceptable levels.

Because the disadvantages of running Access from a file server are so pronounced, I strongly recommend that Access, or at least the runtime engine, be installed on each user's machine.

Strategies for Installing Your Application

Just as there are different strategies for installing Access, there are also various strategies for installing your application, such as the following:

- Install both the application and data on a file server

- Install the data on the file server and the application on each workstation

- Install the application and the data on a machine running Windows 2000 Terminal Services

In other words, after you have created an application, you can place the entire application on the network, which means that all the tables, queries, forms, reports, macros, and modules that make up the system reside on the file server. Although this method of shared access keeps everything in the same place, you will see many advantages to placing only the database's data tables on the file server. The remaining objects are placed in a database on each user's machine, and each local application database is linked to the tables on the network. In this way, users share data but not the rest of the application objects.

20

MULTIUSER AND ENTERPRISE APPLICATIONS

The advantages of doing this are as follows:

- Because each user has a copy of the local database objects, load time and network traffic are both reduced.
- It's very easy to back up data without having to back up the rest of the application objects.
- When redistributing new versions of the application, you don't need to worry about overwriting the application's data.
- Multiple applications can all be designed to use the same centrally located data.
- Users can add their own objects (such as their own queries) to their local copies of the database.

In addition to storing the queries, forms, reports, macros, and modules that make up the application in a local database, I also recommend that you store the following objects in each local database:

- Temporary tables
- Static tables
- Semistatic tables

Temporary tables should be stored in the database that's on each workstation because, if two users are performing operations that build the same temporary tables, you don't want one user's process to interfere with the other user's process. The potential conflict of one user's temporary tables overwriting the other's can be eliminated by storing all temporary tables in each user's local copy of the database.

You should also place static lookup tables, such as state tables, on each workstation. Because the data doesn't change, maintenance isn't an issue. The benefit is that Access doesn't need to pull that data over the network each time it's needed.

Semistatic tables—tables that are rarely updated—can also be placed on the local machine. As with static tables, having these tables in a local database means reduced network traffic and better performance, not only for the user needing the data, but also for anyone sharing the same network wire. Changes made to the semistatic tables can be transported to each workstation by using replication (covered briefly in this chapter and in significant detail in *Alison Balter's Mastering Access 2002 Enterprise Development*).

The configuration described throughout this section is illustrated in Figure 20.1.

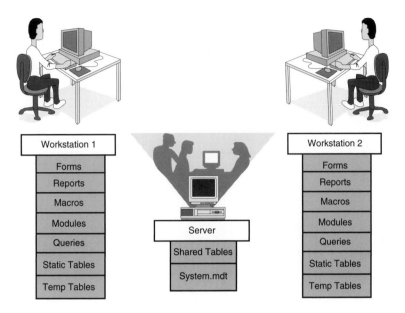

FIGURE 20.1

An example of a configuration with database objects split, storing temporary and static tables locally and shared tables remotely (on the file server).

The final option has recently emerged as a viable alternative for deployment of an Access application. It addresses both bandwidth and centralization issues. With this option, a Windows 2000 machine runs the Windows 2000 Terminal Services. Client machines then access the server machine using the Terminal Server Client Utility. In this scenario, Access, your application, and the data that it accesses, are all installed on the Windows 2000 Server machine. All other machines access the application via user sessions created on the server machine. Keystrokes and mouse events are sent from the client machines to the server machine. The resulting screen image is returned to the client machine. This configuration addresses many of the problems inherent in the two other solutions.

The Basics of Linking to External Data

Linking to external data, including data not stored in another Access database, is covered extensively in Chapter 19, "Using External Data." Three options are available to you:

- Design the databases separately from the start.
- Include all objects in one database; then split them manually when you're ready to distribute your application.
- Include all objects in one database; then split them by using the Database Splitter Wizard.

The first two options are covered in Chapter 19. The last option, the Database Splitter Wizard, is covered here. To split the objects in a database into two separate .MDB files, follow these steps:

1. Open the database whose objects you want to split.

2. Choose Tools|Database Utilities|Database Splitter to open the Database Splitter dialog box, shown in Figure 20.2.

FIGURE 20.2

The Database Splitter Wizard helps you split the data tables that should reside on the server.

3. Click Split Database; this opens the Create Back-end Database dialog box. (See Figure 20.3.)

FIGURE 20.3

Entering a name for the new shared database.

4. Enter the name for the database that will contain all the tables. Click Split. The Database Splitter Wizard creates a new database holding all the tables, and links are created between the current database and the database containing the tables. (See Figure 20.4.)

FIGURE 20.4

The database that has been split.

Understanding Access's Locking Mechanisms

Although the preceding tips for designing network applications reduce network traffic, they in no way reduce locking conflicts. To protect shared data, Access locks either a record or a page of data as the user edits a record. In this way, multiple users can read the data, but only one user can make changes to it. Data can be locked through a form or through a recordset that isn't bound to a form.

Here are the methods of locking for an Access application:

- Record locking
- Page locking
- Table and Recordset locking
- Opening an entire database with Exclusive Access

With Record locking, only the record the user is editing is locked. With Page locking, the 4K page with the record being edited is locked. On the other hand, in Table and Recordset locking, the entire table or recordset with the record being edited is locked. With Database locking, the entire database is locked, unless the user opening the database has opened it for read-only access. In that case, other users can also open the database for read-only access. The ability to get exclusive use of a database can be restricted through security.

It's important to note that the locking scheme you adhere to depends on the source providing the data. If you're using client/server data, you inherit the locking scheme of the particular back end you're using. If you're manipulating ISAM data over a network, you get the type of data locking that the particular ISAM database supports. For example, if you're working with a FoxPro database, you can use Record locking or any other locking scheme that FoxPro supports.

> **NOTE**
>
> Multiuser development and multiuser issues are covered in extensive detail in *Alison Balter's Mastering Access 2002 Enterprise Development.*

Understanding the Client/Server Model

Now that you understand the basics of using Access in a multiuser environment, I am going to take things a step further by discussing client/server applications. *One* of the hot computing terms of the '90s, *client/server* refers to distributed processing of information. A client/server model involves the storage of data on database servers dedicated to the tasks of processing data and storing it.

The client/server model introduces a separation of functionalities. The *client*, or front end, is responsible for presenting the data and doing some processing. The *server*, or back end, is responsible for storing, protecting, and performing the bulk of the data processing.

With its tools that assist in the rapid development of queries, forms, and reports, Access provides an excellent front end for the presentation of back-end data.

For years, most information professionals have worked with traditional programming languages to process and maintain data integrity in the application. This means that data validation rules must be embedded in the programming code. Furthermore, these types of applications are record oriented—that is, all records are read into memory and processed. This scenario has several drawbacks:

- If the underlying data structure changes, every application that uses the data structure must be changed.

- Data validation rules must be placed in *every* application that accesses a data table.

- Presentation, processing, and storage are handled by one program.

- Record-oriented processing results in an extraordinary amount of unnecessary network traffic.

Deciding Whether to Use the Client/Server Model

Client/server technology was not as necessary when there was a clear delineation between mainframe applications and personal computer applications. Today, the line of demarcation has blurred. Personal computer applications are beginning to take over many applications that had been relegated to mainframe computers in the past. The problem is that users still are very limited by the bandwidth of network communications. This is one place where client/server technology can really help.

However, many developers are confused about what client/server architecture really is. Some mistakenly believe that an Access MDB database file stored on a file server acts as a database server. This is not the case. (In fact, I have participated in many debates in which other developers have insisted that Access itself is a database server application. Well, it's not.) Access is a front-end application that can process data stored on a back end. In this scenario, the Access application runs on the client machine accessing data stored on a database server running software such as Microsoft SQL Server. Access does an excellent job acting as the client-side, front-end software in this scenario. The confusion lies in Access's capability to act as a database server.

Many people mistakenly believe that an Access MDB database file stored on a file server acts as a database server. This is not the case. The difference lies in the way that data is retrieved when Access is acting as the front end to a database server versus when the data is stored in an Access MDB file. Suppose that you have a table with 500,000 records. A user runs a query based on the 500,000-record table stored in an Access database on a file server. Suppose that the user wants to see a list of all the Californians who make more than $75,000 per year. With the data stored on the file server in the Access MDB file format, all records would be sent over the network to the workstation, and the query would be performed on the workstation. (See Figure 20.5.) This results in significant network traffic.

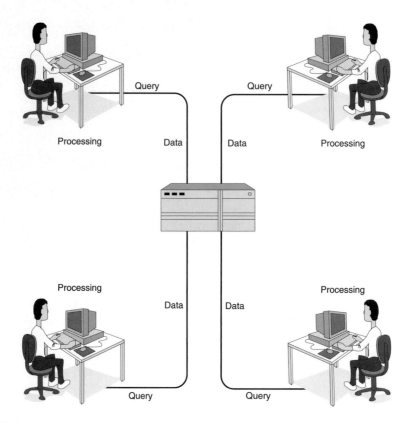

FIGURE 20.5

Access as a front end using data stored in an Access database.

On the other hand, assume that these 500,000 records were stored on a database server such as Microsoft SQL Server. If user runs the same query, only the names of the Californians who make more than $75,000 per year would be sent over the network. In this scenario, only the specific fields requested would be retrieved. (See Figure 20.6.)

What does this mean to you? When should you become concerned with client/server technology and what it can offer you? The following sections present some guidelines as to why you might want to upsize from an Access back end to a SQL Server back end.

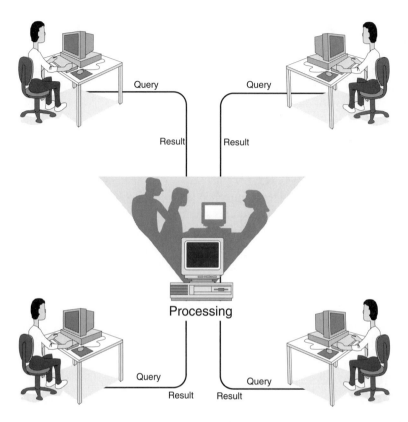

FIGURE 20.6

Access as a front end using a true back end.

Dealing with a Large Volume of Data

As the volume of data in your Access database increases, you probably will notice a degradation in performance. Many people say that 100MB is the magical number for the maximum
size of an Access database, but many back-end database servers can handle databases containing multiple gigabytes of data. Although a maximum size of 100MB for an Access database is
a good general guideline, it is *not* a hard-and-fast rule. You might find that the need to upsize
occurs when your database is significantly larger or smaller than 100MB. The magic number
for you depends on all the factors discussed in the following sections, as well as on how many
tables are included in the database. Generally, Access performs better with large volumes of
data stored in a single table rather than in multiple tables.

Dealing with a Large Number of Concurrent Users

Just as a large volume of data can be a problem, so can a large number of concurrent users. In fact, more than 10 users concurrently accessing an Access database can degrade performance. As with the amount of data, this is not a magical number. I have seen applications with fewer than 10 users where performance is awful, and I have seen applications with significantly more than 10 users where performance is acceptable. It often depends on how the application is designed, as well as what tasks the users are performing.

Demanding Faster Performance

Certain applications demand better performance than other applications. An Online Transaction Processing system (OLTP) generally requires significantly better performance than a Decision Support System (DSS), for example. Suppose that 100 users are simultaneously taking phone orders. It would not be appropriate for the users of the system to ask their customers to wait 15 seconds between entering each item that is ordered. On the other hand, asking users to wait 60 seconds to process a management report that users run once each month is not a lot to ask (although many still will complain about the minute).

Most back-end database servers can use multithreaded operating systems with multiple processors to handle large volumes of user demand; Access cannot.

Handling Increased Network Traffic

As a file server in an organization experiences increasing demands, the Access application simply might exacerbate an already growing problem. By moving the application data to a database server, the overall reduced demands on the network might provide all users on the network with better performance regardless of whether they are using the Access application.

Probably one of the most exaggerated situations I have seen is one in which all the workstations were diskless. Windows and all application software were installed on a file server. All the users were concurrently loading Microsoft Word, Microsoft Excel, and Microsoft PowerPoint over the network. In addition, they had large Access applications with many database objects and large volumes of data. All this was stored on the file server as well. Needless to say, performance was abysmal. You can't expect an already overloaded file server to handle sending large volumes of data over a small bandwidth. The benefits offered by client/server technology can help alleviate this problem.

Implementing Backup and Recovery

The backup and recovery options offered with an Access MDB database stored on a file server simply do not rival the options for backup and recovery on a database server. Any database server worth its salt sports very powerful uninterruptible power sources (UPSs). Many have hot-swappable disk drives with disk mirroring, disk duplexing, or disk striping with parity (RAID Level 5). With disk mirroring and duplexing, data can be written to multiple drives at one time, providing instantaneous backups. Furthermore, some database server tape backup software enables backups to be completed while users are accessing the system. Many offer automatic transaction logging. All these options mean less chance of data loss or downtime. With certain applications, this type of backup and recovery is overkill. With other applications, it is imperative. Although some of what back ends have to offer in backup and recovery can be mimicked by using code and replication, it is nearly impossible to get the same level of protection from an Access database stored on a file server that you can get from a database stored on a database server.

Focusing on Security

Access offers what can be considered the best security for a desktop database. However, it cannot compare with the security provided by most database servers. Database server security often works in conjunction with the network operating system. This is the case, for example, with Microsoft SQL Server and Windows NT Server. The user is given no direct rights to the physical database file; it can be accessed only via an ODBC data source or an ADO connection. Remember that no matter how much security you place on an Access database, this does not prevent a user from seeing or even deleting the entire MDB file from the network disk.

It is very easy to offer protection from this potential problem, and others, on a database server. Furthermore, many back-end application database server products offer field-level security not offered within an Access MDB file. Finally, many back ends offer integrated security with one logon for both the network and the database.

Sharing Data Among Multiple Front-End Tools

The Access MDB file format is proprietary. Very few other products can read data stored in the Access database format. With a back-end database server that supports open database connectivity (ODBC), front-end applications can be written in a variety of front-end application software, all concurrently using the same back-end data.

Understanding What It All Means

You must evaluate the specific environment in which your application will run:

- How many users are there?
- How much data exists?
- What is the network traffic already like?
- What type of performance is required?
- How disastrous is downtime?

- How sensitive is the data?
- What other applications will use the data?

After you answer these and other questions, you can begin to decide whether the benefits of the client/server architecture outweigh the costs involved.

The good news is that it is not an all-or-none decision. Various options are available for client/server applications using Access as a front end. Furthermore, if you design your application with upsizing in mind, moving to client/server technology will not require you to throw out what you have done and start again. In fact, Microsoft provides an upsizing wizard that makes upsizing to a SQL Server database a relatively painless process. How painless depends on numerous factors, including how complex your queries are, whether your queries include VBA functions, and other factors that are covered later in this chapter, and in detail in *Alison Balter's Mastering Access 2002 Enterprise Development*.

The Roles Access Plays in the Application Design Model

This section takes a look at the many different roles Access can take in an application design.

The Front End and Back End as Access MDB Files

Earlier in this book, you learned about using Access as both the front end and the back end. The Access database is not acting as a true back end because it is not doing any processing. Figure 20.7 shows the architecture in this scenario. The Access application resides on the workstation. Access uses the Microsoft Jet Engine to communicate with data stored in an Access MDB database file stored on the file server.

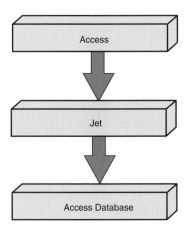

FIGURE 20.7

Access as a front end using an MDB file for data storage.

The Front End as an MDB File Using Links to Communicate to a Back End

In the second scenario, back-end tables can be linked to the front-end application database (.MDB). The process of linking to back-end tables is almost identical to that of linking to tables in other Access databases or to external tables stored in FoxPro, Paradox, or dBASE. And, the linked tables can be treated like any other linked tables. Access uses ODBC to communicate with the back-end tables. (See Figure 20.8.) Your application sends an Access SQL statement to the Access Jet Engine, which translates the statement into ODBC SQL. This ODBC SQL statement is then sent to the ODBC Manager, which locates the correct ODBC driver and passes it the ODBC SQL statement. Supplied by the back-end vendor, the driver translates the statement into the back end's specific dialect. The now back end–specific query is sent to the SQL server and to the appropriate database. As you might imagine, all this translation takes quite a bit of time. Furthermore, ODBC is becoming a technology of the past; it is quickly being replaced by the ADO/OLEDB technology. That is why one of the two alternatives that follow might be a better solution.

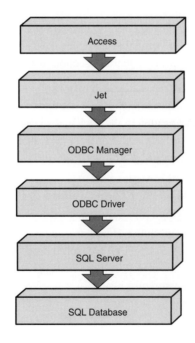

FIGURE 20.8

Access as a front end using links to back-end tables.

The Front End Using SQL Pass-Through to Communicate to a Back End

One of the bottlenecks of using linked tables is waiting for all the translation to happen. Because of this and for the following reasons, you want to bypass the translation process:

- Access SQL might not support some operation that is supported by the native query language of the back end.
- Either the Jet Engine or the ODBC driver produces a SQL statement that is not optimized for the back end.
- You want a process performed in its entirety on the back end.

As an alternative, you can execute a pass-through query written in the syntax specific to the back-end database server. Although the query does pass through the Jet Engine, Jet does not perform any translation on the query. Neither does ODBC. The ODBC Manager sends the query to the ODBC driver, which passes the query to the back end without performing any translation. In other words, exactly what was sent from Access is what is received by the SQL database. Figure 20.9 illustrates this scenario. Notice that the Jet Engine, the ODBC Manager, and the ODBC driver are not eliminated entirely. They are still there, but they have much less impact on the process than they do with attached tables. Pass-through queries are covered in more detail in the "Using Pass-Through Queries" section of this chapter.

As you will see later in this chapter, pass-through queries are not a panacea, although they are very useful. The results of a pass-through query are not updateable, for example. Furthermore, because pass-through queries are written in the back end's specific SQL dialect, you must rewrite them if you swap out your back end. For these reasons and others, pass-through queries generally are used with other solutions.

The Front End Executing Procedures Stored on a Back End

A *stored procedure* is compiled SQL code stored on a back end. It is generally executed using ADO or DAO code. You can also execute a stored procedure using a pass-through query. Regardless of what you call it, the code within the stored procedure is written in the SQL native to the back end on which it is stored, and the stored procedure is executed in entirety on the back end. Stored procedures can return results or can simply execute on the back end without returning any data.

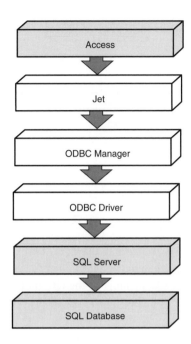

FIGURE 20.9
Access sending a pass-through query to a back-end database.

The Front End as a Microsoft Access Data Project Communicating Directly to a Back End

An additional, very viable solution is available when working with a back-end database server. This involves using a Microsoft Access Data Project (.adp), which was introduced with Access 2000. By using a Microsoft Access Data Project (.adp), you bypass the Jet Engine entirely. An Access project contains only code-based objects such as forms, reports, data access pages, macros, and modules. All tables, views, database diagrams, functions, and stored procedures are stored in a SQL Server database. After you have connected with a SQL Server database, you can easily view, create, modify, and delete SQL Server objects. Figure 20.10 illustrates this scenario. Notice that neither the Jet Engine nor ODBC is involved in the scenario.

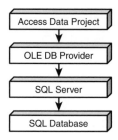

FIGURE 20.10
Access using a Microsoft Access Data Project to communicate to a back end.

Learning the Client/Server Buzzwords

People who talk about client/server technology use many terms that are unfamiliar to the average database developer. To get a full appreciation of client/server technology and what it offers, you must have at least a general understanding of the terminology. Table 20.1 lists the most commonly used terms.

TABLE 20.1   Client/Server Terms

Term	Definition
Column	A field.
DDL	A data definition language used to define and describe the database structure.
Foreign key	A value in one table that must be looked up in another table for validation.
Jet	The native database engine used by Microsoft Access.
ODBC (Open Database Connectivity)	A standard proposed by Microsoft that provides access to a variety of back-end databases through a common interface. In essence, ODBC is a translator.
OLE DB	A new standard for connecting to relational and nonrelational data sources.
DAO (Data Access Objects)	A method of manipulating data. It is being replaced by ADO and was optimized for accessing Jet databases.
ADO (ActiveX Data Objects)	A COM-based object model that you to easily manipulate OLE DB data sources. It is the data access methodology that DAO.
Primary key	A set of fields that uniquely identifies a row.
Row	A record.

TABLE 20.1 Continued

Term	Definition
Schema	A blueprint of the entire database. Includes table definitions, relationships, security, and other important information about the database.
SQL (Structured Query Language)	A type of data manipulation language commonly used to talk to tables residing on a server.
Stored procedures	Compiled SQL statements, such as queries, stored on the database server. Can be called by an application.
Transaction	A set of actions that must be performed on a database. If any one action fails, all the actions are discarded.
Triggers	Pieces of code that execute in response to an action occurring on a table (insert, edit, or delete).

Many books are devoted solely to client/server technology; *Alison Balter's Mastering Access 2002 Enterprise Development* focuses entirely on client/server and Web development using Access 2002. Most magazines targeted at developers contain numerous articles on client/server technology. *Access/VB/SQL Advisor* always offers excellent articles on client/server development. Many of the articles are specifically about client/server connectivity using Access as a front end. *VB Programmer's Journal* often contains useful articles as well. Another excellent source of information is the Microsoft Developer Network CD. Offered by Microsoft as a subscription, it includes numerous articles and white papers on client/server technology, ODBC, and use of Access as a front end to a database server.

Upsizing: What to Worry About

Suppose that your database is using Microsoft Access as both the front end and back end. Although an Access database on a file server might have been sufficient for a while, the need for better performance, enhanced security, or one of the other benefits that a back-end database provides compels your company (or your client's company) to upsize to a client/server architecture. The Access tables already have been created and even contain volumes of data. In this scenario, it might make sense to upsize.

Because all the tables have been designed as Access tables, they must be upsized to the back-end database server. Upsizing involves moving tables from a local Access database (or from any PC database) to a back-end database server that usually runs on Unix, Windows 2000, Windows NT Server, and OS/2 LAN Server or as a Novell NetWare NLM.

Another reason why tables are upsized from Access to a back-end server is that many developers prefer to design their tables from within the Access environment. Access offers a more user-friendly environment for table creation than most server applications.

Because of the many caveats involved when moving tables from Access to a back end, many people opt to design the tables directly on the back end. If you do design your tables in Access, you can export them to the back end and then link them to your local database, or you can use the Upsizing Wizard to greatly facilitate this process. Regardless of the method that you choose, as you export your tables to the database server, you need to be aware of the issues covered in the following sections.

> **NOTE**
>
> If you are updating to a SQL Server database, most of the concerns regarding upsizing are handled by the Upsizing Wizards included as part of Microsoft Access 2000 and Microsoft Access 2002.

Indexes

When exporting a table to a server, no indexes are created. All indexes need to be re-created on the back-end database server. If your database server is running Microsoft SQL Server, you can use the Access Upsizing Wizard for Access 2000 or Access 2002. These wizards create indexes for server tables in the place where the indexes exist in your Access tables.

AutoNumber Fields

AutoNumber fields are exported as Long integers. Because some database servers do not support autonumbering, you have to create an insert trigger on the server that provides the next key value. You also can achieve autonumbering by using form-level events, but this is not desirable. The numbering will not be enforced if other applications access the data. If you are upsizing to Microsoft SQL Server, the Upsizing Wizard for Access 2000 and Access 2002 convert all AutoNumber fields to Identity fields.

Default Values

Default values are not automatically moved to the server, even if the server supports them. You can set up default values directly on the server, but these values do *not* automatically appear when new records are added to the table unless the record is saved without data being added to the field containing the default value. As with autonumbering, default values can be implemented at the form level, with the same drawbacks. If the Upsizing Wizard for Access 2000 or

Access 2002 is used to move the data to Microsoft SQL Server, default values are exported to your server database.

Validation Rules

Validation rules are not exported to the server. They must be re-created using triggers on the server. No Access-defined error messages are displayed when a server validation rule is violated. Your application should be coded to provide the appropriate error messages. You also can perform validation rules at the form level, but they are not enforced if the data is accessed by other means. If the Upsizing Wizard for Access 2000 or Access 2002 is used to move the data to Microsoft SQL Server, validation rules are exported to the server database.

Relationships

Relationships need to be enforced using server-based triggers. Access's default error messages do not appear when referential integrity is violated. You need to respond to, and code for, these error messages in your application. You can enforce relationships at the form level, but as with other form-level validations, this method of validation does not adequately protect your data. If the Upsizing Wizard for Access 2000 or Access 2002 is used to move the data to Microsoft SQL Server, all relationships and referential integrity that you have set up in your Access database are set up within the server database.

Security

Security features that you have set up in Access do not carry forward to the server. You need to re-establish table security on the server. After security is set up on the server, Access is unaware that the security exists until the Access application attempts to violate the server's security. Then, error codes are returned to the application. You must handle these errors by using code and displaying the appropriate error message to users.

Table and Field Names

Servers often have much more stringent rules than Access does regarding the naming of fields. When you export a table, all characters that are not alphanumeric are converted to underscores. Most back ends do not allow spaces in field names. Furthermore, most back ends limit the length of object names to 30 characters or fewer. If you already have created queries, forms, reports, macros, and modules that use spaces and very long field and table names, these database objects might become unusable when you move your tables to a back-end database server.

Reserved Words

Most back ends have many reserved words. It is important to be aware of the reserved words of your specific back end. It is quite shocking when you upsize a table and find that field names you have been using are reserved words on your database server. If this is the case, you need to rename all the fields in which a conflict occurs. Once again, this means modifying all the queries, forms, reports, macros, and modules that reference the original field names.

Case Sensitivity

Many back-end databases are case sensitive. If this is the case with your back end, you might find that your queries and application code don't process as expected. Queries or code that refer to the field or table name by using the wrong case are not recognized by the back-end database and do not process correctly.

Properties

Most properties cannot be modified on remote tables. Any properties that can be modified are lost upon export, so you need to set them up again when the table is exported.

Visual Basic Code

Certain properties and methods that work on Access tables might not work on remote tables. This might necessitate some coding changes after you export your tables.

Proactively Preparing for Upsizing

If you set up your tables and code modules with upsizing in mind, you can eliminate many of the pitfalls discussed previously. Despite any of the problems that upsizing can bring, the scalability of Access is one of its stronger points. Sometimes resources are not available to implement client/server technology in the early stages of an application. If you think through the design of the project with the possibility of upsizing in mind, you will be pleased at how relatively easy it is to move to client/server technology when the time is right. With the Access 2000 and Access 2002 Upsizing Wizards, which are designed to take an Access application and upsize it to Microsoft SQL Server, the process is relatively simple. The upsizing tools for Access 2000 and Access 2002 perform a lot of the work involved in upsizing a database, with just the click of a few buttons.

NOTE

Client/server development and client/server issues are covered in extensive detail in *Alison Balter's Mastering Access 2002 Enterprise Development*.

Introduction to Transaction Processing

Transaction processing refers to the grouping of a series of changes into a single batch. The entire batch of changes is either accepted or rejected as a group. One of the most common implementations of transaction processing is a bank automated teller machine (ATM) transaction. Imagine that you go to the ATM to deposit your paycheck. In the middle of processing, a power outage occurs. Unfortunately, the bank recorded the incoming funds prior to the outage, but the funds had not yet been credited to your account when the power outage occurred. You would not be very pleased with the outcome of this situation. Transaction processing would prevent this scenario from occurring. With transaction processing, the whole process succeeds or fails as a unit.

A group of operations is considered a transaction if it meets the following criteria:

- It is atomic.—The group of operations should finish as a unit or not at all.

- It is consistent.—The group of operations, when completed as a unit, retains the consistency of the application.

- It is isolated.—The group of operations is independent of anything else going on in the system.

- It is durable.—After the group of operations is committed, the changes persist, even if the system crashes.

If your application contains a group of operations that are atomic and isolated, and if, in order to maintain the consistency of your application, all changes must persist even if the system crashes, you should place the group of operations in a transaction loop. With Access 2000 and Access 2002, the primary benefit of transaction processing is data integrity. As you will see in the next section, in versions prior to Access 95, transaction processing also provided performance benefits.

20

MULTIUSER AND
ENTERPRISE
APPLICATIONS

Understanding the Benefits of Transaction Processing

In Access 2.0, there were many marginal benefits of added transaction processing because Access 2.0 did no implicit transaction processing itself. Listing 20.1 shows code that, when run in Access 2.0, writes the data to disk each time the Update method occurs in the loop. These disk writes were costly in terms of performance, especially if the tables were not located on a local machine.

LISTING 20.1   Transaction Processing Using Access Basic as Seen in Access 2.0

```
Sub IncreaseQuantity()

    On Error GoTo IncreaseQuantity_Err
    Dim db As DATABASE
    Dim rst As Recordset

    Set db = CurrentDb
    Set rst = db.OpenRecordset("Select OrderId, _
                Quantity From tblOrderDetails", _
                dbOpenDynaset)

    'Loop through recordset increasing Quantity field by 1
    Do Until rst.EOF
       rst.Edit
       rst!Quantity = rst!Quantity + 1
       rst.UPDATE
       rst.MoveNext
    Loop

IncreaseQuantity_Exit:
    Set db = Nothing
    Set rst = Nothing
    Exit Sub

IncreaseQuantity_Err:
    MsgBox "Error # " & Err.Number & ": " & Error.Description
    Resume IncreaseQuantity_Exit
End Sub
```

NOTE

 This code, and all the code in this chapter, is located in the CHAP20EX.MDB database on the sample code CD-ROM in the basTrans module.

The same code found in Listing 20.1 performs much differently when run in Access 2000 or Access 2002. In addition to any explicit transaction processing you might implement for data-integrity reasons, Access 2000 and Access 2002 do their own behind-the-scenes transaction processing. This implicit transaction processing is done solely to improve the performance of your application. As the processing loop in the IncreaseQuantity routine executes, Access buffers and then periodically writes the data to disk. In a multiuser environment, Jet (implicitly) commits transactions every 50 milliseconds by default. This period of time is optimized for concurrency rather than performance. If you feel that it is necessary to sacrifice concurrency for performance, you can modify a few Windows registry settings to achieve the specific outcome you want. These settings are covered in the next section.

Although implicit transaction processing, along with the modifiable Windows registry settings, generally gives you better performance than explicit transaction processing, it is not a cut-and-dried situation. Many factors impact the performance benefits gained by both implicit and explicit transaction processing:

- Amount of free memory
- Number of columns and rows being updated
- Size of the rows being updated
- Network traffic

If you plan to implement explicit transaction processing solely to improve performance, you should make sure that you benchmark performance using both implicit and explicit transactions. It is critical that your application-testing environment be as similar as possible to the production environment in which the application will run.

Modifying the Default Behavior of Transaction Processing

Before you learn how to implement transaction processing, take a look at what you can do to modify the default behavior of the transaction processing built in to Access 2000 and Access 2002. Three registry settings affect implicit transactions in Access 2000 and Access 2002: ImplicitCommitSync, ExclusiveAsnycDelay, and SharedAsyncDelay. These keys are located in the \HKEY_LOCAL_MACHINE\SOFTWARE\Microsoft\Jet\4.0\Engines\Jet 4.0 registry folder.

20

> **TIP**
>
> You can access the Windows registry using the RegEdit utility. To utilize RegEdit, select the Run option from the Start menu. Then type **RegEdit**.

The ImplicitCommitSync setting determines whether the system waits for a commit to finish before proceeding with application processing. The default is No. This means that the system will proceed without waiting for the commit to finish. You generally won't want to change this setting; using No dramatically improves performance. The danger of accepting the value of No is that you will increase the amount of time during which the data is vulnerable. Before the data is flushed to disk, the user might turn off the machine, compromising the integrity of the data.

The ExclusiveAsyncDelay setting specifies the maximum number of milliseconds that elapse before Jet commits an implicit transaction when a database is opened for exclusive use. The default value for this setting is 2000 milliseconds. This setting does not in any way affect databases that are open for shared use.

The SharedAsyncDelay setting is similar to the ExclusiveAsyncDelay setting. It determines the maximum number of milliseconds that elapse before Jet commits an implicit transaction when a database is opened for shared use. The default value for this setting is 50. The higher this value, the greater the performance benefits reaped from implicit transactions, but also the higher the chances that concurrency problems will result. These concurrency issues are discussed in detail in *Alison Balter's Mastering Access 2002 Enterprise Development*.

In addition to the settings that affect implicit transaction processing in Access 2000 and Access 2002, an additional registry setting affects explicit transaction processing. The UserCommitSync setting controls whether explicit transactions are completed synchronously or asynchronously. With the default setting of Yes, control doesn't return from a CommitTrans statement until the transactions actually are written to disk, resulting in synchronous transactions. When this value is changed to No, a series of changes is queued, and control returns before the changes are complete.

You can modify the values of these registry settings and other Jet settings by using Regedit.exe (the Registry Editor) for Windows 95/98, Windows NT, and Windows 2000. Changes to this section of the registry affect all applications that use the Jet 4.0 Engine. If you want to affect only your application, you can export the Microsoft Jet portion of the registry tree and import it into your application's registry tree. You then can customize the registry settings for your application. To force your application to load the appropriate registry tree, you must set the INIPath property of the DBEngine object.

A much simpler approach is to set properties of the ADO Connection object; you can specify new settings at runtime for all the previously mentioned registry entries as well as for additional entries. A further advantage of this approach is that it will modify (temporarily) registry entries for any machine under which your application runs. Any values you change at runtime temporarily override the registry values that are set, enabling you to easily control and maintain specific settings for each application. This code illustrates how you modify the

ExclusiveAsyncDelay and SharedAsyncDelay settings using properties of the `Connection` object:

```
Sub ChangeOptions()
    Dim cnn As ADODB.Connection
    Set cnn = CurrentProject.Connection

    cnn.Properties("JET OLEDB:Exclusive Async Delay") = 1000
    cnn.Properties("JET OLEDB:Shared Async Delay") = 50
End Sub
```

Implementing Explicit Transaction Processing

Now that you are aware of the settings that affect transaction processing, you are ready to learn how to implement transaction processing. Three methods of the `Connection` object (covered in Chapter 14, "What Are ActiveX Data Objects and Data Access Objects, and Why Are They Important?") control transaction processing:

- `BeginTrans`
- `CommitTrans`
- `RollbackTrans`

The `BeginTrans` method of the `Connection` object begins the transaction loop. The moment `BeginTrans` is encountered, Access begins writing all changes to a log file in memory. Unless the `CommitTrans` method is issued on the `Connection` object, the changes are never actually written to the database file. After the `CommitTrans` method is issued, the updates are written permanently to the database object. If a `RollbackTrans` method of the `Connection` object is encountered, the log-in memory is released. Listing 20.2 shows an example of how transaction processing works under Access 2000 and Access 2002. Compare this to Listing 20.1.

LISTING 22.2 Transaction Processing in Access 2000 and Access 2002 Using `BeginTrans`, Logging, `CommitTrans`, and `RollbackTrans`

```
Sub IncreaseQuantityTrans()
    On Error GoTo IncreaseQuantityTrans_Err
    Dim cnn As ADODB.Connection
    Dim rst As ADODB.Recordset
    Dim boolInTrans As Boolean

    boolInTrans = False
    Set rst = New ADODB.Recordset

    Set cnn = CurrentProject.Connection
    rst.ActiveConnection = cnn
```

LISTING 22.2 Continued

```
    rst.CursorType = adOpenKeyset
    rst.LockType = adLockOptimistic
    rst.Open "Select OrderId, Quantity From tblOrderDetails"

    'Begin the Transaction Loop
    cnn.BeginTrans
        boolInTrans = True
        'Loop through recordset increasing Quantity field by 1
        Do Until rst.EOF
            rst!Quantity = rst!Quantity + 1
            rst.UPDATE
            rst.MoveNext
        Loop
        'Commit the Transaction; Everything went as Planned
    cnn.CommitTrans
    boolInTrans = False

IncreaseQuantityTrans_Exit:
    Set cnn = Nothing
    Set rst = Nothing
    Exit Sub

IncreaseQuantityTrans_Err:
    MsgBox "Error # " & Err.Number & ": " & Err.Description
    'Rollback the Transaction; An Error Occurred
    If boolInTrans Then
        cnn.RollbackTrans
    End If
    Resume IncreaseQuantityTrans_Exit
End Sub
```

This code uses a transaction loop to ensure that everything completes as planned or not at all.
Notice that the loop that moves through the recordset, increasing the Quantity field in each
record by 1, is placed in a transaction loop. If all processing in the loop completes successfully,
the CommitTrans method executes. If the error-handling code is encountered, the
RollbackTrans method is issued, ensuring that none of the changes are written to disk. The
boolInTrans variable is used to determine whether the code is within the transaction loop.
This ensures that the error handler only performs the rollback if an error occurs within the
transaction loop. If the CommitTrans method or the RollBackTrans method is issued without
an open transaction, an error occurs.

Introduction to Replication

Access 95 was the first desktop database that included built-in replication capabilities. Replication has further matured with the introduction of Access 2000 and Access 2002; it's a powerful feature that is becoming increasingly important in today's world of mobile and distributed computing. This section teaches you about replication and how to implement it through both the user interface and code.

Uses of Replication

Data replication is the capability of a system to automatically make copies of its data and application objects in remote locations. Any changes to the original or data changes to the copies are propagated to all other copies. Data replication allows users to make changes to data offline at remote locations. Changes to either the original or the remote data are synchronized with other instances of the database.

The original database is referred to as the *design master*. Changes to definitions of tables or other application objects can be made only at the design master. The design master is used to make special copies called *replicas*. Although there is only one design master, replicas can be made from other replicas. The process of the design master and replicas sharing changes is referred to as *synchronization*. The design master and replicas that participate in the synchronization process are collectively referred to as a *replica set*.

To see an example of data replication at work, suppose that you have a team of salespeople who are out on the road all day. At the end of the day, each salesperson logs on to one of the company's Windows NT servers through DUN (Dial-Up Networking) or RAS (Remote Access Services). Each salesperson's transactions are sent to the server. If necessary, any changes to the server data are also sent to the salesperson. In addition to data being replicated, if the developers in the organization are busily adding forms, reports, and modules to the database's master copy, any changes to the application components are also updated in the remote copies as users log on to the system.

This example illustrates just one of the several valuable uses of replication. In a nutshell, data replication is used to improve the availability and integrity of data throughout an organization or enterprise. The practical uses of data replication are many; they can be categorized into five general areas, explained in the following sections.

Sharing Data Among Offices

In today's global economy, it's the norm for companies to have many offices distributed throughout the country, or even the world. Before Access 95, it was difficult to implement an

Access application that would support sharing data among several offices. However, with replication, each office can have a replica of the database. Periodically throughout the day, each office can synchronize its changes into data at corporate headquarters. How often the synchronization happens depends on the frequency required for data at each location to be current at any given moment.

Sharing Data Among Dispersed Users

Sharing data among dispersed users is illustrated by the salespersons example used earlier. This implementation of replication generally involves mobile users who connect to the network after modifying data out on the road. Because only incremental changes are transferred from the design master (the original) to the replicas (the copies), and from the replicas to the design master, this form of replication makes the mobile computing scenario economically feasible.

Reducing Network Load

Replication can be very effective in reducing network traffic loads. The design master can be replicated onto one or more additional servers. Distributed users can then make changes to one of the additional servers, which significantly improves performance by distributing the processing load throughout the network. Changes made to the data on the additional servers can be synchronized with the main server periodically during the day.

Distributing Application Updates

Replication is an excellent vehicle for distributing application updates. Design changes can be made only to the design master; therefore, as users throughout the organization log on to synchronize with the design master, any structural changes to the application are sent to the user. This is much more efficient and effective than giving every user an entirely new copy of the application database each time a minor change is made to the application's schema.

Backing Up the Data in Your Application

Many people don't think of replication as a means of backing up application data, but replication is extremely well suited for this task. Ordinarily, to back up an Access database, everyone must log off the system, but that's not necessary with replication. The synchronization process can occur periodically during the day while users are still logged on to the system, and all changes are replicated. Not only is this more efficient than backing up the entire database, it also ensures that you can quickly be up and running on a backup server if there's a problem on a main server.

Understanding When Replication Isn't Appropriate

Despite the many positive aspects of replication, it is not appropriate in a few situations, such as when data consistency is critical. If an application requires that data be current at every given moment, it isn't a good candidate for replication. Replication is also not effective when many different users modify a large number of existing records throughout the day. In a situation like this, resolving conflicts that happen when multiple users update the same record wouldn't be practical. Furthermore, you cannot use replication if you are using Visual SourceSafe to manage the development process. Finally, you cannot rename or move design masters, and a design master that becomes corrupted can be difficult to recover.

Understanding the Implementation of Replication

The following steps compose the replication process:

1. Making a database replicable
2. Creating and distributing replicas
3. Synchronizing replicas with the design master
4. Resolving conflicts

These steps can be completed in the following ways:

- Through the Access user interface
- By using the Windows Briefcase
- By using the Replication Manager
- By using ADO code

The steps needed for the replication process, and the alternatives for performing each step, are covered in this chapter. An overview of each alternative is outlined in the following sections.

The Access User Interface

The Access user interface gives you a series of menu items that allow you to perform all the steps of the replication process. The Tools|Replication menu has the following options: Create Replica, Synchronize Now, Partial Replica Wizard, Resolve Conflict, and Recover Design Master. These menu options are covered throughout this chapter.

Briefcase Replication

The Windows Briefcase supplies the foundation Access needs for the replication process. Users can simply drag a database file to the Briefcase to replicate it, make changes to the file while on the road, and synchronize the replica with the design master when they reconnect to the network. This is done because, when Access is installed, it registers a special class ID with the Windows Briefcase. When a database is dragged to the Briefcase, the Briefcase's Reconciler code is called. When the user selects Update Selection or Update All from the Briefcase menu, the Merge Reconciler is called. Briefcase replication is available as an installation option through Windows 95, its successors, and Windows NT 4.0 and later.

The Replication Manager

The Replication Manager is a sophisticated tool that's part of Microsoft Office 2000 and Office 2002 Developer. It's a mandatory player in the replication process when you're managing many replicas. Besides providing basic replication functionality, the Replication Manager lets you schedule the synchronization of replicas. In fact, the Replication Manager allows you to manage and intricately control all aspects of the replication process. The Replication Manager is covered in detail in *Alison Balter's Mastering Access 2002 Enterprise Development*.

ADO Code

Most aspects of the replication process can also be done by using ADO code, which can be used to make a database replicable, create and synchronize replicas, and get and set properties of a replicable database. ADO can easily be integrated with the other methods of replication. Although it requires the most time and effort on your part, ADO code lets you base replication on events rather than time and give your users a custom user interface for the replication process.

Programs That Support Replication Using DAO

Visual Basic 4.0 and later, Excel for Windows 95 and later, and Visual C++ all support replication using Data Access. You can't perform replication with these products by using either the Briefcase or Microsoft Office Developer, however, so it's easier to manage the replication process on a machine that has Access installed.

PRACTICAL EXAMPLES

Getting the Time and Billing Application Ready for an Enterprise Environment

Splitting the application code and data is the first step toward making the Time and Billing Application enterprise ready. Consider placing the application data on the network and the application code on each workstation. If you think that the number of users, required security, or the volume of data stored in the application warrants client/server technology, consider using one or more of the client/server techniques covered in this chapter. If sales people or consultants need disconnected copies of the application and its data on their laptops, consider using replication to synchronize data changes between the users and your master copy of the data. Finally, think about whether any application processes warrant transaction processing. If you feel that client/server technology, replication, or transaction processing is a necessary ingredient to your application, learn more about these techniques from a source such as *Alison Balter's Mastering Access 2002 Enterprise Development*.

Summary

Many people think that the transition of a simple Access application to a multiuser or client/server environment is a simple one. I strongly disagree. There are several things to think about when moving an application from a single-user environment to a multiuser environment and even more things to think about when moving to a client/server environment. The more you think about these potential evolutions when you first design and build your application, the less problems you'll have if your application data has to be upsized.

This chapter exposed you to multiuser techniques. It explained client/server technology and when you need it. It also talked about the various roles that Access plays in the application design model. Finally, you learned about two techniques that are important within an enterprise application: transaction processing and replication.

The chapter is intended to be an introduction to these important topics. All the topics in this chapter are covered in detail in *Alison Balter's Mastering Access 2002 Enterprise Development*.

20

Black-Belt Programming

PART

IV

IN THIS PART

Using ActiveX Controls

IN THIS CHAPTER

Why This Chapter Is Important

A powerful aspect of Access 2002 is its capability to be extensible. In addition to the controls available as part of the product, you can incorporate ActiveX controls on your forms. This means that you aren't limited by what Access supplies, only by the imaginations of third-party developers who design ActiveX controls.

> **NOTE**
>
> Several years ago, Microsoft renamed *OLE controls* to *ActiveX controls*. You will still sometimes see these terms used interchangeably.

ActiveX controls support the OLE 2.0 custom control architecture and provide support for 32-bit operating systems. They have their own code, methods, events, and properties. An ActiveX control's functionality is stored in a file with an .OCX extension. This is why ActiveX controls are often referred to as OCXs. A Calendar OCX control comes with Microsoft Access. Additional OCX controls are included in the Microsoft Office 2002 Developer (MOD) and are available from third-party vendors, such as FMS, DBI Technologies, Database Creations, Crescent, Sheridan, Far Point, and many others.

Two types of ActiveX controls exist. The first is visible at both design time and runtime; after being placed on a form, it provides a front-end interface that allows the user to directly manipulate the object. One example is the Calendar control in Access 2002. The second type of ActiveX control is visible at design time, but not at runtime; this type of control can, for example, give you access to all Windows common dialog boxes, such as Open, Print, and so on. The control itself isn't visible to the user, but its functionality is available to the user at runtime. Another example is a timer control; it operates within the application, triggering event code to run, but it isn't actually visible to the user.

With ActiveX controls, you can easily incorporate more functionality in your applications. For example, if you need to include a calendar on your form, you don't need to worry about how to build your own. Instead, you can include a custom calendar control and modify the calendar's behavior by changing its properties and executing its methods.

Incorporating ActiveX Controls in Access 2002

Before you can incorporate an ActiveX control in your application, you must perform three steps:

1. Install the ActiveX control
2. Register the control
3. Add the control to a form

Installing an ActiveX Control

When you buy an ActiveX control, it generally has an installation program that copies the OCX file to your Windows system directory. The name of this directory can vary depending on whether you're running Windows 95, Windows 98, Windows NT, or Windows 2000 and what you named your Windows directory during your operating system installation.

Registering an ActiveX Control

After you have installed the control, you're ready to register it with Access. Often a control is automatically registered during installation, which is true of the Calendar OCX included with Access, as well as all the OCX controls that come with the Microsoft Office 2002 Developer (MOD). OCX controls are registered in the HKEY_LOCAL_MACHINE\SOFTWARE class in the Windows registry. (See Figure 21.1.) In the figure, the Image List control, registered as ImageListCtrl, is selected.

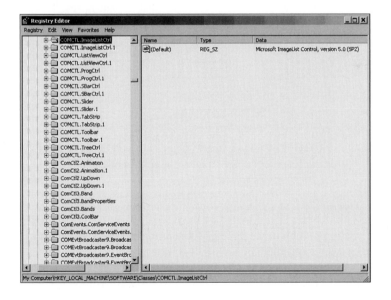

FIGURE 21.1

OCX controls in the Windows registry.

If an ActiveX control isn't registered, you can do so by using the ActiveX Controls dialog box. To open this dialog box, choose Tools|ActiveX Controls. (See Figure 21.2.)

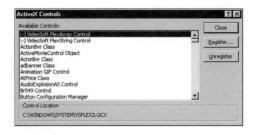

FIGURE 21.2

Use the ActiveX Controls dialog box to register ActiveX controls.

The ActiveX Controls dialog box lists all the ActiveX controls currently registered in Access. To add an ActiveX control to the list, click Register. This opens the Add ActiveX Control dialog box. (See Figure 21.3.)

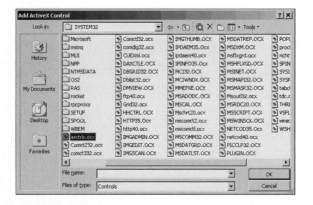

FIGURE 21.3

The Add ActiveX Control dialog box allows you to locate the ActiveX control you want to register.

Make sure that you're pointing to the directory containing the OCX you want to register. The control you're registering must already be installed; if it hasn't been installed, it won't be on the list. Select the OCX you want to register, and click OK. You then return to the ActiveX Controls dialog box, and the control you selected appears on the list of registered controls. You're ready to include the control on a form.

If you no longer plan to use an ActiveX control, you should use the Unregister button, located in the ActiveX Control dialog, which removes the registry entries for controls you don't use.

Adding ActiveX Controls to Forms

After you have registered an ActiveX control, you can include it on your forms. You do this in one of two ways:

- Select the ActiveX control from the toolbox by clicking the More Controls icon.
- Choose ActiveX Control from the Insert menu when you're in Form or Report Design view.

The More Controls tool contains all the ActiveX controls registered by your system. This includes ActiveX controls that are part of Excel, Visual Basic, and any other application that uses ActiveX controls. Some of these controls won't work properly with Access. To determine which controls you can safely include in your application, read the Access Readme file or contact the vendor of the ActiveX control. The More Controls menu is shown in Figure 21.4.

FIGURE 21.4
The More Controls tool shows you all the ActiveX controls registered on your system.

The menu for the More Controls tool shows all the ActiveX controls installed on the system. You can also use the Insert menu to select an ActiveX control from the Insert ActiveX Control dialog box. (See Figure 21.5.) After selecting a control from the Select an ActiveX Control list box, the control is placed on the form. You can move the control around the form and size it as needed.

FIGURE 21.5

Use the Insert ActiveX Control dialog box to add an ActiveX control to a form.

After you have placed an ActiveX control on a form, the control is ready to operate in its default format. If you insert the Calendar OCX control in a form and run the form, it looks like Figure 21.6.

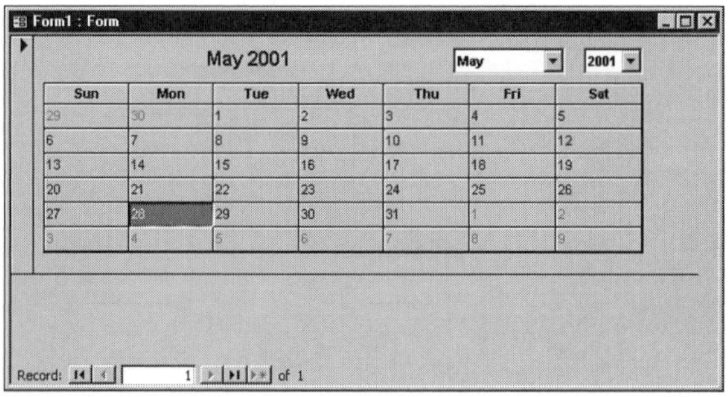

FIGURE 21.6

A Calendar OCX, shown in Form view, with no properties explicitly set.

The Calendar control can display all the months of the year, along with the corresponding days for each particular month. So far, you haven't set any properties for the calendar, nor have you written code to respond to any of the calendar's events. Setting an ActiveX control's properties, executing an ActiveX control's methods, and responding to an ActiveX control's events are covered in the following sections.

Understanding and Managing the Control Reference in Your Access Application

When you insert an ActiveX control on a form, Access automatically creates a reference to the control's Type Library that appears in the References dialog box. (See Figure 21.7.) To invoke the References dialog box, choose Tools|References with the Visual Basic Editor active. Note that the full path to the control is stored in this dialog box. For example, Figure 21.7 shows that the Calendar OCX is stored in C:\Program Files\Microsoft Office\Office. If the OCX is moved, VBA might not be able to resolve the reference. If this happens, you must open the References dialog box and manually remove the check from the reference marked as missing and set a reference to the ActiveX control in its new location.

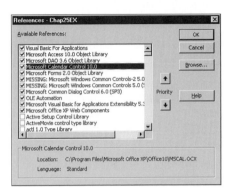

FIGURE 21.7

Use the References dialog box to add and remove library references.

If you're distributing an application with ActiveX controls, the application might or might not work without problems. Access does its best to try to resolve references to ActiveX controls. If the controls are in the Windows\System directory or the directory that Access is installed in, Access can automatically resolve the references, even if the application is installed in a different directory on the user's machine than it was on your machine.

Remember, not only do ActiveX controls need to be referenced, but they also need to be registered in the Windows registry. If you use the Package and Deployment Wizard included with the MOD to distribute your application, the OCXs are automatically registered when the user installs your application. If you don't use the Microsoft Office 2002 Package and Deployment Wizard to distribute your application, you must write code to register the ActiveX control, or the user will have to manually register it.

Setting Properties of an ActiveX Control at Design Time

The methods, events, and properties associated with each ActiveX control differ. They're specific to that control and are determined by the control's author, and they are used to manipulate the control's appearance and behavior. Each control's methods, events, and properties are in a separate .OCX file.

If you don't modify a control's properties, it functions with its default appearance and behavior. Much of the richness of third-party controls comes from the ability to customize the controls by changing their properties at both design time and runtime. Some controls support *data binding*, which lets you store or display data in a control from an underlying field in a table. Furthermore, the ability to respond to an ActiveX control's events lets you respond to the user's interaction with the control, and being able to execute the control's methods lets you manipulate the control.

Figure 21.8 shows some of the Calendar control's many properties. As with any control, most of its properties can be set at design time and modified or read at runtime.

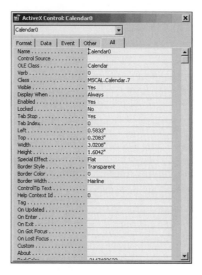

FIGURE 21.8

The Calendar control's Property sheet.

Another way to set properties for a control is to do it graphically by selecting the Custom property from the object's Property sheet, and then clicking the build button. For example, if you select the Custom property from the Calendar control's Property sheet and click the build button, the control's Properties dialog box appears. The properties shown in this dialog box vary for each control.

Figure 21.9 shows the Properties dialog box for the Calendar control. Here, you can modify many of the calendar's attributes, including the first day of the week, whether you want the days of the week to show, and the colors and fonts.

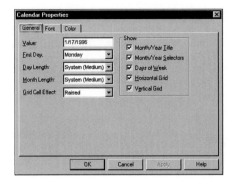

FIGURE 21.9
The Calendar Properties dialog box allows you to set some initial properties for the control.

TIP

You can access a control's Properties dialog box by double-clicking the ActiveX control in the Design view of a form.

Coding Events of an ActiveX Control

Just as the properties of the control can be set or evaluated at runtime, the control's events can be coded, too. To get a list of all the events associated with an ActiveX control, open the Procedure box in the Module window. Make sure that the control name for your ActiveX control is listed in the Object box. Figure 21.10 shows all the events for the Calendar control.

The Calendar control's AfterUpdate event is triggered when the user selects a date from the calendar. The following code changes the value of the txtDateSelected text box to the Value property of the calPickADay control. This code is placed in the Calendar control's AfterUpdate event so that it executes any time the user selects a date on the calendar:

```
Private Sub calPickADay_AfterUpdate()
   txtDateSelected.Value = calPickADay.Value
End Sub
```

 This code—and most of the code in this chapter—is in the CHAP21EX.MDB file on the book's CD-ROM. This example is found in the frmPickADay form.

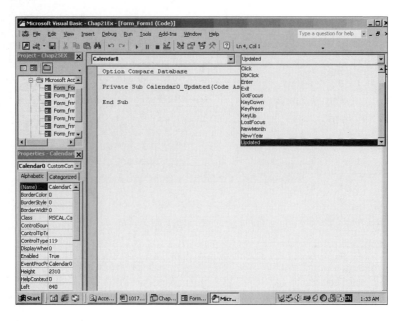

FIGURE 21.10
Viewing the events of the Calendar control.

Using the Calendar Control

The Calendar control is one of the more powerful OCX controls available. Understanding its properties and methods makes it a lot easier to work with; they are covered in the following sections. Most of the examples are found in frmCalPropsAndMethods.

Properties of a Calendar Control

The Day, Month, and Year properties designate the day, month, and year displayed on the calendar. These properties are automatically changed at runtime as the user selects different dates on the calendar. You can modify the values programmatically by using macros or Visual Basic, thereby changing the day, month, or year that's selected.

The Value property is one of the Calendar control's most important properties. It retrieves the selected calendar date or moves the date highlight to a specific day. The following code uses the Value property to display the selected day in a message box:

```
Private Sub cmdDisplayDate_Click()
    'Display the date selected on the calendar
    MsgBox calSelectADay.Value
End Sub
```

The ValueIsNull property lets you indicate that no date is selected on the calendar. This property is used when you want to make sure that the user explicitly selects a date.

The DayFont and DayFontColor properties specify the font and color for displaying the day titles. The DayFont property is further broken down into the properties Name, Size, Bold, Italic, Underline, and Strikethrough. An individual property can be modified like this:

```
calSelectADay.DayFont.Italic = True
```

You can use the With...End With construct to change several font properties at once:

```
With calSelectADay.DayFont
     .Bold = True
     .Italic = True
     .Name = "Arial"
End With
```

The DayFontColor property can be used to easily modify the color of the day titles:

```
calSelectADay.DayFontColor = 16711680
```

The GridFont and GridFontColor properties are similar to the DayFont and DayFontColor properties. GridFont determines the font type and size attributes for the text in the calendar, and GridFontColor indicates the text color in the calendar. For example, the following routine modifies the Bold, Italic, and Name properties of the GridFont property and changes the color of the days displayed on the calendar:

```
Private Sub cmdChangeGridFont_Click()
    'Change attributes of the font on the grid
    With calSelectADay.GridFont
        .Bold = True
        .Italic = True
        .Name = "Arial"
    End With
    calSelectADay.GridFontColor = 8388736
End Sub
```

The DayLength and MonthLength properties designate how you want the day or month titles to be displayed. The available choices for DayLength are Short (0), Medium (1), and Long (2). Short displays the day as one character, Medium displays the day as a three-character abbreviation, and Long displays the full day (for example, Monday). The available choices for MonthLength are Short (0) and Long (2). Short displays the month as a three-character abbreviation, and Long displays the full month name. The following code specifies both the DayLength and MonthLength properties as Short:

```
Private Sub cmdChangeLength_Click()
    'Modify the display of the day and month titles
    calSelectADay.DayLength = 0
    calSelectADay.MonthLength = 0
End Sub
```

The ShowDateSelectors property indicates whether combo boxes appear at the top of the calendar, allowing the user to select a month and year. This property can be set to True or False.

The ShowTitle property indicates whether the month and year are displayed at the top of the calendar.

The GridLinesFormat and GridLinesColor properties specify whether the gridlines are raised, sunken, or flat, and what color they are.

Methods of a Calendar Control

The Calendar control also has several methods, or actions you can take on the Calendar object. The NextDay, PreviousDay, NextWeek, PreviousWeek, NextMonth, PreviousMonth, NextYear, and PreviousYear methods all move the control's Value property forward or backward by the specified period of time.

Other methods of the Calendar control include the following:

- The Refresh method repaints the Calendar control.
- The Today method sets the Value property to the current date.
- The AboutBox method displays the Calendar control's About box.

> **NOTE**
>
> The following examples require controls supplied with Microsoft Office 2002 Developer. You must have MOD 2002 for the following code samples to run. Also, if you have MOD, you can distribute these tools royalty free to your users.
>
> If you have MOD installed and still can't run some of the examples, you might want to check the References dialog box to make sure that the controls are properly referenced.

Figure 21.11 shows how the Calendar control works. As you can see, the form, called frmCalendar, lets the user move from day to day, month to month, or year to year. The user can also move to the current day, or even select a date, and then click the Display Orders for Selected Date command button to view all the orders placed on the selected date.

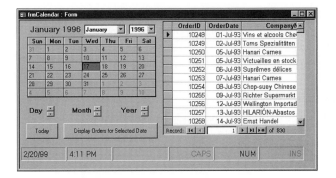

FIGURE 21.11

An example of using the Calendar control.

The code for the Today command button illustrates using the Today method:

```
Private Sub cmdToday_Click()
    'Change the selected date in the calendar control
    'to today's date
    calPickADay.Today
End Sub
```

Because the Today method is issued on the Calendar control, the selected day will become the current date. The code for the Display Orders for Selected Date command button looks like this:

```
Private Sub cmdOrders_Click()
    'Change the recordsource of the form
    'to select only those rows where the order
    'date matches the data selected in the
    'calendar control
    frmOrdersByDate.Form.RecordSource = _
        "Select * from qryOrdersByDate Where OrderDate = #" _
        & calPickADay.Value & "#"
End Sub
```

This code changes the subform's RecordSource to include only those records in which the OrderDate is equal to the selected calendar date. The remainder of the code for the frmCalendar form is discussed in the following section.

Using the UpDown Control

The UpDown control is an excellent tool for incrementing and decrementing values. Used in conjunction with other controls, it can easily act as a means to increment and decrement the other controls' values. For example, on the frmCalendar form, UpDown objects increment and decrement the selected day, month, and year. Like the Calendar control, the UpDown object has its own built-in properties and methods. Although the properties can be modified on the Other tab of the Properties window, it's easier to modify them by using the UpDown properties dialog box.(See Figure 21.12.) To open it, double-click on the UpDown object whose properties you want to modify.

FIGURE 21.12

The UpDown *Properties dialog box.*

The Orientation property, one of the most important for the UpDown object, indicates whether you want the UpDown object to be displayed vertically or horizontally. The two most commonly used events of a UpDown object are the UpClick event and the DownClick event; they specify what happens when the user clicks either button of the control. The following code is placed in the DownClick event of the updnDay UpDown object on frmCalendar. Notice that the code executes a PreviousDay method on the calPickADay control, causing the Calendar control to set the focus to the previous day:

```
Private Sub updnDay_DownClick()
    'Move selected day back one day
    calPickADay.PreviousDay
End Sub
```

The UpClick event of the updnDay control uses the NextDay method of the calPickADay control to cause the focus to shift to the next day:

```
Private Sub updnDay_UpClick()
    'Move selected day forward one day
    calPickADay.NextDay
End Sub
```

The DownClick event of the updnMonth control uses the Calendar control's PreviousMonth method to move focus to the same day in the previous month:

```
Private Sub updnMonth_DownClick()
    'Move selected day back one month
    calPickADay.PreviousMonth
End Sub
```

The `UpClick` event of the updnMonth control uses the Calendar control's `NextMonth` method to move focus to the same day in the next month:

```
Private Sub updnMonth_UpClick()
    'Move selected day forward one month
    calPickADay.NextMonth
End Sub
```

The `DownClick` and `UpClick` events of the updnYear control use the Calendar control's `PreviousYear` and `NextYear` methods to move backward and forward a year in the calendar:

```
Private Sub updnYear_DownClick()
    'Move selected day back one year
    calPickADay.PreviousYear
End Sub

Private Sub updnYear_UpClick()
    'Move selected day forward one year
    calPickADay.NextYear
End Sub
```

As you can see, by combining the different ActiveX controls, you can create exciting, user-friendly, utilitarian applications.

Using the StatusBar Control

You can use the StatusBar control to quickly and easily add professional-looking status bars to your forms, as shown at the bottom of the frmCalendar form in Figure 21.11. The StatusBar in the figure has six panels; the first two have been configured to display the current date and time, and the last three display the status of the Caps, Num, and Ins keys.

Properties can be set for the StatusBar control as a whole or for the individual panels. (See Figure 21.13.) The Style property specifies whether you want the status bar to include multiple panels or only a single panel. The SimpleText property is used only for single-panel status bars; it specifies the text in the panel. Finally, the MousePointer property lets you select the type of mouse pointer that appears when it's placed over the StatusBar control.

Each panel of the StatusBar control has properties that affect what that panel looks like and how it performs. The Index property of the panel is used to identify the particular panel. The panel properties are shown in Figure 21.14. The Style property is an important one; it specifies what information is displayed in the panel. It can be set to Text, `Caps`, `Num Lock`, `Ins`, `Scroll`, `Time`, `Date`, or `Kana Lock` (used for the Japanese character set). When set, the control can automatically sense whether the Caps Lock or other keys are active. The Text property indicates the text displayed in the panel when the Style property is set to `Text`. The value of this property is often modified at runtime to display a specific message to the user. The Alignment property determines whether the information is left-aligned, right-aligned, or centered in the panel, and the Bevel property can be set to None, Inset, or Raised.

FIGURE 21.13

The general properties of the StatusBar control.

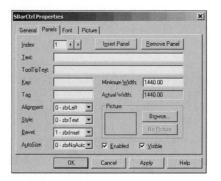

FIGURE 21.14

The StatusBar panel properties.

As you insert and remove panels, each panel is assigned an index, and the Index property is used to refer to a specific panel at runtime, as shown in this example:

```
Private Sub calPickADay_AfterUpdate()
    'If the selected date equals today's
    'date, include the text TODAY!!! in the
    'third panel of the status bar
    If calPickADay.Value = Date Then
        sbrStatus.Panels(3).Text = "TODAY!!!"

    'Otherwise display nothing in the third panel
    'of the status bar
```

```
    Else
        sbrStatus.Panels(3).Text = ""
    End If
End Sub
```

This code evaluates the calPickADay value to see whether it's equal to the current date. If so, the text of the third panel is set to TODAY!!!. Otherwise, the third panel's text is set to a zero-length string.

> **CAUTION**
>
> In the Access world, almost everything is zero-based. Of course, there are exceptions to every rule. The StatusBar control is one of those exceptions—it's one-based. The code in the previous example really does modify the text in the third panel.

Using the Common Dialog Control

The Common Dialog control is actually like many controls in one. It's used to display the standard Windows File Open, File Save As, Font, Color, and Print common dialog boxes. It's a hidden control that doesn't appear at runtime, but whose properties and methods can be manipulated by using VBA code. The frmCommonAndRich form, shown in Figure 21.15, illustrates using several of the common dialog boxes as well as the Rich Textbox control, covered in the next section.

> **NOTE**
>
> The new FileDialog object replaces much of the functionality supplied by the Common Dialog control. It is easy to use and, because it is built in, it is much lighter weight than the Common Dialog control. The FileDialog object is covered in Chapter 9, "Advanced Form Techniques."

The Screen Color and Button Font command buttons illustrate uses of the Common Dialog control. They invoke the Color and Font common dialog boxes, respectively. The code for the Click event of the cmdColor command button looks like this:

```
Private Sub cmdColor_Click()
    'Set flags to show all colors
    dlgCommon.Flags = cdlCCFullOpen
```

```
'Invoke color dialog
dlgCommon.ShowColor

'Change the BackColor property of the
'form to match the selected color
Me.Detail.BackColor = dlgCommon.Color
End Sub
```

FIGURE 21.15

The form used to illustrate common dialog and rich text boxes.

The code begins by setting the Common Dialog control's Flags property, which is used to specify attributes of the common dialog box. The value of `cdlCCFullOpen` indicates that the entire Color common dialog box, including the portion that lets the user create custom colors, is displayed. The `ShowColor` method, when applied to the Common Dialog control, invokes the Color common dialog box. (See Figure 21.16.) The color the user selects is filled into the Color property of the Common Dialog control. This color is used to modify the BackColor property of the form's Detail section.

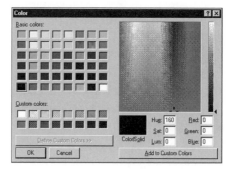

FIGURE 21.16

The Color chooser is part of the Common Dialog control.

The following code uses the `With...End With` loop to change several properties from the Common Dialog control:

```
Private Sub cmdFont_Click()
    Dim ctl As Control

    'Set flags to show only screen fonts
    dlgCommon.Flags = cdlCFScreenFonts

    'Invoke font dialog
    dlgCommon.ShowFont

    'Loop through each control on the form,
    'changing the font properties of the command
    'buttons to the selected font attributes
    For Each ctl In Controls
        If TypeOf ctl Is CommandButton Then
            With ctl
                .FontName = dlgCommon.FontName
                .FontBold = dlgCommon.FontBold
                .FontItalic = dlgCommon.FontItalic
                .FontSize = dlgCommon.FontSize
            End With
        End If
    Next ctl
End Sub
```

The `Click` event of cmdFont first sets the Common Dialog control's Flags property to `cdlCFScreenFonts`. For the Font common dialog box, the value of `cdlCDFScreenFonts` causes the dialog box to list only the screen fonts supported by the user's system. The `ShowFont` method is used to invoke the actual dialog box. (See Figure 21.17.) Using a `With...End With` construct, the code takes each property set in the common dialog box and uses it to loop through the form's Controls collection, modifying the font attributes of each command button.

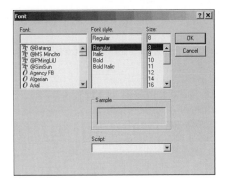

FIGURE 21.17

The Font part of the common dialog box allows you to set several font properties at one time.

The File Open, File Save, and File Print common dialog boxes are covered in the next section.

Using the Rich Textbox Control

The Rich Textbox control allows you to design a text box for writing code that affects the selected text. You can specify the Font, Font Size, Bold, and Italic properties. You can even add bullet points to the selected text. Furthermore, you can save the contents of the Rich Textbox control in a rich text format (RTF) file and later bring it back into the control.

The following code illustrates using several of the Rich Textbox control's properties:

```
Private Sub cmdTextColor_Click()
    'Show the Color dialog
    dlgCommon.ShowColor

    'Change the color of the selected text
    'to the color selected in the dialog
    rtfDocument.SelColor = dlgCommon.Color
End Sub
```

This code uses the Color common dialog box to set the SelColor property of the Rich Textbox control. The selected text appears in whatever color the user selects from the common dialog box.

The Click event of the cmdTextFont command button sets the SelFontName, SelBold, SelItalic, and SelFontSize properties of the Rich Textbox control to the font, style, and size selected in the Font common dialog box:

```
Private Sub cmdTextFont_Click()
    'Set Flags to only show screen fonts
    dlgCommon.Flags = cdlCFScreenFonts

    'Display the Font dialog
    dlgCommon.ShowFont

    'Change the font of the selected text to the
    'font settings designated in the Font dialog
    With rtfDocument
        .SelFontName = dlgCommon.FontName
        .SelBold = dlgCommon.FontBold
        .SelItalic = dlgCommon.FontItalic
        .SelFontSize = dlgCommon.FontSize
    End With
End Sub
```

The selected attributes are applied only to the selected text.

The Rich Textbox control has a method called SaveFile that lets you save the contents of the Rich Textbox control to an RTF file. The code looks like this:

```
Private Sub cmdSave_Click()
    'Designate default settings for the Save dialog
    dlgCommon.Filter = "RTF Files (*.rtf)|*.rtf"

    'Invoke the Save dialog
    dlgCommon.ShowSave

    'If no file is selected, display an error message
    'If a file is selected, save the file with the name and
    'location designated in the dialog
    If dlgCommon.FileName = "" Then
        MsgBox "You Must Specify a File Name", vbExclamation, "File NOT Saved!"
    Else
        rtfDocument.SaveFile dlgCommon.FileName
    End If
End Sub
```

The code begins by setting the Common Dialog control's Filter property; this filters the filenames displayed in the File Save common dialog box. The ShowSave method invokes the Save As common dialog box. (See Figure 21.18.) After the user types in or selects a filename, the Common Dialog control's FileName property is filled in with the name of the file that the user specified. If the user clicks Cancel, the FileName property contains a zero-length string, and the user is warned that the file wasn't saved.

FIGURE 21.18

The Save As common dialog box allows you to enter a name, a location, and an extension to your file.

As mentioned, you can also retrieve the contents of an RTF file into the control. The code looks like this:

```
Private Sub cmdOpen_Click()
    'Set initial values for the Open dialog
    dlgCommon.FileName = ""
    dlgCommon.Filter = "RTF Files (*.rtf)|*.rtf"
    dlgCommon.InitDir = CurDir

    'Display the dialog
    dlgCommon.ShowOpen

    'If the user did not select a file, display a message
    'If the user selected a file, load the file they selected
    If dlgCommon.FileName = "" Then
        MsgBox "You Must Specify a File Name", vbExclamation, "File Cannot Be
Opened!"
    Else
        rtfDocument.LoadFile dlgCommon.FileName
    End If
End Sub
```

The Click event of the cmdOpen command button uses the ShowOpen method to invoke the File Open common dialog box. (See Figure 21.19.) If the user selects a file, the Rich Textbox control's LoadFile method uses the Common Dialog control's FileName property as the name of the file to open.

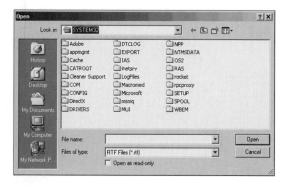

FIGURE 21.19

The Open common dialog box not only lets you specify which files to open, but also allows you to navigate around your computer and network.

Besides being able to open and save the contents of a Rich Textbox control, you can print the control's contents. The Click event of the cmdPrint command button sets the Common Dialog control's Flags property to cdlPDAllPages:

```
Private Sub cmdPrint_Click()
    'Select All in the Print dialog
    dlgCommon.Flags = cdlPDAllPages

    'Show the Print dialog
    dlgCommon.ShowPrinter

    'Print the selected text with the settings
    'selected in the Print dialog
    rtfDocument.SelPrint dlgCommon.hDC
End Sub
```

This selects the All option button in the Print dialog box (and deselects the Pages and Selection option buttons.) The ShowPrinter method displays the Print common dialog box. (See Figure 21.20.) The SelPrint method of the Rich Textbox control is then used to print the selected text with the printer selected in the Print common dialog box.

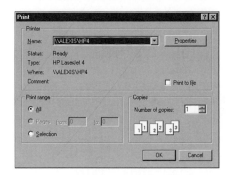

FIGURE 21.20
The Print common dialog box has several options for printing chores.

Using the TabStrip Control

You can use the TabStrip control to conserve screen real estate by displaying data on different "pages" of the same form. The TabStrip control included in the MOD is the same control you're used to seeing in applications such as Microsoft Word and Microsoft Excel. It's easy to implement this control in your own forms. Figure 21.21 shows a form called frmTabbed that uses the TabStrip control.

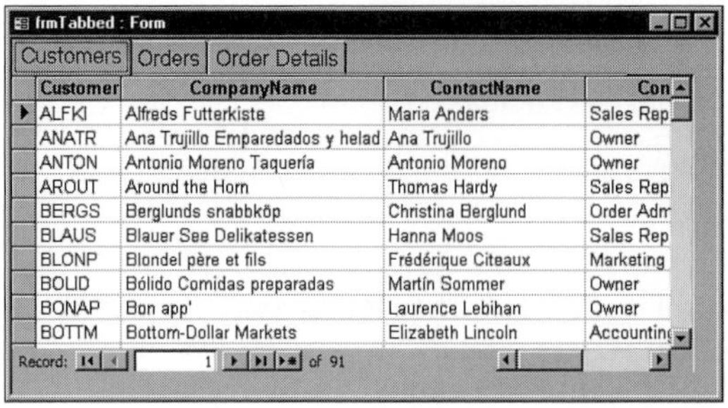

FIGURE 21.21

A form that uses the TabStrip control.

As the user clicks on each tab, the appropriate information displays. For example, if the user selects a customer on the Customers tab, and then clicks the Orders tab, all orders for the selected customer are displayed. If the user selects an order on the Orders tab, and then clicks the Order Details tab, all details about the selected order are displayed. The code looks like this:

```
Private Sub tabSelect_Click()
    'Evaluate which tab is selected
    'Hide and show the appropriate subforms,
    'based on which tab is selected
    Select Case Me!tabSelect.SelectedItem.INDEX
        Case 1
            Me!fsubCustomers.Visible = True
            Me!fsubOrders.Visible = False
            Me!fsubOrderDetails.Visible = False
        Case 2
            Me!fsubOrders.Form.RecordSource = _
                "Select * from tblOrders Where CustomerID = '" _
                & Me!fsubCustomers.Form!CustomerID & "';"
            Me!fsubCustomers.Visible = False
            Me!fsubOrders.Visible = True
            Me!fsubOrderDetails.Visible = False
        Case 3
            Me!fsubOrders.Form.RecordSource = _
                "Select * from tblOrderDetails Where OrderID = " _
                & Me!fsubOrders.Form!OrderID & ";"
            Me!fsubCustomers.Visible = False
            Me!fsubOrders.Visible = False
            Me!fsubOrderDetails.Visible = True
        End Select
End Sub
```

Here's how the code works: After adding a TabStrip control to a form, you can double-click it to view its properties. (See Figure 21.22.) The TabStrip Control Properties dialog box allows you to set properties for the TabStrip control as a whole, as well as for each tab. When the tabs have been added, you can code the TabStrip control's `Click` event to determine what will happen when the user clicks on each tab.

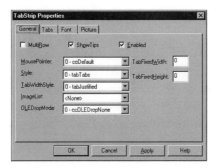

FIGURE 21.22
The TabStrip Control Properties dialog box sets initial properties for the TabStrip control.

> **NOTE**
>
> A Tab control is included as a standard control in the Access toolbox, so you don't need to use the ActiveX TabStrip control in your applications. Third-party vendors have Tab controls with more features than Microsoft's. These are all ActiveX-type controls.

Like the StatusBar control, the TabStrip control is one-based. A `Case` statement evaluates which tab was selected. The frmTabbed form has three subforms: fsubCustomers, fsubOrders, and fsubOrderDetails. When the frmTabbed form is first displayed, only the fsubCustomers subform control is visible. As the user clicks on each tab in the TabStrip control, the appropriate subform is displayed, and the other two subforms are hidden. The `RecordSource` for fsubOrders is modified at runtime to show only orders for the selected customer from fsubCustomers. The `RecordSource` for fsubOrderDetails is modified at runtime to show only the order detail items for the order selected on fsubOrders.

Using the ImageList Control

The TabStrip control can be enhanced by using an ImageList control, which stores images you'll be using in the form. It's populated at design time with these images. The ImageList control is hidden at runtime, but any of its images can be used in your form.

The frmImageList form, shown in Figure 21.23, is similar to the frmTabbed form, except that each tab has an image that comes from the ImageList control called imgPictures. The properties of the imgPictures ImageList control are shown in Figure 21.24. Notice that three pictures have been inserted. The General tab's size has been set to 16×16, and the tabSelect TabStrip control has been modified to include imgPictures as its ImageList under the General properties tab. The index of each picture in the imgPictures ImageList control has been added as the `Image` property for each tab in the TabStrip control; the `Image` property specifies which image in the bound ImageList control should be displayed in the particular tab.

FIGURE 21.23

The frmImageList form, with pictures for tabs.

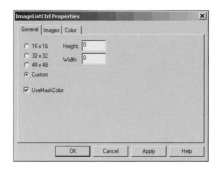

FIGURE 21.24

The properties of the ImageList control.

Licensing and Distribution Issues

Some OCX controls can be distributed freely, but others have differing levels of restrictions. The licensing policies for a particular OCX control are determined by its vendor.

The licensing rules in effect for an OCX can be enforced by law, which means that improper distribution of the control is a crime. Distributing an OCX control without proper licensing is just like copying a software product illegally.

If you have any questions about licensing a third-party control, consult the vendor who created the control. A one-time fee might be required to freely distribute the OCX; in other cases, you might have to pay a royalty for each copy of the control that's distributed. If you aren't sure whether you want to buy a third-party control, you might want to consult the vendor. Many vendors let potential customers try out their products for a limited period of time. In fact, many of the demo versions are available online.

> **NOTE**
>
> Several other ActiveX controls are covered in Chapter 31, "Third-Party Tools That Can Help You to Get Your Job Done Effectively."

PRACTICAL EXAMPLES

Implementing ActiveX Controls

ActiveX controls can be used in many places in your own applications. Use your imagination to determine where controls will enhance the application's usefulness. The following examples illustrate a few potential uses of the ActiveX controls.

Adding a Calendar to the Report Criteria Dialog

One example of an ActiveX control is in the frmReportDateRange dialog box, shown in Figure 21.25. The Calendar control can be used to populate the Beginning Date and Ending Date text boxes.

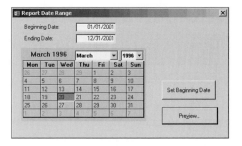

FIGURE 21.25

Adding the Calendar control to the Report Criteria form.

The code for adding the Calendar control looks like this:

```
Private Sub cmdSetDates_Click()
    On Error GoTo cmdSetDates_Error

    If cmdSetDates.Caption = "Set Beginning Date" Then
        BeginDate = calSetDates.Value
        cmdSetDates.Caption = "Set Ending Date"
    Else
        EndDate = calSetDates.Value
        cmdSetDates.Caption = "Set Beginning Date"
    End If

    Exit Sub

cmdSetDates_Error:
    MsgBox "Error # " & Err.Number & ": " & Err.Description
    Exit Sub

End Sub
```

Because the same calendar is used to populate the Beginning Date and Ending Date text boxes, the form has a command button with a caption that toggles. The user can select a date, and then click Set Beginning Date. The BeginDate text box is populated with the value selected on the calendar, and the command button's caption is set to display Set Ending Date. If the command button's caption says Set Ending Date and the user clicks that button, the EndDate text box is filled with the value selected on the calendar, and the command button's caption changes to say Set Beginning Date.

Summary

ActiveX controls greatly extend the capabilities of Access 2002 and enable you to incorporate more functionality into your applications. These controls are easy to use and extremely powerful. In this chapter, you learned how to install, register, and work with ActiveX controls.

Each ActiveX control has its own properties, events, and methods. By modifying properties, reacting to events, and executing methods, you can take advantage of its rich features. Licensing for each ActiveX control varies, so you need to investigate that for each control you want to use to know whether—and under what conditions—you can distribute it to your users.

Automation: Communicating with Other Applications

CHAPTER 22

IN THIS CHAPTER

Why This Chapter Is Important

Windows users have come to expect seamless integration between products. They are not concerned with what product you use to develop their application; they just want to accomplish their tasks. Often, Microsoft Word, Microsoft Excel, or some other product is best suited for a particular task that your application must complete. It is your responsibility to pick the best tool for the job. This means that you must know how to communicate from your application directly to that tool.

All this means is that you can no longer learn only about the product and language that you select as your development tool. Instead, you must learn about all the other available applications. Furthermore, you must learn how to communicate with these applications—a challenging but exciting feat.

ActiveX automation is the capability of one application to control another application's objects. This means that your Access application can launch Excel, create or modify a spreadsheet, and print it—all without the user having to directly interact with the Excel application. Many people confuse automation with the process of linking and embedding. OLE 1.0 gave you the capability to create compound documents, meaning that you can embed an Excel spreadsheet in a Word document or link to the Excel spreadsheet from within a Word document. This capability was exciting at the time and still is quite useful in many situations, but OLE 2.0 (in addition to everything that OLE 1.0 provides) introduced the capability for one application to actually control another application's objects. With Office 97, Microsoft changed the way users refer to OLE. It became known as *automation* and is an industry standard and a feature of the *Component Object Model* (COM).

Just as you can control other applications using automation, you can control the Access application with other applications, such as Excel or a Visual Basic application. This means that you can take advantage of Access's marvelous report writer from your Visual Basic application. In fact, you can list all the Access reports, allow your user to select one, and then run the report—all from within a Visual Basic form.

Defining Some Automation Terms

Before you learn how automation works, you need to understand a few automation terms. Automation requires an automation client and an automation server. The *automation client* application is the one that is doing the talking. It is the application that is controlling the server application. Because this book is about Access, most of the examples in this chapter show Access as an automation client, meaning that the Access application is controlling the other application (Excel, Word, and so on). The *automation server* application is the application being controlled. It contains the objects being manipulated. Excel is acting as an automation server when Access launches Excel, makes it visible, creates a new worksheet, sends the results of a query to the worksheet, and graphs the spreadsheet data. It is Excel's objects that are being controlled, Excel's properties that are being changed, and Excel's methods that are being executed.

Another important component of automation is a *type library*, this is, a dictionary that lists the objects, properties, methods, and events exposed by an automation server application. Type libraries allow the server application's objects, properties, and methods to be syntax checked by the Access compiler. You also can use a type library to get help on another application's objects, properties, and methods from within Access.

An *object model* of an automation server application contains the set of objects that are exposed to automation client applications. The objects within the object model are called *object types*. When you write automation code, you create and manipulate instances of an object type. These instances are called *objects*.

> **CAUTION**
>
> It is important to be aware of the hardware that automation requires. It is common for a developer using a Pentium III with 512M of RAM to create a really slick application, only to find that it won't run on the 32M Pentiums owned by the users. Automation craves RAM. The more, the better! I recommend 128M of RAM or more for applications that use automation. It also is important to recognize that automation is not fast, even on the slickest of machines.

Declaring an Object Variable to Reference Your Application

Automation requires that you create object variables that reference application objects. After you create an object variable, you can query and change the object's properties as well as execute its methods.

You can learn about an object's properties and methods using its object libraries. An *object library* contains a listing of all the properties and methods that an object exposes. To be able to view foreign objects from within Access, you first must establish a reference to that application. After a reference is established, you can view that object's properties and methods using the Object Browser. You also can view any modules and classes that the parent object exposes.

To register an object, the Visual Basic Editor (VBE) must be active. With the code window active, choose Tools|References. The References dialog box appears, as shown in Figure 22.1.

22

AUTOMATION

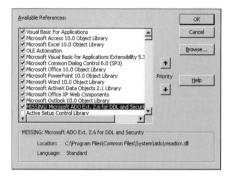

FIGURE 22.1
The References dialog box.

Each time you install a program, the Windows registry is updated. The References dialog box shows you all the objects registered in Windows. (See Figure 22.2.) If you want to link to one of the available objects from within Access, you must enable the check box to the left of the object name. Choose OK. You can browse that object's properties and methods in the Object Browser, as shown in Figure 22.3. As covered in Chapter 8, "Objects, Properties, Methods, and Events Explained," to access the Object Browser, you can choose View|Object Browser, press F2, or click the Object Browser tool while in the Module window. Notice that in Figure 22.3, the Object Browser displays all the classes that belong to the Excel 10.0 object library. The Range class is selected. All the members of the Range class are displayed in the list box at the right. The AutoFill method is selected. Notice that the bottom half of the Object Browser shows all the arguments associated with the AutoFill method of the Range class.

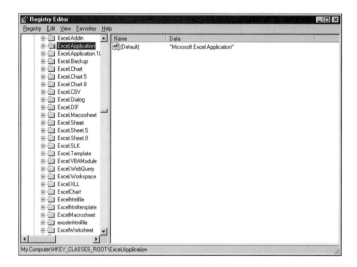

FIGURE 22.2
Registered automation server objects.

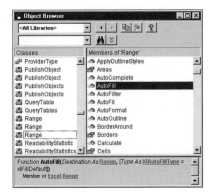

FIGURE 22.3
The Object Browser.

Creating an Automation Object

Before you can talk to an application, you need to know the objects contained within it. You then can use `Dim`, `Private`, or `Public` statements to point to and control various application objects. Each product comes with documentation indicating which objects it supports. You also can view the objects that a product supports by using the Object Browser. After you create an object variable, you can manipulate the object without user intervention.

Declaring an Object Variable

To create an instance of an object, you first must create an object variable that holds a reference to the object. You can do this by using a `Dim` statement:

```
Dim objExcel As New Excel.Application
```

This code creates an object variable pointing to the Excel application object. A new instance of the Excel application is started automatically. This Excel object is part of the Excel application. It can be controlled by VBA using the object variable. Unless instructed otherwise, the instance of Excel is invisible. You can make it visible by using this statement:

```
objExcel.Visible = True
```

Alternatively, you can use two statements to declare and instantiate an object. The code looks like this:

```
Dim objExcel as Excel.Application
Set objExcel = New Excel.Application
```

The `Dim` statement declares an object variable that is ready to be associated with a running instance of Excel. The `Set` statement launches Excel and points the object variable at the new instance of Excel. The advantage of this method is that you can better control when the instance of Excel is actually created. If, for example, the declaration is in the General Declarations section of a form, you can place the Set statement under a command button that is used to launch Excel.

Manipulating an Automation Object

After you create an instance of an object, you are ready to set its properties and execute its methods. You can talk to the object through the object variable you created. Using this object variable, you can get and set properties and execute methods.

Setting and Retrieving Properties

The objects you will be talking to through automation all have properties. *Properties* are the attributes of the object—the adjectives you use to describe the objects. You can use VBA to inquire about the properties of objects and set the values of these properties. Here are some examples:

```
objExcel.Visible = True
objExcel.Caption = "Hello World"
objExcel.Cells(1, 1).Value = "Here I Am"
```

Each of these examples sets properties of the Excel application object. The first example sets the Visible property of the object to True. The second example sets the Caption of the object to "Hello World". The final example sets the Value property of the Cells object, contained within the Excel object, to the value "Here I Am".

Executing Methods

Properties refer to the attributes of an object, and *methods* refer to the actions you take on the object. Methods are the verbs that apply to a particular object type. Here's an example:

```
objExcel.Workbooks.Add
```

This code uses the Add method to add a workbook to the Excel object.

Early Binding Versus Late Binding

Binding is another important automation concept. There are two types of binding available with automation components. They are early binding and late binding. With early binding, you create a reference to a component's type library. This notifies Access of all the library's objects, properties, methods, and events. With late binding, you instantiate objects at runtime without referencing them at design time. VBA does not know anything about the objects that you are creating until runtime.

Most objects that you automate support early binding. You should utilize early binding whenever possible. Early binding has several benefits. Because each object's properties and methods are resolved at compile time, early binding is faster and more efficient. Furthermore, once you create a reference to a type library, all of the library's objects and their properties and methods are available via Intellisense. Finally, online help is available for any type libraries that you have referenced. This means, for example, if you have referenced Excel's library from Access, the process of placing your cursor on an object, property, or method and pressing F1 displays help for the selected item.

Listing 22.1 provides an example of early binding. This code requires that a reference first be made to the Excel object library.

LISTING 22.1 Early Binding Requires that a Reference Be Made to the Appropriate Type Library

```
Sub EarlyBinding()

    'Declare and instantiate an Excel Application object
    Dim objExcel As Excel.Application
    Set objExcel = New Excel.Application

    'Set properties and execute methods of the object
    With objExcel
        .Visible = True
        .Workbooks.Add
        .Range("A1") = "Hello World"
    End With
End Sub
```

CreateObject and GetObject

CreateObject and GetObject are required when using late binding. Because, with late binding, Access is not aware of the server application and its objects, properties, methods, and events, you cannot use a Dim statement and a Set statement to declare and instantiate the server application object. Instead, you must use Dim to declare a generic object variable. You then use a Set statement along with the CreateObject or GetObject function to work with the server object. The CreateObject function launches a new instance of the server object. The GetObject function is similar to CreateObject, but attempts to point a running instance of the requested application. Furthermore, unlike the CreateObject function that receives only one argument as a parameter, the GetObject function receives an optional parameter with the name of the document you want to work with.

Listing 22.2 provides an example of CreateObject and late binding.

LISTING 22.2 The `CreateObject` Function Is Used to Create a Late-Bound Instance of Excel

```
Sub LateBinding()

    'Declare a generic object variable
    Dim objExcel As Object

    'Point the object variable at an Excel applciation object
    Set objExcel = CreateObject("Excel.Application.10")

    'Set properties and execute methods of the object
    With objExcel
        .Visible = True
        .Workbooks.Add
        .Range("A1") = "Hello World"
    End With

End Sub
```

NOTE

Calling `GetObject` doesn't determine if the object is late or early bound. You can declare `Dim objExcel` as Excel.Application, using `GetObject`, and the object will be early bound.

Controlling Excel from Access

Before you attempt to talk to Excel, you must understand its object model. Excel gives you an excellent overview of the Excel object model. You can find this model by searching for "object model" in Excel Help. Each object in the model has hypertext links that enable you to obtain specific help on the object, its properties, and its methods.

After you launch Excel, it launches as a hidden window with a Visible property of `False`. Destroying the Excel object variable does not cause Excel to terminate. To make things even more complicated, each time you use the `New` keyword within the `Dim` or `Set` statement, a new instance of Excel is launched. This means that it is possible for numerous hidden copies of Excel to be running on a user's machine, which can lead to serious resource problems. If you want to use a running instance of Excel, you can omit the `New` keyword. This has its disadvantages as well. Let's say, for example, that the user of your application has created a large spreadsheet and has not saved it recently. Your application uses an existing instance of Excel, creates a new workbook, prints, and then exits without saving. You might find that your user is very angry about the loss of his or her important work. For this reason, I have found it preferable to suffer the potential resource costs and create my own instance of Excel. If you want to launch Excel invisibly, do your work, and get out, make sure that you terminate Excel upon completion of your code.

Before you execute code that relies on a running copy of Excel, it is important to ascertain that Excel launched successfully. The function shown in Listing 22.3 attempts to launch Excel. If it is successful, `True` is returned from the function. Otherwise, `False` is returned from the function.

LISTING 22.3 The `CreateExcelObj` Subroutine

```
Function CreateExcelObj() As Boolean
    'Invoke error handling
    On Error GoTo CreateExcelObj_Err

    'Assume a False return value
    CreateExcelObj = False

    'Attempt to Launch Excel
    Set gobjExcel = New Excel.Application

    'If Excel launches successfully, return true
    CreateExcelObj = True

CreateExcelObj_Exit:
    Exit Function

CreateExcelObj_Err:

    'If an error occurs, display a message and return false
    MsgBox "Couldn't Launch Excel!!", vbCritical, "Warning!!"
    CreateExcelObj = False
    Resume CreateExcelObj_Exit
End Function
```

The routine begins by invoking error handling. It initializes the return value for the function to `False`. The routine then attempts to launch Excel. If it is successful, the public variable `gobjExcel` references the running instance of Excel, and `True` is returned from the function. If an error occurs, the code within the error handler is executed. A message is displayed, and the return value for the function is set to `False`.

NOTE

 You can find this code and most other examples used in this chapter in the CHAP22EX.MDB database located on your sample code CD-ROM. This routine is located in basUtils.

CAUTION

To take advantage of the exciting world of automation, you must install all automation server applications on the user's machine, and the user must possess a full license to the server applications. In fact, you will be unable to compile and run the examples contained in the sample database for this chapter unless you have the server applications loaded on your development machine.

The CreatExcelObj function is called from the Click event of cmdFillExcel command button on the frmSimpleExcel form. The application attempts to talk to the Excel object only if the return value of the function is True, indicating that Excel was loaded successfully.

```
Private Sub cmdFillExcel_Click()
    'If Excel is launched successfully,
    'execute the FillCells routine
    If CreateExcelObj() Then
        Call FillCells
    End If
End Sub
```

If Excel launches successfully, the FillCells subroutine executes, as shown in Listing 22.4.

LISTING 22.4   The FillCells Subroutine

```
Sub FillCells()
   'Declare an Excel Worksheet object
   Dim objWS As Excel.Worksheet

   'Invoke Error Handling
   On Error GoTo FillCells_Err

   With gobjExcel
       'Add a Workbook to the Workbooks collection
       .Workbooks.Add
```

LISTING 22.4 Continued

```
        'Point the Worksheet object at the active sheet
        Set objWS = gobjExcel.ActiveSheet

        'Set the value of various cells in the sheet
        With objWS
            .Cells(1, 1).Value = "Schedule"
            .Cells(2, 1).Value = "Day"
            .Cells(2, 2).Value = "Tasks"
            .Cells(3, 1).Value = 1
            .Cells(4, 1).Value = 2
        End With

        'Select A3 through A4
        .Range("A3:A4").Select

        'Use the AutoFill method to fill the range of A3
        'through A33 with numeric values
        .Selection.AutoFill gobjExcel.Range("A3:A33")

        'Select cell A1
        .Range("A1").Select

        'Make Excel visible
        .Visible = True
    End With

FillCells_Exit:

    Exit Sub

FillCells_Err:
    'If Excel object still set, quit Excel and destroy
    'the object variable
    If Not gobjExcel Is Nothing Then
        gobjExcel.Quit
        Set gobjExcel = Nothing
    End If

    Resume FillCells_Exit
End Sub
```

You can find this relatively simple routine in frmSimpleExcel, which is part of the CHAP22EX.MDB database file. (See Figure 22.4.) It begins by using the Add method on the Workbooks collection of the Excel object to add a new workbook to the instance of Excel. It then uses `Set objWS = gobjExcel.ActiveSheet` to provide a shortcut for talking to the active sheet in the new Excel workbook. Using the `objWS` object reference, it modifies the values of several cells. It then uses the `AutoFill` method to quickly fill a range of cells with data. It returns the cursor to cell `A1`, and the Excel object is made visible. You might wonder what the `AutoFill` method is; it automates the process of filling a range of cells with a pattern of data. Figure 22.5 shows the results. I mention it here not just to tell you what it is, but also to illustrate an important point: You must know the product you are automating and its capabilities. If you are not familiar with the product from a user's perspective, you will find it extremely difficult to work with the product using automation.

FIGURE 22.4

The form used to launch, communicate with, and close Excel.

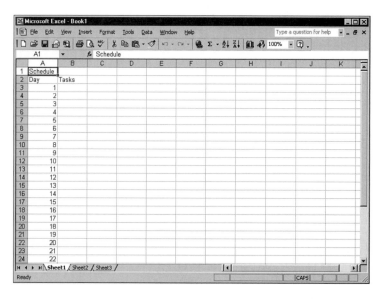

FIGURE 22.5

Using the `AutoFill` *method to populate a range of cells.*

Closing an Excel Automation Object

After the user clicks the Close Excel command button, the CloseExcel subroutine is called, as shown in Listing 22.5. The subroutine first checks to see whether the gobjExcel object variable is still set. If it is, Excel is still running. The DisplayAlerts property of the Excel application object is set to False. This ensures that, when the Quit method is executed, Excel will not warn about any unsaved worksheets. This methodology is acceptable because all work was accomplished using a new instance of the Excel application. If you want to save your work, you should execute the required code before the Quit method is executed.

LISTING 22.5 The CloseExcel Subroutine

```
Sub CloseExcel()

    'Invoke error handling
    On Error GoTo CloseExcel_Err

    'If the Excel object variable is still set,
    'turn of alerts and quit Excel
    If Not gobjExcel Is Nothing Then
        gobjExcel.DisplayAlerts = False
        gobjExcel.Quit
    End If

CloseExcel_Exit:
    'Destroy the Excel object variable
    Set gobjExcel = Nothing
    Exit Sub

CloseExcel_Err:
    'Display error message and resume at Exit routine
    MsgBox "Error # " & Err.Number & ": " & Err.Description
    Resume CloseExcel_Exit
End Sub
```

Creating a Graph from Access

Now that you have learned how to talk to Excel, you are ready to learn how to do something a bit more practical. Figure 22.6 shows a form called frmCreateExcelGraph. The form shows the result of a query that groups the result of price multiplied by quantity for each country. The Create Excel Graph command button sends the result of the query to Excel and produces the graph shown in Figure 22.7. (Listing 22.6 shows the code that produces this graph.)

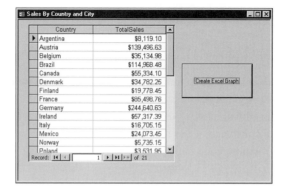

FIGURE 22.6
The form used to create an Excel graph.

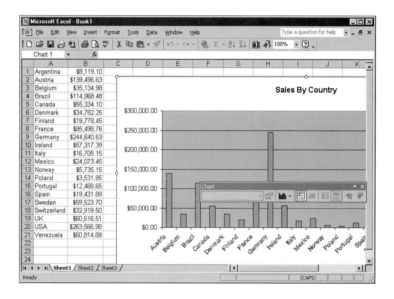

FIGURE 22.7
The result of a query graphed in Excel.

LISTING 22.6   Creating a Graph from Access

```
Private Sub cmdCreateGraph_Click()
    On Error GoTo cmdCreateGraph_Err
    Dim rstData As ADODB.Recordset
    Dim rstCount As ADODB.Recordset
    Dim fld As ADODB.Field
```

LISTING 22.6 Continued

```
Dim rng As Excel.Range
Dim objWS As Excel.Worksheet
Dim intRowCount As Integer
Dim intColCount As Integer

'Display Hourglass
DoCmd.Hourglass True

'Instantiate an ADO recordset and set its Connection
Set rstData = New ADODB.Recordset
rstData.ActiveConnection = CurrentProject.Connection

'Instantiate a second ADO recordset and set its Connection
Set rstCount = New ADODB.Recordset
rstCount.ActiveConnection = CurrentProject.Connection

'Attempt to create Recordset based
'on the result of qrySalesByCount
If CreateRecordset(rstData, rstCount, "qrySalesByCountry") Then

    'If the recordset is created successfully, attempt to launch Excel
    If CreateExcelObj() Then

        'If Excel is launched successfully, add a workbook
        gobjExcel.Workbooks.Add

        'Create a pointer to the Active sheet
        Set objWS = gobjExcel.ActiveSheet
        intRowCount = 1
        intColCount = 1

        'Loop though Fields collection of the recordset,
        'using field names as column headings
        For Each fld In rstData.Fields
            If fld.Type <> adLongVarBinary Then
                objWS.Cells(1, intColCount).Value = fld.Name
                intColCount = intColCount + 1
            End If
        Next fld

        'Send Recordset to Excel
        objWS.Range("A1").CopyFromRecordset rstData, 500

        'Format Data
        With gobjExcel
```

LISTING 22.6   Continued

```
                .Columns("A:B").Select
                .Columns("A:B").EntireColumn.AutoFit
                .Range("A1").Select
                .ActiveCell.CurrentRegion.Select
                Set rng = .Selection
                .Selection.NumberFormat = "$#,##0.00"

                'Add a Chart Object
                .ActiveSheet.ChartObjects.Add(135.75, 14.25, 607.75,
301).Select

                'Run the Chart Wizard
                .ActiveChart.ChartWizard Source:=Range(rng.Address), _
                    Gallery:=xlColumn, _
                    Format:=6, PlotBy:=xlColumns, CategoryLabels:=1,
SeriesLabels _
                    :=1, HasLegend:=1, Title:="Sales By Country", CategoryTitle
_
                    :="", ValueTitle:="", ExtraTitle:=""

                'Make Excel Visible
                .Visible = True
            End With
        Else
            'If Excel not launched successfully, display an error message
            MsgBox "Excel Not Successfully Launched"
        End If
    Else
        'If more than 500 records are in result set, display a message
        MsgBox "Too Many Records to Send to Excel"
    End If

cmdCreateGraph_Exit:
    Set rstData = Nothing
    Set rstCount = Nothing
    Set fld = Nothing
    Set rng = Nothing
    Set objWS = Nothing

    'Turn hourglass off
    DoCmd.Hourglass False
    Exit Sub

cmdCreateGraph_Err:
    'If an error occurs, display a message and return to
```

LISTING 22.6 Continued

```
    'common exit routine
    MsgBox "Error # " & Err.Number & ": " & Err.Description
    Resume cmdCreateGraph_Exit
End Sub
```

> **CAUTION**
>
> If the Common Dialog control is not installed on your machine, or the user's machine, this code will not run. If that is the case, you must remove the reference to the Common Dialog control before running the example. Any examples in the chapter that utilize the Common Dialog control must be modified. The Common Dialog control is included with the Microsoft Office Developer.

22

AUTOMATION

This routine begins by creating several object variables. It then creates two recordsets and sets the ActiveConnection property of each recordset to the connection associated with the current project. It calls a user-defined function called CreateRecordset, located in the basUtils module. The CreateRecordset function receives three parameters: the two recordset object variables and the name of a query. Listing 22.7 shows the CreateRecordset function.

LISTING 22.7 The CreateRecordset Function

```
Function CreateRecordset(rstData As ADODB.Recordset, _
    rstCount As ADODB.Recordset, _
    strTableName As String)
    On Error GoTo CreateRecordset_Err

    'Create recordset that contains count of records in query result
    rstCount.Open "Select Count(*) As NumRecords from " & strTableName

    'If more than 500 records in query result, return false
    'Otherwise, create recordset from query
    If rstCount!NumRecords > 500 Then
        CreateRecordset = False
    Else
        rstData.Open strTableName
        CreateRecordset = True
    End If

CreateRecordset_Exit:
    'Common exit point; destroy the rstCount recordset
```

LISTING 22.7 Continued

```
    Set rstCount = Nothing
    Exit Function

CreateRecordset_Err:
    'Display error message and resume at common exit point
    MsgBox "Error # " & Err.Number & ": " & Err.Description
    Resume CreateRecordset_Exit
End Function
```

This function begins by counting how many records are returned by the query name that is passed. If the number of records exceeds 500, the function returns False; otherwise, the function opens a recordset based on the query name that is passed and returns True. This function ensures that only a reasonable number of records are sent to Excel and that a recordset can be opened successfully.

If the CreateRecordset function returns True, the remainder of the code in the Click event of the cmdCreateGraph command button executes. The routine uses the CreateExcelObj function to launch Excel. If Excel is opened successfully, a new workbook is created. The routine then loops through each field in the Fields collection of the recordset (the result of the query). The values of the cells in the first row of the worksheet are set equal to the names of the fields in the recordset. Next, the routine uses the CopyFromRecordset method of the Excel Range object to copy the contents of the recordset rstData to cell A1 in the active worksheet. The data from each row is placed in a different row within the spreadsheet. The data from each column in a particular row is placed in the various columns of the worksheet. OLE object fields (adLongVarBinary) are excluded from the process.

After all the data in the recordset is sent to Excel, the routine is ready to create a chart. It moves the cursor to cell A1 and then selects the entire contiguous range of data. It adds a chart object to the worksheet and then uses the Chart Wizard to create a chart. Finally, Excel is made visible so that users can see the fruits of their efforts.

Controlling Word from Access

As you discovered in the preceding section, Excel exposes many objects. You can manipulate each of these objects separately, using its own properties and methods. Prior to Office 97, this was not true for Word because Word exposed only one object, called Word.Basic. Microsoft Word 97, Microsoft Word 2000, and Microsoft Word 2002 all sport the Visual Basic for Applications language. Word 97, Word 2000, and Word 2002 expose many objects just as Excel and other Microsoft products do.

Just as with Excel, you can use the Dim statement or Dim as New statement to launch Word. Like Excel, Word launches as a hidden object. The Word application object has a Visible property, which makes the Word object visible. If you create a Word object using automation, Word will not automatically terminate, even if the object variable is destroyed.

Using Word to Generate a Mass Mailing

Figure 22.8 shows the form called frmMergeToWord, which shows the results of running a query called qryMailMerge. After the user clicks the Merge to Word command button, all the records displayed are sent to a Word mail merge and printed. Figure 22.9 shows an example of the resulting document, and Listing 22.8 shows the code that generated this document.

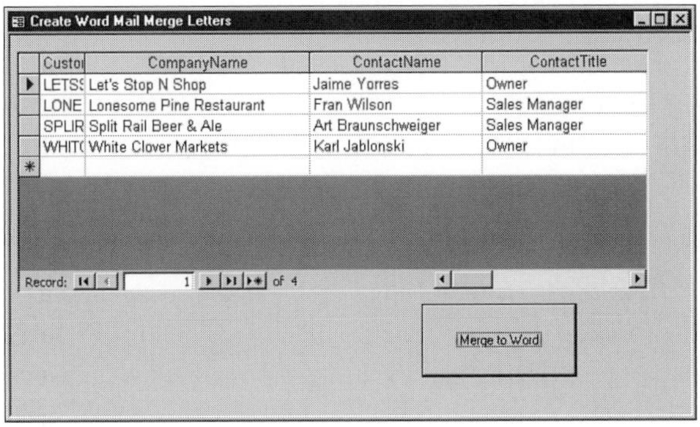

FIGURE 22.8
The data that will be merged to Word.

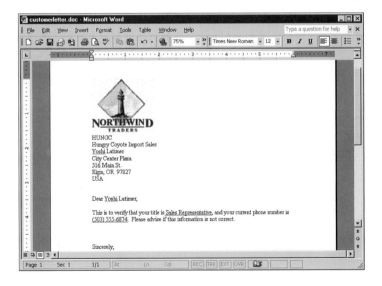

FIGURE 22.9
The result of the mail merge.

LISTING 22.8   Generating a Word Mail Merge Document

```
Private Sub cmdMergeToWord_Click()
    On Error GoTo cmdMergeToWord_Err

    'Turn Hourglass on
    DoCmd.Hourglass True

    'Attempt to create a Word object
    If CreateWordObj() Then

        'If Word object created
        With gobjWord

            'Make Word visible
            .Visible = True

            'Open a document called CustomerLetter in the
            'current folder
            .Documents.Open CurrentProject.Path & _
                "\customerletter.doc"

            'Give the document time to open
            DoEvents

            'Use the MailMerge method of the document
            'to perform a mail merge
            With gobjWord.ActiveDocument.MailMerge
                .Destination = wdSendToNewDocument
                .SuppressBlankLines = True
                .Execute
            End With

            'Send the result of the merge to the print preview
            'window
            .ActiveDocument.PrintPreview    'Preview

            'Make Word visible
            .Visible = True
        End With
    End If

cmdMergeToWord_Exit:
    'Turn hourglass off
```

LISTING 22.8   Continued

```
    DoCmd.Hourglass False
    Exit Sub

cmdMergeToWord_Err:
    'Display error message, destroy Word object and go
    'to common exit routine
    MsgBox "Error # " & Err.Number & ": " & Err.Description
    Set gobjWord = Nothing
    Resume cmdMergeToWord_Exit
End Sub
```

The code begins by presenting an hourglass mouse pointer to the user. This helps to ensure that, if the process takes a while, the user knows that something is happening. It then calls the `CreateWordObj` routine to create a Word object. The `CreateWordObj` routine is similar to the `CreateExcel` routine shown earlier in the chapter. The `Open` method is executed on the Documents collection of the Word object. It opens a document called customerletter in the current folder. The customerletter document already has been set up to do a mail merge with the results of a query called qryMerge. The subroutine sets the Destination property of the `MailMerge` object to a new document. It sets the SuppressBlankLines property to `True`, and then executes the mail merge with the `Execute` method. This merges the results of qryMailMerge and creates a new document with the mail-merged letters. The `PrintPreview` method is executed on the `ActiveDocument` object so that the merged document is printed. Finally, the Visible property of the Word object is set to `True`, making Word visible, and the hourglass vanishes.

Using Word to Overcome the Limitations of Access as a Report Writer

Although in most ways Access is a phenomenal report writer, it does have its limitations. For example, you cannot bold or italicize an individual word or phrase within a text box. This is quite limiting if you need to emphasize something such as a past due amount in a dunning letter. When the document I need to produce appears more like a letter than a report, I often think of Microsoft Word. The document pictured in Figure 22.10 produces a letter that provides information to the recipient of an order. The code shown in Listing 22.9 produces the letter.

22

AUTOMATION

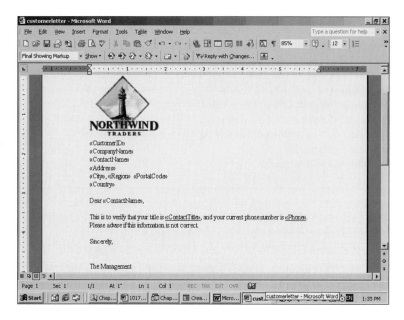

FIGURE 22.10
Order confirmation letter produced in Microsoft Word.

LISTING 22.9   Word Bookmarks Are Used to Indicate Where Inserted Text Is Placed in the Word Template

```
Private Sub cmdSendConfirmation_Click()

    Dim objDocument As Word.Document

    'Launch Word
    If CreateWordObj() Then

        'Make Word visible
        gobjWord.Visible = True

        'Point the Document object at a new document
        'based on the Order.dot template
        Set objDocument = gobjWord.Documents.Add _
            (CurrentProject.Path & "\Order.dot")

        'Populate all of the bookmarks with the order information
        With objDocument.Bookmarks
                .Item("CompanyNameAddress").Range.Text = Nz(Me.txtShipName)
                .Item("Address").Range.Text = Nz(Me.txtShipAddress)
```

LISTING 22.9   Continued

```
                .Item("City").Range.Text = Nz(Me.txtShipCity)
                .Item("Region").Range.Text = Nz(Me.txtShipRegion)
                .Item("PostalCode").Range.Text = Nz(Me.txtShipPostalCode)
                .Item("CompanyName").Range.Text = Nz(Me.txtShipName)
                .Item("Shipper").Range.Text = Nz(Me.txtShipName)
                .Item("ShippedDate").Range.Text = Nz(Me.txtShippedDate)
                .Item("FreightAmount").Range.Text = Nz(Me.txtFreight)

        End With
    End If
End Sub
```

The example first launches Word. It then gets a reference to the a new document based on the Order.dot template. After that, it populates bookmarks in the document with values from the currently displayed order.

Controlling PowerPoint from Access

Believe it or not, even PowerPoint can be controlled using automation. You can create a presentation, print a presentation, or even run a slide show directly from Access.

PowerPoint launches as a hidden window. To make PowerPoint visible, you must set the Visible property of AppWindow to True. Destroying the PowerPoint object variable does not terminate the PowerPoint application.

> **NOTE**
>
> You can find details of the PowerPoint object model in Microsoft PowerPoint Visual Basic Reference in PowerPoint Help. You should review this object model before attempting to communicate with PowerPoint.

The code shown in Listing 22.10 is located under the Click event of the cmdChangePicture command button on frmOLEToPowerPoint, which is shown in Figure 22.11. Figure 22.12 shows the resulting PowerPoint slide.

22

AUTOMATION

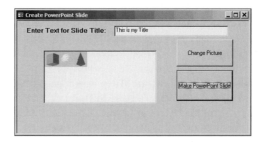

FIGURE 22.11

The form used to create a PowerPoint slide.

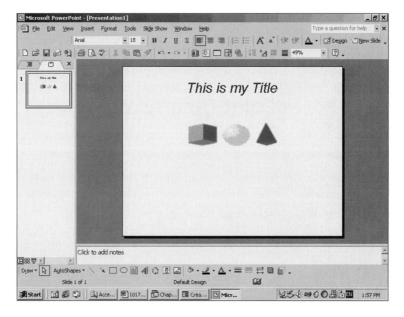

FIGURE 22.12

A PowerPoint slide created using automation.

LISTING 22.10 Select Picture

```
Private Sub cmdChangePicture_Click()
    'Display Open common dialog
    dlgCommon.ShowOpen

    'If the user selected a file, set the SourceDoc
    'property of the OLE control to the selected document
```

LISTING 22.10   Continued

```
    If Len(dlgCommon.Filename) Then
        olePicture.SourceDoc = dlgCommon.Filename

        'Designate that you wish to link to
        'the selected document
        olePicture.Action = acOLECreateLink
    End If
End Sub
```

The code in the Click event of cmdChangePicture invokes the File Open common dialog box so that the user can select a picture to be added to the slide. The Filename property returned from this dialog box is used as the SourceDoc property for the automation object. The new picture then is linked to the automation object.

Listing 22.11 shows the routine that creates the PowerPoint slide.

LISTING 22.11   Creating the PowerPoint Slide

```
Private Sub cmdMakePPTSlide_Click()

    Dim objPresentation As PowerPoint.Presentation
    Dim objSlide As PowerPoint.Slide

    'Ensure that both the title and the picture are selected
    If IsNull(Me.txtTitle) Or Me.olePicture.SourceDoc = "" Then

        MsgBox "A Title Must Be Entered, and a Picture Selected Before
Proceeding"

    Else

        'Create instance of PowerPoint application
        Set mobjPPT = New PowerPoint.Application

        'Make instance visible to user
        mobjPPT.Visible = True

        'Add a Presentation
        Set objPresentation = mobjPPT.Presentations.Add
        'Add a Slide

        Set objSlide = objPresentation.Slides.Add(1, ppLayoutTitleOnly)
```

Listing 22.11   Continued

```
        'Change the Slide Background
        objSlide.Background.Fill.ForeColor.RGB = RGB(255, 100, 100)

        'Modify the Slide Title
        With objSlide.Shapes.Title.TextFrame.TextRange
            .Text = Me.txtTitle
            .Font.Color.RGB = RGB(0, 0, 255)
            .Font.Italic = True
        End With

        'Add the OLE Picture
        objSlide.Shapes.AddOLEObject _
            Left:=200, Top:=200, Width:=500, Height:=150, _
            Filename:=olePicture.SourceDoc, link:=True

    End If

cmdMakePPTSlide_Exit:
    Set objPresentation = Nothing
    Set objSlide = Nothing
    Exit Sub

cmdMakePPTSlide_Err:
    MsgBox "Error # " & Err.Number & ": " & Err.Description
    Resume cmdMakePPTSlide_Exit
End Sub
```

The routine begins by creating an instance of PowerPoint. The instance is made visible. A presentation then is added to the PowerPoint object, and a slide is added to the presentation. The background fill of the slide is modified. The text, color, and italic properties of the title object are customized. Finally, the SourceDoc property of the `olePicture` object is used to create an automation object, which is added to the slide.

Automating Outlook from Access

Microsoft Outlook is a very powerful e-mail client. It is also an excellent tool for both task and contact management. As an application developer, I find many opportunities to automate Outlook from the Access applications that I build. For example, one of my clients sends out mass e-mail mailings to selected groups of his or her customers. I use an Access front end to manipulate customers stored in a SQL Server back end. Included in the front end is a feature that enables the users to generate an e-mail message and then enter the criteria that designates which clients receive the e-mail message. This is one of many examples of how you can integrate the rich features of Access and Outlook.

The form pictured in Figure 22.13 allows the user to select an e-mail template used for a mass mailing. The mailing is sent to all users who meet the criteria entered in a query called qryBulkMail. A more sophisticated example would allow the users to build the query on-the-fly, using a custom query-by-form. The code that allows the user to select an Outlook e-mail template appears in Listing 22.12.

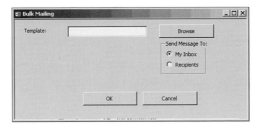

FIGURE 22.13

This form allows the user to select the e-mail template used for a mass mailing.

LISTING 22.12   Selecting the Outlook Template

```
Private Sub cmdBrowse_Click()

    'Filter the Open dialog to Outlook template files
    dlgCommon.Filter = "*.oft"

    'Display the Open dialog
    dlgCommon.ShowOpen

    'Populate txtTemplate with the selected file
    Me.txtTemplate = dlgCommon.FileName
End Sub
```

The code first sets the filter of the Common Dialog control to show only files with the .OFT extension. It then displays the Open dialog. After the user selects a file, the name and path of the file is placed in the txtTemplate text box. The code required to send the mailing is shown in Listing 22.13.

LISTING 22.13   Sending the Outlook Message to the Recipients in the qryBulkMail
ResultSet

```vba
Sub CreateMail()
    ' Customize a message for each contact and then send or save the message
    Dim intMessageCount As Integer

    'Declare and instantiate a recordset object
    Dim rst As ADODB.Recordset
    Set rst = New ADODB.Recordset

    'Open a recordset based on the result of qryBulkMail
    rst.Open "qryBulkMail", CurrentProject.Connection
    intMessageCount = 0

    Set mobjOutlook = CreateObject("Outlook.Application")

    ' Loop through the contacts in the open folder
    Do Until rst.EOF
        ' Check that the contact has an email address.
        If rst("EmailAddress") <> "" Then

            'Create a mail item based on the selected template
            Set mobjCurrentMessage =
mobjOutlook.CreateItemFromTemplate(Me.txtTemplate)

            'Add the email address as the recipient for the message
            mobjCurrentMessage.Recipients.Add rst("EmailAddress")

            ' Send the message or save it to the Inbox
            If Me.optSend = 1 Then
                mobjCurrentMessage.Save
            Else
                mobjCurrentMessage.Send
            End If
            intMessageCount = intMessageCount + 1
        End If
        rst.MoveNext
    Loop

    ' Write the number of messages created to the worksheet
    MsgBox intMessageCount & " Messages Sent"

End Sub
```

First, the code creates a recordset based on qryBulkMail. It then loops through the recordset. As it visits each row in the resultset, it creates an Outlook message based on the designated template. It adds the e-mail address of the current row as a recipient of the e-mail message. It then either saves the message as a draft, or immediately sends it to the designated recipient.

Controlling Access from Other Applications

Many times, you will want to control Access from another application. You might want to run an Access report from a Visual Basic or Excel application, for example. Just as you can tap into many of the rich features of other products (such as Excel) from within Access, you can use some of Access's features from within another program. Fortunately, it is extremely easy to control Access from within other applications.

You can find an overview of the Access object model in Access Help. Unless you are very familiar with the Access object model, you should look at this graphical representation of Access's object model before you attempt to use automation to control Access. Access launches with its Visible property set to False. You can change the Visible property of the application object to True to make Access visible.

The form shown in Figure 22.14 is a UserForm associated with an Excel spreadsheet. It is called frmReportSelect and is part of the Excel spreadsheet called RunAccessReports.xls, included on the sample code CD. The form enables you to select any Access database. It displays a list of all reports in the selected database; you can use this list to preview an Access report or print multiple Access reports.

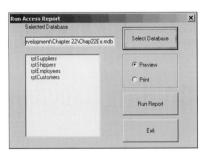

FIGURE 22.14
The UserForm that enables you to print Access reports.

Listing 22.14 shows how this UserForm form accomplishes its work.

Listing 22.14   Creating a Visual Basic Form to Print Reports

```vb
Private Sub cmdSelectDatabase_Click()
    'Set filter property of the Common Dialog control
    dlgCommon.Filter = "*.mdb"

    'Display the open common dialog
    dlgCommon.ShowOpen

    'Ensure that a file was selected
    If dlgCommon.FileName = "" Then
        MsgBox "You Must Select a File to Continue"
    Else

        'Set the text property of the text box to the
        'file selected in the Open dialog
        Me.txtSelectedDB = _
        dlgCommon.FileName

        'Call the ListReports routine
        Call ListReports
    End If
End Sub

Private Sub ListReports()
    On Error GoTo ListReports_Err
    Dim vntReport As Variant

    'If the Access object is not set, instantiate Access
    If mobjAccess Is Nothing Then
        Set mobjAccess = New Access.Application
    End If

    'Open the database selected in the text box
    mobjAccess.OpenCurrentDatabase (Me.txtSelectedDB)

    'Clear the list box
    lstReports.Clear

    'Loop through each report in the AllReports collection
    'of the selected database
    For Each vntReport In mobjAccess.CurrentProject.AllReports
        lstReports.AddItem vntReport.Name
    Next vntReport
```

LISTING 22.14   Continued

```
ListReports_Exit:
    Exit Sub

ListReports_Err:
    MsgBox "Error #" & Err.Number & _
    ": " & Err.Description
    Resume ListReports_Exit
End Sub
```

The cmdSelectDatabase_Click event routine sets the Filter property of the Common Dialog control to Access database files. The ShowOpen method of the Common Dialog control is used to display the File Open dialog to the user. The ListReports routine executes after the user selects a file from the dialog,.

The ListReports subprocedure begins by creating an instance of the Access application. It uses the OpenCurrentDatabase method of the Access object to open the Access database selected by the user in the File Open common dialog box. It then loops through the AllReports collection of the CurrentProject object that is associated with the selected database. It adds the name of each report to the list box.

The routine in Listing 22.15 prints the selected reports.

LISTING 22.15   Creating a New Instance of the Access Application Object

```
Private Sub cmdPrint_Click()
    On Error GoTo cmdPreview_Err
    Dim intCounter As Integer
    Dim intPrintOption As Integer

    'Evaluate whether Print or Preview was selected
    If optPreview.Value = True Then
        intPrintOption = acViewPreview
    ElseIf optPrint.Value = True Then
        intPrintOption = acViewNormal
    End If

    'Make Access Visible
    mobjAccess.Visible = True

    'Loop through the list box, printing the
    'selected reports
    For intCounter = 0 To _
        lstReports.ListCount - 1
```

LISTING 22.15   Continued

```
        If lstReports.Selected(intCounter) Then
            mobjAccess.DoCmd.OpenReport _
            ReportName:=Me.lstReports.List(intCounter), _
            View:=intPrintOption
        End If
    Next intCounter

cmdPreview_Exit:
    Exit Sub

cmdPreview_Err:
    MsgBox "Error #" & Err.Number & _
    ": " & Err.Description
    If Not mobjAccess Is Nothing Then
    mobjAccess.Quit
    End If
    Set mobjAccess = Nothing

    Resume cmdPreview_Exit

End Sub
```

The cmdPrint Click event routine begins by evaluating whether the print or preview option button is selected. The Access application object is made visible. The code then loops through the lstReports list box, printing or previewing each selected report. The OpenReport method is used along with the constant acViewPreview or the constant acViewNormal in order to accomplish this task.

PRACTICAL EXAMPLES

Using Automation to Extend the Functionality of the Time and Billing Application

Many potential applications of automation exist for the Time and Billing application. One of them is discussed in this section.

The form in Figure 22.15 enables users to select a table or query to send to Excel. The form is called frmSendToExcel.

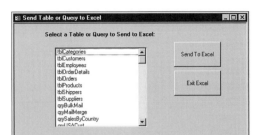

FIGURE 22.15

Exporting a table or query to send to Excel.

The Load event of the form is used to add all the table and query names to the list box. The Load event is shown in Listing 22.16. Notice that the function uses the AllTables and AllQueries collections of the current database to populate the list box, excluding all the system tables.

LISTING 22.16   Adding Table and Query Names to the List Box

```
Private Sub Form_Load()
    Dim vntObject As Variant

    'Loop through each table, adding its name
    'to the list box
    For Each vntObject In CurrentData.AllTables
        If Left(vntObject.Name, 4) <> "MSys" Then
            Me.lstTables.AddItem vntObject.Name
        End If
    Next vntObject

    'Loop through each query, adding its name to
    'the list box
    For Each vntObject In CurrentData.AllQueries
        Me.lstTables.AddItem vntObject.Name
    Next vntObject
End Sub
```

The Click event of the cmdSendToExcel command button sends the selected table or query to Excel. Listing 22.17 shows this code.

Listing 22.17   Sending a Table or Query to Excel

```
Private Sub cmdSendToExcel_Click()
    On Error GoTo cmdSendToExcel_Err
    Dim objWS As Excel.Worksheet
    Dim rstData As ADODB.Recordset
    Dim rstCount As ADODB.Recordset
    Dim fld As ADODB.Field
    Dim intColCount As Integer
    Dim intRowCount As Integer

    Set rstData = New ADODB.Recordset
    rstData.ActiveConnection = CurrentProject.Connection
    Set rstCount = New ADODB.Recordset
    rstCount.ActiveConnection = CurrentProject.Connection

    'Invoke Hourglass
    DoCmd.Hourglass True

    'Try to Create Recordset and Create Excel Object
    If CreateRecordset(rstData, rstCount, lstTables.Value) Then
        If CreateExcelObj() Then

            'Add a Workbook
            gobjExcel.Workbooks.Add

            'Create a reference to the Active Sheet
            Set objWS = gobjExcel.ActiveSheet
            intRowCount = 1
            intColCount = 1

            'Loop through the Fields collection
            'Make each field name a column heading in Excel
            For Each fld In rstData.Fields
                If fld.Type <> adLongVarBinary Then
                    objWS.Cells(1, intColCount).Value = fld.Name
                    intColCount = intColCount + 1
                End If
            Next fld

            'Send Recordset to Excel
            objWS.Range("A2").CopyFromRecordset rstData, 500
            gobjExcel.Range("A1").Select

            'Set up AutoFilter
            gobjExcel.Selection.AutoFilter
```

LISTING 22.17   Continued

```
            gobjExcel.Visible = True
        Else
            MsgBox "Excel Not Successfully Launched"
        End If
    Else
        MsgBox "Too Many Records to Send to Excel"
    End If


cmdSendToExcel_Exit:
    DoCmd.Hourglass False
    Set objWS = Nothing
    Set rstCount = Nothing
    Set rstData = Nothing
    Set fld = Nothing
    Exit Sub

cmdSendToExcel_Err:
    MsgBox "Error # " & Err.Number & ": " & Err.Description
    Resume cmdSendToExcel_Exit
End Sub
```

The routine begins by creating a recordset object using the `CreateRecordSet` function shown in Listing 22.18. It then attempts to launch Excel. If it is successful, it loops through the Fields collection of the recordset resulting from the selected table or query. It lists all the field names as column headings in Excel. Next, it uses the `CopyFromRecordset` method of the range object to copy all the field values to the rows in the Excel worksheet. Finally, it issues the `AutoFilter` method so that the user easily can manipulate the data in Excel, filtering it as necessary. (See Figure 22.16.)

CAUTION

Although extremely easy to use, the `CopyFromRecordset` method of the range object has one major limitation. If the table or query used to populate the recordset being sent to Excel contains an OLE object field, the method will fail. There are two solutions to this problem. The most simple solution is to always base the recordset sent to Excel on a query. Do not include any OLE object fields in the query. A second solution is to use a less elegant alternative to the `CopyFromRecordset` method. Simply loop through the recordset one record at a time. As each record is visited, send it to the appropriate row and column. Because the first method is not only easier to code, but is more optimized, it should be used wherever possible.

22

AUTOMATION

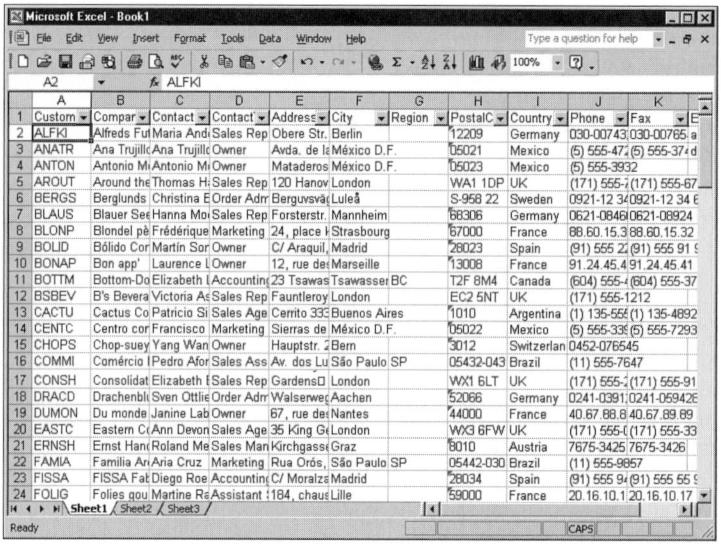

FIGURE 22.16

Using AutoFilter *to analyze data sent to Excel.*

LISTING 22.18   Checking Recordset Size

```
Function CreateRecordset(rstData As ADODB.Recordset, _
   rstCount As ADODB.Recordset, _
    strTableName As String)
    On Error GoTo CreateRecordset_Err

    'Create recordset that contains count of records in query result
    rstCount.Open "Select Count(*) As NumRecords from " & strTableName

    'If more than 500 records in query result, return false
    'Otherwise, create recordset from query
    If rstCount!NumRecords > 500 Then
        CreateRecordset = False
    Else
        rstData.Open strTableName
        CreateRecordset = True
    End If

CreateRecordset_Exit:
    'Common exit point; destroy the rstCount recordset
    Set rstCount = Nothing
    Exit Function
```

LISTING 22.18   Continued

```
CreateRecordset_Err:
    'Display error message and resume at common exit point
    MsgBox "Error # " & Err.Number & ": " & Err.Description
    Resume CreateRecordset_Exit
End Function
```

This routine, found in basUtils, ensures that the recordset is not too large to send to Excel. If the size of the recordset is acceptable, it creates the recordset and returns True.

Summary

Automation enables you to control other applications from your Access application, and it enables other programs to control your Access application. This chapter began by providing an overview of automation and why you might want to use it. It discussed creating an object variable to reference the application you are automating. After the ins and outs of the object variable were explained, you saw numerous examples of manipulating automation objects. You looked at detailed code showing automation involving Excel, Word, Outlook and PowerPoint. Finally, you learned about controlling Access from other applications.

The capability to communicate with other applications has become a prerequisite for successful software development. It is extremely important to be aware of the wealth of tools available. The capability to call on other applications' features is helping to make the world document-centric, rather than application-centric. This means that users can focus on their tasks and not on how they are accomplishing those tasks. Although automation requires significant hardware and also is rather slow, the benefits it provides often are well worth the price.

22

AUTOMATION

Exploiting the Power of the Windows API

IN THIS CHAPTER

Why This Chapter Is Important

One of the richest libraries of programming code functions is supplied by Windows itself. This function library commonly is referred to as the *Windows API* (Application Programming Interface). Fortunately, as a VBA programmer, you can tap into the Windows function library by using these built-in Windows functions in your own VBA modules.

Furthermore, you might discover other *dynamic link libraries* (DLLs) that contain functions that would be useful in your applications. These DLLs also are available to you as long as you are properly licensed to use and distribute them.

A *DLL* is a library of procedures that applications can link to and use at runtime. Functions contained in the Windows API and other DLLs can provide your applications with significant, added functionality. It is often much more efficient to use an external DLL to accomplish a task than to attempt to write a VBA function to accomplish the same task.

Declaring an External Function to the Compiler

To use a DLL function, you must do the following:

- Declare the function to the VBA compiler.
- Call the function.
- Use the return value.

The VBA language is not intrinsically aware of the functions available in external libraries. Declaring a DLL function means making the VBA compiler aware of the name of the function, the library it is located in, the parameters it expects to receive, and the values it expects to return.

If you do not properly declare the library function to the VBA compiler, you receive an error message stating `Sub or Function Not Defined`. User-defined functions and subroutines written in VBA are declared using `Sub` or `Function` keywords. These keywords define the procedures so that VBA can locate the routines when they are called. Functions in a DLL are declared in the same way. After you declare a DLL function to the compiler, Access knows where to locate it, and you can use it throughout your application.

You declare an external function to VBA using a `Declare` statement. You can place `Declare` statements in the Declarations section of a standard module, a standalone class module, or the class module behind a form or report. A `Declare` statement placed in a standard module is immediately available to your entire application. If the `Declare` statement is explicitly declared as private, it is available only to the module in which it was declared. A `Declare` statement placed in the General Declarations section of a standalone class module or the class module behind a form or report is available only after the form or report is loaded or after the class is instantiated. Furthermore, a Declare statement placed in the General Declarations section of a standalone class module or the module behind a form or report can have only private scope.

You can use a Declare statement to declare both subroutines and functions. If the procedure returns a value, you must declare it as a function. If it does not return a value, you must declare it as a subroutine.

A Declare statement looks like this:

```
Private Declare Function GetKeyboardType Lib "user32" _
    (ByVal nTypeFlag As Long) As Long
```

This statement declares a function called GetKeyboardType, which is located in the Windows 9.X or Windows NT System folder in a DLL file called user32. It receives a long integer parameter by value and returns a long integer. Notice that this function was declared as private.

> **NOTE**
>
> Remember that the function name and library name are both case-sensitive. Unless you explicitly include the path as part of the Declare statement, the default system path, the Windows folder, and the Windows System folder are all searched for in the library. Most Windows API functions are contained within the library files user32.exe, gdi32.exe, and kernel32.exe.

> **NOTE**
>
> Do not include unnecessary Declare statements in your applications. Each Declare statement consumes memory, whether or not you use the declaration. A large number of unused Declare statements can dramatically increase the amount of memory and resources required by your application.

Passing Parameters to DLL Functions

You pass parameters to a DLL function just as you pass them to a VBA routine. The only difference is that it is very important that you pass the parameters by reference or by value, as appropriate, and that you always pass the correct data type for each argument. Sending the correct data type means that, if the function expects a long integer value, you shouldn't send a double. Doing so can make your application unstable. Passing by reference versus passing by value is covered in the next section.

Passing by Reference Versus Passing by Value

When a parameter is passed by *reference*, the memory address of the argument is passed to the function. When a parameter is passed by *value*, the actual value of the argument is passed to the function. Unless explicitly told otherwise, VBA passes all parameters by reference. Many library functions expect to receive parameters by value. If such a function is passed a reference to a memory location, it cannot function properly. If you want to pass an argument by value, the ByVal keyword must be placed in front of the argument in the Declare statement. When calling library functions, you must know the types of arguments a function expects to receive and whether the function expects to receive the parameters by reference or by value. Passing an argument by reference rather than by value, or passing the incorrect data type for an argument, can cause your system to become unstable and even can result in a General Protection Fault (GPF) or illegal operation.

Passing String Parameters

String parameters require special handling when being passed to DLL functions. Windows has two ways of storing strings: the BSTR and LPSTR formats. Unless you are dealing with an API call specifically involving object linking and embedding (OLE), the string you are passing to the function is stored in the LPSTR format. DLL functions that receive strings in the LPSTR format cannot change the size of the string they are passed. This means that, if a DLL function is passed a small string that it must fill in with a large value, the function simply overwrites another area of memory with the extra characters. This usually results in a GPF or illegal operation. The following code demonstrates this point and handles the error that is generated:

```
Sub WinSysDir()
    Dim strBuffer As String
    Dim intLength As Integer
    Dim strDirectory As String

    strBuffer = Space$(160)

    intLength = abGetSystemDirectory(strBuffer, Len(strBuffer))
    strDirectory = Left(strBuffer, intLength)
    MsgBox strDirectory
End Sub
```

> **NOTE**
>
> The code here and most of the code in this chapter is located in CHAP23EX.MDB on your sample code CD-ROM.

Notice that the Space$ function is used to store 160 spaces in the string variable strBuffer. Actually, the Space$ function stores 160 spaces, followed by a Null character in the strBuffer variable.

The abGetSystemDirectory Windows API function receives two parameters:

- The buffer that it will fill with the name of the Windows System folder—in this case, strBuffer.

- The length of the buffer that will be filled—in this case, Len(strBuffer). The key here is that the length of the buffer that is passed to the GetSystemDirectory function is more than sufficient to hold the name of the Windows System folder.

The GetSystemDirectory function fills the buffer and returns the length of the string that it actually found. By looking at the left intLength number of characters in the strBuffer variable, you can determine the actual location of the Windows System folder.

The Declare statement for the GetSystemDirectory function looks like this:

```
Declare Function abGetSystemDirectory _
    Lib "kernel32" _
    (ByVal lpBuffer As String, ByVal nSize As Long) _
    As Long
```

Notice the ByVal keyword that precedes the lpBuffer parameter. Because the ByVal keyword is used, Visual Basic converts the string from BSTR to LPSTR format by adding a Null terminator to the end of the string before passing it to the DLL function. If the ByVal keyword is omitted, Visual Basic passes a pointer to the function where the string is located in memory. This can cause serious problems.

23

EXPLOITING THE POWER OF THE WINDOWS API

CAUTION

Windows API calls are fraught with potential danger. To reduce the chances of data loss or database corruption, always save your work before testing a procedure containing an external function call. If the Access application terminates, at least you won't lose your work. In addition, always make sure that your database is backed up. If the Access application terminates and your database is not closed properly, you risk the chance of damage to the database. Regularly backing up ensures that if the database becomes corrupted during testing, you can retrieve the last good version from a backup.

Aliasing a Function

When you declare a function to VBA, you are given the option to alias it, as in the preceding function. To *alias* means to refer to a function by a substitute name. You might want to alias a Windows API function for several reasons:

- A DLL procedure has a name that includes an invalid character.
- A DLL procedure name is the same as a VBA keyword.
- You want to omit the A required by ANSI versions of the API call.
- You want to ensure that you have a unique procedure name in an Access library or application.
- You want to call a DLL procedure referenced by an ordinal number.
- You want to give your API functions a distinctive prefix to prevent conflicts with API declarations in other modules or add-ins.

Reasons for aliasing an API function are discussed in more detail in the following sections.

Function Calls and Invalid Characters

It is not uncommon for a DLL procedure name to contain a character that is not allowed in VBA code, for example, a DLL procedure that begins with an underscore (_). VBA does not allow a procedure name to begin with an underscore. To use the DLL function, you must alias it, as this example shows:

```
Declare Function LOpen _
    Lib "kernel32" _
    Alias "_lopen" _
    (ByVal lpPathName As String, ByVal ReadWrite As Long) _
    As Long
```

Notice that the Windows API function _lopen begins with an underscore. The function is aliased as LOpen for use in the Access application.

DLL Functions with Duplicate Names

The DLL procedure name you want to use might share the same name as a VBA function. You can resolve this conflict only by aliasing the DLL function. The following code aliases a DLL function:

```
Declare Function GetObjectAPI _
    Lib "gdi32" _
    Alias "GetObject" _
    (ByVal hObject As Long, _
    ByVal nCount As Long, _
    lpObject As Any) As Long
```

The `GetObject` function is part of the Windows API and is a VBA function. When you alias the function, there is no confusion as to whether the API or the VBA `GetObject` function is being called.

Eliminating the "A" Suffix Required by ANSI

Many API function calls have both ANSI and Unicode versions. The ANSI versions of the functions end with an "A". You might want to call the ANSI version of a function but prefer to use the name of the function without the "A." You can accomplish this by using an alias, as this code shows:

```
Declare Function FindWindow _
    Lib "user32" Alias "FindWindowA" _
    (ByVal lpClassName As Any, ByVal lpWindowName As String) As Long
```

This `Declare` statement creates an alias of `FindWindow` for the ANSI function `FindWindowA`.

> **NOTE**
>
> *Unicode* is a standard developed by the *International Standards Organization* (ISO). It was developed to overcome the 256-character limit imposed by the ANSI character standard. The ANSI standard uses only 1 byte to represent a character, limiting the number of characters to 256. This standard uses 2 bytes to represent a character, allowing up to 65,536 characters to be represented. Access uses Unicode for string manipulation, which can lead to problems with DLL calls. To overcome this problem, you always should call the ANSI version of the API function (the version of the function that ends with an "A").

23

EXPLOITING THE
POWER OF THE
WINDOWS API

Unique Procedure Names in an Access Library or Module

Sometimes you simply want to ensure that a procedure name in a library you are creating is unique, or you might want to ensure that the code you are writing will not conflict with any libraries you are using. Unless you use the `Private` keyword to declare each procedure, external function declarations are global throughout Access's memory space. This can lead to potential conflicts because Access does not allow multiple declarations of the same external routine. For this reason, you might want to place a unique identifier, such as your initials, at the beginning or end of the function declaration, as in this example:

```
Declare Function ABGetWindowsDirectory Lib "kernel32" _
Alias "GetWindowsDirectoryA" _
(ByVal lpBuffer As String, ByVal nSize As Long) As Long
```

This statement declares the Windows API function GetWindowsDirectoryA in the library kernel32. The function is aliased as ABGetWindowsDirectory. This function was aliased in order to differentiate it from other calls to the GetWindowsDirectoryA function that might share this procedure's scope.

Calling Functions Referenced with Ordinal Numbers

Every DLL procedure can be referenced by an ordinal number in addition to its name. In fact, some DLLs use only ordinal numbers and do not use procedure names at all, requiring you to use ordinal numbers when declaring the procedures. When you declare a function referenced by an ordinal number, you should declare the function with the Alias keyword, as in this example:

```
Declare Function GetAppSettings _
    Lib "Utilities" _
    Alias "#47" () As Long
```

This code declares a function with an ordinal number 47 in the library called Utilities. It now can be referred to as GetAppSettings whenever it is called in VBA code.

Working with Constants and Types

Some DLLs require the use of constants or user-defined types, otherwise known as *structures* or *parameters*. You must place these in the General Declarations section of your module, along with the Declare statements you have defined.

Working with Constants

Constants are used by many of the API functions. They provide you with an English-like way of sending required values to an API function. The constant is used as an alias for a specific value. Here's an example:

```
Global Const SM_CXSCREEN = 0
Global Const SM_CYSCREEN = 1
```

The constant declarations and function declarations are placed in the General Declarations section of a module. When the GetSystemMetrics function is called, the SM_CXSCREEN and SM_CYSCREEN constants are passed as arguments to the function:

```
Sub GetScreenInfo()
   MsgBox "Screen Resolution is : " & _
      GetSystemMetrics(SM_CXSCREEN) & _
      " By " & _
      GetSystemMetrics(SM_CYSCREEN)

End Sub
```

When the `SM_CXSCREEN` constant is passed to the `GetSystemMetrics` function, the horizontal screen resolution is returned; when the `SM_CYSCREEN` constant is passed to the function, the vertical screen resolution is returned.

Working with Types

When working with types, you first must declare the type in the General Declarations section of a module. You then can pass elements of a user-defined type, or you can pass the entire type as a single argument to the API function. The following code shows an example of a `Type` declaration:

```
Type OSVERSIONINFO
    dwOSVersionInfoSize As Long
    dwMajorVersion As Long
    dwMinorVersion As Long
    dwBuildNumber As Long
    dwPlatformId As Long
    strReserved As String * 128
End Type
```

The `Type` structure `OSVERSIONINFO` is declared in the General Declarations section of the module, as shown in Listing 23.1.

LISTING 23.1 Declaring the `Type` Structure `OSVERSIONINFO` in the General Declarations Section of the Module

```
Function GetOSInfo()

    Dim OSInfo As OSVERSIONINFO
    Dim strMajorVersion As String
    Dim strMinorVersion As String
    Dim strBuildNumber As String
    Dim strPlatformId As String

    ' Set the length member before you call GetVersionEx
    OSInfo.dwOSVersionInfoSize = Len(OSInfo)
    If GetVersionEx(OSInfo) Then
        strMajorVersion = OSInfo.dwMajorVersion
        strMinorVersion = OSInfo.dwMinorVersion
        strBuildNumber = OSInfo.dwBuildNumber And &HFFFF&
        strPlatformId = OSInfo.dwPlatformId
        MsgBox "The Major Version Is:  " & _
            strMajorVersion & vbCrLf & _
```

23

EXPLOITING THE
POWER OF THE
WINDOWS API

LISTING 23.1 Continued

```
            "The Minor Version Is:  " & strMinorVersion & vbCrLf & _

            "The Build Number Is:  " & strBuildNumber & vbCrLf & _
            "The Platform ID Is:   " & _
            IIf(strPlatformId = 1, "Win 95 or Win 98", _
            "Win NT") & vbCrLf
    End If
End Function
```

In this listing, the statement `Dim OSInfo As OSVERSIONIFO` creates a `Type` variable. The entire structure is passed to the `GetVersionEx` function (declared in basAPICalls), which fills in the elements of the structure with information about the operating system. This information then is retrieved and stored into variables that are displayed in a message box.

Using the Windows API Text Viewer

As you might imagine, `Declare` statements, constant declarations, and type structures can be time-consuming and difficult to add to your code modules. Fortunately, the Windows API Text Viewer, a tool that ships with Microsoft Office Developer, helps you complete these tasks. It makes it easy for you to add `Declare` statements, types, and constants required by the Windows API function calls to your code. You can launch the Window API Text Viewer as an add-in to the Access 2002 VBE. To do this, follow these steps:

1. Activate the VBE.
2. Select Add-ins|Add-In Manager. The Add-In Manager appears.
3. Select VBA WinAPI Viewer.
4. Click Loaded/Unloaded.
5. Click Load on Startup if you want the API Viewer to be available each time you launch Access.
6. Click OK.
7. Open the Add-Ins menu. WinAPI Viewer should appear.
8. Select WinAPI Viewer from the Add-Ins menu.

When you first launch the Windows API Text Viewer, it appears as shown in Figure 23.1. You can load a text file or a database file containing declares, types, and constants.

FIGURE 23.1

The Windows API Text Viewer.

Loading a Text File

Microsoft Office Developer Edition ships with a file called WIN32API.TXT. You can load and browse this file so that you can obtain `Declare` statements, type structures, and constants easily. To load the WIN32API.TXT file into the Windows API Text Viewer, follow these steps:

1. Choose File|Load Text File. The Select a Text API File dialog box appears, as shown in Figure 23.2.

2. Select a text file to load into the viewer and click Open. The WIN API Text Viewer appears, as in Figure 23.3.

FIGURE 23.2

The Select a Text API File dialog box.

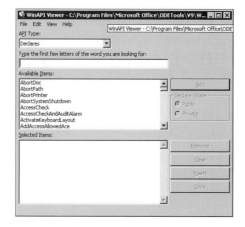

FIGURE 23.3

The WinAPI Viewer after loading a text file.

Loading a Database File

After a text file is converted to a database, you should load the database each time you use the Windows API Text Viewer. To load the database file, follow these steps:

1. Choose File|Load Database File. The Select a Jet Database dialog box appears, as shown in Figure 23.4.

2. Select the database you want to load and click Open.

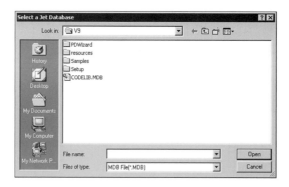

FIGURE 23.4

Use the Select a Jet Database dialog box to specify the database to load into the Text Viewer.

Pasting API Declares, Types, and Constants

Regardless of whether you have loaded a text or a database file, the Windows API Text Viewer appears as shown in Figure 23.5. All the Declare statements for the 32-bit API appear in the

Available Items list box. Select each Declare statement you want to add to your module and click Add. You can use the API Type drop-down list to view and select types or constants. In Figure 23.6, the GetVersionEx and GetWindow Declare statements have been added to the Selected Items list. The SM_CXSCREEN and SM_CYSCREEN constants, as well as the OSVERSIONINFO type, also have been added.

FIGURE 23.5

The Windows API Text Viewer after a file has been loaded.

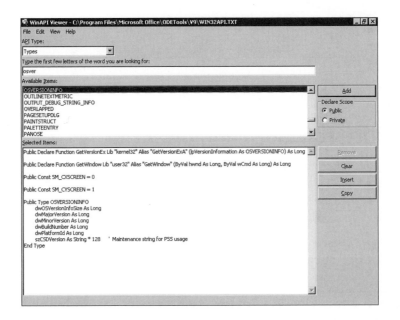

FIGURE 23.6

The Windows API Text Viewer with several items in the Selected Items list.

Follow these steps to add the selected items to a module:

1. In the API Text Viewer, click Copy. The selected declares, constants, and types are placed on the Windows Clipboard.

2. Place your cursor in the module where you want the selected declares, constants, and types to be placed.

3. Click Paste. The selected items are pasted into the module, as shown in Figure 23.7.

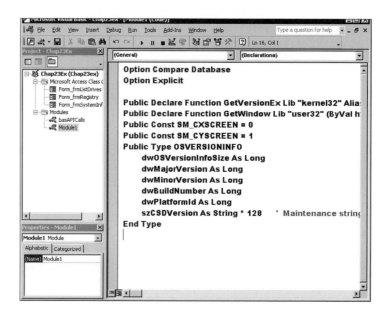

FIGURE 23.7

A module after selected items are pasted into it.

Calling DLL Functions: Important Issues

After a procedure is declared, you can call it just like any VBA function. The main issue is that you must ensure that you are passing correct values to the DLL. Otherwise, the bad call can cause your application to shut down without warning. In fact, external library calls are very tricky. You therefore should always save your work before you test the calls.

Most DLLs expect to receive standard C strings. These strings are terminated with a Null character. If a DLL expects a Null-terminated string, you must pass the string by value. The `ByVal` keyword tells VBA to pass the string as Null-terminated.

Although you must pass strings by value, they actually are received by reference. The `ByVal` keyword simply means that the string is Null-terminated. The DLL procedure actually can modify the value of the string, which can mean problems. As discussed in the "Passing String Parameters" section earlier in this chapter, if you do not preallocate space for the procedure to use, it overwrites any memory it can find, including memory currently being used by your application, another application, or even the operating system. You can avoid this problem by making the string argument long enough to accept the longest entry that you think will be placed into the parameter.

Examining the Differences Between 16-Bit and 32-Bit APIs

You might be familiar with the 16-bit API from earlier versions of Windows, but you must be aware of some issues when working with the 32-bit API. These issues can cause you significant grief:

- Window handles (hWnd properties) are *long integers* in the 32-bit API. They were *integers* in the 16-bit API.

- Function names are *not* case-sensitive in the 16-bit API. They *are* case-sensitive in the 32-bit API.

- When working with the 16-bit API, you should reboot whenever you get a GPF because it is likely that the memory of your computer is corrupted. With the 32-bit API, each program runs in its own virtual machine. Therefore, it often is unnecessary to reboot simply because a GPF occurs.

Using API Functions

The potential uses for API calls are endless. You can use API calls to modify the System menu, obtain system information, or even switch between running applications. In fact, you can accomplish so many things using API calls that entire books are devoted to the topic. The remainder of this chapter covers several of the common uses of API calls.

Manipulating the Windows Registry

Four built-in VBA functions help you manipulate the Windows registry. They include `GetAllSettings`, `GetSetting`, `SaveSetting`, and `DeleteSetting`. These four functions only allow you to manipulate and work with a specific branch of the registry, HKEY_CUR-RENT_USER\Software\VB, and VBA program Settings. There are times when it is necessary to read from or write to other parts of the registry. This is one situation in which the Windows API can really help you out. Using the Windows `RegQueryValueEx` function, you can extract information from registry keys. Using the `RegSetValueEx` function, you can write information to the registry. The declarations for these two functions (found in the basAPICalls module) look like this:

```
'The RegQueryValueExA function is used to
'read information from the Windows registry

Declare Function RegQueryValueEx _
 Lib "advapi32.dll" Alias "RegQueryValueExA" _
 (ByVal hKey As Long, ByVal lpValueName As String, _
 ByVal lpReserved As Long, lpType As Long, _
 lpData As Any, lpcbData As Long) As Long

'The RegSetValueExA function is used to
'write information to the Windows registry

 Declare Function RegSetValueEx _
 Lib "advapi32.dll" Alias "RegSetValueExA" _
 (ByVal hKey As Long, _
 ByVal lpValueName As String, _
 ByVal Reserved As Long, _
 ByVal dwType As Long, _
 lpData As Any, _
 ByVal cbData As Long) As Long
```

Before you use either function, you must first obtain a handle to the registry key you wish to affect. This requires the RegOpenKeyEx function:

```
'The RegOpenKeyExA function is used to
'Return a numeric value that references
'a specific registry key

Declare Function RegOpenKeyEx _
 Lib "advapi32.dll" Alias "RegOpenKeyExA" _
 (ByVal hKey As Long, ByVal lpSubKey As String, _
 ByVal ulOptions As Long, ByVal samDesired As Long, _
 phkResult As Long) As Long
```

Finally, when you are done reading from or saving to the registry, you must use the RegCloseKey function to close the registry key. The declaration for the RegCloseKey function looks like this:

```
'The RegCloseKey fucntion closes the designated
'registry key

Public Declare Function RegCloseKey _
     Lib "advapi32.dll" (ByVal hKey As Long) As Long
```

Listing 23.2 shows how you can use the RegQueryValueEx function to read from the registry.

LISTING 23.2   Using `RegQueryValueEx` to Read Registry Information

```
Private Sub cmdRead_Click()
    Dim strValue As String * 256
    Dim lngRetval As Long
    Dim lngLength As Long
    Dim lngKey As Long

    'Retrieve handle of the registry key
    If RegOpenKeyEx(HKEY_CURRENT_USER, _
        Me.txtKeyName.Value, _
        0, KEY_QUERY_VALUE, lngKey) Then
    End If

    lngLength = 256

    'Retrieve the value of the key
    lngRetval = RegQueryValueEx( _
        lngKey, Me.txtValueName, 0, 0, ByVal strValue, lngLength)
    Me.txtValue = Left(strValue, lngLength)

    'Close the key
    RegCloseKey (lngKey)
End Sub
```

This code is found in frmRegistry in the sample database. Notice that the code first retrieves a handle to the requested registry key. It then uses the `RegQueryValueEx` function to retrieve the designated value from the registry. After the code is complete, it closes the registry key. For example, you could request the value `Last User` from the Software\Microsoft\Office\10.0\Access\Settings registry key. The value stored for the `Last User` setting displays in the txtValue text box.

Listing 23.3 shows how you can use the `RegSetValueEx` function to write to the registry.

LISTING 23.3   Using `RegSetValueEx` to Write Information to the Registry

```
Private Sub cmdWrite_Click()
    Dim strValue As String
    Dim strKeyName As String
    Dim lngRetval As Long
    Dim lngLength As Long
    Dim lngKey As Long

    'Create string with Key name
    strKeyName = Me.txtKeyName.Value & vbNullString
```

LISTING 23.3   Continued

```
'Retrieve handle of the registry key
If RegOpenKeyEx(HKEY_CURRENT_USER, _
    strKeyName, _
    0, KEY_WRITE, lngKey) Then
End If

'Create string with string to store
strValue = Me.txtValue.Value & vbNullString

'Create variable with length of string to store
lngLength = Len(Me.txtValue) + 1

'Save the value to the key
lngRetval = RegSetValueEx( _
    lngKey, Me.txtValueName, 0, REG_SZ, _
    ByVal strValue, lngLength)

'Close the key
RegCloseKey (lngKey)

End Sub
```

The routine first opens a handle to the designated registry key. It then calls the `RegSetValueEx` function, passing the handle, the value you wish to modify, the type of data the key contains, and the new value. Finally, it closes the registry key.

CAUTION

I generally do not make a practice of writing information to the Windows registry. If you write to an important registry key, and make a mistake, you can render the Windows operating environment unusable.

NOTE

Listing 23.3 shows you how to write to a registry key that contains a string. To write to a registry that expects a DWORD value, you must use the `REG_DWORD` constant rather than the `REG_SZ` constant.

Getting Information About the Operating Environment

By using Windows API calls, you can get volumes of information about the system environment, including the type of hardware on which the application is running, the amount of memory that exists or is available, and the operating system version under which the application is running. It is handy and professional to include system information in your application's Help About box. It also is important to include this system information in your error handling and logging because such information can help you diagnose the problem. This is discussed in Chapter 16, "Error Handling: Preparing for the Inevitable."

Figure 23.8 shows a custom About dialog box that includes system environment information. This form uses several Windows API calls to get the system information displayed on the form.

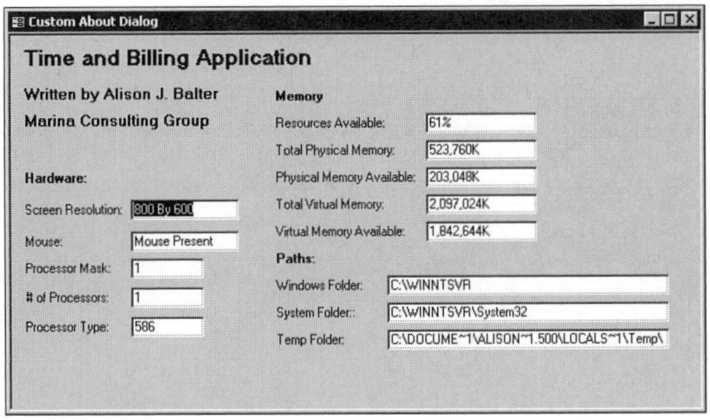

FIGURE 23.8

A custom About dialog box illustrating the capability to obtain system information from the Windows API.

Before any of the DLL functions required to obtain this information can be called, all the functions need to be declared to the compiler. This is done in the General Declarations section of the module basUtils. Any constants and type structures used by the DLL calls also must be included in the General Declarations section. Listing 23.4 shows what the General Declarations section of basAPICalls looks like.

LISTING 23.4   The General Declarations Section of basAPICalls

```
Option Compare Database
Option Explicit

Public Const MAX_PATH = 160
```

LISTING 23.4   Continued

```
'The function GetVersionEx gets information about '
'the version of operating system that is currently '
'running.  The information is filled into the type
'structure OSVERSIONINFO.

Declare Function abGetVersionEx _
   Lib "kernel32" _
   Alias "GetVersionExA" _
   (lpOSInfo As OSVERSIONINFO) As Boolean

Type OSVERSIONINFO
   dwOSVersionInfoSize As Long
   dwMajorVersion As Long
   dwMinorVersion As Long
   dwBuildNumber As Long
   dwPlatformId As Long
   strReserved As String * 128
End Type

'The GetSystemMetrics function utilizes three constants to
'determine whether a mouse is present, and to determine
'the width and height of the screen.

Const SM_CXSCREEN = 0
Const SM_CYSCREEN = 1
Const SM_MOUSEPRESENT = 19

Declare Function abGetSystemMetrics _
   Lib "user32" _
   Alias "GetSystemMetrics" _
   (ByVal nIndex As Long) As Long

'The GlobalMemoryStatus function retrieves information
'about current available memory.  It points to a type
'structure called SYSTEM_INFO, filling in its elements
'with relevant memory information.

Type MEMORYSTATUS
   dwLength As Long
   dwMemoryLoad As Long
   dwTotalPhys As Long
   dwAvailPhys As Long
   dwTotalPageFile As Long
   dwAvailPageFile As Long
```

LISTING 23.4   Continued

```
   dwTotalVirtual As Long
   dwAvailVirtual As Long
End Type

Declare Sub abGlobalMemoryStatus _
   Lib "kernel32" _
   Alias "GlobalMemoryStatus" _
   (lpBuffer As MEMORYSTATUS)

'The GetSystemInfo function returns information about
'the system.  It fills in the type structue SYSTEM_INFO
'with relevant information about the system.

Type SYSTEM_INFO
   dwOemID As Long
   dwPageSize As Long
   lpMinimumApplicationAddress As Long
   lpMaximumApplicationAddress As Long
   dwActiveProcessorMask As Long
   dwNumberOrfProcessors As Long
   dwProcessorType As Long
   dwAllocationGranularity As Long
   dwReserved As Long
End Type

Declare Sub abGetSystemInfo Lib "kernel32" _
   Alias "GetSystemInfo" _
   (lpSystemInfo As SYSTEM_INFO)

'The function GetWindowsDirectory retrieves the name of the
'directory within which windows is running

Declare Function abGetWindowsDirectory _
   Lib "kernel32" _
   Alias "GetWindowsDirectoryA" _
   (ByVal lpBuffer As String, _
   ByVal nSize As Long) As Long

'The GetSystemDirectory function retrieves the name of the
'directory in which the Windows system files reside.

Declare Function abGetSystemDirectory _
   Lib "kernel32" _
   Alias "GetSystemDirectoryA" _
```

LISTING 23.4   Continued

```
    (ByVal lpBuffer As String, _
    ByVal nSize As Long) As Long

'The GetTempPath function retrieves the name of the
'directory where temporary files are stored

Declare Function abGetTempPath _
    Lib "kernel32" _
    Alias "GetTempPathA" _
    (ByVal nBufferLength As Long, _
    ByVal lpBuffer As String) As Long

'The GetCommandLine Function retrieves the command
'line for the current process

Declare Function abGetCommandLine _
    Lib "kernel32" _
    Alias "GetCommandLineA" () _
    As String
```

As you can see, several type structures, constants, and Declare statements are required to obtain all the information that appears on the form. When the form (frmSystemInformation) is opened, all the Windows API functions are called, and the text boxes on the form are filled with the system information. The Open event of the form frmSystemInformation calls a subroutine called GetSysInfo, which is shown in Listing 23.5.

LISTING 23.5   The GetSysInfo Subroutine

```
Sub GetSysInfo(frmAny As Form)
    Dim intMousePresent As Integer
    Dim strBuffer As String
    Dim intLen As Integer
    Dim MS As MEMORYSTATUS
    Dim SI As SYSTEM_INFO
    Dim strCommandLine As String

    frmAny.txtScreenResolution = abGetSystemMetrics(SM_CXSCREEN) & _
    " By " & abGetSystemMetrics(SM_CYSCREEN)
    intMousePresent = CBool(abGetSystemMetrics(SM_MOUSEPRESENT))
    frmAny.txtMousePresent = IIf(intMousePresent, "Mouse Present", _
    "No Mouse Present")

    'Set the length member before you call GlobalMemoryStatus
    MS.dwLength = Len(MS)
```

LISTING 23.5   Continued

```
abGlobalMemoryStatus MS
frmAny.txtMemoryLoad = MS.dwMemoryLoad & "%"
frmAny.txtTotalPhysical = Format(Fix(MS.dwTotalPhys / 1024), _
"###,###") & "K"
frmAny.txtAvailablePhysical = Format(Fix(MS.dwAvailPhys / 1024), _
"###,###") & "K"
frmAny.txtTotalVirtual = Format(Fix(MS.dwTotalVirtual / 1024), _
"###,###") & "K"
frmAny.txtAvailableVirtual = Format(Fix(MS.dwAvailVirtual / 1024), _
"###,###") & "K"

abGetSystemInfo SI
frmAny.txtProcessorMask = SI.dwActiveProcessorMask
frmAny.txtNumberOfProcessors = SI.dwNumberOrfProcessors
frmAny.txtProcessorType = SI.dwProcessorType


strBuffer = Space(MAX_PATH)
intLen = abGetWindowsDirectory(strBuffer, MAX_PATH)
frmAny.txtWindowsDir = Left(strBuffer, intLen)

strBuffer = Space(MAX_PATH)
intLen = abGetSystemDirectory(strBuffer, MAX_PATH)
frmAny.txtSystemDir = Left(strBuffer, intLen)

strBuffer = Space(MAX_PATH)
intLen = abGetTempPath(MAX_PATH, strBuffer)
frmAny.txtTempDir = Left(strBuffer, intLen)
```

```
End Sub
```

23

EXPLOITING THE
POWER OF THE
WINDOWS API

Now take a look at this subroutine in detail. The subroutine calls the function GetSystemMetrics (aliased as abGetSystemMetrics) three times. The first time, it is sent the constant SM_CXSCREEN, and the second time, it is sent the constant SM_CYSCREEN. These calls return the horizontal and vertical screen resolutions. When passed the constant SM_MOUSEPRE-SENT, the GetSystemMetrics function returns a logical True or False indicating whether a mouse is present.

The GlobalMemoryStatus API call fills in a structure with several pieces of information regarding memory. The elements of the structure are filled with the memory load, total and available physical memory, and total and available virtual memory.

The GetSystemInfo API call also provides you with valuable system information. It fills in a structure with several technical tidbits, including the active processor mask, the number of processors, and the processor type.

Finally, the function calls GetWindowsDirectory, GetSystemDirectory, and GetTempPath. These three functions return the Windows folder, System folder, and temp file path, respectively. Notice that buffer space is preallocated before each call. Because each call returns the length of the folder name retrieved, you then take the characters on the left side of the buffer for the number of characters specified in the return value.

Determining Drive Types and Available Drive Space

Often, it is necessary to determine the types of drives available and the amount of space free on each drive. Fortunately, Windows API functions are available to help you to accomplish these tasks. The frmListDrives form lists the type of each drive installed on the system and the amount of free space on each drive, as shown in Figure 23.9. The declarations that are required for the APIs are shown in Listing 23.6.

FIGURE 23.9

The frmListDrives form, showing the type of each drive installed on the system and the amount of free space on each drive.

LISTING 23.6   API Declarations

```
'The GetDriveType Function returns an integer
'indicating the drive type

Public Const DRIVE_UNKNOWN = 0
Public Const DRIVE_UNAVAILABLE = 1
Public Const DRIVE_REMOVABLE = 2
Public Const DRIVE_FIXED = 3
Public Const DRIVE_REMOTE = 4
```

LISTING 23.6   Continued

```
Public Const DRIVE_CDROM = 5
Public Const DRIVE_RAMDISK = 6

Declare Function abGetDriveType _
    Lib "kernel32" _
    Alias "GetDriveTypeA" _
    (ByVal nDrive As String) _
    As Long

'The GetDiskFreeSpace Function determines the amount of
'free space on the active drive

Declare Function abGetDiskFreeSpace _
    Lib "kernel32" _
    Alias "GetDiskFreeSpaceA" _
    (ByVal lpRootPathName As String, _
    lpSectorsPerCluster As Long, _
    lpBytesPerSector As Long, _
    lpNumberOfFreeClusters As Long, _
    lpTotalNumberOfClusters As Long) _
    As Long
```

The Click event of the cmdListDrives command button located on frmListDrives calls a subroutine called GetDriveInfo, sending it the txtDrives text box. Listing 23.7 shows the GetDriveInfo procedure.

LISTING 23.7   The GetDriveInfo Procedure

```
Sub GetDriveInfo(ctlAny As Control)
    Dim intDrive As Integer
    Dim strDriveLetter As String
    Dim strDriveType As String
    Dim strSpaceFree As String

    'Loop through all drives
    For intDrive = 65 To 90 'A through Z
        strDriveLetter = (Chr(intDrive) & ":\")
        'Get Drive Type
        strDriveType = TypeOfDrive(strDriveLetter)
        'Get Space Free
        strSpaceFree = NumberOfBytesFree(strDriveLetter)
        ctlAny.Value = _
            ctlAny.Value & _
            Left(strDriveLetter, 2) & _
```

LISTING 23.7   Continued

```
         " - " & strDriveType & _
         IIf(strDriveType <> "Drive Doesn't Exist", _
            strSpaceFree, "") & _
         vbCrLf
   Next intDrive

End Sub
```

The routine loops through all available drive letters. For each drive letter, two user-defined functions are called: TypeOfDrive and NumberOfBytesFree. Listing 23.8 shows the TypeOfDrive function.

LISTING 23.8   The TypeOfDrive Function

```
Function TypeOfDrive(ByVal strDrive As String) As String
   Dim intDriveType As Integer
   Dim strDriveType As String

     intDriveType = abGetDriveType(strDrive)
     Select Case intDriveType
       Case DRIVE_UNKNOWN
          strDriveType = "Type Unknown"
       Case DRIVE_UNAVAILABLE
          strDriveType = "Drive Doesn't Exist"
       Case DRIVE_REMOVABLE
          strDriveType = "Removable Drive"
       Case DRIVE_FIXED
          strDriveType = "Fixed Drive"
       Case DRIVE_REMOTE
          strDriveType = "Network Drive"
       Case DRIVE_CDROM
          strDriveType = "CD-ROM"
       Case DRIVE_RAMDISK
          strDriveType = "RAM Disk"
     End Select
     TypeOfDrive = strDriveType
End Function
```

The TypeOfDrive function receives a drive letter as a parameter. It calls the Windows API function GetDriveType to determine the type of drive whose drive letter was passed to the function. The GetDriveType function returns a numeric value that indicates the type of the specified drive. The returned value is evaluated with a case statement, and text representing the drive type is returned from the function.

The `NumberOfBytesFree` function determines how many bytes are free on a particular drive, as shown in Listing 23.9.

LISTING 23.9   The `NumberOfBytesFree` Function

```
Function NumberOfBytesFree(ByVal strDrive As String) As String
    Dim lngSectors As Long
    Dim lngBytes As Long
    Dim lngFreeClusters As Long
    Dim lngTotalClusters As Long
    Dim intErrNum As Integer

    intErrNum = abGetDiskFreeSpace(strDrive, lngSectors, _
    lngBytes, lngFreeClusters, lngTotalClusters)
    NumberOfBytesFree = " with " & _
        Format((CDbl(lngBytes) * CDbl(lngSectors)) * _
        CDbl(lngFreeClusters), "#,##0") & _
        " Bytes Free"
End Function
```

This function receives a drive letter as a parameter. It then calls the `GetDiskFreeSpace` Windows API function, sending it the drive letter and several long integers. These long integers are filled in with the information required to determine the number of bytes free on the specified drive.

After the type of drive and number of bytes free are determined, the `GetDriveInfo` procedure concatenates the information with the text contained in a text box on the frmListDrives form. If the drive specified is unavailable, the amount of available disk space is not printed.

Summary

External libraries, referred to as *dynamic link libraries* (DLL), open up the entire Windows API as well as other function libraries to your custom applications. Using external libraries, your applications can harness the power of functions written in other languages, such as C, Delphi, or Visual Basic. In this chapter, you learned how to declare API functions, type structures, and constants, and how to call Windows API functions. Using the techniques that you learned, you can easily extend beyond the power of Access, harnessing the power of the operating system environment.

23

EXPLOITING THE
POWER OF THE
WINDOWS API

Creating Your Own Libraries

IN THIS CHAPTER

Why This Chapter Is Important

As your knowledge of the VBA language expands and you become more proficient as a VBA programmer, you probably will develop functions and subroutines that you would like all your databases to share. Without the use of library databases, the code in each of your databases is an island unto itself. Although the functions and subroutines within your code modules can be called from anywhere in the same database, these procedures cannot be called from a different database.

Without a shared library of code and other standard objects, you will find yourself copying routines and other database objects from one database to the next. The library database can be used by all your applications and distributed to all your users. A library database is just like any other database; it is simply a collection of procedures and objects that you want to share among numerous databases. The only difference between the library database and other databases is in the way the database is referenced. Instead of opening a library database to use it, you reference it from another database.

Access is highly dependent on library databases. The Table Wizard, Form Wizard, Report Wizard, Database Wizard, Database Splitter, Database Analyzer, and Database Documenter are all examples of tools that reside in library databases. In fact, all the wizards, builders, and menu add-ins you are accustomed to using while developing your applications are all contained within library databases. These tools are covered in Chapter 25, "Using Builders, Wizards, and Menu Add-Ins." This chapter focuses on creating library databases and placing generic functions in a library database to make them available to all your application databases.

Preparing a Database to Be a Library

Creating a library database involves two steps:

1. Writing the functions and creating the objects to be included in the library
2. Loading the database as a library

You begin by creating the generic objects you want to share among your applications. To load the database as a library, you must reference it from another database. This process is covered in the next section.

Before you can reference a database as a library, you need to think about how to construct the database so that it best serves you as a library. Although a library database is just a normal database, planning the design of the library is integral to its success and usefulness. Improper planning can cause anything from extra memory being required to the database malfunctioning.

Structuring Code Modules for Optimal Performance

Library databases contain the general functions that you use in most of your applications. Because of the way Access loads code modules, you must structure your library databases effectively in order to achieve optimal performance.

Access 2.0 loaded all code modules the moment the application was loaded. This meant that, when developing an Access 2.0 application, it was not particularly important how you structured your subroutines and functions within the various modules of the database. This situation changed dramatically with Access 95 and all versions that followed it, all of which load code modules only if they are needed. In Access 95 and later, if no procedures within a particular module are called, the module is never loaded into memory. On the other hand, if a single subroutine or function is called or if a public variable is referenced, the entire module is loaded. Therefore, it is crucial that you structure your modules to minimize what is loaded into memory, using these techniques:

- Separate frequently used procedures from those that are called infrequently.
- Place in the same module procedures that are used together.
- Place in their own modules procedures that are called rarely.
- If the same procedure is called by routines in more than one module, consider duplicating the routine and placing a copy of it in each module. This method prevents an entire module from loading just because a single routine within it is called.
- Place in the same module procedures within a call tree. This is necessary because Access looks at the potential call tree when it loads a module. If a procedure in one module is called from a procedure in another module, both modules are loaded into memory.

Although you generally want to load into memory as little as possible, the opposite is true for commonly used functions. By placing frequently used procedures in the same module, you ensure that they are loaded into memory and can be accessed quickly when they are called. This improves the performance of your application.

Writing Library Code That Runs

Code that runs perfectly within a normal database might not run as expected when it is part of a library database. Good examples are the `CurrentProject` object and the `CurrentDB` function. As you have seen throughout this book, the `CurrentProject` object is an object that refers to the current ADP project or Access database (mdb). The `CurrentDB` function is a commonly used function that enables you to reference the current database. You would think that both the `CurrentProject object` and the `CurrentDB` function reference the database in which the code is running, but this is actually not the case. They specifically reference the database that is active in the user interface. If a library function refers to either `CurrentProject` or `CurrentDB`, it does not refer to itself; instead, it refers to the application database that is calling the library function. If you want to refer to the library database, you must use the CodeProject object or the CodeDB function. The CodeProject object and the CodeDB function always refer to the database in which the code is running. You must decide whether CurrentProject, CurrentDB, CodeProject, or CodeDB is applicable for each situation.

Compiling the Library

Compiling a library database before you distribute it ensures optimal performance. If library code is not compiled, it will compile each time it is accessed, which significantly degrades the performance of your application. The compilation process and its benefits are discussed in detail in Chapter 17, "Optimizing Your Application." After you complete all changes to the library database, select Debug|Compile. You must choose this command each time you make changes to the library database.

Creating a Reference

A *reference* is Access's way of locating a library database so that it can use the code in it. You can establish references in four ways:

- Create a library reference
- Create a runtime reference
- Create an explicit reference
- Use VBA code

> ### Tip
>
> Much of the text that follows refers to the Windows registry. You can access the Windows registry using the RegEdit utility. To utilize RegEdit, select the Run option from the Start menu, and then type RegEdit.

Creating a Library Reference

You create a library reference by adding the library to the Menu Add-ins section of the Windows registry, as shown in Figure 24.1. The Menu Add-ins section is located in the HKEY_LOCAL_MACHINE\SOFTWARE\Microsoft\Office\10.0\Access\Menu Add-Ins key. This type of reference is limited because it allows the functions of the library database to be invoked only as an add-in. Add-ins are covered in more detail in Chapter 25.

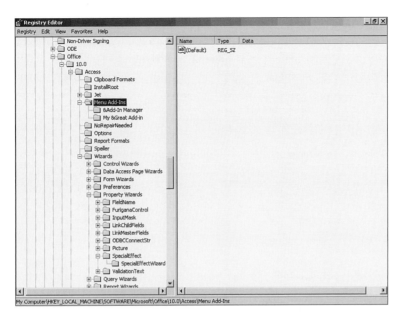

FIGURE 24.1
Viewing the Menu Add-ins section of the Windows registry.

Creating a Runtime Reference

Creating a runtime reference involves establishing a reference to the library at runtime using the Run method of the Application object. This method of creating a reference actually opens the library database and executes the specified function. It uses OLE automation to accomplish this task.

The major advantage of this technique is that the library code is not loaded into memory until it is used. Furthermore, this technique does not require that additional modules in the call stack be loaded into memory unless they are called explicitly. Creating a runtime reference does have a few disadvantages, though:

- The library database must have an MDA extension.
- The library database must be located in the path specified in the AddInPath key in the Windows registry. The AddInPath key is located in the HKEY_LOCAL_MACHINE\SOFTWARE\Microsoft\Office\10.0\Access\Wizards subdirectory of the Windows registry, as shown in Figure 24.2.

Calling a Function from a Library at Runtime

The code in Listing 24.1 illustrates how to call a function in a library. Notice that the IsLoaded function is being called from the library. This code is located in the CHAP24EX.MDB database on the sample code CD-ROM.

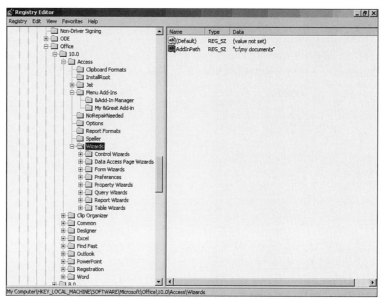

FIGURE 24.2
Viewing the AddInPath key of the Windows registry.

LISTING 24.1   Calling a Function in a Library

```
Sub AppRun()
    If Application.Run("Chap24Lib.IsLoaded", "frmCustomers") Then
        MsgBox "Customers Form is Loaded"
    Else
        MsgBox "Customers Form is NOT Loaded!!"
    End If
End Sub
```

Listing 24.1 uses the Run method of the Application object to call a function called IsLoaded, which is located in the CHAP24LIB.MDA library. This file must be referenced with an explicit reference or be located in the directory specified in the AddInPath key of the Windows registry. Notice the explicit reference to the library name in which the function is located. When using this method of loading a library (without an explicit reference), the library name must be specified.

Using the LoadOnStartup Key

You can add a LoadOnStartup key to the Windows registry. This key provides a means for Access to load a type library when the database is loaded. A type library is not an actual module, but more of a blueprint of what the module looks like. It displays the functions and constants for a specific module. This is helpful because Access can look up functions without having to actually load the module in which the function is located. This key is not automatically created for you. To create the LoadOnStartup key and add an entry to it, follow these steps:

1. Choose Run from the Windows Start menu.

2. Type **RegEdit** and click OK; this launches the registry Editor.

3. Open the Registry tree until you see
   HKEY_LOCAL_MACHINE\SOFTWARE\Microsoft\Office\10.0\Access\Wizards.

4. Click the Wizards entry.

5. Choose Edit|New|Key. A new key is added.

6. Type **LoadOnStartup** as the name of the new key.

7. With LoadOnStartup selected, choose Edit|New|String Value.

8. Type the full name and path of the library as the name of the new string value.

9. Choose Edit|Modify.

10. Type **rw** for the value.

Figure 24.3 shows an example of a completed entry that references the library in the c:\Libraries directory: CHAP24LIB.MDA.

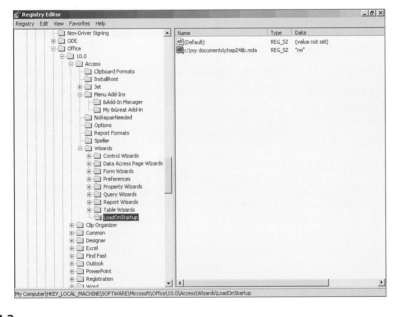

FIGURE 24.3

Referencing a library using the Registry Editor.

The module and procedure lists of library databases listed under the LoadOnStartup key are loaded when Access is started. When you use the Run method (discussed in the "Creating a Library Reference" section), Access searches for the specified procedure in the loaded or referenced libraries. If it does not find the procedure, Access searches any databases listed in the LoadOnStartUp key and then locates and loads the required library.

As you can see, the LoadOnStartUp key can reap the benefits of `Application.Run` by using the type library. The functions can be checked without loading the actual module until it is referenced explicitly through code.

NOTE

The LoadOnStartUp key is not a panacea. Loading the type library when Access is loaded does slow down the initial load time for your application. Furthermore, the memory occupied by the type information is used regardless of whether the library functions actually are accessed. You must decide whether either of these facts is an issue.

Creating an Explicit Reference

The most common type of reference by far is an *explicit reference*. This type of reference is created from any code module in the database referencing the library. To create an explicit reference, follow these steps:

1. Choose a module from the database container window and click the Design button to open the Design view of the module.

2. Choose Tools|References from the VBE menu. The References dialog box appears, as shown in Figure 24.4.

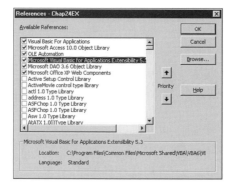

FIGURE 24.4
The References dialog box.

3. Click the Browse button.

4. Select Microsoft Access Databases (*.mdb) or Add-ins (*.mda) from the Files of Type drop-down.

5. Locate the library database you want to reference.

6. Click Open to close the Add References dialog box.

7. Click OK to close the References dialog box.

When you add a library database to the References dialog box, Access loads the database as a library when you make a call to the library from your code. You can call a library routine just as you would call any subroutine or function. You then can use code in the library database to open forms and other objects stored in the library. Access does not actually load the library database into memory until code in the active application database calls a function or subroutine that is located in the library.

Explicit library references impose a few limitations:

- The references you add in a database are available only to that database. Therefore, you must add the library reference to each application database that needs to use the library.

- The explicit path to the reference is stored in the database. This means that, if the library is moved, the reference cannot be resolved. Exceptions to this rule are covered later in this section.

When a function is called that is in a library that Access cannot locate, the message shown in Figure 24.5 appears. The References dialog box shows the library is missing, as shown in the sixth line of the `Available References` list box in Figure 24.6.

FIGURE 24.5

A warning message indicating that the library database cannot be located.

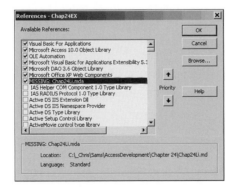

FIGURE 24.6

The References dialog box with a library flagged as missing.

Although Access might not be able to find a library database that has been moved, it does its best to resolve library references. By default, Access looks in these places to attempt to resolve a library reference:

- The absolute path of the library
- The relative path to the library
- The current folder
- The directory where Access is installed
- The Windows path (Windows and Windows\System folders)
- The PATH environment variable
- The path located in the RefLibPaths key of the Windows registry

A couple of these locations require further explanation. If the library is not located in exactly the same location on the user's machine as it is on your machine, the relative path to the library is searched next. This means that, if the library is placed in the same directory as the database that is referencing it, or in the same relative location, the library database is found. Suppose your application database is located in c:\AccessApps\Sales. The library database is located in c:\AccessApps\Sales\Libraries. The user installs the application in c:\SalesApp with the library installed in c:\SalesApp\Libraries. In this case, Access can resolve the reference to the library.

Another trick when dealing with library databases is to use the RefLibPaths key of the Windows Registry. If a key called RefLibPaths exists in the Windows registry, Access also searches the paths specified under RefLibPaths in an attempt to resolve any references. To use this trick, follow these steps:

1. Create a RefLibPaths key under the HKEY_LOCAL_MACHINE\SOFTWARE\Microsoft\Office\10.0\Access subdirectory, if it does not already exist.
2. With the key selected, choose Edit|New|String Value.
3. Type the name of the library database as the name of the new string value.
4. Choose Edit|Modify.
5. Type the name of the path containing the library as the value.
6. Repeat steps 2 through 5 for each library you are referencing.

This is a good method to use if you will be distributing an application containing several library databases. You can select a location for the library databases and then reference that location in the Windows Registry. You even can create the registry entries programmatically by using Windows API calls or the VBA SaveSetting statement. Figure 24.7 shows the RefLibPaths key with an entry for the Chap24Lib.mdb library.

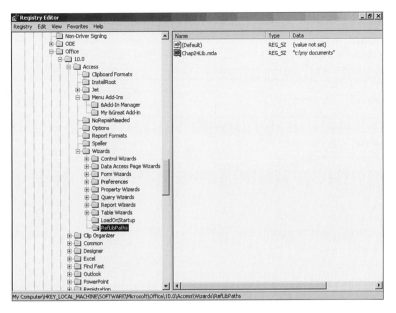

FIGURE 24.7
The RefLibPaths key of the Windows registry.

> **TIP**
>
> You can use the Packaging Wizard to create the RefLibPaths key in the Windows Registry. This is the easiest way to create the RefLibPaths entry, but it requires that you distribute your application using the Packaging Wizard.

Creating a Reference Using VBA Code

With Access 2000 came the capability to create library references using VBA code. You use the `AddFromFile` method to accomplish this task. The `AddFromFile` method is applied to the References collection, which is similar to other collections used within Access, and provides a hook to the references associated with a database. The `AddFromFile` method of the References collection accepts a string as a parameter. The string contains the name of the library reference you are adding. Listing 24.2 shows the code to pass in a library name and then add a reference to it.

LISTING 24.2 Locating and Referencing Libraries in Code

```
Function CreateLibRef(strLibName as String)
    Dim ref As Reference
    On Error GoTo CreateLibRef_Err
    'Create new reference
    Set ref = References.AddFromFile(strLibName)
```

24

CREATING YOUR
OWN LIBRARIES

LISTING 24.2   Continued

```
    CreateLibRef = True
Exit_CreateLibRef:
    Exit Function
CreateLibRef_Err:
    Dim intAnswer As Integer
    Dim strLocation As String
    intAnswer = MsgBox("Library Not Found, Attempt to Locate?", _
        vbYesNo, "Error")
    If intAnswer = vbYes Then
        strLocation = InputBox("Please Enter the Location of the Library")
        Resume
    Else
        CreateLibRef = False
        GoTo Exit_CreateLibRef
    End If

End Function
```

The routine begins by invoking an error handler. A reference object is then set to the result of the `AddFromFile` method being executed on the References collection. If the `AddFromFile` method executes successfully, the reference is created, and the function returns a `True` condition. Otherwise, the user is asked whether he wants to locate the library database. If he responds affirmatively, he is prompted for the location of the library database and the code attempts once again to establish the reference. If he opts not to supply a location, the routine terminates, returning a `False` condition.

Debugging a Library Database

You can open a library database and test it just like any other database. Although you always should begin testing the library functions this way, it also is important that you give the database a test drive as a library. In other words, after you eliminate any bugs from the database, you should reference it from another database and test it as a library database.

If you need to make changes to a library database while accessing it from another database, you can do so easily by following these steps:

1. Make sure that the library database is referenced from Tools|References.
2. Click the Object Browser tool from the Module Design window.
3. From the Project/Library drop-down menu, select the library database that contains the code you want to modify. (See Figure 24.8.)

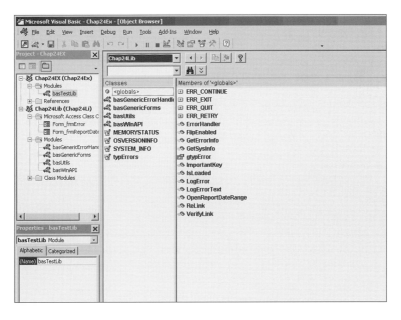

FIGURE 24.8

Using the Object Browser to modify a library database.

4. Select the class you want to modify from the Classes list box.

5. Select the member you want to modify from the Members list box.

6. Click View Definition (the button with the arrow pointing toward the box), or double-click the member whose code you want to view. You are placed in the correct module and procedure of the library database. You now can make changes to the code in the database as required.

Securing an Access Library

Many people develop Access libraries for mass distribution in the retail market. Whether you are marketing a library database or just distributing it within your organization or to your clients, I highly advise you to consider securing your library code. This protects the library code from being modified or copied by unauthorized individuals. It also avoids the headache of some user who tries to alter the code and then calls you for support. Security issues are covered in detail in Chapter 27, "Database Security Made Easy."

Building a Library for Your Application

Now that you are familiar with library databases and what they offer, try extracting all the generic functions from an application and placing them in a library database. This section presents a step-by-step roadmap for accomplishing this task.

NOTE

This process already has been completed for CHAP24.MDB. The associated library database is called CHAP24LIB.MDA. If you want to complete this process as an exercise, copy CHAP24.MDB and complete the outlined steps.

To extract the generic functions from the Time and Billing application and place them in a library database, follow these steps:

1. Create a new database that will become the library database. Import the basUtils, basGenericErrorHandler, and basWinAPI modules as well as the frmError form into the library database.

2. Remove two routines from basUtils within the library database: RunReport and GetCompanyInfo. Assume that these routines are specific to the application database and should not be moved to become a part of the library.

3. Choose Debug|Compile to ensure that you do not get any compile errors in the library database.

4. Open the application database.

5. Remove basGenericErrorHandler, basWinAPI, and frmError from the application database.

6. Remove six subroutines from basUtils in the application database: IsLoaded, FlipEnabled, ImportantKey, AreTablesAttached, LastOccurence, and TryAgain.

7. Choose Tools|References to reference the library database.

8. Choose Debug|Compile to ensure that you do not get any compile errors in the application database.

9. Test the application to ensure that it runs successfully. To properly check all aspects of the application, you need to introduce an error to test the error-handling routines. Rename the CHAP24DATA.MDB database to test the linking routines.

You should move one more database element to the library database: the Report Selection Criteria form. This form is generic and can be used by many of the applications you create.

Follow these steps to move the frmReportDateRange form to the library database:

1. Open the library database and import the frmReportDateRange form.

2. Create a module called basGenericForms and add the OpenReportDateRange subroutine to the module. Because you cannot open a form in a library database directly, you must create a routine within the library database that opens the form.

3. Open the application database and remove the frmReportDateRange form.

4. Modify the appropriate objects within the application database like this:

```
Sub OpenReportDateRange(strOpenArg As String)
    DoCmd.OpenForm "frmReportDateRange", , , , , acDialog, _
        strOpenArg
End Sub
```

You must modify three reports in the application database to accommodate the movement of the frmReportDateRange form to a library database: rptProjectBillingsByWorkCode, rptClientBillingsByProject, and rptEmployeeBillingsByProject. The Open event of rptProjectBillingsByWorkCode should be modified to look like this:

```
Private Sub Report_Open(Cancel As Integer)
    Call OpenReportDateRange("rptProjectBillingsByWorkCode")
    If Not IsLoaded("frmReportDateRange") Then
        Cancel = True
    End If
End Sub
```

Instead of opening the form directly, which would not work because the form is in a library database, you must call the OpenReportDateRange library routine to open the form. The strOpenArg parameter to the OpenReportDateRange subroutine is used as the OpenArgs parameter for the frmReportCriteria form. You must make similar changes to the rptClientBillingsByProject and rptEmployeeBillingsByProject reports. You should modify the Open event of the rptClientBillingsByProject report to look like Listing 24.3.

LISTING 24.3　Modifying the Open Event of the rptClientBillingsByProject Report

```
Private Sub Report_Open(Cancel As Integer)
    Call OpenReportDateRange("rptClientBillingsByProject")
    If Not IsLoaded("frmReportDateRange") Then
        Cancel = True
    Else
        Select Case Forms!frmReportDateRange!optDetailLevel.Value
            Case 1
```

24

CREATING YOUR
OWN LIBRARIES

LISTING 24.3 Continued

```
                Me.Caption = Me.Caption & " - Summary Only"
                Me!lblTitle.Caption = Me.lblTitle.Caption & " - _
                    Summary Only"
                Me.Detail.Visible = False
            Case 2
                Me.Caption = Me.Caption & " - Detail Only"
                Me!lblTitle.Caption = Me.lblTitle.Caption & " - _
                    Detail Only"
                Me.GroupHeader0.Visible = False
                Me.GroupFooter1.Visible = False
                Me!CompanyNameDet.Visible = True
            Case 3
                Me.Caption = Me.Caption & " - Summary and Detail"
                Me!lblTitle.Caption = Me.lblTitle.Caption & _
                " - Summary and Detail"
                Me!CompanyNameDet.Visible = False
        End Select
    End If
End Sub
```

Modify the Open event of the rptEmployeeBillingsByProject report to look like this:

```
Private Sub Report_Open(Cancel As Integer)
    Call OpenReportDateRange("rptEmployeeBillingsByProject")
    If Not IsLoaded("frmReportDateRange") Then
        Cancel = True
    End If
End Sub
```

After you move the generic features of the application to the library database, you can try to build another application database and use the same library features.

Summary

Library databases enable you to create libraries of code, forms, reports, and other objects that will be shared by multiple databases. Library databases facilitate the application development process by enabling you to easily centralize the development of common code libraries. You also can use these databases to incorporate add-ins, wizards, and builders into your applications and development environment (covered in Chapter 25).

This chapter began by defining a library database. It then walked you through all the steps required to prepare a database to become a library database. The chapter discussed the several methods to reference a library database, highlighting the pros and cons of each.

After you reference a library database, the debugging process begins. This chapter highlighted how easy it is to debug an Access 2002 library database. Finally, it provided you with practical examples of how you can use library databases in your applications.

Library databases can greatly facilitate the application development process, enabling you to easily implement sophisticated functionality in all your applications. Although the process of designing library databases can be intimidating at first, a well-planned library database can shave hours off the application development and maintenance processes.

24

CREATING YOUR
OWN LIBRARIES

Using Builders, Wizards, and Menu Add-Ins

IN THIS CHAPTER

Why This Chapter Is Important

Add-ins are tools that extend the functionality of Access. They enhance the Access environment by making difficult tasks easier, automating repetitive tasks, and adding enhanced functionality. You can design add-ins for yourself or for others in your organization to use. You even might want to distribute add-ins as part of your application so that your users can build their own database objects. If you are really ambitious, you might decide to build an add-in for sale in the Access third-party market.

Microsoft Access supports three types of add-ins: builders, wizards, and menu add-ins. Each has its own advantages and uses. When you begin the process of designing an add-in, you must decide whether it will be a builder, wizard, or menu add-in. This decision affects how you design the add-in as well as how you install it. This chapter defines and shows you how to design and install each type of add-in.

Using Builders

A *builder* is an add-in that helps users construct an expression or another data element. Builders most often are used to help users fill in a property of a database object. Builders generally consist of a single dialog box that appears after the user clicks the ellipsis to the right of the property on the Property sheet. An example of a builder is the Expression Builder that appears when users are setting the control source of a text box on a form. Access supports three types of builders:

- Property builders
- Control builders
- Expression builders

Looking at Design Guidelines

When designing your own builder, the design should be consistent with that of the builders included in Access. You therefore must learn about the standards for an Access builder. To design builders that are consistent with the built-in builders, keep a few guidelines in mind:

- Set the AutoCenter property of the Builder form to Yes.
- Remove record selectors and navigation buttons.
- Remove scrollbars.
- Be consistent about the placement of objects on the form. Place the OK and Cancel buttons in the same place in each builder you create, for example.
- Design the forms as dialog boxes.

Creating a Builder

Now that you are familiar with some general design guidelines for builders, you are ready to design your first builder. What a builder does is completely up to your imagination. For illustration, this section begins with a simple builder that prompts users to select the special effect for a text box. Three overall steps are required to create the builder:

1. Write a builder function.

2. Design a builder form.

3. Register the builder.

The following sections go over each of these steps in detail.

Writing a Builder Function

 The *builder function* is the function Access calls each time the builder is launched. The function launches the builder form and then returns a value to the appropriate property. Listing 25.1 is an example of a builder function. It is located in CHAP25LIB.MDA in the basBuilders module on the accompanying CD-ROM.

LISTING 25.1   Creating a Builder Function

```
Function SpecialEffect(strObject As String, _
          strControl As String, _
          strCurrentValue As String)

   On Error GoTo SpecialEffect_Err

   'Open the special effect form, passing it the special
   'effect currently selected
   DoCmd.OpenForm FormName:="frmSpecialEffect", _
              WindowMode:=acDialog, _
              OpenArgs:=strCurrentValue

   'If the user selects a special effect and clicks OK, the
   'form remains open but hidden.  Return a value based on
   'which special effect the user selected
   If SysCmd(acSysCmdGetObjectState, acForm, _
          "frmSpecialEffect") = acObjStateOpen Then
      Select Case Forms!frmSpecialEffect.optSpecialEffect.Value
         Case 1
            SpecialEffect = "Flat"
         Case 2
            SpecialEffect = "Raised"
         Case 3
            SpecialEffect = "Sunken"
```

LISTING 25.1   Continued

```
        Case 4
            SpecialEffect = "Etched"
        Case 5
            SpecialEffect = "Shadowed"
        Case 6
            SpecialEffect = "Chiseled"
    End Select

    'Close the form when done
    DoCmd.Close acForm, "frmSpecialEffect"
Else

    'If the user clicks cancel, return the original value
    'for the special effect
    SpecialEffect = strCurrentValue
End If

SpecialEffect_Exit:
    Exit Function

SpecialEffect_Err:
    MsgBox "Error # " & Err.Number & ": " & Err.Description
    Resume SpecialEffect_Exit
End Function
```

A builder function must receive three preset arguments and must return the value that will become the value for the property being set. The three preset arguments follow:

- strObject—The name of the table, query, form, report, or module on which the builder is operating
- strControl—The name of the control to which the property applies
- strCurrentValue—The current property value

Although the names of the arguments are arbitrary, their data types, positions, and content cannot be changed. Access automatically fills in the values for the three arguments.

The SpecialEffect function opens the form called frmSpecialEffect in Dialog mode, passing it the current value of the property as the OpenArgs value. Figure 25.1 shows the frmSpecialEffect form.

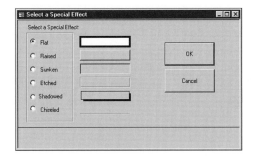

FIGURE 25.1

The Special Effect builder form.

The following code is located in the Click event of the cmdOkay command button on the form:

```
Private Sub cmdOK_Click()
    Me.Visible = False
End Sub
```

Notice that the code sets the Visible property of the form to False. The code placed behind the cmdCancel command button looks like this:

```
Private Sub cmdCancel_Click()
    DoCmd.Close
End Sub
```

This code closes the frmSpecialEffect form.

After the user clicks OK or Cancel, the code within the SpecialEffect function continues to execute. The function uses the SysCmd function to determine whether the frmSpecialEffect form is loaded. You also can use the user-defined IsLoaded function to accomplish this task. If the frmSpecialEffect form still is loaded, the user must have selected a special effect and clicked OK. Because the form still is open, the function can determine which option button the user selected.

The Case statement within the SpecialEffect function evaluates the value of the optSpecialEffect option group found on the frmSpecialEffect form. It sets the return value for the function equal to the appropriate string, depending on the option button that the user of the builder selects. If the user selects the second option button (with a value of 2), for example, the SpecialEffect function returns the string "Raised". After the option button value is evaluated and the return value is set, the frmSpecialEffect form no longer is needed, so it is closed.

If the user chooses Cancel from the frmSpecialEffect form, the SysCmd function returns False, and the return value of the SpecialEffect function is set equal to strCurrentValue, the original property value. The property value therefore is not changed.

Designing a Builder Form

Although you have seen the code behind the `Click` event of the OK and Cancel buttons on the frmSpecialEffect form, you have not learned about the design of the form or the idea behind this builder. Ordinarily, when the Special Effect property is set from the Property window, no wizard exists to assist with the process. Although the process of setting the Special Effect property is quite simple, the main problem is that it is difficult to remember exactly what each special effect looks like. The custom special effect builder is designed with this potential problem in mind. It enables users of the builder to see what each special effect looks like before deciding which effect to select.

The properties of the form are quite simple. The Modal property of the form is set to `Yes`. The record selectors, navigation buttons, and scrollbars are removed. The AutoCenter property of the form is set to `True`. Six text boxes are included on the form. The special effect of each text box is set to a different style. An option group is included on the form. This group has a different value, depending on which option button is selected. The Default property of the OK command button is set to `Yes`, making the OK button the default choice. The Cancel property of the Cancel command button is set to `Yes`, ensuring that if the user presses Esc, the code behind the Cancel button executes. The code behind the `Click` events of the OK and Cancel buttons were shown in the preceding section. Listing 25.2 shows one more piece of code that enhances this builder.

LISTING 25.2   Enhancing the Builder

```
Private Sub Form_Load()
    'Set the Value of the Option Group
    'To the Current Value of the Property
    Select Case Me.OpenArgs
        Case "Flat"
            Me.optSpecialEffect.Value = 1
        Case "Raised"
            Me.optSpecialEffect.Value = 2
        Case "Sunken"
            Me.optSpecialEffect.Value = 3
        Case "Etched"
            Me.optSpecialEffect.Value = 4
        Case "Shadowed"
            Me.optSpecialEffect.Value = 5
        Case "Chiseled"
            Me.optSpecialEffect.Value = 6
End Select
End Sub
```

This subroutine is placed in the Load event of the builder form. It sets the value of the option group to the current value of the property (passed in as an OpenArg).

Although the frmSpecialEffect form is not particularly exciting, it illustrates quite well that you can design a form of any level of complexity to facilitate the process of setting a property value. So far, though, you have not provided an entry point to the builder. If you select the Special Effect property, no ellipsis appears. You do not yet have access to the builder.

Registering a Builder

Before you can use a builder, you must register it in one of two ways:

- Manually add the required entries to the Windows registry.
- Set up the library database so that the Add-in Manager can create the Windows registry entries for you.

Manually Adding Entries to the Windows Registry

Adding the required entries to the Windows registry involves four steps:

1. If no registry key exists for the property for which you are designing a builder, add the property as a subkey under Property Wizards.
2. Add an additional subkey for the builder.
3. Add four predefined registry values for the key.
4. Set the proper data value for each value name.

The four value names that must be created for the subkey are Can Edit, Description, Function, and Library. Table 25.1 describes these value names for the registry subkey.

TABLE 25.1 Values for the Registry Subkey

Value Name	Value Type	Purpose
Can Edit	DWORD	Allows the builder to operate on and modify an existing value
Description	String	Specifies a subkey description that appears in the dialog box, which is invoked automatically if more than one builder exists for a property
Function	String	Name of the builder function
Library	String	Name of the library containing the builder function

Now that you have an overview of the steps involved in the process, you are ready to walk through the steps in detail. The following steps set up the builder called SpecialEffect, which is contained in the library database CHAP25LIB.MDA in the folder c:\My Libraries:

1. To invoke the Registry Editor, choose Start|Run from the task bar. Type **regedit** and click OK. This invokes the Registry Editor.

2. Locate the HKEY_LOCAL_MACHINE\SOFTWARE\Microsoft\Office\10.0\Access\Wizards \Property Wizards key, as shown in Figure 25.2.

FIGURE 25.2

The Property Wizards Registry key.

3. Determine whether a subkey exists with the name of the property for which you are creating a builder (in this case, SpecialEffect). If so, skip to step 6.

4. Choose Edit|New|Key.

5. Type the property name as the name for the new key (in this case, **SpecialEffect**).

6. With the new key selected, choose Edit|New|Key again.

7. Type a descriptive name for your builder (in this case, **SpecialEffectBuilder**).

8. Choose Edit|New|DWORD Value.

9. Type **Can Edit** as the value name.

10. Choose Edit|New|String Value.

11. Type **Description** as the value name.

12. Choose Edit | New | String Value.

13. Type **Function** as the value name.

14. Choose Edit | New | String Value.

15. Type **Library** as the value name.

16. Double-click the Can Edit value name. The Edit DWORD Value dialog box appears, as shown in Figure 25.3.

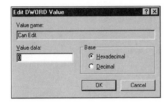

FIGURE 25.3

The Edit DWORD Value dialog box.

17. Enter **1** for the Value data and click OK.

18. Double-click the Description value name. The Edit String dialog box appears, as shown in Figure 25.4.

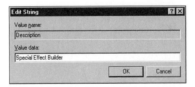

FIGURE 25.4

The Edit String dialog box.

19. Enter the description you want the user of the builder to see if more than one builder is assigned to the property (in this case, **Special Effect Builder**). Click OK.

20. Double-click the Function value name. Enter the name of the builder function (in this case, **SpecialEffect**). Click OK.

21. Double-click the Library value name. Enter the name and location of the library database (in this case, **C:\My Libraries\chap25lib.mda**). You do not have to enter the path if the library is located in the Access folder.

Figure 25.5 shows the completed registry entries. The builder now should be ready to use. To test the builder, you need to exit and relaunch Access. If all the registry entries are created successfully, you can use the builder. To test the builder, open any database (other than the library database), create a new form, and add a text box. Select Special Effect from the Format tab of the Properties window. An ellipsis appears to the right of the Special Effect drop-down arrow, as shown in Figure 25.6. If you click the ellipsis, the builder form appears. Select a special effect and click OK. The special effect you selected now appears in the Special Effect property.

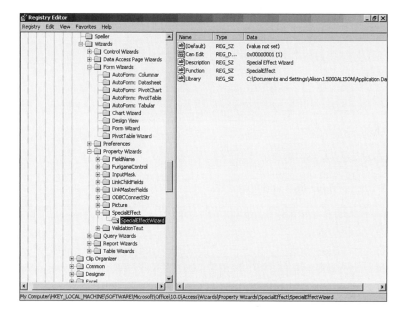

FIGURE 25.5

The completed registry entries required to add the builder.

FIGURE 25.6

Using the custom builder.

NOTE

If you do not exactly follow the format for the value names, the message `Invalid add-in entry for 'SpecialEffectBuilder'` appears, as shown in Figure 25.7. You must correct the registry entry.

FIGURE 25.7

This error message appears if the registry entry is invalid.

Automating the Creation of Registry Entries

The alternative to editing the Windows registry manually is to set up the library database so that the Add-in Manager can create the registry entries for you. This involves adding a table to the library database. The table must be called USysRegInfo. Follow these steps:

1. Show the system tables. (Tables that begin with USys or MSys are considered system tables and, by default, are hidden.) With the library database open, choose Tools|Options. From the View tab, click System Objects. Click OK. Figure 25.8 shows the database with Tables selected in the Objects list.

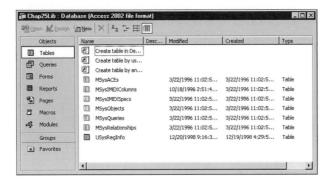

FIGURE 25.8

The Tables tab with system objects visible.

2. Import an existing USysRegInfo tableby right-clicking within the database window and selecting Import. Using the Import dialog box, move to the \Program Files\Microsoft Office\Office10 folder and locate the ACWZMAIN.MDE file. This is a library file that ships with Access. Select the ACWZMAIN.MDE file and click Import. The Import Objects dialog box appears, as shown in Figure 25.9.

3. Locate and select the USysRegInfo table and click OK. A copy of the USysRegInfo table is added to your library database.

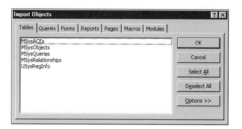

FIGURE 25.9

Using the Import Objects dialog box to add the USysRegInfo table to your library database.

4. Double-click to open the USysRegInfo table in the database window.

5. Delete any existing entries in the table.

6. Add specific entries to the USysRegInfo table. Figure 25.10 shows these entries, and Table 25.2 explains them. Close the table.

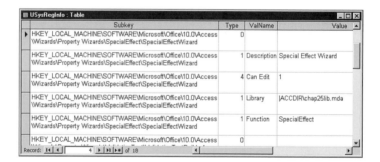

FIGURE 25.10

The completed table with entries for registry.

7. Open the database that references the add-in.

8. Choose Tools|Add-ins|Add-in Manager. The Add-in Manager dialog box appears, as shown in Figure 25.11.

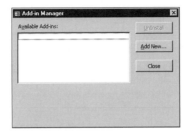

FIGURE 25.11

The Add-in Manager dialog box.

9. Click the Add New button to launch the Open dialog box. Here, you can browse for your add-in or select it from within the default folder.

10. Locate the add-in that you want to add and click Open. The add-in you select is added to the Add-in Manager dialog box and is selected for you.

11. Click Close. You now are ready to use the add-in.

TABLE 25.2   The Structure of the USysRegInfo Table

Field Name	Description
SubKey	Name of the subkey value in the registry where the value you are adding is located
Type	Type of subkey value you are creating (String, Binary, or DWORD)
ValName	Value name for the entry
Value	Value associated with the value name

Using Wizards

A *wizard* consists of a series of dialog boxes that provide a step-by-step interface for creating a database object. The wizard shields users from the complexities of the process. You probably are familiar with wizards such as the Form Wizard, the Report Wizard, and the Database Wizard. Access 2002 supports the development of several types of custom wizards:

- Table wizards
- Query wizards
- Form wizards
- Report wizards
- Data Access Page wizards

25

USING BUILDERS, WIZARDS, AND MENU ADD-INS

- Property wizards
- Control wizards

Looking at Design Guidelines

Wizard design guidelines are almost identical to builder design guidelines. The main difference is that wizards generally present the user with multiple modal dialog boxes, whereas a builder generally consists of a single modal dialog box. All the data requirements for the wizard must be met before the user can close the last dialog box.

Creating a Wizard

 Creating a wizard is more complex than creating a builder. A wizard generally requires a multipage form and code that creates database objects. Consider a wizard that creates a simple form. The wizard comprises two modal dialog boxes, shown in Figures 25.12 and 25.13. The first dialog box asks the user for a form caption, form name, and message to appear on the new form. The second dialog box enables the user to add OK and Cancel buttons to the form. The multipage form and all the code that enables it to work are in the CHAP25LIB.MDA database on the accompanying CD-ROM.

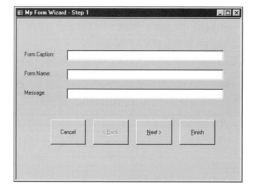

FIGURE 25.12

Step 1 of the custom Form Wizard.

Each page of the wizard contains code to ensure that it operates successfully. The form is called frmGetFormInfo. The first page of this multipage form gives the user the opportunity to choose the next action: Cancel, Next, or Finish. The code for the Cancel button looks like this:

```
Private Sub cmdCancel1_Click()
    DoCmd.Close
End Sub
```

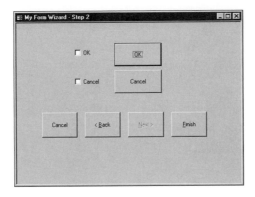

FIGURE 25.13

Step 2 of the custom Form Wizard.

This code closes the wizard form. No other actions are taken because the process is being canceled. If the user clicks Next, this code executes:

```
Private Sub cmdNext1_Click()
   DoCmd.GoToPage 2
   Me.Caption = "My Form Wizard - Step 2"
End Sub
```

This code moves to the second page of the form and changes the caption of the form to indicate that the user is on step 2 of the wizard. The code under the Finish button looks like this:

```
Private Sub cmdFinish1_Click()
   If CreateCustomForm() Then
      MsgBox "Form Created Successfully"
      DoCmd.Close
   Else
      MsgBox "Unable to Create Form"
   End If
End Sub
```

This code calls a function called `CreateCustomForm`, which is responsible for building the actual form. The details of the `CreateCustomForm` function are discussed later in this section. If the function returns `True`, the wizard form is closed, and a message is displayed indicating that the process was successful. Otherwise, a message is displayed indicating that the form was not created successfully, and the user remains in the wizard. The second page of the form contains similar subroutines. The code under the Back button looks like this:

```
Private Sub cmdBack2_Click()
   DoCmd.GoToPage 1
   Me.Caption = "My Form Wizard - Step 1"
End Sub
```

This code moves back to the first page of the form. If the user chooses Cancel, this code executes:

```
Private Sub cmdCancel2_Click()
    DoCmd.Close
End Sub
```

This code closes the form, taking no further action. If the user clicks Finish, the Click event code of the cmdFinish2 command button executes:

```
Private Sub cmdFinish2_Click()
    Call cmdFinish1_Click
End Sub
```

This code calls the code under the Click event of the cmdFinish1 command button.

The CreateCustomForm function (located in the basWizards module of the library database), as seen in Listing 25.3, contains the code that actually builds the new form.

LISTING 25.3 The CreateCustomForm Function Builds the Form

```
Function CreateCustomForm() As Boolean

    On Error GoTo CreateCustomForm_Err

    Dim frmNew As Form
    Dim ctlNew As Control

    'Create a New Form and Set Several of Its Properties
    Set frmNew = CreateForm()
    frmNew.Caption = Forms!frmGetFormInfo.txtFormCaption
    frmNew.RecordSelectors = False
    frmNew.NavigationButtons = False
    frmNew.AutoCenter = True

    'Create a Label Control on the New Form
    'Set Several of Its Properties
    Set ctlNew = CreateControl(frmNew.Name, acLabel)
    ctlNew.Caption = Forms!frmGetFormInfo.txtLabelCaption
    ctlNew.Width = 3000
    ctlNew.Height = 1000
    ctlNew.Top = 1000
    ctlNew.Left = 1000

    'Evaluate to See if the User Requested an OK Command Button
    'If They Did, Add the Command Button and Set Its Properties
    'Add Click Event Code for the Command Button
```

LISTING 25.3   Continued

```
If Forms!frmGetButtons.chkOK.Value = -1 Then
    Set ctlNew = CreateControl(frmNew.Name, acCommandButton)
    ctlNew.Caption = "OK"
    ctlNew.Width = 1000
    ctlNew.Height = 500
    ctlNew.Top = 1000
    ctlNew.Left = 5000
    ctlNew.Name = "cmdOK"
    ctlNew.Properties("OnClick") = "[Event Procedure]"
    frmNew.Module.InsertText "Sub cmdOK_Click()" & vbCrLf & _
        vbTab & "DoCmd.Close acForm, """ & _
        Forms!frmGetFormInfo.txtFormName & _
        """" & vbCrLf & "End Sub"
End If

'Evaluate to See if the User Requested a Cancel Command Button
'If They Did, Add the Command Button and Set Its Properties
'Add Click Event Code for the Command Button
If Forms!frmGetButtons.chkCancel.Value = -1 Then
    Set ctlNew = CreateControl(frmNew.Name, acCommandButton)
    ctlNew.Caption = "Cancel"
    ctlNew.Width = 1000
    ctlNew.Height = 500
    ctlNew.Top = 2000
    ctlNew.Left = 5000
    ctlNew.Name = "cmdCancel"
    ctlNew.Properties("OnClick") = "[Event Procedure]"
    frmNew.Module.InsertText "Sub cmdCancel_Click()" & vbCrLf & _
        vbTab & "MsgBox(""You Canceled!!"")" & vbCrLf & "End Sub"
End If

'If the User Entered a Form Name, Save the Form
If Not IsNull(Forms!frmGetFormInfo.txtFormName) Then
    DoCmd.Save , Forms!frmGetFormInfo.txtFormName
End If

'Return True If No Errors
CreateCustomForm = True
Exit Function

CreateCustomForm_Err:
    MsgBox "Error # " & Err.Number & ": " & Err.Description
    CreateCustomForm = False
    Exit Function
End Function
```

The code begins by creating both form and control object variables. The form object variable is set to the return value from the `CreateForm` function. The `CreateForm` function creates a new form object. Several properties of the new form object are set: Caption, RecordSelectors, NavigationButtons, and AutoCenter. Next, the function uses the `CreateControl` function to create a new label. A reference to the new label is called ctlNew. The Caption, Width, Height, Top, and Left properties of the new label are set. If the user indicated that he or she wanted an OK button, a new command button is created. The Caption, Width, Height, Top, Left, Name, and Properties properties are all set. The `InsertText` method is used to insert code for the `Click` event of the command button. If the user requested a Cancel button, the same properties are set. Finally, if the user indicated a name for the new form, the `Save` method is used to save the new form object.

> **NOTE**
>
> Several functions exist to create and delete forms, reports, form controls, and report controls. You can use ADO code to create, modify, and delete tables and queries. Using the functions and ADO code, you can manipulate database objects any way you want. ADO is covered in Chapter 14, "What Are ActiveX Data Objects and Data Access Objects, and Why Are They Important?"

Getting the Wizard Ready to Go

Like a builder, a wizard needs to be added to the Windows registry before it can be used. You can do this by modifying the registry directly or by adding entries to the USysRegInfo table. Figure 25.14 shows the completed registry entry for the custom Form Wizard.

Notice that the function name is `MyCustomForm`. This is the entry point to the wizard. The Library key designates the name of the library add-in database containing the entry point function. The Description key specifies what appears in the New Object dialog box. Finally, the Index key designates the order in which the wizard is displayed in the list in the New Object dialog box. The `MyCustomForm` function, located in the basWizards module, simply calls the frmGetFormInfo form, initiating the wizard process:

```
Function MyCustomForm(strRecordSource As String) As Variant
   DoCmd.OpenForm FormName:="frmGetFormInfo", WindowMode:=acDialog
End Function
```

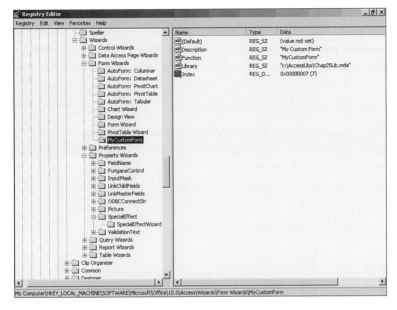

FIGURE 25.14

Registry entries for the custom Form Wizard.

Using Menu Add-Ins

A *menu add-in* is a general-purpose tool that enables you to perform a task that generally affects multiple objects or Access itself. The Database Splitter and Database Documenter are examples of menu add-ins. You access menu add-ins through the Add-ins submenu of the Tools menu.

Looking at Design Guidelines

Menu add-ins are available to the user whenever the Tools menu is available. Menu add-ins are not context sensitive like wizards and builders. Therefore, they should in no way rely on what the user is doing at a particular moment.

Creating a Menu Add-In

Creating a menu add-in is just like creating a wizard. The difference is in how you install the add-in. The menu add-in must be registered under HKEY_LOCAL_MACHINE\SOFTWARE \Microsoft\Office\10.0\Access\Menu Add-Ins. You can accomplish the registration process by modifying the registry directly or by using the USysRegInfo table. Figure 25.15 shows the registry with the correct entries to run the Form Wizard, created earlier in this chapter, as an add-in. Figure 25.16 shows how you can automate the registration process by using the USysRegInfo table. Three entries are included in the USysRegInfo table. All three entries designate the proper place in the registry tree to add the new key. The first entry contains the

25

USING BUILDERS,
WIZARDS, AND
MENU ADD-INS

subkey and a type of zero. The second entry contains the value name `Expression` and the name of the entry point function as the value. Notice that the expression name is preceded by an equal sign (=) and is followed by parentheses. The quotation marks within the parentheses are required because this particular entry-point function requires an argument. The third and final entry contains the value name `Library` and the name of the library as the value. This is all you need to do to turn a wizard into a menu add-in.

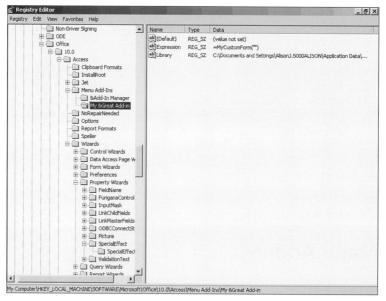

FIGURE 25.15

Registry entries for the menu add-in.

USysRegInfo : Table

Subkey	Type	ValName	Value
HKEY_LOCAL_MACHINE\SOFTWARE\Microsoft\Office\10.0\Access \Menu Add-ins\My &Great Add-in	0		
HKEY_LOCAL_MACHINE\SOFTWARE\Microsoft\Office\10.0\Access \Menu Add-ins\My &Great Add-in	1	Expression	=MyCustomForm("")
HKEY_LOCAL_MACHINE\SOFTWARE\Microsoft\Office\10.0\Access	1	Library	|ACCDIR\Chap25Lib.mda

Record: 1 of 18

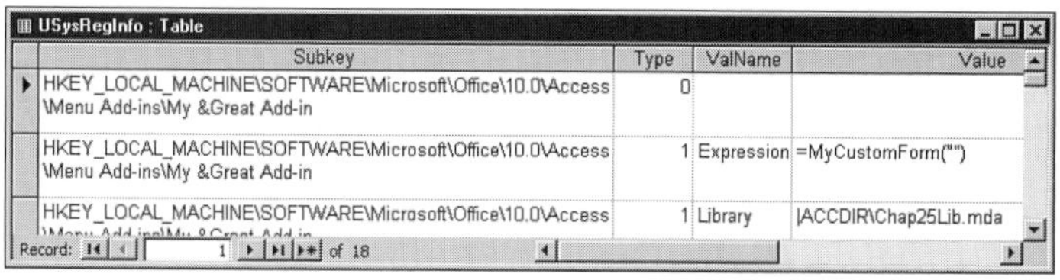

FIGURE 25.16

The USysRegInfo entries for the menu add-in.

PRACTICAL EXAMPLES

Designing Your Own Add-Ins

The types of builders, wizards, and menu add-ins that you create depend on your specific needs. To reinforce what you have learned, this section includes the step-by-step process for creating a builder to help you add validation text messages. When you invoke the builder, the Choose Builder dialog box shown in Figure 25.17 appears. This dialog box appears because you will design two builders: one that enables the user to select from a list of polite messages and another that enables the user to select from rude messages. If the user selects Polite Validation Text Builder, the dialog box in Figure 25.18 appears. If the user selects Rude Validation Text builder, the dialog box in Figure 25.19 appears.

FIGURE 25.17

The Choose Builder dialog box.

FIGURE 25.18

The polite messages builder.

FIGURE 25.19

The rude messages builder.

The first entry-point function is located in basBuilders and is shown in Listing 25.4.

LISTING 25.4   The First Entry-Point Function

```
Function ValidTextPolite(strObject As String, _
            strControl As String, _
            strCurrentValue As String)

    On Error GoTo ValidTextPolite_Err

    'Open the Builder form
    DoCmd.OpenForm FormName:="frmPolite", _
                WindowMode:=acDialog, _
                OpenArgs:=strCurrentValue

    'If the user selected a message and clicked OK,
    'return the selected text to the caller
    If SysCmd(acSysCmdGetObjectState, acForm, _
            "frmPolite") = acObjStateOpen Then
        Select Case Forms!frmPolite.optPolite.Value
            Case 1
                ValidTextPolite = "The Incorrect Value Was Entered"
            Case 2
                ValidTextPolite = "The Computer Cannot Comprehend Your Entry"
            Case 3
                ValidTextPolite = "I'm Sorry, Could You Please Try Again"
            Case 4
                ValidTextPolite = "Please Make Another Selection"
            Case 5
                ValidTextPolite = "Amount Too High"
            Case 6
                ValidTextPolite = "Amount Too Low"
        End Select

        'Close the form
        DoCmd.Close acForm, "frmPolite"

    'If the user clicked cancel, return the original value
    Else
        ValidTextPolite = strCurrentValue
    End If

ValidTextPolite_Exit:
    Exit Function

ValidTextPolite_Err:
    MsgBox "Error # " & Err.Number & ": " & Err.Description
    Resume ValidTextPolite_Exit
End Function
```

The `ValidTextPolite` function receives all the parameters required by a builder function. The function opens frmPolite modally, passing it the current validation text value of the selected control as the `OpenArg`. If the user selects a value from the frmPolite form and clicks OK, the selected value is evaluated, and the appropriate text is returned from the `ValidTextPolite` function. The return value becomes the validation text of the selected control. Listing 25.5 shows the `Load` event of frmPolite.

LISTING 25.5   The Load Event of frmPolite

```
Private Sub Form_Load()
    'Set the Value of the Option Group
    'To the Current Value of the Property
    Select Case Me.OpenArgs
        Case "The Incorrect Value Was Entered"
            Me.optPolite.Value = 1
        Case "The Computer Cannot Comprehend Your Entry"
            Me.optPolite.Value = 2
        Case "I'm Sorry, Could You Please Try Again"
            Me.optPolite.Value = 3
        Case "Please Make Another Selection"
            Me.optPolite.Value = 4
        Case "Amount Too High"
            Me.optPolite.Value = 5
        Case "Amount Too Low"
            Me.optPolite.Value = 6
    End Select

End Sub
```

This code ensures that the value of the option button on the frmPolite form reflects the text that currently is entered in the Validation Text property of the current control. The `ValidTextRude` entry-point function is similar to `ValidTextPolite`. Listing 25.6 shows the `ValidTextRude` entry-point text function; it is located in basBuilders.

LISTING 25.6   The `ValidTextRude` Entry-Point Function

```
Function ValidTextRude(strObject As String, _
            strControl As String, _
            strCurrentValue As String)

    On Error GoTo ValidTextRude_Err
```

LISTING 25.6   Continued

```
    'Open the Builder form
    DoCmd.OpenForm FormName:="frmRude", _
                   WindowMode:=acDialog, _
                   OpenArgs:=strCurrentValue

    'If the user selected a message and clicked OK,
    'return the selected text to the caller
    If SysCmd(acSysCmdGetObjectState, acForm, _
            "frmRude") = acObjStateOpen Then
       Select Case Forms!frmRude!optRude.Value
          Case 1
             ValidTextRude = "Get a Clue Dude"
          Case 2
             ValidTextRude = "What the Heck do You Think You're Doing?"
          Case 3
             ValidTextRude = "Give Me a Break!!"
          Case 4
             ValidTextRude = "I'm a Computer, I'm not an Idiot!!"
          Case 5
             ValidTextRude = "Read the Manual Dude"
          Case 6
             ValidTextRude = "You Really Think I Believe That?"
       End Select

       'Close the form
       DoCmd.Close acForm, "frmRude"

    'If the user clicked cancel, return the original value
    Else
       ValidTextRude = strCurrentValue
    End If

ValidTextRude_Exit:
   Exit Function

ValidTextRude_Err:
   MsgBox "Error # " & Err.Number & ": " & Err.Description
   Resume ValidTextRude_Exit
End Function
```

The Load event of frmRude is similar to the Load event of frmPolite, as Listing 25.7 shows.

Listing 25.7   The Load Event of frmRude

```
Private Sub Form_Load()
    'Set the Value of the Option Group
    'To the Current Value of the Property
    Select Case Me.OpenArgs
        Case "Get a Clue Dude!"
            Me.optRude.Value = 1
        Case "What the Heck Do You Think You're Doing"
            Me.optRude.Value = 2
        Case "Give Me a Break!!"
            Me.optRude.Value = 3
        Case "I'm a Computer, I'm not an Idiot!!"
            Me.optRude.Value = 4
        Case "Read the Manual Dude"
            Me.optRude.Value = 5
        Case "You Really Think I Believe That?"
            Me.optRude.Value = 6
    End Select

End Sub
```

To create the builder, design both forms so that they look like the ones in Figures 25.18 and 25.19. Include code for the Load event of each form as listed previously. The code behind the OK button of each form sets the Visible property of the form to False. The code behind the Cancel button on each form closes the form. Make sure that you name the option groups optPolite and optRude so that the code runs properly for each form. You can place the two entry-point functions, ValidTextPolite and ValidTextRude, in any code module in the library database. The last step involves registering the two builders. The entries in USysRegInfo, shown in Figure 25.20, accomplish the task of registering the builder the first time that the add-in is selected through the Add-ins dialog box. This table is located in CHAP25LIB.MDA.

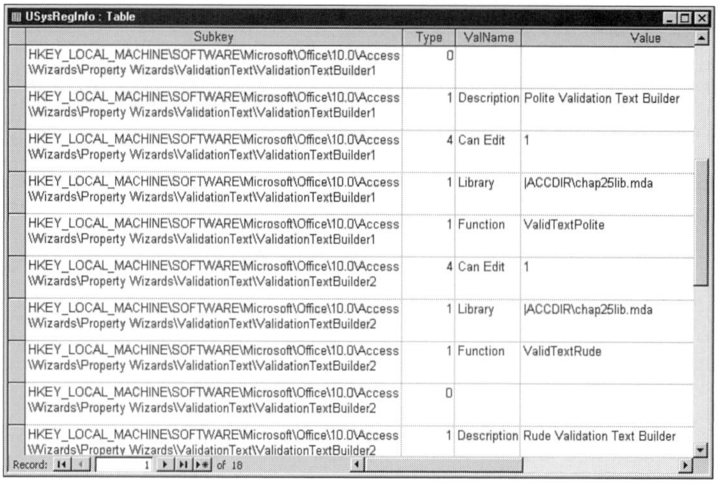

FIGURE 25.20
Registry entries for the polite and rude builders.

Summary

By creating builders, wizards, and add-ins, you can enhance the development environment for yourself and your users. You even can add wizards so that your users can build their own queries, forms, or reports on-the-fly without a full copy of Access. Your wizard simply needs to prompt the user for the appropriate information and then build the objects to his specifications. What you can do with wizards, builders, and add-ins is limited only by your imagination.

An Introduction to Access and the Internet/Intranet

IN THIS CHAPTER

Why This Chapter Is Important

The Internet is part of our everyday lives. The Internet's penetration into the life of an Access developer is no exception. Almost every Access 2002 object can be saved as HTML. Furthermore, Access 2000 introduced a new object type called data access pages. Using data access pages, you can quickly and easily create a Web view of your data. Data access pages are extremely flexible and scalable. The simplest data access page can be created as easily as any Access form. On the other hand, using the Microsoft Script Editor (MSE), you can turn your data access pages into powerful Web pages. Probably the biggest downside of data access pages is that they must be viewed on a machine with Internet Explorer 5 or above, and Microsoft Office installed. This makes data access pages an excellent candidate for intranet applications, but not for Internet applications.

Saving Database Objects as HTML

Probably one of the most basic but powerful features in Access is the capability to save database objects as HTML (HyperText Markup Language) documents. Table data, query results, form datasheets, forms, and reports can all be published as HTML. Each of these objects is covered in the following sections.

Saving Table Data as HTML

When saving table data to HTML, you can store it in the HTML file format so that it can be easily published on the Web. Just follow these steps:

1. Click Tables in the Objects list of the Database window.
2. Click to select the table whose data you want to save as HTML.
3. Choose File|Export to open the Export Table dialog box.
4. Use the Save As Type drop-down list to select HTML documents.
5. Enter a filename and select a location for the HTML document.
6. Click Export to finish the process.

The file is exported to HTML and can be viewed from any Web browser. (See Figure 26.1.) You can also view the HTML source, as shown in Figure 26.2.

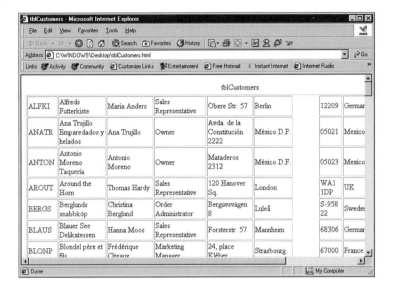

FIGURE 26.1

The tblCustomers table saved as HTML.

FIGURE 26.2

Viewing the source of the tblCustomers table's HMTL file.

Saving Query Results as HTML

The capability to save query results as HTML means you don't need to save all fields and all records to an HTML file. In fact, you can even save the results of Totals queries and other complex queries as HTML. Saving the result of a query as HTML is similar to saving a table as HTML:

1. Click Queries in the Objects list of the Database window.
2. Click to select the query whose results you want to save as HTML.
3. Choose File|Export to open the Export Query dialog box.
4. Use the Save As Type drop-down list to select HTML documents.
5. Enter a filename and select a location for the HTML document.
6. Click Export to finish the process.

Saving Forms as HTML

Only a form's datasheet can be saved as HTML because an HTML file is a static file. It doesn't change as the data in the database changes, nor can the data in the HTML file be modified. To save a form's datasheet as HTML, follow these steps:

1. Click Forms in the Objects list of the Database window.
2. Click to select the form whose results you want to save as HTML.
3. Choose File|Export to open the Export Form dialog box.
4. Use the Save As Type drop-down list to select HTML documents.
5. Select a filename and location for the HTML document.
6. Click Export; this opens the HTML Output Options dialog box.
7. Select an optional HTML template that's applied to the HTML document. By selecting an HTML template, you can easily maintain a consistent look for your Web publications. Select the type of encoding that you wish to use, and click OK.

Saving Reports as HTML

Reports and their formatting can be saved as HTML, too, which is an elegant way to publish data on an Internet or intranet site. To publish a report as HTML, just follow these steps:

1. Click Reports in the Objects list of the Database window.
2. Click to select the report whose results you want to save as HTML.
3. Choose File|Export to open the Save As dialog box.
4. Use the Save As Type drop-down list to select HTML documents.

5. Select a filename and location for the HTML document.

6. Click Export to open the HTML Output Options dialog box.

7. Select an optional HTML template that's applied to the HTML document. Select the type of encoding you wish to use and click OK.

Figure 26.3 shows a report published as HTML. Because the report is a multipage report, several HTML files are generated. Each page of the report is linked, and the user can easily navigate from page to page by using the First, Previous, Next, and Last hyperlinks automatically generated during the export process.

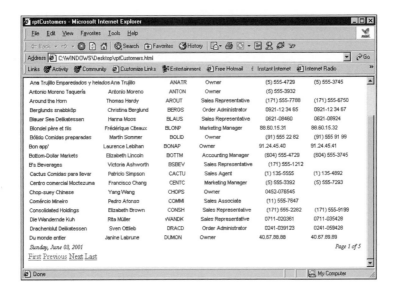

FIGURE 26.3
Viewing the rptCustomersWeb report as HTML.

Linking to HTML Files

Just as you can link to dBASE tables, Paradox tables, or ODBC data sources, you can also link to HTML files by following these steps:

1. Right-click within the Database window and select Link Tables; this opens the Link dialog box.

2. Use the Files of Type drop-down list to select HTML documents.

3. Select the HTML file you want to link to and click Link. The Link HTML Wizard appears. (See Figure 26.4.)

4. In the wizard's first step, indicate whether the first row of data contains column head-ings. You can also see Access's proposed layout for the linked table.

FIGURE 26.4
The first step of the Link HTML Wizard.

5. Click Advanced to designate specifics about the linked table. The Link Specification dia-log box opens. (See Figure 26.5.) Here you can select which fields you want to include in the linked table, date delimiters, and other specifics of the linked file. Make your selections and click OK.

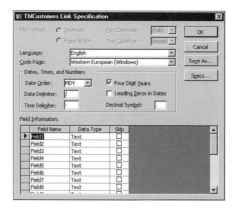

FIGURE 26.5
In the Link Specification dialog box, you designate specifics about the linked table.

6. Click Next to proceed with the Link HTML Wizard. In the next step, you select a field name and data type for each field in the HTML file. Make your selections and click Next.

An Introduction to Access and the Internet/Intranet

CHAPTER 26

1021

26

AN INTRODUCTION
TO ACCESS AND
THE INTERNET

7. In the wizard's last step, you supply a table name for the linked table. Make your selection and click Finish.

8. You then see a message that the table linked successfully. The table appears in the Database window with a special icon indicating that it's an HTML file. (See Figure 26.6.)

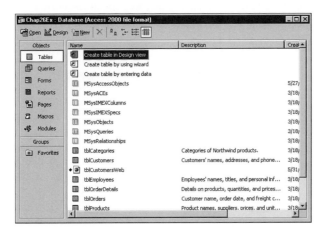

FIGURE 26.6

The Database window with a linked HTML document.

The linked HTML file can be browsed, queried, and reported on just like any other table. However, none of the data in the linked file can be modified.

Importing HTML Files

The data in an HTML file can be imported so that it becomes exactly like any other Access table; follow these steps to import an HTML file:

1. Right-click within the Database window and select Import; this opens the Import dialog box.

2. Use the Files of Type drop-down list to select HTML documents.

3. Select the HTML file you want to import and click Import to open the Import HTML Wizard. This wizard is almost identical to the Link HTML Wizard.

4. In the wizard's first step, you indicate whether the first row of data contains column headings. You can also see Access's proposed layout for the imported table.

5. Click Advanced to designate specifics about the imported table. The Import Specification dialog box opens. Here you can select which fields you want to include in the imported table, date delimiters, and other specifics of the imported file. Make your selections and click OK.

6. Click Next to go to the next step. Here, you have the choice of importing the data into a new table or adding it to an existing table. Make your selection and click Next.

7. In the next step, select a field name and data type for each field in the HTML file. You can also designate whether you want Access to create an index for the field and even whether you want to exclude the field entirely. Make your selections and click Next.

8. Next, the wizard lets you designate a primary key for the imported table. If you prefer, you can have Access supply the primary key. (See Figure 26.7.) Make your selection and click Next.

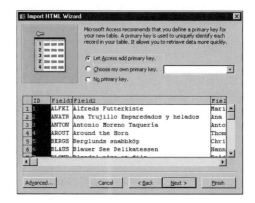

FIGURE 26.7

Designating a primary key for your new table.

9. In the wizard's last step, supply a table name for the linked table. If you're concerned about whether the imported table is normalized, you can have Access launch the Table Analyzer after the import is finished. Make your selections and click Finish.

10. You then see a message that the table imported successfully; it appears in the Database window just as any other Access table does.

Understanding Data Access Pages

Data access pages were introduced with Access 2000. In Access 2000, they were considered version 1 technology and were somewhat challenging to work with. Data access pages have improved significantly in Access 2002. Using data access pages, you can quickly and easily create a Web view of your data. Data access pages are extremely flexible and scalable. The simplest data access page can be created as easily as any Access form. On the other hand, using the Microsoft Script Editor (MSE), you can turn your data access pages into powerful Web pages. Probably the biggest downside of data access pages is that they must be viewed on a machine with Internet Explorer 5, or above, and Microsoft Office Web Components installed. This makes data access pages an excellent candidate for intranet applications, but not for Internet applications.

An Introduction to Access and the Internet/Intranet

CHAPTER 26

1023

26

AN INTRODUCTION
TO ACCESS AND
THE INTERNET

> **TIP**
>
> Data access pages can be run over the Internet or an intranet if the client has IE5/Office Web Components.

Creating Data Access Pages

Data access pages are created in one of the following four ways:

- Using AutoPage
- Using a wizard
- From an existing Web page
- From scratch

Creating a Data Access Page Using the AutoPage Feature

To create a data access page using AutoPage, follow these steps:

1. Click Pages in the list of objects in the Database window.
2. Click the New button in the Database window. The New Data Access Page dialog box appears.
3. Choose the table or query on which the data access page will be based.
4. Select AutoPage: Columnar from the list of options for creating a data access page (see Figure 26.8).

FIGURE 26.8

The New Data Access Page dialog box allows you to select the method you want to use to create a data access page.

5. Click OK. The data access page is created (see Figure 26.9).

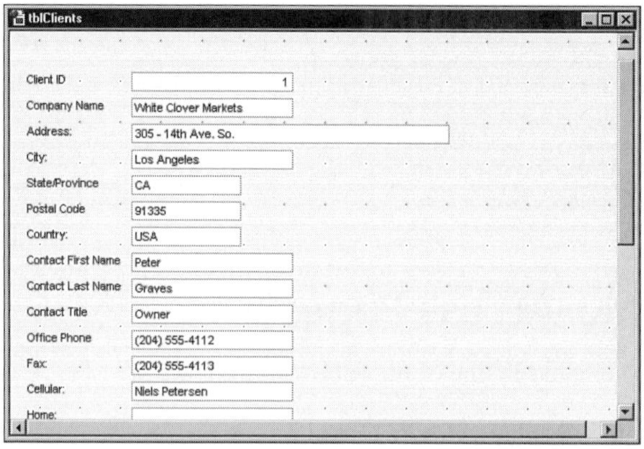

![tblClients data access page]

FIGURE 26.9

A data access page based on the tblClients table using the AutoPage feature.

Creating a Data Access Page Using a Wizard

To create a data access page using a wizard, follow these steps:

1. Click Pages in the list of objects in the Database window.

2. Double-click the Create Data Access Page By Using Wizard option. The Page Wizard appears (see Figure 26.10).

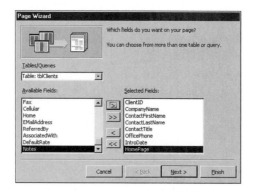

FIGURE 26.10

Selecting the table or query and the fields that you want to include in the data access page.

3. Select the table or query on which you want to base the data access page. In Figure 26.11, the tblClients table is selected.

4 Select the fields that you want to appear on the data access page. In Figure 26.11 the ClientID, CompanyName, ContactFirstName, ContactLastName, ContactTitle, OfficePhone, IntroDate, and HomePage fields are selected. Click Next to continue.

5. Add any desired grouping levels to the page (see Figure 26.11). In Access 2000, the created page was rendered not editable when grouping was applied. Fortunately, this is no longer the case in Access 2002! Click Next to continue.

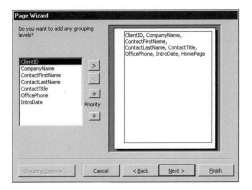

FIGURE 26.11
Adding grouping levels to a data access page.

6. Select a sort order for the records included on the page (see Figure 26.12). In the figure, the page is sorted by the ContactLastName field combined with the ContactFirstName field. Click Next to continue.

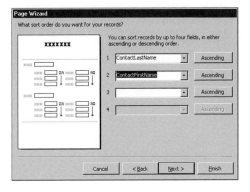

FIGURE 26.12
Selecting a sort order for the records on a page.

7. The last page of the wizard asks you for a title for the page. You can also opt to apply a theme to the page. Enter the title, select whether you want to apply a theme, and then designate whether you want to open the page or modify the page's design. Click Finish to complete the process. If you clicked the check box to apply a theme to the page, the Theme dialog box appears (see Figure 26.13). Select a theme and click OK. Figure 26.14 shows the completed page in Design view. Figure 26.15 shows the completed page in Page view.

FIGURE 26.13

The Theme dialog box allows you to apply a theme to the page.

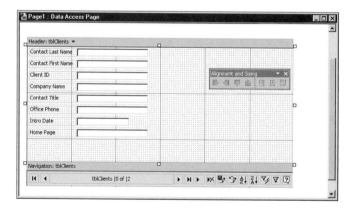

FIGURE 26.14

A completed data access page in Design view.

An Introduction to Access and the Internet/Intranet

CHAPTER 26

1027

26

AN INTRODUCTION
TO ACCESS AND
THE INTERNET

FIGURE 26.15

A completed data access page in Page view.

Data access pages are *not* stored in your database file or project. Instead, data access pages are saved as HTML files. To save a data access page, follow these steps:

1. Click Save on the toolbar. The Save as Data Access Page dialog box appears. (See Figure 26.16.)

FIGURE 26.16

The Save as Data Access Page dialog box allows you to select a name and location for the saved HTML document.

2. Enter the name of the HTML document. In the figure, the name is entered as dapClients. Click Save.

3. A dialog box appears, suggesting that the connection string should point to a UNC path. Doing so ensures that the data behind the page is available over the network.

Although the data access page is saved as a separate document, it appears in the Database window (see Figure 26.17). Notice in the figure that a ToolTip appears, indicating the name and location of the saved HTML document. When the data access page is opened from within Microsoft Access, it appears as a window within the Access environment. To view the page as it will appear in a browser, right-click the page in the Database window and select Web Page Preview.

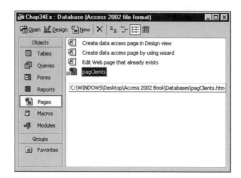

FIGURE 26.17

A completed data access page appears as an object in the Database window.

Creating a Data Access Page from an Existing Web Page

You might already have an HTML document that you have created. Fortunately, Access 2002 allows you to base a new data access page on an existing HTML document. To create a data access page from an existing Web page, follow these steps:

1. Click Pages in the list of objects in the Database window.
2. Double-click the Edit Web Page That Already Exists wizard option. The Locate Web Page dialog box appears (see Figure 26.18).

FIGURE 26.18

The Locate Web Page dialog box allows you to open an existing HTML document for editing within the Access Environment.

3. Select an existing HTML document and click Open. You can now edit the page right within the Microsoft Access environment.

Creating a Data Access Page from Scratch

Although the Data Access Page Wizard is very powerful, there are times when you will want to build a data access page from scratch. To do this, follow these steps:

1. Click Pages in the list of objects in the Database window.

2. Double-click the `Create Data Access Page In Design View` option. A blank data access page appears (see Figure 26.19).

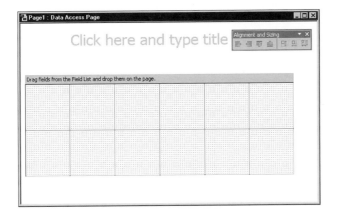

FIGURE 26.19

When the Create Data Access Page in Design View option is used, a blank data access page appears.

3. Add controls to the data access page and set their properties.

You might wonder how to associate a table from your database with a data access page that you build from scratch. The process differs somewhat from the process of associating a form with data. The process is as follows:

1. Click the Field List tool on the toolbar. The Field List window appears (see Figure 26.20).

2. Notice that the Field List window shows two expandable lists: one with the tables in the database, and the other with the queries in the database. (See Figure 26.21.)

3. To add all fields from an existing table or query to the data access page, drag an entire table or query from the field list to the data access page.

FIGURE 26.20
The Field List window allows you to easily add table and query fields to your data access pages.

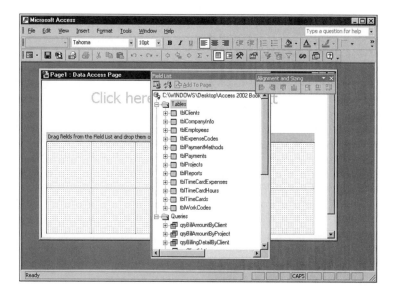

FIGURE 26.21
The expanded Field List window shows you all the tables and queries within the current database.

4. To add specific fields from a table or query to the data access page, expand the field list to display the desired table or query, and then drag and drop individual fields to the data access page. In Figure 26.22, selected fields have been added from the tblEmployee table to the data access page.

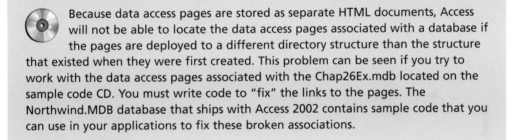

FIGURE 26.22

A data access page containing selected fields from the tblEmployees table.

NOTE

Because data access pages are stored as separate HTML documents, Access will not be able to locate the data access pages associated with a database if the pages are deployed to a different directory structure than the structure that existed when they were first created. This problem can be seen if you try to work with the data access pages associated with the Chap26Ex.mdb located on the sample code CD. You must write code to "fix" the links to the pages. The Northwind.MDB database that ships with Access 2002 contains sample code that you can use in your applications to fix these broken associations.

Modifying Important Properties of a Data Access Page

Just as a form or report has properties, so does a data access page. Many of the properties are similar to those of forms and reports. The most important properties are discussed in this section.

To modify the properties of a data access page, you must first make sure that the page is selected. The easiest way to select the page is to click its title bar. Among the most important properties of a data access page are its Data properties. These appear in Figure 26.23, and the most important properties are discussed here.

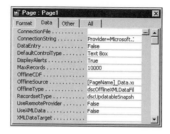

FIGURE 26.23

The Data properties of a data access page allow you to control the behavior of the data underlying the data access page.

The ConnectionFile Property

The ConnectionFile property designates the name of the Office Database Connection (.odc) file or the Microsoft Data Link (.udl) file that connects a data access page to its data source. Using an ODC or UDL file, you can easily modify the source of the data underlying a data access page without having to make changes to the page itself.

To enter the ConnectionFile property, click the ellipsis within the property. The Select Data Source dialog box appears. (See Figure 26.24.) Here you can select an existing ODC or UDL file, or create a new file.

FIGURE 26.24

The Select Data Source dialog box allows you to select an existing ODC or UDL file, or to create a new one.

1. Click New Source to create a new ODC file. The Data Connection Wizard launches. (See Figure 26.25.)

FIGURE 26.25
The Data Connection Wizard walks you through the steps to create an ODC file.

2. Select Microsoft SQL Server to connect to a SQL Server database, or select Other/Advanced to connect to another type of data. Click Next.

3. The dialog box that appears varies based upon the type of data you selected in the previous step. If you want the page to connect to data in a Microsoft Access database, select Other/Advanced. The Data Link Properties dialog box, shown in Figure 26.26, appears.

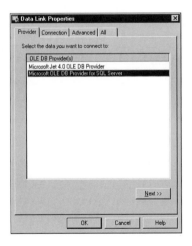

FIGURE 26.26
The Data Link Properties dialog box allows you to choose a data provider.

4. Select Microsoft Jet 4.0 OLEDB Provider and click Next. The wizard prompts you for the database name.

5. Enter the database name and click Test Connection. Click OK to close the Data Link Properties dialog box. The wizard shows you the tables and queries located in the selected database (see Figure 26.27). Click Next.

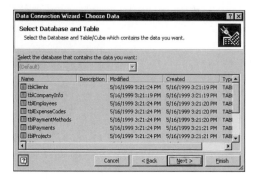

FIGURE 26.27

The Data Connection Wizard connects to the database and shows you all tables and queries contained in the database.

6. Enter a name and an optional file description for the ODC file (see Figure 26.28). Click Finish.

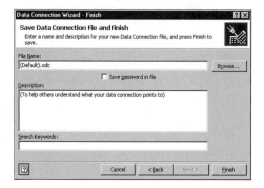

FIGURE 26.28

The Data Connection Wizard prompts you to name the ODC file. You can also enter a description to assist people when selecting an existing ODC file.

7. Select the newly created ODC file in the Select Data Source dialog box. The name and location of the ODC file is entered into the ConnectionFile property.

The ConnectionString Property

The ConnectionString property sets an ADO connection string to be used to connect to a database. The string contains all information required to connect to the data source underlying the page.

An Introduction to Access and the Internet/Intranet

CHAPTER 26

1035

26

AN INTRODUCTION
TO ACCESS AND
THE INTERNET

The DataEntry Property

Another important property is the DataEntry property. By default, the DataEntry property is `False`. This means that, when the data access page is viewed from within Microsoft Access or within a browser, all records in the underlying data source are available. When changed to `True`, records can be added, but existing data cannot be seen (see Figure 26.29).

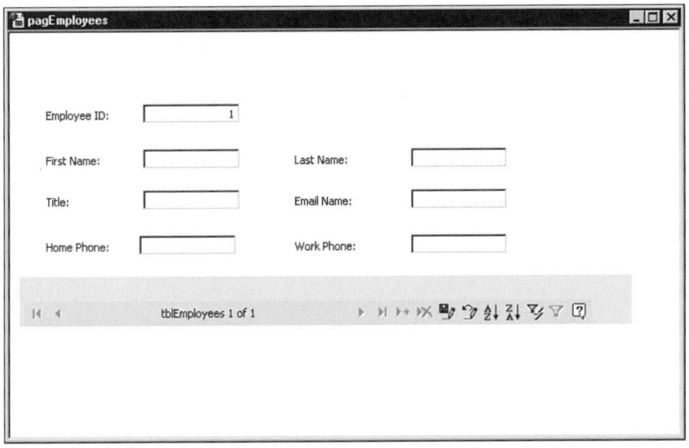

FIGURE 26.29
The DataEntry property allows you to specify whether existing records are available.

The MaxRecords Property

The MaxRecords property allows you to designate the number of records that a connection sends to the local computer. If this property is not set properly, extremely large volumes of data can travel over the Internet or over an intranet to the user's browser. This can cause severe performance problems. It is therefore a good idea to set this number to the maximum number of records that you feel are appropriate for a user to retrieve.

The RecordsetType Property

The RecordsetType property can be set to `dscUpdatableSnapshot` or to `dscSnapshot`. With `dscUpdatableSnapshot` the data in the resulting data access page can be edited. If you select `dscSnapshot`, the data is rendered view-only.

The UseRemoteProvider Property

The UseRemoteProvider property determines whether the data source control uses the Microsoft Remote Data Services provider for data connections. This property can be set to `True` only for pages that are read from a Microsoft Internet Information Server (IIS) using an

HTTP or HTTPS (secure) address. When used, the Microsoft Remote Data Services provider fetches data by passing the HTTP or HTTPS request to Microsoft Internet Information Server. IIS makes the OLE DB connection to the database.

Modifying the Record Navigation Control Properties

By default, the record navigation control on a data access page allows you to perform the following tasks:

- Moving to the next, previous, first, and last record
- Moving to a new record
- Deleting an existing record
- Saving changes to a record
- Cancelling changes made to a record
- Sorting in ascending or descending order
- Filtering data shown on the data access page

There are times when it is not appropriate for all these features to be available. To customize the properties of the record navigation control, you must first select it. To do this, click the control while in Design view of the page.

The RecordSource Property

Probably the most important property of a record navigation control is its RecordSource property, which is located on the Data tab of the Properties window. It is used to designate the table or query that underlies the data access page.

First, Previous, Next, and Last Buttons

You can easily add and remove buttons from the Navigation control. Simply right-click the control and select Navigation Buttons. A fly-out menu appears. (See Figure 32.30.) The First, Previous, Next, and Last options allow you to designate whether the First, Previous, Next, and Last buttons appear on the record navigation control. Selecting the availability of these buttons determines how the user can move through records included in the data access page. You can determine the availability of each button individually. For example, you can opt to include the Previous and Next buttons, but not the First and Last buttons.

An Introduction to Access and the Internet/Intranet

CHAPTER 26

1037

26

AN INTRODUCTION
TO ACCESS AND
THE INTERNET

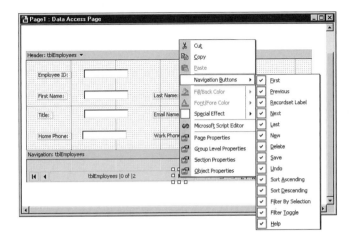

FIGURE 26.30
The Navigation menu allows you to customize the functionality of the Navigation control.

The New Button

Selecting or deselecting the New option allows you to determine whether the new button appears on the record navigation control. If included, the user clicks this button to add a new record to the data underlying the data access page. If excluded, unless you provide your own custom add button, the user is unable to add new records from within the data access page.

The Delete Button

Selecting or deselecting the Delete option allows you to determine whether the Delete button appears on the record navigation control. If included, the user clicks this button to delete the current record. If excluded, unless you provide your own custom delete button, the user is unable to delete records from within the data access page.

The Save Button

Selecting or deselecting the Save option allows you to determine whether the Save button appears on the record navigation control. If included, the user clicks this button to commit changes made to the controls on the data access page. If excluded, the user can save data by moving to another record after making her changes.

The Undo Button

Selecting or deselecting the Undo option allows you to determine whether the Undo button appears on the record navigation control. If included, the user clicks this button to undo changes made to the current record. If excluded, the user can still undo changes to a record using his Escape key.

The Sort Ascending and Sort Descending Buttons

Selecting or deselecting the Sort Ascending and Sort Descending options allows you to determine whether the Sort Ascending and Sort Descending buttons appear on the record navigation control. If included, the user clicks within the field that she wants to sort on and then clicks the appropriate button to sort in ascending or descending order. The data sorts by the field that the user selected. If excluded, the user is unable to sort the data contained within the data access page.

The ShowToggleFilterButton Button

Selecting or deselecting the Filter By Selection and Filter Toggle options allow you to determine whether each of these filter-related buttons appears on the record navigation control. To use the Filter By Selection button, the user clicks within the field he wants to filter on and then clicks the Filter By Selection tool. The data underlying the data access page is filtered based on the contents of the current field for the current record. For example, in Figure 26.31, the data is filtered so that just the system analysts appear. The Filter Toggle button is used to remove the selected filter. If the Filter By Selection button is excluded from the record navigation control, the user is unable to filter the data underlying the data access page (unless you provide this functionality via a custom command button).

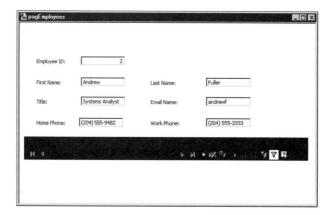

FIGURE 26.31

The Filter By Selection *option allows you to filter the data shown in the data access page.*

An Introduction to Access and the Internet/Intranet

CHAPTER 26

1039

26

AN INTRODUCTION
TO ACCESS AND
THE INTERNET

Creating Grouped Data Access Pages

Grouping records on a data access page is similar to grouping records on a report. Grouped data access pages have the following advantages over grouped reports:

- Current data is always displayed within the data access page.
- Unlike reports, data access pages are interactive. This means that, using a grouped data access page, a user can filter, sort, and view just the records she wants.
- When grouped data access pages are sent via e-mail, the recipient is presented with current data each time he opens the message.

To create a grouped data access page, follow these steps:

1. Click Pages in the list of objects in the Database window.
2. Double-click the Create Data Access Page by Using Wizard option. The Page Wizard appears.
3. Select the table or query on which you want to group the data (the "one" side).
4. Select the fields from the first table or query that you want to appear on the data access page.
5. Select the table or query on which you want to base the "many" side of the data access page.
6. Select the fields from the second table or query that you want to appear on the data access page. In Figure 26.32, the ProjectName field is selected from the tblProjects table (the one side of the relationship). The DateWorked, BillableHours, and BillingRate fields are selected from the tblTimeCardHours table. Click Next to continue.

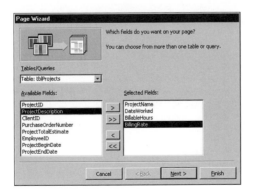

FIGURE 26.32
To create a grouped data access page, first select fields from multiple tables.

7. Select the fields you want to group by. In Figure 26.33, the data is grouped by the ProjectName field. Click Next.

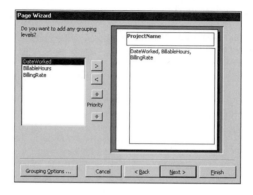

FIGURE 26.33

The data access Page Wizard allows you to designate the fields in which the data is grouped.

8. Select how you want the data to be sorted within the grouping. Click Next.

9. Enter the title for the page and click Finish.

The resulting page appears in Figure 26.34. As you can see, the data automatically appears collapsed. Furthermore, only one project name (the one side of the relationship) appears at a time. Finally, because the data is derived from multiple tables, the resulting data access page is not editable. Fortunately, all these aspects of a grouped data access page are easily modified via properties of the group.

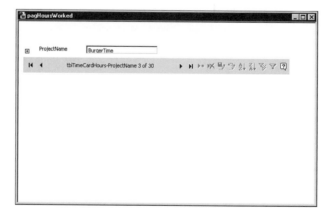

FIGURE 26.34

A grouped data access page shows the data collapsed while displaying only one group at a time.

An Introduction to Access and the Internet/Intranet

CHAPTER 26

1041

26

AN INTRODUCTION
TO ACCESS AND
THE INTERNET

To access the properties of a group, you must right-click the group and select Group-Level properties. The properties of the group are shown in Figure 26.35. When the ExpandedByDefault property is set to Yes, it automatically displays the data within a grouping (see Figure 26.36). The DataPageSize property allows you to designate the maximum number of records to show at a time for a particular grouping level. In Figure 26.37, the DataPageSize property of the second-level grouping is set to 3. This means that up to three detail records appear within each grouping level.

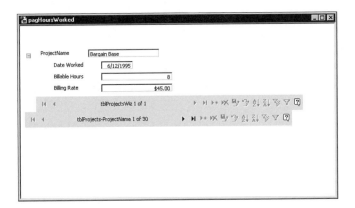

FIGURE 26.35

Using the properties of a group, you can control group attributes.

FIGURE 26.36

The Expanded-By-Default property of a group allows you to designate whether data at a group level automatically appears in an expanded format.

The Unique Table property designates the editable table in a page based on multiple tables. The property is found in the Header properties for the detail section of the page. Enter the name of the table whose data you want to edit. In Figure 26.38, the tblTimeCardHours table is designated as the unique table.

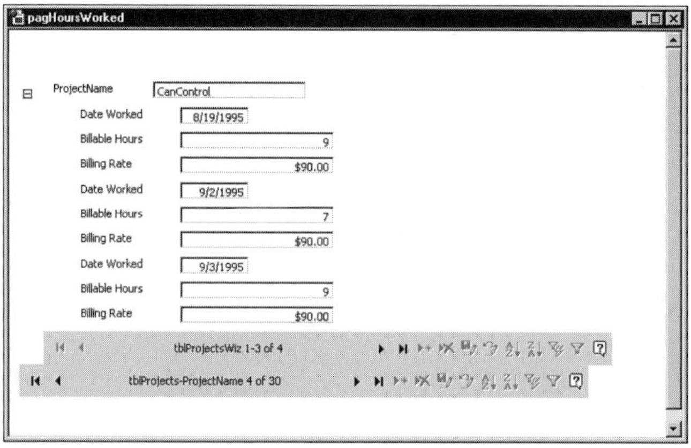

FIGURE 26.37

The DataPageSize property of a group allows you to designate the maximum number of detail records that appear at a time within a particular group.

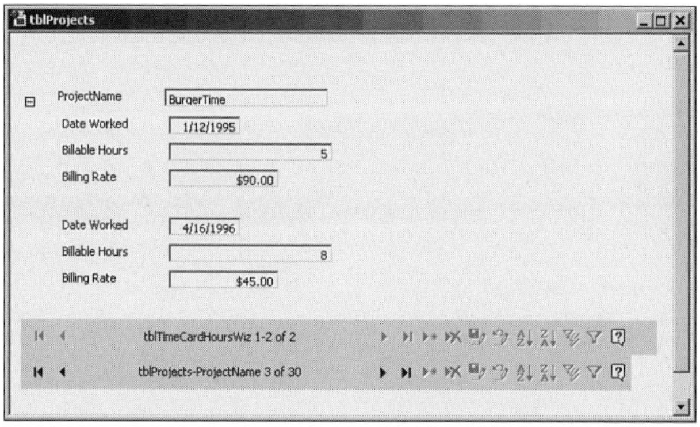

FIGURE 26.38

To render data in a page based on multiple tables as editable, you must designate a unique table.

Augmenting Data Access Pages with VBScript

One of the powers of data access pages is in the ability to customize them beyond what the data access page designer allows. The Microsoft Script Editor (MSE) allows you to create scripts that extend the functionality of your data access pages. Using the MSE, you create scripts behind the events of objects on the data access page.

An Introduction to Access and the Internet/Intranet

CHAPTER 26

1043

26

AN INTRODUCTION
TO ACCESS AND
THE INTERNET

To open the MSE and create script behind a data access page, follow these steps:

1. Create a data access page.
2. Use the Toolbox tool on the toolbar to display the toolbox. (See Figure 26.39.)

FIGURE 26.39
Using the Toolbox, you can add controls to your data access page.

3. Add a control, such as a command button, to the data access page. Use the ID property to rename the control, if desired.
4. Right-click the control and select Microsoft Script Editor. The Microsoft Development Environment (MDE) appears. (See Figure 26.40.) If you did not install Web Scripting when you installed Microsoft Access, you will need to install it for this feature to be available.

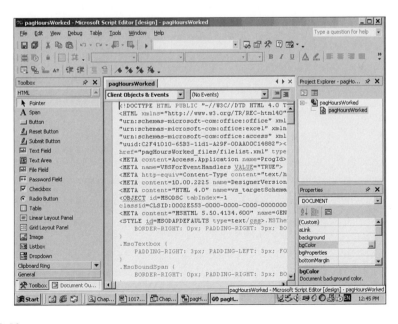

FIGURE 26.40
The Microsoft Script Editor allows you to write code in response to events generated within your data access pages.

5. Activate the HTML window. (See Figure 26.40.)

6. Use the object drop-down on the left of the HTML window to locate the object that you just added.

7. Use the event drop-down on the right of the HTML window to designate the event that you wish to write code for. A script block is created with a stub for the object and event. In Figure 26.41, a script block is inserted for the `onclick` event of the command button called cmdSayHello.

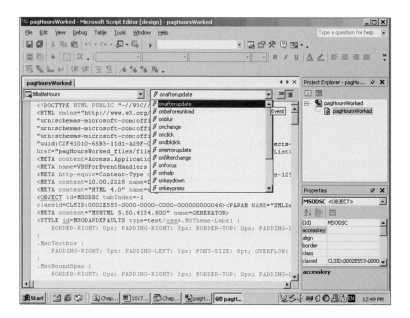

FIGURE 26.41

The HTML window allows you to select an object and an event associated with the object.

8. Write code that executes in response to the event. In Figure 26.42, the `MsgBox` statement is used to display the message `"Hello"` when someone clicks the cmdSayHello command button.

An Introduction to Access and the Internet/Intranet

CHAPTER 26

1045

26

AN INTRODUCTION
TO ACCESS AND
THE INTERNET

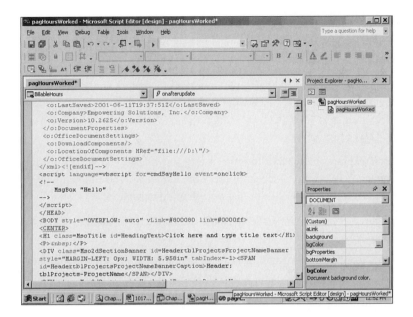

FIGURE 26.42

VBScript code that displays the message `"Hello"` *when the* `onclick` *event of the cmdSayHello command button occurs.*

Important Data Access Page Events

As you have seen, scripts included for data access pages are written in event handlers attached to objects on a page. As in an Access form, an event handler (or event routine) is a subroutine or function that is automatically triggered in response to something happening to an object. Some important events that you can code at the document (page) level include the following:

- The `OnRowEnter` event of the `Document` object fires after the current record changes but before fields are populated for the new record.

- The `OnRowExit` event of the `Document` object occurs before the current record changes. This event is commonly used to perform record-level validations.

- The `BeforeCollapse` event of a section occurs before the section is collapsed.

- The `BeforeExpand` event of a section occurs before a section is expanded.

- The `BeforeNextPage`, `BeforePreviousPage`, `BeforeFirstPage`, and `BeforeLastPage` events of the page navigation control occur before the navigation control navigates to the next, previous, first, and last pages, respectively. All these events can be canceled by setting the `info.return` value of the event to `False`.

- The Current event fires after a section becomes the current section.
- The DataPageComplete event fires when all data binding is completed after a page open, navigation, or expansion.

As with the events of a form or a report, it is important to explore and learn about the events of a page so that you know where to place your code.

VBScript Versus VBA

Because Internet Explorer 5.0 cannot interpret VBA, scripts that you write must be in the VBScript language. VBScript is a subset of the VBA language. The following are important differences between VBA and VBScript that you should be aware of:

- All variables are variants in VBScript. This means that Dim statements in VBScript cannot include types.
- Arguments (parameters) to subroutines and functions in VBScript cannot have types.
- Many built-in functions available in VBA are not available in VBScript.
- Intrinsic constants such as vbYesNo are not available in VBScript. If you want to include constants in your code, you will have to declare them yourself.

VBScript Versus JavaScript

Scripts that you write behind your data access pages can be written in either VBScript or in JavaScript. If you are accustomed to writing VBA code, you will probably find VBScript much easier to learn than JavaScript. On the other hand, if you are experienced at developing Web pages using JavaScript, you will probably want to continue writing your scripts in JavaScript. The following are some important differences between VBScript and JavaScript:

- VBScript is better supported by the data access page object model. This means that certain page events are not recognized if coded in JavaScript.
- JavaScript is case-sensitive, making it more difficult to write than VBScript.

Summary

It's easy to integrate Access with the Internet or with an intranet. Access enables you to easily publish database objects to the Web and import HTML data from the Web. In fact, you can even create dynamic Web pages and build forms that display and update live data directly from a browser! Access 2002 helps bring your data to the continually evolving information super-highway—the possibilities are endless!

Adding Polish to Your Application

IN THIS PART

Database Security Made Easy

IN THIS CHAPTER

Why This Chapter Is Important

After you design and develop a sophisticated application, you should ensure that the integrity of the application and the data it maintains are not violated. Microsoft Access gives you several options for securing your database. These options range from a very simple method of applying a password to the entire database, to applying varying levels of security to each and every object in the database. The more intricate your security solution, the more difficult it is to implement. Fortunately, you can tailor the complexity of the security you implement to the level of security required by each particular application.

Implementing Share-Level Security: Establishing a Database Password

The simplest, yet least sophisticated, method of implementing security is to assign a password to the overall database. This means that every person who wants to gain access to the database must enter the same password. After a user gains access to the database, all the database's objects are available to that user. This type of security is referred to as *share-level security*.

Share-level security is the simplest and quickest security to set up. With almost no effort, the database and its objects are secured. This method of security is quite adequate for a small business in which the administrators of the database want to ensure that no unauthorized people can access the data, but that each authorized person has full access to all its objects.

To assign a database password, follow these steps:

1. Open the database to which you want to assign a password by selecting Open Exclusive from the Open drop-down of the Open dialog.

2. Choose Tools|Security|Set Database Password. The Set Database Password dialog box appears, as shown in Figure 27.1.

3. Type and verify the password and click OK. The password is case sensitive.

FIGURE 27.1

The Set Database Password dialog box.

After you assign a password to a database, users are prompted for a password each time they open the database. The Password Required dialog box appears each time the database is opened, as Figure 27.2 shows.

FIGURE 27.2

The Password Required dialog box.

After users enter a valid password, they gain access to the database and all its objects. In fact, users even can remove the password by choosing Tools|Security|Unset Database Password. The Unset Database Password dialog box only requires that users know the original password. (See Figure 27.3.)

FIGURE 27.3

The Unset Database Password dialog box.

Although these passwords are extremely easy to understand and implement, they also are extremely unsophisticated. As you can see, users either have or do not have access to the database, and it is very easy for any user who has access to the database to modify or unset its password.

> ## CAUTION
>
> If you forget the password associated with a database, it is not easy to gain access to the database and its objects. It therefore is extremely important that you carefully maintain a list of the passwords associated with each database. On the other hand, it is not impossible to break the security set on an Access database. In fact, there are Web sites that will remove Access database security for a fee! This means that, if security is of the utmost importance to you or your users, Access database security might not be the appropriate solution for you. To ensure that your data is secure, you can store it in a Microsoft SQL Server database. A client/server database such as Microsoft SQL Server offers you a much more robust security model than that available with the MDB file format.

> **Note**
>
> To assign a password to a database, users must be able to open the database exclusively. You can grant or deny users the right to open a database exclusively by using the User and Group Permissions dialog box. Assigning rights that permit or deny users or groups exclusive open rights is covered in the "Step 11: Assigning Rights to Users and Groups" section of this chapter.

Encrypting a Database

Before moving on to the more sophisticated methods of securing a database, it is important that you understand what any method of security does and does not provide for you. No matter how well you learn about and implement the techniques in this chapter, you will not be protected against someone attempting to read the data contained in your database. Even after you secure a database, someone with a disk editor can view the contents of the file. Although the data in the file will not appear in an easy-to-read format, the data is there and available for unauthorized individuals to see.

You might be feeling discouraged and asking yourself, "Why bother with security?" Do not despair! Fortunately, Access enables you to encrypt a database, rendering the data in the database indecipherable in word processors, disk utilities, and other products capable of reading text. When a database is encrypted, it is much more difficult to decipher any of its data.

A database can be encrypted using the standard Access menus or by writing a VBA subroutine. In either case, the database you are encrypting must not be open. To encrypt a database using Access's standard menus, follow these steps:

1. Choose Tools | Security | Encrypt/Decrypt Database.
2. The Encrypt/Decrypt Database dialog appears. Select the file you want to encrypt and click OK.
3. You are prompted for the name of the encrypted database. If you select the same name as the existing file, Access deletes the original decrypted file after it determines that the encryption process is successful.

> **Note**
>
> You cannot encrypt a database to itself if it is open. You must first close the database and then select Tools | Security | Encrypt/Decrypt Database.

NOTE

It is always a good idea to back up the original database before you begin the encryption process. This ensures that if something goes awry during the encryption process, you won't lose your data.

NOTE

You also can encrypt or decrypt a database file by using code. This is covered in Chapter 28, "Advanced Security Techniques."

When you encrypt a database, the entire database (not just the data) is encrypted. As you access the data and the objects in the database, Access needs to decrypt the objects so that users can use them. When users are finished accessing the objects, Access then encrypts them again. Regardless of the method of encryption you use, the encrypted database degrades performance by about 15%. Furthermore, encrypted databases usually cannot be compressed by most disk-compression software utilities because compression software usually relies on repeated patterns of data. The encryption process is so effective at removing any patterns that it renders most compression utilities ineffective. You need to decide whether this decrease in performance and the inability to compress the database file is worth the extra security that encryption provides.

Establishing User-Level Security

For most business environments, share-level security is not sufficient. Therefore, it is necessary to take a more sophisticated approach toward securing the objects in your database. User-level security enables you to grant specific rights to users and groups in a workgroup. This means that each user or group can have different permissions on the same object. With this method of security, each user begins by entering a username and password. The Jet Engine validates the username and password and determines the permissions associated with the user. Each user maintains his or her own password, which is unrelated to the passwords of the other users.

In this method of security, users belong to groups. You can assign rights at the group level, the user level, or both. Users inherit the rights of their least restrictive group. This is highlighted by the fact that security is always on. By default, all users get rights to all objects because every user is a member of the group called Users. By default, this group is given all rights to all objects. If you have not implemented security, all users are logged on as the Admin user, who is a member of the Users group and the all-powerful Admins group. The Jet Engine determines that the Admin user has no password and therefore does not display an opening logon screen. Because members of the Users and Admins groups get rights to all objects by default, it appears as though no security is in place.

With user-level security, you easily can customize and refine the rights to different objects. One set of users might be able to view, modify, add, and remove employee records, for example. Another set of users might be able to only view employee information. The last group of users might be allowed no access to the employee information, or they might be allowed access only to specific fields (such as name and address). The Access security model easily accommodates this type of scenario.

The major steps to implementing user-level security follow (each step is developed in detail later in the chapter):

1. Use the Workgroup Administrator to establish a new system database.
2. Start Access and change the Admin user's password to a non-Null password.
3. Create a new user who will be the administrator of the database.
4. Make the user a member of the Admins group.
5. Exit and restart Access, logging on as the new system administrator.
6. Remove the Admin user from the Admins group.
7. Assign a password to the new system administrator.
8. Open the database you want to secure.
9. Run the Security Wizard.
10. Create users and groups consisting of members of the workgroup defined by the system database.
11. Assign rights to users and groups for individual objects.

NOTE

Many of the steps previously outlined can be accomplished using the User-Level Security Wizard. Although the Security Wizard is a powerful tool, it does not provide the same level of flexibility afforded to you when you perform the steps yourself. In this chapter, I therefore focus on performing the steps without the Security Wizard and then cover it in detail in the section "Step 9: Running the Security Wizard." Throughout the chapter, I designate which steps the Security Wizard performs.

Step 1: Creating a Workgroup

The first step to establishing user-level security involves setting up a workgroup. Then you can define groups and users who belong to that workgroup and assign rights to those groups and users. Groups and users are defined only in the context of a specific workgroup. Think of a workgroup as a group of users in a multiuser environment who share data and applications.

When you establish a new workgroup, Access creates a *workgroup information file.* The workgroup information file contains tables that keep track of

- The name of each user and group
- The list of users who make up each group
- The encrypted logon password for each user who is defined as part of the workgroup
- Each user's and group's unique *security identifiers* (SIDs)

A SID is a machine-generated binary string that uniquely identifies each user or group. The system database contains the names and SIDs of the groups and users who are members of that particular workgroup and, therefore, share a system database.

All application databases can share the same workgroup file, or you can maintain separate workgroup files for different application databases.

Understanding the Workgroup: The System.mdw File

The default name for the workgroup information file is System.mdw. Each application database is associated with a specific workgroup information file. This combination of the information stored in the workgroup information file and the information stored in the database grants or denies individual users access to the database or to the objects in it. Multiple databases can share the same workgroup information file.

You can create many workgroup information files. The name of the workgroup information file currently being used is stored in the Windows registry. You can view it under HKEY_CURRENT_USER in the key called \HKEY_ Software\Microsoft\Office\10.0\Access\Jet\4.0\Engines\. (See Figure 27.4.)

27

DATABASE SECURITY MADE EASY

TIP

You can access the Windows registry using the RegEdit utility. Select the Run option from the Start menu, and then type **RegEdit**.

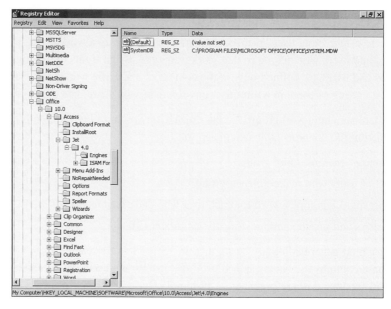

FIGURE 27.4

Viewing the current system information file in the Windows registry.

Establishing a Workgroup

One way to establish a new workgroup is to use the Workgroup Administrator. Prior to Access 2002, the Workgroup Administrator was a separate program that you executed outside Microsoft Access. With Access 2002, the Workgroup Administrator is finally integrated into the product. To launch the Workgroup Administrator, select Tools|Security|Workgroup Administrator.

The Workgroup Administrator dialog box is shown in Figure 27.5.

FIGURE 27.5

The Workgroup Administrator dialog box.

From the Workgroup Administrator dialog box, you can create a new workgroup or you can join one of the existing workgroups. If you click Create, you see the Workgroup Owner Information dialog box shown in Figure 27.6.

FIGURE 27.6

The Workgroup Owner Information dialog box.

In the Workgroup Owner Information dialog box, you can enter a name, an organization, and a case-sensitive workgroup ID that will uniquely identify the workgroup to the system. If you do not establish a unique workgroup ID, your database is not secure. As you will see, anyone can find out your name and organization. If you do not establish a workgroup ID, anyone can create a new system information file with your name and company, rendering any security that you implement totally futile.

It is important that you record and store all workgroup information in a very safe place so that you can re-create it in an emergency. After entering the workgroup owner information, click OK. The Workgroup Information File dialog box appears, prompting you for the name and location of the workgroup information file, as shown in Figure 27.7.

FIGURE 27.7

The Workgroup Information File dialog box.

After you type the name of a new workgroup file and click OK, you are asked to confirm the information, as shown in Figure 27.8. You are given one final opportunity to change any information. Click OK to confirm the information. Next, you are notified that the workgroup has been created successfully. You then can click Exit to close the Workgroup Administrator.

You can use the Security Wizard, covered later in this chapter, to create a new workgroup information file. The Security Wizard prompts you for the information necessary to create the workgroup information file. It doesn't matter whether you opt to create a workgroup information file using the Workgroup Administrator, or with the Security Wizard, the results will be the same.

FIGURE 27.8

The Confirm Workgroup Information dialog box.

Joining a Different Workgroup

If different groups of users in your organization work with entirely different applications, you might find it appropriate to create multiple workgroup information files. In order to access a database that has been secured properly with a specific workgroup information file, the database must be accessed while the user is a member of that workgroup. If the same user requires access to more than one database, each associated with a different workgroup information file, it might be necessary for the user to join a different workgroup. This can be accomplished by using the Workgroup Administrator or by using a desktop shortcut that associates a specific database with a workgroup file. Desktop shortcuts are covered in Chapter 32, "Distributing Your Application." To join a different workgroup using the Workgroup Administrator, follow these steps:

1. Launch the Workgroup Administrator.

2. Click the Join button. The Workgroup Information File dialog box appears.

3. Locate the name of the workgroup file you want to join. You can click the Browse button to help you locate the workgroup file.

4. Click OK. You are notified that you successfully joined the workgroup, as Figure 27.9 shows.

5. Click OK to close the Workgroup Administrator.

FIGURE 27.9

Confirmation that a workgroup was joined successfully.

Step 2: Changing the Password for the Admin User

After creating a new workgroup, you are ready to change the logon for the workgroup by adding a password for the Admin user. This is necessary so that Access will prompt you with a Logon dialog box when you launch the product. If Admin has no password, the Logon dialog box never appears, and you will never be able to log on as yourself.

To change the password for the Admin user, launch Access and select Tools|Security|User and Group Accounts. The User and Group Accounts dialog appears. It does not matter what database you are in when you do this. In fact, you do not need to have any database open because the password that you are creating applies to the workgroup information file rather than to a database.

The User and Group Accounts dialog box enables you to create and delete users and assign their group memberships. It also enables you to create and delete groups and invoke a logon password for Microsoft Access.

CAUTION

It is important to understand that, even if you access this dialog box from a specific database, you are setting up users and groups for the entire workgroup. This means that, if you assign a password while you are a member of the standard SYSTEM.MDW workgroup, and others on your network share the same system workgroup file, everyone on your network is prompted with a logon dialog box when they attempt to launch Microsoft Access. If you do not want this to occur, you must create a new system workgroup file before establishing security.

When you are sure that you are a member of the correct workgroup and are viewing the User and Group Accounts dialog box, you are ready to assign a password to the Admin user. Click the Change Logon Password tab of the User and Group Accounts dialog box to select it, as shown in Figure 27.10.

Assign a new password and verify it. (There is no old password unless you think of the old password as blank.) Then click Apply to establish a password for the Admin user. You are now ready to create a new user who will administrate the database.

If you choose to use the Security Wizard to secure your database, it changes the password for the Admin user. This ensures that the Logon dialog appears when the workgroup file created by the Security Wizard is used.

FIGURE 27.10

The Change Logon Password tab of the User and Group Accounts dialog box.

Step 3: Creating an Administrative User

After you assign a password to Admin, you are ready to create a new administrative user. You accomplish this from within the User and Group Accounts dialog. Access comes with two pre-defined groups: the Admins group and the Users group. The Admins group is the System Administrator's group account. This group automatically contains a member called Admin. Members of the Admins group have the irrevocable power to modify user and group member-ships and clear user passwords, so anyone who is a member of the Admins group is all power-ful within your system. The Admins group must contain at least one member at all times.

It is extremely important to create a unique workgroup ID from the Workgroup Administrator. Otherwise, members of other workgroups can create their own workgroup files and grant them-selves permissions to your database's objects. Furthermore, it is important to ensure that the Admin user does not own any objects and is not given any explicit permissions. Because the Admin user is the same across all workgroups, all objects that Admin owns or has permissions to are available to anyone using another copy of Microsoft Access or Visual Basic.

The system also comes with a predefined Users group. This is the default group composed of all user accounts. All users automatically are added to the Users group and cannot be removed from this group. The Users group automatically is given all permissions to all objects. As with the Admin user, the Users group is the same across all workgroups. It therefore is extremely important that you take steps to remove all rights from the Users group, thereby ensuring that the objects in the database are secured properly. Fortunately, the Security Wizard, covered later in this chapter, accomplishes the task of removing all rights from the Users group. Because rights cannot be removed from the Admins group and the Admin user is the same across all workgroups, another user must be created. This new user will be responsible for administrating the database.

To create a new user to administrate the database, click the Users tab of the User and Group Accounts dialog box. If you closed the dialog box after the last step, choose Tools|Security| User and Group Accounts. Just as when you assigned a password for the Admin user, it does not matter which database you are in when you do this; it is only important that you are a member of the proper workgroup. Remember that you are defining a user for the workgroup— not for the database. The Users tab of the User and Group Accounts dialog box is shown in Figure 27.11.

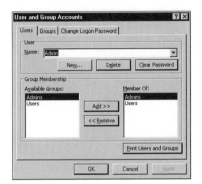

FIGURE 27.11
The Users tab of the User and Group Accounts dialog box.

To establish a new administrative user, click New. The New User/Group dialog box appears, as shown in Figure 27.12.

FIGURE 27.12
The New User/Group dialog box.

The New User/Group dialog box enables you to enter the username and a unique personal ID. This personal ID is not a password. The username and personal ID combine to become the encrypted security identifier (SID) that uniquely identifies the user to the system. Users create their own passwords when they log on to the system.

The Security Wizard allows you to create one or more administrative users for your database. In fact, the Security Wizard automatically creates a user called Administrator. This user becomes the owner of the database.

Step 4: Making the Administrative User a Member of the Admins Group

The next step is to make the new user a member of the Admins group. To do this, select the Admins group from the Available Groups list box, and then click Add with the new user selected in the Name drop-down list box. The new user should appear as a member of the Admins group, as shown in Figure 27.13.

FIGURE 27.13

Adding the new user to the Admins group.

If you use the Security Wizard, the user called Administrator is automatically added to the Admins group. Of course, you can also add other users to the Admins group.

Step 5: Exiting Access and Logging On as the System Administrator

You now are ready to close the User and Group Accounts dialog box and exit Access. Click OK. Exit Access and attempt to run it again. After attempting to open any database (or if you created a new database), you are prompted with the Access Logon dialog box shown in Figure 27.14.

FIGURE 27.14

The Access Logon dialog box.

Log on as the new system administrator. You do not have a password at this point; only the Admin user has a password. It still does not matter which database is open.

Step 6: Removing the Admin User from the Admins Group

Before you continue, you should remove the Admin user from the Admins group. Remember that the Admin user is the same in every workgroup. Because the Admins group has all rights to all objects in the database (including the right to assign permissions to and remove permissions from other users and objects), if you do not remove Admin from the Admins group, your database will not be secure. To remove the Admin user from the Admins group, follow these steps:

1. Select Tools|Security|User and Group Accounts.
2. Make sure the Users tab is selected.
3. Select the Admin user from the Name drop-down list box.
4. Select Admins from the Member Of list box.
5. Click Remove. The User and Group Accounts dialog box appears as shown in Figure 27.15.

FIGURE 27.15

Removing Admin from the Admins group.

If you use the Security Wizard to secure your database, the Admin user is automatically removed from the Admins group. In fact, the Security Wizard does not make the Admin user a member of any group besides Users (the group to which all users must be members).

Step 7: Assigning a Password to the System Administrator

Now that you are logged on as the new Administrator, you should modify your password. If you have closed the User and Group Accounts dialog, choose Tools|Security|User and Group

Accounts. Click the Change Logon Password tab. Remember that you can assign a password only for the user whom you are logged on as.

One of the really cool aspects of the Security Wizard is that it allows you to assign passwords for all users who are members of the workgroup. This saves you a lot of time and effort when establishing a large number of users.

Step 8: Opening the Database You Want to Secure

After all this work, you finally are ready to actually secure the database. Up to this point, it did not matter which database you had open. Everything you have done so far has applied to the workgroup rather than to a particular database. Open the database you want to secure. At the moment, the Admin user owns the database, and members of the Users group have rights to all objects in the database.

Step 9: Running the Security Wizard

Unless you are creating a brand new database after you perform all the preceding steps, the first thing you should do to secure an existing database is to use the Security Wizard. The Security Wizard allows you to perform the following tasks:

- Join an existing workgroup or create a new workgroup information file
- Designate the database objects you want to secure
- Assign a password for the Visual Basic project
- Select from predefined groups that the wizard creates
- Assign desired rights to the Users group
- Create users
- Assign users to groups
- Create a backup, unsecured copy of your database

To run the Security Wizard, choose Tools|Security|User Level Security Wizard. The first step of the Security Wizard dialog box appears, as shown in Figure 27.16.

> **NOTE**
>
> You cannot run the Security Wizard if you have set a Visual Basic Environment (VBE) password for the project. You must unlock the VBE project before running the wizard. VBE passwords are covered in the later section "Securing VBA Code with a Password."

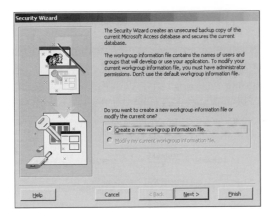

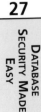

FIGURE 27.16

The first step of the Security Wizard prompts you to select an existing workgroup file or create a new workgroup information file.

The first step of the Security Wizard prompts you to select an existing workgroup information file or create a new workgroup information file. Click Next to proceed to the second step of the Security Wizard (pictured in Figure 27.17). The second step prompts you to provide required information about the workgroup information file that you are creating. You are asked to enter a File name, a WID (Workgroup Identifier), your name, and your company name. You can designate the new workgroup file as the default workgroup file on your computer, or you can have Access create a shortcut to the secured database, including the name and path to the workgroup file.

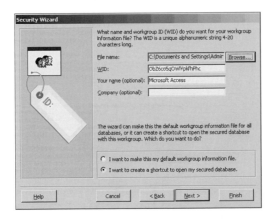

FIGURE 27.17

The second step of the Security Wizard prompts you to enter required information about the workgroup file.

The third step of the Security Wizard, shown in Figure 27.18, allows you to select the objects you want to secure. Notice that you can secure all objects, or you can opt to secure specific tables, queries, forms, reports, or macros. Modules, including the code behind forms and reports, are secured separately.

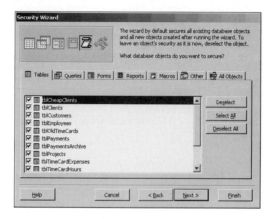

Figure 27.18

The third step of the Security Wizard allows you to select the objects you want to secure.

The fourth step of the Security Wizard, pictured in Figure 27.19, allows you to easily create group accounts. If your security needs match those predefined by one of the default groups, you can save yourself a significant amount of time by allowing the Security Wizard to create the necessary groups for you. An example of a predefined group is read-only users who can read all data but cannot modify data or the design of database objects. Another predefined group is for project designers who can edit all data and the design of application objects but cannot modify the structure of tables or relationships.

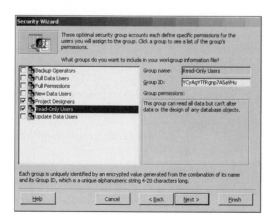

Figure 27.19

The fourth step of the Security Wizard allows you create groups from a list of predefined group accounts.

In the fifth step of the Security Wizard, shown in Figure 27.20, you designate what permissions, if any, you want to grant to the Users group. It is important to remember that *all* users are members of the Users group. Therefore, any permissions that you grant to the Users group are granted to all the users of your application. As a general rule, I recommend not granting any rights to the Users group. It is better to assign rights to other groups and then make specific users members of those groups.

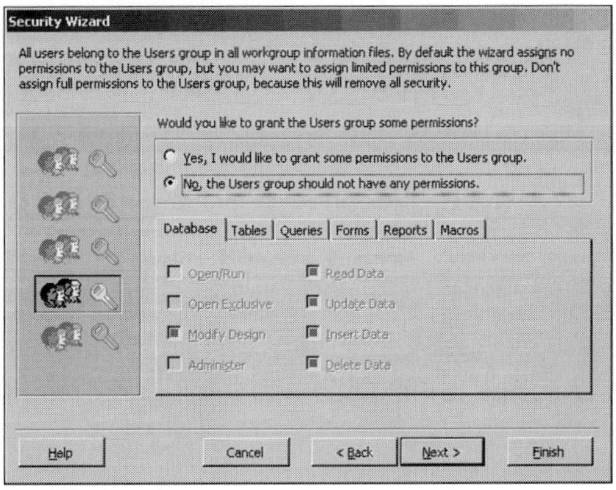

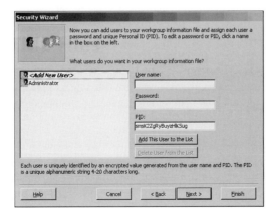

FIGURE 27.20
In the fifth step of the Security Wizard, you can grant specific rights to the Users group.

The sixth step of the Security Wizard allows you to define the users who will use your database. In this step of the wizard, you supply each user's name, a password, and a unique Personal ID, or PID, and then click the Add This User to the List button. (See Figure 27.21.) To delete a user, click that user and then click the Delete User from List button. Click Next when you are finished defining all users.

FIGURE 27.21
The sixth step of the Security Wizard allows you to define the users of your database.

In the next step of the Security Wizard, you assign the users created in step six to the groups designated in step four. To assign a user to a group, click Select a User and Assign the User to Groups. Next select a user from the Group or User Name drop-down. Then click to add the selected user to any of the predefined groups. (See Figure 27.22.)

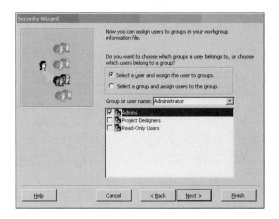

FIGURE 27.22

The seventh step of the Security Wizard allows you to assign users to groups.

The final step of the Security Wizard prompts you to enter the name of the backup copy of the unsecured database. After you click Finish, the existing database is secured, and the original unsecured database is given the name designated for the backup.

The owner of a database cannot be changed and always has rights to everything in the database. Because Admin is the owner of the database and is the same in all workgroups, Access must copy all the database objects to a new, secure database owned by the new user. The wizard is intelligent enough to create a new secure database with the original database name and create a backup with the name that you designate. Access in no way modifies the existing, unsecured database. When the process is completed, the security report shown in Figure 27.23 appears.

Upon completion of its steps, the Security Wizard provides you with a report containing detailed information about the workgroup it created, the objects it secured, and the groups and users it created. The new copy of the database is owned by the new system administrator. All rights have been revoked from the Users group.

When you close the report, you are prompted to save it as a snapshot so that you can view it again later. Because the report contains valuable information about the workgroup and the secured database, I strongly suggest that you save the report in a very safe place. Armed with the information contained in the report, a savvy user could violate the security of your database.

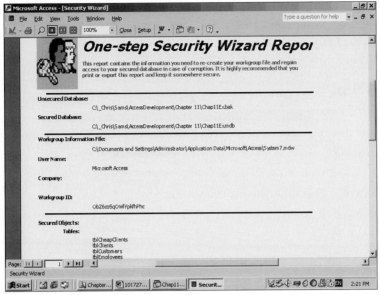

FIGURE 27.23
The One-step Security Wizard Report is the result of a successfully completed Security Wizard process.

Step 10: Creating Users and Groups

Any time after you establish and join a workgroup, you can establish the users and groups who will be members of the workgroup. Users represent individual people who will access your database files. Users are members of groups, which are categories of users who share the same rights. Rights can be assigned at the user level or at the group level. Administratively, it is easier to assign all rights at the group level. However, this involves categorizing access rights into logical groups and then assigning users to those groups.

If groups have been set up properly, the administration of the system is greatly facilitated. If rights of a category of users need to be changed, they can be changed at a group level. If a user is promoted and needs additional rights, you can make that user a member of a new group. This is much easier than trying to maintain separate rights for each user.

You can add, modify, and remove users and groups by using front-end interface tools, as well as through VBA code. This chapter covers how to maintain users and groups using the front-end interface tools. Chapter 28, "Advanced Security Techniques," covers how to maintain users and groups by using code.

Regardless of how you choose to define groups and users, you generally should create groups and then assign users to the appropriate groups. It is important to evaluate the structure of the organization as well as your application before you begin the mechanical process of adding the groups and users.

Adding Groups

To add a new group, follow these steps:

1. Make sure that you are a member of the correct workgroup. With or without any database open, select Tools|Security|User and Group Accounts.
2. Click the Groups tab of the User and Group Accounts dialog box.
3. Click New. The New User/Group dialog box appears.
4. Type the name of the group and enter a PID that uniquely identifies the group.
5. Click OK.
6. Repeat steps 3 through 5 for each group you want to add.

CAUTION

The *personal identification* (PID) is a case-sensitive, alphanumeric string that can be from four to 20 characters in length. In combination with the user or group name, the PID uniquely identifies the user or group in a workgroup. Personal identification numbers should be stored in a very safe place. In the hands of the wrong person, access to the PID can lead to a breach of security. On the other hand, if the database is damaged and an important PID is not available, the data and objects in the database will not be accessible, even to the most legitimate users.

Adding Users

To add users through the user interface, follow these steps:

1. Choose Tools|Security|User and Group Accounts.
2. Click the Users tab if it is not already selected.
3. Click New. The New User/Group dialog box appears.
4. Enter the name of the user and the PID associated with the user. Remember that this is not a password; instead, it combines with the username to create a unique identifier for the user.
5. Click OK.
6. Repeat steps 3 through 5 for each user you want to define.

Assigning Users to the Appropriate Groups

Before you proceed with the final step, assigning rights to users and groups, you should make each user a member of the appropriate group. A user can be a member of as many groups as you choose, but remember that each user gets the rights of his or her most forgiving group. In other words, if a user is a member of both the Admins group and a group with read-only access to objects, the rights of the Admins group prevail. To assign each user to the appropriate groups, follow these steps:

1. Choose Tools|Security|User and Group Accounts.
2. Click the Users tab if it is not already selected.
3. From the Name drop-down list box, select the user for whom you want to create group membership(s).
4. Double-click the name of the group to which you want to add the user, or single-click the group and click the Add button.
5. Repeat steps 3 and 4 for each user to whom you want to assign a group membership.

Figure 27.24 shows a user named Dan, who has been added to the Full Permissions group.

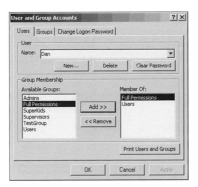

FIGURE 27.24

Assigning a user to the appropriate group.

> **NOTE**
>
> Remember that the users and groups you create are for the workgroup as a whole—not just for a specific database.

Step 11: Assigning Rights to Users and Groups

So far, you have created groups and users, but you haven't given any of your groups or users rights to objects in the database. The key is to assign specific rights to each group, and then to make sure that all users are members of the appropriate groups. After that, you can assign each group specific permissions to the objects in your database. User and group information is maintained in the system database; permissions for objects are stored in system tables in the application database (MDB) file. After you establish a workgroup of users and groups, you must assign rights to specific objects in your database by following these steps:

1. Make sure the database containing the objects you want to secure is open.

2. Choose Tools|Security|User and Group Permissions. The dialog box shown in Figure 27.25 appears. Notice that as you click on each user in the User/Group Name box, as indicated by the check boxes in the Permissions section of the dialog box, you see that only the Administrator has rights to any objects. The Security Wizard automatically removed all permissions from the user named Admin. If you select the Groups option button, you see that only the Admins group has any rights. (If you have previously run the Security Wizard and added other users and groups they will have rights as well.)

Figure 27.25

The User and Group Permissions dialog box.

3. To assign rights to a group, select the Groups option button. All the available groups appear in the User/Group Name box.

4. From the Object Type drop-down list, select the type of object you want to secure.

5. From the Object Name list box, select the names of the objects to which you want to assign rights. You can select multiple objects by pressing the Ctrl and Shift keys.

6. Enable the appropriate Permissions check boxes to select permissions for the objects. The types of available permissions are discussed in the text that follows.

7. Repeat steps 4 through 6 for all objects to which you want to assign rights.

NOTE

It is recommended that you assign groups the rights to objects and then simply make users members of the appropriate groups. Notice that you can use the Object Type drop-down list to view the various types of objects that make up your database.

In order to assign permissions appropriately, it is important that you understand the types of permissions available and what each type of permission allows a user to do. Table 27.1 lists the types of permissions available.

TABLE 27.1   Assigning Permissions

Permission	Allows User To
Open/Run	Open a database, form, or report, or run a macro.
Open Exclusive	Open a database with exclusive access.
Read Design	View tables, queries, forms, reports, macros, and modules in Design view.
Modify Design	View and change the design of tables, queries, forms, reports, macros, and modules.
Administer	Set the database password, replicate the database, and change startup properties (when the user has administer permission of a database). Have full access to the object and its data (when the user has administer permission of a database object—such as a table, query, form, report, macro, or module). Assign permissions for that object to other users (when the user has administer permissions for an object).
Read Data	View the data in a table or query.
Update Data	View and modify table or query data. Cannot insert and delete records, however.
Insert Data	Add records to a table or query.
Delete Data	Delete records in a table or query.

Some of these permissions implicitly include associated permissions. A user cannot update data in a table if he or she does not have the rights to read the data and the design of the table in which that data is located, for example.

Securing VBA Code with a Password

In earlier versions of Access, securing a form or report meant that the code behind it was also secure. With Access 2000 and Access 2002, that is not the case. User-level security does not secure your code. It secures only the forms and reports that refer to the code. This means that denying a user modify design rights to a form prevents them from adding, deleting, or modifying controls on the form, but does not prevent them from modifying the code behind the form.

To secure the code in your application's form, report, standard, and class modules, you must first activate the VBE. Then select Tools|Properties. Click to activate the Protection tab. If you do not want unauthorized users to view the code behind your forms, reports, modules, and class modules, click to select Lock Project for Viewing. Then enter and confirm a password. After you lock the project for viewing, you are prompted for a password once each session. Developers must supply a valid password to view or modify VBA code for the project.

Providing an Additional Level of Security: Creating an MDE

Access 2000 and Access 2002 offer an additional level of security through the creation of an MDE file. An *MDE (compiled database) file* is a database file with all editable source code removed. This means that all the source code behind the forms, reports, and modules contained in the database is eliminated. An MDE file offers additional security because the forms, reports, and modules in an MDE file cannot be modified. Other benefits of an MDE file include a reduced size and optimized memory usage. To create an MDE file, follow these steps:

1. Open the database on which the MDE file will be based.
2. Choose Tools|Database Utilities|Make MDE File. The Save MDE As dialog box appears.
3. Select a name for the MDE and click OK.

Before you dive into MDEs, it is important that you are aware of the restrictions they impose. If you plan ahead, these restrictions probably will not cause you too many problems. On the other hand, if you enter the world of MDEs unaware, they can cause you much grief. You should consider these restrictions:

- The design of the forms, reports, and modules in an MDE file cannot be viewed or modified. In fact, new forms, reports, and modules cannot be added to an MDE. It therefore is important to keep the original database when you create an MDE file. This is where you will make changes to existing forms, reports, and modules and add new forms, reports, and modules. When you are finished, you simply rebuild the MDE.

- Because you must rebuild the MDE every time changes are made to the application, the front-end/back-end approach is best when dealing with MDE files. This means that the tables are contained in a standard Access database, and the other objects are stored in the MDE file. You therefore can rebuild the MDE without worrying about the reconciliation of data.

- You cannot import or export forms, reports, or modules to or from an MDE.

- You cannot change code by using properties or methods of the Access or VBA object models because MDEs contain no code.

- You cannot change the database's VBA project name.

- You cannot convert an MDE to future versions of Access. It is necessary to convert the original database and then rebuild the MDE file with the new version.

- You cannot add or remove references to object libraries and databases from an MDE file. Also, you cannot change references to object libraries and databases.

- Every library database that an MDE references also must be an MDE. This means that if Database1 references Database2, which references Database3, all three databases must be stored as MDEs. You first must save Database3 as an MDE, reference it from Database2, and then save Database2 as an MDE. You then can reference Database2 from Database1, and finally save Database1 as an MDE.

- A replicated database cannot be saved as an MDE. The replication first must be removed from the database. This is accomplished by removing the replication system tables and properties from the database. The database then can be saved as an MDE and the MDE can be replicated and distributed as a replica set. Any time changes must be made to the database, they must be made to the original database, resaved as an MDE file, and then redistributed as a new replica set.

- Any security that applies to a database will follow through to an MDE file created from it. To create an MDE from a database that already is secured, you first must join the workgroup information file associated with the database. You must have Open/Run and Open Exclusive permissions to the database. You also must have Modify Design and Administer permissions to all tables in the database, or you must own all tables in the database. Finally, you must have Read Design permissions on all objects contained in the database.

- If error handling is not added to code within an MDE, and an error occurs, no error message appears.

- If you want to remove security from the database, you must remove the security from the original database and rebuild the MDE.

As long as you are aware of the restrictions associated with MDEs, they can offer many benefits. In addition to the natural security they provide, the size and performance benefits MDEs offer are significant.

> **TIP**
>
> A great use for MDEs is for demo versions of your applications. Performance of MDEs is excellent, but more importantly, by using VBA code, MDEs can easily be rendered both time- and data-limited.

Securing a Database Without Requiring Users to Log On

In a simple security model, it might be appropriate for all users to have the same rights to all objects in the database. In that scenario it doesn't make sense to require users to log on. To eliminate the log on dialog while ensuring that specific objects are secure:

1. Open the database you wish to secure.

2. Run the Security Wizard. If you wish an object to be available to users, grant the appropriate permissions to the Admin account. Clear the permissions for any objects you don't want users to have access to.

3. Make sure that Admin's password is cleared. This will keep the Login dialog from appearing.

Once Admin's password is cleared, users are not prompted to log on, and they are automatically logged on as the Admin user. They therefore are granted any rights given to the Admin user and are denied any rights removed from the Admin user.

Looking at Special Issues

Although the discussion of security so far has been quite thorough, a couple of issues surrounding the basics of security have not yet been covered. They include additional issues with passwords, understanding how security works with linked tables, understanding and working with object ownership, and printing security information. These topics are covered in this section.

Passwords

When you create a user, no password is assigned to the user. Passwords can be assigned to a user only when that user has logged on to the system. The System Administrator cannot add or modify a user's password (the exception to this is when using the Security Wizard). It is important to encourage users to assign themselves a password the first time they log on to the system. Using VBA code, the users can be forced to assign themselves a password. This is covered in Chapter 28. Alternatively, the administrator of the database can log on as each user, assigning each a password.

Although you cannot assign a password to a user or modify the user's password, you can remove a user's password. This is necessary when a user forgets his or her password. To clear a user's password, follow these steps:

1. With or without a database open, choose Tools|Security|User and Group Accounts.

2. From the Names drop-down list, select the user whose password you want to clear.

3. Click Clear Password.

Security and Linked Tables

When you design your application with two databases (one for tables and the other for the remainder of the application objects), it is necessary for you to secure both databases. Securing only the linked tables is not sufficient!

A potential problem still exists. If a user has access to add, delete, and modify data from your application, that user can open the database containing the data tables from outside your application and modify the data without going through the forms and reports you designed. One solution to this problem is to revoke all rights from the tables. Base all forms and reports on queries that have the Run Permissions property set to Owner's. This provides users with the least opportunity to modify the data from outside your system. This technique is covered in more detail in Chapter 28.

Ownership

Remember that the user who creates the database is the database's owner. This user retains irrevocable rights to the database. You cannot change the owner of a database; you can change only the ownership of objects in the database. There is a workaround that allows you, in effect, to change the owner of the database. If you have rights to the database's objects, you can create a new database and import all the objects from the other database. You can accomplish this by using the Security Wizard.

By default, the creator of each object in the database is its owner. To change the ownership of an object in the database, follow these steps:

1. With the appropriate database open, choose Tools|Security|User and Group Permissions.

2. Click the Change Owner tab to select it, as shown in Figure 27.26.

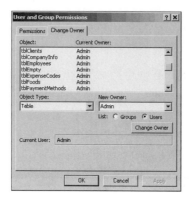

FIGURE 27.26

Changing an object's ownership.

3. From the Object Type list box, select the objects whose ownership you want to change. You can press Ctrl and Shift to select multiple objects.

4. Select the Groups or Users option button.

5. Select the name of the group or user who will become the new owner of the objects.

6. Click Change Owner.

7. Repeat steps 3 through 7 for all objects that you want to assign to new owners.

Printing Security

You can print a list of each user and the groups he or she is a member of by following these steps:

1. With the appropriate database open, choose Tools|Security|User and Group Accounts.

2. Click Print Users and Groups. The Print Security dialog box appears, as shown in Figure 27.27.

3. Select the Both Users and Groups, Only Users, or Only Groups option button.

4. Click OK.

FIGURE 27.27

The Print Security dialog box.

NOTE

You can print the rights to different objects by using the Database Documenter. This is covered in Chapter 29, "Documenting Your Application."

PRACTICAL EXAMPLES

Securing the Time and Billing Application

Now that you have learned the steps involved in properly securing an Access database, you can apply the steps to the Time and Billing application:

1. Launch the Workgroup Administrator. Click the Create button to create a new work-group.

2. Enter your name and organization. Enter `TimeBillApp` as the Workgroup ID, as shown in Figure 27.28. Click OK.

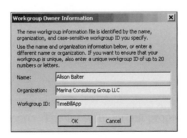

FIGURE 27.28

Entering information for a new workgroup.

3. Call the workgroup database `Time.MDW`. Click OK. Confirm the path to the new work-group, as shown in Figure 27.29.

FIGURE 27.29

Confirming a name and path for a new workgroup information file.

4. Choose Tools|Security|User and Group Accounts.

5. Click New and add a user named PCGuru. Give PCGuru a personal ID of HeadCheese, as shown in Figure 27.30. Click OK.

FIGURE 27.30

Entering the name and personal ID of a new user.

6. Click Add to add PCGuru to the Admins group, as shown in Figure 27.31.

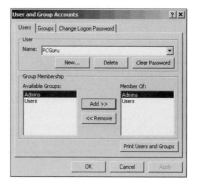

FIGURE 27.31

Adding a user to a group.

7. Click the Change Logon Password tab to select it.

8. Assign a new password of NoPower to the Admin user and click Apply.

9. Click the Users tab.

10. From the Name drop-down list, select Admin.

11. Remove Admin from the Admins group, as shown in Figure 27.32.

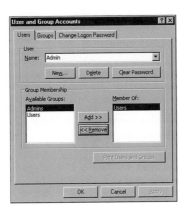

FIGURE 27.32

Removing a user from a group.

12. Exit and restart Access. Open the Chap27 database and log on as PCGuru (with no password).

13. Choose Tools|Security|User and Group Accounts.

14. Click the Change Logon Password tab to select it.

15. Assign PCGuru the password of TheGuru and click OK.

16. Choose Tools|Security|User-Level Security Wizard.

17. Select Modify My Current Workgroup Information File. Click Next.

18. Click Next, accepting that you want to secure all objects.

19. Click to add the groups Read-Only Users and Update Data Users. Click Next.

20. Click Next to accept that the Users group should not have any permissions.

21. Add the following users: Dan, Alexis, Brendan, Gaby, Hugo, and Sonia. Assign any personal IDs and passwords that you want. Click Next.

22. Add Dan, Alexis, and Gaby to the Update Data group. Add Brendan and Hugo to the Read-Only Users group. Add Sonia to the Admins group. Click Next.

23. Enter a name for the backup copy of your database and click Finish.

24. Exit Access and log back on as each of the various users. Attempt to read, modify, add, and delete records from the tblClients and tblProjects tables. Ensure that security has been implemented as planned.

Don't forget that if the tables are linked, you need to go into the linked database to secure those tables.

Summary

The security system in Access 2002 is quite robust but also somewhat complex. Using Access security, you can fully secure a database and all its objects. As a developer, you might want to prevent people from modifying the objects in your database. Furthermore, you might want to restrict certain users from viewing certain data, using specific forms, or running certain reports.

This chapter walked you through all the steps required to properly secure a database. It began by showing you how to set up a database password and how to encrypt a database. It then covered all the details of implementing user-level security.

Invoking user-level security first involves using the Workgroup Administrator to set up a workgroup. You then must create an administrative user and make that user a member of the Admins group. Next, you change the password for the Admin user and remove the Admin user from the Admins group. You then exit Access, log on as the System Administrator, and assign yourself a password. All these steps were covered in detail in this chapter. In addition, this chapter walked you through using the Security Wizard to perform many necessary tasks, such as changing the owner of the database from Admin to the new Administrator and revoking all permissions from the Users group. This ensures that the database is truly secure. The final step is to assign permissions for groups and/or users to the objects that reside in your newly secured database. The chapter also covered this very powerful process.

Advanced Security Techniques

IN THIS CHAPTER

Why This Chapter Is Important

You might not always be available to set up security for the users of your application. Of course, one alternative is to make sure that they purchase their own copies of Access and then to instruct them on how to maintain security implementing the user interface. Access security is very complex, though, so this solution is not particularly practical. In fact, if you are distributing your application to a large group of users, this option is an impossibility. Fortunately, you can build in to your application code the capability to maintain all aspects of security directly. It is important that you provide your administrative users with the capability to establish and maintain security for their workgroups. This involves building a front-end interface to all the security functionality provided by Access. Behind the scenes, you can use ActiveX Data Object (ADO) code to implement the security functionality.

Maintaining Groups Using Code

Chapter 27, "Database Security Made Easy," discusses the importance of creating logical groups of users and then assigning rights to those groups. The administrator of your application might want to add or remove groups after you have distributed your application. You can use ADO code to create and manage group accounts at runtime.

Adding a Group

You add a group using the Append method of the Groups collection. The Groups collection is part of the ADOX Catalog object. Figure 28.1 shows a form that enables users to add and remove groups.

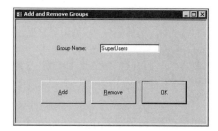

FIGURE 28.1

This form enables administrative users to add and remove groups.

 This form is named frmMaintainGroups and is included in the CHAP28EX.MDB database located on the sample code CD-ROM. Listing 28.1 shows the code under the Add button.

LISTING 28.1   Adding a Group

```
Private Sub cmdAdd_Click()
   Dim boolSuccess As Boolean
   If IsNull(Me.txtGroupName) Then
      MsgBox "You Must Fill In Group Name Before Proceeding"
   Else
      boolSuccess = CreateGroups()
      If boolSuccess Then
         MsgBox "Group Created Successfully"
      Else
         MsgBox "Group Not Created"
      End If
   End If
End Sub
```

This code tests to ensure that entries have been made for the Group Name. If so, the CreateGroups function is called. Based on the return value from CreateGroups, the user is notified whether the group was created successfully. Listing 28.2 uses the Append method of the Groups collection to add a new group to the workgroup.

LISTING 28.2   The CreateGroups Function Adds a Group

```
Function CreateGroups() As Boolean

   On Error GoTo CreateGroups_Err

   Dim cat As ADOX.Catalog

   CreateGroups = True

   Set cat = New ADOX.Catalog
   cat.ActiveConnection = CurrentProject.Connection

   'Append group to the Groups collection
   'of the Catalog object
   cat.Groups.Append (Me.txtGroupName)

CreateGroups_Exit:
   Set cat = Nothing
   Exit Function

CreateGroups_Err:
   MsgBox "Error # " & Err.Number & ": " & Err.Description
   CreateGroups = False
   Resume CreateGroups_Exit
End Function
```

The function uses a Catalog variable. The Catalog variable is part of the Microsoft ADO Extension for DDL and Security (ADOX). You must reference the ADOX library before you can use the Catalog variable. The example sets the ActiveConnection property of the Catalog variable to the connection associated with the current project. After the connection is established, the Append method of the Groups collection of the Catalog object is used to append the group. The Append method of the Groups collection receives one parameter, the name of the group. The Append method, when applied to the Groups collection, adds a new group to the catalog. The function uses the value in txtGroupName as the name of the group to add. After running this routine, you can verify that a new group has been added to the work-group by choosing Tools|Security|User and Group Accounts. The newly created group should appear in the group drop-down list on the group page.

Removing a Group

The code to remove a group is very similar to the code required to add a group. Listing 28.3 shows the code under the cmdRemove command button.

LISTING 28.3   Removing a Group

```
Private Sub cmdRemove_Click()
    Dim boolSuccess As Boolean
    If IsNull(Me.txtGroupName) Then
        MsgBox "You Must Fill In Group Name Before Proceeding"
    Else
        boolSuccess = RemoveGroups()
        If boolSuccess Then
            MsgBox "Group Removed Successfully"
        Else
            MsgBox "Group Not Removed"
        End If
    End If
End Sub
```

This routine ensures that the group name has been filled in and then calls the RemoveGroups function. An appropriate message is displayed, indicating whether the group was removed successfully. Listing 28.4 shows the RemoveGroups function.

LISTING 28.4   The RemoveGroups Function Removes a Group

```
Function RemoveGroups()
    On Error GoTo RemoveGroups_Err

    Dim cat As ADOX.Catalog
```

LISTING 28.4 Continued

```
    RemoveGroups = True

    Set cat = New ADOX.Catalog
    cat.ActiveConnection = CurrentProject.Connection

    'Delete group from the Groups collection
    'of the Catalog object
    cat.Groups.Delete Me.txtGroupName.Value

RemoveGroups_Exit:
    Set cat = Nothing
    Exit Function

RemoveGroups_Err:
    If Err.Number = 3265 Then
        MsgBox "Group Not Found"
    Else
        MsgBox "Error # " & Err.Number & ": " & Err.Description
    End If
    RemoveGroups = False
    Resume RemoveGroups_Exit

End Function
```

The RemoveGroups function uses the Delete method of the Groups collection of the Catalog object, taking the value in txtGroupName as the name of the group to remove. If the group does not exist, an error number 3265 results. An appropriate error message appears.

Using Code to Maintain Users

Not only might you want to maintain groups using code, but you might also want to maintain users with code. You can employ ADO to create and manage user accounts at runtime. The frmMaintainUsers form shown in Figure 28.2 illustrates this process.

FIGURE 28.2
This form enables administrative users to add and remove users.

Adding Users

You add a user with the Append method of the Users collection of the Catalog object. The frmMaintainUsers form, also contained in CHAP28EX.MDB, contains a command button named cmdAddUsers that adds a user. Listing 28.5 shows the code for this.

LISTING 28.5 Adding a User

```
Private Sub cmdAdd_Click()
   Dim boolSuccess As Boolean
   If IsNull(Me.txtUserName) Then
      MsgBox "You Must Fill In User Name Before Proceeding"
   Else
      boolSuccess = CreateUsers(Me.txtUserName.Value, _
         Nz(Me.txtPassword.Value, ""))
      If boolSuccess Then
         MsgBox "User Created Successfully"
      Else
         MsgBox "User Not Created"
      End If
   End If
End Sub
```

This code checks to ensure that the username has been filled in and then calls the CreateUsers function shown in Listing 28.6.

> **NOTE**
>
> The CreateUsers function, along with all the other functions included in this chapter, is found in the Chap28Ex.mdb sample database.

LISTING 28.6 The CreateUsers Function Creates a User

```
Function CreateUsers(UserName as String, _
   Password as String) As Boolean

   On Error GoTo CreateUsers_Err

   Dim cat As ADOX.Catalog

   CreateUsers = True
```

LISTING 28.6   Continued

```
    Set cat = New ADOX.Catalog
    cat.ActiveConnection = CurrentProject.Connection

    'Add User to the Users collection
    'of the Catalog object
    cat.Users.Append UserName, Password

CreateUsers_Exit:
    Set cat = Nothing
    Exit Function

CreateUsers_Err:
    MsgBox "Error # " & Err.Number & ": " & Err.Description
    CreateUsers = False
    Resume CreateUsers_Exit
End Function
```

This routine creates a `Catalog` variable. It sets the ActiveConnection property of the `Catalog` object to the connection associated with the current project. It then invokes the `Append` method of the Users collection of the `Catalog` object to add the user to the catalog. The values in the `txtUserName` and `txtPassword` controls are passed to the `Append` method as arguments. The `Append` method adds the user to the collection of users in the catalog.

Assigning Users to a Group

So far, you have added a user, but you have not given the user group membership. Next, take a look at how you can add a user to an existing group. Listing 28.7 shows the code behind the `cmdAssign` button on the frmMaintainUsers form.

LISTING 28.7   Assigning a User to a Group

```
Private Sub cmdAssign_Click()
    Dim boolSuccess As Boolean
    If IsNull(Me.txtUserName) Or IsNull(Me.txtGroupName) Then
        MsgBox "You Must Fill In User Name and Group Name Before Proceeding"
    Else
        boolSuccess = AssignToGroup(Me.txtUserName.Value, _
            Me.txtGroupName.Value)
        If boolSuccess Then
            MsgBox "User Successfully Assigned to Group"
        Else
            MsgBox "User Not Assigned to Group"
        End If
    End If
End Sub
```

This code makes sure that both the `txtUserName` and `txtGroupName` text boxes are filled in and then calls the `AssignToGroup` function, which attempts to assign the user to the specified group. Listing 28.8 shows the `AssignToGroup` function.

LISTING 28.8   The `AssignToGroup` Function Assigns a User to a Group

```
Function AssignToGroup(UserName as String, _
   GroupName as String)
   On Error GoTo AssignToGroup_Err

   Dim cat As ADOX.Catalog
   Dim usr As ADOX.User

   AssignToGroup = True

   Set cat = New ADOX.Catalog
   cat.ActiveConnection = CurrentProject.Connection

   'Attempt to append group to the Groups
   'collection of the Catalog object
   cat.Groups.Append GroupName

   'Add the user to the specified Group    Set usr = cat.Users(UserName)
   usr.Groups.Append GroupName

AssignToGroup_Exit:
   Set cat = Nothing
   Exit Function

AssignToGroup_Err:
   Select Case Err.Number
       Case -2147467259 'Group already exists
           Resume Next
       Case 3265
           MsgBox "Group Not Found"
       Case Else
           MsgBox "Error # " & Err.Number & ": " & Err.Description
   End Select
   AssignToGroup = False
   Resume AssignToGroup_Exit

End Function
```

This code creates a `Catalog` object variable and a `User` object variable. The ActiveConnection property of the `Catalog` object is set to the Connection property of the current project.

The `Append` method of the Groups collection of the `Catalog` object is used to add the group to the Groups collection of the catalog. If the group already exists, the resulting error is ignored. A `Set` statement points the `User` object at the user specified as the `UserName` input parameter to the function. Finally, the `Append` method of the Groups collection of the User object adds the user to the group supplied by the value specified as the `GroupName` parameter.

Removing Users from a Group

Just as you will want to add users to groups, you also will want to remove them from groups. The code in Listing 28.9 is located under the `cmdRevoke` command button on the frmMaintainUsers form.

LISTING 28.9   Removing a User from a Group

```
Private Sub cmdRevoke_Click()
   Dim boolSuccess As Boolean
   If IsNull(Me.txtUserName) Or IsNull(Me.txtGroupName) Then
     MsgBox "You Must Fill In User Name and Group Name Before Proceeding"
   Else
      boolSuccess = RevokeFromGroup(Me.txtUserName.Value, _
         Me.txtGroupName.Value)
      If boolSuccess Then
         MsgBox "User Successfully Removed from Group"
      Else
         MsgBox "User Not Removed to Group"
      End If
   End If
End Sub
```

This code ensures that the name of the user and group are filled in on the form and then calls the `RevokeFromGroup` function, which is shown in Listing 28.10.

LISTING 28.10   The `RevokeFromGroup` Function Removes a User from a Group

```
Function RevokeFromGroup(UserName as String, _
   GroupName as String)
    On Error GoTo RevokeFromGroup_Err

   Dim cat As ADOX.Catalog

   RevokeFromGroup = True

   Set cat = New ADOX.Catalog
   Dim usr As ADOX.User
```

28

**ADVANCED
SECURITY
TECHNIQUES**

LISTING 28.10 Continued

```
    cat.ActiveConnection = CurrentProject.Connection

    'Delete the user from the specified group
    Set usr = cat.Users(UserName)
    usr.Groups.Delete GroupName

RevokeFromGroup_Exit:
    Set cat = Nothing
    Exit Function

RevokeFromGroup_Err:
    If Err.Number = 3265 Then
        MsgBox "Group Not Found"
    Else
        MsgBox "Error # " & Err.Number & ": " & Err.Description
    End If
    RevokeFromGroup = False
    Resume RevokeFromGroup_Exit

End Function
```

This procedure establishes a Catalog object and points its Connection property to the connection associated with the current project. It establishes a User object and points it to the user specified in the UserName input parameter. It then removes the specified user from the group using the Delete method of the Groups collection of the User object. Notice that the Item of the Users collection referenced is specified in the parameter UserName, which is passed from the text box txtUserName. The group that the user is deleted from is specified by the parameter GroupName, which is passed from the txtGroupName text box.

Removing Users

Sometimes you want to remove a user entirely. The cmdRemove command button on the frmMaintainUsers form accomplishes this task, as shown in Listing 28.11.

LISTING 28.11 Deleting a User

```
Private Sub cmdRemove_Click()
    Dim boolSuccess As Boolean
    If IsNull(Me.txtUserName) Then
        MsgBox "You Must Fill In User Name Before Proceeding"
    Else
        boolSuccess = RemoveUsers(Me.txtUserName.Value)
        If boolSuccess Then
```

LISTING 28.11 Continued

```
        MsgBox "User Removed Successfully"
    Else
        MsgBox "User Not Removed"
    End If
  End If
End Sub
```

This code needs only a username to proceed. If a username has been supplied, the RemoveUsers function is called, as shown in Listing 28.12.

LISTING 28.12 The RemoveUsers Function Deletes a User

```
Function RemoveUsers(UserName as String)
   On Error GoTo RemoveUsers_Err

   Dim cat As ADOX.Catalog

   RemoveUsers = True

   Set cat = New ADOX.Catalog
   cat.ActiveConnection = CurrentProject.Connection

  'Remove a user from the Users collection
   cat.Users.Delete UserName

RemoveUsers_Exit:
   Set cat = Nothing
   Exit Function

RemoveUsers_Err:
   If Err.Number = 3265 Then
      MsgBox "User Not Found"
   Else
      MsgBox "Error # " & Err.Number & ": " & Err.Description
   End If
   RemoveUsers = False
   Resume RemoveUsers_Exit

End Function
```

The RemoveUsers function issues the Delete method on the Users collection of the catalog. This removes the user from the workgroup.

Listing All Groups and Users

Figure 28.3 shows an enhanced version of the frmMaintainUsers form. It is named frmMaintainAll. The frmMaintainAll form, located in CHAP28EX.MDB, enables an administrator to add and remove users, assign users to groups, and assign passwords to users. The Group Name and User Name text boxes in Figure 28.2 have been replaced with combo boxes so that the user can view and select from existing users and groups.

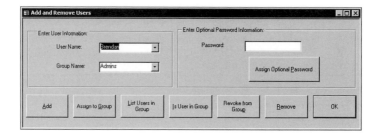

FIGURE 28.3
This form enables administrative users to maintain users, groups, and passwords.

Listing All Groups

The ListGroups function loops through each Group object in the Groups collection. As it loops, it uses the AddItem method of the combo box to add the name of the group to the combo box received as a parameter to the function.. The AddItem method is covered in detail in Chapter 9, "Advanced Form Techniques." Listing 28.13 gathers a list of existing groups in the workgroup.

LISTING 28.13   The ListGroups Function Creates a List of All Groups

```
Function ListGroups(cboAny As ComboBox)

    Dim cat As ADOx.Catalog
    Dim grp As ADOx.Group

    Set cat = New ADOx.Catalog
    cat.ActiveConnection = CurrentProject.Connection

    'Loop through each Group in the Groups collection,
    'Adding the name of each group to the
    'combo box passed as a parameter
    For Each grp In cat.Groups
        cboAny.AddItem grp.Name
    Next grp
End Function
```

Listing All Users

Listing all users is very similar to listing all groups, as shown in Listing 28.14.

LISTING 28.14   The `ListUsers` Function Creates a List of All Users

```
Function ListUsers(cboAny As ComboBox)

    Dim cat As ADOx.Catalog
    Dim usr As ADOx.User

    Set cat = New ADOx.Catalog
    cat.ActiveConnection = CurrentProject.Connection

    'Loop through each User in the Users collection,
    'Adding the name of each user to the
    'combo box passed as a parameter
    For Each usr In cat.Users
        cboAny.AddItem usr.Name
    Next usr
End Function
```

This code loops through each `User` object in the Users collection. It adds the name of each user to the combo box.

Listing Users in a Specific Group

Sometimes it is necessary to print a list of users in a specific group. Listing 28.15 illustrates this process.

LISTING 28.15   The Code in the `cmdListUsers_Click` Event Lists All the Users in the Group Selected in the cboGroupName Combo Box.

```
Private Sub cmdListUsers_Click()
    Dim cat As ADOX.Catalog
    Dim usr As ADOX.User
    Dim strUsers As String

    Set cat = New ADOX.Catalog
    Set cat.ActiveConnection = CurrentProject.Connection

    'Loop through each user object in the Users collection
    'of the Group selected in the cboGroupName combo box
    For Each usr In cat.Groups(Me.cboGroupName.Value).Users
        strUsers = strUsers & usr.Name & vbCrLf
```

28

ADVANCED SECURITY TECHNIQUES

LISTING 28.15   Continued

```
    Next usr

    MsgBox strUsers
End Sub
```

The code loops through each User object in the Users collection of the group selected in the cboGroupName combo box. As it loops, it builds a string with the name of the user.

Determining Whether a User Is a Member of a Specific Group

You can easily determine whether a user is a member of a specific group. The process is illustrated in Listing 28.16.

LISTING 28.16   The cmdIsUserInGroup_Click Event Displays Whether the User Selected in the cboUserName Combo Box Is a Member of the Selected Group

```
Private Sub cmdIsUserInGroup_Click()
    Dim cat As ADOX.Catalog
    Dim usr As ADOX.User
    Dim boolInGroup As Boolean

    'If an error occurs, continue processing
    On Error Resume Next

    Set cat = New ADOX.Catalog
    Set cat.ActiveConnection = CurrentProject.Connection

    'Attempt to retrieve the Name property of the User selected
    'in the Users combo box as part of the Group selected in the
    'Group combo box
    boolInGroup = (cat.Groups(Me.cboGroupName.Value) _
        .Users(Me.cboUserName.Value).Name = _
        Me.cboUserName.Value)

    'Display message with success or failure
    If boolInGroup Then
        MsgBox "User in Group"
    Else
        MsgBox "User Not in Group"
    End If
End Sub
```

Advanced Security Techniques

CHAPTER 28

1097

28

ADVANCED
SECURITY
TECHNIQUES

The code attempts to retrieve the Name property of the user selected in the cboUserName combo box as a member of the group selected in the cboGroupName combo box. If the user is not a member of the group, an error occurs. The code then compares the Name property to the value in the cboUserName combo box. The comparison returns True if the user is in the group, and False if the user is not in the group. The appropriate message is displayed to the user.

Working with Passwords

Many times, the administrative user needs to add, remove, or modify users' passwords. By using the user interface, you can modify only the password of the user currently logged in; by using code, however, you can modify any user's password, as long as you have administrative rights to do so.

Assigning Passwords to Users

The frmMaintainAll form enables the administrative user to assign a password to the user selected in the combo box. Listing 28.17 shows the code to assign a new password for a user.

LISTING 28.17   Changing a User's Password

```
Private Sub cmdPassword_Click()
   Dim boolSuccess As Boolean
   If IsNull(Me.cboUserName.Value) Then
      MsgBox "You Must Fill In User Name and Password Before Proceeding"
   Else
      boolSuccess = AssignPassword()
      If boolSuccess Then
         MsgBox "Password Successfully Changed"
      Else
         MsgBox "Password Not Changed"
      End If
   End If
End Sub
```

This routine ensures that a username has been entered and then calls the AssignPassword function, located in the frmMaintainAll form, as shown in Listing 28.18.

LISTING 28.18   The AssignPassword Function Changes a User's Password

```
Function AssignPassword()
   On Error GoTo AssignPassword_Err

   Dim cat As ADOX.Catalog
   Dim usr As ADOX.User
```

LISTING 28.18 Continued

```
    Set cat = New ADOX.Catalog
    cat.ActiveConnection = CurrentProject.Connection

    AssignPassword = True

    'Use ChangePassword method of the User object
    'to change the password associated with the user
    'selected in the combo box
    Set usr = cat.Users(Me.cboUserName.Value)
    usr.ChangePassword _
        "", Nz(Me.txtPassword.Value)

AssignPassword_Exit:
    Set cat = Nothing
    Exit Function

AssignPassword_Err:
    MsgBox "Error # " & Err.Number & ": " & Err.Description
    AssignPassword = False
    Resume AssignPassword_Exit

End Function
```

The AssignPassword function points the User object at the user selected in the cboUserName combo box. It then uses the ChangePassword method of the User object to change the password associated with that user. The first parameter, the old password, is left blank intentionally. Members of the Admins group can modify anyone's password but their own without having to know the old password. The second parameter, the new password, is the value entered in the txtPassword text box. The Nz function sets the new password to a zero-length string if the administrative user did not supply a new password.

Listing Users Without Passwords

Many times, an administrative user simply wants to obtain a list of all users who do not have passwords. This list can be obtained quite easily by using VBA code and the ADOX library. Figure 28.4 shows the frmMaintainPasswords form, which is located in the CHAP28EX.MDB database.

When the form is loaded, the list box uses a callback function to display a list of all users who do not have passwords. Listing 28.19 shows the code for the frmMaintainPasswords form.

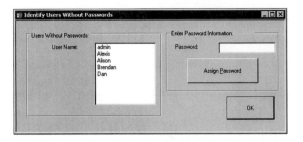

FIGURE 28.4

This form enables administrative users to view users without passwords.

LISTING 28.19   Locating Users Without Passwords

```
Function ListUsers()

   On Error GoTo ListUsers_Err

   Dim cat As ADOX.Catalog
   Dim cnn As ADODB.Connection
   Dim usr As ADOX.User
   Dim boolNoPass As Boolean

   Set cat = New ADOX.Catalog
   cat.ActiveConnection = CurrentProject.Connection

   For Each usr In cat.Users
      boolNoPass = True
      Set cnn = New ADODB.Connection
      cnn.Open CurrentProject.Connection, usr.Name, ""
      If boolNoPass Then
         Me.lstUserName.AddItem usr.Name
      End If
   Next usr

ListUsers_Exit:
   Set cat = Nothing
   Set usr = Nothing
   Exit Function

ListUsers_Err:
   If Err.Number = -2147217843 Then
      boolNoPass = False
      Resume Next
   Else
```

LISTING 28.19   Continued

```
        MsgBox "Error # " & Err.Number & ": " & Err.Description
        Resume ListUsers_Exit
    End If
End Function
```

The meat of the code is in the For...Each loop. The code loops through each user in the Users collection. It begins by setting the value of the boolNoPass flag to True. It creates a new catalog and attempts to log on to the new catalog by using the Name property of the current user object and a password that is a zero-length string. If an error occurs, the error-handling code sets the boolNoPass flag to False. The –2147217843 error means that the password was not valid, indicating that the user must have a password because the logon was not successful. If the logon was successful, the user must not have a password and therefore is added to the list box.

Ensuring That Users Have Passwords

You might want to ensure that users who log on to your application have a password. You can accomplish this by using the code in Listing 28.20.

LISTING 28.20   Ensuring That Your Application's Users Have Passwords

```
Function AutoExec()
    Dim cat As ADOX.Catalog
    Dim usr As ADOX.User
    Dim strPassword As String

    Set cat = New ADOX.Catalog
    cat.ActiveConnection = CurrentProject.Connection
    Set usr = cat.Users(CurrentUser)
    On Error Resume Next
    usr.ChangePassword "", ""
    If Err.Number = 0 Then
        strPassword = InputBox("You Must Enter a Password _
            Before Proceeding", "Enter Password")
        If strPassword = "" Then
            DoCmd.Quit
        Else
            usr.ChangePassword "", strPassword
        End If

    End If
    AutoExec = True
End Function
```

The `AutoExec` function can be called from the startup form of your application. It points a `User` object variable to `CurrentUser`. It accomplishes this by using the return value from the `CurrentUser` function as the user to look at in the Users collection. The `CurrentUser` function returns a string containing the name of the current user.

When an object variable is pointing at the correct user, the code attempts to set a new password for the user. When modifying the password of the current user, both the old password and the new password must be supplied to the `ChangePassword` method of the `User` object. If the old password is incorrect, an error occurs. This indicates that the user has a password and nothing special needs to happen. If no error occurs, you know that no password exists, so the user is prompted for a password. If the user does not supply a password, the application quits. Otherwise, a new password is assigned to the user.

> **NOTE**
>
>
> You can find an example of the usefulness of this function in the basUtils module in the Chap28ExNoPass.MDB database located on your sample code CD-ROM.

> **NOTE**
>
> A user can hold down the Shift key to bypass the code found in Listing 28.20. To keep this from happening, you must programmatically set the AllowBypassKey property of the database to `False`.

Assigning and Revoking Permissions to Objects Using Code

 Often, you will want to assign and revoke object permissions using code. Once again, you easily can accomplish this by using ADO code. The form in Figure 28.5 is named frmTableRights and is located in the CHAP28EX.MDB database.

The code in Listing 28.21 assigns view rights for the table selected in the Select a Table list box to the group selected in the Group Name drop-down list.

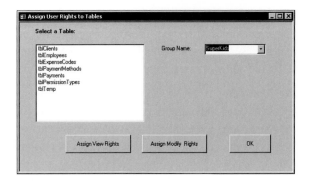

FIGURE 28.5

This form enables administrative users to assign rights to tables.

LISTING 28.21   Assigning View Rights

```
Private Sub cmdViewRights_Click()
    Dim cat As ADOX.Catalog

    Set cat = New ADOX.Catalog
    cat.ActiveConnection = CurrentProject.Connection

    cat.Groups(Me.cboGroupName.Value).SetPermissions _
        Me.lstTables.Value, _
        ObjectType:=adPermObjTable, _
        Action:=adAccessSet, _
        Rights:=adRightRead
End Sub
```

The SetPermissions method of the Groups object is used to establish the permissions for the table. The rights for the table are granted to the group specified in the cboGroupName combo box. The table to which the rights are granted is designated in the lstTables list box. The object type to which the rights are assigned is designated in the ObjectType parameter. The constant adPermObjTable is used to specify the object type as a table. The Action parameter is used to designate the type of action being taken. The constant adAccessSet is used to indicate that the rights are being established. The Rights parameter is used to specify the rights being granted. The constant adRightRead is used to assign read rights to the table. Table 28.1 lists some of the permission constants for queries and tables.

TABLE 28.1 Permission Constants for Queries and Tables

Permission Constant	Grants Permission To
adRightDelete	Delete rows from the table or query.
adRightInsert	Insert new rows into the table or query.
adRightReadDesign	Read the definition of the table or query.
adRightUpdate	Modify table or query data.
adRightRead	Read data stored in the table or query. Also, implicitly grants read permission to the definition of the table or query.
adRightWriteDesign	Alter the definition of the table or query.
adRightWithGrant	Grant permissions for the object.
adRightFull	All rights to the object.

Listing 28.22 shows an example in which the adRightRead constant is combined with the adRightUpdate constant using a bitwise OR. The adRightUpdate constant does not imply that the user also can read the table definition and data. As you might guess, it is difficult to edit data if you cannot read it. You therefore must combine the adRightRead constant with the adRightUpdate constant in order to allow the user or group to read and modify table data.

LISTING 28.22 Modifying User Rights

```
Private Sub cmdModifyRights_Click()
    Dim cat As ADOX.Catalog

    Set cat = New ADOX.Catalog
    cat.ActiveConnection = CurrentProject.Connection

    cat.Groups(Me.cboGroupName.Value).SetPermissions _
        Me.lstTables.Value, _
        ObjectType:=adPermObjTable, _
        Action:=adAccessSet, _
        Rights:=adRightRead Or adRightUpdate
End Sub
```

Determining Whether a Group Has Permission to an Object

It is useful to be able to determine if a user has permissions to an object. This is easy to accomplish using the ADOX object library. The code appears in Listing 28.23.

LISTING 28.23   Determining User Permissions to an Object

```
Private Sub cmdHasPermission_Click()
    Dim boolCanRead As Boolean
    Dim cat As ADOX.Catalog
    Dim grp As ADOX.Group

    Set cat = New ADOX.Catalog
    cat.ActiveConnection = CurrentProject.Connection

    'Determine if the Group selected in the cboGroupName combo box
    'has the permissions selected in the cboPermissions combo box
    'to the table selected in the lstTables list box
    Set grp = cat.Groups(Me.cboGroupName.Value)
    boolCanRead = ((grp.GetPermissions(Me.lstTables.Value, _
        adPermObjTable) _
        And Val(Me.cboPermissions.Value)) = _
        Val(Me.cboPermissions.Value))
    MsgBox boolCanRead
End Sub
```

The code points a `Group` object at the group selected in the cboGroupName combo box. It then uses the `GetPermissions` method of the `Group` object to retrieve the permissions the group has on the specified table. The `GetPermissions` method receives the name of the object whose permissions you want to retrieve, as well as a constant designating the type of object. `GetPermissions` returns a long integer indicating all the permissions for an object. Each bit of the integer indicates a different permission or right. You evaluate a specific permission using a bitwise `AND`, along with a constant for that particular permission. This masks off the bits for the specific permission that you are interested in. When compared to the same bits, the expression evaluates `True` if the group has the permissions, and `False` if it does not. Refer to Table 28.1 for a list of some of the permissions that you can test for.

The code in Listing 28.23 evaluates whether a group has one type of rights to the selected table. You can evaluate one type of rights at a time, or you can test for several rights simultaneously. The code in Listing 28.24 evaluates the Users group to see if members have Read, Update, Insert, and Delete rights to the table selected in the lstTables list box.

LISTING 28.24   Determining Whether a Group Has Multiple Permissions to an Object

```
Private Sub cmdHasMultiple_Click()
    Dim boolRights As Boolean
    Dim cat As ADOX.Catalog
    Dim grp As ADOX.Group
```

LISTING 28.24   Continued

```
Set cat = New ADOX.Catalog
cat.ActiveConnection = CurrentProject.Connection

'Determine if the Group selected in the cboGroupName combo box
'has Read, Update Insert and Delete permissions
'to the table selected in the lstTables list box
Set grp = cat.Groups(Me.cboGroupName.Value)
boolRights = ((grp.GetPermissions(Me.lstTables.Value, _
    adPermObjTable) _
    And (adRightRead Or _
    adRightUpdate Or _
    adRightInsert Or _
    adRightDelete)) = _
    (adRightRead Or _
    adRightUpdate Or _
    adRightInsert Or _
    adRightDelete))
MsgBox boolRights

End Sub
```

The example combines rights using a bitwise OR. The expression returns True only if the selected group has *all* rights designated (Read, Update, Insert, and Delete).

Determining Whether a User Has Permission to an Object

The code in Listings 28.23 and 28.24 showed how you can evaluate an object to determine whether a particular group has rights to it. The process to determine if an individual user has rights to an object is almost identical. It is shown in Listing 28.25.

LISTING 28.25   Determining Whether a User Has Permissions to an Object

```
Private Sub cmdUserHasPermission_Click()
    Dim boolCanRead As Boolean
    Dim cat As ADOX.Catalog
    Dim usr As ADOX.User

    Set cat = New ADOX.Catalog
    cat.ActiveConnection = CurrentProject.Connection

    'Determine if the User selected in the cboUserName combo box
    'has the permissions selected in the cboPermissions combo box
    'to the table selected in the lstTables list box
```

LISTING 28.25 Continued

```
Set usr = cat.Users(Me.cboUserName.Value)
boolCanRead = ((usr.GetPermissions(Me.lstTables.Value, _
    adPermObjTable) _
    And Val(Me.cboPermissions.Value)) = _
    Val(Me.cboPermissions.Value))
MsgBox boolCanRead


End Sub
```

The code in Listing 28.25 points a User object at the user selected in the cboUserName combo box. It then uses the GetPermissions method of the User object to retrieve the permissions the user has on the specified table. The GetPermissions method receives the name of the object whose permissions you want to retrieve, as well as a constant designating the type of object whose permissions you wish to retrieve. GetPermissions returns a long integer indicating all the permissions for an object. Each bit of the integer indicates a different permission or right. You evaluate a specific permission using a bitwise AND, along with a constant for that particular permission. This masks off the bits for the specific permission that you are interested in. When compared to the same bits, the expression evaluates True if the user has the permissions, and False if she does not.

Determining Whether a User Has Implicit Rights to an Object

If a user is not explicitly assigned rights to an object, she might have implicit rights to the object. *Implicit rights* exist if a group that the user belongs to has rights to the object. The code in Listing 28.26 evaluates whether a user has implicit rights to the object.

LISTING 28.26 Determining Whether a User Has Implicit Rights to an Object

```
Private Sub cmdImplicit_Click()
    Dim boolCanRead As Boolean
    Dim cat As ADOX.Catalog
    Dim usr As ADOX.User
    Dim grp As ADOX.Group

    Set cat = New ADOX.Catalog
    cat.ActiveConnection = CurrentProject.Connection

    'Determine if the User selected in the cboUserName combo box
    'has the permissions selected in the cboPermissions combo box
    'to the table selected in the lstTables list box
```

LISTING 28.26 Continued

```
    Set usr = cat.Users(Me.cboUserName.Value)
    boolCanRead = ((usr.GetPermissions(Me.lstTables.Value, _
        adPermObjTable) _
        And Val(Me.cboPermissions.Value)) = _
        Val(Me.cboPermissions.Value))

    'If the user does not have permissions, see if any group they
    'belong to has permissions
    If Not boolCanRead Then
        For Each grp In usr.Groups
            boolCanRead = ((grp.GetPermissions(Me.lstTables.Value, _
                adPermObjTable) _
                And Val(Me.cboPermissions.Value)) = _
                Val(Me.cboPermissions.Value))
            If boolCanRead Then
                Exit For
            End If
        Next grp
    End If

    MsgBox boolCanRead

End Sub
```

The code first evaluates if the user has the designated rights for the object. If the user does not have rights to the object, the code loops through each group that the user is a member of. If it finds the designated rights for any group that the user is a member of, it exits the loop, returning True.

Setting Permissions to New Objects

Earlier in the chapter, you learned how to set permissions for existing objects. You might also want to programmatically assign the permissions a user is granted for new objects. The process is shown in Listing 28.27.

LISTING 28.27 Determining Whether a Group Has Permissions to an Object

```
Private Sub cmdNewObjects_Click()
    Dim cat As ADOX.Catalog

    Set cat = New ADOX.Catalog
    cat.ActiveConnection = CurrentProject.Connection
```

28

ADVANCED
SECURITY
TECHNIQUES

LISTING 28.27   Continued

```
    'Uses the SetPermissions method with a zero-length
    'string for the Name parameter, and adInheritObjects
    'for the Inherit parameter to assign Read rights to all
    'new tables
    cat.Groups(Me.cboGroupName.Value).SetPermissions _
        "", _
        ObjectType:=adPermObjTable, _
        Action:=adAccessGrant, _
        Rights:=adRightRead, _
        Inherit:=adInheritObjects
End Sub
```

The code uses the SetPermissions method of the Group object to assign permissions to the group. Notice that the first parameter to the SetPermissions object, the Name parameter is a zero-length string. The Name parameter, along with the adInheritObjects value for the Inherit parameter, dictates that the rights being assigned apply to new objects.

Manipulating Database Permissions

I've covered how to assign permissions to the objects in a database. Often you will want to programmatically grant or remove rights to the database. You can programmatically determine whether a user or group can open the database, open the database exclusively, and more. The code in Listing 28.28 assigns rights for the database to the group selected in the cboGroupName combo box.

LISTING 28.28   Manipulating Database Permissions

```
Private Sub cmdDatabaseRights_Click()
  Dim cat As ADOX.Catalog

    Set cat = New ADOX.Catalog
    cat.ActiveConnection = CurrentProject.Connection

    'Uses the SetPermissions method with an
    'ObjectType of adPermObjDatabase, an
    'Action of adAccessGrant, and Rights of
    'adRightRead to assign Open rights for the group
    cat.Groups(Me.cboGroupName.Value).SetPermissions _
        "", _
        ObjectType:=adPermObjDatabase, _
        Action:=adAccessGrant, _
        Rights:=adRightRead
End Sub
```

The code uses the SetPermissions method of the group object to assign rights for the database to the group selected in the cboGroupName combo box. Notice the name parameter is a zero-length string. The ObjectType parameter is adPermObjDatabase, and the Rights are set to adRightRead. These parameters grant open rights for the database to the selected group.

Encrypting a Database Using Code

Chapter 27 showed how you can encrypt a database by using the user interface. If a database is not encrypted, it is not really secure because a savvy user can use a disk editor to view the data in the file. If you have distributed your application with the runtime version of Access and you want to give your user the ability to encrypt the database, you must write ADO code to accomplish the encryption process. The code looks like this:

```
Sub Encrypt(strDBNotEncrypted As String, strDBEncrypted As String)
    Dim je As New JRO.JetEngine

    je.CompactDatabase SourceConnection:="Data Source=" _
     & strDBNotEncrypted & ";", _
        DestConnection:="Data Source=" & strDBEncrypted & _
        "; Jet OLEDB:Encrypt Database=True"
End Sub
```

This subroutine receives two parameters. The first is the name of the database that you want to encrypt. The second is the name you want to assign to the encrypted database. The CompactDatabase method is issued on the JetEngine object. This method receives two parameters: the name of the original database to encrypt and the name for the new encrypted database. Notice that the data source for the destination includes information indicating that you want to encrypt the database being compacted.

Accomplishing Field-Level Security Using Queries

In itself, Access does not provide field-level security. You can achieve field-level security by using queries, though. Here's how it works. You do not provide the user or group with any rights to the table that you want to secure. Instead, you give the user or group rights to a query containing only the fields that you want the user to be able to view. Ordinarily, this would not work because, if users cannot read the tables underlying a query, they cannot read the data in the query result.

The trick is in a query option named WITH OWNERACCESS OPTION. The WITH OWNERACCESS OPTION of a query grants the user running the query the rights possessed by the owner of the query. The Staff group, for example, has no rights to the tblEmployees table. The Supervisors group has Read Design, Read Data, and Update Data permissions to the tblEmployees table.

The qryEmployees query is owned by the Supervisors group, as shown in Figure 28.6.
Figure 28.7 shows the query itself. Notice in Figure 28.7 that the Run Permissions property has
been set to `Owner's`. Figure 28.8 shows the resulting SQL. Notice the `WITH OWNERACCESS`
`OPTION` clause at the end of the SQL statement. When any member of the Staff group (who has
no other rights to tblEmployees) runs the query, that member inherits the Supervisor group's
ability to read and modify the table data.

FIGURE 28.6

The query owned by the Supervisors group.

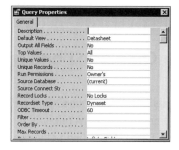

FIGURE 28.7

The Design view of a query with `Run Permissions` *set to* `Owner's`.

FIGURE 28.8

The SQL view of a query with `Run Permissions` *set to* `Owner's`.

Prohibiting Users and Groups from Creating Objects

You might want to prevent the members of a workgroup from creating new databases or creating specific database objects. Preventing users from creating databases or other objects can be accomplished only by using VBA code.

Prohibiting Users and Groups from Creating Objects

You might want to prohibit users from creating specific types of objects. For example, you might want to prevent them from creating new tables, queries, or other objects in your application or data database file. Listing 28.29 illustrates this process.

LISTING 28.29   Prohibiting Users from Creating Other Objects

```
Sub NoTables(strGroupToProhibit)
   On Error GoTo NoTables_Err
    Dim cat As ADOX.Catalog

    Set cat = New ADOX.Catalog
    cat.ActiveConnection = CurrentProject.Connection
    cat.Tables.Refresh

    cat.Groups(strGroupToProhibit).SetPermissions Null, _
        adPermObjTable, adAccessDeny, adRightCreate


NoTables_Exit:
   Set cat = Nothing
   Exit Sub

NoTables_Err:
   MsgBox "Error # " & Err.Number & ": " & Err.Description
   Resume NoTables_Exit

End Sub
```

The code uses the SetPermissions method of the Groups collection of the Catalog object to set permissions for new tables. The parameters used in the example deny table creation rights for the group specified in the call to the function.

Accomplishing Prohibited Tasks by Logging On as a Different User

Although you might not want particular users to be able to accomplish particular tasks, you might at times want to go behind the scenes and accomplish the task for them. As you saw in the preceding section, you can prohibit a user or group from creating new tables and queries. This is fine, except when you run into a situation in which your code requires that a temporary table be created. In this situation, you can temporarily log on as a different user, perform the process, and then log off.

Securing Client/Server Applications

It is important to understand that security for client/server applications must be applied on the back-end database server. You can request logon IDs and passwords from users at runtime and pass them to the database server as part of the connection string, but Access security itself does nothing in terms of interacting with client/server data. Any errors returned from the back end must be handled by your application.

Security and Replication

Database security cannot be implemented on replicated databases. Only user-level security can be implemented. All the replicas inherit the security applied to the Design Master. Replicate only the database file. Never replicate the security information file (System.mdw). Instead, make sure that exactly the same security information file is available at each location where the replica is used. You can do this by copying the file to each location.

A user must have administrator permission on a database to perform the following tasks:

- Converting a nonreplicable database into a replicable database
- Making a replica of the Design Master
- Making a local object replicable
- Making a replicable object local

Implementing Security with SQL

Access 2000 introduced the ability to implement security using SQL. This was accomplished by adding ANSI SQL-92 extensions to Jet 4.0. This section shows you how you can perform common security tasks using SQL.

Maintaining Users with SQL

Just as you can maintain users with ADOX code, you can also maintain them using SQL. The CREATE USER, ADD USER TO, DROP USER FROM, and DROP USER statements will create users, add users to groups, remove users from groups, and remove users, respectively. These statements are all covered in the following sections.

Using SQL to Add a User

The CREATE USER statement is used to add a user to a workgroup. Listing 28.30 illustrates the process.

LISTING 28.30   Using SQL to Create a User

```
Private Sub cmdAddUser_Click()
    Dim cnn As ADODB.Connection
    Set cnn = CurrentProject.Connection

    cnn.Execute "CREATE USER " & Me.txtUser

    Set cnn = Nothing
End Sub
```

Notice that the Execute method of the Connection object is used to execute the CREATE USER statement. The code creates a user with the name designated in the txtUser text box. Two optional parameters are available with the CREATE USER statement. They are the password and the PID. Listing 23.31 illustrates the use of these optional parameters.

LISTING 28.31   Using SQL's CREATE USER Statement to Assign and Password and a PID

```
Private Sub cmdAddUser_Click()
    Dim cnn As ADODB.Connection
    Set cnn = CurrentProject.Connection

    cnn.Execute "CREATE USER ALEXIS GREATKID ABCDE"

    Set cnn = Nothing
End Sub
```

The example creates a user named ALEXIS with a password of GREATKID and a PID of ABCDE.

Using SQL to Add a User to a Group

The ADD USER TO statement adds a user to a group. Listing 28.32 provides an example.

28

LISTING 28.32 Using SQL to Assign a User to a Group

```
Private Sub cmdAddToGroup_Click()
    Dim cnn As ADODB.Connection
    Set cnn = CurrentProject.Connection

    cnn.Execute "ADD USER " & Me.txtUser & _
            " TO " & Me.txtGroup

    Set cnn = Nothing
End Sub
```

The ADD USER TO statement adds the user specified in the txtUser text box to the group designated in the txtGroup text box. Once again, the Execute method of the Connection object is
used to execute the SQL statement.

Using SQL to Remove a User from a Group

The DROP USER FROM statement is used to remove a user from a group. Listing 28.33 provides
an example.

LISTING 28.33 Using SQL to Remove a User from a Group

```
Private Sub cmdRemoveFromGroup_Click()
    Dim cnn As ADODB.Connection
    Set cnn = CurrentProject.Connection

    cnn.Execute "DROP USER " & Me.txtUser & _
            " FROM " & Me.txtGroup

    Set cnn = Nothing
End Sub
```

The DROP USER FROM statement is provided with the name of the user you want to drop and the
group he is to be dropped from. The statement is executed using the Execute method of the
Connection object.

Using SQL to Remove a User

The DROP USER statement is used to remove a user from the workgroup. An example is provided in Listing 28.34.

LISTING 28.34   Using SQL to Remove a User from a Workgroup

```
Private Sub cmdRemoveUser_Click()
    Dim cnn As ADODB.Connection
    Set cnn = CurrentProject.Connection

    cnn.Execute "DROP USER " & Me.txtUser

    Set cnn = Nothing
End Sub
```

Notice that the DROP USER statement with the keyword FROM removes a user from a group. Without the keyword FROM, the user is removed from the workgroup.

Using SQL to Change a Password

The ALTER USER statement is used to modify a password. The process is shown in Listing 28.35.

LISTING 28.35   Using SQL to Modify a Password

```
Private Sub cmdChangePassword_Click()
    Dim cnn As ADODB.Connection
    Set cnn = CurrentProject.Connection

    cnn.Execute "ALTER USER " & Me.txtUser & _
            " PASSWORD " & _
            IIf(IsNull(Me.txtOldPassword), "''", _
                Me.txtOldPassword) & " " & _
            Me.txtNewPassword

    Set cnn = Nothing

End Sub
```

Notice that the ALTER USER statement requires both the old password and the new password. If the old password is blank, you must pass a zero-length string as the parameter value for the old password.

Maintaining Groups with SQL

Just as you can maintain users with SQL code, you can also maintain groups. The CREATE GROUP and DROP GROUP statements are used to add and remove groups.

Using SQL to Add a Group

The CREATE GROUP statement is used to create a group. The statement receives an optional PID, a unique identifier for the group. Listing 28.36 provides an example.

LISTING 28.36   Using SQL to Add a Group

```
Private Sub cmdAddGroup_Click()
    Dim cnn As ADODB.Connection
    Set cnn = CurrentProject.Connection

    cnn.Execute "CREATE GROUP " & Me.txtGroup & _
            " " & Me.txtPID

    Set cnn = Nothing

End Sub
```

Using SQL to Remove a Group

The DROP GROUP statement is used to remove a group. An example appears in Listing 28.37.

LISTING 28.37   Using SQL to Remove a Group

```
Private Sub cmdRemoveGroup_Click()
    Dim cnn As ADODB.Connection
    Set cnn = CurrentProject.Connection

    cnn.Execute "DROP GROUP " & Me.txtGroup

    Set cnn = Nothing
End Sub
```

Using SQL to Assign and Remove Permissions

The SQL GRANT and REVOKE statements are used to assign and remove permissions. Listing 28.38 provides an example of granting rights to an object.

LISTING 28.38   Using SQL to Grant Rights to an Object

```
Private Sub cmdAssignPermissions_Click()
    Dim cnn As ADODB.Connection
    Set cnn = CurrentProject.Connection
```

LISTING 28.38   Continued

```
cnn.Execute "GRANT SELECT ON TABLE tblClients TO " & _
    Me.txtGroup

Set cnn = Nothing

End Sub
```

The code in Listing 28.38 grants select rights to the tblClients table for the group designated in the txtGroup text box. Listing 28.39 shows how a REVOKE statement is used to remove user or group rights to an object.

LISTING 28.39   Using SQL to Revoke Rights to an Object

```
Private Sub cmdRemovePermissions_Click()
    Dim cnn As ADODB.Connection
    Set cnn = CurrentProject.Connection

    cnn.Execute "REVOKE SELECT ON TABLE tblClients FROM " & _
        Me.txtGroup

    Set cnn = Nothing

End Sub
```

Listing 28.39 removes select rights for the tblClients table from the group designated in the txtGroup text box.

DAO and Security

In addition to ADOX and SQL, DAO (Data Access Objects) can also be used to implement security. Because DAO is an older technology whose days are numbered, implementing security with DAO is not covered in this text. Full coverage of security implementation using DAO is included in *Alison Balter's Mastering Access 97 Development*.

Choosing Between ADOX, SQL, and DAO

Determining whether to use ADOX, SQL, or DAO to implement security can be a tough decision. Because DAO is supported primarily for backward compatibility, I do not recommend it for new development. Choosing between ADOX, SQL, and DAO involves comparing the methods, and determining what is important to you. Table 28.2 provides a list of features provided by each technology. You should carefully evaluate each feature and decide which implementation of security is appropriate for you.

28

ADVANCED
SECURITY
TECHNIQUES

TABLE 28.2 ADOX and SQL Comparison

Feature	ADOX	SQL
Adding users and groups	Full support	Full support
Other account maintenance	Full support	Full support
Granting and revoking permissions	Full support	Full support
Querying permissions	Full support	No support
Managing ownership	Full support	No support
Backward compatibility	None	None
Future support	Definitely	Likely
Ease of use	Simpler than DAO	Very simple
SQL Server compatibility	Works with SQL Server; doesn't work with all other databases	Better support than ADOX

PRACTICAL EXAMPLES

Applying Advanced Techniques to Your Application

The advanced techniques you build into your applications depend on how much responsibility you want to give the application for implementing security. You might want to implement security from outside the application rather than build it directly into the application. You can add all the forms contained in CHAP28EX.MDB directly into your applications if you want. Also, you can add the code in the AutoExec routine (covered in the section "Ensuring That Users Have Passwords") into your applications so that you force users running the application to assign themselves a password.

Summary

The security features available in Access are extremely rich. Being able to implement security using both code and the user interface gives you immense power and flexibility when implementing security in your application.

This chapter began with a look at maintaining users and groups using code. Next, you learned about using code to assign and maintain passwords, as well as determining whether a user has a password. You also learned about assigning and revoking permissions to objects using code, as well as many other advanced techniques that give you full control over security in your application.

Security requires a lot of planning and forethought. You must make decisions about what groups to define and which rights you will assign to each group. Also, you must decide what features you will build in to your application using VBA code. This chapter illustrated how you can build all aspects of security directly into the user interface of your application.

28

ADVANCED SECURITY TECHNIQUES

Documenting Your Application

IN THIS CHAPTER

Why This Chapter Is Important

Back in the days of mainframes and very formal centralized management information systems (MIS) departments, documentation was a mandatory requirement for the completion of an application. Today, it seems as though all types of people are developing applications: administrative assistants, CEOs, sales managers, MIS professionals, and so on. To make matters worse, many of us who consider ourselves MIS professionals never received any formal systems training. Finally, the demand to get an application up and running and then to move on to the next application is more prevalent than ever. As a result of all these factors, it seems that documentation has gone by the wayside.

Despite all the reasons why documentation doesn't seem to happen, it is as important to properly document your application today as it was in the mainframe days. Documentation provides you and your users with these benefits:

- It makes the system easy for you and others to maintain.
- It helps state the purpose and function of each object in the application.

This chapter covers the various ways in which you can document your application objects and code.

Preparing Your Application to Be Self-Documenting

Fortunately, Access ships with an excellent tool to assist you with the process of documenting your database: the Database Documenter. Although this tool can be used without any special preparation on your part, a little bit of work as you build the components of your application can go a long way toward enhancing the value of the Database Documenter's output.

Documenting Your Tables

The Database Documenter prints all field and table descriptions entered in the design of a table. Figure 29.1 shows a table in Design view. Notice the descriptions for the ClientID and StateProvince fields. These descriptions provide additional information that is not readily obvious from looking at the field names. The Table Properties window also contains a Description property. This property is included in the table's documentation when it is printed in the Database Documenter.

Entering a table description also assists you and the users of your database when you are working with the tables in the database. Figure 29.2 shows the Database window after table descriptions are entered. The description of each table appears in the Database window.

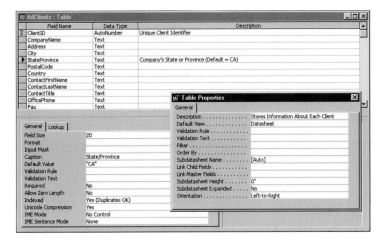

FIGURE 29.1

Documenting a table by including descriptions of each field and using the Table Properties dialog box.

NOTE

Table descriptions appear only if Details is selected as the format for the objects in the Database window.

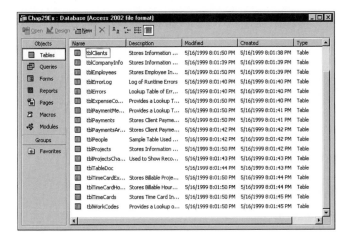

FIGURE 29.2

The Database window with table descriptions.

Documenting Your Queries

Just as you can enhance the output that the Database Documenter provides for tables, you also can enhance the output it provides for queries. Figure 29.3 shows the Query Properties window. The Description property is filled in with a detailed description of the purpose of the query. Figure 29.4 shows the description of an individual column in a query. Both the query and field descriptions are included in the output provided by the Database Documenter.

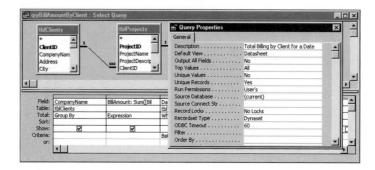

FIGURE 29.3

Documenting a query using the Description property.

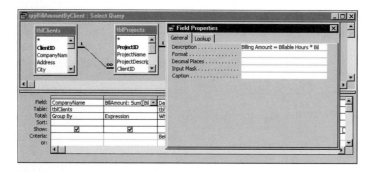

FIGURE 29.4

Documenting a column in a query.

Documenting Your Forms

Documentation is not limited to table and query objects. A form also has a Description property. It cannot be accessed from the Design view of the form, though. To view or modify the Description property of a form, follow these steps:

1. Make the Database window the active window.

2. Right-click the form for which you want to add a description.

3. Choose Properties. The Object Properties dialog box appears, as shown in Figure 29.5.

4. Enter a description in the Description text box.

5. Click OK. The description you entered appears in the Database window, as shown in Figure 29.6, and it also appears in the output from the Database Documenter.

FIGURE 29.5

You can use the Object Properties dialog box to document each object in the database.

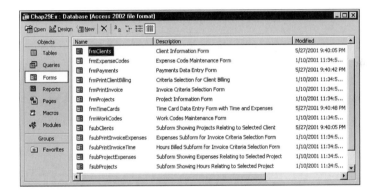

FIGURE 29.6

The Database window with a description of a form.

Documenting Your Reports

Reports are documented in exactly the same manner as forms. Reports have a Description property that must be entered in the Object Properties dialog box. Remember that to access this dialog box, you right-click the object in the Database window and then choose Properties.

Documenting Your Macros

Macros can be documented in significantly more detail than forms and reports. You can document each individual line of the macro, as shown in Figure 29.7. Not only does this provide documentation in the Database Documenter, but also macro comments become code comments when you convert a macro to a Visual Basic module. In addition to documenting each line of a macro, you can add a description to the macro. As with forms and reports, to accomplish this, right-click the macro from the Database window and choose Properties.

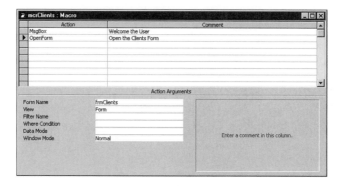

FIGURE 29.7

Documenting a macro by including a description of what each line of the macro does.

Documenting Your Modules

I cannot emphasize enough how important it is to document your modules with comments. Of course, not every line of code needs to be documented. I document all areas of my code that I feel are not self-explanatory. Comments assist me when I revisit the code to make modifications and enhancements. They also assist anyone who is responsible for maintaining my code. Finally, they provide the user with documentation about what my application is doing. Comments print with your code modules, as shown later in this chapter in the section "Using the Database Documenter." As with the other objects, you can right-click a module to assign a description to it.

Using Database Properties to Document the Overall Database

In addition to enabling you to assign descriptions to the objects in the database, Microsoft Access enables you to document the database as a whole. You do this by filling in the information included in the Database Properties window. To access a database's properties, choose File|Database Properties or right-click the title bar of the Database window and choose

Database Properties. The Database Properties dialog box appears, as shown in Figure 29.8. As you can see, it is a tabbed dialog box; tabs include General, Summary, Statistics, Contents, and Custom.

FIGURE 29.8

The Database Properties window showing the General properties of a database.

Descriptions of the tabs in the Database Properties dialog box follow:

- **General**—The General tab displays general information about your database. This includes the date the database was created, when it was last modified, when it was last accessed, its location, its size, its MS-DOS name, and its file attributes. None of the information on the General tab can be modified.

- **Summary**—The Summary tab, shown in Figure 29.9, contains modifiable information that describes the database and what it does. This tab includes the database title, its subject, and comments about the database. It also includes the *hyperlink base*—a base address used for all relative hyperlinks inserted in the database. This can be an Internet address (URL) or a filename path (UNC).

- **Statistics**—The Statistics tab contains statistics of the database, such as when it was created, last modified, and last accessed.

- **Contents**—The Contents tab, shown in Figure 29.10, includes a list of all the objects contained in the database.

- **Custom**—The Custom tab enables you to define custom properties associated with the database. This is useful when you are dealing with a large organization with numerous databases, and you want to be able to search for all the databases containing certain properties.

29

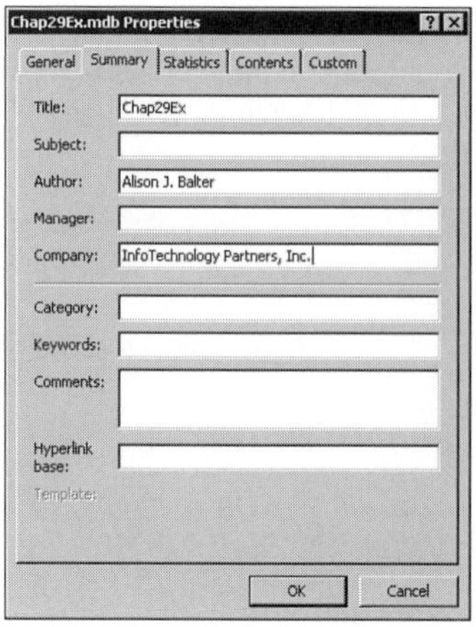

FIGURE 29.9

The Summary tab of the Database Properties window.

FIGURE 29.10

The Contents tab of the Database Properties window.

Using the Database Documenter

The Database Documenter is an elegant tool that is part of the Access application. It enables you to selectively produce varying levels of documentation for each object in your database. To use the Database Documenter, follow these steps:

1. Make sure that the Database window is the active window.

2. Choose Tools|Analyze|Documenter. The Documenter dialog box appears, as shown in Figure 29.11.

FIGURE 29.11

You can use the Database Documenter dialog box to designate which objects you want to document.

3. Click the appropriate tab to select the type of object you want to document. To document a table, for example, click the Tables tab.

4. Enable the check box to the left of each object that you want to document. You can click the Select All command button to select all objects shown on a tab.

5. Click the Options button to refine the level of detail provided for each object. Depending on which object type is selected, different options are displayed. Database Documenter options are covered in the next section of this chapter.

6. Repeat steps 3–5 to select all database objects that you want to document.

7. Click OK when you are ready to produce the documentation.

TIP

To document all objects in the database, click the All Object Types tab and then click Select All.

CAUTION

Access can take quite a bit of time to produce the requested documentation, particularly if numerous objects are selected. For this reason, you should not begin the documentation process if you will soon need your computer to accomplish other tasks. While Access is processing this task, switching to another application becomes difficult if not impossible—how difficult depends on the amount of RAM installed on your system, as well as the type of processor (CPU) installed on your computer and its speed.

29

DOCUMENTING
YOUR
APPLICATION

After you select all the desired objects and options and click OK, the Object Definition window appears. You can use this Print Preview window to view the documentation output for the objects you selected. (See Figure 29.12.) This Print Preview window is just like any other Print Preview window; you can view each page of the documentation and send the documentation to the printer.

FIGURE 29.12

The Object Definition Print Preview window.

Using the Documenter Options

By default, the Database Documenter outputs a huge volume of information for each selected object. Each control on a form is documented, for example, including every property of the control. It is easy to produce 50 pages of documentation for a couple of database objects. Besides being a tremendous waste of paper, this volume of information is overwhelming to review. Fortunately, you can refine the level of detail provided by the Documenter for each category of object you are documenting. Just click the Options button in the Database Documenter dialog box.

Figure 29.13 shows the table definition options. Notice that you can specify whether you want to print table Properties, Relationships, and Permissions by User and Group. You also can indicate the level of detail you want to display for each field: Nothing; Names, Data Types, and Sizes; or Names, Data Types, Sizes, and Properties. For table indexes, you can opt to include Nothing; Names and Fields; or Names, Fields, and Properties.

FIGURE 29.13
You can use the Print Table Definition dialog box to designate which aspects of a table's definition will be documented.

If you select the Queries tab in the Documenter dialog box and then click Options, the Print Query Definition dialog box appears, as shown in Figure 29.14. Here, you can select the level of detail to be output for the selected queries. You can choose whether to include Properties, SQL, Parameters, Relationships, and Permissions by User and Group for the query. You also can select the level of detail for each column of the query and for the indexes involved in the query.

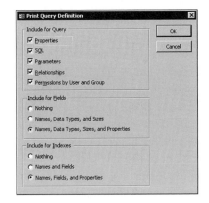

FIGURE 29.14
You use the Print Query Definition dialog box to designate which aspects of a query's definition are documented.

The Form and Report options are similar to one another. Figure 29.15 shows the Print Form Definition dialog box. Here, you can specify whether you want to print Properties, Code, and Permissions by User and Group for a form. For each control on the form, you can choose to print Nothing, the Names of the controls, or the Names and Properties of the controls. The Print Report Definition dialog box offers the same options. Both dialog boxes offer a Properties button, used to designate the categories of properties that are printed. You can opt to print Other properties, Event properties, Data properties, or Format properties.

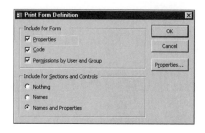

FIGURE 29.15
You use the Print Form Definition dialog box to designate which aspects of a form's definition are documented.

For macros, you can choose whether you want to print macro Properties, Actions and Arguments, or Permissions by User and Group. For modules, you can choose to view Properties, Code, and Permissions by User and Group.

As you can see, the Database Documenter gives you great flexibility in the level of detail it provides. Of course, if you haven't filled in the properties of an object (for example, the description), it does you no good to ask the Documenter to print those properties.

Producing Documentation in Other Formats

After you produce the documentation and it appears in the Object Definition Print Preview window, you can output it to other formats. From the Print Preview window, choose File | Export. The Export Report dialog box appears, as shown in Figure 29.16. Notice that you can output the documentation to Microsoft Excel, HTML, Text Files, a Rich Text Format file, a Snapshot format, or XML. Enter the filename, select Save As Type, and then click Export. If you select the Autostart check box, the Documenter creates the file and then launches you into the appropriate application, depending on your registry entries. If Microsoft's Internet Explorer (IE) is the application associated with the file extension HTML, for example, Autostart launches IE with your Documenter output loaded when you output to an HTML file. Similarly, if you choose a Microsoft Excel file format and Excel is associated through the registry with XLS file types, Autostart launches Excel with the output loaded in Excel when the process is complete. The same holds true for the other file types—RTF and TXT and their respective registry associations, which usually are Word and Notepad.

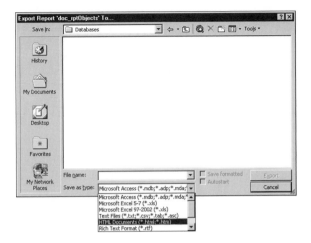

FIGURE 29.16
You use the Export Report dialog box to designate the type of file to which the object definition will be output.

Writing Code to Create Your Own Documentation

Most of the time, the options provided by the Database Documenter are sufficient. At times, you won't like the format the Database Documenter selects—or, more important, you might want to document properties of the database objects not available through the user interface. In these situations, you can choose to enumerate the database objects using code and output them to a custom report format.

Using ADOX (ADO Extensions for DDL and Security), you can enumerate any of the objects in your database. Listing 29.1 shows an example.

LISTING 29.1   Using ADOX to Enumerate the Table Objects in a Database

```
Sub EnumerateTables()

    Dim conn As New Connection
    Dim adoCat As New ADOX.Catalog
    Dim adoTbl As New ADOX.Table
    Dim strSQL As String

    DoCmd.SetWarnings False
    Set conn = CurrentProject.Connection
    adoCat.ActiveConnection = conn

    For Each adoTbl In adoCat.tables
        If adoTbl.Type = "Table" Then
```

LISTING 29.1 Continued

```
            strSQL = "INSERT INTO tblTableDoc" _
                & "(TableName, DateCreated, LastModified) " _
                & "Values (""" & adoTbl.Name & """, #" _
                & adoTbl.DateCreated & "#, #" _
                & adoTbl.DateModified & "#) "

            conn.Execute strSQL
        End If
    Next adoTbl
    DoCmd.SetWarnings True
End Sub
```

> **NOTE**
>
> For the code in Listing 29.1 to run, you must first set a reference (via Tools|
> References) to the Microsoft ADO Ext 2.6 for DDL and Security library.

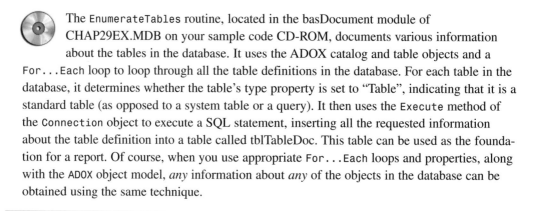 The `EnumerateTables` routine, located in the basDocument module of CHAP29EX.MDB on your sample code CD-ROM, documents various information about the tables in the database. It uses the ADOX catalog and table objects and a `For...Each` loop to loop through all the table definitions in the database. For each table in the database, it determines whether the table's type property is set to "Table", indicating that it is a standard table (as opposed to a system table or a query). It then uses the `Execute` method of the `Connection` object to execute a SQL statement, inserting all the requested information about the table definition into a table called tblTableDoc. This table can be used as the foundation for a report. Of course, when you use appropriate `For...Each` loops and properties, along with the ADOX object model, *any* information about *any* of the objects in the database can be obtained using the same technique.

PRACTICAL EXAMPLES

Applying What You Learned

Practice using various options in the Database Documenter for your own applications. As you change the options for each object type, view the output differences. If you are particularly ambitious, try writing some code to enumerate the objects of the database.

Summary

Documentation is a necessary part of the application development process; fortunately, Microsoft Access makes it very easy. This chapter covered the object Description properties Access provides, as well as the extremely powerful Database Documenter. The chapter also highlighted how you can create your own documentation using ADOX and custom reports. Using any combination of the techniques covered in the chapter, you can produce very complete documentation for all aspects of your application.

Maintaining Your Application

IN THIS CHAPTER

Why This Chapter Is Important

Although you don't need to do too much to maintain an Access database, you must know about an important technique to ensure that your databases are maintained as effectively as possible. The technique, which you should be familiar with, is compacting. *Compacting* a database means removing unused space from a database (MDB file). The compact process and the ways you can accomplish it are covered in this chapter.

Compacting Your Database

As you and the users of your application work with a database, the database grows in size. In order to maintain a high state of performance, Access defers the removal of discarded pages from the database until you explicitly compact the database file. This means that as you add data and other objects to the database and remove data and objects from the database, the disk space that was occupied by the deleted objects is not reclaimed. This not only results in a very large database (MDB) file, but it also ultimately degrades performance as the physical file becomes fragmented on disk. Compacting a database accomplishes these tasks:

- Reclaims all space occupied by deleted data and database objects.

- Reorganizes the database file so that the pages of each table in the database are contiguous. This improves performance because, as the user works with the table, the data in the table is located contiguously on the disk.

- Resets counter fields so that the next value will be one more than the last *undeleted* counter value. If, while testing, you add many records that you delete just prior to placing the application in production, compacting the database resets all the counter values back to 1.

- Re-creates the table statistics used by the Jet Engine when queries are executed and marks all queries to be recompiled the next time they are run. These are two very important related benefits of the compacting process. If indexes have been added to a table or the volume of data in the table has been dramatically changed, the query won't execute efficiently. This is because the stored query plan Jet uses to execute the query is based on inaccurate information. When the database is compacted, all table statistics and the plan for each query are updated to reflect the current state of the tables in the database.

TIP

It is a good idea to defragment the hard drive that a database is stored on before performing the compact process. The defragmentation process ensures that as much contiguous disk space as possible is available for the compacted database.

In earlier versions of Access, the repair process was a separate utility from the compact process. With Access 2000 and Access 2002, there is no longer a separate repair process. The compact and repair processes both occur when a database is compacted. When you open a database in need of repair, you are prompted to compact it.

To compact a database, you can use one of five techniques:

- Use commands provided in the user interface.
- Click an icon you set up for the user.
- Set up the database so that it is compacted whenever you close it.
- Use the `CompactDatabase` method of the JetEngine object.
- Use the `CompactRepair` method of the Application object.

Regardless of which method you select for the compact procedure, the following conditions must be true:

- The user performing the procedure must have the rights to open the database exclusively.
- The user performing the procedure must have `Modify Design` permission for all tables in the database.
- The database must be available to be opened for exclusive use. This means that no other users can be using the database.
- The drive or network share that the database is located on cannot be read—only.
- The file attribute of the database cannot be set to read-only.
- Enough disk space must be available for both the original database and the compacted version of the database. This is true even if the database is compacted to a database by the same name.

It is a good idea to back up the database before attempting to compact it. It is possible for the compact process to damage the database. Also, do not use the compact process as a substitute for carefully following backup procedures. The compact process is not always successful. Nothing is as foolproof as a fastidiously executed routine backup process.

30

MAINTAINING
YOUR
APPLICATION

> **NOTE**
>
> If, at any time, Access detects that a database is damaged, you will be prompted to repair the database. This occurs when you attempt to open, compact, encrypt, or decrypt the damaged database. At other times, Access might not detect the damage. Instead, you might suspect that damage has occurred because the database behaves unpredictably. This is when you should first back up and then perform the compact process, using one of the methods covered in this chapter.

Using the User Interface

Access provides a fairly straightforward user interface to the compact operation. To compact a currently open database, choose Tools|Database Utilities|Compact and Repair Database. The database then is closed, compacted, and reopened.

To compact a database other than the currently open database, follow these steps:

1. Close the open database.

2. Choose Tools|Database Utilities|Compact and Repair Database. The `Database to Compact From` dialog box appears, as shown in Figure 30.1.

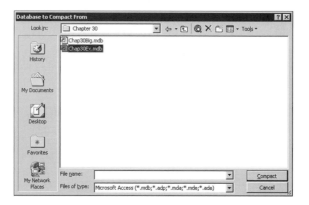

FIGURE 30.1

The Database To Compact From dialog box.

3. Select the database you want to compact and click Compact. The `Compact Database Into` dialog box appears, as shown in Figure 30.2.

FIGURE 30.2

The Compact Database Into dialog box.

4. Select the name for the compacted database. This can be the same name as the original database name, or it can be a new name (if you are compacting a database to the same name, make sure that it is backed up). Click Save.

5. If you select the same name, you are prompted to replace the existing file. Click Yes.

Using a Shortcut

To give users a very simple way to compact a database, you can create an icon that performs the compact process. This is accomplished using the /Compact command-line option, which compacts the database without ever opening it. The shortcut looks like this:

```
c:\MSOffice\Access\Msaccess.e XE c:\Databases\TimeAndBilling.MDB /Compact
```

This syntax can be followed by a space and the name of a destination database if you do not want the current database to be overwritten by the compacted version. If you do not include a path for the destination database, it is placed in the My Documents folder by default. The shortcut can be created automatically for you using the Setup Wizard that ships with the Office 2002 Developer. This is covered in Chapter 32, "Distributing Your Application."

To create a shortcut, follow these steps:

1. Open the folder where your application is installed.

2. Right-click the application (MDB) icon for your database.

3. Choose Create Shortcut.

4. Right-click the shortcut you just created.

5. Choose Properties.

6. Click the Shortcut tab.

7. Modify the shortcut to appear with the syntax shown in the previous example.

Compacting Whenever a Database Closes

Using the environmental setting `Compact on Close`, you can designate that specific databases should be compacted whenever they are closed. A database is compacted upon close only if Access determines that the size will be reduced by at least 256KB. To set the `Compact on Close` environmental setting:

1. Open the database that you want to affect. Select Tools|Options.

2. Click the General tab of the Options dialog.

3. Click the `Compact on Close` check box.

NOTE

Although set in Tools|Options, the `Compact on Close` setting applies only to the database that is open when the option is selected. This allows you to selectively designate which databases are compacted when they are closed.

CAUTION

Remember that all the conditions that must be met for a database to be compacted apply when the database is designated to compact on close. For example, if other users are in the database when someone tries to close it, the user trying to close the database will receive an error.

Using the `CompactDatabase` Method of the JetEngine Object

Using the `CompactDatabase` method, you can compact a database using code. The `CompactDatabase` method is performed on a member of the Microsoft Jet and Replication Objects (JRO), the `JetEngine` object. It receives a source connection string and a destination connection string as parameters. These connection strings are used to designate the source and destination databases, respectively. The `Source Connection` and `Destination Connection` parameters are also used for the following purposes:

- To change the locale of the database
- To encrypt or decrypt the database
- To convert the database from an older Jet version to a new version
- To specify the user ID and password

The Locale Identifier property of the `Destination Connection` parameter determines the collating order in which the data in the compacted database will be sorted. This option is used when you are working with a database in which the data is stored in another language, and you want the data to be collated in a particular language.

The Jet OLEDB:Encrypt Database property of the `Destination Connection` parameter specifies whether you want the compacted database to be encrypted. If you do not specify this property, the compacted database will have the same encryption status as the original source database.

The Jet OLEDB:Engine Type property of the `Source Connection` parameter designates the version of the source database to open. The Jet OLEDB:Engine Type property of the `Destination Connection` parameter indicates the version of the new database. If omitted, the version of the source and destination databases is the same.

Finally, the User ID and Password properties of the `Source Connection` parameter enable you to supply the name of the user and the user's password for a database that is password protected.

The following code, contained in the basCompactDB module of Chap30Ex.MDB, compacts and encrypts a database called Chap30Big.MDB:

```
Sub CompactDB()
    Dim je As New JRO.jetengine
    Dim strFilePath As String

    'Store path of current database in a variable
    strFilePath = Left(CurrentDb.Name, InStrRev(CurrentDb.Name, "\"))

    'If destination database exists, delete it
    If Len(Dir(strFilePath & "Chap30Small.mdb")) Then
        Kill strFilePath & "Chap30Small.mdb"
    End If

    'Use the CompactDatabase method of the JetEngine
    'object to compact the database
    je.CompactDatabase SourceConnection:= _
        "Data Source=" & strFilePath & "Chap30Big.mdb", _
        DestConnection:="Data Source=" & strFilePath & "Chap30Small.mdb; " & _
        "Jet OLEDB:Encrypt Database=True"

End Sub
```

30

MAINTAINING
YOUR
APPLICATION

The compacted database is called Chap30Small.MDB. During the compact process, the database is also encrypted.

In order for this code to execute successfully, remember that the Chap30Big database must be closed, and the user running the code must have the right to open the database exclusively. Furthermore, the user must have `Modify Design` Permissions for all tables in the database. Finally, because the `CompactDatabase` method is performed on the JRO JetEngine object, you must include a reference to the Microsoft Jet and Replication Objects 2.1 Library. This library is not referenced by default when you create a new Access database. You must use Tools | References to reference it.

Using the `CompactRepair` Method of the Application Object

An alternative to the JetEngine object is a method new to the Access 2002 Application object. The `CompactRepair` method simplifies the process shown in the previous section:

```
Sub CompactDBApp()
    Dim strFilePath As String

    'Store path of current database in a variable
    strFilePath = Left(CurrentDb.Name, InStrRev(CurrentDb.Name, "\"))

    'If destination database exists, delete it
    If Len(Dir(strFilePath & "Chap30Small.mdb")) Then
        Kill strFilePath & "Chap30Small.mdb"
    End If

    'Use the CompactRepair method of the application object
    'to compact and repair the database
    Application.CompactRepair strFilePath & "Chap30Big.mdb", _
        strFilePath & "Chap30Small.mdb", True

End Sub
```

The code, located in basMaintenance, declares a string variable. The `Left` and `InstrRev` functions extract the current path from the Name property of the `CurrentDB` object. If the designation file is located in the current folder, it is deleted. The `CompactRepair` method of the Application object compacts and repairs the database into the designated destination database. The `CompactRepair` method receives three parameters. The first is the name and location of the source database, the second is the name and location of the destination database, and the third is whether you want the operation to be logged.

Converting an Access Database

Access 2002 makes it much easier to interact with other versions of Access. Access 2002 allows you to open, read, and update Access databases stored in the Access 2000 file format, without converting the files to the Access 2002 file format! Furthermore, Access 2002 allows you to easily convert files stored in the Access 2002 file format to either the Access 97 or the Access 2000 file format.

To convert an Access 2002 database to a format compatible with an earlier version of Access, select Tools|Database Utilities|Convert Database|To Access 2000 File Format or Tools|Database Utilities|Convert Database|To Access 97 File Format.

As mentioned earlier, Access 2000 files are fully operational in Access 2002. If you wish to convert an open database stored in the Access 2000 file format to the Access 2002 file format, select Tools|Database Utilities|Convert Database|To Access 2002 File Format.

Prior to Access 2002, when problems occurred during the conversion process, users were left wondering exactly what had gone awry. Access 2002 addresses this problem. If errors occur while converting from earlier versions of Access to the Access 2002 file format, a table is created listing each error. You can easily use the data in this table to handle the conversion problem gracefully.

A new Access 2002 method makes it easy to programmatically convert an Access database from one version to another. The code looks like this:

```
Sub ConvertAccessDatabase()
    Dim strFilePath As String

    'Store current file path into variable
    strFilePath = Left(CurrentDb.Name, InStrRev(CurrentDb.Name, "\"))

    'Delete destination database if it exists
    If Len(Dir(strFilePath & "Chap30V97.mdb")) Then
        Kill strFilePath & "Chap30V97.mdb"
    End If

    'Convert source database to Access 97 file format
    Application.ConvertAccessProject strFilePath & "Chap30Big.mdb", _
        strFilePath & "Chap30V97.mdb", _
        DestinationFileFormat:=acFileFormatAccess97
End Sub
```

To begin, the code declares a string variable. The built-in Left and InStrRev functions are used to extract the path associated with the current database and place it in the strFilePath variable. If the destination database exists in the current folder, it is deleted.

30

The `ConvertAccessProject` method of the `Application` object is used to convert the `Chap30Big.mdb` database, located in the current folder and stored in the Access 2002 file format, to the `Chap30V97.MDB` database, located in the current folder and stored in the Access 97 file format.

> **NOTE**
>
> Constants exist for the `ConvertAccessProject` method that allow you to convert to the Access 2002, Access 2000, Access 97, Access 95, and Access 2.0 file formats.

Detecting Broken References

Prior to Access 2002, it was difficult to locate and diagnose broken references. Access 2002 offers BrokenReference, a new property of the Application object that rectifies this problem. If broken references are found, the property evaluates to `True`. If no broken references are found, it evaluates to `False`. Querying the BrokenReference property is much more efficient than looping through each reference to determine if it is intact. The code looks like this:

```
Sub DetectBrokenReference()
    'Display whether or not database contains a broken reference
    MsgBox Application.BrokenReference
End Sub
```

Summary

The compact process should be performed regularly—especially on databases containing your application data. The compact process provides major benefits in terms of both performance and conservation of disk space. The more activity that occurs on a database, the more frequently it should be compacted. Although the compact process should be considered an important part of the database maintenance process, remember that there is absolutely no substitute for proper backup techniques.

In addition to compacting your database, it is important to understand the database conversion options available to you. Databases can be converted from one version to another using either the user interface or code. Finally, whereas it was an arduous, time-consuming process to detect broken references prior to Access 2002, the new BrokenReference property makes this process much easier, by reporting whether or not all database references are intact. Using all of the techniques covered in this chapter should save you a lot of time and effort in maintaining and working with your databases.

Third-Party Tools That Can Help You to Get Your Job Done Effectively

CHAPTER 31

IN THIS CHAPTER

Why This Chapter Is Important

Although Access is a very powerful product, both the development and runtime environments lack numerous features. Fortunately, Microsoft left both Access and the development environment open enough to allow third-party vendors to step in and fill important gaps. Several third-party vendors have created tools to enhance both the development and runtime environments of Microsoft Access. The biggest challenge in working with third-party tools is ensuring their reliability and stability. Although there are many reputable third-party vendors of Access tools out there, I have found the products produced by FMS, Inc. and DBI Technologies to be particularly useful. The products produced by these companies save countless hours of development time for me and my development team, and they enhance the applications that we build. This chapter covers my favorite third-party tools produced by these vendors.

Total Access CodeTools

Total Access CodeTools, produced by FMS, Inc., is by far my favorite third-party product. In a nutshell, Total Access CodeTools automates many of the more mundane development tasks. This helps you to get your job done more quickly and allows you to focus on the fun and exciting aspects of application development. Total Access CodeTool's features are divided into the following categories:

- Code Cleanup
- Code Delivery
- Code Builders
- Coding Tools
- Standards Management

My favorite Total Access CodeTools feature is Code Cleanup. If you've ever inherited a code-intensive database, you'll appreciate this feature. The Code Cleanup feature in Total Access CodeTools automates the process of adding error handling and comments to the procedures that you build. It helps you to standardize code indentations, apply your variable naming convention, and sort the procedures that you write. All these features help you to write code that is more readable, robust, and maintainable.

Figure 31.1 shows the cleanup options available. Notice that you can use Code Cleanup to add module, procedures, and property comments. You can also use Code Cleanup to add Error Handling to your application procedures. Figure 31.2 shows the Standards dialog box. This dialog box allows you to customize the cleanup style, error handling, comments, naming conventions, and other options used when cleaning up your application code.

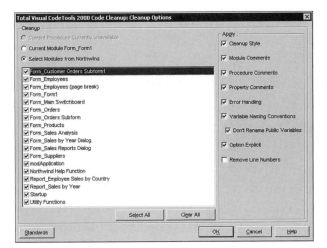

FIGURE 31.1

The Cleanup Options dialog box allows you to designate what tasks Code Cleanup performs.

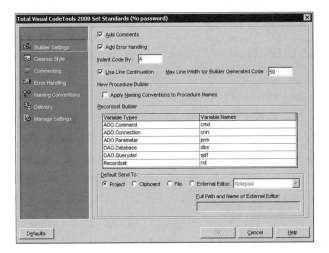

FIGURE 31.2

The Standards dialog box allows you to customize how error handling, comments, naming conventions, and other cleanup tasks are performed.

Total Access CodeTools also helps you with Code Delivery, which can get your application ready for deployment. The Code Delivery features include the ability to add line numbering to the code that you write, which helps you to identify the line on which a runtime error occurred. This significantly simplifies the process of fixing bugs. Total Access CodeTools allows you to remove comments, blanks lines, stop statements, and debug statements from code. The resulting compressed code requires less memory and runs more efficiently.

Figure 31.3 shows the Delivery Options dialog box. This powerful dialog box allows you to designate the specifics of the process. For example, you can specify whether you want the process to remove Debug statements from your code.

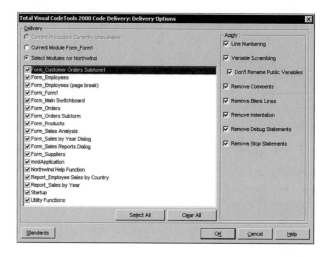

FIGURE 31.3

The Delivery Options dialog box allows you to customize what delivery options are performed.

The other features included in CodeTools include a procedure builder, property builder, SQL builder, recordset builder, message box builder, and more. The tool is so comprehensive that there are too many options to describe in this chapter. I strongly recommend that you download a demo copy of this very powerful product from http://www.fmsinc.com and try it. I'm sure that you will find it well worth the price of admission!

Total Access Analyzer

FMS, Inc. also produces Total Access Analyzer. Its uses include database documentation and analysis. Total Access Analyzer allows you to quickly and easily generate documentation for tables, fields, indexes, relationships, queries, views, database diagrams, stored procedures, forms, reports, controls, data access pages, macros, modules, command bars, users, groups, security, and more! You can view the documentation onscreen in a Tree view, or you can easily output it to a printer.

Total Access Analyzer also performs extensive analysis of your database to generate cross-reference information showing where your objects, fields, and code are used. The hierarchical diagrams are particularly powerful for understanding a database. It also detects a wide variety of problems to help you find more than 100 types of bugs, and provides suggestions and performance tips for debugging. For instance, queries or forms might use a field that no longer exists, or you might want to know which queries or variables aren't used, so that you can delete them. The field consistency analysis is also helpful to make sure that you define the same field name identically across all your tables. FMS has incorporated much of its "Best Development Practices" into Total Access Analyzer, so that you can find and fix problems quickly. In fact, many organizations insist on running Total Access Analyzer against their databases before they deploy them. After all, why let your users experience a crash when Total Access Analyzer can detect the crash before it occurs?

I find that clients are impressed and comforted when I provide them with detailed documentation about the applications that I build. Total Access Analyzer is an easy-to-use tool that quickly generates documentation sure to impress just about any boss or client.

Figure 31.4 shows the first step of the Documentation Wizard. In this step, you select the objects that you want to document. The second step of the wizard, pictured in Figure 31.5, allows you to designate all the documentation options. Options include what cross-references you want to generate, as well as whether you want to document database security. I am particularly impressed with the cross-reference features available in Total Access Analyzer. My favorite feature is the ability to generate detailed cross-references between the VBA code in your database. The final step of the wizard, pictured in Figure 31.6, allows you to perform the documentation process, or schedule it for a later time.

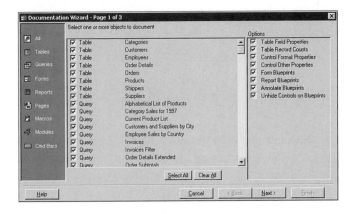

FIGURE 31.4

The first step of the Documentation Wizard allows you to designate the objects you want to document.

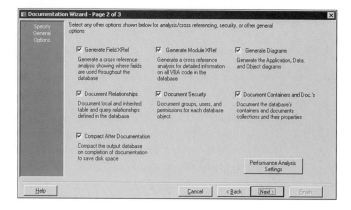

FIGURE 31.5

The second step of the Documentation Wizard allows you to designate documentation options.

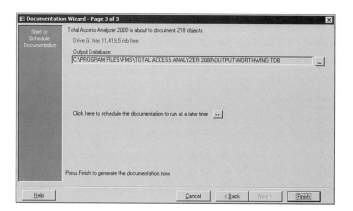

FIGURE 31.6

The final step of the Documentation Wizard allows you to perform the documentation process or to schedule it for a later time.

I find the completed documentation to be professional and easy to work with. Figure 31.7 provides an example of the completed documentation on screen. Notice that you can view a summary, the code, a cross-reference, reported errors, suggestions, and a performance analysis for the selected procedure. Figure 31.8 shows an example of a printed report that provides a modules reference of what each procedure calls. This report is invaluable when debugging a complex application.

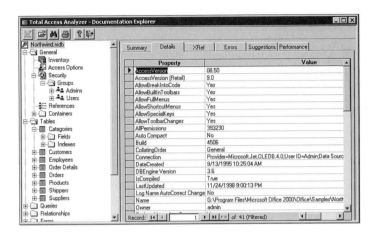

FIGURE 31.7

The onscreen documentation provides you with a plethora of information.

Total Access Analyzer 2000
Database: Northwind.mdb

Procedure Calls
Sorted By Calling Module and Procedure

Monday, May 14, 2001
Time: 11:36:00 AM User: Admin

Calling Module Type and Name / Calling Procedure Name	Line #	Referenced Procedure Name and Parameters	Referenced Module Type and Name
Form: Form1			
cmdCloseAccess_Click	14	CloseAccess	Module: mod Application
cmdCloseDB_Click	20	CloseCurrentDatabase	Module: mod Application
cmdHide Show DB_Click	30	HideDatabaseWindow fShow	Module: mod Application
cmdTest_Click	39	DebugCleanup	Module: mod Application
	42	GetAccessProfile ()	Module: mod Application
	46	GetCurrentUserName ()	Module: mod Application
	48	GetWorkgroupFile ()	Module: mod Application
	51	SetMousePointer ampHorizontalResize	Module: mod Application
	54	GetMousePointer	Module: mod Application
	55	SetMousePointer ampDefault	Module: mod Application
	58	SetupBars True, True	Module: mod Application
	61	StatusMessageClear	Module: mod Application
	64	StatusMessageSet "TVSB Test"	Module: mod Application
	67	StatusMeterInit "Init Meter", 1000	Module: mod Application
	71	StatusMeterUpdate lngCounter	Module: mod Application
	76	StatusMeterClose	Module: mod Application
Form: Orders Subform			
Form_BeforeDelConfirm	13	IsLoaded ("Orders Subform")	Module: Utility Functions
Form_BeforeUpdate	32	IsLoaded ("Orders Subform")	Module: Utility Functions
ProductID_BeforeUpdate	89	IsLoaded ("Orders Subform")	Module: Utility Functions
Form: Sales Reports Dialog			
Preview_Click	57	PrintReports acPreview	Form: Sales Reports Dialog
Print_Click	68	PrintReports acNormal	Form: Sales Reports Dialog
Form: Suppliers			
Form_Close	66	IsLoaded ("Product List")	Module: Utility Functions
	67	IsLoaded ("Products")	Module: Utility Functions

Page: 1

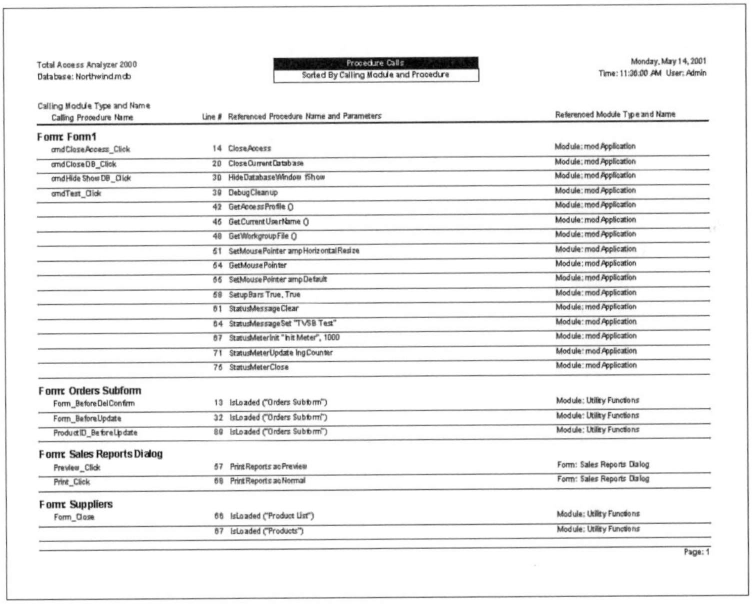

FIGURE 31.8

The printed reports are numerous. Each one provides you with invaluable information.

Total Visual Agent

For your Access databases to run optimally and not grow larger and larger over time, you need to periodically perform database compaction. It also goes without saying that you should back up your data.

Fortunately, FMS, Inc. produces a product, Total Visual Agent, that handles these administrative chores. This powerful product allows you to automatically manage and maintain the databases and applications that you create. It allows you to schedule the process of compacting, backing up, and repairing your databases. You cannot perform these important tasks during the day when users are in the applications that you build. Using Total Visual Agent, you can schedule these tasks to be performed in the middle of the night when no one is using the applications. I often use this wonderful tool to schedule complex management reports to run in the middle of the night. Total Visual Agent runs the reports when no one is in the system. This means that processing involved in creating the reports does not degrade the performance of users trying to get their jobs done during the day. Furthermore, the reports are ready waiting for the users when they arrive at the office in the morning.

Total Visual Agent also allows you to track database statistics, create rolling archives, extract data and write it to other databases, run macros and command line actions, and more.

Total Visual Agent maintains an audit log of every task it performs and can even send an e-mail message to the system administrator if something goes wrong.

Figure 31.9 shows the Total Visual Agent Manager. This is where you create scheduled events and add databases to the events. The Add Database to Event dialog box lets you designate which databases are included in a scheduled event. After adding a database to a scheduled event, you can designate which actions you want to perform on the database (see Figure 31.10).

Once you have created schedules and designated the work you want Total Visual Agent to perform, you are ready to sit back and let the program do its work. At any time, you can view a history of events that have occurred. You can also easily add and modify schedules and actions as necessary. A 30-day, fully functional demo is available from the FMS Web site at www.fmsinc.com.

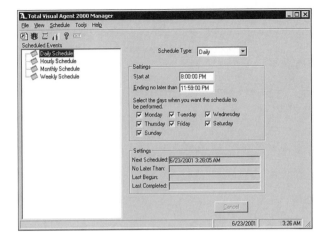

FIGURE 31.9
Total Visual Agent Manager allows you to create scheduled events and add databases to the events.

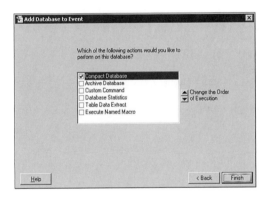

FIGURE 31.10
You can easily designate which actions you want to perform on a database.

Total Access Components

A wide variety of ActiveX controls are available in the Visual Basic market, but many of them do not work in Access. ActiveX controls extend the functionality of Access and let you add features you'd otherwise not be able to get in Access.

Total Access Components, another FMS product, provides a useful collection of ActiveX controls, specifically designed for use within Access forms and reports. The product includes 27 ActiveX controls. The controls shipped with the product include the following:

- About box
- AVI
- Bitmap effects
- Borders
- CD player
- Clipboard
- Clock
- Common dialog boxes
- Digital display
- Enhanced buttons
- Gauge
- Icon menu
- Ini file
- Marquee
- Notes
- Pop-up menu
- Progress meter
- Registry
- Resizer
- Slider
- Spin button
- Splitter
- System info
- Tab strip
- Text effects
- Timer
- Multimedia controls
- Wave

The form resizer and splitter bars are particularly powerful and let you easily add these features to your forms. The visual controls such as rotated text, enhanced tabs, marquees, and bitmap animation also give your databases a professional touch. A royalty-free runtime license lets you distribute these controls to all of your users.

Figures 31.11 and 31.12 show examples from the demo database that ships with Total Access Components. The examples incorporated in the sample database illustrate the rich array of controls included in the product. The sample database provides you with well-documented sample code that you can drop right into the applications that you build. I think that you will find the controls to be both powerful and easy to use.

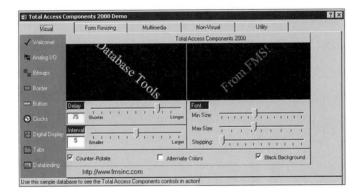

FIGURE 31.11

The Visual Controls tab of the sample database shows you many of the visual controls included in the product.

FIGURE 31.12

The Multimedia tab shows you how easy it is to incorporate AVI files in the applications that you build.

Total Access Statistics

As you accumulate more and more data in Access, you'll find a greater need to analyze it. Access queries perform some basic analysis, but if you need to generate statistical results such as percentiles, regressions, t-tests, frequency distributions, and so on, you're stuck.

Rather than exporting your data to another program, try Total Access Statistics from FMS to perform a wide range of data analysis right inside Access. The product includes a Statistics Wizard to perform parametric, group, and non-parametric analysis and more. The results are placed in Access tables that you can integrate into your forms and reports. It even includes a royalty-free runtime distribution license so you can distribute the analysis with your database.

Figure 31.13 shows the Total Access Statistics Main Menu. This is where you select the type of analysis you want to perform. Once you click New, a wizard launches. The wizard walks you through all the steps required to perform the selected analysis.

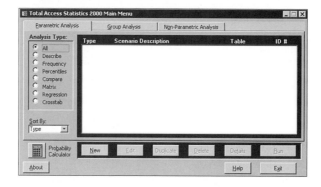

FIGURE 31.13
The multimedia Total Access Statistics Main Menu allows you to designate the type of analysis you want to perform.

Total Access Detective

If you've ever made changes to two copies of the same database, or if your users have made changes that they wanted you to integrate back into the "master" copy, you know how difficult it is to determine what actually changed.

Fortunately, Total Access Detective, produced by FMS, Inc., provides you with an excellent comparison wizard for Microsoft Access. Using the powerful tool, you can easily compare any two objects in one database or any two databases with each other. This is extremely beneficial in a multideveloper environment where different developers are making changes to different database objects. Total Access Detective assists you with the process of merging changes made by multiple developers.

After you have run the Comparison Wizard, you will be able to identify changes in properties, controls, fields, indexes, macro line, and code. Total Access Detective can even compare two versions of the same table to identify their data differences.

Figure 31.14 shows the Comparison Wizard. It walks you through the process of selecting and comparing two database objects. After you click the Do Comparison button, Total Access Detective analyzes the objects and identifies their differences. Figure 31.15 illustrates an example of the results.

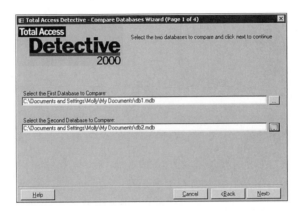

FIGURE 31.14
The Comparison Wizard initiates the process of comparing two databases.

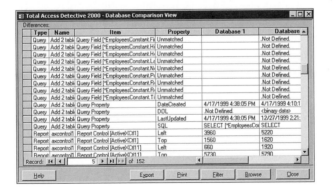

FIGURE 31.15
The results show all differences between the two objects.

Total Visual SourceBook

Total Visual SourceBook is any developer's best friend. This incredible tool provides you with a code library of more than 40 categories, 150 classes and modules, 2,300 procedures, and 85,000 lines of code. Every major category of application development is included:

- Error Handling
- Printing
- XML
- Math Routines
- Soundex
- File and Disk Operations
- Password Encryption
- String Handling
- Date and Time Functions
- And Much More!!!!

The code library alone is worth many times the price of this tool. If that is not enough, you can use Total Visual SourceBook as a repository for all the user-defined functions that you build. You can add your own categories and functions. This tool goes a long way toward promoting reuse and consistency within a development environment.

Figure 31.16 shows the VBA Date and Time functions with the AgeCalc routine selected. Notice that the window contains a Code tab, a Notes tab, an Example tab, and a Details tab. The Code tab, shown in Figure 31.16, shows the selected procedure. The Notes tab, pictured in Figure 31.17, contains important notes about the procedure. The Example tab, shown in Figure 31.18, gives examples of how the procedure is used. The Details tab provides other important procedure details such as dependencies that the selected procedure has on other procedures.

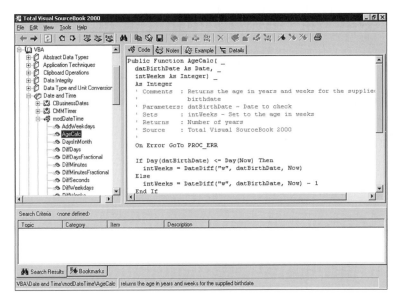

FIGURE 31.16
The Code tab shows the code behind the selected procedure.

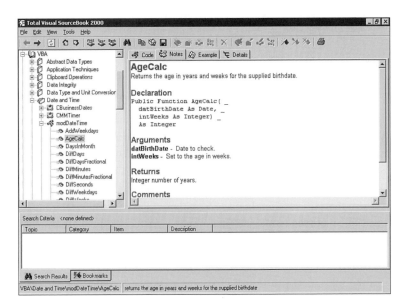

FIGURE 31.17
The Notes tab contains important notes about the selected procedure.

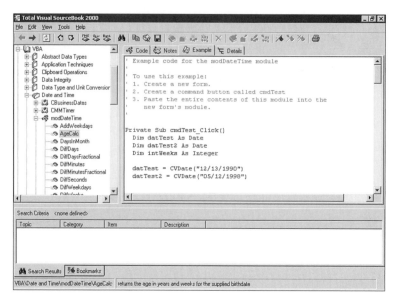

FIGURE 31.18
The Example tab provides excellent examples of how the selected function is used.

Total Access Memo

Memo fields in Access are limited to one font and one point size and no paragraph settings. In many situations, this is way too limiting for users accustomed to Windows word processors. Fortunately, FMS's Total Access Memo product addresses this need.

Total Access Memo is not designed to replace Word, but, if you have a few memo fields that could use rich text format (RTF), it's a great solution. The Total Access Memo control is added to Access forms and reports. Using this full-featured control, you can format the font and character style of selected text in the text box. Furthermore, you can easily export text to an RTF file. Additional features of the control include unlimited undo and redo, bullet points, paragraph alignment and margins, custom line spacing, tabs, color, graphics, and more. A royalty-free runtime license is included so you can add rich text memo fields to your database and distribute it to others.

Figure 31.19 illustrates the sample database that ships with Total Access Memo. Notice the text box at the top of the form. Many different attributes are applied to sections of text within the text box. The example illustrates how very flexible the Total Access Memo control is. The sample database ships with a rich library of source code that programmatically manipulates the Total Access Memo control. You can easily use this source code within the applications that you build.

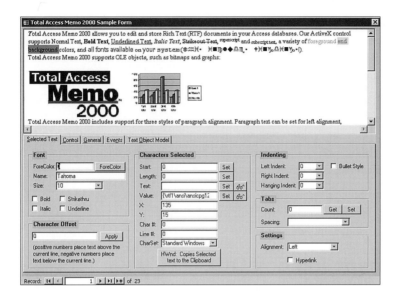

FIGURE 31.19

Total Access Memo is a very flexible ActiveX control that allows you to easily apply the font, character style, and other attributes to the text within it.

Solutions::Explorer

Solutions::Explorer, produced by DBI Technologies, provides five ActiveX controls. All the controls are designed to allow the developer to easily add navigation functionality to the applications that he or she builds. The five controls include

- ctButton
- ctExplorer
- ctFile
- ctFrame
- ctHypLnk

ctButton provides a command button that supports transparency. This allows you to mimic Internet Explorer by including transparent backgrounds and transparent bitmaps.

ctExplorer is an extremely powerful navigational control. It combines a Tree view, List view, HTML view, listbar, tabs, and splitter bar into a single component. This makes it amazingly easy to create multiple views within a single document. Notice that you can drill down within an area to see the different homes in that area. You can then view a general description, a detailed description, financial information, and pictures of the selected home. The description in the example is an HTML document, whereas the detailed description is stored in a Microsoft Word document and the financial information is stored in Microsoft Excel. ctExplorer makes it amazingly easy to display the content of these disparate documents within a single simple interface.

ctFile provides an easy way to display the File Common Dialog box. It sports special properties that augment the functionality of the standard common dialog box. The ctFrame component helps you to create boxes, title bars, and container objects with a variety of border effects. Finally ctHypLnk is a caption component that allows a user to open a document. In essence, it is a label that acts like a hyperlink.

As you can see, Solutions::Explorer includes several valuable components. The product ships with a sample database that highlights the use of each component and provides sample code that you can use in the applications that you build.

Component Toolbox OCX

The Component Toolbox OCX, another DBI Technologies product, provides you with a toolbox of more than 50 ActiveX components. These components help you to create richer and more professional applications. Component Toolbox OCX includes a comprehensive tutorial that walks you through working with the controls included in the product. It also includes sample applications and source code illustrating the use and programmatic interactivity of all the ActiveX controls. A clock control, calculator control, gauge control are just a few of the many controls that ship with the product. A sample database showcases the use of the controls and provides you with sample code that you can incorporate in your own applications.

Solutions::Schedule

Solutions::Schedule is also produced by DBI Technologies. It is a collection of nine ActiveX controls that allow you to add scheduling to the applications that you build. The controls include a Scheduler, Tabs Strip, Drop-down Month Calendar, Date Mask-edit, and Tips control. The sample application allows the user to easily add, edit, and delete appointments. It even incorporates drag-and-drop technology so that you can add and modify appointments by dragging them around the control.

Solutions::PIM Professional

Solutions::PIM Professional is a collection of 17 ActiveX components that allow you to quickly and easily build personal information management (PIM) and personal scheduling into the applications that you create. The tool includes Calendars, Day View, Multi-column Day View, Week View, and Alarm controls. All controls are designed to work together. The Multi-column Day View control allows you to set a person's schedule over a period of several days.

You can also view several people's schedules over a single day. The Enhanced List control is used to display e-mail messages or to-do lists. The ActiveX controls included in Solutions::PIM Professional are demonstrated in the sample database that ships with the product.

PRACTICAL EXAMPLES

Using Third-Party Tools with the Time and Billing Application

The Time and Billing application can benefit from these tools in many ways. You can use Total Access Code Tools to add comments and error handling to the application, and to prepare it for distribution. You can use Total Access Analyzer to test the application for efficiency and to document its objects and their dependencies. Once you deploy the application, you can use Total Access Agent to schedule maintenance and backup activities. You can use Total Access Components, and the products from DBI Technologies to spice up the look and feel of the application and augment the functionality of Access' built-in controls.

Summary

You can use third-party tools to enhance both the development and runtime environments of your Access applications. In terms of the development environment, third-party tools can be used to add error handling, comments, and naming standards to the code that you write, as well as to facilitate the process of building SQL statements, property procedures, and other logical constructs. ActiveX controls are used to greatly enhance the functionality of your forms and reports, and to improve the overall user experience in working with your application.

I find that third-party tools produced by reputable vendors are worth significantly more than the price that you pay for them! The tools from my two favorite vendors of third-party Access tools are available at `www.fmsinc.com` and `www.dbi-tech.com`. In fact, once you begin to use some of the tools out there, I believe that you will never again be able to write Access applications without them.

Distributing Your Application

IN THIS CHAPTER

Why This Chapter Is Important

Many developers are responsible for designing applications that are distributed to many users. The most basic distribution option is to require each user to purchase a copy of Access and then simply provide each user with a copy of the database (MDB) files required for the application. The developer then can go to each user and configure the application appropriately.

Although distributing an application by copying it to each user's machine does not require much specialized knowledge on the part of the developer, it generally is not very practical. For example, in many situations, the developer is distributing an application to users dispersed throughout the country or even the world. Many Access applications are mass marketed to hundreds or even thousands of users. In these situations, it is mandatory to use a professional setup program to properly install the application. For these reasons, most developers distribute their applications using the Packaging Wizard, an important component of the Microsoft Office Developer Edition.

Introducing the Packaging Wizard

The Packaging Wizard enables you to easily create distribution disks containing all the files necessary to run your application. The Packaging Wizard creates a highly professional-looking setup program that your users will run when they want to install your application. Using the Packaging Wizard, they can customize what is included with your application. You can even provide your users with the familiar Standard, Compressed, and Custom options that they have come to know from installing other Microsoft products.

Loading the Packaging Wizard Add-In

Before you can use the Packaging Wizard, you must activate the Packaging Wizard add-in. To do this:

1. Activate the VBE (Visual Basic Development Environment).
2. Select Add-in Manager from the Add-in menu. The Add-in Manager dialog box appears.
3. Select Packaging Wizard.
4. Check the Loaded/Unloaded check box.
5. Check Load on Startup if you want the wizard to be loaded each time that you launch Access.
6. Click OK. The Packaging Wizard should now appear as an option under the Add-in menu.

Distributing Your Application to Run with a Full Copy of Access

Many developers distribute their applications to end users who own and have installed Microsoft Access. These users might be responsible for designing their own ad hoc queries and reports. It is important that you, the developer, properly secure your application for these users, provide them your application with only the functionality you want included, and present your application with professional polish.

Many of the topics in this chapter apply to your application, whether you are distributing the application to users with the Access runtime version or with the full copy of Access. You probably should include a switchboard, custom menu bars, and custom toolbars in your application whether, for example, you are distributing your application with the runtime version or for use under the full version of Access.

Using Full Versions Versus Runtime Versions of Access

Many people have the misconception that using the Packaging Wizard and distributing your application using the Access runtime version somehow means that the application is compiled. This is not the case at all! In fact, if you do not properly secure the database, anyone can install his or her own copy of Access and modify the application's data and other objects just as you can. Using the Packaging Wizard and distributing your application with the Access runtime version does not modify the database in any way. It simply gives you the license to freely distribute the engine required to run your application.

Actually, the engine is not even a modified version of the Access executable! The MSACCESS.EXE file that you distribute is the same as the MSACCESS.EXE that you use to build your application. When you create installation disks for your users with the Packaging Wizard, the installation process copies the same MSACCESS.EXE file to the installation disks. So how can there be any difference between the retail and runtime versions of Access?

When the user installs your application, the installation process copies the MSACCESS.EXE to the user's machine. During this process, the installation program checks a Windows Registry licensing key to see whether the user owns a copy of Access. If the licensing key indicates that the user does not own a copy of Access, or if the key does not exist, the licensing key (which is a set of numbers and letters) is updated to indicate that the user will be using the runtime version of the product. When Access executes and the runtime licensing key is found, the product launches in runtime mode.

When the runtime licensing key is found, Access behaves differently than it does when the full licensing key is found. If you are not aware of the differences, you will be quite surprised when certain aspects of your application no longer function as expected. The following is a list of the limitations of the runtime versions of the product:

- The Database window is hidden.
- Design views are hidden.
- Built-in toolbars are not supported.
- Some menu items are not available.
- Certain keys are disabled.

Hidden Database Window

When users launch your application using the runtime version of Access, the Database window is not visible. It's actually there, but it is hidden because its colors are set to the same colors as the Windows background color. This means that you can interact with the Database window using code, but the users of your application will be unable to interact with the Database window directly.

The fact that the Database window is hidden tends to be a double-edged sword. On one hand, it prevents most users from modifying the objects in your application. On the other hand, it puts the responsibility on you to build a complete interface for your application. Remember that, for you as a developer, the Database window is a starting point. You must provide a different starting point and navigational tools for your users to maneuver throughout your application.

Hidden Design Views

The users of your application won't have direct access to any design views, which means that they are unable to create or modify tables, queries, forms, reports, macros, or modules. You still can get to all this functionality through code, though. You can build a wizard that enables your users to define all aspects of a query or some other object, for example, and then build the query (or other object) using ADO (ActiveX Data Objects) code. Again, this helps protect your application from novice users, but it puts the pressure on you to ensure that your application provides its users with all the functionality they need.

Built-In Toolbars Not Supported

All built-in toolbars are completely unavailable with the runtime version of Access, which means that you must design your own toolbars and attach them to your forms and reports as appropriate. This is covered in the "Adding Custom Menus and Toolbars" section of this chapter.

Unavailable Menu Items

Built-in toolbars are not supported at all when using the runtime version of Access. Menus are simply modified after the runtime key is found. Many menu items are hidden in the runtime version. These hidden menu items prevent users from making changes to your application.

Although many of the menu commands are hidden from the user, they can be accessed by using the DoMenuItem command. In other words, the functionality is there, but it is simply hidden from your users.

Disabled Keys

Several keystrokes are unavailable to your users when they run your application with the runtime version of Access. Table 32.1 lists these keystrokes.

TABLE 32.1   Disabled Keys

Keys	Function
Ctrl+Break	Halts macro and code execution
Shift (when opening the database)	Prevents execution of the AutoExec macro and ignores Startup properties
Alt+F1/F11	Displays the Database window
F12	Displays the Save As dialog box
Shift+F12	Saves a database object
Ctrl+G	Displays the Debug window
Ctrl+F11	Toggles between custom and built-in toolbars

As you can see, these are keys that you would rarely, if ever, want your users to use. You might consider the disabling of these keystrokes a positive side effect of using the runtime version of the product.

Preparing Your Database for Use with the Access Runtime Version

Several steps are required to prepare your database for use with the Access runtime version. Although many of these steps are mandatory when distributing your application with the runtime version, they also are good as a general practice when developing a polished application. To prepare your application for use with the Access runtime version, follow these steps:

- Create the application.
- Create Help files and associate the Help topics with the application's objects, if desired.

- Test and debug the application.
- Run and test the application with the /Runtime command line argument.
- Run the Packaging Wizard.
- Deploy the application.
- Package and distribute the application.

Creating the Application

You must be concerned about several things when designing an application for use with the Access runtime version. Although the following items are niceties in any application, they are a mandatory aspect of developing an application for use with the Access runtime version:

- Build the application around forms.
- Build error handling into the application.
- Build custom menus and toolbars into the application.
- Set startup options for the application.
- Properly secure the application.

Building the Application Around Forms and Menus

The first step when creating the application with runtime distribution in mind is to build the application around forms and menus. This means that everything in the application needs to be form and menu driven. Your application generally should begin by displaying a Main Switchboard, or a startup form with a main menu. The user then can navigate from the Main Switchboard to additional switchboards, such as a Data Entry Switchboard, Reports Switchboard, Maintenance Switchboard, and so on.

An alternative is to display the most commonly used form when the application launches. Menu and toolbar items are used to navigate to other parts of your application. For example, if the application's main purpose is to maintain membership information for a union, the startup form could be the membership form. Other forms, such as the member payments form, could be accessed via a menu attached to the membership form. This second option is my personal favorite.

Building Error Handling into the Application

It is imperative that you build error handling into your application. If an error occurs when someone is using the runtime version of Access and no error handling is in place, an error message is displayed, and the user instantly is returned to the Windows desktop. Therefore, it is crucial that you build error handling into all your routines. Creating a generic error handler to assist you with this task is covered in Chapter 16, "Error Handling: Preparing for the Inevitable."

Adding Custom Menus and Toolbars

As mentioned earlier in this chapter, limited versions of the standard Access menus are available under the Access runtime version, but toolbars are not available at all. You therefore must provide your users with whatever menu bar and toolbar functionality the application requires.

As discussed in Chapter 9, "Advanced Form Techniques," you can attach a menu bar to a form using the Menu Bar property of the form. When a specific menu bar is associated with a particular form or report, the menu appears whenever the form or report becomes the active window. It generally is easier to base a form or report's menu on one of the standard Access menus and then add or remove menu items as appropriate.

You must build each toolbar that you want to use with your application. As covered in Chapter 9, you can specify the toolbar that you want to be visible with your form or report by using the Toolbar property of the form or report. At times, you might prefer to control the toolbars that display by using code. By using this method, you can give the users access to your own toolbars or custom toolbars. Listing 32.1 shows the code placed in the `Activate` event of the form or report.

LISTING 32.1   Code for the `Activate` Event

```
Private Sub Form_Activate()
On Error GoTo Err_Form_Activate
    Call ToolBarShow("tbrMainForm", True)
    Me.fsubClients.Requery

Exit_Form_Activate:
    Exit Sub

Err_Form_Activate:
    MsgBox Err.Description
    Resume Exit_Form_Activate
End Sub
```

The `Activate` event of the frmClients form calls a user-defined procedure called `ToolbarShow`. It passes the `ToolbarShow` routine two parameters: the name of the toolbar it will affect and a Boolean variable indicating whether you wish to hide or show the specified toolbar. Listing 32.2 shows the `ToolBarShow` routine.

LISTING 32.2   The `ToolBarShow` Routine

```
Sub ToolBarShow(strToolbar As String, fShow As Boolean)
  DoCmd.ShowToolbar strToolbar, _
        IIf(fShow, acToolbarYes, acToolbarNo)
```

32

DISTRIBUTING
YOUR
APPLICATION

LISTING 32.2   Continued

```
    DoCmd.ShowToolbar "Form View", _
            IIf(fShow, acToolbarNo, acToolbarWhereApprop)
End Sub
```

The `ToolBarShow` routine handles both the showing and hiding of custom toolbars. It receives a string and a Boolean variable. The `ShowToolbar` method, contained in the `DoCmd` object, makes the toolbars visible or hidden. The command does this by taking the name of the toolbar and a Boolean value (both are passed in as parameters) and toggling the visible property for that toolbar to `True` for visible or `False` for hidden, depending on which was passed into the function. If you pass the `ToolBarShow` routine the string `tbrMainForm` and the Boolean `True`, for example, it shows the `tbrMainForm` toolbar.

In case the application will run in both the retail and runtime versions of Access, you should ensure that the standard toolbar is hidden when the form is active. The second `ShowToolbar` method indicates that the Form View toolbar will be hidden if you are displaying the custom toolbar and will be shown, where appropriate, if you are hiding the custom toolbar. The `Deactivate` event of the form looks like this:

```
Private Sub Form_Deactivate()
    Call ToolBarShow("tbrMainForm", False)
End Sub
```

This routine hides the `tbrMainForm` toolbar and shows the Form View toolbar where appropriate.

Clearly, it is important that you perform all the menu and toolbar handling required by your application. This ensures that all menu bars and toolbars are available when they should be, and *only* when they should be.

Setting Startup Options

Access 2000 and Access 2002 provide you with several startup options that enable you to control what happens to your application when it is loaded. Table 32.2 lists each option in the Startup dialog box.

TABLE 32.2   Startup Options

Option	Function
Application Title	Sets the `AppTitle` property, which displays a custom title in the application title bar.
Application Icon	Sets the `AppIcon` property, which displays a custom icon in the application title bar.

TABLE 32.2   Continued

Option	Function
Menu Bar	Sets the `StartupMenuBar` property, which specifies the custom menu bar displayed by default when the application is loaded.
Allow Full Menus	Sets the `AllowFullMenus` property, which allows or restricts the use of Access menus.
Allow Default Shortcut Menus	Sets the `AllowShortcutMenus` property, which allows or restricts the use of standard Access shortcut menus (menus accessed with a right-click).
Display Form/Page	Sets the `StartupForm` property, which specifies the form displayed when the application is loaded.
Display Database Window	Sets the `StartupShowDBWindow` property, which determines whether the Database window is visible when the application is opened.
Display Status Bar	Sets the `StartupShowStatusBar` property, which determines whether the status bar is visible when the application is opened.
Shortcut Menu Bar	Sets the `StartupShortcutMenuBar` property, which specifies that a menu bar be displayed by default as the shortcut (right-click) menu bar.
Allow Built-in Toolbars	Sets the `AllowBuiltInToolbars` property, which indicates whether built-in toolbars are available to your users.
Allow Toolbar/Menu Changes	Sets the `AllowToolbarChanges` property, which determines whether your users can customize toolbars in the application.
Use Access Special Keys	Sets the `AllowSpecialKeys` property, which determines whether the user can use keys such as F11 to display the Database window, Ctrl+F11 to toggle between custom and built-in toolbars, and so on.

32

DISTRIBUTING YOUR APPLICATION

> **NOTE**
>
> Notice the Use as Form and Report Icon property available when an Application icon is designated. When checked, the icon designated as the Application icon is used as the icon for forms and reports.

As you might have guessed, many of these options apply only when you are running the application under the full version of Access (as opposed to the runtime version.) You do not need to set the Display Database Window property, for example, if your application will be running only under the runtime version of Access. The Database window is never available under the runtime version of the product, so Access ignores this property when the application is run under the runtime version. Nevertheless, I like setting these properties to ensure that the application behaves as I want it to under *both* the retail and runtime versions of the product.

All the properties can be set by using the Startup dialog box or by using code. If you use code, you must make sure that the property exists for the `Database` object before you set it. If the property does not exist, you must append the property to the `Database` object.

Only users with Administer permission for the database can modify the Startup properties. If you want to ensure that certain users cannot modify the startup options of the database, you must make sure that they do not have Administer permissions.

 As part of setting startup options for your database, you should determine what code, if any, is run when the application is loaded. You can accomplish this in one of two ways. You can start the application with an AutoExec macro and then issue a RunCode action to execute a VBA procedure. The other option is to designate a Startup form for the application and then call a custom routine from the `Open` event of the Startup form. I *always* use the second option because it provides you with more control, and you can include error handling in the code module behind the startup form, whereas an AutoExec macro cannot contain error handling. The code shown in Listing 32.3 is called from the `Open` event of the Startup form for the Time and Billing application. This code, and the rest of the code in this chapter, is located in the CHAP32.MDB database file on the sample code CD-ROM.

LISTING 32.3   Setting Options from a Startup Form Routine

```
Private Sub Form_Open(Cancel as Integer)
    'Turn the hourglass on
    DoCmd.Hourglass True

    'Display the splash screen
    DoCmd.OpenForm "frmSplash"

    'Verify links and attempt to relink if necessary
    If LinkTables Then

        'If linking successful, load company info
        Call GetCompanyInfo
    Else
```

LISTING 32.3   Continued

```
        'If linking unsuccessful, close the splash screen
        'and Quit
        DoCmd.Close acForm, "frmSplash"
        Cancel = True
        DoCmd.Quit
    End If

    'Turn hourglass off
    DoCmd.Hourglass False
End Sub
```

32

This routine, placed in the Open event of the startup form, first displays an hourglass. It uses the OpenForm method to open a form called frmSplash. The routine calls a user-defined function that ensures that the database tables are linked successfully. This LinkTables routine is covered in the "Automating the Process of Linking to Tables" section of this chapter. If the LinkTables function returns False, the frmSplash form is closed, and the application is exited. As long as the tables' links have been established successfully, the routine proceeds to call a routine called GetCompanyInfo, where it loads frequently used information into a type structure. The hourglass mouse pointer is removed, and the splash screen is unloaded after it reaches a timer value.

Securing the Application

Don't fool yourself! Remember that the runtime version of Access in no way secures your application. It simply provides you with royalty-free distribution. You must perform all the same measures to secure your application under the runtime version of Access that you perform under the retail version of the product. The bottom line is that you must take measures to secure your application if you want it and its data to be secure. The basics of security are covered in Chapter 27, "Database Security Made Easy." The intricacies of security are covered in Chapter 28, "Advanced Security Techniques." Distributing your application as an MDE (compiled database) provides an additional level of security while improving performance and decreasing the size of the database file. MDE files are covered in the next section.

Distributing Your Application as an MDE

The process of creating an MDE file compiles all modules, removes all source code from your database, and compacts the destination database. All code will run, but the user will be unable to modify forms, reports, and modules. Besides protecting the objects in your database, this process reduces the size of the database and some of the overhead associated with it, thereby improving application performance. Creating and distributing an MDE file is not as simple as it might appear at first glance. Chapter 27 covers the process of creating an MDE file and the important issues that surround this file format.

Adding Custom Help to the Application

To add polish to your application and ensure that the help you provide to your users applies to what they are looking at in your application, you must provide a custom Help file. In essence, adding help to your application involves first creating Help files. You then must add help to the various objects in your application. There are many excellent tools available that can assist you in this.

Testing and Debugging the Application

Before you even bother trying to run your application under the runtime version, you should fully test and debug the application under the retail version of the product. When you are fairly confident that you have all the kinks worked out of the application, you are ready to test it in the runtime environment.

Running and Testing the Application with the `/Runtime` Command-Line Switch

If you have the Microsoft Office 2002 Developer tools installed, Microsoft provides a very easy way to test an application and see how it will perform under the runtime version of Access without having to actually create distribution disks. You can do this by using the `/Runtime` command-line switch. The `/Runtime` switch forces Access to load in runtime mode. Here's how it works:

```
c:\program files\microsoft office\office\msaccess.exe
➥c:\databases\chap32.mdb /runtime
```

After you load the application with the `/Runtime` switch, you should once again test all aspects of the application. At times, you might want to test to see whether the application has been launched with the runtime or retail version of the product. You can accomplish this with the following code:

```
If Not SysCmd(acSysCmdRuntime) _
     And CurrentUser <> "Admin" Then
     MsgBox "You aren't allowed here"
End If
```

The `SysCmd` function, when passed the constant `acSysCmdRuntime`, checks to see whether the application was launched using the runtime version of Access. In this case, if the program was run with the retail version of Access and `CurrentUser` is not `Admin`, a message is displayed, indicating that the user is not allowed. Of course, you easily could modify this routine to check for other users and to quit the application if an unauthorized person attempts to launch the application without the runtime version of the product.

> **TIP**
>
> If you want to simulate the runtime environment on the machine of a user who has Access installed, you must copy the file mso9rt.dll to the directory on the user's machine called \program files\common files\microsoft shared\vba\vba6.

> **NOTE**
>
> The Packaging Wizard was unavailable at the time of this writing. Some of this text may therefore be inaccurate. For an update of this section, please visit http://www.samspublishing.com and enter the ISBN for this book in the search box.

Running the Packaging Wizard

After you have fully tested and prepared your application for distribution, you are ready to run the Packaging Wizard. The Packaging Wizard walks you through all the steps required to build distribution disks that include all the components your application needs to run. You launch the Packaging Wizard from VBE, as follows:

1. Activate the VBE.

2. Select Packaging Wizard from the Add-ins menu. The Packaging Wizard starting dialog box appears.

3. The Packaging Wizard starting dialog box provides you with an introduction to the Packaging Wizard and what it does. Click Next to proceed to the next step.

Identifying Application and Package Information

The first step of the wizard, gives you the opportunity to

- Designate the file you wish to package

- Name the package that you are creating

- Rename, delete, and duplicate packaging scripts

Identify the file you want to package, and supply a package name. Then click Next.

Supplying Application Information

The second step of the wizard, allows you to specify application information. You must supply

- The application title
- Your company name
- Version information
- The setup language

Click Next when ready to continue.

List of Files to Search for Dependency Information

The third step of the wizard, enables you to designate all files that you want to scan for dependency information. This information is used to ensure that all necessary files are included in the package. Click Add File to add any additional files that you wish to scan. Click Next when done.

Inclusion of the Runtime

The fourth step of the wizard, enables you to determine whether the Access Runtime is included with the packaged application. If you opt to include the Access Runtime, you can designate whether you want to include system files and Internet Explorer 5.1. Finally, you can designate the language of the Access runtime that you wish to include. Click Next to continue.

Modifying Installation Locations

The fifth step of the Packaging Wizard allows you to designate where to install each file in the package. For each file, indicate where to place the file, and whether it is shared by other applications. Click Next when done.

Inclusion of Database Components

The sixth step of the wizard enables you to select the database components you want to include with your package.

Selecting Start Menu Items to be Created

In the seventh step of the Packaging Wizard, you can designate Start menu groups and items that are created during the installation process. Click New Folder to create a new folder and New Shortcut to create a new shortcut. If you click a shortcut and click Properties, the Start Menu Item Properties dialog box appears. Designate the Name, Command Line, Start In path, Database information, and Profile information for the item. Click OK to return to the Start Menu Shortcuts step of the wizard. Click a shortcut and click Remove to remove a shortcut. Click Next when you're finished designating all options.

Choosing a File to Run When the Installation Is Complete

The eighth step of the Packaging Wizard allows you to specify a command to execute when the installation is complete. For example, you can designate that you want Access to open a ReadMe file when the installation of the application is complete.

The Final Step

The final step of the Packaging Wizard prompts you either to build the setup program, or to save the package script without building it. Select the appropriate option and click Finish.

Deploying the Application

Before you can begin installing the application on workstations, you must deploy your project's packages to a distribution site. Once again, this is accomplished using the Packaging Wizard. Complete the following steps:

1. From the opening window of the Packaging Wizard, select Deploy.

2. In the first step of the wizard, you select the package to deploy. Click Next when ready.

3. The second step enables you to designate the type of deployment you want to perform. You can deploy to a folder, or via the Web. The steps that follow differ, depending on your selection. Click Next after you make your selection.

4. If you select Folder, the third step of the Packaging Wizard prompts you to designate where you want to deploy the package. You can deploy locally, or to a network. Make your selection and click Next.

5. In the final step, designate a name for the deployment script. This script is used for future deployments of the package. When ready, click Finish.

6. When the process is complete, a Deployment report appears. Click Save Report if you want to save the report. Click Close when done. You are returned to the opening screen of the Packaging Wizard.

Distributing the Application

The most important thing you must do when packaging and distributing your application is test the application on a machine that has never had a copy of Access or any Access runtime application installed. This ensures that your application includes all required components. I like to keep a "virgin" machine available for testing my application setups. Here's what I do:

1. Use Symantec Ghost to create an image of the operating system drive on the test machine.

2. Install my application.

3. Test my application.

4. Restore from the Ghost image.

By following these steps, I ensure that I always have a "clean" machine on which to test my application. Obviously, it is imperative that you test *all* aspects of your application on the machine on which you performed the installation from your setup disks.

> **TIP**
>
> Several third-party software packages are available to help you to back up and restore your Windows installation easily. My favorite program is Ghost, available from Symantec.

When you are ready to test the Setup process, follow these steps:

1. Select Run from the Windows Start menu.

2. In the Run dialog box, locate the Setup files that the Deploy portion of the Packaging Wizard created. Click OK.

3. After being notified of the setup's progress, the Application Setup dialog box appears.

4. Click OK to continue.

5. Select a location for the application installation.

6. Click the command button to install the application to the specified directory. The Choose Program Group dialog box appears. Select a program group and click Continue.

The installation process is completed. If you opted during the Packaging Wizard to create desktop shortcuts, they are created automatically when the Setup program is executed.

Looking at Other Issues

Two additional issues have not yet been covered regarding the distribution of your application. The first involves ensuring that the application database can establish any links that it has to external tables. The second involves the prospect of using replication to effectively distribute changes to your application.

Automating the Process of Linking to Tables

Access hard-codes locations for table links. This means that, if you install your application on another machine, the tables will not link successfully unless the other machine has exactly the same folder structure as you do on your machine. The code shown in Listing 32.4 checks to see whether the required tables are available. If they are not found in the expected location, the routine attempts to locate them in the same folder that holds them in the application database. If they still cannot be found, the user is given an opportunity to locate the files. If they *still* cannot be found, the application terminates.

LISTING 32.4   The LinkTables Routine

```
Sub LinkTables()
    On Error GoTo LinkTables_Err:

        Dim objFileDialog As FileDialog
        Dim strFileName As String

        'Determine if links are ok
        If Not VerifyLink Then

            'If links not ok, attempt to link with default file name
            'in the current folder
            If Not ReLink(CurrentProject.FullName, True) Then

                'If still unsuccessful, allow user to locate the data database
                MsgBox "You Must Locate Tables to Proceed" & vbCrLf & _
                    "The Tables are Located in the Chap32Data Database" & _
                    vbCrLf & _
                    "in the Directory Where You Placed the Sample Files"

                Set objFileDialog = Application.FileDialog(msoFileDialogOpen)

                With objFileDialog
                    .Show
                    .AllowMultiSelect = False
                    strFileName = .SelectedItems(1)
                End With

                'Attempt to relink with the database the user selected
                If Not ReLink(strFileName, False) Then

                    'If still unsuccessful, display message to the user and
                    'return false from this routine
                    MsgBox "You Cannot Run This App Without Locating Data
Tables"
                    LinkTables = False
                Else

                    'User successfully designated new location; return True
                    LinkTables = True
```

LISTING 32.4 Continued

```
                End If
        Else

            'Data database located with default name in the same location
            'as the application database; return True
            LinkTables = True
        End If
    Else

        'Table links not broken; return True
        LinkTables = True
    End If

Exit Function

LinkTables_Err:
    MsgBox "Error # " & Err.Number & ": " & Err.Description
    Exit Function

End Sub
```

 The routine begins by executing a function called `VerifyLink`. The `VerifyLink` function is shown in Listing 32.5 and is found in the FinalLibrary.MDA file on the sample code CD. It first creates an ADOX `Catalog` object. It sets the `ActiveConnection` property of the `Catalog` object to the `Connection` property of the `CurrentProject`. The `CurrentProject` object returns a reference to the database using the library, rather than to the library itself. The heart of the routine is the `For...Next` loop. It loops through each `Table` object in the Tables collection of the `Catalog` object. If the table is linked, it attempts to reference the first field in the table. If an error occurs, the table link must be broken. The error number is non-zero, and the routine exits the `For...Next` loop. Because the function returns whether or not the error number is equal to zero, `False` is returned if an error occurs, and `True` is returned if no error occurs.

LISTING 32.5 The `VerifyLink` Function

```
Function VerifyLink() As Boolean
    'Verify connection information in linked tables.

    'Declare Required Variables
    Dim cat As ADOX.Catalog
    Dim tdf As ADOX.Table
    Dim strTemp As String
```

LISTING 32.5   Continued

```
'Point Database object variable at the current database
Set cat = New ADOX.Catalog

With cat
    Set .ActiveConnection = CurrentProject.Connection

    'Continue if links are broken.
    On Error Resume Next

    'Open one linked table to see if connection
    'information is correct.
    'For Each tdf In .Tables
    '     If tdf.Type = "LINK" Then
    '         strTemp = tdf.Columns(0).Name
    '         If Err.Number Then
    '             Exit For
    '         End If
    '     End If

    'Next tdf

    'If code above is too slow, this is the
    'less conservative alternative
    For Each tdf In .Tables

        If tdf.Type = "LINK" Then
            strTemp = tdf.Columns(0).Name
            Exit For
        End If

    Next tdf


End With

VerifyLink = (Err.Number = 0)

End Function
```

If the VerifyLink function returns a False, the Relink function is executed. The Relink function is shown in Listing 32.6. It receives two parameters. The first parameter is the name of the database to which the function will attempt to link. The second parameter is a Boolean variable that designates whether the database is considered the default database.

The function begins by modifying the status bar. It then creates a `Catalog` object and an instance of a custom class called `DBInfo`. The ActiveConnection property of the `Catalog` object is set equal to the Connection property of the current project. Next the FullName property of the `DBInfo` class is set equal to the name of the file that is passed as a parameter to the function. The `DBInfo` class extracts the path and the filename from the full filename. Just as with the `VerifyLink` function, the `ReLink` function uses a `For...Next` loop. As it loops through each table in the database, it attempts to establish a link to a database with the name passed as a parameter to the `Relink` function.

This is where the `DefaultData` parameter comes into play. The first time that the `LinkTables` routine calls the `Relink` function, it passes the name and path of the application database as the first parameter, and `True` for the second parameter. The `Relink` function then attempts to link to a database located in the same folder as the application database, but with the word *Data* appended to the end of the filename. For example, if the application database is named Membership, the `Relink` function looks for a database called MembershipData in the same location as the application database. If it is successful, it returns `True`, and, if it is unsuccessful, it returns `False`. I use this method to attempt to re-establish the link because I commonly place both the application and data databases on a client's network, both in the same folder. When I do this, I employ a naming convention where the data database has the same name as the application database, but with the word *Data* appended to it.

If no data database with the expected filename is found in the folder where the application database is located (`False` was returned from the `Relink` function), the `LinkTables` routine uses the FileDialog object to display a `File Open` dialog box. This gives the user the opportunity to locate the data database. The filename and path that the user selects in the dialog box is passed to the `Relink` routine, along with `False` as the second parameter. Because the user has selected the file that he believes contains the data, there is no reason to append the word *Data* onto the filename. Once again the `Relink` routine loops through the Tables collection of the `Catalog` object, attempting to re-establish the broken links. If successful, it returns `True`, and, if unsuccessful, it returns `False`. If `False` is returned from the second call to the `Relink` function, the `LinkTables` routine exits the Access application.

LISTING 32.6   The Relink Function

```
Function ReLink(strDir As String, DefaultData As Boolean) _
    As Boolean

    Dim cat As ADOX.Catalog
    Dim tdfRelink As ADOX.Table
    Dim oDBInfo As DBInfo
    Dim strPath As String
    Dim strName As String
```

LISTING 32.6 Continued

```
Dim intCounter As Integer
Dim vntStatus As Variant

'Update status bar
vntStatus = SysCmd(acSysCmdSetStatus, "Updating Links")

Set cat = New ADOX.Catalog
Set oDBInfo = New DBInfo

With cat

    'Use File Information class to extract the application
    'database file name
    .ActiveConnection = CurrentProject.Connection
    oDBInfo.FullName = strDir
    strPath = oDBInfo.FilePathOnly
    strName = Left(oDBInfo.FileName, InStr(oDBInfo.FileName, ".") - 1)

    'Disable error handling
    On Error Resume Next

    'Update progress meter
    Call SysCmd(acSysCmdInitMeter, "Linking Data Tables", .Tables.Count)

    'Loop through each table, attempting to relink
    For Each tdfRelink In .Tables
        intCounter = intCounter + 1
        Call SysCmd(acSysCmdUpdateMeter, intCounter)
        If .Tables(tdfRelink.Name).Type = "LINK" Then
            tdfRelink.Properties("Jet OLEDB:Link Datasource") = _
                strPath & strName & IIf(DefaultData, "Data.Mdb", ".mdb")
        End If

        'If an error occurs, exit the loop
        If Err.Number Then
            Exit For
        End If
    Next tdfRelink
End With

'Remove the progress meter
Call SysCmd(acSysCmdRemoveMeter)

'Clear the status bar
vntStatus = SysCmd(acSysCmdClearStatus)
```

LISTING 32.6   Continued

```
    'Return whether or not an error occurred
    ReLink = (Err = 0)

End Function
```

Using Replication to Efficiently Distribute Your Application

You might not want to rebuild and redistribute Setup disks each time you change the design of your application database. Not only is this time-consuming, but also it is difficult to ensure that each user runs the Setup process in order to obtain the application database. If your organization is networked, it generally is much more effective to distribute application updates using replication. This involves making changes to the Design Master and then synchronizing with a hub after the changes are completed and tested properly. Replication is covered briefly in Chapter 20, "Developing Multiuser and Enterprise Applications," and in detail in *Alison Balter's Mastering Access 2002 Enterprise Development*.

PRACTICAL EXAMPLES

Distributing the Time and Billing Application

To complete your applications and prepare them for distribution, switchboards should be added to assist the user with the process of navigating throughout the application. Error handling should be built in to most of the application's routines. Custom toolbars and menu bars should be added to the application's forms and reports. Startup options must be set. Make sure that you test the application under the runtime version of the product. You must then properly secure the application to meet the specific needs of your organization and to build the Setup disks.

Summary

The process of preparing an application for distribution actually starts in the planning stages of the application. It involves everything from providing a means by which the users of the application can navigate from task to task, to preparing the distribution disks. It also involves important steps such as properly securing the application to ensure that the integrity of its data and objects are maintained, and building in a solid error handler to ensure that all errors are handled gracefully. Remember that whether your users will be running your application using the retail or runtime version of Access, by using the techniques you learned in this chapter, you can add professional polish and pizzazz to any application.

Appendixes

PART
VI

IN THIS PART

Table Structures

This appendix gives you a complete listing of all the tables included in the Time and Billing application. Each table includes the following

- A list of the field names, types, and lengths of each field in the table
- A detailed list of the properties associated with each field in the table

The tblClients Table

This table stores pertinent information about each client, such as the company name, contact name, and phone numbers.

TABLE A.1   The tblClients Table

Field Name	Type	Size (Bytes)
ClientID	Number (Long)	4
CompanyName	Text	50
ContactFirstName	Text	30
ContactLastName	Text	50
ContactTitle	Text	50
ContactTypeID	Number (Long)	4
ReferredBy	Text	30
AssociatedWith	Text	30
IntroDate	Date/Time	8
DefaultRate	Currency	8
Notes	Memo	(Varies)
Miles	Number (Long)	4
TermTypeID	Number (Long)	3
HomePage	Hyperlink	

TABLE A.2   The Field Properties for Each Field in the tblClients Table

Property	Value
ClientID	**Number (Long)**
AllowZeroLength	False
Attributes	Fixed size, auto-increment
Caption	Client ID
CollatingOrder	General

TABLE A.2 Continued

Property	Value
ClientID	**Number (Long)**
Column Hidden	False
ColumnOrder	Default
ColumnWidth	Default
OrdinalPosition	0
Required	False
SourceField	ClientID
SourceTable	tblClients
CompanyName	**Text**
AllowZeroLength	False
Attributes	Variable length
Caption	Company Name
CollatingOrder	General
ColumnHidden	False
ColumnOrder	Default
ColumnWidth	Default
DisplayControl	Text Box
OrdinalPosition	1
Required	True
SourceField	CompanyName
SourceTable	tblClients
AllowZeroLength	length
CollatingOrder	
ColumnHidden	
ColumnOrder	
ColumnWidth	
DisplayControl	
OrdinalPosition	
SourceField	
SourceTable	

Table A.2   Continued

Property	Value
CompanyName	**Text**
AllowZeroLength	length
CollatingOrder	
ColumnOrder	
ColumnWidth	
DisplayControl	
OrdinalPosition	
SourceField	
SourceTable	
AllowZeroLength	length
CollatingOrder	
ColumnHidden	
ColumnOrder	
ColumnWidth	
DefaultValue	
DisplayControl	
OrdinalPosition	
SourceField	
SourceTable	
AllowZeroLength	length
CollatingOrder	
ColumnHidden	
ColumnOrder	
ColumnWidth	
DisplayControl	
OrdinalPosition	
SourceTable	
AllowZeroLength	length
CollatingOrder	
ColumnHidden	
ColumnOrder	
ColumnWidth	
DisplayControl	

TABLE A.2   Continued

Property	Value
CompanyName	**Text**
OrdinalPosition	
SourceField	
SourceTable	
ContactFirstName	**Text**
AllowZeroLength	False
Attributes	Variable length
Caption	Contact First Name
CollatingOrder	General
ColumnHidden	False
ColumnOrder	Default
ColumnWidth	Default
DisplayControl	Text Box
OrdinalPosition	7
Required	False
SourceField	ContactFirstName
SourceTable	tblClients
ContactLastName	**Text**
AllowZeroLength	False
Attributes	Variable length
Caption	Contact Last Name
CollatingOrder	General
ColumnHidden	False
ColumnOrder	Default
ColumnWidth	Default
DisplayControl	Text Box
OrdinalPosition	8
Required	False
SourceField	ContactLastName
SourceTable	tblClients

TABLE A.2   Continued

Property	Value
ContactTitle	**Text**
AllowZeroLength	False
Attributes	Variable length
Caption	Contact Title
CollatingOrder	General
ColumnHidden	False
ColumnOrder	Default
ColumnWidth	Default
DisplayControl	Text Box
OrdinalPosition	9
Required	False
SourceField	ContactTitle
SourceTable	tblClients
ContactTypeID	**Long Integer**
AllowZeroLength	False
Attributes	Fixed size
Caption	Contact Type ID
CollatingOrder	General
ColumnHidden	False
ColumnOrder	Default
ColumnWidth	Default
DataUpdatable	False
DecimalPlaces	Auto
DisplayControl	Text Box
OrdinalPosition	6
Required	False
AllowZeroLength	length
CollatingOrder	
ColumnHidden	
ColumnOrder	
ColumnWidth	

TABLE A.2 Continued

Property	Value
ContactTypeID	**Long Integer**
DisplayControl	
InputMask	
SourceField	
SourceTable	
AllowZeroLength	length
CollatingOrder	
ColumnHidden	
ColumnOrder	
ColumnWidth	
DisplayControl	
InputMask	
OrdinalPosition	
SourceField	
SourceTable	
AllowZeroLength	length
CollatingOrder	
ColumnHidden	
ColumnOrder	
ColumnWidth	
DisplayControl	
InputMask	
OrdinalPosition	
SourceField	
SourceTable	
AllowZeroLength	length
CollatingOrder	
ColumnOrder	
ColumnWidth	
DisplayControl	
InputMask	
OrdinalPosition	

Table A.2   Continued

Property	Value
ContactTypeID	**Long Integer**
SourceField	
SourceTable	
AllowZeroLength	length
CollatingOrder	
ColumnHidden	
ColumnOrder	
ColumnWidth	
DisplayControl	
OrdinalPosition	
SourceField	
SourceTable	
ReferredBy	**Text**
AllowZeroLength	False
Attributes	Variable length
Caption	Referred By
CollatingOrder	General
ColumnHidden	False
ColumnOrder	Default
ColumnWidth	Default
DisplayControl	Text Box
OrdinalPosition	15
Required	False
SourceField	ReferredBy
SourceTable	tblClients
AssociatedWith	**Text**
AllowZeroLength	False
Attributes	Variable length
Caption	Associated With
CollatingOrder	General

TABLE A.2 Continued

Property	Value
AssociatedWith	**Text**
ColumnHidden	False
ColumnOrder	Default
ColumnWidth	Default
DisplayControl	Text Box
OrdinalPosition	16
Required	False
SourceField	AssociatedWith
SourceTable	tblClients
IntroDate	**Date/Time**
AllowZeroLength	False
Attributes	Fixed size
Caption	Intro Date
CollatingOrder	General
ColumnHidden	False
ColumnOrder	Default
ColumnWidth	Default
DefaultValue	=Date()
OrdinalPosition	17
Required	True
SourceField	IntroDate
SourceTable	tblClients
ValidationRule	<=Date( )
ValidationText	Date Entered Must Be On Or Before Today
DefaultRate	**Currency**
AllowZeroLength	False
Attributes	Fixed size
Caption	Default Rate
CollatingOrder	General
ColumnHidden	False

Table A.2   Continued

Property	Value
DefaultRate	**Currency**
ColumnOrder	Default
Column Width	Default
DecimalPlaces	255
DefaultValue	150
Format	Currency
OrdinalPosition	18
Required	False
SourceField	DefaultRate
SourceTable	tblClients
ValidationRule	Between 75 and 200
ValidationText	Rate must be between 75 and 200
Notes	**Memo**
AllowZeroLength	False
Attributes	Variable length
CollatingOrder	General
ColumnHidden	False
ColumnOrder	Default
ColumnWidth	Default
OrdinalPosition	19
Required	False
SourceField	Notes
SourceTable	tblClients
HomePage	**Hyperlink**
AllowZeroLength	False
Attributes	Variable length
Caption	Home Page
CollatingOrder	General
ColumnHidden	False

TABLE A.2 Continued

Property	Value
HomePage	**Hyperlink**
ColumnOrder	Default
ColumnWidth	Default
OrdinalPosition	20
Required	False
SourceField	HomePage
SourceTable	tblClients
Miles	**Long Integer**
AllowZeroLength	False
Attributes	Fixed size
CollatingOrder	General
ColumnHidden	False
ColumnOrder	Default
ColumnWidth	Default
DataUpdatable	False
DecimalPlaces	Auto
DisplayControl	Text Box
OrdinalPosition	17
Required	False
SourceField	Miles
SourceTable	tblClients
TermTypeID	**Long Integer**
AllowZeroLength	False
Attributes	Fixed size
Caption	Term Type ID
CollatingOrder	General
ColumnHidden	False
ColumnOrder	Default
ColumnWidth	Default
DataUpdatable	False

TABLE A.2   Continued

Property	Value
TermTypeID	**Long Integer**
DecimalPlaces	Auto
DisplayControl	Text Box
OrdinalPosition	18
Required	False
SourceField	TermTypeID
SourceTable	tblClients

The tblClientAddresses Table

This table stores the addresses for a client. One client can have multiple addresses. Each address has a specific address type.

TABLE A.3   The tblClientAddresses Table

Field Name	Type	Size (Bytes)
AddressID	Long Integer	4
ClientID	Long Integer	4
Address1	Text	50
Address2	Text	50
City	Text	30
StateProvince	Text	20
PostalCode	Text	20
Country	Text	20
AddressTypeID	Long Integer	4

TABLE A.4   The Field Properties for Each Field in the tblClientAddresses Table

Property	Value
AddressID	Long Integer
AllowZeroLength	False
Attributes	Fixed size, auto-increment
Caption	Address ID

TABLE A.4 Continued

Property	Value
CollatingOrder	General
ColumnHidden	False
ColumnOrder	Default
ColumnWidth	Default
DataUpdatable	False
OrdinalPosition	1
Required	False
SourceField	AddressID
SourceTable	tblClientAddresses
ClientID	**Long Integer**
AllowZeroLength	False
Attributes	Fixed size
Caption	Client ID
CollatingOrder	General
ColumnHidden	False
ColumnOrder	Default
ColumnWidth	Default
DataUpdatable	False
DecimalPlaces	Auto
DisplayControl	Text Box
OrdinalPosition	2
Required	False
SourceField	ClientID
SourceTable	tblClientAddresses
Address1	**Text**
AllowZeroLength	False
Attributes	Variable length
Caption	Address 1
CollatingOrder	General
ColumnHidden	False

TABLE A.4   Continued

Property	Value
Address1	**Text**
ColumnOrder	Default
ColumnWidth	Default
DataUpdatable	False
DisplayControl	Text Box
IMEMode	0
IMESentenceMode	3
OrdinalPosition	3
Required	False
SourceField	Address1
SourceTable	tblClientAddresses
UnicodeCompression	True
Address2	**Text**
AllowZeroLength	False
Attributes	Variable length
Caption	Address 2
CollatingOrder	General
ColumnHidden	False
ColumnOrder	Default
ColumnWidth	Default
DataUpdatable	False
DisplayControl	Text Box
IMEMode	0
IMESentenceMode	3
OrdinalPosition	4
Required	False
SourceField	Address2
SourceTable	tblClientAddresses
UnicodeCompression	True

TABLE A.4   Continued

Property	Value
City	**Text**
AllowZeroLength	False
Attributes	Variable length
CollatingOrder	General
ColumnHidden	False
ColumnOrder	Default
ColumnWidth	Default
DataUpdatable	False
DisplayControl	Text Box
IMEMode	0
IMESentenceMode	3
OrdinalPosition	5
Required	False
SourceField	City
SourceTable	tblClientAddresses
UnicodeCompression	True
StateProvince	**Text**
AllowZeroLength	False
Attributes	Variable length
Caption	State/Province
CollatingOrder	General
ColumnHidden	False
ColumnOrder	Default
ColumnWidth	Default
DataUpdatable	False
DisplayControl	Text Box
IMEMode	0
IMESentenceMode	3
OrdinalPosition	6
Required	False
SourceTable	tblClientAddresses
UnicodeCompression	True

TABLE A.4   Continued

Property	Value
PostalCode	**Text**
AllowZeroLength	False
Attributes	Variable length
Caption	Postal Code
CollatingOrder	General
ColumnHidden	False
ColumnOrder	Default
ColumnWidth	Default
DataUpdatable	False
DisplayControl	Text Box
IMEMode	0
IMESentenceMode	3
OrdinalPosition	7
Required	False
SourceField	PostalCode
SourceTable	tblClientAddresses
UnicodeCompression	True
Country	**Text**
AllowZeroLength	False
Attributes	Variable length
CollatingOrder	General
ColumnHidden	False
ColumnOrder	Default
ColumnWidth	Default
DataUpdatable	False
DisplayControl	Text Box
IMEMode	0
IMESentenceMode	3
OrdinalPosition	8
Required	False
SourceField	Country

Table A.4   Continued

Property	Value
Country	**Text**
SourceTable	tblClientAddresses
UnicodeCompression	True
AddressTypeID	**Long Integer**
AllowZeroLength	False
Attributes	Fixed size
Caption	Address Type ID
CollatingOrder	General
ColumnHidden	False
ColumnOrder	Default
ColumnWidth	Default
DataUpdatable	False
DecimalPlaces	Auto
DisplayControl	Text Box
OrdinalPosition	9
Required	False
SourceField	AddressTypeID
SourceTable	tblClientAddresses

The tblAddressTypes Table

This table stores the valid address types. It relates to the tblClientAddresses table and is a lookup table for the AddressTypeID stored in the tblClientAddresses table.

Table A.5   The tblAddressTypes Table

Field Name	Type	Size (Bytes)
AddressTypeID	Long Integer	4
AddressType	Text	50

TABLE A.6   The Field Properties for Each Field in the tblAddressTypes Table

Property	Value
AddressTypeID	**Long Integer**
AllowZeroLength	False
Attributes	Fixed size, auto-increment
Caption	Address Type ID
CollatingOrder	General
ColumnHidden	False
ColumnOrder	Default
ColumnWidth	Default
DataUpdatable	False
OrdinalPosition	1
Required	False
SourceField	AddressTypeID
SourceTable	tblAddressTypes
AddressType	**Text**
AllowZeroLength	False
Attributes	Variable length
Caption	Address Type
CollatingOrder	General
ColumnHidden	False
ColumnOrder	Default
ColumnWidth	Default
DataUpdatable	False
DisplayControl	Text Box
IMEMode	0
IMESentenceMode	3
OrdinalPosition	2
Required	False
SourceField	AddressType
SourceTable	tblAddressTypes
UnicodeCompression	True

The tblClientPhones Table

This table stores the phone numbers for a client. One client can have multiple phone numbers. Each address has a specific phone type.

TABLE A.7 The Field Properties for Each Field in the tblClientPhones Table

Field Name	Type	Size (Bytes)
PhoneID	Long Integer	4
ClientID	Long Integer	4
PhoneNumber	Text	50
PhoneTypeID	Long Integer	4

TABLE A.8 The Field Properties for Each Field in the tblClientPhones Table

Property	Value
PhoneID	**Long Integer**
AllowZeroLength	False
Attributes	Fixed size, auto-increment
Caption	Phone ID
CollatingOrder	General
ColumnHidden	False
ColumnOrder	Default
ColumnWidth	Default
DataUpdatable	False
OrdinalPosition	1
Required	False
SourceField	PhoneID
SourceTable	tblClientPhones
ClientID	**Long Integer**
AllowZeroLength	False
Attributes	Fixed size
Caption	Client ID
CollatingOrder	General
ColumnHidden	False

A

TABLE STRUCTURES

TABLE A.8   Continued

Property	Value
ClientID	**Long Integer**
ColumnOrder	Default
ColumnWidth	Default
DataUpdatable	False
DecimalPlaces	Auto
DisplayControl	Text Box
OrdinalPosition	2
Required	False
SourceField	ClientID
SourceTable	tblClientPhones
PhoneNumber	**Text**
AllowZeroLength	False
Attributes	Variable length
Caption	Phone Number
CollatingOrder	General
ColumnHidden	False
ColumnOrder	Default
ColumnWidth	Default
DataUpdatable	False
DisplayControl	Text Box
IMEMode	0
IMESentenceMode	3
OrdinalPosition	3
Required	False
SourceField	PhoneNumber
SourceTable	tblClientPhones
UnicodeCompression	True
PhoneTypeID	**Long Integer**
AllowZeroLength	False
Attributes	Fixed size

TABLE A.8 The Field Properties for Each Field in the tblClientPhones Table

Property	Value
PhoneTypeID	**Long Integer**
Caption	Phone Type ID
CollatingOrder	General
ColumnHidden	False
ColumnOrder	Default
ColumnWidth	Default
DataUpdatable	False
DecimalPlaces	Auto
DisplayControl	Text Box
OrdinalPosition	4
Required	False
SourceField	PhoneTypeID
SourceTable	tblClientPhones

The tblPhoneTypes Table

This table stores the valid phone types. It relates to the tblClientPhones table and is a lookup table for the PhoneTypeID stored in the tblClientPhones table.

TABLE A.9 The tblPhoneTypes Table

Field Name	Type	Size (Bytes)
PhoneTypeID	Long Integer	4
PhoneType	Text	50

TABLE A.10 The Field Properties for Each Field in the tblPhonesTypes Table

Property	Value
PhoneTypeID	**Long Integer**
AllowZeroLength	False
Attributes	Fixed size, auto-increment
Caption	Phone Type ID
CollatingOrder	General

A

TABLE STRUCTURES

TABLE A.10   Continued

Property	Value
PhoneTypeID	**Long Integer**
ColumnHidden	False
ColumnOrder	Default
ColumnWidth	Default
DataUpdatable	False
OrdinalPosition	1
Required	False
SourceField	PhoneTypeID
SourceTable	tblPhoneTypes
PhoneType	**Text**
AllowZeroLength	False
Attributes	Variable length
Caption	Phone Type
CollatingOrder	General
ColumnHidden	False
ColumnOrder	Default
ColumnWidth	Default
DataUpdatable	False
DisplayControl	Text Box
IMEMode	0
IMESentenceMode	3
OrdinalPosition	2
Required	False
SourceField	PhoneType
SourceTable	tblPhoneTypes
UnicodeCompression	True

The tblCorrespondence Table

The tblCorrespondence table contains a history of correspondence made to a particular client. It relates to the tblClients table.

TABLE A.11 The tblCorrespondence Table

Field Name	Type	Size (Bytes)
CorrespondenceID	Long Integer	4
ClientID	Long Integer	4
Description	Text	50
Notes	Memo	-
DateSent	Date/Time	8
CorrespondenceTypeID	Long Integer	4
ConsultantID	Long Integer	4
Document	OLE Object	-

TABLE A.12 The Field Properties for Each Field in the tblCorrespondence Table

Property	Value
CorrespondenceID	**Long Integer**
AllowZeroLength	False
Attributes	Fixed size, auto-increment
Caption	
Correspondence ID	
CollatingOrder	General
ColumnHidden	False
ColumnOrder	Default
ColumnWidth	Default
DataUpdatable	False
OrdinalPosition	1
Required	False
SourceField	CorrespondenceID
SourceTable	tblCorrespondence
ClientID	**Long Integer**
AllowZeroLength	False
Attributes	Fixed size
Caption	Client ID
CollatingOrder	General

TABLE A.12   Continued

Property	Value
ClientID	**Long Integer**
ColumnHidden	False
ColumnOrder	Default
ColumnWidth	Default
DataUpdatable	False
DecimalPlaces	Auto
DisplayControl	Text Box
OrdinalPosition	2
Required	False
SourceField	ClientID
SourceTable	tblCorrespondence
Description	**Text**
AllowZeroLength	False
Attributes	Variable length
CollatingOrder	General
ColumnHidden	False
ColumnOrder	Default
ColumnWidth	Default
DataUpdatable	False
DisplayControl	Text Box
IMEMode	0
IMESentenceMode	3
OrdinalPosition	3
Required	False
SourceField	Description
SourceTable	tblCorrespondence
UnicodeCompression	True
Notes	**Memo**
AllowZeroLength	False
Attributes	Variable length

TABLE A.12 Continued

Property	Value
Notes	**Memo**
CollatingOrder	General
ColumnHidden	False
ColumnOrder	Default
ColumnWidth	Default
DataUpdatable	False
IMEMode	0
IMESentenceMode	3
OrdinalPosition	4
Required	False
SourceField	Notes
SourceTable	tblCorrespondence
UnicodeCompression	True
DateSent	**Date/Time**
AllowZeroLength	False
Attributes	Fixed size
Caption	Date Sent
CollatingOrder	General
ColumnHidden	False
ColumnOrder	Default
ColumnWidth	Default
DataUpdatable	False
IMEMode	0
IMESentenceMode	3
InputMask	99/99/0000
OrdinalPosition	5
Required	False
SourceField	DateSent
SourceTable	tblCorrespondence

TABLE A.12   Continued

Property	Value
CorrespondenceTypeID	**Long Integer**
AllowZeroLength	False
Attributes	Fixed size
Caption	Correspondence Type ID
CollatingOrder	General
ColumnHidden	False
ColumnOrder	Default
ColumnWidth	Default
DataUpdatable	False
DecimalPlaces	Auto
DisplayControl	Text Box
OrdinalPosition	6
Required	False
SourceField	CorrespondenceTypeID
SourceTable	tblCorrespondence
ConsultantID	**Long Integer**
AllowZeroLength	False
Attributes	Fixed size
Caption	Consultant ID
CollatingOrder	General
ColumnHidden	False
ColumnOrder	Default
ColumnWidth	Default
DataUpdatable	False
DecimalPlaces	Auto
DisplayControl	Text Box
OrdinalPosition	7
Required	False
SourceField	ConsultantID
SourceTable	tblCorrespondence

TABLE A.12 Continued

Property	Value
Document	**OLE Object**
AllowZeroLength	False
Attributes	Variable length
CollatingOrder	General
ColumnHidden	False
ColumnOrder	Default
ColumnWidth	Default
DataUpdatable	False
OrdinalPosition	8
Required	False
SourceField	Document
SourceTable	tblCorrespondence

The tblCorrespondenceTypes Table

This table stores the valid correspondence types. It relates to the tblCorrespondence table and is a lookup table for the CorrespondenceTypeID stored in the tblCorrespondence table.

TABLE A.13 The tblCorrespondenceTypes Table

Field Name	Type	Size (Bytes)
CorrespondenceTypeID	Long Integer	4
CorrespondenceType	Text	50

TABLE A.12 The Field Properties for Each Field in the tblCorrespondenceTypes Table

Property	Value
CorrespondenceTypeID	**Long Integer**
AllowZeroLength	False
Attributes	Fixed size, auto-increment
Caption	Correspondence Type ID
CollatingOrder	General
ColumnHidden	False

TABLE A.12   Continued

Property	Value
CorrespondenceTypeID	**Long Integer**
ColumnOrder	Default
ColumnWidth	Default
DataUpdatable	False
OrdinalPosition	1
Required	False
SourceField	CorrespondenceTypeID
SourceTable	tblCorrespondenceTypes
CorrespondenceType	**Text**
AllowZeroLength	False
Attributes	Variable length
Caption	Correspondence Type
CollatingOrder	General
ColumnHidden	False
ColumnOrder	Default
ColumnWidth	Default
DataUpdatable	False
DisplayControl	Text Box
IMEMode	0
IMESentenceMode	3
OrdinalPosition	2
Required	False
SourceField	CorrespondenceType
SourceTable	tblCorrespondenceTypes
UnicodeCompression	True

The tblTerms Table

This table stores the valid term types. It relates to the tblClients table and is a lookup table for the TermTypeID stored in the tblClients table.

A

TABLE A.15   The tblTerms Table

Field Name	Type	Size (Bytes)
TermTypeID	Long Integer	4
TermType	Text	50

TABLE A.16   The Field Properties for Each Field in the tblTerms Table

Property	Value
TermTypeID	**Long Integer**
AllowZeroLength	False
Attributes	Fixed size, auto-increment
Caption	Term Type ID
CollatingOrder	General
ColumnHidden	False
ColumnOrder	Default
ColumnWidth	Default
DataUpdatable	False
OrdinalPosition	1
Required	False
SourceField	TermTypeID
SourceTable	tblTerms
TermType	**Text**
AllowZeroLength	False
Attributes	Variable length
Caption	Term Type
CollatingOrder	General
ColumnHidden	False
ColumnOrder	Default
ColumnWidth	Default
DataUpdatable	False
DisplayControl	Text Box
IMEMode	0
IMESentenceMode	3

TABLE A.16   Continued

Property	Value
TermType	**Text**
OrdinalPosition	2
Required	False
SourceField	TermType
SourceTable	tblTerms
UnicodeCompression	True

The tblContactTypes Table

This table stores the valid contact types. It relates to the tblClients table and is a lookup table for the ContactTypeID stored in the tblClients table.

TABLE A.17   The tblContactTypes Table

Field Name	Type	Size (Bytes)
ContactTypeID	Long Integer	4
ContactType	Text	50

TABLE A.18   The Field Properties for Each Field in the tblContactTypes Table

Property	Value
ContactTypeID	**Long Integer**
AllowZeroLength	False
Attributes	Fixed size, auto-increment
Caption	Contact Type ID
CollatingOrder	General
ColumnHidden	False
ColumnOrder	Default
ColumnWidth	Default
DataUpdatable	False
OrdinalPosition	1
Required	False
SourceField	ContactTypeID
SourceTable	tblContactType

TABLE A.18   The Field Properties for Each Field in the tblContactTypes Table

Property	Value
ContactType	**Text**
AllowZeroLength	False
Attributes	Variable length
Caption	Contact Type
CollatingOrder	General
ColumnHidden	False
ColumnOrder	Default
ColumnWidth	Default
DataUpdatable	False
DisplayControl	Text Box
IMEMode	0
IMESentenceMode	3
OrdinalPosition	2
Required	False
SourceField	ContactType
SourceTable	tblContactType
UnicodeCompression	True

A

TABLE STRUCTURES

The tblCompanyInfo Table

This table stores information about your company, including address and default payment terms.

TABLE A.19   The tblCompanyInfo Table

Field Name	Type	Size (Bytes)
SetupID	Number (Long)	4
CompanyName	Text	50
Address	Text	255
City	Text	50
StateProvince	Text	20
PostalCode	Text	20
Country	Text	50

TABLE A.19 Continued

Field Name	Type	Size (Bytes)
PhoneNumber	Text	30
FaxNumber	Text	30
DefaultPaymentTerms	Text	255
DefaultInvoiceDescription	Memo	(varies)

TABLE A.20 The Properties of Each Field Included in the tblCompanyInfo Table

Property	Value
SetupID	**Number (Long)**
AllowZeroLength	False
Attributes	Fixed size, auto-increment
Caption	SetupID
CollatingOrder	General
ColumnHidden	False
ColumnOrder	Default
ColumnWidth	Default
OrdinalPosition	0
Required	False
SourceField	SetupID
SourceTable	tblCompanyInfo
CompanyName	**Text**
AllowZeroLength	False
Attributes	Variable length
Caption	Company Name
CollatingOrder	General
Column Hidden	False
ColumnOrder	Default
ColumnWidth	Default
DisplayControl	Text Box
OrdinalPosition	1
Required	False

TABLE A.20   Continued

Property	Value
CompanyName	**Text**
SourceField	CompanyName
SourceTable	tblCompanyInfo
Address	**Text**
AllowZeroLength	False
Attributes	Variable length
CollatingOrder	General
ColumnHidden	False
ColumnOrder	Default
ColumnWidth	Default
DisplayControl	Text Box
OrdinalPosition	2
Required	False
SourceField	Address
SourceTable	tblCompanyInfo
City	**Text**
AllowZeroLength	False
Attributes	Variable length
CollatingOrder	General
Column Hidden	False
ColumnOrder	Default
ColumnWidth	Default
DisplayControl	Text Box
OrdinalPosition	3
Required	False
SourceField	City
SourceTable	tblCompanyInfo

Table A.20   Continued

Property	Value
StateProvince	**Text**
AllowZeroLength	False
Attributes	Variable length
Caption	State/Province
CollatingOrder	General
Column Hidden	False
ColumnOrder	Default
ColumnWidth	Default
DisplayControl	Text Box
OrdinalPosition	4
Required	False
SourceField	StateProvince
SourceTable	tblCompanyInfo
PostalCode	**Text**
AllowZeroLength	False
Attributes	Variable length
Caption	Postal Code
CollatingOrder	General
ColumnHidden	False
ColumnOrder	Default
ColumnWidth	Default
DisplayControl	Text Box
InputMask	00000\-9999
OrdinalPosition	5
Required	False
SourceField	PostalCode
SourceTable	tblCompanyInfo
Country	**Text**
AllowZeroLength	False
Attributes	Variable length

TABLE A.20   Continued

Property	Value
Country	**Text**
CollatingOrder	General
ColumnHidden	False
ColumnOrder	Default
ColumnWidth	Default
DisplayControl	Text Box
OrdinalPosition	6
Required	False
SourceField	Country
SourceTable	tblCompanyInfo
PhoneNumber	**Text**
AllowZeroLength	False
Attributes	Variable length
Caption	Phone Number
CollatingOrder	General
Column Hidden	False
ColumnOrder	Default
ColumnWidth	Default
DisplayControl	Text Box
InputMask	!\(999") "000\-0000
OrdinalPosition	7
Required	False
SourceField	PhoneNumber
SourceTable	tblCompanyInfo
FaxNumber	**Text**
AllowZeroLength	False
Attributes	Variable length
Caption	Fax Number
CollatingOrder	General
ColumnHidden	False

A

TABLE STRUCTURES

Table A.20   Continued

Property	Value
FaxNumber	**Text**
ColumnOrder	Default
ColumnWidth	Default
DisplayControl	Text Box
InputMask	!\(999") "000\-0000
OrdinalPosition	8
Required	False
SourceField	FaxNumber
SourceTable	tblCompanyInfo
DefaultPaymentTerms	**Text**
AllowZeroLength	False
Attributes	Variable length
Caption	Default Payment Terms
CollatingOrder	General
ColumnHidden	False
ColumnOrder	Default
ColumnWidth	Default
DisplayControl	Text Box
OrdinalPosition	9
Required	False
SourceField	DefaultPaymentTerms
SourceTable	tblCompanyInfo
DefaultInvoiceDescription	**Memo**
AllowZeroLength	False
Attributes	Variable length
Caption	Default Invoice Description
CollatingOrder	General
ColumnHidden	False

TABLE A.20   Continued

Property	Value
DefaultInvoiceDescription	**Memo**
ColumnOrder	Default
ColumnWidth	Default
OrdinalPosition	10
Required	False
SourceField	DefaultInvoiceDescription
SourceTable	tblCompanyInfo

The tblEmployees Table

This table includes relevant employee information, such as name, address, and billing rate.

TABLE A.21   The tblEmployees Table

Field Name	Type	Size (Bytes)
EmployeeID	Number (Long)	4
FirstName	Text	50
LastName	Text	50
Title	Text	50
EmailName	Text	50
Extension	Text	30
Address	Text	255
City	Text	50
StateOrProvince	Text	20
PostalCode	Text	20
Country	Text	50
HomePhone	Text	30
WorkPhone	Text	30
BillingRate	Currency	8

TABLE A.22   The Properties of Each Field Included in the tblEmployees Table

Property	Value
EmployeeID	**Number (Long)**
AllowZeroLength	False
Attributes	Fixed size, auto-increment
Caption	Employee ID
CollatingOrder	General
OrdinalPosition	0
Required	False
SourceField	EmployeeID
SourceTable	tblEmployees
FirstName	**Text**
AllowZeroLength	False
Attributes	Variable length
Caption	First Name
CollatingOrder	General
OrdinalPosition	1
Required	False
SourceField	FirstName
SourceTable	tblEmployees
LastName	**Text**
AllowZeroLength	False
Attributes	Variable length
Caption	Last Name
CollatingOrder	General
Ordinal Position	2
Required	False
SourceField	LastName
SourceTable	tblEmployees
Title	**Text**
AllowZeroLength	False
Attributes	Variable length

TABLE A.22   Continued

Property	Value
Title	**Text**
CollatingOrder	General
OrdinalPosition	3
Required	False
SourceField	Title
SourceTable	tblEmployees
EmailName	**Text**
AllowZeroLength	False
Attributes	Variable length
Caption	Email Name
CollatingOrder	General
OrdinalPosition	4
Required	False
SourceField	EmailName
SourceTable	tblEmployees
Extension	**Text**
AllowZeroLength	False
Attributes	Variable length
CollatingOrder	General
OrdinalPosition	5
Required	False
SourceField	Extension
SourceTable	tblEmployees
Address	**Text**
AllowZeroLength	False
Attributes	Variable length
CollatingOrder	General
OrdinalPosition	6
Required	False

TABLE A.22   Continued

Property	Value
Address	**Text**
SourceField	Address
SourceTable	tblEmployees
City	**Text**
AllowZeroLength	False
Attributes	Variable length
CollatingOrder	General
OrdinalPosition	7
Required	False
SourceField	City
SourceTable	tblEmployees
StateOrProvince	**Text**
AllowZeroLength	False
Attributes	Variable length
Caption	State/Province
CollatingOrder	General
OrdinalPosition	8
Required	False
SourceField	StateOrProvince
SourceTable	tblEmployees
PostalCode	**Text**
AllowZeroLength	False
Attributes	Variable length
Caption	Postal Code
CollatingOrder	General
InputMask	00000-9999
OrdinalPosition	9
Required	False

TABLE A.22 Continued

Property	Value
PostalCode	**Text**
SourceField	PostalCode
SourceTable	tblEmployees
Country	**Text**
AllowZeroLength	False
Attributes	Variable length
CollatingOrder	General
OrdinalPosition	10
Required	False
SourceField	Country
SourceTable	tblEmployees
HomePhone	**Text**
AllowZeroLength	False
Attributes	Variable length
Caption	Home Phone
CollatingOrder	General
InputMask	!(999) 000-0000
OrdinalPosition	11
Required	False
SourceField	HomePhone
SourceTable	tblEmployees
WorkPhone	**Text**
AllowZeroLength	False
Attributes	Variable length
Caption	Work Phone
CollatingOrder	General
InputMask	!(999) 000-0000
OrdinalPosition	12
Required	False

TABLE A.22 Continued

Property	Value
WorkPhone	**Text**
SourceField	WorkPhone
SourceTable	tblEmployees
BillingRate	**Currency**
AllowZeroLength	False
Attributes	Fixed size
Caption	Billing Rate
CollatingOrder	General
DecimalPlaces	2
Format	Currency
OrdinalPosition	13
Required	False
SourceField	BillingRate
SourceTable	tblEmployees

The tblErrorLog Table

This table logs all application errors encountered while using the Time and Billing application, including error number and the name of the routine and module where the error occurred.

TABLE A.23 The tblErrorLog Table

Field Name	Type	Size (Bytes)
ErrorSeq	Number (Long)	4
ErrorDate	Date/Time	8
ErrorTime	Date/Time	8
UserName	Text	30
ErrorNum	Number (Integer)	2
ErrorString	Text	30
ModuleName	Text	50
RoutineName	Text	50

Table A.24   The Properties and Values Associated with Each Field in the tblErrorLog Table

Property	Value
ErrorSeq	**Number (Long)**
AllowZeroLength	False
Attributes	Fixed size, auto-increment
CollatingOrder	General
ColumnHidden	False
ColumnOrder	Default
ColumnWidth	Default
Description	Unique identifier for the error
OrdinalPosition	0
Required	False
SourceField	ErrorSeq
SourceTable	tblErrorLog
ErrorDate	**Date/Time**
AllowZeroLength	False
Attributes	Fixed size
CollatingOrder	General
ColumnHidden	False
ColumnOrder	Default
ColumnWidth	Default
Description	Date that the error occurred
Format	Medium date
OrdinalPosition	1
Required	False
SourceField	ErrorDate
SourceTable	tblErrorLog
ErrorTime	**Date/Time**
AllowZeroLength	False
Attributes	Fixed size
CollatingOrder	General

TABLE A.24   Continued

Property	Value
ErrorTime	**Date/Time**
ColumnHidden	False
ColumnOrder	Default
ColumnWidth	Default
Description	Time that the error occurred
Format	Long Time
OrdinalPosition	2
Required	False
SourceField	ErrorTime
SourceTable	tblErrorLog
UserName	**Text**
AllowZeroLength	False
Attributes	Variable length
CollatingOrder	General
ColumnHidden	False
ColumnOrder	Default
ColumnWidth	Default
Description	Name of the user
DisplayControl	Text Box
OrdinalPosition	3
Required	False
SourceField	UserName
SourceTable	tblErrorLog
ErrorNum	**Number (Integer)**
AllowZeroLength	False
Attributes	Fixed size
CollatingOrder	General
ColumnHidden	False
ColumnOrder	Default
ColumnWidth	Default

TABLE A.24   Continued

Property	Value
ErrorNum	**Number (Integer)**
DecimalPlaces	255
DefaultValue	0
Description	VBA Error Code
DisplayControl	Text Box
OrdinalPosition	4
Required	False
SourceField	ErrorNum
SourceTable	tblErrorLog
ErrorString	**Text**
AllowZeroLength	False
Attributes	Variable length
CollatingOrder	General
Column Hidden	False
ColumnOrder	Default
ColumnWidth	Default
Description	VBA Error Description
DisplayControl	Text Box
OrdinalPosition	5
Required	False
SourceField	ErrorString
SourceTable	tblErrorLog
ModuleName	**Text**
AllowZeroLength	False
Attributes	Variable length
CollatingOrder	General
ColumnHidden	False
ColumnOrder	Default
ColumnWidth	Default
Description	Module in which the error occurred

TABLE A.24   Continued

Property	Value
ModuleName	**Text**
DisplayControl	Text Box
OrdinalPosition	6
Required	False
SourceField	Module
SourceTable	tblErrorLog
RoutineName	**Text**
AllowZeroLength	False
Attributes	Variable length
CollatingOrder	General
ColumnHidden	False
ColumnOrder	Default
ColumnWidth	Default
Description	Routine in which the error occurred
DisplayControl	Text Box
OrdinalPosition	7
Required	False
SourceField	Routine
SourceTable	tblErrorLog

The tblErrors Table

This table gives you information about how your application should respond to error numbers.

TABLE A.25   The tblErrors Table

Field Name	Type	Size (Bytes)
ErrorNum	Number (Long)	4
Response	Number (Long)	4

TABLE A.26   The Properties and Values Associated with Each Field in the tblErrors Table

Property	Value
ErrorNum	**Number (Long)**
AllowZeroLength	False
Attributes	Fixed size
CollatingOrder	General
ColumnHidden	False
ColumnOrder	Default
ColumnWidth	Default
DecimalPlaces	255
DefaultValue	0
Description	Number of the error
DisplayControl	Text Box
OrdinalPosition	0
Required	False
SourceField	ErrorNum
SourceTable	tblErrors
Response	**Number (Long)**
AllowZeroLength	False
Attributes	Fixed size
CollatingOrder	General
ColumnHidden	False
ColumnOrder	Default
ColumnWidth	Default
DecimalPlaces	255
DefaultValue	0
Description	Action to take
DisplayControl	Text Box
OrdinalPosition	1
Required	False
SourceField	Response
SourceTable	tblErrors

A

TABLE STRUCTURES

The tblExpenseCodes Tables

This table contains all the valid expense codes used in the Time and Billing application.

TABLE A.27   The tblExpenseCodes

Field Name	Type	Size (Bytes)
ExpenseCodeID	Number (Long)	4
ExpenseCode	Text	30

TABLE A.28   The Field Properties of the tblExpenseCodes Table

Property	Value
ExpenseCodeID	**Number (Long)**
AllowZeroLength	False
Attributes	Fixed size, auto-increment
Caption	Expense Code ID
CollatingOrder	General
OrdinalPosition	0
Required	False
SourceField	ExpenseCodeID
SourceTable	tblExpenseCodes
ExpenseCode	**Text**
AllowZeroLength	False
Attributes	Variable length
Caption	Expense Code
CollatingOrder	General
OrdinalPosition	1
Required	False
SourceField	ExpenseCode
SourceTable	tblExpenseCodes

The tblPaymentMethods Table

This table lists the valid payment methods.

TABLE A.29 The tblPaymentMethods Table

Field Name	Type	Size (Bytes)
PaymentMethodID	Number (Long)	4
PaymentMethod	Text	50
CreditCard	Yes/No	1

TABLE A.30 The Field Properties of the tblPaymentMethods Table

Property	Value
PaymentMethodID	**Number (Long)**
AllowZeroLength	False
Attributes	Fixed size, auto-increment
Caption	Payment Method ID
CollatingOrder	General
OrdinalPosition	0
Required	False
SourceField	PaymentMethodID
SourceTable	tblPaymentMethods
PaymentMethod	**Text**
AllowZeroLength	False
Attributes	Variable length
Caption	Payment Method
CollatingOrder	General
OrdinalPosition	1
Required	False
SourceField	PaymentMethod
SourceTable	tblPaymentMethods

TABLE A.30   Continued

Property	Value
CreditCard	**Yes/No**
AllowZeroLength	False
Attributes	Fixed size
Caption	Credit Card?
CollatingOrder	General
Format	Yes/No
OrdinalPosition	2
Required	False
SourceField	CreditCard
SourceTable	tblPaymentMethods

The tblPayments Table

This table stores client payment information, such as the amount and date of payment for particular projects.

TABLE A.31   The tblPayments Table

Field Name	Type	Size (Bytes)
PaymentID	Number (Long)	4
ProjectID	Number (Long)	4
PaymentAmount	Currency	8
PaymentDate	Date/Time	8
CreditCardNumber	Text	30
CardholdersName	Text	50
CreditCardExpDate	Date/Time	8
PaymentMethodID	Number (Long)	4

TABLE A.32   The Field Properties of the tblPayments Table

Property	Value
PaymentID	**Number (Long)**
AllowZeroLength	False
Attributes	Fixed size, auto-increment

TABLE A.32 Continued

Property	Value
PaymentID	**Number (Long)**
Caption	Payment ID
CollatingOrder	General
ColumnHidden	False
ColumnOrder	Default
ColumnWidth	Default
OrdinalPosition	0
Required	False
SourceField	PaymentID
SourceTable	tblPayments
ProjectID	**Number (Long)**
AllowZeroLength	False
Attributes	Fixed size
Caption	Project ID
CollatingOrder	General
ColumnHidden	False
ColumnOrder	Default
ColumnWidth	Default
DecimalPlaces	255
DisplayControl	Text Box
OrdinalPosition	1
Required	False
SourceField	ProjectID
SourceTable	tblPayments
PaymentAmount	**Currency**
AllowZeroLength	False
Attributes	Fixed size
Caption	Payment amount
CollatingOrder	General
Column Hidden	False

Table A.32   Continued

Property	Value
PaymentAmount	**Currency**
ColumnOrder	Default
ColumnWidth	Default
DecimalPlaces	2
Format	Currency
OrdinalPosition	2
Required	False
SourceField	PaymentAmount
SourceTable	tblPayments
PaymentDate	**Date/Time**
AllowZeroLength	False
Attributes	Fixed size
Caption	Payment date
CollatingOrder	General
ColumnHidden	False
ColumnOrder	Default
ColumnWidth	Default
Format	Short date
InputMask	99/99/00
OrdinalPosition	3
Required	False
SourceField	PaymentDate
SourceTable	tblPayments
CreditCardNumber	**Text**
AllowZeroLength	False
Attributes	Variable length
Caption	Credit Card #
CollatingOrder	General
ColumnHidden	False
ColumnOrder	Default

TABLE A.32   Continued

Property	Value
CreditCardNumber	**Text**
ColumnWidth	Default
DisplayControl	Text Box
OrdinalPosition	4
Required	False
SourceField	CreditCardNumber
SourceTable	tblPayments
CardholdersName	**Text**
AllowZeroLength	False
Attributes	Variable length
Caption	Cardholder Name
CollatingOrder	General
ColumnHidden	False
ColumnOrder	Default
ColumnWidth	Default
DisplayControl	Text Box
OrdinalPosition	5
Required	False
SourceField	CardholdersName
SourceTable	tblPayments
CreditCardExpDate	**Date/Time**
AllowZeroLength	False
Attributes	Fixed size
Caption	Card Exp. Date
CollatingOrder	General
ColumnHidden	False
ColumnOrder	Default
ColumnWidth	Default
Format	Short date
InputMask	99/99/00

TABLE A.32   Continued

Property	Value
CreditCardExpDate	**Date/Time**
OrdinalPosition	6
Required	False
SourceField	CreditCardExpDate
SourceTable	tblPayments
PaymentMethodID	**Number (Long)**
AllowZeroLength	False
Attributes	Fixed size
Bound Column	1
Caption	Payment Method ID
CollatingOrder	General
Column Count	3
Column Heads	False
ColumnHidden	False
ColumnOrder	Default
ColumnWidth	Default
ColumnWidths	0;1440;0
DecimalPlaces	255
DisplayControl	Combo Box
LimitToList	True
ListRows	8
ListWidth	1
OrdinalPosition	7
Required	False
RowSource Type	Table/Query
RowSource	SELECT DISTINCTROW tblPaymentMethods.* FROM tblPaymentMethods ORDER BY tblPaymentMethods.PaymentMethod;
SourceField	PaymentMethodID
SourceTable	tblPayments

The tblProjects Table

This table stores information about each project, including a cost estimate and important dates.

TABLE A.33   The tblProjects Table

Field Name	Type	Size (Bytes)
ProjectID	Number (Long)	4
ProjectName	Text	50
ProjectDescription	Memo	n/a
ClientID	Number (Long)	4
PurchaseOrderNumber	Text	50
ProjectTotalEstimate	Currency	8
EmployeeID	Number (Long)	4
ProjectBeginDate	Date/Time	8
ProjectEndDate	Date/Time	8

TABLE A.34   The Field Properties of the tblProjects Table

Property	Value
ProjectID	**Number (Long)**
AllowZeroLength	False
Attributes	Fixed size, auto-increment
Caption	Project ID
CollatingOrder	General
ColumnHidden	False
ColumnOrder	Default
ColumnWidth	Default
OrdinalPosition	0
Required	False
SourceField	ProjectID
SourceTable	tblProjects
ProjectName	**Text**
AllowZeroLength	False
Attributes	Variable length

TABLE A.34 Continued

Property	Value
ProjectName	**Text**
Caption	Project Name
CollatingOrder	General
ColumnHidden	False
ColumnOrder	Default
ColumnWidth	Default
DisplayControl	Text Box
OrdinalPosition	1
Required	True
SourceField	ProjectName
SourceTable	tblProjects
ProjectDescription	**Memo**
AllowZeroLength	False
Attributes	Variable length
Caption	Project Description
CollatingOrder	General
ColumnHidden	False
ColumnOrder	Default
Column Width	Default
OrdinalPosition	2
Required	False
SourceField	ProjectDescription
SourceTable	tblProjects
ClientID	**Number (Long)**
AllowZeroLength	False
Attributes	Fixed size
Bound Column	1
Caption	Client ID
CollatingOrder	General
ColumnCount	2

TABLE A.34   Continued

Property	Value
ClientID	**Number (Long)**
ColumnHeads	False
ColumnHidden	False
ColumnOrder	Default
ColumnWidth	Default
ColumnWidths	;14400
DecimalPlaces	255
DefaultValue	0
DisplayControl	Combo Box
LimitToList	True
ListRows	8
ListWidth	1
OrdinalPosition	3
Required	True
RowSourceType	Table/Query
RowSource	SELECT DISTINCTROW [tblClients].[ClientID], [tblClients].[CompanyName] FROM [tblClients];
SourceField	ClientID
SourceTable	tblProjects
PurchaseOrderNumber	**Text**
AllowZeroLength	False
Attributes	Variable length
Caption	Purchase Order Number
CollatingOrder	General
Column Hidden	False
ColumnOrder	Default
ColumnWidth	Default
DisplayControl	Text Box
OrdinalPosition	4

TABLE A.34   Continued

Property	Value
PurchaseOrderNumber	**Text**
Required	False
SourceField	PurchaseOrderNumber
SourceTable	tblProjects
ProjectTotalEstimate	**Currency**
AllowZeroLength	False
Attributes	Fixed size
Caption	ProjectTotalEstimate
CollatingOrder	General
ColumnHidden	False
ColumnOrder	Default
ColumnWidth	Default
DecimalPlaces	255
DefaultValue	0
Format	Currency
OrdinalPosition	5
Required	False
SourceField	ProjectTotalEstimate
SourceTable	tblProjects
EmployeeID	**Number (Long)**
AllowZeroLength	False
Attributes	Fixed size
Caption	Employee ID
CollatingOrder	General
ColumnHidden	False
ColumnOrder	Default
ColumnWidth	Default
DecimalPlaces	255
DefaultValue	0
DisplayControl	Text Box

TABLE A.34 Continued

Property	Value
EmployeeID	**Number (Long)**
OrdinalPosition	6
Required	False
SourceField	EmployeeID
SourceTable	tblProjects
ProjectBeginDate	**Date/Time**
AllowZeroLength	False
Attributes	Fixed size
Caption	Project Begin Date
CollatingOrder	General
ColumnHidden	False
ColumnOrder	Default
ColumnWidth	Default
OrdinalPosition	7
Required	False
SourceField	ProjectBeginDate
SourceTable	tblProjects
ProjectEndDate	**Date/Time**
AllowZeroLength	False
Attributes	Fixed size
Caption	Project End Date
CollatingOrder	General
ColumnHidden	False
ColumnOrder	Default
ColumnWidth	Default
OrdinalPosition	8
Required	False
SourceField	ProjectEndDate
SourceTable	tblProjects

The tblTimCardExpenses Table

This tables stores necessary information for billable project expenses, such as the date and amount of the expense.

TABLE A.35   The tblTimeCardExpenses Table

Field Name	Type	Size (Bytes)
TimeCardExpenseID	Number (Long)	4
TimeCardID	Number (Long)	4
ExpenseDate	Date/Time	8
ProjectID	Number (Long)	4
ExpenseDescription	Text	255
ExpenseAmount	Currency	8
ExpenseCodeID	Number (Long)	4

TABLE A.36   The Field Properties of the tblTimeCardExpenses Table

Property	Value
TimeCardExpenseID	**Number (Long)**
AllowZeroLength	False
Attributes	Fixed size, auto-increment
Caption	Time Card Expense ID
CollatingOrder	General
ColumnHidden	False
ColumnOrder	Default
ColumnWidth	Default
OrdinalPosition	0
Required	False
SourceField	TimeCardExpenseID
SourceTable	tblTimeCardExpenses
TimeCardID	**Number (Long)**
AllowZeroLength	False
Attributes	Fixed size
Caption	Time Card ID

TABLE A.36   Continued

Property	Value
TimeCardID	**Number (Long)**
CollatingOrder	General
ColumnHidden	False
ColumnOrder	Default
ColumnWidth	Default
DecimalPlaces	255
DisplayControl	Text Box
OrdinalPosition	1
Required	False
SourceField	TimeCardID
SourceTable	tblTimeCardExpenses
ExpenseDate	**Date/Time**
AllowZeroLength	False
Attributes	Fixed size
Caption	Expense Date
CollatingOrder	General
ColumnHidden	False
ColumnOrder	Default
ColumnWidth	Default
Format	Short date
InputMask	99/99/00
OrdinalPosition	2
Required	False
SourceField	ExpenseDate
SourceTable	tblTimeCardExpenses
ProjectID	**Number (Long)**
AllowZeroLength	False
Attributes	Fixed size
BoundColumn	1
Caption	Project ID

TABLE A.36   Continued

Property	Value
ProjectID	**Number (Long)**
CollatingOrder	General
ColumnCount	3
ColumnHeads	False
ColumnHidden	False
ColumnOrder	Default
ColumnWidth	Default
ColumnWidths	0;1020;3156
DecimalPlaces	255
DisplayControl	Combo Box
LimitToList	True
ListRows	8
ListWidth	3
OrdinalPosition	3
Required	False
RowSourceType	Table/Query
RowSource	SELECT DISTINCTROW tblProjects.* FROM tblProjects ORDER BY tblProjects.ProjectName;
SourceField	ProjectID
SourceTable	tblTimeCardExpenses
ExpenseDescription	**Text**
AllowZeroLength	False
Attributes	Variable length
Caption	Expense Description
CollatingOrder	General
ColumnHidden	False
ColumnOrder	Default
ColumnWidth	Default
Display Control	Text Box
OrdinalPosition	4
Required	False

TABLE A.36   Continued

Property	Value
ExpenseDescription	**Text**
SourceField	ExpenseDescription
SourceTable	tblTimeCardExpenses
ExpenseAmount	**Currency**
AllowZeroLength	False
Attributes	Fixed size
Caption	Expense Amount
CollatingOrder	General
ColumnHidden	False
ColumnOrder	Default
ColumnWidth	Default
DecimalPlaces	2
Format	Currency
OrdinalPosition	5
Required	False
SourceField	ExpenseAmount
SourceTable	tblTimeCardExpenses
ExpenseCodeID	**Number (Long)**
AllowZeroLength	False
Attributes	Fixed size
Bound Column	1
Caption	Expense Code ID
CollatingOrder	General
ColumnCount	2
ColumnHeads	False
ColumnHidden	False
ColumnOrder	Default
ColumnWidth	Default
ColumnWidths	0;2880
DecimalPlaces	255

TABLE A.36   Continued

Property	Value
ExpenseCodeID	**Number (Long)**
DisplayControl	Combo Box
LimitToList	True
ListRows	8
ListWidth	2
OrdinalPosition	6
Required	False
RowSourceType	Table/Query
RowSource	SELECT DISTINCTROW tblExpenseCodes.* FROM tblExpenseCodes ORDER BY tblExpenseCodes.ExpenseCode;
SourceField	ExpenseCodeID
SourceTable	tblTimeCardExpenses

The tblTimeCardHours Table

This table stores a record of billable hours for a project, including dates and billing rates.

TABLE A.37   The tblTimeCardHours Table

Field Name	Type	Size (Bytes)
TimeCardDetailID	Number (Long)	4
TimeCardID	Number (Long)	4
DateWorked	Date/Time	8
ProjectID	Number (Long)	4
WorkDescription	Text	255
BillableHours	Number (Double)	8
BillingRate	Currency	8
WorkCodeID	Number (Long)	4

TABLE A.38   The Field Properties of the tblTimeCardHours Table

Property	Value
TimeCardDetailID	**Number (Long)**
AllowZeroLength	False
Attributes	Fixed size, auto-increment
Caption	Time Card Detail ID
CollatingOrder	General
ColumnHidden	False
ColumnOrder	Default
ColumnWidth	Default
OrdinalPosition	0
Required	False
SourceField	TimeCardDetailID
SourceTable	tblTimeCardHours
TimeCardID	**Number (Long)**
AllowZeroLength	False
Attributes	Fixed size
Caption	Time Card ID
CollatingOrder	General
ColumnHidden	False
ColumnOrder	Default
ColumnWidth	Default
DecimalPlaces	255
DisplayControl	Text Box
OrdinalPosition	1
Required	False
SourceField	TimeCardID
SourceTable	tblTimeCardHours
DateWorked	**Date/Time**
AllowZeroLength	False
Attributes	Fixed size
Caption	Date Worked

TABLE A.38   Continued

Property	Value
DateWorked	**Date/Time**
CollatingOrder	General
Column Hidden	False
ColumnOrder	Default
ColumnWidth	Default
Format	Short date
InputMask	99/99/00
OrdinalPosition	2
Required	False
SourceField	DateWorked
SourceTable	tblTimeCardHours
ProjectID	**Number (Long)**
AllowZeroLength	False
Attributes	Fixed size
Bound Column	1
Caption	Project ID
CollatingOrder	General
ColumnCount	3
ColumnHeads	False
ColumnHidden	False
ColumnOrder	Default
ColumnWidth	Default
ColumnWidths	0;1020;3156
DecimalPlaces	255
DisplayControl	Combo Box
LimitToList	True
ListRows	8
ListWidth	3
OrdinalPosition	3
Required	False
RowSourceType	Table/Query

TABLE A.38   Continued

Property	Value
ProjectID	**Number (Long)**
RowSource	SELECT DISTINCTROW tblProjects.* FROM tblProjects ORDER BY tblProjects.ProjectName;
SourceField	ProjectID
SourceTable	tblTimeCardHours
WorkDescription	**Text**
AllowZeroLength	False
Attributes	Variable length
Caption	Work Description
CollatingOrder	General
ColumnHidden	False
ColumnOrder	Default
ColumnWidth	Default
DisplayControl	Text Box
OrdinalPosition	4
Required	False
SourceField	WorkDescription
SourceTable	tblTimeCardHours
BillableHours	**Number (Double)**
AllowZeroLength	False
Attributes	Fixed size
Caption	Billable Hours
CollatingOrder	General
ColumnHidden	False
ColumnOrder	Default
ColumnWidth	Default
DecimalPlaces	255
DisplayControl	Text Box
OrdinalPosition	5
Required	False

TABLE A.38   Continued

Property	Value
BillableHours	**Number (Double)**
SourceField	BillableHours
SourceTable	tblTimeCardHours
BillingRate	**Currency**
AllowZeroLength	False
Attributes	Fixed size
Caption	Billing Rate
CollatingOrder	General
ColumnHidden	False
ColumnOrder	Default
ColumnWidth	Default
DecimalPlaces	2
Format	Currency
OrdinalPosition	6
Required	False
SourceField	BillingRate
SourceTable	tblTimeCardHours
WorkCodeID	**Number (Long)**
AllowZeroLength	False
Attributes	Fixed size
Bound Column	1
Caption	Work Code ID
CollatingOrder	General
ColumnCount	2
ColumnHeads	False
ColumnHidden	False
ColumnOrder	Default
ColumnWidth	Default
ColumnWidths	0;2880

TABLE A.38   Continued

Property	Value
WorkCodeID	**Number (Long)**
DecimalPlaces	255
DisplayControl	Combo Box
LimitToList	True
ListRows	8
ListWidth	2
OrdinalPosition	7
Required	False
RowSourceType	Table/Query
RowSource	SELECT DISTINCTROW tblWorkCodes.* FROM tblWorkCodes ORDER BY tblWorkCodes.WorkCode;
SourceField	WorkCodeID
SourceTable	tblTimeCardHours

The tblTimeCards Table

This table stores time card information for each employee.

TABLE A.39   The tblTimeCards Table

Field Name	Type	Size (Bytes)
TimeCardID	Number (Long)	4
EmployeeID	Number (Long)	4
DateEntered	Date/Time	8

TABLE A.40   The Field Properties of the tblTimeCards Table

Property	Value
TimeCardID	**Number (Long)**
AllowZeroLength	False
Attributes	Fixed size, auto-increment
Caption	Time Card ID
CollatingOrder	General

TABLE A.40   Continued

Property	Value
TimeCardID	**Number (Long)**
ColumnHidden	False
ColumnOrder	Default
ColumnWidth	Default
OrdinalPosition	0
Required	False
SourceField	TimeCardID
SourceTable	tblTimeCards
EmployeeID	**Number (Long)**
AllowZeroLength	False
Attributes	Fixed size
BoundColumn	1
Caption	Employee ID
CollatingOrder	General
ColumnCount	3
ColumnHeads	False
ColumnHidden	False
ColumnOrder	Default
ColumnWidth	Default
ColumnWidths	0;2000;700
DecimalPlaces	255
DisplayControl	Combo Box
LimitToList	True
ListRows	8
ListWidth	2
OrdinalPosition	1
Required	False
Row Source Type	Table/Query
Row Source	SELECT tblEmployees.EmployeeID, [LastName] & ", " & [FirstName] AS EmployeeName, tblEmployees.BillingRate FROM tblEmployees ORDER BY [LastName] & ", " & [FirstName];

TABLE A.40   Continued

Property	Value
EmployeeID	**Number (Long)**
SourceField	EmployeeID
SourceTable	tblTimeCards
DateEntered	**Date/Time**
AllowZeroLength	False
Attributes	Fixed size
Caption	Date Entered
CollatingOrder	General
ColumnHidden	False
ColumnOrder	Default
ColumnWidth	Default
Format	Short date
InputMask	99/99/00
OrdinalPosition	2
Required	False
SourceField	DateEntered
SourceTable	tblTimeCards

The tblWorkCodes Table

This table supplies valid work codes for the application.

TABLE A.41   The tblWorkCodes Table

Field Name	Type	Size (Bytes)
WorkCodeID	Number (Long)	4
WorkCode	Text	30

TABLE A.42 The Field Properties of the tblWorkCodes Table

Property	Value
WorkCodeID	**Number (Long)**
AllowZeroLength	False
Attributes	Fixed size, auto-increment
Caption	Work Code ID
CollatingOrder	General
OrdinalPosition	0
Required	False
SourceField	WorkCodeID
SourceTable	tblWorkCodes
WorkCode	**Text**
AllowZeroLength	False
Attributes	Variable length
Caption	Work Code
CollatingOrder	General
OrdinalPosition	1
Required	False
SourceField	WorkCode
SourceTable	tblWorkCodes

Naming Conventions

This appendix gives you suggestions for naming variables and other database objects. The suggested standards are based on the Reddick VBA Naming Conventions (RVBA).

When creating variable names, it's important to make the type and intended use of each variable clear and self-documenting. Here are a few rules to follow:

- Remember to always make variable names mixed case, with each word or abbreviation in the variable name capitalized.
- Don't use underscore characters in your variable names.
- Abbreviate variable names only when it's necessary.
- Make the beginning of each variable name describe the type of data it contains.

Following these conventions will go a long way toward keeping your code concise and readable. The format for an object is

`[prefixes]tag[BaseName[Suffixes]]`

A *prefix* appears in lowercase and is used to indicate additional information, such as the scope of a variable. The *tag* also appears in lowercase. It is a short set of characters that indicates the type of an object. Use the *BaseName* to indicate what the object represents. Capitalize the first letter of each word in the *BaseName*. *Suffixes*, when used, provide additional information about the meaning of the *BaseName*. An example of a name for an object is

`mstrFirstName`

Use the prefix `m` to indicate that the variable appears at the module level. The tag `str` indicates that the variable contains a string. The BaseName `FirstName` indicates that the variable holds a first name. Table B.1 recommends prefixes for Access object tags.

TABLE B.1   Recommended Prefixes for Access Object Tags

Prefix	Control Type	Example
app	appInfoBase	Application
chk	CheckBox	chkReadOnly
cbo	ComboBox	cboLanguages
cmd	CommandButton	cmdRefreshTable
ctl	Control	ctlAny
ctls	Controls	ctlsAll
ocx	CustomControl	ocxCalendar
dap	DataAccessPage	dapCustomers
dcm	DoCmd	dcmOpenForm
fcd	FormatCondition	fcdOverDue

TABLE B.1 Continued

Prefix	Control Type	Example
fcds	FormatConditions	fcdsRules
frm	Form	frmDataEntryView
frms	Forms	frmsClientsAndOrders
hyp	Hyperlink	hypCustomers
img	Image	imgHeadShot
lbl	Label	lblShowAllCheckBox
lin	Line	linDivider
lst	ListBox	lstLastTenSites
bas	Module	basErrorControl
ole	ObjectFrame	oleWorksheet
opt	OptionButton	optReadOnly
fra	OptionGroup (frame)	fraColorSchemes
brk	PageBreak	brkTopOfForm
pal	PaletteButton	palBackgroundColor
prps	Properties	prpsActiveForm
shp	Rectangle	shpHidableFrame
ref	Reference	refExcel
refs	References	refsApps
rpt	Report	rptOrders
rpts	Reports	rptsTodaysChanges
scr	Screen	scrSecondSplashScreen
sec	Section	secOrderDetail
fsub	Subform	fsubBillableHours
rsub	SubReport	rsubTopFiveSales
tab	TabControl	tabCustomer
txt	TextBox	txtAdditionalNotes
tgl	ToggleButton	tglShowFormatting

B

NAMING
CONVENTIONS

Table B.2 lists prefix tags for standard variable types, as well as the storage space required by each.

TABLE B.2   Standard Variable Data Type Tags

Prefix	Data Type	Storage	Example
byte or byt	Byte	1 Byte	byteArray
bool or f	Boolean	2 bytes	boolSecurityClear
int	Integer	2 bytes	intLoop
lng	Long	4 bytes	lngEnv
sng	Single	4 bytes	sngValue
dbl	Double	8 bytes	dblValue
cur	Currency	8 bytes	curCostPerUnit
dat	Date and Time	8 bytes	datStartTime
obj	Object	Varies	objActiveObject
str	String	1 byte per character	strFirstName
stf	String (fixed length)	10 bytes + 1 byte per char	stfSocNumber
var	Variant	16 bytes + 1 byte per char	varInput

Access 2002 provides the ActiveX Data Objects Library. Table B.3 lists the recommend tags for ADO.

TABLE B.3   Recommended ADO Tags

Prefix	Object Type
cmn or cmd	Command
cnn or cnx	Connection
err	Error
errs	Errors
fld	Field
flds	Fields
prm	Parameter
prms	Parameters
prp	Property
prps	Properties
rst	Recordset

The Jet Engine uses objects you might need to refer to in VBA code. Table B.4 lists the Data Access Objects (DAO) object types and their standard naming prefixes.

TABLE B.4   Jet Object/Collection Prefixes

Prefix	Object Type
cnt	Container
cnts	Containers
db	Database
dbs	Databases
dbe	DBEngine
doc	Document
docs	Documents
err	Error
errs	Errors
fld	Field
flds	Fields
grp	Group
grps	Groups
idx	Index
idxs	Indexes
prm	Parameter
prms	Parameters
pdbe	PrivDBEngine
prp	Property
prps	Properties
qry (or qdf)	QueryDef
qrys (or qdfs)	QueryDefs
rst	Recordset
rsts	Recordsets
rel	Relation
rels	Relations
tbl (or tdf)	TableDef
tbls (or tdfs)	TableDefs
usr	User

B

NAMING
CONVENTIONS

TABLE B.4   Jet Object/Collection Prefixes

Prefix	Object Type
usrs	Users
wrk	Workspace
wrks	Workspaces

In addition to the standard notations for variables, there are variable notations for scope and lifetime. These should be placed at the beginning of the variable, before any other prefix. Table B.5 lists the scope and lifetime prefixes.

TABLE B.5   Prefixes for Scope and Lifetime

Prefix	Description
(None)	Local variable, procedure-level lifetime
s	Local variable, program-level lifetime (static variable)
m	Private (module) variable, program-level lifetime
g	Public (global) variable, program-level lifetime

Table B.6 lists general naming convention tags for the Database window objects.

TABLE B.6   Tags for Database Window Objects

Prefix	Object Type
tbl	Table
qry	Query
frm	Form
rpt	Report
mcr	Macro
dap	DataAccessPage
bas	Module

There are two sets of naming conventions you can use when naming specific database window objects: Either use the prefix for the general object prefix from the table, or supply one of the more descriptive tags listed in Table B.7.

TABLE B.7   Tags for Specific Database Window Objects

Prefix	Suffix	Object Type
tlkp	Lookup	Table (lookup)
qsel	(none)	Query (select)
qapp	Append	Query (append)
qxtb	XTab	Query (crosstab)
qddl	DDL	Query (DDL)
qdel	Delete	Query (delete)
qflt	Filter	Query (filter)
qlkp	Lookup	Query (lookup)
qmak	MakeTable	Query (make table)
qspt	PassThru	Query (SQL pass-through)
qtot	Totals	Query (totals)
quni	Union	Query (union)
qupd	Update	Query (update)
fdlg	Dlg	Form (dialog)
fmnu	Mnu	Form (menu)
fmsg	Msg	Form (message)
fsfr	Subform	Form (subform)
rsrp	SubReport	Form (subreport)
mmnu	Mnu	Macro (menu)

INDEX

SYMBOLS

A

listings

M

Q